ABNORMAL PSYCHOLOGY

CURRENT PERSPECTIVES

FIFTH EDITION

ABNORMAL PSYCHOLOGY

CURRENT PERSPECTIVES

RICHARD R. BOOTZIN
University of Arizona

JOAN ROSS ACOCELLA

RANDOM HOUSE
NEW YORK

Fifth Edition

98765432

Copyright © 1972, 1977, 1980, 1984, 1988 by
Random House, Inc.

**Library of Congress Cataloging-in-Publication
Data**

Bootzin, Richard R., 1940–
  Abnormal psychology.

  Bibliography: p.
  Includes indexes.
  1. Psychology, Pathological. I. Acocella, Joan
Ross, 1945–   . II. Title. [DNLM:
1. Psychopathology.   WM 100 B7235a]
RC454.B577 1988   616.89   87–12810

ISBN 0–394–36859–2

Manufactured in the United States of America

Cover and Book Design: Glen M. Edelstein

Sculpture by Linda Peer, courtesy of the artist.

Photo by Ken Karp.

PREFACE

The fifth edition of *Abnormal Psychology: Current Perspectives* preserves—and improves on—the strengths of the fourth edition. The multi-perspective approach, which recognizes all the major viewpoints on psychological disorder, has been retained and updated. The newly issued revised edition of the American Psychiatric Association's *Diagnostic and Statistical Manual of Mental Disorders* (usually referred to as *DSM-III-R*) is fully integrated into the text. This brings *Abnormal Psychology: Current Perspectives* up to date with the most influential and widely used diagnostic tool in the field, and it is an important feature of this new edition. The research orientation of this edition has again been strengthened. Throughout the book, recent research findings have been added—many of them reflecting exciting new discoveries about the causes of particular disorders.

One of our major goals in preparing this edition was to augment and strengthen our discussion of the neuroscience perspective. Because of the ever-increasing importance of research into the biological causes of abnormality, we have increased our coverage of the neuroscience perspective to a full chapter (Chapter 5). In this chapter we describe both the broad ideas and methods of the field and some of the specific techniques it has contributed to the study of abnormal behavior. We hope that our discussion here, whether of genetic studies, biochemical research, or of new techniques in brain imaging—including some of the most significant findings of the past few years—will be both illuminating and exciting.

We continue to concern ourselves not only with the scientific aspects of abnormal psychology in this edition, however, but with its human aspects as well. Recognizing the crucial role of social support in preventing and in treating the various disorders, we have expanded our discussion of the role of the family as an aid to the troubled person. And recognizing that this influence works both ways, we have considered the stress that disordered behavior—whether its cause is schizophrenia, alcoholism, or Alzheimer's disease—can place on a family. We have also considered larger social issues: Has "deinstitutionalization" been a success? How has society's treatment of mentally ill defendants changed in the aftermath of the John Hinckley case? And so on.

Finally, we have done a good deal of work to make the book—as its subtitle suggests—truly *current*. From changing patterns of drug abuse to the explosion of cognitive research on depression to increasing concern about child abuse, we have brought every chapter up to date.

REVISION OVERVIEW

The following is an overview of what is new in this edition, in addition to changes brought about by *DSM-III-R:*

Chapter 1 (history) reflects current research in the history of abnormality, which questions the idea that earlier ages routinely treated the disturbed as "possessed" or as witches. The picture is a far more subtle one than most texts acknowledge.

Chapter 2 (psychodynamic perspective) has added discussion of influential trends in post-Freudian psychology. Highlighted are Margaret Mahler and object relations theory and Heinz Kohut's theory of narcissism.

Chapter 3 (behavioral perspective) contains expanded information on the cognitive behavioral perspective and its developing therapies.

Chapter 4 (humanistic-existential and sociocultural perspectives) now contains a discussion of the contributions of Rollo May.

Chapter 5 (neuroscience perspective) is a new chapter devoted to genetic, neurological, and biochemical research, including new brain imaging methods.

Chapter 6 (research methods) is devoted to familiarizing students with research procedures and problems in abnormal psychology.

Chapter 7 (diagnosis and assessment) has an expanded discussion of computer assessment and the issues associated with it.

Chapter 8 (anxiety, somatoform, and dissociative disorders) has new research on panic disorders.

Chapter 9 (psychological stress and physical disorders) has been extensively revised to reflect the dramatic increase in research in this field.

Chapter 10 (mood disorders) covers another area in which there has been a great deal of exciting new research. Our chapter reflects this activity by including new research on cognitive theories of depression and an expanded neuroscience section. It also contains new material on dysthymia, cyclothymia, and seasonal affective disorder.

Chapter 11 (personality disorders) now contains descriptions of all the personality disorders listed in *DSM-III-R*. It also describes the controversy about two newly proposed disorders.

Chapter 12 (addictive disorders) describes the treatment approach known as relapse prevention and adds information on compulsive gambling.

Chapters 14 and 15 (schizophrenia and paranoia) have new research on communication within families and expanded coverage of recent research in neuroscience.

Chapter 16 (organic disorders) contains additional information on Alzheimer's disease and its impact on victims and their families.

Chapter 17 (childhood and adolescent disorders) includes new material on the problem of child abuse and on the prevention of childhood disorders.

Chapter 18 (autism) has been reorganized and rewritten to reflect recent research on autism and severe developmental disabilities.

Chapter 19 (retardation) covers new information in legal decisions relating to institutional care and the new early intervention programs that seek to help retarded babies and young children develop their abilities. It takes up the question of dual diagnosis, recognizing that many retarded children have other disorders as well. It also has expanded coverage of the emotional and social problems of the retarded adult.

Chapter 20 (psychotherapy) has an increased focus on commonalities across therapies and includes recent research on the evaluation of therapies.

Chapter 21 (other forms of treatment), a newly reorganized chapter, includes a comparison of drug treatment with psychotherapy, together with information on the impact of the deinstitutionalization movement and its successes and failures.

Chapter 22 (legal issues) has an update of the recent court decisions affecting commitment and patients' rights.

PEDAGOGY

Each chapter begins with an outline that offers the student a concise overview of the chapter. Important terms within each chapter are in boldface so that they can be quickly identified. These terms are defined not only in the text when they first appear, but also in the full-scale glossary at the end of the book. At the end of each chapter there is a summary section, which allows the reader to review the material already covered. References cited in this edition range from classic citations to the newest research, which is only now making its major impact in the field. The references are compiled in an extensive reference section at the end of the text. For this fifth edition, a complete review was undertaken of the illustrations. More than half of the photographs were changed in order to complement better the text. And many are now in color to make the text more attractive.

SUPPLEMENTS

The *Study Guide to Accompany Abnormal Psychology, Fifth Edition,* is intended to help students understand the vocabulary and concepts of abnormal psychology. Each chapter corresponds to a chapter in the text and contains an outline of major concepts, learning objectives, a study outline, exercises testing key terms and concepts, practice multiple-choice questions, and essay questions.

The *Casebook in Abnormal Psychology* by John Vitkus, Barnard College, is a compilation of case studies illustrating a wide range of clinical problems and amplifying the concepts presented in the text. Each case study, based on real-life patients, includes a description of the presenting complaint, a detailed personal history, analysis of treatment, and discussion. The case treatments reflect a broad spectrum of approaches including the humanistic, neuroscience, psychodynamic, behavioral, and eclectic perspectives.

A new *Test Bank,* with over 1,300 multiple-choice questions that are both factual and applied, and are referenced to the text page on which the correct answer can be found, has been written exclusively for *Abnormal Psychology,* Fifth Edition. A **computerized test bank** is available for the IBM PC/PC-XT (or true compatibles) and Apple IIe/2c computers. The *Instructor's Manual* offers instructors chapter outlines, lecture topics, essay questions and answers, and an annotated video/film list and references. The *Instructor's Manual* and *Test Bank* are published as one volume.

ACKNOWLEDGMENTS

We would like to thank those talented people who worked with us on the editorial, design, and production stages: Barry Fetterolf, Mary Falcon, Alison Husting, Judith Kromm, Bob Greiner, Glen Edelstein, Andy Roney, Kathy Bendo, and Leonora Morgan. We wish to thank especially Betty Gatewood for her work in developing this current edition; she has brought skill, dedication, and sensitivity to this project.

The breadth of coverage of abnormal psychology is so great that we asked a number of specialist consultants and reviewers to assist us. We are indebted to the following people for their help:

Specialist Consultants

Amedeo Giorgi, Director of Research, Saybrook Institute in San Francisco, is a specialist in existential psychology. Dr. Giorgi assisted with the presentation of the humanistic-existential perspective.

Joseph LoPiccolo, professor and chairman, department of psychology, University of Missouri, is a specialist in sexual function and dysfunction. Dr. LoPiccolo assisted with the sexual disorders chapter in this edition and in the previous third and fourth editions.

Theodore Millon, professor at the University of Miami, Coral Gables, is a specialist in personality disorders. Dr. Millon assisted with the chapter on personality disorders.

Steven Reiss, professor of psychology at the University of Illinois, Chicago, is a specialist in the treatment of emotional disorders of the retarded. Dr. Reiss assisted with the chapter on mental retardation in this edition and in the fourth edition.

Lawrence Squire, professor of psychology at the Veterans Administration Medical Center, San Diego, and University of California/San Diego, is a specialist in neuropsychology. Dr. Squire reviewed the neuroscience perspective sections throughout.

George Stricker, professor and dean, the Derner Institute at Adelphi University, is a specialist in clinical psychology. Dr. Stricker assisted with the psychodynamic perspective chapter and reviewed the psychodynamic perspective sections throughout.

Howard Ulan, an attorney for the Pennsylvania Department of Public Welfare, who also has a Ph.D. in psychology, is a specialist in mental health law. Dr. Ulan supervised the preparation of the legal issues chapter for the third, fourth, and fifth editions.

Charles Wenar, professor of psychology at Ohio State University, is a specialist in developmental psychology. Dr. Wenar assisted with the chapter on the disorders of childhood and adolescence.

Steven Zarit, professor at the University of Southern California, Los Angeles, is a specialist in clinical neuropsychology. Dr. Zarit assisted with the organic brain disorders chapter.

Reviewers

Lauren B. Alloy, Northwestern University

David H. Barlow, State University of New York at Albany

Barbara E. Brackney, Eastern Michigan University

James Calhoun, University of Georgia

Karen Chapin, University of Detroit

Joseph Culkin, Queensborough Community College

Robert Dies, University of Maryland

Jerome Frieman, Kansas State University

Stuart Golann, University of Massachusetts/Amherst

Martin Harrow, Michael Reese Hospital and Medical Center, Chicago, Illinois

Phillip Kendall, Temple University

Richard Leavy, Ohio Wesleyan University

Brendan Maher, Harvard University

Joanne Marengo, Michael Reese Hospital and Medical Center, Chicago, Illinois

David Mostofsky, Boston University

Christopher Potter, Harrisburg Area Community College

Clive Robins, New York University

Kathryn K. Rileigh, Pembroke State University

Sidney H. Schnoll, M.D., and Ph.D., Medical College of Virginia

Sandra Wilcox, California State University/Dominquez Hills

Lorna Wing, Institute of Psychiatry, Maudley Hospital, London, England

We hope that this new edition of *Abnormal Psychology* will make the student not only more knowledgeable, but also more understanding. For in describing what we know so far about why people act as they do, we have attempted to present this complex subject from a human perspective. "Abnormal" is a relative term, the meaning of which has changed many times over the centuries. We offer a balanced approach to the standards against which abnormality is defined. We also present the causal theories in a balanced fashion. This approach is intended to impress upon the student the dynamic character of the field: its openness to dispute, to movement, and to change. We hope that the book will also encourage students to appreciate the interconnection between mind and body, which is perhaps the central theme of this book.

R. R. B.

J. R. A.

CONTENTS

BOXES

Abnormal Behavior: Yesterday and Today

A century ago, if a father "disciplined" his misbehaving son with a vicious beating, most of his neighbors would not have considered this treatment unusual; today we would think the man guilty of child abuse. Likewise, today many people place their aging parents in nursing homes, where they are deprived of their accustomed surroundings, of companionship, and of any useful role to perform—a practice that would have been considered extraordinary a hundred years ago.

Ideas about acceptable behavior change over time, sometimes slowly, sometimes more rapidly. Similarly, ideas about psychological abnormality change from century to century and from society to society. "Abnormality," "madness," "lunacy"—by whatever name—is a relative concept. We begin our exploration of abnormal psychology by considering what "abnormality" has meant and what it means today.

ABNORMAL BEHAVIOR AND SOCIETY

Defining Abnormal Behavior

When we ask how a society defines psychological abnormality, what we are asking is where that society draws the line between acceptable and unacceptable patterns of thought and behavior. Acceptability is gauged by a variety of measuring sticks, but perhaps the most commonly used is the society's norms.

1

One way we define abnormal behavior is by asking whether it violates a norm—a socially imposed standard of acceptable behavior. The vagueness of this definition presents problems, however: where exactly is the line between mere eccentricity and truly abnormal behavior? (Adolahe/Southern Light)

Norm Violation   Every human group lives by a set of **norms**—rules that tell us what it is "right" and "wrong" to do, and when and where and with whom. Such rules circumscribe every aspect of our existence, from our most far-reaching decisions to our most prosaic daily routines.

Consider, for example, the ordinary act of eating. Do we eat whatever we want, wherever and whenever we want it? We do not. Eating is governed by norms as to what is "good for us" to eat, how often we should eat, how much we should eat, and where we should eat. Eating at a rock concert is fine, but eating at a symphony concert is not. Furthermore, there are rules as to when and where certain things can be eaten. Drinking wine with dinner is acceptable; drinking wine with breakfast would be considered rather odd. Hot dogs at a barbecue are fine; hot dogs at a banquet are not.

Some cultures even have strict rules about whom one can eat with. Certain tribes, for instance, prohibit eating in the presence of blood relatives on the maternal side, since eating makes one vulnerable to being possessed by a devil, and such devils are more likely to appear when one is in the presence of one's maternal relatives.

To outsiders, such norms may seem odd and unnecessarily complicated, but adults who have been raised in the culture and who have assimilated its norms through the process of socialization simply take them for granted. Far from regarding them as folkways, they regard them as what is right and proper. And consequently they will tend to label as abnormal anyone who violates these norms.

In a small, highly integrated society, there will be little disagreement over norms. In a large, complex society, on the other hand, there may be considerable friction among different groups over the question of what is right and proper. For example, the Gay Liberation movement may be conceptualized as the effort of one group to persuade the society as a whole to adjust its norms so that homosexuality will fall inside rather than outside the limits of acceptability.

In a sense, the use of norms as a standard for judging mental health may seem inappropriate. Norms are not universal and eternal truths; on the contrary, as we have seen, they vary across time and across cultures. Therefore, they seem a weak basis for applying the label "abnormal" to anyone. Furthermore, whether or not adherence to norms is an appropriate criterion for mental health, it may be called an oppressive criterion. It enthones conformity as the ideal pattern of behavior and it stigmatizes the nonconformist. For norms contain value judgments. People who violate them are not just doing something unusual; they are doing something wrong. Yet despite these objections, norms remain a very important standard for defining abnormality. Though they may be relative to time and place, they are nevertheless so deeply ingrained that they *seem* absolute, and hence anyone who violates them appears abnormal.

Important as norms are, they are not the only standard for defining abnormal behavior. Other criteria are statistical rarity, personal discomfort, maladaptive behavior, and deviation from an ideal state.

Statistical Rarity   From a statistical point of view, abnormality is any substantial deviation from a statistically calculated average. Those who fall within the "golden mean"—those, in short, who do what most other people do—are normal, while those whose behavior differs from that of the majority are abnormal.

This criterion is used in some evaluations of psychological abnormality. The diagnosis of mental retardation, for instance, is based in large part on statistical accounting. Those whose tested intelligence falls below an average range for the population (and who also have problems coping with life—which, with intelligence far lower than the average, is likely to be the case) are labeled retarded (see Figure 1.1). However, careful statistical calculations are not always considered necessary in order to establish deviance. In the extreme version of the statistical approach,

any behavior that is simply unusual would be judged abnormal.

The statistical-rarity approach makes defining abnormality a simple task. One has only to measure the individual's performance against the average performance; if it falls outside the average range, it is abnormal. However, there are obvious difficulties with this approach. As we saw earlier, the norm-violation approach can be criticized for exalting the shifting values of social groups. Yet the major weakness of the statistical-rarity approach is that it has *no* values; it lacks any system for differentiating between desirable and undesirable behaviors. In the absence of such a system, it is the average behavior that tends to be considered the ideal. Such a point of view is potentially very dangerous, since it discourages and denigrates even valuable deviations from the norm. For example, not only mentally retarded people but also geniuses—and particularly geniuses with new ideas—may be considered candidates for psychological treatment. Of course, most users of the statistical-rarity approach acknowledge that not all deviations from the average should be identified as abnormal, yet the focus on the norm does have discomforting implications.

Personal Discomfort   An alternative criterion for defining abnormality is personal discomfort. If people are content with their lives, then their lives are of

FIGURE 1.1
The distribution of IQ scores in the United States. More than 78 percent of the population scores between 84 and 116 points. Using the statistical approach to abnormality, diagnosticians designate as mentally retarded those falling below approximately 68 points. As the figure indicates, this group is statistically rare, representing only about 2 percent of the population.

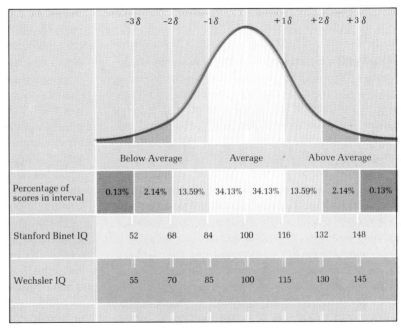

	-3δ	-2δ	-1δ		+1δ	+2δ	+3δ
	Below Average			Average		Above Average	
Percentage of scores in interval	0.13%	2.14%	13.59%	34.13%	34.13%	13.59%	2.14%	0.13%
Stanford Binet IQ		52	68	84	100	116	132	148
Wechsler IQ		55	70	85	100	115	130	145

no concern to the mental health establishment. If, on the other hand, they are distressed over their thoughts or behavior, then they require treatment.

This is a more "liberal" approach than the two we have just discussed, in that it makes people the judges of their own normality, rather than subjecting them to the judgment of the society or the diagnostician. And this is the approach that is probably the most widely used in the case of the less severe psychological disorders. Most people in psychotherapy are there not because anyone has declared their behavior abnormal but because they themselves are unhappy.

Reasonable as it may be in such cases, the personal-discomfort criterion has obvious weaknesses as a comprehensive standard for defining abnormal behavior. The same behavior pattern may cause very different degrees of dissatisfaction in different people. If we focus on dissatisfaction, we are left with no stable criterion for evaluating the behavior itself. The lack of an objective standard is especially problematic in the case of behaviors that cause serious harm or are socially disruptive. Is teenage drug addiction to be classified as abnormal only if the teenager in question expresses dissatisfaction with this way of life? Furthermore, even if a behavior pattern is not necessarily harmful, it may still merit psychological attention in the absence of personal distress. People who believe that their brains are receiving messages from outer space may inflict no great pain on others and may report no unhappiness with their lives, yet in the eyes of most people they would appear to be in need of psychological treatment.

Maladaptive Behavior   A fourth criterion for defining a behavior as abnormal is maladaptiveness. Here the question is whether the person, given that behavior pattern, is able to meet the demands of his or her life—hold down a job, deal with friends and family, pay the bills on time, and the like. If not, the pattern is abnormal. This standard overlaps somewhat with that of norm violation. After all, many norms are rules for adapting our behavior to our own and our society's requirements. (To arrive for work drunk is to violate a norm; it is also maladaptive, in that it may get you fired.) The maladaptiveness standard is also connected to that of personal discomfort, for it is often the consequences of maladaptive behavior (e.g., lost jobs) that cause us discomfort. At the same time, the maladaptiveness standard is unique in that it concentrates on the practical matter of getting through life with some measure of success.

This practical approach makes the maladaptiveness standard a useful one. Those whose behavior makes them unable to cope with the everyday demands of life would seem obvious candidates for psychological help. Furthermore, the maladaptiveness standard is favored by many professionals for its elasticity—because it focuses on behavior *relative to life circumstances,* it can accommodate many different styles of living. But as with the personal-discomfort criterion, this liberalism is purchased at the cost of values, and it raises certain moral questions. Are there not, for example, certain kinds of circumstances to which we should *not* adapt? Can we say that the behavior of Germans who adapted poorly to Hitler's regime—who became depressed or rebellious, losing jobs and friends as a result—was abnormal? This question raises another: Just how liberal is the maladaptiveness standard? Like the norm-violation standard, it does seem to favor conformity, since, in general, those who adapt well are those who "fit in."

Deviation from an Ideal   As we shall see in later chapters, several psychological theories describe an ideally well-adjusted personality, any deviation from which is interpreted as abnormal to a greater or lesser degree. Since the ideal is difficult to achieve, most people are seen as being poorly adjusted at least part of the time. One may strive to achieve the ideal, but one seldom makes it.

In light of such theories, many people may judge themselves to be abnormal, or at least in need of psychological treatment, even though they have no particularly troubling behavioral symptoms. For example, a woman may have a number of friends and a reasonably satisfying job and yet consider herself a candidate for psychotherapy because she lacks something—an intimate relationship with another person, a sense of realizing her full potential—that is held up as a criterion for mental health by one or another theory. This standard is obviously related to the personal-discomfort standard; the source of the personal discomfort—and hence of the presumed need for treatment—may be a failure to achieve an ideal.

The shortcomings of the deviation-from-an-ideal approach are again obvious. First, a person who falls short of an ideal does not necessarily merit the label "abnormal" or require treatment. The pursuit of ideal adjustment can add to people's troubles, making them feel seriously inadequate, whereas they may simply be imperfect, like all human beings. Second, psychological theories are as relative to time and place as social norms, and they change even more quickly. Thus if norms are a weak foundation for the evaluation of mental health, theoretical ideals are even weaker. (And at least social norms ask only for the possible.) Nevertheless, the need to achieve something more than ordinary adjustment has propelled many people into psychotherapy in recent years—and especially into group therapies oriented toward what is called "personal growth."

In sum, behavior may be identified as abnormal in a variety of ways, no one of which is foolproof. In practice, the judgment of abnormality, whether by professional diagnosticians or by family and neighbors, is usually based on a combination of standards. The person's happiness, relation to social norms, and ability to cope—and also the society's ability to cope with him or her—are all taken into account in varying degrees.

Explaining Abnormal Behavior

As we have just seen, defining abnormal behavior is a complex task. The same is true of the problem of explaining abnormal behavior—that is, identifying its causes. Since antiquity, Western society has developed theories of abnormal behavior. Not only do the theories vary with the kinds of abnormality they seek to explain; they often compete with each other to explain the same abnormality—and the entire problem of abnormal behavior. These various explanations have a common base in that they are all naturalistic. That is, in keeping with a secular and scientific age, they seek to account for abnormal behavior in terms of natural events—disturbances in the body or disturbances in human relationships. Beyond this, however, they differ considerably, and since they will figure importantly in the succeeding chapters of this book, it is worth examining them briefly at this point.

The Medical Model   According to what is loosely called the **medical model** (or *disease model*), abnormal behavior is like a disease: each kind of abnormal behavior, like each disease, has specific *causes* and a specific *set of symptoms* (a "syndrome"). In its strictest sense, the medical model also implies that the abnormal behavior is **biogenic**—that is, it results from some malfunction within the body. However, even those who do not think that all abnormal behavior is biologically *caused* may still reflect the assumptions

of the medical model if they consider "symptoms" the products of underlying causes.

Biogenic theories of abnormal behavior have been with us since ancient times. In the Middle Ages and the Renaissance they coexisted with supernatural theory, the belief that abnormal behavior was caused by God or, more often, the devil. But in the eighteenth and early nineteenth centuries, religious explanations went into decline, and theories of biological causation predominated. Since abnormal behavior was considered an illness, it was thought to be the exclusive province of medicine. It was within the framework of these assumptions that the modern discipline of abnormal psychology developed in the nineteenth century. Most of the major early theoreticians of abnormal psychology, regardless of their specific theories, were medical doctors who saw abnormality as illness.

This newly dominant medical approach was soon rewarded by a series of extremely important breakthroughs. Several previously unexplained behavior patterns were found to result from identifiable brain pathologies—infection, poisoning, and the like. Such discoveries brought immense prestige to the organic theory of abnormal behavior. Medicine, it was assumed, would ultimately conquer madness. And on this assumption, madness was increasingly turned over to the medical profession.

At the same time, there remained many patterns of abnormal behavior—indeed, the majority—for which no medical cause had been discovered. Yet because researchers were confident that such causes would eventually be found (and because abnormal behavior was by now the province of medicine), these patterns were treated *as if* they were organically based. In other words, they were treated according to a medical "model." (In scientific terms, a "model" is an analogy.) This meant not only that abnormal behavior should be handled by physicians, in hospitals, and by means of medical treatments (for instance, drugs); it also meant that the entire problem of deviant behavior should be conceptualized in medical terms. Today, even those who seriously question the medical model still find themselves using such terms as "symptom," "syndrome," "pathology," "mental illness," "mental disorder," "patient," "therapy," "treatment," and "cure," all of which are derived from the medical analogy (Price, 1978). Although this book is not based on the medical model, such terms will occur here repeatedly. They are almost unavoidable.

A number of psychologists and other researchers in abnormal psychology, however, have pointed out that the medical model is merely an analogy. Most forms of abnormal behavior, in fact, have *not* been proved to be biologically caused, and some critics have argued that it is wrong to think of them as illnesses. Perhaps the most prominent critic of the medical model is the American psychiatrist Thomas Szasz. In a book titled *The Myth of Mental Illness* (1961), Szasz claims that most of what the medical model calls mental illnesses are not illnesses at all, but rather "problems in living" manifested in deviations from moral, legal, and social norms. To label these deviations "sick" is, according to Szasz, not only a falsification of the conflict between the individual and the society but also a dangerous sanctification of the society's norms. In addition, the "sick" label deprives individuals of responsibility for their behavior (they are sick—they can't help it) and relegates them to a passive role that genuinely impedes their return to normal behavior.

On the other hand, recent research into the possible biological causes of certain kinds of abnormal behavior has produced some intriguing findings—suggesting that biological disturbance does accompany some forms of psychological disturbance. In this book we will survey some of these findings, which we have grouped together as the **neuroscience perspective** within abnormal psychology. Like the medical model, the neuroscience perspective focuses on the biological components of abnormal behavior. However, it does not suggest that all or even most abnormal behavior patterns are merely symptoms of biological abnormalities, or even that such patterns are best treated in a medical setting. Rather, neuroscience concentrates on the biological aspects of a disorder in an effort to understand its characteristics. To offer an analogy, a person who feels sad may cry. One way to study this phenomenon is to analyze the thoughts that accompany the sadness; another is to analyze the physiology of weeping. To do the latter—which is what neuroscientists do—is not to say that tears cause or contribute to sadness (though they may). It is simply to choose one level of analysis, the organic. Thus neuroscience has retained the medical model's organic focus of study without expanding it into an all-embracing medical approach to abnormal behavior.

A Multiperspective Approach: Psychological and Biological Perspectives   In contrast to the medical model are the strictly psychological theories of abnormal behavior. Such theories attribute disturbed behavior patterns not to biological malfunction but to relatively intangible psychological processes resulting from the individual's interaction with the environment. Thus disturbed behavior may be explained by a cruel or negligent upbringing, by exposure to traumatic events, by inaccurate social perceptions, or by too much stress.

There are dozens of competing psychological explanations of abnormal behavior. Some focus on a single behavior pattern, others on abnormal behavior as a whole. Some concentrate on the patient's childhood, others on his or her present state. Nevertheless, in all this multiplicity of theories it is possible to identify a few fairly unified "perspectives"—broad schools of thought based on the same fundamental assumptions. In this book we will refer repeatedly to three psychological perspectives:

1. *The psychodynamic perspective,* which assumes that abnormal behavior issues from unconscious psychological conflicts originating in childhood.

2. *The behavioral perspective,* which holds that a primary cause of abnormal behavior is inappropriate learning, whereby maladaptive behaviors are rewarded and adaptive behaviors are not rewarded.

3. *The humanistic-existential perspective,* which maintains that abnormal behavior results from a failure to accept oneself, to take responsibility for one's actions, and to pursue personal goals.

In addition to these psychological viewpoints, we will pay close attention to the organic approach just described:

4. *The neuroscience perspective,* which analyzes abnormal behavior in terms of its biological components.

Each of these perspectives has made substantial contributions to the study of abnormal psychology. And each, likewise, has substantial shortcomings as a comprehensive approach to human behavior. The four perspectives will be discussed in detail in Chapters 2, 3, 4, and 5.

Treating Abnormal Behavior

Whatever the explanation of abnormal behavior, most societies feel that something must be *done* about such behavior. How do human groups arrive at a way of treating the deviant in their midst?

This process depends on many factors. One is the structure and nature of the society. In a small, traditional community, where deviant persons can be looked after, they may remain at home, and their odd ways will be seen as a problem for the family rather than for the society. Typically, they will be prayed over, relieved of heavy responsibilities, and treated with mixed kindness and ridicule. A large technological society, on the other hand, will tend to isolate deviants so as to prevent them from disrupting the functioning of the family and the community.

A second factor influencing the treatment of abnormal behavior, or at least the objective of such treatment, is the criterion by which it is identified. The standard of normality against which abnormality is defined—adherence to norms, average performance, personal satisfaction, adequate "coping," theoretical versions of ideal adjustment—will be the goal of treatment.

The specific treatment procedures typically follow from the society's explanation of abnormal behavior. If, as has been the case in some societies, bizarre behavior is interpreted as resulting from possession by evil spirits, then the logical treatment is any procedure recognized as useful in drawing out such spirits— prayer, special baths, special potions, or whatever. If, in keeping with the medical model, abnormal behavior is assumed to be the result of organic pathology, then the appropriate treatment is medical interventions—drugs, hospitalization, or perhaps even surgery. Or if abnormal behavior is interpreted according to recent psychological theories, it will be treated via psychological therapies. When previous learning is thought to be the problem, the appropriate procedure is considered to be a new learning program, designed to reward appropriate behavior. When unconscious childhood conflicts are held responsible, the appropriate treatment is thought to be a "talk" therapy, aimed at provoking the memory to reveal the ancient wound. In sum, the explanation of abnormal behavior dictates its treatment.

How abnormal behaviors are defined, explained, and treated in our society is the subject of this book. Our modern conceptions of abnormal psychology are not new, however. They are the result of centuries of trial and error in dealing with what each century has defined as deviant. Accordingly, in the next section of this chapter we will present a brief history of Western society's interpretation of abnormal behavior. Then, in the final section, we will examine the assumptions on which this book's presentation of abnormal psychology will be based.

CONCEPTIONS OF ABNORMAL BEHAVIOR: A SHORT HISTORY

Ancient Societies: Deviance and the Supernatural

We know little about the handling of deviant behavior in prehistoric or ancient societies. However, what we do know suggests that our early ancestors regarded deviant behavior, like most other things they did not understand, as the product of remote or supernatural forces—the movements of the stars, the vengeance of God, the operation of evil spirits. This idea seems to have endured for many centuries. References to possession can be found in the ancient

A trephined skull from the Stone Age. Note the evidence of healing around the trephine. (The American Museum of Natural History)

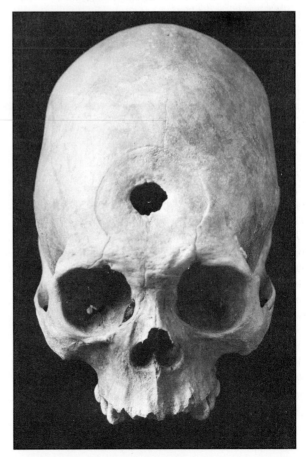

Trephining: Therapy or Surgery?

Among the Stone Age skulls that have been unearthed by archaeologists in Europe and South America are many that are marked by holes. Apparently the holes were purposely cut. Some of these skulls also show evidence of healing around the *trephine,* or hole, indicating that Stone Age people at least occasionally survived this crude surgery.

Trephining, as this ancient practice is called, was long interpreted by some psychologists as evidence of the acceptance of supernatural theories of mental illness on the part of prehistoric societies. According to this view, our Stone Age ancestors believed that mental illness was caused by evil spirits lodged in the head, and that they would be able to escape if a hole were cut in the skull of the "possessed" person.

Recently a more prosaic explanation of trephining has been proposed: that it may have served only to remove bone splinters and blood clots resulting from blows to the head (Maher and Maher, 1985a). Trephining was used for this purpose as late as the eighteenth century, and there is reason to believe that it served that purpose in the Stone Age as well.

To begin with, the Paleolithic stone axes that have survived would have been quite capable of delivering bone-crushing blows, and many of the trephined skulls do show evidence of trauma, usually fracture. Second, if trephining was performed as a ritual procedure to release evil spirits, it would be reasonable to expect trephined skulls from the same time and place to have the hole in the same location on the head, whereas in fact the placement of the hole varies, except that it seems to occur mainly in those parts of the head that would be most vulnerable to blows. Finally, if this operation was related to mental illness, we would not expect to find more trephined skulls of one sex than of the other or of any particular age group, since mental illness in the Stone Age, as in ours, presumably occurred with equal frequency in both sexes and in all age groups. But trephined skulls are usually those of adult males—in other words, the segment of the population most likely to be swinging axes at one another.

This does not mean that Stone Age societies did not attribute mental illness to possession by malevolent spirits. They well may have done so, as later societies did. But trephining is arguably not evidence of such supernatural beliefs.

records of the Chinese, the Egyptians, the Greeks, and the Hebrews. The Bible mentions demonic possession in a number of places. In the New Testament, Jesus is reported to have drawn out devils from the possessed.

The accepted cure for possession was to coax or force the evil spirits out of their victim. This practice, called **exorcism,** involved a wide variety of techniques, ranging from the mild to the brutal. Prayer, noisemaking, and the drinking of special potions appear to have sufficed in some cases. In more difficult cases, the possessed person might be submerged in water, whipped, or starved in order to make the body a less comfortable habitation for the devil. It was once thought that some were even subjected to surgery to permit the devils to escape (see the box above on trephining). Not surprisingly, some people died from exorcistic treatments.

It should not be imagined, however, that all ancient deviants were thought to be housing devils or, even if they were, that they were subjected to elaborate exorcisms. In the absence of solid evidence, it is reasonable to assume that even among highly superstitious peoples, abnormal behavior was often handled in an undramatic way. For example, the person might simply be sent home to rest and given special mention in the community's prayers. Such action is common in small, traditional societies today, and it was probably common in many ancient societies as well.

The Greeks and the Rise of Science

Among the ancient Greeks, psychological disturbance was still widely explained in supernatural terms, as a punishment sent by the gods. However, it is among the Greeks (and also the Chinese) that we begin to see the gradual evolution of a naturalistic approach to abnormal behavior. The earliest surviving evidence of this new approach to abnormal behavior is found in the writings attributed to the Greek physician Hippocrates (c. 460–c. 360 B.C.). In opposition to current supernatural theories, Hippocrates set about to prove that all illness, including mental illness, was due to natural causes. He had little patience with supernatural explanations. For example, in his treatise on epilepsy, known at the time as the "sacred disease," he made the following curt observation: "If you cut open the head, you will find the brain humid, full of sweat and smelling badly. And in this way you may see that it is not a god which injured the body, but disease" (cited in Zilboorg and Henry, 1941, p. 44).

Hippocrates' achievement was threefold. First, he set himself the novel task of actually *observing* cases of mental disturbance and of recording his observations in as objective a manner as possible. Consequently, it is in his writings that we encounter, for the first time in Western scientific literature, empirical descriptions of such mental disorders as phobia, epilepsy, and postpartum psychosis.

Second, Hippocrates developed one of the first organic, or biological, theories of abnormal behavior. Though he recognized that external stress could have a damaging psychological effect, it was primarily internal processes that he held responsible for mental disturbance. To modern science some of his theories appear rather crude. Hysteria,* for example, he attributed to a wandering uterus. (The uterus at that time was thought to be unanchored in the female body and thus free to float about.) Likewise, he believed that various personality disorders were due to an imbalance among four **humors,** or vital fluids, in the body: phlegm, blood, black bile, and yellow bile. An excess of phlegm rendered people phlegmatic—that is, indifferent and sluggish. An excess of blood gave rise to rapid shifts in mood. Too much black bile made people melancholic, and too much yellow bile made them choleric—irritable and aggressive. Primitive as some of these theories may seem, they foreshadowed and in many ways made possible today's physiological and biochemical research in abnormal psychology.

Third, Hippocrates was apparently the first West-

ern scientist to attempt a unified classification of abnormal mental states. He classified mental disorders into three categories: mania (abnormal excitement), melancholia (abnormal dejection), and phrenitis (brain fever).

Hippocrates' great contributions were in the areas of theory and methodology. He made no important advances specifically in the cure of mental disorder. However, his treatment methods were considerably more humane than those of the exorcistic tradition, and this in itself was a significant advance. His treatment for melancholia, for example, involved rest, exercise, a bland diet, and abstinence from sex and alcohol. Since such a regimen could be most easily followed under supervision, he often moved patients into his home, where he could watch them.

This trend toward a gentler and more dignified treatment was supported by Hippocrates' younger contemporary, the philosopher Plato (429–347 B.C.). Though still adhering to a quasi-supernatural theory of mental disorder, Plato insisted that the care of the mentally disturbed should be a family responsibility and that they should not be held accountable or be punished in any way for their irrational acts. Such thinking led to the establishment, in later Greek civilization, of retreats for the mentally ill. In Alexandria, for example, special temples dedicated to the god Saturn were set aside as asylums where the mentally ill could recover with the help of rest, exercise, music, and other therapeutic measures.

The Middle Ages and the Renaissance: Natural and Supernatural

With the decline of Greek civilization and the growth of the Roman Empire, the enlightened Hippocratic approach to mental disorder survived for yet a few more centuries. In the first century B.C., Asclepiades, a Greek physician practicing in Rome, was the first to differentiate between chronic and acute mental illness. Furthermore, he described the characteristics that distinguished hallucination, delusion, and illusion and explained how these characteristics could be used as diagnostic signs. Galen (A.D. 129–c. 199), another Greek physician who practiced in Rome, codified the organic theories of his predecessors and made significant advances in anatomical research. It was Galen, for example, who first showed that the arteries contained blood—not air, as was commonly thought. Af-

---

*Hysteria involves the involuntary loss or impairment of some normal function, physical or psychological (e.g., sight, sense of touch, memory), with no demonstrable organic cause. The hysterical disorders, which diagnosticians now call the somatoform and dissociative disorders, will be discussed in Chapter 8.

In the Middle Ages and the Renaissance, abnormal behavior was often taken as evidence of the devil's work. This late-fifteenth-century painting portrays St. Catherine of Siena casting the devil out of a possessed woman. The devil is pictured as a tiny imp fleeing from the woman's head. Even at this time, though, mental illness was sometimes viewed as a natural phenomenon. (The Bettmann Archive)

ter the death of Galen, however, little progress was made.[*] Eventually, with the fall of Rome to the invading tribes from northern Europe in the fifth century, the study of mental illness, together with most other branches of science, was laid aside. And when, in the Middle Ages, Europe began to experience a revival of learning, and hence of naturalistic theories of mental illness, these theories nevertheless resurfaced within a setting of unquestioning religious belief.

Medieval Theory and Treatment   Like everything else medieval, the treatment of the mentally ill in the Middle Ages must be viewed within the context of the Christian church. Unlike the religion of the Greeks, which glorified the human body, the early Christian church held that earthly life was simply a prelude to the true life: life after death. As for the body, it was merely the perishable container of the eternal soul. It is therefore no surprise that as the

church gained power, deviant behavior was often explained in terms of superhuman forces—usually the devil.

Again, cures for possession ranged from the gentle to the grim. Some of the afflicted were taken to shrines, prayed over, and sprinkled with holy water. Others were starved and flogged, to harass the devil within. Barbarous as the latter treatments may seem to us now, they were regarded as quite proper by most people, including the humane and the educated, and not only in the Middle Ages, but well into the Renaissance. The wise and mild-mannered Sir Thomas More, later sainted, wrote to a friend about his handling of a lunatic: "I caused him to be taken by the constables and bound to a tree in the street before the whole town, and there striped [whipped] him until he waxed weary. Verily, God be thanked, I hear no more of him now" (cited in Deutsch, 1949, p. 13). It should be added, however, that we do not know how many of the people thus treated were in fact psychologically disturbed. Obviously, some were mentally ill, but others were probably local eccentrics or simply socially undesirable types.

At the same time, it is clear that many cases of mental illness were approached not as supernatural

---

[*] This discovery led to the practice of bleeding the mentally disturbed, hoping to restore the proper balance among the humors of the body. Bleeding persisted as a treatment for emotional and physical disorders into the nineteenth century.

Paracelsus—a sixteenth-century Swiss physician—and other Renaissance thinkers thought that madness was caused by the movements of the moon and the stars. Indeed, the modern terms "lunacy" and "lunatic" are derived from the Latin word *luna,* meaning "moon." This seventeenth-century engraving shows a group of women, crazed by the full moon, dancing in the town square. (The Bettmann Archive)

visitations but as natural phenomena resulting from physical or emotional mishaps. For example, a recent search of English legal records has shown that when medieval officials examined people who were allegedly deranged in order to decide how they should be provided for, the officials often recorded natural, common-sense explanations for the derangement. One man, examined in 1291, was said to have lapsed into insanity after a "blow received on the head." The uncontrollable violence of another man, examined in 1366, was reportedly "induced by fear of his father" (Neugebauer, 1978). These are the kinds of causes that might be cited today. Likewise, the *Encyclopedia of Batholomaes,* written by an English monk in the early thirteenth century and widely used in European universities for the next three hundred years, traced psychological disturbance to physical and emotional sources. It is fair to assume that none of these writers doubted that the cause was ultimately supernatural, but the intervening, direct causes were natural.

Furthermore, whether insanity was attributed to natural or supernatural forces, there is evidence that once it occurred, it was often viewed as a form of illness. Windows of medieval churches show the saints curing the insane alongside the lame, the blind, and the leprous. Apparently many of the insane were admitted to the same hospitals as other sufferers. For example, the deed of Trinity Hospital, founded in Salisbury, England, in the fourteenth century, provides for an institution in which, along with the treatment of other patients, "the mad are kept safe until they are restored to reason" (Allderidge, 1979, p. 322).

The Witch Hunts   The Renaissance, stretching from the fifteenth to the seventeenth centuries, has long been regarded as a glorious chapter in the history of Western culture. However, it is during this same period that we encounter one of the ugliest episodes in European history: the witch hunts. Ever since the eleventh century, the church had been beleaguered by heresies, demands for economic and religious reform, and other types of protest and insurrection. It is likely that some of the "witches" of the Middle Ages were simply people who were causing annoyance to the local church authorities. As opposition to the church mounted during the early Renaissance, such counterattacks occurred with increasing frequency and brutality. People were accused not just of being in league with the devil but of committing heinous acts—eating children, staging sexual orgies, and the like. The charges soon spread, creating a climate of fear and hysteria in which anyone who behaved strangely, or who behaved in a way that someone in power did not like, stood in danger of being tried and executed for witchcraft.

The witch hunts soon received full endorsement from the church. In 1484 Pope Innocent VIII issued a papal bull declaring the church's intention of rooting out the offenders. Soon afterward, he appointed church officials, called inquisitors, the seek out witches and ensure that they were appropriately punished. It is estimated that from the middle of the fifteenth century to the end of the seventeenth, 100,000 people were executed as witches. During the seventeenth century, as many as 20,000 witches may have been put to death in Scotland alone (Deutsch, 1949). The hunting down of witches became a social and religious duty. Neighbors reported neighbors. Priests turned in their own parishioners. Everyone was suspect.

Renaissance Theory and Treatment   It has been argued (e.g., Spanos, 1978) that the witch hunts may have had little connection with the history of mental illness, as most of the accused were not mentally ill. In large communities, witch hunting apparently had less to do with bizarre behavior than with political and economic interests. That is, the trials were used to eliminate political rivals, to confiscate property, and to suppress heresy. In smaller communities, however, the accused were often poor, old, socially marginal women or simply socially disreputable types—"fornicators, blasphemers, thieves, ill-tempered persons, and the like" (Spanos, 1978, p. 423)—and some of the mentally ill no doubt fell into this group.

The fact that the mentally ill suffered from the witch hunts is also clear from the writings of those who protested against the craze. Among the chief arguments that these writers marshal against the Inquisition is that many of its victims, far from being in league with the devil, are simply deranged. For example, the German physician Johann Weyer (1515–1588), the first medical practitioner to have developed a special interest in mental illness, published in 1563 a treatise declaring that those who were being burned and tortured as witches were actually mentally unbalanced and not responsible for their actions. Weyer was soon followed by an Englishman named Reginald Scot, who in 1584 published his *Discovery of Witchcraft,* a scholarly work pointing out, among other arguments, the evidence of mental illness in those being persecuted by the witch hunters.

It seems likely, then, that some of the "witches" of the Renaissance were psychologically disturbed. At the same time, the evidence suggests that the majority of the deranged were of little interest to the witch hunters. Instead, they were regarded, much as in the Middle Ages, as sick people whose problems might be explained in natural terms (Neugebauer, 1978) and whose care, in any case, had to be seen to by the community. Some were apparently kept in almshouses (institutions for the poor), others in general hospitals. Indeed, London's Bethlehem Hospital, founded in 1247, was given over almost exclusively to the insane by the fifteenth century. It is also in the Renaissance that we see, at least in England, the first major efforts to institutionalize the practice of community care (Allderidge, 1979)—that is, supervision of the mentally ill within the community but outside the hospital. The "poor laws" of seventeenth-century England required that "lunaticks," along with the aged, the blind, and other unfortunates, be provided for by their local government or parish. Such provision was not always ideal. People who were violent, for example, could be lawfully imprisoned. They could also, by law, be chained and beaten, as such treatment was considered one way of restoring their reason. But many of the approaches arrived at in Renaissance England were exactly the kinds we are using today. Some patients, for example, were kept at home, while money for their maintenance or for the relief of their families was paid out of parish funds. Homeless patients might be boarded with a succession of families in the community. The legal records of a seventeenth-century English county include an order for the care of such a person:

> It is ordered that Daniell Hancox a poore Ideott who was borne in Weston . . . and is now in the care and custody of William Mulliner gent[lemen] on[e] of the Inhabitants there shalbe forthwith Clothed by and out of the stock of money given to the Inhabitants there to that purpose. And it is further ordered that the said Daniell shalbe forthwith removed from the said Mr. Mulliner and be kept and provided for by the Inh[ab]itants of the said parish from house to house as heretofore hee hath beene there mainteyned and kept (quoted by Allderidge, 1979, p. 327).

Community home care also existed during the fifteenth century in Belgium. Psychologically disturbed individuals who traveled to visit the shrine at Gheel often remained and lived with the residents. This tradition continued so that even today, hundreds of psychologically disturbed individuals live in private homes in Gheel (Aring, 1974). As we shall see, the practice of housing the psychologically disturbed with willing families in their own communities is one that is being experimented with in the United States, as well.

The Eighteenth and Nineteenth Centuries: The Supremacy of Science

The Reform of the Asylums   The practice of hospitalizing the psychologically disturbed is a very old one. In Arabian countries, general hospitals provided wards for the mentally ill as early as the eighth century (Mora, 1980). As we have seen, some European hospitals of the Middle Ages and Renaissance also accepted mental patients. The first hospital exclusively for the insane opened in Moslem Spain in the early fifteenth century. This example was eventually followed elsewhere. Mental hospitals were founded in London, Paris, Vienna, Moscow, Philadelphia, and other major cities. More and more of the insane were institutionalized, if not in public hospitals, then in smaller, privately owned "madhouses," which began to flourish in the eighteenth century.

Most of these institutions were opened with the best of intentions, and some of them did offer both decent care and some form of treatment. Many others, however, were little better than prisons. Allderidge (1979, p. 331) describes the conditions in one English madhouse around 1815:

> Part of the accommodation consisted of six cells about 9′ by 5′, opening on to a passage which in turn looked out on to a pigsty and dung-heap. The walls were unplastered, damp greenstone; there was no light or ventilation except when the cell doors were opened; three cells were floored only with bare earth. The patients were chained to beds consisting of long boxes raised from the ground and filled with straw. Of the fourteen male patients, only one was not confined in irons.

Though the madhouses were notorious, conditions in many of the public hospitals were equally horrifying. In London's Bethlehem Hospital, mentioned earlier, patients lay howling in chains while the curious public bought tickets to see them perform. (The word *bedlam,* meaning chaos and confusion, is derived from the name of this hospital.) In other hospitals, patients were chained, caged, starved, preyed upon by rats, left for years lying naked in their own excrement, and, as at Bethlehem, displayed in their misery for the amusement of the public (Foucault, 1965).

The first serious efforts to improve treatment in the large hospitals began in the late eighteenth century. In 1789, Vincenzo Chiarugi, superintendent of the newly opened Ospedale di Bonifazio, a hospital for the mentally ill in Florence, published regulations stressing the need for humane treatment, ordering that the patients be provided with work and recre-

A nineteenth-century technique (*left*) for treating depression: the unhappy person was spun in a rotating chair.

A precursor of the strait jacket (*above*), this nineteenth-century crib was used to restrain violent patients. (The Bettmann Archive)

ation, and forbidding the use of restraint (e.g., chains) unless absolutely necessary (Maher and Maher, 1985b). But the most famous instance of reform, roughly contemporary with Chiarugi's, took place at La Bicêtre, a large hospital in Paris. This effort was due in large part to a layman with no special training, Jean-Baptiste Pussin, who was superintendent of the hospital's "incurables" ward from 1784 to 1802. Upon taking his post, Pussin laid down new rules. One was that the staff was forbidden to beat the patients. As Pussin later recalled, this innovation caused a near-insurrection on the part of the staff: "The attendants tried to rebel against me, saying that they were not safe. . . . But, despite their clamors, I persisted in my resolve and, to reach my goal, I was forced to dismiss almost all of them in turn when they disobeyed" (quoted by Weiner, 1979, p. 1133). Even more shocking was Pussin's decision to unchain a group of patients who, having been declared "furious," had lain in shackles for years (some of them for decades). Without their chains, these patients could now move about on the grounds, take the fresh air, and feel some sense of personal liberty. As Pussin had hoped, many of them became more manageable.

Pussin's reforms were extended by Philippe Pinel (1745–1826), who became chief physician of La Bicêtre's ward for the mentally ill in 1793. (Pinel, in fact, has usually received credit for Pussin's innovations.) Pinel's position was that the mentally ill were simply ordinary human beings who had been deprived of their reason by severe personal problems; to treat them like animals was not only inhumane but also obstructive to recovery. Pinel replaced the dungeons in which the patients had been kept with airy, sunny rooms and did away with violent treatments such as bleeding, purging, and cupping (blistering the skin with small hot cups). Furthermore, he spent long hours talking with the patients, listening to their problems, and giving them comfort and advice. He also kept records of these conversations and began to develop a case history for each patient. This practice of record keeping, introduced by Pinel, was an extremely important innovation, for it allowed practitioners to chart the characteristic *patterns* that emerge in the course of various disorders. Knowledge of these patterns has become the basis for the classification of disorders, for research into their causes, and for treatment.

Later Pinel, with the help of Pussin, reorganized the ward for the mentally ill at another large hospital in Paris, La Salpêtrière, along the same lines. After Pinel's retirement, his student and successor, Jean Esquirol (1772–1840), continued the reform movement, founding ten new mental hospitals in various parts of France, all based on the humane treatment developed by Pussin and Pinel.

At the same time that Pussin and Pinel were working at La Bicêtre, a Quaker named William Tuke was attempting similar reforms in northern England. Con-

Philippe Pinel supervises the unchaining of the inmates at La Salpêtrière, the hospital he directed after his work at La Bicêtre. The reforms of Pussin, Pinel, and Tuke led to a widespread movement called moral therapy. (Rapho/Photo Researchers)

vinced that the most therapeutic environment for the mentally ill would be a quiet and supportive religious setting, Tuke moved a group of mental patients to a rural estate which he called York Retreat. There they talked out their problems, worked, prayed, rested, and took walks through the countryside. Not surprisingly, York Retreat's recovery rate was high.

Though vigorously resisted by Pinel's and Tuke's contemporaries, these new techniques eventually became widespread, under the name of **moral therapy.** Based on the idea that the mentally ill were simply ordinary people with extraordinary problems, moral therapy aimed at restoring their "morale" by providing a pleasant and relaxed environment in which they could discuss their difficulties, live in peace, and engage in some useful employment. More than anything else, moral therapy aimed at treating patients like human beings. And apparently this approach was extremely successful. Contemporary records show that during the first half of the nineteenth century, when moral therapy was the only treatment provided by mental hospitals in Europe and America, at least 70 percent of those hospitalized either improved or actually recovered (Bockoven, 1963).

The Reform Movement in America   The foremost figure in the development of the American mental health establishment was Benjamin Rush (1745–1813), born in the same year as Pinel and known as the "father of American psychiatry." A famous doctor and a remarkable man he was a signer of the Declaration of Independence, a member of the Continental Congress, surgeon general to the Continental Army, treasurer of the United States Mint, and founder of the first free medical dispensary and the first antislavery society in America—Rush advanced the cause of mental health by writing the first American treatise on mental problems (*Medical Inquiries and Observations upon the Diseases of the Mind,* 1812), by organizing the first medical course in psychiatry, and by devoting his attention, as the foremost physician at Philadelphia Hospital, exclusively to mental problems.

In retrospect, Rush's theories seem primitive: he believed that mental illness was due to an excess of blood in the vessels of the brain, produced in response to overexcitement. The treatments to which this theory led him seem even more primitive. To relieve the pressure in the blood vessels, he relied very heavily on bleeding. Another of his favorite practices, aimed at slowing the flow of blood to the brain, was to strap patients into a device called the "tranquilizer"

or to drop them suddenly into ice-cold baths. These procedures, however, were clearly intended not to torture but to cure, and were accompanied by a number of very humane practices. For example, Rush recommended that doctors regularly bring little presents such as fruit or cake to their patients. He also insisted that Philadelphia Hospital hire kind and intelligent attendants—people who could read to patients, talk to them, and share in their activities. In sum, Rush contributed a great deal to American psychiatry, lending it his prestige and moving it in the direction of a humane therapy.

The task of extending these reforms was taken up by a Boston schoolteacher named Dorothea Dix (1802–1887). At the age of forty Dix took a job teaching Sunday school in a prison. There she had her first contact with the gruesome conditions suffered

Dorothea Dix, nineteenth-century reformer, campaigned for humane treatment of the disturbed and was instrumental in the establishment of public mental hospitals. (The Granger Collection)

by the mentally ill. Soon she was traveling across the country, visiting the squalid jails and poorhouses in which the mentally ill were confined and lecturing state legislators on their duty to these miserable and forgotten people. To the Massachusetts legislature she spoke as follows:

> I come to place before the Legislature of Massachusetts the condition of the miserable, the desolate, the outcast. I come as the advocate of helpless, forgotten, insane and idiotic men and women . . . of beings wretched in our prisons, and more wretched in our Alms-Houses.
>
> I proceed, Gentlemen, briefly to call your attention to the state of Insane Persons confined within this Commonwealth, in *cages, closets, cellars, stalls, pens: Chained, naked, beaten with rods,* and lashed into obedience (quoted in Deutsch, 1949, p. 165).

Dix extended her campaign across the United States, to Canada, and to Scotland. She was directly responsible for the founding and funding of thirty-two mental hospitals.

The Decline of Moral Therapy   Dix's reforms had one unfortunate result that she could not have anticipated: they contributed to the decline of moral therapy (Foucault, 1965). As hospital after hospital opened, there were simply not enough advocates of moral therapy to staff them. Indeed, there were not enough staff of any kind, for though the state governments were willing to build mental hospitals, they still did not consider mental health as important as physical health. This meant less money for mental hospitals, and less money meant less staff. At the same time, the patient populations of these hospitals grew year by year, so that soon the patient–staff ratio was such as to preclude altogether the sort of tranquil atmosphere and individual care essential to moral therapy. Walled off in somber isolation in rural areas, the new mental hospitals also helped the public to unlearn the lesson that Pinel and Tuke had worked so hard to teach: that the mentally ill were simply ordinary people. To the public mind, these huge fortresses seemed to conceal some dark horror, and the mentally disturbed were once again seen as freakish, dangerous, and alien.

But there were other reasons for the decline of moral therapy (Bockoven, 1963). To begin with, the first generation of its advocates—practitioners such

as Pinel and Tuke—were not succeeded by an equally powerful second generation. As a new movement, moral therapy needed influential leaders, and no such leaders came forth after its founders died. Second, by the turn of the century, many of the indigent patients who filled the mental hospitals were Irish Catholic immigrants, against whom there was considerable prejudice. The Protestant establishment might be willing to pay for these patients' hospitalization, but not for the luxury of moral therapy.

Finally, the growth of the state mental hospital system occurred at the same time as the rise of the medical model. The early successes of the medical model convinced psychiatric professionals that their efforts should be directed toward biological research rather than toward creating the total therapeutic environments typical of moral therapy. The medical model also convinced them that patients should not be released until they were "cured," so that, as the years passed, more and more beds were occupied by chronic, long-term patients, who never got better and never left.

Thus moral therapy fell into disuse. Recovery rates dropped considerably and did not rise again for several decades (Bockoven, 1963; Dain, 1964). More and more of the people who suffered from mental disturbance were put into large and usually grim public hospitals. This situation continued until the middle of the present century, when the phenothiazines, a new class of antipsychotic drugs, were introduced. Sedatives, or calming medications, had been given to mental patients for decades. But the phenothiazines were far more effective, and they have been the major factor in reducing the number of institutionalized patients in recent years. Patients who previously might have been locked away for long periods now moved to open wards or halfway houses, or into the community itself. The use of drugs, which is proving to be a milestone in the history of treatment, will be discussed in detail in Chapter 20. It should be noted here, however, that the widespread acceptance of these drugs in recent years has lent even more support to the medical model.

Foundations of Modern Abnormal Psychology

In the late nineteenth century, as the new mental hospitals were opening throughout the United States, the study of abnormal psychology was rapidly expanding in both Europe and America. New theories were being introduced and tested, while opposing theories arose to challenge them. At the same time, theorists were developing new ways of classifying and studying abnormal behavior.

The Experimental Study of Abnormal Behavior   In 1879, Wilhelm Wundt, a professor of physiology at the University of Leipzig, Germany, established a laboratory for the scientific study of psychology—that is, the application of scientific experimentation, with precise methods of measurement and control, to human thought and behavior. The opening of Wundt's laboratory is often cited as the beginning of modern psychology. It was also a critical step in the development of abnormal psychology, for the methods taught by Wundt were soon applied to abnormal as well as normal behavior.

Among Wundt's students was the German researcher Emil Kraepelin (1856–1926), who eventually established his own psychological laboratory, devoted primarily to the study of **psychopathology,** or abnormal psychology. There Kraepelin and his students investigated how psychopathology was related to movement, to fatigue, to emotion, to speech, and to memory. They also studied the effects of drugs on different kinds of psychological abnormality (Maher and Maher, 1979).

Kraepelin's example was followed elsewhere. In 1904 the first American laboratory for experimental work with mental patients opened at the McLean Hospital in Massachusetts. Other hospitals soon established laboratories of their own, and experimental abnormal psychology made substantial strides in the first two decades of the century. Thereafter, it fell behind somewhat, as a result of the rising popularity of psychodynamic theory, which, at least in its early years, did not lend itself to experimental study. But in the 1950s the experimental branch of abnormal psychology once again became influential and productive, and it has remained so ever since, providing, as we shall see, some of the most important current findings in the field.

Kraepelin and Biogenic Theory   Biogenic theory, as we have seen, originated in ancient times and persisted, though sometimes obscured by supernaturalism, through the Middle Ages and Renais-

sance. Then, in the late eighteenth and early nineteenth centuries, when medical research was making rapid advances, it again became dominant. The first systematic presentation of the biogenic theory of mental disturbance was made by a German psychiatrist, Wilhelm Griesinger, in the mid-nineteenth century. But it was Kraepelin, the founder of experimental abnormal psychology, who first placed the medical model in the forefront of European psychiatric theory. In his *Textbook of Psychiatry* (1883), Kraepelin not only argued for the central role of brain pathology in mental disturbance but furnished psychiatry with its first comprehensive classification system, based on the biogenic viewpoint. He contended that mental illness, like physical illness, could be classified into separate pathologies, each of which had a different organic cause and each of which could be recognized by a distinct cluster of symptoms, called a **syndrome.** Once the symptoms appeared, the mental disturbance could be diagnosed according to the classification system. And once it was diagnosed, its course and outcome could be expected to resemble those seen in other cases of the same illness, just as one case of mumps can be expected to develop and turn out like other cases of mumps.

Kraepelin's organic theory and his classification system received wide publicity and generated high hopes that the hitherto impenetrable mysteries of mental illness might be shown to have concrete, chemically manageable organic causes. At the same time, the neurological and genetic components of psychopathology were gaining attention through the writings of another famous follower of Griesinger, Richard von Krafft-Ebing (1840–1902), who emphasized organic and hereditary causation in his *Textbook of Psychiatry* (1879) and in his pioneering encyclopedia of sexual disorders, *Psychopathia Sexualis* (1886). It was from the work of these early theorists that the modern medical model of mental disturbance evolved.

As we noted earlier, the medical model in its early days produced brilliant results. By the turn of the century, neurological research was progressing so rapidly that it seemed that the hopes raised by Kraepelin might at last be in the process of fulfillment. The senile psychoses, the toxic psychoses, cerebral arteriosclerosis, mental retardation—one mental syndrome after another was linked to a specific brain pathology. The most stunning success of all, however, was the discovery, through the work of Krafft-Ebing and other scientists, that **general paresis,** a mysterious mental syndrome involving the gradual and irreversible breakdown of physical and mental functioning, was actually an advanced case of syphilis, in which the syphilitic microorganisms had passed through the bloodstream and into the central nervous system and the brain.

This discovery had an immense impact on the mental health profession and helped to establish the medical model in the lofty position it still occupies today. However, at the same time that neurological research was nourishing biogenic theory, other findings were laying the foundation for a comprehensive **psychogenic theory,** the theory that psychological disturbance is due primarily not to organic dysfunction but to emotional stress.

Mesmer and Hypnosis   The history of modern psychogenic theory begins with a colorful and controversial figure, Franz Anton Mesmer (1733–1815). Mesmer, an Austrian physician, subscribed to the belief that heavenly bodies influenced psychological states. According to Mesmer, the movement of the planets controlled the distribution of a universal magnetic fluid, and the shiftings of this magnetic fluid were responsible for the health or sickness of mind and body. Furthermore, he was convinced that this princi-

ple of "animal magnetism" could be used in the treatment of hysteria, a common complaint at the time, especially in women.

Mesmer's therapy for his hysterical patients was rather exotic. The patients would enter a room and seat themselves around a huge vat containing bottles of various fluids from which iron rods protruded. The lights were dimmed and soft music was played. Then Mesmer himself appeared, "magnetic" wand in hand, and passed from patient to patient, touching various parts of their bodies with his hands, with his wand, and with the rods protruding from the vat, in order to readjust the distribution of their magnetic fluids.

The most striking aspect of this treatment is that it seems in many cases to have worked. Nonetheless, Mesmer's theory of "animal magnetism" was investigated by a special commission and declared invalid. Yet even the investigating physicians noted in their reports what has since been recognized as Mesmer's great contribution to abnormal psychology: the discovery of the power of suggestion to cure mental disorder. Mesmer is now acknowledged to have been the first practitioner of **hypnosis** (originally known as "mesmerism"), an artificially induced trance in which the subject becomes highly susceptible to suggestion. Mesmer was eventually barred from practice in Vienna and Paris, but mesmerism continued to be practiced by others.

Early hypnosis, or "mesmerism." Soft music and dim light were used to soothe patients, easing their way into a trancelike state in which they would be susceptible to the power of suggestion. (The Bettmann Archive)

The Nancy School   Some years after Mesmer's death, his findings were reexamined by two enterprising French physicians, Ambrose-Auguste Liébeault (1823–1904) and Hippolyte-Marie Bernheim (1840–1919), both practicing in Nancy, a city in eastern France. For four years Bernheim had been treating a patient, with no success. Finally, after hearing that a certain Dr. Liébeault was having considerable success with unconventional methods, Bernheim sent the patient to him. When the patient returned shortly afterward completely cured, Bernheim naturally called on Liébeault to ask what he had done. What Liébeault had done was simple: he had hypnotized the patient and then had told him, while he was under hypnosis, that when he awakened, his symptoms would be gone (Selling, 1940).

Bernheim was persuaded, and thereafter the two physicians worked as a team. Together they discovered that hysteria could not only be cured but also induced by hypnosis. For example, if a hypnotized

Jean-Martin Charcot, a nineteenth-century French neurologist, was active in the crucial debate over whether hysteria—and other psychological disorders—had emotional or organic origins. (Morath/Magnum)

subject were told that he or she had no feeling in the hand—as is the case in **glove anesthesia,** a form of hysteria—the hand could then be pricked with a needle without producing any response from the subject. On the basis of such findings, Liébeault and Bernheim evolved the theory that hysteria was actually a form of self-hypnosis and that other mental disorders might also be due entirely to psychological causes.

This view eventually won a number of adherents, who became known as the "Nancy school." The Nancy school soon came under direct attack by a formidable challenger, Jean-Martin Charcot (1825–1893), a famous Parisian neurologist who at that time was director of La Salpêtrière Hospital. Charcot had also experimented with hypnosis but had eventually abandoned it and was convinced that hysteria was due to actual organic damage. The debate between the Paris school, consisting of Charcot and his supporters, and the Nancy school was one of the earliest major academic debates in the history of modern psychology. Eventually the insurgent Nancy school triumphed, and Charcot himself was later won over to the psychogenic theory of hysteria. However, the ramifications of this debate extended far beyond the specific problem of hysteria, for it raised the possibility that any number

of psychological disorders might in fact be due to emotional states rather than to organic causes.

Breuer and Freud: The Beginnings of Psychoanalysis   One of the many students of Charcot was Sigmund Freud (1856–1939), a young Viennese physician who had come to Paris to study under the great neurologist. Later Freud became acquainted with the methods of Liébeault and Bernheim as well, and when he returned to Vienna, he went to work with a physician named Josef Breuer (1842–1925), who at that time was also experimenting with the use of hypnosis. A few years earlier Breuer had treated a woman, later known to medical history as "Anna O.," who was troubled by hysterical paralysis, inability to eat, and various disturbances of sight and speech. Somewhat by chance, Breuer discovered that under hypnosis the patient was able to discuss her problems quite uninhibitedly, and that after doing so, she obtained some relief from her symptoms. Breuer, quick to recognize the therapeutic value of this emotional purging, called it the "cathartic method," or "talking cure" (Jones, 1953).

Together Breuer and Freud experimented extensively with "talking cures." They soon became convinced that hysteria and other disorders were caused by "unconscious" conflicts that could be drawn out under hypnosis; once aired, the conflicts would lose their power to maintain the symptoms. In 1895 Breuer and Freud published their findings in a volume titled *Studies in Hysteria.* This book, in which the authors put forth their theory of the unconscious, has become a milestone in the history of psychology.

Later, working independently, Freud abandoned hypnosis. To begin with, not everyone could be hypnotized. Furthermore, Freud had found that he could obtain the same result—the loosening of inhibitions—by a technique that he called **free association:** patients were asked to relax on a couch and simply to pour out whatever came to mind. Patients were also encouraged to talk about their dreams and their childhood. Freud then interpreted this material to the patient on the basis of the theories he was gradually constructing as to the nature of the unconscious mind. To this form of therapy, in which the patient is cured through the gradual understanding of unconscious conflicts, Freud gave the name **psychoanalysis.**

The development of his theories of the unconscious (which will be explained in Chapter 2) occupied the remainder of Freud's long and fruitful career. These theories, because of their novelty, were regarded with extreme skepticism by many of his contemporaries and did not become influential in the field of mental health until the 1920s. Since that time, however, they have become the basis for the entire psychodynamic perspective and have exerted a massive influence on all areas of twentieth-century thought.

A MULTIPERSPECTIVE APPROACH

In our discussion so far, we have seen a wide variety of perspectives on abnormal behavior. In the remainder of this book we will attempt to take a broad approach, combining the insights and discoveries of several perspectives. This approach rests on four basic assumptions. The first is that *human behavior can be studied scientifically.* That is, scientists can observe objectively both behavior and the environment in which it occurs. From these observations they can draw conclusions as to the causes of behavior, and knowing these causes, they can predict and influence behavior.

Second, this book will proceed on the assumption that *most abnormal behavior is the product of both psychological and biological processes.* The unobservable events of the mind, such as attitudes, memories, and desires, are unquestionably involved in most forms of psychopathology. And psychopathology, in turn, is connected to biological events: the secretion of hormones by the glands, the movement of electrical impulses across the brain, and so forth. How these events hook together in the web of causation—which is the primary cause, which the result, and whether the results have in turn caused other results, both psychological and biological—is, as we shall see, a maddeningly complex question.

The third assumption of this book is the *integrity of the individual.* Human behavior may be discussed in general terms, and it may be traced to certain social and biological determinants. Nevertheless, it still issues from individuals, each of whom has a unique set of memories, desires, and expectations, and each of whom has some ability to control his or her behavior.

Finally, we assume that *human behavior is highly complex* and that allowance must be made for this complexity. People's emotions must be taken into account along with their physical makeup, their cultural environment, and their personal history. Furthermore, individuals must be seen not as either normal or abnormal but as complicated beings with a wide range of behaviors, each of which may fall in a different spot on a continuum ranging from the most adaptive and fulfilling to the most defeating and distressing. Finally, to add to the complexity, those behaviors that are the most defeating—the most "abnormal"— must be seen as issuing from the same causes and as following the same principles as the most normal behaviors. In short, all people have reasons for the things they do, and though their actions may vary widely, their reasons are usually quite similar. We all experience such feelings as attraction and loathing, hope and despair, self-love and self-contempt. And though these feelings may be translated into an infinitely wide range of behaviors, we still cannot afford to isolate any one of these behaviors as freakish or alien.

Working from this comprehensive approach, we shall stress in the following chapters the four current psychological perspectives on human behavior that we described earlier: the psychodynamic, behavioral, humanistic-existential, and neuroscience perspectives. Each of these viewpoints is narrower and more specific than the broad approach we have just defined, and more often than not they disagree with one another. But taken together, they provide a comprehensive and many-faceted view of human psychology as it is understood today.

The plan of this book is as follows. Chapters 2, 3, 4, and 5 will examine the four major perspectives, along with a few less comprehensive viewpoints. Chapters 6 and 7 will cover research methods and diagnostic assessment, respectively. Chapters 8 through 19 will describe the most common categories of abnormal psychology and will discuss the theories and treatments offered by the different perspectives with regard to these disorders. Chapters 20 and 21 will review the general methods of treatment developed by the major perspectives. Finally, Chapter 22 will examine some current legal and ethical issues in abnormal psychology.

SUMMARY

Psychological abnormality is a concept that varies from century to century and from society to society. A society may use several approaches to define psychological abnormality. Possibly the most common is norm violation: a behavior that most people regard as wrong or improper is considered abnormal. Other approaches classify a behavior as abnormal when it is statistically rare, when it brings personal discomfort to the individual who exhibits it, when it is maladaptive, or when it deviates from a theoretical ideal. Each of these approaches has its drawbacks, and in practice abnormal behavior is usually identified on the basis of a combination of these criteria.

Just as there are many definitions of abnormality, there are many ways to explain it. According to the medical model, abnormal behavior is like a disease. Even if it is not actually biogenic, or the result of organic dysfunction, it should be conceptualized and treated medically. Among the various psychological approaches to abnormality, the psychodynamic perspective assumes that abnormal behavior originates in unconscious childhood conflicts; the behavioral perspective holds that abnormality is caused by inappropriate conditioning; and the humanistic-existential perspective attributes abnormal behavior to a failure to accept or take responsibility for oneself. The recently

developed neuroscience perspective, like the medical model, focuses on the organic components of abnormal behavior, but it does not insist that abnormal behavior is merely symptomatic of biological abnormality or that treatment must be medical.

The treatment of abnormal behavior typically depends on the nature of the society, the criterion by which abnormality is defined, and the society's explanation of abnormal behavior.

The earliest societies seem to have regarded abnormal behavior as the product of supernatural forces. An accepted method of dealing with disturbing behavior was to drive out evil spirits by various forms of exorcism, although much abnormality was probably treated in less dramatic ways. A more scientific approach to abnormality evolved in ancient Greece; the physician Hippocrates observed and recorded cases of mental disturbance, developed an organic theory of abnormal behavior, attempted to classify abnormal mental states, and adopted humane methods of treatment. His approach survived until the fall of the Roman Empire in the fifth century A.D.

In the Middle Ages, abnormal behavior was often attributed to demonic possession, and cures ranged from prayers and other gentle measures to starvation and flogging. However, abnormality was often regarded as a naturally caused phenomenon. In the Renaissance, thousands of people—many of whom exhibited abnormal behavior—were executed as witches. But most of the deranged were probably of no interest to the witch hunters; they were kept in hospitals or institutions for the poor, generally under horrible conditions.

Though hospitalization of the insane became more common in the eighteenth and nineteenth centuries, little effort was made to improve treatment until the reforms of Vincenzo Chiarugi in Florence and of the better-known Frenchmen Jean-Baptiste Pussin and Philippe Pinel at La Bicêtre, a Paris asylum, in the late eighteenth century. The leaders of this reform movement in nineteenth-century America were Benjamin Rush and Dorothea Dix. These reformers advocated moral therapy, or improving the morale of the mentally ill through peaceful living, useful employment, and dignified treatment.

Although remarkably successful, moral therapy declined in the late nineteenth century, partly because of the rise of the medical model. Wilhelm Wundt and his student Emil Kraepelin were pioneers in applying scientific methods to the study of human thought and behavior, and the work of Kraepelin and others brought the medical model to the forefront. At the same time, psychogenic theories, which attribute mental disorder to emotional stress, also began to gain prominence. The controversial work of Franz Anton Mesmer, who discovered the power of suggestion to cure some mental disorders, laid the groundwork for psychogenic theory.

Mesmer's efforts were expanded upon by the members of the Nancy school, notably Ambrose-Auguste Liébeault and Hippolyte-Marie Bernheim, and later the rival Paris school, under Jean-Martin Charcot. Sigmund Freud, a student of Charcot, and Josef Breuer became convinced that mental disorders were caused by "unconscious" conflicts that, once revealed under hypnosis, could be resolved. But Freud later abandoned hypnosis, replacing it with his technique of free association, and developed his pioneering theory of psychoanalysis.

This book will take a broad approach to abnormal behavior which draws on several perspectives. This approach rests on the assumptions that human behavior can be studied scientifically, that most abnormal behavior is the product of both psychological and biological processes, that human behavior issues from each individual's uniqueness and ability to control his or her behavior to some degree, and that human behavior is highly complex. The perspectives that will be stressed are the psychodynamic, the behavioral, the humanistic-existential, and the neuroscience. Though they often conflict with one another, these perspectives offer a comprehensive and multidimensional view of contemporary abnormal psychology.

Historical and Theoretical Perspectives

The Psychodynamic Perspective

The **psychodynamic perspective** is a school of thought that encompasses a group of theories and therapies united by a common concern with the dynamics, or interaction, of forces lying deep within the mind. Different theorists emphasize different aspects of mental dynamics, but almost all psychodynamic theorists agree on three basic principles. First is that of psychic determinism: that much of our behavior is not freely chosen, but, on the contrary, is determined by the nature and strength of intrapsychic forces. Second is the belief that such forces operate, for the most part, unconsciously—in other words, that the true motives of our behavior are largely unknown to us. Third, most psychodynamic thinkers assume that the form these forces take is deeply affected by early childhood experience.

The founding father of the psychodynamic perspec-

tive was Sigmund Freud, a neurologist by training, who began his practice in Vienna at the end of the nineteenth century. At this time the most common complaints brought to the neurologist were physical disorders—such as paralysis—for which no physical cause could be found. As we saw in Chapter 1, the idea that the origin of such disorders might be psychological rather than physiological had already been proposed by Liébeault and Bernheim, and various psychological treatments—hypnosis, Breuer's "cathartic method"—were being attempted. Convinced by this approach, Freud at the beginning of his career set himself the task of discovering the specific psychological causes involved and of working out an effective cure. Within a few years (1894) he had put forth the idea that these disorders with no apparent physical cause, called *hysteria* at that time, involved a

Sigmund Freud, the father of psychodynamic theory.
(National Library of Medicine)

defense against unbearable memories or ideas. (The hand may be "paralyzed," for example, to overcome an urge to strike out.) From this seed grew his theory of **psychoanalysis,** which was to occupy him for the rest of his life and by which, ultimately, he sought to explain not just hysteria but the whole of human behavior, normal and abnormal.

The psychodynamic perspective is by no means bounded by Freud's theory. It is a large and living school of thought, by now nearly a century old, built of proposals and counterproposals, propositions and refinements, contributed by many thoughtful theorists besides Freud. It is impossible, however, in the space of this chapter to give appropriate coverage to all who made significant contributions to the psychodynamic perspective.[*] Furthermore, Freud's theory, however much it has been challenged and revised, is still the foundation on which all later psychodynamic

thought has been based. Therefore this chapter will give first and fullest consideration to Freud—that is, to the most "classical" psychodynamic position. Then we will describe the ways in which later theorists have revised and expanded this view. Finally, we will discuss the arguments for and against the psychodynamic perspective.

BASIC CONCEPTS OF FREUDIAN THEORY

The Depth Psychology Hypothesis

The key concept of psychoanalysis, and Freud's most important contribution to psychology, is the **depth psychology hypothesis,** the idea that almost all mental activity takes place unconsciously. According to Freud, the mind is divided into two levels. At the surface is the **perceptual conscious,** consisting of the narrow range of mental events of which the individual is aware at any given instant. Beneath the perceptual conscious lies the **unconscious,** consisting of all the psychological materials (memories, desires, fears, etc.) that the mind is not attending to at that moment.

The unconscious, in turn, is divided into two levels, depending on the retrievability of its contents. Materials that are normally unconscious but still easily retrievable are said to belong to the **preconscious.** If, for example, you are asked the date of the French Revolution and say "1789," you have called this date up from the preconscious. According to Freud, however, by far the greater part of unconscious mental contents is not readily accessible to consciousness, and it was this vast repository of hidden materials, called the *unconscious proper,* that was Freud's primary interest. Although in Freud's schema the unconscious includes both the preconscious and the unconscious proper, he tended in his writings to use the term *unconscious* to mean solely the unconscious proper. We will do the same.

It was Freud's belief that the things we forget do not in fact drop out of the mind. They simply go into the unconscious. Furthermore, much of this "forgotten" material does not passively fade from retrievable memory, as we might forget the phone number of a friend we have lost touch with. Rather, it is actively forgotten, forced out of consciousness, because it is disturbing to us—a process called **repres-**

---

[*] Neither is it possible to do justice to Freud's views in one short chapter. He was an extraordinarily prolific writer; the English edition of his collected writings, known as *The Standard Edition of the Complete Psychological Works of Sigmund Freud* (London: Hogarth Press, 1953–1974), fills twenty-four volumes. Furthermore, Freud constantly revised and refined his ideas throughout his long life. The reader should be aware that what is presented in this chapter is a condensation of a complex and extensive collection of theories.

sion. These censored materials may erupt into consciousness when psychological controls are relaxed—for example, under hypnosis, under anesthesia, and above all in dreams. But during our normal waking hours the contents of the unconscious are kept tightly sealed from our awareness. At the same time—and this is the crucial point—these unconscious materials always play some role in determining our behavior. When we like one movie rather than another or marry one person rather than another, we do so not only for the reasons that we tell ourselves and our friends, but also because of events from our past that are now hidden from us—a fascinating and disturbing notion. From this it follows that if we are unhappy with our behavior and want to change it, we have to unearth from the unconscious the repressed memories and associated conflicts that are causing the problems. And that, precisely, is the goal of psychoanalytic therapy: as Freud himself put it, "to make the unconscious conscious."

The Necessity of Interpretation

If Freud is correct in his archeological, or "topographic," conception of the human mind—that is, that the origins of our behavior are buried deep in the psyche—then psychology, in its search for causes, cannot confine itself simply to observing surface behavior. Rather, it must *interpret* behavior, decode it, revealing the intrapsychic motives. This method, interpretation, was the primary tool of Freud's theory-building and of his therapy. In all human behavior—actions, dreams, jokes, works of art—he saw two layers of meaning: the **manifest content,** or surface meaning, and the **latent content,** or true, unconscious meaning. The goal of his theoretical writings was to reveal, via interpretation, the latent content: unconscious forces that cause people to say what they say, dream what they dream, live as they live. Freud did not claim that unconscious forces alone motivate behavior. He argued rather that behavior is "multidetermined"—that it has many contributing causes, including unconscious forces, and that those forces have to be uncovered if behavior is to be truly understood (or changed). In his therapy, this analysis of behavior took the form of *interpretation:* he would lead patients to an understanding of their feelings and actions by pinpointing what he saw as their operative unconscious motives.

"Readings" of behavior can of course be faulty.

Worse yet, it is difficult to find out scientifically whether or not they *are* faulty. However, as many psychological writers have pointed out (e.g., Bruner, 1973; Erdelyi and Goldberg, 1979; Neisser, 1967; Norman, 1976), some decoding process, whether or not it is called "interpretation," is indispensable to human communication and is used not just by Freudian theorists but by all of us, every day. When we "get" a joke, what we get is the connection between its surface meaning and its real, unstated meaning. When someone you have asked for a date replies that she is busy for the next month, you naturally understand her to mean not that she is actually booked every night for the next thirty-one days but that she does not wish to go out with you. And the ability to get along in human society depends on our reading beneath such statements. Interpretation, then, was by no means a Freudian innovation. What was innovative in Freud's position was, first, his offering of interpretation as a potentially *scientific* method; and, second, his use of interpretation to identify *unconscious* motives for our behavior (as when we "forget" to do things we don't want to do). In the next section we shall see what Freud's use of interpretation led him to hypothesize about the human mind.

The Structural Hypothesis: Id, Ego, and Superego

Some years after his formulation of the depth psychology hypothesis, Freud constructed a second, and complementary, psychic schema. As we have seen, the defining characteristic of psychodynamic theory, as handed down from Freud, is its concern with the interaction of forces within the mind. In 1923 Freud proposed a simple preliminary model, the so-called **structural hypothesis.** This hypothesis holds that the mind can be divided into three basic forces: the id, the ego, and the superego. These three forces are continually interacting with one another, and since each has a different goal, that interaction often takes the form of conflict.

The Id   At birth, according to Freud's hypothesis, the energy of the mind is bound up entirely in primitive biological drives, to which Freud gave the collective term **id.** The id is the foundation of the psychic structure and the source from which the later developments of ego and superego must borrow their energy.

The force of the id dominates much of the behavior of infants and small children. This child simply *wants* his teddy bear and neither understands nor cares about the logical reasons he cannot have it. (Kenneth Garrett/Woodfin Camp & Associates)

The drives that make up the id are of two basic types, sexual and aggressive—the former above all.* Freud saw the sexual drive as permeating the entire

---

* On the matter of basic drives, as on other points, Freud changed his theory several times. In his early writings, he proposed that there were two basic drives, the sexual drive and the ego (or self-preservation) drive. Then, from about 1914 until 1920, he concluded that self-preservation was merely an aspect of the sexual drive, which Freud now felt was the sole driving force of the personality. Finally, after 1920, he elevated aggression to the status of a basic drive, along with sex—a position he took at least in part in response to the horrors of World War I. But in all these stages of his thought, the primacy of the sexual drive is a constant.

personality and subsuming, in addition to actual erotic behavior, a wide range of other life-sustaining pursuits, such as the need for food and warmth, the love of friends and family, and the impulse toward creativity. These and other positive desires, in Freud's view, were extensions and transformations of a basic sexual drive, which he named the **libido** and which he saw as the major source of psychic energy.

The id has two important characteristics. First, it operates entirely on what Freud called the **pleasure principle.** That is, it is utterly hedonistic, seeking only its own pleasure or release from tension and taking no account of logic or reason, reality or morality. Hungry infants, for example, do not ask themselves whether it is time for their feeding or whether their mothers may be busy doing something else; they simply want food, and so they cry for it. According to Freud, we are, at some level, still hungry infants, no matter how old we are.

Second, thought patterns directed by the id take on a primitive form that Freud called **primary process thinking.** In this style of thinking, as in the operations of the pleasure principle, reality and logic play no role. Different time periods are collapsed into one; an image may represent both itself and its opposite; above all, the image may be mistaken for the real thing. Infants, Freud speculated, think in this way. So do adults when they dream, when they are engaged in artistic creation, and when they succumb to severe mental disorders such as schizophrenia.

The Ego   While the id can imagine what it wants, it has no way of determining which means of dealing with the world are safe and which are not. To fulfill these functions, the mind develops a new psychic component, the ego. Deriving its energy from the id, the **ego** mediates between the id and the forces that restrict the id's satisfactions, namely, reality and the superego. (The superego is described below.) The ego may be said to appear after the child is about six months old, though ego functions begin to develop shortly after birth and emerge slowly over a period of years.

While the id operates on the pleasure principle, the ego operates on the **reality principle,** the most important feature of which is the concern for safety. When the id signals its desire, the ego locates in reality a potential gratifier for the desire, anticipates the consequences of using that gratifier, and then either reaches out for it or, if the consequences could be dangerous, delays the id's satisfaction until a more appropriate means of gratification can be found.

Let us imagine, for example, a three-year-old girl playing in her room. The id signals that aggressive impulses seek release, and the girl reaches for her toy hammer. The ego then goes into action, scanning the environment. The girl's baby brother is playing nearby. Should she clobber him over the head with her hammer? The ego, which knows from experience that this will result in the painful consequence of a spanking, says no and continues the scanning process. Also nearby is a big lump of clay. The ego determines that no harm will come from pounding the clay, and so the girl proceeds to bang away at it.

This mediating process obviously requires more sober calculations than those of which the id is capable. While the id uses primary process thinking, the ego uses **secondary process thinking,** a more advanced style of thinking that takes into account reason, logic, and the distinctions among different times, objects and people, and situations. According to Freud, it is from the ego's weighing of these considerations in order to serve the id that the mind develops and refines all of its higher functions: language, perception, learning, discrimination, memory, judgment, and planning. All these are ego functions.

The Superego   Imagine that three years later the same girl once again sits with hammer in hand looking for something to pound. Again she considers her brother's head, and again she rejects that outlet. This time, however, she rejects it not because it would result in a spanking but because it would be "bad." What this means is that the child has developed a superego.

The **superego** is that part of the mind that represents the moral standards of the society as interpreted by the parents. As a consequence of the resolution of the Oedipus complex, which we will discuss shortly, the child internalizes the parents' standards, and these standards come together to form the third psychic component, which, like the ego, gets its energy from the id. This new superego, which is approximately equivalent to what we call "conscience," takes no more account of reality than the id does. Instead of considering what is realistic or possible, it embraces an abstract **ego ideal** (a composite picture of values and moral ideals) and, in keeping with that ideal, demands that the sexual and aggressive impulses of the id be stifled and that moral goals be substituted instead. It is then the job of the ego to find a way to satisfy the id without eliciting censure (experienced as "remorse" or "guilt") from the superego.

Thus in the fully developed psychic structure the ego has three fairly intransigent parties to deal with: the id, which seeks only the satisfaction of its irrational

The superego develops as the child begins to internalize the parents' standards of right and wrong. (Joel Fishman/Photo Researchers)

and amoral demands; the superego, which seeks only the satisfaction of its rigid ideals; and reality, which offers only a limited range of objects for satisfying the id and which metes out stern punishment for unwise choices.

While there is no exact congruence between the components of the depth psychology hypothesis and those of the structural hypothesis, there is a rough correspondence between the two systems. The id, ego, and superego all have roots in the unconscious. However, id impulses are totally confined to the unconscious. Superego processes often take place at the unconscious level, but they may also operate in the preconscious and perceptual conscious. Ego functions likewise occur at all three levels, but of necessity the ego tends to operate at the higher levels—for, as we have seen, its role is to mediate between reality and the superego and id.

When we consider the structural hypothesis, it is important to keep in mind that id, ego, and superego are not *things* in the mind or even parts of the mind, but simply names that Freud gave to broad categories of intrapsychic forces. It is difficult, in discussing these categories, not to speak of them as if they were actual entities—the id screaming for gratification, the superego demanding the opposite, and the ego running back and forth between them, arranging compromises. But these are metaphors, nothing more. Freud himself explicitly warned against overliteral conceptualizations of psychic structure: "Do not mistake the scaffolding for the building" (1900, p. 536). Id, ego, and superego are highly simplified explanatory devices for highly complex psychological processes.

The Dynamics of the Mind

As we have seen, each of the three structural components of the psyche has its own exclusive functions. Hence these three forces are often in conflict with one another. Most of the time ego functions keep the conflict at a manageable level, by making sure that the id, superego, and reality are all given their due. At times, however, either the id or the superego will muster new strength and threaten to overwhelm the ego's controls, resulting in unacceptable feelings or behavior. In response to this threat, the individual experiences an emotion that Freud called anxiety.

Anxiety   **Anxiety,** akin to what most of us call "fear," is a state of psychic distress that acts as a signal to the ego that danger is at hand. Anxiety can have its source in reality, as when you confront a burglar in your bedroom. Or—and this of course was Freud's major concern—anxiety can originate in internal dynamics, in an id impulse that threatens to break through the ego's controls and cause the person to be punished, either by the superego (in the form of guilt) or by reality.

Anxiety can be managed in a number of ways. If, for example, a pregnant woman is afraid of childbirth, she can calm her fears by going to childbirth classes and learning how to control labor pains. However, the ego's solutions are not always so straightforward. Indeed, most anxiety is not even experienced consciously. It is kept closeted in the unconscious, and the danger dealt with, through the ego's employment of what are called defense mechanisms.

Defense Mechanisms   The ego has a tendency to distort or simply to refuse to acknowledge a reality (whether external or internal) that would arouse unbearable anxiety. This tactic is called a **defense mechanism.** We all use defense mechanisms all the time. If we did not, we would be psychologically disabled, for the facts they conceal—of the hungers of the id, of the condemnations of the superego, of the deepest traumas and darkest "sins" of childhood—would produce intolerable anxiety if they were constantly bubbling up into the conscious mind. The defense mechanisms, then, serve an invaluable adaptive function. They allow us to avoid facing what we cannot face and thus to go on with the business of living.

For this convenience, however, we pay a price. The more we turn away from anxiety-provoking realities, denying or distorting the truth, the less we are in touch with reality in general, and the less we are able to deal with it constructively. When defense mechanisms require that we never leave the house or—to use a more ordinary example—that we play "helpless" when situations become difficult, then we are sacrificing our adaptive capacities. Furthermore, it must be kept in mind that it is the ego that engineers these defenses. If most of the ego's energy is tied up in the job of maintaining defenses, then the ego will have little strength left for its other functions, such as perception, reasoning, and problem solving,

The Psychodynamic Perspective Interprets Paranoia

"They're out to get me," says a man to his therapist. "They" may be the couple down the street, the police, perhaps all Catholics, Protestants, or Jews. Whoever "they" are, the patient is convinced that they want him and will pursue him until he is caught. He imagines plots against him. He is being watched and secretly manipulated by evil forces. The enemy knows his thoughts, habits, and whereabouts at all times.

People with fears and delusions of this sort are generally diagnosed as *paranoid*. Freudian analysts who encounter a person suffering from paranoia try to understand the conflicts underlying the person's fears. Consider, for example, the case of N.:

> This patient continually rails against homosexuals, whom he detests with a violent passion. After a brief, unsuccessful marriage, followed by impotence, he began to experience delusions of persecution, according to which the CIA and the FBI were continually observing him with the ultimate purpose of getting him to submit to the sexual advances of Richard Nixon. He gave up all attempts at heterosexual sex, because he "would not make love in public," i.e., in front of the lurking agents. He soon came to understand also that his impotence had been imposed on him, via laser rays, by Nixon's agents. Satellites specifically sent up for this purpose began to bombard him with homosexual messages. Finally he constructed a special protective hat fitted with a highly complex electrical jamming device. He wore this hat continually, at home and in public places, including restaurants and work (he was soon dismissed). Even so, the messages that he should submit to Nixon increased in intensity and began to "penetrate" at times. Around this period he took all his jackets to a tailor and had the tailor sew up the slits (or flaps) in the back of the jackets. He implored his male acquaintances to do likewise, lest they be taken for "slot-jacket ass panderers." He deplored tight dungarees because they revealed buttocks too openly and therefore constituted a disgraceful invitation to sodomy. He complained that the CIA was spreading rumors

> that he was a homosexual, indeed, they had contrived to find a "double" for himself and a friend and photographed them—the doubles—in "disgusting" homosexual acts, all for the purpose of blackmail, so that he might submit to the homosexual importunings of the "anarcho-communist sodomite" Gerald Ford, who, as he now came to realize, was really "behind" the conspiracy (Nixon, it now turned out, was just a "front"). Ford, he believed, succeeded in having his landlord evict him from his apartment, so that he would be forced to live in the local YMCA among "faggots." This was meant to be a "softening-up" tactic (Erdelyi and Goldberg, 1979, p. 372).

What can be the meaning behind this patient's confused thoughts? Are they to be taken literally? Certainly, N. consciously hated homosexuals. He even began to talk about "destroying them." Is this simply a case of a man fearing retribution from people he hates? For the Freudian, a face-value acceptance of a patient's complaints is never enough; in fact, such a reading often contradicts the true explanation of a problem. A psychodynamic explanation of any disorder is always based on the *interpretation* of symptoms. What unconscious conflicts, then, are being masked by N.'s fear and hatred of homosexuals?

First, recall the defense mechanism known as *projection,* in which a person projects onto others his or her own unacceptable desires or impulses. Unable to entertain these thoughts or wishes in the conscious mind because of the unbearable anxiety they cause, the person attributes them to others. In this case, a psychodynamic interpretation would suggest that N. was actually *attracted* to homosexuals, but such feelings were so repulsive and anxiety-provoking that he banished them from consciousness. Instead of feeling himself attracted to men, he imagined that other men were attracted to him.

Underlying this defense mechanism, according to Freudians, lies the "true" conflict. What N. really fears is not that the homosexuals will get him, but that he will become one himself, succumbing to taboo impulses that he feels but must deny.

all of which are essential to adaptive functioning. Defense mechanisms, then, are adaptive up to a point. Beyond that point, they become self-defeating, as when a country devotes so many of its resources to defense that it can no longer afford essential services.

The basic defense mechanisms described by Freud and his followers (e.g., A. Freud, 1946) are as follows.

REPRESSION   In the process of repression, as we have already seen, unacceptable id impulses are pushed down into the unconscious and thereby forgotten. Thus, for example, a girl who is sexually attracted to her father will simply remove this intolerable thought from her consciousness. It may come up again in her dreams, but when she awakens, the dreams too will be repressed.

One of the earliest of Freud's conceptualizations, repression is the most fundamental defense mechanism of psychodynamic theory. It is on the basis of this mechanism that Freud constructed his symbolic readings of human behavior, whereby a person's actions are viewed as masked representations of the contents of his or her unconscious. And Freud evolved his technique of psychoanalysis expressly for the purpose of dredging up this repressed material, in the belief that once the person faced these banished memories and desires, they would cease to cause anxiety and thus would lose their power to force the person into maladaptive behaviors in the effort to relieve that anxiety.

Repression is fundamental also in that it is the basis of all the other defense mechanisms. In every one of the defenses that we will describe in the following paragraphs, the "forbidden" impulse is first repressed; then, instead of acting on that impulse, the individual engages in some substitute behavior that serves either as an outlet for the impulse or as an additional protection against it, or both.

PROJECTION   In the mechanism of **projection,** unacceptable impulses are first repressed, then attributed to others. Thus an internal threat is converted into an external threat. For example, a man threatened by his own homosexual inclinations may complain that other men are constantly making sexual overtures to him. This stratagem relieves his anxiety about his own attraction to men and simultaneously enables him to throw the "guilt" onto others.

DISPLACEMENT   **Displacement,** like projection, involves a transfer of emotion. In this case, however, it is not the source of the emotion that is switched but the object of the emotion. Afraid to display or even to experience certain feelings against whoever has aroused them, the person represses the feelings. Then, when the opportunity arises, he or she transfers them to a safer object and releases them in full force on this new object. A good example of displacement can be found in a story by James Joyce titled "Counterparts." In it a man who has been subjected to various defeats and humiliations all day long goes home and beats his young son on the pretext that the boy let the fire go out.

Displacement is a defense mechanism that involves the transfer of a repressed emotion to a substitute for the actual object of emotion. It may assume positive or negative forms. A man who is afraid to show anger toward his boss, for example, may displace it destructively by attacking another person or an object. (George W. Gardner)

RATIONALIZATION   Most defenses occur not in isolation but in combination (Erdelyi, 1985). In the example just cited, the pretext that the man used for beating his son illustrates another defense mechanism, **rationalization.** A person who engages in rationalization offers socially acceptable reasons for something that he or she has actually done (or is going to do) for unconscious and unacceptable reasons. Rationalization is one of the most common defenses. While much of our behavior may be motivated by irrational and infantile needs, as Freud claimed, we still feel required to explain it to ourselves and others in rational, grown-up terms. When we do so, we are rationalizing.

ISOLATION AND INTELLECTUALIZATION   In a related move, we engage in **isolation** when we avoid unacceptable feelings by cutting them off from the events to which they are attached, repressing them, and then reacting to the events in an emotionless manner. Isolation, which might be called the Mr. Spock syndrome, is a common refuge of patients in psychotherapy. Eager to tell the therapist what the problem is but unwilling to confront the feelings surrounding the problem, patients will relate the facts in a calm, detached fashion as Mr. Spock in "Star Trek" would do. ("Yes, my mother's death caused me considerable distress"), whereas it is actually the feelings, more than the facts, that need to be explored.

Isolation is often accompanied by **intellectualization:** the person achieves further distance from the emotion in question by surrounding it with a smoke-screen of abstract intellectual analysis ("Yes, my mother's death caused me considerable distress. Young children find it difficult to endure separation, let alone final separation, from their mothers," etc.).

DENIAL   **Denial** is the refusal to acknowledge the existence of a potential external source of anxiety. In some cases, the person will actually fail to perceive something that is obvious. For example, a person who is diagnosed as terminally ill may go on planning a lengthy vacation trip to be made when he or she is well again. In more subtle cases, what the person fails to see is not the facts but their meaning. Thus parents of a retarded child may go on for a long period telling themselves and others that the child doesn't talk because he is shy or his older siblings don't give him a chance.

REACTION FORMATION   A person who engages in **reaction formation** represses the feelings that are arousing anxiety and then vehemently professes the exact opposite of those feelings. Thus someone who claims to be disgusted by the sexual promiscuity of the young may be demonstrating a reaction formation against his or her own sexual impulses.

REGRESSION   **Regression** involves a return to a developmental stage that one has already passed through. Unable to deal with its anxiety, the ego simply abandons the scene of the conflict, reverting to an earlier, less threatening stage, when gratification was easier to come by. Regression is a good example of the fact that defense mechanisms can vary from relatively harmless means of self-comfort to signs of severe psychological disturbance. In its extreme aspect, regression can involve a total breakdown of physical and mental functioning: the regressed adult may be reduced to a babbling, helpless creature who has to be fed and toileted like a baby. On the other hand, well-adjusted adults often resort to minor regressive behaviors—whining, making childish demands, getting drunk—simply to take the edge off the pressures they are experiencing at the moment.

SUBLIMATION   **Sublimation,** the transformation and expression of sexual or aggressive energy into more socially acceptable forms, differs from all other defense mechanisms in that it can be truly construc-

Freudian theory would regard "dancing cheek to cheek" as a sublimation—a socially acceptable public expression of sexual impulses. (José Fernandez/ Woodfin Camp & Associates)

tive. The skill of a great surgeon, for example, may represent a sublimation of aggressive impulses. Likewise, Freud hypothesized that many of the beautiful male and female nudes created by Renaissance painters and sculptors were the repositories of sublimated sexual impulses. Indeed, Freud saw civilization itself as the result of thousands of years of sublimation (Lindzey et al., 1973).

The Stages of Psychosexual Development

Freud (1905) saw the child as motivated primarily by sexual drives.[*] In his view, the development of the personality was a process of **psychosexual development,** a series of stages in each of which the child's central motivation was to gratify the drive for pleasure in various bodily zones: the mouth, the anus, and the genitals, in that order. The characteristics of the adult personality were a consequence of the ways in which these id strivings were handled at each stage of development. For at each stage the child is forced to deal with a conflict between his or her own drive for gratification and the restrictions (in the form of weaning, toilet training, etc.) that the social environment places on that gratification. Both undergratifi-

In the oral stage, the first of Freud's psychosexual stages, the mouth is the focus of the child's pleasure. (Joel Gordon)

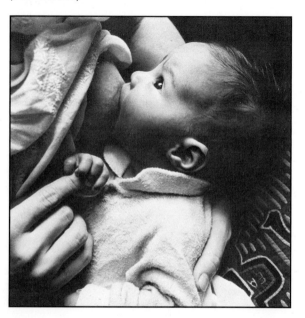

cation and overgratification can engender anxiety, and anxiety can lead to maladaptive adult behavior.

Freud's developmental schema is one component of his theory that has been heavily revised. We will discuss below the differing theories of Erik Erikson and Margaret Mahler in regard to the critical events of childhood. But Freud's remains the classical formulation, and he was the first to state the principle on which all the others are based: that young children's experiences have a determining influence on their adult lives.

The Oral Stage   The first year of life constitutes the **oral stage,** in which, as the name indicates, the mouth is the primary focus of id strivings. Infants must suck in order to live; accordingly, they are equipped at birth with the impulse to suck. Soon, however, they are using their mouths to satisfy not only their hunger but also their libidinal and aggressive impulses. Breast, bottle, thumb, pacifier, blankets, toys—infants suck, mouth, bite, and chew whatever they can find in their search for oral stimulation. And according to Freud, the various actions involved in these oral exercises—sucking in, holding on, spitting out, and closing—serve as prototypes for later personality traits such as acquisitiveness, tenacity, and destructiveness.

The Anal Stage   In the second year of life, the child shifts his or her libidinal attention from the mouth down to the other end of the alimentary canal, the anus. In the **anal stage** the major sources of physical pleasure are the retaining and expelling of feces. In the retention of feces, the pleasurable stimulus is the mild pressure of the feces against the walls of the rectum, while in the expulsion of feces, the pleasure is the reduction of tension as this pressure is relieved.

---

[*] Of all Freud's theories, this was the one that was most profoundly shocking and repulsive to the Victorian society in which he lived. (In 1910, when his theories were brought up by a participant at a meeting of German neurologists and psychiatrists, another participant declared, "This is not a topic for discussion at a scientific meeting; it is a matter for the police!") Again, however, it should be kept in mind that Freud used the term *sexual* in an extremely broad sense. Had he not used this adjective to describe the infant's pleasure in feeding, for example, his ideas about the importance of this infantile gratification would have been much more readily accepted. But to Freud the use of the term was necessary to indicate that the pleasure of feeding was tied to the same instincts as adult sexual pleasure.

Unlike the oral pleasures of the first year, however, the child's anal pleasures are barely established before they are interfered with, through the process of toilet training. Traditionally, Freudian theorists have regarded toilet training as a crucial event, since it is children's first confrontation with a systematic effort on the part of parents and society to control their impulses. Suddenly their retentive and expulsive pleasures are brought under regulation. They are told when, where, how, and so forth. Caught between these reality-imposed demands and the id's demands for its own timetable of gratification, the ego may experience considerable conflict and anxiety. And as in the oral stage, such anxiety can engender personality problems.

The Phallic Stage   In the **phallic stage,** which extends from the third to the fifth or sixth year, the focus is shifted to the genitals, and sensual pleasure is derived from masturbation, the manipulation of the genitals. During this period, **narcissism,** erotic preoccupation with one's own body, is assumed to be particularly intense, since for the first time the child is deriving pleasure not from sensations associated with automatic and life-sustaining body processes, such as sucking and excretion, but from a willed manipulation of his or her own body. Partly because of this erotic self-sufficiency, the child in the phallic stage begins to develop a strong sense of self, of independence and autonomy, as opposed to the extreme dependence characteristic of earlier stages.

The phallic stage is held to be particularly crucial to psychological development because it is this stage that is the scene of the **Oedipus complex,** the most important determinant of the child's future sexual adjustment. In Greek legend, King Oedipus had the misfortune to discover that he had killed his father and married his mother. Likewise, according to Freud (1905), all children during the phallic stage long to dispose of the parent of the same sex and to take possession of the parent of the opposite sex. In boys, this incestuous desire arouses what Freud called **castration anxiety**—the child's fear that his father will punish him for his forbidden wishes by cutting off the guilty organ, his penis. This fear is supposedly confirmed by the boy's observations of female anatomy. Lacking penises, girls seem to him castrated, and he fears the same fate for himself. To allay his castration anxiety, he eventually represses the incestuous desire that aroused it.

At the same time girls, observing that, unlike boys,

In Freud's view, the Oedipus complex occurs when the child enters the phallic stage of psychosexual development and begins to compete with the same-sex parent for "possession" of the opposite-sex parent. (Nancy Durrell McKenna/Photo Researchers)

they have been born without penises, experience a condition Freud (1905) called **penis envy.**[*] While the boy's castration anxiety causes him to repress his longing for his mother, the girl's penis envy impels

---

[*] It has been pointed out that such concepts as castration anxiety and penis envy reflect an unjustified assumption that to be born without a penis is cause for bitter disappointment. This assumption, along with such terms as "phallic stage," reflects the degree to which Freud's theories are based on male biology and male psychology—a bias that has made Freud a target of criticism from feminists. Of course, in most societies, those with penises *do* have favored status, and it is this, rather than the organ itself, that may be the focus of female envy (Horney, 1967).

her toward her father. If she can have him, then at least vicariously she can obtain the desired organ.

In time, however, the girl's oedipal desires, like the boy's, are resolved. Rather than war against the parent of the same sex for the unattainable object, both boys and girls settle for **identification** with the same-sex parent. Since they can't beat them, they join them, incorporating the parent's values, standards, sexual orientation, mannerisms, and so forth. And it is through the incorporation of the parent's moral values in the process of identification that the child develops a superego.

Latency and the Genital Stage   Between the ages of six and twelve, the child goes through the **latency** period, in which, as the term indicates, sexual impulses seem latent. While the libido hibernates, the child's attention is redirected toward the mastery of developmental skills. After this period of presumably asexual behavior, sexual strivings are reawakened as the child enters puberty. Now, however, sexual functioning undergoes a highly significant change. During the oral, anal, and especially the phallic stages, children's sexual strivings are, as we have seen, narcissistic. Their central erotic love objects are their own bodies, and other people—particularly the mother—are loved to the extent that they contribute to this self-directed physical pleasure. In puberty, on the other hand, children begin rechanneling some of this libidinal energy directly toward other people, and not just as adjuncts of their bodily pleasure but as individuals in their own right. As puberty advances, this altruistic love eventually merges with the more instinctual libidinal energies to produce mature sexual functioning, in which tenderness mingles with the primitive sexual hunger. This final phase of development, called the **genital stage,** ends with the attainment of mature sexuality, which to Freud meant not only heterosexual love but also maturity in a broad sense: independence, resourcefulness, the ability to work, and so forth.

Normal and Abnormal Behavior

Having outlined the fundamental principles of Freudian theory, let us now draw out from these principles Freud's conceptualization of normal and abnormal personality functioning.

Normal Personality Functioning   To begin with, Freudian theory views the normal personality as containing strong irrational elements. For centuries enlightened people had viewed mental disorder as a loss of one's *reason:* the sane person was rational, and the insane person was irrational. In contrast, Freud saw both the sane and the insane as motivated at bottom by the irrational id, with its reckless drives for pleasure and aggression.

Second, adult functioning is, to a large degree, molded by events that occurred long before adulthood is ever reached. As we have seen, extreme anxiety at any one of the psychosexual stages can result in behavioral abnormalities. But this is only the extreme case. According to Freud, the most ordinary traits of the adult personality—whether we are diligent or lazy, gregarious or solitary, even-tempered or volatile—are determined by our success in satisfying our drives before the age of six.

Finally, the normal personality, according to Freud's theory, is characterized by a balance among the three psychic components of id, ego, and superego. While id strivings may be the generator of behavior, the form that behavior takes is dictated by the ego and superego. This does not mean that the id, ego, and superego coexist in perfect harmony. On the contrary, they are continually conflicting, and power is continually shifting among them. In times of stress, the ego may be weakened, in which case the defenses will operate poorly, leaving us with a good deal of anxiety. Or, under the influence of alcohol, the superego's functioning may become weak and thus allow id impulses the upper hand. When the superego's functioning returns to normal, the psyche may be afflicted with guilt. But these are simply normal ups and downs. Once shaken, the balance of power among the three psychic components is again restored, and the person is once again able to satisfy the demands of the id and at the same time to meet the requirements both of reality and of morality.

Abnormal Personality Functioning   Like normal functioning, abnormal functioning is motivated primarily by irrational drives and determined by childhood experiences. Indeed, one of the central principles of psychoanalytic theory is that normal and abnormal behavior lie on a continuum—abnormality, then, is a difference in degree, not in kind. Dreams, fantasies, works of art, abnormal symptoms, hallucinations—these are simply different stops on the same road. The behavior of schizophrenics and of the doctors who care for them issue from the same source.

What, then, is the difference between normal and abnormal? It lies in the crucial matter of energy balance among id, ego, and superego. In the abnormal personality the distribution of energy among the three components of the psyche either has developed in a lopsided fashion or has been knocked askew as a result of some trauma, deficit, or disturbance in pregenital psychosexual development. We have already noted that anxiety over impulse gratification in childhood can engender psychological problems. One such pathological process Freud called **fixation:** aspects of the adult personality remain fixed, or "frozen," at the anxiety-ridden stage, still acting out in symbolic fashion the impulse in question. Thus the victim of harsh toilet training may grow up "anal-retentive," that is, stingy and compulsively neat. Such one-for-one formulas have been largely rejected by later psychodynamic theorists. Similarly, anxiety can bring about regression: the individual abandons some elements of ego or superego maturity and returns to an earlier stage. Improper resolution of the Oedipus complex may leave the individual with superego problems. Conversely, an extremely stern and punitive upbringing can shift too much of the id's energy to the superego and cause the ego's power to be depleted through constant repression of id demands.

Once the balance among the three structural components is disrupted, any number of symptoms may occur. If the superego is weakened, aggressive id impulses may gain the upper hand, producing the sort of amoral, opportunistic individual that we will discuss in Chapter 11 under the heading of "antisocial personality." Or, if the superego becomes dominant, defenses may become exaggerated to the point where they seriously impair normal functioning. For example, a man who has to rely heavily on projection may end up imagining that everyone is "out to get him"— a condition that, if extreme, could be diagnosed as paranoia.

While the variety of symptoms is infinite, most of them have one thing in common: no matter what component is strengthened, the ego is usually weakened (if it was not already underdeveloped to begin with). And since our contact with reality is only as strong as our egos, any draining of ego strength—whether from the task of repressing an inordinate amount of material or from the task of erecting and maintaining defenses—will result in an impairment of our ability to adapt to reality. Appointments will be missed; new

situations will become terrifying; minor difficulties will become major calamities. As these troubles build, a vicious cycle is set up: the troubles create further conflict, which in turn further weakens the ego, which in turn further reduces our ability to adapt to reality.

Many people find themselves in such a state at some point in their lives, when they are under severe emotional stress; once the stress is lifted, the defenses are relaxed, and the ego bounces back. In some cases, however, the conflict continues, creating more and more anxiety, which in turn creates more and more rigid defenses, in the form of behaviors that drastically impede the individual's adaptive functioning. Suddenly a woman who commutes to work can no longer drive. Suddenly a student finds that he no longer has the strength to get out of bed and go to class. Such people may be dismayed by their behavior, but they cannot alter it; it somehow protects them from facing the source of their unconscious anxiety—a protection that is all-important. Such conditions Freud called **neuroses.**

In extreme cases, the ego's strength may be severely depleted (or again, severely underdeveloped from the start), in which case adaptive functioning is drastically curtailed. Defenses break down, flooding the psyche with id impulses and attendant anxiety. Emotions are cut loose from external events. Speech loses its coherence. Inner voices are mistaken for outer voices. Imaginary people appear at the window, and real people are treated as if they did not exist. This condition of ego collapse, known as **psychosis,** is the furthest reach of the structural imbalance that Freud considered the foundation of abnormal behavior.

THE DESCENDANTS OF FREUD

While Freud's theory was at first greeted with considerable skepticism by most of his contemporaries, it eventually gave rise to an entire new school of thought: the psychodynamic perspective. From many countries young people came to Vienna to be analyzed by Freud and his followers, taking back with them the new theory and disseminating it throughout Europe and the United States. As it spread, however, Freudian theory changed. Many of Freud's pupils and their pupils were highly original thinkers in their own right. And though accepting many of his basic premises, they extended and modified his views, creating numerous subschools of psychodynamic thought.

Post-Freudian thinking took off in many different directions. Three trends, however, are especially noteworthy. The first is the pronounced emphasis on the ego. Freud, while by no means ignoring the ego, gave special attention to the role of the id. In general, later contributors to psychodynamic thought shifted the spotlight from the id to the ego. That is, they deemphasized sex, instincts, and determinism and emphasized goals, creativity, and self-direction. Second, the post-Freudian thinkers tended to view the child's social relationships as the central determinant of normal and abnormal development. Again, this is hardly a subject that was ignored by Freud; the Oedipus complex, for example, is nothing if not a social drama. Nevertheless, Freud always viewed social interactions in relation to the strivings of the id. Later theorists, deemphasizing the id, moved social interaction to center stage. Finally, later theorists tended to extend the period of critical developmental influences. While in Freud's schema psychosexual development runs from birth through puberty, his emphasis was on the phallic stage, and especially on the Oedipus complex. Many subsequent writers have placed greater stress on infancy, while others see critical developmental junctures occurring well into adulthood.

Of the major post-Freudian thinkers, we will consider two of Freud's original students who dissented from his ideas—Carl Jung and Alfred Adler; two theorists outside psychoanalysis proper who built on Freud's ideas—Harry Stack Sullivan and Karen Horney; and two psychoanalysts who were pioneers in "ego psychology"—Heinz Hartmann and Erik Erikson. Finally, we will discuss two recent contributors, Margaret Mahler and Heinz Kohut, who explored the psychology of earliest childhood.

Carl Gustav Jung

Freud's most cherished pupil, the Swiss psychiatrist Carl Gustav Jung (1875–1961), broke with him early in his career, claiming that Freud's theory was unduly negative and reductive. The main focus of the disagreement was the nature of the libido. Whereas Freud saw the energy of the psyche as primarily sexual, Jung viewed the libido as a much broader force, comprising an autonomous "spiritual instinct" as well as a sexual instinct. There was a corresponding division in the two men's views of the unconscious. To Freud, the unconscious is a regressive force, pulling us back into infantile, id-directed behavior. To Jung, the unconscious is also a creative force. Jung (1935) argued, moreover, that the mind contains not just the "personal unconscious" posited by Freud (that is, biological drives and childhood memories) but also a **collective unconscious,** a repository of "archetypes," or symbols, expressive of universal human experiences. This set of symbols, shared by all humankind, is the source of mythology and art, whose unity across cultures is explained by their common origin. As the theory of the collective unconscious suggests, Jung was powerfully drawn to the aspects of mental life that are beyond the rational, such as religion, mysticism, and the occult—preoccupations that Freud and his more orthodox followers regarded as unscientific.

Jung's therapeutic practices also differed from Freud's. He saw psychotherapy as a process of integrating opposing tendencies (for instance, masculinity and femininity, extraversion and introversion) within the self. This integration, whereby the patient "becomes who he really is," Jung called "individuation" (Roazen, 1974). Thus both Freud and Jung valued insight, but for different purposes. In Freudian therapy the goal of insight is control: the rational ego taking control of the irrational id and directing it to constructive ends. In Jung's approach, the purpose of insight is to discover and express all parts of the self, a process that Jung assumed would naturally lead to constructive ends.

Carl Gustav Jung, a student of Freud's. Jung took a broader and more positive view of the unconscious than Freud did, claiming that it is creative and includes not only the personal but also the collective unconscious, a set of universal human symbols. (Henri Cartier-Bresson/ Magnum)

Alfred Adler

Another member of Freud's inner circle who eventually broke with him was Alfred Adler (1870–1937). Like Jung, Adler believed that Freud had placed undue emphasis on the sexual drive. In Adler's view, the primary motivator of behavior is not sexuality but an aggressive drive for dominance. Adler postulated that all human beings are born with a crippling sense of inferiority (it was Adler who coined the term *inferiority complex*) and that much of human behavior can be explained as an effort to compensate for that imagined handicap by gaining power over others. In his emphasis on this struggle to cope and succeed, Adler helped to shift the focus of psychodynamic theory from the id to the ego.

Adler's most important contribution, however, was his concern with the social context of personality. Psychological disturbance, he claimed, has its roots not so much in early childhood experiences as in the person's present circumstances. Most important of all are the person's social circumstances. It is relationships with others that determine and indeed define psychological health. The mature person is one who can overcome the self-absorbed power struggle and devote himself or herself selflessly to others. An active socialist, Adler was concerned not just with intimate social relationships but with society in general, which he hoped to serve through psychiatric means.

Harry Stack Sullivan

The study of psychological disorder as a social phenomenon was carried forward by the American psychiatrist Harry Stack Sullivan (1892–1949). Like Adler, Sullivan claimed that psychological problems both stem from and are defined by interpersonal problems. Particularly crucial, in his view, is the parent–child relationship. Children of rejecting parents develop severe anxiety about themselves—anxiety that makes it almost impossible for them, as they grow up, to weather the threats to the self that are part of almost any close relationship. Other people simply become too threatening, and the frightened individual responds either by rigid self-protecting behaviors (neurosis) or by withdrawing completely from the world of other people (psychosis). But regardless of its severity, psychological disturbance is an anxiety-motivated flight from human relationships.

Alfred Adler, also a student of Freud's. Adler emphasized the importance of viewing human beings in a social context, differing with Freud's heavy stress on the role of biological drives. (The Granger Collection)

Aside from his elaboration of the social theory of psychopathology, Sullivan made two important contributions to the psychodynamic perspective. First, he pointed out the critical role of the self-concept. Sullivan argued that, as children, each of us develops a "self-system," made up largely of other people's appraisals of us. If those appraisals are harsh, we may come to screen out large portions of our experience, labeling them "not-me" in order to spare ourselves anxiety. Such overreliance on denial, in Sullivan's view, leads directly to psychological disturbance.

Sullivan's other major contribution was in the treatment of severe mental disturbance, an area in which Freud and his early followers felt that psychoanalysis could be of little help. Sullivan was the first analyst to report significant success in the long-term psychoanalytic treatment of psychotics, and the warm, supportive approach that he developed for this purpose has served as a model for later psychodynamic treatments of psychosis.

Karen Horney

In line with Adler and Sullivan, Karen Horney (1885–1952) deemphasized Freud's instinct theory in favor of a social analysis of psychopathology: "Neuroses," as she put it, "are an expression of a disturbance in human relationships" (1945, p. 47). In her schema, psychological disturbance develops as follows: bad parenting, whether punitive or overindulgent, negligent or overprotective, leaves the child with "basic anxiety," a perception of the world as a hostile place. As protection against this perceived threat, the individual develops a "neurotic trend," or basic strategy

Karen Horney differed from Freud's instinct theory by promoting the view that neurotic patterns of individual behavior are responses to disordered social relationships and societal structures. (Culver Pictures)

for dealing with other people, the most common strategies being helplessness, hostility, and isolation. Whichever one the individual chooses, however, it will clash with competing needs. An attitude of hostility, for instance, will leave unsatisfied the person's underlying need for love, just as a stance of helplessness will clash with a suppressed desire for domination. And it is this conflict among opposing attitudes toward other people that engenders psychological disturbance.

Like Adler, Horney was concerned not just with intimate social ties but with larger social structures, whose flaws, in her view, helped to create psychological disorders. For example, the thesis of her book *The Neurotic Personality of Our Time* (1937) was that industrial societies such as the United States, by promoting competition and materialism, tend to create a specific and increasingly common neurotic pattern, marked by conflicts over aggression and by an inordinate craving for affection combined with a difficulty in giving affection.

Heinz Hartmann

Aside from the social analysis of personality, the important trend in post-Freudian psychoanalytic theorizing is an increasing emphasis on ego functions. A milestone in this line of thought was Heinz Hartmann's *Ego Psychology and the Problem of Adaptation* (1939). Freud, as we have seen, tended to regard the ego merely as the handmaiden of the id. It derives its energy from the id, and its role is to serve the id by finding realistic ways of satisfying id strivings. Against

this limited view of the ego's functioning, Hartmann (1894–1970) argued that the ego develops independently of the id and has its own autonomous functions—functions, in other words, that serve *ego* strivings, such as the need to adapt to reality, rather than id strivings. In particular, the mind's cognitive (mental-processing) operations, such as memory, perception, and learning, are, in Hartmann's view, "conflict-free" expressions of the ego. The id and the superego may help induce a child to go to school, for example, but only a relatively pure ego motivation can explain how the child learns to solve an algebra problem or translate a sentence into Latin. From this proposition it follows that Freud overemphasized the role of conflict in mental life. If, in many of its basic operations, the ego is working for itself rather than mediating battles between the id and the superego or the id and reality, then the life of the mind also has a "conflict-free sphere."

Hartmann's ideas were instrumental in the founding of a whole new school of **ego psychology,** which has had a tremendous influence on psychoanalytic theory since World War II. Earlier, psychoanalytic writings concentrated on the id and the conflicts engendered by id strivings. Today they tend to focus on the ego and the interplay between its conflict-solving functions, particularly the defenses, and its conflict-free, autonomous functions, particularly cognitive processes. This shift has had the effect of bringing psychoanalysis closer to other branches of psychology, where cognitive processes have been commanding more and more attention in the past few decades.

Erik Erikson

An important extension of the new ego psychology and of the social analysis of personality was the theory of development put forth by Erik Erikson (1902–). To Erikson, the major drama of development is the formation of the **ego identity,** an integrated, unique, and autonomous sense of self. The ego identity is the product of what Erikson calls **psychosocial development.** Like Freud's theory of psychosexual development, of which it is a deliberate revision, Erikson's psychosocial development proceeds through a series of chronological stages. But these stages differ in important ways from Freud's psychosexual stages (see Figure 2.1). In the first place, there are more

FIGURE 2.1

Erikson views life as a succession of biological stages, each having its own developmental conflict whose resolution has lasting effects on personality. Erikson's psychosocial stages represent an extension and expansion of Freud's psychosexual stages, with parallels between the first four stages of each theory. (After Erikson, 1950)

Stage	1	2	3	4	5	6	7	8
Maturity								Ego Integrity vs. Despair
Adulthood							Generativity vs. Stagnation	
Young Adulthood						Intimacy vs. Isolation		
Puberty and Adolescence					Identity vs. Role Confusion			
Latency				Industry vs. Inferiority				
Locomotor-Genital			Initiative vs. Guilt					
Muscular-Anal		Autonomy vs. Shame, Doubt						
Oral Sensory	Basic Trust vs. Mistrust							

of them. To Freud, the personality is essentially formed by the age of six or seven; to Erikson, personality development is a process that extends from birth to death. The second difference is the pronounced social emphasis of Erikson's theory, proclaimed in the term *psychosocial*. While Freud saw the individual psyche in near isolation except for the influence of parents and siblings, Erikson sees personality development as deeply affected not only by the family but also by many other social agents; teachers, friends, spouses, and the like all do their part in molding the individual.

Third and most important is the central role of the ego in Erikson's developmental progression. Freud's psychosexual stages have to do with challenges to id strivings; Erikson's psychosocial stages have more to do with challenges to the ego. At each stage there is a crisis—a conflict between the individual and the expectations now imposed by society. The ego is then called upon to resolve the crisis by learning new adaptive tasks. In the second year, for example, the child is faced with toilet training, a challenge that may lead to a new sense of self-reliance or, if the training is poorly handled, to feelings of shame and self-doubt. Likewise, from the third to the fifth years, when the challenge confronting the child is that of separating from the mother, a successful resolution will lead to a new sense of initiative, whereas a troubled separation will foster guilt.

Through this process of conflict resolution, the ego identity—the image of oneself as a unique, competent, and self-determining individual—is gradually formed. Or, if the ego fails to master the crisis, this failure will hamper identity formation and may generate psychological disorders. Erikson believes, however, that a failure at one stage does not guarantee failure at future stages. In his scheme, the ego is a strong, resilient force, and there is always a second chance. Erikson's theory is thus far more hopeful than Freud's scheme, where a serious childhood trauma can handicap a person for life. In general, recent psychoanalytic thinking, because of its emphasis on the adaptive, problem-solving ego, is more optimistic than earlier psychoanalytic formulations, with their stress on the self-seeking, tyrannical id.

Margaret Mahler

Even more important than the ego as an organizer of recent psychodynamic thought is the concept of object relations. In psychodynamic terminology, "objects" are the people to whom one is attached by strong emotional ties. For the child, obviously, the chief object is the primary caretaker, usually the mother. And according to the **object relations theorists,** the most powerful determinant of psychological development is the child's interaction with the mother.

A very influential member of this school was probably Margaret Mahler (1897–1985). As she indicated when she titled her book *The Psychological Birth of the Human Infant* (Mahler et al., 1975), Mahler was concerned primarily to chart the process by which infants separate themselves psychologically from their mothers. Mahler saw newborns as having no sense whatever of their own existence apart from their mothers. Then, at around five months, begins the long and sometimes wrenching process of **separation–individuation.** In the first of its four phases, "differentiation" (five to twelve months), babies, aided by their sharpening cognitive faculties, begin to distinguish between their own bodies and that of the mother. Then comes "practicing" (twelve to eighteen months), in which the child, now able to walk, can and does escape from the mother—an experience that brings a pleasing sense of autonomy—but returns to her frequently for "emotional refueling" (Mahler, 1979). Next comes a painful moment of truth, the "rapprochement" phase (eighteen to twenty-four months). Children now realize with horror what has happened: that they have lost the primal fusion with the mother, or, as they see it, that they have lost the mother. At the same time, paradoxically, they are increasingly impelled toward independence. Thus they swing back and forth between pushing the mother away and clinging to her desperately. This ambivalence is resolved in the final "object constancy" phase (twenty-four to thirty-six months), in which the child internalizes the image of the mother (who thus becomes fixed, or constant, in the mind—no longer truly losable) and, thus anchored, consolidates his or her individuality.

This outline, like our earlier description of Freud's developmental schema, sketches the ideal scenario. In real life, separation–individuation can be disturbed by many factors, above all by the mother, if she hurries the child into independence or resists the toddler's growing separateness. And like Freud, Mahler felt that the individual's success in these early stages determines his or her psychological future, for the features of this first and crucial relationship will be repeated in later intimate relationships.

Heinz Kohut

Like Mahler, Heinz Kohut (1913–1981) was interested primarily in the psychological consequences of the parent–child relationship. In his practice as a therapist Kohut encountered a great many patients who, though they shared similar problems—extreme demandingness and self-importance covering a very fragile self-esteem—seemed to fit no diagnostic category. He referred to this syndrome as **narcissistic personality disorder** (see Chapter 11), and from his work with these patients he built his so-called **self psychology.**

Kohut proposed that the development of the **self,** or core of the personality, depends on the child's receiving two essential psychological supports from the parents. One is the confirmation of the child's sense of vigor and "greatness." The other is a sense of calmness and infallibility: the feeling that there is nothing that the child can't handle, that everything will be all right. Parents communicate these things through the most ordinary daily behavior—by exclaiming over the ceramic soap dish that the child made in school, by assuring the child, when he or she is nervous or upset, that everything will be all right. But whether parents do in fact communicate these things depends on the strength of their own self-esteem:

> If the parents are at peace with their own needs to shine and to succeed . . . , then the proud exhibitionism of the budding self of their child will be responded to acceptingly. . . . The proud smile of the parents will keep alive a bit of the original omnipotence, to be retained as the nucleus of the self-confidence and inner security about one's worth that sustain the healthy person throughout his life. (Kohut and Wolf, 1978, p. 417).

Likewise, if the parents feel strong, then they are free to confirm the child's fantasy of infallibility. But some parents cannot provide these supports, and the result, for the child, is a damaged self. Thus Kohut's theory, like Mahler's, differs from Freud's both in its interpersonal character and in its emphasis on cognitive and emotional rather than biological needs. Kohut and Mahler also placed the critical events of early childhood well before the oedipal stage, again in contrast to Freud.

Kohut felt that an ill-developed self could account for a wide range of disorders (e.g., psychosis, sexual deviance, drug and alcohol addiction), but the syndrome he felt was most closely associated with disturbances of the self was narcissistic personality disorder—now, thanks to him, a common term in psychology. Kohut also developed a treatment method for narcissistic personalities, based on his view that therapists, instead of trying to suppress exaggerated demands for approval, must help such patients discover the childhood roots of the problem, as in Freudian psychoanalysis, and to accept and express the unfulfilled narcissistic needs of their childhood. In this way, Kohut felt, these patients would come at last to approve of themselves.

EVALUATING THE PSYCHODYNAMIC PERSPECTIVE

Psychodynamic Theory versus the Medical Model

Since Freud was trained in medicine, it is no surprise that the theoretical perspective he founded has ties to the medical model. The Freudian view of behavioral abnormalities as the surface symptoms of an underlying psychic disturbance is very close to the medical model's approach to maladaptive behavior patterns as the symptoms of an underlying organic dysfunction. Furthermore, the determinism of some psychoanalytic theories, which view people as victims of their pasts, corresponds to the determinism of the medical model, which views the mentally ill as victims of their bodies.

However, Freud himself went to great pains to differentiate his theory from the medical view. He claimed that a medical education was of no use whatsoever to the psychoanalyst—"The analyst's experience lies in another world from that of pathology, with other phenomena and other laws" (1926, p. 119)—and he urged the training of lay (nonphysician) analysts.[*] Furthermore, he insisted that psychoanalysis could offer nothing comparable to a medical cure. (In an often cited passage, he said that the most that psychoanalysis could do was convert neurotic misery into ordinary human unhappiness.) Actually, despite its parallels with medicine, the psychodynamic per-

spective is the oldest of the purely psychological approaches to abnormal behavior. Freud's theory was the first systematic interpretation of the mind to regard abnormal behavior not as a moral, religious, or organic problem, but as a psychological problem—a problem in the history of the individual's emotional life.

Criticisms of Psychodynamic Theory

Freud's theories were no sooner enunciated than they were attacked. And today the psychodynamic perspective remains controversial.

Lack of Experimental Support   The most common criticism of the psychodynamic position is that most of its claims have never been tested in scientifically controlled experiments. Freud evolved his theories on the basis of **clinical evidence**—that is, observations of patients in therapy—and today psychodynamic writers still tend to rely on case studies to support their formulations. The problem with case studies is that their accuracy is always questionable. For instance, we can never know to what degree Dr. Smith's ideas and expectations colored his patients' responses and his reporting of those responses. Furthermore, in the psychodynamic view, the relationship between behavior and mental processes is so complicated and indirect that clinical evidence can sometimes be taken to mean whatever the writer wants it to mean. For example, if a six-year-old boy expresses great love for his mother, this can be interpreted as evidence of oedipal attachment. However, if the same six-year-old boy expressed great hatred for his mother, this too could be interpreted as an expression of oedipal attachment, through reaction formation.

The reason psychodynamic writers have depended on clinical evidence rather than controlled experiments is that most of the phenomena they deal with are too complex to be testable by current experimental techniques (Erdelyi and Goldberg, 1979). Furthermore, most of these phenomena are unconscious, and hence inaccessible to direct testing. However, it *is* possible to determine whether the relationships that Freud proposed—the connection, for example, between oral preoccupations and dependency, or between anal preoccupations and compulsive orderli-

---

[*] A *psychoanalyst* (or *analyst*), a person who has received advanced training in the theory and practice of psychoanalysis, is not necessarily a *psychiatrist,* or a physician trained in the medical specialty of psychiatry. (A *psychologist* is a practitioner who holds a doctorate in psychology.)

Psychodynamic Theory and Feminine Development

It is a curious fact that Freud's entire theory of feminine psychology is built on his observation that girls do not have a penis. According to Freud, the moment a child notices this basic anatomical difference, he or she begins to become, psychologically as well as biologically, a male or a female. For the little girl, the realization that she has no penis produces ineradicable jealousy, or "penis envy." This is the beginning of her long slide into inferiority. As Freud puts it, "The discovery that she is castrated is a turning point in a girl's growth" (1974, p. 105). He might have said *the* turning point," for starting with the notion of penis deprivation and penis envy, Freud constructs an elegant chain of reasoning leading directly to female inferiority.

The process may be summarized as follows. Because she lacks a penis, the girl's oedipal conflict takes a form different from the boy's. Already "castrated," she is barred from the healthy process of experiencing and then overcoming castration anxiety. Furthermore, her choice of her father as a love object is a negative rather than a positive choice. Like the boy, she originally preferred her mother, but once she discovers that her mother, like her, is an amputee and is even responsible for bringing her into the world

so poorly equipped, she turns to her father out of resentment against her mother. Thus her oedipal experience lacks both the stable heterosexual orientation and the cathartic resolution of the boy's oedipal crisis. And as a result, her superego (the fruit of a successfully resolved Oedipus complex) is stunted. Throughout her adult life she remains narcissistic, vain, lacking in a fully developed sense of justice, and, above all, envious. In short, she is morally inferior, for she can never overcome either her bitterness over her castration or the need to compensate for her lack of a penis. Furthermore, she is culturally inferior, since the ability to contribute to the advance of civilization depends on the mechanism of sublimation, which in turn depends on a strong, mature superego—the very thing she lacks. According to Freud, there is only one contribution that women have made to civilization, the art of weaving, a practice unconsciously motivated by woman's desire to conceal her "genital deficiency" (1974, p. 111).

Thus, while men, legitimized by their penises, go out to do the work of justice and civilization, women, as inferior creatures, must content themselves with substitutes. If a woman is lucky, she will be rewarded with that ultimate penis substitute, a baby. And if

ness—actually exist. As it turns out, some of Freud's most fundamental ideas have been supported by research (Fisher and Greenberg, 1977). Experiments have shown, for example, that dreams do allow people to vent emotional tension; children do go through a period of erotic interest in the parent of the opposite sex, accompanied by hostile feelings toward the same-sex parent; and people who experience unusual anxiety over anal imagery do tend to show what Freud regarded as the "anal" traits of orderliness and stinginess. In other cases, however, the evidence contradicts Freud. For example, there is little or no support for his claim that dreams represent wish fulfillment

or that women regard their bodies as inferior to men's because they lack penises. (Indeed, most of Freud's conclusions regarding specifically female sexuality have been contradicted [Fisher and Greenberg, 1977].) However, the important point is that psychodynamic theory is not closed to empirical testing and that in some cases it holds up well under such testing. Indeed, even without the intention of testing psychodynamic theory, experimental psychologists have turned up evidence in support of many of Freud's positions—for example, that most of our mental contents are unconscious (Miller, 1956); that under normal conditions some of our unconscious mental con-the baby should turn out to be a boy, "who brings the longed-for penis with him" (1974, p. 107), all the better.

To sum up: woman is morally feeble, culturally unproductive, and somehow "other"—a variation on the standard of masculinity, a deviation from the norm. Thus, the little girl's perception of herself as castrated, and her consequent envy, is responsible for her inferiority.

The opposition to this theory was first put forward in 1926 by Karen Horney, who retorted that Freud was in a poor position to know what little girls think. According to Horney (1967), it is not little girls who perceive their condition as degraded. Rather, it is little boys—and the men they eventually become—who see their penisless counterparts as mutilated and deficient and who thus have created the self-fulfilling prophecy that has doomed womankind to inferiority.

More recently, psychodynamic thinkers have proposed some sharply revised ideas of feminine development—ideas that have abandoned the entire concept of penis envy. What these thinkers have in common with Freud is the notion that the young child's attachment to its mother is of crucial importance to masculine or feminine development, and that this attachment has a very different meaning for girls than for boys. One influential theorist, Nancy Chodorow (1978), stresses the differences between girls' and boys' early childhood environment. For both, the mother is the primary love object during early infancy. However, the girl's task is to internalize the feminine role, while the boy's task is to renounce an identification with femininity and differentiate from it in order to become masculine. Boys, therefore, place a premium on separation and individuation. Girls, on the other hand, are not as motivated to differentiate themselves, and, consequently, have more difficulty with separation and individuation.

Another theorist in this mode is Carol Gilligan, the author of an influential book on girls' moral development (1982). Like Chodorow, she sees boys' needs to separate from their mothers as responsible for a personality difference observable in adult men and women:

> For boys and men, separation and individuation are critically tied to gender identity since separation from the mother is essential for the development of masculinity. For girls and women, issues of femininity or feminine identity do not depend on the achievement of separation from the mother or on the progress of individuation. Since masculinity is defined through separation while femininity is defined through attachment, male gender identity is threatened by intimacy while female gender identity is threatened by separation. Thus males tend to have difficulty with relationships, while females tend to have problems with individuation (p. 8).

In this view, the key crisis of early childhood is not the oedipal conflict, but Margaret Mahler's "separation–individuation" crisis. Girls, according to this theory, do *not* grow up into morally inferior penis enviers. They may, however, grow into adulthood with a greater need for close human attachments than many men have.

tents are accessible to us while others are not (Tulving and Pearlstone, 1966); and that most of the causes of our behavior are inaccessible to us (Nisbett and Ross, 1980; Nisbett and Wilson, 1977).

Dependence on Inference A second, related criticism of the psychodynamic approach is that it depends heavily on inference. When, in typing, the word *mob* comes out *mom,* does this mean we are preoccupied by feelings about our mothers? If I leave my umbrella at your house, does this really mean I want to come back? If a person is sexually prudish, does this mean that she is beset by anxiety over sexual longings?

In defense of such interpretations, it should be pointed out that they are seldom made on the basis of one piece of evidence alone. A responsible psychoanalyst, faced with a prudish patient, might suspect sexual anxiety but would not draw this conclusion unless there were other, supporting indications. Furthermore, the fact that interpretation may be in error does not mean that we can afford to eliminate it from psychology. Most human communications require interpretation—a truth that is now being taken into account even by the behavioral psychologists, once the severest critics of psychodynamic interpretation (see Chapter 3).

Unrepresentative Sampling and Cultural Bias
Another point on which psychodynamic theory has been criticized is that it is based on the study of a very limited sample of humanity. In the majority of Freud's published cases, at least, the patients were upper-middle-class Viennese women between the ages of twenty and forty-four (Fisher and Greenberg, 1977). Though these people were adults, Freud drew from them his theories regarding the child's psyche. (He never studied children in any systematic way.) Though they had serious emotional problems, he drew from them his theories regarding normal development. Though they lived in a time and place where overt expressions of sexuality (especially by women) were uniformly frowned upon, he concluded that their sexual preoccupations were typical of all human beings. Later investigators, it should be noted, have tested Freud's theories with children, with psychologically normal people, with lower-class people, with people raised in less repressive environments, and with people living in nonindustrial societies, and have argued that these theories do in fact describe the human species in general. Nevertheless, critics are still skeptical about the universal applicability of a set of theories based on such a special sample of humanity.

There is also the matter of Freud's own life circumstances and his consequent personal biases. Freud lived in a highly repressive society where social-class distinctions were rigidly observed, where the family was dominated by the father, and where women's opportunities were strictly limited. That these social facts influenced his patients' thoughts is unquestionable. In addition, as Erich Fromm (1980) pointed out, they may have influenced Freud's interpretation of that evidence, leading him to see more repression, more sexual motivation, and more "penis envy" than are actually the universal properties of the human psyche. They may also help to explain the extreme conservatism of Freud's thought, his assumption that psychological health is defined by our abilitiy to "fit in" and to perform the role assigned to us by society.

Reductive Interpretation of Life   Finally, it has been argued that psychodynamic theory has handed down to the twentieth century an incomparably dismal vision of human life—a vision in which the human being is a creature driven by animal instincts beyond his or her control; in which the individual is virtually helpless to change the self after the die is cast in the early years of life; in which works of art are largely substitutes for relief of sexual and aggressive impulses; in which acts of great heroism or generosity are actually disguised outgrowths of baser motives; and in which all that the average individual can know of his or her own mind is the surface, while behavior issues from the murky pool of repressed thoughts that lie beneath that surface.

Many of these positions, it should be recalled, have been substantially modified by later psychodynamic theorists. Furthermore, even if that were not the case, it is not the duty of science to produce a comforting picture of life, only a true one. Freud, as it happens, found much to admire in the human psyche he envisioned. As he put it, "one can only characterize as simple-minded the fear . . . that all the highest goods of humanity, as they are called—research, art, love, ethical and social sense—will lose their value or their dignity because psychoanalysis is in a position to demonstrate their origin in elementary and animal instinctual impulses" (1963, p. 50). If the ego could fashion civilization out of the base materials provided by the id, then the ego was a heroic force indeed. However, many thinkers, unable to share Freud's double vision, have argued that his reductive interpretation of life is both unsound and destructive.

The Contributions of Psychodynamic Theory

In answer to such criticisms, it must be pointed out that psychodynamic theory has made enormous contributions to the modern treatment of abnormal behavior and to modern thought in general. In the first place, it has directed the attention of the twentieth century to the inner life—to dreams, to fantasies, to memory, and to the motives underlying behavior. This intensified subjectivity has extended far beyond the limits of psychology. Indeed, it has changed the face of art, literature, history, and education in our century. Furthermore, psychodynamic theory, while deterministic, still holds out the hope that by acquainting ourselves with our inner lives, we can exercise greater control over our destinies. In short, it has pointed out the adaptive value of self-knowledge.

Second, psychodynamic theory has helped to de-mythologize mental disorder. By showing that the most bizarre and "crazy" behaviors have their roots in the same impulses and in the same developmental processes as the most adaptive and "sane" behaviors, Freud contributed greatly to the modern effort to treat the mentally disturbed as human beings rather than as freaks. Furthermore, by pointing out what he called the "psychopathology of everyday life"—the ways in which irrational and unconscious impulses emerge in dreams, in jokes, in slips of the tongue, in our ways of forgetting what we want to forget—Freud showed that the mentally disturbed have no monopoly on irrationality. This aspect of psychodynamic theory helped to establish the concept of mental health as a continuum ranging from adaptive to maladaptive rather than as a dichotomy of "sick" and "healthy."

Finally, to the treatment of mental problems Freud contributed the technique of psychoanalysis, which helps patients to confront and understand their unconscious impulses and thus to gain greater mastery over their actions. However, Freud's major contribution to modern psychological treatment is probably not orthodox psychoanalysis, which is now relatively rare, but rather the wide variety of other therapies that grew out of psychoanalysis. These include family therapy, marital therapy, group therapy, and above all the highly flexible, once-or-twice-a-week, psychodynamically based psychotherapy that is probably the most widely used form of psychological treatment in the United States today. Even therapists who reject Freud's theory altogether reveal his influence in the consulting room. The now-traditional technique of a one-to-one patient–therapist relationship aimed at increasing the patient's self-knowledge—a technique that underlies almost every known form of psychotherapy—was essentially a Freudian invention.

While modern thinkers are still arguing with Freud, no one can deny his impact on the contemporary conceptualization, assessment, and treatment of abnormal behavior. It is Freudian theory that is responsible for the widespread assumption that abnormal behavior stems from events in the individual's past and that it occurs in response to unconscious and uncontrollable impulses. In terms of psychological assessment, the popular "projective" tests (e.g., inkblot tests), in which the person is asked to interpret various pictures and symbols, are interpreted according to the Freudian notion that behavior is symbolic and that what a person reads into a picture or an event is actually a

reading of his or her own psyche. As for psychological treatment, there is, as we just saw, almost no form of psychotherapy in use today that does not bear Freud's imprint.

The impact of psychodynamic theory has been felt far beyond the limited field of professional psychology. Ordinary citizens, though they may never have read a word by Freud, often show no hesitation in explaining their friends' quirks in terms of childhood difficulties, in regarding their own children's development as crucial prefigurations of their adult lives, and in using such terms as *repressed, rationalization,* and *ego*—terms coined by Freud to explain the human psyche. Psychodynamic theory has thus colored not only scientific but also popular thinking. In truth, Freud radically altered the Western conception of the human mind. The same cannot be said of any other psychological theorist.

SUMMARY

The psychodynamic perspective focuses on the interactions of such forces as desires, impulses, anxieties, and defenses within the mind. Psychodynamic theorists tend to believe that these processes occur without the individual's awareness.

Sigmund Freud's theory of psychoanalysis provided the foundation for the psychodynamic perspective. The key concept of Freud's theory is the depth psychology hypothesis, the idea that almost all mental activity takes place unconsciously. Freud divided the mind into two levels, the perceptual conscious and the unconscious, which in turn consists of the preconscious (normally unconscious but retrievable material) and the unconscious proper, which contains much material that has been actively forgotten, or repressed. Freud stated that the goal of psychoanalytic therapy is "to make the unconscious conscious."

To achieve this objective, Freud relied on interpreting, or decoding, the manifest or surface meaning of human behavior to reveal its latent content, or true, unconscious meaning. The use of interpretation as a scientific method to identify unconscious processes was a major innovation of Freudian practice.

To complement the depth psychology hypothesis, Freud later proposed the structural hypothesis, which divides the mind into three forces—the id, ego, and superego—that continually interact and often conflict. The id is present at birth and consists of primitive biological drives—of which the most important is the libido, or sexual drive—that establish the basis of the psychic structure. It operates on the pleasure principle and uses primary process thinking, ignoring reason, reality, and morality. The ego develops somewhat later and mediates between the id and the real world, operating on the reality principle, with its concern for safety. It uses secondary process thinking, which takes into account reason, logic, and the distinctions among different times, objects and people, and situations. The superego, which develops last, represents the moral standards of society as interpreted by the parents. It is roughly equivalent to "conscience," and its role is to prohibit behavior that falls short of a moral ideal.

Anxiety results when the ego senses danger. Freud distinguished among reality anxiety (a threat from the outside world), moral anxiety (guilt or shame caused by the superego), and neurotic anxiety (danger from the id's impulses). Most anxiety is not experienced consciously but is kept closeted in the unconscious and expressed only through the ego's use of the defense mechanisms—repression, projection, displacement, rationalization, isolation (intellectualization), denial, reaction formation, regression, and sublimation.

Freud viewed personality development as a process of childhood psychosexual development from the oral stage to the anal stage and then to the phallic stage. Anxiety connected with undergratification or overgratification at any of these stages can lead to maladaptive adult behavior. The phallic stage is especially crucial because it is the time when a child is faced by the Oedipus complex, or desire to do away with the same-sex parent and possess the opposite-sex parent. This conflict is usually resolved by identification with the same-sex parent. Latency and the genital stage, in which mature sexuality is attained, are the final stages of psychosexual development.

Freud believed that both normal and abnormal behavior result from the interactions of the id, ego, and superego. Abnormal behavior can result when the three components are in a state of imbalance and the ego is weakened or when an unresolved childhood conflict produces acute anxiety, or neurosis. Anxiety over impulse gratification can lead to fixation in the adult personality. In extreme cases, adaptive functioning breaks down and the ego collapses, a condition called psychosis.

Freud's theories were extended and modified by a number of other thinkers. Post-Freudian theorists tended to deemphasize sexuality, the id, and the phallic stage of development; they emphasized instead self-direction and social relationships. Carl Gustav Jung believed that the libido and the unconscious contain broader and more positive forces than they do in Freud's view, and he argued for the existence of a collective unconscious, or set of symbols shared by all humankind. His brand of psychotherapy involved individuation, or integration of opposing forces. Alfred Adler claimed that all human behavior is an attempt to overcome an inferiority complex and that social relationships are the key to psychological health.

Harry Stack Sullivan agreed with Adler that psychological problems are caused by interpersonal ones and stressed the parent–child relationship. He pointed out the importance of the self-concept; he was also the first analyst to report success in treating psychotics over the long term. Karen Horney also believed in the social root of psychological disorders, attributing them in part to society as a whole, not just to immediate social relationships.

Heinz Hartmann shifted emphasis from the id to the ego and its functions. His ideas became the foundation of ego psychology and provide a bridge between classical psychoanalytic theory and cognitive psychology. Erik Erikson extended this trend by emphasizing the formation of ego identity through the process of psychosocial development, a series of stages that extends not just through childhood but until death.

Margaret Mahler and Heinz Kohut emphasized the child's relations and emotional ties to the parent. Mahler, an object relations theorist, focused on the early process of separation–individuation, which occurs in four phases between the ages of five months and three years. Kohut developed self psychology and invented the diagnostic category of narcissistic personality disorder. Although Mahler's and Kohut's theories are consistent with Freud's view that early childhood experience determines the adult's psychological health or disturbance, their views are broader, balancing emotional, cognitive, and interpersonal needs against purely biological ones in the developing self.

Although it corresponds in some ways to the medical model, psychodynamic theory was the first theory to explain behavioral and mental disorders in terms of the individual's emotional history. It has been attacked on a variety of grounds—its lack of experimental support, dependence on inference, unrepresentative sampling of case histories, and reductive view of human life. However, psychodynamic theory has made crucial contributions to twentieth-century thought, focusing attention on inner life, enabling the mentally disturbed to be treated as human beings, and giving rise to a wide range of therapies.

The Behavioral Perspective

Perhaps the most fundamental assumption of psychodynamic theory is that what you see is not what you've got. Behavior and even feelings, insofar as they are conscious, are only the surface. The truth lies beneath, in inner and, usually, remote causes. It is in this matter of causative focus that behavioral psychology, the second major perspective we will consider, departs most radically from psychodynamic thought. For the behaviorists, the most important causes of behavior are *proximal* causes, causes that lie close to the behavior itself and can therefore be readily identified (Kaplan, 1974; Bootzin and Max, 1980).

As in many other quarrels among the various perspectives, the difference is a matter of emphasis. Nev-

ertheless, it is a very big difference. Faced with a student who is depressed following a poor showing on an exam, a psychodynamic theorist would not ignore the fact of the exam, but would consider it a jumping-off point for more fundamental explorations: How did failure during childhood affect his relationship with his parents? And what are the chances that his true emotion is not perhaps depression but something that the depression is covering—anger, for example, at his parents? Faced with the same student, the behavioral theorist would not ignore childhood experiences with failure, but would be more interested in current experiences: What did the student say to himself before the exam, and after? What circumstances in his environment may have caused the failure, and what current perceptions and circumstances may now be operating to encourage the response of depression?

This difference in focus between psychodynamic and behavioral theorists is reflected in their methods. Psychodynamic theorists, interested in the inner reaches of the psyche, must frequently forgo scientific verifiability. The behaviorists' proximal focus, by contrast, is in part the *result* of their insistence on scientific method.

The behavioral approach to specific patterns of abnormal behavior will be discussed in the chapters dealing with those patterns. The purpose of the present chapter is to outline the history of behavioral psychology, its basic assumptions, and its general interpretation of normal and abnormal behavior, along with the current movement toward the study of cognitive influences on behavior.

THE BACKGROUND OF BEHAVIORISM

Freud's was only one of many psychological theories in the late nineteenth century that depended on **introspection,** the study of the mind by analysis of one's own thought processes. Originating in Europe, the introspective method soon spread to the United States, where it became the dominant trend in academic psychology. It was in reaction to this trend that behaviorism arose, claiming that the causes of behavior need not be sought in the depths of the mind but could be found in the immediate environment, in stimuli that elicited, reinforced, and punished

Ivan Pavlov, the Russian neurophysiologist who discovered the conditioned reflex. Pavlov received the Nobel Prize in 1904. (Culver Pictures)

certain responses. The explanation, in other words, lay in **learning,** the process whereby behavior changes in response to the environment.

In fact, learning had long been recognized as an important influence on human character. But it was not until the early twentieth century that scientists began to uncover the actual mechanisms of learning, thereby laying the theoretical foundation for behaviorism. The contributions of four particular scientists were especially crucial.

Pavlov: The Conditioned Reflex

In conducting research with dogs, Ivan Pavlov (1849–1936), a Russian neurophysiologist, found that if he consistently sounded a tone at the same time that he gave a dog food, the dog would eventually salivate to the sound of the tone alone. Thus Pavlov discovered a basic mechanism of learning, the **conditioned reflex:** if a neutral stimulus (e.g., the tone) is paired with a nonneutral stimulus (e.g., the food), the organism will eventually respond to the neutral stimulus as it does to the nonneutral stimulus.

The implications of this discovery were truly revolutionary. Whereas it had always been assumed that human beings' reactions to their environment were the result of complicated subjective processes, Pavlov's finding raised the possibility that many of our responses, like those of the dogs, were the result of a simple learning process. In other words, our loves and hates, our tastes and distastes might be the consequences of nothing more mysterious than a conditioning process whereby various things in our environment became "linked" in our minds to other things that we responded to instinctively, such as food, warmth, and pain. As we shall see, this extraordinary notion became a fundamental principle of behavioral psychology.

Pavlov contributed not only to the theory but also to the methodology of behaviorism. He was part of a school of Russian neurophysiologists, including Ivan Sechenov (1829–1905) and Vladimir Bechterev (1857–1927), who rejected the introspective approach to psychology in favor of the strictly objective, experimental approach that was eventually to become the hallmark of behaviorism (Kazdin, 1978a). But Pavlov and his colleagues simply pursued this methodology; they did not turn it into a manifesto for a new psychology. This role fell to a younger man, an American.

Watson: The Founding of Behaviorism

It is John B. Watson (1878–1958), an American psychologist, who is credited with founding the behavioral movement. This honor has been bestowed on him not because Watson made major contributions to the theory of behaviorism but rather because he publicized the empirical method and made it the battle cry for a new school of psychology, aggressively opposed to subjective approaches.

In a now-famous article, "Psychology as the Behaviorist Views It," Watson made his position clear: "Psychology, as the behaviorist views it, is a purely objective, experimental branch of natural science which needs introspection as little as do the sciences of chemistry and physics" (1913, p. 176). Watson argued that introspection was, if anything, the province of theology. In any case, it had no place in psychology. The province of psychology was behavior—that is, observable and measurable responses to specific stimuli. And the goal of psychology was the prediction and control of behavior.

Watson supported his rejection of the introspective method by demonstrating, in a classic experiment, that a supposedly subjective emotion such as fear could, like the salivation response of Pavlov's dogs, result from a simple, objective conditioning process. With the help of one of his colleagues, Rosalie Rayner, Watson conditioned a fear of rats in an eleven-month-old boy, Albert B. (Watson and Rayner, 1920). Before the experiment, Albert had no fear of laboratory rats. On the contrary, he liked them and was used to playing with them. On the first day of the experiment, the boy was shown a white rat. As he reached for it, Watson struck an iron bar with a hammer, producing a very loud noise. The first time this happened, Albert was simply startled. As it happened again and again, he began to show signs of fright—crying, falling over, and crawling away from the rat. After seven pairings of the rat and the noise, Albert reacted in the same manner to the rat alone, without the noise. Thus a strong conditioned fear reaction had been established. Later tests showed that without further conditioning, Albert produced the same frightened behaviors in response to a variety of stimuli similar to the rat: a rabbit, a dog, a sealskin coat, a bearded Santa Claus mask. In commenting on these results, Watson argued that many of our "unreasonable" fears are established in the same way that Albert's was—through conditioning.

John B. Watson, the founder of the behaviorist movement. He argued for an empirical approach to the study of human behavior, and in his experiment with Albert B., he demonstrated that human emotions could be generated through observable conditioning processes. (Culver Pictures)

Thorndike: The Law of Effect

Another psychologist of Watson's time was Edward Lee Thorndike (1874–1949), whose early experiments with animals had a decisive influence on learning theory. Unlike Pavlov and Watson, who had studied the relationship between stimuli that preceded behavior, Thorndike was interested in the impact of such stimuli as *consequences* of behavior. If an organism is repeatedly presented with a pleasant or painful stimulus after making a given response, how will the stimulus affect the response?

In one experiment Thorndike placed a hungry cat in a box equipped in such a way that if the cat pulled a cord or pressed a lever, the door of the chamber flew open. When the cat escaped through the door, it was given a piece of salmon to eat. Thorndike noted the time it took for the cat to escape on each successive trial. In early trials the pattern was irregular. Sometimes the cat escaped quickly; on other occa-

Edward L. Thorndike contributed to behavioral theory through his formulation of the law of effect, which established the importance of rewards in the learning process. (National Library of Medicine)

sions it took a long time. Gradually, however, the pattern became more regular and the escape time shorter and shorter, so that finally when the cat was placed in the box, it almost immediately made the desired response, escaped, and received the food.

Thorndike concluded that the reason the cat had learned the proper escape response was that this response had become associated with the food, which was the consequence of escaping. From this conclusion Thorndike formulated what he called the **law of effect,** which stated that responses that led to "satisfying" consequences were strengthened and therefore were likely to be repeated, while responses that led to "unsatisfying" consequences were weakened and therefore were unlikely to be repeated.

Though Thorndike used objective methods in his experiments, Watson did not consider him a behaviorist, for he used subjective terms such as "satisfying" and "unsatisfying" to describe his observations. For the early behaviorists, all references to inferred mental states were unscientific and therefore to be avoided. Yet despite its subjective wording, Thorndike's law of effect had laid down another fundamental principle of learning: the importance of reward in the learning process.

Skinner: The Control of Behavior

Following the pioneering discoveries of Pavlov and Thorndike, many prominent psychologists—including Edwin Guthrie (1886–1959), Edward Chase Tolman (1896–1961), Clark Hull (1884–1952), and B. F. Skinner (1904–   )—contributed to the development of learning theory. Of these, the one who has had the most decisive influence on the behavioral perspective has been Skinner.

Skinner's major contribution was to refine Thorndike's discoveries and to demonstrate their application to everyday life. Like Watson, Skinner was interested in the control of behavior, and he saw in Thorndike's law, which he renamed the **principle of reinforcement,** the basic mechanism for predicting and controlling human behavior. Skinner (1965) pointed out that our social environment is filled with reinforcing consequences, which mold our behavior as surely as the piece of salmon molded the behavior of Thorndike's cat. Our friends and families control us with their approval or disapproval. Our jobs control us by offering or withholding money. Our schools control us by passing us or failing us and thus affecting our access to jobs. In short, in all the areas of our lives our

B. F. Skinner, the articulate spokesman of modern behaviorism, has done much to refine and extend earlier conceptualizations, demonstrating their applicability to everyday life. (Camilla Smith)

actions are determined by their connection with pleasant or unpleasant consequences. Thus Skinner finally stated what Pavlov's research had merely suggested: that much of our behavior is based not on internal contingencies but on external contingencies. Furthermore, precisely because they *are* external, these contingencies can be altered to change our behavior. As we shall see, this is a fundamental principle of behavioral treatment in abnormal psychology.

Early Cognitive Theorists

Most of the early behaviorists concentrated exclusively on the relationship between behavior and external events, avoiding any reference to **cognition**—that is, mental processes such as emotion, thought, expectation, and interpretation. There is nothing in Pavlov's writings about what occurred in the minds of the dogs between the sound of the tone and the response of salivation, nor does Watson make any reference to the mental processes underlying Albert B.'s change of heart concerning rats. These investigators did not deny that learning involved cognitive events, but they regarded such events as nothing more than byproducts of external events. Cognition had no *causal* role in learning, and therefore it could be safely ignored.

This stimulus-response, or S R, position was endorsed by most learning theorists. Other theorists, however, questioned the exclusion of cognitive events. How is it, the latter asked, that a group of human beings, all presented with the same stimulus (for example, the announcement that the theater they are in is on fire), can produce so many different responses? Some other factor, in addition to the stimulus, must be contributing to the formation of the response. Presumably, that other factor was cognition: the mental processing of the stimulus.

Some psychologists, including Edward Tolman, went so far as to contest the very principle of reinforcement. According to this line of thought, human beings learn not by reinforcement of trial-and-error responses but by perceiving the relationship among various elements of the task. Reinforcement, Tolman argued (1948), affected learning by creating expectancies, inner "predictions" as to which responses would lead to rewards and punishments in which situations. But as for the responses themselves, they were

These people on a ride are being exposed to the same stimulus, but their responses are very different. Cognitive theorists attribute these differences in response to the way in which each person's mind processes the stimulus. (David Woo/Stock, Boston)

learned through mental processes independent of reinforcement. Tolman and Honzig (1930) demonstrated this principle by showing that if rats were given a chance to explore a maze, first with no reinforcement, then later, when reinforcement was available, these rats would run the maze faster than other rats that had not had an opportunity to explore the apparatus. In other words, the rats had learned something without being rewarded for it.

Thus behaviorism no sooner evolved a comprehensive S-R theory than it also produced a cognitive challenge to that theory. As we shall see, this friendly quarrel within the behavioral school has produced valuable results in the form of refined theories and advances in treatment.

THE ASSUMPTIONS OF BEHAVIORAL PSYCHOLOGY

Before we go on to discuss the mechanisms of learning, it will be useful to review briefly the basic assumptions of behaviorism as it developed in the hands of the scientists whose work we have just discussed.

The Study of Behavior

The first assumption is that the task of psychology is, as Watson claimed, the study of behavior—that is, the study of the responses that an organism makes to the stimuli in its environment. Such stimuli may come from outside us—from the people, objects, and events in our external environment. However, they may also be internal, such as back pain, which may elicit the response of going to the bathroom to take a pill, or the thought "Oops, I forgot to take my pill," which will elicit the same response. Likewise, responses may be external (e.g., pounding a table in anger) or internal (e.g., the thought "I'm not going to show her I'm angry"). And they can range from the simplest reflex, such as a blinking of the eyes in response to bright light, to a highly complex chain of actions such as hitting a baseball or writing an essay.

The Empirical Method

A second basic assumption has to do with methodology. According to classical behaviorism, both stimuli and responses are objective, empirical events that can be observed and measured, and that *must* be observed and measured in order to qualify as scientific evidence. Hence behavioral studies since the time of Pavlov have always attempted to include careful measurement of responses. Indeed, one of the major innovations of Pavlov's research was that he not only observed the dogs' responses but also quantified them as to *magnitude* (the amount of saliva that occurred in response to the stimulus) and *latency* (the amount of time it took for the salivation response to occur after the presentation of the stimulus). Another very important measurement is *rate,* the frequency with which a response occurs within a given period of time. Such measures have become the basic tools of behavioral research.

The Prediction and Control of Behavior

A third assumption, again formulated by Watson, is that the goal of psychology is the prediction and control of behavior. In declaring this goal, Watson placed behavioral psychology in direct alignment with the natural sciences, whose object is to discover and apply general laws. Just as a botanist can predict that a cactus will grow only in warm, dry weather, and could control the development of a sickly cactus by moving it from Massachusetts to Arizona, so the behaviorist attempts to predict how human beings will respond under different sets of environmental conditions and to control those responses by controlling the environmental stimuli that affect them.

For the behaviorist working in a laboratory, under carefully controlled environmental circumstances and with experimental animals whose conditioning history is known, prediction and control are a fairly easy matter. But when the behaviorist moves out of the laboratory into the world at large and attempts to deal with human beings, prediction and control become more difficult. For the environmental stimuli of everyday life are infinitely more varied, complex, and uncontrollable than those of the laboratory. Furthermore, the responses of human beings are far more complicated—and their conditioning histories far less knowable—than those of the white rat. One might predict, for example, that a hungry boy, when called to dinner, might go directly to the dinner table. But if the boy has come to associate dinnertime with his parents' quarreling, then he may be just as likely to lock himself in his room as to go to the dinner table. In keeping with cognitive theory, many behaviorists would now argue that these more nebulous variables—associations, thoughts, feelings—can also be pinpointed, just like the dinner call. In any case, the behavioral position is that human responses to various kinds of stimuli can be stated as general laws and that when a response is interfering with a person's adjustment, that response can be changed by careful alteration of the stimuli in question.

The Importance of Learning

The final basic assumption of behaviorism is that the major ingredient in behavior is learning. As we saw in the preceding section, behavioral psychology was founded on learning theory. The two are not synonymous, for behaviorism is method as well as theory. Behavioral psychology might best be defined as the application of learning theory and other experimentally derived principles to human behavior (Begelmann, 1975; Bootzin, 1975). Still, the behaviorists definitely regard learning as the central component of behavior, and it is primarily in terms of learning theory that they attempt to explain both normal and abnormal behavior.

These four assumptions are the pillars of classical behaviorism. As we just saw in the last example, they have been modified somewhat in keeping with cognitive theory. Indeed, merely by studying mental processes, the cognitive wing of behaviorism flies in the face of Watson's insistence that psychologists focus exclusively on observable phenomena. Furthermore, most cognitive theorists would now question the assertion that environmental stimuli control learning. Following Tolman, they would say that environmental stimuli merely control performance—that is, the likelihood of the organism's producing the response in any given set of circumstances. Learning, on the other hand, is the product of mental events. Despite these objections, however, the cognitive theorists still share the empirical tradition of behaviorism and try to study thoughts with as much precision and objectivity as if they were salivary responses. In general it can be said that the basic assumptions of classical behaviorism still function as guiding principles, if not as iron laws, for modern behaviorism.

THE MECHANISMS OF LEARNING

Respondent Conditioning

According to classical behavioral theory, all behavior falls into two classes, respondent and operant. **Respondent behavior**—behavior that occurs reflexively, or automatically, in response to specific stimuli—consists of **unconditioned responses** and **conditioned responses.** Unconditioned responses are simple responses, such as blinking or salivation, that occur automatically when elicited by certain stimuli. However, as we have seen, it is possible, through the pairing of stimuli, to condition an organism so that it will show the same response to a new stimulus,

one that would not naturally have elicited the response. The learning of such a conditioned response is called **respondent conditioning** (or **classical conditioning**). The classic example is the one we have already discussed: Pavlov's dog experiment. Since a hungry dog will naturally salivate when presented with food, the food is designated as an **unconditioned stimulus** (UCS) and the natural response of salivation as the **unconditioned response** (UCR). And since the dog's salivation to the tone was the result of conditioning, the tone is called the **conditioned stimulus** (CS) and the salivation to the tone alone the **conditioned response** (CR).

Generalization and Discrimination   An extremely important aspect of respondent behavior is the process of **generalization,** whereby once an organism has been conditioned to respond in a certain way to a particular stimulus, it will respond in the same way to similar stimuli without further conditioning. In other words, the conditioned response automatically "spreads," or generalizes, to things that resemble the conditioned stimulus. Once again, we have already seen the classic example: Albert B.'s spontaneous fear of rabbits, dogs, sealskin coats, and Santa Claus masks once he was conditioned to fear the white rat. Likewise, Pavlov noted that once a dog had been conditioned to salivate upon hearing a tone of a certain sound frequency, tones of similar but different frequencies could also elicit salivation without having been paired with food. By the same process, a person who, as a child, had a beloved cocker spaniel and a mother with a Southern accent may go through life automatically feeling warmly toward all cocker spaniels and women with Southern accents.

The effects of generalization can be limited by the process of **discrimination**—that is, learning to distinguish among similar stimuli and to respond only to the appropriate one. Pavlov, for instance, found that if the food was consistently paired with only one tone, while similar tones were always presented without food, then the effects of generalization would be effaced, and the dog would learn to salivate only at the sound of the tone that had been paired with food. Likewise, people learn to discriminate between similar stimuli—between a yellow banana and a green banana, between jaywalking on a country road and jaywalking on a six-lane highway—when one of these stimuli is found to be rewarding and the other is not.

Preparedness

Why are people so much more afraid of snakes than of automobiles when they are, in our society at least, so much more likely to be killed in a car accident than bitten by a serpent? Some investigators have suggested that human beings—and other mammals—seem instinctively prepared, or biologically predisposed, to make certain associations (Seligman, 1971). Have millions of years of evolution biologically prepared us to fear snakes—and to like and approach or dislike and avoid other specific stimuli? Or is the brain a "general-purpose associator," so that we learn to fear or dislike certain objects only through respondent conditioning?

The actual evidence in regard to preparedness is mixed. Some researchers claim that we discriminate between potentially harmful and harmless stimuli that are paired with an unconditioned fear stimulus, but others disagree. One group of experimenters found that subjects were just as likely to acquire a fear of flowers as of snakes when pictures of these objects were paired with an electric shock as the UCS. However, the experimenters had a much harder time extinguishing the fear of snakes in their subjects than the fear of flowers (Öhman et al., 1985). In another experiment, pictures of snakes or of flowers were established as safety signals for the *absence* of electric shock (McNally and Reiss, 1982). The problem the researchers encountered in extinguishing the fear of snakes seems to support preparedness theory, but the successful use of this stimulus as a safety signal argues against it.

The validity of preparedness was also tested in a clinical setting when researchers examined the records of sixty-nine phobic and eighty-two obsessional patients treated in a London hospital and then rated the patients' phobias on the basis of their supposed evolutionary significance. Examiners reasoned that phobias supporting the concept of preparedness should prove to be easily learned yet difficult to extinguish—but this was not the case (DeSilva et al., 1977). Records of onset and treatment showed that although snake phobias are easily acquired, they are also easily treated. In a subsequent study of forty-nine phobics, preparedness of the phobia was found to be unrelated to suddenness of onset, age at onset, duration of treatment, severity of anxiety, or severity of disruption to the patient's life (Zafiropoulou and McPherson, 1986).

Preparedness, then, fails to explain why people develop phobias in response to stimuli that have no

Operant Conditioning

While respondent behavior is confined to simple, automatic responses, **operant behavior,** the second class of behavior, can range in complexity from small, uncomplicated acts such as flipping a light switch to extremely intricate sequences of actions such as building a house. The essential difference between respondent and operant behavior is implied in the two names: in respondent behavior the organism simply responds to a stimulus, whereas in operant behavior the organism operates upon the environment—in short, *does something*—in order to achieve a desired result. An easy (although, technically speaking, not totally accurate) way of distinguishing between the two is to think of respondent behavior as involuntary and of operant behavior as voluntary (Skinner, 1965).[*] If someone has a coughing fit (respondent behavior) during a funeral service, we don't blame the person, because we recognize the behavior as involuntary. But if some one does a crossword puzzle (operant behavior) during the service, we do consider this action improper, since we see it as voluntary.

---

[*] Twenty years ago, the voluntary-versus-involuntary distinction, as applied to operant and respondent behavior, was generally accepted. However, it has since been discovered that many areas of respondent behavior once considered involuntary—such as changes in heart rate and blood pressure—can in fact be brought under voluntary control if the person is allowed to monitor his or her functioning in this area through a process called *biofeedback* (Miller, 1969). Biofeedback and its contributions to abnormal psychology will be discussed in Chapter 9.

evolutionary significance or why their fears of objects that do carry such significance respond so readily to treatment. But the theory does help to explain why almost all of us take fright at certain stimuli even before conditioning and why we—and many other species as well—often make selective associations in experiments in respondent conditioning. In a series of experiments, John Garcia and his colleagues (Garcia et al., 1968, 1972) demonstrated that rats too are selective. When rats became ill after eating distinctively flavored food, they almost invariably developed an aversion to any food of that flavor, tending to "blame" the food for their illness even though it was induced by drugs or X-rays administered several hours after the rats had eaten. However, rats subjected to externally administered pain, such as electric shock, that was paired with the conditioned stimulus of the same odd-flavored food failed to make the association and were willing to taste and eat the food again. The rats seemed biologically prepared to associate selectively, avoiding a specific type of CS (the novel food) after experiencing a specific type of UCR (gastric rather than external pain). In other experiments, taste-aversion conditioning has been used to protect grazing lambs from coyotes (Gustavson et al., 1974) and wolves (Garcia et al., 1977). After eating lamb meat laced with lithium chloride and other emetic agents, the predators eat other natural prey, such as rabbits, but avoid lambs altogether.

Human beings seem just as likely as other mammals to associate illness and nausea with new flavors they have sampled. Young cancer patients who ate Mapletoff, a distinctively flavored ice cream, before undergoing chemotherapy—a treatment frequently followed by attacks of nausea—rejected the flavor 3 to 1 when offered the choice again several months later. A control group of cancer patients, who had not had chemotherapy after eating ice cream, were equally divided in the second trial, choosing Mapletoff as often as another flavor (Bernstein, 1978).

Selective associations—for example, between novel flavors and subsequent stomach upset—certainly have survival value and probably have developed, as preparedness theory suggests, over the course of evolution. And the kinds of preparedness favored by evolution depended on the environmental hazards we and other mammals faced. Early humans who feared snakes presumably lived longer than those who did not. Even though the fear of snakes was easily treated in phobic patients in their snake-free London environment, we would not assume that desensitization or other treatments to extinguish fears of rats or scorpions would be very successful with people previously conditioned to avoid them—in rat-infested tenements or in public bathhouses in the tropics. Whenever we describe a stimulus as neutral or the brain as a "general-purpose associator," we would do well to keep in mind that even before conditioning most people seem to know on some level whether certain stimuli are friends or foes.

Unlike respondent behavior, all operant behavior is the result of conditioning. In **operant conditioning** (sometimes referred to as **instrumental conditioning**), an organism learns to associate certain results with certain actions that it has taken. If the results are desirable, then the organism will repeat those actions, and if they are not desirable, it will avoid repeating them. This, of course, is Thorndike's law of effect, and the best example is Thorndike's cat. After a few accidental pressings of the lever, resulting in the rewards of an open door and piece of fish, the cat eventually learned to associate these rewards with the pressing of the lever. Consequently, it began to press the lever as soon as it was put in the box. However, if pressing the lever had resulted in an electric shock, it would have learned, by the same operant-conditioning process, to associate this

aversive (that is, painful or unpleasant) stimulus with the pressing of the lever and thus to avoid pressing it.

In the course of human development, operant conditioning goes on every day. Part of the reason children learn to speak is that speaking allows them to communicate their needs and desires to others. They learn to stop wetting their pants because wet pants bring parental disapproval. As they get older, they learn social skills—how to decline an invitation to a party they don't want to attend, how to ask someone for a date, how to respond to an insult—because such skills allow them to deal effectively with other people.

Operant versus Respondent Conditioning   As the previous discussion suggests, respondent and operant conditioning teach us two different and complementary components of behavior. In general, it is through respondent conditioning—years and years of learned associations between previously neutral stimuli and pleasant or unpleasant stimuli—that we acquire our values, our ideas about what we like and don't like. And in general, it is through operant conditioning—as many years of being rewarded or punished for different actions—that we acquire our skills, our ways of getting what we like and avoiding what we don't like. Walking, speaking, reading, writing, riding a bicycle, playing a musical instrument, throwing a football—we master all these skills by stringing operant responses together. But the reason we care to master them at all is that they satisfy desires developed through respondent conditioning.

A good way to grasp the difference between the two types of learning is to try to imagine either one without the other. People equipped with a variety of respondents but no operants would be sensitive but helpless. Loving lasagne, they would be incapable of getting in the car and going to an Italian restaurant; hating to get wet, they would not know how to come in out of the rain. By contrast, people equipped with operants but no respondents would be robots—all skills and no desires. Though capable of getting to an Italian restaurant or of coming in out of the rain, they would have no motivation to do so; someone else would have to press the button. Both of these anomalies are equally hard to imagine, for in actual experience the products of respondent and operant learning are inextricably mixed, the one providing the spice of life—our joys and sorrows—the other providing our ways of getting through life.

Reinforcement

Were it not for the fish, Thorndike's cat would not have learned to press the lever. Were it not for the paycheck, most of us would not go to work. In all cases, according to classical behaviorism, behavior is learned by being reinforced.

As Skinner has pointed out, the world is full of reinforcers, positive and negative—food, traffic tickets, birthday presents, head colds, people who amuse us, people who annoy us. The simplest type of reinforcer, the **primary reinforcer,** is one to which we respond instinctively, without learning. For example, *primary positive reinforcers* include such basic requirements as food, water, warmth, and sex, while *primary*

negative reinforcers include the termination or avoidance of such automatically aversive stimuli as bright lights, extreme heat or cold, and electric shock.

However, most of the reinforcers to which we respond are not the simple primary reinforcers but rather **conditioned reinforcers** (also called **secondary reinforcers**), stimuli to which we have learned to respond by associating them with primary reinforcers. For example, a newborn baby places no value on its parents' approval. What the baby does value is being fed and held, and it is by associating the parents with these primary reinforcers that the baby learns to respond to the parents themselves and their approval as conditioned positive reinforcers, and to respond to their disapproval as a conditioned negative reinforcer. Money is another good example of a conditioned reinforcer. We respond to it positively because it is associated with past reinforcers and signals the future delivery of further reinforcers.

Modes of Reinforcement   Reinforcement operates on behavior in four basic ways. In **positive reinforcement** a response is followed by a positive reinforcer, with the result that the response increases in frequency. Suppose that a child who is afraid of the dark makes it through the night without invading her parents' bedroom. Her parents reward her by saying, "Good girl!" and giving her pancakes for breakfast. If the child then makes it through the succeeding nights without incident, we can say that positive reinforcement has occurred, with the parents' approval acting as a conditioned positive reinforcer and the pancakes acting as a primary positive reinforcer. It is important to note that positive reinforcement, along with the other forms of reinforcement, occurs only if the stimulus in question actually changes the frequency of the response. Reinforcement, by definition, works; reinforcers, by definition, influence behavior. If the approval and the pancakes do not impel the child to further efforts to master her fear, they have not acted as positive reinforcers, and positive reinforcement has not taken place.

A second type of reinforcement that operates to increase the frequency of behavior is **negative reinforcement.** In this case, however, what promotes the response is not the presentation of a pleasant stimulus but *the avoidance or removal of an aversive stimulus.* (Negative reinforcement should not be confused with punishment, the suppression of a response

Everyday experience demonstrates that food—perhaps especially free food—exerts a powerful attraction on most people. Classical behaviorists agree that food and other primary reinforcers evoke a simple, instinctive response that does not involve learning. (Ellis Herwig/The Picture Cube)

through the presentation of an aversive stimulus. This mechanism will be discussed shortly.) To understand negative reinforcement, let us imagine that a student fails to study for an exam and consequently receives an F (conditioned negative reinforcer). If he or she then studies for the next exam and thereby avoids a further exposure to this aversive stimulus, the response of studying for exams will probably increase, having been reinforced by the student's relief over escaping failure.

This process, also called **avoidance learning,** can teach us some very useful behaviors, as in the example just cited. However, behaviorists feel that it may also be responsible for many patterns of abnormal behavior. For example, the little boy who is bitten by a dog may afterward simply run the other way whenever he sees a dog, and every time he flees, the reduction of his fear once the dog is out of sight will reinforce the escape response. As a result, the dog phobia will be maintained indefinitely. The only thing that can relieve it is a series of good or at least neutral contacts with dogs, but since the boy avoids dogs altogether, he has no chance of making such contacts.

While positive and negative reinforcement have the effect of promoting a response, the two remaining modes of reinforcement, extinction and punishment, act to eliminate and suppress responses. **Extinction** involves the removal of the reinforcement that is maintaining a response, with the result that the response gradually dies out. Thus if Thorndike, after teaching the cat to press the lever, had rearranged the box so that pressing the lever no longer resulted in the opening of the door, then the cat, after a number of attempts with no results, would eventually have ceased to press the lever. Extinction is no doubt partially responsible for the normal child's gradual abandonment of infantile behaviors. When tears are no longer met with comforting and "cute" mispronunciations are no longer reinforced by "Isn't she sweet!" these habits are likely to extinguish.

Finally, there is **punishment,** in which a response is followed by an aversive stimulus, or by the termination or omission of a positive stimulus, with the result that the frequency of the response decreases. For example, when we smack a dog with a newspaper (primary punishment) for chewing on the furniture, or yell "No! No!" (conditioned punishment) at a child

Identifying Reinforcers: The Premack Principle

How do we decide what will be reinforcing to any particular individual? To behavior therapists, this is an important question, for in order to increase any given behavior, they have to find some way of reinforcing that behavior. One solution would be to depend on primary reinforcers—food, for example. But food for one person is not food for another person. Some people adore soft drinks, while others find them cloying and unwholesome. Furthermore, the power of a primary reinforcer will vary with the degree of deprivation that has preceded it. Ten minutes after a heavy dinner, even a glutton may refuse food.

A useful rule for identifying reinforcers has been suggested by the psychologist David Premack (1965). This rule, called the Premack Principle, states that *any high-probability behavior can be used to reinforce a low-probability behavior.* In other words, anything that you tend to do often can be enlisted as a reinforcer to help you do things that you do seldom but wish you did more. Behavioral psychologists use this rule in designing therapy programs, and you can use it on yourself.

Consider your daily activities. What are the things that you do regularly? Do you watch the news on television every night? Read the paper every morning on the bus? Have a cup of coffee between your two o'clock class and your four o'clock class? These may seem relatively unglamorous activities, but if you engage in them regularly, then for you they are probably reinforcing. And if so, you can increase some other behavior by making these reinforcers contingent upon the performance of that behavior.

Let us assume, for example, that you do stop for a cup of coffee every afternoon. Also assume that you don't do exercises in the morning, although you wish you did. Thus, in order to increase your rate of exercising, you allow yourself the afternoon coffee only on days when you have already done all your exercises in the morning.

The Premack Principle is useful in that it calls attention to reinforcers that we might otherwise ignore. (You might not imagine, for example, that your reading assignments in history are reinforcing, but if they are the assignments that always get done, while French and economics tend not to get done, then they can probably be used as reinforcers to encourage you to do French and economics. Just make a rule that French and economics must be completed before you start history.) Furthermore, these humble, everyday reinforcers are often of more value in helping people to change their behavior than other, more elaborate reinforcers, such as milkshakes or movies, which can become expensive, fattening, and impractical.

who is flushing a towel down the toilet, we are trying to use punishment, and if the child and the dog thereafter indulge less frequently in these behaviors, we have succeeded. However, stimuli that may appear to be aversive sometimes make no dent whatsoever in the frequency of the responses they follow, either because they are not actually aversive for the person concerned or because their effects are canceled out by conflicting reinforcers. (For example, an especially rebellious child may derive more pleasure than pain from his mother's distress, in which case a scolding from her will simply cause him to misbehave with increased relish.) The pleasantness or aversiveness of any given reinforcer varies from individual to individual and from situation to situation. For this reason, reinforcement is defined by its effect—a change in the frequency of the response—rather than by the seemingly positive or negative value of the stimulus.

Shaping

Particularly important in learning is a process called **shaping,** which involves the reinforcement of successive approximations of a desired response until it finally achieves the desired form. Imagine, for example, that you are doing an experiment in which you want to train a pigeon to peck at a disk on the side of its cage. One thing you might do is wait for the pigeon to make the response, at which point you could reinforce it. However, if you use this strategy, you might have to wait by the side of the cage for years, since the chances that this response will occur spontaneously are small. Instead, what you can do is shape the response, first by reinforcing any movement on the side of the cage nearest the disk, then by reinforcing only those movements that the pigeon makes specifically in the direction of the disk, then by reinforcing only pecking-like movements in the direction of the disk. Finally, when the bird at last pecks at the disk, you reinforce this response and stop reinforcing all other responses—with the result that they will extinguish.

The process of shaping is extremely important in the development of many of our skills. Imagine a child learning to dive. First she sits on the edge of the pool, puts her head down, and just sort of falls into the water. For this first step she receives a pat on the back (positive reinforcement) from the swimming teacher. Then she may start from a standing position and even hazard a little push as she takes off. This effort will be reinforced by further approval from the teacher, by the pleasure of a smoother descent into the water, and by her own feelings of achievement. Soon she will be ready for the diving board and then for fancier and fancier dives, with external and internal rewards at every step of the way. Thus throughout the process there is positive reinforcement of successive approximations of the diving response, while other responses—for example, the child's belly flops—are extinguished.

Modeling

We have omitted one aspect of the child's diving lesson. It is probable that the swimming teacher would dive into the pool to show the child the proper technique and would then reward the child with approval if she could imitate this technique. This type of learning—learning through imitation—is known in the vocabulary of behaviorism as **modeling** (Bandura and Walters, 1963; Rosenthal and Bandura, 1978).

As in the diving lesson, so in human development in general, modeling normally accompanies shaping—that is, we are rewarded for successive approximations of a model response. But the converse is not necessarily true. Many children get no pats on the

Modeling, which is controlled by internal processes, can occur without reinforcement: In order to be reproduced, a behavior simply has to be observed. Thus, by observing his father's golf stroke, this boy can improve his own. (Menschenfreund/Taurus Photos)

back as they are learning how to dive; they simply watch someone else do it, and suddenly they too are doing it. A striking characteristic of modeling is that unlike many other forms of learning, it can—and often does—occur without reinforcement, or at least without external reinforcement (Rosenthal and Bandura, 1978). The discovery of this fact gave an immense push to the cognitive position within behaviorism. Clearly, if modeling is not controlled by external reinforcements, then it must be controlled by internal processes, processes occurring within the mind. And by extension, the same might well be true of other kinds of learning.

The fact that modeling can occur without reinforcement is extremely important in human development. Many of the skills that we have to learn in life are

The Mechanisms of Learning

	Definition	Example
Respondent conditioning	Pairing a neutral stimulus with a non-neutral stimulus until the organism learns to respond to the neutral stimulus as it would to the nonneutral stimulus	A baby learns to love its mother because of the cuddling and the food she provides
Operant conditioning	Rewarding or punishing a certain response until the organism learns to repeat or avoid that response in anticipation of the positive or negative consequences	A girl learns not to lose her homework because she knows from experience that her teacher will be angry if she does
Positive reinforcement	Increasing the frequency of a behavior by rewarding it with a positive reinforcer	Students are praised by parents for doing well in school
Negative reinforcement	Increasing the frequency of a behavior by removing an aversive stimulus in response to that behavior	You learn to take aspirin for headache after doing so results in relief of the headache
Extinction	Decreasing the frequency of a behavior by removing the reinforcers that are maintaining that behavior	You refuse to lend your lecture notes to a friend who constantly cuts classes and then inconveniences you by borrowing your notes
Punishment	Decreasing the frequency of a behavior by subjecting the organism to an aversive stimulus in response to that behavior	A child who runs into the street is spanked
Generalization	Spontaneously transferring a conditioned response from the conditioned stimulus to similar stimuli	A woman, after having been raped, begins to fear all men
Discrimination	Learning to confine a response only to particular stimuli	A boy learns, via aversive encounters with his mother, that fingerpainting on the back porch is fine, whereas fingerpainting on the living room rug is not fine
Shaping	Reinforcing successive approximations of a desired response until that response is gradually achieved	A child is taught to make her bed by being praised first for pulling up the covers and smoothing them down, then for pulling up the covers, smoothing them down, and tucking them in
Modeling	Learning by imitation	A boy bangs at the piano keys after watching an adult play the piano

exceedingly complex, made up of many different responses that are performed simultaneously and sequentially. If we had to be reinforced for each successive response—for each step in boiling an egg, for example—then the acquiring of such skills would be a long and tedious process. However, because modeling seems to be self-powered to a large degree, people who have watched someone else boil an egg can, without further ado, produce the same sequence of responses. Of course, once the imitator performs these behaviors, they must prove reinforcing in some way—either externally or internally—in order to be repeated. But the fact that they can be produced whole without prior rewarding of successive steps makes modeling an incomparably efficient form of learning, without which human beings would be considerably less competent than they are.

COGNITIVE BEHAVIORISM

Early on, as we have seen, traditional, S-R behaviorism bred a dissenting school of cognitive theorists, some arguing that mental events had to be taken into account as mediators between stimulus and response, others going so far as to claim that learning was itself a mental event. In recent years the two schools have in some measure merged, with cognitive theorists becoming more interested in classic methods of behavior change while behaviorists have become more concerned with cognition (Kendall and Hollon, 1979). This combined movement, known as **cognitive behaviorism,** has become more and more influential. The central claim of the cognitive behaviorists is that cognition affects behavior independently of the stimulus—indeed, that people's actions are often responses not so much to external stimuli as to their own individual mental processing of those stimuli. These theorists claim that though cognitive events are not objectively observable, they are learned responses, and thus are subject to the same laws as other behavior.

Cognitive Appraisal

The cognitive behaviorists hold that between stimulus and response comes the all-important process of **cognitive appraisal,** whereby the person evaluates the stimulus in light of his or her own memories, beliefs, and expectations before reacting. It is this internal processing that accounts for the wide differences in individual responses to the same external stimulus. Faced with a banana split, one person may attack it with gusto; a second person, in whom this stimulus calls up thoughts regarding the social desirability of being thin, may pick at the sundae more delicately; a third person, for whom this stimulus arouses fears regarding the medical dangers of butterfat and refined sugar, may extract the banana, eat that, and walk away. Likewise, two people giving a lecture may react quite differently to the stimulus of seeing several members of the audience get up and walk out in the middle of the talk. One may say to himself, "Oh, I must be boring them to tears. I knew I would make a bad lecturer." And to this **interpretation of the stimulus** (or cognitive appraisal) he will respond by becoming anxious, perspiring, and perhaps stumbling over his words. Another lecturer, with a more positive view of herself and her speaking skills, interprets the people's departure as due to circumstances external to herself: "They must have a class to catch. Too bad they have to leave; they will miss a good talk" (Meichenbaum, 1975, p. 358). And she will proceed, unruffled, with her lecture.

In other words, what determines the response is not the stimulus itself but the person's interpretation of the stimulus. Or, as the Greek philosopher Epictetus put it, "men are disturbed not by things but by the views they take of them"—a maxim that the cognitive behaviorists are fond of quoting.

Cognitive Variables Affecting Behavior   What types of processes are involved in cognitive appraisal? Walter Mischel (1973, 1979) has proposed that there are five basic categories of cognitive variables that help to determine individual responses to a given stimulus:

1. *Competencies.* Each of us has a unique set of skills, acquired through past learning, for dealing with various situations. If person A has learned to respond to pushiness by giving in, while person B has learned to stand up for herself, then these two people will react differently when someone squeezes in front of them in the checkout line at the supermarket.

2. *Encodings.* Each of us has a special way of perceiving and categorizing experience. If a

Cognitive behaviorists believe that our cognitive appraisal of our competence affects our behavior in various situations. A person who has learned athletic skills in childhood will feel confident about participating in sports and is not likely to fear or avoid them. (Bruce Coleman)

woman who strongly supports the feminist agenda finds a copy of *Penthouse* under her teenage son's bed, she may have a talk with the boy on the injustice of viewing women as sex objects. Another woman may say to herself, "Boys will be boys," and push the magazine back under the bed.

3. *Expectancies.* Through learning, each of us forms different expectations as to which circumstances are likely to lead to rewards and punishments. A child who last year ate too much cotton candy at the circus and vomited on her new dress may turn down an invitation to go to the circus again this year, whereas another child would eagerly accept.

4. *Values.* Each of us, as a result of learning, places different values on different stimuli. A person raised in a large city may go on calmly reading his newspaper when the man sitting next to him on the bus begins talking to himself out loud. A person raised in a small, well-behaved community might get up nervously and change seats.

5. *Plans.* Through learning we also formulate plans and rules that guide our behavior. When faced with an opportunity to embezzle funds, a bank

employee whose goal is to become bank manager might report the situation to his superior. Another employee, who hates the bank and plans to move on, might take the money and leave town the next morning.

Another prominent behavioral psychologist, Albert Bandura (1977, 1982), also sees behavior as regulated primarily by cognition, but whereas Mischel divides the cognitive territory into five categories of variables, Bandura has concentrated on one category, expectations. Bandura distinguishes between two types of expectations: (1) outcome expectations, expectations that a given behavior will lead to a certain outcome; and (2) efficacy expectations, expectations that one will be able to execute that behavior successfully. Bandura claims that efficacy expectations are the chief determinant of coping behavior, and that they in turn are determined primarily by performance feedback from prior experience. Imagine, for example, that a woman who is afraid of flying must fly to a distant city for a job interview. Here the outcome expectation is the woman's judgment as to how likely it is that the plane will get her to her destination. In this case, the outcome expectation is quite high. But whether or not she will actually make the reservation depends more on her efficacy expectation, her confidence as to whether she will actually be able to get on the plane and make the trip without incident. That confidence, in turn, depends on how well she has managed similar stressful situations in the past (performance feedback from prior experience).

Self-Reinforcement

If the chief determinants of behavior lie in thought processes, then presumably reinforcement is one of those processes. Cognitive behaviorists agree with the classic position that behavior is molded by rewards and punishments, but they claim that the most potent rewards and punishments come not from the external environment but from the mind—in the form of self-approval and self-criticism. In some cases this cognitive reinforcement can lead to external reinforcement ("I just made it through that frightening plane trip— I think I'll go buy myself a steak"), but more often it remains on the cognitive level, in the form of simple self-congratulation and increased self-esteem. And on that level it can exert a tremendous impact on behavior.

This mechanism of cognitive self-reinforcement may account for the fact that modeling often occurs without external reinforcement. Conceivably, the imagined prospect of being like the admired model— teacher, mother, older brother, local football star— is sufficiently rewarding to fuel the response of imitation. In any case, it is clear that cognitive processes play a central role in modeling. After all, modeled behaviors may be "learned"—that is, stored in the mind—years before they are actually performed. In disciplining their children, for example, parents often fall back on the same methods, whether spankings or patient explanations or sending the child to his room, that their parents used with them twenty or thirty years before. Such learning suggests not merely that behavior is "influenced" by cognition but that it is in fact the product of a vast mental machinery in which years of stimuli and their associations are coded, sifted, modified, and stored for future use.

Other Cognitive Theories

Beyond cognitive behaviorism, there exists within psychology an independent cognitive perspective, only some of whose principles and procedures have been adopted by the behaviorists (Kihlstrom and Nasby, 1981). In the next section of this chapter we will examine the behavioral interpretation of abnormal behavior. First, however, we will look at two cognitive theories that have greatly influenced the cognitive behaviorists' view of abnormality.

Self-Defeating Thoughts   A more radical variant of the cognitive behaviorists' position is the theory that the primary cause of such emotional disorders as anxiety and depression is self-defeating thoughts. An influential proponent of this view is Albert Ellis (1958), who argues that when people behave inappropriately, they do so because they are operating on mistaken assumptions—what Ellis calls "irrational beliefs." If, for example, a woman believes that she must be loved and approved of by everyone or that it would be catastrophic for her to make a mistake (which, according to Ellis, are two of the most common irrational beliefs), then she will spend inordinate amounts of time trying to please others or compulsively checking and rechecking her work. As a result, her behavior will appear odd and inappropriate. Furthermore, it will allow no expression of her true preferences and interests—a sacrifice that will eventually give rise to feelings of acute frustration.

In a similar vein, Aaron Beck and his colleagues (Beck et al., 1979; Bedrosian and Beck, 1980) propose that depression is simply the behavioral response to an attitude or cognition of hopelessness. Whereas most theorists hold that the belief that all is hopeless is a symptom or result of the emotional condition called depression, Beck, with classic cognitive reasoning, reverses this causal relationship, making the depressed feelings the result of the cognition of hopelessness. (Beck's theory of depression will be discussed more fully in Chapter 10.)

Information Processing   While self-defeating thoughts constitute an explanatory theory of specific disorders, information processing is a broader area of cognitive research, concerned with how the human mind takes in, stores, and uses information from the environment. Nevertheless, many of the findings of information-processing research have proved useful in the study of abnormal behavior.

Cognitive researchers have learned, for example, to make a distinction between what they call automatic and controlled processing of information. Automatic processing requires little attention and yields quick, well-learned responses that remain stable over time. Controlled processing, on the other hand, occurs in novel situations and requires time and effort as the mind integrates new information and devises a response. When a child comes crying to a parent with a skinned knee, for example, the parent will engage in automatic processing—not a lot of thought, but rather a quick succession of responses: consoling words, soap and water, bandage. But when, at age fourteen, the same child begins moping, coming in late from school, and spending considerable time locked in his room, the parent, lacking any "formula" for this new problem, will have to engage in controlled processing. Many abnormal behavior patterns, such as phobias and other anxiety responses, can be viewed as the result of inappropriate automatic processing, and therapists have had some success in teaching people with these problems to convert to controlled processing (Kanfer and Hagerman, 1985).

Another information-processing concept relevant to abnormal psychology is that of the schema. A **schema** is a structured body of information that is stored in the mind and helps the person to organize and process new information. A self-schema, as the term indicates, is the individual's schema regarding his or her self. Many researchers now believe that a distorted self-schema may be a central component of depression, causing people to process relatively neutral information (a flat tire, a rained-out picnic) as applying to them and indeed as evidence of their inadequacy (Davis, 1979; Derry and Kuiper, 1981).

ABNORMAL BEHAVIOR AS A PRODUCT OF LEARNING

Earlier we saw how the mechanisms of learning operate in normal human development. Personality development, in the behavioral view, is simply the result of the interaction between our genetic endowment and the types of learning to which we are exposed by our environment. And according to the behaviorists, this is as true of abnormal development as it is of normal development.

Consider a problem that has arisen among cancer patients. Once they have undergone chemotherapy and experienced the extreme nausea that accompanies it, they often become nauseated at the mere

sight of a hospital, a doctor, or a nurse (Redd et al., 1985; Burish et al., 1985). This is the same simple respondent conditioning process that established the fear of rats in Albert B. In this case, the chemotherapy is the UCS, the chemotherapy-produced nausea, the UCR, the stimuli associated with the chemotherapy (nurse, doctor, hospital) the CS, and the nausea in the face of these stimuli the CR. The "spread" of the nausea to associated medical stimuli—a nurse on a television program, for example—is the result of generalization.

Other kinds of abnormal patterns may also be the products of learning. We have already seen how negative reinforcement can help to explain the maintenance of phobias: if children who have been bitten by a dog proceed to avoid all dogs, then their fear of dogs will persist indefinitely. Similarly, depression may be due in part to extinction: if significant positive reinforcements are withdrawn—a job lost, a marriage ended—many of a person's behaviors will simply extinguish, and he or she will become inactive, withdrawn, and dejected—in short, depressed. Likewise, modeling may contribute to a variety of abnormal behaviors. There is little question that the example of parents and peers is important in the development of alcoholism and other kinds of drug abuse.

With these learning theories cognitive behaviorists would not disagree. They would simply say that in most cases the abnormal behavior is a response not to the stimulus but to the mental processing of the stimulus. In regard to the extinction theory of depression, for example, cognitive behaviorists would argue that it is not simply or even primarily the loss of positive reinforcements that causes the depression but the person's negative meditations on these losses: "He was right to fire me," "No wonder she left," "I'm not competent," "I'm unattractive."

Contemporary behaviorists tend increasingly to support integrative theories of abnormal behavior, theories that combine S-R mechanisms with cognitive behaviorism, information processing, and other factors to produce a complex picture of causality. The extinction theory of depression, for example, arose in the 1970s, with P. M. Lewinsohn as its leading proponent. Today Lewinsohn claims that neither extinction theory nor competing cognitive theories such as Beck's are sufficient to account for depression. Instead, he and his colleagues (1985) have put forth a vicious-cycle theory involving many components, with stress leading to a disruption of ordinary behavior patterns, leading to reduced positive reinforcement (extinction theory), leading to increased self-awareness and self-criticism (altered self-schema), leading to feelings of hopelessness, leading to self-defeating behaviors that occasion further stress, thus taking the person through the cycle again. Such explanations, favoring complexity over simplicity and attempting to incorporate all recent experimental findings, represent the coming of age of behavioral theory of abnormality.

Despite their complexity, it is important to note that such theories still concentrate on proximal causes. In the behavioral view, psychopathology need not be explained by any "underlying" condition; it is the product of the same learned behaviors and cognitions that lead to normal behavior. As a corollary, behaviorists tend to avoid using such terms as *normal* and *abnormal,* since these terms imply a clear distinction between something healthy and something sick. Instead, behaviorists see the range of human responses as a continuum, all the responses being united by the same principles of learning. At one end of the continuum we can indeed identify responses that make it difficult for people to conduct their lives successfully, but these responses do not differ qualitatively from more adaptive responses. Hopelessness, as we just saw, may develop through the same mechanisms as hopefulness; an irresistible urge to wash one's hands every hour may be acquired in the same way as more conventional hand-washing behavior. Hence behaviorists, instead of designating such patterns *abnormal,* prefer the term *maladaptive.*

Likewise, behaviorists have traditionally been skeptical of the usefulness of labeling people according to diagnostic categories (e.g., phobia, schizophrenia, paranoia), since these categories, with their resemblance to medical diagnoses (e.g., pneumonia, tuberculosis, cancer), seem to imply the medical model. That is, they suggest disease states—a suggestion that runs directly counter to the behaviorists' belief in the continuity of normal and abnormal. To the behaviorists, what is needed is not to put diagnostic labels on people but simply to specify as clearly as possible what the maladaptive behavior is, what environmental stimuli may be eliciting and maintaining it, and how these stimuli may be rearranged in order to alter it (Ullmann and Krasner, 1975; Wilson and O'Leary, 1980).

In applying this sort of analysis to psychological abnormalities, the behaviorists do not claim that all such abnormalities are the result of learning alone, but only that learning may be an important contribution

and that, *whatever the cause,* relearning may help to alter the behavior. For example, no one would claim that the basic cause of mental retardation is faulty learning, yet many mentally retarded people have been helped by behavior therapies.

Types of Maladaptive Behavior

Four categories that behaviorists use in describing maladaptive behaviors focus directly on the specific behavior and its contingencies, whether environmental or cognitive. These four categories are behavior deficit, behavior excess, inappropriate stimulus control, and inadequate reinforcing systems.

Behavior Deficit   When a person engages in a particular behavior much less frequently than the society expects, behavior with the result that the individual's social, intellectual, or practical skills are impaired, the person is said to have a **behavior deficit.** Examples include a high school student's unwillingness to answer a question in class and a man's inability to engage in sexual intercourse with his wife. Some children fail to acquire proper toilet habits, speech, or the ability to engage in cooperative play. Likewise, some adults are totally withdrawn, avoiding any social interaction. All such patterns indicate behavior deficits, and the behaviorist's aim in treating them is to increase the frequency of the behavior that is currently being avoided.

Behavior Excess   A **behavior excess,** as the name indicates, is the opposite of a behavior deficit. Here the behavior occurs at a higher frequency than is adaptive according to the standards of the society. The woman who constantly talks to herself out loud; the hyperactive child who cannot sit still in class but is constantly in motion and in a state of intense excitement; the man who must get out of bed and check all the locks in the house exactly twenty times each night before he can go to sleep—these people's responses are called behavior excesses, and the behaviorist's goal is to decrease their frequency.

Inappropriate Stimulus Control   **Inappropriate stimulus control** is a disruption in the relationship between stimulus and response. Either a response occurs in the absence of any appropriate stimulus, as when a person interprets other people's harmless conversations as plots against his life, or a stimulus fails to elicit the appropriate response, as when a person deprived of food for long periods still refuses to eat or when a person cannot fall asleep in his or her own bedroom. In the case of a behavior involving inappropriate stimulus control, the behaviorist's objective is the establishment of proper discrimination.

Inadequate Reinforcing Systems   Some maladaptive behaviors may be seen as a result of the person's having a system of reinforcements different from that of the average person. In short, the person hears a different drummer, often to his or her great discomfort. In such a situation, the behavior is said to be due to an **inadequate reinforcing system.** A number of variant sexual patterns fall into this category. In fetishism, for example, some special object has taken the place of conventional erotic stimuli in the person's system of reinforcements. Other examples are the sexual sadist, who is positively reinforced by seeing other people suffer, and the masochist, who is positively reinforced by having pain inflicted upon himself or herself. In dealing with a maladaptive behavior that is the result of an inadequate reinforcing system, the behaviorist attempts to deactivate inappropriate reinforcers and condition the individual to respond to new, more appropriate reinforcers.

Behavior Therapy

The most decisive influence of the behavioral perspective has been in the area of treatment (Rimm and Masters, 1979; Wilson and O'Leary, 1980). The various techniques that behaviorists have used to treat specific problems will be brought up in various chapters throughout this book, and the subject of **behavior therapy** as a whole will be discussed in Chapter 20. Here, however, we can introduce the topic by saying that behavior therapy concentrates on the behavior itself and attempts to alter it via the same types of learning that presumably engender behavior in the first place—positive reinforcement, negative reinforcement, extinction, punishment, discrimination, generalization, modeling, and so forth.

One of the earliest attempts at behavior therapy was a now-famous experiment by Mary Cover Jones

(1924). What Jones did was essentially the reverse of Watson's respondent conditioning experiment with Albert B. Whereas Watson had instilled a fear of furry animals in Albert by pairing the animals with an aversive stimulus, Jones eliminated a fear of furry animals in a boy named Peter by pairing the animals with a pleasant stimulus. She first got the child busy eating candy and then introduced a rabbit into the room at some distance from where the boy was sitting. On successive occasions the rabbit was brought closer and closer, again while the child was eating, and eventually he was able to touch it without exhibiting any fear. The rabbit was thus paired with the pleasant stimulus of the candy so that eventually it took on pleasant associations. At the same time, whatever unpleasant consequences the child expected from his encounter with the rabbit did not take place, with the result that the fear, lacking reinforcement, was extinguished.

A somewhat later example of treatment via respondent conditioning is **systematic desensitization,** a technique developed by the psychiatrist Joseph Wolpe (1958, 1973) for relieving anxiety. In this procedure, patients imagine their anxiety-eliciting stimuli (e.g., dogs, exams, women) under conditions that inhibit the development of anxiety—usually a state of deep muscle relaxation. Through repeated pairings of the stimulus with the relaxed state, the stimulus gradually loses its power to arouse anxiety. This technique has had a major influence on the development of behavior therapy and has now been incorporated into behavioral treatments for a vast range of problems, from sexual dysfunction to alcoholism—indeed, any problem in which anxiety is thought to play an important role.

Operant conditioning has also been widely used in behavior therapy. A striking example was a case in which speech was reinstated in two mute schizophrenic adults largely through shaping (Isaacs et al., 1960). Chewing gum was used as the major reinforcer. At first the patients were given the gum even if they simply looked at it. Later they were rewarded only for vocalization (e.g., "eeh," "aah," any sound they chose to make), then only for imitating the experimenters' words, then only for answering questions. To make the speaking response generalize beyond the experimental situation, ward personnel were instructed to respond to the patients during the rest of the day only if they verbalized their needs. Through this painstaking, systematic program, the two patients—one of whom had not spoken for nineteen years, the other for fourteen years—once again began communicating verbally.

Today behavioral treatment, particularly for depression and anxiety, often includes **cognitive restructuring,** a process in which the therapist, through modeling and other methods, teaches patients to revise their interpretations of events. Recall the example, earlier in the chapter, of the two people giving speeches. The first person would be a good candidate for cognitive restructuring, through which he would be trained to say to himself what the second person said ("Too bad they have to leave") upon seeing people exit in the middle of his lecture.

Behavior therapy has had very impressive success with a wide range of disorders: phobia, depression, insomnia, conduct disorders (delinquency), and also such health-related problems as overeating, smoking, and hypertension. Such successes do not necessarily support the behaviorists' claim that learning is the source of abnormal behavior: the fact that conditioning can eliminate a response does not prove that the response was acquired through conditioning. Nevertheless, even if they tell us nothing about cause, such treatments still constitute an impressive contribution on the part of the behavioral movement. In the first place, because they are carefully documented in terms of specific procedures and specific results, they can be replicated by other scientists. Second, and most important, many of these behavioral treatments clearly *work*. And sometimes they have worked with precisely those patients, such as autistic children, who are hardest to reach through the more subjective therapies.

EVALUATING BEHAVIORISM

Behavioral Theory versus Other Theories

As we pointed out earlier, the basic tenets of behaviorism constitute a direct challenge to both the medical model and psychodynamic theory. Behaviorists have been among the most outspoken critics of the medical model (Bandura, 1969; Mischel, 1968; Ullmann and Krasner, 1975). Where the medical model sees illness, behaviorists see variations in learning history. Where the medical model sees qualitative differences between normal and abnormal, the behaviorists see only quantitative differences. Where the medical model favors diagnostic labels, behaviorism regards them with caution.

The behaviorists' quarrels with psychodynamic theory have been outlined at the opening of our chapter. Psychodynamic theory attributes abnormal behavior to deep-seated unconscious processes; behavioral theory, to observable learning processes. Because the object of its study is by definition hidden, psychodynamic theory must rely on inference and interpretation. Behaviorism avoids such methods and attempts to be as scientific as possible. The one approach is subjective; the other aims for maximum objectivity.

The medical model and psychodynamic theory are not just scientific constructs; they are theoretical outgrowths of some of our most deeply ingrained beliefs—for example, the belief that the psychologically disturbed are "different" from the rest of us (medical model) and that psychological disturbance has its roots in the depths of the psyche (psychodynamic theory). Hence the disagreements between behaviorism and these two schools of thought are not just quibbles over details. Though the behaviorists shy away from grand philosophical claims, the fact remains that their theory of behavior constitutes a drastic revision of Western thought on the subject of human life. And as such, it has been severely criticized.

Criticisms of Behaviorism

Oversimplification   A primary objection is that behaviorists have grossly oversimplified human life. In particular, the behaviorists' technique of reducing human existence to small, measurable units of behavior has been criticized as a naive simplification, and one that distorts the very data they are measuring (London, 1969). Furthermore, critics claim that by excluding the inner life from consideration, classical behaviorists have chosen to ignore everything that distinguishes a human being from an experimental animal. As Arthur Koestler (1968) has argued, if mental events are to be banned from psychology, then the only thing left for psychology to study is rats. And indeed, as we have seen, many behavioral principles have been evolved from animal experimentation. Critics have asked whether such principles are truly applicable to human beings.

Actually, as we noted earlier, the behaviorists have never denied the existence of mental events. (Indeed, some of the most traditional behavioral treatment methods rely on mental events—e.g., the imagining of feared stimuli in systematic desensitization.) What the classical behaviorists denied was that mental events *caused* behavior. The cognitive behaviorists, as we have seen, dissent from this position and in consequence have drawn severe criticism from some traditional behaviorists (e.g., Ledwidge, 1978; Wolpe, 1978), who regard the study of mental events as a threat to behaviorism's empirical method. In response, the cognitive behaviorists argue that subjective experiences can be studied without sacrificing objectivity. Michael Mahoney (1974), for example, makes a distinction between "methodological behaviorism," the emphasis on objective observation, and what he calls "metaphysical behaviorism," the ideological rejection of subjective experience as an object of scientific study. Mahoney claims that cognitive behaviorists can adhere to methodological behaviorism without having their hands tied by metaphysical behaviorism. For example, thoughts, in the form of "mental sentences," can be counted and recorded like external events. And this is exactly what the cognitive behaviorists do.

It might be said, then, that cognitive behaviorism in some measure constitutes a response to the charge of oversimplification—behaviorism mending its ways. But in fact the cognitive behaviorists' view of mental events is in some ways as "simple" as the classical behaviorists' view of external events. The idea that the workings of the mind can be reduced to brief "self-sentences" and that a single "self-sentence" can serve to explain a behavioral response—with no consideration of conflicting wishes and impulses—makes cognitive behaviorism seem as superficial as classical behaviorism in the eyes of many adherents of a more subjective psychology.

Determinism   The second major focus of criticism is the deterministic emphasis of behaviorism (one of the few points on which it agrees with psychodynamic theory). According to the classical behaviorists, most human behavior is the product of respondent and operant conditioning. Thus it is not free will but rather the stimuli in our environments that determine what we will do with our lives.

Skinner, for example, argues that the notion of human freedom is simply obsolete and should be abandoned:

The free inner man who is held responsible for the behavior of the external biological organism is only a prescientific substitute for the kinds of causes which are discovered in the course of a scientific analysis. All these alternative causes lie *outside* the individual. . . . These are the things that make the individual behave as he does. For them he is not responsible, and for them it is useless to praise or blame him (1965, pp. 447–448).

If we follow this idea to its conclusion, there is no foundation whatsoever for any kind of legal system, for any religious belief, or for any moral code. Law, religion, and morality are all based on the notion that we are capable of choosing between right and wrong, whereas according to Skinner, whatever we do—whether we treat other people kindly or brutally, whether we behave ourselves or lie, cheat, and steal—we do these things because our conditioning history has programmed us to do them. Needless to say, such ideas have been coldly received by modern thinkers, especially humanistic and existential theorists, who still cling to the view that each human being is a unique and free individual.

Again, cognitive behaviorism may appear to represent a concession on this point. The great value that the cognitive behaviorists assign to mental events seems to rescue human beings from the passive position to which they are relegated in traditional behavioral theory—the position of merely *reacting*—and restore to them, or at least to their cognitions, a determining influence over their behavior. However, while the cognitive behaviorists do see mental events as having a causal role in behavior, those mental events are not regarded as the workings of a free will. On the contrary, they are products of the same learning mechanisms as overt responses.

The same logic applies to Albert Bandura's recent concept of "reciprocal determinism" (1978, 1984)—that whereas environmental stimuli determine our responses, we in turn determine those stimuli by filtering and selecting our environments. This idea too seems to give some power back to the person. We don't just react; we choose what we will react to. Yet Bandura would not argue that our ways of filtering and selecting are guided by free will; they too are products of learning. Thus what Bandura and the cognitive behaviorists have done is to insert some plausible intermediate steps between stimulus and response, yielding a determinism that is more complex.

The Issue of "Control"   Finally, the word *control,* as used by the behaviorists, often makes people uneasy. Skinner in particular aroused some fears with his descriptions of how all behavior is controlled by environmental reinforcers and how we could lead happier lives if we simply admitted we were controlled and set about designing better reinforcement programs. Such "behavioral engineering," as critics noted, could conceivably become the basis of a totalitarian regime, in which people were coerced not by force but by reinforcement.

Actually, the term *control,* in the behavioral vocabulary, does not mean coercion. It means predictability, the adherence to scientific laws. For example, a child learning to ride a bicycle is subjecting herself to "control." As she practices, she will gradually eliminate those responses that lead to falling down, and she will increase the frequency of those responses that keep her balanced. Though no one is coercing her, her behavior is nevertheless being "controlled" by its consequences (Bootzin, 1975).

Nevertheless, the mere fact that behaviorists feel they can identify the factors that control our behavior has caused some critics to worry that such knowledge, in irresponsible hands, might lead to coercion. Actually, psychology in general could arouse the same concern, for all psychologists attempt to identify the factors that cause human beings to behave as they do. It is only because the behaviorists have focused on external variables—those, in other words, that can be manipulated—that they have been the primary object of "mad scientist" suspicions.

The Contributions of Behaviorism

There is also much that can justly be said in favor of behaviorism. In the first place, the objectivity of behavioral research is not a virtue to be slighted. Indeed, a major problem with all the other psychological perspectives is that their statements on human behavior are often vague, based more on inference than on fact, and open to the charge of bias. In contrast, the behaviorists' findings are expressed much more concisely and as much as possible are based on actual, measurable evidence, with the result, as we have noted earlier, that they can easily be retested by other professionals. The value of such precision has not gone unnoticed. Almost all psychological re-

search is now behavioral in method. That is, it is based on experimentation and on objective measurement, and if inferred constructs are used, they are defined in terms of concrete behaviors.

Second, while the behaviorists are accused of doing away with individualism, it can be argued that individualism is safer with the behaviorists than it is with psychologists of other schools of thought. For unlike many other psychologists, the behaviorists recognize a broad range of responses as legitimate and are very sensitive to the adverse effects of labeling people as "abnormal."

Finally, it bears repeating that the treatment methods developed by the behaviorists have produced some extremely promising results. Behavior therapy takes less time, is less expensive, and in many cases has been found more effective than other forms of treatment. In addition, substantial contributions have been made in education, business, and sports physiology through the application of behavioral principles. And while the successful applications of behavioral principles in no way constitute proof of behavioral learning theories, such success is obviously an achievement in itself—and one that no psychological perspective can afford to do without, no matter how convincing its theories.

SUMMARY

The behavioral perspective was developed in the early twentieth century as a way to study psychology empirically, with stress on proximal rather than distal causes of behavior. Its foundation was the discovery of the mechanisms of learning, whereby behavior changes in response to interaction with the environment. Ivan Pavlov's research with dogs revealed one of these mechanisms—the conditioned reflex, or the training of an organism to respond to a neutral stimulus in the same way it would to a nonneutral one. His work raised the possibility that complex human responses were simply the result of a conditioning process.

John B. Watson was the first to publicize behaviorism, arguing that psychology is a natural science that has no use for introspection. He conditioned a fear of rats in a baby boy to demonstrate that many of our "unreasonable" fears are produced in a similar way.

Edward Lee Thorndike developed the law of effect, which states that responses that lead to "satisfying" consequences are strengthened and likely to be repeated, while responses that lead to "unsatisfying" consequences are weakened and unlikely to be repeated. B. F. Skinner renamed this law the principle of reinforcement and viewed it as the basic mechanism for predicting and controlling human behavior.

Early cognitive behaviorists argued that the stimulus-response position overlooked the way in which the human mind processes stimuli and failed to explain why different people respond to the same stimulus in different ways.

The basic assumptions of classical behaviorism are that psychology's task is the study of behavior, or the responses an organism makes to the stimuli in its environment; that its methodology should be empirical, based on measurement; that behavior can be controlled and predicted; and that the major component of behavior is learning. These four assumptions have been modified somewhat by cognitive theory to include the influence of mental events on learning.

According to classical behaviorists, all behavior is either respondent or operant. Respondent behavior occurs reflexively in response to specific stimuli, and through respondent conditioning a conditioned response can be learned. Important processes in respondent behavior are generalization, or the spread of a conditioned response to stimuli that resemble the conditioned stimulus, and discrimination, or learning to distinguish among similar stimuli and respond only to the appropriate one. In operant behavior, the organism operates on its environment in order to achieve a desired result. All operant behavior is conditioned, and in operant (instrumental) conditioning, the organism learns to associate certain results with certain actions it has taken.

Reinforcement is a key mechanism of learning. Primary reinforcers are those to which we respond instinctively. Most reinforcers, though, are conditioned, or secondary; we associate them with primary ones. In positive reinforcement, a response is followed by a positive reinforcer, which increases the frequency of that response. In negative reinforcement, or avoidance learning, the response is promoted by the avoidance or removal of an aversive stimulus. Extinction involves the removal of the reinforcement that is maintaining a response so that the response will die out.

Punishment is the presentation of an aversive stimulus following a response so that the frequency of the response decreases.

Shaping involves the reinforcement of successive approximations of a desired response until it is finally achieved. It usually occurs in combination with modeling, or learning through imitation.

Cognitive behaviorists claim that mental processes affect behavior independently of the stimulus. They add two other basic mechanisms of learning—the individual's interpretation, or appraisal, of a stimulus and his or her self-reinforcement of rewards and punishments. Appraisals that affect behavior depend on individual competencies, encodings, expectancies, values, and plans. According to Albert Bandura, efficacy—as opposed to outcome—expectations determine a person's coping behavior. Self-reinforcement theory claims that self-approval and self-criticism are more potent reinforcers than external stimuli. The cognitive behavioral view of abnormality has been influenced both by the specific theory that self-defeating thoughts lead to anxiety and depression and by the broader discipline of information processing, from which cognitive behaviorists take the concepts of inappropriate automatic processing (in phobias and anxiety disorders) and distorted self-schema (in depressive disorders).

Behaviorists see both normal and abnormal behavior as the products of the interaction between our genetic endowment and the types of learning to which we are exposed. They believe that maladaptive learning is a major contributor to psychological abnormality and that relearning may help to alter the behavior. Cognitive behaviorists view abnormal behavior as a response to the ways a person processes or appraises the stimulus, not to the external stimulus itself. Cognitive behavioral theories of abnormality, including Lewinsohn's vicious-cycle theory of depression, are thus more complex than S-R causal explanations.

There are four categories of maladaptive behavior in the behaviorist view—behavior deficit, behavior excess, inappropriate stimulus control, and inadequate reinforcing systems. Behavior therapy attempts to alter specific responses through the same types of learning that engendered them initially. Systematic desensitization, in which anxiety is reduced when the anxiety-causing stimulus is paired with a relaxed state, is an example of a behavior therapy. Behavioral treatment of depression and anxiety today may include cognitive restructuring, in which patients learn to revise their appraisals. Disorders and problems that respond to behavior therapy include phobias, depression, insomnia, delinquent behavior, and smoking.

Behaviorism presents a challenge to both the medical model and the psychodynamic perspective. In fact, it presents a view of human life that differs drastically from most Western thought on the subject. As a result, it has been criticized as an oversimplification of human experience, as a deterministic theory that denies the existence of free will, and as a possible means of coercion. Nevertheless, behaviorism has made contributions to the study of human behavior: it emphasizes experimentation and objective measurement in psychology; it recognizes a broad range of responses as legitimate and is sensitive to the effects of labeling people as abnormal; and its treatment methods take less time, cost less, and are often more effective than other therapies.

CHAPTER 4

The Humanistic-Existential and Sociocultural Perspectives

The psychodynamic and behavioral perspectives, while opposed on many points, do agree in at least one respect: both of them try to break down human behavior into separate components and to identify cause-and-effect relationships between those components—a method akin to that of the natural sciences. Botanists, when they see a rosebush put forth a new flower, regard this phenomenon as the result of a chain of discrete chemical reactions, each causing the next and ultimately producing the rose. Likewise, both behavioral and psychodynamic theorists, when they look, for example, at a severely depressed person, try to reduce the depression to specific, naturalistic causes, whether learning experiences or problems in psychosexual development.

The humanistic and existential perspectives arose in direct opposition to this approach. According to the humanists and existentialists, to study human behavior in the manner of the natural sciences is to ignore much of what is important about human life: that it is subjective, not naturalistic; that it is experienced as a unity, not as a series of separate components; that it occurs within a context, not as an isolated phenomenon; that it takes place over time and thus cannot be frozen into a formula of past causes and present results.

Finally, the humanists and existentialists want psychology to take account of the primary factor underlying these truths: human consciousness. We do not know whether rosebushes have "thoughts" about the roses they produce. But we know that human beings are keenly aware of themselves—a fact that drastically affects and complicates their behavior. Humanists and existentialists want to make sure that this crucial difference between human beings and other forms of life is made part of psychological science.

In addition to humanistic-existential psychology, this chapter will cover the sociocultural perspective, which seeks the causes of abnormal behavior in the society at large. The sociocultural perspective is less comprehensive than the psychodynamic, behavioral, or humanistic-existential approach. That is, instead of offering a theory of human behavior in general, it is more a collection of limited theories dealing with some specific aspect of psychological disorder, such as diagnosis. This is why we discuss it after, and more briefly than, the other three psychological perspectives. Such placement is not meant to imply that the sociocultural approach is less important than the others. As we shall see, some disorders cannot be discussed without reference to their social context.

THE HUMANISTIC-EXISTENTIAL PERSPECTIVE

While it is convenient for the purpose of clarity to speak of a unified **humanistic-existential perspective,** humanistic and existential psychology can only loosely be defined as a single school of thought, or even as two schools of thought. Rather, what we are dealing with in this section is a group of highly individual theorists. Nevertheless, since they share some basic assumptions, it is possible to speak—as we shall in this chapter—of a humanistic-existential perspective. At the same time, in order to do justice to the individualism that marks this perspective, our discussion of the theory will focus not on a general view but on the view of six representative theorists: the humanists Carl Rogers and Abraham Maslow and the existentialists Rollo May, Viktor Frankl, J. H. van den Berg, and R. D. Laing.

The Background

The humanistic and existential perspectives are relatively recent entries into psychological theory, having emerged in the 1950s and 1960s. It was at this time that Western thinkers began to express serious alarm over modern technology's threat to human values— a crisis to which psychodynamic and behavioral psychology, with their deterministic theories, seemed

to offer no answer. To address this problem, there arose the so-called Third Force in psychology. Comprised of a number of theories—most prominently, the humanistic and existential—the Third Force was an effort to revamp the science in such a way as to reaffirm human values, above all, individuality and personal freedom.

Though new to modern psychology, the ideas behind the humanistic and existential perspectives have been part of Western philosophy since at least the nineteenth century. The two perspectives arrived at these ideas, however, by very different paths.

The Background of Humanistic Psychology

Humanistic psychology, basically an American phenomenon, took shape in the decade after World War II as both a protest movement and a program for the future of psychology. In this period the American workplace was undergoing rapid and bewildering changes. People were being replaced by machines; tasks were becoming narrower and more specialized. As a result, people began to feel alienated from their jobs. Workers, it appeared, were merely replaceable parts in the big machine of society. The depersonalization of the workplace seemed to have spread to the psychology laboratory, where most research was being done either on animals or on human functions isolated from the human being as a whole. Impersonal observers measuring the responses of anonymous creatures and stating their conclusions in terms of a statistical average that represented no single living person—is this, asked the humanists, what we want from the study of the human mind?

The humanists thus sought to restore to psychology those aspects of distinctly human experience that they felt were being ignored. One such aspect, in their opinion, was people's *innate* capacity for creativity and goodness. This idea—that human beings, if they are not overly restricted by their society, will naturally pursue the good—had been part of Western thought since it was first promulgated in the late eighteenth century by the French philosopher Jean-Jacques Rousseau. The humanists incorporated it into modern psychology.

A second fundamental concern of the humanists was the "self-concept," our mental portrait of ourselves, according to which we judge and interpret our behavior and experience. The notion of self-concept was first introduced in the late nineteenth century by the American philosopher and psychologist William

James. Later, in the 1930s, George Herbert Mead, an American sociologist, pointed out the crucial role of social relationships in the development of the self-concept. As we shall see, the humanists have carried on this line of investigation, studying how the self-concept develops and how it affects people's abilities to fulfill their inborn potential.

The Background of Existential Psychology
While humanistic psychology arose in the United States, existential psychology grew out of European existentialism, a philosophical movement of the late nineteenth and early twentieth centuries represented by such thinkers as Søren Kierkegaard (1813–1855), Edmund Husserl (1859–1938), Martin Heidegger (1889–1976), Karl Jaspers (1883–1969), Maurice Merleau-Ponty (1908–1961), and Jean-Paul Sartre (1905–1980). Like humanism, existentialism was a response to dehumanization, but on a more global scale. Beginning in the late eighteenth century, Western thought underwent a severe crisis. With the rise of industrialization, the fall of the European empires, and the challenge to religion posed by Darwin's theory of natural selection, the ideologies that people had trusted and the social structures in which they had found their place were swept away—a devastation capped by World War I, in which millions of lives were lost for no apparent reason in the view of many.

Human beings, it seemed, had been cut adrift in a world no longer understandable. Many kinds of knowledge competed for their belief, but no one of them seemed "true" in the way of the old truths.

This was the crisis that gave birth to existential philosophy. The existentialists did not seek to brighten the picture. On the contrary, it was they who enunciated the problem, claiming that the human condition was by nature one of uncertainty and anxiety. This discomforting vision, shared by existential psychology, is based on what these writers regard as three fundamental facts of human life.

One is the contingency of human existence—the fact that having been born, we are slated to die. Second is the frailty of human reason. This fact, like that of death, is one that people prefer not to confront. In order to get along in life, most of us need to think of ourselves as rational beings. But the evidence of twentieth-century history—two world wars, the vast exterminations perpetrated by Hitler and Stalin, the current threat of a "no-win" nuclear war—would seem to support the existentialists' assertion that reason is not a given, but rather a constant struggle, against heavy odds. A final "fact of life" stressed by the existentialists is estrangement, the individual's sense of being cut off and alone. Existentialist literature—Sartre's *Nausea,* Albert Camus' *The Stranger,* Antoine de Saint-Exupéry's *Little Prince*—is full of lonely heroes trying to make contact with the world or with

Existentialism sees human reason as a fragile barrier against the irrational impulses that sometimes burst through and cause such atrocities as the slaughter of millions of suspected dissidents by the Pol Pot regime in Cambodia in the 1970s. (Wally McNamee/Woodfin Camp & Associates)

Another basic tenet of existential philosophy is that each person is alone and must struggle to make contact with other people and with the world. (Allan Price/Photo Researchers)

others. In the existentialist view, such estrangement, like death and the frailty of reason, is not something that can be remedied, but something that must be accepted and navigated. Human beings *are* alone. No one else can make their choices for them, nor can anyone else absorb the risks that those choices entail.

With all this facing of painful truths, existentialism may seem a uniquely tragic view of human life. Along with anguish and doubt, however, the existentialists hold out the hope of a highly meaningful life. With no surviving systems of received truth to support or explain it, existence itself becomes a complex and heroic adventure. This can be seen in three basic principles of existential thought.

The first is the indissoluble unity of human consciousness and the world—a unity that the existentialists call **being-in-the-world.** From the seventeenth century to our own day, science has tended to make a split between subjective phenomena and objective phenomena, concentrating on the latter to the exclu-

sion of the former. In opposition to this tradition, the existentialists argue, first, that the subjective life cannot be excluded from any branch of knowledge that concerns itself with human beings and, second, that there *is* no split between subjective and objective. There is no mental experience that is not an experience of the world, and there is no knowable world apart from our mental experience of it. Thus human consciousness is placed at the center of all knowledge.

A second major theme of existentialist philosophy is **authenticity.** Being-in-the-world means, among other things, living constantly under the pressure of other people's expectations. A foremost concern of the existentialists is the tendency of human beings to deny large parts of their experience, screening out thoughts and desires that are deemed "unacceptable" by parents, friends, and society at large. Such self-censorship may temporarily assuage the anxiety of estrangement, but eventually it produces a painfully divided personality: a false outer self covering an isolated and denied inner self. To avoid this split, people must constantly strive to live "authentically"—that is, to accept the full range of their mental experience. This does not mean acting on every impulse. If a man feels the desire to kill someone, the existentialists do not recommend that he indulge this wish. What is important is that he acknowledge its existence—recognize that he is capable of a wish to kill. The existentialists argue that only by being aware of and accepting our feelings, no matter how unacceptable they may be to others, can we lead real lives and make meaningful choices.

Through living authentically, we grow as human beings. Hence the third theme of existentialism: the emphasis on the present and future as opposed to the past. Life, according to the existentialists, is not a predictable outcome of the past. On the contrary, it is a continual **becoming,** a dynamic process of day-to-day self-creation. This means, first, that human beings are responsible for their lives; they cannot blame their problems on past misfortunes. Second, it means that science too should not treat human beings as finished products, the results of past causes. People are open-ended processes, not products, and therefore must be studied within the dimension of time.

Underlying Assumptions

To subject such ideas as *authenticity* and *becoming* to scientific study may seem a difficult matter, but according to the humanists and existentialists, science must adapt its methods to its subject matter—in this case, human life—rather than vice versa. Early in the twentieth century the German philosopher Wilhelm Dilthey emphasized the distinction between the "natural sciences," which treat their subject matter as material "things," and the "human sciences," which treat their subject matter as subjective, dynamic processes. As we noted at the opening of this chapter, the psychodynamic and behavioral schools of psychology developed, to some extent, in imitation of the natural sciences. By contrast, the humanists and existentialists argue that psychology should be converted into a human science, by focusing on specifically human characteristics. This implies a set of assumptions altogether different from that of behavioral and psychodynamic theory. Though with differing emphases, the humanists and existentialists would agree on four basic premises.

The Phenomenological Approach "Can we be sure . . . that we are seeing the patient as he really is, knowing him in his own reality; or are we seeing merely a projection of our own theories about him?" This question, posed by the existential theorist Rollo May (1959, p. 3), points to one of the central assumptions of humanistic and existential psychology: that the therapist must enter into the patient's world. This method, known as the **phenomenological approach,** means listening with maximum empathy to everything that the patient is communicating about his or her experience. To do this, therapists must avoid attending only to evidence that fits their own theoretical biases. Nor should they necessarily try to dig below the patient's statements in order to drag up the "real" truth. Their primary duty is to "tune in" to the patient's mental life, to see the world through the patient's eyes.

It must be stressed that humanistic-existential theorists embrace the phenomenological method not because they are warm, sympathetic types but because of a firm philosophical and indeed scientific conviction that this is the only authentic approach to human experience. Phenomenology was an important philosophical movement of the early twentieth century, and its basic discovery—that all knowledge is subjective and therefore cannot be considered apart from the mind doing the "knowing"—has been incorporated into much of modern culture. That it has not yet been fully incorporated into psychology is, in the humanistic-existential view, a sign of backwardness.

The Uniqueness of the Individual Because each person perceives the world in a special way and participates in his or her own "self-creation," each person is unique. According to the humanistic-existential perspective, to reduce the individual to a set of formulas, whether behavioral or psychodynamic, is to see only a very limited portion of his or her being. While human behavior may follow certain rules, such rules can never define a human life, for each person is an utterly singular entity.

Human Potential The humanists, like the existentialists, see the individual as a process rather than a product. For both, human life is a matter of growth through experience. Hence the humanistic-existential perspective places great emphasis on human potential—the ability of individuals to become what they

The humanistic-existential perspective affirms the potential of human beings to overcome almost any obstacle in order to be and do their best. (Pat Canova/ Bruce Coleman)

want to be, to fulfill their capabilities, and to lead the lives best suited to them.

Freedom and Responsibility   The humanistic-existential perspective is unique in its insistence on the freedom of the individual. The lives of human animals, like those of all the other animals, are affected by external events beyond their control. But unlike other animals, human beings are gifted (and burdened) with self-awareness. Their self-awareness allows them to transcend their impulses and to *choose* what they will make of the "givens" of their existence. By so doing, they make their own destinies.

The corollary of this freedom is that people are also responsible for their destinies. What we are, we have ourselves created. Authentic or inauthentic, fulfilling or nonfulfilling, our existence is the result of our own free choosing.

Humanistic Psychology

As we have seen, the basis on which humanistic psychology rests is an emphatically positive vision of the human being. Whereas Freud saw the individual as motivated, at bottom, by the selfish and irrational id, which had to be constantly checked by the forces of society, humanists hold that if individuals are allowed to develop freely, without undue constraints, they will become rational, socialized beings. Furthermore, they will become *constructive* beings, intent on fulfilling not only their biological needs but also some higher vision of their capabilities. Of the humanists who have built their psychological theories on this optimistic foundation, the most influential have been Carl Rogers (1902–1987) and Abraham Maslow (1908–1970).

Rogers: The Organism and the Self   Unlike psychodynamic theorists, who see behavior as motivated by three opposing forces in the personality, Carl Rogers sees all behavior as motivated by a single overriding factor, the actualizing tendency. The actualizing tendency is the desire to preserve and enhance oneself. On one level, it includes the drive simply to stay alive, by eating, keeping warm, and avoiding physical danger. On a higher level, the actualizing tendency also includes people's desire to test and fulfill their capabilities: to expose themselves to new experiences, to master new skills, to quit boring jobs and find more exciting ones, to meet new people, and so on. This process of exploring and fulfilling one's potential is called **self-actualization.**

In the course of pursuing self-actualization, people engage in what Rogers calls the **valuing process.**

Carl Rogers on Listening

Carl Rogers, the founder of client-centered (or "person-centered") therapy, was once asked to give a lecture describing what *communication* meant in his kind of therapy. The following excerpt, in which he describes the importance of truly hearing another person, illustrates the client-centeredness of this humanistic therapy.

> When I say that I enjoy hearing someone, I mean, of course, hearing deeply. I mean that I hear the words, the thoughts, the feeling tones, the personal meaning, even the meaning that is below the conscious intent of the speaker. Sometimes too, in a message which superficially is not very important, I hear a deep human cry that lies buried and unknown far below the surface of the person.
>
> So I have learned to ask myself, can I hear the sounds and sense the shape of this other person's inner world? Can I resonate to what he is saying so deeply that I sense the meanings he is afraid of yet would like to communicate, as well as those he knows?
>
> I think, for example, of an interview I had with an adolescent boy. Like many an adolescent today he was saying at the outset of the interview that he had no goals. When I questioned him on this, he insisted even more strongly that he had no goals whatsoever, not even one. I said, "There isn't anything you want to do?" "*Nothing. . . .* Well, yeah, I want to keep on living." I remember distinctly my feeling at that moment. I resonated very deeply to this phrase. He might simply be telling me that, like everyone else, he wanted to live. On the other hand, he might be telling me—and this seemed to be a definite possibility—that at some point the question of whether or not to live had been a real issue with him. . . . I didn't know for certain what the message was. I simply wanted to be open to any of the meanings that this statement might have, including the possibility that he might at one time have considered suicide. My being willing and able to listen to him at all levels is perhaps one of the things that made it possible for him to tell me, before the end of the interview, that not long before he had been on the point of blowing his brains out. This little episode is an example of what I mean by wanting to really hear someone at all the levels at which he is endeavoring to communicate (Rogers, 1980, pp. 8–9).

Experiences that are perceived as enhancing to oneself are valued as good and are therefore sought after; experiences perceived as not enhancing are valued as bad and are consequently avoided. In other words, people know what is good for them. As we shall see, this assumption of the innate soundness of the individual's judgment is an important factor in Rogerian therapy.

Whether people will actually trust the valuing process and *do* what is good for them depends on the interaction of two factors that Rogers sees as the basic units of the personality: the organism and the self. The *organism* is our total perception of our experience, both internal and external. The *self* is our image of ourselves, akin to what others call the self-concept. And the degree of self-actualization that we achieve depends on *the degree of congruence between the self and the organism.* If the image of the self is flexible and realistic enough to allow us to bring into our consciousness and to evaluate all the experiences of the organism, then we are in an excellent position to identify and pursue those experiences that are most enhancing. The nature of the self is thus

Carl Rogers, influential spokesman for humanistic psychology and developer of the technique of client-centered therapy. (The Bettmann Archive)

In order to become self-actualizing, Carl Rogers maintained, a child needs the positive regard of his or her parents. (Barbara Pfeffer/Peter Arnold)

the crucial factor in self-actualization. (Accordingly, Rogers' system is known as the "self" theory.)

What determines whether the self will be flexible or rigid, realistic or unrealistic? The decisive factor is childhood experience. As children become aware of themselves, they automatically develop the need for what Rogers calls **positive regard**—that is, affection and approval from the important people in their lives, particularly their parents. Invariably, however, positive regard comes with strings attached: the child must be mild-mannered, aggressive, boyish, girlish, or whatever to be loved. And these extraneous values, dictating which of the child's self-experiences are "good" and which are "bad," are incorporated into the child's self as **conditions of worth.** If the conditions are few and reasonable, then the child can still develop a self flexible enough so that he or she can entertain a variety of experiences and judge independently which are enhancing and which are not. If, however, the conditions of worth are severely limiting, screening out large portions of the experience of the organism, then they will seriously impede self-actualization.

The latter situation is, according to Rogers, the source of abnormal behavior. The problem is essentially one of perception—the self's perception of the experience of the organism. On the one hand, the organism, motivated by its actualizing tendency, perceives the internal and external environment in all its variety. On the other hand, the self, cramped by unrealistic conditions of worth, attempts to filter out whatever organismic experiences do not conform to those conditions. For example, a girl who is valued by her parents to the degree that she is gentle and docile may spend the rest of her life denying to herself that she ever experiences anger. Rogers quotes a letter from a woman who, after just such a childhood, finally discovered her denied hostility:

> So *much hurt and anger* came out of me that I *never really knew existed.* I went home and it seemed that an *alien* had taken over. . . . . I continued to feel this way until one night I was sitting and thinking and I realized that this alien was the *me* that I had been trying to find (1980, p. 210).

If, as in the case of this woman, important thoughts and emotions are totally denied, so that the real person becomes an actual alien to the mind, then the process of self-actualization simply comes to a halt. Immobilized by anxiety and rechanneling all energies to the defense of the self, the person ceases altogether to engage freely in experience. The result is abnormal behavior.

To untie this knot, Rogers has developed a technique that he calls **client-centered therapy** (Chapter 20).* Briefly, what the client-centered therapist does is to create for the patient a warm and accepting atmosphere, by mirroring whatever feelings the patient expresses, by attempting to perceive the patient's world as he or she does, and most of all, by offering the patient unconditional positive regard—respect and approval, with no conditions of worth. (See the box on p. 83.) In such an atmosphere, the patient is released from the necessity of defending an unrealistic self-image and can at last confront feelings and experiences that are inconsistent with the self—a process that will result in the broadening of the self to include the total experience of the organism. The self and the organism are thereby brought back into congruence, and the patient is free to "*be,* in a more unified fashion, what he organismically *is*" (Rogers, 1955, p. 269). Thus freed, the patient can once again proceed with self-actualization.

Maslow: The Hierarchy of Needs   Like Rogers, Abraham Maslow starts out with the premises that human beings are basically good and that all their behavior issues from a single master motive, the drive toward self-actualization. Maslow's special contribution to the humanistic program is his concept of the **hierarchy of needs,** a series of needs that must be met, one by one, in the process of development before the adult can begin to pursue self-actualization. (See Figure 4.1).

Maslow proposes five levels of needs, each of which must be satisfied before the individual can proceed to the next level. First are the *biological* needs, the need for physical comfort and survival. Second are the *safety* needs, the need for a stable and predictable environment. The third level is the need for *belongingness and love*—that is, warm relationships with friends and family. At the fourth level are the *esteem* needs, which impel the individual to seek the respect of others and eventually to create an internal fund of self-

esteem. Finally, having fulfilled the needs for survival, safety, love, and esteem, the individual can proceed to the fifth level and begin fulfilling the need for *self-actualization*. This ultimate goal Maslow defines "as ongoing actualization of potentials, capacities and talents, as fulfillment of mission, as a fuller knowledge of, and acceptance of, the person's own intrinsic nature, as an increasing trend toward unity, integration or synergy within the person" (cited in *Psychosources,* 1973, p. 140). As is obvious from this definition, self-actualization for Maslow, as for Rogers, is a process that is never completed, but rather a continual growing that ends only with death.

For children to progress through the hierarchy of needs, they must have a warm, accepting environment in which those needs can be fulfilled. Given such an environment, they can pass from one level to the next until, having reached adulthood, they have arrived at the point where they can devote themselves to self-actualization. If, however, children's environments are loveless, unstable, or demeaning, then as adults they will still be concentrating on fulfilling whatever lower need remains unsatisfied and will be incapable of progressing to the higher rungs. For example, an unfulfilled need for love will prevent us from developing self-esteem. Low self-esteem, in turn, may keep us back from seeking a more challenging job—in other words, from pursuing self-actualization. To Maslow, such situations are the essence of abnormal behavior.

It should be noted that this represents a unique outlook on psychopathology. What Maslow is concerned with is not really abnormality, but rather the failure to progress beyond the minimum acceptable standards of normality. According to Maslow, a man might hold down a job, take care of his children, differentiate between the real and the imaginary, and yet still feel lonely, alienated, and ineffectual—a situation Maslow calls "the psychopathology of the normal." Human beings, Maslow argues, require a great deal more than mere "adjustment." Hence psychology should address itself not just to repairing "breakdowns" but also to helping people live rich, creative lives. This preoccupation with self-fulfillment—shared, as we have seen, by Rogers—is highly typical of humanistic psychology. And it is that preoccupation more than anything else that sets the humanistic school apart from other schools of abnormal psychology, most of which are chiefly concerned with actual psychopathology.

---

* "Client-centered" was Rogers' original term for his therapy, and since it is the familiar term, it is the one that will appear in this book. Rogers later began to call his approach *person*-centered rather than *client*-centered to indicate his belief that the same principles apply in all human interaction, not just in the relations between therapist and client.

Abraham Maslow denounced the existing formulations of psychology as pessimistic, negative, and limited because they did not view human beings as dynamic, creative, holistic organisms. (Ted Polumbaum)

Existential Psychology

As we have seen, existential psychology is an outgrowth of European existential philosophy, with its emphasis on the difficulty of living authentically in the modern world. In the existentialist view, human beings, in their rush to obtain the material comforts offered by modern technology, have lost their ties to church, region, and family—the very structures that formerly gave direction and meaning to life. Caught in the midst of a vast and amoral technological society, people are left with no values to protect them against the demands for social conformity. They do not choose; they follow. And the result, as we have seen, is the denial of the true self. According to the existentialists, this condition, which they call *alienation,* is a sort of spiritual death, in which the individual is haunted by a sense of the meaninglessness of life and by terror over the inevitability of death.

As a means of ministering to this anguish of the spirit, existential psychology has gained considerable attention in the last two decades. The movement has no single spokesman. We will focus on the theories of four of its major contributors, the Europeans Viktor Frankl, J. H. van den Berg, and R. D. Laing, along with the American psychologist Rollo May.

May: The Ontological Context   The existential perspective was introduced into the United States

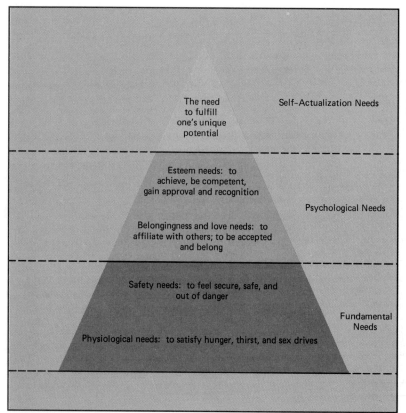

The need to fulfill one's unique potential

Self-Actualization Needs

Esteem needs: to achieve, be competent, gain approval and recognition

Belongingness and love needs: to affiliate with others; to be accepted and belong

Psychological Needs

Safety needs: to feel secure, safe, and out of danger

Physiological needs: to satisfy hunger, thirst, and sex drives

Fundamental Needs

FIGURE 4.1
Maslow's hierarchy of needs. According to Maslow, fundamental needs must be satisfied before a person is free to progress to psychological needs, and these in turn must be satisfied before a person can turn to self-actualization needs.

by Rollo May (1905–   ), and he remains its foremost American interpreter. May accepts many basic principles formulated by other perspectives, such as neurosis, anxiety, and defense. His uniqueness lies in his insistence that such facts have meaning only in the *ontological context*—that is, only in the context of the living being of the patient. In May's view, therapists, when confronted with a patient, must ask themselves, "What are the essential characteristics that constitute this patient as an existing person, that constitute this self as a self?" (1961, p. 74). One such characteristic—in all people, May claims—is the need to preserve a center, a stable foundation for existence. And abnormality, in his view, is often merely a stratagem for protecting that center in the face of perceived threats. The person "shrinks" the range of his or her world, stops knowing or doing certain things, in order to secure the center. It is, as May puts it, "a way of accepting *nonbeing* . . . in order that some little *being* may be preserved" (1961, p. 75)—a formulation not unlike Rogers', except that the emphasis is on being rather than self-actualization.

To minister to this problem, the therapist must appeal to another ontological characteristic, self-consciousness, the ability to see oneself as a subject, as a person who has his or her own world. By dint of affirming the patient completely and also by meeting the patient on common ground, as an existing human being, the existential therapist fights for the full emergence of the patient's self-consciousness. This is a halting and fear-laden process, for in all our "worlds"

there is much that we would rather not know. Furthermore, seeing ourselves as having a world that is purely our own means accepting both responsibility and aloneness. Yet, in keeping with the general existential position, May holds that psychological freedom depends entirely on such acceptance.

As this therapeutic method suggests, May has been in the forefront of the humanistic-existential campaign to make psychology deal with the whole person rather than with isolated functions. He cites, for example, the case of a highly "repressed" patient of his who suffered from hysterical tenseness of the larynx, a problem that conveniently inhibited her speech. A previous therapist had told her that

> she was too proper, too controlled. She reacted
> with great upset and immediately broke off the
> treatment. Now, technically speaking, he was
> entirely correct; existentially, he was entirely
> wrong. What he did not see . . . was that this
> very properness, this overcontrol, far from being
> things that Mrs. Hutchens wanted to get over,
> were part of her desperate attempt to preserve
> what precarious center she had. As though she
> were saying, "If I opened up, if I communicated, I
> would lose what little space in life I have" (1961, p.
> 75).

May's emphasis on the whole person is merely part of his insistence that psychology must stop trying to explain the human condition in terms of processes that humans share with other animals: "what makes a horse a horse are not the elements it shares with

Commuters and other people who must follow a rigid daily routine experience the pressure to conform that, according to the existentialists, breeds alienation. (Dan Brinzac/Peter Arnold)

the dog but what constitutes distinctively, 'horse' " (1961, p. 79). Likewise what makes a human being human is not learning or instincts—characteristics that we share with the horse—but those elements that are uniquely human, above all, self-consciousness.

Frankl: The Search for Meaning   A student of Freud, Viktor Frankl (1905–   ), unlike Freud, was unable to escape from the Nazis and spent the years 1942 to 1945 in concentration camps. Imprisoned along with him were his parents, his brother, and his wife, all of whom died in the camps. From this harrowing experience Frankl evolved the basic tenets of his theory. In the camps, he observed that those prisoners who were able to survive psychologically, resisting despair, were those who could find some spiritual meaning in their suffering. This observation led Frankl to the conclusion that traditional psychology, in dealing with human beings only in their biological and psychological dimensions, was omitting an all-important third dimension: the spiritual life.

It is this emphasis on spiritual meaning that is the central feature of Frankl's existential theory. According to Frankl, the prime motive of human behavior is not the will-to-pleasure or the will-to-power, as psychodynamic theory would have it, but rather the **will-to-meaning**—the struggle of human beings to find some reason for their troubled, complicated, and finite existence. They can discover such meaning only by experiencing *values*. And they discover values through work, through love of other people and of the world, and through confrontation with their own suffering.

Frankl views this process of pursuing values as a moral duty: "Ultimately, man should not ask what

the meaning of life is, but rather he must recognize that it is *he* who is asked. In a word, each man is questioned by life, and he can only respond by being responsible" (1962, p. 101). Those who avoid the pursuit of values also avoid the role of responsibility offered to them by the spiritual life and thus remain the puny, driven creatures that human beings appear to be from the viewpoint of science. Through the discovery of meaning, on the other hand, people rise above whatever forces attempt to control their lives.

When people cannot discover meaning, they experience **existential frustration,** which, in Frankl's view, is a major source of abnormal behavior. To deal with existential frustration, Frankl has evolved a treatment strategy that he calls **logotherapy** (from the Greek word *logos,* denoting "word" or "thought"), aimed at addressing spiritual problems in the philosophical terms appropriate to such problems. The role of the therapist in logotherapy is to confront patients with their responsibility for their existence and help them choose values. This demanding process is softened by the nature of the patient–therapist relationship. As Frankl views it, this relationship is an existential partnership in which the therapist, by intuiting the patient's world, explores that world with him or her. The two of them then work together to correct the flaws in the patient's approach toward life so that he or she can once again take up the task of seeking meaning through values (Frankl, 1975b).

van den Berg: The Lived World   The writings of the Dutch psychiatrist J. H. van den Berg (1914–   ) exemplify existential psychology's basic principle of being-in-the-world, along with the corollary that people can be understood only via the phenomenological approach. Van den Berg (1971, 1974) has put forth a theory of history based on the unity of the individual mind with its environment, and particularly with its sociocultural context. In his view, the history of art, literature, science, education, technology—in short, human expression—is a function of dynamic changes, over the centuries, in the relationship of the individual to the sociocultural milieu.

The same holds true, van den Berg claims, for the history of psychopathology. Society, by allowing or not allowing certain modes of expression, gives shape to our discontents. Thus every society, in every period, fosters its own characteristic neuroses. (Accordingly, van den Berg [1971] thinks the neuroses

Viktor Frankl is the foremost proponent of the existential perspective, which emphasizes people's need to search for meaning and value in life. (Raimondo Borea)

should be renamed "socioses.") The trend of Western society in the last two centuries has been toward increasing pluralism, fragmentation, and individuality—in other words, a loosening of the bonds among the various parts of society and between the individual and the society. This process, in turn, is reflected in the modern psyche, where we find, first, a breaking up of the self into numerous "selves" and, second, a pronounced feeling of loneliness and isolation. Van den Berg's hypothesis is supported to some extent by the current rise in the so-called borderline and narcissistic disorders (Chapter 11), which are characterized primarily by a sense of fragmentation of the self and by an inability to form lasting relationships with others.

Van den Berg's major contribution to treatment has been his elaboration of the phenomenological approach. To understand and treat troubled people, he insists, you must first obtain a faithful description of their "lived world," including their view of themselves, of the objects and people in their world, and of the passage of time. Because of the unity of self and world, people's descriptions of their world will also be descriptions of themselves. As van den Berg puts it:

> The patient is ill; this means that his *world* is ill, literally that *his objects are ill,* however unusual this may sound. When the psychiatric patient tells us what his world looks like, he states, without detours and without mistakes, what he is like (1972, p. 46).

Laing: The False and the True Self

Like the other existential theorists we have discussed, the British psychiatrist R. D. Laing (1927–   ) strongly advocates the phenomenological approach. Laing, however, defines himself specifically as a "social phenomenologist." To him, the central fact of our being-in-the-world is our personal relationships, and what determines our behavior is our experience of the behavior of those close to us:

> The task of social phenomenology is to relate my experience of the other's behavior to the other's experience of my behavior. Its study is the relation between experience and experience. Its true field is interexperience (1970, p. 17).

Much of this "interexperience," in Laing's view, is not a pretty sight. The existential conceptualization of the modern mind as a divided entity—the false self covering the true, unexpressed inner self—is essentially Laing's, and he blames the split on the falsity of modern social communication. The family in particular, by surrounding us with "double messages" and by requiring us to stifle our feelings and pursue meaningless goals, consistently discourages authentic behavior in favor of empty conventionalism. Thus, by the time we reach adulthood, we are utterly cut off from our true selves. Seemingly normal, we are actually deeply impaired psychologically—"half-crazed creatures more or less adjusted to a mad world" (1967, p. 58).

Like "normal" behavior, abnormal behavior, according to Laing, is a function of relationships. Indeed, he claims that psychopathology is something that occurs not in a person but in a relationship. Laing has concentrated on schizophrenia, one of the severest forms of psychological disturbance. Schizophrenia, he writes, is not so much a disorder as "a special strategy that a person invents in order to live in an unlivable situation" (1979, p. 115). Certain people, when faced with extraordinary interpersonal stresses—perhaps combined, as Laing concedes, with a biochemical handicap (Sedgwick, 1982)—find themselves no longer able to maintain the false self that society requires of them. Hence they retreat from reality, plunging into their own inner worlds. This maneuver causes them to produce the kind of behavior that we call schizophrenic. At the same time, it offers them the opportunity to relocate their true selves and to heal the split between the inner and the outer self, thereby carrying them far beyond the pseudonormality of those who never make this plunge.

Thus schizophrenia, in Laing's view, is a last-ditch struggle for true sanity, the sanity of authentic living. Accordingly, the last thing schizophrenics need is conventional psychotherapy, the kind of therapy that would aim at retraining them to resume their false selves. Rather, what they require is a supportive, sympathetic environment in which to pursue their inner voyage, with all the disorganized and regressive behavior that entails. (In the therapy programs designed by Laing and his followers, patients were allowed, even encouraged, to scream, smear feces on the walls, and so forth.) By passing through these regressive stages, Laing argues, schizophrenics may eventually rediscover and make peace with their true selves, reemerging into reality with the capability for creativity and for authentic behavior that was sacrificed in the process of creating the false self.

Comparing Humanism and Existentialism

As we have pointed out, humanistic psychology and existential psychology are similar enough in their basic assumptions to warrant discussion of a single humanistic-existential perspective. Both schools use the phenomenological approach, both are deeply concerned with human values—above all, individuality—and both stress people's capacity for growth, their freedom to choose their lives, and their responsibility for those choices. Furthermore, both see abnormal behavior as not reducible to forces outside of human consciousness (biological drives or environmental influences), and they both understand abnormality to be difficulty in relating to the world or others. However, the humanists have tended to emphasize the role of self-actualization, while the existentialists have stressed the search for authenticity, the struggle to establish and act according to one's own values. And this difference in interpretation gives rise to other subtle differences between the two approaches.

First, humanists focus on the individual—each person's needs, perceptions, and goals—and studiously avoiding holding the individual up to any external standard. It is the "inner" person that is the primary frame of reference (see Figure 4.2). The existentialists, in contrast, insist on viewing the individual within the context of the human condition and attempt to deal with the larger moral and philosophical questions involved in that relationship.

Second, because of their greater interest in the individual's being-in-the-world, the existentialists are generally more rigorous than the humanists in their

FIGURE 4.2

The search for a more authentic and meaningful life is a prime concern of the humanistic-existential perspective. (Drawing by Weber; © 1982 The New Yorker Magazine, Inc.)

"My wife and I are deeply in love, my children are a delight, my career is exciting, I find solace and inspiration in my religion, I'm as healthy as anybody I know. But, still, something is missing."

THE HUMANISTIC-EXISTENTIAL AND SOCIOCULTURAL PERSPECTIVES   91

use of the phenomenological approach. The humanists tend to confine their sharing of the patient's world to empathy; their effort is to "tune in" to the patient's feelings, to "be with" the patient. The existentialists, on the other hand, attempt to elicit an actual picture of what the world is like for the patient—to see his or her world, in detail, from the inside. This process requires a temporary abandonment of their own world-view, something many of them try to achieve by stating their theoretical assumptions at the outset of therapy and then, insofar as they are able, laying those assumptions aside.

Third, the aim of humanistic therapy is to free patients to satisfy their needs and desires. Each person's responsibility is only to himself or herself, though it is assumed that because people are innately good, they will not harm others in the process of self-actualization. The aim of existential therapy, on the other hand, is to develop patients' spiritual lives, a process that includes patients' realizing their responsibility to others and their responsibility to fulfill a rather lofty vision of human life.

Fourth, humanistic psychology is unremittingly optimistic. All the humanists' emphasis is on freedom, hope, potential, and what they see as the clear possibility of self-fulfillment. The existentialists, in contrast, do not hold out any hope for total fulfillment. Indeed, they place great emphasis on the sorrows and frustrations built into life: the threats to freedom, the anguish of choice, the problem of anxiety, the terror of death. As we have seen, Frankl's whole system is in a way based on the challenge of transcending suffering, while Laing's theory is based on the challenge of rescuing some part of the true self from the onslaughts of a crazed world. To these thinkers, freedom is a matter of struggle. For freedom carries with it responsibility: as Frankl says, life expects something from *us* (1955). Nor does fulfillment of this responsibility guarantee self-actualization. Rather, the reward of accepting responsibility is a sort of philosophical peace treaty with the human condition, whereby individuals can rescue their dignity as human beings.

The Impact of the Humanistic-Existential Perspective

As a relatively new approach—and one, furthermore, that arose in direct opposition to established approaches—the humanistic-existential perspective has still had only a limited impact on traditional psychological theory and practice. Nevertheless, some humanistic and existential concepts have made their way into psychodynamic and behavioral psychology. In recent years, for example, many psychodynamic theorists have abandoned the notion of the therapist as a neutral participant in therapy and have begun instead to analyze the ways in which therapists, as individuals with their own emotional histories and their own world-views, influence the course of therapy. This shift is undoubtedly due in part to the humanistic-existential concept of the therapeutic relationship as a partnership. There are other traces of influence as well. Many therapists now emphasize to patients that they will still be accepted even if they behave in self-destructive ways—an obvious borrowing from Rogers' idea that the therapist must provide unconditional positive regard. The existential technique of confronting patients with their responsibility for their own lives has also been appropriated by many psychodynamic and behavioral therapists.

However, the greatest impact of humanistic and existential therapy has been not in the area of the traditional one-to-one patient–therapist relationship but rather in the rapid proliferation of group therapies since the 1950s. Group therapy can take any number of forms—Gestalt therapy, sensitivity training, psychodrama, encounter groups, marathon groups, and so on. (The most common of these therapies will be discussed in Chapter 20.) A large part of the group therapy movement, however, is based on humanistic-existential assumptions: that the therapist–patient relationship should be an existential partnership rather than a parent–child type of interaction; that interpersonal relations in the here and now must constitute a central focus of treatment; and that therapy should foster growth rather than simply repair maladjustment.

Another important byproduct of humanistic-existential psychology has been the search for untapped human potential through altered states of consciousness, achieved via meditation, yoga, hypnosis, hallucinogenic drugs, and other means (Tart, 1975). Such "transpersonal" therapies, while they include the existentialists' philosophical emphasis and the humanists' faith in individual potential, nevertheless represent an important departure from mainstream humanistic-existential psychology. The humanists and especially the existentialists have always sought to help people lead more authentic and meaningful lives within the context of the normal human condition. The goal of the transpersonal therapies, on the other hand, is to help people, in some measure, to transcend that condition, through special states of enlightenment (Fadiman, 1980).

Comparing the Humanistic-Existential Perspective with Other Perspectives

The humanistic-existential perspective and the medical model differ radically. The humanists—and, in some measure, the existentialists—feel that people themselves must be the judges of whether their behavior stands in need of adjustment. (In this respect they resemble what Chapter 1 called the "personal-discomfort" approach to abnormal behavior.) Furthermore, the humanistic-existential theorists believe that patients must "cure" themselves; the role of the therapist is primarily to provide an environment conducive to such "self-cure." The medical model, in contrast, looks primarily to cultural norms—what we could call typical behavior—as the measure of whether a person's responses are abnormal. And if they are judged to be abnormal, then all efforts are aimed at locating the internal dysfunction that is causing the trouble; the patient's will and judgment have little role in the therapy. In sum, both the humanists and the existentialists are "client-centered" in psychological assessment as well as in treatment; medical psychology is society-centered in assessment and body-centered in treatment.

The relationship between the humanistic-existential and psychodynamic perspectives is intimate and complicated. Many humanistic and existential theorists, such as Frankl, began as psychodynamic therapists and have retained certain basic assumptions of psychodynamic theory. Rogers' and May's idea that abnormality is the result of the screening out of experience in order to preserve some psychological anchor (the "self," the "center") is an obvious adaptation of Freud's theory of defense, for example. Likewise, the humanistic-existential theorists, like their psychodynamic predecessors and contemporaries, believe that the key to therapeutic change is insight (London, 1964). In psychodynamic therapy, however, the insights are provided mainly by the therapist and are presumably interpretations of repressed material from the patient's past history. Furthermore, this material is brought to light not so that the patient can act on it but so that the ego's energy can be redirected from

the task of repression toward more constructive defenses, such as sublimation. In humanistic-existential therapy, on the other hand, the insights are supposed to come from patients themselves, as they explore, along with the therapist, their *present* world. The patient's statements, while they may not be taken at face value, are seen as a version of the truth; in any case, they are not read as symbols of hidden truths. Finally, the goal of insight is not to construct a better defense system or any sort of defense system but rather to fill in the missing pieces of a self that is seen as intrinsically directed toward wholeness and which can then follow its natural drive toward positive goals.

The humanistic-existential perspective shares certain assumptions with the behavioral approach as well. Along with the behaviorists, humanists see faulty learning as an important source of abnormal behavior. And like the behaviorists, humanists and existentialists concentrate not on the past but on the present, in the effort to help people find better ways of functioning. These areas of agreement are small, however, compared with the great and fundamental differences between the two schools. Whereas the humanists and existentialists see the human being as a free agent and focus on the patient's subjective world, behaviorists see human functioning as determined and are wary of inferences about people's subjective experience. The behaviorists are even more wary of the philosophical inquiries that distinguish the humanistic-existential perspective. Behaviorists, for example, will discuss values (e.g., Mischel, 1979), but whereas the existentialists speak of values as being inherent in human life, the behaviorists conceptualize them as learned cognitive variables. Finally, the two perspectives differ radically in their therapeutic approaches. As we have seen, the humanistic-existential perspective uses insight as the prime tool of therapy. The behaviorists, on the other hand, try to alter behavior by altering the individual's learning experiences.

Evaluating the Humanistic-Existential Perspective

The primary criticism of the humanistic-existential perspective is that it is unscientific, even antiscientific. The main source of information in humanistic therapy, for example, is simply what the therapist thinks about what the patient thinks about his or her own life.

The existentialists, with their philosophical inquiries, are perhaps even less scientifically precise. In some cases, the perspective seems actually to ignore scientific evidence. According to the behaviorists, for example, the humanistic-existential insistence on free will is directly contrary to the assumptions of mainstream science. Another questionable matter is the phenomenological approach. How can therapists verify that they are in fact perceiving the patient's inner world—or, even if they are, that such empathy is actually of therapeutic value?

To these charges humanistic-existential theorists reply that the scientific methods being demanded of them are borrowed from natural science and therefore are inadequate for the study of human behavior (Giorgi, 1970). In their view, as we have seen, what psychology needs is a new, "human" science—one that can take into account such fundamental human matters as will, values, goals, and meaning—and that is what they are trying to construct. Their argument, in other words, is that they are being scolded for failing to use the wrong tool. They would add (and many would agree) that it is questionable whether the therapeutic situation can actually be judged by scientific standards. Because of its many intangibles, therapy has often been described more as art than as science.

It should also be said that whatever their scientific status, humanistic-existential theorists are tackling problems that are of urgent concern to human beings and that psychology can therefore ill afford to ignore. Free will, for example, may be a scientifically questionable concept, yet the fact remains that most people (including most scientists, in their daily lives) do believe they have free will, and when they congratulate themselves on their achievements, or worry about their future, or wonder whether to order steak or chicken, they are operating on that belief. In view of its power, should the idea of free will be dismissed by psychology because it is scientifically unverifiable? Particularly in the twentieth century, when people have fewer restrictions and fewer firm values than ever before, the conviction of free will can be especially strong, and utterly bewildering. With this contemporary problem the humanistic-existential perspective is better equipped to deal than other perspectives. Indeed, it can be argued that humanistic-existential theory is the only one to have taken modern history seriously.

Finally, as we have mentioned in connection with Maslow, the humanistic-existential perspective can be credited with calling attention to the "constructive" side of human psychology. While psychodynamic and behavioral theories are typically devoted to "repair" work, humanistic and existential psychology, in attempting to help people discover values or fulfill untapped potential, is more ambitious.

THE SOCIOCULTURAL PERSPECTIVE

The sociocultural perspective explains abnormal behavior not so much in terms of the individual psyche as in terms of the society. According to this view, it is the society at large that causes abnormal behavior; furthermore, once a person begins to behave abnormally, the society actually encourages this behavior, thus hindering any "cure." The sociocultural perspective embraces two interrelated theories—one straightforward, one more subtle.

Psychopathology as the Product of Social Pathology

The more straightforward position is that psychological ills are the result of social ills. While we may single out this or that person as being psychologically disturbed, such individual disturbances are merely symptoms of general disturbances in the society. The economic recession of the late 1970s and early 1980s provided abundant evidence for this hypothesis. As unemployment rose, admissions to mental hospitals, suicides, and deaths from stress-related ailments such as heart disease and cirrhosis of the liver rose significantly as well (Pines, 1982).

Sociocultural theorists have also pointed to the many injustices built into our society—poverty, discrimination against minority groups and women, the lack of any valuable or respected role for the aged—as further instances of the cultural provocation of psychological disturbance. In addition to experiencing more stress, the poor are less likely to have the personal resources and social support to cope with stress (Dohrenwend and Dohrenwend, 1981). It should come as no surprise if a poor, ill-educated, and jobless teenager acts "wild" or if a lonely and idle eighty-year-old woman is depressed. And rather than probe their psyches for the underlying psychological cause

Sociocultural theorists maintain that the stresses of living in an impoverished environment can give rise to psycho-pathology; thus, social ills create psychological ills. (Harvey Stein)

of these behavioral abnormalities, we should address ourselves to the obvious social causes.

Psychopathology as a Social Institution

The second major sociocultural position is that what we call psychological abnormality is simply an artifact, or artificial creation, of our culturally accepted ways of handling people who violate social norms. As we saw in Chapter 1, the definition of abnormal behavior depends upon which society is doing the defining. It is on this fact that the second sociocultural theory rests. Adherents of this theory claim that we may label people mentally ill not because of anything intrinsically pathological in their behavior but simply be-

cause they have violated social norms—a situation that the society cannot tolerate and that it handles by labeling and treating the people in question as if they were "sick." We have already mentioned this argument and its foremost proponent, Thomas Szasz (1961), in Chapter 1, under the criticisms of the medical model. Szasz's basic point is that mental illness is simply a convenient myth. Deviations from norms are signs not of illness but of "problems in living." However, we do not know how to deal with people who have problems in living; furthermore, we perceive them as a threat to the social structure. Therefore we label them as sick—a solution that allows us to deny any validity to their problem and, if the deviation is serious enough, to shut them up in mental hospitals, where they can no longer interfere with the workings of the society.

The Process of Labeling   This theory has generated some interest in the process whereby people become labeled as mentally ill. How does the society choose which deviants it will designate as sick? And why do the people accept the label?

One theorist who has considered these questions at length is Thomas Scheff (1966, 1975). Scheff agrees with Szasz that the "mentally ill" are simply people who have been labeled as such. His analysis of the labeling process is as follows. Deviant behavior, whatever its cause, is extremely common. Most of it is transitory and is ignored by the society. However, certain forms of deviance, for one reason or another, come to the attention of the mental health establishment and are singled out as "mental disorders." Once singled out and labeled in this way, the individual is placed in the **social role** of the "mentally ill" person. And it is extremely likely that he or she will accept that role, for as with any other social role (e.g., teacher, student, wife, husband), the society provides strong rewards for behavior consistent with the role and strong punishments for behavior inconsistent with the role. If, for example, a man who has once been labeled "mentally ill" tries to rejoin the world of the sane, he will find much to deter him—rejections from employment agencies, raised eyebrows from people who know about his "past," and so forth. In other words, the rewards that are generally available to sane people are denied to him. If, on the other hand, he accepts the mentally ill role, he is offered a number of rewards: attention, sympathy, and a life free of responsibilities. Thus, according to Scheff, most people who are designated mentally ill ultimately embrace the role and settle back into what has been called the "career" of the mental patient (Goffman, 1959b), fulfilling its duties (i.e., to act crazy and not to try going "straight") and receiving its rewards. In short, the label becomes a self-fulfilling prophecy.

Labeling and Social Class   What *kinds* of behavior are most likely to earn a person the label of mentally ill? What do those socially learned stereotypes of mental illness consist of? A famous group of studies, the so-called New Haven studies (Hollingshead and Redlich, 1958; Myers and Bean, 1968), throw some light on this question, suggesting not only that psychological disturbance is a social phenomenon but that it is closely related to social class.

What the New Haven studies found was that when people of lower socioeconomic levels suffered from behavior disturbances, they were more likely than middle-class people to be placed in state mental hospitals. The reasons were twofold. First, the lower-class people could not afford private outpatient care. Second, they tended to manifest their unhappiness in aggressive and rebellious behaviors. And these behaviors, while acceptable to other lower-class people as "normal" signs of frustration, appeared unacceptable—indeed, genuinely bizarre—to the mental health professionals who were diagnosing them, since those professionals came from higher socioeconomic brackets and accordingly had different ideas about what constituted normal responses to stress. Hence persons with lower socioeconomic backgrounds were more likely to be labeled as psychotic and to be hospitalized as a result. In contrast, people of higher socioeconomic levels tended not to be hospitalized, not only because they could pay for outpatient care but also because their "style" of deviance (e.g., withdrawal and self-deprecation) seemed to the doctors, coming from the same social class, less bizarre. Consequently, these people were diagnosed as neurotic—a label that carries much less stigma—and with the help of regular therapy were able to return to their daily lives. Unlike the hospitalized and "psychotic" poor, they were not given a "sick" role to fill and thus were more likely to improve. In sum, socioeconomic differences not only determine who is considered severely abnormal but by doing so can seriously affect the individual's chances for improvement (Braginsky et al., 1969).

Evaluating the Sociocultural Perspective

Almost no one in the mental health field would dispute the first theory outlined above: socioeconomic conditions *do* contribute to psychological disturbance. The only question is one of emphasis. Whereas sociocultural theorists claim that socially engendered stress is the primary cause, other theorists say that it is secondary to other factors, such as personal resources or family conflict. In turn, most sociocultural theorists readily concede the influence of personal resources and family discord but argue that these are often the result of social disadvantage.

The second theory—that psychological abnormality is a cultural artifact, maintained through labeling—is far more controversial. Differential labeling is not the only possible explanation for the disproportionate numbers of lower-class people who are diagnosed as psychotic. The phenomenon could be accounted for more simply via the socioeconomic-stress theory: since the poor have to cope with more serious stresses, they have more serious breakdowns. Another possible explanation is that severely disturbed people slip downward on the socioeconomic ladder—they tend to lose their jobs, for example—so that whatever their original socioeconomic status, they are members of the lower class by the time they are diagnosed (Dunham, 1965).

A third hypothesis has to do with differing attitudes toward psychological disturbance. There is evidence that lower-class people are more resistant than the middle class to the idea that they are psychologically disturbed and therefore are more likely to reach a diagnostician only after their symptoms have become severe enough to be described as psychotic (Gove, 1982). In short, labeling is only one of several possible factors underlying the correlation between diagnosis and social class.

Even aside from its connection with social class, labeling theory is now being called into question. The theory was developed in the 1950s, when mental hospital stays tended to be long, thus fostering both the stigma and the social role attached to mental patient status. Today, on the other hand, mental hospital stays are far briefer, and accordingly there is less evidence of persisting stigma (Gove, 1982) and less inducement to role-taking. Thus the necessary conditions for labeling have to some extent been removed, yet the prevalence of mental disorder has remained about the same. Since the reduction of hospitals stays was motivated in part by an effort to prevent labeling, labeling theory has, ironically, suffered from its own acceptance.

SUMMARY

Humanistic-existential psychology, which arose in the 1950s in reaction to the determinism of psychodynamic and behavioral theory and in response to the spiritual problems of mid-twentieth-century life, takes a uniquely nonmechanical view of human existence. The humanistic and existential perspectives share an emphasis on human individuality and self-awareness, capacity for growth, freedom to choose one's fate, and responsibility for one's decisions. The two perspectives and related theories are called the Third Force in psychology. The humanistic movement in psychology can be traced to post–World War II disillusion with automation and depersonalization in America. The roots of existential psychology lie largely in Europe, where the reaction to dehumanization that the existential movement represented both came earlier (after World War I) and addressed a more broadly philosophical crisis in the history of ideas.

Humanistic psychology sees human beings as basically good, rational, and socially oriented. It sees consciousness and self-consciousness as uniquely human and on this ground distinguishes human behavior from the behavior of other forms of life. According to this philosophy, the prime motivation in human life is the drive toward self-actualization, the fulfillment of one's capabilities. Abnormal behavior results from a blocking of self-actualization, either because of an incongruence between an individual's experience and his or her self-image (Carl Rogers' theory) or because of a failure to satisfy basic needs (Abraham Maslow's theory). For both of these theorists, a healthy personality is not defined simply by the absence of psychopathology. Rather, it is characterized by an openness to the experiences and challenges that lead to self-fulfillment.

Existential psychology stresses the concept of being-in-the-world (that is, the individual's relatedness to the world and his or her constant state of interaction with others); the struggle to live authentically, by one's own principles, in the face of demands from others; and the importance of the individual's present and future as opposed to the past. Rollo May, who introduced the existential perspective to the United States, argues that facts have no meaning outside the ontological context—the patient's living self and consciousness of self. Thus therapy emphasizes the whole person, not isolated functions, processes, or behaviors. Like Rogers and other theorists, May believes that the key to therapeutic change is to foster insight in the patient. Viktor Frankl, a psychiatrist and leading existential theorist, argues that the search for meaning in life is the essence of a healthy personality. For Frankl, this task is a lifelong struggle; those who avoid it will end up feeling helpless and frustrated. Frankl points to existential frustration as a major source of abnormal behavior. Two other European psychiatrists who share Frankl's view are J. H. van den Berg and R. D. Laing. Laing takes a more radical approach than Frankl, arguing that society causes psychopathology by forcing people to develop false selves and to deny their true selves.

Though similar enough to be united in a single perspective, humanistic psychology and existential psychology have certain differences. The humanists place greater emphasis on the individual and on the satisfaction of needs and desires, while the existentialists focus more on the individual's relation to the human condition as a whole and on the question of individual responsibility.

The humanistic-existential perspective has influenced psychodynamic and behavioral psychology in several ways. Many therapists, for example, have become more interested in the way their own personalities influence the course of therapy. It is also more common now for therapists to challenge patients to assume responsibility for their own lives. The major influence of humanistic-existential psychology has been on the development of group therapies.

While criticized for its heavy reliance on the concept of the self and for its use of inferred constructs, the humanistic-existential perspective has been justly credited with focusing on major human concerns and with stressing the positive aspects of human psychology.

The sociocultural perspective holds that the ills in society at large cause abnormal behavior in individuals. Further, the behavior we call "abnormal" is often not pathological but merely a violation of social norms. Society attaches the label "sick" to those who violate certain social norms.

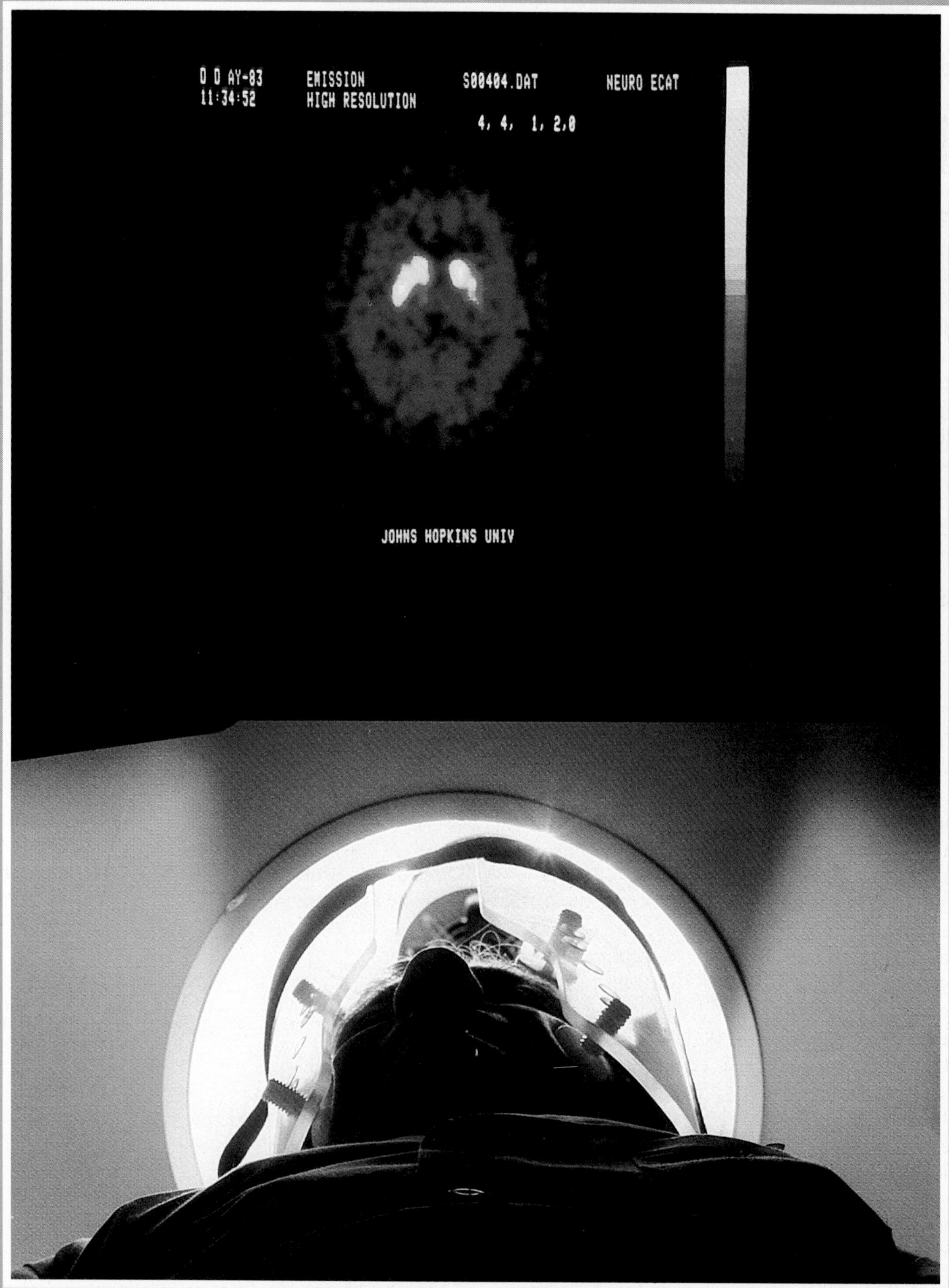
0 D AY-83
11:34:52
EMISSION
HIGH RESOLUTION
S00404.DAT
4, 4, 1, 2,0
NEURO ECAT
JOHNS HOPKINS UNIV

CHAPTER 5

The Neuroscience Perspective

THE BIOLOGICAL BASES OF BEHAVIOR

Behavior Genetics
The Central Nervous System
The Peripheral Nervous System: Somatic and Autonomic
The Endocrine System

EVALUATING THE NEUROSCIENCE PERSPECTIVE

Long before recorded history, people associated abnormal behavior with things going on inside the head. As the brain does not permit easy access, however, theories about the organic bases of abnormal behavior remained for centuries in the realm of speculation. Today such speculation is being informed by concrete evidence. With the help of advanced technology, researchers can now flip a switch and see a moving picture of a living brain as it is functioning, and can search these pictures for blood clots, tumors, and other possible causes of emotional or behavioral problems.

The brain, then, is no longer the dark territory that it used to be. The same is true of other biological functions that affect our thoughts and emotions. Perhaps the greatest source of optimism and excitement in the field of abnormal psychology in the last two decades has been the tremendous advance in the study of the biological bases of behavior. And this advance in turn has led to a tremendous rise in prestige for the neuroscience perspective, the source of these breakthroughs.

The neuroscience perspective focuses on the organic determinants of behavior. It is not a single, general theory, but rather a collection of specific theories about specific pathologies. Most of these theories will be dealt with in the chapters that discuss those syndromes. The purpose of the present chapter is to describe the kinds of biological mechanisms—the genes, the nervous system, the endocrine system—now being investigated by biological researchers in abnormal psychology and thus to lay the groundwork for the theories that we will consider in later chapters.

THE BIOLOGICAL BASES OF BEHAVIOR

Fundamental to the neuroscience perspective is the issue of the relationship between the physical and psychological aspects of our functioning—the so-called **mind-body problem,** first discussed in the early seventeenth century by the French philosopher René Descartes. While the psychological perspectives we have examined so far regard human behavior primarily as a function of the relationship between the mind and the social environment, biological researchers focus on the relationship between the mind and its *organic* environment, the body. In this view they are certainly justified. Though most of us tend to regard our minds as things apart from our bodies, the fact is that what we call the mind is actually a function of our physical being, especially of the brain and the nervous system. Thus physical and mental functioning cannot realistically be considered apart from each other.

Actually, it has long been recognized that certain abnormal behavior patterns, such as epilepsy, are caused by organic factors. This book devotes two entire chapters (Chapters 16 and 17, "Organic Brain Disorders" and "Mental Retardation") to such patterns. But in recent years researchers have come increasingly to suspect—indeed, to show—that organic factors are involved in, and possibly important causes of, disorders *not* traditionally considered organic, such as anxiety and depression. It is on the factors involved in this new research that we will focus in this chapter.

Behavior Genetics

Every cell in the human body contains a mass of threadlike structures known as **chromosomes.** Coded on the chromosomes are all the instructions, inherited from the parents at the moment of conception, as to what proteins the body should produce. The proteins in turn determine what the body will become: brown-eyed or blue-eyed, tall or short, brown-skinned or light-skinned. The individual units in which this information is carried are called **genes.** In some cases, a given trait is controlled by a single gene. But the vast majority of human traits are **polygenic,** the products of the interaction of many genes.

It has long been known that genetic inheritance influences not only physical traits, such as eye color, but also behavior. What is not known is the *extent* to which genes control behavior. This is the famous nature–nurture question, and it is as unresolved in abnormal psychology as it is in any other branch of psychology. Researchers in **behavior genetics,** as this subfield is called, have methods of determining whether a behavioral abnormality is subject to genetic influence. But establishing the degree of genetic influence is a much thornier matter. As we just saw, most traits are controlled by the subtle interaction of many genes—and affected, furthermore, by other factors in the body chemistry. Thus the relationship of genes to traits is not a single link but a vast net of influences.

Because of these complexities, it is only in the past three decades that researchers have begun to make any genuine progress in relating genetics to behavior disturbances. To date, genetic defects have been shown to be directly responsible for a few forms of abnormality—for example, Down's syndrome (a type of mental retardation). However, the research suggests that such clear-cut cases of direct genetic causation are rare. Instead, most genetically influenced disorders seem to fit what is called the **diathesis-stress theory.** According to this theory, certain genes or gene combinations give rise to a **diathesis,** or constitutional predisposition, to a disorder. If this diathesis is then combined with certain kinds of environmental stress, abnormal behavior will result. Studies within the past thirty years seem to indicate that just as a tendency to develop diabetes, heart disease, and certain types of cancer can be genetically transmitted, so can a predisposition to certain kinds of behavioral disturbances (McBroom, 1980; Rosenthal, 1971). Research in this area has focused particularly on schizophrenia, and as we shall see in Chapter 15, we now have firm evidence that genes do in fact play a role in the development of this form of psychosis. There is also evidence of genetic influence in certain forms of depression.

The Mechanics of Genetic Studies   To understand the genetic evidence, one must understand the methods by which it is obtained. Every human being is born with a unique **genotype**—that is, a highly individual combination of genes representing the biological inheritance from the parents. This genotype interacts with the individual's environment to determine the **phenotype**—that is, the individual's equally unique combination of observable characteristics. The entire purpose of behavior genetics is to separate the two tangled threads of genotype and environment and thus to discover to what extent different psychological disorders are due to genetic inheritance rather than environmental influence. This is done via three basic types of studies: family studies, twin studies, and adoption studies.

FAMILY STUDIES   Family studies are based on our knowledge that different types of family relationships involve different degrees of genetic similarity. All children receive half their genes from one parent and half from the other. Thus parents and children are 50 percent identical genetically. Likewise, any two siblings have approximately 50 percent of their genes in common. Aunts and uncles, one step further removed, are approximately 25 percent identical genetically to a given niece or nephew. And first cousins, yet another step removed, have approximately 12.5 percent of their genes in common.

With these percentages in mind, the genetic researcher puts together a substantial sample of families containing one diagnosed case, referred to as the **index case** or **proband case,** of the disorder in question. Then the researcher studies the other members of each family—grandparents, parents, children, grandchildren, siblings, aunts and uncles, cousins—to determine what percentage of individuals in each of these relationship groups merits the same diagnosis as the index case. When all the families have been examined in this way, the percentages for each relationship group are averaged, so the researcher ends up with an average percentage of siblings sharing the index case's disorder, an average percentage of aunts and uncles bearing the index case's disorder, and so on down the line. If it should turn out that these percentages roughly parallel the percentages of shared genes—if, for example, siblings prove approximately twice as likely as aunts and uncles to share the index case's disorder—then this evidence would strongly suggest that predisposition to the disorder in question might be transmitted genetically. If you turn ahead to Figure 15.1 (p. 387), you will see a graph summarizing family studies of schizophrenia. The figures clearly suggest that the more closely one is related to a schizophrenic, the more likely one is to develop schizophrenia.

Such evidence, however, only suggests it does not prove—genetic transmission. While a person has more genes in common with siblings than with aunts and uncles, he or she also has much more of the environment in common with siblings than with aunts and uncles. Therefore, if a person is more likely to share a psychological disorder with siblings than with aunts and uncles, this differential could easily be the result of shared environment (same parents, same schools, same neighborhood) rather than shared genes.

TWIN STUDIES The genes-versus-environment confusion is less troublesome in twin studies. Here the basic technique is to compare monozygotic and dizygotic twins. **Monozygotic (MZ) twins,** also called **identical twins,** develop from a single fertilized egg and therefore have exactly the same genotype; they are always of the same sex, have the same eye color, share the same blood type, and so on. In contrast, **dizygotic (DZ) twins,** also called **fraternal twins,** develop from two eggs fertilized by two different sperm. Therefore DZ twins, like any pair of siblings, have only approximately 50 percent of their genes in common; like ordinary siblings, one may be female and the other male, one blue-eyed and one brown-eyed, and so forth. Thus while monozygotic twins are as likely as dizygotic twins to share the same environment, they have approximately twice as many genes in common.

From this configuration one can guess the research design. The researcher assembles one group of index cases, each of whom is an MZ twin, and a second group of index cases, each of whom is a DZ twin. All of the **co-twins** (the twins of the index cases) are then examined to discover how many of them are **concordant**—that is, share the same disorder—with their index twin. If the researcher should discover that the concordance rate for the MZ twins is considerably greater than that for the DZ twins, then this would be substantial evidence that predisposition to the disorder is genetically transmitted. And that in fact is what has been discovered in the case of schizophrenia: a concordance rate three to five times higher for MZ twins than for DZ twins. Even more than the family studies, this is strong evidence for a hereditary factor in schizophrenia.

Twin studies are beautifully simple in design but not in practice, the chief problem being that MZ twins are rare. It is no easy task, for example, to assemble an adequate sample of paranoid schizophrenics all of whom are MZ twins. Furthermore, the question of environmental influence cannot be altogether eliminated from twin studies, since MZ twins, so similar physically and always of the same sex, may be raised in more similar ways than DZ twins.

ADOPTION STUDIES Adoption studies represent an attempt at decisively separating the evidence of genetic influence from that of environmental influence. As we have seen, as long as two relatives share the same environment—live under the same roof, pet the same dog, fight the same family fights—the fact that they share the same psychological disorder cannot be attributed with certainty to genetic influence. But if, through adoption, the environmental tie were broken, then any significant similarities in psychological history should be entirely the result of the genetic tie. For example, if infants who were born of severely disturbed mothers and adopted into other families at birth developed that same psychological disorder at approximately the same rate as infants born of *and* raised by mothers suffering from that disorder, then the disorder must, to some extent, be in the genes. Likewise, if a pair of MZ twins who were separated at birth and raised in different homes still showed a substantially higher concordance rate for a given disorder than DZ twins raised together or separately, then this would constitute the firmest possible evidence for genetic transmission.

It is just such mother–child pairs and twin pairs that are the object of adoption studies. The adopted twin studies are the less important of the two, because the samples are so small. (If it is difficult to assemble a group of MZ twins all of whom are paranoid schizophrenic, imagine the difficulty of putting together a group of MZ twins all of whom are paranoid schizophrenic *and* have been raised apart from their co-twins.) The mother–child adoption studies are somewhat easier to do, since a severely disturbed mother is likely to give up her child for adoption. Several such studies have been done, and as we shall see in Chapter 15, they now constitute our best evidence for the genetic transmission of a tendency toward schizophrenia.

The Central Nervous System

If behavioral abnormalities do result from some form of biological malfunction, then the likely place to look for such malfunction is the nervous system. The **nervous system** is a vast electrochemical conducting network that extends from the brain through the rest of the body. Its function is to carry information, in the form of electrical impulses, from the brain to the rest of the body and back.

The nervous system has many divisions (see Figure 5.1), but its headquarters is the **central nervous system (CNS),** consisting of the brain and spinal cord. Of all the parts of the nervous system, the CNS is the one primarily responsible for the storage and transmission of information. Through the spinal cord the brain sends its instructions to the muscles ("Take that pot off the stove"); again through the spinal cord, the skin and the muscles send back to the brain information about the outside world ("The pot handle is too hot"); the brain processes this information and then, through the spinal cord, sends back further messages ("Get a potholder"). In this way the CNS controls all human behavior, from the cooking of dinner to the writing of a book to the blinking of an eye.

Logically, when there is a problem in the CNS, there is a problem in behavior. As we shall see in Chapter 16, any damage to the brain, whether from injury or disease, can cause a massive revolution in the personality. Recent research, however, has concentrated more on subtle chemical changes that may be implicated in psychopathology.

Neurons   As anyone who has ever tried alcohol or marijuana knows, alterations in body chemistry can have significant effects on thought, emotion, perception, and behavior. This is because the chemicals of the body control the passage of information through the nervous system.

Like every other part of the body, the nervous system is made up of cells specifically adapted for its functions. Nerve cells, called **neurons,** have four characteristic structural features (see Figure 5.2):

1. The *cell body,* which contains the nucleus. The chemical reactions that take place in the cell

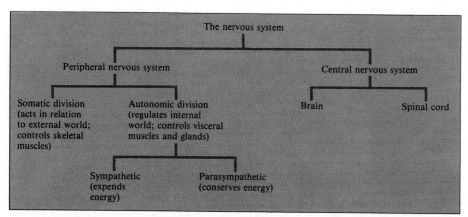

FIGURE 5.1
Diagram of the relationships among the parts of the nervous system

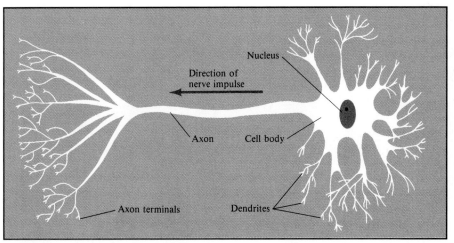
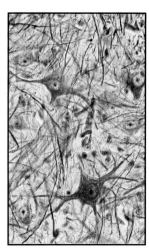

FIGURE 5.2
A diagram (*left*) and a photomicrograph (*right*) of a neuron, or nerve cell. (Photomicrograph: Biophoto Associates/ Science Source/Photo Researchers)

body provide the energy and the chemicals needed for the transmission of signals.

2. The *dendrites,* short fibers branching out from the cell body. In most neurons, it is the dendrites that receive signals from other neurons.

3. The *axon,* a long fiber stretching outward from the cell body. This is the passageway through which signals are transmitted down the neuron, on their way to other neurons or to the muscles and glands.

4. The *axon terminals,* the axon's branchlike endings, each with a button-like structure at its tip. It is through these buttons at the ends of the axon terminals that the impulse is transmitted to the next neuron.

The typical pathway is as follows. Receiving, through its dendrites, an electrical impulse from a neighboring neuron, the neuron passes that impulse down its axon to the end of an axon terminal. There it must leap a small gap, called the **synapse,** between the terminal button and the dendrite of the neuron that is to receive the impulse. This leap is accomplished by chemicals known as neurotransmitters. Other types of connections—axon to cell body and axon to axon—similarly facilitate or inhibit transmission.

Neurotransmitters   Stored in small sacs within the terminal buttons, the **neurotransmitters** act as the messengers from one neuron to the next. When an electrical impulse reaches the terminal button, the neurotransmitter is squirted into the synapse, flooding the gap and making contact with the dendrite of the next neuron. Molecules within the neurotransmitter fit into corresponding receptors on the surface of the dendrite, and this reaction causes a change in voltage in the receiving neuron. The impulse is thus transmitted.

The neurotransmitters, then, are the critical links from neuron to neuron, and therefore it is no surprise that studies of possible neurological malfunction in the psychologically disturbed have implicated, above all, the neurotransmitters. Scientists have been aware of the existence of neurotransmitters only since the 1920s, and research involving their relation to psychological disorders is now one of the most exciting areas of investigation in abnormal psychology. It is not yet known how many kinds of neurotransmitters exist in the human body—probably more than fifty. Among those that have been identified so far, the ones that may have an important role in psychopathology are the following (Snyder, 1980; Cooper et al., 1986):

1. *Acetylcholine.* The first neurotransmitter discovered, acetylcholine is involved in transmitting nerve impulses to the muscles throughout the body. It may also be involved in certain sleep disorders and in Alzheimer's disease (a form of senility).

2. *Dopamine.* This substance seems to be crucially involved in the regulation of motor behavior.

Imaging Brain Structure and Function

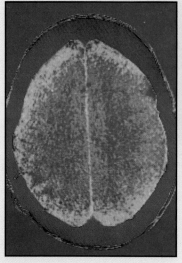

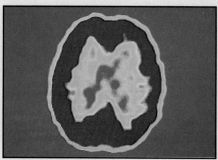

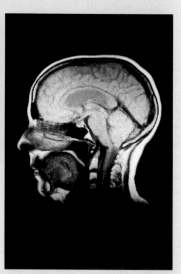

Images of a normal brain generated by CT scan (left,) PET scan (center), and MRI (right). (Dan McCoy/Rainbow)

Can a system explain itself? Logicians have constructed proofs that it cannot—and perhaps we will never completely explain the complex systems of the brain and all its functions. Yet the neurosciences are pioneering investigations into the mind's organic basis and environment and laying the groundwork for knowledge that should prove, in the next century, to be the most exciting in the history of science. For abnormal psychology, findings today are tentative, and hypotheses are only as good as the methods available to test them. Investigating brain function and structure without disturbing them requires sophisticated imaging technologies. New techniques that allow diagnosticians to "see" inside the brain

Excess dopamine activity is thought to be related to schizophrenia, as we shall see in Chapter 15.

3. *Enkephalins.* These substances seem able to act upon the opiate receptors in the brain (the parts that are affected by opium or related drugs). As such, they may be the body's "natural drugs."

4. *GABA* (gamma-amino-butyric acid). GABA is a neurotransmitter that works almost exclusively in the brain, inhibiting neurons from "firing," or sending impulses.

5. *Glycine.* This substance is involved in metabolic functions throughout the body and seems, like GABA, to work as an inhibitory neurotransmitter in the brain.

6. *Glutamic acid.* Also involved in metabolism, glutamic acid stimulates brain neurons to fire.

7. *Histamine.* Well known for its role in allergic reactions in the body, histamine in the brain is concentrated in the areas that are related to the emotions. Its precise function is as yet unknown.

8. *Norepinephrine.* This substance is involved in transmitting impulses to the autonomic nervous system, producing "fight or flight" responses, such as increased heart rate and blood pressure.

9. *Serotonin.* This neurotransmitter handles a good deal of impulse transmission within the brain. Imbalances in serotonin and norepinephrine may be involved in severe depression, a theory we shall examine in Chapter 10.

Four key neurotransmitters that may be related to abnormal behavior are acetylcholine, dopamine, norepinephrine, and serotonin. Although they account

without surgically invading it include computerized tomography (CT), positron emission tomography (PET), and magnetic resonance imaging (MRI), or nuclear magnetic resonance (NMR).

CT and MRI scans give information about the brain's structures; PET yields images of brain activity, or function. All three techniques process data about the brain and display it as either static or moving images on a monitor screen. The CT scan passes X-rays through cross sections of the brain and measures the radioactivity at the other side. By detecting differences in tissue density at discrete locations, it reveals tumors or injuries that may be related to language disorders, loss of memory, and other symptoms of specific behavioral abnormalities. The PET scan detects abnormal brain activity by monitoring a radioactive tracer substance as it travels through the blood vessels of the brain, and the computerized scanner displays a moving picture in which color contrasts reveal differences in metabolism. Thus, it is possible to tell which parts of the brain are most active as the individual engages in different cognitive tasks. The PET scan of brain cross sections can show evidence of degenerative disorders, epilepsy, stroke, and the actual site activity of psychoactive drugs. MRI, a newer imaging technique, provides more precise pictures of brain structures than CT scans, and from different vantage points. For MRI, the patient is enclosed in a magnetic field, and radio waves are used to detect abnormalities in brain tissue. The image is so precise that it looks like a black and white photograph of the brain.

Neuroscientists are using these techniques to test several new hypotheses about the organic basis of abnormal behavior. Evidence from CT scans suggests that enlarged ventricles—cavities in the brain that carry cerebrospinal fluid—may contribute to schizophrenia. Although some negative findings argue against this hypothesis, recent research supports it (Reveley, 1985; Seidman, 1983). MRI images of the brains of schizophrenics show smaller frontal lobes, cerebrums, and craniums (Andreason et al., 1986), suggesting that early developmental abnormalities could have retarded both brain and skull growth. PET scans suggest that a lower level of activity in the left hemisphere may help to explain schizophrenia (Buchsbaum et al., 1982), a theory that is not necessarily inconsistent with the frontal-lobe hypothesis if the left-hemisphere frontal lobe is affected.

Theories about the organic basis of schizophrenia and other disorders remain tentative, and evidence from CT, PET, and MRI needs to be correlated with data obtained by other methods. Postmortem analysis helps to confirm some of the hypotheses that are based on the high-technology, noninvasive brain scans. Postmortem exams have confirmed, for example, that the brains of schizophrenics do tend to have enlarged ventricles and to weigh less than the brains of nonschizophrenics (Brown et al., 1986). Future research into the organic causes of abnormal behavior will be aimed at finding new links in the chain of evidence that now leads from malfunctions in neurotransmitters and other elements of brain biochemistry and structure to the observed behavior of people afflicted with psychoses.

for a small percentage of all nerve impulse transmission, their role seems to be important.

In treating those disorders in which neurotransmitter imbalances seem to be involved, physicians have tried to correct those imbalances with drugs that interfere with the neurotransmitter at any one of several stages. As Figure 5.3 shows, neurotransmitters begin as amino acids in the bloodstream; they are then converted into neurotransmitters in the axon terminal before they are used in firing. Thus drugs may be used in an attempt to increase the level of the constituent amino acid in the bloodstream, or to facilitate its conversion in the axon terminal, or to prolong the stay of the neurotransmitter in the synapse, whether by blocking its re-uptake into the axon terminal or by other means. But these are very delicate manipulations, still in the experimental stages. Indeed, as we shall see, in some cases researchers still do not know whether the neurotransmitter in question needs to be increased or decreased.

The Anatomy of the Brain   While behavior may be affected by chemical reactions at the finest level of brain activity, we also know that many behavioral abnormalities are related to the gross structure of the brain, and therefore a knowledge of the anatomy of the brain is essential to an understanding of psychopathology.

Covering the brain is an intricate, convoluted outer layer of "gray matter" called the *cerebral cortex* (see Figure 5.4). The external surface of the cerebral cortex has many *sulci* (fissures) and *gyri* (ridges between sulci), which are "landmarks" in studying the brain. A major sulcus called the *longitudinal fissure* divides the brain along the midline into two symmetrical, mirror-image cerebral hemispheres, the right and left

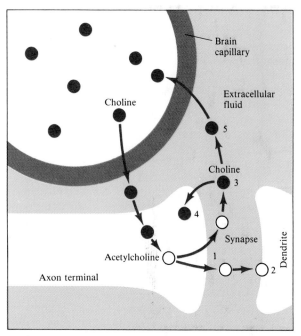

FIGURE 5.3

The life cycle of a neurotransmitter. Neurotransmitters are made from amino acids contained in the protein we take in as food. The amino acids circulate in the bloodstream. To get from the capillaries (blood vessels) of the brain to the brain cells, where they are converted into neurotransmitters, the amino acid molecules must cross the "blood–brain barrier." Here, for example, a molecule of the amino acid choline crosses through the capillary wall, enters the extracellular fluid, and is taken up by a neuron. In the neuron it is converted into acetylcholine and stored in the axon terminal. When the neuron fires, the acetylcholine is released into the synapse (1). There it either reacts with the dendrite of an adjoining neuron, thereby transmitting a signal (2), or is converted back into choline (3), which may then be taken up by the neuron again (4) or may reenter the extracellular fluid and the bloodstream (5).

brain, connected by the *corpus callosum,* a band of nerve fibers. Each hemisphere is further divided into four lobes. The *central sulcus* (or *fissure of Rolando*) divides the cortex into the *frontal lobe* and the receptive cortex, made up of the *parietal, temporal,* and *occipital lobes.* Another major fissure, the *lateral sulcus* (or *fissure of Sylvius*), runs along the side of each hemisphere, separating the temporal lobe from the frontal and parietal lobes.

The functions of these different lobes of the brain have been the subject of much research and debate. The frontal lobes are a particular enigma, but at present it appears that they are related essentially to lan-

guage ability, to the regulation of fine voluntary movements, and to the ordering of stimuli and sorting out of information. In addition, the frontal lobes serve as a comparator organ—that is, they somehow allow the individual to look at his or her behavior and evaluate its appropriateness and the way it is being perceived. This enables the person to behave differently when feedback suggests the need. The frontal lobes also serve to overcome psychological inertia (that is, they help tell the person when to start and stop any particular action). Knowing the proper time to stop or change course is crucial to socially appropriate behavior. Damage to frontal-lobe structures often results in odd behavior, since the impaired person has lost an important part of self-awareness.

The temporal lobes control auditory perception and some part of visual perception; furthermore, they clearly have some role in memory, for damage to the temporal lobes generally involves memory loss. The parietal lobes are the center of intersensory integration (e.g., the ability to visualize a cow upon hearing a "moo") and of motor and sensory-somatic functions. Damage to the parietal lobes frequently results in spatial disorientation and in loss of control over gross-motor behavior (e.g., walking). Finally, the occipital lobes appear to control visual discrimination and visual memory.

A cross section of the brain reveals further important structural features: the *hypothalamus,* which controls body temperature, metabolism, and appetite and helps regulate emotions; the *thalamus,* which relays sensory messages to the appropriate parts of the brain; the *cerebellum,* involved in posture, physical balance, and fine-motor coordination; the *pons,* a major relay station connecting the cerebellum with other areas of the brain and with the spinal cord; and the *medulla,* which regulates such vital functions as heartbeat, breathing, and blood pressure. The *brainstem* includes the pons, the medulla, and the *reticular formation,* which regulates sleep and arousal. Within the brain there are *ventricles,* cavities filled with cerebrospinal fluid.

Several of these brain structures are now the focus of intense study by researchers in abnormal psychology. Both enlarged ventricles and unusually small frontal lobes have been associated with schizophrenia. Temporal-lobe malfunction may be responsible for the memory loss seen in Alzheimer's disease. The appetite-control function of the hypothalamus is being investigated in relation to obesity. These theories will be discussed in Chapters 9 and 16.

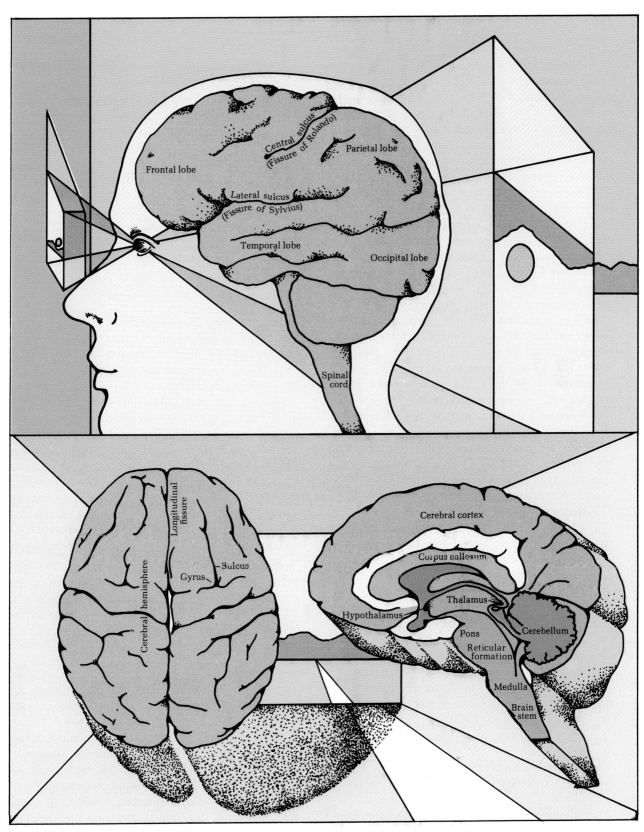

FIGURE 5.4
The anatomy of the brain

LATERALIZATION: RIGHT AND LEFT BRAIN   Another matter researchers are now investigating is **lateralization,** the localization of functions in one hemisphere of the brain or the other. Though the right and left hemispheres are roughly mirror images of one another, they have different specialties. To begin with, each controls movement on one side of the body—the opposite side. (Thus severe damage to the right hemisphere will usually cause paralysis to the left side of the body, and vice versa.) Furthermore, the two halves seem to be associated with different kinds of abilities.

The left hemisphere appears to be the speech center for right-handed people. Research has found, for example, that almost no right-handed person can speak if his or her left hemisphere is temporarily disabled by a barbiturate injection (Kupferman, 1981). Among left-handed people, 20 to 40 percent also rely primarily on the left hemisphere for speech. This localization extends to different speech functions: speech comprehension is apparently headquartered in the temporal lobe, speech production in the frontal lobe. Such divisions are important in the study of the **aphasias,** organically based language disorders. And researchers are now investigating the possibility that schizophrenia, which typically involves disordered speech, may be related to dysfunction in the left hemisphere (Buchsbaum et al., 1982; Flor-Henry, 1976; Flor-Henry et al., 1983).

The right hemisphere seems to be specialized for spatial skills, visual imagery, musical abilities, and also the expression and comprehension of emotion. Such findings have led some writers to propose that the right brain is the center of creativity and subjectivity, as opposed to the more practical, reality-oriented left brain. This is a great oversimplification, yet research has shown that people with right-brain damage do have difficulty interpreting emotions. This finding in turn suggests that such emotional disorders as depression and anxiety may be organically linked to the right hemisphere (Flor-Henry, 1976; Flor-Henry et al., 1983; Golden et al., 1983).

The Peripheral Nervous System: Somatic and Autonomic

While the central nervous system is the high command of the body's information network, the **peripheral nervous system,** a network of nerve fibers leading from the CNS to all parts of the body, is what carries out the commands. The peripheral nervous system has two branches. One is the **somatic nervous system,** which senses and acts on the external world. The somatic nervous system relays to the brain information picked up through the sense organs, and it also transmits the brain's messages to the skeletal muscles, which move the body. The actions mediated by the somatic nervous system are actions that we think of as voluntary: picking up a telephone, crossing a street, tying one's shoes.

The second branch of the peripheral nervous system is the autonomic nervous system, and it is this branch that is of special interest to abnormal psychology.

The Autonomic Nervous System   While the somatic nervous system activates the skeletal muscles, the **autonomic nervous system (ANS)** controls the smooth muscles, the glands, and the internal organs. Thus while the somatic division directs our more purposeful responses to environmental stimuli, such as crossing a street when the light turns green, the autonomic division mediates our more automatic responses, such as increased heart rate if we come close to being run over as we cross the street. Because the functions of the ANS tend to be automatic, it used to be known as the "involuntary" nervous system. And though we now know that many autonomic functions can be brought under voluntary control, it is still true that these functions—the regulation of heartbeat, respiration, blood pressure, pupil dilation, bladder contraction, perspiration, salivation, adrenaline secretion, and gastric-acid production, to name only a few—are generally carried out without our thinking about them.

THE SYMPATHETIC AND PARASYMPATHETIC DIVISIONS The role of the ANS is to adjust the internal workings of the body to the demands of the environment. Like the central and the peripheral nervous systems, the ANS is subdivided into two branches—the sympathetic division and the parasympathetic division—which are structurally and functionally distinct (Figure 5.5). The **sympathetic division,** consisting of the nerve fibers that emanate from the middle of the spinal cord, mobilizes the body to meet emergencies. To return to the example of crossing the street, a person who sees a car headed straight for him at high speed automatically experiences a sudden increase in sympa-

FIGURE 5.5

The autonomic nervous system. The fibers of the autonomic nervous system connect the central nervous system to the smooth muscles, glands, and internal organs. The ANS has two branches, sympathetic and parasympathetic. The sympathetic division's fibers emerge from the middle of the spinal cord, in the thoracic and lumbar regions, and pass through a chain of nerve fibers and cell bodies known as the sympathetic ganglia. They govern mobilization for activity. The parasympathetic division's fibers emerge from the medulla region of the brainstem and from the bottom of the spinal cord. They govern metabolic slowdown and energy replenishment. The two divisions work in opposition, but together they innervate most of the internal organs and regulate those functions that tend to be automatic— pupil dilation, for example, and saliva flow.

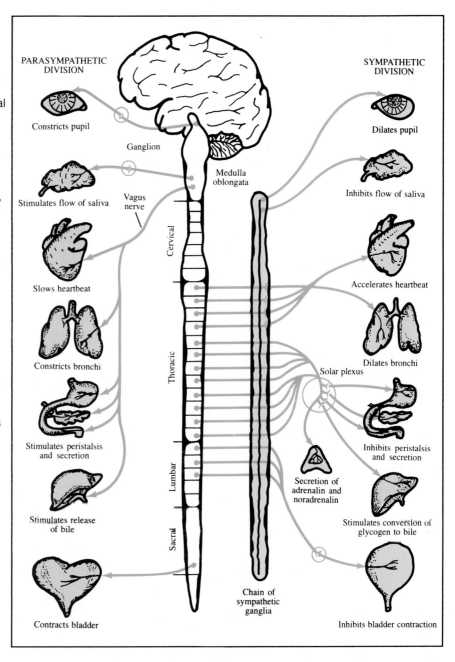

PARASYMPATHETIC DIVISION

Constricts pupil

Ganglion

Stimulates flow of saliva

Vagus nerve

Slows heartbeat

Constricts bronchi

Stimulates peristalsis and secretion

Stimulates release of bile

Contracts bladder

Medulla oblongata

Cervical

Thoracic

Lumbar

Sacral

Chain of sympathetic ganglia

SYMPATHETIC DIVISION

Dilates pupil

Inhibits flow of saliva

Accelerates heartbeat

Dilates bronchi

Solar plexus

Inhibits peristalsis and secretion

Secretion of adrenalin and noradrenalin

Stimulates conversion of glycogen to bile

Inhibits bladder contraction

thetic activity, which in turn produces a number of physiological changes. The heart beats faster and pumps out more blood with each beat. The blood vessels near the skin and those that lead to the gastrointestinal tract constrict, increasing blood pressure and slowing digestion. At the same time, the blood vessels serving the large muscles—the muscles that will be needed for action—dilate, so that they receive more blood. The pupils of the eyes also dilate, making vision more acute. Adrenaline is pumped into the blood, and this in turn releases blood sugar from the liver so that it can be used by the muscles. Breathing becomes faster and deeper so as to take in an increased oxygen supply. The effect of all these changes is to prepare the body for quick action. Of course, sympathetic arousal is not always so intense, but regardless of its intensity, the result is to adjust internal conditions so that the organism can make maximum use of whatever energy it has stored within it.

The **parasympathetic division,** which consists of nerve fibers emerging from the top and bottom of the spinal cord (Figure 5.5), is essentially opposite in function to the sympathetic division. While the latter gears up the body to use its energy, the parasympathetic division slows down metabolism and regulates the organs in such a way that they can do the work of rebuilding their energy supply. Thus, while sympathetic activity increases heart rate, parasympathetic activity decreases it; while sympathetic activity inhibits digestion, parasympathetic activity promotes it, and so on.

Because of its connection to arousal, the ANS is critically important in regard to stress-related disorders such as ulcer, headaches, hypertension, and insomnia. As we shall see, the theory now dominant in the study of these disorders is that something has gone wrong in the regulation of the cycle connecting the brain to the ANS to the organ in question as they operate together in response to environmental demands.

The Endocrine System

Closely integrated with the central nervous system is the **endocrine system,** which is responsible for the production of **hormones,** chemical messengers that are released into the bloodstream by the endocrine glands and that affect sexual functioning, physical growth and development, the availability of energy, and also emotional responses. The headquarters of the endocrine system is the hypothalamus, which, as we saw, lies at the center of the brain. Just below the hypothalamus is the pituitary gland, called the "master gland" because it regulates hormone secretion by the other glands of the body.

Hormones play an important part in certain highly specific disorders. For example, cretinism, a now-rare form of mental retardation, is due to failure on the part of the thyroid gland. In addition, researchers suspect that dysfunction in a number of different glands may be implicated in severe depressions.

EVALUATING THE NEUROSCIENCE PERSPECTIVE

The neuroscience perspective presents certain methodological problems. When we find that a biochemical abnormality is associated with a particular disorder, we cannot assume that the abnormality *caused* the disorder. It is quite possible that both the biochemical abnormality and the disorder are caused by some other, unknown factor. Yet people often leap at biological discoveries as if the cause *were* now revealed and the disorder shortly to be eliminated through simple medical means (the "wonder drug").

Furthermore, the neuroscience approach raises several ethical questions. If certain disorders do involve a hereditary factor (as schizophrenia, for example, seems to), can we prohibit people suffering from these disorders from having children, or should we caution them that in doing so they may be passing on the disorder? Should we attempt to "repair" their defective genes by genetic engineering, when and if technology makes that possible?

A second ethical concern is that recent neuroscience research may lead to a newly "medicalized" psychology—one in which most psychological problems are treated with psychoactive drugs. Although effective drugs have been one of the greatest contributions of research in neuroscience, they may also cause nondrug therapies to be nudged aside, perhaps inappropriately. Drugs can be very helpful, of course, but they can also be a too-quick solution to psychological disturbance. Behavioral abnormalities may be a signal that something is wrong in the patient's life. For example, a woman who is suffering from anxiety because of a soured marriage or a dreary job may calm down if given tranquilizers. But the "success" of this treatment poses the danger that the interpersonal problem, never having been addressed, will reassert itself once again in the future. In other words, symptom relief, which the neuroscience perspective is good at providing, may be mistaken for cure, to the detriment of other perspectives and consequently of sufferers of the symptoms.

It should be added, on the other side, that biological researchers tend to be careful scientists and very rarely make single-cause claims without abundant evidence. Nor can the fact that their discoveries may raise ethical problems be held against them. It is up to society to address these problems.

But the strongest argument for the neuroscience perspective is simply the new hope that it has held out. Schizophrenia and depression ruin lives. If neuroscientists should in fact discover that such disorders are rooted in neurotransmitter malfunction, and if such findings aided in the prevention and cure of these disorders, no one could argue with the result. Actually, it is doubtful that biochemical abnormalities will be found to be the sole cause of these major disorders.

As noted, researchers today favor the diathesis-stress model: an innate predisposition *plus* severe environmental stress. If the diathesis-stress model is borne out by further research, the different perspectives will work together on genetic, organic, developmental, and psychological causes.

Finally, in support of the neuroscience perspective, it bears repeating that psychological problems cannot realistically be considered apart from the body—and the brain is part of the body. Even the nature–nurture dichotomy is an oversimplification. Learning, or nurture, *modifies* the brain, changes it biologically (Kandel, 1983). Thus the question is not one of studying nature in addition to nurture. Biological researchers are studying the *products* of nurture and nature.

Summary

In the neuroscience perspective, a collection of specific theories about the organic basis of behavior, physical and mental functions cannot be separated. Genetic factors, the central and peripheral nervous systems, and the endocrine system are all biological functions that interact with each other and with environmental influences to determine behavior.

Behavior genetics is a subfield of psychology that attempts to determine the degree to which specific disorders are inherited. Although only a few disorders, such as Down's syndrome, have a clear-cut genetic cause, many disorders, including schizophrenia, result from the interaction of environmental stressors and an inherited diathesis, or predisposition, to the disorder. Through family, twin, and adoption studies, behavior geneticists try to assess heritability. An individual's observable characteristics, or phenotype, show the combined results of experience and underlying genotype. Family studies help to determine the degree of influence of the genotype by comparing percentages of genes shared by family members—for example, siblings share about 50 percent—with percentages of shared disorder, or concordance. Although family studies suggest that closer relatives of the index, or proband, case are more likely than more distant relatives to be predisposed to schizophrenia, these correlational studies do not prove heritability. Twin studies give stronger evidence that schizophrenia is inherited. Although monozygotic (MZ), or identical, twins and dizygotic (DZ), or fraternal, twins generally share the same environment, MZ twins, who share all their genes, are more than twice as likely (three to five times as likely) as DZ twins, who share half their genes, to share the disorder of schizophrenia. Adoption studies attempt to separate and weigh the relative influence of environment and genetic predisposition. It is thought that similarities between related individuals reared in different environments may be caused by genetic predisposition. Small samples of MZ twins reared apart along with larger mother–child samples offer the best evidence for the genetic transmission of schizophrenia.

The central nervous system (CNS), consisting of the brain and spinal cord, controls behavior by processing, transmitting, and storing information. Nerve cells, or neurons, which consist of the cell body, dendrites, axon, and axon terminals, receive and transmit electrical impulses along the neural pathway. The neuron receives the impulse through the dendrites, passes it down the axon to the terminals, then sends it across the synapse lying between the terminal and the dendrites of another nerve cell. Neurotransmitters are the critical chemical links between neurons and effect the transmission of impulses across the synapse. Among at least fifty neurotransmitters that are thought to operate along neural pathways, nine are implicated in various psychological disorders and four play a critical role in psychopathology: acetylcholine, dopamine, norepinephrine, and serotonin. Neurotransmitters begin as amino acids in the bloodstream and are converted at the axon terminals just before the impulse is fired across the synapse. Drugs used to correct a suspected malfunction of the body's neurotransmitters operate by increasing amino acid levels, facilitating conversion, or prolonging the action of neurotransmitters at the synapse.

The external surface of the cerebral cortex—the intricate gray matter covering the brain—is formed of fissures (sulci) and ridges (gyri). The longitudinal fissure divides the brain along the midline into two symmetrical hemispheres, each containing four lobes with differentiated functions. Regulatory structures include the hypothalamus, thalamus, cerebellum, and brainstem, a structure containing the pons, medulla, and reticular formation. Ventricles filled with cerebrospinal fluid occur throughout the brain. Psychological disorders have been traced to dysfunctions in many of these structures as well as to dysfunctions related to brain lateralization. Aphasias are organically based language disorders; some researchers suspect that schizophrenia, which is characterized by disordered speech, may be partly explained by left-hemisphere dysfunction. It is also suspected that right-hemisphere dysfunction may contribute to such emotional disturbances as anxiety and depression.

The peripheral nervous system consists of the somatic nervous system and the autonomic nervous system (ANS). The somatic division activates skeletal muscles and controls such purposeful behavior as crossing a street on the green signal. The ANS activates smooth muscles, glands, and internal organs and controls such automatic responses as heart rate, respiration, and the release of adrenaline (to name only a few). The ANS functions to adjust the body to changing environmental demands through its sympathetic and parasympathetic branches. Sympathetic arousal prepares us for quick action in emergencies— for example, increasing heart rate, respiration, and blood sugar (through the release of adrenaline). The parasympathetic division slows metabolism and helps to restore the system to equilibrium. The ANS is associated with such stress-related disorders as hypertension, ulcers, and insomnia.

The endocrine system influences emotional states, sexual functioning, physical development, and level of available energy by releasing hormones into the bloodstream from the hypothalamus, pituitary gland, and other endocrine glands. Glandular dysfunction may be partly responsible for severe depressive disorders.

The neuroscience perspective presents problems of both causality and ethics. Finding that a genetic predisposition or chemical imbalance accompanies a given disorder does not mean that the organic factor is the only or even the principal cause of the disorder. Ethical concerns include questions of prevention (in genetic counseling) and of intervention (in genetic engineering), as well as concerns that the neuroscience approach could lead to a "medicalized" psychology that treats only symptoms. The strongest argument in favor of the neuroscience perspective is the hope it holds for people with severe depression, schizophrenia, and other disabling disorders. Even for these disorders, however, researchers favor the diathesis-stress model, which studies the combined influences of environmental stress and biochemical factors.

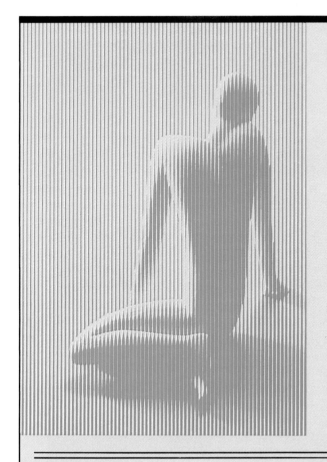

Research Methods in Abnormal Psychology

Though it is doubtful that Isaac Newton really stumbled on the law of gravitation by being hit on the head by a falling apple, the principle behind the story is sound. Scientific discovery often occurs in a very unmethodical way, through accidents, hunches, and intuition. The earliest antidepressant drug, for example, was developed by accident. Called iproniazid, it was first introduced as a treatment for tuberculosis. Actually it did little to repair the lungs of the patients on whom it was tested, but strange to say, it made them suddenly cheerful and optimistic. The drug was then tested, quite successfully, with depressives. Iproniazid has since been discarded (it was found to cause liver damage), but its discovery led to the development of other, safer treatments for depression.

Discovery, then, is a process of groping. It is creative and disorderly. The verification of a discovery, on the other hand, is as orderly as scientists can make it. This chapter describes the general principles of scientific research. First we will examine the characteristics of the scientific method. Then we will look at the research designs that scientists have found most useful in the study of abnormal behavior.

CHARACTERISTICS OF THE SCIENTIFIC METHOD

Skeptical Attitude

More than anything else, scientists are skeptical. Not only do they want to see it before they believe it; they want to see it again and again, under conditions of their own choosing. Scientists come to be skeptical because they recognize two important facts. First, they know that behavior is complex, that there are often many factors behind any psychological phenomenon. They also know that it is usually quite difficult to identify those factors. Explanations are often premature: not enough factors may have been considered. While it may seem that a child's asthma attacks always follow an emotional upset, for example, chances are good that cat hair, pollen levels, and the child's history of respiratory infection are also involved. Single-cause explanations are inherently appealing—the mind craves clarity—but in the study of behavior they are rarely accurate.

The second reason for skepticism is that science is a human endeavor. People make mistakes. The powers of human reasoning are not always to be trusted. Therefore, scientists are almost always skeptical of "new discoveries" and extraordinary claims—until they can be repeated under controlled conditions.

Objectives

The scientific method is intended to meet three objectives: description, prediction, and understanding. **Description** is the defining and classifying of events and their relationships. To be useful, a description must have **reliability**—that is, it must be able to stand the test of repeated measurements. It must also have **validity:** it must measure what it claims to be measuring. (These two concepts will be exam-

Research into the workings of the brain is increasing our understanding of the biological as well as the psychological causes of many abnormal conditions, such as schizophrenia. (Christopher Springmann/The Stock Market)

ined more closely in Chapter 7.) Assessment techniques have been developed to provide reliable and valid descriptions of a wide range of concepts, from typing skill to depression.

A description of events and their relationships often serves as a basis for **prediction.** If a description of schizophrenia (a disorder in which the person's thoughts and language are severely disturbed) notes that children of schizophrenic parents are ten times more likely to become schizophrenic than children of nonschizophrenic parents, it can reasonably be predicted that there is a causal relationship between the two factors.

However, successful prediction doesn't always depend on being able to pinpoint a cause. In the case of schizophrenia, for example, the fact that children of schizophrenic parents are at risk for schizophrenia does not tell us whether this relationship is due to genes, to nongenetic biological dysfunction, or to family dynamics. Nevertheless, it is still useful to know that these children are at risk, for such knowledge can help in the development of treatments and preventive measures.

Should we ever find out what measure of responsibility can be assigned to each of the factors thought to lead to schizophrenia, we will have achieved the third goal of the scientific method: **understanding,** the identification of the cause or causes of a phenomenon. Before causality can be demonstrated, three conditions must be met. First is the **covariation of events:** if one event is to be the cause of another, the two events must vary together—that is, when one changes, the other must also change. Second is a **time–order relationship:** the presumed cause must occur *before* the presumed effect. The final condition is the **elimination of plausible alternative causes:** the proposed causal relationship can be accepted only after other likely causes have been ruled out.

Covariation and time order are sometimes difficult to establish. But it is usually even harder to determine that changes in behavior are the result *solely* of changes in the proposed causal factor.

Internal and External Validity   In trying to eliminate plausible alternative explanations, a scientist is often faced with a problem called *confounding.* **Confounding** occurs when two or more causal factors are exerting an effect on the same thing at the same time, thus interfering with accurate measurement of

Any population reflects demographic differences—that is, members vary in age, sex, race, and so on. Random sampling is the best technique available for ensuring that the characteristics of the population as a whole are adequately reflected in the research sample. This representativeness, in turn, helps to ensure a study's external validity. (Mark Antman/The Image Works)

the causal role of either one. For example, suppose a group of investigators is trying to understand the mental confusion that characterizes schizophrenia. The investigators might compare the word associations of hospitalized schizophrenic patients with the word associations of people chosen from the general population. Chances are that they would find that when the patients spoke they produced chains of associations, with each association linked to the one immediately before it but not tied to an overall theme. In the statements of the nonpatient group, on the other hand, the investigators would probably find a central theme unifying the sets of associations, as in normal conversation. (See Chapter 14 for a further discussion of schizophrenic language.) The investigators in our hypothetical study presumably would want to link any differences in word associations between the two groups to the mental disorder for which the first group was hospitalized.

However, the patient population in this study would probably differ from the nonpatient population in many ways other than mental condition. For example, the patients would probably be receiving drug treatment. Their diet too might be substantially different from nonpatients'. Diet and drug differences between the two groups thus *confound* the patient–nonpatient difference. That is, any differences in word associations between the patients and the nonpatients could be caused by the mental disorder, the drugs, the diet,

some combination of these factors, or even some other difference between the groups. When factors are confounded, it is generally impossible to determine the one factor that is responsible for differences in performance. When *no* confounding takes place, a research study is said to have **internal validity.**

The internal validity of a study can be distinguished from its external validity. **External validity** involves the extent to which research results can be generalized. **Generalizability**—the ability of a finding to be applied to different populations, settings, and conditions—in turn depends on the **representativeness** of the sample from which the findings were gathered: the degree to which this sample's essential characteristics match those of the population under discussion. An internally valid study may show, for example, that schizophrenic patients at a certain hospital respond better to one drug than to another. But if the schizophrenic patients in that hospital are not representative of schizophrenic patients in general—if, let's say, they come primarily from the upper middle class—then the findings cannot be generalized.

The representativeness of a sample depends on how carefully the subjects, settings, and conditions of the study have been selected. The best way to achieve a representative sample is to use random sampling. A **random sample** is one in which every element of the population has an equal likelihood of being included. Given that the sample is large enough, random sampling ensures that the characteristics of the sample will generally match the characteristics of the population.

Experimental Procedures

The scientific method is put to use—or should be—every time researchers perform an experiment. In any well-conducted experiment, the key elements are the development of a hypothesis, the formulation of operational definitions, and the establishment of methods of control.

Development of a Hypothesis   Research often begins with the development of a testable hypothesis. A **hypothesis** is a tentative explanation for behavior; it attempts to answer the questions "How?" and "Why?" In discussing the scientific method, some writers leave the impression that hypotheses are issued from some centralized location where scientists come to pick them up. In fact, hypotheses are *discovered* through the efforts of individual investigators, and discovery, as we have pointed out, is a creative process—perhaps the one area of scientific endeavor in which skepticism is out of place. Neal Miller (1972) describes the state of mind required:

> During the discovery or exploratory phase, I am interested in finding a phenomenon, gaining some understanding of the most significant conditions that affect it, and manipulating those conditions to maximize the phenomenon and minimize the "noise" that obscures it. During this phase I am quite free-wheeling and intuitive—follow hunches, vary procedures, try out wild ideas, and take shortcuts. During it, I am usually not interested in elaborate controls; in fact, I have learned to my sorrow that one can waste a lot of time on designing and executing elaborate controls for something that is not there (p. 348).

But as we also noted in our introduction, the romance of discovery is followed by the rigors of testing. For a hypothesis to be scientifically useful, it must be possible to *disconfirm* it—that is, to show that it is *not* true. This aspect of a hypothesis is called *testability* (also *falsifiability*).

Operational Definitions   If hypotheses are to be testable, concepts must be clearly defined. In science, definitions that provide a set of specific criteria to identify a concept are called **operational definitions.** An operational definition of depression, for example, might include loss of interest in activities, loss of energy, poor appetite, and insomnia, among other things. Once the criteria for defining a "depressed" individual have been established, there can be no argument, among those who have accepted this definition, as to what "depression" means. Thus an important byproduct of operational definitions is that they facilitate communication: all researchers who accept a given operational definition know they're talking about the same thing.

Methods of Control   In setting up experiments to test their hypotheses, researchers often need to control events that might influence the behavior they are studying. An experiment usually involves the *manipulation* (deliberate changing) of one or more factors and the *measurement* of the effects of the manipulation on behavior.

INDEPENDENT AND DEPENDENT VARIABLES   The factors the researcher controls or manipulates are called the **independent variables.** The factors used to measure the effect (if any) of the independent variables are called **dependent variables.** If the hypothesis is to receive a fair trial, the experiment must be internally valid: that is, the only possible cause for any obtained outcome must be the independent variable. The internal validity of a study is ensured if **control techniques** are used properly. The three methods of control are manipulating, holding conditions constant, and balancing. These three methods can be illustrated by a hypothetical experiment. Let us say that we are going to examine the effect of alcohol consumption on tension.

In the simplest of experiments, the independent variable is *manipulated* at two levels. These two levels usually represent the presence and absence of some treatment. The condition in which the treatment is *present* is commonly called the *experimental* condition; the condition in which the treatment is *absent* is called the *control* condition. In the experimental condition in our hypothetical research project, subjects are given 0.5 grams of alcohol per kilogram of body weight. The alcohol is administered as a mixture of vodka and tonic water. In the control condition, subjects are given the tonic water plain—no vodka. The alcohol is thus the independent variable; its presence or absence is manipulated by the researcher. The dependent variable is the subject's heart rate, which is the operational definition of tension in this study.

Other factors in the experiment that could influence the subjects' performance are controlled by *being held constant.* For instance, the instructions given for performing the tasks in the experiment, the tone of voice used by the experimenter in giving these instructions, the setting and the length of time in which the subjects are allowed to consume the drink, and other factors that can be held constant are identical in the two conditions. When factors that could be independent variables are held constant, no confounding is possible. Therefore, the researcher can be reasonably sure that the experiment has only one independent variable.

At least one set of factors cannot be held constant in this or any other experiment—namely, the characteristics of the subjects tested. Researchers control factors that are not manipulated and that cannot be held constant by *balancing* the influence of these factors among all the conditions. The most important balancing technique, **random assignment,** involves assigning subjects randomly to the different groups in the experiment. For example, if our hypothetical researchers assigned all the male subjects to the vodka group and all the female subjects to the no-vodka group, sex differences would confound the experiment. If, however, the subjects were assigned randomly—by drawing lots, for example—then the researchers could assume that the two groups were equivalent on all measures other than the independent variable. (Note the difference between random assignment and random sampling, described earlier. In random sampling, subjects are chosen at random from a population, the goal being representativeness. In random assignment, already-chosen subjects are sorted at random into different experimental groups, the goal being balance among the groups.)

In a properly conducted experiment, then, all variables other than the independent variable are either held constant or balanced. If it were not for the manipulation of the independent variable (the consumption of an alcoholic or nonalcoholic drink), the groups would be expected to perform similarly. Therefore, if the groups perform *differently,* the researchers can assume that the independent variable is responsible for the difference.

MINIMIZING THE EFFECTS OF EXPECTATIONS   A further problem in conducting experiments is that both the experimenter and the subjects may *expect* a certain outcome, and may act accordingly. For example, if subjects know that they are drinking alcohol, they are likely to expect certain effects: that they will feel relaxed, giddy, and so on. If subjects respond according to these expectations, called **demand characteristics,** it will be difficult to determine the effect of the alcohol. Similarly, the experimenter may have expectations that shape his or her behavior: subjects who have received alcohol may be treated differently from those who have not. For example, the experimenter may read the instructions more slowly to the "drinkers." The experimenter's observations of behavioral results may also be biased by the knowledge of the experimental conditions. For instance, the experimenter, in observing the "drinking" group, may be more likely to notice any unusual motor movements or slurred speech. The term used to describe these biases is **experimenter effects.**

Researchers have developed procedures to control for both demand characteristics and experimenter effects. One is the use of **placebo control groups.** A *placebo* (from the Latin word meaning "I shall please") is a substance that looks like a drug or other active substance but that is actually an inert, or inactive, substance. In our alcohol example, a placebo control group would receive a drink that would look, smell, and taste like the alcoholic drink, but would contain no alcohol. Thus if "alcoholic" effects could be noted in these subjects' behavior after they had had their drinks, the experimenters would know that the subjects' expectations played an important role in their behavior.

Placebo control groups are traditionally used for evaluating drug treatments, but they have also been used to assess various forms of psychotherapy. While other groups will undergo specific therapies, the placebo control group will receive a "theoretically inert" treatment (O'Leary and Borkovec, 1978). That is, they will be taken through some procedure that, while sufficiently complicated to seem like a treatment, is nevertheless unrelated to any recognized form of therapeutic intervention. If, as has happened, this group shows improvement comparable to that of subjects receiving recognized treatments, experimenters will at least be alerted to the fact that therapeutic outcome is being affected by nonspecific (non-theory-related) factors, such as expectations.

Another way to minimize the influence of subjects' and experimenters' expectations is to use a **double-blind** procedure. In this technique, both the subject and the observer are kept unaware (blind) of what treatment is being administered. In our alcohol study, we could achieve double-blind control by having two researchers: one to prepare the drinks and to code

In a double-blind study, the experimental substance and the placebo control are administered from coded bottles so that neither the experimenters nor their subjects know until afterward which subjects received which substance. This procedure helps to prevent the expectations of both the experimenters and the subjects from affecting the research results. (Sarah Putnam/The Picture Cube)

each drink in some way, and a second researcher to pass them out, recording that subject 1 got a glass marked *x,* subject 2 got a glass marked *y,* and so on. As long as the first researcher did not know who got what drink and the second researcher did not understand the coding system, neither of them would know, when they got to the stage of observing the subjects' behavior, who was a "drinker" and who was not. The drinkers would be identified only later, when the code was compared with the record of who got what.

STATISTICAL INFERENCE   There is one very important distinction between the control provided by holding conditions constant and that provided by balancing. When we hold some factor constant, we eliminate all variation due to that factor. Balancing through random assignment does not eliminate the differences among subjects; it simply attempts to distribute these differences equally among the groups participating in the experiment. But even with balancing, differences will remain among subjects within each group. This measure of uncontrollable variation due to individual differences is called **error variation.** Because of error variation, the researcher cannot say with complete certainty that differences between experimental groups are due to the independent variable, or to the independent variable alone.

To help solve this problem, researchers may use **statistical inference.** Statistical inference is induc-

tive and indirect. It is inductive because we draw *general* conclusions about populations on the basis of *specific* samples we test in our experiments. It is indirect because it begins by assuming the **null hypothesis**—which, as the name implies, is the assumption that the independent variable *has had no effect.* Then we use probability theory to determine the likelihood of obtaining the results of our experiment if the null hypothesis were true (that is, the likelihood of obtaining these results if the independent variable had had no effect). If this likelihood is small (conventionally, less than 5 times out of 100, or 0.05), we judge the result to be "statistically significant," reject the null hypothesis, and conclude that the independent variable did have an effect.

Perhaps you can appreciate the process of statistical inference by considering the following dilemma. A friend says he will toss a coin to see who pays for the meal you just had at a restaurant. Your friend just happens to have a coin ready to toss. Now, it would be convenient if you could *directly* test to see if your friend's coin were biased. The best you can do, however, is to test your friend's coin *indirectly* by assuming that it is not biased and seeing if you consistently get outcomes that differ from the expected 50–50 split of heads and tails. If the coin does not follow the ordinary 50–50 split, you might surmise that your friend is trying to get you to pay for the meal. Similarly, researchers would like to test any obtained result directly for significance, but the best they can do is to compare their outcome to the expected outcome under conditions involving chance variation alone.

Statistical inference, like any tool, can be and is misused. At times researchers seem to forget that the statistical significance of a finding does not guarantee the internal validity of an experiment. Although we may be tempted to accept an interpretation if it is based on a statistically significant finding, we must remember that our ability to draw appropriate conclusions depends most of all on the internal validity of the study. And internal validity, as we have seen, depends on whether the investigator has been able to exert sufficient control to eliminate alternative explanations.

One illustration of a statistically significant finding in a confounded experiment is the famous "executive monkey" study (Brady, 1958), which will be discussed in Chapter 9. In this study four pairs of monkeys were wired to receive electric shocks every twenty seconds. In each pair, however, one monkey, the so-called executive monkey, could turn off the coming shock if at any time in the intervening twenty seconds it pressed a lever near its hand. The second monkey in each pair, called the "yoked" monkey, had no such control. It simply received whatever shocks the executive received. The results of this study were not only statistically significant, they were dramatic. All four executive monkeys developed ulcers and died, while the yoked monkeys showed no signs of ulcer. The conclusion seemed clear: being in charge is stressful and can be hazardous to health.

After several attempts to replicate this finding had failed, however, researchers began to look more closely at the procedures followed in the original experiment. Rather than being randomly assigned, the four executive monkeys had been selected because, on a preliminary test, they had shown higher rates of responding than their yoked partners. Subsequent research has shown that higher response rates are associated with an increased likelihood of developing ulcers (Weiss, 1977). In fact, the more recent research findings suggest that being in charge *decreases* the likelihood of developing ulcers. The original research clearly contributed to our understanding of an important problem, but it also showed that we must pay close attention to the procedures that are used in producing a statistically significant outcome.

Another problem with statistical inference is that it is always possible to produce statistically significant findings merely by reducing error variation. Error variation can be automatically reduced by controlling procedures in such a way that a large number of factors are held constant. In "sensitive" experiments of this kind, very small average differences may be statistically significant. At the same time, the external validity of such findings may be so small as to render them useless in practical terms. A therapist reading about a new treatment wants to know not just whether the effect on his or her patients will be statistically significant, but whether it will be *substantial.* Thus information about the strength of a treatment (the likelihood of its effectiveness) is more important for the clinician than is the treatment's statistical significance (Yeaton and Sechrest, 1981). This does not mean that tests of statistical significance are a waste of time. In some cases, they are a crucial protection against mistaking chance conjunctions for important relationships. But statistical significance is a minimum standard, beyond which the finding's *clinical significance*—can it be used? will it work?—remains to be shown.

RESEARCH DESIGNS

Research designs are the tools experimenters use to test hypotheses. Each design has its advantages and disadvantages. Asking a researcher whether one design is better than another is like asking a carpenter whether a screwdriver is better than a hammer. Which tool is best depends on the job to be done.

Correlational Research Designs

In abnormal psychology, both ethical and practical considerations influence our choice of research method. For example, if we were interested in whether a traumatic event such as major surgery can cause depression, we could not ethically perform surgery on a randomly selected group of introductory psychology students and compare them with another, unmolested group of students to see which group was more likely to get depressed. Similarly, if we were interested in the relationship between divorce and emotional disorders, we could not randomly assign some people to get divorced.

A common approach to this research dilemma is to examine groups that have been "treated naturally." That is, people who have had surgery can be compared with those who have not had surgery; people who have chosen to get a divorce can be compared with those who have chosen to stay married. Because subjects in these studies are selected from existing,

The Correlation Coefficient: A Measure of Predictive Strength

The correlation coefficient (r) is a measure of how well we can predict one variable if we know the value of another variable. For example, we might want to know how accurately we could predict students' success in college on the basis of their SAT scores. The correlation coefficient has two characteristics, a direction and a magnitude.

The *direction* can be either positive or negative. A positive correlation indicates that as the value of one variable (X) increases, the value of the other variable (Y) also increases (see diagram A). The correlation between SAT scores and success in college should be a positive one. In a negative correlation, as the value of X increases, the value of Y decreases (see diagram B). The higher a person's social class, the *less* likely that person is to be admitted to a mental hospital; social class and admission to mental hospitals are negatively correlated. Diagram C shows what happens when two variables are neither positively nor negatively correlated: as the value of X increases, the value of Y changes unpredictably. Because we have no ability to predict Y on the basis of X, the correlation coefficient in this situation is zero. The relationship between intelligence and mental illness represents a zero correlation; we could not predict the likelihood that a person would become mentally ill by knowing the person's IQ.

The *magnitude* of the correlation coefficient can range from 0 to 1.00. A value of $+1.00$ indicates a perfect positive correlation and a value of -1.00 indicates a perfect negative correlation. Values between 0 and 1.00 indicate predictive relationships of intermediate strength. Remember, the sign of the correlation signifies only its direction; an r value of -0.46 indicates a stronger relationship than an r of $+0.20$.

One final word of caution: the correlation coefficient represents only the *linear* relationship between two variables. The linear correlation of X and Y in diagram D is zero, but the two variables are obviously related. A curvilinear relationship like that shown in diagram D exists between level of arousal and performance. Performance first increases with increasing arousal but then declines when arousal exceeds an optimal level.

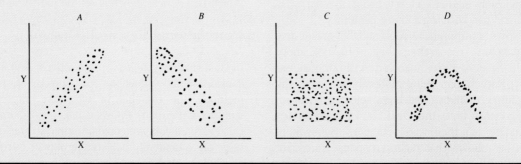

natural groups, the designs are called **natural group designs.** The purpose of such studies is to see whether these natural treatments result in other differences between the groups. For example, studies have shown that people who are separated or divorced are much more likely to receive psychiatric care than are those who are married or widowed, or who have remained single (Bloom et al., 1978). Such studies involve looking for correlations between subjects' characteristics and their performance; such designs are therefore called **correlational research designs.**

Correlational research designs are highly effective in meeting the first two objectives of the scientific method, description and prediction. Unfortunately, serious problems arise when the results of correlational studies are used as a basis of causal inference. People have a tendency to assume that all three conditions for a causal inference (covariation of events, a time–order relationship, and elimination of plausible alternative causes) have been met when really only the first condition, covariation, has been met. The most common measure of covariation used by psychologists is the correlation coefficient (see the box on p. 122). For instance, the finding that divorced people are more likely than married people to receive psychiatric care shows that these two factors are correlated. This finding could be taken to mean that divorce causes emotional disorders that lead to psychiatric care. Before reaching this conclusion, however, we must be sure that the time–order condition has been met—namely, that divorce *preceded* the emotional disorder. Perhaps those who suffer from emotional disorders are more likely to get divorced, because of the strain placed on the relationship by the disorder. In other words, a demonstration of covariation offers no indication of the *direction* of a causal relationship.

Nor does covariation eliminate plausible alternative causes. The fact that two factors covary does not mean that one is the cause of the other. Perhaps they are both dependent on another factor altogether—a situation called the **third-variable problem.** In our example, perhaps the situation is not that divorce causes emotional disorder or vice versa but rather that in our sample both are caused by the stresses of poverty. The directionality and third-variable problems make it a treacherous enterprise to infer causation from correlations.

One possible solution to the third-variable problem is to match the subjects on other potentially relevant factors. The divorced and nondivorced subjects could be matched, for example, on income level. The idea, of course, is to end up with two groups that differ only on the dimension of interest, divorce. In a sense, matching is an application of the control technique of holding conditions constant. One problem with this approach is that matching may lead to such a restriction of the people included in the study that the groups may no longer be representative of the general population. If you were to compare the emotional disorders of college students with those of elderly people who had been matched for general health and amount of education, you would probably be studying a very unrepresentative group of elderly people. A more serious problem with matching, however, is that the number of potentially relevant factors is usually so large that it's impossible to select two or more groups that are equal in all characteristics except the one of interest. In the divorce study, one might want to control many factors besides income—for example, educational level, religion, ethnic origin, number of

children. Nonetheless, matching can be useful. If a relationship between divorce and the need for psychiatric care persisted after divorced and married groups were matched on income level, then the researcher could reasonably conclude that income level alone was not responsible for the difference.

Sometimes the best way to eliminate a potentially confounding factor is to go ahead and test it. For instance, a correlational study of biochemical differences between patients and nonpatients might show that the patient group had more of one particular enzyme in their bodies. This finding could be used to support a biochemical explanation of their disorder. On the other hand, the enzyme difference could be the result not of biochemical malfunction but of diet or drug differences between the two groups. To eliminate this question, the researcher could have patients and nonpatients follow a special diet (for example, a high- or a low-protein diet) so that the influence of diet on the enzyme difference between the two groups could be evaluated. If differences in diet had contributed to the *original* enzyme difference, then the enzyme difference between patients and nonpatients should vary with changes in diet. If it does not, then the researchers can probably assume that diet is not confounding their findings.

Longitudinal or Developmental Studies

One type of correlational research design is sufficiently distinct to warrant separate discussion. In these studies (called **longitudinal** or **developmental studies**), the behaviors of the same subjects are studied on several different occasions over what is usually an extended period of time. Because the same people are tested several times, it is possible to specify more precisely the time–order relationship between factors that covary. In addition, researchers can use longitudinal studies to deal with the third-variable problem and thereby eliminate some alternative possible causes for observed differences. For example, economic stress may vary over the years, and if this factor is responsible for the relationship between divorce and mental disorder, then divorce and mental disorder should vary with changes in economic stress.

Mednick and his associates (Mednick, 1970; John et al., 1982) have provided one of the best illustrations of the use of the longitudinal design in abnormal psychology. These investigators have been studying the development of children whose mothers were schizophrenic. Because the disorder seems to have some genetic component, these children are at high risk for schizophrenia. (The research is described in greater detail in Chapter 15.) Two of the findings of this longitudinal project are especially noteworthy. First, schizophrenic mothers whose children also became schizophrenic were more severely disturbed than were schizophrenic mothers whose children did not become schizophrenic. Second, the mothers of the high risk children who became schizophrenic were hospitalized—and thus separated from their families—while their children were young.

Although longitudinal designs are more powerful than conventional correlational designs, they too present problems when it comes to inferring causation. To say that the child's schizophrenia is related to the severity of the mother's schizophrenia and to the timing of her hospitalization is not necessarily to say that separation from the mother or the degree of her psychopathology *caused* the disorder in the child. Once again, the problem rests with the *direction* of the causal relationship. Perhaps the children who were later diagnosed as schizophrenic were already, in their early years, sufficiently affected to cause increased emotional distress in their mothers, which in turn could have caused these mothers to be more severely disturbed and to be hospitalized sooner. Longitudinal studies, then, do not eliminate the question of causality, but they do enable researchers to gain a more complete picture of the time course of the development they are investigating.

Epidemiology and Population Surveys

Epidemiology is the study of the incidence and prevalence of disease in a population. **Incidence** is the number of new cases of a disorder reported during a specific time period—a year, for example. **Prevalence** is the frequency of a disorder in a particular population. Epidemiological studies often involve a survey of the population of interest. For example, Costello (1982) interviewed a random sample of nearly five hundred Canadian women to obtain information on the prevalence of fears and phobias in women. Such studies tell us, to begin with, how common a disorder is. They may also point researchers to significant relationships between this disorder and other variables, such as age, sex, or the prevalence of *another* disorder. These findings in turn help us to identify groups at risk and to describe the course of the disorder.

Population surveys, like other research designs, are prone to certain pitfalls. The most serious concern is that descriptions of a population based on a sample are critically dependent on the representativeness of the sample. As we noted earlier, *representativeness* refers to the extent to which the sample matches the essential characteristics of the population. Random sampling is the best technique currently available to ensure representativeness. Random sampling produces representativeness, however, only when all the selected respondents take part in the survey. For instance, 16 percent of the women selected by Costello (1982) refused to participate in the study. We have no way of knowing whether these women would be more likely or less likely to have fears and phobias than were the women who agreed to participate. Perhaps the nonparticipants were generally more fearful and thus were unwilling to talk to a stranger. Or perhaps they were generally *less* fearful and thus able to be assertive in refusing to be questioned. Although there is no hard-and-fast rule as to an acceptable response rate, the representativeness of a survey is threatened whenever the response rate is less than 100 percent.

A second problem facing survey researchers is that respondents often feel pressure to respond in socially desirable ways. When talking to an interviewer, we may not want to admit, for example, that we are afraid of dogs. This pressure for **social desirability** may threaten the validity of the survey data. Finally, survey responses, like other retrospective data, are subject to the selectiveness of human memory. A depressed person who is filling out a survey may be more likely to remember negative events from the past. In contrast, a happy person may be inclined to present an overly rosy view of his or her history. While clearly not without problems, epidemiological surveys represent an effective means of gathering information about large populations by studying relatively small numbers of individuals.

The Case Study

Psychology, as a *nomothetic* (law-establishing) discipline, seeks to develop broad generalizations, universal "laws" that apply to wide populations. In consequence, psychological research frequently involves the study of a large group of subjects and emphasizes the "average" performance of the group. Such studies, however, cannot capture the actual "feel" of human life: vivid, concrete, and personal. This short-

The case study, like any other method of idiographic research, is based on extensive, one-to-one interviews. (Nancy Bates/ The Picture Cube)

coming has led some psychologists, notably Gordon Allport (1961), to argue that research based on groups must be supplemented by **idiographic research,** research built on the individual. A major form of idiographic research is the case study method, a **case study** being an intensive description and analysis of a single individual.

In its classic form, the case study describes the psychological treatment of the person in question. Such studies have been instrumental in encouraging clinical innovation. The vividness of the case study is itself inviting—clinicians can imagine themselves implementing the same procedure—and the amount of detail included in the typical case study instructs clinicians as to how, exactly, the treatment is applied. Freud's famous case studies—Little Hans (1909), Anna O. (1895), the Rat-Man (1909)—did as much as his general writings to gain followers for his new method. Likewise D. W. Winnicott's case studies (1958) of short-term psychotherapy with children encouraged clinicians to experiment with these techniques. The same has been true of behavioral treatment. One of the crucial factors in the spread of behavioral therapy in the past twenty years was the publication, in 1965, of Leonard Ullmann and Leonard Krasner's *Case Studies in Behavior Modification,* a collection of accounts of single-case applications of what were then relatively new behavioral treatments.

The case study is also an effective means of describing rare phenomena. Certain kinds of psychopathology

occur so infrequently that assembling a group to study becomes impossible—hence the case study. Multiple personality, a condition in which the person alternates between two or more separate personalities, is a rarity of this sort; and we have learned much from famous case studies such as *Sybil* (Schreiber, 1974) and *The Three Faces of Eve* (Thigpen and Cleckley, 1957).

Case studies also can advance scientific thinking by providing a "counterinstance": a case that violates a widely accepted principle (Kazdin, 1980). Twenty years ago, for example, it was generally agreed that the human brain acted as a single unit—an assumption that was then challenged by the results of an operation on a patient suffering from uncontrollable epilepsy (Bogen et al., 1965). In an attempt to alleviate the violent seizures accompanying this disorder, surgeons severed the corpus callosum, the major brain pathway between the two hemispheres, thus disrupting the unity of the patient's normal consciousness. The outcome of this "split brain" was, in the words of one researcher, a "patient with two minds" (Gazzaniga, 1972, p. 311). Although the patient behaved normally, careful testing revealed that it was literally possible for the right brain to know something that the left brain did not, and vice versa.

While case studies sometimes disconfirm assumptions, in other instances they offer tentative support for a theory under debate. Particularly convincing are case studies that provide an "extreme test" of a theory. Consider, for example, the theory that human

Genie: A Tragic Test Case of the Effects of Deprivation

The case study of Genie, a "modern-day wild child," offers both testimony to the survivability of the human spirit and insight into the consequences to a child of untreated parental psychopathology. Genie's birth had been unwanted by her father, who had a history of child abuse and of violence toward his wife. He had placed an earlier child in the garage when he became exasperated and irritated by the child's crying. The child died of pneumonia and exposure at age 2½ months. When Genie was 14 months old her mother took her to see a pediatrician because of a fever. The physician thought she showed signs of retardation but could not assess her development adequately because of the fever. However, the doctor's statement appeared to give the father justification for his subsequent behavior. The mother, who was becoming blind and who feared the father would kill her (the mother), became a bystander to the cruel treatment of Genie that followed. Excerpts from Genie's case study reveal the extreme cruelty of the father's actions and the degree of her social isolation.

> In the house Genie was confined to a small bedroom, harnessed to an infant's potty seat. Genie's father sewed the harness, himself; unclad except for the harness, Genie was left to sit on that

chair. Unable to move anything except her fingers and hands, feet and toes, Genie was left to sit, tied-up, hour after hour, often into the night, day after day, month after month, year after year. At night, when Genie was not forgotten, she was removed from her harness only to be placed into another restraining garment—a sleeping bag which her father had fashioned to hold Genie's arms stationary (allegedly to prevent her from taking it off). In effect, it was a straitjacket. Therein constrained, Genie was put into an infant's crib with wire mesh sides and a wire mesh cover overhead. Caged by night, harnessed by day, Genie was left to somehow endure the hours and years of her life.

Hungry and forgotten, Genie would sometimes attempt to attract attention by making noise. Angered, her father would often beat her for doing so. In fact, there was a large piece of wood left in the corner of Genie's room which her father used solely to beat her whenever she made any sound. Genie learned to keep silent and to suppress all vocalization; but sometimes, desperate for attention or food, Genie would use her body or some object to make noise. Her father would not tolerate this either, and he often beat her with his wooden stick on these occasions as well. During these times,

language develops through exposure to normal speech during a "critical period" of childhood, extending from about age two to the onset of puberty (Lenneberg, 1967). In this view, natural language acquisition cannot take place after puberty. Of course, most humans acquire language long before puberty, and no researcher would try to test this theory by isolating a person until the age of fourteen or fifteen. However, a "natural" test of this theory was provided by the discovery of a child called Genie, who had been subjected to extreme isolation from birth to age thirteen (Curtiss, 1977). Genie's history and its relevance to the critical-period hypothesis are summarized in the box above.

The limitations of the case study method are quite obvious. Because numerous variables are not con-

trolled, cause-and-effect conclusions can rarely be drawn; too many plausible alternative causes remain uneliminated. Likewise, it is impossible to generalize safely from one individual. Who can say that the progress of a dog phobia in patient X, or one's response to a given drug or talk therapy, is representative of phobics in general? Yet, case studies do have the unique advantage of vividness. In reading a case study—especially an account of a "textbook case," a person who sums up the characteristics of a disorder—one can actually form a mental picture of what that condition is like. In view of these strengths and weaknesses, case studies are generally regarded as most valuable when they are used to *complement* other, specifically nomothetic research (Kazdin, 1980). That is the way they will be used in this book.

and on all other occasions that her father dealt with Genie, he never spoke to her. Instead, he acted like a wild dog. He made barking sounds, he growled at her, he let his nails grow long and scratched her, he bared his teeth at her; and if he wished to merely threaten her with his presence, he stood outside the door and made his dog-like noises—to warn her that he was there and that if she persisted in whatever she was doing, he would come in and beat her. That terrible noise, the sound of her father standing outside her door growling or barking or both, was almost the only sound Genie heard during those years she was imprisoned in her room.

This was Genie's life—isolated, often forgotten, frequently abused (many details of horrible abuse are omitted here), physically restrained, starved for sensory stimulation. Thus minimally exposed to humanity, and most of that the most hideous of human behavior, Genie grew into a pitiful creature.

Genie's father was convinced that Genie would die. He was positive that she would not live past the age of twelve. He was so convinced of this that he promised his wife that if the child did live beyond twelve, the mother could seek help for Genie. But age twelve came and went; Genie survived, but the father reneged on his promise. The mother, too blind to even dial the phone and forbidden under threat of death to contact her own parents (who lived in the area), felt helpless to do anything.

Finally, when Genie was 13½-years-old, Genie's mother, after a violent argument with her husband in which she threatened to leave unless he called

her parents, succeeded in getting her husband to telephone her mother. Later that day Genie's mother took Genie and left her home and her husband.

They escaped to the grandmother's home, where she and Genie stayed for three more weeks. During the third week, Genie's mother was advised to apply for aid to the blind. Taking Genie with her, she inadvertently went to the family aids building, where an eligibility worker, upon seeing Genie, sensed that something was terribly wrong. The worker alerted her supervisor immediately, and the two of them questioned the mother. What they saw and heard caused them to call the police. The police took Genie into custody; charges were brought against the parents. On the day of the trial the father killed himself. He left a suicide note stating, "The world will never understand."

Genie was admitted into the hospital for extreme malnutrition. She had been discovered, at last (Curtiss, 1977, pp. 5–6).

Genie had never developed language, although she apparently could understand a few words spoken to her. Therefore, she faced the task of learning her first language at the age of thirteen. Not having been exposed to significant natural language during her development, Genie offered a test of the critical-period hypothesis of language development. After much time and work, Genie did show some progress in language development, but her speech never resembled "normal" language. Her case, therefore, was judged to support Lenneberg's critical-period hypothesis (Curtiss, 1977).

Analogue Experiments

In studying abnormal behavior, researchers sometimes try to reproduce under controlled conditions the essential features of naturally occurring psychopathology or its treatment. Such studies are called **analogue experiments,** in that the experimental situation is analogous to "real life" and thus can serve as a model of how psychopathogy develops and how it can be alleviated. For instance, Watson and Rayner's (1920) conditioning of eleven-month-old Little Albert (Chapter 3) was the first attempt to induce psychopathology in a human subject under laboratory conditions (Abramson and Seligman, 1977). By demonstrating that the pairing of the rat with a very loud noise resulted in Albert's fear of white rats, Watson and Ray-

ner provided evidence that naturally occurring phobias could be acquired through classical conditioning.

One major advantage of analogue research is that it permits the kinds of control necessary to identify causal relationships and therefore has high internal validity. A typical experimental procedure is to assign subjects randomly to groups and then to manipulate systematically a variable that is thought to cause a behavior disorder. Some recent laboratory studies of depression provide examples of this technique. Hiroto and Seligman (1975), for instance, presented one group of college students with solvable cognitive problems and another group with unsolvable problems before measuring all the students' performance on some unrelated tasks. Students who had been given the unsolvable problems did not do as well on the later

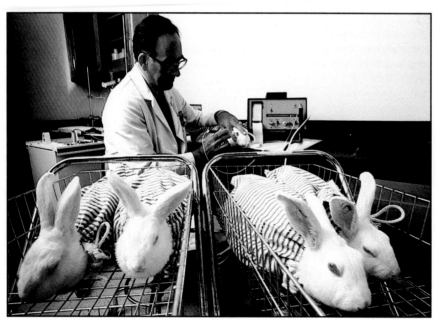

Some analogue experiments use animals where it would be impossible or unethical to use human subjects. The animals' responses can legitimately be regarded as analogous to the reactions of humans and often increase our knowledge without harming the experimental animals—as here, where rabbits are being used in a study of the effects of marijuana on the eyes. However, the use of animals, especially in unnecessary replications of previous research, is becoming increasingly controversial. (Hank Morgan/Photo Researchers)

tasks as did the students who had worked with the solvable problems. Similar performance deficits have been observed in people who are depressed, and these results have been viewed as supporting the theory that depression is a form of "learned helplessness" (Seligman, 1981). (See Chapter 10.)

Another advantage of analogue research is that in the "artificial" analogue setting the experimenter can test variables that could not be manipulated with genuinely distressed subjects. To cause ordinary college students to become briefly depressed, as was done in the experiment just described, is ethically permissible, but one cannot risk making depressed people more depressed.

An interesting form of analogue research is the therapy outcome experiment (Kazdin, 1986; Vanden-Bos, 1986), aimed at determining whether clients improve as a direct result of psychotherapy and, if so, which types of therapy benefit them most. In such an experiment, some clients will be assigned to a psychodynamic talk therapy, for example, others to systematic desensitization, and still others to a waiting-list control group; and after a period of time improvement in the three groups will be measured and compared (Sloane et al., 1975). Such research does not actually reproduce the conditions of real-life therapy, nor can it hope to do so. As the experimental clients are carefully screened, they are not necessarily representative of ordinary clinical clients. Furthermore, the knowledge that they are part of an experiment may lead them to behave differently from the usual client. Therapists, too, will be behaving differently. As their goal is to assess specific therapeutic methods, they will adhere to those methods more strictly than therapists usually do in clinical practice, where they often combine and modify techniques according to temperament and experience. Here as elsewhere, then, an analogue experiment is only an analogue, something *like* the real thing; it is not a reproduction of the real thing (Kazdin, 1978b).

A dilemma faced by human analogue research is that experimental manipulations that produce more than trivial effects are ethically prohibited, while trivial consequences are not usually convincing analogues to severe pathologies (Suomi, 1982). To state the problem more concretely, failure to complete a set of unsolvable laboratory problems may be trivial compared with real precursors of depression, such as the death of a close friend, but researchers cannot kill people's friends in order to produce a better analogue. This problem can be partially solved by development of animal models of psychopathology. For example, uncontrollable electric shock has been used with animal subjects as an analogue of the types of stressful experiences that are thought to cause ulcers and depression (Weiss, 1977, 1982). We saw this technique in the executive monkey experiment.

Animal models offer several advantages (Suomi, 1982). Not only can researchers more closely mimic the severity of naturally occurring events; they can also gain almost complete control over the subject's developmental history (for example, diet and living conditions) and even, through controlled breeding, its genetic endowment. Many important variables, therefore, can be held constant and thus eliminated as possible explanations for behavior change. Further, many behavioral and physiological procedures considered too intrusive to be used with human subjects (sampling brain neurotransmitters or cerebrospinal fluid, for example) can be performed on animals. And since laboratory animals develop more rapidly and have shorter life spans than do human subjects, the long-term consequences of pathology and effectiveness of treatment can be assessed relatively quickly. Animal models have been developed for drug addiction, minimal brain dysfunction, and various other forms of mild to severe psychopathology (Maser and Seligman, 1977).

Though analogue experiments cannot be exactly like the real thing, they can come close to it, and it is on the degree of likeness that they are evaluated: How close to reality did they come? This evaluation in turn depends on how much we currently know about the real thing in question (Suomi, 1982). We still do not know the causes of many psychological disorders, let alone the cures. (This is what the researchers are trying to find out.) Consequently, many models can be validated only partially—in terms of the symptoms they reproduce, for instance. Yet even though experimenters may, by manipulating certain variables, reproduce the symptoms of a naturally occurring disorder, they still have not proved that the naturally occurring disorder issues from those same variables (Abramson and Seligman, 1977). Research has shown, for instance, that laboratory-induced fears, such as that of Little Albert, do not always resemble naturally occurring phobias (Marks, 1977). Thus the essential features of phobia acquisition have not been completely captured by the laboratory models. When animal subjects are used, a nagging question is always present: Just how similar is the behavior of any other animal species to that of the human species? In addition, it is unlikely that all forms of human psychopathology can be induced in animals.

The internal validity provided by analogue experiments must be weighed against the cost to external validity. As a general rule, experimental procedures that increase internal validity tend to decrease or limit external validity (Kazdin and Rogers, 1978). Nevertheless, the search for causal relationships is best served by the tightly controlled investigations that tend to increase internal validity.

Single-Case Experimental Designs

Multiple-group experiments, particularly those in which subjects are randomly assigned to experimental conditions, are often considered the best means of establishing cause-and-effect relationships. Nevertheless, they have been criticized as having certain disadvantages for research in abnormal psychology (e.g., Hersen and Barlow, 1976). For example, ethical problems arise when researchers withhold a potentially beneficial treatment from subjects in order to provide a "control" group that satisfies the requirements of internal validity. Furthermore, it is sometimes difficult to assemble enough appropriate subjects for a group experiment. Finally, it has been pointed out that the average response of a group of subjects may not be representative of any one subject. Therefore, critics of multiple-group techniques have argued that single-case experimental designs are more appropriate for applied research.

The **single-case experiment** resembles its cousin the case study in focusing on behavior change in one person; however, it differs from the traditional case study in that it methodically varies the conditions surrounding the person's behavior and continuously monitors the behavior under those changing conditions. When properly carried out, the single-case experimental design has considerable internal validity.

The first stage of a single-case experiment is usually an observation, or *baseline,* stage. During this stage, a record is made of the subject's behavior before any intervention. A typical measure is frequency of behavior over some unit of time, such as an hour, a day, or a week. For example, a record might be made of the number of tantrums thrown by a child or the number of headaches reported by a migraine sufferer per week. The goal of the baseline record is to tell us what the behavior would be like if treatment were not provided.

Once behavior is shown to be relatively stable—that is, once there is little fluctuation between recording intervals—an intervention is introduced. The effect of the treatment is ordinarily evaluated by comparing baseline behavior with after-intervention behavior. In other words, how does the behavior change following the experimental treatment? Tests of statistical significance are only rarely used in this type of research. Single-case designs are most often carried out by practitioners of behavior modification (Chapter 3), and interventions are therefore usually based on learning principles.

While several different experimental designs are

available to the researcher (Kazdin, 1980), the most commonly used are the ABAB and multiple-baseline designs.

ABAB Design   The **ABAB design** seeks to measure the effectiveness of a treatment by demonstrating that the person's behavior changes systematically with alternating conditions of no treatment and treatment. In this design, an initial baseline stage (A) is followed by a treatment stage (B), a return to baseline (A), and another treatment stage (B). Because treatment is removed during the second A stage and any improvement in behavior is likely to be reversed, this design is also referred to as a *reversal design.* If behavior, after improving in the first treatment stage, reverts to baseline when the treatment is withdrawn and then improves again in the final treatment stage, it is fair to assume that the treatment was responsible for the behavior change. On the other hand, if only one baseline and one treatment stage were used (an AB design), any improvement in the B stage might reasonably be seen as a coincidence, reflecting perhaps a spontaneous change occurring at the same time the treatment was introduced.

Kelly and Drabman (1977) used an ABAB design when they tried to modify a socially undesirable behavior in a three-year-old retarded girl. For most of her life, the subject, Susan, had had a habit of repeatedly sticking out her tongue. The clinicians were concerned that, left untreated, this behavior would become even more persistent and would make it difficult for Susan to be accepted by other people.

Baseline observations were made of the frequency of Susan's tongue thrusts during daily ten-minute sessions. Then came the treatment: a mildly aversive stimulus, lemon juice, was squirted on Susan's tongue whenever she stuck it out. Treatments lasted ten minutes and continued for nine sessions. Treatment was then withdrawn for sixteen sessions. Finally, a second treatment stage was instituted, for another sixteen sessions. A follow-up was conducted six months after the end of the ABAB treatment. Figure 6.1 shows the changes in Susan's behavior through alternating baseline and treatment conditions. As the graph demonstrates, the lemon juice was successful in eliminating tongue thrusting, and the six-month follow-up revealed no recurrence.

The ABAB design may pose certain ethical problems when treatment is withdrawn. Although Susan's behavior would not be judged as life-threatening or particularly debilitating, there are certain behaviors—such as head-banging in severely disturbed children—for which it would not be appropriate to halt treatment once its effectiveness had been demonstrated. In such cases, other single-case experimental designs must be considered.

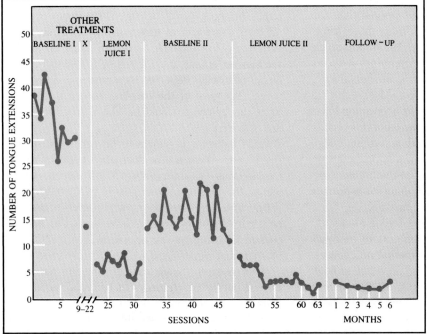

FIGURE 6.1
The ABAB procedure helped Susan, a retarded three-year-old, learn to stop sticking out her tongue. As the graph shows, squirting lemon juice on her tongue discouraged her habit. When the lemon juice treatment was temporarily halted (Baseline II), her tongue thrusting started up again. (During sessions 9 through 22, several treatment strategies were explored "without lasting success" before lemon juice was used [Kelly and Drabman, 1977]).

FIGURE 6.2
Dyer, Christian, and Luce (1982) used the multiple-baseline design to see whether encouraging autistic children to pay attention to instructions before performing a discrimination-learning task would help them do better on the task. The multiple-baseline design has an important advantage over the ABAB design: it does not require the experimenter to temporarily halt treatment that seems to be helpful.

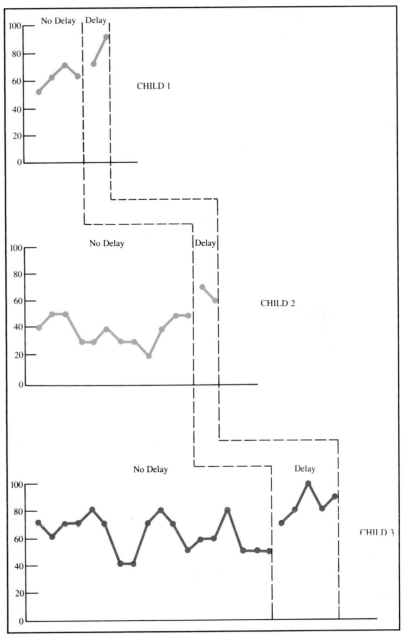

Multiple-Baseline Designs   An experimental design that does not depend on removing treatment or reversing a positive effect is the **multiple-baseline design.** In this procedure, the same treatment is aimed successively at several targets—usually several subjects, or several behaviors in one subject, or several situational variants for one behavior. When the design is used *across subjects,* for example, a baseline is first established for each subject; then the intervention is introduced first for one subject, then for the next, and so on. If the intervention is responsible

for changing behavior, then presumably an effect will be observed in each subject immediately following treatment. Like the ABAB design, the multiple-baseline design rules out alternative explanations for behavior change by demonstrating that behavior responds *systematically* to the introduction of the treatment.

Dyer, Christian, and Luce (1982) used a multiple-baseline design to see whether children suffering from autism (Chapter 18) could be taught to "look before they leaped" in performing discrimination-learning tasks. Teachers of autistic children have often observed that many such children seem to respond to a task before attending to its requirements. It was felt that this tendency could be remedied by use of a "response-delay" procedure, which requires the child to wait a predetermined amount of time before responding. The procedure was tried on three autistic children. In practical terms it generally meant holding the child's hands for several seconds after he or she was presented with a discrimination problem.

Multiple baselines for performance on the discrimination-learning tasks were established for the three children. Intervention was introduced first with one child, then with the second, and finally with the third. An examination of the behavioral records (Figure 6.2) shows that each child's discrimination learning immediately improved with the response-delay treatment.

Other variations on the multiple-baseline procedure include designs *across behaviors,* in which different behaviors are observed in the same person, and designs *across situations,* in which the same behavior is observed in different situations (Kazdin, 1980). In a multiple-baseline design across behaviors, for example, independent baselines are obtained for different behaviors. Intervention is directed first at one behavior, then at another, and so forth. A causal relationship between an intervention and behavior change is assumed if each behavior responds directly to treatment. In a multiple-baseline design across situations, baselines are established for a behavior in different situations (in the home and in the clinic, for example). The intervention is introduced first in one situation and then in another. As with the other forms of this design, the researcher looks to see if behavior changes systematically follow treatment.

Many researchers combine the multiple-baseline and reversal designs. This procedure was followed with the autistic children described above, and predictably, their gains were lost when the response-delay treatment was interrupted. Other design possibilities include the use of two or more forms of the multiple-baseline procedure in combination—for example, observation of behavior both across subjects and across situations. Many different strategies can be used to establish causal relationships in the context of a single-case experiment.

Limitations of the Single-Case Design   Like the traditional case study, the single-case experiment design is weak in external validity. As each person is unique, it can be argued that there is no way of knowing whether the effect of a particular treatment on one person can predict its effect on other people. This problem may not be as serious as it appears, for two reasons (Kazdin, 1978b). First, the kinds of learning-based treatments usually used in single-case studies are often ones that produce dramatic and sizable changes in behavior. If such treatments work for one person, chances are that they will have at least some effect on others. Second, the efficiency with which data can be collected from one subject often makes it easy to repeat the procedures with other subjects. Therefore while generalizability is in no way guaranteed by the single-case design, it can easily be tested. Moreover, external validity can be enhanced by use of a single *group* of subjects in a single-case experimental design, such as ABAB. Then it is possible to draw conclusions about the effect of the experimental variable not just on the individual subjects but on the population from which the sample was drawn.

Summary

The scientific method provides a basis for developing theories of abnormal behavior as well as a means to test those theories. It is also used to determine whether particular therapeutic approaches are effective in treating clients. The scientific method is characterized by the skeptical attitude of those who use it, by the objectives it is intended to meet (description, prediction, and understanding), and by the specific procedures used to meet those objectives (hypothesis testing, definition formulation, and methods of control). Careful description of phenomena often serves as the basis of prediction, which is an essential part of psychological assessment.

The most difficult objective of scientific research is understanding what causes a phenomenon. Understanding is achieved only when three conditions have been demonstrated: covariation of events, a time–order relationship, and the elimination of plausible alternative causes. People often think that causality has been established when only one condition has been met—for example, covariation of events. Research that fails to eliminate alternative explanations is said to be confounded. Only when no confounding is present is a study internally valid.

The external validity of research depends on our ability to generalize, or apply, the findings to different populations, settings, and conditions. External validity increases as the representativeness of a sample increases. The best way to achieve a representative sample is to use a random sampling procedure.

Research often begins with the development of a testable, or falsifiable, hypothesis. Generally, a hypothesis is tested in an experiment that uses three control techniques: manipulating the independent variable, holding all other variables constant, and balancing uncontrollable factors—the personal characteristics of the subjects being tested—among all conditions. Holding conditions constant rules out the effect of those conditions, but balancing through random assignment may still produce some error variation. Special problems of control also arise from expectations on the part of subjects (demand characteristics) and researchers (experimenter effects). Placebo control groups and double-blind procedures may help avoid these problems.

Research results are often evaluated through statistical inference. The null hypothesis is assumed and is rejected only if there is a statistically significant likelihood that the independent variable had an effect. In the context of therapy, however, clinical significance (the effectiveness of a treatment outside the laboratory) is more important than statistical significance.

Many different research designs are used to investigate abnormal behavior. Correlational or natural group designs examine whether systematic differences exist between groups of people who have been treated "naturally." A serious problem in evaluating the results of correlational studies is to determine the direction of the causal relationship and to eliminate possible third variables that may cause differences between groups. Longitudinal, or developmental, studies examine the behavior of an individual over time. Although this design does not solve the problem of causality, it is more powerful than a correlational design because assumptions of covariation and time–order relationships can be more easily tested. Epidemiological studies examine the incidence and prevalence of a behavioral disorder in a population. Such studies can help to determine whether the frequency of a particular disorder is related to other variables, including the demographic characteristics of the population and the prevalence of other disorders in that popula-

tion. Major concerns in population surveys are the representativeness of the sample and the fact that survey responses are affected by social desirability and selective memory.

The case study method is the intensive description and analysis of a single individual. Case studies offer an opportunity for clinical innovation and can provide either a counterinstance that disconfirms a general scientific principle or tentative support for a psychological theory. The usefulness of the case study is limited because investigators can usually not draw cause-and-effect conclusions from it or apply their findings to other individuals.

Analogue experiments attempt to reproduce under controlled conditions the essential features of naturally occurring psychopathology or its treatment. They allow the kind of control that is generally prohibited for ethical or practical reasons but that often enables researchers to establish causal relationships. Analogue experiments with animal subjects can closely approximate natural treatments, and they allow the use of intrusive behavioral and physiological measures; moreover, data can be obtained in a relatively brief period because of the short life span of many animals. The emphasis on internal validity in analogue or laboratory experiments, however, often leads to the criticism that they are low in external validity.

Single-case experimental designs monitor behavior change following an intervention that was introduced after a baseline (no-treatment) observation. Evidence for a causal relationship is obtained if the person's behavior changes systematically with the introduction of the treatment. The ABAB, or reversal, design seeks to confirm a treatment effect by showing that behavior changes systematically with alternating conditions of no treatment (A), treatment (B), a return to baseline (A), and another treatment (B). Because improvement in behavior may be reversed when treatment is withdrawn at the second A stage, ethical considerations frequently suggest a multiple-baseline procedure, in which a treatment is introduced at different intervals across subjects, behaviors, or situations. Two or more multiple-baseline procedures used in combination can establish causal relationships in the single-case design, and external validity can be improved by the use of a group rather than a single subject; conclusions can then be drawn from the group about the population it represents.

Diagnosis and Assessment

M ost of this book is devoted to the common categories of abnormal behavior. As categories, such disorders are relatively easy to discuss. We chart the symptoms, give illustrative case histories, weigh the possible causes, and review the suggested treatments. It is only in the vocabulary of psychology, however, that these abnormal behaviors exist as categories. In reality, they are the complex and ambiguous things that people do and say. And the first job of the mental health profession is to look at what the person says and does and to make some sense out of his or her behaviors. This process is called **psychological assessment,** which may be defined as the collection, organization, and interpreta-tion of information about a person and his or her situation.

Psychological assessment is not a recent invention. Throughout history people have been developing systems for sorting individuals into categories in order to predict how they will behave. The first assessment system was probably astrology, developed by the ancient Babylonians and later disseminated to Egypt, Greece, India, and China (McReynolds, 1975). Initially the stars were read only for clues about matters of public concern—wars, floods, crop failure. By the fifth century B.C., however, astrology was also being used as the basis of personal horoscopes, revelations of individual character and destiny.

Around the same time, ancient Greece produced another assessment procedure—physiognomy, the interpretation of character according to physique and bearing. Physiognomy may have been responsible for the first psychological test. It is reported that the Greek philosopher Pythagoras (sixth century B.C.) screened candidates for his religious cult not just by questioning them verbally but also by subjecting them to a physiognomic examination, in which the form and bearing of the candidates' bodies, along with their facial features and expressions, were "read" as indicators of their character.

Later centuries produced their own systems of assessment, from Hippocrates' four humors to Kraepelin's medical classification scheme (Chapter 1). An important thing to note about all these assessment systems is that each is based on an implicit theory of human behavior. To the astrologists, behavior was determined not by will, learning, or parentage, but by the positions of the stars at one's birth. To the physiognomists, behavior was the product of a consistent underlying personality—one that could be determined on the basis of physical features. Similarly, modern assessment procedures are outgrowths of psychological theories, which, like all theories, are revised from decade to decade. Thus with assessment—as with definitions, explanations, and treatments of abnormal behavior—we are looking at something that is relative and changing, the product of each generation's effort to make sense of human behavior.

In this chapter we will first discuss the issues surrounding assessment: what it aims to do, how well it succeeds, and what can cause it to fail. Then we will describe the most commonly used assessment techniques and, finally, their relation to the major psychological perspectives.

ASSESSMENT: THE ISSUES

Why do people undergo psychological assessment? In what cases, and why, does such assessment involve diagnostic labeling? How useful are diagnostic labels? How can we tell a good assessment technique from a bad one? What extraneous factors can influence assessment? These are not questions that can be answered simply. As we shall see, the entire enterprise of assessment—to say nothing of individual assessment methods—is surrounded by disagreement and controversy.

Why Assessment?

Different assessment techniques have been developed for different purposes. Basically, however, all psychological assessment has two goals. The first is **description**—to render an accurate portrait of personality, cognitive functioning, and behavior. This goal would be important even if there were no such thing as abnormal psychology. Science aims to describe, and psychology, the science of human personality and behavior, aims to describe personality and behavior, simply for the sake of increasing our understanding of reality. However, such descriptions may also be needed for practical purposes, and this is definitely the case in abnormal psychology. A clear picture of the person's problem must be obtained before any decision can be made about treatment.

This brings us to the second goal of psychological assessment: **prediction.** Again, prediction need serve no practical purpose. The mere desire to advance human knowledge could motivate a psychologist to try to predict, for example, whether children of divorced parents are likely to become divorced themselves or whether boys actually grow up to be more aggressive than girls. Such predictions are, in fact, scientific **hypotheses,** and assessment is our only method of testing them.

But predictions based on psychological assessment also have an important practical application: they aid decision making. People are given psychological tests to help them decide on a profession, to determine who will go to which college, to screen job applicants, and so forth. Within the clinical context—that is, the context of abnormal behavior—people are assessed to determine what kind of behavior they might be likely to display and what kind of treatment they require. Should this child be put in a special-education program? Should her parents be called in for family therapy? Would that patient benefit from drugs? Should he be hospitalized—even against his will? Needless to say, these are critical questions, as answers may determine the direction of the individual's entire future. Patients must also be reassessed to determine which treatments actually work. Was the drug helpful? Did family therapy relieve the problem? It is these questions that clinical assessment tries to answer.

Psychiatric Diagnosis

In nonclinical contexts, assessment may involve no labeling. One person is chosen for the job or admitted to the college, the others are not, and that is all. Clinical assessment, however, often includes **diagnosis,** in which the person's problem is classified within one of a set of recognized categories of abnormal behavior and labeled accordingly. By far the most common form of diagnosis is **psychiatric diagnosis,** in which the patient's problem is classified within the taxonomy of psychological disturbances developed by the psychiatric profession.

The Classification of Abnormal Behavior All sciences classify—that is, they order the objects of their study by identifying crucial similarities among them and sorting them into groups according to those similarities. Botanists, for example, classify plants according to species. Astronomers classify heavenly bodies according to color, size, and temperature. Physicians classify diseases according to the organ or system affected. And mental health professionals classify mental disorders according to patterns of behavior, thought, and emotion.

As we saw in Chapter 1, the classification of abnormal behavior appears to have begun with Hippocrates. But the first truly comprehensive classification system for severe mental disorders was developed by Kraepelin in the late nineteenth century. All later systems were influenced by Kraepelin's taxonomy. Eventually, in 1952, the American Psychiatric Association (APA) published its own version of the system, under the title *Diagnostic and Statistical Manual of Mental Disorders,* or *DSM.* Since that time, the *DSM* has undergone several revisions. A new and heavily revised third edition, known as *DSM-III,* was published in 1980, and *DSM-III* has in turn been fine-tuned in a more recent revision, *DSM-III-R,* published in 1987.[*] (The *DSM-III-R* listing of diagnostic categories may be seen in the box on pp. 138–139.)

---

[*] Another classification system that should be noted is the mental disorders section of the World Health Organization's *Ninth Revision of the International Classification of Diseases,* or *ICD-9.* Though it is less detailed than *DSM-III-R* and is used primarily for statistical purposes, *ICD-9* is important as the only international classification system for psychological disturbance.

Hospital personnel must often deal with people who are obviously disturbed or behaving strangely. If such a person is to be helped, the on-the-spot, informal evaluation must eventually be supplemented by a careful, formal assessment and diagnosis made by mental health professionals. (Robert Goldstein/Medichrome/The Stock Shop)

The Practice of Psychiatric Diagnosis It is the *DSM* that provides the foundation for psychiatric diagnosis. Each of the *DSM* categories is accompanied by a description of the disorder in question. To arrive at a diagnosis, the assessor compares the behavior of the patient with these descriptions. The patient is then labeled in accordance with the description that he or she "fits" best. The purpose is to provide a description of the patient's problem, along with a **prognosis**—that is, a prediction of its future course. It is hoped that accurate diagnosis will also lead to progress in identifying causes and designing appropriate treatments.

DSM-III-R Classification of Psychological Disorders

The following is an abbreviated list of the diagnostic categories appearing in *DSM-III-R:*

DISORDERS USUALLY FIRST EVIDENT IN INFANCY, CHILDHOOD, OR ADOLESCENCE

Developmental Disorders

Mental Retardation

Mild mental retardation
Moderate mental retardation
Severe mental retardation
Profound mental retardation
Unspecified mental retardation

Pervasive Developmental Disorders

Autistic disorder
Pervasive developmental disorder NOS*

Specific Developmental Disorders

Academic skills disorders
 Developmental arithmetic disorder
 Developmental expressive writing disorder
 Developmental reading disorder
Language and speech disorders
 Developmental articulation disorder
 Developmental expressive language disorder
 Developmental receptive language disorder
Motor skills disorder
 Developmental coordination disorder
 Specific developmental disorder NOS

Other Developmental Disorders

Developmental disorder NOS

Disruptive Behavior Disorders

Attention-deficit hyperactivity disorder
Conduct disorder
 group type
 solitary aggressive type
 undifferentiated type
Oppositional defiant disorder

Anxiety Disorders of Childhood or Adolescence

Separation anxiety disorder
Avoidant disorder of childhood or adolescence
Overanxious disorder

Eating Disorders

Anorexia nervosa
Bulimia nervosa
Pica
Rumination disorder of infancy
Eating disorder NOS

Gender Identity Disorders

Gender identity disorder of childhood
Transsexualism
Gender identity disorder of adolescence or adulthood, nontranssexual type
Gender identity disorder NOS

Tic Disorders

Tourette's disorder
Chronic motor or vocal tic disorder
Transient tic disorder
Tic disorder NOS

Elimination Disorders

Functional encopresis
Functional enuresis

Speech Disorders Not Elsewhere Classified

Cluttering
Stuttering

Other Disorders of Infancy, Childhood, or Adolescence

Elective mutism
Identity disorder
Reactive attachment disorder of infancy or early childhood
Stereotype/habit disorder
Undifferentiated attention-deficit disorder

ORGANIC MENTAL DISORDERS

Dementias Arising in the Senium and Presenium

Primary degenerative dementia of the Alzheimer type, senile onset
 with delirium
 with delusions
 with depression
 uncomplicated
Primary degenerative dementia of the Alzheimer type, presenile onset
Multi-infarct dementia
Senile dementia NOS
Presenile dementia NOS

Psychoactive Substance-Induced Organic Mental Disorders

Alcohol
 intoxication
 idiosyncratic intoxication
 Uncomplicated alcohol withdrawal
 withdrawal delirium
 hallucinosis
 amnestic disorder
 Dementia associated with alcoholism
Amphetamine or similarly acting sympathomimetic
 intoxication
 withdrawal
 delirium
 delusional disorder
Caffeine
 intoxication
Cannabis
 intoxication
 delusional disorder
Cocaine
 intoxication
 withdrawal
 delirium
 delusional disorder
Hallucinogen
 hallucinosis
 delusional disorder
 mood disorder
 Posthallucinogen perception disorder
Inhalant
 intoxication
Nicotine
 withdrawal
Opioid
 intoxication
 withdrawal
Phencyclidine (PCP) or similarly acting arylcyclohexylamine
 intoxication
 delirium
 delusional disorder
 mood disorder
 organic mental disorder NOS
Sedative, hypnotic, or anxiolytic
 intoxication
 Uncomplicated sedative, hypnotic, or anxiolytic withdrawal
 withdrawal delirium
 amnestic disorder
Other or unspecified psychoactive substance
 intoxication
 withdrawal
 delirium
 dementia
 amnestic disorder
 delusional disorder
 hallucinosis
 mood disorder
 anxiety disorder
 personality disorder
 organic mental disorder NOS

Organic Mental Disorders associated with Axis III physical disorders or conditions, or whose etiology is unknown

Delirium
Dementia
Amnestic disorder
Organic delusional disorder
Organic hallucinosis
Organic mood disorder
Organic anxiety disorder
Organic personality disorder
Organic mental disorder NOS

PSYCHOACTIVE SUBSTANCE USE DISORDERS

Alcohol
  dependence
  abuse
Amphetamine or similarly acting
    sympathomimetic
  dependence
  abuse
Cannabis
  dependence
  abuse
Cocaine
  dependence
  abuse
Hallucinogen
  dependence
  abuse
Inhalant
  dependence
  abuse
Nicotine
  dependence
Opioid
  dependence
  abuse
Phencyclidine (PCP) or similarly
    acting arylcyclohexylamine
  dependence
  abuse
Sedative, hypnotic, or anxiolytic
  dependence
  abuse
Polysubstance dependence
Psychoactive substance
    dependence NOS
Psychoactive substance abuse
    NOS

SCHIZOPHRENIA

Schizophrenia
  catatonic
  disorganizod
  paranoid
  undifforontiated
  residual

DELUSIONAL (PARANOID) DISORDER

Delusional (Paranoid) disorder

PSYCHOTIC DISORDERS NOT ELSEWHERE CLASSIFIED

Brief reactive psychosis
Schizophreniform disorder
Schizoaffective disorder
Induced psychotic disorder
Psychotic disorder NOS (Atypical
    psychosis)

MOOD DISORDERS

Bipolar Disorders

Bipolar disorder
  mixed
  manic
  depressed
Cyclothymia
Bipolar disorder NOS

Depressive Disorders

Major Depression
  single episode
  recurrent
Dysthymia (or Depressive neurosis)
Depressive disorder NOS

ANXIETY DISORDERS (or Anxiety and Phobic Neuroses)

Panic disorder
  with agoraphobia
  without agoraphobia
Agoraphobia without history of panic
    disorder
Social phobia
Simple phobia
Obsessive compulsive disorder (or
    Obsessive compulsive neurosis)
Post-traumatic stress disorder
Generalized anxiety disorder
Anxiety disorder NOS

SOMATOFORM DISORDERS

Body dysmorphic disorder
Conversion disorder (or Hysterical
    neurosis, conversion type)
Hypochondriasis (or
    Hypochondriacal neurosis)
Somatization disorder
Somatoform pain disorder
Undifferentiated somatoform
    disorder
Somatoform disorder NOS

DISSOCIATIVE DISORDERS (or Hysterical Neuroses, Dissociative Type)

Multiple personality disorder
Psychogenic fugue
Psychogenic amnesia
Depersonalization disorder (or
    Depersonalization neurosis)
Dissociative disorder NOS

SEXUAL DISORDERS

Paraphilias

Exhibitionism
Fetishism
Frotteurism
Pedophilia
Sexual masochism
Sexual sadism
Transvestic fetishism
Voyeurism
Paraphilia NOS

Sexual Dysfunctions

Sexual desire disorders
  Hypoactive sexual desire disorder
  Sexual aversion disorder
Sexual arousal disorders
  Female sexual arousal disorder
  Male erectile disorder
Orgasm disorders
  Inhibited female orgasm
  Inhibited male orgasm
  Premature ejaculation
Sexual pain disorders
  Dyspareunia
  Vaginismus
Sexual dysfunction NOS

Other Sexual Disorders

Sexual disorder NOS

ADJUSTMENT DISORDER

Adjustment disorder
  with anxious mood
  with depressed mood
  with disturbance of conduct
  with mixed disturbance of
    emotions and conduct
  with mixed emotional
    features
  with physical complaints
  with withdrawal
  with work (or academic)
    inhibition
Adjustment disorder NOS

PSYCHOLOGICAL FACTORS AFFECTING PHYSICAL CONDITION

Psychological factors affecting
    physical condition

PERSONALITY DISORDERS

Paranoid
Schizoid
Schizotypal
Antisocial
Borderline
Histrionic
Narcissistic
Avoidant
Dependent
Obsessive compulsive
Passive aggressive
Personality disorder NOS

V CODES FOR CONDITIONS NOT ATTRIBUTABLE TO A MENTAL DISORDER THAT ARE A FOCUS OF ATTENTION OR TREATMENT

Academic problem
Adult antisocial behavior
Borderline intellectual functioning
Childhood or adolescent antisocial
    behavior
Malingering
Marital problem
Noncompliance with medical
    treatment
Occupational problem
Parent-child problem
Other interpersonal problem
Other specified family circumstances
Phase of life problem or other life
    circumstance problem
Uncomplicated bereavement

---

* NOS = not otherwise specified.

Source: *Diagnostic and Statistical Manual of Mental Disorders*, Third Edition (Revised). Washington, D.C.: American Psychiatric Association, 1987. Reproduced with permission.

The medical basis of this procedure is obvious from the name alone. Psychiatric diagnosis is unquestionably tied to the medical model, the practice of treating abnormal behaviors as if they were symptoms of organic dysfunction. In view of this connection, one might expect psychiatric diagnosis to be used on a very limited basis, for as we saw in Chapter 1, many mental health professionals strongly object to the medical model. Yet in fact, psychiatric diagnosis is used constantly by mental health professionals of all persuasions, for reasons that are largely practical. Psychology, like any other discipline, needs a vocabulary, not only for the sake of research but simply for the sake of discussion. The *DSM* provides such a vocabulary, and when mental health professionals use it, they are using psychiatric diagnosis. Furthermore, psychology is tied in with many other institutions in our society, and all of these institutions require the use of diagnostic labels. To get funding for its special-education program, a school system has to say how many mentally retarded or autistic children it is handling. When hospitals and clinics apply for funds, they have to list the number of schizophrenics, alcoholics, and so on that they are treating. Insurance companies require a diagnosis before they will pay the bills. And so diagnosis is practiced, and its vocabulary—that of the *DSM*—has become our society's primary means of communicating about abnormal behavior.

Criticisms of Psychiatric Diagnosis   While it is widely practiced, psychiatric diagnosis is also widely criticized. Perhaps the major focus of criticism is the tie with the medical model. As we noted in Chapter 1, Szasz (1961) and many other writers have vigorously attacked the medical model, and they have attacked psychiatric diagnosis on the same grounds—namely, that its purpose is to give psychiatrists control over other people's lives. In addition to this argument, three other criticisms of psychiatric diagnosis merit consideration.

The first is that it falsifies reality by implying that most abnormal behavior is qualitatively different from normal behavior. If you look in *DSM-III-R* and see the category "dream anxiety disorder," you may think that this condition is different in kind from your own periods of bad dreams. In fact, it is probably different only in degree, or perhaps not different at all except that the person with "dream anxiety disorder" went

for treatment (and therefore received a diagnosis) whereas you did not. Likewise, most forms of psychopathology are simply the far end of a long continuum from normal to abnormal, with many gradations in between. The truth, in other words, is far less clear-cut than the diagnostic system.

A second criticism is that diagnosis gives the illusion of explanation. For example, the statement "He hallucinates because he is schizophrenic" *seems* to have explanatory value. In fact, it has none whatsoever, for "schizophrenic" is simply a term that has been made up to describe a certain behavior pattern involving hallucinations—a behavior pattern of which the cause is unknown. Likewise, "depression," "phobia," "paranoia," and other diagnostic labels are simply descriptive terms, not explanations. This fact is often forgotten.

A third criticism is that diagnostic labeling is actually harmful to people. As humanistic-existential theorists would be the first to point out, the label obscures the person's individuality, inviting therapists to treat the "phobia" or "depression" rather than the human being. In addition, diagnostic labels can do concrete harm, damaging people's personal relationships, making it hard for them to get jobs, and in some cases even depriving them of their civil rights. (In many states, people classified as "psychotic" may be hospitalized against their will, and once committed, they forfeit many of their legal rights.) Furthermore, as we saw in Chapter 4, sociocultural theorists such as Scheff (1975) claim that diagnostic labels encourage people to settle back into the "sick" role and embark upon careers as mental patients.

These three criticisms can be applied to any diagnostic method—indeed, to most assessment methods. But because psychiatric diagnosis interacts with social values, it is at that system that they are most often directed. According to some writers, the shortcomings of psychiatric diagnosis are so serious that the system should be abandoned altogether. Rosenhan (1975), for example, maintains that a diagnostic system must demonstrate that its benefits (in indicating appropriate treatments, for instance, or leading researchers to causes) outweigh its liabilities in order to justify its use; since causes and treatments have not yet been discovered for so many of the *DSM* categories, these diagnostic labels should be discarded. To this argument the supporters of psychiatric diagnosis reply that research cannot proceed without diagnosis. Spitzer, for example, has responded to Rosenhan's argument as follows:

Is Rosenhan suggesting that prior to the development of effective treatments for syphilis and cancer, he would have decried the use of these diagnostic labels? Should we eliminate the diagnoses of antisocial personality, drug abuse, and alcoholism until we have treatments for these conditions whose benefits exceed the potential liabilities associated with the diagnosis? How do we study the effectiveness of treatments for these conditions if we are enjoined from using the diagnostic categories until we have effective treatments for them (1976, p. 469)?

Research, in other words, depends on diagnosis. It is only by diagnosing patients and thus analyzing groups of people with similar problems that researchers can find out whether their problems *do* have a common cause and what treatments can help them.

Yet in order to aid research, diagnosis must be consistent and meaningful. It must *mean* something—and it must mean the same thing to everyone—that a patient is labeled "schizophrenic" or "paranoid" or "phobic." In this respect, psychiatric diagnosis has, in the past, made a poor showing. Earlier editions of the *DSM* offered relatively brief and vague descriptions of the disorders they listed. Consequently there was a good deal of inconsistency in diagnosis. What some diagnosticians called "schizophrenia" others called "depression"; what some called "anxiety neurosis" others called "personality disorder." As a result, diagnostic groups were disappointingly heterogeneous. That is, the symptoms of the patients assigned to many of the categories were not similar enough to make the label truly useful for description or prediction. Furthermore, the *DSM* explicitly or implicitly ascribed numerous disorders to causes that had not been definitely established, thus further complicating diagnosis and impeding research.

DSM-III-R   *DSM-III* and its recent revision, *DSM-III-R,* are in large part an effort to remedy these problems. Let us examine this document.

SPECIFIC DIAGNOSTIC CRITERIA   First, the criteria for diagnosis are highly detailed and specific, including the following:

1. *Essential features* of the disorder: those that "define" it.

2. *Associated features:* those that are usually present.

3. *Diagnostic criteria:* a list of symptoms (taken from the lists of essential and associated features) that *must* be present for the patient to be given this diagnostic label.

4. Information on *differential diagnosis:* how to distinguish this disorder from other, similar disorders.

In addition, the descriptions offer information on the course of the disorder, age at onset, degree of impairment, complications involved, predisposing factors, prevalence, sex ratio, and family pattern (that is, whether the disorder tends to run in families). The most important feature of the descriptions, however, is the highly specific quality of the diagnostic criteria. A typical *DSM-III-R* description of a disorder may be seen in the box on pages 138–139.

FIVE AXES OF DIAGNOSIS   A second important feature of *DSM-III-R* is that it requires the diagnostician to give a substantial amount of information about patients, evaluating them on five different "axes," or areas of functioning:

> *Axis I—Clinical syndrome:* the diagnostic label for the patient's most serious psychological problem, the problem for which he or she is being diagnosed.
>
> *Axis II—Personality disorders (adults) or developmental disorders (children and adolescents):* any accompanying long-term disorder not covered by the Axis I label.[*]
>
> *Axis III—Physical disorders:* any medical problem that may be relevant to the psychological problem.
>
> *Axis IV—Psychosocial stressors:* current sources of stress (e.g., divorce, retirement, pregnancy)

---

[*] Axis II is confined to disorders that generally date from childhood. They are separated from the Axis I "clinical syndromes" to give the diagnostician a chance to note not just the primary problem (Axis I) but also any subtler, chronic condition (Axis II) that accompanies the primary problem and perhaps contributes to it. In some instances, a chronic condition *is* the patient's primary problem, in which case it is still listed on Axis II but is marked "principal diagnosis."

On Being Sane in Insane Places

Can the sane be distinguished from the insane with current diagnostic methods? In an attempt to answer this question, D. L. Rosenhan (1973) set up an experiment whereby eight psychologically stable people, with no history of mental disorder, would try to get themselves admitted to mental hospitals. The eight "pseudopatients"—three psychologists, a psychiatrist, a graduate student in psychology, a pediatrician, a painter, and a housewife—presented themselves at separate hospitals in five states. They all went under assumed names, and those involved in mental health lied about their professions. Otherwise they gave completely accurate histories, adding only one false detail: each of them claimed that he or she had been hearing voices that seemed to say something like "hollow," "empty," or "thud."

The pseudopatients' greatest fear in embarking on their experiment was that they would be unmasked as frauds and thrown out of the hospital, much to their embarrassment. They had no reason to fear. With only one exception, they were diagnosed as schizophrenic, and without exception they were all admitted as mental patients.

Once they were admitted, the pseudopatients made no further reference to the voices. They be-

haved completely normally, except that they made special efforts to be courteous and cooperative. Yet not a single one of them was ever exposed as a fraud. In Rosenhan's opinion, the staff simply assumed that because these people were in a mental hospital, they were disturbed. This assumption persisted despite the fact that all the pseudopatients spent a good part of the day taking copious notes on what went on in the ward. Far from being judged as a sign of normality, the note taking was either ignored or interpreted as an indication of pathology. On one pseudopatient's hospital record the nurse recorded, day after day, this same symptom: "Patient engages in writing behavior" (p. 253). The genuine mental patients were apparently not so easy to fool. According to Rosenhan, they regularly accused the pseudopatients of being completely sane and speculated out loud that they were either journalists or professionals sent in to check up on the hospital.

Without ever having had their "insanity" questioned, each of the patients was eventually discharged. Their stays ranged from seven to fifty-two days, with an average of nineteen days. Upon discharge, they were classified not as being "cured" or as showing no behavior to support the original

that may have contributed to the patient's psychological problem. The diagnostician should note whether the stressor is acute (of recent onset) or enduring and rate its severity on a scale of 1 to 6.

Axis V—Global assessment of functioning: a rating, on a scale of 1 to 90, of the patient's current adjustment (work performance, social relationships, use of leisure time) and of his or her adjustment during the past year.

Thus a hypothetical patient's diagnosis might be as follows:

Axis I: Major depressive episode

Axis II: Avoidant personality disorder

Axis III: Diabetes

Axis IV: Loss of job, acute (5). Marital conflict, enduring (4)

Axis V: Current—major impairment (40). In past year—moderate difficulty (60)

Thus instead of simply writing down "depression," today's diagnostician must create a little portrait, the features of which may then be useful in devising a treatment program. Furthermore, it is hoped that these five-part diagnoses will help researchers in their explorations of connections between psychological disorders and other factors, such as stress and physical illness.

UNSPECIFIED ETIOLOGY   A final important feature of *DSM-III-R* is that it avoids any suggestion as to the cause of a disorder unless the cause has been definitely established. This feature represents a change

diagnosis, but rather as having psychosis "in remission." In other words, their "insanity" was still in them and might reappear.

The evidence of this study leads Rosenhan to conclude that while there may in fact be a genuine difference between sanity and insanity, those whose business it is to distinguish between them are unable to do so with any accuracy whatsoever. The focus of his criticism is the fact that once the pseudopatients were admitted and began behaving normally, their normality was not detected. In his view, the reason for this is that in diagnosis the initial evaluation—which, as in this case, may be based on a single symptom—distorts all future evaluations of the patient, making it impossible for diagnosticians to see the person otherwise than in the role of "schizophrenic" or whatever he or she has been labeled. As a result, the sane cannot be distinguished from the insane.

This conclusion has been contested by a number of other investigators. Spitzer (1976), for example, argues that the fact that the pseudopatients were able to lie their way into the hospital is no proof that the diagnostic system is invalid. (If a person swallows a cup of blood and then goes to an emergency room and spits it up, and if the physician on duty diagnoses the person's condition as a bleeding ulcer, does this mean that the diagnostic criteria for bleeding ulcer are invalid?) As for the pseudopatients' psychiatric normality going undetected once they were in the hospital, Spitzer again argues that this is no reflection on the diagnostic system. People are not diagnosed solely on the basis of how they are behaving at the moment but also on the basis of their past behavior. The slate is not wiped clean every morning. If a person reports having repeated hallucinations and then reports no further hallucinations for two weeks, this does not necessarily—or even probably—mean that no psychiatric abnormality exists, much less that none ever existed. In the absence of alcoholism or other drug abuse, hallucination is ordinarily a sign of severe psychological disturbance; for a diagnostician to discount this symptom simply because it had not appeared for a few weeks would be extremely careless. Indeed, as Spitzer points out, the fact that the hospitals released the pseudopatients in an average of nineteen days actually shows a rather rapid response to their failure to produce any further symptoms. And the fact that they were released as being "in remission," an extremely rare diagnosis, suggests that the hospital staff recognized that they were atypical, if not faked, cases; in any case, they were not just lumped together with all other diagnosed schizophrenics.

The controversy over Rosenhan's experiment is simply part of the longstanding controversy over psychiatric diagnosis in general. Although debate about the merits of any diagnostic system is inevitable, and though any system can be used well or poorly, it is still useful—and necessary—to work at the development of a reliable and valid taxonomy.

of policy that necessitated some substantial changes in the classification system when it was introduced in the 1980 edition of the *DSM*. The term *neurosis,* for example, was dropped altogether, as it implies a Freudian theory of causation (i.e., that the disorder is due to unconscious conflict). The new manual simply names the disorders and describes them as clearly and specifically as possible; their causes, if they are not known, are not speculated upon.

The major goal of the 1980 revision was to resolve the difficulty mentioned above: diagnostic groups created according to the earlier *DSM* categories were too heterogeneous to be helpful in the search for causes and treatments. In the vocabulary of psychological assessment, what the *DSM* now attempts to do is improve the reliability and validity of psychiatric diagnosis. Reliability and validity have already been discussed briefly in Chapter 6. They are important criteria to be met by *any* assessment procedure; but we will examine these two concepts by considering how they apply to psychiatric diagnosis.

Assessing the Assessment: Reliability and Validity

Reliability   The **reliability** of any measurement device is the degree to which its findings can stand the test of repeated measurements. Thus, in its simplest sense, reliability is a measure of the consistency of such a device under varying conditions. A 12-inch ruler is expected to produce the same measurements whether it is used today or tomorrow, in Wisconsin or South Dakota, by you or by me. Likewise, a psychological assessment technique, to be considered reliable, must produce the same results under a variety of circumstances.

DSM-III-R on Major Depressive Episode

The following is the description and diagnostic criteria for major depressive episode. Note that the detailed description is supplemented by a list of extremely precise diagnostic criteria:

The essential feature of a Major Depressive Episode is either depressed mood (or possibly, in children or adolescents, an irritable mood) or loss of interest or pleasure in all, or almost all, activities, and associated symptoms, for a period of at least two weeks. The symptoms represent a change from previous functioning and are relatively persistent, that is, they occur for most of the day, nearly every day, during at least a two-week period. The associated symptoms include appetite disturbance, change in weight, sleep disturbance, psychomotor agitation or retardation, decreased energy, feelings of worthlessness or excessive or inappropriate guilt, difficulty thinking or concentrating, and recurrent thoughts of death, or suicidal ideation or attempts. The diagnosis is made only if it cannot be established that an organic factor initiated and maintained the disturbance and the disturbance is not the normal reaction to the loss of a loved one (Uncomplicated Bereavement). In addition, the diagnosis is not made if the disturbance is superimposed on Schizophrenia, Schizophreniform Disorder, Delusional Disorder, or Psychotic Disorder NOS, or if the criteria for Schizoaffective Disorder are met.

A person with depressed mood will usually describe feeling depressed, sad, hopeless, discouraged, "down in the dumps," or some colloquial equivalent. In some cases, although the person may deny feeling depressed, the presence of depressed mood can be inferred from others observing that the person looks sad or depressed.

Loss of interest or pleasure is probably always present in a Major Depressive Episode to some degree, and is often described by the person as not being interested in usual activities as previously, "not caring anymore," or, more rarely, a painful inability to experience pleasure. The person may not complain of loss of interest or pleasure, but family members generally will notice withdrawal from friends and family and neglect of avocations that were previously a source of pleasure.

Appetite is frequently disturbed, loss of appetite being the more common, but increased appetite sometimes being evident. When loss of appetite is severe, there may be significant weight loss or, in the case of children, failure to make expected weight gains. When appetite is markedly increased, there may be significant weight gain.

Sleep is commonly disturbed, the more frequent complaint being insomnia, but sometimes hypersomnia. The insomnia may involve difficulty falling asleep (initial insomnia), waking up during sleep and then returning to sleep only with difficulty (middle insomnia), or early morning awakening (terminal insomnia). Hypersomnia may involve sleeping for a longer period of time than is usual, daytime sleepiness, or taking excessive naps. Sometimes the sleep disturbance, rather than the depressed mood or loss of interest or pleasure, is the main symptom that brings the person into treatment (see Sleep Disorders, p. 297).

Psychomotor agitation takes the form of inability to sit still, pacing, hand-wringing, pulling or rubbing of hair, skin, clothing, or other objects. Psychomotor retardation may take the form of slowed speech, increased pauses before answering, soft or monotonous speech, slowed body movements, a markedly decreased amount of speech (poverty of speech), or muteness. A decrease in energy level is almost invariably present, and is experienced as sustained fatigue even in the absence of physical exertion. The

There are three criteria for reliability in psychological assessment:

1. **Internal consistency.** Do different parts of the test yield the same results?

2. **Test-retest reliability.** Does the test yield the same results when administered to the same person at different times?

3. **Interjudge reliability.** Does the test yield the same results when scored or interpreted by different judges?

Each of these three criteria applies with particular force to certain kinds of tests. Test-retest reliability is most important in assessments of stable individual-difference characteristics (e.g., IQ tests), while inter-

smallest task may seem difficult or impossible to accomplish.

The sense of worthlessness varies from feelings of inadequacy to completely unrealistic negative evaluations of one's worth. The person may reproach himself or herself for minor failings that are exaggerated and search the environment for cues confirming the negative self-evaluation. Guilt may be expressed as an excessive reaction to either current or past failings or as exaggerated responsibility for some untoward or tragic event. The sense of worthlessness or guilt may be of delusional proportions.

Difficulty in concentrating, slowed thinking, and indecisiveness are frequent. The person may complain of memory difficulty and appear easily distracted.

Thoughts of death (not just fear of dying) are common. Often there is the belief that the person or others would be better off dead. There may be suicidal thoughts, with or without a specific plan, or suicide attempts.

Note: A "Major Depressive Syndrome" is defined as criterion A below.

A. At least five of the following symptoms have been present during the same two-week period and represent a change from previous functioning; at least one of the symptoms is either (1) depressed mood, or (2) loss of interest or pleasure. (Do not include symptoms that are clearly due to a physical condition, mood-incongruent delusions or hallucinations, incoherence, or marked loosening of associations.)

(1) depressed mood (or can be irritable mood in children or adolescents) most of the day, nearly every day, as indicated either by subjective account or observation by others

(2) markedly diminished interest or pleasure in all, or almost all, activities most of the day, nearly every day (as indicated either by subjective account or observation by others of apathy most of the time)

(3) significant weight loss or weight gain when not dieting (e.g., more than 5 percent of body weight in a month), or decrease or increase in appetite nearly every day (in children, consider failure to make expected weight gains)

(4) insomnia or hypersomnia nearly every day

(5) psychomotor agitation or retardation nearly every day (observable by others, not merely subjective feelings of restlessness or being slowed down)

(6) fatigue or loss of energy nearly every day

(7) feelings of worthlessness or excessive or inappropriate guilt (which may be delusional) nearly every day (not merely self-reproach or guilt about being sick)

(8) diminished ability to think or concentrate, or indecisiveness, nearly every day (either by subjective account or as observed by others)

(9) recurrent thoughts of death (not just fear of dying), recurrent suicidal ideation without a specific plan, or a suicide attempt or a specific plan for committing suicide.

B. (1) It cannot be established that an organic factor initiated and maintained the disturbance

(2) The disturbance is not a normal reaction to the death of a loved one (Uncomplicated Bereavement)

Note: Morbid preoccupation with worthlessness, suicidal ideation, marked functional impairment or psychomotor retardation, or prolonged duration suggest bereavement complicated by Major Depression.

C. At no time during the disturbance have there been delusions or hallucinations for as long as two weeks in the absence of prominent mood symptoms (i.e., before the mood symptoms developed or after they have remitted).

D. Not superimposed on Schizophrenia, Schizophreniform Disorder, Delusional Disorder, or Psychotic Disorder NOS.

Source: *Diagnostic and Statistical Manual of Mental Disorders*, Third Edition, Revised, Washington, D.C.: American Psychiatric Association, 1987, pp. 218–223.

nal consistency is most important in tests that use many items to measure a single characteristic (e.g., a sixty-item test for anxiety). In psychiatric diagnosis, the most crucial criterion is interjudge reliability, the degree of agreement among different diagnosticians as to what specific disorder any given patient has.

As we indicated earlier, in the past this rate of agreement has been extremely low. Indeed, Spitzer and Fleiss (1974), in a review of research on the reliability of psychiatric diagnosis, found that interjudge reliability was satisfactory in only *three* diagnostic categories: mental retardation, organic brain syndrome, and alcoholism. And these are broad categories. When diagnosticians were called upon to make finer distinctions—assigning patients not only to "schizophrenia," for example, but also to subcategories within that category—the degree of agreement fell even lower (Schmidt and Fonda, 1956). In one study, for example, a number of psychologists and psychiatrists were asked to evaluate a series of simulated patient profiles and to assign each "patient" to a subcategory of schizophrenia; the resulting rate of agreement between any two judges assigned the same profile was a dismally low 25 percent (Blashfield, 1973).

DSM-III (1980), with its highly detailed and specific diagnostic criteria, solved this problem to some degree. In one study, for example, 251 clinicians, including psychologists, social workers, nurses, and physicians, were given a training workshop in the use of the *DSM-III* criteria and then were asked to diagnose patients on the basis of videotaped interviews. The rate of overall exact agreement among the diagnosticians was 74 percent, a comparatively good score (Webb et al., 1981). Yet when the *DSM-III* categories were used as the bases for diagnoses of some disorders, notably the personality disorders (Chapter 11), interjudge reliability was still poor (Mellsop et al., 1982; Drake and Vaillant, 1985). This is one problem that the 1987 revision of the manual set out to solve. As we shall see when we examine the personality disorders, the criteria for these diagnoses have now been made highly specific.

Increased interjudge reliability is not achieved without costs, however. As Blashfield and Draguns (1976) have pointed out, reliability is not the only consideration in creating a diagnostic system. Ideally, the system should also have high "coverage"—that is, most cases of abnormal behavior should qualify for one or another of its categories. Earlier editions of the *DSM* achieved high coverage by having loose diagnostic criteria; because the behavioral descriptions were so broad, almost any patient could be made to fit somewhere. The later editions, with their stricter criteria, have lower coverage, with the result that more patients are swept into residual, or catchall, categories such as "psychotic disorder not otherwise specified." In other words, the diagnostic groups are probably purer, but they are also smaller, while a substantial percentage of patients remain effectively undiagnosed.

Validity   Whereas *reliability* refers to the consistency of a measuring instrument under varying conditions, **validity** refers to the extent to which the test measures what it is supposed to measure. Do people who score high on a typing test really type better

than people who score low? If so, the test is valid.

As with reliability, there are several kinds of validity. Because the major purpose of any assessment system is to describe and predict behavior, we will discuss the two kinds of validity that are most relevant to psychiatric diagnosis: descriptive validity and predictive validity (Blashfield and Draguns, 1976).

DESCRIPTIVE VALIDITY   The **descriptive validity** of an assessment device is the degree to which it provides significant information about the current behavior of the people being assessed. A frequent criticism of psychiatric diagnosis is that it has little descriptive validity—that it doesn't tell us very much about the people diagnosed. Many mental health professionals would agree with this criticism. The question is: How much descriptive validity *does* it have? Some critics would say none. Proponents of this view point to the fact, mentioned earlier, that people assigned to the same diagnostic group may in fact behave quite differently, while people assigned to different diagnostic groups may show many of the same behavioral oddities. The classic demonstration of this fact was a study of the relationship between the symptoms and diagnoses of 793 patients diagnosed by hospital psychiatrists (Zigler and Phillips, 1961). Rating the patients on a variety of symptoms, the investigators found, for example, that the manic-depressives and the neurotics were equally likely to be self-deprecating and almost equally likely to be depressed; that physical complaints were almost equally common in the manic-depressives, the neurotics, and the schizophrenics; that the occurrence of hallucinations was approximately the same in the manic-depressives and in those diagnosed as having personality disorders; and that there were numerous other similarities among differently labeled patients. In view of this overlap, critics ask: What is the descriptive value of the diagnostic labels?

Yet there is some question whether this evidence can actually be interpreted as a sign of poor descriptive validity. Psychiatric diagnosis does not claim to produce groups that are completely homogeneous; this would be impossible, for no two people have the same behavior pattern, normal or abnormal. Nor does it claim that a symptom typical of one diagnostic group will not be found in other groups. Like any other scientific taxonomy, psychiatric classification groups individual cases not according to individual characteristics but according to *patterns* of characteristics—patterns in which there is invariably some duplication of individual characteristics (Spitzer, 1976). Three people may have high fevers, yet if their symptom pictures differ in other ways—one having a runny nose, another being covered with red spots, another having swollen cheeks—they will be diagnosed as having different diseases. Likewise, three people may have hallucinations, yet if they differ in other important respects—one having a long history of alcohol abuse, the second showing severe depression, and the third believing that his thoughts are being broadcast so that everyone in the room can hear them—then they are likely to be given three different diagnoses: alcoholism, depression, and schizophrenia, respectively. In other words, research would have to show that the *pattern* of symptoms—not just individual symptoms—is substantially different within categories and substantially similar between categories before psychiatric diagnosis could be said to have poor descriptive validity.

PREDICTIVE VALIDITY   An assessment tool with high descriptive validity is one that helps us describe the person's current behavior; an assessment method with high **predictive validity** is one that helps us answer important questions about that behavior. In abnormal psychology, the most important questions are cause, prognosis, and treatment. Thus the predictive validity of a psychiatric diagnosis is the extent to which it helps us to discover what caused the patient's behavioral abnormality, what course it will take, and what type of therapy it might respond to.

Some diagnostic labels have high predictive validity in some respects. We know, for example, that people diagnosed as manic or schizophrenic are likely to respond to certain specific drugs. Likewise, we know that people diagnosed as either manic or depressive will probably recover within a fairly short time even if they are not treated—and that they will probably have further episodes of mood disturbance from time to time. Diagnostic labels offer few hints, however, as to the course of less severe disturbances or the treatment they will respond to. And diagnosis is of little help in identifying the cause of practically any disturbance.

It is possible that the limited predictive ability of psychiatric diagnosis is due primarily to its poor reliability. While an assessment technique that has high reliability may have low validity,[*] the reverse is not true. To have high validity, a system must have high

reliability. The improved reliability of the recent editions of the *DSM* may result in improved validity. In one study, for example, the records of 134 patients, all potential candidates for a diagnosis of schizophrenia, were examined. The patients were diagnosed according to four different sets of criteria, one of which was *DSM-III.* Follow-up records were also available in which the patients were interviewed on an average of 6.5 years after the initial interview. Of the four sets of criteria, *DSM-III* was the most accurate in predicting which of the patients continued to show poor adjustment (Helzer et al., 1981). Other studies (e.g., Zimmerman et al., 1986) found that *DSM-III* is not as valid as other criteria for some diagnoses. In *DSM-III-R,* an effort was made to improve the validity of less accurate diagnostic categories.

Problems in Assessment

The reliability and validity of any assessment tool can be affected by a number of problems, some having to do with the administration of the measure, others with its interpretation. One such problem is the assessor—his or her personal manner and how it affects the person being assessed (Masling, 1960; Mischel, 1968). If a diagnostician tends to be very formal and businesslike during a diagnostic interview, the subject—particularly a child or a troubled adult—may respond in a guarded and apprehensive way. If the diagnostician interprets this behavior as a reflection of paranoid or depressive leanings and diagnoses accordingly, it may be impossible for people who later treat the patient to know that the "paranoia" or "depression" was primarily a response to the diagnostician. Even attributes that the examiner cannot control, such as physical appearance, race, and sex, may affect the subject's performance.

Assessors affect examination results more directly through their interpretation of the evidence. Subjects present many different sorts of information; diagnosticians must filter all of it through their own minds,

---

[*] For example, astrology has high reliability. People can be grouped according to birth date with great consistency and accuracy. But in order to have high validity as well, these groupings would have to reflect what the astrologers claim they reflect—namely, individual personality traits. Since there is no evidence that they do, the system has low validity.

selecting what seems most important. In the selection process, they are bound to be guided to some extent by their own biases. For example, some diagnosticians favor certain diagnoses over others. Indeed, there have often been marked differences in diagnosis between hospitals, between communities, and between countries. For years, what was called depression in England was often called schizophrenia in the United States (Cooper et al., 1972). Likewise, one hospital may have long experience treating manic episodes, while a neighboring hospital has equally long experience with paranoid schizophrenia—largely because those are the diagnostic labels favored by their respective staffs. On a more comprehensive level, many critics feel that diagnosticians in general have a "pathological bias"—a tendency to see sickness instead of health. Diagnosticians often have neither the tools nor the training to assess areas of strength, whereas they are carefully trained to spot signs of weakness or deviance. Consequently, it is weakness and deviance that they tend to find (Soskin, 1954; Taft, 1955; Hartlage et al., 1984). (See the box on pp. 142–143.)

Finally, pragmatic considerations may interfere with accurate evaluation. When psychological treatment is paid for through company insurance, word of the patient's "condition" stands a chance of reaching the ears of his or her co-workers. Anticipating such gossip, diagnosticians may apply a label that indicates a milder disturbance than they feel the patient actually has. In other instances, they may exaggerate a patient's disturbance—again for practical reasons. The Veterans Administration, for example, pays higher benefits to veterans diagnosed as psychotic than to those with less severe diagnoses. Thus when a patient's financial circumstances are particularly bad, psychiatrists may favor the evidence for psychosis.

The recent editions of the *DSM* attempt to minimize these interferences in various ways, principally by making the criteria for a diagnosis very specific and by establishing a fixed decision rule for each diagnosis, stating, for example, that four out of eight listed symptoms must be present for a given diagnosis to be made. But such rules raise their own questions. Who knows whether three symptoms are enough, or whether five should be the minimum? Furthermore, aside from "defining" characteristics, no effort has been made to rank the symptoms according to their importance. In the diagnosis of major depressive episode, weight loss is counted equally with feelings of worthlessness, whereas it is doubtful that they are equally central to the disorder. (See the box on pp. 144–145.)

But even if the diagnostic system were flawless, there would still be a problem, because a certain percentage of diagnosticians simply do not follow the

Assessment techniques must be geared to the status and capabilities of the subject. Children are likely to be unwilling or unable to respond to an assessor's questions in a formal diagnostic interview. The assessor will probably find it more effective to let a child's concerns emerge spontaneously through play in an informal setting. (Alan Carey/ The Image Works)

FIGURE 7.1
Assessment is subject to certain
interferences, as this cartoon shows.
(© 1957 United Feature Syndicate, Inc.)

rules. A study of *DSM-III* diagnoses made by psychiatrists and graduating psychiatric residents found that 48 percent of the psychiatrists' patients and 36 percent of the residents' patients did not satisfy the diagnostic criteria for the disorders ascribed to them (Jampala et al., 1986). Many therapists whose patients tend to have the normal run of middle-class sorrows fall back repeatedly on certain diagnoses (anxiety disorder and adjustment disorder are particular favorites) that they feel are specific enough to satisfy the insurance company but "harmless" and vague enough not to invade the patient's privacy. Consequently they may seldom even open the diagnostic manual.

METHODS OF ASSESSMENT

Current assessment techniques fall into four general categories: the interview, psychological tests, situational observation, and laboratory measures.

The Interview

Of all the methods of assessment, the **interview,** consisting of a face-to-face conversation between subject and examiner, is the oldest, the most commonly used, and the most versatile. It may be highly structured, with the subject answering a prearranged sequence of questions, or it may be unstructured, giving subjects the chance to describe their problem and their thoughts about it in their own way and at their own speed. Likewise, the evaluation method varies from structured to unstructured. Even after a highly structured question-and-answer session, examiners may rely primarily on their own subjective impressions in evaluating subjects. Alternatively, they may follow a detailed manual to score subjects' responses, giving one point for one type of response, two points for another type of response, and so forth.

The degree of structure in the interview and the questions asked will depend on the interviewer's purpose. If the aim is simply to put the client at ease, in an effort to promote confidence and candor, then the structure will be loose. This is usually the case, for example, with the intake interview at the beginning of psychotherapy. However, interviewers often have a clear idea of what kind of information they need— whether to provide a diagnosis or to make a treatment recommendation or simply to screen a job applicant— and cannot waste too much time obtaining it. Therefore, most interviews have some definable structure that guides the subject to give the kind of information the interviewer wants.

The major pitfall of assessment by interview is that it can give uncontrolled play to interviewers' subjectiv-

Computer Testing and Psychological Assessment

Psychological tests today are frequently scored—and even administered and interpreted—by computer. Psychologists, psychiatrists, and a growing number of other health-care practitioners, including family physicians, are among the users of the new technology. Patients or clients taking IQ or projective tests or other personality inventories can enter their responses more quickly on a keyboard than they could on an answer sheet. Examinees also seem better able to attend to items presented one at a time on the screen. They are neither discouraged nor distracted by the hundreds of questions that lie ahead in the old-style examination booklets. The new programming also permits adaptive testing: the computer can select the appropriate sequence and type of items to be presented in response to answers given to key questions early in the test. Whether it is designed to present items and record answers in a prearranged order or to adapt its presentation to the client's responses, the software for psychological assessment does what computer science is expected to do in all its applications: save time and money, permit compilation and comparison of hundreds or thousands of records, and correct for those biases in judgment that human beings seem unable to avoid.

But can these advantages be harnessed for psychological assessment? *Assessment* is the key issue, for it means a great deal more than *testing*. A computer can test a person's traits as efficiently as a solar telescope can scan for sunspots, but only the clinician or astronomer can interpret the data in order to make reasonable predictions about the kind of behavior or weather that is likely to occur. Testing is only the first step in a complicated process that will yield a valid and predictive finding.

The first problem with today's computerized clinical interpretations is that they remain unvalidated. Because they are based on actuarial data, they cannot take into account the unique history of each respondent. The neatly printed pages that issue from the

---

ity and biases, both as they conduct the interview and as they evaluate it. Political, cultural, and even personal biases are likely sources of interference. Interviewers, like most of the rest of us, have feelings about blacks and whites, women and men, handsome people and plain people, even tall people and short people, and such feelings can influence the results of the interview.

For this reason, a fairly structured interview and scoring system are often recommended, even though the subject's responses and the interviewer's intuitive powers are thereby restricted. When the purpose of the interview is diagnosis, and particularly when the diagnosis is to be used in research—for example, to assemble a group of schizophrenics for the study of a new drug—researchers use highly structured interviews. One such interview is the Schedule for Affective Disorders and Schizophrenia, or SADS (Endicott and Spitzer, 1978), which, with its own special scoring system, has proved highly reliable (Andreasen et al., 1982). Another is the Diagnostic Interview Schedule,

or DIS, of the National Institute of Mental Health (Robins et al., 1981), which provides diagnoses by computer according to the *DSM* and other criteria. Such diagnostic tools do not have high "coverage," but that is not their purpose. Their goal is to give diagnoses as precisely as possible, so that when a team of researchers says that the new drug worked or didn't work with a group of schizophrenics, they can be fairly certain that it was in fact tested on a group of schizophrenics.

Psychological Tests

More structured than the normal interview, the **psychological test** is a standard procedure in which individuals are presented with a series of stimuli to which they are asked to respond. Such a test, like the highly structured interview, gives the subject little freedom in responding, but because of its restrictive quality, the psychological test can be scored more

computer may appear valid and objective but may have far less predictive value than the user—too frequently untrained in psychological assessment—expects. The second problem is the practitioners themselves. Even if more valid computer assessments are developed, they can have little predictive value if the users of these instruments remain untrained in clinical interpretation. The simple fact is that a computer-generated interpretation cannot take account of individual differences. Given two identical scores or findings, for example, interpretation—the final step in all assessment techniques—must rely on the "natural or human context" to permit predictions of behavior (Matarazzo, 1986). If a nineteen-year-old black male college student and a fifty-year-old white female textile worker get the same readout, that seemingly objective interpretation has obvious limitations. Only a professionally trained clinician can complete the assessment process, weighing test results against each respondent's unique life experiences. The third problem with computerized testing introduces the issue of ethics. After all, tests are given and results reviewed so that they can be put to some use. The central question here is invasion of privacy. Even if we can develop software that provides interpretations better able to be validated and even if users become better trained in the subtleties of assessment, the increased use of computerized interpretations of personality and intelligence scores is bound to invite both lawsuits and government intervention. According to Matarazzo, practitioners as well as developers and sellers of assessment software "will learn through incisive questioning in courts of law who is at fault when harm has been done to a patient by the use of such impersonal clinical interpretations" (1986).

This is not to say that computer testing—once its limitations are understood—should be abandoned or that research should not continue. Interpretations of the MMPI and other testing instruments are useful and can be made more valid through research and development. In 1986 the APA published *Guidelines for Computer-Based Tests and Interpretations* to help correct the problems we have outlined here. The pamphlet addresses the issues of validity and ethics, and it warns and instructs users untrained in clinical interpretation about the limits and appropriate uses of test instruments in the process of assessment. As in other applications of computer technology, the instant availability of the products is probably responsible for instances of their blind use. As Thoreau aptly observed, "a man needs only to be turned around once with his eyes shut in this world to be lost." The lesson for those who practice assessment is to slow down long enough to put prediction back in its proper place—following understanding.

---

easily and more objectively. In fact, many psychological tests are scored by computer. (See the box on p. 150.)

For decades the dominant method of psychological testing has been the **psychometric approach.** The aim of this method is to locate stable underlying characteristics, or **traits** (e.g., anxiety, passivity, aggression, intelligence), that presumably exist in differing degrees in the entire population. Because it assumes the existence of stable traits and aims to measure them, the psychometric method considers response variability due to situational influences to be simply a source of error and makes every effort to screen out such influences. For example, instead of leaving it to examiners to give the test instructions in their own words—words that might vary in substance and tone from one examiner to the next—most psychological tests now provide extremely precise directions that the examiner reads aloud to the subjects, as anyone who has taken a standardized test in school may recall.

There are many different kinds of psychological tests. We shall examine only the most important categories: intelligence tests, projective personality tests, self-report personality inventories, and tests for organic impairment.

Intelligence Tests   **Intelligence tests** were the first of the psychological assessment techniques to be widely used. Modern intelligence tests are based on the work of Alfred Binet, the French psychologist who in 1905 introduced the first intelligence test into the French school system to help teachers determine which children should go on to higher education. Since revised by Lewis Terman of Stanford University and now known as the Stanford-Binet Intelligence Scale, the test measures a child's ability to recognize objects in a picture, to remember a series of digits, to define simple words, to complete sentences in a logical fashion, and so forth. There is also an adult version of the test, with comparable tasks scaled to adult abili-

The Wechsler Intelligence Scales measure a number of dimensions of intelligence, including Performance IQ. In the testing segment shown here, the subject is being timed as he tries to reproduce a block pattern. (Dan McCoy/Rainbow)

ties. The subject's final score on the test is rendered as an **intelligence quotient,** or **IQ.**

Another widely used series of intelligence tests consists of the Wechsler Intelligence Scales. Developed by the American psychologist David Wechsler, these tests, unlike the Stanford-Binet tests, yield not only a general IQ but also a Verbal IQ, measuring verbal ability, knowledge, and comprehension, and a Performance IQ, measuring problem solving and intelligence in a manner that does not depend upon verbal ability (see Figure 7.2). When Verbal IQ is being assessed, adults might be asked how many days there are in a year or how many state capitals there are in the United States. When Performance IQ is being assessed, they might be asked to transcribe a code or to reproduce a design with colored blocks. There are three Wechsler tests: the Wechsler Adult Intelli-

gence Scale—Revised (WAIS—R), the Wechsler Intelligence Scale for Children—Revised (WISC—R), and the Wechsler Preschool and Primary Scale of Intelligence (WPPSI), each geared to the group specified.

EVALUATION OF INTELLIGENCE TESTS   Intelligence tests have come under heavy attack in recent years. Their power is very great. Not only do they play an important part in the diagnosis of mental retardation and organic brain damage, but unlike all other psychological tests, they are routinely given to schoolchildren across the country, and often they have a serious impact on those children's futures. IQ scores can determine whether students are placed in "special education" or "gifted" classes and what high schools and colleges they attend. These decisions in turn determine the quality of education they will receive and the kinds of jobs they will be able to get as adults. Yet whether these crucial scores are actually a valid measure of intelligence—that is, overall mental ability—is questionable.

As Wechsler (1958) himself pointed out, intelligence is not an existing *thing,* such as heart rate or blood pressure, that can be objectively quantified. Rather, it is an inferred construct. We infer the quality of intelligence from what we consider correct behavior in response to various problems. Thus our estimate of a person's intelligence will depend on what we consider important problems and what we deem appropriate responses to such problems. Basically, the kinds of problems posed by the intelligence tests and the answers that are counted correct are the kinds of problems meted out by our current educational system and the answers which that system deems correct. In other words, what the intelligence tests measure—and measure fairly accurately—is the likelihood of the subject's succeeding in our society's educational

FIGURE 7.2
These test items are similar to those included in the various Wechsler intelligence scales. (Top left) A sampling of questions from five of the verbal subtests; (top right) a problem in block design, one of the performance subtests in which the subject is asked to arrange the blocks to match a pattern on a card; and (bottom) another example of a performance subtest in which the subject is required to put together puzzle pieces to form an object such as a duck. (Reproduced by permission of The Psychological Corporation, New York.)

Paraphrased Wechslerlike Questions

General Information
1. How many wings does a bird have?
2. How many nickels make a dime?
3. What is steam made of?
4. Who wrote "Paradise Lost"?
5. What is pepper?

General Comprehension
1. What should you do if you see someone forget his book when he leaves his seat in a restaurant?
2. What is the advantage of keeping money in a bank?
3. Why is copper often used in electrical wires?

Arithmetic
1. Sam had three pieces of candy and Joe gave him four more. How many pieces of candy did Sam have altogether?
2. Three men divided eighteen golf balls equally among themselves. How many golf balls did each man receive?
3. If two apples cost 15¢, what will be the cost of a dozen apples?

Similarities
1. In what way are a lion and a tiger alike?
2. In what way are a saw and a hammer alike?
3. In what way are an hour and a week alike?
4. In what way are a circle and a triangle alike?

Vocabulary
This test consists simply of asking, "What is a _____?" or "What does _____ mean?" The words cover a wide range of difficulty or familiarity.

system. Whether this is an index of intelligence depends on one's definition of intelligence.

Many people feel that the IQ tests' definition is too narrow. Gardner (1984), for example, has developed a "theory of multiple intelligences," identifying seven kinds of intelligence: linguistic, logical-mathematical, spatial, musical, bodily-kinesthetic, intrapersonal (self-knowledge), and interpersonal (knowledge of others). In his view, IQ tests, by measuring only the first two, dismiss the greater part of human capabilities. Others have argued, more pointedly, that what intelligence tests measure is not intelligence but rather a knowledge of white middle-class culture, for that is what constitutes intelligence in the eyes of the white middle-class psychologists who make up the tests (Williams, 1970). On these grounds, minority-group leaders have objected strenuously to IQ testing, seeing it as a means for keeping minority children on the lower rungs of the educational system. At one time, for example, there were four times as many blacks and three times as many Hispanics, proportionately, as there were white English-speaking students in special-education classes in California (Albee, 1978). The use of tests to place students in such classes is now being challenged in the courts, but the issue will probably not be settled until it reaches the Supreme Court.

Projective Personality Tests   **Projective personality tests** are based on the psychodynamic assumption that people's true motives, because they are largely unconscious, must be drawn out indirectly. Accordingly, projective tests expose subjects to ambiguous stimuli into which they must "read" meaning. Whatever meaning they give to the stimulus is thought to contain clues to their unconscious processes—clues that the interviewer must interpret. Murstein (1961) has further pointed out that the projective tests assume (1) that no response is accidental, so every response is interpretable; (2) that the subject is unaware of what he or she is revealing; and (3) that verbal responses to the test parallel the subject's behavior in the social environment.

THE RORSCHACH   Most famous of the projective tests is the Rorschach Psychodiagnostic Inkblot Test (Rorschach, 1942), in which subjects are asked to respond to ten cards, each showing a symmetrical inkblot design. The designs vary in complexity and

shading, becoming increasingly colorful as the sequence progresses. The test is administered in three phases. In the first phase, the *free association* phase, subjects are asked to describe as specifically as possible what each card reminds them of. The second phase, called the *inquiry* phase, involves questioning the subject as to which characteristics of each inkblot contributed to the formation of his or her impression of that inkblot. A final, optional phase, called *testing the limits,* consists of telling subjects what other people usually say about a particular card and asking them to point out which characteristics of each inkblot would call forth that response.

As we pointed out earlier, highly unstructured interviewing methods may be combined with highly structured scoring methods. This is the case with the Rorschach. The subjective material elicited by the inkblots is generally evaluated according to a detailed manual indicating how specific responses are to be interpreted (Beck, 1961; Exner, 1978, 1982, 1986). For example, an important aspect of the evaluation depends on the extent to which the subject's responses represent what is called "good form"—that is, how plausible the subject's interpretation of a picture is in view of the shapes contained in it and how closely the subject's interpretation matches that of most other people in response to that picture. Consider, for example, the inkblot in Figure 7.3, which might reasonably be interpreted as a flower or a particularly elaborate insect. Many other readings are plausible as well, but if a subject claimed that what he or she saw in this picture was a small boy crouching in a corner—something that actually contradicts the form of the inkblot—then the interviewer might conclude that the response reflected an inner conflict and distortion of reality (or that the subject was not taking the test seriously).

The examiner also weighs the content of the subject's responses. If a certain theme keeps reappearing in the subject's interpretations, then, depending on the nature of the theme, the examiner may take it as a clue to underlying psychopathology. Water, for example, may be interpreted as a sign of alcoholism; eyes, of paranoid suspiciousness; and so forth.

THE TAT AND CAT   A second projective technique that enjoys wide popularity is the Thematic Apperception Test, or TAT (Morgan and Murray, 1935). In this test the subject is presented with up to thirty pictures in black, white, and shades of gray. Unlike

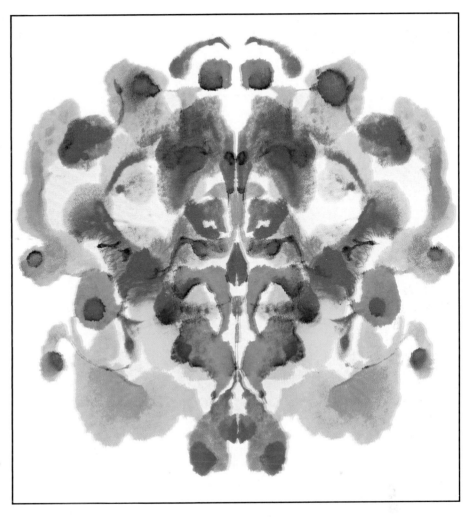

FIGURE 7.3
An inkblot card similar to those that make up the Rorschach test. In this test, the subject is asked what he or she "sees" in the design, and why.

the ambiguous inkblots of the Rorschach, the TAT pictures show a person, or possibly two or three people, doing something. The scenes are ambiguous enough to allow for a variety of interpretations, yet they nudge the subject in the direction of certain kinds of associations. (For example, the picture at left in Figure 7.4, showing a man in business clothes coming through a door, might tap the subject's feelings about his or her father.) Some researchers (e.g., Rapaport et al., 1968) claim that certain cards are particularly useful in eliciting specific kinds of information, such as the presence of underlying depression, suicidal thoughts, or strong aggressive impulses.

As with the Rorschach, subjects go through the cards one by one. With each card they are asked to describe what has led up to the scene presented in the picture, what is going on in the picture itself,

what the characters are thinking and feeling, and what the final outcome will be. Like the Rorschach, the TAT includes an inquiry phase to clarify ambiguous responses. Then, through a complex scoring system, the subject's responses are converted into an interpretation of his or her unconscious conflicts and motivations. A children's version of this test, the Children's Apperception Test, or CAT (Bellack, 1954), follows the same principles as the TAT except that the scenes focus on situations particularly relevant to children's concerns, such as feeding, toileting, and rivalry.

EVALUATION OF PROJECTIVE TESTS   Of all the varieties of psychological testing, the projective techniques incontestably allow subjects the greatest freedom in

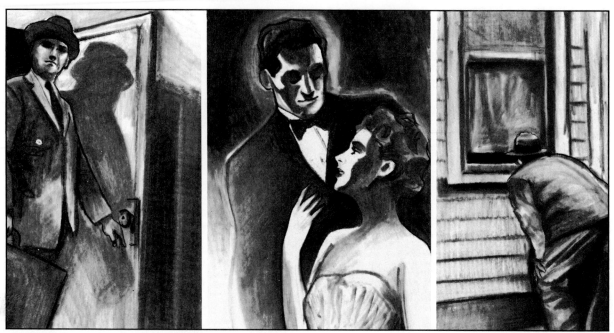

FIGURE 7.4
Pictures similar to those used in the Thematic Apperception Test (TAT). In this test, the subject is asked to describe what is going on in the pictures.

expressing themselves. However, these tests also allow the interviewer the greatest freedom in interpreting the subject's responses, and herein lies the major problem with this type of test. Opponents of the projective tests claim that the chain of inference leading from the subject's response to the interviewer's report is simply too long, too complex, and too subjective, with the result that the report may tell more about the interviewer than about the subject. This argument has been supported by numerous studies (e.g., Datel and Gengerelli, 1955; Howard, 1962; Little and Shneidman, 1959) revealing the poor interjudge reliability of the projective tests. And as may be expected when a method lends itself to many different clinical interpretations, many researchers have found the validity of the projective tests to be disturbingly low (Chapman and Chapman, 1969; Mischel, 1968; Nunnally, 1978). It was partly in response to such findings that empirically based scoring systems were developed for the projective tests. The Exner scoring system for the Rorschach is a highly detailed procedure in which the subject's responses are reduced to a numerical pattern, which is then compared with patterns derived from a variety of normative groups. Whatever the scientific standing of projective testing, its supporters claim that this is the only assessment method open and flexible enough to provide

information about the subject's unconscious processes and that such information, even if its validity is hard to document, is still useful to the clinician. Many clearly agree, for both the Rorschach and the TAT are among the ten most frequently used psychological tests (Lubin et al., 1984).

Self-Report Personality Inventories   Self-report personality inventories, unlike the projective tests, ask the subjects direct questions about their feelings and personal characteristics. Such a test may instruct subjects to rate a long list of descriptive statements—such as "I am afraid of the dark" or "I prefer to be alone most of the time"—according to their applicability to themselves. Or the test may consist of a list of things or situations that subjects are asked to rate according to whether they are appealing or frightening. In any case, in the self-report inventory, as the name indicates, subjects assess themselves. This self-assessment may not be taken at face value by the psychologist interpreting the test, but it is given some weight.

THE MMPI   The most widely used self-report personality inventory is the Minnesota Multiphasic Personality Inventory, or MMPI (Hathaway and McKinley, 1943). This test was developed to simplify the process of differential diagnosis of psychiatric patients by comparing their statements about themselves with those provided by groups of already diagnosed patients—schizophrenics, paranoids, depressives, and so on. Thus it is important to note that the diagnosis is not derived directly from the subject's self-description. A person who answers yes to such statements as "Voices speak to me in the night" or "Someone is pouring dirty thoughts into my head" is not automatically diagnosed as schizophrenic. Rather, the diagnosis depends on whether responses to these and other statements show a *pattern* similar to that seen in the MMPI responses of already diagnosed schizophrenics.

The test items range from statements of workaday vocational and recreational preferences to descriptions of genuinely bizarre thoughts and behaviors. We have already given a few examples of the latter. Other items similar to those on the MMPI checklist would be:

"I go to a party every week."

"I am afraid of picking up germs when I shake hands."

"I forgive people easily."

"I sometimes enjoy breaking the law."

The test items were originally put together from a variety of sources—psychiatry textbooks, directions for psychiatric and medical interviews, and previously published personality tests (Hathaway and McKinley, 1940). These items were tried out on groups of hospitalized depressives, schizophrenics, and so on, and then given to normal individuals. Only those items on which the pathological groups substantially diverged from the normal groups were retained. In the end, the test was made up of 550 statements, yielding a rating of the subject on ten clinical scales. The following are the ten scales, along with the characteristics that might be inferred from a high score on any one of them:

Hypochondriasis: anxious over bodily functioning

Depression: hopeless

Hysteria: immature, suggestible, demanding

Psychopathic deviate: amoral, unscrupulous, rebellious

Masculinity-femininity: characterized by traits and interests typically associated with the opposite sex

Paranoia: suspicious, jealous

Psychasthenia: fearful, lack of confidence

Schizophrenia: withdrawn, disorganized in thought processes

Hypomania: impulsive, distractible

Social introversion: shy, self-effacing

In addition to the clinical scales, the MMPI uses three control scales designed to measure the validity of the subject's responses. The L (Lie) scale indicates the degree to which the subject appears to be falsifying responses in order to appear in a more favorable light. For example, if a subject has answered yes to some extremely improbable statement, such as "I can't remember ever having lied to anyone," then this response would boost his or her score on the L scale. The F scale is a measure of the subject's carelessness in responding. Included on the MMPI are a number of statements that are rarely endorsed. The more of these statements that a subject endorses, the higher the score on the F scale, indicating that he or she may be checking off items at random or may be trying to appear disturbed. A third control scale, the K scale, indicates to what degree the subject has responded with unusual defensiveness or unusual candor. A person's scores on several clinical scales will be corrected by the addition of the K-scale score, or a proportion of it.

The usual procedure for evaluating an MMPI is to arrange the subject's scores on the various scales in numerical order, from the highest to the lowest score, and then to interpret the pattern of scores by comparison with patterns seen in normal and pathological groups, rather than to interpret any one scale separately. Some clinicians do draw diagnostic conclusions from scores on individual scales. A clinician may assume, for example, that a person who scores high on the depression scale is a good candidate for the psychiatric diagnosis of depression—that is, that he or she will show not only sadness but also guilt, lack of motivation, sleeping and eating problems, and other symptoms of depression. Such one-scale diagnoses are apparently not very meaningful, however. In a review of several studies on the relationship between specific symptoms and individual MMPI scales, Hedlund (1977) found that although many of the scales were related to the expected symptoms, these symptoms were usually related to several (in some cases, almost all) of the other scales as well. Thus scores on individual scales cannot, in general, yield sound diagnoses. Indeed, there is some doubt as to whether even the pattern of scores is a valid source of diagnostic information. The major value of the MMPI is probably in communicating the degree of overall disturbance (mildly troubled, deeply troubled, etc.) rather than in pinpointing the exact nature of the disturbance—depression, schizophrenia, or whatever.

EVALUATION OF THE MMPI   Even as a measure of the degree of disturbance, the MMPI is by no means an infallible instrument. Although it was designed to minimize the inherent inaccuracies of a self-report technique, and although the L, F, and K scales allow the clinician to make some corrections in the subject's self-portrait, no one pretends that all distortion can be detected. In clinical situations, where people taking the MMPI are usually doing so because they know they have problems and want someone to help them, deliberate falsification is less likely than in other situations (for example, the screening of job applicants). Nevertheless, people may describe themselves inaccurately without knowing that they are doing so.

A good deal of attention has been given to the problem of **response sets**—that is, test-taking attitudes that lead subjects to shade their responses in one direction or another, often unintentionally. One such response set is the **social desirability set,** which leads subjects to ascribe to themselves qualities that will make them look good. This problem can be controlled to some degree, but not entirely eliminated, by the use of the L scale (Edwards, 1953). Another response set that can distort an MMPI profile considerably is the **acquiescence set,** which makes subjects tend to agree with a statement whether it applies to them or not (Jackson and Messick, 1961).

Thus MMPI scores may be more a reflection of the patient's response set than a source of clinically useful information. It has also been argued that little accuracy can be hoped for from a test created on the basis of psychiatric diagnosis, since psychiatric diagnosis has proved so unreliable in the past. In response to this criticism, it should be noted that the pathological groups on whose responses the test was standardized included only patients whose diagnosis was agreed on by a number of psychiatrists. However,

the major argument in support of the MMPI is that since it can be scored by computer, it is an extremely convenient and time-saving method of screening patients. Indeed, the computers that now analyze the answer sheets and make up the profiles can do so in less than one and a half seconds. In addition to saving time, computer scoring is more reliable and makes it easy for examiners to compare one subject's results with those of previously tested subjects (Butcher, 1978). Furthermore, although the MMPI is not immune to error, it has been found to agree substantially with personality descriptions derived from elaborate case histories (Little and Shneidman, 1954).

The MMPI is currently undergoing its first major revision. Out-of-date items have been deleted or rewritten and new normative samples are being tested with the intention of increasing the validity and usefulness of the MMPI.

THE MCMI   While the MMPI is used in a wide variety of contexts, a newer self-report test, the Millon Clinical Multiaxial Inventory, or MCMI (Millon, 1982), is intended specifically to aid in the diagnosis of disorders in the *DSM,* and particularly of the personality disorders. The personality disorders (Chapter 11) are long-standing patterns of maladaptive thought and behavior. Unlike most other disorders, they do not disrupt the person's life; they are part of that life—and as such, they are hard to diagnose. The MCMI is an effort to solve this problem. The test is a 175-item true-false inventory that yields ratings on twenty clinical scales, all of which correspond to *DSM* categories, including the personality disorders. The correspondence between the *DSM* criteria and the MCMI is not exact (Widiger et al., 1985). Millon has relied on his own research, especially with regard to the personality disorders, as well as on the diagnostic manual. But as intended, the MCMI does a better job than other self-report inventories in identifying the patterns described in the *DSM* (Millon, 1985a,b).

THE Q-SORT   Also designed for a specific purpose is the Q-sort (Butler and Haigh, 1954), which aims at measuring a person's self-concept. In this test, subjects are given a pile of cards, each of which describes a certain personal quality (e.g., "Is well-liked," "Evades responsibility," "Works diligently"). They are then asked to sort the cards into nine piles, ranging from those that they feel are most descriptive of themselves to those that they feel are least descriptive of themselves. Often this procedure is followed by a second step, in which subjects re-sort the cards in order to describe their "ideal selves," the kind of person they would *like* to be. Repeated Q-sorts have been used to measure changes in self-concept as a result of therapy. Humanistic therapists have shown, for example, that discrepancies between real and ideal Q-sorts often decrease as psychotherapy progresses—a fact that makes the Q-sort useful in determining whether a therapeutic procedure is having any success (Rogers, 1959; Rogers and Dymond, 1954).

Other investigators have been using the Q-sort as a research tool to gain further information on selected groups of people (Block, 1961). For example, if children who delay gratification in a particular situation are given a Q-sort, some conclusions may be drawn about the personality characteristics needed to defer gratification in that setting (Bem and Funder, 1978).

Psychological Tests for Organic Impairment
As we have seen in earlier chapters, psychological disturbance may be due to neurological problems rather than, or as well as, "life" problems. Thus a major task of psychological assessment is to distinguish biogenic from psychogenic cases and, in biogenic cases, to determine where and what the neurological problem is.

Certain pencil-and-paper tests have proved valid measures of neurological damage. One device that is widely used to screen patients for "organicity" (i.e., neurological malfunction) is the Bender Visual-Motor Gestalt Test (Bender, 1938). Here the subject is shown nine simple designs, each printed on a separate card, and is asked to reproduce the designs on a piece of paper. If certain errors, such as rotation of the figures or rounding of the corners, consistently appear in the subject's drawings, the examiner is likely to suspect neurological impairment. (See Figure 7.5.) In some cases the test involves a second phase, in which the examiner asks the subject to reproduce the designs from memory. Failure to reproduce more than two designs is generally viewed as further evidence of impairment.

Some clinicians also use projective techniques, primarily the Rorschach and various figure-drawing tests, to diagnose organicity. Responses that are consistently primitive and poorly formed may be taken as signs of organic damage. However, while projective devices can provide reliable general information about

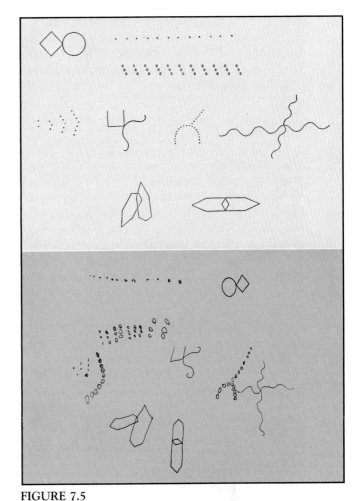

FIGURE 7.5
(Top) The nine figures of the Bender Visual-Motor Gestalt Test. (Bottom) Reproductions of the Bender drawings done by a ten-year-old boy with an average IQ show evidence of his diagnosed brain damage. Characteristics of the boy's drawings such as the reversal of the square and the circle in the first figure and the rotation of the last figure strongly suggest organic impairment.

organicity, they cannot determine the specific location or magnitude of the suspected tissue damage.

More helpful in providing specific information is a coordinated group of tests called the Halstead-Reitan Neuropsychological Battery. These tests are based on our (still imperfect) knowledge of which areas of the brain control which intellectual and motor functions. The subject is confronted with a variety of tasks—several performance measures, including those of the Wechsler Adult Intelligence Scale, along with tests of perception and rhythm, a test measuring the subject's ability to fit various wooden forms into receptacles of the same shapes while blindfolded, and so forth—each of which is designed to assess the functioning of a specific portion of the brain. Failure at any one of these tasks can thus help the diagnostician to pinpoint the site of the neurological damage.

Laboratory Tests

While psychological measures can be of help in diagnosing organicity, the primary means of detecting such problems is direct testing of the structure and function of the nervous system through laboratory methods. A standard test is the **electroencephalogram,** or **EEG,** in which the electrical activity in the brain cells is picked up by electrodes attached to the skull and recorded in oscillating patterns called

Nuclear magnetic resonance, or NMR, utilizes magnetic fields to reveal excellent images. It has become a valuable tool in the diagnosis of organic brain abnormality. (Gabe Palmer/The Stock Market)

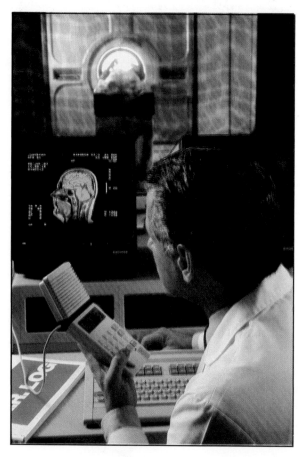

brain waves. The EEG can detect tumors and injuries in the brain. Recently researchers have discovered more sophisticated means of testing for organicity, such as **computerized axial tomography,** or **CT,** which is essentially a series of computer-enhanced X-rays of the brain, and **positron-emission tomography,** or **PET,** which involves injecting the patient with a radioactively labeled sugar solution and then tracing the progress of the radioactive particles through the brain. Both techniques have already produced new findings with regard to schizophrenia (Weinberger et al., 1982; Buchsbaum et al., 1982, 1984). An even newer method is **nuclear magnetic resonance,** or **NMR.** Through the use of magnetic fields, NMR yields a highly precise picture of the brain from more vantage points than other methods (see also Chapter 5).

Laboratory tests can also be used to identify psychogenic disorders. There is an intimate relationship between emotion and physiological functioning. When a person's hostility level rises, so may the blood pressure. When a person's anxiety level rises, so may the activation level of the sweat glands. Such changes can be monitored by physiological recording devices such as the **polygraph,** a machine equipped with a number of sensors, which, when attached to the body, can pick up subtle physiological changes. These fluctuations, in the form of electrical impulses, are amplified within the polygraph and activate pens that then record the changes on a continuously moving roll of paper. When sensors are attached to the scalp, the result is an EEG. When the sensor measures changes in the electrical resistance of the skin, the result is a reading of **galvanic skin response (GSR).** When the sensor is used to pick up subtle changes in the electrical activity of muscles, the result is an **electromyograph (EMG).** The polygraph can also measure a number of other physiological responses, such as heart rate, blood volume, and blood pressure.

All these measures can be used as indicators of emotional responses to specific stimuli and thus may aid in the process of assessment. For example, patients with high blood pressure may be fitted with a portable blood-pressure recorder so that they can take their own blood pressure at regular intervals during the day, at the same time recording in a notebook what they are doing at the time of each reading. When the two records are compared and elevations in blood pressure correlate consistently with some specific environmental stimulus, such as the family dinner hour, then the diagnostician has at least some preliminary clues as to the source of the patient's stress.

In other cases, physiological tests may be required to pinpoint the actual nature of the patient's problem. The EEG, for example, can be invaluable in determining whether patients who complain of insomnia do in fact have what psychologists and physicians call insomnia or whether they are suffering from some other sleep disorder. For example, people who complain of insomnia may actually have sleep apnea, a respiratory disorder in which breathing repeatedly stops for ten seconds or more during the night. Since sleep apnea causes extreme daytime tiredness, both patient and doctor may assume that the problem is insomnia. Often it is only by means of an all-night EEG recording that sleep apnea can be detected.

Observation in Natural Settings

As we noted earlier, the psychometric approach aims to measure what are presumed to be the individual's stable personality characteristics. Supporters of this approach would not deny that behavior is influenced by **situational variables,** the environmental stimuli that precede and follow any given action. No one disputes, for example, that children who are coddled by their parents after temper tantrums are likely to have more temper tantrums. Nevertheless, adherents of the psychometric approach assume that behavior issues primarily from **person variables,** the individual's stable traits.

In the last few decades this theory has been challenged by a number of behavioral psychologists, who take essentially the reverse position. They acknowledge that human actions are determined in part by person variables (interpreted as learned patterns of thought and behavior rather than as "traits"). But they claim that the major determinants of behavior are the situational variables—the physical and social settings in which the behavior takes place. From this point of view, it follows that abnormal behavior cannot be accurately assessed in a clinician's office, where the individual is removed from the people and places that form the context of his or her life. Rather, people must be observed in their natural settings—the classroom, the home, wherever the diagnostician can unobtrusively follow them.

Actually, a diagnostician need not subscribe to behavioral theory in order to value this method of assessment. It has been used for a very long time by clinicians of many persuasions, especially in treating children. Its value is that it allows the diagnostician to pinpoint circumstances that elicit the problem behavior—information that is useful no matter what the behavior is ultimately ascribed to. Consider, for example, a child who is having discipline problems in school. An observer may be sent into the classroom to analyze precisely what environmental conditions provoke her outbursts—teasing by other children, difficult academic tasks, or whatever. Once this information is collected, the diagnostician is in a better position to determine what the child's problem actually is. Likewise, observers can go into the home to assess problems that appear to be specific to the family environment (e.g., Reid, 1978).

Like interviews, observation may be structured or unstructured. At one extreme, the observer may simply follow the persons being measured wherever they go, watching them respond to whatever stimuli they encounter (e.g., Barker and Wright, 1955). At the other extreme, the setting may be geared toward one particular stimulus. A new assessment technique in marital therapy, for example, is essentially to stage a quarrel in the therapist's office. Each partner fills out a questionnaire separately, so that their areas of disagreement can be pinpointed. Then they discuss one of these differences in front of the therapist, who can then see how they handle conflict with each other (Boals et al., 1982).

Direct observation has a number of advantages over other assessment techniques. For one thing, it does not depend on self-report, which, as we have seen, may be extremely inaccurate. While the parents of an aggressive boy may state that he is *always* making trouble, and while the child may report that he makes trouble only when someone hits him or takes his things, the observer has a better chance of finding out where the truth lies. Second, observation cuts down on assessment errors caused by the subject's response to the examiner or by the examiner's interpretive flights of fancy. Finally, observation tends to provide *workable* answers to behavioral problems. Whereas a projective test may show that a child's aggressive behavior is due to oedipal conflicts, situational observation may reveal that his aggression surfaces only during certain kinds of interaction with his mother—a variable that is much easier to deal with than oedipal conflict. Furthermore, if oedipal conflict does exist, it is possible that adjustment of the mother–child interaction will help resolve it.

Observation is not without its problems, however.

In the first place, it requires an immense investment of time, not only in the observation itself but also in the training of observers so that criteria are thoroughly understood and so that ratings of behavior are reliable and unbiased. Second, the presence of observers may be "reactive"; that is, the person being observed may act differently because he or she is being observed.[*] "Problem" children (and "problem" parents and teachers) often show speedy improvement once they realize they are being watched by a person with a clipboard. A partial solution to both these problems has been to use recording equipment rather than human beings to do the actual observing. Unlike a human observer, a tape recorder or a camera can be set up to operate continuously, with the result that the people being observed eventually forget its presence and resume their accustomed behavior. Furthermore, the information stored in such recording devices can be scored at the convenience of the diagnostician.

THEORETICAL PERSPECTIVES ON ASSESSMENT

As we have seen in preceding chapters, the various psychological perspectives, while acknowledging that abnormal behavior may have many different types of causes, nevertheless have clear ideas as to which is the most *important* type of cause. And not surprisingly, each perspective tends to choose assessment methods that focus on that sort of cause.

The Psychodynamic Approach

As we saw in Chapter 2, two basic assumptions of psychodynamic theory, as derived from Freud, are (1) that people's behavior is determined primarily not by their will or by their current environment but by their inborn drives and their psychosexual history, and (2) that these latter factors, kept in check by defenses, operate unconsciously in motivating behavior. Proceeding on these two assumptions, psychodynamic assessment procedures attempt to place the subject in a free atmosphere, so that defenses will be relaxed and unconscious material will reveal itself.

This assessment strategy involves two basic techniques. The first is the **depth interview,** in which subjects are encouraged to talk about their childhood and also about their current lives as candidly as possible. The second major psychodynamic assessment tool is the projective test. This technique, as we have seen, gives the subject some stimulus to respond to, but at the same time keeps the stimulus vague enough so that it will not restrict the subject's responses to a specific context and thereby allow his or her defenses to remain intact. The hoped-for result is that, faced with this ambiguous stimulus, the subject will be forced to fall back on imagination and thus to project onto the image whatever is foremost in the unconscious.

These psychodynamic assessment techniques may be said to have the same virtues and vices as psychodynamic theory itself. On the one hand, they represent one method of tapping the inner reaches of the personality, levels that lie below the individual's surface behaviors. On the other hand, they tend to accord the status of fact to assumptions that cannot be empirically validated—assumptions regarding the primacy of sexual and aggressive drives, the determining influence of psychosexual development, the importance of oedipal conflicts, and so forth. Furthermore, psychodynamic theory assumes, as we have seen, that any response is interpretable in terms of unconscious motivation.

What these criticisms come down to is a serious concern regarding the faith that psychodynamic assessment places in the clinician's subjective judgment. In situations such as the depth interview and projective testing, the clinician is asked to take whatever information the subject has produced, organize it into a coherent picture—a "personality"—and then, on that basis, to make predictions about the subject's future. But there are many possible pitfalls along this route. First, the clinician's picture of the individual may be inaccurate. Second, the clinician's theory about the relationship between personality and future behavior may be wrong. Third, even if the assessment

---

[*] While some investigators have tried to solve this problem by observing surreptitiously, such tactics are both ethically questionable and extremely difficult to carry out. Even children, in general, do not take long to sense that they are being watched. Still, in some cases a psychologist who has come to a classroom to observe a specific child will be introduced to the class as the teacher's "helper" for that day. Or an observer will appear, unintroduced, in a classroom or hospital dayroom, so that the people know that someone is being observed but do not know who.

of the individual was correct and the theory sound, the type of behavior being predicted (e.g., will this child's antisocial behavior diminish if he is moved to a foster home?) may be subject to influences that lie beyond the person's control.

In other words, the odds ranged against the predictive validity of clinical judgment are heavy, and many studies (e.g., Goldberg, 1959; Holtzman and Sells, 1954; Meehl, 1954) have shown such validity to be low. An interesting recent example was a follow-up study of psychiatric predictions about the future adjustment of four successive classes (1946–1949) of first-year medical students at the University of Chicago. On the basis of psychiatric interviews, each student was rated as having a good, guarded, or poor prognosis with regard to academic, professional, and personal adjustment. Then, thirty-five years later, the subjects were tracked down, and on the basis of a detailed questionnaire, they were rated on current adjustment. How well were the predictions borne out? Not very well. Overall, those who had been rated as having a poor prognosis had not fared as well in life as those with good prognoses, but actually most of the subjects had fared very well indeed and showed little sign of emotional impairment. Aldrich (1986), who conducted this study, concludes that the original interviewers paid too much attention to signs of possible disturbance—a good example of the "pathological bias" mentioned earlier—and too little attention to the students' capacity for change and coping.

The problem of clinical judgment plagues mental health workers of all persuasions. But of all the psychological perspectives, the psychodynamic is the one that relies most heavily on inference and interpretation, and therefore this problem is especially pertinent to psychodynamic approaches to assessment.

The Behavioral Approach

Unlike psychodynamic theorists, who see behavior as controlled by intrapsychic forces, the behaviorists, as we have seen in Chapter 3, regard behavior as issuing primarily from people's interaction with their environment. Thus when people report that their actions or feelings are distressing to them, the behaviorist, in assessing the problem, will concentrate on determining with the greatest possible accuracy what it is in the environment that is reinforcing the maladaptive response (Wilson and O'Leary, 1980).

Because they see behavior as changing in relation to the environment, behaviorists place little faith in such stable-trait-oriented assessment methods as the projective tests and the MMPI. Indeed, behaviorists are generally not interested in interpreting human actions as *signs* of anything else—underlying traits, intrapsychic conflicts, or even psychological disorders (hence their avoidance of diagnostic labeling). Rather, they view behaviors as *samples,* specimens of a particular person's typical responses in particular situations. In dealing with a patient who complains of shyness, for example, a behavioral clinician would not care greatly whether such behavior was a sign that the trait "introversion" was particularly pronounced in this person. The behaviorist would simply regard the patient's social behavior as a sample of a particular response pattern and would concentrate on finding out what concrete stimuli—and, in keeping with the new cognitive behaviorism, what thoughts—were eliciting and maintaining that response pattern. The main tools for obtaining such information are interviews, self-monitoring diaries, and direct observation.

An interview conducted by a behaviorist bears little relation to the depth interview favored by psychodynamic clinicians. Generally, a behavioral assessment interview takes the form of a **functional analysis,** which involves a systematic dissection of the person's complaint: what precisely the problem behavior is, how it developed, what the person has done to try to combat it, and—most important of all—the changes in the environment that precede, accompany, and follow the behavior. In addition, the interviewer will try to get some idea of the person's strengths and preferences, since such elements help to determine an appropriate treatment program. In such an interchange, the subject's remarks are assumed to be fairly accurate statements of the problem rather than veiled clues to its underlying dynamics.

To supplement information gathered in the interview, many behavioral examiners will ask subjects to keep a self-monitoring diary of their problem behaviors. For example, a woman who is afflicted with vague anxieties would be asked to note down when her anxiety occurs and what circumstances surround these episodes. If the diary should reveal, for instance, that her anxiety regularly occurs when she is taking the bus home from work, then this correlation will provide a starting point for determining the stimuli that are maintaining the anxiety in this and other situations. In keeping with the trend toward cognitive behaviorism, self-monitoring diaries are also used to identify thoughts, images, and maladaptive problem-solving strategies that underlie psychological problems (Kendall and Hollon, 1981). In this case, the woman with the anxiety condition would be asked to record, on the spot, what thoughts passed through her mind each time the feelings of anxiety struck.

Finally, a widely used behavioral assessment method is direct observation of the problem behavior. As described earlier, the behaviorist may observe the subject in the school, work, or home environment in order to identify the discriminative stimuli that trigger the maladaptive responses. Or the behavior sampling may take place in the clinical situation itself, as when married couples are asked to discuss points of disagreement in front of the therapist.

In evaluating the behavioral approach to assessment, we should note first of all that this approach generally fulfills very well its stated objective—that is, the detailed and concrete analysis of the problem behavior and the environmental conditions that support the behavior. On the negative side, behavioral assessment is subject to the same objection that has been leveled at behavioral theory in general, that it is reductive and superficial: that it treats human beings as if they were on a par with white rats and that it attends only to the symptoms, ignoring the underlying causes. In answer to this criticism, behavioral clinicians argue that a technique that works for human beings should not be discarded because it also works for white rats, and that if problems can be solved by attention to environmental contingencies, then there is no need for speculation as to unverifiable underlying causes.

The Humanistic-Existential Approach

Like behaviorists, humanists and existentialists avoid labeling in the assessment process, but for a different reason: they consider diagnostic labels an affront to the patient's individuality. The central focus of humanistic-existential psychology, as we saw in Chapter 4, is precisely this matter of individuality, the uniqueness of each human being and the validity of his or her unique perceptions. And the central aim of humanistic-existential therapy is to restore to patients their power as individuals, the power to be true to themselves.

In accordance with this orientation, humanistic-existential assessment procedures are aimed at helping both the therapist and the patient become more fully aware of precisely what the patient's self really is.

Any assessment instrument may be used, but it will not be used in the usual way. Therapists try to set aside their own preconceptions and let the client use the instrument as a way of informing the therapist about his or her own subjective experience (Dana, 1982). The client may even be asked to talk about what the experience of taking the test is like. Some procedures, such as the Q-sort, have been favored by humanists. This procedure, described above, has been used extensively by Carl Rogers and other humanists to measure patients' self-concepts. Personality inventories have also been developed to reflect some of Frankl's concepts—for example, the Purpose-in-Life Test (Crumbaugh and Maholick, 1964).

Reliance on an interview or on a method such as the Q-sort—procedures in which there are no "right" answers, only revealing ones—has a distinct advantage. First, such an approach focuses on obtaining a clear picture of the individual in all his or her idiosyncratic reality rather than on forcing the personality into a theoretical mold. Second, of all the assessment procedures that we have discussed, these techniques are probably the least contaminated by pathological bias. The major weakness of this phenomenological approach to assessment is that it must assume that what patients say in interviews or in a Q-sort is true, at least for themselves. Hence no account is taken of the possibility of intentional or semi-intentional distortion. Humanistic-existential clinicians respond to this criticism by claiming that is better to err in the direction of empathy than in the direction of skepticism. Whatever elusive "truth" is served by skepticism is worth far less than the renewed stength the patient derives from having his or her inner world confirmed by the therapist's belief in it.

The Neuroscience Approach

Given its focus on the organic components of behavior, the neuroscience perspective naturally favors assessment methods that reveal organic structure and function. A good deal of the excitement that has surrounded this perspective in recent years has been due to the development of more sophisticated organic tests, particularly such imaging procedures as the CT and PET scans and NMR. For years the brain was unexplored territory; one might speculate on its functions and malfunctions, but with little empirical support. Now, with such things as PET scan images of the actual itinerary that glucose takes as it travels through a given brain, there is ground for theory building, and therefore theories and research have proliferated.

Progress is slow, however, and despite the new procedures, our knowledge of the brain and its relation to behavior is still very elementary. Therefore neuropsychological assessment still depends heavily on psychological tests, such as the Halstead-Reitan Battery, that reveal performance deficits.

SUMMARY

Psychological assessment has two goals. The first is to describe the personality and behavior of the person being assessed. The second is to predict unknown variables relevant to the person's psychological functioning. Prediction serves such practical purposes as job screening and career choice; in the clinical context, it helps to determine the best treatment for the individual.

Clinical assessment often involves psychiatric diagnosis, the labeling of the subject in accordance with one of the categories of abnormal behavior listed in the *DSM,* the *Diagnostic and Statistical Manual of Mental Disorders* of the American Psychiatric Association. While psychiatric diagnosis has been widely criticized, it is necessary for research. If diagnostic labels are to aid research, however, they must provide useful information. Diagnosis on the basis of past editions of the *DSM,* with their loose diagnostic criteria, has proved weak in this respect. Psychiatric diagnosis is based on the medical model, which views abnormal behaviors as symptoms of some underlying organic dysfunction, and has been criticized for three shortcomings. First, psychiatric diagnosis implies falsely that most abnormal behavior is qualitatively different from normal behavior. Second, diagnostic labels are tautological, that is, the labels merely describe behavior; they do not explain it. Third, diagnostic labels ignore human individuality and in some cases may deprive people of their civil rights. *DSM-III,* the 1980 edition of the diagnostic manual, offered, among other new features, highly specific diagnostic criteria, in an effort to make diagnostic labels more meaningful. The newly revised *DSM-III-R* of 1987 aims to increase further the reliability and validity of psychiatric diagnosis.

The usefulness of any assessment method depends

on (1) its reliability, that is, its consistency under varying conditions; and (2) its validity, the extent to which it measures what it is supposed to measure, a factor that depends in turn on its reliability. Diagnosis based on past editions of the *DSM* has had extremely low interjudge reliability and, perhaps for this reason, limited validity, especially predictive validity. The highly specific diagnostic criteria of *DSM-III* increased the system's reliability, and the 1987 revision is expected to increase interjudge reliability even in regard to the personality disorders, on which diagnosticians have tended to disagree in the past. Reports on the reliability and validity of *DSM-III* criteria, however, indicate mixed results.

Several possible problems may interfere with accurate assessment. Every psychological assessment is influenced by the assessor. A clinician's behavior and appearance may influence a subject's responses and behavior. Diagnosticians' evaluations will also be influenced by their own biases. The flexibility of diagnostic categories in the recent editions of the *DSM* may help to reduce diagnostic error, but it is impossible to eliminate it completely.

There are four common methods of assessment. The first is the interview, which may be structured and conducted in a variety of ways. A second technique is the administration of psychological tests, which include intelligence tests (e.g., the Stanford-Binet and Wechsler scales); projective personality tests (e.g., Rorschach, TAT, self-report personality inventories such as MMPI and Q-sort); and tests for organic impairment (e.g., Halstead-Reitan Neuropsychological Battery). Recent developments in psychological testing include a reevaluation of the scope and components of intelligence tests and the introduction of a new self-report test, the MCMI, in efforts to improve psychiatric diagnosis based on the *DSM* categories, especially the eleven categories of personality disorder. A third method is laboratory testing of such physiological indicators as blood pressure, brain waves, and galvanic skin response, which can provide clues to the subject's emotional reactions to various stimuli. Nuclear magnetic resonance (NMR) is a new scanning technique that yields more complete information about the brain. Finally, direct observation of subjects in their own environments is intended to identify the environmental determinants of their behavior. Direct observation can reveal the situational factors that give rise to a given behavior, whereas projective tests can only key a subject's response to preconceived and unobservable causes, such as the Oedipus complex or an anxiety syndrome. Although observation may identify biases in subjects' self-reports, it introduces the problem of reactive behavior—people tend to react differently when they know they are being observed.

An examiner's choice of assessment technique is often tied to his or her theoretical orientation. Psychodynamic clinicians tend to favor the depth interview and projective techniques, both of which require a great deal of interpretation by the examiner. Studies have shown that clinical assessments based on the depth interview have relatively low predictive validity. Follow-ups on subjects who performed better than expected suggest that the early assessments were pathologically biased, overemphasizing signs of distur-

bance and underemphasizing people's adjustment and coping skills. Behavioral assessment, in contrast, avoids subjective interpretations and relies instead on functional analytic interviews, behavioral checklists, and situational observation. Finally, humanistic-existential assessment generally relies on a loosely structured interview and on techniques that reveal the person's unique ways of perceiving the self and others. The examiners tend to make more positive predictions and avoid the pathological bias. The neuroscience approach depends on procedures for detecting brain functions and relating such neural functions to behavior. Knowledge of the brain is still in its infancy, and the refinement of causal theories therefore awaits further research.

PART 3

The Emotional Disorders

CHAPTER 8

Anxiety, Somatoform, and Dissociative Disorders

Richard Benson, age thirty-eight, applied to a psychiatrist for therapy because he was suffering from severe and overwhelming anxiety which sometimes escalated to a panic attack. . . . During the times when he was experiencing intense anxiety, it often seemed as if he were having a heart seizure. He experienced chest pains and heart palpitations, numbness, shortness of breath. . . .

. . . The intensity of the anxiety symptoms was very frightening to him and on two occasions his wife had rushed him to a local hospital because he was in a state of panic, sure that his heart was going to stop beating and he would die. . . .

Mr. Benson had had a chronic problem of bladder and kidney infections when he was a child [when suffering from these infections, he had great difficulty controlling his bladder; furthermore, urination was intensely painful], but he had had no further infections since the age of eleven. Nevertheless, he had continued his childhood practice of always making sure that he knew exactly where a bathroom was located whenever he was in an unfamiliar place. He indicated a fear that he would wet his pants if he could not find a bathroom immediately when he had an urge to urinate. The client stated that he still felt extremely anxious when he did not have direct access to a bathroom, but over the past few months [since his promotion to a new job] his anxiety had become more intense and had generalized to many other circumstances. . . .

. . . [In the new job] he was no longer able to spend most of the working day at his desk. He had to meet with persons in their offices and he was sometimes involved in conferences in unfamiliar buildings that lasted an hour or more. It was more difficult for him to find a bathroom in his immediate vicinity and if he did not locate a rest room before he began conferring with someone, he felt an overwhelming need to urinate. He was extremely fearful that he would embarrass himself by wetting his pants and he eventually had to make some excuse in order to leave the conference and urinate in a rest room. The client revealed that he had also begun to feel trapped when someone engaged him in conversation, and he occasionally experienced a sensation of panic. Even if he knew the location of a bathroom, he did not feel that he was free to leave the room as long as someone was talking to him. He also feared that he would be trapped in his car by heavy traffic, or that his car would stall in a tunnel or on a bridge. . . .

Mr. Benson reported that he had derived great enjoyment from bicycle riding with his children on the weekend. However, he became more and more reluctant to go cycling because many of the trails the children urged him to go on did not have bathroom or medical facilities available. . . . [Since the advent of the panic attacks, he had become as concerned about availability of a doctor as about bathrooms.] He eventually gave up cycling even on familiar trails with hospitals nearby, because he was afraid that the rest room facilities would be in use if he had a sudden urge to urinate. . . .

After suffering through an episode of severe anxiety, the client said that he was unable to eat and he could not go to work the next day. He took a sick leave from his job five weeks after the anxiety attacks began, because he was intensely anxious in most interpersonal situations. He found it difficult to be out of the house even during the short time it took to do an errand at a neighborhood store and he therefore tried to stay home as much as possible (Leon, 1977, pp. 113–188).

R ichard Benson's problem is anxiety, a state of fear and apprehension that affects many areas of functioning. The focus of anxiety varies widely. For Benson, it was urination; more commonly, it is failure or rejection or enclosed places; for others, the anxiety is unfocused. Whatever its form, anxiety involves three basic components:

1. *Subjective reports* of tension, apprehension, sense of impending danger, and expectations of inability to cope.

2. *Behavioral responses* such as avoidance of the situation at hand, impaired speech and motor functioning, and impaired performance on complex cognitive tasks.

3. *Physiological responses* including muscle tension, increased heart rate and blood pressure, rapid breathing, dry mouth, nausea, diarrhea, and frequent urination.

Anxiety is part and parcel of human existence. All people feel it in moderate degrees, and in moderate degrees it is an adaptive response. In the words of one researcher, "Without it, we would probably all be asleep at our desks" (Stephen M. Paul, quoted in Schmeck, 1982). We would also expose ourselves to considerable trouble and danger. It is anxiety that impels us to go for medical checkups, to return our library books, to slow down on a slippery road, and thus to lead longer and more productive lives. But while most people feel anxiety some of the time, some people feel anxiety most of the time. And for these people it is not an adaptive response. Rather, it is a source of extreme distress, relievable only by strategies that limit freedom and flexibility.

The main sections of this chapter will focus on three categories of psychological disorders:

1. *Anxiety disorders,* characterized either by manifest anxiety or by behavior patterns aimed at warding off anxiety.

2. *Somatoform disorders,* characterized by complaints or symptoms of physical disorder for which there is no demonstrable organic cause.

3. *Dissociative disorders,* characterized by a splitting off of some psychological function from the rest of the conscious mind.

Until recently, these disorders were grouped under a single diagnostic heading, known by the familiar name *neurosis.* This term was coined in the eighteenth century by a Scottish physician, William Cullen. To Cullen, neurosis was an organic disorder, a general affliction of the nervous system that produced various forms of bizarre "nervous" behavior. The term stuck, and so did its biogenic meaning. Throughout the nineteenth century, people who were demonstrably "sane" but nevertheless engaged in rigid and self-defeating behaviors were labeled neurotic and were thought to be the victims of some unidentified neurological dysfunction. Then, beginning around the turn of the century, this biogenic view of neurosis was gradually replaced by Freud's psychogenic view. Freud kept the term but discarded the explanation. To him neurosis was due not to organic causes but rather to anxiety. As repressed memories and desires threatened to break through from the unconscious to the conscious mind, anxiety occurred as a "danger signal" to the ego. And neurotic behavior was either the expression of that anxiety or a defense against it.

This theory was widely accepted and formed the basis of the classification of the neuroses in the *DSM*. *DSM-II*, for example, introduced the neuroses as follows: "Anxiety is the chief characteristic of the neuroses. It may be felt and expressed directly, or it may be controlled unconsciously and automatically by . . . various . . . psychological mechanisms" (1968, p. 39)—Freud's view exactly.

In the past few decades, however, there has been growing opposition to this view, particularly from behaviorists. The basic criticism is that anxiety is actually observable in only a few of the so-called neuroses. For example, in what is called conversion disorder, involving the involuntary loss of some sensory or motor function (e.g., vision, hearing, ability to walk), the individual may show no distress at all. Psychodynamic theorists generally feel that such conversion reactions are anxiety-reducing defenses—a theory that would explain the patient's blasé attitude—but this is an inference, not an observable fact. And many other psychologists (e.g., Ullmann and Krasner, 1975) argue that a reliable classification system cannot be based on inference.

There have been other objections as well. For one thing, anxiety, like intelligence (Chapter 7), is an inferred construct, based on a number of measures: subjective reports of distress, behavioral avoidance, physiological signs. Yet these measures do not always agree (Lang, 1970; Rachman, 1978). Patients may show extensive physiological signs, for example, without complaining of any particular emotional distress, so that two researchers, both talking about anxiety, may actually be talking about different things if one is relying primarily on physiological measures and the other on subjective reports. Hence the use of the global term *anxiety,* unless its meaning is carefully specified, may impede rather than advance progress in the study of these disorders.

Finally, anxiety is not limited to so-called neurotics. As we noted earlier, "normal" people feel it too. So do psychotics, depressives, and sexual deviants (Nathan et al., 1969). This universality makes anxiety even more difficult to use as a diagnostic criterion. If everyone experiences it, what is it that distinguishes the neurotic from the nonneurotic?

In view of these problems, *DSM-III* and *DSM-III-R* abandoned the practice of gathering all the so-called neurotic disorders into a single, anxiety-based category. Instead, these disorders are now classified according to the behavior patterns they involve. And since there are several such behavior patterns, there are now several major categories in place of what was once the single major category of neurosis.

In the process, the term *neurosis,* as a diagnostic label, has been discarded. Though lamented by some, this is probably a constructive step. The diagnostic manual is designed to be used by mental health professionals of all theoretical persuasions. Therefore the use of a term that implies a psychodynamic interpretation is not appropriate. However, the term has not been abandoned altogether. It continues to be found in psychodynamic writings. And mental health professionals of many persuasions continue to use it as an indication of the *severity* of a psychological disorder, "neurosis" indicating the milder disturbances and "psychosis" the more debilitating ones.

Thus anxiety disorders, somatoform disorders, and dissociative disorders are now no longer subdivisions of neurosis; they are independent categories. Nevertheless, they still have at least two basic features in common. First, they leave "reality contact" relatively unimpaired. People with these disorders may misinterpret or overreact to certain stimuli related to their psychological problems, but in general they see the same reality that the rest of us see. Second, because they do not sever contact with reality, these are usually "ambulatory" disorders. In most cases, people burdened by these conditions still go about their daily rounds, studying or working, carrying on fairly reasonable conversations, engaging in relationships with other people, and so on. They may cope poorly, but they cope. These two features summarize the meaning of "neurotic" as an indicator of severity.

In this chapter, we will first describe the basic features of the anxiety, somatoform, and dissociative disorders. Then we will examine the different theoretical perspectives on these forms of psychological disturbance.

ANXIETY DISORDERS

Anxiety can be experienced in a variety of ways. There are, however, three basic patterns. In generalized anxiety disorder and panic disorder, the anxiety is unfocused; either it is with the person continually or it descends "out of nowhere," unconnected to any special stimulus. In phobic disorder, on the other hand, the fear is aroused by one particular object or situation. Finally, in obsessive-compulsive disorder, anxiety occurs if the person does *not* engage in some thought or behavior that otherwise serves no purpose and may in fact be unpleasant and embarrassing.

Without treatment, agoraphobia can become so severe that the victim dares not venture outside the home for months, or sometimes years, at a time. (Bettye Lane/ Photo Researchers)

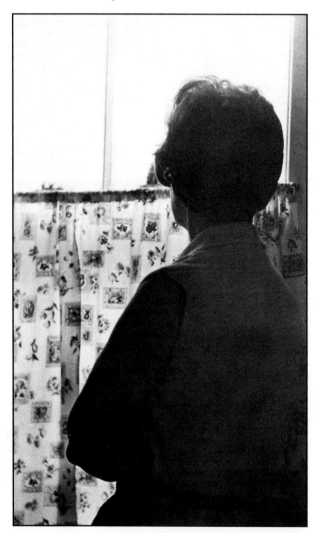

Panic Disorder

We have already seen, in the case of Richard Benson, the general features of a panic attack. In a **panic attack,** anxiety mounts to an almost unbearable level. The person sweats, feels dizzy, trembles, shivers, and gasps for breath. The pulse quickens and the heart pounds. The world seems unreal. Above all, there is a feeling of inescapable doom; the person may feel that he or she is about to die or go insane or commit some horrible act. Such attacks usually last several minutes, though they may continue for hours. When the attack subsides, the person feels exhausted, as if he or she had survived a traumatic experience—which is in fact the case.

In many instances, panic attacks occur in the absence of an identifiable stimulus. It is this independence of any specific provocation that makes panic attacks so mysterious and so terrifying. Most victims of the disorder report one or more stressful life events within six months of the first attack (Roth, 1959; Uhde et al., 1985), and attacks are more likely to come when the person is tense (Liebowitz et al., 1985). But for the most part the attacks are unpredictable, and therefore unmanageable. Victims of panic disorder cannot go anywhere—to the movies, the grocery store, a restaurant—without fearing that they may have an attack in front of everyone, and with help nowhere to be found.

Consequently, some may in fact cease to go anywhere—a complication of panic disorder called agoraphobia. Literally, **agoraphobia** means fear of open places. Actually, what the agoraphobic fears is leaving home. This disorder is often preceded by a phase of panic attacks. Eventually, the person becomes so afraid of having an attack, especially in a public place, that he or she begins to stay closer and closer to home. Some agoraphobics refuse to leave home unless someone goes with them; others refuse to leave home at all, becoming completely housebound. At the end of the case of Richard Benson we saw an incipient agoraphobia, preceded as usual by panic attacks and based on a fear of further attacks.

Not all cases of panic disorder lead to agoraphobia. Conversely, some agoraphobics do not have panic disorder. What keeps the latter at home is the fear not of a panic attack but of some other incapacitating symptom, such as dizziness, cardiac problems, or loss of bladder or bowel control, which they cannot bear the thought of suffering in the aisle of a grocery store.

Panic disorder, with or without agoraphobia, tends to make its appearance in late adolescence or early adulthood and is reasonably common, affecting about 1 percent of the population. Agoraphobia is more common, with a prevalence rate of 3 to 6 percent (Myers et al., 1984). Also common is the occasional panic attack. In a survey of 186 Canadian extension students, 34 percent reported having had one or more panic attacks in the previous year (Norton et al., 1985). Also subject to occasional panic attacks are the victims of all kinds of anxiety disorders. In one study, 83 percent of 108 patients complaining of anxiety had had at least one panic attack (Barlow et al., 1985).

Phobic Disorders

Phobic disorders involve two factors: (1) a **phobia,** or intense fear of some object or situation which, as the individual realizes, actually poses no major threat; and (2) avoidance of the phobic stimulus. In some cases, the phobic stimulus is something that seems utterly harmless. Often, however, the stimulus is one that carries a very slight suggestion of danger—something that a child, for example, might be afraid of, such as dogs, insects, snakes, or high places. (Many phobias do in fact begin in childhood.) Nonphobic people may also avoid these things. Many people, for example, distinctly prefer not to step out onto fire escapes and would never touch a snake, no matter how harmless. The difference between these reactions and a phobic reaction is, first, one of severity. While the normal person may feel apprehension at the sight of a snake, the snake-phobic person willl show intense anxiety, along with its usual physiological signs: escalated heart rate, sweating, and so forth. (In the extreme case, the phobic stimulus may precipitate a panic attack.) Second, because of the severity of the anxiety response, phobic people, unlike others, must design their lives so that they avoid the thing they fear.

Phobias are fairly common, affecting up to 13 percent of the general population (Myers et al., 1984).

Among the more frequently seen types are **acrophobia,** fear of heights; **claustrophobia,** fear of enclosed places (e.g., elevators, crowded subways); and animal phobias, particularly for dogs, snakes, mice, and insects. The most common phobias are the animal phobias (Agras et al., 1969; Costello, 1982), but many people with these conditions do not seek help.

Another category of phobia is **social phobia,** which causes the person to be afraid to perform certain actions when exposed to the scrutiny of others. Common objects of social phobia are public speaking, eating in public, and using public bathrooms. Clinicians sometimes report other, more idiosyncratic phobias, such as the case of an opera singer whose phobia was specific to singing one musical note, two Cs above middle C, though she could sing higher notes. Once, in a public performance, her voice had cracked while she was singing this note, and thereafter she avoided any score that included it—a condition that, needless to say, interfered with her career and eventually brought her into treatment.

Though the woman's condition is an extreme case, it illustrates the basic problem with phobia: that it restricts people's choices, forcing them into rigid and narrow channels of behavior. Furthermore, it erodes self-esteem: to flee from a cocker spaniel is a humiliating experience. However, the degree of impairment depends heavily on the degree to which the phobic stimulus is a usual factor in the individual's normal round of activities. Dog-phobic people are in a bad position, for dogs are everywhere. Fear of air travel might be more debilitating to a business executive than to a suburban housewife. In other cases, the phobic stimulus is so rare a factor in the person's environment that it has little or no effect on daily activities. For example, a city dweller with a phobia for snakes need only avoid going to the zoo. That is why many people with animal phobias are able to get by without treatment.

Generalized Anxiety Disorder

As the name suggests, the main feature of **generalized anxiety disorder** is a chronic state of diffuse anxiety. *DSM-III-R* defines the syndrome as unrealistic and excessive worry about two or more life circumstances—a college student, for example, might dwell nervously on his grades and on his social life—but usually the anxiety spreads far beyond two situations, leaving the person in a state of constant tension, a condition that Freud called "free-floating anxiety." People with generalized anxiety disorder are continually waiting for something dreadful to happen, either to themselves or to those they care about. Eventually they may also develop secondary anxiety—that is, anxiety about their anxiety—fearing that their condition will cause them to develop ulcers, lose their jobs, alienate their spouses, go crazy, be hospitalized, and so forth.

This subjective condition spills over into cognitive and physiological functioning. The person finds it hard to concentrate, make decisions, and remember commitments. Letters go unmailed; appointments are missed; it may take a half hour to scrutinize a menu. At the same time, chronic muscle tension and heightened arousal in the nervous system give rise to numerous physiological complaints. People with this disorder may develop muscular aches, nervous twitches, headaches, breathing difficulties, clammy hands, racing pulse, tingling feelings in their hands and feet, indigestion, insomnia. In other words, they have pervasive "jitters."

While generalized anxiety disorder sounds as though it might be the "resting state" of panic disorder, research suggests that they are two entirely separate syndromes. To begin with, there is evidence, as we shall see, of a genetic component in panic disorder, but not in generalized anxiety disorder. Second, it has been found that while the symptoms of four out of five victims of panic disorder will increase if the victims are induced to hyperventilate (some will have panic attacks), this procedure is much less likely to increase anxiety in people with generalized anxiety disorder (Rapee, 1986). Both findings point to a much stronger organic component in panic disorder than in generalized anxiety disorder.

Obsessive-Compulsive Disorder

An **obsession** is a thought or an image that keeps recurring to the mind, though the individual may consider it senseless or even unpleasant. Similarly, a **compulsion** is an action that a person feels compelled to repeat again and again, though he or she has no conscious desire to do so. The person feels that he or she has not voluntarily produced the obsessions or compulsions; rather, they have simply forced their way in and taken over. People suffering from either obsessions or compulsions—or, as is usually the case,

from both—are said to have **obsessive-compulsive disorder.**

Mild obsessions strike many of us from time to time. We may dwell repeatedly on some song lyric, or our thoughts may keep running back to a story we read in the paper or to the question of whether we remembered to leave out food for the cat before going to work. But these minor obsessions pass, and we go on about our business. Pathological obsessions, on the other hand, do not pass; they recur day after day. Furthermore, they often have a prurient or violent quality, which makes them even more demoralizing to the people who have them. A mother may become obsessed with the idea of drowning her baby in its bath, or a man may become obsessed with the fear that he will masturbate in public. Predictably, people with such obsessions are usually swamped by guilt.

Compulsions, though they may be as irrational and disruptive as obsessions, tend to be more "acceptable" in content. Indeed, they generally have overtones of duty and caution. Compulsives tend to fall into two categories (Rachman and Hodgson, 1980). First are those with checking rituals—people who are compelled to interrupt their activities again and again to go and make sure they have done something that they were supposed to do. Some people, for example, no sooner get into bed than they have to get up and make certain they have locked the front door or, worse yet, all the doors and windows in the house— a process that may be repeated seven or eight times until, exhausted and still uncertain, they at last fall asleep. The second group consists of people with cleaning rituals, such as compulsive hand washers, who are typically obsessed with the idea that they are contaminated. Whatever their routine, compulsives become extremely anxious if they are prevented, or try to prevent themselves, from engaging in it. And therefore, tiresome and humiliating though it may be, they give in to it.

At its worst, obsessive-compulsive disorder can be completely disabling, as the person's life is given over to obeying the compulsion. Such was the situation in the following case. The patient was nineteen years old, and the account was provided by his father:

> When George wakes in the morning, . . . he feels that his hands are contaminated and so he cannot touch his clothing. He won't wash in the bathroom because he feels that the carpet is contaminated

and he won't go downstairs until he is dressed. Consequently, I have to dress him, having first cleaned his shoes and got out a clean shirt, underclothes, socks and trousers. He holds his hands above his head while I pull on his underpants and trousers and we both make sure, by proceeding very cautiously, that he doesn't contaminate the outside of his clothing. Any error or mishap and he will have to have clean clothes because he must avoid at all costs passing on the contamination to others. George then goes downstairs, washes his hands in the kitchen and thereafter spends about twenty minutes in the toilet. . . . I then have to stand in the doorway and supervise him, my main function being to give reassurance that he has not done anything silly to contaminate his clothing. Thankfully he is now managing on some occasions to cope in the toilet without my close supervision but I still have to be on call so that I can help him if he starts to panic for any reason. Incidentally, I have to put newspapers down on the floor of the toilet and change them daily to make sure that his trousers never come into contact with any contaminating substances. If he only wants to urinate then my task is made easier. I simply have to check his trousers and boots for splashes, sometimes getting down on my hands and knees with a [flashlight]. . . . Recently he has been checking that there are no pubic hairs on the floor and he asks me to get down on my hands and knees to check the floor meticulously. Basically he has to be completely sure that there is no contamination around because if he is not sure then he will start to worry and ruminate about it later on. He has to be completely sure and therefore needs a second opinion. As soon as he has zipped up his trousers I have to march in with a pad soaked in antiseptic and give the zip a quick once-over. When he washes his hands after toileting, he meticulously scrubs each finger and methodically works his way up as far as his elbow. I used to have to watch him at every step of the way but now he only calls me in occasionally. Sometimes he will have washed and dried his hands and then decides that he is not sure whether he washed properly. At this stage I usually have to supervise him so that when he is finished he is absolutely certain that the job has been done perfectly without missing a square inch of contamination (Rachman and Hodgson, 1980, pp. 66–67).

This was merely the patient's morning routine. The rest of the day followed a similar course.

"Out, damned spot." Lady Macbeth's unshakable conviction that King Duncan's blood remains on her hands, even after extensive cleaning, can be seen as an instance of obsessive-compulsive disorder. (Culver Pictures)

Obsessive-compulsive disorder, with a prevalence of about 1 to 2 percent (Myers et al., 1984), should not be confused with the far more common problems of excessive drinking, eating, or gambling. We often hear people speak, for example, of "compulsive gamblers" or "compulsive eaters." These activities, however, are not compulsions. By definition, a compulsion is not engaged in as an end in itself, but to relieve the distress attendant upon *not* engaging in it. "Compulsive eaters" and "compulsive gamblers," while they may be pained by the *consequences* of these excesses, do nevertheless pursue eating and gambling as ends in themselves.

The stresses of combat can build up and culminate in the condition known as posttraumatic stress disorder. This syndrome was especially common and long-lasting among veterans of the Vietnam War, but the majority of victims eventually recovered. (David Burnett/Contact Press Images)

A more justifiable confusion is between obsessive-compulsive disorder and mood disturbance. Not just "unsavory" obsessions but most obsessions and compulsions are accompanied by guilt, depression, and feelings of helplessness—a fact that has led to controversy over whether this syndrome should be classified as a mood disorder (Chapter 10) rather than an anxiety disorder. It is possible that obsessive-compulsives belong in a separate category altogether, overlapping both the anxiety and mood disorders (Insel et al., 1985).

Posttraumatic Stress Disorders

Posttraumatic stress disorders are acute psychological reactions to intensely traumatic events—events much more disturbing than most ordinary human troubles.[*] Such events include assault, rape, natural disasters such as earthquakes and floods, accidents such as airplane crashes and fires, and wartime traumas such as torture and bombing. Predictably, most of our knowledge of posttraumatic stress disorders comes from war survivors—people who lived through Nazi concentration camps, the bombing of Hiroshima, or simply the day-to-day agonies of combat in World War II and the Korean and Vietnam wars.

Because posttraumatic stress disorder is normally characterized by anxiety, *DSM-III-R* classifies this syndrome under the anxiety disorders. They differ from other anxiety disorders, however, in that the source of stress is an external event of an overwhelmingly painful nature, so that the person's reaction, though it may resemble other anxiety disorders, seems to some degree justified and "normal."

Justified or not, posttraumatic stress disorders can be extremely debilitating. Victims may go on for days, weeks, or months reexperiencing the traumatic event, either in pained recollection or in nightmares. In some cases, stimuli reminiscent of the event may cause the patient to return psychologically to the scene of the disaster and go through it, in his or her mind, all over again. At the same time, victims of these disorders show a diminished responsiveness to their present surroundings, a sort of "emotional anesthesia." They may find it difficult, for example, to respond to affection—a source of great pain to families of returning soldiers—or to interest themselves in things that they cared for before the trauma. Typically, they also suffer physical symptoms—insomnia, decreased sex drive, and heightened sensitivity to noise—so that they may jump out of their seats at the sound of a door opening. In addition, they may

---

[*] In *DSM-III-R* psychological reactions to more ordinary traumas, such as the death of a parent or a heavy business loss, are classified separately, as *adjustment disorders*.

experience depression, anxiety, and intense irritability, exploding over the slightest frustration.

Not all people exposed to intensely traumatic experiences develop such symptoms. Many soldiers, for example, go through grueling combat experiences and emerge with nothing more than a few bad dreams. Not surprisingly, the likelihood of developing posttraumatic stress disorder seems to depend to some degree on one's psychological strength before the trauma. It also depends on the nature of the trauma. Traumas caused by human actions, such as combat, tend to precipitate more severe reactions than natural disasters such as floods, earthquakes, or hurricanes. And in the case of community disasters, such as floods or earthquakes, the greater the threat of death and the larger the population affected, the greater the likelihood of severe posttraumatic stress disorder (Gleser et al., 1981).

Symptoms of posttraumatic stress disorder generally appear shortly after the trauma. In some cases, however, there is an "incubation period"; for days or even months after the event the person is symptom-free, and then, inexplicably, the traumatic reaction begins to surface. In the usual case, symptoms clear up by themselves within about six months; some, however, may linger for years. For example, a survey found that of the 2.7 million American military personnel who served in the Vietnam War, somewhere between 500,000 and 700,000 are still suffering from posttraumatic stress disorder (Walker and Cavenar, 1982). That is 20 to 25 percent, a shockingly high number.

Combat   From World War I to World War II to the Korean and Vietnam wars, traumatic reactions to combat have been known by a succession of names: "shell shock," "combat fatigue," "combat exhaustion," and so forth. Actually, no one term is fitting, for stress reactions to combat differ markedly from one person to another. Some soldiers succumb to depression, curling up in their bunks unable to move. Others experience anxiety, which escalates to panic attacks. Whatever the response, the precipitating stimulus is usually the same: a close escape from death, often with the added horror of seeing one's companions killed. Such traumas, however, are usually preceded by months or years of accumulated stress: fear, deprivation, cold, heat, and numerous brushes with death. Many soldiers seem to succumb not so much to a single trauma as to this constant piling up of stress.

Indeed, many show no effects until they have returned to civilian life and are suddenly surprised by nightmares and nervous tremors.

We have already mentioned the inordinately high rate of persistent posttraumatic stress disorder among Vietnam veterans: an estimated 20 to 25 percent. This may be a conservative figure. In two further surveys (Wilson, 1977; Frye and Stockton, 1982), 40 to 50 percent of Vietnam combat veterans were still reporting moderate to strong symptoms of posttraumatic stress disorder ten years later—a problem, it should be added, not just for them but for their families as well. (A recent study found that Vietnam posttraumatic stress disorder patients had more difficulty expressing themselves to their partners and were more likely to be physically aggressive toward them than other people seeking outpatient help [Carroll et al., 1985].) In view of the dimensions of the problem, the Veterans Administration in 1980 began to accept posttraumatic stress disorder, as defined by *DSM-III,* as a potentially compensable disability.

Why should this war have left its veterans more traumatized than other wars? According to one study (Figley, 1979), certain characteristics of the Vietnam conflict made it particularly damaging psychologically. To begin with, soldiers were shipped to Vietnam simply as masses of recruits rather than in organized combat groups, and, once there, they were transferred frequently. As a result, they had little chance to develop a sense of group identity, which provides psychological protection against stress. Second, opposition to the war on the part of the American citizenry bred feelings of purposelessness in the soldiers while they were in Vietnam and of betrayal once they were home. Third, the lack of an all-out attempt to win the war aggravated the troops' confusion and sense of purposelessness. Fourth, military psychiatry was apparently inadequate. While early reports indicated low rates of psychiatric casualties, later studies revealed that many psychological disorders were masked by the inordinately high rate of drug use among the soldiers in Vietnam (Figley, 1979). Finally, removal from combat was extremely abrupt. Some soldiers went from the firing lines to their living rooms in a matter of two or three days, with no chance to make a reasonable transition to civilian life.

Civilian Catastrophe   Disaster, of course, is not confined to wartime. There are "civilian catastrophes" as well. Victims of a plane crash, fire, or flood, of assault or rape or hijacking, are also subject to post-traumatic stress disorder.

According to some writers, victims of severe physical trauma show a definite pattern of responses known as the **disaster syndrome.** In the first phase, the *shock stage,* they are stunned and dazed, frequently to the point of immobility. In extreme cases, there may be disorientation and memory loss as well. During the second stage, the *suggestibility stage,* they become passive and are willing to take orders from almost anyone. At this point, they may begin to express concern for other people involved in the incident. During the *recovery stage,* they begin to pull themselves together and to approach their situation in a more rational way. However, they may still show signs of generalized anxiety and may go on recounting their experience to others again and again (Raker et al., 1956). The psychological effects of a disaster may persist for many months, as the box on the Hyatt Regency catastrophe indicates.

The initial shock stage has been described in numerous accounts of human responses to disasters. One such account is *Everything in Its Path* (1976), a study by the sociologist Kai Erikson (son of Erik Erikson—Chapter 2) of the survivors of a devastating flood. One day in 1972, at the top of a mountain hollow called Buffalo Creek in West Virginia, a makeshift dam burst, and over 100 million gallons of mud poured down onto the communities below. Within hours 125 people were dead, while thousands of others had watched their homes and belongings wash away. In the survivors' descriptions of their immediate reactions to the flood, the most prominent feeling is not sorrow or fear but simply numbness. The initial shock stage is also documented in a study of survivors of the Hiroshima bombing (Lifton, 1967). This reaction has been called "psychic numbing."

Another important component of the survivor's psychology is guilt. Many people, having barely escaped some disaster, begin to feel deep remorse that their lives were spared, as if by taking up a place on the survivor list, they had forced others to die. This guilt was another theme reiterated by the survivors of Buffalo Creek:

> One of our very close friends stayed drunk for almost five months because he could still hear his brother and sister screaming for their mother and his mother screaming "God help us" when the water hit them. Sometimes he talks with me about it and I get the impression that he feels bad because he lived through it all. He is only twenty years of age, but I guess sometimes he feels like a thousand years old (Erikson, 1976, p. 171).

A similar sense of guilt has been observed in Hiroshima and concentration-camp survivors and in combat troops. Along with sorrow and fear, it is one of

People who suddenly lose their homes in a tornado may display the sequence of reactions that has been called the disaster syndrome—first shock, then suggestibility, and finally recovery. (David Woo/Stock, Boston)

Posttraumatic Stress Disorder: After the Hyatt Regency

On July 17, 1981, two "skywalks" in the Hyatt Regency Hotel in Kansas City, Missouri, collapsed, killing 113 people and injuring 200 others. This catastrophe proved to have lasting emotional effects on those who survived. A year after the ordeal, a study of 103 survivors and rescue workers showed that although many of the initial reactions to the calamity—such as loss of appetite, difficulty concentrating, insomnia, and fatigue—eventually diminished, others lasted for months.

The study, conducted by Charles Wilkinson, a psychiatrist and the associate dean of the School of Medicine, University of Missouri, Kansas City, revealed that all but two of the survivors suffered significant aftereffects, such as repeated recollections of the event, recurrent dreams and nightmares, hypersensitivity to sudden noises, fear of overhead structures, extreme fatigue, anger, and guilt (Brody, 1982b).

Sixty percent of the survivors interviewed experienced undue fatigue; more than half had recurrent dreams—often nightmarish; nearly half had trouble concentrating; a quarter, a loss of appetite; a quarter, diminished sexual desire; and a quarter, feelings of isolation and detachment from others. Many of these symptoms are typical of depression, Wilkinson noted. Feelings of guilt and anger were especially common.

The study underscored the fact that one needn't be physically injured in such a disaster to be hurt by it. In fact, Wilkinson found that the injured had *fewer* symptoms of emotional ill health than did those who escaped injury or who served as rescue workers. "It's as if the injured had already paid their debt," he noted.

Although nearly all cities have emergency rescue plans in case of major disaster, few consider the emotional devastation that such calamities engender. Yet the emotional scars often outlast the physical injuries. Though no comprehensive mental health plan existed in Kansas City before the accident, its mental health centers organized the world's first "shrink-in," as one official termed it, within two days. Dozens of psychotherapists volunteered their services at meetings held throughout the area. The centers opened their doors to the public for twelve weeks, and group therapy sessions were held day and night. No files were kept on participants, to reduce the possibility of the stigma associated with mental illness. Many of the sessions were held in nonmedical settings, such as schools and churches, for the same reason.

To encourage people to make use of the support groups, local celebrities talked freely about their emotional anguish in the media. "We took a preventive approach," said Richard Gist, director of the Kansas City Association for Mental Health. "We let people know they were having normal feelings about an abnormal experience and that it was important to accept those feelings, express them to others and have others accept them." Gist believed that this swift, aggressive intervention prevented the development of more severe reactions later on: "The literature suggests that about 15 percent of those involved in the disaster should have needed professional psychotherapy within a year of the event. At most, only 3 percent . . . had to seek formal treatment" (Gist and Stolz, 1982).

the agonies against which "psychic numbing" defends the mind (Lifton, 1967).

The responses of the survivors of Hiroshima and the Nazi death camps are the extreme case, for these people suffered not only extreme physical peril but also the deaths of their families and friends, the loss of their homes, the obliteration of their whole world. Survivors of less complete disasters (e.g., near-death in a fire or automobile accident), who can go home to their families and their accustomed surroundings,

tend to recover more quickly and more completely. Yet even these people, after getting over the acute phase of the traumatic reaction, may suffer what is called **posttraumatic syndrome,** in which they no longer show extreme anxiety or depression but are simply irritable and have difficulty concentrating and resuming their former daily routine. In this last stage, which may last for months, individuals may also avoid social activities and spend many hours ruminating about the traumatic event.

SOMATOFORM DISORDERS

The primary feature of the **somatoform disorders** is, as the name suggests, that psychological conflicts take on a somatic, or physical, form. Some patients complain of physical discomfort—stomach pains, breathing problems, and so forth. Others show an actual loss or impairment of some normal physiological function; suddenly they are unable to see or swallow or move their right leg. In either case, there is no organic evidence to explain the symptom, while there *is* evidence (or at least a strong suspicion) that the symptom is linked to psychological factors.

There are several types of somatoform disorder, and in some cases the differences among them are subtle. We shall discuss three forms: hypochondriasis, somatization disorder, and conversion disorder.

Hypochondriasis

The primary feature of **hypochondriasis** is a gnawing fear of disease—a fear maintained by constant

The typical hypochondriac, constantly afraid of becoming ill, keeps an arsenal of medications on hand for self-diagnosis and self-treatment. (Ray Ellis/Photo Researchers)

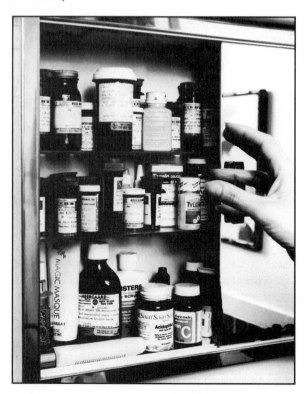

misinterpretation of physical signs and sensations as abnormal. Hypochondriacs have no real physical disability; what they have is a conviction that a disability is about to appear. Hence they spend each day watching for the first signs of its onset. Such signs usually do not take long to appear. One day the heart will skip a beat, or the body will register some new ache or pain. This is then interpreted by the hypochondriac as the first sign of a disease that is now at work throughout his or her body. Often, when they appear at the doctor's office, hypochondriacs have already diagnosed their condition, for they are usually avid readers of articles on health in popular magazines. And when the medical examination reveals that they are perfectly healthy, they are typically incredulous. Soon they will be back in the doctor's office with reports of further symptoms, or they may simply change doctors. Some go through several doctors a year. Others will resort to "miracle" cures, or they will try to cure themselves, either by pursuing strenuous health regimens or by dosing themselves with pills, of which they typically have large collections.

It should be emphasized that hypochondriacs do not fake their "symptoms." They truly feel the pains they report; they are sincerely afraid that they are about to succumb to some grave disease; and they suffer terribly as a result. Insofar as they cannot be reassured by the medical evidence, their fears are irrational. However, these fears do not have the bizarre quality of the disease delusions experienced by psychotics, who will report that their feet are about to fall off or that their brains are shriveling. Hypochondriacs tend to confine their anxieties to more ordinary syndromes, such as heart disease or cancer, and will generally focus on a single disorder.

Somatization Disorder

A second somatoform pattern is **somatization disorder** (previously known as Briquet's syndrome), characterized by numerous and recurrent physical complaints that have persisted for several years and have caused the person to seek medical help but for which no medical basis can be found. Somatization disorder resembles hypochondriasis in that it involves symptoms with no demonstrable physical cause. Yet the two disorders differ in the focus of the patient's distress. What motivates the hypochondriac is the fear of disease, usually a specific disease; the "symptoms" are troubling not so much in themselves but because they indicate the presence of that disease. In contrast, what bothers the victim of somatization disorder is actually the "symptoms" themselves. There is also a difference in their approach to the "symptoms." Whereas hypochondriacs may try to be scientific, measuring their blood pressure several times a day and carefully reporting the results, victims of somatization disorder usually describe their symptoms in a vague, dramatic, and exaggerated fashion. Finally, the two disorders differ in the number of complaints. Hypochondriacs, as noted, often fear one particular disease, and therefore their complaints tend to be fairly limited. In somatization disorder, on the other hand, the complaints are many and varied. Indeed, *DSM-III-R* requires thirteen different kinds of complaints for this diagnosis to be given. Among the common complaints are headache, heart palpitations, breathing difficulty, nausea, dizziness, deafness, blurred vision, double vision, stomach pain, back pain, and chest pain.

In addition to the distress caused by their imagined symptoms, people with somatization disorder may develop genuine symptoms as a result of unnecessary hospitalization, surgery, and medication. In one case (Pitman and Moffett, 1981), a male patient had averaged one hospitalization per year for the preceding thirty-nine years. During one hospital stay, for a presumed back injury, a doctor had told him that back trouble sometimes leads to sexual problems. Soon the patient began to experience intermittent impotence; by the time of the study, at age fifty-eight, he had been sexually inactive for twenty years. During another hospitalization, unnecessary back surgery left him with a permanent impairment. In the course of his hospital stays and doctors' visits, he was also given a variety of drugs. Further hospitalizations were required for drug overdose.

This case is typical in all respects except the sex of the patient. In contrast to hypochondria, which affects men and women equally, somatization disorder is more common in women than in men. But even among women it is a rare disorder, affecting only two or three women per thousand (Myers et al., 1984).

Conversion Disorder

In hypochondriasis and somatization disorder, there is no physical disability, only fear of or complaints about illness or disability. In **conversion disorder,** on the other hand, there is an actual disability: the loss or impairment of some motor or sensory function. Conversion symptoms vary considerably, but among the most common are blindness, deafness, paralysis, and anesthesia (loss of sensation)—often partial but sometimes total. Like the "symptoms" involved in hypochondriasis and somatization disorder, conversion symptoms are not supported by the medical evidence, but neither are they faked. They are involuntary responses, not under the person's conscious control. At the same time, they contradict the medical facts. Upon examination, for example, the eyes will be found to be perfectly free from defect or damage, and yet the person is unable to see. In this, conversion disorders can be distinguished from what have been called the psychophysiological ("psychosomatic") disorders, such as ulcers, in which there is an observable medical dysfunction. (These disorders will be discussed in Chapter 9.)

Conversion disorder, formerly known as **hysteria,** has played a central role in the history of psychology. As we saw in Chapter 1, it was described by Hippocrates, who believed that it was confined to women—particularly childless women—and was due to the wanderings of a uterus that was not being put to its proper use. (The Greek word for uterus is *hystera;* hence the term *hysteria.*) Idle and frustrated, the uterus traveled around inside the body, creating havoc in various organ systems. The cure that Hippocrates prescribed was marriage.

In the nineteenth century, hysteria served as the focal point for debate between psychogenic and biogenic theory. Indeed, it may be said that psychodynamic theory grew out of the study of hysteria. It was the cure of this disorder through hypnosis—first by Mesmer, then by Liébeault and Bernheim, then by Josef Breuer and his young friend Sigmund Freud—that laid the foundation for the theory of the unconscious. Ironically, Freud's explanation of hysteria stressed the same factor as Hippocrates': sexual conflict. Today, many psychologists reject the sexual interpretation, but it is generally agreed that conversion disorders are the result of *some* psychological conflict. Indeed, conversion disorder is the one syndrome for which *DSM-III-R* asserts a specific psychological cause rather than simply offering a behavioral description. According to the *DSM-III-R* definition, this disorder "is apparently an expression of a psychological conflict or need" (*DSM-III-R,* 1987, p. 257). The manual goes on to cite—but does not explicitly endorse—an essentially psychodynamic explanation of the syndrome. According to this explanation, the conversion symptom serves two important psychological purposes. First, it blocks the individual's awareness of internal conflict; this is called the **primary gain.** In addition, it confers the **secondary gain** of excusing the individual from responsibilities and attracting sympathy and attention.

One reason many psychologists accept the conflict-resolution hypothesis is that many conversion patients (about one-third) seem completely unperturbed by their symptoms—a response known as **la belle in-différence,** or "beautiful indifference." Whereas most people would react with horror to the discovery that they were suddenly half-blind or could no longer walk, "indifferent" conversion patients are undismayed. Typically, they are eager to discuss their symptoms, and will describe them in the fullest and most vivid terms, but they do not seem particularly eager to part with them. This paradoxical reaction has been interpreted by psychodynamic theorists as a sign of the relief that patients experience once their newfound disability supplies a defense against unconscious conflicts and thereby reduces their anxiety.

Conversion disorders represent something of a philosophical paradox. On the one hand, the patient's body appears to be in good health. Biologically, conversion patients *can* do whatever it is that they say they can't do. And often they can be made to do it, either by trickery or under hypnosis or drugs. Further evidence for their lack of organic pathology is that the symptoms are often selective. Conversion "epileptics," for example, seldom injure themselves or lose bladder control during attacks, as true epileptics do. Likewise, in conversion blindness, patients rarely bump into things. Furthermore, victims of conversion blindness, when given visual discrimination tests, will often perform much worse than if they had answered merely at random—a result indicating that they *are* receiving visual input (Sackeim et al., 1979). In short, all evidence points to the conclusion that the conversion patient's body is capable of functioning properly. On the other hand, conversion patients by definition are *not* consciously refusing to use parts of their body. The response is involuntary. Where, then, is the connection between body and consciousness severed? At present, we do not know.

The following case illustrates some characteristic features of this disorder:

> After a minor industrial accident, Ari, a twenty-seven-year-old Israeli, developed paralysis in both legs—a condition for which no organic cause could

be found. The paralysis seemed quite genuine. When pins were pushed into the patient's legs up to the groin, he showed no response whatsoever. Nevertheless, he moved his legs during sleep.

There were several possible explanations for this case. Ari was due shortly to report for military service, and unlike the army, the hospital was an extremely pleasant place. Patients were offered movies, television, and excellent food, and after dinner there was much socializing, which Ari seemed to enjoy. Finally, as a disabled person, Ari would be entitled to a government pension.

Ari's therapists began treatment by making the disability less rewarding. They informed him that because his condition was not organic, he would not be entitled to a pension. They then told him that for the next several weeks he would have to go to bed at eight o'clock, since they were going to give him a drug that required a great deal of sleep. The core of the treatment, however, was the "drug." They told him that it was a new medication that had been very successful in curing paralyzed American veterans of the Vietnam War. Actually, it was a placebo, which the doctors were hoping would work by the power of suggestion and at the same time provide a face-saving mechanism—a way of getting well without having to face the implication that he had been well all along.

As the investigators relate, the drug did its job: "Approximately one hour after his first treatment, a nurse excitedly called us to Ari's room. We rushed to his bedside, where we found that a crowd of staff and patients had gathered. Ari was sitting up, smiling, beads of perspiration on his forehead, tears rolling down his face; he had what appeared to be a look of genuine euphoria. He stated that he was in pain, kept pointing to his toes, and then moved them slightly" (p. 261). On the second day he could move his toes easily. On the fourth day he could walk without crutches. On the sixth day he could do cartwheels. On the seventh day he was discharged from the hospital (adapted from Goldblatt and Munitz, 1976).

With conversion disorder, differential diagnosis is both important and tricky. First, *malingering*—the conscious faking of symptoms in order to avoid some responsibility—must be ruled out. Since diagnosticians cannot read minds, this distinction is sometimes hard to make. However, malingerers are usually cautious and defensive when questioned about their symptoms, since they are afraid of being caught in a lie. Conversion patients, on the other hand, are typically candid and naive and, as we noted, will sometimes talk eagerly and at length about their disabilities.

Second and more difficult is the task of ruling out an actual organic disorder. In some cases, the symptoms constitute "neurological nonsense," as Charcot put it—that is, they directly contradict what we know about the nervous system. For example, in **glove anesthesia,** patients report that the entire hand is numb, from the tips of the fingers to a clear cutoff point at the wrist (see Figure 8.1)—in other words, the area covered by a short glove—whereas if they were suffering from a true neurological impairment, the area of numbness would run in a narrow stripe from the lower arm through one or two of the fingers. Furthermore, the line of demarcation between sensitive and insensitive areas would be much less precise, with some intermediate areas of semisensitivity.

These, however, are the easier cases. In others, the symptoms are uncannily similar to those of true organic disorders. Nevertheless, there may still be certain signs that suggest conversion disorder. These include:

1. *Rapid appearance of symptoms, especially after some psychological trauma.* Organic disorders tend to surface more gradually.

2. *La belle indifférence.* Organic patients are more likely to be upset over their symptoms.

3. *Selective symptoms.* If "paralyzed" legs move during sleep, the paralysis is presumably not organic.

These criteria, in addition to specialized medical tests, are usually the basis for the diagnosis of conversion disorder. However, they are not foolproof—a fact that research has made painfully clear. In one study, the later medical records of fifty-six patients diagnosed as having conversion disorder were compared with the records of fifty-six patients diagnosed as suffering from anxiety or depression. In the "conversion" group, 62.5 percent had since developed signs of organic brain disorder, compared with only 5.3 percent of the anxiety/depression group (Whitlock, 1967). In a more recent study (Watson and Buranen, 1979), involving forty cases diagnosed as conversion, 25 percent were found, in a ten-year follow-up, to have been misdiagnosed; in most cases, the true problem, again, was organic brain disorder. Clearly, a substantial proportion of "conversion disorders" are in fact neurological disorders in their early stages, when they are hardest to detect.

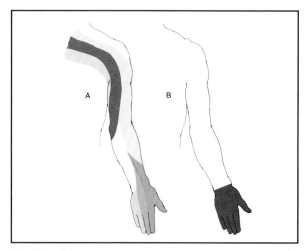

FIGURE 8.1

A patient who complained of numbness in the hand might be diagnosed as suffering from conversion disorder if the area of the hand affected showed that a disorder of the nervous system was not responsible. The skin areas served by nerves in the arm are shown in A. The "glove anesthesia" shown in B could not result from damage to these nerves.

Conversion disorder is described as rare by many authorities. It is possible, however, that what is rare is merely the *diagnosis* of conversion disorder. Conversion patients, after all, believe they have a medical, not a psychological, problem; therefore they go to physicians, not to psychotherapists. As we have noted, differential diagnosis is quite tricky. Furthermore, many physicians may associate conversion disorder with the more dramatic and bizarre symptoms of late-nineteenth-century hysteria—glove anesthesia, inability to swallow, paralysis, and the like—thus allowing the more ordinary cases, such as back trouble and blurred vision, to slip by unnoticed. In short, it seems likely that just as many "conversion disorders" are actually organic, so many conditions diagnosed as organic are actually conversion disorders (Jones, 1980). One researcher estimates that 20 to 25 percent of all patients admitted to hospital general medical services are conversion cases (Engel, 1970). Another study, of students in a naval aviation academy, found that 16 percent of those reporting to the health service had conversion symptoms (Mucha and Reinhardt, 1970). Interestingly, almost three-quarters of these cases involved impaired vision, the very thing to disqualify one from flying. The researchers theorized that in situations where failure is unacceptable—as in an elite naval aviation school—the rate of conversion disorders will rise accordingly.

DISSOCIATIVE DISORDERS

As the name indicates, the **dissociative disorders** involve the dissociation, or splitting apart, of components of the personality that are normally integrated. As a result, some psychological function—identity, memory, control over motor behavior—is screened out of consciousness. We shall examine three dissociative syndromes: amnesia, fugue, and multiple personality.

Psychogenic Amnesia

As we shall see in Chapter 16, **amnesia,** the partial or total forgetting of past experiences, often appears in organic brain syndromes. However, it may also occur without organic cause, as a response to psychological stress. In addition to medical tests for organic pathology, there are several ways of distinguishing between biogenic and psychogenic amnesia. (Note the similarity between these criteria and those for conversion disorder.) First, psychogenic amnesia tends to appear suddenly, following a severe psychological trauma, such as the death of one's parent; it also remits suddenly. Second, amnesia is often selective; the "blank" period tends to include events that most people would want to forget—either a precipitating trauma, as just noted, or perhaps an unacceptable action such as an extramarital affair. Third, psychogenic amnesiacs are often much less disturbed than those around them over their condition—an indifference that, as in conversion disorder, suggests relief from conflict. Finally, because the events forgotten in psychogenic amnesia are simply screened out of consciousness rather than lost altogether (as is the case in organic amnesia), they can often be recovered under hypnosis.

There are four patterns of psychogenic amnesia. First and most common is **localized amnesia,** in which all events occurring during a circumscribed period of time are blocked out. For example, a man who has survived a fire in which the rest of his family died might ring down the curtain on everything that happened from the time of the fire until three days later. Second and less common is **selective amnesia,** in which the person makes "spot" erasures, forgetting only certain events that occurred during a circumscribed period of time. In the above case, for example, the man might recall the fire engines coming and the ambulance taking him to the hospital, but forget seeing his children carried out of the house before he went to the hospital and identifying their bodies a day later. Third is **generalized amnesia,** in which the person forgets his or her entire past life; though this is the kind that tends to turn up in novels and movies, it is actually rare. Finally, another rare pattern is **continuous amnesia,** in which the person forgets all events after a specific period and up to the present, including events that occur *after* the onset of the amnesia. For example, if the amnesia begins on Monday, the individual will not know on Wednesday what he or she did on Tuesday, to say nothing of prior events. While some patterns are more common than others, amnesia in general is rare. However, its incidence tends to spiral among victims of war and natural disasters. Indeed, many of the reported cases of amnesia were soldiers in World War I and World War II.

Predictably, confusion and disorientation almost always accompany amnesia, especially generalized and continuous amnesia, in which all or much of the individual's past is blacked out. Typically, patients in these categories do not know who or where they are, do not recognize family or friends, and cannot tell you their name, address, or anything else about themselves. Nevertheless, habits, tastes, and basic learned abilities generally remain intact. People who disliked spinach will go on disliking it during the amnesia. They will also be able to read and write, add and subtract. Often they can execute even more specialized tasks. Typists will still be able to type, and carpenters to build cabinets, though they will not know that they once did this for a living.

Some psychogenic amnesias continue for the rest of a person's life. Most, however, remit abruptly and spontaneously anywhere from a day to several years after the onset.

Psychogenic Fugue

A condition related to amnesia is **psychogenic fugue,** in which the individual takes a sudden, unexpected trip or excursion, forgetting his or her identity

A person in a fugue state, fleeing from an intolerable life situation, not only forgets his or her identity but travels to a new place and takes on a new identity. (Dan McCoy/Rainbow)

and assuming a new identity. Fugue, then, is a sort of traveling amnesia, but it is more elaborate than amnesia. While amnesiacs, in their confusion, may wander about aimlessly, fugue patients are purposeful in their movements. Furthermore, while amnesiacs may also forget their identity, fugue patients go one step further and manufacture a new identity.

The length and elaborateness of fugues vary considerably. Some patients may go no farther than the next town, spend the day in a movie house, check into a hotel under a new name, and recover by morning. Such relatively subdued adventures are the usual pattern. In rare cases, however, patients will travel to foreign countries, assume an utterly new identity, fabricate a detailed past history, and pursue a totally new life for months or even years. During fugue, patients will appear fairly normal to observers. When at last they "wake up" (which, as in amnesia, occurs

suddenly), they will be completely amnesic for the events that occurred during the fugue. The last thing they remember is leaving for work that morning; as for how they got to where they are, they have no idea.

Like amnesia, fugue is generally rare, but more common in wartime and after natural disasters. Again like amnesia, it tends to occur after a severe psychological trauma and—as the term (derived from the Latin word for "flight") suggests—seems to function as an escape from unbearable psychological stress. The following case shows both the precipitating trauma and the escape motivation:

Bernice L., a middle-aged housewife, had been raised in a stern, loveless, and fanatically religious home. She grew up shy and anxious, but when she went away to college, she began to "bloom" a bit.

This was largely the work of her roommate, a pretty and vivacious girl by the name of Rose P., who introduced Bernice to her friends, encouraged her to develop her talent for the piano, and in general drew her out. In their junior year, however, their friendship suffered a crisis. Rose became engaged to a young man with whom Bernice too promptly fell in love. When the man married Rose, Bernice fell into a severe depression. She returned home for a while, but at her parents' insistence, she eventually went back to school.

Upon graduation, Bernice married a young clergyman for whom she felt little attraction but whom her parents approved of. They had two children and eventually settled in a small, dull town not unlike her childhood home. Bernice had few satisfactions in life other than her children and her happy memories of her first two years in college. Then, when she was thirty-seven years old, her younger and favorite child, a musically talented boy, died. The next day she disappeared, and for four years she could not be traced.

Later, with the help of a therapist, Bernice recalled some of the events of those four years. Totally amnesic for her past life, she had returned to her old college town. There, under the name of Rose P., she began giving piano lessons, and within two years she became assistant director of the local conservatory of music. She made a few friends, but she never spoke of her past life, for it was still a complete blank to her. Then one day she was recognized by a woman who had known both her and Rose P. during college. Bernice's husband, now a minister in Chicago, was located, and under protest she was returned to him.

In therapy, Bernice's amnesia was finally dispelled. She reassumed her old identity, readjusted to her husband, who proved patient and sympathetic, and settled down to a normal life in Chicago (adapted from Masserman, 1961, pp. 35–37).

Multiple Personality

Perhaps the most bizarre of the dissociative disorders is **multiple personality,** in which the individual alternates between two or more distinct personalities, each well integrated and well developed, with its own tastes, habits, memories, and learned behaviors. (Sometimes called "split personality," multiple personality should not be confused with schizophrenia,

which is an altogether different disorder. See Chapter 14.) The first case of multiple personality to receive extensive professional attention—the case of "Miss Beauchamp," who may have had as many as seventeen personalities—was reported by Prince in 1905. Ever since, this disorder has held a certain fascination for the public, as shown by the immense popularity of Thigpen and Cleckley's *The Three Faces of Eve* (1957), both book and movie, and by the best seller *Sybil* (Schreiber, 1974), about a girl with sixteen personalities. However, the amount of attention this disorder has received is disproportionate to its prevalence. It is a rare condition.

There are many different patterns of multiple personality—patterns that become more complicated as the number of personalities increases. In the simplest form, called **alternating personality,** two identities alternate with one another, each having amnesia for the thoughts and actions of the other. A second pattern involves one or more dominant personalities and one or more subordinate ones. While the dominant personality is ostensibly controlling the person's behavior, the subordinate personality, fully aware of the thoughts and actions of the dominant personality, continues to operate subconsciously and to make its presence felt now and then through various covert means. In such cases, the subordinate personality is said to be **coconscious** (Prince, 1905) with the dominant personality. When the coconscious personality finally surfaces, it can discuss in detail the interesting problems of the other personality. Of such a type was the celebrated case described in *The Three Faces of Eve* (1957):

> Eve White was the original dominant personality. She had no knowledge of the existence of her second personality, Eve Black, although Eve Black had been alternating with Eve White for some years. Whenever Eve Black surfaced, all that Eve White could report was that she had "black-outs." Eve Black, on the other hand, was coconscious with Eve White, knew everything that she did, and would talk about her with flippancy and contempt. Eve White was bland, quiet, and serious—a rather dull personality. Eve Black, on the other hand, was carefree, mischievous, and uninhibited. She would "come out" at the most inappropriate times, leaving Eve White with hangovers, bills, and a reputation in local bars that she could not explain. During treatment, there emerged a third personality, Jane, who was coconscious with both Eve White and Eve

A Case of Multiple Personality: Billy Milligan

In 1977, a man named William Stanley Milligan was arrested for the rapes of three women in Columbus, Ohio. Two of the women positively identified him as the Ohio State University "campus rapist"; the other victim tentatively identified him. Fingerprints found at the scene of one of the crimes matched those of Milligan, who was out on parole after serving time for robbery. It seemed to be an open-and-shut case. But not until Milligan twice tried to commit suicide in jail while awaiting trial did it occur to his lawyers that he might need psychiatric help.

The report of the examining psychologists and psychiatrists profoundly altered the nature of the case. At the time of the trial they had identified at least ten different personalities somehow coexisting within Milligan. These included the core personality, "Billy"; Authur, an emotionless, self-taught Englishman, who dominated the other personalities; Ragen, a Yugoslavian with extraordinary strength, an associate of criminals and addicts, who was known as the protector of women and children and the "keeper of hate"; Allen, an eighteen-year-old manipulator and con artist; Tommy, age sixteen, a belligerent and antisocial personality, a landscape painter, and an escape artist; Danny, fourteen, a timid painter of still lifes; eight-year-old David, who "absorbed" the pain and suffering of the others; Christene, a three-year-old English girl; Christopher, her thirteen-year-old troubled brother; and Adalane, nineteen, an introverted lesbian.

The astonishing range of talents and dispositions manifested by these personalities showed up from time to time in Billy's jail experience. For instance, after his second suicide attempt he was placed in solitary confinement in a straitjacket. When his jailers looked in on him, they found him fast asleep with the straitjacket under his head as a pillow. Presumably, Tommy, the escape artist, had effected his release.

Billy was eventually found not guilty by reason of insanity—the first case of a multiple personality being acquitted of a major crime under that plea. Milligan was also the first Ohio defendant to come under a new state law that called for treating a person acquitted of a crime by reason of insanity as a mental patient, not as criminally insane. Accordingly, he was sent to the Athens (Ohio) Mental Health Center, where he was placed under the care of David Caul, a psychiatrist who had experience in treating cases of multiple personality.

Caul soon discovered that there were *more* than ten personalities; there were, in addition, thirteen personalities called "undesirables" by Arthur because they rebelled against his control. Among others, these personalities included a thug with a Brooklyn accent, a snob, a small-time criminal, an impostor, and a practical joker. Finally, there was the Teacher—the fusion of all twenty-three alter egos. Described as "Billy all in one piece," the Teacher had total recall of the events in Billy's life. In his sessions with Caul, Billy's personalities fused more and more into one competent person. Soon he was allowed unattended trips into town and weekend furloughs. These privileges, however, provoked anger and resentment among Columbus citizens, who still feared Billy's potential for violent behavior.

Under the glare of unfavorable publicity and open public hostility, Billy's personalities once again defused. Aggressive personalities came to the fore, causing Billy to be sent to a maximum-security institution for the criminally insane. Here he was treated as a psychopathic schizophrenic rather than a multiple personality. His lawyers are now trying to obtain his release to a less restrictive environment, where he can resume treatment for multiple personality.

Even though several able and experienced psychiatrists have testified that Billy's disorder is multiple personality, traceable to traumatic abuse he suffered as a boy at the hands of his stepfather, many professionals and laypeople alike suspect that Billy Milligan is faking. Such suspicion is typical of this disorder, and is sometimes justified. But it is difficult to see how one person could carry off acting out so many roles on such a consistent basis and in such a convincing manner. Still, as one journalist has noted, "Only time will tell whether Milligan has played the world for a fool or is one of its saddest victims" (quoted in Keyes, 1981, p. xiii).

Source: Daniel Keyes, *The Minds of Billy Milligan*, N.Y.: Random House, 1981.

Black, though she had no memory of their activities up to the time of her appearance. More mature than the other two, Jane seemed to have emerged as the result of the therapeutic process.

Eve's problems with multiple personalities did not stop in 1957 with the publication of *The Three Faces of Eve*. In 1975, a woman called Chris Sizemore, an apparently normal and unremarkable middle-aged housewife from Fairfax, Virginia, revealed that she was "Eve" and that Eve Black, Eve White, and Jane were only three of the many personalities with which she had struggled throughout her life. Indeed, Mrs. Sizemore had manifested twenty-one separate identities, each with its own speech patterns, habits, preferences and moral code. The personalities invariably came in sets of three, with considerable conflict among them. "If I had learned to sew as one personality and then tried to sew as another, I couldn't do it. Driving a car was the same. Some of my personalities couldn't drive" (Nunes, 1975, p. 4).

In the early years, a particular personality would dominate for a period of several days. Later, Mrs. Sizemore's personality would change at least once a day. The transition from one personality to another was usually marked by a sudden and very painful headache. The headache would last for about ten seconds, during which Mrs. Sizemore was conscious of nothing. When the pain disappeared, a new personality would be in control.

Mrs. Sizemore reported that she is now recovered (Sizemore and Pittillo, 1977), a fact she ascribed to the eventual realization that all of her different personalities were truly parts of herself, and not invaders from the outside. Whatever the cause, Mrs. Sizemore has been able to stay with one stable personality for an extended period. "You don't know how wonderful it is," she said, "to go to bed at night and know that it will be you that wakes up the next day" (Nunes, 1975, p. 4).

As with Eve, many cases of multiple personality seem to involve personalities that are polar opposites: one conformist, duty-doing, "nice" personality and one rebellious, impulsive, "naughty" personality. In this respect, multiple personalities seem to be extreme cases of the normal conflict between self-indulgence and restraint—or, as the Freudians would put it, between id and superego—that all human beings experience in some measure. It is relevant to note that most victims of multiple personality report sexual molestation and severe physical abuse during childhood (Greaves, 1980), for such traumas would be likely to intensify internal conflicts. Such was the case

with Billy Milligan, whose story is told in the box on page 187. Abused children may attempt to distance themselves from the horrible reality of being assaulted by developing different personalities.

In the past decade, there has been a marked increase in the number of reported multiple-personality patients. Because of the dramatic nature of multiple personality and the media attention it receives, some individuals may begin to describe their inner conflicts in terms of different personalities. The fact that most cases of multiple personality have turned up in the United States, where public interest in this disorder seems greatest, and that therapists have often used hypnosis in getting multiple-personality patients to switch from one personality to another raises the possibility that the power of suggestion, along with the patient's desire to please the therapist, may have played some role in transforming severe but less exotic emotional problems into more interesting "multiple personalities" (Rycroft, 1978).

Yet multiple personality undoubtedly does exist, leaving mental health professionals with the job of distinguishing the true cases from the false. Eich (1986) has proposed that one criterion might be the nature of the accompanying amnesia. In true multiple personality, amnesia is usually asymmetrical: material learned by the primary personality is remembered by all of the secondary personalities, but material learned by a secondary personality is not known to the other secondary personalities or to the primary personality. In false multiple-personality cases, on the other hand, "amnesia" is usually symmetrical—that is, material learned by one personality is unknown to all other personalities.

PERSPECTIVES ON THE ANXIETY, SOMATOFORM, AND DISSOCIATIVE DISORDERS

In Chapters 2, 3, 4, and 5 we presented a general overview of the psychodynamic, behavioral, humanistic-existential, and neuroscience approaches to abnormal behavior. In the present section, we shall see how adherents of each of these perspectives would interpret and treat anxiety, somatoform, and dissociative disorders. (Since treatment will be discussed in detail in Chapters 20 and 21, our coverage of the various treatments for these disorders will be brief.)

The Psychodynamic Perspective: Neurosis

The psychodynamic view of the anxiety, somatoform, and dissociative disorders is difficult to summarize, for the simple reason that these disorders, known as the neuroses[*] in the psychodynamic vocabulary, have been the major focus of psychodynamic writing. The books and articles offering different psychodynamic interpretations of the neuroses could, and do, fill whole libraries. Our discussion of the psychodynamic perspective on these disorders represents only the most general outline.

The Roots of Neurosis   It is a fundamental concept of psychodynamic theory that anxiety is at the root of neurosis. Freud, as we have seen, argued that anxiety stemmed not just from external threats but also from internal ones, in the form of unacceptable id impulses attempting to break through into consciousness and behavior. Predictably, it is this latter type of anxiety that psychodynamic theory sees as the major source of neurosis. The problem with neurotics is that the cold war among the various components of their psyches has turned into open battle. The id pushes in one direction, toward the conscious awareness and enactment of its sexual or aggressive impulse. And the ego, knowing that the id impulse is unacceptable in terms of both reality and the superego's ideals, works in the opposite direction, pushing the impulse back into the unconscious through repression and other defense mechanisms. As we noted in Chapter 2, this push and counterpush goes on all the time in normal lives and usually works well enough so that anxiety over the id impulse is never experienced consciously. In some cases, however, the anxiety is so intense that it *is* experienced consciously, with debilitating results. Or it is kept at bay only through the employment of extremely rigid defense mechanisms. It is these situations that, according to the psychodynamic position, constitute neurotic behavior.

In cases where anxiety is experienced chronically and directly, without elaborate defense, what we see is generalized anxiety disorder. The cause is re-

pressed, but the anxiety leaks through. In the panic attack, the cause—that is, the id impulse—moves closer to the boundaries of the conscious mind; the ego responds with desperate efforts at repression, and a state of maximum conflict ensues. Once the ego regains the upper hand and the impulse is once again safely repressed, the attack passes.

Usually, however, the defenses marshaled against anxiety are considerably more elaborate than ordinary repression, and it is these defenses that appear as the symptoms of neurotic disorder. In phobic disorders, for example, displacement may be at work. The classic illustration of such displacement in phobia is Freud's case of "Little Hans" (1909). Hans was a five-year-old boy who refused to go out into the street for fear that a horse would bite him. Freud's interpretation of the phobia was that Hans was caught up in a fierce oedipal struggle, in which his strong attachment to his mother was accompanied by extreme hostility toward his father. As usual in oedipal conflicts, the hostility was accompanied by intense anxiety that the father would retaliate by castrating the boy. Therefore Hans displaced his fear and hostility onto horses (a logical substitution, since his father would sometimes play "horsie" with him) and by avoiding horses was able to relieve his anxiety.

In amnesia, and in all dissociative disorders involving amnesia, psychodynamic theorists see total repression at work. However, psychodynamic theory would suggest that in fugue and particularly in multiple personality, the individual acts out the unconscious impulse, directly or symbolically, in the dissociative state while the ego protects itself from consciousness of the forbidden impulse by maintaining amnesia for the episode.

Obsessive-compulsive disorder may be interpreted in a number of ways, depending on the nature of the obsession or compulsion. In the case of a man who is obsessed with the fear that he will kill his wife in her sleep, for example, psychodynamic theory would suggest that the unconscious aggressive impulse has in fact made its way into the conscious mind. On the other hand, cleanliness rituals and obsessions with germs would be interpreted as a combination of fixation and reaction formation, the ego defending itself against the anal desire to soil, to play with feces, and to be generally messy and destructive.

In hypochondriasis and somatization disorder, psychodynamic theory would see a strong element of regression. According to this view, patients with such disorders defend themselves against the anxieties of

---

[*] Since psychodynamic writers call these disorders "neuroses" and those who have them "neurotics," we shall do the same in discussing the psychodynamic perspective.

adult life by regressing to the state of a sick child, where they hope to receive extra attention, support, and "babying." As we saw earlier, these extra satisfactions that the neurotic receives in the form of comforting and relief from responsibilities are called secondary gains. The primary gain, in hypochondriasis, somatization disorder, and all other neuroses, is the relief of anxiety through the use of the defense mechanism.

Finally, in conversion disorder, the conversion symptom serves simultaneously to block awareness of the forbidden impulse and to express it, by incapacitating some part of the body related to that impulse. Paralysis, for example, might be a defense against the expression of murderous anger. Likewise, a person with glove anesthesia may be reacting to an urge to masturbate or to guilt over past episodes of masturbation. Here, as in hand-washing rituals, we see what Freud meant when he said that neurotic symptoms have symbolic significance. Because the symptom is a defense against a specific impulse, it serves as a clue to the nature of the impulse.

Treating Neurosis   We have seen that according to psychodynamic theory the job of maintaining elaborate defenses monopolizes and exhausts the ego, so that it has little energy left for the constructive role of furthering the individual's work and personal relationships. The goal of psychodynamic therapy is to remedy this situation by exposing and neutralizing the material that the ego is spending its energy to repress. The assumption is that once the terrors of the unconscious are confronted, they will lose their power to terrify. In other words, if patients can face and understand their repressed conflicts, the ego will be liberated from the all-consuming task of masking these conflicts and can devote itself to more useful and creative tasks.

Orthodox psychoanalysis uses two basic techniques to achieve this goal. The first is **free association.** Here the patient lies back on a couch and simply says whatever comes to mind, without the censorship of reason, logic, or "decency." Unconscious material will eventually surface and will be interpreted by the therapist—that is, the therapist will point out how the patient's remarks indicate this or that unconscious preoccupation. The second technique is **dream interpretation,** whereby patients report their dreams as accurately as possible and the therapist explores with the patient the elements of the dreams

as symbols of unconscious wishes and conflicts. Free association is traditionally a part of dream interpretation; the patient free-associates to the content of the dream. In other forms of psychodynamic therapy—far more common today than classical psychoanalysis—underlying conflicts are excavated in a more conventional manner, with patients sitting face to face with the therapist and simply discussing their problems as frankly as possible.

It is assumed that when the therapist begins touching sensitive parts of the patient's unconscious, the patient will begin to show **resistance,** arguing with the therapist, changing the subject, missing appointments, and so forth. Because resistance is an unconscious process, this too must be interpreted to the patient. A final and critical component of psychodynamic therapy is analysis of the **transference.** Presumably, patients transfer to their therapists the love and also the hostility that as children they felt for their parents. These emotions, again, are interpreted to the patient, in the effort to clarify conflicts left over from the parent–child relationship.

In treating patients with dissociative disorders and posttraumatic stress disorders, the therapist may also use hypnosis. Under hypnosis the patient is encouraged to recall the traumatic experiences to which he or she has been subjected. This unleashing of the traumatic memory relieves some portion of the patient's anxiety. Then the patient and therapist work together to analyze the patient's defenses against this anxiety.

The Behavioral Perspective: Learning to Be Anxious

As mentioned earlier, behavioral researchers have often challenged the psychodynamic argument that anxiety is at the root of all these disorders. Behaviorists distinguish between observable anxiety, as in the anxiety disorders, and inferred anxiety, as in the conversion reactions and dissociative disorders. Behavioral theory and treatment have focused primarily on disorders in which anxiety is observable.

How We Learn Anxiety   The behaviorists have put forth a number of theories to explain the anxiety disorders. One is that these disorders are engendered through avoidance learning, a two-stage process proposed by Mowrer (1948) and described briefly in Chapter 3. The process is as follows:

Stage 1: In the course of the person's experience, some neutral stimulus is paired with an aversive stimulus and thus, through respondent conditioning, becomes anxiety-arousing.

Stage 2: The person avoids the conditioned stimulus, and since this avoidance results in relief from anxiety (i.e., negative reinforcement), the avoidance response, via operant conditioning, becomes habitual.

Imagine, for example, a man who periodically gets drunk and beats his young daughter. Soon the signs of the father's drinking (CS) will become paired in the child's mind with the pain of the beating (UCS), and she will experience anxiety (CR) at the first sign that her father is intoxicated. Eventually this anxiety may generalize to the father as a whole, drunk or sober, in which case he himself becomes the CS. She therefore avoids him, and every time she does so, her anxiety is relieved, thus reinforcing the avoidance response. In time, the anxiety may further generalize—to all men who drink or indeed to men in general. Again she responds with avoidance, and again avoidance produces negative reinforcement in the form of anxiety relief. Needless to say, this process may later result in serious psychological difficulties.

In the view of many behaviorists, the disorders that we have discussed in this chapter are variations on this avoidance-reinforced anxiety. Agoraphobia, as we have seen, often develops as a way of avoiding having a panic attack in public. In simple phobia, the avoidance strategy is less global—one need not stay confined to the home in order to avoid air travel—but in both cases the avoidance is presumably "stamped in" by negative reinforcement. In obsessive-compulsive disorder, the anxious person has found that some action, such as hand washing, reduces his or her anxiety. The action thus becomes a form of avoidance, strengthened once again through negative reinforcement. Consequently, however painful or inconvenient, it develops into a habit.

The avoidance-learning theory focuses entirely on empirical evidence—concrete stimulus, observable response—without concern for the *thoughts* that may be involved in anxiety. Many studies, however, indicate that such an explanation is insufficient. To begin with, a painful stimulus need not be concrete in order

to arouse anxiety. Cognitive events such as mental images and verbal self-statements can also engender anxiety responses. Furthermore, the stimulus need not be experienced directly. People can also acquire anxiety responses vicariously, by watching others react with pain to a given stimulus. In laboratory studies, even monkeys have learned to be afraid just by watching other monkeys respond with fear to an unfamiliar object (Cook et al., 1985; Mineka et al., 1984). In human beings, not even observation is required. To feel fear while walking through a high-crime neighborhood, you do not have to have seen someone mugged in that part of town. You need only have heard or read that that neighborhood is dangerous (Bootzin and Max, 1980).

What all this suggests is that cognitive processes such as memory and expectation play an important role in the acquisition of anxiety responses. Such processes may also determine the behavioral *response* to anxiety. Albert Bandura (1977, 1982) has shown that the best predictor of avoidance behavior is not the amount of anxiety experienced but rather "efficacy expectations"—people's expectations, based on past performance, as to how well they will be able to cope with the situation. Many actors and dancers, for example, regularly suffer intense stage fright, to the point of vomiting before performances. Yet still they go onstage, presumably because they know from experience that they can still put on a good performance despite their anxiety.

A recent theory related to efficacy expectations is the "fear of fear" interpretation of panic disorder (Barlow, in press). In this view, the physiological changes that accompany the panic attack—increased heart rate, sweating, and so forth—become conditioned stimuli for further panic attacks: when these changes start to occur, even for ordinary reasons, the person begins to feel afraid of a coming attack, and in a classic spiral, the fear intensifies the physiological reactions and vice versa until the attack occurs. This fear of fear can be seen in many kinds of anxiety disorder, but above all in panic disorder (Reiss et al., 1986).

Posttraumatic stress disorders are viewed by behaviorists as responses to extremely aversive situations that cannot be avoided, so that escape from anxiety is impossible. For the prisoner of war, for example, there is no way of avoiding the fear of death or punishment that marks his daily existence. And the "psychic numbing" that POWs often manifest would be interpreted by the behaviorist as the only possible means of escape remaining to them—psychological escape. Similarly, behaviorists would say that for the person whose livelihood or family or both are wiped out in a flood, the sudden deprivation of normal positive reinforcements results in the extinction of normal behaviors, leaving the person inert and depressed.

In somatoform and dissociative disorders there is less observable anxiety, and behaviorists are likely to interpret these disorders as the result of the person's adopting a social role that is reinforced by its consequences (Ullmann and Krasner, 1975). For a man who must report for military duty, a conversion paralysis may be a highly rewarding condition, as in the case of Ari, presented above. Likewise, a self-doubting violinist who develops a hysterical cramp in her bowing arm salvages her self-esteem and spares herself bad reviews, poor ticket sales, and difficulties in getting concert engagements. In dissociative reactions such as amnesia and fugue, many consequences are dramatically changed for the better as a result of the loss of memory for painful events.

Unlearning Anxiety   We have already mentioned in Chapter 3 the behaviorists' pragmatic approach to treatment. Behavioral therapy does not concern itself greatly with how the symptoms arose. Instead, it simply aims at removing them.

For the anxiety disorders the behaviorists have evolved a set of related techniques aimed at reducing the anxiety through graduated exposure to the feared stimulus. One classic technique is **systematic desensitization** (Wolpe, 1973), already described briefly in Chapter 3. In this technique, patients draw up a "hierarchy of fears"—a list of increasingly anxiety-arousing situations culminating in the situation they most fear (e.g., holding a snake, being pressed against other people in a crowded elevator). Then they are taught to relax their muscles as completely as possible, and in this state of relaxation they imagine the situations in their hierarchy one by one, progressing from the least feared to the most feared over a number of therapy sessions. By the end of the treatment, if it is successful, they are able to imagine their most anxiety-arousing stimulus and still remain relaxed—a response that in most cases will generalize to the real-life situation.

A variation on this technique, called **in vivo desensitization,** involves leading patients through their hierarchies in the real-life situations themselves. For example, a dog-phobic person, usually in the company of the therapist, will first look at pictures of dogs, then listen to a dog barking in the next room, then enter a room where there is a caged dog, then go within ten feet of the dog, and so on, until at last he or she is able to remain relaxed in the presence of dogs.

In the treatment of phobias and obsessive-compulsive disorder, the therapist will often combine modeling with the sort of practicing just described. With a compulsive hand washer, for example, the therapist would first model the act of touching something "unclean," then encourage the patient to do it as well, with the stipulation that he or she must not resort to the ritual. With repetition, this procedure desensitizes the patient to the fear and thus makes the ritual unnecessary (Rachman and Hodgson, 1980).

Modeling also provides an opportunity for therapists to teach patients new cognitive strategies, by alerting them to self-defeating thoughts that they may engage in and by showing them how to combat such thoughts. For instance, in the procedure just described, the therapist might say out loud, while touching the "unclean" matter, "I can't do this. This problem has been with me for years, and there's no way of solving it now." Then the therapist would "answer" such thoughts: "If other people can do it, so can I. There's nothing lethal about this stuff. It's just soft and sticky." Later, when patients are on their own and are assailed by self-defeating thoughts, they will have some way of answering them (Meichenbaum, 1977).

While the last method addresses cognitive processes directly, cognitive factors such as attitudes, personal goals, and mental images also mediate the other techniques. On a more concrete level, all these treatment strategies depend both on respondent conditioning (the pairing of the feared stimulus with a new, relaxed response) and on operant conditioning, in the form of extinction (the removal of the reward of anxiety relief via avoidance) and in the form of positive reinforcement (praise from the therapist plus the simple and potent reward of success).

Reinforcement can also be manipulated more directly. Brady and Lind (1968), for example, report treating a conversion blindness by reinforcing the patient for gradually "seeing" more and more. On the other hand, maladaptive symptoms can be extinguished by removing the reinforcements that are maintaining them. As was demonstrated in the case of Ari, conversion patients may improve considerably once they are deprived of reinforcement such as financial compensation and release from work obligations (Sackeim et al., 1979). Anxiety disorders too may involve some positive reinforcement and consequently may be alleviated by the elimination of such reinforcement. In the case of George, the obsessive-compulsive, the exceedingly elaborate anticontamination ritual obviously depended to some extent on the father's collaboration, which, as a form of attention, was probably reinforcing to the patient. With such a case, the behavioral therapist might well begin by instructing the father not to participate in the ritual.

The Humanistic-Existential Perspective: The Individual and Society

Like psychodynamic theorists, humanistic-existential theorists see the disorders we have discussed in this chapter as stemming from anxiety over intrapsychic conflicts. What is unique about the humanistic-existential approach is that it conceptualizes this anxiety not simply as an individual problem but, in a larger sense, as the predictable outcome of conflicts between the individual and the society. Carl Rogers (1961), for example, insisted that as long as societies thwart the natural goodness of human beings, oppose their innate drive for self-actualization, and frustrate their search for meaning, anxiety and psychological disturbance are inevitable.

The Impaired Self-Concept   According to the humanists, the seat of anxiety is the self-concept. In administering the Q-sort (Chapter 7), humanistic psychologists have found that patients entering therapy tend to have lofty notions of what they would like to be and negative views of what they actually are. In other words, there is a great discrepancy between the self-concept and the ideal self. The humanists see this discrepancy as the result of a hostile and rejecting upbringing. The child grows up being told that he or she *should* be many fine things and falls pitifully short of these ideals. Hence the deep split between the self-concept and the ideal self. Yet the individual goes on striving for actualization, and the conflict between this effort and the restrictive self-concept is what produces anxiety. The person may also manufacture elaborate defenses (e.g., conversion disorders, fugue) against his or her anxiety. Even more important than the symptoms, however, is the retardation of personal growth. To integrate new experiences and to generate new goals, people must be able to see themselves as being many different things and as capable of being many more things. Thus a narrow and negative self-concept makes self-actualization impossible. More than anything else, "neurotics" are people who are blocked in their growth.

Existential theorists would emphasize not so much the drive for self-actualization as the drive for authenticity. According to this view, "neurotics" are simply people who are not as successful as others in being inauthentic. While others have actually forgotten their true selves, "neurotics" are still aware of the split between the true self and the false, conforming self that society forces them to adopt. Hence their anxiety. And this anxiety further impedes their ability to make authentic decisions.

Rebuilding the Damaged Self   Although humanistic-existential therapists are quite individual in their approaches, they all emphasize the fact that the responsibility for change lies with the client. All the therapist can do is create an emotional environment in which change may take place.

One of the most popular humanistic treatment approaches is **client-centered therapy,** designed by Carl Rogers (1951). In Rogers' view (1980), what psychologically troubled people most need is not to be analyzed, judged, or advised, but simply to be "heard"—that is, to be truly understood and respected by another human being. Therefore, the primary effort of client-centered therapists is to apply all their powers of attention, intuition, and empathy to the task of grasping what the client is actually feeling. To show that they have understood, they "mirror" the feelings, restating them to the client. This gives clients the sense that their inner life has some validity. It also helps them to expand their self-concept, incorporating into it *all* their feelings and experiences instead of sorting them into separate mental pigeonholes of "what I am" (bad, weak) and "what I should be" (good, strong). Rogers (1951) demonstrated that this mirroring process, along with the "unconditional regard" that the therapist gives the client, does in fact improve the self-concept.

Existential therapies for "neurotic" patients are perhaps even less directive than humanistic therapies. In recent years there has been an increasing push toward a completely phenomenological approach, with therapists attempting to exclude from the therapeutic situation all their own preconceptions, even their convictions about authenticity, freedom, and other pillars of existential theory. As we saw in Chapter 4, some existential therapists will state their theoretical principles at the outset of therapy and then, insofar as they are able, lay them aside—a technique called "bracketing." The idea is to remove any last impediment to the therapist's full empathic participation in the patient's subjective world.

As for more specific techniques, the existentialists, like the humanists, are less concerned with symptoms than with restoring the patient's sense of wholeness and freedom. For example, in a technique called **paradoxical intention,** originated by Viktor Frankl (1975a), patients are told to indulge their symptoms, even to exaggerate them. A person with a checking compulsion, for example, might be encouraged to spend the entire day doing nothing but checking the doors to see if they are locked. In this way, the person comes to learn that the symptom can be controlled; if the behavior can be performed more frequently, it can also be performed less frequently. Furthermore, through deliberate enactment, the person masters his or her *fear* of the symptom, a fear that can be very important in maintaining the disorder.

The Neuroscience Perspective: Heredity and Biochemistry

Genetic Research   Evidence for a genetic component in most of the anxiety, somatoform, and dissociative disorders is not particularly strong. Generalized anxiety disorder does seem to run in families. For example, a study comparing the relatives of 112 individuals with anxiety disorder with the relatives of 110 controls found that 18 percent of the parents, siblings, and children of the anxiety disorder group could be diagnosed as having anxiety disorder, as compared with 3 percent of the relatives of the control group (Noyes et al., 1978). But as we have seen, family studies provide the least valid of genetic evidence. Twin studies of the combined "neurotic" disorders have turned up a concordance rate of 53 percent in MZ twins versus 40 percent in DZ twins (Rosenthal, 1970), but this is not a persuasive differential. (Remember that in a disorder with a strong genetic basis, we would expect to find the concordance rate in MZ twins to be at least double that in DZ twins.)

The only disorder discussed in this chapter for which there is compelling genetic evidence is panic disorder. Not only is it more likely to be shared among relatives than other anxiety disorders (Noyes et al., 1986), but Torgersen (1983) found a concordance rate of 31 percent in MZ twins as opposed to 0 percent in DZ twins. This finding suggests that panic disorder may have an organic foundation, and one that is genetically transmitted.

The Role of Neurotransmitters   For years it has been known that anxiety can often be relieved by such drugs as Valium and Librium, which belong to a chemical group called the benzodiazepines. But how the benzodiazepines actually affect the brain's chemistry remained a mystery. Then, in 1977, it was discovered that the benzodiazepines attach to certain specific receptors on the neurons of the brain. (Receptors are the sites on the dendrite that, by interacting with neurotransmitters released from adjacent neurons, permit electrical impulses to pass from one neuron to the next; see Chapter 5.) This finding suggests that the brain may have a natural chemical, similar to the benzodiazepines, that regulates anxiety. It follows, then, that abnormalities in this chemical—too high a level, too low a level—may underlie the anxiety disorders.

Whatever the chemical process in question, we know that it involves a neurotransmitter called GABA (gamma aminobutyric acid), for it is GABA that is activated by the benzodiazepines (Costa, 1985). GABA is an inhibitory neurotransmitter; that is, once activated, it turns *off* the affected neurons. This, presumably, is the chemical basis of the benzodiazepines' ability to control anxiety: they signal GABA to shut off a certain measure of the brain's electricity.

It is doubtful, however, that this process underlies all anxiety conditions, for only certain types of anxiety, those experienced as generalized tension, are responsive to the benzodiazepines. Other anxiety conditions, such as panic disorder, are more responsive to antidepressant drugs. This finding points to two conclusions. First, the chemical basis of panic disorder is probably different from that of generalized anxiety—a conclusion already suggested by the genetic evidence. In other words, there is apparently more than one kind of anxiety, at least biochemically. Second, panic disorder may be more closely related to depression biochemically than to generalized anxiety. We know that the antidepressants in question affect the neuro-

Anxiety and the Middle-Aged Brain

When is brain deterioration good news? According to some researchers, the decreased incidence of anxiety disorders in middle-aged individuals may be the result of deterioration in the locus coeruleus, a portion of the medulla oblongata.

The medulla oblongata has long been known to control such functions as breathing and heart rate and to produce the neurotransmitters epinephrine (adrenaline) and norepinephrine. The locus coeruleus in particular appears to be responsible for norepinephrine production—some 70 percent of all cells with receptors for this hormone are located there. Although the locus coeruleus is a tiny mass at the base of the brain, it has extensive connections to many other parts of the nervous system.

Normally the locus coeruleus acts as a sort of alarm system, producing increased amounts of norepinephrine in the face of stress and of real or imagined danger. High activity levels in the locus coeruleus are characteristic of panic attacks, for example, and low activity levels may be associated with reckless behavior.

Apparently, however, the locus coeruleus undergoes a number of changes in middle age that lessens the amount of anxiety an individual experiences. Au-topsies of people aged 40 to 60 indicate that the cells of the locus coeruleus begin to lose their bluish color after 40. (Although the importance of pigmentation in the locus coeruleus is not known exactly, this coloring is not found in the brains of children [Stilling, 1846].) The cells of the locus coeruleus also become clogged in middle age with neuromelanin, thought to be a waste product of norephinephrine. This excess of neuromelanin initially slows the cells' functioning and eventually kills them. As a result, norephinephrine production declines sharply in middle age. At the same time, there is an increase in the production of monoamine oxidase, an enzyme that breaks down norephinephrine, thereby reducing further the amount of norepinephrine available to the brain.

As norephinephrine declines, so does anxiety. Many middle-aged people report feeling less worried and more self-assured than when they were younger. Of particular interest to psychotherapists is the decline of drug addiction, bulimia, and anxiety disorders such as panic attacks in patients over age 40. Indeed, according to Dr. Stephen Roose, a psychiatrist at the New York State Psychiatric Institute, "As these cells [of the locus coeruleus] die, diseases that are pathologies of this brain system seem to burn out."

transmitters norepinephrine and serotonin, which have been repeatedly implicated in depression. But since these drugs can also alleviate panic disorder, norepinephrine and serotonin are probably involved in anxiety as well as in depression (Hoehn-Saric, 1982).

Whatever the specific biochemical processes involved, these findings have given new impetus to research on neurotransmitters. As we noted in Chapter 5, neurotransmitters are now the object of intense study by researchers investigating the organic aspects of psychopathology. Previously, such research was focused primarily on schizophrenia and other psychotic conditions. The newfound connection between neurotransmitters and anxiety states will both broaden and intensify this line of investigation.

SUMMARY

The anxiety, somatoform, and dissociative disorders are associated with persistent anxiety. These disorders have two basic features in common: they leave "reality contact" relatively unimpaired, and they are "ambulatory," rarely requiring hospitalization.

The components of anxiety are indicated by self-reports of tension and fear; behavioral responses such as avoidance and impaired motor and speech functioning and cognitive performance; and physiological responses, including increased blood pressure and heart rate, rapid breathing, and muscle tension. Although *DSM-III-R* classifies several of the so-called neurotic disorders according to behavior patterns rather than to Freud's psychogenic criteria, behavioral and other measures of anxiety do not always agree, and anxiety remains an inferred construct.

There are three basic patterns of anxiety disorder. People with panic disorder suffer from panic attacks—brief episodes of acute anxiety with accompanying physiological stress—in the absence of a specific stimulus. Agoraphobia, or fear of leaving the home (literally, fear of open places), affects 3 to 6 percent of the population and may or may not accompany panic disorder, which affects about 1 percent of the population. Phobic disorders are characterized by (1) a phobia, or intense fear of an object or situation the person knows to be harmless or only slightly harmful, and (2) avoidance of the phobic stimulus. Phobic people panic when exposed to the feared stimulus, and to escape such feelings they generally avoid the thing they fear, often restricting their activities in order to do so. Phobias affect up to 13 percent of the population.

People suffering from generalized anxiety disorder feel anxious most of the time without knowing why. They have trouble making decisions and may develop physical symptoms. Generalized anxiety disorder is considered a separate syndrome from panic disorder, which is believed to have a genetic, organic basis.

People suffering from obsessive-compulsive disorder are bothered by thoughts (obsessions) or actions (compulsions) that they seem unable to control. Checking and cleaning rituals are the most common compulsive behaviors.

Posttraumatic stress disorders may be traced to traumatic external events. Victims typically reexperience the event for long periods of time, show diminished responsiveness to their present surroundings, develop physical symptoms, and may suffer from depression, anxiety, and irritability. Combat and civilian catastrophes may trigger posttraumatic stress disorder, depending on the person's previous psychological adjustments to less severe traumas.

Somatoform disorders result from psychological conflicts that take on a physical form. The three major forms are hypochondriasis, somatization disorder, and conversion disorder. Hypochondriacs, while physically healthy, are convinced that they are suffering from some disability or are about to contract some dread disease. People suffering from somatization disorder are bothered by numerous physical symptoms (at least 13, according to *DSM-III-R*) for which no organic cause can be found. People with conversion disorder, formerly called hysteria, suffer the actual loss or impairment of some motor or sensory function—disorders that are neither faked nor supported by medical evidence. It is generally agreed that conversion disorders result from some psychological conflict, but studies indicate that many apparent conversion disorders are really organic brain disorders in their early stages.

Dissociative disorders involve the splitting apart of components of the personality that are normally integrated. Three dissociative disorders are amnesia, fugue, and multiple personality.

Psychogenic amnesia, a response to psychological stress, tends to occur suddenly and is often selective as to the forgotten events. The most common pattern of psychogenic amnesia is localized amnesia, in which all events during a circumscribed period are blocked out. Less common forms include selective amnesia (certain events are forgotten), generalized amnesia (one's entire past life is forgotten), and continuous amnesia (all events after a specific period are forgotten).

In fugue, the person takes a sudden, unexpected trip away from home and assumes a new identity, forgetting about his or her past identity. Like amnesia, fugue seems to function as an escape from unbearable psychological stress.

An individual with multiple-personality disorder alternates between two or more distinct personalities. The simplest pattern consists of alternating personalities; two identities alternate with one another, each having amnesia for the thoughts and actions of the other. Another pattern involves one or more subordinate personalities that are coconscious with one or more dominant personalities. Multiple personality is a rare disorder, but its incidence has increased with public interest. Recent attempts to distinguish between true and false cases suggest that true cases of the disorder are characterized by asymmetrical amnesia.

Adherents of different psychological perspectives offer different interpretations of and treatments for the anxiety, somatoform, and dissociative disorders. A fundamental concept of the psychodynamic view is that anxiety is at the root of neurosis; the form that neurotic behavior takes depends on the individual's response to anxiety. In all neuroses, the relief of anxiety is sought through various defense mechanisms. The goal of psychodynamic therapy is to expose unconscious material that the ego is struggling to repress, in order to liberate the ego for more constructive tasks. Free association is a basic technique and is used in conjunction with dream interpretation. The therapist also interprets to the patient his or her unconscious processes of resistance and transference.

Behaviorists have often challenged psychodynamic interpretations of the role of anxiety in psychological disorder. Behaviorists focus on disorders in which anxiety is observable rather than inferred. According to behaviorists, avoidance is a response learned to relieve anxiety; for example, agoraphobia is a strategy to avoid panic attacks in public. Avoidance learning is the major source of anxiety and is a two-stage process: (1) through respondent conditioning, a neutral stimulus becomes anxiety-arousing; (2) the avoidance response relieves anxiety through negative reinforcement and becomes habitual. Behavior therapy is aimed at removing symptoms of disorder, not determining their cause. Behavioral techniques include systematic desensitization, in vivo desensitization, modeling, and operant conditioning.

Humanistic-existential theorists ascribe the disorders to intrapsychic conflicts, but the anxiety is seen as the outcome of conflicts between the individual and society. According to the humanists, the source of neurosis is the discrepancy between the self-concept and the real self. If the way we perceive ourselves is very different from the way we would like to be, we feel incapable of meeting life's challenges, and anxiety results. Despite individual differences, all humanistic-existential therapies stress the individual's responsibility for change.

The neuroscience perspective seeks biochemical links to anxiety. Recent evidence suggests that brain chemistry and neurotransmitters influence some forms of anxiety. Except for panic disorder, the evidence for a genetic factor in the disorders discussed in this chapter is weak.

CHAPTER 9

Psychological Stress and Physical Disorders

MIND AND BODY

Autonomic Reactions to Stress
Psychological Events and Physical Illness:
   A Disregulation Model

PHYSICAL DISORDERS ASSOCIATED WITH PSYCHOLOGICAL FACTORS

Ulcer
Obesity
Essential Hypertension
Headache
Asthma

Insomnia
Cancer

PERSPECTIVES ON STRESS-RELATED PHYSICAL DISORDERS

The Behavioral Perspective
The Psychodynamic Perspective
Personality Theories
The Sociocultural Perspective
The Neuroscience Perspective

The idea of **psychophysiological** (or "psychosomatic") **disorders**—illnesses that are influenced by emotional factors—is familiar to most people. Many of us have been told by our doctors that in order to cure our headaches or skin rash or ulcers, we need not a pill but a vacation—or a different attitude toward life.

Abnormal psychology has also long recognized that medical disorders can be affected by emotional states. Recently, however, the relationship between psychological stress and physical illness has undergone a major reevaluation. To begin with, it is now believed to be far more important than it was once thought to be. Researchers used to believe that only certain disorders (asthma, ulcer, hypertension, migraine, etc.) were strongly influenced by psychological states. Accordingly, earlier editions of the *DSM* listed these

conditions as the "psychophysiological disorders." Now evidence suggests that almost any physical disorder, from cancer to the common cold, can be to some extent "psychophysiological." Hence recent editions of the *DSM* no longer contain a list of specifically psychophysiological disorders. Instead, there is one comprehensive category, "psychological factors affecting physical condition," the implication being that such factors may affect any physical condition (*DSM-III-R,* p. 333).

In current theory the role of stress in physical illness has not only broadened; it has become far more complex. Researchers now recognize that even if an illness is caused by a purely physical factor, that illness in turn *causes* emotional stress. Surveys of medical patients have found, for example, that as many as a third have depressive symptoms and that about 20 percent of people in the hospital, for whatever illness, have a diagnosable depressive syndrome (Rodin and Voshort, 1986). There is no question that these emotional factors in turn affect the course of the illness—how serious it will become, whether and how quickly the patient will recover. In sum, many professionals are coming to believe that physical illness can no longer be studied apart from psychological factors.

This more *holistic,* or unified, concept of body and mind has led to the development of a new research discipline, **behavioral medicine** (also called *health psychology*). Three major historical trends have met in behavioral medicine. The first is the above-mentioned trend toward holistic thinking: the recognition that our way of living and state of mind affect our physical well-being. The second is the acknowledgment that the science of psychology, with its accumulated wisdom regarding emotional and intellectual functioning, has much to contribute to the study and cure of physical illness. The third is the discovery that certain treatments pioneered by behavioral psychology, such as biofeedback and relaxation training, can help to relieve stress-related physical ailments.

In this chapter we will first discuss the main issue underlying stress-related disorders: the relationship between mind and body—how they interact and by what route emotional stress may produce bodily damage. Then we will examine some physical disorders in which emotional stress is often implicated. Finally, we will review the major theoretical perspectives on these disorders.

MIND AND BODY

What is the relationship between the mind and the body? Philosophers and scientists have been debating this question—the **mind-body problem**—for centuries, and it is yet to be resolved. Logically, it would seem that mind and body are essentially the same thing or, at most, two aspects of the same thing. "Mind," after all, is simply an abstract term for the workings of the brain. And the brain not only is part of the body but is directly connected by nerves to all other parts of the body. Therefore whatever is going on "mentally" inside a person is also going on physically, and vice versa. Yet the fact remains that most of the time we are completely unaware of the activity going on in our brains. We are conscious only of the *effects* of that activity—effects that we think of as "mental," not physical. This is undoubtedly one

reason why we tend to regard the mind as something apart from the body (Schwartz, 1978).

Whatever the reason, the prevailing opinion for centuries has been that mind and body are two independent entities—interrelated, perhaps, but still independent. This dualistic conception of mind (or soul) and body is often attributed to the Greek philosopher Plato, in the fifth century B.C., but it undoubtedly reaches much further back, to the efforts of prehistoric peoples to explain death. In death, they observed, the body remained, yet it was no longer alive. Something, then, must have departed from it. That something—the mind or soul or spirit—was clearly separate from the body.

Incorporated into the Jewish and Christian religions, this dualistic image of mind and body was handed down from ancient times to the Middle Ages and the Renaissance. In the early seventeenth century, the French philosopher René Descartes described mind and body as independent entities—the mind spiritual, the body physical. Descartes' influential theories, together with the discoveries of Galileo and Sir Isaac Newton, laid the foundation of modern scientific rationalism. In this view, nature was a vast, self-powered machine. To explain the operation of the machine, one did not have to resort to philosophical or religious concepts. On the contrary, nature could and *must* be explained only by reference to its internal parts—that is, only through empirical evidence, things that could be directly observed and measured. Thus a line was drawn between matters that could be studied scientifically and matters that could not. The mind, with its intangible thoughts and emotions, fell on one side of this line, the body on the other. And physicians from that point on were trained to confine themselves to the latter. The belief that the workings of the body could affect the mind was never abandoned; throughout the eighteenth and nineteenth centuries the most prominent theories of psychological disorder were still organic theories. But the converse—that the workings of the mind could affect the body—was seldom considered. Organic illness had to be traceable to strictly organic (and therefore empirically observable) causes.

In the late nineteenth century, with the discovery by Louis Pasteur and other scientists that germs cause disease, mind-body dualism was greatly reinforced. Before Pasteur's discovery, many common illnesses, such as tuberculosis and cholera, remained unexplainable. Then, with the development of the germ theory, it was shown that these diseases, too, could be accounted for according to the mechanistic model—with the germ as the monkey wrench thrown into the machine. With this added support, the belief that physical phenomena must be explained according to physical causes, with no reference to nonempirical events, hardened into a rule.

There were, of course, some exceptions to the rule. Over the years, physicians repeatedly noted a connection between certain disorders, such as ulcers and high blood pressure, and psychological tension. And so a list of psychophysiological disorders gradually evolved, the same list that was included in the early editions of the *DSM*. Yet these disorders were regarded as the exceptions. All the thousands of remaining organic illnesses known to medicine were assumed to be due to strictly organic problems.

Only in our own century has this assumption been called into question, by mounting evidence of psychological influence over organic processes. In the sixties it was discovered that physiological functions such as blood pressure and heart rate, which were once considered completely involuntary (i.e., the province of the body, not of the mind), could be controlled voluntarily. And if the mind could affect the beating of the heart or the constriction and dilation of blood vessels, why could it not also affect such processes as the growth of cancer cells and the progress of an infection? In fact, there is now much evidence—by no means conclusive, but very suggestive—that psychological factors do play a role in cancer, infections, and many other illnesses traditionally regarded as purely organic. In the face of this evidence, many physicians are now beginning to doubt the long-entrenched separation of mind and body. The same trend is affecting the mental health professions, as can be seen in the *DSM*. As we noted earlier, the list of psychophysiological disorders has been replaced by a single broad category of "psychological factors affecting physical condition"—a category that can apply to *any* physical condition. Kept apart for centuries, mind and body are now increasingly being considered as one.

In this chapter we will take the position that mind and body are a unity. What we may experience as a mental event, such as sadness, is also, whether we realize it or not, a physical event. Likewise, physical events, such as the firing of neurons in the brain, trigger mental events. It is not so much that the one causes the other as that they cannot, in truth, be separated. As one researcher put it, the words *psychological* and *physical* refer not to different phenomena but to different ways of talking about the same phenomenon (Graham, 1967, p. 52).

Autonomic Reactions to Stress

What are the physiological changes associated with emotion? To attempt an answer we must look again at the autonomic nervous system (ANS). As we saw in Chapter 5, the ANS controls the smooth muscles, the glands, and the internal organs, regulating a wide variety of functions—among them heartbeat, respiration, blood pressure, bladder contraction, perspiration, salivation, adrenaline secretion, and gastric-acid production—to allow the body to cope with the ebb and flow of environmental demands. In general, the sympathetic division mobilizes the body to meet such demands by speeding up heart rate, constricting the blood vessels near the skin (and thereby raising blood pressure), increasing adrenaline flow, and so forth. And in general, the parasympathetic division reverses these processes, returning the body to a resting state so that it can rebuild the energy supply depleted by sympathetic activity (see Figure 5.5, p. 109).

Determinants of Autonomic Response   Because it mediates between environmental stress and such crucial biological functions as respiration, digestion, and blood circulation, the ANS has been a major object of study for researchers investigating the relationship between psychological processes and physical disorders. Several decades ago, W. B. Cannon (1936) proposed that stress results in a massive activation of the entire sympathetic division: increased heart rate and blood pressure, fast breathing, heavy adrenaline flow, dilated pupils, inhibited salivation and digestion. Regardless of the nature of the stress or of the individual, the physiological response, according to Cannon, was the same generalized sympathetic arousal. That hypothesis has been confirmed in broad outline. On the basis of extensive research, Hans Selye (1956, 1974) described a "general adaptation syndrome" which divides the body's reaction into three successive stages: (1) alarm and mobilization—a state of rapid, general arousal in which the body's defenses are mobilized; (2) resistance—the state of optimal biological adaptation to stress; and (3) exhaustion and disintegration—a stage reached when the body loses its ability to cope with prolonged stress.

General arousal in reaction to stress, however,

does not explain why some people respond to such stress by developing ulcers, others migraine, and others high blood pressure. The question is still not completely answered. In addition to general arousal, there are highly specific patterned responses that vary in accordance with the nature of both the stress and the individual.

STIMULUS SPECIFICITY   One of the earliest indications that the kind of stress the person is exposed to will result in a specific pattern of physiological response came from a rather bizarre experiment involving the direct observation of a human stomach at work (Wolf and Wolff, 1947). In 1947 a patient named Tom who had experienced severe gastrointestinal damage underwent surgery, and in the course of the operation a plastic window was installed over his stomach so that its internal workings could later be observed. In subsequent sessions with Tom, the investigators found that his flow of gastric juices decreased when he was exposed to stimuli that aroused his anxiety and increased when he was exposed to stimuli that aroused his anger. Thus this experiment not only showed that gastric activity (and by extension ulcer) was related to emotional states, as researchers had long suspected; it also established the principle of **stimulus specificity**—that different kinds of stress produce different patterns of physiological response.

This principle has since been confirmed by other investigators. Fear and anger, it has been found, have significantly different effects not only on gastric activity but also on heart rate, blood pressure, muscle tension, respiration rate, and numerous other physiological functions (Ax, 1953; Schwartz et al., 1981). Likewise, changes in heart rate in response to stress may vary depending on whether the stressor requires that the person block out environmental stimuli, as in performing mental arithmetic problems, or attend closely to environmental stimuli, as in listening to a dramatic tape (Lacey, 1959; Lacey et al., 1963). In short, the way the ANS reacts depends on what it is reacting to.

INDIVIDUAL RESPONSE SPECIFICITY   ANS response depends not only on the nature of the stressor but also on the nature of the person. As a result of genes or of learning (probably both), people appear to have characteristic patterns of autonomic response, which carry over from one type of stress to another—a phenomenon called **individual response specificity.** The first hint of this fact came in an experiment in which a group of people with histories of cardiovascular complaints (e.g., high blood pressure) and a group of people with histories of muscular complaints (e.g., backache) were both exposed to the same painful stimulus. Though the stressor was the same, the "cardiovascular" group responded with greater changes in heart rate than the "muscular" group, while the "muscular" group showed greater changes in muscle tension than the "cardiovascular" group (Malmo and Shagass, 1949). In other words, the subjects seemed to favor one or another physiological system in responding to stress. The same was later found to be true of people with no history of physical complaints, and of stressors other than pain.

There is an apparent contradiction between individual response specificity and stimulus specificity. If individuals have characteristic patterns of response that carry over from stressor to stressor, how can response vary significantly according to the nature of the stressor? This seems improbable only if we think of autonomic response as a simple process, which it is not. It is an extremely complex process, in which a large number of variables influence the final response. The two variables in question—the individual and the stressor—have been shown to operate simultaneously (Engel, 1960; Engel and Bickford, 1961). As we saw above, the flow of gastric juices tends to increase with anger and decrease with anxiety; here we see stimulus specificity. The *degree* of increase and decrease, however, will be subject to individual response specificity. That is, "gastric reactors" may show extreme increases and decreases; "cardiac reactors," on the other hand, may show only mild gastric changes, concentrating instead on heart-rate changes.

We know, then, that both the nature of the stressor and the nature of the individual determine to some extent the nature of autonomic responses. What we don't yet know is whether they also determine the nature of the physical disorders that people develop—and if so, how. In the effort to solve this problem, Gary Schwartz (1977) has proposed a model for understanding stress-related physical disorders.

Psychological Events and Physical Illness: A Disregulation Model

The central concept in Schwartz's model is that of negative feedback. **Feedback** is the process in which information is returned to a system in order to regulate that system. When we are driving a car, for example, the speedometer gives us feedback as to how fast we are going and thereby helps us regulate the relationship between the local speed limit and the amount of pressure that we put on the gas pedal. **Negative feedback** is simply a specific kind of feedback in which the turning *on* of one component of a system leads to the turning *off* of another component, in order to regulate the system.

Consider, for example, a room equipped with a thermostat connected to a furnace. The thermostat is set at 65 degrees, and the temperature of the room is 65 degrees. But it is stuffy, so we open a window slightly, and the room temperature soon drops to 60 degrees. The thermometer attached to the thermostat picks up this information, and the thermostat automatically activates the furnace, which then works at high speed until the room temperature once again rises to 65 degrees. At this point, the thermometer once again gives a message to the thermostat—the message that the room is now properly heated—and the thermostat accordingly turns off the furnace for the time being (Figure 9.1). Thus in this system, information is carried (1) from the control center (the thermostat) to the operations center (the furnace), and then (2) *back* from the operations center to the control center, so that when the proper balance has been restored in the system, the control center can turn off what it has turned on in order to regain that balance. The second part of this process (represented by a dashed line in Figure 9.1) is called a *negative feedback loop.*

As Schwartz points out, negative feedback loops are critical in the regulation of bodily processes (see Figure 9.2). For example, in response to environmental stress, the nervous system may elevate the blood pressure. Blood pressure that rises too high, however, activates pressure-sensitive cells called baroreceptors surrounding the blood vessels. The baroreceptors then send the message back to the nervous system, which in turn lowers the blood pressure. Likewise, when something delicious is put before us on a plate, this environmental stimulus excites the nervous system to turn on the flow of gastric juices in the stomach. Later, when we have eaten and are full, internal feedback mechanisms relay this information to the nervous system, which then turns off the gastric juices.

According to Schwartz's model, it is when these internal regulatory systems fail to operate properly that diseases develop. Hence he calls his model a **disregulation model.** The fault, Schwartz claims, may lie with excessive environmental demands, or it may be due to some flaw in the regulatory system. In either case, what should have been regulation becomes disregulation, and the result is physical disorder.

Disregulation can occur at any of four stages. (The stages are marked in Figure 9.2.)

FIGURE 9.1

An everyday example of a *negative feedback loop:* the thermostat turns the furnace on when an opened window causes the room to cool. When the thermometer rises to 65°, the thermostat turns the furnace off. The second part of this sequence (represented by the dashed lines) is the negative feedback loop.

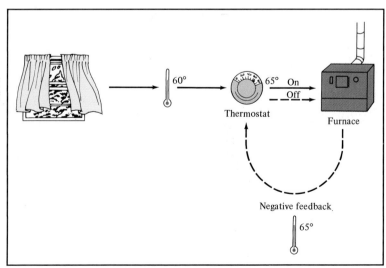

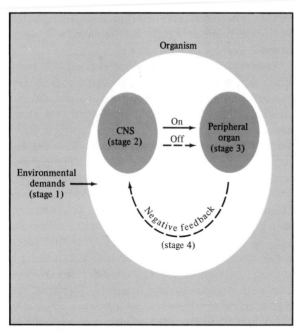

FIGURE 9.2

Negative feedback loops are critical to proper regulation of the activities of the body. These processes ensure that our internal organs "turn on" and "turn off" as they should. According to Schwartz, diseases develop when our internal regulatory systems fail to operate properly. This disregulation can occur at one or more of the four stages shown. (Adapted from Gary E. Schwartz, "Psychosomatic Disorders and Biofeedback: A Psychobiological Model of Disregulation," in *Psychopathology: Experimental Models,* ed. Jack D. Maser and Martin E. P. Seligman. San Francisco: W. H. Freeman, 1977.)

Stage 1: Environmental Demands   The demands placed on the person by the environment may be so great that he or she is forced to ignore negative feedback from the body. To return to the thermostat example, suppose we opened another window every time the thermostat was about to give the "turn-off" signal to the furnace. In such a circumstance, the furnace would probably break down in short order. And so will the stomach or heart if environmental stress forces us continually to ignore negative feedback so that we overwork the system.

Stage 2: Information Processing in the Central Nervous System   Even if environmental demands are not unreasonable, the brain may be programmed, either by genes or by learning, to respond inappropri-

ately either to those demands or to the body's negative feedback. (This would be an instance of individual response specificity.) If, in our example, the thermostat (the heating system's brain) were defective, it might overrespond to the stimulus of the open window, or it might ignore the negative feedback when the proper temperature was restored. In either case, it would have the furnace running too high and would thus put it under great strain. By the same token, people who have learned to ignore negative ("I am full") feedback from their stomachs are likely to become overweight.

Stage 3: The Peripheral Organ   Even if environmental demands are not excessive and the central nervous system (CNS) is processing information smoothly, the peripheral organ may be incapable of responding in an appropriate manner to the brain's instructions. If the furnace were defective, it might raise itself to a white heat (or fail to go on at all) in response to the signal from the thermostat. Likewise, if a person, through genetic inheritance or disease, has developed a defective heartbeat-pacing mechanism, then CNS instructions that would produce the appropriate response in a normal heart might cause this heart to begin beating abnormally fast or slowly.

Stage 4: Negative Feedback   Finally, even if environmental demands, CNS information processing, and the functioning of the peripheral organ are all normal, a problem may develop in the negative feedback loop. If we wrapped insulation around the thermometer attached to the thermostat, it would not get the message that the room temperature had returned to 65 degrees. And lacking this negative feedback, it would keep the furnace burning at top speed. Similarly, some people who have chronically high blood pressure may be born with or may develop defective baroreceptors, which would keep their brains from getting proper negative feedback—the message to lower the pressure.

Like the proverbial chain, this four-part regulatory system is only as strong as its weakest link. When a problem occurs at one of the stages, the entire regulatory process is disrupted. Furthermore, it is not just one function, such as heart rate, that is disrupted; it is the entire system of which that function is a part. Thus a disregulated heart rate means a disregulated cardiovascular system; a disregulated flow of gastric juices means a disregulated gastrointestinal system, and so forth.

An advantage of the disregulation model is its versatility. It can take into account stimulus specificity, since environmental stressors may be associated with specific regulatory systems. It can also take into account individual response specificity, since CNS information processing, along with the functioning of the peripheral organ and of the negative feedback loop, may vary from individual to individual. Furthermore, the model can cover *any* physical disorder, including those that can be attributed to a primarily organic cause, for the environmental stressor may be a germ or a blow on the head as well as a final exam or an argument with one's mother.

The prime virtue of Schwartz's model, however, is its conceptualization of disorder as part of a *system.* An easy but often only temporarily effective approach to disorder is to treat the symptom, as when we take aspirin for pain. The disregulation model suggests that the symptom is a message of systemic dysfunction, and consequently that the system must be analyzed before we can know what it is that actually requires the treatment. Schwartz's model is thus less an explanation than a description of the complex interrelationships that underlie physical disorder.

PHYSICAL DISORDERS ASSOCIATED WITH PSYCHOLOGICAL FACTORS

We will describe six of the more serious and more common syndromes commonly associated with psychological stress: ulcer, obesity, essential hypertension, headache, asthma, and insomnia. Finally, we will examine recent evidence of psychological influences in cancer.

Ulcer

Disorders of the gastrointestinal system, the system of organs through which our food passes, are probably the most common afflictions of humanity (Hill and Kern, 1977). And of the gastrointestinal disorders, one of the most common is ulcer. There are millions of ulcer sufferers in the United States today,

and the incidence is reportedly increasing at a rate of over 2 percent a year (Eisenberg, 1978). Ulcers are far more common in some groups than in others. They are found with greater frequency in men than in women, more often in the middle-aged than in other age groups. Overall, however, approximately 10 percent of the population will develop ulcers during their lifetimes (Whitehead and Bosmajian, 1982).

An **ulcer** can be described as an open sore, anywhere from the size of a pinhead to the size of a quarter, in the wall of any part of the digestive system. Ulcers usually develop either in the stomach, in which case they are called *gastric ulcers,* or in the duodenum (the area lying between the stomach and the small intestine), in which case they are referred to as *duodenal ulcers*. One of the first symptoms of an ulcer is usually a burning sensation in the stomach. Eventually, once the lesion, or actual tissue damage, appears, the stomach discomfort turns to actual pain, which may be very intense. If the lesion gets larger, there may be vomiting. Finally, if blood vessels have broken, there will be hemorrhaging in the stomach and vomiting of blood.

How do ulcers develop? Both the duodenum and the stomach have an inner lining of mucus that protects them from the corrosive effects of the gastric juices that the stomach secretes to break down food. In some cases, however, this protection fails. The acid in the gastric juices eats through the mucosal lining and begins "digesting" the wall of the stomach or duodenum—hence the ulcer.

There is strong evidence that duodenal ulcers are associated with excess secretions of gastric juices (Dragstedt, 1967). Gastric ulcers, on the other hand, seem to be associated with some weakness in the mucosal lining as well as with abnormalities in gastric secretions. Exactly what causes these conditions we do not know, but psychological stress is almost certainly one factor, at least in the abnormal rates of gastric secretion. As we saw earlier, Tom, the patient with the plastic window in his stomach, responded to stress with clear changes in gastric secretions—increased secretion when he was angry and decreased secretion when he was anxious (Wolf and Wolff, 1947). The connection between ulcers and psychological stress is illustrated in the following clear-cut case:

> Mr. R. M., a retired mailman, had been happily married for fifty-eight years. Then, when his wife died, he moved in with his son and daughter-in-law. This arrangement proved unhappy for all

Several interesting animal studies have been carried out to determine what specific kinds of stress are most likely to cause ulcers. Perhaps the best known is a series of experiments by Brady and his colleagues (1958), which we described briefly in Chapter 6. These researchers installed four pairs of monkeys in an apparatus that was wired to give them electric shocks every twenty seconds for six hours. However, the first monkey of each pair—Brady called it the "executive" monkey—could turn off any one of the scheduled shocks if it pressed a lever located near its hand during the twenty-second interval between the shocks. The second monkey, called the "yoked" monkey, could do nothing; its fate depended entirely on the executive monkey. Brady's hypothesis was that the yoked monkey, helpless to control its well-being, would develop ulcers. As it turned out, it was the executive monkey that developed (and invariably died of) ulcers. The researchers concluded that it was not just stress from the shocks that produced ulcers; both monkeys, after all, experienced the same number of shocks. Rather, the cause was the stress of having to make decisions, the burden of responsibility—a conclusion that dovetailed nicely with the popular assumption that ulcers tended to strike people in responsible, high-level positions (hence "executive" monkey).

However, several attempts to replicate the results of these experiments failed (e.g., Foltz and Millet, 1964)—a problem that was certainly due in part to the fact that Brady's monkeys were not randomly assigned to the "executive" and "yoked" roles. Brady chose as his executives the monkeys that, on a pretest, had showed higher response rates. As was later established, higher response rates are related to a susceptibility to ulcers.

In the meantime, other studies indicated that Brady's original hypothesis—that lack of control would lead to ulceration—was closer to the truth. Kahn (1969), for example, found that ulcers were more common in discontented blue-collar workers than in business executives on the rise. But the most striking findings came from a series of experiments similar to Brady's. In these experiments (Weiss, 1971), pairs of rats were placed in an apparatus similar to that of Brady's monkeys, and as with the monkeys, the "executive" rat could prevent or terminate the shock (in this case by turning a wheel) while the "yoked" rat, having no control, simply had to endure whatever shocks the executive rat received. However, the ex-

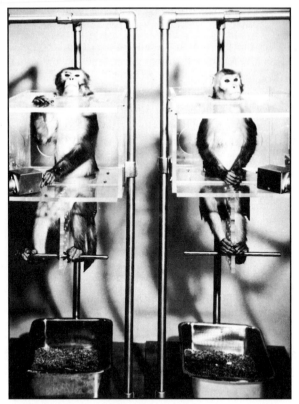

The experimental setup in Brady's "executive" monkey experiments. A shock was delivered to one foot of each monkey at twenty-second intervals for a period of six hours. Shock to both monkeys could be avoided or terminated if the monkey on the left (the "executive") pressed a lever; the monkey on the right had no control over the shock. In these experiments, the "executive" monkey always developed and died of perforated ulcers; the control monkey showed no ulceration. The constant need to make "decisions" apparently led to increased gastric secretions that resulted in ulceration. Further investigation revealed that the secretion of gastric acids increased in the "executive" following, not during, the six-hour session. Brady's results suggested that the stress of responsibility may cause ulcers. (Jospeh V. Brady)

concerned. Six weeks before Mr. M.'s admission to the hospital, he had an argument with his daughter-in-law about the meals she served. Finally, the daughter-in-law told Mr. M. that she would allow him to remain in the house only if he prepared his own meals or ate in a restaurant. Very soon thereafter Mr. M. began having stomach pains fifteen to thirty minutes after every meal. When he finally sought treatment, it was discovered that he had a large stomach ulcer, apparently of recent origin (adapted from Hofling, 1968).

ecutive rat, unlike the executive monkey, received a warning signal before the shock. Under these conditions the executive rat developed far *less* ulceration than the second rat. In a later experiment, a tone was sounded after the executive rat had made the appropriate (i.e., shock-stopping) response, and again the executive rat showed much less ulceration than the second rat.

In comparing his results with Brady's, the experimenter, Jay Weiss (1977), pointed out that in addition to the nonrandom assignment of Brady's monkeys, two crucial variables seemed to account for the difference: the number of responses and the amount of feedback. Brady's executive monkey was pressing the lever repeatedly but never had any immediate feedback indicating that these responses were actually achieving the desired result. The executive rat, on the other hand, could postpone its response until the warning signal sounded. Furthermore, once the signal sounded and the response was made, the rat knew immediately—because the threatened shock did not come and, in the later experiment, because the tone sounded as well—that the response had been effective. Weiss's findings suggest that the best defense against ulcers in a stressful situation is the ability to direct one's coping attempts to a predictable threat and to know immediately, via feedback, that these responses were successful. If this is so, then the problem for Brady's executive monkeys was not that they had too much responsibility but that they had responsibility without a sense of control. As we shall see, a sense of control is regarded by the behaviorists as a crucial protection against stress.

It should be noted that both Brady's and Weiss's experiments focus on stage 1 of Schwartz's model—the kind of environmental stress that produces disregulation. However, many researchers feel that stage 2, CNS information processing, may also be critical in the development of ulcers. That is, some people may have a hereditary or learned tendency to make gastric responses to stressors that other people would either respond to with another system or simply ignore (Walker, 1983).

Obesity

Eating behavior, like the internal functions of the gastrointestinal system, is regulated by feedback loops. In highly simplified terms, the sequence is as follows. When the body is in need of nourishment, it sends hunger signals to the brain. Then, as we eat, other internal signals alert the brain that the body is satiated, at which point we put down our forks. This, in any case, is the normal regulatory cycle. However, it too can succumb to disregulation. The feedback may fail to reach the brain (Schwartz's stage 4), or the brain may receive the feedback but still respond inappropriately (stage 2). In either case, the cycle is thrown off, and the person either fails to eat when the stomach signals hunger or goes on eating when the stomach signals satiety.

The first of these two patterns of disregulation—chronic failure to eat, to the point of extreme malnutrition—is known as **anorexia nervosa.** Because it normally begins in adolescence, we will postpone our discussion of it until Chapter 17, which deals with childhood and adolescent disorders. We turn our attention now to the second and far more familiar pattern, obesity.

Obesity is a socially defined condition. Strictly speaking, the term refers to an excessive amount of fat on the body, but every culture has its own idea of what is excessive. What would have been regarded as a healthy adult in the late nineteenth century we would now call a fat person; conversely, to nineteenth-century eyes, the thinness of today's fashion models would seem abnormal and ugly. Our society, actually, is caught in a curious paradox. Perhaps in no other society has thinness been so highly prized, and perhaps in no other society has obesity been so prevalent. Somewhere between 15 and 50 percent of American adults are more than 20 percent overweight. The prevalence of obesity increases with age and is highest among lower socioeconomic groups (Brownell, 1982).

Obesity is not good for the body—it puts a strain on the heart and other organs—but does this fact permit us to label it as an "abnormal" condition? Certainly not by the statistical-rarity criterion, as we have just seen. However, it might be defined as such according to the norm-violation criterion, the norm being thinness. Above all, the "abnormality" of obesity would be related to the personal-discomfort criterion. In many sectors of our society, obesity is viewed as "a state verging on crime" (Rodin, 1977). As a result, the obese suffer not only the consequences of their socially defined unattractiveness—consequences ranging from a mild sense of inferiority to extreme social and sexual maladjustment—but they must also suffer the sense of responsibility for their condition.

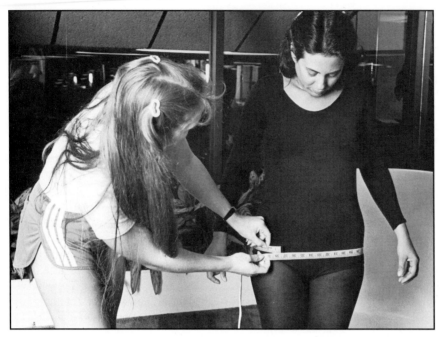

Society's emphasis on thinness causes many people to be concerned about their weight even when it's unnecessary. (S. Oristaglio/Photo Researchers)

This is personal discomfort of the first order, and one that brings many people into therapy.

What causes obesity? In part, the reasons are directly physiological. There is increasing evidence that excess weight is not necessarily due to excess eating. Many obese people eat moderately and still remain fat, while many thin people can "eat anything" and still stay thin—an injustice of which overweight people often complain. In such cases, the controlling variables are apparently activity level and metabolic rate, the rate at which the body converts food into energy (Thompson et al., 1982). And while activity level can be altered by exercise programs, metabolic rate is in large measure genetically determined. Furthermore, once a person becomes overweight, the added pounds *further* lower the metabolic rate. (That is, once the weight is gained, fewer calories are needed to keep it on than were needed to put it on [Sims et al., 1973].) To make matters worse, dieting also lowers the rate of metabolism, with the result, ruefully noted by many dieters, that one can count calories religiously and still not lose weight (Rodin, 1981). In sum, certain bodies are apparently born to carry more fat than other bodies, and trying to counteract such a tendency, at least by dieting, is to some extent swimming against the stream.

Yet obesity is due not to physiology alone, but to an interaction of physiological and psychological factors. A number of studies indicate that obese people are far more responsive than others to any food-relevant stimulus: the taste of food (Nisbett, 1968); the sight and smell of food (Schachter, 1971; Rodin, 1981); the clock indicating that it is mealtime (Schachter and Gross, 1968); and, presumably, television commercials and magazine advertisements. In terms of Schwartz's model, this overresponsiveness would constitute disregulation at stage 2. Other experiments suggest that overweight people may also have a problem at stage 4: the transmission of feedback regarding hunger and satiety from the stomach to the brain. When normal people are asked how hungry they are, their answers correlate strongly with the frequency of their stomach contractions; when overweight people are put to the same test, the correlation is much weaker (Stunkard and Koch, 1964).

It is hard to say, however, whether the disregulation observed in these experiments was actually due to obesity. Most overweight people are dieters, and recent research suggests that whatever disregulation they show may be the result not of excess weight but of dieting. Several experiments have found that obese people who are not dieters do not show overresponsiveness to food cues (Herman and Mack, 1975; Hibscher and Herman, 1977; Ruderman and Wilson, 1979). On the other hand, overresponsiveness and many of the other peculiarities said to characterize the eating behavior of the obese *are* found in people who are of normal weight but are chronic dieters (Klajner et al., 1981). There is now solid evidence that chronic dieting may lead to disregulation. People who, whether or not they are overweight, have been kept from their normal eating pattern are more likely to engage in binge eating (Wardle, 1980), are more likely to eat in response to emotional stimuli (Baucom and Aiken, 1981; Herman and Polivy, 1975; Ruderman, 1985), and are more likely to go on eating once they have violated the dietary restraint (Herman and Mack, 1975; Hibscher and Herman, 1977)—facts that will sound familiar to anyone who has been on a diet. This disregulation may eventually lead to the chronic pattern of binge eating known as bulimia (Polivy and Herman, 1985). Bulimia will be discussed, with anorexia, in Chapter 17.

In view of such findings, along with the physiological evidence described above, many physicians are now deemphasizing dieting in favor of exercise. Exercise presumably does not interfere with the regulatory cycle that controls eating. On the other hand, it does burn up calories, suppress the appetite, and increase the metabolic rate, so that even when one is not exercising, calories are being burned faster. In addition to more exercise, many experts feel that what our society needs is a broader definition of physical attractiveness, so that beauty is not confined to the skinniest end of the spectrum of human body types. Many moderately heavy people have nothing wrong with them, either physically or psychologically.

Essential Hypertension

Of all the physical disorders commonly associated with psychological stress, chronically high blood pressure, known as **hypertension,** is by far the most common and the most dangerous. An estimated 15 percent of the population of the United States suffers from this cardiovascular disorder (Hypertension Detection and Follow-Up Program Cooperative Group, 1979), which in turn predisposes them to two other, deadly cardiovascular disorders: heart attack and "stroke" (Kannel et al., 1968). Untreated hypertensives have an average life expectancy of between fifty and sixty years, compared with seventy-one years for the population at large (Lyght, 1966).

The connection between hypertension and other cardiovascular disorders is a good illustration of the principle, stated earlier, that disregulation in one part of a physiological system is disregulation of the system

One cause of hypertension may be environmental stress. A major source of such stress is working with dangerous equipment on a regular basis. (Ethan Hoffman/Archive Pictures)

as a whole. The function of the cardiovascular system, consisting of the heart and the peripheral blood vessels, is to pump blood through the body, carrying nutrients where they are needed and carrying wastes where they can be disposed of. Every heartbeat represents a contraction of the heart; with each contraction, blood is pushed out of the heart and through the blood vessels. At the same time, the blood vessels are contracting and dilating in response to internal and external stimuli. The blood pressure—that is, the pressure that blood exerts on the walls of the blood vessels—is a function of several variables, but one of the most important, at least in chronic hypertensives, seems to be the degree of constriction in the blood vessels (Forsyth, 1974). When a normal person's blood pressure rises too high, the baroreceptors convey this information to the brain, which then relaxes the constricted vessel walls. In hypertensives, however, this regulatory mechanism somehow fails to work, with the result that the blood vessels remain chronically constricted and hence the blood pressure chronically high.

Why does this happen? In a small percentage of cases, approximately 10 to 15 percent, hypertension is linked to an identifiable organic cause, usually kidney dysfunction (Shapiro and Goldstein, 1982). In the remaining cases, known as **essential hypertension,** there is no known organic cause. Many different factors have been suggested, from genetic abnormalities to repressed anger. As Schwartz (1977) has pointed out, these proposed causes can be classified according to the stage in which the regulatory cycle is disturbed:

Stage 1: Environmental Demands   It is possible that essential hypertensives are to some extent victims of the principle of stimulus specificity. That is, their condition may be due to the fact that their environments are particularly rich in the kinds of stressors that tend to increase blood pressure. What kinds of stressors would these be? Danger is one possibility. Researchers have noted that when animals are placed in an environment where they must be constantly watchful in order to avoid painful stimuli, they tend to respond with high blood pressure (Herd et al., 1974). Likewise, human beings have bouts of high blood pressure when placed in situations requiring constant alertness against the threat of danger (Gutmann and Benson, 1971). In light of these findings, it is interesting to note that essential hypertension

is twice as common among blacks as it is among whites. While this disparity may be a function of genes, one might also hypothesize that blacks as a group are exposed to greater threats—the threat of job loss, the threat of physical harm in ghetto neighborhoods—than whites.

Stage 2: CNS Information Processing   Essential hypertension may also be due in part to individual response specificity. In other words, genes or experience may have programmed the brain to respond to different kinds of stress with increases in blood pressure. In support of the genetic hypothesis, it is known that hypertension runs in families (Zinner et al., 1971), and though this tendency might be explained as the product of learning rather than of genetic inheritance, the fact that rats can be bred for hypertension (Jones and Dowd, 1970), along with the finding that very young children sometimes show hypertension, suggests that genes do play a role in its development.

Learning hypotheses tend to focus on how the person learns to handle feelings of aggression. It was long ago suggested that hypertensives are generally people who have difficulty venting anger (Alexander, 1939), and subsequent experiments have shown that normal subjects, when angered, do show elevated blood pressure, which remains elevated if the anger is suppressed but returns to normal if the anger is expressed (Diamond, 1982). It is possible, then, that children raised in environments where displays of aggression are frowned on may become conditioned to associate feedback from their baroreceptors with the temptation toward aggression and to suppress both (Schwartz, 1977).

Recent research, however, has focused less on anger than on the simple matter of daily coping with controllable stress. In such research, some difficult but not impossible task is generally imposed on high-risk subjects. One group assumed to be at risk for hypertension includes people with at least one hypertensive parent, and many studies have shown that such people, when confronted with demanding behavioral and cognitive tasks, do experience greater cardiovascular reactions than people without a family history of hypertension (Steptoe, 1984). Another and probably more valid high-risk group consists of people who have had mildly elevated blood pressure in childhood or early adulthood; these people, too, react to laboratory tasks and controllable stress with high blood pressure (Steptoe et al., 1984). The problem, then, may lie not with the stressor—after all, even the best of lives contain a large measure of controllable stress—but with the individual. If so, these individuals need to design their lives and their responses to stress somewhat better than the rest of us.

Stage 3: The Peripheral Organ   It has been suggested that chronic hypertension may eventually produce structural changes in the blood vessels, so that they can no longer dilate properly. In other words, the brain is transmitting the right instructions, but the blood vessels are no longer capable of obeying them (Forsyth, 1974; Schwartz, 1977).

Stage 4: Negative Feedback   Chronically high blood pressure may also, in time, affect the operation of the baroreceptors. Under the strain of chronically high pressure, the baroreceptors may eventually adapt to this stimulus and thus cease to respond to it in such an extreme manner. Or they may simply wear down. In either case, they would cease to send the appropriate "high-pressure" signals to the brain.

It seems unlikely that any one of these forms of disregulation *alone* would be sufficient to produce chronic hypertension. In combination, however, they might tip the balance. For example, a combination of congenitally weak baroreceptors with a learned tendency to overreact to stress—or a combination of a highly stressful environment with a learned or genetic tendency to respond to stress with changes in blood pressure—might be sufficient to create trouble at other stages as well, so that what was once a regulatory cycle would become a "disregulatory cycle," the disturbance at each stage reinforcing the disturbances at successive stages. The result would be chronic hypertension.

The following case is a good illustration of the aggression-inhibiting personality that some experts believe may be associated with hypertension:

> A fifty-year-old municipal employee had been born into a restrained family, where the domineering mother never allowed him to express anger. He grew up earnest and compliant, in contrast to his independent, self-reliant older brother, who did well in business. At age thirty-six, he married a school

teacher, temperamentally similar to his mother, who emphasized his limitations, made him take speech training, and refused to divulge the amount of her salary to him. She and his mother were not congenial; he observed, "I was caught between two strong women." His hypertension was first recognized when his job as a meter inspector, which he had held for twenty-eight years, was threatened because of political change.

> In the clinic, he was given strong reassurance and support, and he was encouraged to express his feelings freely. Moreover, long discussions of his recollections and of his relations to his mother were undertaken. His wife was called in and her support was enlisted. As he became increasingly relaxed and self-confident during treatment, he was successful in defying his boss at work, and he noted that his wife was "softening up." His blood pressure remained normal for the next four years, except for brief episodes of elevation associated with specific threats. On one occasion, his blood pressure rose to 165/110 during a discussion of his more successful brother. On another occasion, a less marked rise in blood pressure occurred following a psychological testing procedure that he felt revealed inadequacies in him (Wolf, 1977, pp. 223–224).

Because high blood pressure produces no immediate discomfort, many hypertensives are unaware of their condition, with the result that it may go untreated for years. Furthermore, those who are aware that they have hypertension are often unaware that circumstances in their family life or work environment may be aggravating it. Like the aforementioned baroreceptors, they have adapted to the stress and therefore no longer see it as stressful. Often it takes some kind of crisis—a situation in which blood pressure and environmental pressures simultaneously increase dramatically—before such patients will take seriously the connection between their blood pressure and their way of life, and consider changing the latter.

Headache

Headaches may accompany any number of other physical disorders. When chronic headache is the major or only symptom, however, it is often thought to be related to psychological stress. Stress-related headaches seem to be of two types. **Muscle-contraction headaches,** also known as **tension head-**

The Physiological Error Called Migraine

A migraine, as any person who has experienced one can testify, is very different from an ordinary headache. When migraines occur frequently, the disorder can become disabling. Novelist Joan Didion, in an essay on migraine, gives this account of her own experience:

> Three, four, sometimes five times a month, I spend the day in bed with a migraine headache, insensible to the world around me. Almost every day of every month, between these attacks, I feel the sudden irrational irritation and the flush of blood into the cerebral arteries which tell me that migraine is on its way, and I take certain drugs to avert its arrival. If I did not take the drugs, I would be able to function perhaps one day in four. The physiological error called migraine is, in brief, central to the given of my life. When I was 15, 16, even 25, I used to think that I could rid myself of this error by simply denying it, character over chemistry. "Do you have headaches *sometimes? frequently? never?*" the application forms would demand. "Check one." Wary of the trap, wanting whatever it was that the successful circumnavigation of that particular form could bring (a job, a scholarship, the respect of mankind and the grace of God), I would check one. "*Sometimes,*" I would lie. That in fact I spent one or two days a week almost unconscious with pain seemed a shameful secret, evidence not merely of some chemical inferiority but of all my bad attitudes, unpleasant tempers, wrongthink.
>
> For I had no brain tumor, no eyestrain, no high blood pressure, nothing wrong with me at all: I simply had migraine headaches, and migraine headaches were, as everyone who did not have

aches, range from mild to severe and are usually described by their sufferers as an aching or tightness around the neck or head. In most cases, the pain is felt on both sides of the head, either at the front or back of the head or at the back of the neck (Haynes, 1981). **Migraine** headaches are more intense and are usually localized on one side of the head. A migraine attack further differs from a muscle-contraction headache in that it is often preceded by an **aura**—a subjective sensation alerting the person that the headache is about to begin—and is more likely than the muscle-contraction headache to be accompanied by other somatic disturbances, such as dizziness, fainting, nausea, and vomiting. Migraine attacks range from bearable discomfort to complete immobilization and last anywhere from several hours to several days.

As the more severe condition, migraine has been the object of more research than muscle-contraction headaches. Such research has focused primarily on stages 1 and 2 of the disregulation cycle: what specific kind of stress might bring on a migraine and what specific kind of person might respond to stress with migraine. Neither question has as yet been satisfacto-rily answered. However, the physiological basis of the disorder is now fairly clear.

Like hypertension, migraine is a cardiovascular disorder. It appears to be due to the following sequence of events. First, the blood vessels in the brain constrict as a result of stress. Then, once the stress is relieved, the arteries leading to the brain dilate, and more blood is delivered to the area than can be comfortably accommodated. The result of this dramatic change in blood flow is a sharp, painful, throbbing sensation in the head—in short, the migraine. Thus it is not actually stress but rather the period of relief after stress that ushers in the headache. This helps to explain why migraine attacks often occur at night or early in the morning, when the person has rested after a stressful day. In contrast, muscle-contraction headaches are apparently due directly to constriction of the blood vessels. In response to stress, the muscles of the head and neck contract; this causes the neighboring blood vessels to constrict, which in turn produces the head pain.

Migraine appears to be a common disorder. It is estimated that 12 million Americans experience mi-

them knew, imaginary. I fought migraine then, ignored the warnings it sent, went to school and later to work in spite of it, sat through lectures in Middle English and presentations to advertisers with involuntary tears running down the right side of my face, threw up in washrooms, stumbled home by instinct, emptied ice trays onto my bed and tried to freeze the pain in my right temple, wished only for a neurosurgeon who would do a lobotomy on house call, and cursed my imagination.

It was a long time before I began thinking mechanistically enough to accept migraine for what it was: something with which I would be living, the way some people live with diabetes. Migraine is something more than the fancy of a neurotic imagination. It is . . . [a] complex of symptoms, the most frequently noted but by no means the most unpleasant of which is a vascular headache of blinding severity, suffered by a surprising number of women, a fair number of men (Thomas Jefferson had migraine, and so did Ulysses S. Grant, the day he accepted Lee's surrender), and by some unfortunate children as young as two years old. . . .

Migraine gives some people mild hallucinations, temporarily blinds others, shows up not only as a headache but as a gastrointestinal disturbance, a painful sensitivity to all sensory stimuli, an abrupt overpowering fatigue, a strokelike aphasia, and a crippling inability to make even the most routine connections. When I am in a migraine aura (for some people the aura lasts fifteen minutes, for others several hours), I will drive through red lights, lose the house keys, spill whatever I am holding, lose the ability to focus my eyes or frame coherent sentences, and generally give the appearance of being on drugs, or drunk. The actual headache, when it comes, brings with it chills, sweating, nausea, a debility that seems to stretch the very limits of endurance. That no one dies of migraine seems, to someone deep into an attack, an ambiguous blessing. . . .

From "In Bed," *The White Album* by Joan Didion. New York: Simon and Schuster, 1979.

graines either regularly or on occasion, as a function of stress (Adams et al., 1980). It is also known that the incidence of migraine is about twice as high in women as in men. The fact that women usually do not begin experiencing these attacks until adolescence and that the headaches normally subside after menopause has led to speculation concerning the possible influence of hormonal factors associated with the appearance and disappearance of the menstrual cycle, but no firm connection has as yet been established.

Asthma

Asthma has been the focus of considerable attention, not only because of its high prevalence—about 3 percent of the general American population suffer from it—but also because it is one of the few stress-related physical disorders common in young children. Approximately one-third of all asthmatics are under the age of sixteen (U.S.D.H.E.W., 1970).

Asthma is a disorder of the respiratory system, the function of which is to bring air in and out of the lungs, so that the body can take in oxygen and give off carbon dioxide. During an asthma attack the body's air passageways narrow, and the constriction causes coughing, wheezing, and general difficulty in breathing. Asthma attacks may last for only a few minutes or for several hours. They also vary considerably in their intensity. Some attacks are mild; in others, bronchial spasms cause the air passageways to become so constricted that the person has immense difficulty getting air in and out of the lungs. Wheezing and coughing uncontrollably, the asthmatic feels that he or she is suffocating, literally at the point of death. This is a terrifying experience. It can also be a dangerous one. A series of severe attacks can cause a progressive deterioration of the bronchial system, so that mucus accumulates and the muscles lose their elasticity. In such a weakened condition, the bronchial system loses its ability to fight back, and any further attack may indeed prove fatal. However, very few asthmatics die of the disorder.

Asthma is normally divided into two classes: allergic and nonallergic. Some asthmas are, at least in part, allergies—reactions to specific irritants such as pollen, molds, and animal dander. Nonallergic asthmas may stem from a variety of organic disorders, the most common causes being respiratory infections such as pneumonia and whooping cough. Indeed, the first asthma attack usually follows closely upon a respiratory infection (Alexander, 1981). However, there are many cases for which no organic cause, allergic or otherwise, can be found and for which no medical therapy proves truly effective. Such cases are often suspected to be psychogenic.

The psychogenic theory of asthma is quite old. Indeed, asthma was one of the cornerstones of "psychosomatic" theory in general, particularly in psychodynamic quarters. Yet systematic research has failed to show that psychological factors are a primary cause of asthma. There is even some doubt about psychological stress as a secondary cause—that is, as a trigger for attacks, whatever the original cause of the condition. Attempts to induce attacks in asthma sufferers by exposing them to emotion- and stress-inducing stimuli have resulted in slightly decreased air flow, but no actual attacks (e.g., Weiss et al., 1976).

Our best evidence for a psychological factor in asthma is an experiment by Luparello and his associates (1971). In what the investigators claimed was a study of air pollution, each of forty asthmatics and forty normal subjects was given five substances to inhale. The asthmatics were told that they were inhaling irritants known to be related to their previous attacks. The normal subjects were told that they were inhaling five progressively stronger concentrations of air pollutants, and that they might respond with breathing problems. Actually, all of the subjects were inhaling nonallergenic saline vapors. The normal subjects proved quite resistant to the power of suggestion; none of them showed any pathological reactions. By contrast, one-third of the asthmatic group developed constricted airways, and twelve of the forty proceeded to have full-scale attacks.

Still, this does not prove that in those cases the asthma was entirely or even largely psychogenic. It is more likely that the subjects were showing a short-term conditioning effect. That is, since in the past their expectation of having an attack was followed by an attack, the raising of that expectation by the experimenters was sufficient to bring on the attack. (If so, the response would probably have extinguished after a few trials.) As we shall see, conditioned stimuli can produce elaborate physiological responses, but that does not mean that those responses are *typically*

elicited by those stimuli, let alone that they were first established by those stimuli.

This is not to say that psychological problems are not associated with asthma. The disorder itself may lead to psychological problems, particularly in children who are overprotected because of their condition. And even if the disorder is clearly biogenic, such psychological ramifications may aggravate it.

Insomnia

Insomnia, the chronic inability to sleep, is rarely discussed in textbooks on abnormal psychology except as a symptom of other, more pervasive disorders, such as depression. Yet for an extremely large number of people, sleeplessness is the sole complaint, and one that occasions severe physical and psychological distress.

According to epidemiological surveys, the manufacture and sale of sleeping pills is now big business. In 1975, over $60 million was spent in the United States on drugstore prescriptions for sleeping pills, and this figure does not include hospital-dispensed sedatives or over-the-counter medications. It is estimated that in this country somewhere between 14 and 25 percent of the population have sleeping problems. There is no way of establishing, however, what proportion of these people would report insomnia as their only psychological problem. We do know that women tend to report sleep disturbances more often than men. We also know that sleep disturbances increase for both sexes with age. In 1977, for example, people over the age of sixty accounted for close to 40 percent of all sleeping pill prescriptions, though they made up only 15 percent of the population (Institute of Medicine, 1979).

There are three broad patterns of disturbed sleep. Some people take an extremely long time to fall asleep; others fall asleep easily but awaken repeatedly during the night; others fall asleep easily but wake up much too early in the morning (e.g., 3 or 4 A.M.) and are unable to fall asleep again. At some point in our lives, each of us has probably experienced one or another of these difficulties. The term *insomnia* is generally applied only if the problem persists and the person's daily functioning is clearly disturbed— by fatigue, irritability, inability to concentrate, and so forth—as a result.

Sleep disturbance is almost always a source of concern for the person experiencing it, and this concern leads to what is called *anticipatory anxiety* (a problem that, as we shall see, is also a major factor in sexual dysfunction). The minute the person gets into bed, or even while undressing, he or she begins to worry: Will I be able to sleep? Will it be like last night? How will I get through work again on three hours' sleep? And since worry of any kind impedes sleep, the person probably *will* have another night like last night. Hence insomnia qualifies as a classic example of the vicious cycle.

Insomnia can stem from many factors, including drugs, alcohol, caffeine, nicotine, stress and anxiety, physical illness, psychological disturbance, inactivity, poor sleep environment, and poor sleep habits (Boot-zin et al., 1983). There is evidence that poor sleepers are more likely to be psychologically disturbed than good sleepers (Monroe, 1967; Coursey et al., 1975), but again, we cannot safely conclude that psychological disturbance is a cause rather than a result of the sleep disorder. It has also been observed that many poor sleepers show abnormally high levels of physiological arousal during sleep. Their hearts beat faster than those of good sleepers, their temperature is higher, their peripheral blood vessels constrict more often, and they move more frequently during their sleeping hours (Monroe, 1967).

Overarousal may also help to explain one curious fact about insomniacs—that is, that they often report that it takes them longer to fall asleep than other measures indicate. In one study, for example, a group of insomniacs who reported that it took them an average of fifty-nine minutes to fall asleep actually fell asleep in an average of fifteen minutes according to EEG sleep criteria (Schwartz et al., 1963). In other words, they showed a brain-wave pattern associated with being asleep in *one-fourth* the amount of time that they had estimated. Actually, EEG sleep criteria, based on brain-wave patterns, are simply operational definitions. People who are "asleep" by EEG criteria will often, if you wake them up and ask them if they were asleep or awake, say that they were awake. Still, this happens far more often with insomniacs than with good sleepers (Borkovec et al., 1981). And by measures other than the EEG, some of these insomniacs *are* awake. In one experiment, a group of insomniacs "slept" (by EEG criteria) while, every four or five minutes, a voice on a tape, speaking at normal volume, said a letter of the alphabet. If awakened and asked to repeat the last letter spoken, some of

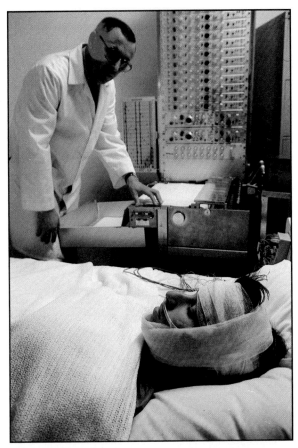

Many sleep researchers today are focusing on the problem of insomnia, which afflicts millions of people. (Roy Morsch/The Stock Market)

the subjects were able to give the right answer (Engle-Friedman et al., 1985). Such evidence suggests that at least for some insomniacs, the critical problem may be hypervigilance. That is, they are less able to turn off the sounds of the night while asleep than the rest of us. The problem may be less a failure to sleep than a failure to rest during sleep.

Most sleep-inducing drugs currently on the market are ineffective when used over a long period. And those in the barbiturate family are unsafe as well as ineffective. (We shall discuss barbiturates in Chapter 12.) Hence there is a great need for treatments that can "compete" with drugs. Insight therapy may be helpful for those whose insomnia is part of a larger psychological problem, but for those whose major or only problem is insomnia, the best route now available

Life Changes and Physical Ailments

After studying the recent histories of people with medical problems, Holmes and Holmes (1970) have concluded that many illnesses, not just the commonly recognized psychophysiological disorders, can be precipitated by the stress accompanying changes—negative or positive—in one's life. To measure the impact of different kinds of changes, Holmes and Rahe (1967) have developed the Social Readjustment Rating Scale, which rates each kind of potentially stressful event in terms of "life change units" (LCUs).

Life Event	LCUs
Death of spouse	100
Divorce	73
Marital separation	65
Jail term	63
Death of close family member	63
Personal injury or illness	53
Marriage	50
Fired at work	47
Marital reconciliation	45
Retirement	45
Change in health of family member	44
Pregnancy	40
Sex difficulties	39
Gain of new family member	39
Business readjustment	39
Change in financial state	38
Death of close friend	37
Change to different line of work	36
Change in number of arguments with spouse	35
Mortgage over $10,000	31
Foreclosure of mortgage or loan	30
Change in responsibilities at work	29
Son or daughter leaving home	29
Trouble with in-laws	29
Outstanding personal achievement	28
Wife begins or stops work	26
Begin or end school	26
Change in living conditions	25
Revision of personal habits	24
Trouble with boss	23
Change in work hours or conditions	20
Change in residence	20
Change in schools	20

Life Event	LCUs
Change in recreation	19
Change in church activities	19
Change in social activities	18
Mortgage or loan less than $10,000	17
Change in sleeping habits	16
Change in number of family get-togethers	15
Change in eating habits	15
Vacation	13
Christmas	12
Minor violations of the law	11

The more LCUs you compile in a short period of time, the more prone you are to disease. In one sample Holmes found that of those who had absorbed more than 300 LCUs during a one-year period, 86 percent experienced some serious health problem, whereas health changes were found in only 48 percent of those who had scored between 150 and 300.

Other studies have found associations between life stress and a wide variety of disorders. For example, life stress has been found to be associated with broken bones (Tollefson, 1972) and, as mentioned in the text, with the onset of cancer in children (Jacobs and Charles, 1980). However, these studies involved retrospective analyses: the scale was administered after the illness began. Such retrospective studies cannot demonstrate that stress *caused* the illness. Although no prospective studies in which LCUs are measured first and subjects are then observed for symptoms of illness have been done on cancer, such relationships have been found for minor diseases. For example, in studies of the armed services, recent life change levels predicted the symptoms of minor illness within a year (Rahe and Arthur, 1978). And in a well-controlled study of streptococcal throat infections, throat cultures were taken from each family member in the study at least every three weeks for one year. Families were interviewed periodically to rate each person's level of stress. Investigators found that respiratory infections were four times more likely to follow a family crisis than to precede it (Meyer and Haggerty, 1962).

is probably behavioral therapy, which typically combines relaxation training with procedures aimed at strengthening the habit of falling asleep at bedtime (Bootzin and Engle-Friedman, 1987).

Cancer

For years it was believed that whatever physical disorders might be associated with psychological stress, cancer was not one of them. Then, a few decades ago, researchers began to discover what seemed to be correlations between susceptibility to cancer and certain kinds of psychological characteristics. One researcher, Caroline Bedell Thomas, gave psychological tests to a large sample of medical students in 1946 and then recontacted them every year to check on their health. By 1977, forty-eight of her subjects had developed cancer, and according to Thomas, those subjects showed a marked tendency toward emotional restraint, the "bottling up" of strong feelings, whether positive or negative. In subsequent studies of people already suffering from cancer, other researchers have found that those who were able to express negative feelings—fear, horror, anger—about the disease were more likely to survive it than the more stoical types (Rogentine et al., 1979). Besides emotional restraint, other psychological variables suspected as possible contributors to cancer are a sense of "helplessness/hopelessness" and, possibly as a cause thereof, the experience of severe personal loss (Jemmott and Locke, 1984). One study found that of four hundred cancer patients, 72 percent had suffered the loss of an important personal relationship within eight years prior to the diagnosis of cancer, compared with 10 percent of a control group within a comparable period (Le Shan, 1966). Likewise, a study of children with cancer found that a significant percentage had undergone serious life changes, often involving the loss of an important relationship, within a year prior to the diagnosis (Jacobs and Charles, 1980).

Recent animal studies seem to support the proposed relationship between the growth of cancer and the experience of helplessness in the face of stressful events. In one study, Sklar and Anisman (1979) implanted tumor cells in rats and then divided the rats into three groups. One group received electric shocks that they could escape by pressing a bar. The second group received inescapable shocks, and the third group, no shocks. The experimenters found that the tumors grew more quickly in the rats given inescapable shocks than in either of the other groups. In a more recent study, with much the same design, the cancer cells were implanted in smaller doses, so that the animals' immune systems could conceivably combat them. The results were quite striking: the rats given the inescapable shocks were only half as likely to reject the cancer and were twice as likely to die of it as the escapable-shock and no-shock groups (Visintainer et al., 1982).

It is important to note that the proposition being tested in these experiments is not that stress *causes* cancer but that it influences the course of cancer, by draining the strength of the immune system. This interaction between psychological factors and the immune system, mediated by the central nervous system, is now the focus of a rapidly developing subspecialty, **psychoneuroimmunology.** Psychoneuroimmunologists have established that stress does directly affect the immune system (Laudenslager et al., 1983). They have also found that mental imagery can alter the workings of the immune system. In one study, highly hypnotizable subjects increased their immune response when, under hypnosis, they were given the suggestion that their white blood cells were "powerful sharks" destroying "weak germs" (Hall, 1983).

These findings suggest that psychological factors not only influence the development of cancer but may be enlisted in its treatment. Several researchers are now investigating this possibility. Perhaps the best-known psychological therapy for cancer patients is that developed by Carl and Stephanie Simonton, in which patients are encouraged to visualize defensive forces within their bodies attacking and devouring the cancer cells. The idea is to restore the patient's sense of control, a psychological change that presumably will lead to actual immunological control over the cancer. The Simontons have reported some surprising successes with "incurable" patients, as have other researchers (e.g., Le Shan, 1966) who have taken somewhat different approaches.

Such therapies are offered not as replacements for drug and radiation therapy but as strategies to be used in conjunction with these medical procedures. Even so, many physicians distrust them, claiming that they raise hopes that will only be dashed. Opponents also feel that such psychological theories and therapies tend to burden incurable cancer patients with responsibility for the disease. The patients not only must die; they must die feeling that their failure to recover is their fault—a fate doubly cruel. Indeed, the possibility of psychological factors in the development of cancer is still a matter of speculation, and much more research will be needed before such a connection is widely accepted, let alone therapies based on it.

PERSPECTIVES ON STRESS-RELATED PHYSICAL DISORDERS

Predictably, psychological theories of stress-related physical disorders are concerned primarily with stages 1 and 2 of the disregulation model: the types of stressors to which the person is and has been exposed, and the manner in which the brain processes new stimuli as a result of past experience. There are also sociocultural theories, which tend to focus exclusively on one aspect of stage 1—the demands that the society at large places on the individual. Finally, there are neuroscience theories, which emphasize the pos-

This laboratory rat was trained through operant conditioning to regulate its vascular functioning so that one ear flushed while the other ear paled. This is one of several recent studies showing that what were once considered involuntary responses can sometimes be taught by operant conditioning. (Bernard Gotfryd/Newsweek Magazine)

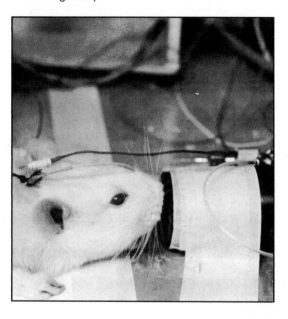

sibility of organic predisposition to disregulation at stages 2, 3, and 4. It should be pointed out that all these theories are compatible with the disregulation model; they merely emphasize different stages as the site of the disregulation.

The Behavioral Perspective

The Conditioning of Disregulation   For years, as we have seen, it was generally accepted that autonomic responses were involuntary. Therefore, if conditioning were involved in the disregulation of these responses, it would have to be respondent conditioning, for operant conditioning requires that the organism be capable of voluntarily modifying its response in order to obtain rewards or avoid punishments. It is possible to explain a physical disorder in terms of respondent conditioning. Imagine, for example, that a child tends to respond to an allergen such as dust with asthma attacks. If certain neutral stimuli were consistently paired with the experience of inhaling dust, then those stimuli could also become precipitants of attacks. Such explanations did not seem sufficient, however. First, if we assume that in many cases the conditioned stimuli were presented *without* the unconditioned stimulus (the dust), then the conditioned response would have been difficult to acquire or would have been extinguished. Of course, it might conceivably be maintained by rewards; indeed, it seemed quite plausible that asthma, for example, was reinforced to some degree by rewarding consequences (getting attention from mother, being able to stay home from school). But this could not be, for the autonomic response was *involuntary* and therefore not subject to operant conditioning.

Then, in the sixties, a number of research reports suggested that autonomic responses were in fact under some kind of voluntary control. Two investigators found that subjects could change their heart rate in order to avoid electric shock (Frazier, 1966; Shearn, 1962). In the late sixties a series of now-classic studies with rats showed that not only heart rate but also blood pressure and urine formation could be modified through operant conditioning (Miller, 1969). One rat was even taught to dilate the blood vessels in one ear and at the same time to constrict the blood vessels in the other ear in response to a cue (Di Cara and Miller, 1968). Clearly, some autonomic responses could not only be controlled but controlled with great precision.

This discovery had two important consequences. First, it helped to explain how learning could operate in the development of physical disorders: if the disorder had any rewarding consequences, then these consequences might be maintaining the disorder through operant conditioning. Second, whether or not voluntary control was involved in the development of the disorder, it could be enlisted to relieve disorder.

Biofeedback Training   Since these early experiments, it has been found that the physiological responses underlying most of the disorders we have discussed in this chapter can be partially controlled if patients are first trained to recognize these responses in their bodies—to know what it "feels like" when their heart rate or blood pressure, for example, goes up and down. Given this information, the patient can then *make* it go up and down. This type of training is known as **biofeedback training.** A hypertensive patient, for example, will be fitted with an apparatus that beeps as his blood pressure rises; a migraine patient will be hooked up to a machine that shows waves on a screen indicating the constriction and dilation of the blood vessels in her head. The patients, in other words, are given immediate feedback on their bodily functioning and then somehow, through a process that we do not yet understand, they begin to exert control over this functioning—a control that it is hoped will extend beyond the biofeedback laboratory, into their daily lives. Such training is usually combined with other techniques, particularly relaxation training, in order to facilitate the patient's relaxation response.

Biofeedback training has been used most effectively with tension headaches, migraine headaches, and muscle retraining following strokes or spinal cord injuries (Olton and Noonberg, 1980). Disappointingly, it has not been especially effective with hypertension, producing results no better than relaxation training alone.

Biofeedback can teach people not only how to relieve stress but to identify the aspects of their lives that are generating stress. In one program, for example, hypertensives were given blood-pressure feedback while they talked about various aspects of their lives. By hearing the machine beep whenever they began to discuss their marriages or jobs or whatever, they learned what areas of their lives were causing their stress problems. This feedback gave them the information necessary to identify the areas in which

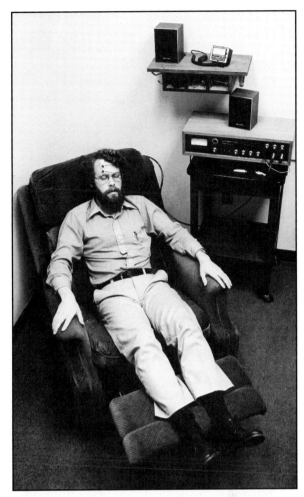

With the use of biofeedback devices, subjects can monitor their own biological processes. Here, via electrodes attached to the skull, the subject picks up the rhythm of his brain-waves and, in time, can learn to control them. (Ken Robert Buck & University Hospital, Boston/Stock, Boston)

they needed to cope more effectively in order to lower their blood pressure (Lynch et al., 1982).

It should be noted that biofeedback fits nicely into Schwartz's disregulation model. Many of the medical treatments for physical disorders serve to enhance disregulation. Drugs, for example, bypass the body's own regulatory capabilities and simply suppress the body's signals. (And in the process of regulating one system, they often disregulate other systems—a phenomenon that we call *side effects.*) Biofeedback, on the other hand, retrains patients to "listen" to their bodies and exercise their own natural capabilities to restore regulation (Schwartz, 1977).

Predictability and Control   As with anxiety, so with stress: the cognitive behaviorists have pointed out that there is more to the process than simply stimulus and response. Two variables that seem to be particularly important in stress reactions are the predictability of the stressful stimulus and the individual's control over the stimulus.

As research has shown, predictable stimuli are less stressful than unpredictable stimuli. This principle was borne out during the London blitz of World War II. Londoners, who were bombed regularly and frequently, experienced very few serious stress reactions, whereas people in the countryside, who were bombed far less frequently but unpredictably, often responded with severe anxiety (Vernon, 1941). That predictability can affect the conversion of stress into physical illness was shown in Jay Weiss's ulcer experiments with rats (1977), described earlier. As we noted, the ability of many of the "executive" rats to survive the experiment without ulceration was probably due not only to their control of the shock but also to its predictability—the fact that it was always preceded by a warning signal.

However, their control of the shock was probably even more important. Crucial as predictability is in protecting the organism against stress, control is apparently even more crucial (Thompson, 1981). Remember the rats who were implanted with the cancer cells. Remarkably, the rats who were able to control the shock were as likely to reject the cancer as those who received no shock (Visintainer et al., 1982). This phenomenon is presumably related to Bandura's theory of "efficacy expectations" and their effect on anxiety levels (Chapters 3 and 8). As common sense would suggest, the subjective stressfulness of an experience depends less on how dangerous or painful it is than on how effective we expect to be in defending ourselves against the pain or danger. Thus a self-confident bomber pilot may feel far less stress flying over enemy lines than a nervous person taking his first airplane trip.

These cognitive principles have been put into practice in so-called stress management programs (Meichenbaum and Jaremko, 1983). The goal of such programs is to pinpoint the cognitive and environmental sources of the patient's stress and then to build up the skills that he or she needs in order to cope with those stressors. If the person's problem is a feeling of being pushed around by others, for example, assertiveness training may be given, to teach the person how to avoid being pushed around. Likewise, people who feel overwhelmed by demands on their time may be given help with time management. Most patients are also instructed in muscle relaxation, either through the contracting-and-relaxing technique (see Chapter 20) or through meditation.

The Psychodynamic Perspective

Psychodynamic theorists, as we have seen, regard most behavior as symptomatic of buried emotional content. Thus it comes as no surprise that the psychodynamic school was the first to recognize that psychological difficulties might contribute significantly to physical illness. Traditionally psychodynamic theorists have referred to stress-related physical disorders as *organ neuroses*. As the term suggests, psychodynamic theory regards these disorders as caused by the same mechanisms, and treatable by the same therapy, as the anxiety, somatoform, and dissociative disorders.

Organ Neuroses   Like the anxiety, somatoform, and dissociative disorders, such physical disorders as asthma, hypertension, and ulcer are regarded by psychodynamic theorists as related to disturbances in psychosexual development—disturbances that generate conflicts in the unconscious. As in the other "neuroses," the conflict produces anxiety, and anxiety is met with defense. In the "organ neuroses," however, the defense leads to some somatic expression of the conflict (e.g., increased gastric secretion), which in turn leads to physical illness (e.g., ulcer).

Early psychodynamic theorists argued in addition that the symptom was a covert expression of the conflict—that an ulcer, for example, was related to an oral conflict, colitis to an anal conflict, and so forth. But the current view is far less tidy. While psychodynamic theorists do regard the "choice of symptom" in conversion disorders as a clue to the underlying problem (Chapter 8), they tend to see the "organ neuroses" as far less specific to the nature of the conflict.

Psychodynamic theorists regard family interactions as central in the etiology of stress-related physical disorders, as of all other psychological disorders. And they may be correct, for these disorders tend to run in families. Migraine, hypertension, asthma, and ulcer are all more common in families of people with these disorders than in the population at large. However, this could be a function of shared genes rather than, or as well as, of shared emotional distress.

Many psychodynamic theorists, particularly the more orthodox ones, employ an extremely broad definition of stress-related physical disorders. For example, in a book devoted to what was then called psychosomatic medicine, Dunbar (1935) had much to say about the unconscious wishes of people who are accident prone. Freud himself took the position that in the course of human behavior, there was no such thing as an accident. Likewise, psychodynamic theorists have proposed that the unconscious may be implicated in many disorders that others consider purely organic, such as tuberculosis (Weiss and English, 1943). Most physicians would regard this as overinterpretation. However, as we have seen, recent research supports the position that all physical conditions involve psychological processes, although perhaps not the specific psychological processes postulated by psychodynamic theory.

Aside from recommending medical care when it is needed, psychodynamic therapists treat stress-related physical disorders no differently from any other anxiety-based disorder. The general goal is to identify the buried conflict, either—in orthodox psychoanalysis—by dream analysis and free association or—in modified psychodynamic therapies—by face-to-face discussion of problems and their roots in the past.

Personality Theories

Several decades ago, psychodynamic theorists attempted to link "symptom choice" not only to the nature of the conflict but also to personality type— an approach that appealed to many nonpsychodynamic theorists as well. Dunbar (1935), on the basis of interviews with patients, sketched a number of such personality portraits. Eczema sufferers were self-punitive, frustrated, helpless, and hungry for affection; they were the children of conscientious but emotionally distant parents. Migraine patients were hardworking, conscientious, perfectionistic, and committed to a variety of "good causes." Similarly, Alexander (1939) described hypertensives as inhibited in the expression of aggressive feelings—a handicap that made them envious, ineffective, and self-demeaning, which in turn led to further inhibition of aggression. Later studies, however, tended to discredit this trait-cluster approach. Though classic cases do turn up—inhibited

Type A personalities, according to Friedman and Rosenman, keep themselves under unremitting pressure. These people—driven, impatient, and unable to relax—are much more likely to have heart attacks than people who can "take it easy." (Arthur Tress)

hypertensives, perfectionistic migraine sufferers—the population of patients with each of these disorders seems to be quite heterogeneous.

Nevertheless, the search for traits and attitudes that may predispose people to specific disorders continues. An example is the book *Type A Behavior and Your Heart* (1974), by Friedman and Rosenman. The thesis of this book is that hypertension, along with other cardiovascular disorders, tends to strike a specific kind of personality, which they call Type A. Unlike Alexander's inhibited hypertensives, Friedman and Rosenman's Type A people are aggressive achievers. They talk, walk, and eat rapidly, and are highly impatient. They fidget in frustration if kept waiting by an elevator or a traffic light. They finish other people's sentences for them. They pride themselves on getting things done in less time than other people, and they measure their own performance by rigorous standards. In short, they keep themselves under unremitting pressure—pressure that eventually takes its toll on their cardiovascular systems.

In an impressive longitudinal study, 2,249 male executives between the ages of thirty-nine and fifty-nine were evaluated and followed for nine years (Rosenman et al., 1975). Approximately half of them were identified as Type A and the other half as Type B (the more relaxed, patient executive). Of the 257 men who had heart attacks during the nine years, 178 were Type A while only 79 were Type B—a striking 2-to-1 differential. Further studies have shown that two particular components of the Type A pattern, impatience and competitive drive, are particularly predictive of heart disease (Matthews et al., 1977). It seems, actually, that the cardiovascular systems of Type A people may be overresponsive to competitive stress. In one study, Type A and Type B college students were asked to play computer ping-pong. At a certain point, the experimenters began to drop derogatory remarks about the subjects' performance. These criticisms led to increases in blood pressure, heart rate, and adrenaline secretion in the Type A's but not in the Type B's (Glass et al., 1980). Similar cardiovascular changes were seen in Type A's, but not in Type B's, when they were asked to compete with one another in solving timed mental arithmetic problems (Williams et al., 1982).

This persuasive evidence has led to a series of programs designed to teach Type A's to cope with stress in a more Type B fashion, and thus prevent heart disease. One such project assembled 1,035 male and female patients who had suffered a heart attack within the previous six months. A third were assigned to Type A behavioral counseling and another third to cardiac counseling, having to do with diet, exercise, and medication. The remaining third served as the control group. After three years the recurrence of heart attacks was lowest in the Type A counseling group and highest in the control group (Friedman et al., 1982; Thoresen et al., 1982). This finding suggests that heart disease is related to Type A behavior and that Type A's can control heart disease by altering their behavior.

The Sociocultural Perspective

Several theorists claim that a major source of disregulation is to be found at stage 1, in the pressures that society places on the individual. In a provocative volume titled *Man's Presumptuous Brain* (1961), Albert Simeons argues that many physical disorders stem from a basic conflict between social mores and biological instincts. The instinct on which Simeons focuses is the "fight-or-flight" response: the state of intense sympathetic arousal, described earlier, in which heart rate and respiration rate increase, digestion slows, adrenaline is pumped into the blood,

and so forth, in response to a serious threat. This response presumably evolved, both in our species and in other species, because it was adaptive: it prepared the body to take quick action in the face of danger. According to Simeons, however, cultural evolution has now made this response maladaptive for human beings. While other animals can still fight or flee, human beings are taught to "reason" with their enemies, resist quietly, "stay cool," or try some other civilized strategy. Unfortunately, these indirect solutions, even if they take care of the threat, are much less efficient than direct physical action in returning the body to a state of balance. The arousal remains bottled up inside the body and, according to Simeons, fosters physical disorders.

Weiss's studies with rats provide some support for this hypothesis. When given electric shocks to their tails, rats will instinctively fight with one another. Weiss and his colleagues (1976) found that rats that were shocked together, so that they could attack and even seriously wound one another, developed much less stomach ulceration than rats that were shocked alone, with no one to attack. Thus the freedom to make an aggressive response does help to prevent stress-related disorders in rats, and possibly in human beings as well.

Another aspect of modern industrial society that may contribute to stress-related disorders is the disruption of marriage and the family. Every year the number of single-person households in the United States creeps upward. The number of unmarried people is of course far greater. And according to an impressive array of findings, these people, in attempting to live without regular social support, are depriving themselves of potent protection against illness. There is considerable evidence that social support helps people to recover from injury and disease (Cohen and Wills, 1985; Meyerowitz, 1980; Silver and Wortman, 1980; Sklar and Anisman, 1981). There is even more evidence that people without social support are more prone to disease. Among the leading causes of premature death in our society are heart disease, cancer, strokes, cirrhosis of the liver, hypertension, and pneumonia. For every one of these disorders, without exception, premature death rates are significantly higher in the unmarried than in the married, among both men and women. In the case of heart disease, our society's major killer, the death rate, depending on age group, is anywhere from two to five times higher among the divorced, the single, and the widowed than among the married (Lynch, 1977). While the lack of an intimate relationship may predispose people to disease, the *loss* of such a relationship may be an even greater health hazard. Recall the findings, described earlier, on the high percentage of cancer patients whose diagnosis had followed soon after the loss of an important relationship.

In addition to the breakup of the family, other broad changes in our society appear to be affecting the susceptibility of certain groups to stress-related disorders. For example, ulcers were once four times as prevalent among men as among women. This ratio has now been reduced to about 2 to 1, presumably because more women are now doing the same work as men and are therefore exposed to the same stressors. As women become a larger and larger percentage of the work force and increasingly assume jobs of great responsibility, it is possible that the sex differential will disappear altogether. Likewise, if the fact that blacks are twice as likely as whites to develop hypertension is due to the stresses of being a disadvantaged minority rather than to genes (or to a salt-heavy diet, another possibility), this ratio may also be equalized as opportunities are equalized.

At one time it was thought that stress-related physical complaints were the exclusive property of industrialized cultures—a testament to the psychological burdens of industrialization. Cross-cultural studies do indicate that these complaints are much less common in nonindustrial societies, but because of the generally high mortality rates in these societies, such data are difficult to interpret.

In sum, while the evidence is disputable, there is some indication that both socialization and specific sociocultural patterns create psychological pressure that can be converted into physical disorders. Again, these sociocultural stressors should not be regarded as *the* cause, but rather as one among several contributing causes.

The Neuroscience Perspective

As we noted earlier, such disorders as ulcer, asthma, and hypertension are probably due not to stress alone but to stress operating on bodies that are predisposed to these disorders by certain variations in their functioning. The effort of biological researchers has been to identify those variations—a line of investigation that is still in its early stages.

Genetic Predisposition   As we have seen, stress-related physical disorders tend to run in families—a fact that suggests genetic causation. It is known, for example, that the incidence of ulcers among the brothers of ulcer sufferers is twice as high as it is in the normal population (Gregory and Rosen, 1965). In itself, this is certainly no basis on which to conclude that people inherit a tendency to develop ulcers. Growing up in the same family, two brothers might easily *learn* the same maladaptive way of coping with stress. However, other evidence indicates that learning is not the whole story. For one thing, there is a correlation between ulcers and blood type, an inherited characteristic. People with type O blood are more likely to develop ulcers than people with other blood types (Berg, 1969; Evans et al., 1968). Second, one researcher, examining thirty-four pairs of monozygotic twins and seventy-eight pairs of dizygotic twins, found a 50 percent concordance rate for peptic ulcers in the MZ twins, as opposed to 14 percent in the DZ twins (Eberhard, 1968). Third, it is apparently possible to breed ulcer-prone rats. In one experiment, a large number of rats were exposed to stress and then examined for ulcers. Those that developed ulcers were subsequently inbred, and their offspring were put through the same test and selection process. This procedure was repeated through six generations. The result was a group of rats all of which, without exception, developed ulcers after twelve hours of physical restraint. Another group of rats, not bred for ulcer susceptibility, were also subjected to twelve hours of restraint; of these only 20 percent developed ulcers (Sines, 1959, 1963).

Genes may play a role in hypertension as well. As we saw earlier, people with at least one hypertensive parent show greater cardiovascular reactions to stress than people without a family history of hypertension. This evidence is supported by twin studies, which have found exaggerated reactivity to be more commonly shared between MZ twins than between DZ twins or siblings (Rose and Chesney, 1986). Since we know from longitudinal studies that people with heightened cardiovascular reactivity are at risk for hypertension (Falkner et al., 1981), early identification and treatment of stress-reactive people should help to prevent this disorder.

Somatic Weakness   In view of the differences in our genetic endowments and physiological histories—

diet, illness, accident, and so on—it is unlikely that any two human beings have an equivalent set of organ systems. According to the theory of **somatic weakness,** a psychophysiological complaint is most likely to develop in a person's weakest or most vulnerable organ system. This theory, then, focuses on stage 3 of the disregulation model. Consider, for example, a person with a strong digestive system, an average vascular system, and a weak respiratory system. Severe stress of any kind would be likely to have a damaging effect on the respiratory system, possibly in the form of asthma. There is some evidence in support of this hypothesis. Rees (1964), for example, has shown that 80 percent of the asthmatic children he studied had previously suffered from respiratory ailments. Likewise, as we saw earlier, chronic hypertensives seem to show structural changes in the walls of their blood vessels—changes that apparently are a decisive factor in making the condition chronic. Possibly a stronger vascular system might have bounced back, even under conditions of severe stress.

SUMMARY

The mind-body problem—that is, the problem of the relationship between mental and physical processes—has for centuries been a subject for debate. Until recently, scientists tended to regard mind and body as separate entities, and therefore distinguished between psychological and physical (or organic) illnesses. While scientists acknowledged the existence of certain psychophysiological illnesses—illnesses due in part to psychological stress—most illnesses were thought to be purely organic. More recent research suggests that mind and body are in fact a unity and that *any* physical disorder may be affected by psychological stress. Accordingly, recent editions of the *DSM* have replaced the list of psychophysiological disorders with a single category, "psychological factors affecting physical condition." Researchers now take a more holistic view, recognizing that physical illness can cause psychological stress and that emotional factors in turn affect the course of physical illness. Behavioral medicine, or health psychology, favors the holistic approach and applies the science of psychology and the techniques of behaviorism to the study and treatment of stress-related physical disorders.

The physiological changes associated with emotion play an important role in the development of these disorders. The role of the autonomic nervous system (ANS), which connects the central nervous system (CNS) to the smooth muscles and the internal organs, is to adjust the body's "automatic" functions to the demands of the environment. The ANS has two divisions: (1) the sympathetic division, which mobilizes the body to meet environmental challenges or demands by increasing heart rate, blood pressure, and adrenaline flow, and (2) the parasympathetic division, which generally reverses these processes to permit the body to rebuild energy resources depleted by sympathetic activity. Although one division may be more active than the other at a given moment, both are constantly in operation, and both react to stress. The precise reaction patterns of the two divisions of the ANS are of interest to researchers studying stress-related physical disorders. In addition to the general arousal pattern described in Selye's "general adaptation syndrome" model—arousal, resistance, and exhaustion—there appear to be highly specific responses that vary according to the nature of the stress (stressor specificity) and the individual (individual response specificity).

Any given physiological function is regulated by a complex cycle of reactions. According to Schwartz's negative-feedback or "disregulation" model, this cycle consists of four stages: (1) the environment makes a demand on the organism; (2) the demand is processed by the brain (CNS), which then sends a message (via the ANS) to the peripheral organ to adjust its functioning to the environmental demand; (3) the peripheral organ makes the adjustment; (4) when the adjustment has been made, negative feedback—the message that whatever the brain turned on it should now turn off—is sent back (again via the ANS) from the peripheral organ to the brain, so that the brain can then make the necessary *re*adjustment. Physical disorders result when this regulatory cycle is disturbed. The disregulation may be due to excessive environmental demands (stage 1), faulty CNS information processing (stage 2), malfunctioning in the peripheral organ (stage 3), or inappropriate negative feedback (stage 4). The disregulation model thus views disorder as part of a system and symptoms as messages of dysfunction in that system.

In studying such stress-related physical disorders as ulcers, obesity, essential hypertension, headache (including migraine), asthma, insomnia, and even cancer, researchers have focused on different stages of the regulatory cycle as the primary site of disregulation. However, any given case of any one of these disorders is probably the result of breakdown at several stages. Essential hypertension, for example, may be caused by several interactive factors, including a threatening environment (stage 1), a tendency to inhibit anger or aggression (stage 2), structural changes in the peripheral blood vessels (stage 3), and lack of feedback from baroreceptors (stage 4); insomnia may in many cases be essentially a problem of overarousal; and the development of cancer may be influenced by stress, through its direct effects on the immune system.

Most psychological research on stress-related physical disorders focuses on disregulation at stages 1 and 2 (the types of stressors and the way the brain processes new stimuli as the result of past experience). Behavioral theorists emphasize the role of respondent and operant conditioning; in other words, they find that conditioning is involved in the disregulation of autonomic responses. Behavioral therapists treat stress-related physical disorders through biofeedback training, in which patients are taught to recognize and control autonomic responses, and through stress management, in which they are helped to pinpoint the source of stress and develop appropriate coping skills. Psychodynamic theorists emphasize the role of unconscious conflicts and family interactions; treatment consists of insight therapy. Other investigators have explored the possibility that certain clusters of personality traits, certain attitudes toward stress, and certain types of social demands may make people prone to specific physical disorders; Type A behavior, for example, is characteristic of a personality construct that is related to heart disease. The sociocultural view focuses on disregulation at stage 1, where social factors such as the breakdown of the family become stressors. Finally, it is generally acknowledged that biological predisposition plays a role in the development of many stress-related physical disorders. Physiological and neuroscience researchers focus on stages 2, 3, and 4 to identify the hereditary, biochemical, and other organic variations that may predispose individuals to specific disorders.

The Mood Disorders

Some of us respond to stress by going into a "high"—becoming feverishly active, going out a great deal, plowing through unusual amounts of work, and generally feeling excited, a bit reckless, and quite pleased with ourselves. Most of us have also known the opposite state, a mood of dejection in which nothing seems worthwhile, least of all ourselves. In other words, **mania** and **depression,** in mild and temporary forms, are part of ordinary human existence. For some people, however, such mood swings become so prolonged and extreme as to disrupt their lives. These conditions are known as the **mood disorders** (also called *affective disorders,* "affect" meaning emotion).

The mood disorders have been recognized and written about since the beginning of the history of medicine. Both mania and depression were described in detail by Hippocrates in the fourth century B.C. And as early as the first century A.D., the Greek physician Aretaeus observed that manic and depressive behaviors sometimes occurred in the same person and seemed to stem from a single disorder. In the early nineteenth century, Philippe Pinel (1801) wrote a compelling account of depression, using the Roman emperor Tiberius and the French king Louis XI as illustrations. Depression has also been vividly described by some of its more famous victims. In one of his recurring episodes of depression, Abraham Lincoln wrote, "If what I feel were equally distributed to the whole human family, there would not be one cheerful face on earth." Winston Churchill also spoke of his struggles with what he referred to as "the mad dogs of depression."

Even though they have been scrutinized by scientists for centuries, these debilitating extremes of mood still remain something of a mystery. What is known about them will be outlined in the first part of this chapter. In the second section of the chapter we shall turn our attention to suicide, which is often the result of depression.

CHARACTERISTICS OF MANIC AND DEPRESSIVE EPISODES

One of the most characteristic features of the mood disorders is their episodic quality. Within a few weeks, or in some cases within a few days, a person who has been functioning normally is plunged into despair or scaling the heights of mania. Once the episode has run its course, the person may return to normal or near-normal functioning, though he or she is likely to have further episodes of mood disturbance. The nature of the episode (whether it is depressive or manic), its severity, and its time course determine the diagnosis and often the treatment as well—matters that we will discuss below. For now, let us examine more closely the typical features of manic and depressive episodes. It should be kept in mind that we are describing here the severest forms of the disturbance.

Manic Episode

The typical **manic episode** begins rather suddenly, over the course of a few days. It may last from several days to several months, and then usually ends as abruptly as it began. *DSM-III-R* (p. 217) describes the prominent features of the manic episode as follows:

1. *Elevated, expansive, or irritable mood.* The mood change is the essential, "diagnostic" feature of a manic episode. Typically, manics feel wonderful, see the world as a wonderful place, and have limitless enthusiasm for whatever they are doing or plan to do. This expansiveness is usually mixed with irritability. From the heights of their euphoria, manics often see other people as slow, doltish spoilsports and can become quite hostile, especially when someone tries to interfere with their behavior. In some cases irritability may be

the manic's dominant mood, with euphoria either intermittent or simply absent.

2. *Hyperactivity.* The expansive mood is usually accompanied by restlessness and increased activity—physical, social, occupational, and often sexual.

3. *Talkativeness.* Manics tend to talk loudly, rapidly, and constantly. Their speech is often full of puns, irrelevant details, and jokes that they alone find funny.

4. *Flight of ideas.* Manics often have racing thoughts. This is one reason why they speak so rapidly—to keep up with the flow of their ideas. Manic speech also tends to shift abruptly from one topic to the next.

5. *Inflated self-esteem.* Manics tend to see themselves as extremely attractive, important, and powerful people, capable of great achievements in fields in which they may in fact have no talent whatever. Thus they may begin composing symphonies, designing nuclear weapons, or calling the White House with advice on how to run the country.

6. *Sleeplessness.* The manic episode is almost always marked by a decreased need for sleep. Manics may sleep only two or three hours a night and yet have twice as much energy as those around them.

7. *Distractibility.* Manics are easily distracted. While doing or discussing one thing, they will notice something else in the environment (e.g., a magazine cover, the clothing of a passer-by) and abruptly turn their attention to that instead.

8. *Reckless behavior.* The euphoria and grandiose self-image of manics often lead them into flamboyant and ill-advised actions: buying sprees, reckless driving, careless business investments, sexual indiscretions, and so forth. They usually become quite indifferent to the needs of others and think nothing of yelling in restaurants, calling friends in the middle of the night, or spending the family savings on a Cadillac.

For a condition to merit the diagnosis of manic episode, it must be severe enough either to have caused the person to be hospitalized or to have interfered

Everyone is capable of an occasional outburst of mania—behaving giddily, going on a shopping spree, and the like. A true manic episode, however, results in hospitalization or serious interference with work or social relationships. (Alan Carey/The Image Works)

seriously with his or her work or social relationships. The following account describes a clear-cut case:

> Terrence O'Reilly, a single 39-year-old transit authority clerk, was brought to the hospital in May, 1973, by the police after his increasingly hyperactive and bizarre behavior and nonstop talking alarmed his family. He loudly proclaimed that he was not in need of treatment, and threatened legal action against the hospital and police.
>
> The family reported that a month prior to admission Mr. O'Reilly took a leave of absence from his civil service job, purchased a large number of cuckoo clocks and then an expensive car which he planned to use as a mobile showroom for his wares, anticipating that he would make a great deal of money. He proceeded to "tear around town" buying and selling the clocks and other merchandise, and when he was not out, he was continuously on the phone making "deals." He rarely slept and, uncharacteristically, spent every evening in neighborhood bars drinking heavily and, according to him, "wheeling and dealing." Two weeks before admission his mother died suddenly of a heart attack. He cried for two days, but then his mood began to soar again. At the time of admission he was $3000 in debt and had driven his family to exhaustion with his excessive activity and

overtalkativeness. He said, however, that he felt "on top of the world" (Spitzer et al., 1983, p. 115).

Major Depressive Episode

The course of a **major depressive episode** follows a smoother curve than that of a manic episode. Though in some cases a severe psychological trauma may plunge the individual into depression overnight, the onset is usually gradual, occurring over a period of several weeks or several months. The episode itself typically lasts longer than a manic episode and then ends, as it began, slowly and gradually.

As in a manic episode, the person entering a depressive episode undergoes profound changes in most aspects of his or her functioning—not just mood, but also motivation, thinking, and physical and motor functioning. The following are the characteristic features of the major depressive episode as described by *DSM-III-R* (p. 222):

1. *Depressed mood.* Almost all severely depressed adults report some degree of sadness or unhappiness, ranging from a mild melancholy to total hopelessness. This dejection may be described by the individual as utter despair,

Depression can often be "read" in a person's posture and expression: the head hangs, the shoulders stoop, and movements are infrequent and sluggish. (Charles Harbutt/Archive)

loneliness, or simply boredom. Mildly or moderately depressed people may have frequent crying spells; more severely depressed patients often state that they feel like crying but cannot. Deeply depressed people generally regard their condition as irreversible; they cannot help themselves, nor can anyone possibly help them. This way of thinking has been characterized as the **helplessness-hopelessness syndrome.**

2. *Loss of pleasure or interest in usual activities.* Aside from depressed mood, the most common characteristic of a major depressive episode is reduced motivation. (One or the other of the two features must be present for this diagnosis to be given.) Whatever the depressed person used to do—work, take care of the children, talk to friends, go to the movies—no longer seems worth doing. Typically, sex drive is also greatly reduced. The onset of this pervasive apathy was described by one woman as follows:

> I began not to be able to manage as far as doing the kinds of things that I really had always been able to do easily, such as cook, wash, take care of the children, play games, that kind of thing. . . . Another thing that was very frightening to me was that I couldn't read any more. And if awakened early . . . earlier than I needed to, I sometimes would lie in bed two hours trying to make myself get up because I just couldn't put my feet on the floor. Then when I did, I just felt that I couldn't get dressed. And then, whatever the next step was, I felt I couldn't do that.*

At first, the reduced gratification from activities involving social responsibilities may be compensated for by an increase in such passive recreational activities as lying in bed watching television or reading magazines. As the depression deepens, however, even such withdrawal responses cease to give pleasure. Severely depressed patients may experience a complete "paralysis of the will"—an inability to mobilize themselves to do anything, as in the above quotation.

3. *Disturbance of appetite.* Most depressives have poor appetite and lose weight; some, however, especially those who have previously been dieters, react by eating more and putting on weight (Polivy and Herman, 1976).

4. *Sleep disturbance.* Insomnia is an extremely common feature of depression. Awakening too early and then being unable to get back to sleep is the most characteristic pattern, but depressed people may also have trouble falling asleep initially, or they may awaken repeatedly throughout the night. In some cases, the sleep disturbance, like the appetite disturbance, takes the form of excess rather than deficiency, with the patient sleeping fifteen hours a day or more.

---

* Source: "Depression: The Shadowed Valley," from the series *The Thin Edge,* © 1975 by the Educational Broadcasting Corporation.

5. *Psychomotor retardation or agitation.* Depression can usually be "read" immediately in the person's motor behavior and physical bearing. In the most common pattern, called **retarded depression,** the patient seems overcome by a massive fatigue and shows little spontaneous activity. Posture is stooped, movement is slow and deliberate, gestures are kept to a minimum, and speech is low and halting, with long pauses before answering. In severe cases, depressives may fall into a mute stupor. More rarely, the symptoms may take the opposite form, called **agitated depression,** marked by incessant activity and restlessness—hand wringing, pacing, fidgeting, complaining, and moaning.

6. *Loss of energy.* The depressive's reduced motivation is usually accompanied by a sharply reduced energy level. Without having done anything, he or she may feel exhausted all the time.

7. *Feelings of worthlessness and guilt.* Depressives are dismayed not only by life but also by themselves. Typically, they regard themselves as deficient in whatever attributes they value most: intelligence, physical attractiveness, health, social skills. Their frequent complaints about loss—whether of love, material goods, money, or prestige—may also reflect their sense of personal inadequacy. Such feelings of worthlessness are often accompanied by a profound sense of guilt. Depressives exaggerate their present and past failings and seem to search the environment for evidence of problems that they have created. If a child has trouble with schoolwork or the car has a flat tire, it is their fault.

8. *Difficulties in thinking.* In depression, mental processes, like physical processes, are usually slowed down. Depressives tend to be indecisive, and they often report difficulties in thinking, concentrating, and remembering.

9. *Recurrent thoughts of death or suicide.* Not surprisingly, in view of their emotional state, many depressives have recurrent thoughts of death and suicide. Often they will say that they (and everyone else) would be better off if they were dead, and as we shall see, some depressed people do in fact kill themselves.

The following case illustrates some features of a major depressive episode:

Paula Stansky was a 57-year-old woman, widow and mother of four children, who was hospitalized on the psychiatry service of a large county hospital near her home because, according to her children, she was refusing to eat and take care of herself.

The patient lived in a small, five-room woodframe row house with her two younger, unmarried children, aged 18 and 22. She was described as a usually cheerful, friendly woman who took meticulous care of her home. . . . About two months prior to her hospitalization, however, her younger children reported a change in their mother's usual disposition, for no apparent reason. She appeared more easily fatigued, not as cheerful, and lackadaisical about her housework. Over the course of the next few weeks, she stopped going to church and canceled her usual weekly bingo outing with neighborhood women. As the house became increasingly neglected and their mother began to spend more time sleeping or rocking in her favorite chair, apparently preoccupied, the younger children called their married brother and sister for advice.

Her 26-year-old son, who lived in a nearby town, became worried when his mother canceled the regular Sunday family dinner. He recalled a similar period about ten years previously, when he was a teenager, when his mother had gone to a hospital for about three weeks.

When her son, in response to the telephone call, arrived at her house, Ms. Stansky denied that anything was wrong. She claimed to be only tired, "possibly the flu." For the ensuing week, her children tried to "cheer her up," but with no success. After several days had gone by without her taking a bath, changing her clothes, or eating any food, her children put her in the car and drove her to the hospital emergency room where she was admitted.

On admission, Ms. Stansky was mostly mute, answering virtually no questions except correctly identifying the hospital and the day of the week. She cried periodically throughout the interview, but only shook her head back and forth when asked if she could tell the interviewer what she was feeling or thinking about. She was agitated, frequently wringing her hands, rolling her head toward the ceiling, and rocking in her chair. Her clothes were loosely fitting; her hair was in disarray. The history from her children indicated that during the past week she had been waking up at 3:00 A.M., unable to fall back to sleep. She also seemed to them to have lost considerable weight. Her weight on admission was 125 pounds, down from her usual weight of 140 to 150 pounds (Spitzer et al., 1983, p. 118).

MOOD DISORDERS: INDIVIDUAL SYNDROMES

Major Depression

People who undergo one or more major depressive episodes, with no intervening manic episodes, are said to have **major depression.** It is generally agreed that this disorder constitutes a major health problem. In the United States the prevalence of major depression is about 1 to 2 percent for men and somewhere between 3 and 4.6 percent for women (Myers et al., 1984). The lifetime risk—that is, the percentage of Americans who will experience major depression at some point in their lives—is 8 to 12 percent for men and 20 to 26 percent for women (Boyd and Weissman, 1981). In this country, depression is second only to schizophrenia (Chapter 14) in frequency of first and second admissions to mental hospitals. In outpatient clinics, depression is by far the most frequent diagnosis, accounting for as much as one-third of the patient population (Woodruff et al., 1975).

Certain groups within the population are more susceptible than others. The lower socioeconomic classes show a disproportionately high prevalence of major depression. So do women. As the above statistics indicate, women are at least twice as likely as men to be diagnosed as depressive—a fact that investigators have tried to account for with theories ranging from hormonal differences between the sexes to the changing social role of women. On the other hand, it is possible that the explanation lies in diagnostic procedures. A study of mental disorders among the Amish people of Pennsylvania found that while mood disorders were the most common form of psychological disturbance in the community, there was no difference between men and women in the prevalence of these disorders. The investigators speculate that the same may be true in the general population, the difference being that among the general population mood disorders in men are often masked by, and diagnosed as, alcoholism—a confusion that cannot occur among the Amish, since they have no alcoholism (Egeland and Hostetter, 1983).

It was once thought that susceptibility to mood disorders also varied with age, the middle-aged and the elderly being the high-risk groups. Today, however, many clinicians feel that depression is equally common among young adults, adolescents, children, and even infants, though the symptom picture differs from age

More than twice as many women as men are diagnosed as depressed, for reasons that are still being investigated. (Ed Lettau/ Photo Researchers)

group to age group. In depressed infants, the most striking and alarming sign is failure to eat. In older children, depression may manifest itself primarily as apathy and inactivity; alternatively, it may take the form of severe separation anxiety, in which the child clings frantically to parents, refuses to leave them long enough to go to school, and is haunted by fears of death (or of the parents' death). In adolescents, the most prominent symptoms may be sulkiness, negativism, withdrawal, complaints of not being understood or appreciated, and perhaps antisocial behavior and drug abuse as well (Cantwell, 1982; Gallemore and Wilson, 1972)—in other words, an exaggeration of normal adolescent problems. In the elderly, apathy and difficulties in thinking (e.g., memory loss, mild disorientation) may be the most obvious signs. In sum, depression, like any other psychological state, expresses itself differently at different stages of life.

In about 50 percent of the cases, the first major depressive episode is also the last. For the remaining 50 percent, the depression will return, perhaps many times. The course of recurrent depression varies considerably. For some people, the episodes come in clusters; for others, they are separated by years of normal functioning. In some cases, the frequency of the episodes tapers off with age; in others, the depressions come more often as the person gets older. In most cases of recurrent depression, the individual's adjustment between episodes is approximately normal. However, about one-fifth of recurrent depressives, usually those with frequent episodes, never truly return, between episodes, to **premorbid adjustment**—that is, the level of functioning that was normal for them before the onset of the disorder. This is not surprising. Depressive episodes erode self-confidence, disrupt family and marital relationships, interfere with progress in school or at work, and alter other people's expectations of the depressed person—all of which make it difficult for people coming out of a depressive episode to resume their former lives. Thus the episode itself may set up the conditions for further episodes.

The following case shows how vast a personality change this disorder can bring about:

> E. D., aged 60, was admitted to the hospital because he was depressed, ate insufficiently, and believed that his stomach was "rotting away." The patient [in the premorbid state] was described as a friendly, sociable individual, not quarrelsome, jealous, or critical, and with a sense of humor. He was considered even-tempered, slow to anger, tender-hearted, and emotional.
>
> At 51 the patient suffered from a depression and was obliged to resign his position. This depression continued for about nine months, after which he apparently fully recovered. He resumed his work but after two years suffered from a second depression. Again he recovered after several months and returned to a similar position and held it until two months before his admission. At this time he began to worry lest he was not doing his work well, talked much of his lack of fitness for his duties, and finally resigned. He spent Thanksgiving Day at his son's in a neighboring city, but while there he was sure that the water pipes in his own house would freeze during his absence and that he and his family would be "turned out into the street." A few days later he was found standing by a pond, evidently contemplating suicide. He soon began to remain in bed and sometimes wrapped his head in the bedclothing to shut out the external world. He declared that he was "rotting away inside" and that if he ate, the food would kill him. He urged the family not to touch the glasses or towels he used lest they become contaminated.
>
> On arrival at the hospital, he appeared older than his years. He was pale, poorly nourished, and dehydrated, with his lips dry, cracked, and covered with sores. His facial expression and general bearing suggested a feeling of utter hopelessness. He was self-absorbed and manifested no interest in his environment. When urged to answer questions, there was a long delay before he attempted to reply, but he finally spoke briefly, hesitatingly, and in a low tone. He occasionally became agitated and repeatedly said, "Oh, Doctor, why did I ever get into anything like this? Doctor, I am all filled up! I can't get anything through me—what am I going to do? Oh, dear! Oh, dear!" In explaining his presence in the hospital, he said he realized he had been sent by his family because they believed he would be benefited by the treatment, but added, "I don't know how they sent me here when they had not the means. My wife cannot pay for me, and by this time she must have been put out of the house" (Kolb, 1982, pp. 375–376).

Bipolar Disorder

Whereas major depression is confined to depressive episodes, **bipolar disorder,** as the name suggests, involves both manic and depressive episodes. In the usual case, bipolar disorder will first appear in the form of a manic episode. The subsequent episodes

Genetic Links to Bipolar Disorders

The Old Order Amish of Lancaster, Pennsylvania, are quiet, hard-working pacifists as a rule. Indeed, so unusual is it to find a bragging, violent, or deeply depressed individual in this community that the Amish have an expression to describe the problem: "Siss im blut"—"It's in the blood." A recent study seems to bear out their conclusion.

Scientists have long known that manic depression has some biological component. If one identical twin is afflicted with a bipolar disorder, the other has an 80 percent chance of suffering the disorder as well. But the second of fraternal twins has only a 20 percent likelihood of such mental disturbance (Kolata, 1986a). Now a recent report by Janice Egeland and her colleagues has linked bipolar disorder to a specific gene for the first time (Egeland et al., 1987).

Egeland has been studying the Amish for many years. From a scientific standpoint, they are ideal subjects. Not only are drug abuse, alcoholism, and poverty rare among the Amish, but they have large families (7 children on average) and are a closed genetic pool—all 12,000 Amish in Lancaster County are descended from 30 couples who emigrated from Europe in the early 1700s. The meticulous geneological records kept by the Amish also proved invaluable to researchers, who were able to trace all 26 suicides among the Amish since 1880 to just four families.

After taking blood samples from every member of one 81-member clan, scientists isolated the deoxyribonucleic acid (DNA) that makes up the 23 chromosomes—the genetic code of each person. They next used restriction enzymes to slice the DNA into segments. Then molecular probes were employed to seek out the one segment (genetic marker) so closely related to the gene for bipolar disorders that the two are inherited together. They found an apparent marker for manic depression on chromosome 11. Moreover, when they compared the chromosomes of the 19 family members diagnosed as suffering from psychiatric (primarily bipolar) disorders to those of the 62 family members considered psychiatrically well, they consistently found a discrepancy at chromosome 11.

Analysis of the genealogies of afflicted individuals led researchers to conclude that the responsible gene was "dominant with incomplete penetrance." Inheritance of a dominant gene from either parent makes an individual highly prone to express the traits involved. But because the penetration is incomplete in the case of the gene on chromosome 11, not all those who inherit the gene actually suffer from bipolar disorders. David Pauls and his colleagues at the Yale University School of Medicine estimate that a maximum of 63 percent of those who inherit the gene actually exhibit the symptoms of the disorder, which suggests that environmental factors may also play a role in development of manic depression (Kolata, 1986a).

While the findings of Egeland et al. provide an exciting new path for researchers hoping to understand the causes of—and thus locate better cures for—bipolar disorders, they are only a starting point. Because the study was limited to one large family, it may not be borne out by wider tests. In fact, British studies of six non-Amish families with histories of manic depression found no link between the disease and chromosome 11. Rather than viewing these results as negating the Amish study, however, many scientists see them as support for the idea that bipolar disorders are a group of related disorders with a variety of genetic—and environmental—causes that await identification.

may occur in any of a variety of patterns. The initial manic episode may be followed by a normal period, then by a depressed episode, then a normal period, and so forth. Or one episode may be followed immediately by its opposite, with normal intervals occurring only between such manic–depressive pairs. In rare cases, called the *cycling type,* mood may shuttle back and forth between mania and depression for long periods, with no intervals of normal functioning. Another rare pattern is the *mixed type,* in which depressive and manic symptoms appear simultaneously. For example, the person may show manic hyperactivity and yet weep and threaten suicide at the same time.

The addition of manic episodes is not the only characteristic that differentiates bipolar disorder from major depression. The two syndromes differ in many important respects (Depue and Monroe, 1978; Hirschfeld and Cross, 1982). First, bipolar disorder is much less common than major depression, affecting an estimated 0.4 to 0.8 percent of the adult population

(Myers et al., 1984). Second, the two disorders show different demographic profiles. Unlike major depression, bipolar disorder occurs in the two sexes with equal frequency, and while major depression is more prevalent among the lower classes, bipolar disorder is more prevalent among higher socioeconomic groups. Third, people who are married or have intimate relationships are less prone to major depression but have no advantage with respect to bipolar disorder. Fourth, people with major depression tend to have histories of low self-esteem, dependency, and obsessional thinking, whereas the premorbid personality of people with bipolar disorder is typically more normal. Fifth, whereas major depression can occur at any time of life, bipolar disorder usually has its onset before the age of thirty. Sixth, the course of the two disorders is somewhat different: in bipolar disorder, episodes are generally briefer and more frequent than in major depression. Finally, bipolar disorder is more likely to run in families than major depression. On the basis of these clues, many researchers think that the two disorders, similar as they may appear, spring from different causes. Later in this chapter we will examine the genetic evidence for this view.

Since the first episode of bipolar disorder tends to be manic, a person undergoing a manic episode, with no previous history of mood disorder, will usually be classified as having bipolar disorder, the expectation being that the person will eventually have a depressive episode. Occasionally, however, no depressive episode occurs. Instead, the person recovers and has no further periods of mood disturbance, or—even more rarely—has a series of manic episodes with no intervening depressive episodes. Such cases, it seems, should not be called bipolar disorder, since they have only one "pole." Nevertheless, they are classified as bipolar disorder, since aside from the absence of depressive episodes they resemble the classic bipolar disorder. (They respond to the same medications as bipolar disorder, there tends to be a family history of bipolar disorder, and so on.) Indeed, some researchers suspect that these exclusively manic disorders are simply cases of insufficient follow-up. Presumably, if the follow-up were thorough enough, it would reveal that in such cases the missing depressive episode did eventually occur.

The following case history illustrates the remarkable mood swings characteristic of bipolar disorder:

M. M. was first admitted to a state hospital at the age of 38, although since childhood she had been characterized by swings of mood, some of which had been so extreme that they had been psychotic in degree. At 17 she suffered from a depression that rendered her unable to work for several months, although she was not hospitalized. At 33, shortly before the birth of her first child, the patient was greatly depressed. For a period of four days she appeared in coma. About a month after the birth of the baby she "became excited" and was entered as a patient in an institution for neurotic and mildly psychotic patients. As she began to improve, she was sent to a shore hotel for one night and on the following day signed a year's lease on an apartment, bought furniture, and became heavily involved in debt. Shortly thereafter, Mrs. M. became depressed and returned to the hospital in which she had previously been a patient. After several months she recovered and, except for relatively mild fluctuations of mood, remained well for approximately two years.

She then became overactive and exuberant in spirits and visited her friends, to whom she outlined her plans for reestablishing different forms of lucrative business. She purchased many clothes, bought furniture, pawned her rings, and wrote checks without funds. She was returned to a hospital. Gradually her manic symptoms subsided, and after four months she was discharged. For a period thereafter she was mildly depressed. In a little less than a year Mrs. M. again became overactive. . . . Contrary to her usual habits, she swore frequently and loudly, created a disturbance in a club to which she did not belong, and instituted divorce proceedings. On the day prior to her second admission to the hospital she purchased 57 hats

During the past 18 years this patient has been admitted and dismissed from the hospital on many occasions. At times, with the onset of a depressed period, she has returned to the hospital seeking admission. At such times she complained that her "brain just won't work." She would say, "I have no energy, am unable to do my housework. I have let my family down; I am living from day to day. There is no one to blame but myself." During one of her manic periods, she sent the following telegram to a physician of whom she had become much enamored: "To: You; Street and No.: Everywhere; Place: the remains at peace! We did our best, but God's will be done! I am so very sorry for all of us. To brave it through thus far. Yes, Darling—from Hello Handsome. Handsome is as Handsome does, thinks, lives and breathes. It takes clear air, Brother of Mine, in a girl's hour of need. All my love to the Best Inspiration one ever had" (Kolb, 1982, pp. 376–377).

Dysthymia and Cyclothymia

There are many people who are chronically depressed or who chronically pass through depressed and expansive periods but whose condition is nevertheless not debilitating enough to merit the diagnosis of major depression or bipolar disorder. Such "subsyndromal" patterns are known as dysthymia and cyclothymia.

Dysthymia is a mild, persistent depression. Dysthymics are typically morose, introverted, overconscientious, and incapable of fun (Akiskal, 1983). In addition, they often show the low energy level, low self-esteem, suicidal ideation, and disturbances of eating, sleeping, and thinking that are associated with major depression, though their symptoms are not so severe or so numerous. The syndrome is approximately as prevalent as major depression and, like major depression, is twice as common in women as in men (Myers et al., 1984).

Cyclothymia, like dysthymia, is chronic. For years, the person never goes longer than a few months without a phase of moderately manic or depressive behavior. Because the pattern is mild and persistent, as in dysthymia, it becomes a way of life. In their manic periods, which they come to depend on, cyclothymics will often work long hours without fatigue—indeed, with their mental powers newly sharpened and creative—before lapsing back into a normal or depressed state.

Both dysthymia and cyclothymia may persist for a lifetime. In this sense they are like the personality disorders, the subject of our next chapter. But in a certain number of cases they will crystallize into a major mood disorder, cyclothymia into bipolar disorder and dysthymia into major depression or bipolar disorder (Akiskal et al., 1983; Depue et al., 1981). Because of this risk factor, the two syndromes have recently become the focus of efforts to find out what it is that predisposes people to the major mood disorders.

Dimensions of Mood Disorders

In addition to the important distinction between bipolar and major depressive disorder, there are certain "dimensions," or points of differentiation, that researchers and clinicians have found useful in classifying mood disorders. We shall discuss two such dimensions: psychotic-neurotic and endogenous-reactive.

Psychotic versus Neurotic   As we saw in Chapter 8, psychological disorders may be described, in terms of severity, as either psychotic or neurotic—a distinction that has traditionally hinged on the matter of reality contact, the ability to perceive and interact with one's environment in a reasonably efficient manner. Neurotics, as we noted, may be seriously incapacitated, but they can seldom be characterized as out of contact with reality. In **psychoses,** such as schizophrenia, on the other hand, the individual's perception of reality is drastically distorted. Many psychotics have **hallucinations,** or false sensory perceptions, and suffer from **delusions,** or false beliefs. Others simply withdraw into their own private world. In either case, the psychotic's sense of reality is so severely impaired that he or she cannot achieve even the most marginal adaptive functioning. For this reason, psychotics, unlike neurotics, are usually hospitalized.

The neurotic-psychotic distinction is often applied to depression. In psychotic depression, hallucinations, delusions, or extreme withdrawal effectively cut the tie between the individual and the environment and preclude adaptive functioning. We have already seen a good example of psychotic depression in the case of E. D. (p. 233), with his delusional belief that his stomach was rotting and that he contaminated the things he touched. Manic episodes can also have psychotic features. Many manics show thought disorders similar to those of schizophrenics, including illogical thinking, incoherence, and loosening of associations—that is, jumping from one subject to another with no apparent linkage (Harrow et al., 1986). M. M.'s letter to her doctor (p. 235) qualifies as evidence of psychotic-level thought disturbance.

Neurotic-level mood disorders may also wreak havoc on people's lives, but reality contact remains unbroken. People with these disorders still know what is going on around them and can still function to some degree—carry on a fairly reasonable conversation, find their way to the therapist's office, and so forth. Many cases of major depression and bipolar disorder remain at this level, and dysthymia and cyclothymia are by definition nonpsychotic.

In view of these important distinctions, should we conclude that neurotic and psychotic mood disorders are two different entities altogether? The traditional position is that they are. For example, Kraepelin (Chapter 1), in his original classification system, listed all incapacitating mood disorders under the heading "manic-depressive psychosis," which he considered an organic illness quite distinct from the less extreme mood disturbances that we would now call neurotic. Many theorists still hold to this position.

Others, however, argue that the distinction between neurotic and psychotic depression is quantitative rather than qualitative (Beck, 1967; Kendell, 1968). This theory, known as the **continuity hypothesis,** rests on the idea that depression appears, above all, to be an exaggerated form of everyday sadness. According to the proponents of the continuity hypothesis, psychotic depression, neurotic depression, dysthymia, and normal "blues" are simply different points on a single continuum. The more severe the disorder, the more symptoms the person is likely to experience (Beck, 1967), but there is no justification for attaching different diagnostic labels to the different levels of severity. The finding that dysthymics and cyclothymics are at risk for more severe mood disorders gives some support to the continuity hypothesis. And *DSM-III-R* in some measure reflects this position. Though diagnosticians are expected to note whether a patient's behavior is psychotic, all mood disorders, whether neurotic or psychotic, are grouped together.

A depressive episode can be triggered by grief over the death of a loved one. (Costa Manos/Magnum)

Endogenous versus Reactive   The proponents of the continuity hypothesis tend to believe that all mood disorders are in large part psychogenic. Those who hold to the Kraepelin tradition, on the other hand, generally believe that only the neurotic forms are psychogenic; the psychotic forms they regard as biogenic.

Basic to the latter point of view is a second dimension of mood disorder: the endogenous-versus-reactive dimension. Originally, these terms were intended to indicate whether or not a depression was preceded by a precipitating event, such as a death in the family or the loss of a job. Those that were linked to such an event were called **reactive;** those that were not were called **endogenous** (literally, "coming from within"). According to adherents of Kraepelin's position, neurotic depressions were generally reactive and therefore psychogenic, while psychotic depressions were generally endogenous and therefore biogenic.

As it turns out, however, the distinction is not so tidy. It is often difficult to determine with certainty whether a depression has been triggered by a specific event. Friends and family may be unaware of psychological traumas the patient has suffered, while patients themselves may forget or jumble the events leading up to the onset of the depression. What has happened, as a result, is that the endogenous-reactive dimension has been retained but has been loosened from its connection with precipitating events. Instead, the distinction is made primarily on the basis of symptomatology. Patients who show the more "vegetative," or physical, symptoms, such as sleep loss, weight loss, loss of sexual interest, and psychomotor retardation, are generally classified as endogenous, while those whose disturbance is primarily emotional and cognitive are called reactive.

The endogenous-reactive distinction made on the basis of symptoms does seem to describe a genuine difference, one that is confirmed by differences in sleep patterns (Feinberg, 1982) and also in hormone secretion (Carroll et al., 1981; Zimmerman et al., 1986). Furthermore, the distinction is useful in predicting treatment response: cases classified as endogenous are more likely to respond to biological treatments, such as drugs. Finally, the distinction may, at least in part, describe what it was originally

Seasonal Depression: More than Winter Blues

Many people—even quite normal people—find winter a dreary time. When outdoor activity means a struggle with coats and boots, when plans are spoiled by sleet or snow, when darkness descends before five o'clock, it's not surprising that people come down with the blahs.

But for some people winter is not only dreary—it is deeply depressing. In the past few years it has been recognized that people who become depressed only in the winter suffer from a peculiar mood disorder. It has been called **seasonal affective disorder,** or (perhaps appropriately) **SAD.**

The typical SAD victim is a woman (for some reason far more women than men have this problem) who has suffered from wintertime depression for years. Sometimes such people have sought help for their condition in vain; until recently, their descriptions of extreme lethargy, low spirits, and sleepiness during winter were often considered exaggerations of normal winter blues.

What causes SAD? In 1980 Dr. Norman Rosenthal of the National Institute of Mental Health proposed an explanation: during the hours of darkness the pineal gland, a tiny structure at the bottom of the brain, secretes the hormone melatonin, which is associated with drowsiness and lethargy. (Light suppresses the secretion of this hormone.) In normal people, the body's chemical balance is not disturbed by the extra melatonin secreted in winter, but victims of SAD in effect overdose on their own hormone.

If lack of sunlight is the culprit in SAD, the treatment would seem likely to be simply more light. And, in fact, it is. Most SAD victims show marked improvement after only a few days of light therapy. Typically, the person sits for several hours a day in front of a bank of fluorescent lights specially designed to include all the colors of natural daylight. With this simple technique, some people with SAD find that they retain their energy and emotional well-being even through winter's darkest days.

intended to describe. Recent studies do indicate that patients labeled reactive on the basis of symptoms have experienced more stressful life events before the onset of the depression than patients labeled endogenous (Winokur, 1985; Zimmerman et al., 1986). But research has yet to show that the term *endogenous* can be taken literally. If endogenous cases are more biogenic, then we would expect endogenous patients to show a greater family history of depression than reactives. So far, this has not proved to be the case (Andreasen et al., 1986; Zimmerman et al., 1986). One depressive disorder, however, has been convincingly linked to a biological factor, as the box on seasonal depression explains.

Depression is now a focus of intense study on the part of neuroscientists, and it would help them greatly if the more "biological" depressions could be isolated from the reactive cases. Accordingly, *DSM-III-R* requires that cases diagnosed as major depression be subtyped as with or without "melancholia," the criteria for melancholia being the vegetative symptoms. To

increase the likelihood that the diagnosis of depression with melancholia will identify a more biological subgroup, *DSM-III-R* lists biological criteria for melancholia, including prior good response to drugs or electroconvulsive therapy (ECT) and more pronounced depression in the morning.

When depression is preceded by a clear precipitating event, that event often has to do, not surprisingly, with intimate relationships. "Exit events"—death, separation, divorce, a family member's leaving home—rank high among stressors associated with the onset of depression (Paykel, 1979a). By the same token, if the individual has a close personal relationship —this means someone to confide in—the less likely the person is to succumb to depression in the face of stressful life events (Anesheusel and Stone, 1982; Brown, 1979). The same principles hold for people recovering from depression. Stress, and particularly stress connected to exit events, is associated with relapses, and social support, particularly in the form of a confidant, is associated with continued recovery, even in the face of stress (Paykel and Tanner, 1976; Cohen and Wills, 1985).

PERSPECTIVES ON THE MOOD DISORDERS

As depression is far more common than mania and as many theorists regard mania as secondary—that is, a reaction—to depression, theories of mood disorder have concentrated largely on depression alone. As we shall see, theorists who take the neuroscience perspective are the exceptions.

The Psychodynamic Perspective

Reactivated Loss   The first serious challenge to Kraepelin's biogenic theory of mood disorder came from Freud and other early psychoanalytic theorists, who argued that depression was not a symptom of organic dysfunction but a massive defense mounted by the ego against intrapsychic conflict. In his now-classic paper "Mourning and Melancholia" (1917) Freud described depression as a response to loss (real or symbolic), but one in which the person's sorrow and rage in the face of that loss are not vented but remain unconscious, thus weakening the ego. This formulation was actually an elaboration of a theory put forth by one of Freud's students, Karl Abraham (1911, 1916). Abraham had suggested that depression arises when one loses, or feels one has lost, a love object toward whom one had ambivalent (that is, both positive and negative) feelings. In the face of the love object's desertion, one's negative feelings turn to intense anger. At the same time, one's positive feelings give rise to guilt, a feeling that one failed to behave properly toward the now-lost love object. Because of this guilt—and also because of early memories in which the primary love object was symbolically "eaten up," or incorporated, by the infant—the grieving person turns his or her anger inward rather than outward, thus producing the self-hatred and despair that we call depression.

While "anger in" still figures importantly in traditional psychoanalytic discussions of depression, modern psychodynamic theorists have greatly expanded and revised this early position. There are now many psychodynamic theories of depression, yet they do share a certain number of core assumptions (Stricker, 1983). First, it is generally believed that depression is rooted in some very early defect, often the loss or threatened loss of a parent (Bowlby, 1973). Second, this primal wound is reactivated by some recent loss, which may be clear-cut (e.g., death, divorce) or more subtle (e.g., being passed over for a promotion). Whatever the precipitating event, the person is plunged back into the infantile trauma. Third, a major consequence of this regression is a sense of helplessness and hopelessness—a reflection of what was the infant's actual powerlessness in the face of harm. Feeling incapable of controlling his or her world, the depressive simply withdraws from it. Fourth, many theorists, while perhaps no longer regarding anger as the hub of depression, do feel that ambivalence toward introjected objects (that is, love objects who have been "taken in" to the self) is fundamental to the depressive's emotional quandary. Fifth, it is widely agreed that loss of self-esteem is a primary feature of depression. Otto Fenichel (1945) described depressives as "love addicts," trying continually to compensate for their own depleted self-worth by seeking comfort and reassurance from others. This leads to the sixth common assumption of psychodynamic theories, that depression has a functional role. It is not just something that people feel but something that they *use,* particularly in the form of dependency, in their relationships with others.

This last, interpersonal aspect of depression has been the object of some study in recent years. Depression, it has been found, can function as a way of forcing "caring" behavior from people who, in the depressive's view, no longer care enough. Instead of love, however, what the depressive is likely to get from his or her put-upon family or friends is shallow reassurance of the "now, now" variety or, worse, antipathy and withdrawal, which simply aggravates the depressed person's feeling of rejection (Coyne, 1976a). Depression, then, is a cry for help, but one that rarely works.

Repairing the Loss   In keeping with its basic orientation—and with the known fact that depressive symptoms usually remit by themselves in time—psychodynamic therapy is aimed not at the symptoms but at the person. Long-term psychodynamic treatment generally strives to uncover the presumed childhood roots of the current depression and to unknot and explore the ambivalent feelings toward the lost object, both primal and current.

As we have noted, however, today's psychodynamic theorists tend to be more directive than their predecessors, and more concerned with the patient's present circumstances as opposed to the past. Furthermore, the early-defect hypothesis is by no means confirmed (Crook and Eliot, 1980). While depressives are more likely than controls to have experienced the death of a parent, particularly the father, in childhood (Barnes and Prosen, 1985), the fact remains that most depressives have *not* experienced parental death in childhood.

For these various reasons, psychodynamic therapists now focus less on childhood trauma than on the current cause of the depression and on how the patient uses the depression in his or her dealings with others. This pragmatic approach is even more pronounced in short-term therapy. Klerman and his colleagues (1979) have produced a manual for a twelve- to sixteen-session treatment in which therapist and patient identify the core problem—the four most common categories being grief, interpersonal disputes (e.g., a failing marriage), role transition (e.g., retirement), and lack of social skills—and then actively attack that problem together.

The Humanistic-Existential Perspective

Predictably, humanistic and existential theorists approach depression from a phenomenological base. That is, no matter how distorted the depressives' perceptions of themselves and of the world may seem, these perceptions are accepted as a subjectively true picture of their particular "here and now."

Depression as a Response to Inauthenticity
Existentialists would interpret depression as a response to something quite genuine: a sense of "nonbeing," resulting from a failure to live completely and authentically. If depressives speak of their guilt feelings, the existentialist, along with the humanist, would say that they *are* guilty, because they are failing to make choices, fulfill their potential, and take responsibility for their lives (May, 1958). In sum, depression is an understandable reaction to an inauthentic existence.

One aspect of this inauthenticity may be fear of aloneness. As we have seen, depressives are often dependent people, and depression is often precipitated by the loss of an important relationship. Thus loneliness may be an important constituent of depression. From the existential point of view (Moustakas, 1961, 1972, 1975), loneliness is not something to be avoided or treated. On the contrary, it is the human condition and should be accepted and used as a means to personal growth. However, like most other articles of existentialist faith, the value of loneliness is hard for people to accept. Instead, they react to their solitary state by becoming anxious and engaging in wasteful, superficial social activities that nevertheless do not allay their fears. According to the existentialists, this futile struggle to avoid aloneness may be a contributor to depression.

Confronting Existence   In treating depression, the existential therapist tries to help patients see that their emotional pain is an authentic reaction—one that they should accept, value, and learn from. What is to be learned is, first, that one can never attain personal satisfaction by always acceding to the expectations of others. One must formulate one's own values and act upon them. Second, if fear of loneliness is a factor in the depression, the patient must learn to confront this loneliness, accept it as a condition of existence, and value it as a spur to the pursuit of unique personal goals.

The Behavioral Perspective

Like the psychodynamic perspective, the behavioral perspective on mood disorders is a collection of theories. We shall discuss the two major approaches, one focusing on external reinforcers and the other on cognitive processes.

Extinction   Many behaviorists regard depression as the result of extinction (Ferster, 1965, 1973; Lazarus, 1968; Lewinsohn, 1974). As one proponent of this view puts it, depression is "a function of inadequate or insufficient reinforcers" (Lazarus, 1968, p. 84). That is, once behaviors are no longer rewarded, the person ceases to perform them. He or she becomes inactive and withdrawn—in short, depressed.

What causes the reduction in reinforcement? Lewinsohn (1974) has pointed out that the amount of positive reinforcement a person receives depends on

In the behavioral view, depression is less likely to occur in people who have access to reinforcing stimuli, such as friends and social activities, which help to keep them from becoming inactive and withdrawn. (Frank Siteman/Stock, Boston)

three broad factors: (1) the number and range of stimuli that are reinforcing to that person; (2) the availability of such reinforcers in the environment; and (3) the person's skill in obtaining reinforcement. Sudden changes in a person's environment may affect any one of these factors. A new and reluctant retiree, for example, may find that the world outside the office holds few things that are truly reinforcing. Or a man whose wife has recently died may find that whereas he had the social skills to make a success of marriage, he is at a loss in the dating situation. In their new circumstances, these people simply do not know how to obtain reinforcement, and therefore they withdraw into themselves. Such withdrawal is all the more likely in the case of people who have recently absorbed a number of painful changes in their lives. For the student who has just lost his girlfriend, been placed on academic probation, and had his car stolen, staying in bed may be a welcome relief, providing powerful negative reinforcement for further withdrawal.

A number of studies by Lewinsohn and his colleagues have produced results consistent with the extinction hypothesis. For example, one objection to this hypothesis has been the widely held assumption that depressives are *resistant* to reinforcement; it is not that they lack sources of pleasure, but rather that they have lost the ability to experience pleasure. Lewinsohn and his colleagues have found, however,

that a person's mood fluctuates with the number of pleasant and unpleasant events experienced (Lewinsohn and Graf, 1973; Lewinsohn and Libet, 1972; Lewinsohn et al., 1979) and that even severely depressed people, if they learn to decrease the frequency of unpleasant events and increase the frequency of pleasant activities, will show an elevation of mood (Lewinsohn et al., 1980b). There is also some empirical support for Lewinsohn's claim that depression may be due to lack of skill in obtaining reinforcement. Focusing on the matter of social reinforcement, studies have shown that depressives are much less adept than controls at interacting with others (Youngren and Lewinsohn, 1980) and are more likely to elicit negative reactions from people they interact with (Coyne, 1976b; Gotlib and Robinson, 1982). This lack of social skill, whether or not it existed before the depression, would contribute to maintaining it.

Learned Helplessness   In a more cognitive interpretation, Seligman (1975) has suggested that depression may be understood as analogous to the phenomenon of **learned helplessness** in animals. This phenomenon was first demonstrated with laboratory dogs. After exposing a number of dogs to inescapable electric shocks, Seligman and his colleagues found that when the same dogs were later subjected to escapable shocks, they either did not initiate escape responses or were slow and inept at escaping. The investigators concluded that during the first phase of the experiment, when the shocks were inescapable, the dogs had learned that the shock was *uncontrollable*—a lesson that they continued to act upon even in the second phase of the experiment, when it was possible to escape the shocks (Maier et al., 1969).

After further research on learned helplessness in animals and humans, Seligman noted that this phenomenon closely resembles depression in its symptoms, hypothesized cause, and treatment (Table 10.1, p. 000). On the basis of this resemblance, he proposed that depression, like learned helplessness, was the result of inescapable or seemingly inescapable traumas, which served to teach the individual that he or she lacked control over reinforcement and therefore discouraged any adaptive responses. Note the difference between this theory and extinction theory. In the latter, the crucial factor is an objective environmental condition, a lack of positive reinforcement; in the former, the crucial factor is a subjective cognitive process, the *expectation* of lack of control over rein-

forcement. One should also note the connection between Seligman's theory and the psychodynamic theory of early loss.

There are certain weaknesses in the learned helplessness model of depression. As Seligman and his colleagues themselves point out, the model may explain the passivity characteristic of depression but it does not explain the equally characteristic sadness and guilt. Nor does it account for the fact that different cases of depression vary considerably in intensity and duration. To fill these gaps, the investigators have refined the theory. According to their more recent formulation, depression depends not simply on a belief in lack of control over reinforcement but also on the *attribution* of this lack of control—that is, the causes to which the people in question attribute it. Only people who see their lack of control as due to causes that are (1) permanent rather than temporary, (2) internal (part of their personality) rather than external (part of their environment), and (3) generalized over many areas of their functioning rather than specific to one area of functioning are likely to become severely depressed (Abramson et al., 1978). Thus what

TABLE 10.1	FEATURES COMMON TO LEARNED HELPLESSNESS AND DEPRESSION	
	Learned Helplessness	Depression
Symptoms	Passivity	Passivity
	Difficulty learning that responses produce relief	Negative cognitive set
	Dissipates in time	Dissipates in time
	Lack of aggression	Introjected hostility
	Weight loss, appetite loss, social and sexual deficits	Weight loss, appetite loss, social and sexual deficits
	Norepinephrine depletion	Norepinephrine depletion
	Ulcers and stress	Ulcers (?) and stress
		Feelings of helplessness
Cause	Learning that responding and reinforcement are independent	Belief that responding is useless
Cure	Directive therapy: forces exposure to responses that produce reinforcement	Recovery of belief that responding produces reinforcement
	Electroconvulsive shock	Electroconvulsive shock
	Time	Time
	Norepinephrine stimulants (?)	Norepinephrine stimulants (?)
Prevention	Immunization by mastery over reinforcement	

Source: Adapted from Seligman, 1975, p. 106.

was originally a cognitive-learning formulation has been refined to be an even more explicitly cognitive formulation.

In the past few years this new formulation has been widely tested, with mixed results. On the positive side, some researchers have found that depressed patients are more likely than controls to explain negative events by means of the kinds of attributions listed above (Raps et al., 1982), and others have found that attributional style can actually help to predict who, in a given sample, will become depressed when exposed to stress (Golin et al., 1981; Kayne et al., in press; Metalsky et al., 1982; O'Hara et al., 1982). The latter findings have led to a proposal that there is a subtype of depression, "hopelessness depression," based in large measure on attributional style (Abramson et al., in press). At the same time, other studies have found no relationship between attributional style and depression (Brewin, 1985; Lewinsohn et al., 1981; Hammen and de Mayo, 1982; Devins et al., 1981; Persons and Rao, 1985). However, these latter studies did find that depression was related to certain other cognitive variables: expectancies, self-esteem, irrational beliefs, and—in keeping with the original learned-helplessness theory—degree of perceived control. In sum, it seems clear that cognitive factors do play a role in depression. What is not clear is which cognitive variables are involved and whether they actually predispose a person to depression or are merely a consequence of the disorder.

Increasing Reinforcement   In keeping with the extinction theory of depression, behavioral treatment usually focuses on increasing the patient's rate of reinforcement. Fensterheim (1975), for example, describes what is essentially a project for the relearning of pleasure. First, patients are urged to imagine a gratifying action—eating an ice cream cone, reading a detective story, anything that seems remotely appealing to them. Then they must make an "appointment" with themselves to perform this action, and when the time of the appointment arrives, they must perform the action, whether or not they feel like it. Patients repeat this process a number of times, all the while keeping a record of their responses to their "pleasure excursions." The goal is not only to increase the patients' contact with reinforcers but also to retrain them in the experience of pleasure.

Another important thrust in the behavioral treatment of depression is **social-skills training.** As we have seen, depressives are not popular with others—a problem that social-skills training aims to remedy directly by teaching basic techniques for engaging in satisfying social interactions. Patients are shown how to initiate a conversation, how to keep eye contact, how to make small talk, how to give a compliment, how to end a conversation—in other words, the nuts and bolts of socializing. Such behaviors are often modeled for patients, after which they are practiced through role playing, the therapist, for example, pretending to be a guest at a party with whom the patient must open a conversation. Patients may also be given **assertiveness training,** which teaches them how to deal with situations in which they tend to let themselves be taken advantage of—how to refuse an unreasonable request, how to send back an overdone steak, and so forth.

Most behavioral treatments for depression are multifaceted, using the techniques described above, together with others, in combination. For example, Lewinsohn and his colleagues (1980b) have put together a treatment that includes self-monitoring of mood and activities, training in positive coping self-statements, and a variety of techniques for decreasing unpleasant experiences and increasing pleasant experiences: relaxation, time management, parenting, coping skills, and social skills. Such comprehensive therapies, combining behavioral and cognitive techniques, have had reasonably good success. In one comparison of a multifaceted behavioral program with psychotherapy, drug therapy, and relaxation training (McLean and Hakstian, 1979), the behavioral program, which focused on enhancing communication skills, social interaction, decision making, and cognitive self-control, was shown to be more effective than the other treatments at the end of a ten-week treatment period. Upon three-month follow-up, the gains made in the behavioral program were still holding, though at this point the differences in effectiveness among the four therapies were less marked.

The Cognitive Perspective

As we have seen earlier in this chapter, depression involves a number of changes: emotional, motivational, cognitive, and physical. Cognitive theorists hold that the critical variable is the cognitive change. We have already seen this reasoning in the learned-helplessness theory of depression. Here and in all cognitive formulations, it is the way people *think* about themselves that gives rise to the other factors involved in depression.

Beck, one of the major proponents of this approach, evolved his theory from findings that the hallucinations, delusions, and dreams of depressed patients often contain themes of self-punishment, loss, and deprivation (Beck and Valin, 1953; Beck and Hurvich, 1959). In Beck's view (1967, 1976), this negative bias—the tendency to see oneself as a "loser"—is the fundamental cause of depression. If a person, because of childhood experiences, develops a cognitive "schema" in which the self, the world, and the future are viewed in a negative light, that person is then predisposed to depression. Stress can easily activate the negative schema, and the consequent negative perceptions merely serve to strengthen the schema. For example, the sadness that results from the depressive's persistently negative interpretations of experience is in turn interpreted as further evidence of objective hopelessness. Hence the negative cognitive set becomes progressively more dominant as the depression deepens.

Recent research supports Beck's claim that depressives have an idiosyncratically negative schema, at least as regards the self. In one study, three groups of people—a clinically depressed group, a group with other psychological disorders, and a normal group—were asked to rate a series of words on how closely each word applied to them. Later, when asked to recall as many of the words as possible, the depressed group remembered more of the negative words that they had earlier judged to be self-descriptive than did the other two groups (Derry and Kuiper, 1981). In another study, patients who were consistently depressed either in the morning or in the evening were asked to relate memories. In general, the patients produced more negative memories and fewer positive memories during the hours when they were depressed than during the hours when they were not depressed (Clark and Teasdale, 1982). Other studies indicate that depressives selectively attend to and remember more negative than positive information about themselves (Kuiper et al., 1987). Still other research suggests that depressives may have more than one style of being negative. A study of depressed patients found two distinct negative self-schemas, one centered on dependency, the other on self-criticism. For those with dependency self-schemas, it was stressful life events—in other words, situations in which their dependency would be most keenly felt—that led to depression. For those with self-criticism

schemas, it was failure that tended to trigger depression (Hammen et al., 1985).

An interesting finding is that while depressives may be more pessimistic than the rest of us, their pessimism is sometimes more realistic than our optimism. Lewinsohn and his co-workers (1980a) put a group of depressives and two control groups through a series of social interactions and then asked the subjects (1) how positively or negatively they reacted to the others and (2) how positively or negatively they thought the others reacted to them. As it turned out, the depressives' evaluations of the impression they had made were more accurate than those of the other two groups, both of whom tended to assume that they had made more positive impressions than in fact they did. As the authors concluded, "To feel good about ourselves we may have to judge ourselves more kindly than we are judged" (1980b, p. 212). We may also have to judge ourselves more capable than we are. Alloy and Abramson (1979) found that depressives, in doing an experimental task, were far more accurate in judging how much control they had than nondepressed subjects, who tended to overestimate their control when they were doing well and to underestimate it when they were doing poorly. Thus, in certain respects it may be that normal people, not depressives, are cognitively biased—but that such an optimistic bias is essential for psychological health.

Perhaps the best evidence for the cognitive underpinnings of depression comes from studies showing that depressed states can be induced by cognitive manipulation. Velten (1968), for example, found that a person would become depressed by simply reading a list of depressing statements aloud. Alloy and her colleagues (1981) found that when euphoric moods were induced in depressed subjects through cognitive means, the subjects developed the same "illusion of control" that was seen in the normal subjects in Alloy and Abramson's task experiment (1979), described above. By the same token, when depressed moods were induced in nondepressed subjects, the subjects showed the same "depressive realism" that depressed subjects showed in that experiment.

Again, while these studies strongly suggest that cognitive variables play a role in depression, it is by no means clear that this role is causal. As we have seen before, however, a factor need not be causal, let alone proved causal, in order to be useful in treatment. Beck and his colleagues (1979) have developed a multifaceted therapy that includes both behavioral assignments and cognitive retraining, the latter aimed at helping clients to identify and correct negative biases. For example, the following procedure is used to attack the client's dysfunctional thoughts directly.

First the destructive thoughts are identified; then the client learns to "answer" them with more realistic thoughts. Sometimes clients are asked to write down their negative thoughts—when they occur, how they feel when such thoughts come to mind, and so on—according to a list such as the following:

1. Briefly describe an upsetting situation.
2. Identify the emotions associated with it.
3. List the corresponding automatic thoughts.
4. Provide rational responses to the dysfunctional ideation.

(Bedrosian and Beck, 1980, p. 142)

One young man, an unemployed college graduate who was deeply troubled by feelings of failure, used the above list to identify and counter his negative thoughts, and made the following list:

1. Sitting around in kitchen, watching television.
2. Depressed, sad, angry, and tired.
3. I will never find a job; I will never have a career. I have no friends or lovers. I can't snap out of my depression. I may never be happy.
4. I've just begun looking for a job. It takes time. I don't have to find a career immediately. I will make friends as I become more outgoing. People have liked me before. As I learn to solve my problems, I may find some contentment.

(Bedrosian and Beck, 1980, pp. 142–143)

In some encouraging evaluations, cognitive therapies have been shown to be even more effective than drug therapy, both at the end of treatment and at a one-year follow-up (Kovacs et al., 1981; Rush et al., 1977; Simons et al., 1986).

The Neuroscience Perspective

Although many researchers consider environmental stress a contributing cause of mood disorders, recent genetic studies, along with biochemical and neurophysiological research, suggest that organic dysfunctions may also play an important role.

Genetic Research   Family studies have shown that first-degree relatives (that is, immediate family members—parents, siblings, and children) of people with bipolar mood disorders are far more likely than other people to develop this disorder. In contrast to a 0.4 to 0.8 percent prevalence of bipolar disorder in the general population, first-degree relatives of bipolar patients show a 10 to 20 percent prevalence (Rosenthal, 1970; Stenstedt, 1952). Although unipolar patients are found among the relatives of bipolar patients, the reverse seldom occurs. That is, relatives of unipolar patients are seldom found to have bipolar disorder (Depue and Monroe, 1978). This is further support for the theory that the two syndromes spring from different causes.

As we know, it is difficult in family studies to separate environmental from genetic influence. However, twin studies also support the role of genetic inheritance in the mood disorders. In a review of genetic research on mood disorders in twins, Allen (1976) found that the concordance rate for bipolar disorder was 72 percent among monozygotic twins as compared with 14 percent among dizygotic twins. The concordance rate for unipolar disorder was 40 percent among monozygotic twins as compared with 11 percent among dizygotic twins. The difference between the bipolar and unipolar concordance rates among monozygotic twins (72 percent versus 40 percent) indicates that genetic factors may be more important in bipolar than in unipolar disorder—a finding that has been confirmed by later twin studies (Torgersen, 1986).

But the most impressive evidence comes from adoption studies, which suggest heritability for *both* bipolar and unipolar mood disorders. In a study of the biological and adoptive parents of bipolar adoptees as compared with the biological and adoptive parents of normal adoptees, Mendlewicz and Rainer (1977) found a 31 percent prevalence of mood disorders in the biological parents of the bipolar adoptees as opposed to 2 percent in the biological parents of normal adoptees—a striking difference. A more recent study (Wender et al., 1986), this time of the biological and adoptive parents, siblings, and half-siblings of adoptees with a broad range of mood disorders, found that the prevalence of unipolar depression was eight times greater—and the suicide rate *fifteen* times greater—in the biological relatives of the index cases than in the biological relatives of normal adoptees. Taken together, these two studies constitute firm support for some genetic component in both bipolar and unipolar mood disorder.

Given that organic factors are probably implicated in the mood disorders, the next question is: *What* organic factors? This is the question that neurophysiological and biochemical researchers are attempting to answer.

Neurophysiological Research   According to neurophysiological researchers, the basic problem lies in the central nervous system. One theory is that depression may be due to a malfunction of the hypothalamus, a portion of the brain known to regulate mood. Since the hypothalamus affects not only mood but also many other functions that are typically disrupted in the course of a depression, such as appetite and sexual interest, some researchers (e.g., Kraines, 1966) suggest that the hypothalamus may be the key to depressive disorders. The fact that depressives may also show disturbances in the functioning of the gonads and of the pituitary, adrenal, and thyroid glands, all of which are affected by the hypothalamus, lends support to this hypothesis (Sachar, 1976).

Biochemical Research   As we saw in Chapter 5, chemical substances within the body are intimately involved in the actions of the nervous system. Hence, if there is something neurologically wrong with depressives, the problem may be biochemical. At present there are two major biochemical theories.

HORMONE IMBALANCE   The first theory is that depression has to do with hormone imbalance. As we just saw, some researchers suspect that depression is due to a general malfunction of the hypothalamus. However, the problem may lie less with the general functioning of the hypothalamus than with one specific function: the control of hormone production. The hypothalamus regulates the pituitary gland, and both the hypothalamus and the pituitary control the production of hormones by the gonads and the adrenal and thyroid glands. There is substantial evidence that in depressives there is some irregularity in this process. In the first place, depressives often show abnormal hormone levels. Second, people with abnormal hormone activity often show depression as a side effect. But perhaps the best evidence is that depression can sometimes be effectively treated by altering hormone levels. In certain cases, for example, induced changes in thyroid output have aided in recovery from depression; in others, estrogen, a sex hormone, has proved an effective treatment (Prange et al., 1977).

Hormone imbalances appear to be particularly characteristic of endogenous depressions—and, indeed, can be used to help differentiate between endogenous and reactive cases, via a new, still experimental technique called the **dexamethasone suppression test,** or **DST.** Dexamethasone is a drug that in normal people suppresses the secretion of the hormone cortisol for at least twenty-four hours. However, endogenously depressed patients, who seem to secrete abnormally high levels of cortisol (Depue and Kleiman, 1979), manage to resist the drug's effect. This is the basis for the DST. Depressed patients are given dexamethasone, and then their blood is tested at regular intervals for cortisol. Those whose cortisol levels return to high levels within twenty-four hours despite the drug are classed as endogenous (Carroll et al., 1981).

An important finding in the research on hormone imbalances is that such imbalances occur both in major depression and in depressive episodes of bipolar disorder. Genetic research, as we have noted, suggests that major depression and bipolar disorder are two distinct syndromes, with different causes. For this reason, it seems unlikely that the hormonal abnormalities common to both syndromes constitute a primary cause. Similarly, although the DST does differentiate depressed patients from normal people and patients with chronic disorders, it is not as effective at differentiating depressed patients from acute psychotic patients (Arana et al., 1985). This may mean that hormonal abnormalities are largely a consequence of depression and acute psychosis. At the same time, the fact that hormones can sometimes relieve depression suggests that in certain, perhaps atypical cases, hormone imbalance may in fact play a causal role.

NEUROTRANSMITTER IMBALANCE   The second important area of biochemical research has to do with the neurotransmitters norepinephrine and serotonin. According to one theory, called the **catecholamine hypothesis,**[*] increased levels of norepinephrine produce mania, while decreased levels produce depression (Schildkraut, 1965). The only way to test this hypothesis directly would be to analyze brain-tissue samples of manics and depressives to determine whether their norepinephrine levels are in fact abnor-

---

[*] This theory is so called because norepinephrine belongs to a group of structurally similar molecules called the *catecholamines*.

mally high and low, respectively. Since this cannot be done without damage to the brain, we have to rely on indirect evidence. That evidence consists of animal-research findings that drugs and other treatments that relieve depression or produce mania increase the level of norepinephrine in the brain, while drugs that produce depression or alleviate mania reduce the level of norepinephrine in the brain (Schildkraut, 1972).

This research is spurred by the hope that the action of the drugs will tell us something about the process by which mood disorders develop in the first place. As we saw in Chapter 5, the neurotransmitters carry electrical impulses from one neuron to the next in the brain. When an impulse travels down a neuron and reaches its end, this neuron, the so-called *presynaptic* neuron, releases the neurotransmitter into the synapse that lies between it and the next, or *postsynaptic,* neuron. The neurotransmitter is then taken up by the postsynaptic neuron, thereby transmitting the impulse, or it is taken back up into the presynaptic neuron. (See Figure 5.3, p. 106.)

The drugs most commonly used for depression, the **tricyclics** (Chapter 21), generally work by blocking the reuptake of norepinephrine by the presynaptic neuron. Superficially, this suggests that depression may be due to too rapid reuptake, or perhaps to inadequate secretion. However, the picture is probably far more complicated than that. To begin with, some newer (and effective) tricyclics do not work by blocking reuptake; they increase norepinephrine levels by more subtle means (McNeal and Cimbolic, 1986). Furthermore, the fact that tricyclics generally take two weeks to start to relieve symptoms suggests that their success has to do not with immediate effects, such as blocking reuptake, but with long-term effects—specifically, the readjustment of regulatory mechanisms. We know, for example, that when the reuptake of norepinephrine is blocked, the presynaptic neuron responds by releasing more norepinephrine into the synapse, and that the receptors on the postsynaptic neuron respond to the increase in norepinephrine by becoming less sensitive to it. This response does not cancel out the effect of blocking reuptake. As we have seen, the tricyclics do work. But they probably work via a gradual recalibration of a highly complicated regulatory cycle (Whybrow et al., 1984).

Nor, as the research suggests, does the system have to do with norepinephrine alone. It has been shown, for example, that L-tryptophan, an amino acid

that increases serotonin levels, is an effective treatment for *both* mania and depression. Taking such findings into account, Prange and his associates in 1974 put forth a combined norepinephrine-serotonin hypothesis with two premises: (1) that a deficiency of serotonin creates a predisposition to mood disorder; and (2) that given the serotonin deficiency, too high a level of norepinephrine will produce mania, while too low a level of norepinephrine will produce depression. Later, in view of the accumulating evidence of excess thyroid activity in depressives, this hypothesis was revised (Whybrow and Prange, 1981) to include the involvement of thyroid hormones. So, for the time being, the picture simply gets more complicated.

We can summarize the biochemical findings as follows. At this point it seems indisputable that norepinephrine, serotonin, and thyroid activity are all involved in the mood disorders, and the most compelling current theories differ only in the emphasis they give to each of these three factors. No doubt they are all involved, and the same can be said of genetic and neurological factors. It is quite possible, for example, that a person could be born with a particular genetic makeup that would cause a biochemical malfunctioning resulting in a central nervous system disorder resulting in depression. What we know of the interdependence of the various organs of the body makes such a sequence highly plausible. Indeed, what is most likely is that mood disorders are due to a complex interaction of genetic, neurophysiological, biochemical, developmental, cognitive, and situational variables (Whybrow et al., 1984)

Whatever the neuroscience perspective ultimately contributes to uncovering the cause of mood disorders, it has already contributed heavily to their treatment. Probably the most common therapy for patients with mood disorders, whether or not they are receiving other kinds of treatment, is drugs—generally lithium carbonate for bipolar disorder and the tricyclic antidepressants for major depression. Another physical treatment, though less widely used, is electroconvulsive ("shock") therapy. These measures will be described more fully in Chapter 21.

SUICIDE

In any consideration of the mood disorders we must include some discussion of suicide. People take their lives for many reasons, but a very common reason is depression. In a study of attempted suicides, 35 to 79 percent were diagnosed as depressive (Weissman, 1974). Another group of researchers found that in their sample of patients who had committed suicide, approximately 80 percent had been depressed before the fatal attempt (Barraclough et al., 1969).

The Prevalence of Suicide

Accurate statistics on the incidence of suicide are difficult to obtain. Many of those who commit suicide prefer to make their deaths look accidental, to spare their families or themselves the shame linked with suicide. Finch, Smith, and Pokorny (1970) estimate that at least 15 percent of all fatal automobile accidents are actually suicides.

National estimates of the number of suicides each year range from 25,000 to 60,000; at least 200,000 more attempt to kill themselves and fail (Epstein, 1974). Further, 2 million living Americans have made suicide attempts—that is, almost 1 percent of the population. Suicide is now one of the most common causes of death in the United States, ranking somewhere between tenth and twelfth. Among young people aged fifteen to twenty-four, it is considered the second most common cause of death. Furthermore, some statisticians argue that if all self-inflicted deaths were recorded, suicide would rank nationally as the fourth or fifth most common cause of death. Whatever the accuracy of the statistics, life-threatening behavior constitutes a serious problem in this country.[*]

Who Commits Suicide?

Certain social variables are correlated with successful and unsuccessful suicide attempts. For example, although three times as many women as men attempt suicide, three times as many men succeed in killing themselves as do women. Statistical studies also show that twice as many single people as married people kill themselves, and that in general the likelihood of a person's committing suicide increases as a function of age, especially for men.

---

[*] It is an even more serious problem in other countries. The suicide rate in the United States is 12.2 per 100,000. Sweden's is 20.8 per 100,000, or close to double our own; Czechoslovakia's is 22.4 per 100,000; and Hungary's, the highest in the world, is 40.7 per 100,000 (de Catanzaro, 1981).

On the basis of these and other findings, Shneidman and Farberow (1970) have put together a demographic summary of suicide. According to these investigators, the *modal suicide attempter* (that is, the person who most commonly attempts suicide and survives) is a native-born Caucasian female, a housewife in her twenties or thirties, who attempts to kill herself by swallowing barbiturates and gives as her reason either marital difficulties or depression. In contrast, the *modal suicide committer* (that is, the person who succeeds in taking his or her own life) is a native-born Caucasian male in his forties or older who, for reasons of ill health, depression, or marital difficulties, commits suicide by shooting or hanging himself or by poisoning himself with carbon monoxide (see Figures 10.1 and 10.2).

Though these generalizations still hold, there have been some recent shifts in suicide-related variables, particularly in regard to age. Perhaps the most striking shift is the decrease, over the past sixty years, in suicide rates among men over sixty (Murphy et al., 1986)—a heartening change that may be due to improved economic and social conditions for retirees. On the other hand, suicide rates among men aged fifteen to thirty-four have increased in the past few decades (Murphy and Wetzel, 1980). Older men are still more likely to kill themselves than younger men, but the gap is narrowing. (See the box on p. 250.)

Is there a type of personality that is predisposed toward suicide? Apparently not. Suicide may be undertaken by any type of person in any of a variety of moods, ranging from the most frenzied to the most sober and calculating. Even so formidable a psychological intelligence as Freud's was not immune to suicidal thoughts. At age twenty-nine, in the throes of love, he wrote to his fiancée: "I have long since resolved on a decision [i.e., suicide], the thought of which is in no way painful, in the event of losing you" (Jones, 1963, p. 85).

Myths about Suicide

Common as it is, suicide is still surrounded by an aura of mystery and by a considerable number of popular misconceptions. One of the most unfortunate myths about suicide is that people who threaten to kill themselves will not carry out the threat; only the "silent type" will pull it off. This is quite untrue. One study found that approximately 70 percent of all suicides had communicated their suicidal intent within

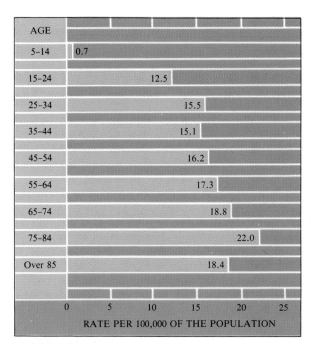

FIGURE 10.1
Suicide Rate by Age. The largest number of suicides occurs among those between 75 and 84 years of age; in this group there are 22.0 deaths per 100,000 of population. (Source: *Vital Statistics Report, Advance Report on Mortality Statistics, 1984.* Washington, D.C.: U.S. Government Printing Office, 1987.)

three months before the fatal act (Stengel, 1964). In other words, when people threaten suicide, they should be taken seriously.

Another myth is that people who attempt suicide and fail are not serious about ending their lives. In this view, a mild self-inflicted injury—a superficial cutting of the wrist, for example—suggests that the would-be suicide was making a histrionic gesture, just faking or looking for sympathy. On the contrary. About 75 percent of all suicides have made a previous attempt or threat (Cohen et al., 1966). Studies show that approximately 2 percent of those who make non-fatal suicide attempts will make a second, successful attempt within one year (Hirsch et al., 1982). With these people, the first attempt may serve as a sort of trial run, enabling them to prepare for a later, more efficient attempt. Another 10 to 39 percent of unsuccessful first-attempters will go on to a second unsuccessful attempt (Hirsch et al., 1982), and some of them, ultimately, to a successful one.

As we have mentioned, the issue of suicide is often obscured by a cloud of mystery. Our emotional reac-

tions to this phenomenon—fear, horror, curiosity, incomprehension, and perhaps attraction as well—give suicide the status of "unmentionable" in the minds of many people, a taboo that is strengthened by the Judeo-Christian prohibition against taking one's own life. Connected with this cultural response is a third myth about suicide: the myth that in conversation with depressed people, suicide is an unmentionable topic. According to this notion, questioning depressives about whether they have suicidal thoughts will either put the idea into their heads or, if it is already there, give it greater force. In opposition to this belief, almost all clinicians agree that encouraging patients to talk about suicidal wishes often helps them to overcome such wishes and also provides the information necessary for therapeutic intervention.

Suicide Prediction

When a person commits suicide, family and friends are often astonished. Such comments as "He seemed to be in such good spirits" or "But she had everything to live for" are typical reactions. And these responses reveal how frequently people in the immediate social environment of suicidal people are oblivious of the clues that they provide. Some suicides, of course, are particularly adept at concealing their intentions. But the majority of suicides do give out signals.

At times, clues to suicidal plans may be detected

FIGURE 10.2
Suicide Rate by Race and Sex. Suicide occurs most frequently among white males, least frequently among nonwhite females. (Source: *Vital Statistics Report, Advance Report on Mortality Statistics, 1984.* Washington, D.C.: U.S. Government Printing Office, 1987.)

	Rate per 100,000	Total
White males	21.3	20,882
White females	5.9	6,120
Black males	10.6	1,432
Black females	2.2	328
	Total suicides:	28,762

RATES PER 100,000 POPULATION
IN SPECIFIED GROUP

Suicide among the Young

Since the mid-1960s, the suicide rate among young people aged fifteen to twenty-four has climbed steadily. Although most adults have had some experience of bereavement or depression that makes them able to understand the suicidal impulse in other adults, suicide in young people is much more difficult to comprehend. How can those who, as the cliché goes, "have their whole life ahead of them" reach the point where they feel they have nothing to live for?

Psychologists and other observers have suggested a number of factors that may be responsible: the rising divorce rate and the effect of parental divorce on adolescents; fears about the future, whether of unemployment or nuclear annihilation; and stresses stemming from school or parental pressure. A recent study (Garfinkel et al., 1982) sought to identify the factors behind young people's attempts to take their own lives. The investigators compared 505 suicide attempters who came to the emergency room of a large children's hospital between 1970 and 1977 with 505 sex- and age-matched controls who were treated at the emergency room, but not for a suicide attempt. Among the attempters, there were three times as many girls as boys, and the girls were older (the

average age was 15.3 years for the girls and 14.7 years for the boys). In comparison with the controls, the suicide attempters had more experience with substance abuse, more history of psychiatric disorder, and more prior psychotherapy. In addition, the families of the attempters had more psychiatric disorder (primarily alcohol and drug abuse), more history of suicide, more paternal unemployment, and more parental absence—whether through death or divorce.

From this picture, we can conclude that suicidal young people often have real problems, and these problems very often have their roots in their parents' problems. For teenagers, these difficulties are multiplied: they are still dependent on their families for love and support that may not be forthcoming, and they are often too young to seek out professional help for themselves. These young people may indeed feel that there is no one to turn to and that death is the only solution. Given the pathology within many families, there is no simple solution to this problem. Hot lines, school counseling services, and free public clinics may perhaps offer some troubled young people—and their families—the help they need to cope with their problems.

in secretive behavior or in a sudden decision to have a will drawn up. Sometimes a suicidal person makes a very direct verbal statement, such as "I don't want to go on living" or "I know I'm a burden to everyone." People who have made the decision to commit suicide may withdraw into an almost contemplative state. They may refrain from conversation or drastically reduce their intake of food. They may sleep more soundly than usual, or they may suffer from insomnia. Often they act as if they were going on a long trip. In what they presume will be their last days of life, suicidal persons frequently give away their most highly valued possessions. Sometimes the expression of suicidal intent is less direct and can be pieced together only in retrospect. For example, a depressed patient leaving the hospital on a weekend pass may say, "I want to thank you for trying so hard to help me."

Since a period of calm may follow a decision to

commit suicide (Keith-Spiegel and Spiegel, 1967), the sudden tranquillity of a previously agitated patient is a danger signal, but it is often misinterpreted as a sign of improvement. Since such people seem better, they may be watched less carefully. And not uncommonly they will use this new freedom to carry out their suicide. In this connection, it should be pointed out that depressives who commit suicide tend to do so as they are coming out of their depression. It is not clear, however, whether they seem less depressed because they have made the decision to commit suicide or whether, being less depressed, they at last have the energy to carry out their suicidal wishes.

Although the individual may appear calm to others, stressful events, particularly of an interpersonal nature, are often associated with suicide. Like the onset of depression, suicide attempts are often preceded by "exit" events. Unlike depressions, however, suicide attempts also tend to be preceded by "entrance" events, such as births, marriages, or the return of a family member (Paykel, 1979b). One study comparing fourteen serious suicide attempters with fourteen depressed controls found more exit events, more uncontrollable events in general, and less "confidant support" in the lives of the suicide attempters than in the nonsuicidal depressives (Paykel, 1979b). The controlling variables are similar, however, and suicide attempters may simply have the extra measure that induces them to act.

Cognitive variables may be among the most useful predictors of who will attempt suicide. A test called the Reasons for Living Inventory (Linehan et al., 1983) asks subjects to rate how important various reasons for living would be if they were contemplating suicide. The reasons fall into six categories: survival and coping beliefs, responsibility to family, child-related concerns, fear of suicide, fear of social disapproval, and moral objections. Of people who took the test, those with strong beliefs in the categories of survival and coping, responsibility to family, and child-related concerns proved the least likely to attempt suicide.

Not surprisingly, the cognitive variable most frequently associated with serious suicidal intent is hopelessness (Beck, 1967; Leonard, 1974). Analyses of suicide notes indicate that for many suicides death seems the only way out of an insoluble problem. In a study comparing notes left by successful suicides with simulated notes written by a well-matched control group, Shneidman and Farberow (1970) found that the writers of the genuine notes expressed significantly more suffering than the control group. Truly suicidal anguish is evidently hard to feign. Interestingly enough, however, the genuine suicide notes also contained a greater number of neutral statements—instructions, admonitions, lists of things to be done after the suicide has taken place, and so forth. Both the ring of authentic hopelessness and the neutral content are illustrated in the following two notes:

Barbara,

I'm sorry. I love you bunches. Would you please do a couple of things for me. Don't tell the kids what I did. When Theresa gets a little older, if she wants to cut her hair please let her. Don't make her wear it long just because you like it that way. Ask your Mom what kind and how much clothes the kids need and then buy double what she says. I love you and the kids very much please try and remember that. I'm just not any good for you. I never learned how to tell you no. You will be much

better off without me. Just try and find someone who will love Theresa and Donny.

Love Bunches—Charlie

P.S. Donny is down at Linda's
Put Donny in a nursery school

Dear Steve:

I have been steadily getting worse in spite of everything and did not want to be a burden the rest of my life.

All my love,
Dad

My brown suit is the only one that fits me.

Not all suicides experience unqualified despair, however. According to Farberow and Litman (1970), only about 3 to 5 percent of people who attempt suicide are truly determined to die. Another two-thirds of the suicidal population do not really wish to die but instead are trying, through the gesture of a suicide attempt, to communicate the intensity of their suffering to family and friends. Finally, about 30 percent of the suicidal population falls into what Farberow and Litman call the "to be or not to be" group—those who are ambivalent about dying.

In short, the vast majority of suicide attempts are made by people who on one level truly wish to live. In trying to dissuade would-be suicides, professionals often make use of this fact, pressing such persons with arguments for staying alive and trying to persuade them to postpone irrevocable action until the crisis has passed. If they can be dissuaded, potential suicides are then usually given some kind of therapy.

PERSPECTIVES ON SUICIDE

The Psychodynamic Perspective

In psychoanalytic terms suicide may seem something of an enigma—a flagrant violation of the powerful life instinct. Yet Freud claimed that psychoanalysis had solved this enigma with the following discovery: people do not have the psychological capacity to violate the life instinct by killing themselves unless in doing so they are also killing a love object with whom they have identified themselves. In other words, suicidal persons are bent not so much on destroying themselves as on destroying another person, a "significant other," whose image they have incorporated into their own psyche. This theory is simply a logical extension of Abraham's and Freud's theory of depression as

Severely depressed people may become so overwhelmed with hopelessness that they take their own lives. Certain that their torments will never cease, they see suicide as "the only way out." (Woodcut by Käthe Kollwitz; Courtesy of the National Gallery of Art, Washington, D.C., Rosenwald Collection.)

"anger in." In the suicide the anger assumes murderous proportions, but since it is directed inward, the murder is perpetrated against the self.

In some of his later writings, Freud theorized that such aggressive impulses issued from a death instinct, a kind of yearning to return to the nothingness we experienced before birth. This theme of the death instinct was picked up by Menninger (1938), who proposed that suicide represented the triumph of people's destructive aspects over their constructive, life-affirming tendencies. According to Menninger, the desire to live depends on the feeling of self-esteem contained in the superego. When self-esteem is reduced, for whatever reasons, suicidal persons regress to the state of the hungry, deserted infant who wishes to annihilate the incorporated love object. By committing suicide, they succeed in annihilating that original love object whose incorporation helped to create the superego.

Much of this anger on which Freud and Menninger place so much emphasis has to do, then, with the loss of the significant other. In psychodynamic theory, object loss, both past and present, plays a significant role in suicide, as in depression. Rejection by signifi-

cant others early in life may cause people to develop defenses against the pain they unconsciously come to expect as adults. If these defenses give way and such a person confuses the overwhelming pain of the early loss with a current rejection or separation, he or she may commit suicide.

Similarly, psychodynamic theorists maintain that some children who are traumatized by an early devastating loss grow up believing that close interpersonal relationships cannot continue over time. They may even develop some kind of internal "time clock" by which they gauge how long they can expect such a relationship to endure before the inevitable separation. These are the people who tend to commit **anniversary suicides,** ending their lives on a date that has some special personal meaning, like their birthday or their wedding anniversary.

Psychodynamic treatment of the suicidal patient tends to follow the same lines as treatment for depression. However, in the case of the potential suicide, psychodynamic therapists typically stress emotional support. They are careful to avoid doing or saying anything that the patient could view as rejection. And in their analysis of the patient's behavior, they are likely to interpret suicidal threats as an appeal for love, whether from the therapist or from others. They also try to help the patient develop more constructive ways of achieving intimacy (Halperin, 1979). One means to this end is family therapy, either in place of or in conjunction with individual counseling. In family therapy, ideally, the patient learns how to ask for and accept the support of others, while the family learns how to provide such support.

The Humanistic-Existential Perspective

The humanists and existentialists place great emphasis on the individual's confrontation with death. Rollo May claims that death is the fact that gives life absolute value. He quotes a person in therapy: "I know only two things—one, that I will be dead someday, two, that I am not dead now. The only question is what shall I do between those two points" (1958, p. 90). In other words, our knowledge of the inevitability of death allows us to take life in earnest and use it to pursue our greatest potential.

Suicide, in this view, is an act of waste and defeat, for it eliminates the possibility of realizing one's potential. Indeed, Boss (1976) claims that all suicides are preceded by "an existential partial suicide" in which the individual withdraws from others, abrogates responsibilities, and ceases to pursue genuine values. Thus the actual suicide is simply the culmination of a series of inauthentic choices.

Humanistic-existential therapy for suicidal patients focuses on bringing them to a full realization of their current existence, in the hope that they will find enough meaning in their lives to begin living more authentically. The therapist also tries to draw patients' attention to their potentialities and thus give them some reason to go on living.

An outgrowth of the humanistic-existential approach has been the establishment of suicide-prevention "hot lines," twenty-four-hour telephone services that suicidal people can call to discuss their troubles with a sympathetic person, usually a volunteer. The usual approach of hot-line personnel is in the Rogerian tradition. That is, their goal is to provide support by "tuning in," thus giving the caller the comfort of feeling that his or her experience has validity—that someone "hears." Hot lines will be discussed more fully in Chapter 21.

The Behavioral Perspective

According to Ullmann and Krasner (1975), self-destruction is the result of a particular shift in the person's pattern of reinforcements. The essential feature of this new "suicidal" pattern is the person's estimate of his or her current life situation as having no adequate source of reinforcement. Thus suicide results from the real, anticipated, or fantasized loss of highly valued reinforcers—job, health, friends, family, and so on.

At the same time that such people expect no further reinforcements from their lives, they may find the thought of death positively reinforcing, in that it will make the people they leave behind feel sorry for them and will punish with remorse those who have hurt them. In other words, such people may see death as bringing them a number of things they want: attention, pity, and revenge.

Thus for the behaviorists a suicide attempt, like depression and indeed like most other behavior, involves a movement away from nonreinforcing situations and toward reinforcing situations. The solution, logically, is to alter the pattern of reinforcement. Behavioral treatment for suicide attempters, as for depressed patients, is generally a multicomponent therapy aimed at teaching patients how to increase their rate of pleasant experiences and decrease their rate of unpleasant experiences. For example, Liberman and Eckman (1981) have reported a successful evaluation of a behavioral program for repeated suicide attempters that comprises social-skills training, anxiety management, and contingency contracting (Chapter 21) with family members regarding family disputes.

The Sociocultural Perspective

One of the first scholars to study suicide scientifically was the French sociologist Emile Durkheim (1897). Durkheim saw suicide not as the act of an isolated individual but as the act of an individual within a society. In his view, whether or not a person commits suicide is determined in large part by the person's adjustment to society, by the stability or instability of that society, and by the network of values and norms with which the society surrounds the individual.

Working on this premise, Durkheim described three "etiological types" of suicide: anomic, egoistic, and altruistic. **Anomic suicide** occurs when the equilibrium of a society is severely disturbed. In this country, for example, the sudden crash of the stock market in 1929 resulted in a rash of suicides. And in Austria suicide rates took a sharp upturn following World War II, possibly because of the stress created by the loss of the war and the occupation by enemy troops (Havighurst, 1969).

Egoistic suicide, a very different classification, results from lack of integration into one's society. Loners with no strong ties to community or family, egoistic suicides are people who have no supportive social network to see them through periods of stress.

In contrast to egoistic suicide, **altruistic suicide** occurs because individuals are totally immersed in the value system of their culture—a value system that tells them that under certain circumstances it is either necessary or at least honorable to commit suicide. In the modern era, this cultural endorsement of suicide has been much more common in Eastern than in Western cultures. Typical examples include the practice of hara-kiri, or ritual disembowelment, in Japan, the suicide missions of the Japanese kamikaze pilots during World War II, and the self-immolation of a number of Buddhist monks protesting the war in Vietnam. The most dramatic example in recent years, however, was the mass suicide of hundreds of followers of the charismatic Jim Jones in Guyana in 1978. Although many residents of Jonestown undoubtedly did commit what Jones called "revolutionary suicide" in the belief that this choice was honorable and worthy, it is impossible to know how many of the victims were coerced into this choice and thus were not suicides at all.

The Neuroscience Perspective

The striking finding, noted above, that biological relatives of adoptees with mood disorders were fifteen times more likely to commit suicide than biological relatives of control adoptees suggests that the association between depression and suicide may have a biological base. On the surface, this would seem self-evident: logically, whatever biochemical problems depressed people have, depressed suicides may have in greater measure—or in the same measure but with fewer environmental supports. It has been proposed, however, that a particular kind of biochemical imbalance, decreased flow of serotonin from the brainstem to the frontal cortex, may be specifically associated with suicide and with impulsive, aggressive behavior. In support of this hypothesis, tests of the cerebrospinal fluid of suicide attempters, particularly those who have chosen violent methods, have found evidence of abnormally low serotonin activity (Edman et al., 1986). In addition, postmortem analyses of suicides have found subnormal amounts of serotonin and also impaired serotonin receptors in the brainstem and frontal cortex (e.g., Mann et al., 1986). Should this hypothesis gain further support, it is possible that in the future we will have special drug therapies for suicide attempters.

SUMMARY

People who suffer from the major mood disorders—disorders of affect, or feeling—experience either mania or depression, which are exaggerations of the same kinds of positive and negative feelings all human beings experience. The symptoms of both mania and depression are distributed across all aspects of human behavior: feeling, thinking, motivation, and physiological functioning. The manic episode is characterized by a change to elevated, expansive, or irritable mood, hyperactivity, talkativeness, flight of ideas, inflated self-esteem, sleeplessness, distractibility, and reckless behavior. The major depressive episode is characterized by depressed mood (the helplessness-hopelessness syndrome), loss of pleasure in usual activities, disturbance of appetite and sleep, psychomotor retardation or agitation, loss of energy, feelings of worthlessness and guilt, difficulties in thinking and remembering, and recurrent thoughts of death or suicide. In major depression, the individual undergoes one or more major depressive episodes with no intervening manic episodes. Victims of bipolar disorder, the other major mood disorder, typically alternate or swing between major depressive and manic episodes. The two major mood disorders also differ in demographic, family history, and case history patterns—a fact that suggests different etiologies for the two syndromes. Two subsyndromal conditions that are chronic but milder forms of the two major syndromes are dysthymia (depression) and cyclothymia (bipolar disorder). Symptoms of both conditions are more moderate (nonpsychotic) and fewer than those of the major syndromes.

Psychologists have also identified certain dimensions of mood disorder—areas in which subtypes can be distinguished from one another. Two of the most commonly used dimensions are psychotic versus neurotic and endogenous versus reactive. In neurotic depression, the individual may be seriously incapacitated but is still able to function and is not out of touch with reality. In psychotic depression, the individual's perception of reality is so drastically distorted that he or she cannot function. In mania, psychotic features may include thought disorders similar to those of schizophrenics. It is not yet firmly established whether neurotic and psychotic depression are different disorders or differ only in severity of symptoms along a continuum. The continuity hypothesis has support in the finding that some cases of dysthymia and cyclothymia (nonpsychotic symptoms) are at risk for the major disorders (whose symptoms are often psychotic). Depressed patients who exhibit biogenic symptoms, such as weight loss and psychomotor retardation, are commonly described as suffering from endogenous depression. Those whose disturbance is primarily emotional are said to manifest reactive depression. The endogenous-reactive distinction finds some support in studies showing that patients who are labeled reactive have experienced more significant stressful events before onset than have endogenous patients, but family history studies so far have not established a genetic factor to bear out the distinction between endogenous and reactive cases.

Freud's psychoanalytic view of depression challenged the earlier biogenic model of mood disorders, explaining depression as a response to loss: aggression or anger toward the lost, introverted love object is turned inward. Many modern psychodynamic theorists preserve the "anger in" hypothesis, seeing depression as rooted in an early trauma that is reactivated by a recent loss and plunges the person into helplessness and hopelessness, ambivalent feelings about the introjected other, and loss of self-esteem. Psychodynamic treatment of the mood disorders stresses not only recall and expression of early hostile feelings but also current causes of depression and the depressed person's problems in relating to other people. From the humanistic-existential perspective, blocked self-actualization and consequent inauthentic living give rise to depression. The existential therapist tries to help the depressed person see that loneliness is part of the human condition and can be channeled into constructive growth. There are two prominent behavioral approaches to depression. According to one view, the extinction hypothesis, depression results from a reduction in and a lack of skill in obtaining positive reinforcement. According to the other view, learned helplessness, depressed people believe that they have no control over reinforcement and attribute their lack of control to aspects of their own personalities. Behavioral treatment for depression focuses on increasing the patient's ability to find gratification in reinforcement. A recent approach of the cognitive perspective sees depression as the function of negative self-schemas that are focused on either dependency or self-criticism. Treatment usually includes both behavioral therapy and cognitive retraining. Finally, in addition to these psychological perspectives, research in neuroscience suggests that genetic factors and neurophysiological and/or biochemical dysfunction may play a part in the etiology of major mood disorders. Adoption studies suggest a genetic factor for both major mood disorders, and one study shows a much higher suicide rate for the biological relatives of index cases. The two major biochemical theories

point to hormone and neurotransmitter imbalances. According to the catecholamine hypothesis, for which we have only indirect evidence, increased levels of norepinephrine produce mania; decreased levels, depression. Tricyclics, drugs commonly used to treat depression, increase norepinephrine levels. Lithium carbonate is used to treat bipolar disorder.

Suicide rates in recent years have decreased for men over sixty and increased for men age fifteen to thirty-four, but older men are still more likely than younger men to take their lives. Suicide, often associated with depression, is surrounded by a number of misconceptions. Research has established that people who threaten suicide often do attempt it; that an unsuccessful suicide attempt in no way rules out a later successful attempt; and that discussing suicidal wishes with depressed patients can be of great therapeutic value, as most suicidal people have highly ambivalent feelings about taking their lives. A sense of hopelessness is the psychological variable most frequently associated with suicidal intent. Cognitive variables, which are assessed in the Reasons for Living Inventory, have proved to be useful predictors of suicide attempts.

Suicide has been interpreted from several perspectives. According to psychodynamic theory, suicidal persons are really trying to destroy another person whom they have incorporated into their own psyches. Therapy is similar to treatment for depression and typically seeks to provide emotional support and to enable patients to find such support in their families. The humanistic-existential therapist tries to help patients see that suicide is an "inauthentic" choice. For the behaviorist, suicide attempts result when valued reinforcers are lost or when the idea of death itself becomes positively reinforcing. The sociocultural perspective recognizes that the instability of the society a person lives in, or the person's failure to adjust to society and its values, contributes significantly to suicidal feelings. The neuroscience perspective is supported by heritability studies that indicate a biological basis for depression and suicide. Physiological tests indicate that decreased flow of serotonin from the brainstem to the frontal cortex may be associated with both suicide and impulsive, aggressive behavior.

PART 4

The Social Disorders

The Personality Disorders

As we saw in Chapter 8, the anxiety, somatoform, and dissociative disorders are serious psychological disturbances that nevertheless do not greatly impair reality contact or, in most cases, make adaptive functioning impossible. People with these disorders still see the same world that others see and still cope with that world, with varying degrees of success. The same is true of the disorders to which we now turn, the **personality disorders.** In other respects, however, the personality disorders are unique. *DSM-III-R* defines them as follows:

> Personality *traits* are enduring patterns of perceiving, relating to, and thinking about the environment and oneself, and are exhibited in a wide range of important social and personal contexts. It is only when *personality traits* are

inflexible and maladaptive and cause either significant functional impairment or subjective distress that they constitute *Personality Disorders.* The manifestations of Personality Disorders are often recognizable by adolescence or earlier and continue throughout most of adult life, though they often become less obvious in middle or old age (1987, p. 335).

As this definition indicates, there are major differences between the personality disorders and the anxiety, somatoform, and dissociative disorders. The latter may appear at any time of life, and when they do, their victims are painfully aware of the problem and usually feel acute distress. Personality disorders, by contrast, are long-standing habits of thought and behavior that have been with the person since childhood or adolescence; consequently, if they cause the

259

person unhappiness, that unhappiness is more like a familiar dull ache than actual pain. Indeed, personality disorders may give less pain to the people who have them than to those who have to deal with them—their co-workers, their children, and so forth. Furthermore, while the anxiety, somatoform, and dissociative disorders involve a specific emotion or behavior—a fear of dogs, a paralyzed limb, a loss of memory—personality disorders are pervasive, coloring much of the person's thought and behavior. As the name indicates, the problem is with the personality as a whole.

There is considerable debate over the value of the personality disorders as diagnostic categories. In the first place, most of these categories have shown less reliability than categories of other disorders. Though diagnosticians generally agree that a given case is one of personality disorder (as opposed to obsessive-compulsive disorder or schizophrenia, for example), they frequently disagree on *which* personality disorder they are confronting. What one calls "schizoid personality disorder" another may call "avoidant personality disorder" or something else. A second problem is that because the diagnosis of personality disorders focuses on long-term functioning rather than current functioning, the diagnostician needs to consider the patient's past. And this retrospective diagnosis gives great play to "bias for consistency"—the tendency to see whatever is consistent with the current problem and to ignore whatever is not—on the part of both patient and diagnostician. Third and perhaps most important is the assumption, clearly stated in the *DSM-III-R* definition, that human beings have stable personality traits that determine their behavior from one situation to another. There is good evidence that human behavior is influenced as much by the person's particular situation at the moment as it is by his or her "personality traits" (Mischel, 1968; Mischel and Peake, 1982). Consequently, many psychologists are suspicious of diagnostic categories based on the notion of fixed traits.

Nevertheless, diagnosticians do see people whose problem does not seem reducible to specific symptoms but is rather a whole orientation to experience—a general "style" of handling problems, treating other people, and thinking about oneself that is as natural to the person, as much a part of who he or she "is," as it is maladaptive and self-defeating. And these people are still diagnosed as having personality disorders.

DSM-III listed eleven personality disorders. *DSM-III-R* has proposed three new personality-disor-

der categories, which are listed in an appendix section. We shall describe two of them, but will devote the most time to antisocial personality disorder, which has been the subject of much more research than the other syndromes (see the box on p. 261).

PERSONALITY DISORDERS: INDIVIDUAL SYNDROMES

Paranoid Personality Disorder

The defining trait of **paranoid personality disorder** is suspiciousness. Suspiciousness is something that we all feel in certain situations and with certain people, often for good reasons. However, paranoid personalities feel suspicious in almost all situations and with almost all people, usually for very flimsy reasons. And when they are confronted with evidence that their mistrust is unfounded, they will simply begin to mistrust the person who brought them the evidence: "So he's against me too!"

Such an attitude of course reflects an impairment in cognitive functioning. Paranoid personalities are constantly scanning the environment for evidence to support their suspicions—and constantly finding such evidence. If two people are talking together near the coffee machine, or if the mail is late, or if the neighbors are blaring music at midnight, this is taken as evidence of personal hostility.

Emotional adjustment is equally hampered. Friendship and love are based on trust—the very thing that paranoid personalities lack. Hence they typically have few friends. They may have an "ally," usually a person in a subordinate position, but eventually they begin to suspect the ally too and switch to another ally—a process that repeats itself time after time. Despite these interpersonal problems, paranoid personalities rarely turn up in the offices of psychologists and psychiatrists, for they see their difficulties as coming from without rather than within. For this reason it is difficult to estimate the prevalence of this disorder.

Despite similarities in name and defining trait, paranoid personality disorder should not be confused with paranoia or paranoid schizophrenia. The latter are psychoses (see Chapter 14)—that is, severely disabling disorders, involving loss of reality contact. By contrast, paranoid personality disorder is not necessarily disabling. This is true of personality disorders

Two New Personality Disorders

DSM-III-R introduces two new categories of personality disorder. These new categories are controversial and have been opposed by some clinicians and researchers. To resolve this controversy, *DSM-III-R* has officially recognized them but has described them in an appendix until further research can establish their validity.

SELF-DEFEATING PERSONALITY DISORDER

Also known as "masochistic" among psychoanalysts, self-defeating personalities seem to be drawn into situations and relationships that will cause them to suffer. Apparently avoiding enjoyable experiences and opportunities for success, people with this personality disorder tend to be self-sacrificing—they give up what they want so that other people can have their way. They are rarely interested in making friends or building relationships with people who seem to like them, preferring those who reject or hurt them.

The major objection to adding the self-defeating personality to *DSM* classifications is the implication that people who are abused (most often women in our society) *want* to suffer, and prefer relationships with people who inflict pain and punishment. This kind of thinking encourages a tendency to "blame the victim"—to see victims as themselves responsible for their suffering, rather than the people who abuse them.

SADISTIC PERSONALITY DISORDER

According to psychoanalytic theory, people whose behavior toward others is cruel and demeaning are often sadistic personalities. They seem to enjoy making other people suffer. Not all sadistic personalities inflict pain through violence. Some hold high positions in business and in academic and other institutions, and wield their power in the form of harsh disciplinary action, unreasonable restrictions, or public humiliation of subordinates.

The clinicians who object to the inclusion of sadistic personality as a *DSM* classification also object to the addition of self-defeating personality disorder. They are concerned about letting people who brutalize others off the hook with a claim of mental disorder.

Sadistic and antisocial personality disorders sometimes coexist in the same person, but they do not typically do so, and the two need to be differentiated in diagnosis. The sadist is aggressive and brutalizing, but usually avoids illegal or socially unacceptable actions; the antisocial personality, by definition, deliberately breaks laws and undermines social and ethical values.

---

in general. In an interesting phrase quoted above, *DSM-III-R* (p. 335) states that personality disorders cause "*either* significant functional impairment *or* subjective distress" (italics added)—not necessarily both. Though people with personality disorders cannot be called well adjusted, some nevertheless may feel no distress, while others may achieve a great deal, despite their self-defeating traits.

Schizotypal Personality Disorder

Schizotypal personality disorder was added to the 1980 edition of *DSM-III* as part of an effort to improve the reliability of the diagnosis of schizophrenia and to study its relation (if any) to other conditions. Diagnostic lines, as we have seen repeatedly, are often hard to draw, and schizophrenia is no exception. In the "classic" case of schizophrenia, the person will appear decidedly odd in many respects: speech, thought, perception, emotion, social behavior, motor behavior, and so on. Yet many cases are not classic ones. The person will seem only marginally odd in a number of respects, or perhaps very odd but only in one respect, such as peculiar mannerisms. In the past, such cases were classified either as subtypes of schizophrenia or, if they were mild, as "schizoid personality disorder," with much overlap among the categories.

Today, with researchers in pursuit of the causes

Delusions involving persecution or jealousy are the hallmarks of paranoid personality disorders. Such extreme, groundless suspiciousness is often the only symptom involved. (Jeff Jacobson/Archive)

of schizophrenia, there is a need to sort these marginal cases into stricter groupings. There is evidence, for example, that people who show marked eccentricities of thought and behavior while failing to qualify for a diagnosis of schizophrenia are nevertheless disproportionately common among the relatives of diagnosed schizophrenics. This finding suggests that these people may be at risk, genetically or otherwise, for schizophrenia (Spitzer et al., 1979). This is apparently not the case, however, with people whose only obvious eccentricity is social withdrawal. Therefore, *DSM-III* and *DSM-III-R* have created for these two patterns two separate categories, schizotypal personality disorder and schizoid personality disorder, respectively.

The person with **schizotypal personality disorder** will seem odd in his or her speech, behavior, thinking, and/or perception, but not odd enough for a diagnosis of schizophrenia. For example, speech may ramble, but never to the point of actual incoherence, as is often the case with schizophrenics. Or the person may report recurrent illusions, such as feeling as if his dead mother were in the room—a situation nevertheless different from that of the schizophrenic, who is likely to report that his dead mother *was* in the room. Schizotypal personalities may also show magical thinking, claiming that they can tell the future, read the thoughts of others, and so on. Partly, no doubt, because of the disbelief inspired by such claims, they tend to be suspicious, aloof, and withdrawn. As we have noted, this pattern seems to be more common in the families of diagnosed schizophrenics than in the population at large.

Schizoid Personality Disorder

While schizotypal personality disorder involves a range of eccentricities, **schizoid personality disorder** is defined by one fundamental eccentricity, a preference for social isolation. According to current thinking, schizoids are deficient in the capacity to experience social warmth or any deep feelings and unable to form attachments. Schizoid personalities rarely marry, have few (if any) friends, seem indifferent to praise or criticism from others, and prefer to be alone. Because of their self-absorption, they may seem vague or absent-minded—"out of it," so to speak. However, they do not show the unusual thoughts, behaviors, or speech patterns that one sees in the schizotypal personality. And unlike schizotypal personalities, they may be quite successful in their work, if it is an occupation that calls for little social contact. On the other hand, schizoid personality disorder may also be common among inhabitants of skid rows.

Avoidant Personality Disorder

Like schizoid personality disorder, **avoidant personality disorder** is marked by social withdrawal. However, the avoidant personality withdraws not out of inability to experience interpersonal warmth or closeness but out of fear of rejection. This new category, based primarily on research by Millon (1981), has as its essential feature a hypersensitivity to any possibility of rejection, humiliation, or shame. Avoidant personalities, though they want to be loved and accepted, expect not to be, and therefore tend to avoid relationships unless they are reassured again and again of the other's uncritical affection. Even then, they remain watchful for any hint of disapproval. For most of us, waiting for a friend who is late is an inconvenience or annoyance. For the avoidant personality, it is an

Most people think of the telephone as a link between themselves and the world, but the avoidant personality—hypersensitive to rejection—is likely to see it as one more channel for humiliation. (Frank Siteman/Jeroboam)

emotional catastrophe: the long-dreaded sign that the friend no longer cares.

Not surprisingly, avoidant personalities generally have low self-esteem, and while this problem may be a cause of their social difficulties, it is also a result. That is, they typically feel depressed and angry at themselves for their social failures, and these feelings further erode their self-esteem—a vicious cycle.

Dependent Personality Disorder

Also marked by low self-esteem is **dependent personality disorder,** of which the defining characteristic, as the name indicates, is dependence on others. Fearful or incapable of making their own decisions, dependent personalities turn over to one or two others—for example, a spouse or a parent—the responsibility for deciding what work they will do, where they will go on vacation, how they will handle the children, what people they will associate with, even

what they will wear. Underlying this self-effacement is a fear of abandonment. Thus the dependent personality, often a woman, will tolerate her husband's infidelities, drunkenness, even physical abusiveness for fear that, should she protest, he will leave her. This passivity breeds a vicious cycle similar to that of the avoidant personality. That is, the more the dependent personality lets others control and abuse her, the more she feels helpless and stupid, and these feelings in turn further discourage her from taking any assertive and self-respecting actions.

Borderline Personality Disorder

The distinguishing feature of **borderline personality disorder** is instability, which usually manifests itself in a number of areas. Borderline personalities are typically unpredictable in their behavior, leading quiet lives one week and then gambling, overdosing on drugs, running up huge bills, or otherwise "cutting loose" at another time. Their emotions may also be marked by abrupt shifts, and particularly by outbreaks of anger and spells of depression, emptiness, and boredom. Expectably, their relationships with others are also subject to frequent ups and downs. This instability may be accompanied by a severe identity disturbance—problems with self-image, gender identity, career choice, long-term goals, the entire question of "Who am I?" Borderline personalities may also have difficulty being alone.

The "borderline" category, although questioned by some diagnosticians as lacking reliability and clear characteristics (Perry and Klerman, 1980), is becoming more generally accepted. The literature on the borderline personality has increased considerably in recent years, discussing causes or origins, clinical symptoms, and treatment (e.g. Gunderson, 1984; Kernberg, 1975; Masterson, 1976; Meissner, 1984; Stone, 1980).

The major characteristic of this disorder, originally formulated by psychoanalytic clinicians, is a lack of cohesiveness, an instability of personality that affects all aspects of living. Attitudes and feelings are erratic, relationships and social life undergo unpredictable changes, and the self-image or identity is shaky.

Some clinicians see the borderline personality as a variant of mood disorders (Chapter 10). In the same sense that the schizotypal personality can be viewed as a less severe variant of schizophrenia, the borderline disorder is seen as a subclinical or premorbid variant of mania and depression (Akiskal, 1981; Klein, 1975). The instability, display of temper, feelings of emptiness, and recurrent threats of suicide suggest an affinity between the borderline and mood disorders.

Histrionic Personality Disorder

The essential feature of **histrionic personality disorder** is self-dramatization—the exaggerated display of emotion. Such emotional displays are often clearly manipulative, aimed at attracting attention and sympa-

The dramatic gesture of this young man, purposely acted out in order to attract attention for no apparent reason, is characteristic of histrionic personality disorder. (James T. Cott/Jeroboam)

thy. Histrionic personalities will "faint" at the sight of blood, will dominate an entire dinner party with the tale of their recent faith healing, will be so "overcome" with emotion during a sad movie that they have to be taken home immediately (thus spoiling their companions' evening), will threaten suicide if a lover's interest cools, and so forth. To themselves, they seem very sensitive; to others, after the first impression has worn off, they usually seem shallow and insincere.

Their interpersonal relationships, then, are usually fragile. Initially, upon meeting a new person, they will seem warm and affectionate. Once the friendship is established, however, they become oppressively demanding, needing their friends to come right over if they are having an emotional crisis, wondering piteously why no one called them after a traumatic visit to the dentist, and generally taking without giving. They are typically flirtatious and sexually provocative, but their characteristic self-absorption prevents them from establishing any lasting sexual bond.

As *DSM-III-R* indicates, the histrionic personality resembles a caricature of femininity—vain, shallow, self-dramatizing, immature, overdependent, and selfish. The disorder is more common in women than in men.

Narcissistic Personality Disorder

The personality syndrome most commonly diagnosed in a number of psychoanalytic centers in recent years has been the so-called narcissistic personality (Millon, 1981). Largely because of the interest of the psychoanalytic community (Lion, 1981), this category was added to *DSM* in 1980. The essential feature of **narcissistic personality disorder** is a grandiose sense of self-importance, often combined with periodic feelings of inferiority (Kernberg, 1975; Kohut, 1966). Narcissistic personalities will brag of their talents and achievements, predict for themselves great successes—a Pulitzer prize, a meteoric rise through the company ranks—and expect from others the sort of attention and adulation due to one so gifted. Yet this apparent self-love is often accompanied by a very fragile self-esteem, causing the person to "check" constantly on how he or she is regarded by others and to react with rage or despair in response to criticism. (Alternatively, in keeping with their self-importance, narcissistic personalities may respond to personal defeats with cool nonchalance.)

This is poor equipment for friendship or love. Narcissistic personalities characteristically demand a great deal from others—affection, sympathy, favors. Yet they give little in return, and tend to show a striking lack of empathy. If a friend calls to say that he has had an automobile accident and cannot go to the party that night, the narcissistic personality is likely to be more concerned over the missed party than over the friend's safety. Narcissistic personalities are also given to exploitation, choosing friends on the basis of what they can get from them. Their feelings about such "friends" tend to alternate between opposite poles of idealization and contempt, often depending on how flattering the friend has been lately. Not surprisingly, in view of these facts, narcissistic personalities tend to have long histories of erratic interpersonal relationships, and it is usually failures in this area that bring them into therapy.

In the past decade or two, a number of articles and books have been written about narcissistic personality disorder from two opposite perspectives: the psychoanalytic and social learning points of view. Best known is the psychoanalytic theory suggesting that such personalities are compensating for inadequate affection and approval from their parents in early childhood (Kernberg, 1975; Kohut, 1972). In the opposite, social learning perspective (Millon, 1969, 1981), this personality disorder stems from unrealistic expectations of what the child will achieve in adulthood, based on an inflated view of his or her talents. Adherents of both theories agree, however, about the basic characteristics of such personalities: they need constant admiration, expect favors from others without reciprocating, and react to criticism with arrogance and contempt.

Obsessive-Compulsive Personality Disorder

The defining characteristic of **obsessive-compulsive personality disorder** is excessive preoccupation with trivial details, at the cost of both spontaneity and effectiveness. Obsessive-compulsive personalities are so taken up with the mechanics of efficiency—organizing, following rules, making lists and schedules—that they cease to be efficient, for they never get anything important done. In addition, they are generally stiff and formal in their dealings with others and are incapable of taking genuine pleasure in any-

thing. For example, they may spend weeks or months planning a family vacation, deciding what the family will see and where they will eat and sleep each day and night, and then derive no enjoyment whatsoever from the vacation itself. Typically, they will spoil it for the others as well by refusing to deviate from the itinerary, worrying that the restaurant will give away their table, and so forth.

This personality disorder should not be confused with obsessive-compulsive disorder (Chapter 8). In the personality disorder, compulsiveness is not confined to a single sequence of bizarre behaviors, such as constant hand washing, but is milder and more pervasive, affecting many aspects of life. Furthermore, while obsessive-compulsive disorder is rare, obsessive-compulsive personality disorder is fairly common (more so in men than in women). As the names indicate, however, the two syndromes bear a family resemblance. Like the rituals involved in obsessive-compulsive disorder, the behaviors of the obsessive-compulsive personality are superficially "proper," careful, and dutiful.

Though some jobs would seem to require a degree of "compulsiveness," people with obsessive-compulsive personality disorder rarely do well in their occupations because they are preoccupied with trivia. What with making lists and organizing their papers, they have no time left for the important work. Furthermore, because of their anxiety over doing things "just right," they generally have tremendous difficulty making decisions.

Passive-Aggressive Personality Disorder

The essential characteristic of **passive-aggressive personality disorder** is an indirectly expressed resistance to demands made by others. At home and at work, passive-aggressive personalities find a way *not* to do what they are expected to do. Yet they never openly state their refusal; rather, they covertly sabotage the job, by procrastinating, dawdling, making errors, or some other means. For example, a man who is left to care for his small child on a Saturday while his wife goes out may pin the diapers on inside out, spill baby powder all over the floor, and "forget" to feed the child. Yet when the wife comes home, he can plead that he was doing his best. Despite the cover of "good intentions," such maneuvers are not appreciated by spouses or employers; ultimately, human beings are judged on their performance, not their stated intentions. Hence passive-aggressive personalities tend to have troubled marriages and spotty job records.

The name of this disorder implies that passive-aggressive maneuvering is a cover less for laziness or job dissatisfaction than for an underlying hostility toward other people. This interpretation is controversial, however. So, indeed, is the category itself. It is arguable that passive-aggressive behavior is the expression not of a "personality trait" but of unhappiness in specific situations and therefore is not pervasive but confined to specific areas of the person's life, such as job performance or sexual behavior. *DSM-III-R* states that this diagnosis does not apply to people who show passive-aggressive behavior in isolated situations in which assertive behavior is discouraged or actually punished (e.g., a job in the military). It is to be given only to those who show pervasive and long-standing passive-aggressive behavior, both on the job and at home.

ANTISOCIAL PERSONALITY DISORDER

People suffering from the personality disorders that we have studied so far may inconvenience their families and friends considerably, but usually they harm themselves more than they harm others. The defining trait of **antisocial personality disorder,** by contrast, is a predatory attitude toward other people—a chronic indifference to and violation of the rights of one's fellow human beings.

While antisocial personality disorder is listed along with the other personality disorders, it is by no means an unusual phenomenon. It is apparently common, affecting about 1 percent of females and 3 percent of males in their teens and twenties among the general population, according to *DSM-III-R*. Furthermore, since antisocial behavior often involves criminal behavior, this disorder raises the whole issue of the relationship between abnormal psychology and crime. For these reasons—and because it is the most reliably diagnosed and the most thoroughly researched of the personality syndromes—we will devote the remainder of this chapter to this disorder.

The Psychiatric Classification of Antisocial Behavior

The question of the relationship between psychological disturbance and **antisocial behavior,** behavior that violates the rights of others, forms an interesting chapter in the history of psychology.[*] Until about two hundred years ago, criminals were generally treated as criminals, with little thought as to their psychological well-being. Then in the eighteenth and nineteenth centuries, such clinicians as Philippe Pinel and Benjamin Rush began to speculate that certain cases of immoral and criminal behavior might be subtle forms of mental illness. In 1835 an English psychiatrist, J. C. Prichard, identified a condition that he called "moral insanity," which he described as "a form of mental derangement in which the intellectual functions appear to have sustained little or no injury, while the . . . moral or active principles of the mind are strangely perverted or depraved" (cited in Preu, 1944, p. 923).

In the late nineteenth century such people came to be called "psychopaths," and in keeping with the biogenic thinking of the period, it was assumed that their problem was a hereditary defect. This "bad seed" theory was widely accepted for many decades. Then, with the rise of sociology in the twentieth century, investigators began instead to stress the influence of social conditions. Accordingly, "psychopaths" were relabeled "sociopaths" (Birnbaum, 1914), the implication being that the ultimate source lay not within the individual but in the individual's relationship to society.

Thus, while its causes were still being disputed, antisocial behavior was absorbed into abnormal psychology. In the beginning, however, perhaps too much was absorbed. Once psychologists learned to see some antisocial behavior as "sick," some of them began to see *all* antisocial behavior as "sick." There were no longer any criminals, just disturbed people. Yet many criminals seem to commit their crimes not

---

[*] It is important to remember that antisocial behavior is not identical with antisocial personality disorder. Just as anxiety is the defining characteristic of anxiety disorder but is not limited to people with this disorder, so antisocial behavior is the defining characteristic of antisocial personality disorder but is not limited to antisocial personalities. Psychologically "normal" people also lie, cheat, and steal.

because of some deep-seated personality disturbance but for simple and relatively understandable reasons—to supplement their incomes, to "fix" someone who cheated them in a drug deal, and so forth. Are these people also to be regarded as psychologically disturbed? In early editions of the *DSM* there was some hedging on this point. In *DSM-III* and *DSM-III-R* there is not. The current diagnostic manual offers two distinct categories, one pathological and one normal. The first is antisocial personality disorder, described above, in which antisocial behavior is presumed to be a function of psychological disturbance. The second is "adult antisocial behavior," listed in the back of the manual under "conditions not attributable to a mental disorder" and reserved for those whose antisocial activities do not seem to be linked to any psychological disturbance.

Thus the pendulum, having swung from one direction to the other, has now settled in the middle. Some people who engage in antisocial behavior are psychologically "normal," and others are not. We shall confine our attention to the second group.

Characteristics of the Antisocial Personality

DSM-III-R's list of criteria for the diagnosis of antisocial personality disorder (*DSM-III-R,* pp. 342–345) can be summarized as five basic points:

1. *A history of illegal or socially disapproved activity beginning before age fifteen and continuing into adulthood.* Usually by the time of puberty—or, in the case of boys, earlier—the person has begun his or her career of antisocial behavior, in the form of truancy, delinquency, theft, vandalism, lying, drug abuse, casual sex, running away from home, and/or chronic misbehavior in school. As adults, antisocial personalities may graduate to prostitution, pimping, drug selling, and other crimes.

2. *Failure to show constancy and responsibility in work, sexual relationships, parenthood, or financial obligations.* Antisocial personalities lack steadiness and a sense of obligation. They tend to walk out on jobs, spouses, children, and creditors.

3. *Irritability and aggressiveness,* including not just street brawls but often abuse of spouse and children.

4. *Reckless and impulsive behavior.* Unlike most "normal" criminals, antisocial personalities rarely en-

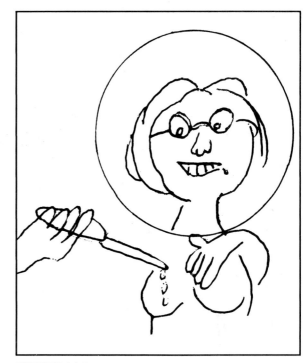

FIGURE 11.1
A hostile, sociopathic patient made this doodle of a bloody knife being plunged into a female breast. On a subsequent occasion only the face within the circle was shown to the patient, and he identified it as his mother's. (Courtesy of C. Scott Moss)

gage in planning. Instead, they tend to operate in an aimless, thrill-seeking fashion, traveling from town to town with no goal in mind, falling into bed with anyone available, stealing a pack of cigarettes or a car, depending on what seems easiest and most gratifying at the moment.

5. *Disregard for the truth.* Antisocial personalities lie frequently. Cleckley (1976) gives the example of a man who, while frequently giving his "word of honor," seemed to have no conception of what honor meant.

In a letter to his wife, at last seeking divorce and in another city, one patient set down dignified, fair appraisals of the situation and referred to sensible plans he had outlined for her security. He then added that specified insurance policies and annuities providing for the three children (including their tuition at college) had been mailed under separate

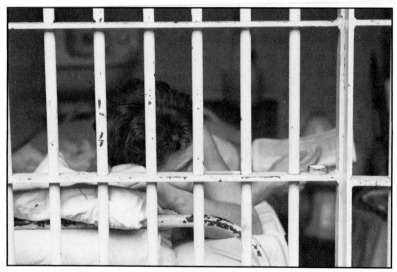

Even confinement in the bleak surroundings of a prison may not keep the antisocial personality from committing further offenses after release. Punishment is a poor "teacher" in such cases; antisocial personalities make few connections between their actions and their consequences. (Owen Franken/Stock, Boston)

cover and would, if she had not already received them, soon be in her hands. He had not taken even the first step to obtain insurance or to make any other provision, and, once he had made these statements in his letter, he apparently gave the matter no further thought (p. 342).

As is almost always the case with *DSM-III-R* criteria, only some, not all, of these characteristics need be present in order for the case to be diagnosed as antisocial personality disorder. However, a history of antisocial behavior during both adolescence and adulthood must be present.

In keeping with the policies of the diagnostic manual, this list confines itself to verifiable behaviors. Other writers, going further, have created more subjective portraits of the antisocial personality. For example, Cleckley, who has treated antisocial personalities for many years, has devoted an entire book, *The Mask of Sanity* (1976), to a description of this disorder. According to Cleckley, antisocial personalities differ from normal people, including "normal" criminals, not only in their actions but also in their emotions, motivations, and thought processes. First, their misdeeds are not just impulsive but almost unmotivated—or rather, not motivated by any understandable purpose. Their behavior, therefore, often has a perverse or irrational quality. Cleckley cites the case of a teenager whose exploits included "defecation into

the stringed intricacies of the school piano, the removal from his uncle's automobile of a carburetor for which he got 75 cents, and the selling of his father's overcoat to a passing buyer of scrap materials" (1976, p. 65). This lack of purposefulness, says Cleckley, is what makes most antisocial personalities unsuccessful criminals.

Second, according to Cleckley, antisocial personalities have only the shallowest emotions. What permits them to ignore what the rest of us would regard as obligations is a lack of love, of loyalty, and, above all, of empathy—an inability to imagine what might be the feelings of the child they have left alone all day in an empty house, the friend whose credit cards they have stolen, and so forth. Nor do they feel anxiety or remorse over such actions, for they are as deficient in guilt as in other basic emotions. In this regard, Zax and Stricker report the case of a boy who had accidentally or otherwise killed a neighborhood child by shooting her in the head:

> He spoke of the incident . . . in a nonchalant, unfeeling way, and was very suave and unnaturally composed in explaining why he was on the ward. He said, "I was showing her the gun. I didn't know it was loaded. She turned her head and it got her in the temple. I told the police that I was very sorry. You're to find out if there is anything mentally wrong with me. I thought I'd have to go to reform school . . ." (1963, p. 240).

A third aspect of Cleckley's portrait is poor judgment and failure to learn from experience. Antisocial personalities, he explains, do not seem to make the connection between their actions and the consequences of those actions. Hence they tend not to learn from experience. Once punished for some action, normal people learn either not to repeat the action or to repeat it in such a way that they will not be caught. In contrast, antisocial personalities may repeat the same offense again and again, and in the same manner, even though they have been punished for doing so.

Finally, according to Cleckley, most antisocial personalities are able to maintain a pleasant and convincing exterior. Because of their lack of anxiety and guilt, they can lie, cheat, and steal with remarkable poise. Therefore, despite repeated offenses, they are still able to convince people of their goodwill.

The Case of Roberta

Though no single human being will conform in every detail to the pattern outlined above, the following case, described by Cleckley, comes close. In Roberta, the subject, we see most of the features outlined by *DSM-III-R* as well as those listed by Cleckley:

> "I can't understand the girl, no matter how hard I try," said the father, shaking his head in genuine perplexity. . . .
>
> He had related, in a rambling but impressive account, how Roberta at the age of ten stole her aunt's silver hairbrush, how she repeatedly made off with small articles from the dime store, the drug store, and from her own home. "At first it seemed just the mischievous doings of a little girl," he said, "a sort of play. . . . You know how children sometimes tell a lot of fanciful stories without thinking of it as lying."
>
> Neither the father nor the mother seemed a severe parent. . . . However, there was nothing to suggest that this girl had been spoiled. The parents had, so far as could be determined, consistently let her find that lying and stealing and truancy brought censure and punishment.
>
> As she grew into her teens this girl began to buy dresses, cosmetics, candy, perfume, and other articles, charging them to her father. He had no warning that these bills would come. Roberta acted without saying a word to him, and no matter what he said or did she went on in the same way. For

> many of these things she had little or no use; some of them she distributed among her acquaintances. In serious conferences it was explained that the family budget had been badly unbalanced by these bills. As a matter of fact, the father, previously in comfortable circumstances, had at one time been forced to the verge of bankruptcy.
>
> In school Roberta's work was mediocre. She studied little and her truancy was spectacular and persistent. No one regarded her as dull and she seemed to learn easily when she made any effort at all. (Her I.Q. was found to be 135.) She often expressed ambitions and talked of plans for the future. These included the study of medicine, dress designing, becoming an author, and teaching home economics in a nearby college. For short periods she sometimes applied herself and made excellent grades, but would inevitably return to truancy. . . .

Roberta was eventually expelled from three successive schools. She then went to work for her father's business, embezzling funds on a regular basis. Periodically she would simply disappear from home for days or weeks. On one such occasion she took off with the intention of finding a soldier friend, whom, as she later explained, she was thinking of marrying. Unable to locate him, she ended up at nightfall in a strange town, and there she had her first sexual experience.

> Not having concluded plans for her next step, she sat for a while in a hotel lobby. Soon she was approached by a middle-aged man. . . . He soon offered to pay for her overnight accommodations at the hotel. She realized that he meant to share the bed with her but made no objection. As well as one can tell by discussing this experience with Roberta, she was neither excited, frightened, repulsed, nor attracted by a prospect that most [young girls] would certainly have regarded with anything but indifference.
>
> The man, during their several hours together, handled her in a rough, peremptory fashion, took no trouble to conceal his contempt for her and her role, and made no pretense of friendliness, much less affection. She experienced moderate pain but no sexual response under his ministrations. After giving her $5.00 with unnecessarily contemptuous accentuations of its significance, he left her in the room about midnight.
>
> Next morning she reached her soldier friend by telephone and suggested that he send her sufficient funds to join him. She had not discarded the idea of

marrying him, nor had she progressed any further toward a final decision to do so. He discouraged her vigorously against coming, refused to send money, and urged her to return home. She was not, it seems, greatly upset by this turn of events, and, with little serious consideration of the matter, decided to go to Charlotte, which was approximately 150 miles distant. . . .

Short of funds during her stay in Charlotte, Roberta drifted into random prostitution. Finally, after three weeks, she was located by her parents, whom she greeted with great affection. Her behavior, however, did not change. Indeed, she went on for years in exactly the same way, with intervals in which her parents would have her hospitalized for psychiatric observation.

> She returned for psychiatric treatment on several occasions, always saying she had been helped and expressing simple but complete confidence that it was impossible for her to have further trouble. Despite her prompt failures she would, in her letters to us at the hospital, write as if she had been miraculously cured:
>
> "You and Doctor —— have given me a new outlook and a new life. This time we have got to the very root of my trouble and I see the whole story in a different light. I don't mean to use such words lightly and, of all things, I want to avoid even the appearance of flattery, but I must tell you how grateful I am, how deeply I admire the wonderful work you are doing. . . . If, in your whole life you had never succeeded with one other patient, what you have done for me should make your practice worthwhile. . . . I wish I could tell you how different I feel. How different I am! . . ." etc. . . .
>
> Though she realized I had been informed of recent episodes quite as bad as those in the past, on several occasions she wrote requesting letters of recommendation for various positions she had applied for or was considering. . . . Roberta seemed sweetly free of any doubt that such recommendations would be given without qualification and in the highest terms of assurance (1976, pp. 46–55).

Antisocial Behavior in Juveniles: The Conduct Disorders

Antisocial behavior is not confined to adults. Juveniles commit an alarming number of crimes, and many arrested juveniles are actually preadolescent. In such a case in New York City, an artist was beaten to death with a tree limb by a gang of six boys to whom he refused to surrender his new bicycle; of the gang, two were sixteen years old, two were fifteen, one was thirteen, and one was twelve.

Antisocial personality disorder, by definition, begins in adolescence. One form juvenile antisocial behavior can take is gang membership, in which members engage in aggression against other gangs or the society at large. (Michael Abramson/Black Star)

Juvenile delinquency comes under the heading of "conduct disorders" in *DSM-III-R* and is grouped not with the personality disorders but with the disorders of childhood and adolescence. Therefore we will deal with this subject more fully when we come to the childhood disturbances (Chapter 17).

Juvenile delinquency raises some very urgent psychological issues. First is the question of cause. What is it that "hardens" children to the point where they can engage in antisocial acts, as it were, before their time? Second is the matter of psychological intervention. Childhood conduct disorders have been shown to be excellent predictors of antisocial behavior in adulthood (Robins, 1979). (As we saw earlier, antisocial personality disorder by definition begins before age fifteen. Therefore all antisocial personalities were once teenagers with conduct disorders.) What psychological remedies could be applied to prevent this progression from taking place?

We have no definitive answers to these questions. However, to the degree that conduct disorders are related to adult antisocial personality disorder, some suggestions can be offered by the different theoretical perspectives on this disorder.

PERSPECTIVES ON THE PERSONALITY DISORDERS

The idea of personality disorder—unified, long-standing, and deeply ingrained traits or trait clusters that handicap the individual in dealing with the world—is essentially a psychodynamic concept, and it is psychodynamic writers who have given it the most attention. However, as we shall see, other perspectives have also made contributions to the study of these disorders. We shall continue to give the most space to antisocial personality disorder, as it is the one most thoroughly studied.

The Psychodynamic Perspective

Character Disorders   According to psychodynamic theory, personality disorders, called "character disorders" in the psychodynamic literature, are rooted in early childhood experiences—as are all psychological disturbances, in this view. Character is defined as a "pattern of adaptation to instinctual and environ-

mental forces that is typical or habitual for a given person" (Meissner et al., 1975). People with character disorders differ from neurotics and psychotics, falling somewhere between the two in adaptive and functional capacities. Neurotics have more intact ego functions and adaptive abilities than people with personality disorders, who are not so dysfunctional as psychotics.

Character disorders, say psychodynamic thinkers, stem from disturbances at certain early stages of psychosexual development. The more severe syndromes, such as the antisocial personality, are believed to originate in the early pre-oedipal one-to-one relationship with the infant's mother or other primary caretaker. A disturbed relationship interferes with the main developmental tasks at this stage: psychological separation from the mother figure in conjunction with a comfortable sense of relatedness to her and a growing ability to perceive oneself and others as unique, complete individuals. Failure to achieve this development leads to a flawed sense of self and difficulty in relating to others as an adult.

The less severe character disorders, such as the obsessive-compulsive personality, are grounded in disturbed parent–child relations in the later oedipal phase. Strong ambivalent reactions to mother and father at this stage of childhood can lead to a rigid and distorted view of the self—one based on needs and fantasies rather than reality.

Normal "coping" behavior is to some extent absent from all personality disorders, and erratic, distorted, or deviant behavior takes its place. The borderline personality, for instance, has a tenuous adaptive capacity that is easily disrupted during times of stress; the antisocial personality is unable to delay gratification; and the dependent personality can cope with environmental demands only in an immature or childlike way. The functional capacities of character-disordered persons may vary with circumstances, in reaction to particular inner and outer stresses. Basically, what defines the character disorders is a pattern of distorted or weakened ego functions—such capacities as perception, memory, language, learning, and motor behavior. Each character disorder shows a pattern of maladaptive behavior in one or more of these areas. One example is the hypervigilant, detailed perception of the environment that is typical of the paranoid personality, whose mode of adaptation to all situations is organized largely around misperception of others' behavior. Disordered personalities act in accordance with their own distorted views of reality, often failing to respond to the actual demands of a particular situation.

Narcissistic personality disorder has recently been the subject of much study and controversy in psychodynamic circles. Otto Kernberg (1975), along with *DSM-III-R,* sees the basic pattern as a combination of grandiosity and feelings of inferiority. In his view, however, it is the sense of inferiority that is primary; the grandiosity is merely a defense against childhood feelings of rage and inferiority. Heinz Kohut (1966, 1972, 1977), on the other hand, sees the grandiosity as primary—the expression of a "narcissistic libido" that for various reasons has evaded the neutralizing efforts of the ego. When the narcissistic personality shows rage and wounded self-esteem, these are reactions to blows to the grandiose self-image.

Predictably, psychodynamic theorists attribute antisocial personality disorder to superego failure. For some reason, the person has failed to acquire adequate superego controls and consequently has little means of resisting the id's demands for instant gratification. Why the failure? As we saw in Chapter 2, the emergence of the superego depends on the child's identification with the parent of the same sex. Presumably, if there is some serious disturbance in the parent–child relationship, or if there *is* no parent–child relationship, such identification may never occur.

This brings us to a common assumption about antisocial personality disorder: that the problem lies in the family. Some theorists hold that the crucial predisposing factor is parental deprivation. It has been demonstrated time and again (Greer, 1964; Oltman and Friedman, 1967; Robins, 1966) that the antisocial personality is much more likely than the average person to have suffered, as a child, the loss of a parent through death, separation, or simple abandonment. Other writers (e.g., McCord and McCord, 1964) claim that the crucial determinant is parental rejection. It should be remembered, however, that these family problems—divorce, separation from parents, rejection by parents—have also been implicated in the etiology of anxiety disorders, depression, schizophrenia, autism, alcoholism, and a host of other disorders. Furthermore, many children of divorced or rejecting parents grow up to be altogether normal. Conversely, many antisocial personalities, such as Roberta, come from apparently normal homes. Robins (1966, 1979), attempting to sort through this confusion, proposes that the critical variable is not family disruption but

the presence of an antisocial parent, and particularly an antisocial father. It is because antisocial parents tend to be rejecting, absent, or divorced that their families are likely to experience disruption. Although there are many determinants of an antisocial personality, Robins stresses that the antisocial qualities of the parents are the primary source of antisocial qualities in the child.

Psychotherapy for Personality Disorders   As we have pointed out, personality disorders are long-standing patterns that often are *not* experienced as acutely distressing. Therefore people with personality disorders tend not to seek treatment. When they do end up in a therapist's office, it is often not on their own initiative, but rather because they have been dragged in, by reason of a spouse's complaints or a child's emotional problems, to marriage counseling or family therapy. In such situations, they are generally resistant to treatment. And even when they do experience sufficient unhappiness to enter treatment on their own, they tend to see the problem as external to them rather than internal—an attitude that bodes ill for insight-oriented therapy.

The treatment of antisocial personality disorder has yielded particularly unimpressive results, and hence the prognosis for antisocial personalities is poor. Characteristically lacking both insight and the desire to change, they are poor candidates for the insight-oriented psychotherapies. Furthermore, whatever the form of therapy, the antisocial personality's emotional poverty and lack of motivation place immense demands on the patience of the therapist (Kolb, 1973)—demands that many therapists would sooner avoid. And while there is some evidence that the family and the society may be partly to blame, families are not easy to change, to say nothing of societies.

Antisocial personalities are most unlikely to enter psychotherapy voluntarily, and when they are treated involuntarily—in prisons, for example—their lack of motivation, along with their characteristic lack of insight, generally dooms the process (Thorne, 1959; Ellis, 1977). Nevertheless, there is some hope that psychodynamic therapy may be effective with conduct disorders (Schuster, 1976). A number of residential programs for adolescents with conduct disorders use psychodynamic techniques in both individual and group therapy. The goal of this therapy is to create a setting in which the adolescent can begin to develop trust in an adult (i.e., the therapist)—the trust that parents failed to inspire—and go on from there to identify with the therapist and incorporate his or her standards. As yet there have been no formal evaluations of the effectiveness of these programs. It should be noted, however, that they are working against formidable odds, in the form of administrative problems. Staff turnover is typically high, for the work is extremely difficult and the funding is always fluctuating. Furthermore, the patient population is constantly shifting, since there is much pressure to move these adolescents out quickly and not "institutionalize" them. Consequently, either the therapist or the patient may be out the door before the two of them have had time to develop a genuinely trusting relationship.

The Behavioral Perspective

Most behaviorists object to the very concept of personality disorder, since it implies fixed traits. That people have stable personality traits—that a person, for example, is either introverted or extroverted, cold or warm, candid or guarded, in most areas of his or her life—is a time-honored and widely held belief. However, it may well be mistaken, according to the research of Walter Mischel. In 1968 Mischel showed that correlations between behavior and personality trait measures such as those obtained by the MMPI (Chapter 7) are generally low. Mischel (1979) acknowledges that people do in fact show some consistency—the result of their learned competencies, encodings, expectancies, values, and plans (Chapter 3). But such consistency is likely to occur not across situations (e.g., extroverted with strangers and with friends) but across time in the same situations (e.g., always highly extroverted with friends, always less extroverted with strangers). When people rate other people's behavior as consistent across situations, they are usually obeying the "bias for consistency" mentioned at the beginning of the chapter. And in following that bias, they are usually guided by what they regard as prototypic behaviors: behaviors that seem to them the "acid test" of the trait in question (Mischel and Peake, 1982). Thus, for example, if a woman is cold as a mother, people will tend to see her as cold in other contexts as well, even when she is not.

These findings suggest to the behaviorists that the stable, cross-situational traits fundamental to the personality disorders are often illusory—in other words, the concept of personality disorder is probably too all-encompassing to have much descriptive validity. To the extent that they discuss these disorders, they discuss them as specific maladaptive responses that occur (1) in response to specific stimuli and (2) as a result of specific reinforcing consequences. And as with other disorders, they would explain them as a function of those eliciting stimuli and reinforcing consequences.

Modeling and Reinforcement   Thus with antisocial personalities, behaviorists focus not on the personality but on the crucial maladaptive behavior—that is, antisocial and aggressive behavior. To identify the sources of this behavior, they, like the psychodynamic theorists, look to the family. They regard the family, however, not as an arena of intrapsychic conflict but as a learning laboratory. In the behavioral view, two learning mechanisms are paramount in the creation of antisocial and aggressive behavior. One is modeling, which, as research has demonstrated, can both teach aggressive behavior and trigger specific aggressive acts (Bandura, 1976). The crucial models are undoubtedly parents and peers. However, the entertainment media probably do their part as well. Many studies indicate that when children watch aggressive acts on film or television, they may imitate the violence they have seen if an appropriate situation arises shortly thereafter.

The second important mechanism is reinforcement. Studies of children who seldom engage in antisocial behavior have shown that the parents of these children consistently reinforce prosocial behavior (e.g., helpfulness, cooperation, affection) and ignore or punish antisocial behavior (Johnson et al., 1973; Snyder, 1977). In the case of parents whose children have conduct disorders, a different pattern emerges. First, when such parents respond to their child, the response tends to be a punishing one. Second, the reinforcement that the parents provide is generally **noncontingent reinforcement.** That is, the nature of the parents' response is not related to whether the child's behavior was prosocial or antisocial; it is simply arbitrary (Synder, 1977). Both these factors—overuse of aversive consequences and noncontingent reinforcement—are vividly illustrated in the following statement by Albert DeSalvo, who came to be known as the Boston Strangler:

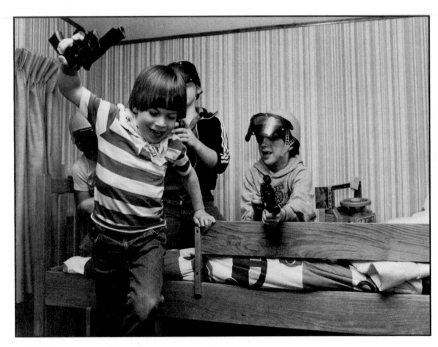

The behavioral perspective regards modeling as the source of antisocial behavior—and as an approach to its treatment. (Judy S. Gelles/Stock, Boston)

My father . . . we used to have to stand in front of him, my brother Frank and me, every night and be beaten with his belt. I can still to this very moment tell you the color of the belt and just how long it was—two inches by 36—a belt with a big buckle on it. We used to stand in front of him every night and get beaten with that damn thing—every night, whether we did anything wrong or not. We were only in the fourth or fifth grade . . . (Frank, 1966, p. 316).

Such parents, according to the behaviorists, not only serve as models for aggression but also teach children that there is no connection between their behavior and the treatment they will receive. Consequently, the children become desensitized to social stimuli such as rules and laws that indicate to people what the consequences of their behavior will be. Rather than heed these stimuli, they simply do as they please, assuming that the outcome of their behavior will be determined not by the nature of that behavior but by some arbitrary force, such as luck.

Finally, it should be added that antisocial behavior may also be learned through direct positive reinforcement. It may win attention from parents and school authorities, while prosocial behavior goes unnoticed.

And it may well increase the child's prestige in his or her peer group, whereas prosocial behavior may be ridiculed by peers.

Behaviorists analyze other personality disorders in the same straightforward fashion. For example, dependent personality disorder might result from a childhood in which assertiveness was repeatedly punished; histrionic personality disorder from parental indulgence of temper tantrums; compulsive personality disorder from consistent rewards for neatness, rule-following, and other "goody-goody" behaviors. Or, as with antisocial personality disorder, parental modeling of the behaviors in question might be as important as rewards and punishments.

New Learning   Behavioral treatment for personality disorders relies on the usual behavioral arsenal: modeling, reinforcement of adaptive behaviors, extinction of maladaptive behaviors. For example, in marital therapy with a couple in which the wife is a dependent personality, the husband would be instructed not to reinforce passivity by taking over decision making. Or, in the case of a histrionic or narcissistic personality, the spouse would be told not to reward the demands for attention. At the same time, rewards *would* be provided for appropriate behaviors.

In the case of antisocial personality disorder, behavioral treatment, like the psychodynamic, has focused on adolescents. There are two major treatment approaches. One is the use of elaborate reinforcement programs within residential or foster-home settings. The best-known of such programs is Achievement Place, founded in Kansas in the mid-1960s and since copied in many other cities (Phillips et al., 1976). The goal of Achievement Place and other programs like it is to create an environment in which prosocial behavior (e.g., completing work and school assignments) is systematically reinforced, while antisocial behavior (e.g., using abusive language) is extinguished. Such programs have proved successful at reducing antisocial behavior while the adolescent is actually living at the treatment center. However, they are apparently no more effective than comparison residential programs at reducing future contacts with the law once the adolescent leaves the center and returns to the less therapeutic environment from which he or she came (Jones, 1978).

The second treatment approach is to keep the adolescent at home and train the *parents* to reinforce prosocial behavior and extinguish antisocial behavior. This, of course, can be done only when parents are highly motivated to help the child and sufficiently in control of their own lives to be able to do so. Where it is possible, however, parent-administered reinforcement may be the most effective means of preventing relapse. Alexander and Parsons (1973) and Reid and Patterson (1976) have reported an impressive number of successes with this approach, but it remains to be tested on a wider basis.

The Sociocultural Perspective

Predictably, sociocultural theorists have addressed themselves primarily to antisocial personality disorder. Most social scientists would agree that the injustices built into our society contribute their fair share to the development of criminal behavior. To what degree might the society also foster antisocial personality disorder? According to Gough (1948),

> there are very definite aspects of our cultural pattern which give [antisocial personalities]

encouragement. In America we put great value on the acquisition of material gain, prestige, power, personal ascendance, and the competitive massing of goods. . . .

> We have very short memories about the origins of some of our great national fortunes, toward the holders of which we hold so much respect. At the other end, of course, our machine civilization tends to level, and strangle individuality, leaving large groups within our culture fearful, anxious, resentful and even occasionally openly hostile. In such an atmosphere [antisocial personality disorder] rises, grows and fattens . . . (pp. 359–366).

This critique summarizes the sociocultural position. While other theorists look to the individual psyche for the explanation of antisocial personality disorder, sociocultural theorists feel that these psychological processes are merely the products of large-scale social processes—processes that ensure the prosperity of certain social groups and the deprivation of others. Accordingly, they argue that psychologists should devote their efforts to changing the society rather than trying to change its victims (Holland, 1978).

Interesting to consider in this connection is the theory of **anomie,** offered by the sociologist Robert K. Merton (1957) to explain crime but possibly useful in explaining antisocial personality disorder as well. Merton claims that societies such as ours—societies in which material luxuries are highly valued and widely displayed but in which only certain groups have access to such luxuries—engender a state of "anomie," or normlessness, in disadvantaged groups. These groups feel that since they cannot acquire the society's rewards by any legitimate means, neither do the society's notions of what is legitimate apply to them. Consequently, according to Merton, they simply go after what they want without consulting any system of rules or values. Such normlessness is a characteristic feature of the antisocial personality, and since a disproportionate number of antisocial personalities come from impoverished backgrounds (McGarvey et al., 1981), it is possible that this disorder is to some extent a product of the forces Merton describes.

More broadly, it could be argued that the values of modern society ("get it while you can," "don't get involved") encourage antisocial behavior patterns. As *DSM-III-R* notes, people with some features of antisocial personality disorder—for example, the disregard for truth, though not the childhood delinquency—may achieve considerable success in public life. And the prominence of such people may breed an atmosphere in which antisocial behavior flourishes.

The Neuroscience Perspective

The neuroscience perspective, like the sociocultural, has concentrated primarily on the antisocial personality. As we mentioned at the beginning of this chapter, the most popular approach to antisocial behavior in the late nineteenth century was the biogenic view. Particularly active in this area of speculation was the Italian school of criminology, led by Cesare Lombroso. Lombroso argued that a tendency toward crime was genetically transmitted, just like blue eyes and red hair, and that the presence of this hereditary taint could be recognized by certain physical characteristics, such as a low forehead and protruding ears. Lombroso's theory of the physically marked "born" criminal was discredited decades ago. Nevertheless, many researchers still believe that genetic and physiological factors may figure, in a more subtle fashion, in the etiology of the antisocial personality.

XYY and Other Genetic Factors   A highly publicized discovery of the mid-1960s was that a certain percentage of violent criminals showed the rare XYY chromosomal abnormality. Almost every cell in the human body is equipped with twenty-three chromosome pairs, one of which determines the sex of the individual. In the female, this sex-related pair is made up of two female (X) chromosomes; thus the female is an XX type. The male, in contrast, carries one female and one male (Y) chromosome and is therefore an XY type. In the 1960s, it was found that a number of male criminals who had committed especially brutal crimes were XYY types—that is, they carried an extra male chromosome (Jacobs et al., 1965). Could it be that the extra Y chromosome produces some biochemical predisposition to violence—for example, an excess of testosterone, the hormone that some believe underlies "male aggressiveness"?

This discovery set off a flurry of chromosomal research on violent criminals. Such efforts were given further impetus when it was reported that Richard Speck, who murdered eight student nurses in Chicago one night in 1966, was an XYY type (Montague, 1968). So far, however, these studies have failed to prove the hypothesis that the XYY type is biochemically predisposed to violence. The XYY type *has* been found to be about fifteen times more common among male criminals than among males in general (Jarvik et al., 1973). Yet the prevalence among male criminals is still very low: about 2 percent. Furthermore, most of the criminals who show the XYY configuration have *not* been convicted of violent crimes (Witkin et al., 1976). Finally, most XYY types are not criminals but are often slightly mentally retarded and generally peace-loving. The XYY research, in other words, has not yielded any solid answers as to what produces a violent criminal, or even an ordinary criminal, and has probably received much more attention than is warranted (Reid, 1981).

Nevertheless, twin and adoption studies have produced evidence that heredity may be implicated in criminal behavior. Using the national birth and criminal registers, Christiansen (1968) studied all twins born in a specified area of Denmark between 1881 and 1910. Of 3,568 twin pairs born during that period, at least one member of 799 pairs later engaged in criminal activity. The concordance rate for monozygotic (identical) twins was 36 percent as compared with 12.5 percent for dizygotic (fraternal) twins. Thus the other member of a monozygotic pair was almost three times more likely to have engaged in criminal behavior than the other member of a dizygotic pair.

This is not conclusive evidence regarding a genetic role, since monozygotic twins, as we have noted, may share a more similar environment than dizygotic twins. The genetic hypothesis is supported, however, by adoption studies showing that children of a criminal parent who are put up for adoption at birth are more likely to engage in criminal behavior in later life than are other matched adoptees (Hutchings and Mednick, 1975; Crowe, 1975). Still, the relationship is small, and the vast majority of adoptees do not engage in criminal behavior no matter what their biological heritage.

The studies discussed thus far have not distinguished between antisocial personalities and others who might engage in criminal activity. One important study has done so. Using the Copenhagen adoption and psychiatric registers, along with police files, Schulsinger (1972) identified adopted infants who later met the criteria for diagnosis as psychopaths (antisocial personality disorder). He then examined the records of both the biological and adoptive relatives of the adoptee and found that biological relatives were four to five times more likely than adoptive relatives to meet the psychopathy criteria. The relationship again was small, indicating that although there is a genetic role, the environmental influence is also substantial.

Physiological Abnormalities If there is a genetic predisposition to antisocial personality disorder, what is it that is inherited? There is reason to believe that antisocial personalities may be the victims of some physiological defect. In the first place, somewhere between 31 and 58 percent of all antisocial personalities show some form of EEG abnormality (Ellington, 1954), the most common abnormality being slow-wave activity, which is typical of the infant and the young child but not of the normal adult (Hare, 1970). This finding has led some investigators to believe that antisocial personality disorder may be the product of "cortical immaturity"—that is, delayed development of the cerebral cortex, the topmost layer of the brain and seat of most of its "higher" functions (Chapter 16). If this is the case, then we might expect antisocial personalities to become better behaved with age; as the person grew older, the brain would finally mature, and consequently antisocial behavior would diminish. This does in fact seem to be true in many cases. Robins (1966), for example, found that one-third of a group of eighty-two diagnosed antisocial personalities showed marked behavioral improvements as they grew older, particularly between the ages of thirty and forty.

But if this cortical immaturity exists, what are its effects? What is the mental function that is impaired? According to one school of thought, it is the capacity for fear. Most of the abnormal slow-wave activity in antisocial personalities comes from the temporal lobe and the limbic system, two parts of the brain that are known to control memory and emotion. This finding suggests that the essential defect in antisocial personality disorder may be an inability to respond normally to fear-inducing stimuli, leading in turn to an inability to inhibit responses that will result in punishment. This suggestion may help to explain the resistance of antisocial personalities to avoidance learning—the fact that they can be punished again and again for the same offenses and still never learn how to avoid this consequence.

Evidence in support of "physiological fearlessness" was first provided by Lykken (1957). He subjected three groups—a group of college students, a group

of nonsociopathic prisoners, and a group of sociopathic (i.e., antisocial) prisoners—to an ingeniously devised test involving the learning of correct responses to a series of twenty problems. The subjects responded by pressing levers on a board. For every correct press, there were three possible incorrect presses, one of which gave the subject a mild electric shock, while the other two simply turned on a red light. Lykken found that all three groups made approximately the same number of errors; in other words, there were no striking differences in intelligence. However, the nonsociopathic prisoners managed to avoid the "shock" errors better than the sociopathic prisoners, thus supporting the hypothesis that lack of anxiety renders the sociopath less adept at avoidance learning. Lykken's findings were later supported by Schachter and Latané (1964), who found that sociopathic prisoners did considerably better on Lykken's test when they had been injected with adrenaline, which promotes anxiety. It seems, then, that the antisocial personality lacks sufficient anxiety to learn—or bother to learn—how to avoid punishment—at least punishment in the form of physical discomfort. Interestingly, Schmauk (1970) found that antisocial personalities were good at avoidance learning when the punishment was loss of money rather than physical pain or social disapproval.

Another finding that strengthens the "physiological fearlessness" hypothesis is that the autonomic nervous system of the antisocial personality seems to operate at a lower level of arousal than that of the normal person. This finding is consistent with the discoveries of Lykken and of Schachter and Latané. In particular, it meshes neatly with the fact that injections of adrenaline, which the body naturally produces in a state of high autonomic arousal, improve the antisocial personality's performance in avoidance learning. According to Hare (1970), autonomic underarousal could explain a number of the antisocial personality's behavioral oddities. In the first place, as we indicated earlier, many antisocial personalities show an unshakable poise, even in situations that would prove extremely unnerving to anyone else (e.g., being interrogated by the police). Possibly the antisocial personality's autonomic nervous system is simply unable to achieve the degree of arousal necessary to produce fear. If so, this factor would in turn account for the antisocial personality's difficulties with avoidance learning. Finally, autonomic underarousal might also help to account for the impulsiveness of the antisocial personality. Quay (1965) has proposed that this impulsiveness is not so much passive—that is, a giving in to impulses—as it is active, a form of thrill seeking. If this is the case, the antisocial personality's quest for stimulation could be a function of the body's need to compensate for autonomic underarousal.

Thus what physiological researchers now have is a cluster of interrelated findings: EEG abnormalities, behavioral improvements with age, poor performance in avoidance learning, improved performance with adrenaline injections, and signs of autonomic underarousal. Individually, each of these findings could be quarreled with. Taken together, however, they constitute an impressive argument for a disorder that has both behavioral and physiological components. This has led some researchers to suggest that many of the characteristics of the antisocial personality may be related to deficits in the areas of the brain that regulate and organize behavior (Gorenstein and Newman, 1980; Gorenstein, 1982). Such research is just beginning, but it may eventually lead to a way to identify a predisposition toward antisocial personality.

SUMMARY

The personality disorders are personality traits that are inflexible and maladaptive and cause either significant impairment of social or occupational functioning or subjective distress. They are characterized by long-standing habits of thought and behavior that have pervaded the individual's personality since childhood or adolescence; a personality disorder may bother the person who has it less than it disturbs those who deal with him or her. In spite of the debate over the value of personality disorders as diagnostic categories, the concept is useful to describe people who have a generally maladaptive "style" of dealing with problems, other people, and themselves.

Paranoid personality disorder is marked by suspicion in almost all situations and of almost all people; it differs from paranoia and paranoid schizophrenia in that it is not a severely disabling psychosis. In schizotypal personality disorder, the person's speech, behavior, thinking, and/or perception seem odd—but not odd enough to be considered schizophrenic. Such a person tends to be suspicious, aloof, and withdrawn.

A somewhat similar disorder is schizoid personality disorder, which is defined primarily by social withdrawal and isolation.

The essential feature of avoidant personality disorder is hypersensitivity to the possibility of rejection, humiliation, or shame; the result is withdrawal due to fear of social contact. Dependent personality disorder is characterized by excessive dependence on others—turning over to another person the responsibility for deciding the course of one's life. Fear of abandonment seems to underlie this passivity.

Borderline personality disorder is distinguished by instability and abrupt shifts in emotion and behavior. This instability is often accompanied by severe identity problems and difficulty in being alone. The dominant feature of histrionic personality disorder is self-dramatization, often as a means to win attention and sympathy. Narcissistic personality disorder is characterized by an exaggerated sense of self-importance, often combined with an underlying feeling of inferiority. Such personalities are demanding and exploitive.

Obsessive-compulsive personality disorder is defined by excessive preoccupation with trivial details, at the cost of spontaneity and effectiveness. The primary trait of passive-aggressive personality disorder is indirect resistance to demands made by others or the sabotaging of tasks that one is expected to perform. Such behavior may indicate underlying hostility.

The most reliably diagnosed and thoroughly researched of these syndromes is antisocial personality disorder, a condition that often involves criminal behavior and danger to others. In the late nineteenth century, antisocial personalities were called psychopaths, and their disorder was attributed to a hereditary defect. With the rise of sociology in the twentieth century, the syndrome became linked to social influences, and its victims were called sociopaths. Today *DSM-III-R* distinguishes between antisocial personality disorder and antisocial activities that are not attributable to a mental disorder.

DSM-III-R lists five general criteria for diagnosing antisocial personality disorder: a history of illegal or socially disapproved activity beginning at puberty or earlier and continuing into adulthood; failure to show constancy and responsibility; irritability and aggressiveness; reckless and impulsive behavior; and disregard for the truth. Of these criteria, only evidence of both adolescent and adult antisocial behavior *must* be present for a diagnosis of antisocial personality disorder to apply. Antisocial criminal acts may be committed by juveniles; *DSM-III-R* lists juvenile delinquency as a "conduct disorder."

The psychodynamic perspective attributes the personality or character disorders to early childhood disturbances at one of the stages of psychosexual development; psychodynamic theorists blame antisocial personality disorder on inadequate superego controls, which normally result from a disturbed relationship with the same-sex parent. Victims of personality disorders, especially antisocial personalities, are unlikely to seek treatment, but there is some hope that psychodynamic therapy may be effective with adolescent conduct disorders.

Advocates of the behavioral perspective generally object to the concept of personality disorders because it implies the existence of stable personality traits—an assumption that most behaviorists do not hold. Behaviorists deal with personality disorders by focusing on specific behaviors, which they see as the result of maladaptive modeling and reinforcement. Behavioral treatment relies on relearning—reinforcement of adaptive behaviors and the extinction of maladaptive behaviors.

Advocates of the sociocultural perspective blame social injustices for most antisocial behavior and argue for changing the society, not individuals. The theory of anomie, or normlessness, among certain disadvantaged groups may be applicable to antisocial personalities.

The neuroscience perspective focuses on genetic and physiological factors that may contribute to antisocial personality disorder, evidenced by research on EEG abnormalities, poor performance in avoidance learning, autonomic underarousal, and other related phenomena.

The Addictive Disorders

To many people the very word *drug* has connotations of danger. Yet most Americans do use some form of **psychoactive drug**—that is, a drug that alters one's psychological state—either occasionally or regularly. While some people go to the trouble of seeking out illegal drugs, most confine themselves to such legal drugs as alcohol, nicotine, and caffeine, which, precisely because they *are* legal, tend not to be looked upon as drugs. Yet the damage done by legal drugs may be as great as, if not greater than, that caused by many illegal drugs.

Psychoactive drugs do not invariably cause harm. When they are prescribed by physicians, they can be very helpful indeed. In many societies, and in subcultures of our own society, they are an integral part of social and religious ritual. Nor is occasional recreational use, in small doses, necessarily the road to

destruction. Certain drugs are an important source of harmless pleasure, as anyone knows who has ever enjoyed a cup of coffee in the morning or a beer at a ball game. It is when drug use becomes habitual and when it begins to erode the person's normal functioning—work, studies, relationships with others—that it is redefined as abuse.

In the past few decades drugs have become a major focus of social concern, as evidenced by the rapid proliferation of alcohol- and drug-treatment centers and of educational programs aimed at the prevention of abuse. Particularly in the mid-eighties, with the appearance in the illegal drug market of "crack," a cheaper, more powerful, and highly addictive form of cocaine, social anxiety escalated feverishly. A nationwide anticrack campaign claimed billboards and television commercials. Efforts were made to mandate urine testing for holders of high-risk jobs in order to detect drug users. In 1986 drug abuse made the cover of *Newsweek* three times in five months. Other news magazines, such as *Time,* also ran cover stories, and a CBS television news special called "48 Hours on Crack Street" reportedly drew 15 million viewers. Yet in the early eighties cocaine use among high school students, the targets of the anticrack campaign, actually increased very little, if at all. Alcohol is still America's number-one drug problem. And social alarm, though it may further prevention, has still not resulted in truly effective treatment for the abusers of any drug.

In this chapter we will first describe the common features of drug dependence. Then we will discuss alcohol and tobacco, the most easily available and widely used drugs in our society. Finally, we will examine other varieties of drugs: depressants, stimulants, hallucinogens, and marijuana. Theories as to the cause and treatment of abuse will also be covered.

Though our chapter will go drug by drug, it is important to keep in mind that in many cases drugs are not used individually. Some drug users like to combine effects, a common combination being marijuana and alcohol. Other drug users switch repeatedly from one drug to another. As a result, the current trend in drug-treatment centers is to deal with patients as people who seek *a* drug experience—any alteration in their state of consciousness—rather than to worry over whether they are alcoholics, heroin addicts, or whatever. Yet despite this trend, information on multiple drug use is still scarce. Hence we will confine our discussion to the individual effects of the various drugs.

THE NATURE OF SUBSTANCE DEPENDENCE

The discussion of drug abuse is hampered by the fact that neither the society nor the mental health profession has yet agreed on a clear and consistent terminology. For years it was customary to distinguish physiological and psychological need. Drug use that had altered the body's chemistry to the point where its "normal" state was the drugged state, so that the body required the drug in order to feel normal, was called **addiction.** By contrast, the psychological dimension of drug abuse—the abuser's growing tendency to center his or her life on the drug—was often called **psychological dependence.** These definitions, however, were not accepted by all profes-

sionals. (Indeed, recent editions of *DSM* reserve the term *dependence* specifically for conditions that involved addiction.) Furthermore, as methods for detecting "withdrawal symptoms" became more precise, researchers discovered that all psychoactive drugs had both physiological and psychological effects; the two could not be separated.

In response to these confusions, *DSM-III-R* (pp. 167–168) has gathered all manifestations of pathological drug use under a single diagnostic category, **psychoactive substance dependence.** The nine criteria include both psychological and physiological consequences, and fulfillment of any three qualifies the drug user for the diagnosis:

1. *Preoccupation with the drug.* A great deal of time is spent in activities necessary to get the substance (e.g., theft), taking the substance (e.g., chain smoking), or recovering from its effects.

2. *Unintentional overuse.* Problem users begin to find repeatedly that they have taken more of the drug than they intended.

3. *Tolerance.* As noted, habitual drug use alters the body chemistry. The body becomes habituated to the drug, so that the usual dose no longer produces the desired effect—a phenomenon called **tolerance.** Some alcoholics, for example, can drink a quart of whiskey a day without seeming intoxicated. As tolerance develops, the person requires larger and larger amounts of the drug in order to achieve the desired biochemical change.

4. *Withdrawal.* With habituation, the body *requires* the drug in order to maintain stability. If the drug level is decreased, the person undergoes **withdrawal symptoms,** psychological and physical disruptions ranging from mild anxiety and tremors to acute psychosis and, in extreme cases, death.

5. *Relief substance use.* The person often takes the drug in order to relieve withdrawal symptoms.

6. *Persistent desire or efforts to control drug use.* Many drug-dependent people try repeatedly to quit, and repeatedly relapse. Drug abuse is a chronic disorder, and complete cures are not common.

7. *A pattern of drug-impaired performance in social or occupational circumstances, or when drug use is dangerous*—for example, failing an exam

because of a hangover or driving under the influence of marijuana.

8. *The abandonment of important social, occupational, or recreational activities for the sake of drug use.* Many of life's major functions—work, friendship, marriage, child rearing—conflict with heavy drug use and may be given up as a result.

9. *Continued drug use despite serious drug-related problems.* Many people go on smoking despite emphysema, or taking narcotics despite a long record of drug-related arrests. This is no longer recreational use.

ALCOHOLISM

For thousands of years alcohol has been the traditional "high" of Western culture. And it can be purchased legally in all but a few parts of the United States, unlike most of the other drugs we will discuss in this chapter. For both of these reasons, alcohol is the most widely used of all the psychoactive drugs. In 1982, 68 percent of those between eighteen and twenty-five years old had had an alcoholic beverage during the month before the survey, as had 57 percent of those over twenty-five (U.S. Bureau of the Census, 1986). Ten percent of the over-fifteen population drink more than 1.0 ounce of absolute alcohol each day. That 1.0 ounce of absolute alcohol can be ob-

tained in either 2.5 ounces of distilled spirits (about two mixed drinks) *or* 7 ounces (about two glasses) of wine *or* 22 ounces (about two cans) of beer. The average yearly consumption of those who drink more than once a month is about 4.4 gallons of distilled spirits *and* 3.7 gallons of wine *and* 45.2 gallons of beer. Substantial as this may seem, it is, statistically, the normal rate of consumption. As for those who drink more, the National Institute on Alcohol Abuse estimates that there are now nearly 18 million alcoholics and alcohol abusers in the United States.

The Social Cost of Alcohol Abuse

It is impossible to measure the damage done to society at large as a result of alcohol abuse. Easier to measure is the amount of money it costs. It is estimated that alcohol-related problems cost the American economy more than $116 billion in 1983 (National Council on Alcoholism, 1986). Most of this economic loss is concentrated in three areas: decreased work productivity, health problems, and motor vehicle accidents.

The largest portion of this loss—about $70 billion—is due to decreased work productivity. Workers with drinking problems are slower and less efficient, lose time on the job (by coming in late with a hangover, taking long lunches with several drinks, leaving early for cocktail hour, and so on), make hasty decisions, cause accidents, and lower the morale of their co-

Drinking and driving are often a lethal combination. Public awareness of this fact is increasing, as a result both of formal publicity campaigns and of such informal reminders as this sign on a car wrecked in an alcohol-related accident and left on the street as a warning to other drivers. (Paul Conklin)

workers. Furthermore, they are more likely to become prematurely disabled and to die young.

In 1981, $15.9 billion was spent for medical treatment costs and support services. In one estimate, each alcoholic employee cost his or her company the equivalent of 25% of their salary (Alcoholism Council of Greater New York, 1987). Approximately half of all occupied beds in American hospitals are filled by people with ailments linked to alcohol consumption (U.S. Department of Health and Human Services, 1981).

Finally, $10 billion is lost annually in alcohol-related motor vehicle accidents (National Safety Council, 1987). Before we comment on the relationship between drinking and driving, it is necessary to clarify the matter of blood alcohol levels. The effects of alcohol on the nervous system—and consequently on the drinker's behavior—are directly proportionate to the amount of alcohol in the bloodstream. This latter factor is called the **blood alcohol level**, which is expressed in terms of the amount of alcohol in relation to a specific volume of blood. Table 12.1 indicates the approximate relationship between alcohol intake and blood alcohol level. Note that there is a sex difference. Women have less body fluid (but more fat) per pound of body weight. Therefore, if a 150-pound woman and a 150-pound man go out and have five drinks apiece, she will have a higher blood alcohol level than he, and consequently will be more intoxicated.

In all states a person with a blood alcohol level of 0.10 percent is considered by law to be intoxicated. As Table 12.2 indicates, a driver with a blood alcohol level of 0.10 percent is less cautious, less alert, and slower to react than a nondrinking driver. A nighttime driver who has had several drinks is also laboring under a severe visual handicap, since it has been shown that visual recovery from glare slows down as blood alcohol level increases (Sekuler and MacArthur, 1977).

The relationship between blood alcohol level and motor vehicle accidents is all too clear. Alcohol is

TABLE 12.1   RELATIONSHIPS AMONG SEX, WEIGHT, ORAL ALCOHOL CONSUMPTION, AND BLOOD ALCOHOL LEVEL

		Blood Alcohol Levels (mg/100 ml)					
Absolute Alcohol (Ounces)	Beverage Intake*	Female (100 lbs.)	Male (100 lbs.)	Female (150 lbs.)	Male (150 lbs.)	Female (200 lbs.)	Male (200 lbs.)
½	1 oz. spirits† 1 glass wine 1 can beer	0.045	0.037	0.03	0.025	0.022	0.019
1	2 oz. spirits 2 glasses wine 2 cans beer	0.09	0.075	0.06	0.05	0.045	0.037
2	4 oz. spirits 4 glasses wine 4 cans beer	0.18	0.15	0.12	0.10	0.09	0.07
3	6 oz. spirits 6 glasses wine 6 cans beer	0.27	0.22	0.18	0.15	0.13	0.11
4	8 oz. spirits 8 glasses wine 8 cans beer	0.36	0.30	0.24	0.20	0.18	0.15
5	10 oz. spirits 10 glasses wine 10 cans beer	0.45	0.37	0.30	0.25	0.22	0.18

* In 1 hour.
† 100 proof spirits.

Source: O. S. Ray, *Drugs, Society, and Human Behavior*, 3rd ed. (St. Louis: Mosby Company, 1983).

implicated in as many as half of all car accidents, and its involvement in fatal car accidents is even higher. A California study of 440 young men killed in motor vehicle accidents found that 81 percent of the bodies had drugs in the bloodstream, and of these, 70 percent had alcohol (Williams et al., 1985). In one out of three fatal adult pedestrian accidents, the *pedestrian* has a blood alcohol level above 0.10 percent. Thus the more you have had to drink—or the more the driver coming toward you has had to drink—the more likely you are to be injured or killed in a car accident.

Even if alcohol abusers are too young to drive, they can still cause serious social damage. Alcohol contributes to the incidence of physical assault and sexual offenses. One careful study of young offenders (Tinklenberg and Woodrow, 1974) found that alcohol use was involved in 30 percent of all the corroborated assaults in which tissue damage occurred and in 30 percent of the deaths. In fact, alcohol use was involved in about half of those physical assaults in which the assailant was under the influence of some drug. In the area of sexual offenses—pedophilia and forcible rape—alcohol use accounted for 90 percent of the drug-related sexual offenses. In commenting on this evidence, Tinklenberg and Woodrow conclude that violence in the adolescent under the influence of alcohol tends to be "a process of enhanced irritability and indiscriminate assaultive tendencies directed toward anyone who might happen to be present" (p. 223).

The Personal Cost of Alcohol Abuse

The Immediate Effects of Alcohol   Pharmacologically, alcohol is a depressant. It slows down and interferes with the transmission of electrical impulses in the higher brain centers, areas that control, organize, and inhibit some of our complex mental processes. And it is precisely because of this release from control that we use alcohol to ease our way in social situations. It helps us relax, stop worrying about what other people think of us, and just have a good time.

By the time the blood alcohol level reaches 0.03 to 0.06 percent, two types of effects occur. First, mood and social behavior change. Some people become depressed and remorseful; others become amorous or belligerent. The second effect is that judgment is impaired. Amorous types will begin making wanton remarks to strangers, belligerent types will start fights, and so forth. As the blood alcohol level contin-

Blood Alcohol Level	Effect
0.05%	Lowered alertness; usually good feeling; release of inhibitions; impaired judgment
0.10%	Less caution; impaired motor function
0.15%	Large, consistent increases in reaction time
0.20%	Marked depression in sensory and motor capability, decidedly intoxicated
0.25%	Severe motor disturbance, staggering; sensory perceptions greatly impaired, smashed!
0.30%	Stuporous, but conscious—no comprehension of world around them
0.35%	Surgical anesthesia; about LD 1, minimal level causing death
0.40%	Probable lethal dose about LD 50

TABLE 12.2   BLOOD ALCOHOL LEVEL: PHYSIOLOGICAL AND PSYCHOLOGICAL EFFECTS

Source: O. S. Ray, *Drugs, Society, and Human Behavior*, 3rd ed. (St. Louis: Mosby Company, 1983).

ues to rise, the depressant effect of alcohol becomes more obvious. People slow down, stumble and trip, and slur their words. Their judgment is further impaired, and they tend to engage in even more reckless behavior. "Depressive" drunks may begin loudly confessing their sins and failures or cease feeling guilty about them altogether. According to some theorists, it is this effect—the release from anxiety over past, present, and future sins, real or imaginary—that alcoholics seek to maintain.

For a long time it was believed that the "bad" behaviors associated with drinking, particularly sexual indiscretion and belligerence, resulted directly from the physiological effect of alcohol on the brain. Presumably alcohol impeded the brain's inhibition functions, and the "real person" came out. But experiments in which the behavior of people who have drunk alcohol is compared with the behavior of people who merely think they have drunk alcohol suggest that the disinhibiting effect has as much to do with expectations—beliefs about what alcohol does to people—as with biochemistry. Increased sexual arousal, in particular, is apparently due more to expectations than to chemical effects (Hull and Bond, 1986). Likewise it appears that beliefs about alcohol's unleashing of immoral and aggressive behavior do much to excuse and maintain such behavior (Critchlow, 1986). The context must also be taken into account—not just the drink, but the fact that we are at a party or in a bar. Barrooms, as we know, are where brawls may occur. Therefore, for those inclined in that direction, the expectations associated with both the drink and the barroom may produce brawling.

As for the widely held belief that alcohol relieves tension (Southwick et al., 1981), this belief is correct, and the effect *does* seem to be based on chemistry. In a test that subjected people to the stress of having to make a favorable first impression on someone of the opposite sex, alcohol reduced the subjects' cardiovascular responsiveness regardless of their expectations (Sher and Walitzer, 1986). Another study found a more complex relationship between alcohol and tension. After a failure experience on an IQ test, subjects were cheered up by alcohol only if it was combined with a distracting activity. Thus alcohol, by slowing information processing, may make it harder for us to dwell on our troubles, but in order actually to prevent such rumination, we must be given something else to do instead (Steel et al., 1986).

The Long-Term Effects of Alcohol Abuse   Because of alcohol's tension-relieving effects, alcohol is often resorted to as a means of coping with, or at least enduring, life's problems. The ironic result is that alcoholics end up with more problems than they had before and fewer resources for dealing with them. Hence they drink more. Hence they have more problems—a classic vicious cycle. In the process, their mental acuteness is lost; memory, judgment, and the power to concentrate are all diminished. They lose both respect and self-respect. They neglect and alienate their friends and family. Often unable to work, alcoholics typically feel guilty toward their families, but at the same time they may take out their problems on the family. Child abuse, for example, is often connected with alcohol abuse. Alcohol also impairs sexual functioning and is one of the leading causes of impotence.

As serious as the psychological consequences are the physiological effects. Habitual overuse of alcohol can cause stomach ulcers, hypertension, heart failure, or brain damage. Another common consequence is cirrhosis of the liver, which is now among the five leading causes of death in several countries (Schmidt, 1977). Alcoholics are also prone to malnutrition. Alcohol is high in calories, which provide energy, but it is devoid of any known nutrient. Because alcoholics frequently eat very little and very unselectively, their protein and vitamin intake is dangerously insufficient. In addition, in extreme cases alcoholics may develop Korsakoff's psychosis (Chapter 16), a severe memory disorder thought to be caused by vitamin B deficiency.

An infrequent but terrifying complication of chronic alcoholism is **delirium tremens,** literally translated as "trembling delirium" and better known as the DTs. This severe reaction is actually a withdrawal symptom, occurring when the blood alcohol level drops suddenly. Deprived of their needed dosage, patients with DTs tremble furiously, perspire heavily, become disoriented, and suffer nightmarish delusions. This condition usually lasts for three to six days, after which the patient may vow never to take another drink—a vow that in many cases is broken shortly after discharge from the treatment center.

The Making of an Alcoholic

As we shall see later in this chapter, there is considerable confusion as to what type of person is likely to become an alcoholic. There is also considerable variability in *how* people become alcoholics, but some common patterns have been noted. While some people become "instant alcoholics," most go through a long period of social drinking during which they discover, and come to rely on, the tension-relieving properties of the drug. As consumption increases, many people begin to experience "blackouts," periods of time in which, under the influence of alcohol, they remain conscious and carry on in a fairly normal fashion but of which they have no memory the following day. The alcoholic-to-be may also, in social situations, begin "sneaking drinks" (e.g., stopping at the bar on the way to the men's room) in order to keep ahead of the others without letting them know. Another serious danger sign is morning drinking, to "get myself going." Eventually such people get drunk whenever they drink. They may also go on "benders," alcoholic binges lasting several days.

Whatever the pattern, most alcoholics eventually find that they are drunk every day and no longer have the ability to abstain. (Some alcoholics remain "spree" drinkers, staying sober for long periods but then, often in response to stress, going on benders.)

Compulsive Gambling

Like alcoholism, drug dependence, and certain eating disorders, compulsive gambling is a progressive impulsive disorder. Without treatment, pathological gamblers are driven into debt, into bankruptcy, and sometimes to suicide. Just as nonalcoholics can turn down a drink at any time, most people can take or leave gambling. For the pathological gambler, however, there is no turning back—the gambler's self-value is tied to the win, and the win is pursued with increasing desperation. Estimates of the prevalance of the disorder in the United States range from 1.1 million (Custer and Milt, 1985) to 9 million (Gamblers Anonymous). The number of people affected by the gambler's behavior is certainly in the millions, for gambling not only depletes the individual's emotional and material resources but also steals from the workplace and devastates the family.

Compulsive gambling generally progresses in a pattern, with predictable crises and accelerated efforts to recoup losses. Men are more likely than women to have the disorder (*DSM-III-R*). The personality traits and social characteristics of both male and female compulsive gamblers include above-average intelligence and education; a need for challenge, stimulation, and risk taking; and competitiveness (Peck, 1986). Loss of control, or bottoming out, can occur from one to twenty years after the onset of the compulsion, but for gamblers over age thirty-five, the time frame is about five years. A few get hooked with the first bet; the compulsive gambler is usually someone who has a substantial win right at the beginning, although some gamblers play compulsively after an initial loss.

In the early stages of the disorder, the gambler tends to win and often continues to win because initial luck is replaced by skillful playing and astute betting strategies. During the winning phase, confidence builds along with excitement and the sense that the gambler is exceptional. At this point the big win occurs—the amount won may exceed a year's salary. The gambler's story almost always includes a big win that sets off the compulsion (Custer and Custer, 1978).

The big win typically introduces the next phase—losing. In the losing phase, the gambler is betting compulsively and "chasing"—betting more and more to get back the money lost, whether he or she is chasing stock options or betting more heavily in casi-

nos, at racetracks, or in private games. Skilled gamblers know that chasing is a loser's or novice player's strategy but cannot stop themselves. The gambler, now betting poorly and more heavily, incurs more and more losses. After income and savings are depleted, the gambler borrows. The irrational belief that he or she will soon win and repay the debt has become part of the gambler's self-concept and sense of value. Most compulsive gamblers report that the initial experience of borrowing brings a feeling akin to that of the big win.

Now the pathological gambler begins to borrow heavily as losses mount—with predictable consequences. Like the alcoholic who hides bottles from spouse and children, the gambler covers up losses, lies to the boss, and manipulates family members and friends as she or he tries to pay off pressing debts while maintaining a stake sizable enough to keep betting. When legal sources dry up, many compulsive gamblers turn to loan sharks and bookies, and some risk death or injury when they can't pay. Divorce, imprisonment, and job loss become increasing threats. With fear of exposure and financial ruin, the compulsive bettor may become paranoid. Some confess their problem to family members and get temporarily or partially "bailed out." The bailout only defers an acceptance of responsibility; for the pathological gambler, the reprieve is like the big win or initial loan (Peck, 1986).

After the bailout and repeated failures to keep promises to stop gambling, desperation, the third and final phase, sets in, and the compulsive gambler spirals down. Gambling continues with "all-consuming intensity and apparent disregard for family, friends, and employment" (Moran, 1970). Eating and sleep disturbances ensue, and symptoms at this stage include depression, irritability, hypersensitivity, and restlessness. Alienated, debt-ridden, exhausted, and welcome nowhere, the compulsive gambler hits bottom. If not yet arrested for criminal activity, the gambler can run, attempt suicide, or seek help.

Many compulsive gamblers recover in self-help groups such as Gamblers Anonymous, but mental health professionals have taken little interest in the problem. With treatment facilities almost nonexistent and compulsive gambling so widespread, people who suffer from this devastating disorder do not get the help they need—despite the fact that it can be treated.

Jellinek (1946), who described many of these patterns, claimed that the total itinerary, from the beginning of heavy drinking to complete defeat by alcohol, took twelve to eighteen years, but for many people the route is shorter.

The following case of Jellinek's illustrates some of the common features of alcoholism:

> This forty-five year-old white male, who works as a construction foreman during his sober periods, completed eight years of education and served two years in the army during the Korean War. He started drinking at the age of eighteen, and although he reports that his drinking has been a problem only for the last ten years, he also admitted that he had been court-martialed three times in the army and had spent six months in the stockade for alcohol-related offenses.
>
> He described himself as a "spree" drinker, but his heavy-drinking episodes now last three to four weeks and occur about six times a year. During these drinking periods, according to his statement, he consumes at least a quart of whiskey, a gallon of wine, and one to three six-packs of beer per day. He has had loss of memory and times of extreme shakes and hallucinations on a "few" occasions. He has had so many arrests for public drunkenness that he cannot even estimate their number. He has also had one arrest for drunk driving. He reports that both of his brothers are also alcoholics. His father drank heavily for years but was dry for the year before his death.
>
> On his first known admission five years ago, the patient denied that he had been drinking heavily and said he had only a few beers a day. He was brought to the hospital by his wife because he was talking to the television, hearing strange music, and seeing bugs and snakes. He was detoxified. On his next admission, two years ago, he said that he had not been working more than a day or two at a time and that his wife supported him by working as a manager at a local department store. . . .
>
> During his second admission he said that he was ready to go into a treatment program, but he managed to miss all of his scheduled appointments and evaluations. He requested a long pass to "look for work," and when he was told that he wasn't ready to leave the hospital, he returned to his room, dressed and left.
>
> A year later his wife brought him to the hospital because she had returned from work to find him unconscious on the floor. His heart was pounding furiously, and he was blood-red in color and gasping for breath. After sobering up in the hospital . . .

> he swore that he was "willing to do anything to get better."
>
> Everyone was convinced, and eight days later he was given a one-day pass to visit his wife before entering the alcohol treatment program. He returned sober from the pass, but he must have brought a bottle with him, since the next morning he was intoxicated and unable to begin the treatment program. He left the hospital two days later against the advice of the staff.
>
> The staff's last contact with this patient took place six months ago, when he was brought to the hospital by ambulance after passing out in a downtown alley. A companion reported that the patient had drunk a case of beer in one hour (which is not possible). He left the hospital three days later and has not yet returned.

There appear to be certain marked differences between male and female alcoholics. First, women usually begin drinking later in their lives, experience their first intoxication later, develop alcoholism later, and come to facilities with shorter histories of drinking problems than do men. In addition, women are more likely than men to cite a stressful event as precipitating the problem drinking. Women are also more likely to have a problem-drinking husband or lover than men are to have a problem-drinking wife or lover. When women drink with someone else, it is likely to be someone close to them, but women tend much more often than men to drink alone. Conversely, men are more likely than women to drink in public places. Women also drink large amounts less often, do less bender and morning drinking, and have shorter drinking bouts. Finally, women more frequently combine other substances with alcohol. The polydrug pattern may include tranquilizers, barbiturates, amphetamines, hypnotics, antidepressants, or nonprescription drugs (Gomberg, 1981). The course of alcoholism has interesting parallels with the course of another devastating behavioral disorder, compulsive gambling (see the accompanying box).

PERSPECTIVES ON ALCOHOLISM

What causes alcoholism? As we shall see in the following section, many theories have been put forth regarding the origins of alcoholism, but no one theory can yet be applied to all the different kinds of alcoholics—

the solitary woman drinking at home, the noisy man at the pinball machine, the Junior Chamber of Commerce Man of the Year, or the derelict on the sidewalk. At this point the only trait that we know for certain to be shared by all alcoholics is the need for alcohol.

As with most other kinds of abnormal behavior, there are probably multiple factors underlying each case of alcoholism. It is also likely that the importance of any one factor will vary from individual to individual.

The Behavioral Perspective

Tension Reduction   From the behavioral perspective, alcoholism is viewed as a powerful habit maintained by many antecedent cues and consequent reinforcers. Several suggestions have been offered as to what the primary reinforcer might be: social approval, ability to engage in relaxed social behavior, avoidance of physiological withdrawal symptoms, reduction of psychological tension. Although all of these factors may be involved, most behavioral theories accept the premise that excessive drinking is motivated primarily by a desire to reduce tension.

According to the tension-reduction hypothesis, the dynamics of alcoholism are as follows. All of us have our share of troubles—anxiety, self-doubt, depression, guilt, annoyance. In the process of trying to reduce our psychological discomfort, some of us will take a drink. Alcohol, as we have seen, can definitely do the job, dulling whatever mental distress we are experiencing. Thus alcohol use becomes associated with the alleviation of psychological pain. Because of this reinforcement, drinking is likely to be repeated. Eventually, of course, excessive drinking may itself create further psychological distress, especially guilt. This distress will in turn be alleviated by more drinking. In this way the individual enters the vicious cycle described earlier.

The tension-reduction hypothesis has received some support from animal research. In a classic study (Conger, 1951), for example, laboratory rats were given an electric shock whenever they came near their food dishes. As a result, the rats showed hesitation, vacillation, and other signs of inner conflict when they approached their food. When they were injected with alcohol, however, they went up to their food dishes with no signs of conflict. Unfortunately, other animal studies based on different experimental designs

have not provided consistent support for the tension-reduction hypothesis.

Studies of humans indicate that alcohol is a much better tension reducer for some people than for others. In one experiment, for example, people were identified as high or low risks for alcoholism on the basis of personality scores. Those who were outgoing, aggressive, impulsive, and antisocial were considered at risk for alcoholism. Although there were no differences in response to stress without alcohol, when given alcohol, the high-risk subjects experienced less cardiovascular arousal in response to stress than did subjects who were considered low risks (Sher and Levenson, 1982). In other words, alcohol protected the high-risk subjects from stress more than it did the low-risk subjects. Perhaps if we can identify early those individuals whose drinking is most reinforced by alcohol's tension-reducing properties, it may be possible to prevent them from abusing alcohol.

The mixed findings on the tension-reduction hypothesis, the fact that individuals vary in the degree of tension reduction, and the additional finding that many people experience *increased* anxiety after drinking (Nathan, 1976) all suggest that tension reduction is a determinant of excessive drinking for only some people in some situations.

A broader theory that has gained some attention in recent years is the "opponent process" theory (Solomon and Corbit, 1974; Solomon, 1980), which offers an explanation not only of addiction to alcohol but also of tolerance and withdrawal. According to this theory, the human brain is organized in such a way that any strong emotional state, whether pleasant or unpleasant, automatically elicits an "opponent process," or opposite state, that serves to counteract and suppress the original state. At first the opponent process is weak, but it is strengthened each time the original state is elicited. Applied to alcohol, this theory suggests that the first few times a person drinks, the state of euphoria and relaxation (state *A*) will be much stronger than the underlying state of tension and irritability (state *B*). But after the person drinks on many occasions, the underlying opponent state is strengthened considerably. This has two consequences: first, state *A* is canceled out, so that the person experiences hardly any "positive" effect while drinking—the phenomenon of *tolerance*. Second, when the effects of the alcohol end (i.e., when state *A* ends), state *B* effects are experienced directly as *withdrawal symptoms*. If the person responds by increasing alcohol intake in order to reduce the effects of state *B,* addiction will occur. In sum, each drinking episode increases the severity of withdrawal symptoms, which causes the person to increase drinking, which strengthens the withdrawal symptoms further, and so on. Again, a circular process.

This theory, however, does not explain why, as so often happens, alcoholics will resume excessive drinking once they have "dried out" and undergone withdrawal. Solomon states that this phenomenon can be accounted for by respondent conditioning. In the course of the drinking cycle, many previously neutral stimuli will become conditioned to either state *A* or state *B.* For example, if a man did most of his drinking in a particular bar, or with a certain group of friends, or upon leaving work, a reencounter with any one of these stimuli will trigger state *A,* which in turn will bring on state *B* and a craving for its antidote, alcohol. Thus even if the alcoholic has not had a drink in months and presumably "knows better," the cycle may begin again.

In our society the stimuli for drinking are everywhere, making it all the more difficult for alcoholics to abstain. (John Banasiak)

Learning Not to Drink   Early behavioral programs for alcoholism relied primarily on aversion conditioning: alcohol was paired with some unpleasant stimulus, usually electric shock or induced nausea. Such programs had some initial success, but also a heavy relapse rate. Only 44 percent of subjects in one large program, for example, were found on follow-up to have remained abstinent (Lemere and Voegtlin, 1950).

The problem with such treatments, presumably, was that while they suppressed the behavior (drinking), they did nothing to alter the conditions that elicited and maintained it. Many alcoholics, one can guess, are people who had inadequate coping skills to begin with—skills that have been further eroded by alcoholism at the same time that stresses (e.g., unemployment, marital conflicts) have been increased. The object of current behavioral programs is to remedy this broad adjustment problem. The alcoholism is still addressed directly. Patients are taught to identify cues and situations that lead to drinking, and through role playing and practicing they are taught alternative responses. But they are also taught new ways of dealing with life: how to solve problems and, by training in relaxation and social skills, how to cope with stress.

Much recent work (e.g., Marlatt and Gordon, 1985) has been aimed specifically at prevention of relapse. Here patients engage in cognitive restructuring to correct mistaken beliefs (e.g., that one lapse means defeat) and learn ways of dealing with slips so that they do not lead to total relapse. Some cognitive therapists have even guided patients through "planned relapses" in order to coach them to combat the defeatist thoughts that tend to follow slips.

The Psychodynamic Perspective

Meeting Emotional Needs with Drink   Psychodynamic theorists hold that alcoholism is the symptom of an unconscious emotional problem. As for what the problem is, there are several theories.

The first is that alcoholism is a reflection of unsatisfied dependency needs. This dependency, in turn, is thought to stem from oral fixation. In other words, people become alcoholics in order to obtain oral gratification and to be cared for by others. There is some evidence that alcoholics may in fact have more intense oral needs than other people. For example, alcoholics are much more likely than nonalcoholics to be heavy cigarette smokers (Maletzky and Klotter, 1974). As for the dependency of the alcoholic, this theory is supported by a wealth of research data (e.g., McCord et al., 1960) and is likely to receive the assent of anyone who has lived with an alcoholic. However, most of the evidence for dependency is retrospective, and prospective studies indicate that the alcoholic's dependency, or at least its overt expression, develops out of the drinking problem rather than vice versa (Vaillant and Milofsky, 1982).

Another motivational theory related to the psychodynamic perspective is directly contrary to the dependency-needs hypothesis: David McClelland and his colleagues (1972) have proposed that what leads people to alcoholism is a drive for power. According to this view, people who feel that they lack control over themselves and their world can obtain from alcohol a renewed sense of confidence and mastery; hence they drink more and more. The aggressiveness commonly seen in alcoholics—and interpreted by the dependency-need theorists as a defense against passivity—is viewed by this school as a direct expression of the power drive. Likewise, the tendency of alcoholics to seek relationships with strong individuals is interpreted as an attempt to "borrow" strength from others, rather than as the expression of a desire to be cared for, as the dependency theory would have it. In a series of studies, McClelland and his colleagues have found a strong correlation between excessive drinking and the yearning for power. One finding was that the ingestion of alcohol leads to an increase in thoughts of winning personal victories over adversaries.

A third theory, this one derived from social psychology, has less to do with deep motivation than with impression management. Jones and Berglas (1978) conceptualize alcoholism as a self-handicapping strategy. In their view, the alcoholic, when placed in a situation likely to lead to failure, will drink in order to have an excuse for failing: "I'd have gotten that raise if it hadn't been for my drinking," or "I'd be able to pass this course if I didn't drink." By reasoning that drinking is at fault, the alcoholic maintains a semblance of self-esteem. Research has found that people do sometimes use alcohol in this manner (Tucker et al., 1981), though it has yet to be shown that this strategy actually leads to alcoholism.

Treatment   Psychodynamic treatment of the alcoholic aims less at the "symptom"—that is, the drinking—than at the underlying psychic cause, since according to psychodynamic theory, the symptom will not be relieved until the unconscious conflict is relieved. Insight-oriented psychodynamic therapies, however, have had poor success rates with alcoholism and are not common forms of treatment. When they are used, the therapist will often recommend that the patient also use some supplementary support system, such as Alcoholics Anonymous.

Group treatment programs based on McClelland's power theory have been implemented in some settings. In one program, alcoholics were given a thirty-five-hour intensive group course in power motivation training (Cutter et al., 1977). The course included self-study, behavioral exercises, simulations, lectures, and discussions—all designed to help the group members learn alternative means for feeling in control of themselves and their world. For example, patients were taught how to resolve interpersonal conflicts, how to give and receive help, how to influence others, and how to relieve their feelings of tension through yoga and meditation. Like most treatments for alcoholism, the program did not have remarkable success. Nevertheless, the improvement rate was higher in those who received the power motivation training in addition to standard hospital treatment than in those who received only the standard hospital treatment (McClelland, 1977).

The Sociocultural Perspective

Do certain social groups produce a disproportionate number of alcoholics? And if so, can we assume that cultural pressures have a role in the development of alcoholism? According to the widely noted study by McCord and his colleagues (1960), the answer is yes. In a follow-up study of young men who had been interviewed carefully as adolescents, these investigators found that the major factors dividing those who became alcoholics from those who did not were social class and ethnic background. The higher the educational and socioeconomic level, the higher the incidence of alcoholism. Among ethnic groups, men of American Indian and Irish extraction were more prone to become alcoholics, while those of Italian and other Latin backgrounds were the least likely. Statistics on alcoholism among American Indians are especially alarming. In one tribe it was found that one-third of the Indians over age twelve and *one-half* of the men over forty drank to excess. For all Indians the death rate from alcoholic cirrhosis is 27 per 100,000, as compared with 6 per 100,000 in the general population (Whittaker, 1982).

Another cultural correlate of alcoholism is religious affiliation. The one religious group that seems particularly resistant to alcohol problems is, predictably, conservative Protestants, who have a notably high percentage of alcohol abstainers and a notably low percentage of heavy drinkers. There are also few alcoholics among Orthodox Jews, who drink wine but in controlled and primarily religious settings (Snyder, 1958). Catholic, Reform Jewish, and liberal Protestant groups all contain a fairly high proportion of alcohol users, with the Catholics leading the other groups in the percentage of heavy drinkers. In all religious groups, it appears that the rate of church attendance correlates highly with abstinence.

Rural residents and small-town dwellers are less likely to drink and less likely to be heavy drinkers than their urban cousins (Cisin and Calahan, 1970). This finding may be related to the fact that environmental stresses and cultural confusion are greater in the city than in the country. Regardless of where one lives, one's culturally ingrained attitudes toward alcohol use will to some degree determine the likelihood of one's becoming alcoholic. Likewise, peer-group behavior appears to be a major determinant of alcohol consumption among adolescents. If a college student lives in a fraternity house where weekends are given over to beer parties, he is likely, no matter what his background, to join in the festivities.

Finally, it should be mentioned that cultural expectations may have something to do with the much higher prevalence of alcoholism among men than among women. Perhaps the pressures on men have been greater. Or perhaps the use of alcohol as a tension reliever has been more culturally acceptable in men than in women. If so, women's entry into the traditionally male work world may account for the rising prevalence of alcoholism among women.

The Neuroscience Perspective

A number of researchers and clinicians believe that the critical predisposing factors in alcoholism are genetically inherited physiological and biochemical abnormalities. One type of genetic evidence comes from cross-cultural studies. It has been reported, for example, that Japanese, Koreans, and Taiwanese respond with obvious facial flushing and clear signs of intoxication after drinking amounts of alcohol that have no detectable effect on Caucasians (Wolff, 1972). Such ethnic differences have led some investigators to conclude that sensitivity to alcohol is related to genetic factors, possibly affecting the autonomic nervous system.

Goodwin and his co-workers (1973) have conducted an even more revealing study with a group of male adoptees. Each of the men in the index group had been separated in infancy from his biological parents, one of whom had been hospitalized at least once for alcoholism. Many more of the index children grew up to have drinking problems and to seek psychiatric treatment than did a matched control group of adoptees whose biological parents were not alcoholic. The adoptive parents of both groups were of comparable socioeconomic standing and had similar proportions of alcoholism and other psychiatric disorders. Hence this study seems to suggest that the critical variable is not environmental (i.e., growing up with an alcoholic parent) but genetic (i.e., having the genes of an alcoholic parent).

Additional support for the existence of a genetic factor comes from findings that the sons and brothers of severely alcoholic men run a 25 to 50 percent risk of becoming alcoholics themselves at some point in their lifetime, and that there is a 55 percent concordance rate for alcoholism in identical twins as compared with 28 percent for same-sex fraternal twins (Schuckit and Rayses, 1979). The fact that the concordance rate for fraternal twins is as high as 28 percent does, however, indicate that there is a substantial environmental component as well.

The question of what the genetic variable might be—that is, what inherited organic abnormality might predispose a person to alcoholism—has been the focus of much biochemical and physiological research. No theory has yet been generally accepted, but researchers have come up with some interesting leads, one of which concerns the metabolism of alcohol. Schuckit and Rayses (1979) found that a high-risk population (men with alcoholic parents or siblings) showed a higher rate of metabolism of alcohol than a control group. There is also evidence that in metabolizing alcohol, heavy drinkers may use an additional pathway, one not used by normal drinkers (Korsten and Lieber, 1985). Thus those at risk for alcoholism may be receiving a larger effective dose of alcohol than those not at risk.

A longitudinal study now in progress in Denmark suggests, however, that the causes are more complicated. The researchers (Schulsinger et al., 1986) are following the progress of 134 sons of alcoholic fathers and 70 matched controls born between 1959 and 1961. So far the researchers have turned up three significant differences between the two groups. First, the high-risk men experienced much more disruption in their family lives, schooling, and social relationships as they were growing up. Second, as children, the high-risk men were rated as more restless and impulsive by their teachers. Third, in school the high-risk men had more reading problems and poorer verbal skills. But one difference that has not yet turned up between the two groups is a difference in the rate of alcoholism. Neither the high-risk nor the control group has yet produced any alcoholics, and both groups contain the same percentage of heavy drinkers. These findings cast doubt on the metabolism theory, for any differences due to metabolism should have shown up by now. (The men are in their late twenties.) At the same time, the differences between the two groups in childhood adjustment may point to a more subtle organic predisposition. Or, as in all family studies, they may be due to environmental rather than organic factors.

Multimodal Treatments

The treatment of alcoholism begins with **detoxification**—that is, getting the alcohol out of the person's system and seeing him or her through the withdrawal symptoms. Detoxification can be done at home, under outpatient care, though it is often undertaken in the hospital. The patient is usually given a tranquilizer, such as Librium, as a substitute for alcohol. Withdrawal to this substitute drug is generally completed in about five to seven days. A high level of vitamins and liquids is administered daily to counter nutritional deficiency and dehydration. Depending on the severity of the alcoholism, an anticonvulsant, such as Dilantin, may be administered to eliminate the possibility of seizures.

Once detoxification is completed, the difficult part of treatment begins—the effort to change the alcoholic from a social dropout, with disrupted interpersonal, family, and job relationships, to an integrated, self-sustaining, coping member of society. This is no easy task. Since rehabilitation touches so many aspects of the alcoholic's life, the better-designed alcohol rehabilitation programs are multimodal. Within a supportive environment, alcoholics are provided with occupational therapy, to help them learn or relearn a hobby;

relaxation training, to teach them how to reduce tension without alcohol; group and individual therapy, to help them learn something about themselves and to show them how to relate to others without drinking; family and marital therapy, to resolve some of the problems at home that may have contributed to and/or resulted from their drinking; and industrial or job-seeking counseling, to get them back to work. These various forms of treatment are given concurrently, and most, if not all, patients participate in them daily.

Sometimes hospital treatment programs supply an additional deterrent to drinking, in the form of a drug called Antabuse. Antabuse (disulfiram) is a chemical that interferes with the normal metabolic processing of alcohol for about two days after the medication is taken. When the Antabuse taker drinks alcohol, a toxic agent accumulates in the bloodstream, causing flushing, increased heart rate, and intense nausea. Antabuse treatment is based on the assumption that it will help alcoholics to avoid impulsive drinking (Baekeland et al., 1971), since if they want to take a drink without becoming violently ill, they must stop taking the Antabuse at least two days in advance. The drug thereby provides artificial support for the patient's "will power." However, the support *is* artificial. Once out of the hospital, many alcoholics simply stop taking the drug.

One part of most successful rehabilitation programs is follow-up. Ex-patients may meet one or more times a week for three to six months, or they may go on meeting indefinitely. This continued contact provides support, reminding ex-alcoholics once again that they need not battle their problem alone—that help is available. Furthermore, the follow-up meetings give them the opportunity to continue working on their problems and to learn additional interpersonal coping skills.

The most widely known of these regular meeting programs is Alcoholics Anonymous, better known as AA. The AA program started in the mid-thirties and has since spread around the world. AA operates on two basic tenets: (1) once an alcoholic, always an alcoholic; and (2) no one can stop drinking without help. AA sees alcoholism as a lifelong problem from which the individual never recovers. Consequently, he or she must abstain completely from alcohol and must rely on AA for comradeship and support in doing so. Such support is provided not only through the meetings but also through AA's famous "buddy system." A member who feels that the urge to drink is becoming overpowering calls AA. One or two members will then come to the caller as soon as possible

Relapse Prevention

For alcoholics, heroin addicts, overeaters, compulsive gamblers (see box), smokers, and others who suffer from addictive disorders, efforts to change the problem behavior fail more often than not: current estimates of relapse rates across the addictive disorders range from 50 to 90 percent (Brownell, 1986). Thus, the problem of relapse has become the major challenge of prevention and treatment programs. How we define *relapse*—as part of a process or as final outcome—has important implications for understanding behavior change. Kelly Brownell and colleagues (1986) distinguish between a *lapse,* or slip, which they view as an event in the process of change, and a *relapse,* which may suggest instead a final outcome, a point of no return. The way the person views a slip, then—as a mistake he or she can learn from or as confirmation that he or she has lost the battle—is a critical cognitive factor in efforts at recovery.

In keeping with this concept, we need to understand relapse and its consequences in light of the stages of change that precede it. One model (Prochaska and Diclemente, 1983, 1984) proposes three stages in the process of changing addictive behavior: (1) decision and commitment, (2) the initial change, and (3) maintaining the change. If a relapse in the third stage is viewed as a step in incremental learning rather than as a failure, it can lead to new efforts to change—beginning at stage 1 and leading eventually to successful maintenance. This view is consistent with Stanley Schachter's (1982) findings that permanent behavior change is more likely to occur after a person has dealt with several relapses. Researchers are now beginning to identify specific factors that lead to relapse. These fall into three categories: individual (intrapersonal), environmental (situational), and physiological.

Not surprisingly, negative emotional states are one of strongest determinants of relapse. These include stress, anger, depression, anxiety, and other negative moods. Such states may account for 30 percent of relapses across the addictive disorders (Cummings, 1980), and they increase the likelihood that a single lapse, or slip, will lead to relapse rather than to renewed efforts to change. Motivation and commitment are also key individual factors. Evaluating an addictive person's level and degree of motivation becomes an important part of treatment, both because people bursting with enthusiasm at the commitment stage

and will stay until the urge passes. In the process, it is believed, they will be helping themselves.

AA is said to be very effective—a claim that is based more on personal testimony than on actual research. The organization appears to have an extremely high dropout rate—as high as 80 percent (Edwards et al., 1967). Of those who remain, AA claims that at least half manage to stop drinking. This claim has not yet been confirmed. One comparative study found that the subjects assigned to AA later encountered more life difficulties and drank more than subjects assigned to other treatment methods (Brandsma et al., 1980). Further comparative studies remain to be done.

The last decade has seen a tremendous growth in residential care for alcoholics. There are alcoholic units in the Veterans Administration hospitals and in the psychiatric and general hospitals. In addition, the United States now has more than four hundred private residential alcoholism-treatment facilities (Moore, 1985), some of them, such as the Betty Ford Center, highly visible. It is questionable, however, whether alcoholics really need to be hospitalized round the clock. Outpatient and day-hospital programs have also been expanding during the last decade, and a review of comparative studies of outpatient and inpatient programs found no difference in relapse rates between the two approaches (Miller and Hester, 1986). It is likely that many people choose full hospitalization because, though it is expensive, it is the only treatment approach their medical insurance will pay for.

Though treatment centers are multiplying, their cure rates are still not encouraging. The few follow-up studies that have been conducted indicate that only

may not be able to maintain motivation for long-term change and because many others may begin the process motivated more by external social pressure than by internal commitment. Thus, both screening for motivation and developing programs to improve it should become part of relapse-prevention plans. Researchers have also found that a person's initial responses to treatment and his or her coping responses—including the important cognitive factor of self-efficacy, or belief that using available skills *will* bring success—are individual factors that can predict later success from a person's early efforts to change behavior.

Environment determinants of relapse include the presence or absence of social support and all the situations the person faces (or avoids) once he or she had decided to change. Studies have shown that interpersonal conflict is a strong predictor of relapse. Just as the stress of conflict can lead to relapse, social support—from family members, people in the work environment, and friends—can increase a person's chances for recovery. Self-help groups, such as Alcoholics Anonymous, Weight Watchers, Overeaters Anonymous, SmokEnders, Gamblers Anonymous, and Narcotics Anonymous, also bring the positive social support that only fellow sufferers can give. These groups also increase coping skills, a critical individual determinant of success or failure. Contingencies are always a danger for people trying to maintain motivation for behavior change. For ex-

ample, social pressure from users or exposure to the drug or activity often precedes a lapse or relapse (Shiffman, 1982). Contingency management—avoidance or control of such external events or cues—therefore becomes an important tool in recovery, especially for alcoholics.

For all these reasons, preventing relapse in the addictive disorders requires better understanding of how individual, environmental, and physiological factors interact during the stages of change. Physiological factors, for example, withdrawal cravings, can lead swiftly to a slip, especially if the person is experiencing anger, depression, or another negative emotion, lacks positive social support, and then is exposed to cues or contingencies—say, he enters a bar, or she goes to a party with former drinking buddies. To avoid such situations and to endure emotional stress without lapsing requires both strong motivation and coping skills.

Researchers are finding out, too, that people with addictive disorders benefit from learning new, "positive" addictions, such as physical exercise. People apparently need new sources of gratification if they are to maintain long-term behavior change. Although existing relapse rates are discouraging, this new focus of relapse prevention—finding ways to boost motivation and self-efficacy by replacing negative addictive behavior with positive behavior, leading to a new, rewarding life style—holds hope for millions of people.

---

about 40 percent of people who enter the more successful programs actually stop drinking permanently. At the same time, such new approaches as relapse prevention offer hope that better treatment programs will ultimately be devised.

TOBACCO DEPENDENCE

Three out of every ten American adults are smokers (U.S. Bureau of the Census, 1986). This makes tobacco dependence the most common form of drug dependence in the United States. Yet discussions of psychoactive drugs often give little if any attention to tobacco, for of all the psychoactive drugs, it is the least destructive *psychologically*. Indeed, it ap-

pears to do no psychological damage whatsoever. The disorder "nicotine dependence," as defined by *DSM-III-R,* refers primarily to those who want to stop smoking but cannot.

Tobacco contains nicotine, which has apparently paradoxical effects on the central nervous system. On the one hand, it stimulates the system by elevating the blood pressure and increasing the heart rate. At the same time, it has a calming effect. This effect is not just psychological—the product of the pleasure of indulging a habit. Animal studies have shown that injections of nicotine reduce aggression. Scientists are currently investigating this complex mix of calming and arousal (Gilbert, 1979). In any case, tobacco does not seem to impair mental functioning. What it impairs is the smoker's health.

In 1964, years of suspicion and research regarding

Many state and local laws have been passed in recent years restricting smoking in public places. Such laws are difficult to enforce because many smokers are unable or unwilling to obey them. (Getsug/Anderson/Photo Researchers)

the hazards of tobacco finally culminated in the famous "Surgeon General's Report" (U.S. Public Health Service, 1964), which presented compelling evidence that smoking was a major contributor to lung cancer, heart disease, emphysema, and other fatal illnesses. Since 1964 further studies have merely confirmed this claim. Those who smoke less than a pack of cigarettes a day have a death rate four times higher than nonsmokers; those who smoke more than a pack a day have a death rate seven times higher than nonsmokers. For certain specific diseases, the risks are even higher. For example, any man who smokes is ten times as likely as a nonsmoker to die of lung cancer (U.S. Department of Health, Education, and Welfare, 1970).

These findings have resulted in legislation banning cigarette advertisements from radio and television and requiring that each pack of cigarettes sold in this country carry an advertisement of its own potentially lethal effects. In recent years there has been a marked increase in antismoking sentiment and agitation. Some forty states now have restrictions on smoking in public places. There are over 800 local ordinances against tobacco use. And the General Services Administration now restricts smoking in federal buildings by federal employees.

The tobacco companies have vigorously opposed antismoking legislation. Nevertheless, there is evidence that the antismoking message has gotten through. A government survey conducted in 1975 revealed that almost everyone now believes that smoking is detrimental to health; 90 percent of the survey population agreed that smoking is harmful, including 80 percent of those who were currently smokers.

At the same time, many people have come to regard smoking not only as dangerous but also as offensive—an infringement of the rights of others. Smokers are finding themselves increasingly the objects of disapproving looks, accusatory coughs, and straightforward requests to put out their cigarettes. And in response, many have quit. The 1975 survey showed that cigarette smoking had declined by several percentage points since 1970, but the overall decline since 1964 (when the government first began to survey the problem) has been even more dramatic. The American Cancer Society conducted a thirteen-year survey that found that 38 percent of the smokers in 1959 had quit by 1972. Of those who continued to smoke, 59 percent switched to brands with less tar and nicotine (Garfinkel, 1979). While many are quitting, fewer are starting: the percentage of high school seniors who smoke daily dropped from 27 percent in 1975 to 21 percent in 1983 (Johnston et al., 1984).

It is clear that tobacco smoking is one of the most potent of all drug habits. A sad example is that of Sigmund Freud. Knowing full well that his practice of smoking as many as twenty cigars a day was weakening his heart and engendering cancerous growths in his mouth and jaw, Freud, after numerous futile attempts to quit, decided that without his cigars he simply could not maintain the psychological strength to continue his work. And so, even after his entire jaw had to be replaced by a clumsy artificial one, he continued smoking as long as his mouth could hold a cigar. Finally, in 1939, after cancer had eaten through his cheek as well, he died. It cannot be said that he died young—he lived to be eighty-three—but his death came only after years of harrowing pain.

Perspectives on Tobacco Dependence

Why tobacco should have such a firm hold over so many people is not at all clear. Explanations from various perspectives are similar to those advanced for alcoholism. Psychodynamic theorists generally regard smoking as another instance of oral fixation. Behavioral theorists see it as a learned habit maintained by a number of reinforcers—the stimulant effects of nicotine, the pleasure associated with inhaling and exhaling smoke, the experience of tension reduction in social situations, the enhanced image of oneself as "sophisticated," or perhaps all of these, the primary reinforcer varying from smoker to smoker (O'Leary and Wilson, 1975). Yet these reinforcers seem rather weak to maintain such a dangerous habit.

Is smoking, then, a physiological addiction? In the past, some researchers have argued that this was the case. Yet the research findings in favor of the addiction hypothesis were ambiguous. Furthermore, there was no evidence of tolerance; many people go on smoking a pack a day for years. And the withdrawal symptoms experienced by those who stopped smoking—irritability, anxiety, restlessness, difficulty in concentrating, decreased heart rate, craving for tobacco, overeating (Hughes and Hatsukami, 1986)—seemed mild compared with those of addictions such as alcohol. Hence most people assumed that smoking was a case of psychological dependence rather than physiological addiction.

In 1978, however, Schachter presented impressive evidence in support of the addiction hypothesis In a number of studies, Schachter and his colleagues found that smoking does not calm smokers or elevate their mood, nor does it improve their performance over that of nonsmokers. On the other hand, *not* smoking, or an insufficient nicotine level in the bloodstream, causes smokers to perform considerably worse than nonsmokers. Schachter concluded that smokers get nothing out of smoking other than avoidance of the disruptive effect of withdrawal, and that it is for this reason—avoidance of withdrawal—that they smoke.

In support of this conclusion, Schachter and his co-workers have good evidence that smokers regulate their nicotine levels in order to ensure that withdrawal symptoms do not occur. In one experiment, smokers increased their cigarette consumption when low-nicotine cigarettes were substituted for their regular, high-nicotine brands. In another experiment, a group of smokers were given vitamin C, which has the effect of lowering the nicotine level in the bloodstream. (Vitamin C acidifies the urine and so increases the rate at which nicotine is excreted.) Once again the subjects compensated by smoking more. Schachter suggests that this mechanism may explain why people smoke more when they are under stress. Stress, like vitamin C, acidifies the urine. Thus smokers under stress would have to increase their nicotine intake in order to maintain their usual nicotine level and thereby fend off withdrawal symptoms.

Treatment programs for smokers tend to report the same results that Freud showed repeatedly with his cigar habit: successful abstention followed by relapse. Mark Twain summed it up neatly. He could stop smoking, he said, with great ease; indeed, he had done so hundreds of times. Many people, of

Children often try cigarettes in an attempt to look and feel more grown up. (Hilde Moray/Photo Researchers)

course, do break the habit for good, and more often than not, they succeed without the help of a formal treatment program (Schachter, 1982).

OTHER PSYCHOACTIVE DRUGS

For the person in search of a potent psychoactive drug other than alcohol, a wide variety of drugs—depressants, stimulants, hallucinogens—can be equally destructive if they are used habitually. Most of these drugs are nothing new. Opium, for example, has been easing people's pain for almost 9,000 years. And indeed, until recently, many of these drugs were sold legally over the counter in the United States. During the nineteenth century countless numbers of self-respecting ladies thought nothing of taking laudanum, a form of opium, to help them sleep. During the Civil War morphine was commonly administered

TABLE 12.3 DRUG ABUSE STATISTICS, 1985*

	Total† (pop. 190,790,000)	
	Ever Used‡	Current User‡
Marijuana & Hashish	61,940,000	18,190,000
Hallucinogens	12,880,000	960,000
Inhalants	12,940,000	1,940,000
Cocaine	22,240,000	5,750,000
Heroin	1,930,000	—
Stimulants	17,610,000	2,690,000
Sedatives	11,540,000	1,710,000
Tranquilizers	14,750,000	2,180,000
Analgesics	12,620,000	2,450,000
Alcohol	164,360,000	113,070,000
Cigarettes	144,510,000	60,280,000

* Revised November 1986
† These estimates are based on the number of people 12 years of age or older who have reported that they have used drugs nonmedically. The numbers are rounded off and they were developed from the *National Household Survey on Drug Abuse, 1985*, for the National Institute on Drug Abuse by the Institute for Survey Research, Temple University.
‡ Ever Used: used at least once in a person's lifetime. Current User: used at least once in the 30 days prior to the survey.

Source: *NIDA Capsules*, the National Institute on Drug Abuse, U.S. Department of Health and Human Services, November 1986.

as a cure for dysentery and other ailments, with the result that many soldiers returned from the war as morphine addicts. At the beginning of this century, the major ingredient in the best-selling cough syrups was a recently discovered miracle drug called heroin. In 1914, however, Congress passed the Harrison Act, making the nonmedical use of the opiates illegal. Marijuana was made illegal in 1937. Likewise, most of the drugs that we will discuss in the remainder of this chapter cannot be legally purchased for recreational purposes. They must be obtained from a doctor or bought illegally. Table 12.3 illustrates the extent to which illegal drug abuse has developed in the United States.

Depressants

As we have seen in the case of alcohol, a **depressant** is a drug that acts on the central nervous system to reduce pain, tension, and anxiety, to relax and disinhibit, and to slow intellectual and motor reactivity. Along with alcohol, the major depressants are narcotics, sedatives, and tranquilizers (such as Librium and Valium). All have a number of important effects in common: tolerance develops; withdrawal symptoms occur; and high dosages depress the functioning of vital systems, such as respiration, and thus may result in death.

Narcotics The **narcotics** are a class of drugs that induce relaxation and reverie and provide relief from anxiety and pain. Included in this group are opium, the derivatives of opium, and chemically synthesized drugs that imitate certain effects of opium.

The grandfather of the narcotics is **opium,** a chemically active substance derived from the opium poppy. Early in the nineteenth century, scientists succeeded in isolating one of the most powerful ingredients in opium. This new narcotic, which they called **morphine** (after the Greek god of dreams, Morpheus), was soon widely used as a pain reliever. As the years passed, however, it became clear that morphine was dangerously addictive. And so scientists went back to work, this time attempting to find a narcotic that would relieve pain without causing addiction. In 1875 this research culminated in the discovery, by Heinrich Dreser (who also discovered aspirin), that a minor chemical change could transform morphine into a new miracle drug, **heroin,** much stronger than morphine and presumably nonaddictive. (This presumption was, of course, cruelly mistaken.) The final entry in our list of narcotics was developed by the Germans during World War II, when they were cut off from their opium supply. A synthetic chemical, **methadone** satisfies the craving for narcotics without producing an equivalent euphoria. For this reason it is now used as a replacement drug in the treatment of heroin addicts. Our discussion will focus on heroin, which is the most widely used illegal narcotic.

It is impossible to give an accurate picture of the extent of illegal narcotics use. Through the early 1970s heroin use increased each year, and in 1972–1973 a reasonable estimate was that there were 600,000 narcotics addicts in the United States. In 1974 it was widely believed that the "epidemic" was over. However, reports indicate that the number of new users continued to increase through 1974 and 1975. Since then, the percentage of heroin users in the country seems to have remained constant, though some changes have been noted in the users. First, the heroin users of the eighties are older than were their counterparts of the sixties and seventies. Second, since 1972 whites have come to outnumber blacks among heroin users. Finally, recent initiates to heroin use it less frequently than did initiates of the sixties and seventies (Kozal et al., 1985).

Heroin is normally taken by injection, either directly beneath the skin ("skin-popping") or into a vein ("mainlining"). The immediate positive effects of mainlining heroin are twofold. First is the "rush," lasting five to fifteen minutes. As one addict described it, "Imagine that every cell in your body has a tongue and they are all licking honey" (Ray, 1983). The second effect is a simple state of satisfaction, euphoria, and well-being, in which all positive drives seem to be gratified and all negative feelings—guilt, tension, anxiety—disappear completely. Unfortunately, from the addict's point of view, this artificial paradise lasts only three to five hours, after which he or she needs another injection.

Such are the positive effects. The negative effects are even more impressive. In the first place, not all people have the honey-licking experience. All users respond initially with nausea, and for some, this response outweighs the euphoric effects.

Second, if heroin use becomes regular, both addiction and tolerance develop. Thus, in order to avoid withdrawal symptoms, the addict has to inject larger and larger doses.

Third, should withdrawal take place, it can be a miserable experience. Withdrawal symptoms begin about four to six hours after the injection and vary in intensity according to the dosage regularly used. The first sign of withdrawal is anxiety. Then the addict enters a period of three to five days during which he or she feels wretched. Specifically, withdrawal symptoms generally include watering eyes, a runny nose, yawning, hot and cold flashes, tingling sensations, increased respiration and heart rate, profuse sweating, diarrhea and vomiting, headache, stomach cramps, aches and pains in other parts of the body, and possibly delirium and hallucinations as well—all this combined with an intense craving for the drug. Though this experience can be very uncomfortable, it is not nearly so devastating as some novels and

For some users, a shot of heroin provides a brief but intense "rush," followed by a euphoric state that lasts three to five hours, after which another injection is needed. For others, nausea is the primary effect. Regular use of heroin leads to both addiction and tolerance, and withdrawal symptoms are very unpleasant. (Arthur Tress)

movies have depicted it, particularly since in the hospital setting drugs are commonly used to relieve the symptoms. Furthermore, unlike withdrawal from alcohol or barbiturates, heroin withdrawal very rarely results in death.

Most people have the notion that repeated exposure to narcotics automatically leads to long-term addiction. However, an alternative view maintains that drug use represents a means of adapting to major stresses in one's life; if these stresses are temporary, the addiction is likely to be also (Alexander and Hadaway, 1982). For instance, many soldiers became addicted to heroin while serving in Vietnam, but few of them continued the habit once they returned home (Bourne, 1974). Similarly, most people who are given opiates in the hospital do not become addicted after they have left the hospital. Those who no longer need to escape major stresses in life appear able to handle withdrawal from narcotics quite well.

Barbiturates   The **barbiturates,** including Nembutal (pentobarbital) and Seconal (secobarbital), are a group of powerful sedative (i.e., calming) drugs whose major effects are to alleviate tension and bring about relaxation and sleep. These drugs are legally prescribed by some physicians as sleeping pills. They are sold illegally on the street as "downers" to provide an alcohol-like experience without the alcohol taste, breath, or expense.

Barbiturates were long the drug of choice for suicide attempts. An overdose first induces sleep and then stops respiration. Furthermore, the overdose need not be made up solely of barbiturates. Both barbiturates and alcohol are depressants, so their combined impact is multiplied in what is called a **synergistic effect.** If a barbiturate is taken with alcohol, the effect is four times as great as that of either of the drugs taken alone (Combs et al., 1980). The person who combines the two drugs runs the risk, intentionally or unintentionally, of becoming a suicide-overdose statistic. This was the cause of the well-publicized deaths of Judy Garland and Marilyn Monroe. Today, partly because of their danger, barbiturates are less widely prescribed, but, as noted, they are still sold illegally and continue to be implicated in many suicides.

The use of barbiturates by the young is generally recreational and sporadic. The true addicts are usually middle-aged women and marginally employed men who do not see themselves as addicts until hospitalization becomes necessary. Typically, such adult addicts begin using barbiturates for the standard reason—to relieve insomnia. As we shall see, however, barbiturates, along with other depressants, tend over time to aggravate rather than relieve sleeping problems. So the person takes more and more of the drug and eventually becomes addicted.

In their effects, which generally last from three to six hours, barbiturates are quite similar to alcohol. Like alcohol, they disinhibit, induce relaxation and mild euphoria, and impair judgment, speech, and motor coordination. Like the alcoholic, the barbiturate addict will exhibit an unsteady gait, slurred speech, diminished intellectual functioning, and confusion. Again like alcohol, the barbiturates, though they are technically depressants, may seem to have a stimulating effect, especially if they are taken with the expectation of "having some fun" rather than of getting to sleep (Wesson and Smith, 1971). Indeed, one of the major concerns of those who study barbiturates is the relationship between aggression and Seconal, a favored barbiturate of the young. We have already mentioned the study conducted by Tinklenberg and Woodrow (1974) on the relationship between drugs and aggression in young men arrested for assault. These young offenders reported that they expected to be more aggressive when they used "reds"—and they were. They took Seconal when they "wanted to have a party." To counteract the sedative-depressant effects of the drug, they literally "fought to stay awake"— that is, they used aggression as a form of stimulation to keep themselves from slowing down. These offenders also reported that after taking Seconal they had less control over their behavior than usual and would persist in an assault even when their opponent was already defeated.

A final area of similarity between barbiturates and alcohol is the matter of withdrawal. Withdrawal from barbiturate addiction is similar to withdrawal from alcohol addiction and is equally unpleasant. Without medical supervision, it can even result in death.

Tranquilizers and Nonbarbiturate Sedatives   Within the last decade, the dangers associated with barbiturates have led to their widespread replacement, as a prescription sleeping medication, by such nonbarbiturate sedatives as Dalmane and Halcion. At the same time, **tranquilizers** (also called *anxiolytics*), such as Tranxene (chlorazepate), Librium (chlordiazepoxide), and Valium (diazepam), which have long been used in the treatment of anxiety disorders and stress-related physical disorders, are also prescribed for insomnia.

All of these drugs have essentially the same problems as the barbiturates, but to a lesser degree. They are habit-forming and they have serious side effects, including drowsiness, breathing difficulties, and impaired motor and intellectual functioning. The elderly are particularly vulnerable to the dangers of these drugs, for they are more likely to have disorders the drugs can aggravate—respiratory disorders and kidney and liver ailments (Institute of Medicine, 1979). Taken in high doses over a long period, these drugs can also create symptoms very close to those of major depression. Finally, like barbiturates, tranquilizers and nonbarbiturate sedatives have a synergistic effect in combination with other depressants, though the risk of accidental suicide is not so great.

As with barbiturates, dependence on nonbarbiturates and tranquilizers is a problem less for the young—these drugs produce little or no "high"—than for the quiet, stay-at-home adult user. Again, dependence typically begins with a sleeping problem. The person takes the drug and initially obtains some relief. After about two weeks of continuous use, however, tolerance develops, and the usual dose no longer produces a good night's sleep. Yet at this point many people go on taking the drug, for two reasons. First, by this time their difficulties in sleeping may not only have returned but be worse than before. Prolonged drug use often creates what is called **drug-induced insomnia,** a pattern of fitful and disrupted slumber, without any deep sleep. Faced with this new problem, many users reason that if they needed pills before in order to sleep, now they *really* need them. Second, these drugs suppress REM (rapid-eye-movement) sleep, the stage of sleep in which dreams occur. If, after a week or two of drug-induced sleep, users try to sleep without the medication, they are likely to experience a "REM rebound"—a night of restless dreaming, nightmares, and extremely fitful sleep—after which they may go back to the drug simply to avoid a repetition of such a miserable night. (Dalmane is the only one of these drugs that suppresses REM but does not produce a REM rebound, because it stays in the bloodstream for more than 24 hours. Therefore, an additional disadvantage of Dalmane is that it produces daytime hang-over and sedation effects.)

Thus although the drug soon loses its effectiveness against the original sleeping problem, the usual solution is not to abandon the drug but rather to take more of it. Once the person increases the dose to about two to three times the normal sleep-inducing dose, addiction begins to develop. And from that point on, the drug becomes a way of life.

Tranquilizers, of course, are taken not just for insomnia but for generalized anxiety—anxiety that is often the result of high-pressure jobs and an overstressful environment. Their association with high achievers helps to account for the lag in public recognition of their danger. In a society distrustful of pleasure but respectful of work, a class of drugs that yields no "party" but instead allows lawyers and business executives to endure their often harrowing schedules is not one that will be high on the public alarm list. For the same reason, many physicians, themselves veterans of years of overwork, recognize and in some measure respect work-induced anxiety in their patients and often prescribe tranquilizers as a "necessary evil." Recently, however, the public has become increasingly aware of the side effects of tranquilizers and of the possibility of their overprescription (Clinthorne et al., 1986).

Stimulants

The **stimulants** are a class of drugs whose major effect, as the name indicates, is to provide energy, alertness, and feelings of confidence. We have already discussed one widely used stimulant, nicotine. Another is caffeine. Far more powerful are the amphetamines, which can be obtained only by prescription or "on the street," and cocaine, which must be bought illegally.

Amphetamines   The **amphetamines** are a group of synthetic stimulants—the most common are Benzedrine (amphetamine), Dexedrine (dextroamphetamine), and Methedrine (methamphetamine)—which dispel any feelings of boredom or weariness. Suddenly users find themselves alert, confident, full of energy, and generally ready to take on the world. The amphetamines depress appetite—hence their use by people with weight problems. They improve motor coordination—hence their use by professional athletes. And they inhibit sleepiness—hence their use by college students preparing for exams. Contrary to campus rumors, however, they do not improve complex intellectual functioning (Tinklenberg, 1971a).

As long as they are taken irregularly and in low or moderate doses, amphetamines do not appear to pose any behavioral or psychological problems. As with most other psychoactive drugs, the problems arise from high doses and habitual use. And once use becomes habitual, tolerance develops, and accordingly higher doses become necessary.

The problems of amphetamine abuse are epitomized in the behavior of "speed freaks"—persons who inject liquid amphetamine into their veins for periods of three to four days, during which they neither eat nor sleep but remain euphorically and intensely active. This heightened activity level can easily lead to paranoid and violent behavior.

Of special importance to the student of abnormal psychology is the clear resemblance between the effects of amphetamine abuse and the symptoms of paranoid schizophrenia (Chapter 14). Under the influence of heavy doses of amphetamines, the individual may express the same delusions of persecution that we see in the paranoid schizophrenic (Bell, 1973; Snyder, 1979). This amphetamine psychosis appears to be unrelated to any personality predispositions and is thus assumed to be the direct result of the drug. As a result of this finding, research is now in progress with both animals and human beings to determine whether paranoid schizophrenia may be caused by the same chemical changes that amphetamines induce in the brain. (This research will be discussed in Chapter 15). It should be noted that amphetamine psychosis is the only drug-induced psychosis that is virtually identical to a clinically observed "functional" psychosis.

Cocaine   Unlike the synthetic amphetamines, **cocaine** is a natural stimulant; it is the active ingredient in the coca plant. Producing feelings of euphoria and omnipotence unsurpassed by any other drug, cocaine is now the "in" stimulant. Its popularity soared in the seventies and has increased since then. More than one in four people between the ages of eighteen and twenty-five report that they have tried cocaine (National Institute on Drug Abuse, 1983). Until recently it was quite expensive, and consequently its regular users tended to be middle- and upper-class white-collar workers and executives. (It was also favored by entertainment celebrities, whose glamour attached itself to the drug.) But with the advent of crack, cocaine is now within the buying power of people on weekly allowances. A vial of crack "rocks" may sell for as little as $10.

In its classic form, cocaine is sold as a powder, which may be smoked, swallowed, or injected but is usually "snorted"—that is, the powder is inhaled into the nostrils, where it is absorbed into the bloodstream through the mucous membranes. A more elaborate procedure is "freebasing," in which the powder is heated with ether—a process that "frees" its base, or most powerful component—and then smoked. Freebasing is dangerous not only in its psychoactive effects, far more potent than those of the ordinary powder, but also because ether is extremely flammable.

Crack is sold in small chunks, or "rocks," which are smoked in a pipe. Like freebase, it is exceptionally powerful, producing in seconds an intense rush, which wears off within a few minutes. The rush produced by a snort of traditional cocaine does not take effect for about eight minutes, lasts about twenty minutes, and is milder than that of crack.

As with amphetamines, tolerance develops with regular use of cocaine, and prolonged heavy use is

Because it was very expensive and was thought to be nonaddictive when it began to be widely used in this country, cocaine acquired a reputation as a glamorous, "safe" drug among its white-collar users. Now, however, the truth about the hazards of cocaine—whether snorted or smoked—is beginning to come out. (Tom Grill/Comstock)

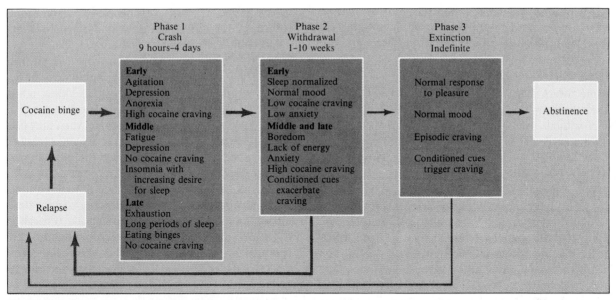

FIGURE 12.1

The three phases of cocaine withdrawal, as charted by Gawin and Kleber (1986). As the symptom lists show, the craving for cocaine disappears in phase 1 only to reappear in phase 2 and then dissipates very gradually. The arrows at the bottom indicate the likelihood of relapse: strong in phase 2, moderate in phase 3.

followed by severe withdrawal symptoms. In a recent study of fourteen "binge" users, Gawin and Kleber (1986) charted the withdrawal symptoms in three distinct phases (Figure 12.1). The first phase, known to cocaine users as the "crash," begins quite horribly. Within a half hour of the final cocaine dose, the person experiences a mounting depression and agitation combined with an intense craving for the drug. These feelings then change to fatigue and an overwhelming sleepiness, which last several days. In the second phase, "withdrawal," the person returns to deceptively normal functioning, which then gives way to a fluctuating state of boredom and listlessness, mixed with anxiety. At this point, strong cocaine cravings return, and the person may begin another binge. If not, the withdrawal phase passes in anywhere from one to ten weeks. It is followed by phase 3, "extinction," in which the person regains normal functioning, though with occasional cocaine cravings, usually in response to some conditioned stimulus (e.g., seeing old cocaine-using friends). Such episodic cravings may recur indefinitely.

Caffeine   When coffee was first introduced to Europe during the Renaissance, many people considered it dangerous because of its stimulating properties. But gradually, because of those very properties and also because people came to like its distinctive taste, the new import caught on. Today millions of people find it hard to get going in the morning without a cup (or more) of coffee. Coffee is also widely used in social rituals. When it is too early in the day to offer a person a drink, coffee is what is normally brought out.

The problem with coffee is that it contains caffeine, a stimulant found also in tea, cola drinks, cocoa, and other forms of chocolate. Like so many other psychoactive substances, caffeine is harmless in small amounts. But in excess—*DSM-III-R* places the cutoff at 250 mg. (about two cups of coffee)—it can cause intoxication, marked by nervousness, excitement, rambling thoughts, motor agitation, insomnia, muscle twitching, a flushed face, an irregular heartbeat, and an increased need to urinate: symptoms that many of us will recognize. Whether or not habitual caffeine users become intoxicated, they may suffer withdrawal symptoms—irritability, moodiness, headache—if they are deprived of their usual dose.

In the course of the health-food movement of the last twenty years, caffeine, along with sugar and saturated fats, has come under increasing suspicion. Food manufacturers, as usual, have been quick to respond. Caffeine-free soft drinks and sophisticated decaffeinated coffees are now widely available, and many people are switching to them.

Hallucinogens

The **hallucinogens** are a class of drugs that act on the central nervous system in such a way as to cause distortions in sensory perception; hence their name, which means "hallucination-producing." Unlike the stimulants or depressants, they achieve their effect without substantial changes in level of arousal. Tolerance develops rapidly to most hallucinogens, but there is no evidence that they are physiologically addictive. There are many hallucinogens, including mescaline, psilocybin, DMT, PCP, and, best known of all, LSD, referred to by pharmacologists as lysergic acid diethylamide and by users as "acid." Despite this variety, rarely can any hallucinogen other than LSD or PCP be bought on the street.

LSD was originally synthesized by a Swiss chemist, Albert Hoffman, in 1938. Five years later, Hoffman reported an interesting experience that he had had after a morning's work in his laboratory:

> Last Friday . . . I was forced to stop my work in the laboratory . . . and to go home, as I was seized by a peculiar restlessness associated with the sensation of mild dizziness. On arriving home, I lay down and sank into a kind of drunkenness which was not unpleasant and which was characterized by extreme activity of imagination. As I lay in a dazed condition with my eyes closed (I experienced daylight as disagreeably bright) there surged upon me an uninterrupted stream of fantastic images of extraordinary plasticity and vividness and accompanied by an intense, kaleidoscope-like play of colours. This condition gradually passed off after about two hours (1971, p. 23).

Hoffman guessed that this experience might have been due to his having ingested some of the new chemical on which he was working. So he purposely swallowed a small amount of LSD and found that he had indeed guessed correctly.

LSD and the other hallucinogens seem to work by interfering with the processing of information in the nervous system. That is their danger and their attraction. They can produce a kaleidoscope of colors and images. They can give the user a new way of seeing things. And they may open up new states of awareness, allowing the user to find out things about the self that were never imagined before. These are potentially attractive benefits. And for the stable, mature individual who uses hallucinogens under controlled, nonthreatening conditions, there is little chance of a negative outcome from the experience (Cohen and Ditman, 1963).

The problem arises with people who are unable to process or accept the new kinds of perceptions induced by hallucinogens. The person whose grasp on reality is not firm, who derives great support from the stability of the surrounding world, or who has emotional problems may suffer negative effects, possibly for years, from any of the hallucinogens.

The hallucinogens are most harmful when they produce a "bad trip," in which the user becomes terrified and disorganized in response to distorted perceptions. Such an experience is not quickly forgotten. For some people, the drug-induced disruption of their relationship with reality is so severe that they require some kind of long-term therapeutic assistance (Frosch et al., 1965). Also, a small percentage of regular LSD users suffer "flashbacks"—spontaneous recurrences, when not under the drug, of hallucinations and perceptual distortions that occurred under the drug—a phenomenon that may disrupt their functioning considerably.

PCP (phencyclidine), or "angel dust," is a hallucinogen that surfaced in the seventies and was widely used, for it was cheap, easily available, and often mixed with (or misrepresented as) other substances. The drug soon acquired a bad reputation. For one thing, overdoses were extremely toxic and extremely common. In one large mental health facility in Washington, D.C., PCP poisoning accounted for one-third of inpatient admissions between 1974 and 1977, outstripping even alcoholism (Luisada, 1977). A more serious risk was PCP's behavioral toxicity, the tendency of users to harm themselves—through burns, falls, drowning, automobile accidents—and also to endanger others as a result of the paranoia and perceptual distortions produced by the drug. These problems discouraged many users, and PCP consumption has been declining steadily since the late seventies.

Marijuana and Hashish

Marijuana and hashish are often classified as hallucinogens, yet they deserve separate treatment. In the first place, their effects are considerably milder than those of the hallucinogens described above. For this reason, they are often referred to as "minor hallucinogens," while LSD, PCP, mescaline, and the others are called "major hallucinogens." Second, although the major hallucinogens may be widely used, the use of marijuana and hashish is far more common. More than one out of every three Americans over the age of twelve has tried marijuana (National Institute on

FIGURE 12.2

The left photograph shows a beautifully precise web spun by a spider under the influence of LSD. In contrast, the erratically executed web at right was constructed by the same spider, at another time, after being given mescaline. A great deal of knowledge about the effects of drugs is gained through research with animals. With human subjects, it is difficult to ascertain the specific effects of agents such as LSD because of variables introduced by nonspecific factors such as the subject's expectations, prior experiences, and situational characteristics.

Drug Abuse, 1983), and many, having tried it, become frequent users. Marijuana use among the young increased dramatically in the 1970s, peaked in 1979 and 1980, and has been declining slowly since then, but it is still America's most popular illicit drug. Besides its "recreational" use, marijuana has medicinal uses: it is effective in combating the nausea produced by cancer chemotherapy and in relieving the ocular pressure of glaucoma.

Marijuana and hashish are both derived from cannabis, a hemp plant that grows, cultivated and wild, in many countries, including the United States. Marijuana consists of the dried and crushed leaves of cannabis. Though it is usually rolled into a cigarette, or "joint," and smoked, it can also be eaten. Hashish, derived from the resin rather than the leaves of cannabis, is about five or six times stronger than marijuana. Like marijuana, it can be eaten, but it is usually smoked in a specially designed pipe.

The active ingredient is the same in both forms: THC (delta 9, tetrahydrocannabinol), which most researchers agree is not physiologically addictive. THC has two consistent physiological effects. The first is an accelerated heart rate. As the dose increases, so does the heart rate, which may go up to 140–150 beats per minute. The second change is a reddening of the whites of the eyes. Both effects disappear as the drug wears off.

The behavioral effects of marijuana have been studied in a variety of situations. The effects of a mild marijuana high on simple behaviors are either nil or minimal. The person can easily turn on the record player, dial a phone number, make a pot of coffee, and so forth. However, as the complexity of the task increases, as speed of response becomes more important, and as a more accurate sense of time and distance is required, the impairment of ability from a single-joint marijuana high becomes more apparent. It has been clearly established that driving under the influence of marijuana is dangerous (Klonoff, 1974).

Having discussed the physiological and behavioral effects, we now come to the major reason for using marijuana and hashish—the psychological effects. These have been summarized by Tinklenberg (1975):

> Initial effects of cannabis at low doses usually
> include euphoria, heightening of subjective sensory
> experiences, alterations in time sense, and the
> induction of a relaxed, laissez-faire passivity. With
> moderate doses, these effects are intensified with
> impaired immediate memory function, disturbed
> thought patterns, lapses of attention, and a
> subjective feeling of unfamiliarity (p. 4).

It should be noted that the latter group of reactions are generally not at all disturbing. The individual simply feels "spaced out"—a not unpleasant experience for most people under relaxed conditions. Many marijuana users report being totally absorbed in their drug experience while it is happening. During these episodes of total involvement, the person's perceptual, imaginative, and cognitive resources are completely engaged (Fabian and Fishkin, 1981).

There is also a negative side to marijuana: it can heighten unpleasant experiences. The drug may intensify an already frightened or depressed mood until the person experiences acute anxiety. This is most likely to happen to an inexperienced user who takes a large dose and is unprepared for its effects (Grinspoon, 1977). At high levels of THC intake, the effects and the dangers are similar to those of LSD. Some people experience sensory distortions, depersonalization, and changes in body image—all of which can result in a panic reaction and a fear of "going crazy." At this point, intervention by a professional or a trained lay therapist becomes necessary, and short-term psychotherapy may eventually be required. It must be emphasized, however, that these severe reactions to the use of THC are the exception, not the rule, and that they occur at the higher dose levels.

Much less clear than the short-term effects of THC use are the long-term effects. Can regular use of marijuana or hashish cause psychological or physiological damage? This question has polarized scientists as well as generations (Maugh, 1982). While many lay people still feel that smoking a single joint can be the first step on the road to complete personality deterioration, for scientists there are essentially four areas of specific concern.

The first has to do with the effect of prolonged heavy marijuana use on the blood levels of the male sex hormone, testosterone. There seems to be general agreement that regular marijuana use (about nine joints a week) for six or more months will result in a reduction of the testosterone level in the blood (Miller, 1975). The degree of testosterone reduction is directly related to the amount of marijuana smoked. However, even the 40 percent reduction in testosterone reported in the original study of this problem (Kolodny et al., 1974) does not seem to be enough to impair significantly the sexual activity of males *with established patterns of sexual activity.* However, variations in sex-hormone level have a greater impact on the sexual activity of men who have not yet stabilized their patterns of sexual behavior. Therefore it is possible, though it has not been proved, that heavy chronic marijuana use by young, sexually inactive men could result in impaired sexual functioning.

The second current question is whether marijuana use suppresses immune reactions—the body's mechanisms for fighting off the invasion of foreign substances such as germs. The evidence is fairly solid that chronic marijuana smoking does in fact impair the functioning of one part of the immune system (Miller, 1975). However, this impairment has yet to show any recognizable clinical effect. Therefore, as with the testosterone problem, the significance of the immune response effect is unclear.

A third concern is the effects of marijuana smoke on the lungs. A report commissioned by the Institute of Medicine (1982) indicates that chronic marijuana use may injure the lungs. Since marijuana smoke contains about 50 percent more carcinogenic hydrocarbon than does tobacco smoke and since laboratory exposure of human lung cells to marijuana smoke produces changes that are characteristic of early cancer, health authorities are concerned that heavy, prolonged marijuana use could lead to lung cancer.

A fourth problem centers on the psychological effect of chronic marijuana use. Some professionals feel strongly that prolonged use of marijuana eventually results in impaired judgment, apathy, and—as with the more potent drugs—a focusing of one's existence on the drug experience. Related to this thinking is the argument that those who begin by smoking marijuana will go on to more dangerous drugs, such as heroin. However, a comparison of the figures on frequency of marijuana use and narcotics use will show that very few marijuana smokers make the transition to narcotics. As for general deficits that may result from prolonged use, the first study of long-term use among Americans found no cognitive effects after more than seven years of extremely heavy use (Schaeffer et al., 1981). Intellectual functioning among these ten adults was above average and virtually identical with that shown in tests they had taken fifteen to twenty years previously. There *is* evidence that the amotivational syndrome (apathy, loss of ambition, difficulty in concentrating) does exist among marijuana smokers, but there is some indication that it may be primarily an accentuation of preexisting behavior patterns (Maugh, 1982).

In sum, the issues are clear, but the answers aren't. Testosterone levels go down, but sexual activity may not. One immune response is suppressed, but there is no observable effect. The personality may be affected, but the evidence is incomplete. The only thing that we know for sure about long-term marijuana smoking is that it increases the likelihood of respiratory ailments. Much more data are needed before the marijuana issue can be reasonably settled.

PERSPECTIVES ON DRUG DEPENDENCE

As we mentioned earlier, the current trend in the study and rehabilitation of drug abusers is to consider these people as a group rather than to distinguish among the alcoholic, the narcotics addict, the barbiturate addict, and so on. Hence the theoretical perspectives that we have discussed in relation to alcoholism tend to apply as well to the abuse of other drugs. The behaviorists would still point to reinforcement; the psychodynamic theorists, to dependency; and so on. In the following section we will examine briefly the biochemical research, personality theories, and social issues pertaining to drug abuse, and the various current approaches to rehabilitation.

Drugs and Brain Chemistry

In the early seventies, scientists discovered that nerve cells in the brain have specific *opiate receptors,* sites to which opiates such as heroin and morphine attach themselves. The fit between the opiates and the receptors was so perfect that researchers suspected the brain must produce some natural substance that the receptors were intended to fit. This suspicion led in 1975 to the discovery of *enkephalins,* brain chemicals that are similar to morphine and that do indeed fit the opiate receptors (Goldstein, 1976). Several of these substances have been given the name *endorphins,* meaning "morphine within."

Endorphins may account for a number of mind-body phenomena that have puzzled scientists for many years. For one thing, they may underlie our natural control of pain and our natural experience of pleasure. It has long been known that stimulation of certain parts of the brain can produce pleasure and help control intractable pain. The stimulation seems to cause the brain to produce more endorphins. (The effectiveness of acupuncture may be due to the same mechanism.) Endorphins may also explain why placebo drugs can relieve pain. Possibly the person's expectation that the drug will relieve pain causes the brain to increase its production of endorphins, which then proceed to kill the pain.

More to the point of this chapter, endorphins may also explain physiological dependence on drugs. It is possible that when external opiates are taken, the brain ceases to produce internal opiates, or endorphins. The person thus becomes entirely dependent on external opiates for the relief of pain and the achievement of pleasure. Withdrawal symptoms, accordingly, occur during the time between the cessation of external opiate consumption and the resumption of internal opiate production.

Recently scientists have discovered that the opiate receptor sites can be occupied by a substance that prevents both opiates and endorphins from attaching themselves to the receptors. One such opiate antagonist is naloxone, which is now being used in experiments to treat addiction. When a person on naloxone takes an opiate, the opiate has no effect—it neither produces a rush nor reduces withdrawal symptoms. The hope is that the repeated experience of taking an opiate without any effect will eventually break the addiction.

Drugs and Personality Factors

Psychologists lately have been intrigued by the question of what personality factors addicts may have in common, or, indeed, whether there are any common factors at all. There is some evidence that personality does in fact play a role in drug abuse. For example, the troops in Vietnam who habitually used heroin tended to drop the habit once they came home, but then many of them got hooked on another, more readily available drug: alcohol. In turn, many alcoholics who stop drinking begin "abusing" caffeine and nicotine by drinking coffee and smoking cigarettes to excess. Thus it seems that certain personality traits may lie behind the tendency toward drug abuse.

What might these traits be? A report by the National Academy of Sciences cites "significant" personality factors that appear to contribute to addiction: impulsive, sensation-seeking behavior; a nonconforming and antisocial personality; a feeling of alienation from society and a lack of respect for social values; and a sense of heightened stress (National Academy of Sciences, 1983). Other similarities found among addicts are depressive tendencies, dependent behavior, and a focus on short-term goals at the expense of long-term ones. Many addicts have been found to have similar family backgrounds, including physical or sexual abuse in childhood and inconsistent parental behavior and expectations.

Still, the author of this report on the "addictive personality," Alan Lang, concludes that "there is no single unique personality entity that is a necessary and sufficient condition for substance use" (quoted in *The New York Times,* January 18, 1983). Drugs affect people in different ways and serve different needs, so it is hard to predict whether a particular personality type will abuse a particular drug. Social factors are also important in the development of addiction. The drug must be readily available and its use promoted or at least tolerated by one's peers. According to the best evidence, the strongest predisposing factor for drug use in the case of adolescents is drug use by peers (Rohr and Densen-Gerber, 1971). Adolescents tend to smoke pot if their friends smoke pot. Drug use by parents also exerts an influence, though it is not as great as that of peers (Kandel, 1973; see the box on adolescent addicts).

For adolescents and young adults, drug use may be related to a period of confusion and transition in their lives. One study (Salzman and Lieff, 1974) of a group of young people who had discontinued heavy use of hallucinogens supports this notion. The subjects reported that they began using hallucinogens at a point when they were facing major life decisions— choosing a career, deciding whether to go to graduate school, and so forth. They discontinued their hallucinogen use when the transitions were finally made. "Drug use ceased as problems resolved. Relationships and goal directions were often clarified, sometimes solidified. Commitments to people and tasks were often established, and the drug experience lost prominence" (p. 332).

For other young people, however, drug use may in fact predict a troubled adulthood. In a longitudinal study of drug use, more than a thousand youths were assessed first at age fifteen or sixteen and then again at age twenty-five. It was found that, at least for this group, early drug use did correlate with later use of the same drug. It also correlated with increased delinquency, unemployment, divorce, abortion, and drug-related health problems (Kandel et al., 1986).

Drugs and Society

The study just cited is only one of many showing that not just alcoholism but addiction to any drug is damaging to the society as well as to the individual. Work productivity declines, medical resources are wasted, and lives are lost in drug-related accidents. Furthermore, the money spent on illegal drugs generally goes into the coffers of organized crime. Finally, there appears to be a clear correlation between the use of addictive drugs and involvement in crime. For the most part, this is not violent crime, but rather shoplifting, burglary, and theft. Narcotics addicts, for example, must come up with a substantial amount of money every day to support their habit. They are generally unemployable, and therefore, unless they are independently wealthy, they must steal: addicts are responsible for millions of dollars' worth of property crimes annually. A study of 354 narcotics addicts (Ball et al., 1983) found that the addicts were four to six times more likely to commit crimes when they were actively addicted than during periods of little or no drug use.[*]

One solution to the problem of addiction-related crime which is often suggested is to legalize the drugs and dispense them to addicts, under medical supervision, at a nominal cost. Such a system has been in effect in Great Britain now for more than fifteen years. Opponents of this approach claim that it will simply encourage addiction, and the apparent increase over the past decade in the number of British addicts seems to support this argument. However, defenders of the British system claim that it is the only reasonable way to prevent addicts from doing as much harm to society as they do to themselves.

Drug Rehabilitation

Most drug rehabilitation begins with withdrawal, which, though a painful experience, is nevertheless generally easier than the task that faces addicts after withdrawal is completed: that of developing the skills and confidence to live a reasonably gratifying life in this society without drugs. As with alcoholism, so with other forms of drug dependence, multicomponent treatments combine job skills training with group, marital, and family therapy and training in relaxation, decision making, and general stress management. Several behavioral programs follow this comprehensive model (Grabowski et al., 1984).

A more radical approach is that of the therapeutic residential community. The best-known of these was Synanon, a California group founded in the late fifties by a former AA member. Synanon based its rehabilitation program on two principles: (1) once an addict, always an addict (note the resemblance to AA doctrine); and (2) the first step in learning new nondrug

---

[*] It should be noted that although marijuana was made illegal in 1937 because it was thought to encourage crime, there is little evidence of any clear relationship between marijuana and crime. Some think that the tranquilizing effect of marijuana may actually discourage crime, particularly violent crime (Tinklenberg, 1971b).

Adolescent Addicts

How do adolescents drift into drug addiction? Flender (1972) has assembled thirteen case histories of young ex-addicts, most of whom were heavily involved with drugs by the age of fifteen. As for why, each had his or her own reasons. But in the accounts of their entry into the drug subculture, two themes do tend to recur. The first is peer pressure—the desire to be part of a group:

> I got into drugs when I was twelve or thirteen years old by trying to be like the older dudes in the neighborhood. I would look up to those fellows of sixteen or seventeen who had the slickest clothes and all the girls. If they used drugs, then I wanted to use drugs. They used drugs (p. 50).

> Trying to get in with a crowd in order to have friends was [one] reason for drugs, probably the most important reason. I began to go steady with this boy I met in high school. He was into shooting speed. At first I was afraid to fool around with it, even by popping pills. But then when I got in with my boyfriend's crowd of people, I felt I had to do what they were doing . . . (p.15).

> I got into drugs, I guess . . . because of things that happened to me like, you know, the way I felt about myself. I was a very, very skinny, ugly little kid.
>
> And it made me feel even worse that the only kids I could hang out with, that would accept me, were the kids who did crazy wild things—like taking drugs. So you can say I started fooling around with drugs . . . when I was about ten. I started by sniffing glue (p. 78).

> I took drugs because of the great need I had to be accepted. And dope fiends very easily accept anyone who's on drugs, no matter what drugs they're on, whether it's heroin or speed or anything (p. 136).

The second major theme in these young people's accounts of how they began using drugs is "problem solving." Like forty-year-olds, fourteen-year-olds take drugs in order to forget their troubles:

> What got me started on heroin was being so disgusted with life. I had left this really bad neighborhood in Denver, where nobody would give you a chance, and come all the way to California. And nobody would give me a chance there either. I just couldn't get a job. They always said they wanted somebody with some experience. Well, how could I get some experience if nobody would hire me for my first job?
>
> So I said, "I don't care. I'm just going to forget about everybody else." And as long as I was on heroin I forgot about everybody else. It really worked, you know (p. 33)?

> It was after I'd gotten out of the unwed mothers' home and given my second baby for adoption that I went from using acid to heroin. I just didn't see any future for myself. First I started sniffing, and then I started shooting it in my arms (pp. 59–60).

> I guess one of the reasons I felt this big need for drugs was because I had a big hang-up about chicks. I was so skinny and ugly, no girl would go for me. Even if we were in a group where there was an extra girl, she wouldn't go for me. She'd go over to somebody else even if he already had a girl, and hang around with the two of them rather than be alone with me (p. 81).

These two factors, peer influence and the need to forget one's troubles, combined with the startling availability of most illegal drugs—on the streets, in the high schools, in the detention centers—make drug abuse appear an easy "solution" for teenagers with a greater-than-average share of adolescent woes.

ways of coping with stress is to learn about oneself. In accordance with the second principle, an integral part of the rehabilitation program was regular attendance at intense, confrontational group therapy sessions.

Though Synanon is now defunct, it served as the model for many surviving communities, such as Gateway House in Chicago and Phoenix House, Daytop Village, and Odyssey House in New York. As with AA, the dropout rates in such communities are reportedly high, and the rehabilitation rate among remaining members is hard to evaluate, for such groups do not always welcome scrutiny by scientific researchers.

The therapeutic communities treat drug abuse as an *adaptation* to stress and concentrate on providing coping skills. Another method of rehabilitation—methadone maintenance—focuses on *exposure* to narcotics and attempts to break the link with withdrawal symptoms. As we have seen earlier in this chapter, methadone is a synthetic narcotic, and like the other narcotics, it is highly addictive. It does not produce the extreme euphoria of heroin, but it does satisfy the craving for heroin and prevent withdrawal symptoms. In short, what methadone maintenance programs do—at best—is to switch individuals from heroin addiction to methadone addiction, thus relieving them of their "doped" behavioral symptoms and at the same time of the necessity of stealing to finance their drug habit. But while methadone maintenance may succeed in taking the addict off heroin, it does not prevent the individual from becoming addicted to alcohol, barbiturates, and other drugs.

Methadone maintenance must be combined with the kinds of help mentioned earlier—stress management, job training, employment assistance—in order to enable addicts to leave the drug culture. Methadone programs often lack the funds, staff, and facilities for such assistance, and consequently methadone maintenance has had only limited effectiveness (Dole and Nyswander, 1976; Sells et al., 1977).

Despite some successes with these programs, there are still thousands of addicts whom we truly do not know how to help. Still, great efforts are being put into the prevention of drug abuse. Drug education is now common in the schools and the workplace. Television commercials show hip young people warning teenagers against drugs, and advertisements in buses and subways tell people who already have drug problems where they can go for help, what number they can call, before they become defeated.

SUMMARY

Psychoactive drugs are substances used either occasionally or regularly to alter one's psychological state. Definitions of drug dependence no longer separate its physiological and psychological dimensions. *DSM-III-R*'s new category "psychoactive substance dependence" lists nine criteria for all forms of dependence, whether the substance is used alone or in combination with others: preoccupation with the drug; unintentional overuse; tolerance (progressively larger doses are needed to achieve the effect); withdrawal symptoms following discontinuance or decreased levels of the substance; use of other substances to avoid or relieve withdrawal symptoms; persistent efforts to control drug use; a pattern of drug-impaired social or work performance; abandonment of social or work activities that interfere with drug use; and continued use despite problems caused by drug dependence.

Alcohol, sanctioned in our society both by custom and by law, is one of the most widely abused drugs; it is currently estimated that 18 million Americans are alcoholics or alcohol abusers. The social and personal costs of alcohol abuse are enormous. Alcohol is a depressant that slows the activity of the higher brain centers, which control or inhibit behavior. People often begin drinking to feel at ease in social situations. Both mood and social behavior change with blood alcohol levels of 0.03 to 0.06 percent, and depressive effects increase with higher doses. Recent studies suggest that people's expectations of alcohol's effects on sexual and aggressive behavior play a stronger role than actual physiological effects, and that alcohol's tension-reducing effect, although based largely on biochemical changes, may also be mediated by cognitive factors.

Alcoholism probably has multiple causes. Behaviorists argue that it results from a variety of antecedent and consequent variables, including the need for anxiety relief. The tension-reduction model does not describe all alcoholics and fails to explain the increased anxiety that many people experience after drinking. The opponent process theory tries to explain withdrawal and tolerance as well as craving: although drinking initially creates a state of relaxation (state *A*), continued use results in the opposite state (state *B*) of irritability. Eventually state *B* predominates, and the alcoholic keeps trying to relieve its symptoms with more alcohol in a vicious cycle. Behavioral treatment no longer relies only on aversion therapy; current programs teach alcoholics alternative responses to stress, such as coping and social skills, both to prevent relapses and to avoid defeatism if a relapse occurs. Psychodynamic theory traditionally explained alcoholism as dependency resulting from oral fixation. Current theories look to the power needs that motivate alcoholics or view alcoholism as a self-handicapping strategy used to justify failure. The sociocultural and neuroscience perspectives suggest cultural or genetic causes. A 55 percent concordance rate for identical twins and observed ethnic differences indicate a genetic factor, and new research suggests differences between alcoholics and normal drinkers in metabolizing alcohol. Longitudinal studies show developmental differences that point to interactive environmental and genetic causes for alcoholism. Treatment begins with detoxification, which may include temporary use of a tranquilizer or use of Antabuse on release. Multimodal rehabilitation approaches that deal with all aspects of the alcoholic's life are most effective and generally include a support group such as Alcoholics Anonymous.

Tobacco use exacts a high toll on health through higher death rates from cancer, heart disease, and other illnesses associated with smoking. In the 1980s fewer people are beginning to smoke, and many are quitting. According to one theory, smokers regulate their nicotine intake in order to avoid withdrawal symptoms, which include irritability, restlessness, anxiety, overeating, and difficulty in concentrating.

The depressants include not only alcohol but narcotics (e.g., opium, morphine, heroin), barbiturates (e.g., Nembutal, Seconal), and tranquilizers (e.g., Librium and Valium). Narcotics, normally taken by injection, provide euphoria and relief from anxiety. They are rapidly addictive; tolerance develops; and withdrawal is extremely uncomfortable.

Barbiturates, legally prescribed as sleeping pills, are sold illegally for their alcohol-like effects: disinhibition, relaxation, and mild euphoria. In some persons, however, their use may prompt aggression. Physiologically, barbiturates can be extremely dangerous. Barbiturate overdoses are often implicated in suicides. Likewise, barbiturate withdrawal can be lethal.

Tranquilizers, which can be useful in treating anxiety disorders and some other conditions, are sometimes abused for their relaxing effects. They can be habit-forming and may have a dangerous synergistic effect when taken with other depressants, such as alcohol. Habitual use may produce drug-induced insomnia, a pattern of disturbed sleep that users try to relieve by increasing the dose, which then leads to addiction.

The stimulants, including caffeine, the amphetamines (e.g., Benzedrine, Dexedrine, Methedrine), and cocaine induce alertness, energy, and feelings of confidence. Amphetamine addicts—colloquially known as "speed freaks"—can become violent; indeed the symptoms of amphetamine abuse are strikingly similar to those of paranoid schizophrenia. Cocaine, which

is usually inhaled but may be swallowed, smoked as freebase, or injected, produces an extravagant, short-lived euphoria. Crack, like freebase, has powerful effects, and its use became a topic of intense public concern in 1986. Amphetamine and cocaine users achieve tolerance and experience severe withdrawal symptoms after prolonged use. The pattern begins with a crash, followed by withdrawal symptoms and extinction. Episodic cravings for the drug may return indefinitely. Excessive use of caffeine (over 250 mg, according to *DSM-III-R*) causes symptoms of agitation, and habitual users may experience such withdrawal symptoms as moodiness, headache, and irritability.

The hallucinogens (e.g., mescaline, psilocybin, DMT, and LSD) produce distortions in sense perception. Although tolerance develops rapidly to most hallucinogens, they are not considered physically addictive. PCP ("angel dust") creates paranoia and behavioral disturbances in addition to hallucinations; its use has been declining since the late 1970s.

Finally, marijuana and hashish, both derived from cannabis, induce psychological effects of euphoria, passivity, intensified sensory perception, impaired memory, and feelings of unfamiliarity. THC, the active ingredient, increases heart rate and reddens the whites of the eyes. Research continues on the long-term effects on the sexual functioning of young, sexually inactive users and on immune reactions, lung function, and psychological acuteness.

Brain chemistry plays a special role in drug dependence. The endorphins—enkephalins, or brain chemicals, similar to morphine—may account for our natural ability to control pain and experience pleasure. (Expectations of pain relief, which are part of the placebo effect, may lead to increased endorphin production.) Dependence on external opiates may be explained by the decrease in natural endorphin levels that follows their use. Personality and social factors associated with drug dependence include sensation seeking, nonconformity, social alienation, stress, dependent behavior, depressive tendencies, focus on short-term goals, and the influence of peers who use or accept the drug. Early drug use does not necessarily predict a troubled adulthood, but longitudinal studies indicate a correlation with later ills. Therapeutic communities view drug dependence as an adaptation to stress and focus on teaching coping skills. Methadone maintenance, which replaces heroin addiction with methadone addiction, needs to be combined with programs that teach occupational and other life skills.

Abnormality and Variation in Sexual Behavior

The most common forms of abnormal sexual behavior involve no harm to one's fellow human beings. Yet there are very few categories of abnormal behavior to which society attaches as much shame as it does to sexual abnormalities. People who are too depressed to get out of bed in the morning may regard themselves as "sick" or "abnormal," but people who cannot perform sexual intercourse as they feel it should be performed, or who derive sexual satisfaction primarily from acts other than sexual intercourse, often feel not only abnormal but shamed, disgraced, devalued as human beings. Self-esteem in our society is intimately tied to what is defined as normal sexual functioning.

In this chapter we will discuss three categories of sexual behavior:

1. *Sexual dysfunction,* the inability to achieve sexual gratification.

2. *Sexual deviations,* abnormalities of sexual attraction or gender identity.

3. *Homosexuality,* sexual activity directed to members of one's own sex.

The first two categories are viewed as abnormalities by both society and the mental health establishment. The third, homosexuality, is no longer regarded by mental health professionals as being, by definition, abnormal, but it is still considered deviant by a large portion of society. Before discussing these behaviors, however, we must first look at our sexual norms and the extent to which they actually reflect our sexual make-up and behavior.

DEFINING SEXUAL ABNORMALITY

The belief that a sexually normal person is one whose sexual goals are confined to coitus (that is, penile–vaginal intercourse) with a member of the opposite sex has a long history in Western moral and religious teaching. While the ancient Greeks not only tolerated but actually glorified homosexuality, the Judeo-Christian tradition that supplanted classical thought has consistently condemned homosexuality. God presumably made clear his attitude toward homosexuals when he rained fire and brimstone on the cities of Sodom and Gomorrah (Genesis 19), where homosexuality was practiced. Further along in the Bible, Leviticus 20:13 spells out the prohibition: "If a man also lies with mankind, as he lieth with a woman, both of them have committed an abomination; they shall surely be put to death; their blood shall be upon them." As for masturbation, God's striking down of Onan, who in Genesis 38:9 "spilled [his seed] on the ground" rather than in the proper place, was taken as a precedent for centuries of religious teaching that masturbation (also called *onanism*) was an abhorrent practice, dangerous to mind and body.[*] Indeed, any sexual

practice that could not result in pregnancy was unequivocally condemned by the early Christian and Jewish religions.

Many scholars have interpreted this stance as the outcome of political necessity. The ancient Jews and the early Christians were persecuted minorities, to whom a population increase was extremely desirable, and the only sexual practice that will yield a population increase is coitus. Today, when most people consider a population increase undesirable, church doctrine on sexual morality continues largely unchanged. Many Christian denominations, along with Orthodox Jews, still forbid any sexual practice that circumvents or replaces coitus.

The widespread view of coitus as the only legitimate route to orgasm is derived not only from religious dogma but also from the writings of mental health experts. Two of the most influential early psychiatric works on sex, Richard von Krafft-Ebing's *Psychopathia Sexualis* (1886) and Havelock Ellis' *Studies in the Psychology of Sex* (1900), condemned masturbation as a psychologically dangerous practice. In Krafft-Ebing's opinion, masturbation halted the development of normal erotic instincts, caused impotence in early heterosexual contacts, and thus led to homosexuality. Both Krafft-Ebing and Ellis regarded homosexuality as a form of psychopathology. In their view, and in Freud's too, the only genuinely healthy, mature, and normal sexual outlet was coitus. Succeeding generations of psychologists and psychiatrists concurred. In *DSM-II,* published in 1968, individuals whose sexual interests were "directed primarily toward objects other than people of the opposite sex [or] toward sexual acts not usually associated with coitus" were classified as suffering from sexual disorders. Thus alternatives to coitus were pronounced evil by the church and were considered abnormal by the mental health establishment.

This rather narrow definition of normal sexual behavior has served for many centuries to help guarantee the continuation of the human species and the survival of the family structure. However, there is little to indicate that human beings are programmed biologically to confine their sexual gratification to coitus. On the contrary, while the sex drive itself is inborn, the direction that it will take is, according to anthropological evidence, a result of socialization. For example, while Western culture considers the female breast an erotic object, many societies consider it sexually neutral. Likewise, while homosexuality is frowned on in our society, in other societies it is not only accepted but actually institutionalized as the

---

[*] Actually, Onan was not masturbating but practicing a primitive form of birth control called *coitus interruptus* (withdrawal immediately before ejaculation). He was struck down because by this act he avoided impregnating the wife of his dead brother, for whom religious law decreed that he provide a child.

Attitudes toward sexuality differ among cultures and vary over time within the same culture. Earlier in this century in our society, for example, women's undergarments covered the body from breast to knee, and advertisements for them were correspondingly modest. Today, in contrast, highly erotic ads for revealing underwear can be encountered literally on any street corner. (Left, The Bettmann Archive; right, Birgit Pohl)

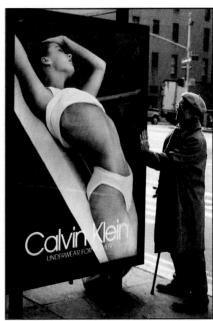

proper sexual outlet for adolescent boys (Ford and Beach, 1951).

As for freedom of sexual expression, an instructive contrast is provided by two small villages, one in Polynesia, one on an island off the coast of Ireland. In the Irish village of "Inis Beag," a researcher (Messenger, 1971) who interviewed the inhabitants over nineteen months found that they had no apparent knowledge of tongue-kissing, male mouth on female breast, female hand on penis, oral–genital contact, premarital coitus, or extramarital coitus. Nudity, which extends to bare feet, is shunned. Intercourse is achieved quickly, with underwear not removed. Female orgasm is apparently unknown. By contrast, on the Polynesian island of Mangaia, "copulation is a principal concern of the Mangaian of either sex" (Marshall, 1971, p. 116). The people begin full-scale sexual activity at about thirteen years, after receiving detailed instruction from older "experts." Sexual technique and sexual anatomy are the object of passionate connoisseurship: "The average Mangaian youth has fully as detailed a knowledge . . . of the gross anatomy of the penis and vagina as does a European physician" (p. 110). For males, the average rate of orgasm at age eighteen is three per night, seven nights a week; at age twenty-eight, two per night, five to six nights a week. Women do better, since the male's goal in intercourse is to bring the woman to orgasm several times before he himself reaches climax.[*] All Mangaian

women are orgasmic. When told that many European and American women do not experience orgasm, the Mangaian will typically ask whether this failing does not impair their health. In short, the definition of what is sexually normal and abnormal in Mangaia is almost completely the reverse of that in "Inis Beag." These two cultures are extremes—perhaps the most sexually permissive and the most sexually repressive societies known to Western research. But they illustrate a crucial point: the sexual instinct, viewed across cultures, is astonishingly flexible.

Within a culture, attitudes toward sexuality may change over time (LoPiccolo and Heiman, 1978). Our own society is far more open about sex today than it was even a few decades ago, for example. Even in less tolerant times, however, sexual behavior does not necessarily conform to declared standards of sexual morality or normality. The famous Kinsey reports (1948, 1953) revealed that many Americans had engaged in culturally prohibited sexual activities. More than 90 percent of the males Kinsey interviewed had masturbated; over 80 percent of the men and 50 percent of the women in his samples had participated in premarital sex; and oral sex was far from uncommon.

---

[*] This finding has been questioned. Marshall interviewed only Mangaian men, who may have exaggerated their sexual prowess and ability to bring women to orgasm.

Then, in 1966, Masters and Johnson published the results of their study of the physiology of sex. They found that men and women were more alike than different in their sexual responses. The Kinsey reports had shocked the public; Masters and Johnson's *Human Sexual Response* found a more receptive audience.

In part because of research, in part because of the general social climate, the 1960s and 1970s brought widespread questioning of traditional sexual morality in the United States. Prohibitions on such activities as premarital sex, masturbation, and oral–genital sex were relaxed. Homosexuality, too, has been reconsidered, not only by the public but also by the mental health establishment. *DSM-III* (1980) removed homosexuality per se from its list of psychosexual disorders. Nor did it specify that sexual activity must involve coitus to be normal.

Nevertheless, the catalog of psychiatrically recognized sexual disorders remains a long one, and the list of sexual behaviors regarded as abnormal by society is even longer. The remainder of this chapter is devoted to these behaviors.

SEXUAL DYSFUNCTION

The lifting of sexual repression in the last two decades has brought a new emphasis on sexual technique and sexual gratification. The enormous popularity of Dr. Ruth Westheimer, who advocates frequent and varied sexual activities in her books, newspaper column, and TV appearances, attests to today's preoccupation with exploring the limits of our sexual capabilities. Whereas twenty years ago people wondered whether what they were doing was right, now they may be asking themselves whether they are doing it right.

This recent interest in sexual gratification has had many beneficial effects. It has eased the flow of information about sex, increased sexual communication between partners, and dispelled anxiety and guilt over harmless sexual practices. At the same time, however, it has ushered in new forms of anxiety and guilt. Many sexually normal men and women now worry about the adequacy of their sexual "performance."

Where the so-called sexual revolution will take us as a society remains to be seen. However, its impact on the field of psychology is already evident in the increasing attention being given to **sexual dysfunc-**

tions, disorders that prevent the individual from having or enjoying coitus (Kaplan, 1974).

Forms of Sexual Dysfunction

William Masters and Virginia Johnson (1970), of the Reproductive Biology Foundation in St. Louis, and Helen Singer Kaplan (1974, 1977), of the Sex Therapy and Education Program at New York Hospital, were pioneers in the study and treatment of sexual dysfunction. When they began their work, studies of sexuality were rare and clinicians who dealt specifically with sexual problems still rarer. In the last decade, however, the number of researchers, therapists, and journals specializing in sexuality has grown enormously. One result has been a more sophisticated understanding of sexual dysfunctions. In the past, any lack of sexual interest or arousal in males was called "impotence"; similarly, the pejorative label "frigidity" was applied to almost every female sexual complaint. Today psychologists recognize a variety of specific difficulties. Following a classification system proposed by Kaplan (1974), *DSM-III-R* groups sexual dysfunctions according to the phase in the sexual response cycle in which they occur:

1. *Disorders of the desire phase.* The first phase of normal sexual response, called the *desire phase,* involves interest in sexual activity. The diagnostic term *hypoactive desire* refers to lack of interest in sex. *Aversion to sex* refers to feelings of disgust, repulsion, anxiety, and other negative emotions toward sex. Patients with the latter type of dysfunction often turn out to be victims of childhood molestation, incest, or rape. Their sexual impairment is, in a sense, a form of posttraumatic stress disorder.

2. *Disorders of the arousal phase.* In the second phase, called the *arousal phase,* feelings of sexual pleasure are normally accompanied by specific physiological changes. The tissues of the man's penis become congested with blood, producing an erection. Similar congestion causes the woman's genitals to swell, while the walls of the vagina secrete lubricant. The absence or weakness of excitement is called **erectile disorder** in men, **female sexual arousal disorder** in women. Within these categories, the *DSM* distinguishes between physiological

responses and the subjective experience of sexual excitement. For example, some men report that they feel highly aroused but do not get an erection. Conversely, some women experience the physiological signs of excitement but do not feel sexually aroused.

3. *Disorders of the orgasm phase.* In the third, or *orgasm,* phase of sexual response, the peaking of sexual pleasure triggers rhythmic contractions of the muscles in the genital region and, in men, simultaneous ejaculation of semen from the penis. If the rapidity of a man's ejaculation interferes with the couple's enjoyment, the problem is called **premature ejaculation.** If, on the other hand, ejaculation is greatly delayed or does not occur at all, the condition is called **inhibited male orgasm.** The delay or absence of orgasm in women is called **inhibited female orgasm.**

Two types of sexual dysfunction do not fit neatly into this three-part typology. One is **dyspareunia,** or pain during intercourse, which may occur in either sex, though it is usually a female complaint. The second is a female disorder, **vaginismus,** in which the muscles surrounding the entrance to the vagina undergo involuntary spasmodic contractions when attempts are made to insert the penis; these contractions make intercourse either impossible or painfully difficult.

Helen Singer Kaplan of the Sex Therapy and Education Program at New York Hospital. Author of *The New Sex Therapy* (1974), Dr. Kaplan has made important contributions to both the theory and technique of treating sexual dysfunction. (Courtesy of Dr. Helen Singer Kaplan)

The *DSM* also distinguishes between problems that are lifelong and those that are acquired. A **lifelong dysfunction** is one that has existed, without relief, since the individual's earliest sexual experiences. A sexual problem is considered to be an **acquired dysfunction** if the response has been normal on at least one occasion (and often on many occasions) but is impaired at the time of diagnosis. Thus a man who has never had an erection sufficient for intercourse has lifelong erectile dysfunction, whereas a man who has responded normally in the past but becomes impotent after he has had an operation or lost his job has acquired erectile dysfunction. Similarly, a **generalized dysfunction** is one that is present in all sexual situations at the time of diagnosis; a **situational dys-**

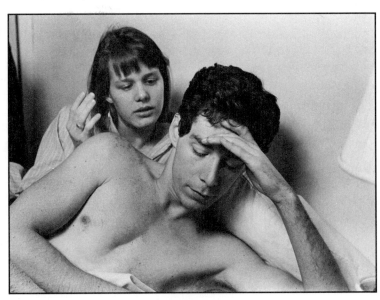

Sexual problems are often thought to result from early life training, in which sexual feelings are associated with shame, disgust, fear of discovery, and anxiety about failure. These associations then thwart sexual responsiveness in the adult. (Harvey Wang)

function, as the term indicates, is one that occurs only in certain situations. A woman with a situational orgastic dysfunction, for example, may be able to achieve orgasm when she is masturbating alone, but not during sexual activity with a partner; a woman who has an absolute orgastic dysfunction never has orgasms.

It should be noted that the term *sexual dysfunction* applies only to problems that persist over time. Occasional, random episodes of "sexual failure" are normal. When an adult is tired, sick, upset, drunk, or simply distracted, sexual responsiveness may be dulled. Nor should the label of sexual dysfunction be applied to the common occurrence of premature ejaculation, erectile dysfunction, or orgastic failure in young people who have not yet established a regular pattern of sexual activity and are so concerned with "doing it right" (or getting to do it at all) that they cannot fully enjoy sex. The myths that sex comes naturally and that a couple should be able to reach the heights of ecstasy under any and all conditions are leading causes of sexual problems. Counseling often reveals that one episode of failure leads to another simply because the first episode created so much anxiety that sexual responsiveness is impaired on the next occasion. The second failure aggravates the anxiety, further undermining sexual performance, and so on, until a regular pattern of sexual failure is established. Furthermore, such anxiety is communicable: sexual anxiety is often found in both members of a couple. Vaginismus and lifelong erectile dysfunction, or orgastic dysfunction and premature ejaculation, are often seen together in a marriage.

PERSPECTIVES ON SEXUAL DYSFUNCTION

The Psychodynamic Perspective: Oedipal Conflict

As we saw in Chapter 2, Freud claimed that mature genital sexuality was the product of successful resolution of the Oedipus complex. Accordingly, psychodynamic theorists tend to attribute sexual dysfunction to unresolved oedipal conflicts. This line of thinking may be seen in the interpretation of impotence offered by Otto Fenichel, a prominent psychoanalyst:

> Impotence is based on a persistence of an unconscious sensual attachment to the mother.

> Superficially no sexual attachment is completely attractive because the partner is never the mother; in a deeper layer, every sexual attachment has to be inhibited, because every partner represents the mother (1945, p. 170).

Similarly, psychoanalytic formulations of orgastic dysfunction tend to stress the role of continued penis envy, and vaginismus has been interpreted as the expression of an unconscious desire to reject or injure the male's envied penis (Fenichel, 1945).

Beyond anecdotal evidence from clinical practice, there is little empirical support for these theories. At the same time, psychodynamic therapy has had some success with sexual dysfunction. In a review of sexually dysfunctional patients treated at one psychoanalytic institute, 77 percent of men with erectile dysfunction either improved or were cured after two years of psychoanalysis (O'Connor and Stern, 1972). The results with other forms of dysfunction were less impressive, however. Furthermore, even if the cure rate were 100 percent, the fact remains that only a tiny percentage of the millions of people who suffer from sexual dysfunction can afford two years of psychoanalysis; nor is it likely that many of them need to (see the box on p. 320).

For many years psychodynamic therapy was the only generally available form of treatment. Certain authorities who took other approaches (Wolpe, 1958; Ellis, 1962) argued that sexual dysfunction, instead of being analyzed as a symptom of underlying conflict, should be attacked directly, by altering either the behavior in question or the attitudes surrounding it. But this was a minority view. Then in 1970 came the landmark publication of Masters and Johnson's *Human Sexual Inadequacy,* outlining a systematic, short-term approach to direct symptomatic treatment. This approach, described in the next section, revolutionized sex therapy.

The Behavioral Perspective

Learned Anxiety and the "Spectator Role"
Behavioral theories of sexual inadequacy have focused consistently on the role of early respondent conditioning in which sexual feelings are paired with shame, disgust, fear of discovery, and especially anxiety over possible failure, all of which then proceed to block sexual responsiveness (Kaplan, 1974; Wolpe, 1969). This is also the position of Masters and Johnson,

though they do not associate themselves with behaviorism or with any other theoretical school. According to Masters and Johnson (1970), any one of a number of painful experiences can cause the individual to worry that he or she will be unable to perform adequately—will not achieve erection, will reach orgasm too quickly or not quickly enough, or whatever. As a result of this anxiety, the worried partner assumes what Masters and Johnson call the "spectator role." That is, instead of simply relaxing and experiencing pleasure, the individual is constantly watching and judging his or her performance. And, with cruel irony, the performance is almost inevitably a failure because the individual's tense and critical attitude blunts his or her responsiveness to sexual stimuli.

As for the factors that first trigger performance anxiety and lead to the adoption of the spectator role, Masters and Johnson point to several possibilities: religious and sociocultural taboos on sexual feelings, particularly in women; disturbance in the marriage; parental dominance of one or the other partner; overuse of alcohol; and, finally, early psychosexual trauma, which can range from molestation and rape to humiliating experiences, illustrated by the following case:

> During the patient's first sexual episode the prostitute took the unsuspecting virginal male to a vacant field and suggested they have intercourse while she leaned against a stone fence. Since he had no concept of female anatomy, of where to insert the penis, he failed miserably in this sexually demanding opportunity. His graphic memory of the incident is of running away from a laughing woman.
>
> The second prostitute provided a condom and demanded its use. He had no concept of how to use the condom. While the prostitute was demonstrating the technique, he ejaculated. He dressed and again fled the scene in confusion (Masters and Johnson, 1970, p. 177).

Direct Symptomatic Treatment   If sexual dysfunction stems from faulty learning, so that sexual arousal comes to be associated with anxiety, then presumably it may be curable through new learning that gradually breaks down and eliminates this association. This idea is the basis of Masters and Johnson's treatment strategy and of most behavioral sex therapies.

First the person is retrained to experience sexual excitement without performance pressure. Training usually takes the form of "sensate focus," or petting,

William Masters and Virginia Johnson, pioneers in sex therapy, emphasize treating the dysfunction itself, rather than exploring its psychic underpinnings at great length. (Bob Levin/Black Star)

exercises. During the period devoted to these exercises, the couple observes a ban on sexual intercourse. Instead, they simply devote a certain amount of time each day to gentle stroking and caressing in the nude, according to instructions given by the therapist. Very gradually, the allowed sexual play is increased, but always without performance demands.

The purpose of sensate focus exercises is not only to allow the couple to rediscover their natural sexual responses, but also to improve their communication. In the course of the exercises, each provides the other with feedback—what feels good, what doesn't feel good. The sharing of such information, aside from its crucial value in allowing the couple to satisfy each other, also serves to deepen their commitment to and trust in each other, which may have been sorely damaged by years of unhappy sex. After a period of sensate focus exercises, the couple is given more specific exercises, aimed directly at the disorder in question.

For premature ejaculation, many therapists prescribe the so-called pause technique (Semans, 1956). In this procedure the woman stimulates the man's penis until he feels ready to ejaculate, at which point he signals her to stop. Once the need to ejaculate subsides, she stimulates him again, until he once again signals her to stop. Repeated many times, this tech-

What Is Normal Sexual Response In a Woman?

Should a woman feel inadequate because intercourse alone is not sufficient to bring her to orgasm? Whether explicitly stated or not, "normal" female sexual response seems to imply that a woman should reach orgasm during intercourse, preferably without manual stimulation. Yet millions of women do not fit this description and so feel deficient. One of the most common complaints women bring to sex therapists is a socially defined dysfunction: they reach orgasm only through manual or oral stimulation of the clitoris, or only when intercourse is combined with such direct stimulation.

The designation of this pattern as abnormal is due in part to our society's moral strictures against masturbation; intercourse may be normal, but "touching" yourself (or being touched) is not. It is also reflected in an old Freudian distinction between "clitoral" and "vaginal" orgasms in which only the woman who has "vaginal" orgasms is sexually normal and psychologically mature.

Many sex researchers feel that this definition of sexual normality should be revised. All orgasms, no matter how they are achieved, constitute the same physical process, and there is no evidence that women who require direct stimulation to reach orgasm are any less healthy or mature than those who do not. Women who reach orgasm during intercourse receive indirect stimulation of the clitoris: their partner's pubis (the bony structure behind the penis) rubs against their genitals, and penile thrusting pulls the clitoral hood back and forth. Many, possibly most, women require the more intense, *direct* stimulation of the clitoris, but the physiological mechanism of the orgasm is identical in both instances.

To say that direct clitoral stimulation is less healthy or normal than indirect stimulation is, in the words of the psychologist Joseph LoPiccolo, "to draw almost mystical distinctions between the male pubis and the male hand" (1977, p. 1239). Thus, according to LoPiccolo,

> a woman who can have coital orgasm if she receives concurrent manual stimulation of her clitoris does not have secondary orgasmic dysfunction; she is normal. Similarly, a woman who regularly has orgasm during manual or oral stimulation by her husband, and who enjoys intercourse even though orgasm does not occur during coitus, is a candidate for reassurance about her normality rather than for sex therapy (1977, p. 1239).

As Helen Singer Kaplan points out (1974), female sexual response, like most human traits, is extremely variable. Women reach orgasm from erotic fantasy alone, from brief foreplay, coitus, manual or oral stimulation of the clitoris without coitus, coitus combined with manual stimulation, or intense stimulation such as that provided by a vibrator. About 10 percent of women never experience orgasm, and although they may justifiably seek professional help if they are distressed by their lack of orgasms, any pattern of response can certainly serve as the foundation for a happy sexual relationship. Of course, any woman who is dissatisfied with her response pattern should seek sex therapy, for the pattern may well be changeable. But those who are satisfied sexually yet worry that they do not fit some definition of "normal" should save their money. There is no single normal pattern.

nique gradually increases the amount of stimulation required to trigger the ejaculation response, so that eventually the man can maintain an erection for a longer time. The "squeeze" technique, in which the woman squeezes the tip of the man's penis when he feels close to ejaculation, has a similar effect.

With erectile dysfunction, the therapist, to eliminate anxiety, may actually tell the patient to try *not* to have an erection while the couple are going through their "petting" exercises. This technique of proscribing the behavior that the patient is trying to accomplish is called *paradoxical instruction*. Forbidden to have an erection, the patient may find himself sufficiently free of anxiety that he begins to respond to the sexual stimuli and thus has the "prohibited" erection. Once this happens, the therapist "permits" the couple, in very gradual stages, to proceed further and further toward intercourse, always with the warning that the techniques "work best" if the man can prevent himself from having an erection. In the end, intravaginal ejaculation is "allowed" only after it has already occurred, because the man could not stop himself (LoPiccolo and Lobitz, 1973).

The most effective treatment for lifelong orgastic dysfunction in women (LoPiccolo and Lobitz, 1973; LoPiccolo and Stock, 1986) begins with education on female sexual anatomy and self-exploration exercises designed to increase body awareness. Then the woman is taught techniques of self-stimulation, perhaps with the aid of an electric vibrator and/or erotic pictures and books. This approach is based on the belief that masturbation enables a woman to identify the "symptoms" of sexual excitation, to discover which techniques excite her, and to anticipate pleasure in sex. When she has achieved orgasm alone, the therapist recommends sensate exercises with her partner, gradually incorporating the "orgasm triggers" she used alone. She may be encouraged to use a vibrator while her partner is present and to engage in the fantasies that arouse her when she is masturbating. Teaching her partner what stimulates her is an essential element of this program. Treatment of women with situational orgastic dysfunction is similar. For women who are averse to sex, these procedures are often combined with systematic desensitization. As with male sexual problems, the goal is to remove the pressure to perform and to encourage instead the simple experience of pleasure.

Masters and Johnson popularized the concept of direct treatment of sexual dysfunction: attacking the symptom itself, without extensive exploration of its psychic roots. But their approach does not ignore psychological components; it is not a strictly behavioral program. They also emphasized treatment of the *couple,* not just the dysfunctional individual. In their program, the first three days of treatment are devoted to extensive interviewing—the wife by a female therapist, the husband by a male therapist, and then vice versa—leading to a round-table meeting of the couple and the therapists. During the interviews the therapist explores the beliefs and experiences that may have led to the present dysfunction. Shame-ridden memories are discussed with comforting matter-of-factness; repressive attitudes are challenged out-

right; the individual is encouraged to appreciate his or her sexuality. The round-table meeting is designed to restore a sense of trusting collaboration between partners. Resentments, fears, and secret memories that may have blocked communication are aired. The couple are encouraged to provide each other with concrete feedback during their exercises and in future meetings with the therapists. (Studies conducted since Masters and Johnson began their program have shown that a male–female therapist team is not essential and that a single therapist may accomplish the same goals [Arentewicz and Schmidt, 1983].)

Multifaceted Treatment

Many contemporary sex researchers are dissatisfied with the theory that sexual dysfunction is caused by faulty learning. As they point out, millions of sexually untroubled individuals have been exposed to learning of this sort. Many people (perhaps most people) were taught that sex was dirty; for many people the first attempt at intercourse was painful and embarrassing, if indeed intercourse was even achieved; and many people have unhappy marriages—yet their sexual functioning remains stubbornly normal. Conversely, in many cases of sexual dysfunction there is no sign of these stressors. Obviously, the cause of sexual dysfunction involves more than bad experiences and repressive attitudes. Consequently, many sex therapists incorporate symptom-directed exercises in a multifaceted program directed also at cognitive, intrapsychic, and "relationship" factors that may be causing sexual dysfunction, or at least helping to maintain it.

Kaplan: Remote Causes   The sex therapists who came after Masters and Johnson have tended to probe psychological factors more systematically and more deeply. Helen Kaplan (1974), for example, argues that sexual dysfunction is probably due to a combination of immediate and remote causes. *Immediate causes* are such factors as performance anxiety, overconcern about pleasing one's partner, poor technique, lack of communication between partners, and marital conflict—the sort of causes on which Masters and Johnson concentrate. Such factors, Kaplan claims, are potent stressors, but in most cases they are not enough to undermine sexual functioning unless they are combined with (or based on) *remote causes* of sexual dysfunction: intrapsychic conflicts that predispose the individual to anxiety over sexual expression. These conflicts are essentially the same as those the psychodynamic theorists blame for sexual dysfunction: infantile needs, deep-seated guilt, and—above all—unresolved oedipal struggles.

On the basis of this theory, Kaplan has devised a combined "direct" and psychodynamic therapy. She agrees with other direct therapists that behavior should be the primary focus of treatment and that unconscious conflicts, even when they are obvious to the therapist, should be bypassed as long as the patient is responding to the direct treatment. However, in some cases the remote causes of sexual dysfunction prevent the patient from responding to therapy. In such cases, Kaplan argues, some brief "insight" therapy is called for. Furthermore, in many instances the direct therapy itself brings to the surface psychological problems that the patient has been blocking through avoidance of normal sexual functioning. Indeed, it is extremely common for patients to progress well in direct therapy until they are just on the edge of reaching their goal, at which point they seem to experience a flood of anxiety and begin to resist treatment. Kaplan interprets this response as a last-ditch attempt to maintain psychological defenses against whatever conflict has been blocking sexual responsiveness. And she claims that at this point psychodynamic exploration and interpretation of the patient's conflict is necessary before one can resume direct therapy.

Systems Theory: The Function of the Dysfunction   Under the influence of Kaplan's writings, many direct therapists now use some psychodynamic techniques. Other therapists confront the psychological components of sexual dysfunction via **systems theory,** the analysis of relationships as systems of interlocking needs. According to the systems theory approach, sexual dysfunction, distressing though it may be to the couple, usually has an important function in their total relationship—that is, it serves psychological needs for both partners (Heiman et al., 1981). Consider, for example, low sexual desire on the part of the man, a problem that is turning up more and more frequently in sex therapy (Kaplan, 1974; Schover and LoPiccolo, 1982; Zilbergeld and Ellison, 1980). Low sexual desire often has a number of causes. If the relationship in question involves conflicts over power and control, with the woman tending to dominate, then the man's lack of interest in sex may be his way of preserving some area of control for himself. At the same time, the woman, though she may complain of the man's sexual indifference, may also be deriving benefits from it. If she has great ambivalence about sex, his "problem" allows her to avoid facing up to her problem. Or if she is angry at him for reasons that she does not understand or can't express, his symptom offers a good target for the displacement of her anger.

According to systems-oriented therapists, such secret payoffs underlie most cases of sexual dysfunction and must be dealt with if the dysfunction is to be relieved. Kaplan, as we have seen, addresses deep psychological issues only if and when the client begins to resist treatment. Systems-oriented therapists, on the other hand, *expect* resistance, since it is predicted by their theory. That is, once the dysfunction starts to disappear, its absence causes chaos in the system, with the result that the patients cling frantically to the dysfunction. Therefore, the therapist generally addresses the "function of the dysfunction" from the beginning of treatment, asking patients to describe the benefits they derive from the problem; warning them that they may feel considerable fear as the problem begins to lessen; analyzing this fear, once it appears, as the product of a shaken system; and helping them to devise a better system. Such analysis, like Kaplan's, is combined with direct treatment.

All these approaches are relatively new, but already they have produced respectable results. The average success rates of programs based on direct treatment, either alone or in combination with the psychological techniques described above, are highest for premature ejaculation (90–95 percent), vaginismus (90–95 percent), and primary orgastic dysfunction (85–95 percent). Success rates are lower for other disorders, but they are still encouraging: secondary orgastic dysfunction, 70–80 percent; secondary erectile dysfunction, 60–80 percent; primary erectile dysfunction, 40–60 percent (Masters and Johnson, 1970; Kaplan, 1974; Hogan, 1978; LoPiccolo and Hogan, 1979).

The Neuroscience Perspective: Differential Diagnosis

In 1970 Masters and Johnson asserted that 95 percent of erectile failures were psychological, not physiological or organic, in origin. Today researchers are not so sure (LoPiccolo, 1985a). In some cases, organic causes are known. Erectile dysfunction may be the result of diabetes, heart disease, kidney disease, or alcoholism. A variety of medical treatments—renal dialysis, tranquilizers, medications for hypertension—can also interfere with erection. Long-term use of oral contraceptives can reduce the female sex drive. Female dyspareunia (pain during intercourse) may be caused by vaginal infections, ovarian cysts, or lacerations or scar tissue resulting from childbirth (Sarrel, 1977). In other cases, organic factors are suspected but not proved. A number of researchers have proposed that sexual dysfunction may be caused by hormonal deficiencies, neurological impairment, or low levels of neurotransmitters.

In the 1970s and early 1980s, sex researchers devoted considerable time to diagnostic tools for differentiating between psychological and organic sexual dysfunction. Some concentrated on devices for measuring vasocongestion in the genital region, others on tests of the sensory threshold in the genital area. Research on "nocturnal penile tumescence" (NPT) attracted a good deal of attention. Men have erections during rapid-eye-movement (REM) sleep, the stage of sleep associated with dreams. NPT research is based on the assumption that if a man has erections while he is asleep, but not during sexual encounters, his problem is primarily psychological in origin. Experience with these diagnostic procedures suggests that diagnosis is not always so straightforward.

Today researchers are questioning the very concept of differential diagnosis (LoPiccolo, 1985a). Many reject the idea that sexual dysfunction must be *either* psychological *or* organic in origin. Rather, they hold that many (if not most) cases of sexual dysfunction involve *both* psychological and physiological factors. A mild organic impairment—perhaps one that cannot be detected by current techniques, or one not yet known to be associated with sexual functioning—may make a person vulnerable to sexual dysfunction. But whether that person actually experiences sexual difficulties may depend on psychological factors, learning, and/or sexual technique. This would help to explain, for example, why some people who have been taught that sex is sinful or who had humiliating early experiences with sex function normally, while others do not. Future research may show that some cases of sexual dysfunction are purely psychological in origin, some primarily organic, and many others the result of interacting organic and psychological factors.

SEXUAL DEVIATIONS

The sexual revolution has expanded our definition of normal sexual behavior. Premarital sex, oral sex, homosexuality—behaviors that were spoken of in whispers, if at all, twenty-five years ago—are now discussed casually by many people. This does not mean, however, that all barriers have fallen. According to *DSM-III-R*—and, it is safe to assume, according to most members of our society—normal sexuality still requires that (1) the person accept his or her own biological gender and (2) the primary focus of sexual attraction be a consenting adult.

A number of recognized sexual patterns deviate from one or the other of these criteria. We shall discuss the following:

1. **Fetishism:** reliance on inanimate objects or on some body part (to the exclusion of the person as a whole) for sexual gratification.

2. **Transvestism:** sexual gratification through dressing in the clothes of the opposite sex.

3. **Transsexualism:** gender identification with the biologically opposite sex.

4. **Exhibitionism:** sexual gratification through display of one's genitals to an involuntary observer.

5. **Voyeurism:** sexual gratification through clandestine observation of other people's sexual activities or sexual anatomy.

6. **Sadism:** sexual gratification through infliction of pain on others.

7. **Masochism:** sexual gratification through pain inflicted on oneself.

8. **Pedophilia:** child molesting—that is, gratification, on the part of the adult, through sexual contacts with children.

9. **Incest:** sexual relations between members of the immediate family.

10. **Rape:** forced sexual intercourse with a nonconsenting partner.

All of the patterns on this list are deviations of attraction[*] (with the exception of transsexualism). What arouses the person is something other than what is commonly considered a normal sexual object or sexual activity. But a distinction must be drawn between those sexual deviations that are essentially "victimless" and inflict no harm on others (fetishism, transvestism, and transsexualism) and those that cause psychological and/or physical damage (sadism, masochism, pedophilia, incest, and rape). Exhibitionism and voyeurism fall between the two: they may or may not cause harm, depending on the circumstances and the participants.

It is important to note that most of these behaviors occur in mild, playful, or sublimated forms in what we may call normal everyday life. The wife who regularly chooses to take her bath while her husband is shaving and the husband who regularly chooses to shave while his wife is taking her bath are engaging in socially allowable exhibitionism and voyeurism. It is only when peeping and exhibiting—or, for that matter, the use of aggressive or of inanimate objects—become the central focus and *sine qua non* of the person's arousal and gratification that they are generally deemed abnormal by the society and by diagnosticians. Similarly, rape fantasies, attraction between family members, and flirtations between adults and children are common enough phenomena. It is only when these impulses are acted upon that they are labeled pathological.

According to available data, most of the deviations that will be treated in this section are all but exclusively male aberrations. Some writers believe this is so because female sexuality is repressed in the process of socialization, and women have little opportunity to develop either truly normal or truly abnormal forms of sexual expression. In addition, most of our data on the prevalence of these deviations come from arrest records, and women are much less likely than men to be arrested, or even reported, for unconventional sexual behavior. These facts, however, do not account for the vastly greater numbers of deviant males of all types. There seems to be a true difference between the sexes in this respect.

_____

[*] *DSM-III-R* categorizes most of these patterns under the heading of *paraphilias* (from the Greek *para,* meaning "beside" or "amiss," and *philia,* meaning "love"), to emphasize that the abnormality lies in the focus of attraction.

Fetishism

Fetishism is a good example of the fact that sexual disorders, like so many other psychological disorders, exist on a continuum ranging from the normal to the abnormal, with many variations in between. It is not unusual, of course, for people to concentrate sexual interest on some particular attribute of the opposite sex. Certain women consider the size of a man's penis to be particularly important, while many men are fascinated by large breasts or a shapely bottom. Other men prefer as sexual partners women who are stylishly dressed, and the sight of a pair of underpants held together with a safety pin can leave them considerably discouraged sexually. In general, however, such people, despite their marked preferences, do not totally disregard the rest of the person and can in fact respond to conventional sexual stimuli.

Further along the continuum we can place the following case, originally reported by Krafft-Ebing in 1886:

> A lady told Dr. Gemy that in the bridal night and in the night following her husband contented himself with kissing her, and running his fingers through the wealth of her tresses. He then fell asleep. In the third night Mr. *X* produced an immense wig, with enormously long hair, and begged his wife to put it on. As soon as she had done so, he richly compensated her for his neglected marital duties. In the morning he showed again extreme tenderness, whilst he caressed the wig. When Mrs. *X* removed the wig she lost at once all charm for her husband. Mrs. *X* recognized this as a hobby, and readily yielded to the wishes of her husband, whom she loved dearly, and whose libido depended on the wearing of the wig. It was remarkable, however, that a wig had the desired effect only for a fortnight or three weeks at a time. It had to be made of thick, long hair, no matter of what colour. The result of this marriage was, after five years, two children, and a collection of seventy-two wigs ([1886] 1965, pp. 157–158).

The question of whether Mr. *X*'s "hobby" deserves the label of pathological is not easy to answer. The wigs were admittedly a necessary prerequisite for his sexual arousal; yet with the help of the wigs, the couple enjoyed an otherwise conventional and satisfactory sexual relationship.

In most of the cases of fetishism that come to the attention of diagnosticians, however, the person's

For a fetishist, sexual preoccupation with objects such as women's shoes replaces any interest in a sexual relationship with another human being. (Lee Snider)

sexual fascination with a single body part or, more commonly, with some type of inanimate object has totally crowded out any interest in normal sexual interplay with another human being. Much of the person's life is occupied with collecting new examples of his favored object.

Common fetishistic objects are fur, women's stockings, women's shoes, women's gloves, and especially women's underpants, but more exotic fetishes have also been reported. Bergler (1947), for example, has cited the case of a man whose major source of sexual gratification was the sight of well-formed automobile exhaust pipes. The fetishist's sexual activity, typically, consists of fondling, kissing, and smelling the fetish, and masturbating in the process.

Transvestism

Similar to the fetishists in being sexually excited by inanimate objects, transvestites go one step further and actually put on their fetish, which is the clothing of the opposite sex. Once cross-dressed, the transvestite typically masturbates privately or has heterosexual intercourse, though he may also enjoy appearing publicly in his costume.

Transvestites usually do not come into conflict with the law, and recent social attitudes toward transvestism seem to range from indifference to curiosity.

Indeed, nightclubs featuring transvestite performers have become increasingly popular. Partly as a result of this social tolerance, there has been little psychological investigation of transvestism. However, some insight into the psychology of the transvestite has been provided by Bentler and his colleagues (Bentler and Prince, 1970; Bentler et al., 1970), who, with the help of a national transvestite organization, administered standardized personality tests to a large sample of male transvestites. These tests revealed what a number of clinicians had already suspected: that as a group, transvestites appear to be no more prone to psychological disturbance than the population at large. Not surprisingly, however, they are prone to marital problems. Some wives will tolerate the husband's cross-dressing and even incorporate it into the sexual relationship. But most women, upon discovering their husbands' transvestism, are very distressed; many such marriages end in divorce. (In these cases, transvestism cannot be considered entirely "victimless.")

Transvestism is thought to be relatively rare, but the reported rarity may be due to lack of public exposure or public alarm. Many transvestites lead quiet, conventional lives, cross-dressing only in their bedrooms and never appearing on talk shows or in therapists' offices. Thus the pattern may be more common than is assumed.

The pattern may also be a less distinct phenomenon

than is assumed. Because of the shared predilection for cross-dressing, transvestites are sometimes confused in the public mind with homosexual "drag queens." For many years it was thought that such confusion was unwarranted—that is, that the two patterns were totally separate, transvestites being predominantly heterosexual (Buckner, 1970). It now seems, however, that there is some overlap between the two categories, with some men starting out as heterosexual transvestites and eventually making the transition to homosexual drag queen. The distinction between transvestism and transsexualism (see below) has also blurred somewhat in recent years, with a number of what seem to be transvestites deciding that they are in fact transsexuals (Prince, 1978). In such cases, the diagnostic lines may be very difficult to draw.

Transsexualism

Unlike transvestites, transsexuals—most of whom, again, are males—believe that they truly *do* belong to the opposite sex. They consider their biological gender a mistake and their genitals ugly appendages. Typically cross-dressing on a regular basis, they do not feel the sexual arousal that the transvestite feels in women's clothes; rather, they feel relaxed, "at home." Indeed, they may feel as strange in men's clothing as a normal man would feel in women's cloth-

Most sex changes by transsexuals are from male to female, but Annie M., at age sixteen (left), underwent surgery for sex reassignment as a man (right, six years after surgery). (AP/Wide World Photos)

ing (Green, 1971). By biological standards, they are usually homosexual, but since they think of themselves as women, in their minds they are heterosexual.

In transsexualism, then, it is not the object of sexual interest but rather the *gender identity* that is askew by conventional standards. The subjective reversal of gender usually dates from early childhood. In a thorough study of fourteen male transsexuals, Money and Primrose (1968) found that without exception all of these men had been branded as "sissies" in childhood and had presented a feminine rather than a masculine appearance. (The reverse is not true: only a minuscule proportion of "sissy" boys grow up to be transsexuals.)

There have been a few reported cases of transsexual "cures"—that is, of transsexuals reoriented toward their biological gender, usually through behavioral techniques—but in general, this pattern has proved resistant to therapy (Abramowitz, 1986). Some transsexuals are content to cross-dress and play the desired gender role. But a great many are convinced that the only way they will find relief from anguish and despair is through sexual transformation. Their lives become a quest for a sympathetic physician who will "change" them to the opposite sex.

The first "sex change" operations were performed in the 1930s, but sex reassignment did not receive much attention until the highly publicized case of Christine Jorgensen, whose successful surgery was reported by Hamburger in 1953. In cases of male-to-female transsexualism, treatment begins with hormone injections to inhibit beard growth and stimulate breast development. Surgery involves the removal of the penis and testicles and the construction of a vagina, which (ideally) allows the individual to experience orgasm through intercourse. In female-to-male sexual reassignment, treatment begins with hormone injections to lower the voice, promote beard growth, stop menstruation, and in some cases enlarge the clitoris. Surgery involves a mastectomy, removal of the ovaries and uterus, and closure of the vagina. In some cases an artificial penis is constructed of tissue and cartilage taken from other parts of the body; in others, the urethra is rerouted through the enlarged clitoris. The penis does not function normally, but may look almost normal and allow the individual to urinate while standing.

By 1977 it was estimated that approximately 2,500 Americans had undergone sex reassignment surgery (Gagnon, 1977). Early positive reports (Benjamin,

1966; Pauly, 1968) were followed by a report from the Gender Identity Clinic at Johns Hopkins University, which concluded that "sex reassignment confers no advantage in terms of social rehabilitation" (Meyer and Peter, 1979, p. 1015). The clinic was closed shortly thereafter. Most follow-up reports suffer from weak methodology (investigator bias, lack of a control group, etc.) (Abramowitz, 1986). The best available evidence indicates that about two-thirds of the transsexuals who undergo surgery experience some improvement in sexual functioning and psychosocial adjustment (Abramowitz, 1986). As most transsexuals have only furtive sexual experiences and poor relationships with family, friends, and co-workers, however, "some improvement" does not necessarily mean that they are happy, successful, well-adjusted individuals after surgery. The life of a transsexual often remains one of loneliness and isolation (Lindemalm et al., 1986). In many cases, the surgery itself is far from successful; severe complications occur in about 50 percent of patients (Lindemalm et al., 1986). Moreover, nearly all studies report at least one "casualty": regret over the operation and a desire to go back, a psychotic episode, hospitalization, or suicide (Abramowitz, 1986). Interestingly, female-to-male reassignments, while rarer, are more often deemed successful than male-to-female reassignments.

Exhibitionism

Exhibitionism and voyeurism are the two sex offenses most often reported to the police. They are usually treated harshly by the courts, on the assumption that if the offender is treated leniently, he will "graduate" to more serious sex crimes. Studies of sex offenders indicate that more than 10 percent of child molesters and 8 percent of rapists began their sex "careers" as exhibitionists (Abel et al., 1984). But most exhibitionists are not dangerous; they do not attempt to have sexual contact with their victims.

Virtually all reported exhibitionists are men—a fact that is surely due in part to the reversed double standard. Should a woman choose to undress regularly in front of a window, male observers are unlikely to report the matter to the police. Also, modern dress codes give women ample opportunity for mild exhibitionism—an advantage not shared by men.

The typical exhibitionist is a young man, sexually inhibited and unhappily married (Mohr et al., 1964). Experiencing an irresistible impulse to exhibit himself, he will usually go to a public place such as a park, a movie theater, or a department store, or simply stroll down a city street, and upon sighting the appropriate victim—typically a young woman, though sometimes a young girl—will show her his penis. The penis is usually, but not always, erect. The exhibitionist's gratification is derived from the woman's response, which is generally horror, fear, and revulsion. Observing the reaction, the exhibitionist experiences intense arousal and either ejaculates immediately, masturbates to ejaculation, or in some cases simply experiences psychic relief. He then flees. Although the exhibitionist may do his victim no physical harm, such an experience can be upsetting for an adult woman and traumatic for a child.

In some cases, exhibitionism occurs as a symptom of a more pervasive disturbance, such as schizophrenia, epilepsy, senile brain deterioration, or mental retardation. But most exhibitionists turn out to be simply shy, submissive, immature men who have uncommonly puritanical attitudes about sex (Witzig, 1968), particularly about masturbation. Furthermore, they often experience feelings of social and sexual inferiority and serious doubts about their masculinity (Blair and Lanyon, 1981). Thus, it has been suggested, they display their genitals for shock value in a desperate effort to convince themselves of their masculine prowess (Blane and Roth, 1967; Christoffel, 1956), all the while arranging the circumstances so that the woman is extremely unlikely to respond positively and thus make sexual demands on them. In the rare instance in which the victim evinces indifference or scorn rather than the expected shock and dismay, the exhibitionist will generally be cheated of his sexual gratification. Indeed, it has been suggested that the best "cure" for exhibitionism would be to educate the public not to respond to it.

Voyeurism

An element of voyeurism, as of exhibitionism, is usually involved in normal sexual activity. In recent years, sexually oriented magazines and explicit movies have provided more or less "acceptable" outlets for those people who derive pleasure from looking. The traditional definition of voyeurism, however, distinguished true voyeurs (or "peeping Toms," as they are sometimes called) as those people for whom the pleasures of looking *replace* normal sexual interplay with another person. Actually, voyeurism often occurs alongside "normal" heterosexuality. Since this is the case, a realistic definition of voyeurism must take into account social sanctions against violating the privacy of others. In practice, then, a voyeur obtains gratification from watching strangers in violation of their sexual privacy. This usually means watching women who are undressing or couples engaged in sex play. The element of risk involved in watching strangers may be a desirable adjunct to the voyeur's pleasure. The danger of being discovered in his perch on the fire escape, balcony, or whatever adds to the sexual thrill of the peeping, which usually leads to masturbation.

Like exhibitionism, voyeurism seems to provide a substitute gratification and a reassurance of power for otherwise sexually anxious and inhibited males. Voyeurs are often withdrawn both socially and sexually, with little in their developmental histories to support the learning of more appropriate interpersonal skills.

Sadism and Masochism

There appears to be an element of aggression in even the most "natural" sexual activity. Aggressive sexual fantasies—of raping or of being raped—are not uncommon. Human beings, like most other mammals, sometimes bite and scratch during intercourse

—behavior that would be considered cruel and aggressive in almost any other context. Conversely, a sexual element often underlies aggression. Both men and women have reported becoming sexually excited at boxing matches and football games or while watching fires or executions—observations that have led some theorists to propose that our society's preoccupation with violence may be sexually motivated.

In sadism and masochism, however, the element of physical cruelty—inflicting and being subjected to it, respectively—assumes a central role in sexual functioning. Both disorders are named for literary figures who publicized the sexual pleasures of cruelty. The term *sadism* is taken from the name of the Marquis de Sade (1740–1814), whose novels included numerous erotic scenes featuring the delights of whipping a woman. Masochism is named for an Austrian novelist, Leopold von Sacher-Masoch (1836–1895), whose male characters tended to swoon with ecstasy when physically abused by women.

Individual patterns of sadism turn up primarily in men. The degree of cruelty may range from sticking a woman with a pin to gruesome acts of mutilation, numerous examples of which may be found in Krafft-Ebing's *Psychopathia Sexualis* ([1886] 1965). Between these two extremes are sadists who bind, whip, bite, and cut their victims. For some, the mere sight of blood or the victim's cries of pain are sufficient to trigger ejaculation; for others, the act of cruelty

The sadomasochistic subculture has given rise to a small industry that supplies leather masks, whips, and other devices used in this form of sexual expression. (Sepp Seitz/Woodfin Camp & Associates)

merely intensifies arousal, which eventually leads to rape. Similarly, the masochist may need to suffer only a mild pain, such as spanking or verbal abuse, or may choose to be chained and whipped. And like the sadist, he or she may reach orgasm through the experience of pain alone, or the abuse stage may serve simply as "foreplay," leading eventually to intercourse. While individual sadists may prey on unwary women or prostitutes, individual masochists usually have to resort to prostitutes, some of whom specialize in catering to masochistic tastes.

However, many cases of sadism and masochism are not individual patterns but dual patterns, in which a sadist and a masochist pair up in a relationship to satisfy their complementary tastes. Such **sadomasochistic** sexual relationships are sometimes found within otherwise conventional marriages. Other sadists and masochists are homosexuals; in fact, there is a substantial so-called S-and-M segment within the homosexual subculture. To serve this population, many underground newspapers and magazines carry advertisements by sadists and masochists seeking partners. Likewise, in many large American cities there are now "sex shops" that specialize in selling sadomasochistic equipment.

Pedophilia

Although sadomasochism may cause injury, at least the participants are consenting adults. Not so with pedophilia (from the Greek, meaning "love of children"). Children, by definition, lack the knowledge and experience to consent to sexual relations. Thus pedophilia involves a flagrant violation of the rights of the child, who may suffer serious psychological damage as a result. The pedophile may (in order of increasing rarity) covertly or overtly masturbate while talking to the child and caressing him or her, stroke the child's genitals, masturbate between the child's thighs, have the child masturbate or "lick" him, or attempt intercourse. He may entice a group of children to participate in sexual activities and pose for pornographic pictures, using peer pressure to maintain secrecy (Burgess et al., 1981).

An estimated 10 to 15 percent of children and adolescents have been sexually victimized by an adult at least once (Lanyon, 1986). Prepubescent children are more likely than older adolescents to be victimized, and girls twice as likely as boys. Although cases of female sexual abuse of children occasionally turn up, they are very rare: most pedophiles are male. The stereotype of the child molester includes a number of myths, however. First, the typical pedophile is not a "dirty old man" who lives on the margins of respectable society. In most cases he is an otherwise law-abiding citizen who may escape detection precisely because he is liked and trusted in the community. Although ranging in age from the teens to the seventies, most pedophiles are in their thirties or forties. Most are also married or divorced men who have children of their own. Second, most child molestation is not committed by strangers lurking about the playground. The offender is usually a friend of the victim and his or her family; indeed, many are related to the victim (see the discussion of incest, below) (Conte and Berliner, 1981). Third, child molestation usually does not entail physical violence. Rather, the offender uses his authority as an adult to persuade the child to acquiesce (Finkelhor, 1979). Finally, child molestation usually is not an isolated event, but consists of repeated incidents. The molestation may begin when the child is quite young and recur continuously or at intervals over five or ten years before it is discovered or broken off (Finkelhor, 1979).

Pedophilia does not follow a single pattern (Finkelhor and Araji, 1986). In some cases it may be associated with arrested psychological development: experiencing himself as a child, with childish emotional needs, the pedophile is most comfortable relating to children. Other pedophiles may be so isolated socially or so timid and shy that they are unable to establish adult heterosexual relationships and turn to children as substitutes. In still other cases, an early experience of arousal with other children may become fixed in the person's mind. The pedophile may have been a victim of childhood molestation himself (de Young, 1982). In an attempt to restore his feeling of control, he reenacts his own victimization.

Children rarely report their victimization to anyone: they are afraid their parents will be angry and blame them. Molestation is discovered when an adult becomes suspicious, the child tells an adult other than his or her parent, or a physician sees signs of sexual abuse (Finkelhor, 1979). But children "tell" adults about their problem in indirect ways (Browne and Finkelhor, 1986). Most studies of child victims report varying degrees and combinations of sleep and eating disorders, fears and phobias, difficulties at school, and inappropriate sexual behavior. The effects do not go away when the abuse stops. Adults who were sexually exploited as children frequently exhibit depression, self-destructive behavior (suicide attempts), feelings of being isolated and stigmatized, and distrust of others. They report problems relating to other adults of either sex, their parents, and even their children. Tragically, women who were abused as children are more likely than other women to be abused by their husbands or other partners as adults. The degree of trauma seems to depend on the type of sex act (intercourse and fellatio are more traumatic than petting) and on the victim's relation to the offender. The negative effects of sexual molestation by a father or stepfather are deeper and longer-lasting than those of abuse by other adults.

Incest

All human societies have—and have had throughout their known histories—a taboo against incest. Explanations of this universal taboo range from the argument that it encouraged families to establish wider social contacts to the contention, supported by scientific studies, that inbreeding fosters genetic defects in offspring.

Despite the taboo, incest does occur. Alfred Kinsey (1948, 1953) reported that only 3 percent of his sample had had incestuous relations. More recent studies indicate the proportion is much higher (10 to 23 percent). One problem with studies of incest is that they are often based on clinical samples (people who sought treatment). Diana Russell's household survey of women in the San Francisco area (1986) was an attempt to correct this bias. Russell found that 16 percent of women in her sample had been victims of incest at least once before age eighteen, 12 percent before age fourteen. Molestation by uncles was most common, followed by first cousins, fathers, and brothers. A quarter of the experiences were rated as "very severe sexual abuse" (actual or attempted intercourse, fellatio, cunnilingus, analingus, or anal intercourse), more than 40 percent as "severe sexual abuse" (genital contact without clothing). The age of victimization ranged from two years to seventeen. In most cases, the molester was at least twenty years older than the victim and lived under the same roof. Often (43 percent of cases) the incestuous assault was not repeated, but twenty-four of the women in the sample reported being molested by more than one relative.

Russell concludes that father–daughter incest is "the supreme betrayal": more than twice as many victims of fathers reported being extremely upset and suffering severe long-term effects as victims of all other incest perpetrators combined. What kind of man would assault his daughter? One who is promiscuous and unselective in his sexual partners? Research suggests not. Cavallin (1966) reports that the typical incestuous father confines his extramarital sexual contacts to his daughter, or perhaps to several daughters, beginning with the eldest. Far from being indiscriminately amoral, such fathers tend to be highly moralistic and devoutly attached to fundamentalist religious doctrines (Gebhard et al., 1965). Father–daughter incest tends to occur in connection with a troubled marriage. The man may abuse his wife as well as his daughter, and turn to the daughter sexually when his wife rejects his advances. The wife may pretend not to notice because she is afraid of her husband's violence, or she may blame her daughter for threatening to break up the family.

Not surprisingly, the impact on the daughter can be profound. The long-term effects reported by incest victims in the Russell survey were similar to those of nonincestuous child molestation: lowered self-esteem, self-blame, and self-hatred; a tendency to be vengeful or passive; emotional coldness and lack of responsiveness; negative feelings about physical closeness; and the belief that other people would think ill of them if the incest were known. Russell contrasts abuse of a child by a close relative with rape of an adult.

> An adult woman is more likely to have experienced trust in intimate relationships, to have a sense of who she is and what sex is before the traumatic attack. In contrast, children's capacity to trust can be shattered. Their sense of who they are and what sex is about is often totally or substantially shaped by the sexually abusive experience (1986, p. 157).

Rape

Rape, forced sexual intercourse with a nonconsenting partner,[*] is not only a sexual deviation but also a

---

[*] There is one category of rape that does not involve actual physical force: **statutory rape,** sexual intercourse with a minor. Though the girl may have consented, she is deemed by law (statute) to be incapable of consent, and therefore the act constitutes rape.

violent crime. More than 75,000 rapes are reported to the police each year (Becker et al., 1983), but this figure represents only a small fraction of the rapes actually committed.

In dealing with rape, we are faced with the question of why a man who presumably could find a willing sexual partner, if only a prostitute, would force himself instead on an unwilling woman and coerce her, kicking and screaming, into an act that is supposed to involve mutual pleasure and affection. There seem to be several answers to this question. Some men apparently resort to rape because they cannot find—or feel they cannot find—a willing sex partner. Like the typical voyeur and exhibitionist, the rapist of this category is described as a timid, submissive male who has grave doubts about his masculinity and is so fearful of rejection that he cannot seek sexual gratification through more acceptable channels (Cohen and Seghorn, 1969). Other rapists are clearly antisocial personalities—people who simply follow their impulses to seize whatever they want and are indifferent to the pain they inflict on others. In still other cases, the element of force may be a necessary prerequisite of sexual arousal, much as cruelty is for the sadist. In many cases, however, the rapist's motivation appears to be more aggressive than sexual. Many rapists were victims of child abuse (Hartogs, 1951; Rada, 1978); for them, hurting and humiliating women is a form of revenge or "identification with the aggressor." But some rapists are no different psychologically from "normal" men. They have adequate sexual relationships and show no pattern of abnormality on tests of psychological functioning (Dean and de Bruyn-Kops, 1982). This finding suggests that many rapes are the result not of psychological disorders but of our cultural emphasis on sex and violence. To some extent, men are socialized to become sexual predators in our society. A comparison of college undergraduates who admitted that they had forced a date to have intercourse (the phenomenon known as "date rape") and undergraduates who had never done so found that the former were "sexually very active, successful, and aspiring"; believed that rape was justified under certain circumstances (if the woman was "loose," a "pickup," or a "tease"); said their best friends would "definitely approve" of coercive tactics with certain women; and felt considerable pressure from their peers to engage in sexual exploits (Kanin, 1985).

With rape, as with pedophilia and incest, psychology must concern itself not only with the perpetrator but also with the victim. In addition to doing physical

Foiling a rapist: two detectives from the Sex Crimes Analysis Unit of the New York City Police Department demonstrate methods of self-defense to women. Rape, unlike most other sexual deviations, can have more serious psychological consequences for the victim than for the perpetrator. (Bettyo Lane)

harm, rapists inflict psychological damage on their victims. One study (Becker et al., 1983) found that rape victims were seven times more likely to suffer from moderate to severe depression than were women who had never been assaulted. Over 60 percent experienced lasting sexual dysfunction (ranging from aversion to inability to become aroused) (Becker et al., 1986). Many reported that their relationships with their partners had deteriorated. And most exhibited high levels of both general and specific rape-related fear. The case of Laura is not unusual.

A 29-year-old attorney, Laura, was assaulted several years ago. She had just graduated from law school and was serving as a law clerk in a large city. One hot summer night she was alone in the house she shared with five other women when she went to bed wearing no clothes. At 1:30 A.M. she awoke to see a figure by her bed going through her wallet. Refusing to answer any of Laura's questions, the figure suddenly jumped on top of her. When Laura realized that the figure was not one of her roommates but rather a strange man, she began to struggle. However, when the man held a silvery metal object to her throat, Laura ceased resisting physically and attempted to talk her way out of the assault. The man told her to "shut up" with a foreign accent and then attempted unsuccessfully to penetrate her vaginally. After about 15 minutes he stopped and put her in the closet. When she could no longer hear the intruder and was certain he had left, Laura tried to call the police on the telephone in her bedroom but found that the cord had been cut. She did call the police on a second telephone in the house. . . . Laura . . . continues to experience great fears related to the assault and is very ashamed of her fears. She insists that she live on a high floor in a building with a doorman. She continues to feel compelled to check every room in her apartment before she locks the door. Every night she puts large boxes in front of her door to make it more difficult for an intruder to enter. Additionally, she insists upon having two telephones with lighted push-button dials in her apartment.

Laura said that all her activities are planned around safety issues. She feels she must be able to take taxicabs or she is unable to go somewhere. She has great difficulty sleeping alone in her apartment and continues to experience insomnia and nightmares (Becker et al., 1983, pp. 252–253).

Women who report a rape to authorities all too often find that the search for justice leads to humiliation. Until quite recently, the laws in many states were designed to protect men from false accusations of rape, not to protect victims of rape. New York State, for example, required that there be a witness to the crime. (Needless to say, there rarely is.) More than 95 percent of rape cases reported to the police do not go to trial, either because identification of the rapist is uncertain or the evidence is insufficient (LoPiccolo, 1986), leaving the woman vulnerable to retaliation. If the case does go to court, the woman may feel that *she,* not the rapist, is on trial. The fact that she gave in to save her life may be used against her. In one recent case, the judge found the defendant innocent of rape on the ground that young women dress provocatively; in another, the judge told

the victim he could not believe her story because she was "the ugliest woman he had ever seen" (LoPiccolo, 1986). The trauma of the trial is thus added to the trauma of the rape.

Fortunately, recent attention to these injustices has led to the establishment of counseling centers for rape victims, special training for police officers who investigate rape cases, and the repeal of many laws that seemed designed to protect rapists from conviction.

PERSPECTIVES ON SEXUAL DEVIATIONS

Both the psychodynamic and the behavioral perspectives tend to interpret a variety of sexual deviations as resulting from the same mechanisms. Hence we will not attempt a complete rundown of etiological theories regarding all the patterns outlined above. Instead, we will summarize what each perspective views as the major causative factors and the most hopeful therapeutic approaches to sexual deviations in general.

The Psychodynamic Perspective

Oedipal Fixation   According to Freudian theory, sexual disorders represent a continuation into adulthood of the diffuse sexual preoccupations of the child. In Freud's words, young children are "polymorphously perverse"—that is, their sexual pleasure has many sources: sucking, rubbing, defecating, "showing off" their sexual equipment, peeping at that of others. These diverse sources of pleasure are brought together in the "mature" heterosexual response. Furthermore, according to Freud, children are capable of any number of defensive maneuvers in attempting to deal with the castration anxiety and penis envy supposedly endemic to the oedipal period. Thus, psychodynamic theorists generally consider sexual deviations to be the result of fixation at a pregenital stage. And in general, with sexual deviations as with sexual dysfunctions, it is the oedipal stage, with its attendant castration anxiety, that is considered the major source of trouble.

Freud theorized that fetishism is a displacement of sexual interest to a safer object. Transvestism is seen as a denial of the mother's presumed castration. Dressed in the clothes of a woman but still equipped with a penis underneath, the transvestite can momentarily convince himself that his mother did not suffer castration after all and that therefore he need not fear the same fate for himself (Nielson, 1960). Similarly, Fenichel (1945) interprets sadism as an attempt, through cruelty and aggression, to take the part of the castrator rather than that of the castrated and thus to relieve anxiety. Indeed, castration anxiety is often seen as paramount in any sexual deviation involving the avoidance of coitus. For the male who fears losing his penis, the thought of coming into contact with the supposedly truncated genitals of the woman and of watching his penis "disappear" inside her raises anxiety to an intolerable level. Hence he defends himself by redirecting his sexual impulses toward a safer outlet, such as a fetish, a child, or vicarious participation in the sexual activities of his neighbors across the way.

Other psychodynamic interpretations of sexual disorders have stressed the individual's inability to disentangle and control his basic id impulses. Thus sadism has been explained as a continuation of the child's confusion of sexual and aggressive impulses. Similarly, masochism may be seen as a redirection onto the self of aggressive impulses originally aimed at a powerful, threatening figure.

Group and Individual Therapy   In individual psychotherapy or psychoanalysis, the procedure with the sexual deviant follows traditional lines. The therapist interprets symbolic remarks, behaviors, and dreams in an attempt to bring the unconscious sexual conflict to the conscious level so that it can be confronted and "worked through." A variation on this technique—group therapy—has been employed as a substitute for imprisonment in the cases of some rapists, pedophiles, and other criminal offenders. The group technique has the obvious advantage of placing the troubled and often deeply remorseful individual in a situation where he can take comfort from the knowledge that he is not "the only one"—a reassurance that can hasten his confrontation of his problem.

Although successful treatment of sexual deviants through group therapy, individual psychotherapy, and psychoanalysis has been reported (e.g., Cohen and Seghorn, 1969), such cases are the exceptions. A sexual deviant may have committed hundreds of offenses before he comes to the attention of authorities. When such men do enter therapy, it is nearly always

because they have been caught and required to enter treatment by the courts. Their motivation to stay out of jail, and hence their motivation to lie to the therapist—to claim that they are responding to treatment, thinking normal sexual thoughts, engaging in normal sexual acts—is often high. But their motivation to change may be very low. Having convinced a therapist (and perhaps themselves) that they are "cured," they often slip back into deviant patterns.

The Behavioral Perspective

Conditioning and Attitudes   The simplest behavioral interpretation of sexual deviations is that the deviation results from a respondent conditioning process in which early sexual experiences, particularly masturbation, are paired with some unconventional stimulus, which then becomes the discriminative stimulus for arousal. This formulation, at least with regard to fetishism, has been given some support by an experiment (Rachman, 1966) in which male subjects were repeatedly shown slides of women's boots in alternation with slides of nude women in explicit erotic poses. Eventually the subjects began to register sexual responses at the signal of the boots alone. The fetishist attraction was, however, weak and easily dissipated. Furthermore, the results of this experiment have never been replicated, despite several attempts—perhaps because it is difficult to produce such a response artificially in adults.

In the case of sadism and masochism, behavioral theorists have noted that sex, aggression, and the experience of pain all involve strong emotional and physiological arousal; hence it has been proposed that the sadist and the masochist are simply persons who never learned to discriminate among the various types of arousal. Another learning theory of masochism is that as a child the masochist may have been cuddled and loved by his parents only after being punished, with the result that love and punishment became paired. Likewise, learning may play some role in the development of transvestism and transsexualism. The case histories of these people often reveal that they were reinforced by being given attention and being told that they were "cute" when they dressed up in their mothers' or sisters' clothes (Rekers and Lovaas, 1974).

Recent behavioral theories of sexual deviation tend to stress cognitive factors as well as, or in preference to, direct conditioning. Albert Bandura (1969), for example, has argued that parents may knowingly or unknowingly model deviant sexual behavior. Other writers emphasize more general processes, such as repressive attitudes toward sex, distorted thinking about male and female roles, and poor social skills (Barlow and Abel, 1976; Blair and Lanyon, 1981). In such formulations, the deviant behavior is not so much the basic disturbance as merely the point of arrival after a long history of cognitive detours from normal sexual functioning.

Unlearning Deviant Patterns: A Multifaceted Approach

New programs for the treatment of sex offenders take the complex nature of sexual deviance into account. A multifaceted approach combines elements of traditional psychotherapy with specific techniques for dealing with sexual issues. The goal is to change the patient's sexual arousal patterns, beliefs, and behavior (LoPiccolo, 1985b).

Treatment begins with steps to bring deviant sexual behavior under temporary control. A man who drinks to reduce his inhibitions may be required to join Alcoholics Anonymous; a child molester is required to stop any job or recreational activities that bring him into contact with children; an incestuous father may be required to move out of his home temporarily.

Behavioral techniques are then used to eliminate deviant arousal. One such technique is called **stimulus satiation.** Suppose the patient is an exhibitionist who is aroused by young girls. He is asked to collect pictures of girls which arouse in him an urge to expose himself, and to arrange them in order from the least to the most exciting. He is also told to collect "normal" sexual stimuli, such as erotic pictures from men's magazines. Then he is instructed to take these materials home and masturbate while looking at the normal stimuli, and to record his fantasies verbally with a tape recorder. Two minutes after he has ejaculated (or after ten minutes if he does not), he must switch to the deviant stimuli, begin masturbating again, and continue for fifty-five minutes, regardless of whether or how often he ejaculates. During this phase he continues to record his exhibitionist fantasies. The patient is required to repeat this procedure three times a week for at least one month, moving from the stimuli that excite him least to those that stimulate him the most. His tapes are analyzed carefully. If his fantasies with normal stimuli are confined to such exhibitionist acts as looking at a *Playboy* centerfold and being looked at by her, he is encouraged to imagine physical contact with her. After ten to fifteen sessions, most

sex offenders find the deviant stimuli boring, uninteresting, even aversive—a turn-off rather than a turn-on (LoPiccolo, 1985b).

Stimulus satiation may be combined with other procedures. In **covert sensitization,** the patient is taught to indulge in a deviant fantasy until he is aroused, then to imagine the worst possible consequences—his wife finds him engaged in sex play with a child, he is arrested in front of his neighbors, the arrest makes headlines, his son attempts suicide, and so on. In **shame aversion therapy,** the patient is required to go through a deviant act—to exhibit himself or, if he is a transvestite, to dress in female clothing—in the therapist's office, while the therapist and the patient's wife observe and comment. (This technique is so distressing that it is used only when other techniques seem to be failing.)

Sex offenders often express distorted beliefs about their activities. Rapists frequently assert that all women have a secret desire to be raped, that a woman who accepts a ride or comes to your apartment wants to have sex with you, and the like; pedophiles, that the child could say no if he or she didn't want to have sex with him; incestuous fathers, that they are "teaching" their daughter about sex in a positive, caring, emotional context. Whether these beliefs cause them to behave in deviant ways or develop afterward as rationalizations, they play a role in maintaining deviant behavior. Multifaceted treatment includes cognitive restructuring, in which the therapist directly challenges the patient's false ideas.

"Normal" fantasies and corrected ideas do not necessarily translate into normal behavior, however. Sex offenders often lack basic social and sexual skills. Treatment of unmarried offenders includes training in conversational skills, eye contact, empathy skills, listening skills, asking for a date, and making tasteful sexual advances. Married sex offenders often report that their sexual relationship with their wife is good or adequate, but further probing usually reveals that sex is infrequent and stereotyped, lacking in playful erotic activities. The couple are taught to do sensate exercises, communicate their desires, and explore new sexual experiences.

Weekly therapy for at least six months is recommended for most sex offenders. Follow-up sessions every two weeks or once a month should continue for another year or year and a half. Thereafter the patient should be reassessed every six months for three to five years. But even this refined, intensive, long-term therapy does not guarantee a "cure."

The Neuroscience Perspective

Since sexual arousal is controlled in part by the central nervous system, it is possible that sexual aberrations may be related to neurological disorders. A number of researchers have investigated this question, but without conclusive results (Rada, 1978; Blumer and Walker, 1975). Whatever its role in etiology, however, there is no question (other than the ethical one) that biology can be employed in the treatment of sexual deviation. In various European countries, both castration and brain surgery have been used with dangerous sex offenders (usually rapists and pedophiles), this "treatment" usually being offered as an alternative to imprisonment. Another route is the administration of various drugs that decrease the level of testosterone, a hormone essential to male sexual functioning (Berlin, 1983). Anti-androgen treatment is widely used in Europe and has been experimented with in the United States as well. That such procedures are controversial need hardly be said. In addition, the sex drive of a person who has had previous sexual experience is under the control more of psychological and cognitive variables than of hormones. Recent findings that the experimental procedures in fact do not work in many cases have increased public and professional opposition to them (Heim, 1981; Schmidt and Schorsch, 1981; Rieber and Sigusch, 1979; Heim and Hursch, 1979).

HOMOSEXUALITY

Technically, the term *homosexuality* (from the Greek word *homos,* meaning "same") means sexual activity directed toward one's own sex. But this narrow definition does not take into account the emotional and psychological dimensions of sexuality. A broader definition of a homosexual person is an individual whose primary erotic and emotional affiliations are with members of the same sex and who sees him- or herself as a homosexual. A homosexual's gender identity conforms to biological sex: the person's perception of him- or herself as a male or female is accurate. The difference between homosexuals and heterosexuals lies not in their gender identity but in their sexual orientation and attraction toward the same sex. Everyday language draws a further distinction between males and females. The term *homosexuality* is generally reserved for males, while female homosexuality (which receives far less attention) is called

lesbianism. (The word is taken from the Greek island of Lesbos, home of the poet Sappho, who in the sixth century B.C. wrote of her love for other women.)

Attitudes toward Homosexuality

Negative attitudes toward homosexuality have a long history in Western societies, as we noted earlier. Judeo-Christian traditions held that the purpose of sexual relations was procreation, not pleasure; homosexuality in particular was condemned. As part of the general trend toward more positive views of sexuality, attitudes toward homosexuality have become more tolerant. By the 1980s, many people had come to think of homosexuality simply as an alternate life style. The term *gay* (originally a code word homosexuals used to imply positive feelings about themselves) came into common use.

Changes in official psychiatric nomenclature have reflected these trends. In its first six printings, *DSM-II* listed homosexuality as a sexual disorder, along with pedophilia, fetishism, sadism, and so forth. Then in 1973 the board of trustees of the American Psychiatric Association voted to drop homosexuality per se from the list. Their report described homosexuality as "a normal form of sexual life" (1974). But they retained a category called "ego-dystonic homosexuality disorder" for individuals who *themselves* reject their sexual inclinations and wish to become exclusively heterosexual. Many psychologists, as well as gay rights groups, argued that homosexuals who reject their own homosexuality do so because they have internalized negative stereotypes; by labeling their sexual orientation a psychological disorder, the mental health establishment reinforced those stereotypes. In 1986 the APA voted to drop homosexuality from *DSM-III-R* and to replace it with a new category, "Psychosexual Disorder Not Otherwise Specified" for persistent and marked distress or confusion about one's sexual orientation.

Public attitudes toward homosexuality today are best described as mixed. A few states, among them Illinois, Connecticut, Texas, and New York, have decriminalized homosexual acts between consenting adults in private. In a 1986 ruling, however, the U.S. Supreme Court upheld a Georgia "sodomy" law prohibiting oral–genital sexual contact. Technically, this ruling applies to anyone, including married couples, although the case in question involved a homosexual act. But heterosexuals are rarely, if ever, prosecuted for what they do in the privacy of their homes; such laws are invoked against homosexuals. The sudden appearance of AIDS (Acquired Immune Deficiency Syndrome) has underscored the split in public attitudes toward homosexuality. AIDS is caused by a blood-borne virus that attacks the immune system and leads to death within two to five years. Although AIDS can also be transmitted by infected blood donors and drug abusers who share unsterilized hypodermic needles, most of the known 21,000 victims in the United States (about 70 percent) are male homosexuals. The AIDS epidemic has inspired many people to donate their time and talent to raise funds for research. But it has convinced others of the evils of homosexuality. Indeed, many people see AIDS as "God's punishment for homosexuality." (If one follows this statement to its logical conclusion, God must love lesbians: 30 percent of AIDS cases involve heterosexuals; female homosexuals have been untouched by the disease.) AIDS has intensified the ongoing debate about whether homosexuals should be protected from discrimination in housing and employment, allowed to teach in the schools, granted custody or even visiting rights with their children after a divorce, and other matters. These debates directly affect the lives of millions of Americans.

The Prevalence of Homosexuality

Virtually nothing was known about the prevalence of homosexuality in the United States until 1948, when Kinsey shocked the American public by reporting that 37 percent of his male sample had had at least one homosexual experience to orgasm after the onset of adolescence, while 18 percent revealed as much homosexual as heterosexual experience. Another 13 percent experienced, but did not act upon, homosexual impulses. Of those men who remained unmarried at the age of thirty-five, 50 percent had engaged in homosexual activity to orgasm since the beginning of adolescence. In all, only 63 percent of Kinsey's sample had had exclusively heterosexual experience, and only 4 percent had exclusively homosexual histories (Kinsey et al., 1948). Kinsey's data on women indicated a much lower incidence of homosexual experience—only 13 percent (Kinsey et al., 1953)—but even this figure was considered startling when it was first published. Kinsey and his associates argued that homosexual and heterosexual orientations should not

be seen as a dichotomy of "them" versus "us," but rather as a continuum, with a large percentage of "us" falling somewhere between the two extremes of exclusive homosexuality and exclusive heterosexuality. This point was often lost in the public uproar.

Kinsey's reports have been criticized on a number of points. In the first place, the sample may be considered unrepresentative because only volunteers, most of whom were white, middle-class, and above average in education, were interviewed. Second, sexual data based on self-reports tend to be viewed with skepticism because many people are not willing to reveal the intimate details of their sex lives to even the most objective interviewer, while others exaggerate their reports. However, other surveys of sexual behavior (Gebhard, 1972; Hunt, 1974) generally confirm Kinsey's findings. About 2 percent of men and 1 percent of women are exclusively homosexual; roughly 75 percent of men and 85 percent of women are exclusively heterosexual; and some 23 percent of men and 14 percent of women have had sexual experience with both sexes.

Despite data to the contrary and Kinsey's warning, we still tend to think of homosexuality and heterosexuality as either/or traits. As a result, **bisexuals,** who have sexual experiences with both sexes, have received little attention. MacDonald (1981) divides this group into four subcategories: bisexuality as a real orientation (people who experience continuing attraction to both sexes); bisexuality as a transitory orientation (usually people who experiment with homosexuality, perhaps in a same-sex setting such as a boarding school, but return to a heterosexual orientation thereafter); bisexuality as a transitional orientation (a relationship that causes a person to change his or her sexual orientation, usually from heterosexuality to homosexuality); and bisexuality as denial of homosexuality (typically, a person who gets married to avoid confronting his or her homosexual interests and/or to escape social stigmatization).

Homosexual Myths and Realities

The issue of homosexuality is surrounded by a good deal of misinformation. One prevailing myth is that homosexuals generally suffer from the type of gender confusion that we have described as typical of the transsexual. Consequently, many people believe that male homosexuals are invariably limp-wristed, effeminate types and that lesbians are generally tough-looking "dykes." The evidence indicates, however, that most homosexuals cannot be distinguished from heterosexuals by their appearance alone.

Another popular misconception is that there is a distinctly homosexual personality type. On the contrary, it appears that homosexuals differ as much from one another in personality make-up as do heterosexuals (Hooker, 1957; Wilson, 1984).

Third, it is widely believed that psychological disturbance is much more prevalent among homosexuals than among heterosexuals. If it was not maladjustment that "drove" them to homosexuality, then their homosexuality, with its attendant guilt, will drive them to maladjustment. Yet several studies have shown that despite the social disapproval they are forced to endure, homosexuals are no more prone to psychopathology than are matched groups of heterosexuals (Hooker, 1957; Saghir et al., 1969; Paul et al., 1982).

Fourth, some people assume that homosexuality as a behavior pattern is especially communicable to children who come into contact with adult homosexuals. However, a study (Green, 1978) found that of thirty-seven children raised in "sexually atypical" households (most of which were headed by female homosexuals), all but one reported preferences for toys, games, clothing, and activities typically associated with their own sex. The older children in the study who reported sexual fantasies or behavior were all heterosexually oriented. A more recent study (Green et al., 1986) compared children of lesbian mothers with children of heterosexual mothers and found no differences in gender identity, popularity, or overall social adjustment. Furthermore, the vast majority of adult homosexuals were not "initiated" or seduced by an older homosexual, but had their first experience with a person of their own age (Bell et al., 1981).

Finally, it is often thought that male and female homosexual relationships mimic heterosexual relationships, with one person playing the active "male" role and the other the passive "female" role. Several studies have found this to be untrue (Saghir and Robins, 1969; Saghir et al., 1969; Peplau, 1981). Most homosexual couples have "best friendships" (with romantic and erotic overtones). By comparison, heterosexual relationships seem far more stereotyped and tradition-bound. Peplau (1981) suggests that homosexual couples might provide role models for heterosexual couples seeking to establish more egalitarian relationships.

What homosexuals do in their sexual interplay can

Many homosexuals live together as couples and construct stable, mutually supportive households. They differ in personality as widely as heterosexuals, are no more prone to psychopathology than heterosexuals, and are generally indistinguishable from heterosexuals in appearance. (Michael Malyszko/Stock, Boston)

be stated without great mystery: their sexual activities are quite similar to those of heterosexuals (with the one exception of penile–vaginal intercourse). As among heterosexuals, foreplay involves touching, kissing, fondling, and tactile stimulation of the genitals. Contrary to stereotypes, the sexual activities of male homosexuals do not center on phallic play alone. Most gay men consider affection and tenderness extremely important and satisfying (Bell and Weinberg, 1978). Achieving orgasm through fellatio is most common, followed by manual stimulation by a partner and anal intercourse. Because AIDS is transmitted through body fluids, some homosexual men now use condoms during oral and anal intercourse to avoid contact with semen (Schecter et al., 1984). Lesbians generally reach orgasm through oral–genital stimulation, manual stimulation by the partner, or rubbing genitals together. Contrary to stereotypes, lesbians rarely use dildos (penis-shaped devices). Nor do they find sex without intercourse unsatisfying. To the contrary, Kinsey found that lesbians experience orgasm more frequently than do heterosexual women, perhaps because they have a greater understanding of a woman's sexual responses.

Homosexual Life Styles

Homosexuals are found in all economic, racial, religious, and occupational groups. Their personalities, relationships, and life styles are as varied as those of heterosexuals. What all homosexuals have in common is the search for sexual and emotional fulfillment with a member of the same sex and the shared experience of prejudice and discrimination (Crooks and Baur, 1987).

There are differences between lesbian and male homosexual life styles. As a general rule, lesbians seek committed, romantic relationships. Most have had fewer than ten sexual partners, and many consider fidelity or monogamy central to their relationship (Thoresen, 1984). Homosexual men are more likely to engage in casual sex, and many have had brief

sexual encounters with hundreds of partners (Bell and Weinberg, 1978). This is hardly surprising: females in our society are socialized to put love before sex, while men learn the reverse. But there are many exceptions to these rules (McWhirter and Mattison, 1984). In a large-scale study of homosexuals in the San Francisco Bay area, Bell and Weinberg identified five basic homosexual categories. "Closed-coupled" homosexuals were at ease with their homosexuality and committed to their current partner. Twenty-eight percent of lesbians and 10 percent of homosexual men fitted into this "happily married" category. "Open-coupled" individuals lived with a primary partner but also engaged in erotic relationships with other partners. About 18 percent of homosexual men and 17 percent of lesbians were in this category. "Functionals" were independent or "single" homosexuals who were deeply involved in the gay world, took a good deal of interest in sex, but had little desire for a committed relationship. Fifteen percent of gay men and 10 percent of lesbians fitted this description. "Dysfunctionals," in contrast, regretted their homosexuality and experienced many problems in daily living. Twelve percent of male homosexuals and 5 percent of lesbians were in this group. Sixteen percent of male homosexuals and 11 percent of lesbians were "asexuals" who reported fewer sexual partners and less interest in

Contrary to myth, the vast majority of children of homosexuals grow up to have a heterosexual orientation. (Catherine Allport)

sex than those in other groups. Asexuals tended to be loners. But these categories did not account for all of the homosexual individuals in the study: 29 percent did not fit into any category.

Despite an increase in social acceptance, all homosexuals face the difficult choice of remaining "in the closet"—that is, keeping their sexual orientation secret and "passing" as a heterosexual—or "coming out"—that is, making their preferences known and facing the consequences. Coming out is a more complex decision than heterosexuals, who never face this choice, might imagine. It means acknowledging one's unconventional preferences, overcoming internalized negative stereotypes about homosexuals, telling one's parents, and often risking one's job, social position, friendships, even custody or visiting rights with one's children. Moreover, this is not a decision a homosexual can make once and for all. The issue of disclosure is repeated every time the person makes a new acquaintance, takes a new job, moves to a new home.

The gay subculture can be an important resource. Most major cities in the United States have gay bars and cafés, education centers, service organizations, professional groups, religious organizations, and political rights groups. In the past, gay bars and baths played an important role in the lives of homosexual men; often they were the only places where such men could be honest about their sexual preferences. In part because of greater social acceptance of homosexuality, in part because of the threat of AIDS, the role of such places is declining. But gay rights groups continue to be important to individuals who encounter discrimination.

PERSPECTIVES ON HOMOSEXUALITY*

The Psychodynamic Perspective

Castration Anxiety and the "Smother Mother"
The classical psychodynamic view of male homosexuality, like that of the sexual disorders described earlier, centers on the problem of unresolved oedipal con-

---

* As we noted earlier, homosexuality has received far more attention than lesbianism, perhaps because our society takes male sexuality more seriously than female sexuality. The theoretical perspectives described here deal primarily with male homosexuality.

flicts. According to this theory, the homosexual is unable to overcome his attachment to his mother and to identify with his father, and thus is unable to proceed to the mature stage of genital sexuality. (Freud expresses his own views in the box on p. 340.) Hence he continues to suffer from acute castration anxiety, and consequently he strenuously avoids contact with female genitals for fear of injury to or loss of his penis. Homosexuality thus develops as a substitute for the heterosexual adaptation that the individual's fears prevent him from achieving but for which, at some level, he still yearns (Bieber, 1976).

This family-centered theory received some support from a famous study in which Bieber and his associates (1962) asked a number of their psychiatric colleagues to fill out detailed questionnaires on the family histories of their homosexual patients. When these investigators analyzed the information they received, they found a frequent occurrence of what might be called the "smother mother" syndrome. Briefly, the pattern involves a disturbed relationship between the parents, with the result that the mother transfers her love to her son and becomes overprotective of him. Meanwhile the father, like a rejected suitor, becomes withdrawn, resentful, and very negative in his interactions with his rival, the son. The mother is either explicitly or subtly seductive with the son but at the same time discourages erotic displays on his part and communicates to him her contempt for the male role in general. Needless to say, such a pattern would hardly be conducive to any successful resolution of the Oedipus complex. Thus Bieber's findings have been hailed as definitive evidence in support of the psychodynamic formulation. And while this evidence is not definitive, such a family theory does seem to merit serious consideration. At the same time it should be noted that the Bieber pattern turns up in the histories of heterosexuals as well, and, conversely, fails to appear in the families of many homosexuals (Bell et al., 1981).

Working through the Conflict   The psychodynamic treatment of homosexuality follows the tradiional route of free association, dream analysis, and "talking out," with special attention, of course, to the confrontation of the oedipal conflicts. Such treatment procedures, particularly with highly motivated patients who are not exclusively homosexual, have had some limited success. However, the question of motivation is a crucial one. Many homosexuals who

A Letter From Freud on Homosexuality

Four years before his death, Freud, by then world-famous, received a letter from an American woman desperately asking for advice regarding her son's "problems." Freud's kindly reply—written, as it was, thirteen years before the publication of the Kinsey report—seems extremely modern in its approach to homosexuality. Predictably, he ascribes this condition to arrested psychosexual development. Note, however, that he adamantly rejects the notion that homosexuality can be classified as either a vice or an illness, suggests that it need not be accompanied by neurosis, is skeptical about the advisability or success of any treatment, and appears to consider the happiness of the woman's son of greater importance than his sexual orientation. After nearly fifty years of research, the most avant-garde psychologists have had little to add to this position.

April 9, 1935

Dear Mrs.——

I gather from your letter that your son is a homosexual. I am most impressed by the fact that you do not mention this term yourself in your information about him. May I question you, why you avoid it? Homosexuality is assuredly no advantage, but it is nothing to be ashamed of, no vice, no degradation, it cannot be classified as an illness; we consider it to be a variation of the sexual function produced by a certain arrest of sexual development. Many highly respectable individuals of ancient and modern times have been homosexuals, several of the greatest among them (Plato, Michelangelo, Leonardo da Vinci, etc.). It is a great injustice to persecute homosexuality as a crime, and cruelty too. If you do not believe me, read the books of Havelock Ellis. [Ellis, a contemporary of Freud, was famous for his seven-volume *Studies in the Psychology of Sex*.]

By asking me if I can help, you mean, I suppose, if I can abolish homosexuality and make normal heterosexuality take its place. The answer is, in a general way, we cannot promise to achieve it. In a certain number of cases we succeed in developing the blighted germs of heterosexual tendencies which are present in every homosexual; in the majority of cases it is no more possible. It is a question of the quality and the age of the individual. The result of treatment cannot be predicted.

What analysis can do for your son runs in a different line. If he is unhappy, neurotic, torn by conflicts, inhibited in his social life, analysis may bring him harmony, peace of mind, full efficiency, whether he remains a homosexual or gets changed. If you make up your mind, he should have analysis with me! I don't expect you will! He has to come over to Vienna. I have no intention of leaving here. However, don't neglect to give me your answer.

Sincerely yours with kind wishes,
Freud

P.S. I did not find it difficult to read your handwriting. Hope you will not find my writing and my English a harder task (quoted in Jones, 1963, p. 490).

seek psychological treatment in order to change their sexual orientation do not actually do so of their own volition. Rather, they are pressured by their families and enter treatment with some reluctance. As indicated in a letter from Freud (see the box above), the goal of psychoanalysis is to improve self-understanding rather than to change sexual orientation.

The Behavioral Perspective

Homosexuality as a Learned Preference   Predictably, most psychologists who follow a learning the-ory interpret homosexuality simply as a learned preference. If we regard most human beings as potentially responsive to stimulation from both males and females, then the development of the individual's sexual orientation will depend upon his or her personal experiences in sexual arousal and satisfaction. Males who have had punishing experiences with females, including their mothers, will tend to avoid females, and if such avoidance is coupled with sexual satisfaction from males, then the situation is clearly conducive to the development of homosexual orientation.

Many elements of this behavioral analysis are in keeping with the psychodynamic theory of the conflict-ridden mother–son relationship. The similarity between these two points of view is nicely illustrated by a study (Evans, 1969) of forty-three male homosexuals, all members of a West Coast homosexual organization. In contrast to a matched group of heterosexuals, the homosexuals recalled themselves during their childhood as frail, clumsy, and nonathletic. Most were afraid of physical injury, tended to play with girls rather than boys, and thought of themselves as loners; they seldom entered into competitive games. The mothers of the homosexuals were likely to be seen as cold and puritanical, demanding of the son's attention, preferring the son to the father in an open and demanding sort of way, interfering with the development of relations with girls during adolescence, and generally encouraging feminine attitudes while discouraging masculine attitudes. The homosexuals spent less time with their fathers, reported more negative feelings toward their fathers, and were in general more afraid that their fathers might harm or injure them.

While certain of these findings are clearly supportive of the psychodynamic position—indeed, they have been taken as further evidence for Bieber's family theory—the findings of this study are also in keeping with the view of homosexuality as a learned predisposition or preference. But a large-scale study by the Kinsey Institute found that the role of parent–child relationships in the development of homosexuality was "grossly exaggerated" and, in particular, that "the connection between boys' relationships with their mothers and whether they become homosexual or heterosexual is hardly worth mentioning" (Bell et al., 1981, p. 184).

Instead of focusing on family relationships, some psychologists emphasize critical learning experiences. According to this view, individuals who learn to masturbate with a same-sex friend or who experience their first orgasm through homosexual interaction are more likely to become homosexual in orientation (Van Wyk, 1984). But this view raises an unanswerable chicken-and-egg question: Does homosexual experience lead to feelings of homosexual attraction, or do feelings of attraction to the same sex make the experience intensely pleasurable?

Learning a New Preference   Traditionally, behavioral therapy for homosexuals has followed essentially the same route as behavioral therapy for sexual deviations. Until recently, many therapists relied on aversion conditioning. Typically, the patient, once aroused by homosexual pictures or fantasies, would be given an electric shock that he could terminate by switching to heterosexual pictures or by verbalizing heterosexual fantasies. Today, however, many behaviorists, along with other therapists, do not try to treat homosexuality per se, having adopted the position that homosexuality is not an illness but a matter of personal choice. For those homosexuals who wish to change their orientation, most modern behavioral therapy typically emphasizes arousal reconditioning (LoPiccolo, 1985a), relying on the masturbation procedure outlined above, and social skills training, aimed at teaching the would-be heterosexual how to meet women with whom to exercise his newly learned arousal pattern.

In *Homosexuality in Perspective* (1979), Masters and Johnson asserted that they had successfully "converted" homosexual men who were unhappy with their orientation to a heterosexual orientation through intensive, short-term treatment consisting of a combination of sensate exercises with a female partner, fantasy satiation (a variation of stimulus satiation), and training in heterosexual skills. They claimed that over 70 percent of the men treated were still functioning as heterosexuals five years after treatment (Schwartz and Masters, 1984). Critics were quick to point out, however, that the men they treated were better described as bisexuals or heterosexuals experiencing sexual problems. Most were in love with a woman before they began treatment, and some were married. Therapy enabled them to add sexual intimacy to emotional intimacy, to align their sexual orientation with their emotional orientation.

The Humanistic-Existential Perspective

Humanistic-existential theory may see homosexuality, male or female, as a lack of authentic choice, but only when homosexuality is part of a total pattern of disturbed functioning. Humanistic psychologists have been in the forefront of the movement to recognize homosexuality as a potentially valid form of sexual expression. Humanists emphasize the risks of a commitment to homosexuality in a society that is so heavily geared to heterosexuality, but they would validate such a choice if it was made with full awareness. In such a case, the humanistic or existential therapist, instead of attempting to reorient the patient to a more socially acceptable pattern, would concentrate on helping the patient to accept responsibility for his choice and to develop honest and fulfilling relationships.

In view of the finding by the Task Force on Homosexuality of the National Institute of Mental Health that only about one-fourth of the people who are exclusively homosexual can effect any change in this pattern through current therapies, the humanistic-existential approach may represent the most pragmatic as well as the most humane treatment of homosexual patients. It has now been endorsed by many psychodynamic and behavioral writers as well. Indeed, Davison (1974), a leading behaviorist, argues that therapists should stop offering treatment for the purpose of altering homosexual orientation, since the mere existence of such treatment serves as a tacit endorsement of the society's condemnation of homosexuality—and a tacit encouragement to homosexuals to regard themselves as "sick." Further, Begelman (1975) has suggested that instead of treating homosexuality, behavior therapists should "make strides in the resolution of the real 'problem': the public derogation of diverse life styles." This is the extreme position. Most therapists are not turning away homosexual patients who wish to become heterosexual. Nevertheless, many therapists of all persuasions have now begun to question such patients closely about their reasons for seeking this change and to offer them the choice of improving their lives as homosexuals rather than looking for new lives as heterosexuals.

The Neuroscience Perspective

The oldest theory of homosexuality is that it is due to genetic or hormonal defects. The scientific support for this formulation is lacking, however. In the case of genetic etiology, Kallmann (1952) originally reported 100 percent concordance rates for homosexuality in monozygotic twins, compared with a concordance rate of less than 15 percent of dizygotic twins. However, later research (Parker, 1964; Pritchard, 1962) has failed to confirm this evidence, and at the moment the genetic theory of homosexuality remains one of the least convincing.

The hormonal theory centers on the role of testosterone, the hormone that is largely responsible for the development of such male secondary sex characteristics as beard growth, deepening of the voice,

and sperm production. According to one hypothesis, abnormally low levels of testosterone may be responsible for the development of homosexuality. Loraine and his co-workers (1971) found less urinary testosterone in homosexual men than in heterosexual men, and more testosterone in lesbians than in heterosexual women. Similarly, Kolodny and his colleagues (1971) found lower plasma testosterone as well as poorer-quality sperm in male homosexuals than in heterosexuals. However, many subsequent studies (e.g., Barlow et al., 1974; Brodie et al., 1974; Gartrell, 1982) have failed to discover consistent hormonal differences between homosexuals and heterosexuals, and at the moment biological theories of homosexuality are not widely accepted.

SUMMARY

The social sanctions on abnormalities and variations in sexual behavior are very stringent. While the human sexual impulse is capable of gratification through a wide range of outlets, Western society tends to regard heterosexual relations as the only normal form of sexual activity.

Sexual dysfunctions may be classified according to the phase of the sexual response cycle in which they occur: hypoactive sexual desire (desire phase); erectile dysfunction and general sexual dysfunction (excitement phase); and premature ejaculation, retarded ejaculation, and orgastic dysfunction (orgasm phase). Two additional disorders are vaginismus and dyspareunia. Masters and Johnson claim that the major source of sexual dysfunction is performance anxiety, while Kaplan maintains that deeper psychological issues are also involved. Theorists who take the systems approach contend that sexual dysfunction usually has an important though unsuspected role in maintaining the couple's relationship. Treatment varies with the form of dysfunction, but the most successful current treatments are based on a formula of increased stimulation and lowered performance demands.

Among the sexual deviations are fetishism, transvestism, transsexualism, exhibitionism, voyeurism, sadism and masochism, pedophilia, incest, and rape. In all but transsexualism, the abnormality involved is one of attraction; what arouses the person is something other than what is generally considered a normal sexual object or activity. These behaviors are reported primarily in males, and many of them are thought to result from feelings of sexual inadequacy, which prevent the male from pursuing more acceptable forms of gratification. Neurological research into the causes of sexual deviation has so far been inconclusive. Psychodynamic theorists emphasize the etiological role of unresolved oedipal conflicts and continuing castration anxiety; behavioral theorists stress the importance of early respondent conditioning, claiming in effect that deviant behavior is learned as other behaviors are.

Advocates of both schools of thought invoke essentially the same mechanisms as explanations of homosexuality. However, homosexuality differs from what we have called the sexual deviations in that it is a much more common pattern and is coming to be viewed by both psychological professionals and society as a legitimate sexual preference. As investigators explore the various coping styles of different types of homosexuals, many myths about homosexuals are disproved. While genetic and hormonal theories of homosexuality remain largely unproved, both the psychodynamic and the behavioral interpretations have received some scientific support, and both schools have had some treatment successes. Most therapists today believe that the best treatment for homosexuals is to help them to accept their orientation and to establish fulfilling homosexual relationships.

Schizophrenia and Paranoia

I n his *Lectures on Clinical Psychiatry* (1904), Emil Kraepelin (Chapter 1) describes the case of a woman he calls the "widow":

> The widow, aged thirty-five, . . . gives full information about her life in answer to our questions, knows where she is, can tell the date and the year, and gives proof of satisfactory school knowledge. It is noteworthy that she does not look at her questioner, and speaks in a low and peculiar, sugary, affected tone. . . . For many years she has heard voices, which insult her and cast suspicion on her chastity. They mention a number of names she knows, and tell her she will be stripped and abused. The voices are very distinct, and, in her opinion, they must be carried by a telescope or a machine from her home. Her thoughts are dictated to her; she is obliged to think them, and hears them repeated after her. She is interrupted in her work, and has all kinds of uncomfortable sensations in her body, to which something is "done." In particular, her "mother parts" are turned inside out, and people send a pain through her back, lay ice-water on her heart,
>
> squeeze her neck, injure her spine, and violate her. . . .
>
> The patient makes these extraordinary complaints without showing much emotion. She cries a little, but then describes her morbid experiences again with secret satisfaction and even with an erotic bias. She demands her discharge, but is easily consoled, and does not trouble at all about her position and her future. Her use of numerous strained and hardly intelligible phrases is very striking. She is ill-treated "flail-wise," "utterance-wise," "terror-wise"; she is "a picture of misery in angel's form," and "a defrauded mamma and housewife of sense of order." They have "altered her form of emotion." She is "persecuted by a secret insect from the District Office. . . ." Her former history shows that she has been ill for nearly ten years (quoted in *DSM-III Casebook*, 1981, pp. 308–309).

The "widow" offers a good illustration of the psychotic. As we have noted previously, the **psychoses** are a class of psychological disorders in which reality contact—the capacity to perceive, process, and respond to environmental stimuli in an adaptive manner—is radically impaired, with the result that the individual sometimes cannot meet even the most ordinary demands of life. The psychoses, then, are the most severe of all the psychological disorders. Most of the conditions that we have discussed in earlier chapters allow for some measure of adaptive functioning. Alcoholics, fetishists, hypertensives, amnesiacs—these people can still, in many cases, look after themselves, earn a living, carry on a reasonable conversation, and so forth. Psychotics in the midst of an acute episode generally cannot. For this reason—and because their behavior is incomprehensible and disturbing to others—they are often hospitalized.

The psychoses are traditionally divided into two broad categories: the **biogenic psychoses,** those associated with known physical conditions (to be covered in Chapter 16), and the **functional psychoses,** those for which no physical basis has been clearly identified and which therefore may be at least partly psychogenic. There are three main groups of functional psychoses:

1. The mood disorders, characterized, as their name indicates, primarily by disturbance of *mood.* (But remember that not all mood disorders are psychotic.)

2. The schizophrenic disorders, considered to be primarily disturbances of *thought.*

3. The delusional disorders, in which the essential, and possibly the only, abnormality is a limited system of *delusions.*

Mood disorders have already been described in Chapter 10. The present chapter will focus on the two remaining types of functional psychoses—the schizophrenic disorders and the delusional disorders—with special emphasis on the former, as they are by far the more common. The purpose of this chapter is simply to describe these disorders. Theories as to cause and treatment will be discussed in Chapter 15.

SCHIZOPHRENIA

Schizophrenia is the label given to a group of psychoses in which deterioration of functioning is marked by severe distortion of thought, perception, and mood, by bizarre behavior, and by social withdrawal. As we saw above, the actual name of the diagnostic category is the *schizophrenic disorders,* a term that emphasizes the diversity of symptoms seen within this diagnostic group. However, the shorter term "schizophrenia" is widely used for the sake of convenience, and we shall use it in this chapter. Nevertheless, the reader should keep in mind that we are most likely dealing not with a single disorder but with a group of disorders, which differ widely not only in symptomatology but probably in etiology as well.

The Prevalence of Schizophrenia

Between 1 and 2 percent of people in the United States have had or will have a schizophrenic episode (Robins et al., 1984). At present, there are about a million actively schizophrenic people in the country (Berger, 1978). Such people occupy about half the beds in United States mental hospitals (President's Commission on Mental Health, 1978). And while many other schizophrenics have been released from the hospital—to smaller facilities or simply into the community—about half of those discharged for the first time return to the mental hospital within two years (Gunderson et al., 1974). Clearly, schizophrenia constitutes an enormous public health problem in our society.

The History of the Diagnostic Category

Though schizophrenia has probably been with us for thousands of years, it is only since the end of the nineteenth century that it has been recognized as a distinct disorder. The first identification of the disorder came in 1896, when Emil Kraepelin proposed that there were three major types of psychosis—manic-depressive psychosis, paranoia, and "dementia praecox." Syndromes that involved delusions, hallucinations, attention deficits, and bizarre motor behavior fell under the heading of dementia praecox (Latin for "premature mental deterioration"). Implied in the term was Kraepelin's belief that the illness normally began in adolescence (hence "premature") and that it involved an irreversible mental deterioration.

Kraepelin's description of the syndrome of dementia praecox has lasted, but the term he gave it did not. In 1911, Eugen Bleuler, a highly influential Swiss psychiatrist, pointed out that "dementia praecox" was actually a poor description of the patients it was supposed to describe. In the first place, the disorder was not always "premature"; many patients did not develop symptoms until well into their adult years. Second, most patients did not proceed to complete mental deterioration. Some remained the same year after year; others improved; others improved and relapsed. Thus, according to Bleuler, "dementia praecox" was a misnomer, and its inappropriateness was preventing psychiatrists from recognizing the disease entity in question. To solve this problem, Bleuler proposed a new term:

> I call the dementia praecox "schizophrenia" from the Greek words *schizein,* meaning "to split," and *phren,* meaning "mind" because the "splitting" of the different psychic functions is one of its most important characteristics. For the sake of convenience, I use the word in the singular although it is apparent that the group includes several diseases ([1911] 1950, p. 8).

Hence the term "schizophrenia," which has since become the commonly accepted label. Because of its association with "splitting," many people misunderstand the term as designating multiple or "split" personality, which, as we saw in Chapter 8, is another syndrome altogether—a dissociative disorder far rarer than schizophrenia. What Bleuler was referring to was *not* a splitting of the personality into two or more distinct personalities but rather a split or disconsonance among different psychic functions within a single personality. In the mind of the schizophrenic, emotions, ideas, and perceptions cease to operate as an integral whole. In a given situation, one set of ideas may dominate the person's behavior while other ideas, equally important for adaptive functioning in that particular situation, seem to have no importance. Furthermore, emotions may be split off from perception and thus seem very inappropriate to a given situation. This loss of integration has been vividly described by one former schizophrenic:

> I have experienced this process chiefly as a condition in which the integrating mental picture in my personality was taken away and smashed to bits, leaving me like agitated hamburger distributed infinitely throughout the universe (Mendel, 1976, p. 8).

Or, in the plainer words of Bleuler, "the personality loses its unity" ([1911] 1950, p. 9). The four fundamental symptoms of schizophrenia noted by Bleuler, along with four secondary symptoms, are described in the accompanying box.

The Symptoms of Schizophrenia

Although there is general agreement on the major symptoms of schizophrenia, some authorities disagree about which are the *fundamental* symptoms. Traditionally, schizophrenia has been regarded as a thought disorder, but as we have noted, the schizophrenic almost invariably manifests other abnormalities as well—in perception, mood, motor behavior, social relationships, orientation to the world in general. Which of these ruptures is primary and which secondary? Are interpersonal relations the fundamental problem, as some believe, or is the schizophrenic's social withdrawal a result of his or her communication problems—caused, in turn, by disrupted thought processes? If schizophrenic patients report that their thoughts are being radio-controlled by outsiders, is this delusion the fundamental problem, or is it just their way of explaining the chaos in their brains? Although *DSM-III-R* does not take a specific stand as to which symptoms are fundamental, it does emphasize the presence of delusions and hallucinations, stating that "at some phase of the illness Schizophrenia always involves delusions, hallucinations, or certain characteristic disturbances in affect and the form of thought" (p. 187). In addition, the disorder must have shown itself continuously for at least six months during some point of the person's life, and it must be accompanied by a disruption of functioning. *DSM-III-R*'s criteria for a diagnosis of schizophrenia are listed in the box on page 353.

In the following section we shall discuss the various symptoms of schizophrenia as separate categories. Keep in mind, however, that in real life they are not separate. Whatever the direction of causality, these various disturbances do undoubtedly influence one another. For example, if thought is disrupted, mood will also be disturbed; if mood is disturbed, one's relation to the external world will be disrupted. It should also be kept in mind that while all schizophrenics do display some of these symptoms some of the time, none display all of the symptoms all of the time. Indeed, some people labeled schizophrenic may behave normally much of the time.

Bleuler's "Four A's"

Many different criteria for diagnosing schizophrenia have been proposed. Eugen Bleuler, who gave the disorder its name, listed four fundamental characteristics, called the "four A's," and four secondary, or accessory, symptoms:

Fundamental Symptoms

1. *Association*—the patient shows evidence of a thought disorder, usually by the way he or she uses language.

2. *Affect*—the patient's emotional responses are blunted or inappropriate.

3. *Ambivalence*—the patient is indecisive and unable to carry on normal goal-directed activities.

4. *Autism*—the patient is withdrawn and self-absorbed.

Secondary Symptoms

1. *Hallucinations*

2. *Paranoid thinking*

3. *Grandiosity*

4. *Hostility and belligerence*

Other diagnosticians (e.g., Schneider, 1959) have emphasized hallucinations and delusions as the key symptoms. Recently interest in Bleuler's system has revived as a result of the findings that antipsychotic drugs have a marked effect on the "four A's" and only a moderate effect on Bleuler's secondary symptoms (see Chapter 15).

Disorders of Thought and Language

I'm a doctor, you know. . . . I don't have a diploma, but I'm a doctor. I'm glad to be a mental patient, because it taught me how to be humble. I use Cover Girl creamy natural makeup. Oral Roberts has been here to visit me. . . . This place is where *Mad* magazine is published. The Nixons make Noxon metal polish. When I was a little girl, I used to sit and tell stories to myself. When I was older, I turned off the sound on the TV set and made up dialogue to go with the shows I watched. . . . I'm a week pregnant. I have schizophrenia—cancer of the nerves. My body is overcrowded with nerves. This is going to win me the Nobel Prize for medicine. I don't consider myself schizophrenic anymore. There's no such thing as schizophrenia, there's only mental telepathy. I once had a friend named Camilla Costello. She was Abbott and Costello's daughter. . . . I'm in the Pentecostal Church, but I'm thinking of changing my religion. I have a dog at home. I love instant oatmeal. When

you have Jesus, you don't need a diet. Mick Jagger wants to marry me. I want to get out the revolving door. With Jesus Christ, anything is possible. I used to hit my mother. It was the hyperactivity from all the cookies I ate. I'm the personification of Casper the Friendly Ghost. I used to go outside asking the other kids to be my friend when I was little. California's the most beautiful state in the Union. I've been there once, by television. My name is Jack Warden, and I'm an actress (Sheehan, 1982, pp. 72–73).

As one expert has noted, "perhaps the single most striking feature about schizophrenics is their peculiar use of language" (Shapiro, 1981, p. 64). That peculiarity is evident in the above quotation of a schizophrenic woman's attempt at conversation in a hospital ward. The disordered language of schizophrenics, with its odd associations and rapid changes of subject, is presumably a clue to their disordered thought processes. Some writers, in discussing the disorder, have tried to distinguish between disturbances of thought and disturbances of language—or between disturbances in the content of thought and disturbances in language and communication—but such distinctions are possible only at a theoretical level. The fact remains that language is nothing if not the expression of thought. Conversely, our primary clue to thought is language. The two functions, then, are interdependent, and for this reason we shall consider them together.

DELUSIONS   A striking characteristic of schizophrenic thought is the presence of **delusions,** firmly held beliefs that have no basis in reality. Delusions may accompany a variety of psychological conditions—mania, depression, organic syndromes, drug overdose, and others. But they are extremely common among schizophrenics. In a sample of 405 schizophrenics, Lucas and his colleagues (1962) found that 71 percent were delusional.

How unshakable schizophrenic delusions can be was illustrated in an experiment conducted some years ago by the psychologist Milton Rokeach. In 1959 Rokeach had three men, each of whom claimed to be Jesus Christ, transferred to the same ward of a hospital in Ypsilanti, Michigan. The following is an excerpt from one of their first encounters:

> "Well, I know your psychology," Clyde said, "and you are a knick-knacker, and in your Catholic church in North Bradley and in your education, and I know all of it—the whole thing. I know exactly what this fellow does. In my credit like I do from up above, that's the way it works."
> "As I was stating before I was interrupted," Leon went on, "it so happens that I was the first human spirit to be created with a glorified body before time existed."
> "Ah, well, he is just simply a creature, that's all," Joseph put in. "Man created by me when I created the world—nothing else."
> —*Did you create Clyde, too?* Rokeach asked.
> "Uh-huh. Him and a good many others."
> At this, Clyde laughed (Rokeach, 1964, pp. 10–11).

Rokeach had the "three Christs" assigned to adjacent beds, a shared table in the dining hall, and similar jobs in the laundry room. He then observed them for two years in order "to explore the processes by which their delusional systems of belief and their behavior might change if they were confronted with the ultimate contradiction conceivable for human beings: more than one person claiming the same identity" (Rokeach, 1964, p. 3). After two years of continuous daily contact, each of the three men remained unmoved in his belief that he alone was Jesus Christ.

The content of schizophrenic delusions is as rich and diverse as the human imagination. However, delusions do tend to fall into certain recognized patterns:

1. *Delusions of persecution:* the belief that one is being plotted against, spied upon, threatened, interfered with, or otherwise mistreated, particularly by a number of parties joined in a conspiracy.

2. *Delusions of control* (also called *delusions of influence*): the belief that other people, forces, or perhaps extraterrestrial beings are controlling one's thoughts, feelings, and actions, often by means of electronic devices that send signals directly to one's brain.

3. *Delusions of reference:* the belief that events or stimuli unrelated to the individual are actually referring specifically to the patient. For example, patients may think that their lives are being depicted on television or in news stories (the case of Laura on pages 369–370 illustrates delusions of reference).

4. *Delusions of sin and guilt:* the belief that one has committed "the unpardonable sin" or inflicted great harm on others. Patients may claim, for example, that they have killed their children.

5. *Hypochrondriacal delusions:* the unfounded belief that one is suffering from a hideous physical disease. The hypochondriacal delusions of schizophrenics differ from the unfounded fears seen in hypochondriasis (Chapter 8) in that they refer not to recognized diseases but to bizarre afflictions. While hypochondriacs will complain of liver disease or brain tumors, for instance, schizophrenics will claim that their livers are being carried away in pieces or that their brains are full of mold.

6. *Nihilistic delusions:* the belief that oneself or others or the whole world has ceased to exist. The patient may claim, for example, that he or she is a spirit returned from the dead.

7. *Delusions of grandeur:* the belief that one is an extremely famous, powerful, and important person. Such delusions may crystallize into a stable delusional identity in which the person maintains that he or she is some renowned historical personage, such as Joan of Arc, Napoleon, or Christ.

Finally, many schizophrenics complain that their thoughts are being tampered with in some way. Such delusions, related to delusions of control, include:

1. *Thought broadcasting:* the belief that one's thoughts are being broadcast to the outside world, so that everyone can hear them.

2. *Thought insertion:* the belief that other people are inserting thoughts, especially obscene thoughts, into one's head.

3. *Thought withdrawal:* the belief that other people are removing thoughts from one's head.

These delusions, as noted earlier, may well represent the patients' effort to explain to themselves the chaotic condition of their thoughts. Many schizophrenics, for example, experience what is called **blocking;** in the middle of talking about something, they suddenly fall silent, with no recollection whatsoever of what they were talking about. This experience, presumably, is as disturbing to a schizophrenic as it would be to anyone else, and one way to explain it is to say that someone is stealing the thoughts out of one's head.

Occasionally it is difficult for the diagnostician to distinguish between what is delusional and what is real. And, no doubt, diagnostic mistakes do occur. Kraft and Babigian (1972) report the case of a woman, Mrs. M., who appeared one day in the hospital emergency room complaining that she had needles in both arms. Upon questioning, the woman revealed that she had spent a total of nine years in psychiatric hospitals. Each of her eight hospitalizations had been precipitated by an episode of self-multilation in which Mrs. M., obeying voices that told her that she was bad and that she should kill herself, had slashed her wrists, thighs, or abdomen. She also reported seven years of alcohol abuse. This history, along with the physical examination, which revealed no needle marks on her arms or any foreign bodies inside the arms, convinced the examining physicians that Mrs. M. was delusional. However, they were thorough enough to

order an X-ray and were very much surprised when it showed that the woman did indeed have a number of needles in both arms. Apparently, in a suicide attempt the year before, she had inserted several sewing needles in each arm, and the needles had remained undetected during three subsequent hospitalizations. It is probable that during these hospitalizations Mrs. M. reported the presence of the needles and that her reports were assumed to be delusional.

LOOSENING OF ASSOCIATIONS   As we saw earlier, it was for the quality of psychological "splitting"—a disconnection between different ideas or different mental functions—that Bleuler named the group of disorders in question schizophrenia. One of the clearest demonstrations of this splitting is the rambling, disjointed quality of schizophrenic speech. Normal speech tends to follow a single train of thought, with logical connections between ideas. In some schizophrenic speech, such connections are abandoned. Ideas jump from one track to another one that is indirectly related, or to one that is completely unrelated, with the result that the person wanders further and further away from the topic. When the problem is severe, speech may become completely incoherent.

We do not know exactly what mental processes cause this confusion in speech, but it is likely that the problem lies in the mind's way of dealing with associations. Although language is the best mirror of thought processes, it is by no means an exact copy of thought. In communicating with one another, people make many mental associations both to the statements of those they are speaking to and to their own statements. Before speaking, however, the person "edits" these associations, selecting the ones that are most relevant to the topic and discarding the others. In the schizophrenic mind, this selection process seems to break down, so that the speaker follows his or her own private train of associations without any editing for relevance.

This does not mean that schizophrenics cannot give a straight answer to a direct question. As Cohen and his co-workers (1974) have pointed out, schizophrenics can make very common primary associations to a given stimulus about as easily as normal people. It is the more subtle secondary associations that many schizophrenics cannot make without becoming confused and incoherent. This phenomenon was illustrated in an experiment conducted by Cohen and his colleagues. A group of normal subjects and a group of schizophrenics were shown two colored disks and

Diagnostic Criteria for a Schizophrenic Disorder

The following are the *DSM-III-R* criteria for the diagnosis of schizophrenia:

A. Characteristic psychotic symptoms of the active phase. Either (1), (2), or (3) [for at least one week (or less if symptoms successfully treated)]:

   (1) two of the following:
      (a) delusions
      (b) prominent hallucinations (throughout the day for several days or several times a week for several weeks, each hallucinatory experience not being limited to a few brief moments)
      (c) incoherence or marked loosening of associations
      (d) catatonic behavior
      (e) flat or grossly inappropriate affect
   (2) bizarre delusions (i.e., involving a phenomenon that the person's culture would regard as totally implausible, e.g., thought broadcasting, being controlled by a dead person)
   (3) prominent hallucinations [as defined in (1)(b) above] of a voice with content having no apparent relation to depression or elation, or a voice keeping up a running commentary on the person's behavior or thoughts, or two or more voices conversing with each other

B. During the course of the disturbance, functioning in such areas as work, social relations, and self-care is markedly below the highest level achieved prior to the disturbance (or when the onset is in childhood or adolescence, failure to achieve expected level of social development).

C. Major depressive or manic syndrome, if present during the active phase of the disturbance (symptoms in A), was brief relative to the duration of the disturbance.

D. Continuous signs of the disturbance for at least six months. The six-month period must include an active phase (of at least one week, or less if symptoms have been successfully treated) during which there were psychotic symptoms characteristic of Schizophrenia (symptoms in A), with or without a prodromal or residual phase, as defined below.

Prodromal phase: A clear deterioration in functioning before the active phase of the disturbance that is not due to a disturbance in mood or to a Psychoactive Substance Use Disorder and that involves at least two of the symptoms listed below.

Residual phase: Following the active phase of the disturbance, persistence of at least two of the symptoms noted below, these not being due to a disturbance in mood or to a Psychoactive Substance Use Disorder.

Prodromal or Residual Symptoms

   (1) marked social isolation or withdrawal
   (2) marked impairment in role functioning as wage-earner, student, or homemaker
   (3) markedly peculiar behavior (e.g., collecting garbage, talking to self in public, hoarding food)
   (4) marked impairment in personal hygiene and grooming
   (5) blunted or inappropriate affect
   (6) digressive, vague, overelaborate, or circumstantial speech, or poverty of speech, or poverty of content of speech
   (7) odd beliefs or magical thinking, influencing behavior and inconsistent with cultural norms, e.g., superstitiousness, belief in clairvoyance, telepathy, "sixth sense," "others can feel my feelings," overvalued ideas, ideas of reference
   (8) unusual perceptual experiences, e.g., recurrent illusions, sensing the presence of a force or person not actually present
   (9) marked lack of initiative, interests, or energy

Examples: Six months of prodromal symptoms with one week of symptoms from A; no prodromal symptoms with six months of symptoms from A; no prodromal symptoms with one week of symptoms from A and six months of residual symptoms.

E. Not due to any Organic Mental Disorder.

F. If a history of Autistic Disorder, the additional diagnosis of Schizophrenia is made only if prominent delusions or hallucinations are also present.

Source: Diagnostic and Statistic Manual of Mental Disorders, Third Edition (Revised). Washington, D.C.: American Psychiatric Association, 1987, pp. 194–195.

were asked to describe one of the colors in such a way that a listener who also had those two colors before him or her could pick out the one being described. When the colors were quite dissimilar, the schizophrenics did about as well as the normals. For example, when one color was red and the other a purple-blue and subjects were asked to describe the latter, responses were as follows:

> Normal Speaker 1: Purple.
>
> Normal Speaker 2: Purple.
>
> Normal Speaker 3: This is purple blue.
>
> Schizophrenic Speaker 1: Blue.
>
> Schizophrenic Speaker 2: Purple.
>
> Schizophrenic Speaker 3: The bluer.
>
> (Cohen et al., 1974, p. 11)

Thus when dealing with a clear difference between red and blue, the schizophrenics, like the normal subjects, could make the simple association between the visual stimulus of the purple-blue disk and the word used to describe that color.

In the next stage of the experiment, however, the two colors were quite similar, requiring that the speaker make subtle associations in order to describe the slight difference between the two. Faced with this task, the normal speakers managed to combine and refine their associations in such a way as to indicate which color they meant. The schizophrenics, on the other hand, began reeling off associations that, while quite vivid, failed to convey the appropriate information:

> Normal Speaker 1: Both are salmon colored. This one, however, has more pink.
>
> Normal Speaker 2: My God, this is hard. They are both about the same, except that this one might be a little redder.
>
> Normal Speaker 3: They both are either the color of canned salmon or clay. This one here is the pinker one.
>
> Schizophrenic Speaker 1: A fish swims. You call it a salmon. You cook it. You put it in a can. You open the can. You look at it in this color. Salmon fish.
>
> Schizophrenic Speaker 2: This is a stupid color of a shit ass bowl of salmon. Mix it with mayonnaise. Then it gets tasty. Leave it alone and puke all over the fuckin' place. Puke fish.
>
> Schizophrenic Speaker 3: Make-up. Pancake make-up. You put it on your face and they think guys run after you. Wait a second! I don't put it on my face and guys don't run after me. Girls put it on them.
>
> (Cohen et al., 1974, p. 11)

FIGURE 14.1
In this painting by a schizophrenic patient, the disjointed bodies and random, mixed phrases illustrate the incoherent and disordered associations of schizophrenic thought.

What is it that pushes schizophrenics off the track? Some investigators propose that once schizophrenics make a given association, they cannot let go of it, as normal people can, and search for a more appropriate association. They get "stuck" on the first association, and the remainder of the response is "chained" off that first association, without any concern for relevance to the topic at hand. In other words, schizophrenics are at the mercy of their associative processes. In the examples just given, for instance, all three of the schizophrenic speakers made a first association—salmon for the first two, pancake make-up for the third—but then, instead of refining it in order to differentiate between the two colors, they went off on trains of private associations to that first thought.

Other investigators have stressed similar causes. For example, Cromwell and Dokecki (1968) suggest that schizophrenics have difficulty "disattending to" a stimulus once it has caught their attention. Indeed, a number of researchers are now suggesting that the entire associational problem may be rooted in a collapse of the normal capacity for selective attention—a hypothesis that we will examine shortly.

Like delusions, associative problems are seen in other psychoses besides schizophrenia, and particularly in mania (Harrow et al., 1986). Indeed, one recent study (Andreasen and Grove, 1986) found that manic speech was even *more* likely than schizophrenic speech to show derailment (the thought gets off track), tangentiality (other thoughts come in "from left field"), incoherence, and illogicality. By contrast, schizophrenics were more likely either not to speak at all or to produce speech marked by poverty of content (as we shall see). In other words, while thought disorder is considered to be the fundamental symptom in schizophrenia, it is not confined to schizophrenia. (Likewise, while mood disorder is the fundamental symptom in mania, it is also seen in schizophrenics.)

POVERTY OF CONTENT   The result of loosened associations is that schizophrenic language may convey very little. Though the person may use many words, all grammatically correct, he or she nevertheless communicates poorly. This **poverty of content** may be seen in the following excerpt from a letter by a schizophrenic patient:

Dear Mother,
I am writing on paper. The pen which I am using is from a factory called "Perry & Co." This factory is in England. I assume this. Behind the name of Perry Co. the city of London is inscribed; but not the city. The city of London is in England. I know this from my school days. Then, I always liked geography. My last teacher in that subject was Professor August A. He was a man with black eyes. I also like black eyes. There are also blue and gray eyes and other sorts, too. I have heard it said that snakes have green eyes. All people have eyes. There are some, too, who are blind. These blind people are led about by a boy. It must be terrible not to be able to see. There are people who can't see and, in addition can't hear. I know some who hear too much. One can hear too much (Bleuler, [1911] 1950, p. 17).

Bleuler, who first published this letter, points out that the only common denominator of the ideas expressed in it is that they are all present in the patient's awareness: London—geography lesson—geography teacher—his black eyes—gray eyes—green snake eyes—human eyes—blind people—deaf people, and so on. The letter says much, and all very properly, but in terms of direct communication, it conveys almost nothing, for it lacks any unifying principle beyond the irresistible linkage of associations.

NEOLOGISMS   As we pointed out earlier, most researchers interpret the confused speech of schizophrenics as the product of confused thinking. However, some writers (e.g., Fish, 1957; Kleist, 1960) have suggested that certain peculiarities of schizophrenic language may result not from radical thought disturbances but merely from an inability to retrieve commonly agreed-upon verbal symbols. That is, what schizophrenics have to say may be reasonable enough; they simply cannot find the right words with which to say it.

This hypothesis might account for the rare appearance in schizophrenic speech of words and phrases not found in even the most comprehensive dictionary. These usages, called **neologisms** (literally "new words"), are sometimes formed by combining parts of two or more regular words. Or the neologism may involve the use of common words in a unique fashion. In either case, what is interesting about neologisms is that while sometimes they are totally unintelligible, at other times they manage to communicate ideas quite clearly and vividly, as may be seen in the following transcript. (Possible intended meanings are indicated in brackets.)

Dr.: Sally, you're not eating supper tonight. What's the problem?

Pt.: No, I had belly bad luck and brutal and outrageous. [I have stomach problems, and I don't feel good.] I gave all the work money. [I paid tokens for my meal.] Here, I work. Well, the difference is I work five days and when the word was [when I am told to work] but I had escapingly [I got out of some work]. I done it for Jones. He planned it and had me work and helped me work and all and had all the money. He's a tie-father. [He's a relative.] Besides generation ties and generation hangages [relationships between family generations—the way generations hang together] . . . he gave love a lot. I fit in them generations since old-fashion time [since long ago]. I was raised in packs [with other people] . . . certain times I was, since I was in littlehood [since I was a little girl] . . . she said she concerned a Sally-twin [my twin sister]. She blamed a few people with minor words [she scolded people], but she done goodship [good things]. I've had to suffer so much. I done it United States long.

Dr.: Sally, is there anything else you want to tell me before you go?

Pt.: Well, I expect there's a lot of things, but I would know what they were, especially the unkind crimery [the bad things].*

CLANGING   Another oddity sometimes found in the speech of schizophrenics (and, again, of manics as well) is **clanging,** the juxtaposition of words that have no relation to one another beyond the fact that they rhyme or sound alike. Clanging may be related to the associational problem discussed above. In this case, however, the basis for the associations is sound rather than sense. Hence clanging speech is often closer to nonsense verse than to rational communication.

The following is a transcript of a conversation between a doctor and a schizophrenic patient who was particularly adept at clanging. (About half of all his daily speech was rhymed.) As the transcript shows, clanging often involves neologisms:

Dr.: How are things going today, Ernest?

Pt.: Okay for a flump.

Dr.: What is a flump?

Pt.: A flump is a gump.

Dr.: That doesn't make any sense.

Pt.: Well, when you go to the next planet from the planet beyond the planet that landed on the danded and planded on the standed.

Dr.: Wait a minute. I didn't follow any of that.

Pt.: Well, when we was first bit on the slit on the rit and the man on the ran or the pan on the ban and the sand on the man and the pan on the ban on the can on the man on the fan on the pan. [All spoken very rhythmically, beginning slowly and building up to such a rapid pace that the words could no longer be understood.]

Dr.: What's all that hitting your head for . . . and waving your arms?

Pt.: That's to keep the boogers from eatin' the woogers.

WORD SALAD   In some cases, schizophrenic language seems to show a complete breakdown of the associational process, so that it becomes impossible for the listener to trace any links between successive words and phrases. This extreme situation is illustrated in the following statement, made by the same patient whose clanging we quoted above:

It's all over for a squab true tray and there ain't no music, there ain't no nothing besides my mother and my father who stand alone upon the Island of Capri where there is no ice, there is no nothing but changers, changers, changers. That comes like in first and last names, so that thing does. Well, it's my suitcase, sir. I've got to travel all the time to keep my energy alive.

Appropriately, this type of speech, in which words and phrases are combined in what appears to be a completely disorganized fashion, is referred to as **word salad.** Unlike neologisms, word salad betrays no effort to communicate. Nor does it appear to reflect a train of tangential associations, as when associations are merely loosened. Nor are the words even connected on the basis of sound, as in clanging. Word salad, then, is the ultimate in schizophrenic "splitting." Nothing is related to anything else, and therefore the message has no communicative value.

Disorders of Perception   There is considerable evidence that schizophrenics perceive the world differently from other people. In the first place, schizo-

---

* Unpublished case examples in this chapter are from the clinical files of Dr. Richard Hagen, Florida State University, Tallahassee, Florida.

phrenics consistently *report* perceptual abnormalities. In a comparative study of newly admitted schizophrenic and nonschizophrenic patients, Freedman and Chapman (1973) found that the schizophrenics reported a significantly greater number of changes in their perceptual functioning, including visual illusions, disturbingly acute auditory perception, inability to focus attention, difficulty in identifying people, and difficulty in understanding the speech of others. Schizophrenics have also reported olfactory changes, complaining that their own body odor is more pronounced and more unpleasant, that other people smell stronger, and that objects smell funny (Hoffer and Osmond, 1962).

Second, these reports are confirmed by standard laboratory perceptual tests, which indicate that schizophrenics do poorly on perceptual tasks such as size estimation (Strauss et al., 1974), time estimation (Johnson and Petzel, 1971; Petzel and Johnson, 1972), and **proprioceptive discrimination** (Ritzler and Rosenbaum, 1974)—that is, discrimination of the orientation of their bodies in space. Among the many perceptual oddities reported by schizophrenics, two are of special concern: the breakdown of selective attention and the experience of hallucinations.

BREAKDOWN OF SELECTIVE ATTENTION   As we noted earlier, there is some dispute over what is the *basic* pathology in schizophrenia—the one symptom from which the other symptoms arise—but a number of experts now believe that the answer has to do with attention (Maher, 1977; Maher and Maher, 1979). Normal people, without thinking about it, exercise selective attention. That is, they decide what they want to focus on in the environment and then concentrate on that, with the result that sensory data from the thing they are interested in register forcibly in the mind while extraneous data (the sound of the air conditioner in the classroom, the earrings on the student in the front row) are confined to the edge of consciousness.

The fact that schizophrenics seem unable to exercise this normal selection process was remarked upon by Kraepelin and Bleuler. Today, almost a century later, many researchers feel that this particular deficit may underlie most of the remainder of schizophrenic symptomatology. McGhie and Chapman, two major proponents of this hypothesis (1961), ask us to imagine what would happen in the mind if selective attention broke down:

Consciousness would be flooded with an undifferentiated mass of incoming sensory data, transmitted from the environment via the sense organs. To this involuntary tide of impressions there would be added the diverse internal images, and their associations, which would no longer be coordinated with incoming information. Perception would revert to the passive and involuntary assimilative process of early childhood, and, if the incoming flood were to carry on unchecked, it would gradually sweep away the stable constructs of a former reality (1961, p. 105).

In consequence, the individual would presumably see an altered world, make odd associations, produce bizarre speech, experience inappropriate emotions—and, it is easy to imagine, work out strange beliefs and strange behavior patterns as a defense against the sensory overload. In other words, the result would be what we call schizophrenia. Some of McGhie and Chapman's patients testify to their attention problems in simple and poignant terms:

Things are coming in too fast. I lose my grip of it and get lost. I am attending to everything at once and as a result I do not really attend to anything (p. 104).

My thoughts get all jumbled up. I start thinking or talking about something but I never get there. Instead I wander off in the wrong direction and get caught up with all sorts of different things that may be connected with the things I want to say but in a way I can't explain. People listening to me get more lost than I do (p. 108).

HALLUCINATIONS   Added to the perceptual problems of schizophrenics is the fact that many of them perceive things that are not there. Such perceptions, occurring in the absence of any appropriate external stimulus, are called **hallucinations.** Most of us are able, with varying degrees of vividness, to hear imagined voices, to form pictures "in the mind's eye," and even to re-create experiences of taste, touch, and smell in the absence of primary stimulation. But when we do so, we are aware (1) that we are controlling these sensory imaginings and (2) that they are products of the imagination rather than responses to actual external stimuli. Hallucinations, by contrast, are not conjured up or created at will; they occur spontaneously. Furthermore, while many schizophrenics do recognize that the voices they hear are "only in my head," many others are unsure as to

FIGURE 14.2
This drawing of a visual hallucination was made by a young schizophrenic woman while she was actually experiencing the hallucination. She reportedly saw herself "threatened on all sides by hideously grimacing heads of monsters, large birds and the like who wanted to tear her to bits." (Source: J. H. Plokker, *Artistic Self-Expression in Mental Disease: The Shattered Image of Schizophrenics.* I. Findlay, tr., The Netherlands: Mouton & Co., 1964, p. 170.)

whether their hallucinations are real or imagined, and a fair percentage—presumably the more severely psychotic (Buss, 1966)—are in fact convinced that their hallucinations are perceptions of objectively real events.

The common clinical observation is that auditory hallucinations are the most frequent, followed by visual hallucinations, followed by hallucinations involving the other senses.[*] These frequencies have been confirmed by research. For example, in one study of a random sample of one hundred schizophrenics, 50 percent reported auditory hallucinations, while only 9 percent reported visual hallucinations (Malitz et al., 1962).

Mintz and Alpert (1972) have offered an explanation for this pattern of frequencies. These writers point out that according to research, 10 percent of the normal population are able to experience vivid visual imagery, while 48 percent are able to experience vivid auditory imagery. These figures are very close to the percentages of schizophrenics who report visual

and auditory hallucinations—9 percent and 50 percent, respectively, according to the study cited above (Malitz et al., 1962). Hence the distribution of vivid imagery among the sensory modalities is the same for schizophrenics as for normal people. Accordingly, Mintz and Alpert have proposed that schizophrenics differ from normal people not in the fact that they have imagined sensory experiences or in the frequency or modality of those experiences, but simply in the inability to *distinguish* between those sensory experiences that are responses to actual external stimuli and those that are not. In short, schizophrenics have impaired reality testing. And thus we call their sensory imagery, which they mistake for objective reality, by a different name: "hallucinations."

Disorders of Mood   While schizophrenia is considered to be a disturbance primarily of thought, it often involves disturbances of mood as well. However, schizophrenic mood abnormalities differ from those of psychotic mood disorders in two important respects. First, as we saw in Chapter 10, the mood disorders involve either deep depression or manic elation, or an alternation between the two; in schizophrenia, on the other hand, what we usually see is either a lack of affect or affect that is inappropriate

---

[*] The type of hallucination affects the diagnosis. Visual hallucinations suggest organic psychosis, particularly toxic psychosis (Chapter 16) or alcoholism (Chapter 12). Olfactory hallucinations sometimes occur in epilepsy.

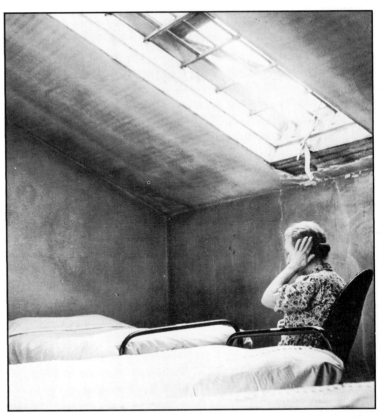

Hallucinations, especially auditory ones in which they "hear voices," are a common perceptual problem of schizophrenics. (Jerry Cooke/Photo Researchers)

to the immediate context.* Second, whereas the mood disorders may involve sudden and extreme reversals of affect, the schizophrenic is unlikely to undergo sustained mood shifts.

Two types of mood abnormality are commonly seen in schizophrenics. One is a reduced emotional responsiveness, known as **blunted affect** or **flat affect,** depending on the degree of apathy. Patients with blunted affect show little emotion. Those with flat affect show no emotion; their faces remain expressionless, their voices monotonous, regardless of what they are saying or what is going on around them. Second, many schizophrenics display **inappropriate affect;** in other words, their emotional responses seem totally unsuitable to the immediate context. For example, a patient may giggle while relating a painful childhood memory or begin yelling angrily when given a present.

Disorders of Motor Behavior   The variety of unusual behaviors manifested by schizophrenics seems limited only by the boundaries of behavior itself. The following portrait of a schizophrenic ward shows a typical mix of behaviors that might be observed daily in hundreds of schizophrenic wards throughout the country.

> In the day room Lou stands hour after hour, never saying a word, just rubbing the palm of his hand around and around on the top of his head. Jerry spends his day rubbing his hand against his stomach and running around a post at the same time. Helen paces back and forth, her head down, mumbling about enemies who are coming to get her, while Vic grimaces and giggles over in the corner. Virginia stands in the center of the day room

---

* Some people, however, do have either a manic or a major depressive episode while at the same time showing the symptoms of schizophrenia. This intermediate syndrome is called **schizoaffective disorder** and has an intermediate prognosis. That is, schizoaffective patients fare somewhat better than schizophrenics, on the average, and somewhat worse than mood-disorder patients (Harrow and Grossman, 1984).

vigorously slapping her hand against the fullness of her dress, making a rhythmical smacking sound which, because of its tireless repetition, goes unnoticed. Nick tears up magazines, puts bits of paper in his mouth, and then spits them out, while Bill sits immobile for hours, staring at the floor. Betty masturbates quietly on the couch, while Paul follows one of the young nurse's aides on her room check, hoping to get a chance to see up her dress as she leans over to smooth a bed. Geraldine is reading her Bible; Lillian is watching television; and Frank is hard at work scrubbing the floor.

In some cases, such as the last three in this example, schizophrenic motor behavior appears perfectly normal. In other cases, such as those of Betty and Paul, it is abnormal only insofar as it is inappropriate to the setting. However, certain repetitive motor behaviors, such as the head-rubbing, dress-smacking, and paper-tearing in the above case, are clearly abnormal. The act of engaging in purposeless actions repetitively for hours is called **stereotypy.**

Schizophrenics sometimes show frenetically high levels of motor activity, running about, thrashing their arms, upsetting furniture, and generally expending a good deal of energy. Much more common, however, is the opposite: marked inactivity. In the extreme case, schizophrenics may lapse into a catatonic stupor, not moving or speaking for days on end. (Catatonic behavior will be discussed later in this chapter.)

Social Withdrawal   As we shall see, an early sign of schizophrenia is emotional detachment—a lack of attention to or interest in the goings-on of the external world. Preoccupied with their own thoughts, schizophrenics gradually withdraw from involvement with the environment. Above all, they withdraw from in-

FIGURE 14.3
Paintings by schizophrenic patients that suggest the disturbance of affect and sense of self that are often present with the disorder. (Top) A painting done by a young schizophrenic man in the early stages of the disorder. The sad, partially faceless woman alone in the desert suggests his loss of identity and the pain of social withdrawal. (Middle) A schizophrenic's painting of the earth being split apart by lightning—perhaps the patient's effort to picture his internal disintegration. (Bottom) The partly hidden ghostlike figure painted by this patient suggests depersonalization and loss of identity.

volvement with other people. Note that in spite of the wide range of behaviors, both usual and unusual, taking place on the ward described above, there is one behavior that is strikingly absent: interpersonal interaction. Rarely do schizophrenic patients engage in small talk. Rarely do they address one another except to ask for a cigarette or a light. Usually they act as if the others did not exist.

Social withdrawal is particularly marked in the chronic schizophrenic, the type of patient in the ward described above. Duke and Mullins (1973), for example, found that chronic schizophrenics preferred greater interpersonal distance—that is, more space between themselves and the person standing or sitting next to them—than either nonschizophrenic psychiatric patients or a group of normal people. Other investigators have found that schizophrenics tend to look at other people less than do normal people (Rutter, 1973; Rutter and Stephenson, 1972) and tend to avoid the gaze of anyone looking directly at them (Harris, 1968).

Recall our earlier discussion of the schizophrenic's breakdown in selective attention and consequent sensory overload. Could it be that in avoiding the gaze of others, schizophrenics are not specifically fending off social attentions but simply trying to reduce their sensory load in general? To answer this question, one investigator compared the amount of time three different groups of subjects—schizophrenics, nonschizophrenic psychiatric patients, and normal people—spent looking either at a television program or at a person who was trying to engage them in conversation and was looking directly at them. No differences were found between the normal people and the nonschizophrenic patients. The schizophrenics, in comparison, spent considerably less time looking at the person and considerably more time looking at the television program (Williams, 1974). Thus it seems that schizophrenic gaze avoidance is in fact "person avoidance" and not just "stimulus avoidance."

This does not mean, however, that the social withdrawal of schizophrenics is unrelated to their attentional problems. Actually, the two are probably intimately related. The mental havoc that presumably results from the attention deficit would make communication very difficult, and as we have seen, schizophrenics communicate poorly. One does not have to make oneself understood to a television set; to a human being, one does. Therefore schizophrenics, knowing from experience that people tend not to understand them—indeed, may treat them very curtly

or abusively—may favor the television set or anything other than another human being.

Other Symptoms   In addition to the symptoms described above, two others are often seen in schizophrenia: *disturbance in the sense of self* and *lack of volition.* These problems are associated with the withdrawal just mentioned. Many schizophrenics, though apparently self-preoccupied, seem at the same time uncertain as to who they are, and they may dwell on this question. In addition, schizophrenics typically show a disturbance in volition, sometimes lapsing into complete inactivity. They lack the interest or drive to engage in normal goal-directed activities (putting their clothes on properly, completing a chore), and instead, if they are active, often engage in the bizarre motor behavior described earlier.

The frightening world of the schizophrenic is vividly described in the box on page 364.

The Course of Schizophrenia

Like some other psychological disorders, schizophrenia seems to follow a regular course, or progression of stages, through time. The course of the disorder has traditionally been divided into three phases.

The Prodromal Phase   The onset of schizophrenia usually occurs during adolescence or early adulthood. In some cases, it is very sudden. In a matter of days, the individual is transformed from a reasonably well-adjusted person into a hallucinating psychotic. In other cases, there is a slow, insidious deterioration of functioning that may go on for years before any clearly psychotic symptoms appear. This gradual downhill slide is known as the **prodromal phase.**

During the prodromal phase, incipient schizophrenics generally become withdrawn and socially isolated. Often they cease to care about their appearance or hygiene, forgetting to bathe, sleeping in their clothes, and so on. Performance in school or at work begins to deteriorate; the person shows up late, if at all, and seems careless and inattentive. At the same time, the person's emotions begin to seem shallow and inappropriate. Eventually family and friends (by this time, former friends) will note a change in personality. Sometimes, however, the disorder proceeds so gradually that it is not remarked upon until the person

Lack of interest in the external world—especially in social contact with other people—is one of the early manifestations of schizophrenia. (David E. Kennedy/Texa-Stock)

begins dressing in odd ways, collecting garbage, talking to himself or herself, or engaging in some other unmistakably bizarre behavior. By this time the person may be entering the active phase.

The Active Phase   In the **active phase,** the patient begins showing prominent psychotic symptoms—hallucinations, delusions, disorganized speech, severe withdrawal, and so forth. The symptoms outlined earlier in this chapter describe the active phase of schizophrenia. As we noted, however, no one patient is likely to show all of those symptoms.

The Residual Phase   Just as onset may occur almost overnight, so may recovery—or "complete remission," as it is known in the schizophrenia literature. Ordinarily, however, what recovery there is is gradual. In most patients, the active phase is followed by a **residual phase,** in which behavior is similar to that seen during the prodromal phase. Blunted or flat affect is especially common in this period. Speech may still ramble, hygiene may still be wanting, and

though outright hallucinations and delusions may have dissipated, the person may still have unusual perceptual experiences and odd ideas, claiming, for example, to be able to tell the future or to control events through magical thinking. In consequence, running a household or holding down a job would still be difficult for most schizophrenics in the residual phase.

In some cases, the residual phase ends with a return to completely normal functioning. This outcome, unfortunately, is not common. Many patients remain impaired to some degree, and many go on to have further psychotic (i.e., active-phase) episodes, with increasingly impaired functioning between episodes. An extensive long-term follow-up study of more than 1,000 schizophrenics by Manfred Bleuler (1978)—the son of Eugen Bleuler—found that approximately 10 percent of the schizophrenics remained so for the rest of their lives, 25 percent returned to and maintained normal functioning, and 50 to 65 percent alternated between the residual phase and a recurrence of an active phase. Other long-term studies have produced similar findings (Ciompi, 1980; Vaillant, 1978). Interestingly, a large international study sponsored by the World Health Organization suggests that course and prognosis vary from country to country. Charting the progress of 1,202 psychotic patients, most of them schizophrenic, in eight countries, the researchers found that it was in the developing countries—Nigeria, India, Colombia—that psychotic episodes were briefest and long-term prognosis most positive; in the more industrialized countries—the United States, the United Kingdom, the USSR, Denmark, and Czechoslovakia—long-term outcomes were poorer (Sartorius et al., 1978).

The Dimensions of Schizophrenia

Early research in schizophrenia simply compared groups of undifferentiated schizophrenics with groups of normal people. But these studies found that the schizophrenic groups were far too heterogeneous for the purposes of certain kinds of research. Hence investigators began searching for dimensions along which more homogeneous subgroups of schizophrenics could be formed. Among the dimensions of schizophrenia that have since been proposed, the three that have received the most attention are the process-reactive dimension, the positive-negative symptoms dimension, and the paranoid-nonparanoid dimension.

The Process-Reactive or Good-Poor Premorbid Dimension   As we noted, there is considerable variation in the onset of schizophrenia. Some patients go through an extended prodromal phase. Others seem to have no prodromal phase at all; almost overnight, they go from normal functioning to full-blown psychosis. This dimension of variation has traditionally been known as the **process-reactive dimension.** Those cases in which onset is gradual are called **process schizophrenia;** those in which onset is sudden and apparently precipitated by some traumatic event are called **reactive schizophrenia.**

This dimension has a long history, beginning with Kraepelin and Eugen Bleuler. These two theorists believed that the onset of the psychoses provided a good clue to their etiology. The biogenic psychoses, since they were the result of some abnormal physiological *process,* would presumably have a gradual onset over a long period of time. The functional psychoses, since they were *reactions* to traumatic experiences, would be sudden in onset. Hence the terms "process" and "reactive." Today many researchers view the

process-reactive dimension more as a continuum than as a dichotomy. Indeed, some now prefer to avoid the terms "process" and "reactive" altogether and to classify patients instead on the basis of *good versus poor premorbid adjustment*—that is, on the basis of their adjustment before the onset of the active phase. In practice, this dimension is much the same as the process-reactive dimension, minus the etiological connotations. To describe onset is to describe premorbid adjustment, and vice versa.

Although there is some disagreement over the usefulness of the process-reactive dimension, there is fairly general agreement on what the terms describe. The process (or poor-premorbid) case typically involves a long history of inadequate social, sexual, and occupational adjustment. Process schizophrenics typically did not belong to a group of friends in school, did not date regularly during adolescence, did not continue their education after high school, never held a job for longer than two years, and never married (Kantor et al., 1953; Ullmann and Krasner, 1975). Furthermore, there appears to have been no precipitating event—no sudden change such as a divorce or the loss of a job—immediately preceding the active phase. Rather, what the history usually reveals is a gradual eclipse of thoughts, interests, emotions, and activities, until at last the person becomes so withdrawn that he or she is hospitalized.

In contrast, histories of reactive (or good-premorbid) schizophrenics are apparently normal. The patient fitted in at home and at school, had friends, dated, and got along well in general. The onset of the schizophrenic symptoms usually occurs after a clear precipitating event and is sudden and spectacular, often involving hallucinations and delusions. Such patients also tend to show extreme panic and confusion, for they are as surprised and horrified as anyone else over what has happened to them.

Premorbid adjustment has been useful in predicting which patients will recover and which will not (Garmezy, 1970). Poor-premorbid schizophrenics are more likely to have longer hospitalizations and are less likely to be discharged than good-premorbid patients. It is this factor that allows the terms "chronic" and "acute" to be used, for all practical purposes, almost interchangeably with "poor premorbid" and "good premorbid" (or "process" and "reactive"). As the terms are generally defined, *chronic* refers to patients who have long-standing severe deficits. Often such patients are hospitalized for years. *Acute* usually

"I Feel Like I Am Trapped inside My Head, Banging Desperately against Its Walls"

The following first-person account of schizophrenia, written by a young woman during a lucid interval, suggests some of the problems characteristic of this disorder:

Can I ever forget that I am schizophrenic? I am a ghost within myself, a spirit no one knows. Long ago when they locked us up forever, perhaps they were not so wrong. What good is physical freedom if the human feelings are trapped, unable to escape? . . .

The most wearing aspect of schizophrenia is the fierce battle that goes on inside my head in which conflicts become irresolvable. I am so ambivalent that my mind can divide on a subject, and those two parts subdivide over and over until my mind feels like it is in pieces, and I am totally disorganized. At other times, I feel like I am trapped inside my head, banging against its walls, trying desperately to escape while my lips can utter only nonsense. . . .

Recently, my mind has played tricks on me, creating The People inside my head who sometimes come out to haunt me and torment me. They surround me in rooms, hide behind trees and under the snow outside. They taunt me and scream at me and devise plans to break my spirit. The voices come and go, but The People are always there, always real.

Life for most schizophrenics is a nightmare full of fears and doubts about oneself and about reality; they have a distorted view of that most profound question of how they relate to the world around them. Boundaries become unclear and other people are frightening and not to be trusted. Thus, the very thing which could bring relief—closeness to other people—is shunned as something horrible and dangerous. . . .

Living day to day is a challenge because it is just simply *hard* for schizophrenics to live in a world that is so troublesome to them. My fears are so intense that before I do most things I must pass through a "wall of terror" that stands between myself and my goal. Leaving the house, talking to someone, or taking a walk can create panic, simply because I do not feel like part of the world. It is a foreign place to me. Since my childhood I have felt like an outsider looking in.

Schizophrenia is not just an illness, it is a way of life, and it is a life constantly disrupted by symptoms. . . .

In my experience, the best source of relief is other people who are sensitive enough to understand me and patient enough to help me through my times of unreality. . . .

refers to patients who are in the midst of the short-term active phase of their first schizophrenic episode.

The Positive-Negative Symptoms Dimension The good-poor premorbid dimension seems to parallel another dimension, that of positive versus negative symptoms. **Positive symptoms,** characterized by the presence of something, include hallucinations, delusions, bizarre or disorganized behavior, and positive thought disorder such as incoherence.

Negative symptoms, characterized by the absence of something, include poverty of speech, flat affect, withdrawal, apathy, and attentional impairment (Andreasen and Olsen, 1982; Strauss et al., 1974). Patients with negative symptoms are more likely to have had poor-premorbid adjustment, longer hospitalization, and more cognitive dysfunction (Andreasen and Olsen, 1982).

These findings have led to increased speculation that there may be two biologically distinct types of schizophrenia, of which the one with negative symptoms is more like Kraepelin's original dementia prae-cox. One team of researchers (Crow et al., 1982) has distinguished two such types: Type I, which is characterized by positive symptoms, tends to respond to medication, whereas Type II, characterized by negative symptoms (and associated with enlarged brain ventricles), does not respond to medication. The "dopamine hypothesis," a biochemical theory of schizophrenia that will be discussed in Chapter 15, seems to apply only to Type I patients (Haracz, 1982).

Other research has linked sex differences to these dimensions of schizophrenia (Lewine, 1981). It has been found that onset of schizophrenia and hospitalization tend to occur earlier in men than in women. Men are most at risk under the age of twenty-five; women are most at risk over the age of twenty-five. Men are also more likely to be withdrawn and to exhibit negative symptoms; women are more likely to have affective and positive symptoms. In addition, men have generally poorer premorbid adjustment than do women. These findings suggest that men and women may be differentially at risk for different types of schizophrenia, with men more susceptible to process, poor-premorbid, Type II schizophrenia and women more susceptible to reactive, good-premorbid, Type I schizophrenia.

The Paranoid-Nonparanoid Dimension   Like the process-reactive dimension, the **paranoid-nonparanoid dimension** has been used by investigators to reduce the wide variety of schizophrenic symptomatologies by sorting them into manageable subgroups. On this dimension the criterion of classification is the presence (paranoid) or absence (nonparanoid) of delusions of persecution and/or grandeur. Although some studies have found the paranoid-nonparanoid dimension to be independent of the process-reactive dimension (e.g., Johannsen et al., 1963; Zigler and Levine, 1973), other studies have presented evidence of a relationship between the two dimensions. Buss, for instance, points out that in general, paranoid schizophrenics, like reactive schizophrenics, "are more intact intellectually, perform better in a variety of tasks, and have a higher level of maturity" (1966, p. 230). Not surprisingly, in view of these findings, the first hospitalization is later (Zigler and Levine, 1981), the length of hospitalization is briefer, and the number of rehospitalizations fewer for paranoid schizophrenics (Strauss, 1973). Thus the paranoid-nonparanoid dimension, like the process-re-

active, the good-poor premorbid, and the positive-negative symptoms, has had prognostic value and may aid in the development of theories about etiology. (Paranoid schizophrenia will be discussed more fully in the following section.)

The Subtypes of Schizophrenia

Ever since the days of Kraepelin and Eugen Bleuler, schizophrenia has been divided into subtypes. Patients were described not merely as schizophrenic but as catatonic schizophrenics, paranoid schizophrenics, and so forth. These subtypes are often problematic for the diagnostician, for although they are based on behavioral signs, such signs may change from week to week. If, upon intake, a patient with other schizophrenic features claims that he is an eminent person bedeviled by enemies, he will probably be classified as paranoid schizophrenic. But if, two weeks later, he no longer speaks of the enemies but will not move from his chair, should he be reclassified as a catatonic schizophrenic?

Despite the difficulties, subtype diagnoses may ultimately be of great value. As we saw in Chapter 7, the process of sorting patients into relatively restrictive diagnostic groups is essential to research. Though at present we do not know whether different schizophrenic symptomatologies issue from different causes and call for different treatments, we can never find out unless we study groups of patients with similar symptomatologies. And this means sorting them into subtypes.

DSM-III-R lists five subtypes. One of these, the "undifferentiated" type, is a miscellaneous category, used for patients who do not fit into any of the other categories or who fit into more than one. Since many patients have aspects of more than one subtype, undifferentiated schizophrenia is a commonly employed diagnosis. A second category, the "residual" type, is for patients who have passed beyond the active phase. This leaves three categories that actually describe active-phase symptomatology: disorganized, catatonic, and paranoid schizophrenia.

Disorganized Schizophrenia   What *DSM-III-R* now calls **disorganized schizophrenia** has traditionally been known as **hebephrenic schizophrenia.** "Hebephrenic" comes from the name of the Greek goddess of youth, Hebe, and the reference is to the childish behaviors typical of this subtype. Gig-

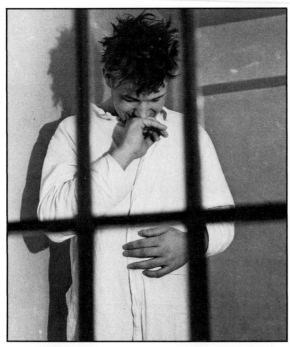

Disturbance of affect is illustrated by this young man, who constantly laughs and giggles. Such inappropriate affect is characteristic of individuals who are diagnosed as disorganized schizophrenics. (Benyas Kaufman/Black Star)

gling wildly, making funny faces, and assuming absurd postures, the disorganized schizophrenic often resembles nothing so much as a normally silly seven-year-old boy trying to get a rise out of his parents. Even neologisms, so often a part of the hebephrenic's speech, are typical of young children's attempts to express themselves.

According to *DSM-III-R* two symptoms are especially characteristic of disorganized schizophrenia. First is a pronounced incoherence of speech; it is the disorganized schizophrenic, for example, who is most likely to produce neologisms, clang associations, and word salad. Second is disturbed affect, usually in the form of inappropriate giggling and constant silliness. Though these two symptoms may define the subtype, most disorganized schizophrenics run the gamut of the symptoms described earlier in this chapter as characteristic of schizophrenia in general. Their motor behavior is strikingly odd. Disorders of thought and perception are prominent, including delusions and

hallucinations which often focus on sex, religion, persecution, or bodily harm but which are not organized around a single theme, as are genuinely paranoid imaginings. Furthermore, most disorganized schizophrenics are severely withdrawn, utterly caught up in their own private worlds, and at times almost impervious to whatever is happening around them. With this wide array of bizarre characteristics, the disorganized schizophrenic, of all the varieties of the psychologically disturbed, is the one who best fits the popular stereotype of a "crazy" person.

Despite their apparent retreat from reality, many disorganized schizophrenics have a certain knowing quality about them and tend to perform their antics only for carefully chosen audiences. For example, the word salad and clang associations quoted earlier in this chapter were produced by a disorganized schizophrenic who would perform these verbal antics only if an attentive staff member was nearby. Furthermore, it was obvious to anyone listening to him that the patient took real pride in the speed and facility with which he could pour forth his gibberish. There are also other indications that disorganized schizophrenics are often keenly aware of what is going on around them. White and Watt (1973) report that when a young psychiatrist decided to live for two weeks as a patient in a schizophrenic ward, his play-acting was quickly detected by a disorganized patient, who at the end of the doctor's second day on the ward "came over to the doctor, put his hand protectively on his shoulder and confided with mock earnestness, 'You know, Doc, I think you're much better already.'"

The onset of disorganized schizophrenia is usually gradual and tends to occur at a relatively early age. The distinguishing mark of the onset—withdrawal into a realm of bizarre and childlike fantasies—is illustrated in the following case:

> Doris, Sam's wife, reported that she was bothered by his behavior at times but she attributed it to the pressure of business. . . . As Doris said, "What hurt me most was the feeling I began to get more and more of the time that I was losing contact with him. It was as if he were drifting away from me and I didn't know what to do about it. I would talk to him for a while, but when I looked at him, I would realize he wasn't listening. He was off somewhere lost in thought and never heard a word I said. Then he began to do scary and creepy things. I would wake up in the middle of the night and he would be gone. Once I found him sitting on the grass in the middle of the backyard at 4:00 A.M. and he didn't

seem to know where he was or what was going on. He was confused, but he was all right the next day and never mentioned what had happened the night before. . . ."

About three weeks later, Sam was arrested at 3:00 A.M. in a small town about 40 miles from where he lived. The police report said that he was driving through town at nearly 85 miles an hour when he was stopped and that he told the arresting officers that he was trying to "get up escape velocity for a trip to Mars." . . .

Some of the ideas Sam spoke about freely to doctors and fellow patients were extremely bizarre. At one time he was convinced he was Robin Hood, for example. He had not notified anyone of this sudden shift in his identity and it was discovered only [after] he leaped from a perch atop a door and landed on the back of an unsuspecting attendant who had just entered the room (McNeil, 1970, p. 98).

It should not be assumed, however, that the fantasy life of disorganized schizophrenics is playful fun. Along with Robin Hood, a number of grim horrors people the private worlds of these patients. Enemies stalk them through the night, and voices accuse them of sexual crimes. McNeil, who reported the case of Sam, has commented on this darker aspect of the disorganized schizophrenic's imaginings:

There is no exact replica of a hebephrenic experience in normal existence. Probably the closest match is the occasional bizarre, frightening, nonsensical nightmare that sometimes awakens us in a cold sweat in the dark of night. In a nightmare we are entangled in delusions, hallucinations, and distorted logic. But we wake up to a rational, ordered life. The hebephrenic is caught in a nightmare from which he may never awaken (1970, p. 99).

Catatonic Schizophrenia

There was no family history of mental illness in the case of F. C. He had been an average scholar but introspective and solitary at school, with no liking for games and no hobbies. He became a millworker at the age of 15 and was "more a boy for home, never keen on girls." He served in the Army during the Second World War and had some sort of transient mental breakdown, of which no records are available. After demobilization he was idle for six months; he appeared depressed and mixed up,

seemed to take no interest in things around him and did not even respond to questioning. Then he had a job for six months, but was dismissed and again hung around the house, making no attempt to seek further employment. Thereafter he became even more dull and apathetic, looked vacant and faraway, refused to get out of bed or take food. He declared that . . . some unknown individual was "making him think about things," and that he himself was a "riddle of bones." In the year following his demobilization from the Army he was admitted to a mental hospital, aged 23 years.

In hospital at first he lay in bed with an occasional vacant smile, and refused food. . . . He complained of hearing buzzing noises, sounds like someone squealing, and voices which he could sometimes understand but whose messages he could not remember, and he described flashes of light and shadows in the middle of the room. He expressed the belief that the doctors and nurses could manipulate their shadows, and that there was another person in his bed. Often he could not be engaged in conversation, sat vacantly by the hour and had both to be taken to his meals and pressed to eat. At times he was incontinent, chewed the end of his tie and hoarded rubbish. For weeks on end he would be in a state of stupor or near to it. . . . Then a period of excitement would intervene, when for days or weeks on end he would be hyperactive and talk a great deal in a disjointed and usually incoherent way. At these times he would strike out impulsively at the nursing staff. On occasion he clowned in a crude way and would walk on his hands (Henderson and Gillespie, 1969, pp. 278–279).

This patient was diagnosed as catatonic primarily on the basis of what might be called his nonbehavior—the slowing down of motion and eventual cessation of all adaptive responses. Once a common disorder but now quite rare (Morrison, 1974), **catatonic schizophrenia** has as its distinguishing feature a marked disturbance in motor behavior. Sometimes this disturbance takes the form of **catatonic stupor,** or complete immobility, usually accompanied by **mutism,** the cessation of speech; the patient may remain in this condition for weeks, as in the case just described. Some catatonics assume extremely bizarre postures during their stupors—a phenomenon known as **catatonic posturing.** They may also show **waxy flexibility,** a condition in which their limbs, like those of a rubber doll, can be moved around and "arranged" by another person and will remain in whatever position is imposed. However, catatonia is not limited to de-

Disturbances in motor behavior are prominent symptoms in catatonic schizophrenia. Patients may cease to move altogether, sometimes taking on bizarre postures. (Lawrence Frank)

his already anxiety-ridden and dangerous situation" (1970, p. 100). Whatever the psychological basis, it should be kept in mind that an extraordinary expenditure of energy is required to hold for hours the bizarre postures that catatonics often assume.

Furthermore, although catatonics, in their statue-like poses, seem utterly cut off from reality, this too may be deceptive. As with the disorganized schizophrenic, there are indications that catatonics may be well aware of what is going on around them. For example, many patients show what is called **catatonic negativism;** that is, they not only will refuse to do what is requested of them but will consistently do just the opposite, indicating that they understand very well the nature of the requests.

Paranoid Schizophrenia   Though Kraepelin's term "dementia praecox" lasted only briefly, his descriptions of various aspects of the disorder continue to prove remarkably accurate. The following description of **paranoid schizophrenia,** written by Kraepelin more than three-quarters of a century ago, dramatically captures the most prominent features of the disorder.

> The patients . . . divulge a *host of delusions,* almost entirely of persecution; people are watching them, intriguing against them, they are not wanted at home, former friends are talking about them and trying to injure their reputation. These delusions are changeable and soon become *fantastic.* The patients claim that some extreme punishment has been inflicted upon them, they have been shot down into the earth, have been transformed into spirits, and must undergo all sorts of torture. Their intestines have been removed by enemies and are being replaced a little at a time; their own heads have been removed, their throats occluded, and the blood no longer circulates. They are transformed into stones, their countenances are completely altered. . . .
>
> *Hallucinations,* especially of hearing, are very prominent during this stage; fellow-men jeer at them, call them bastards, threaten them, accuse them of horrible crimes. . . . Occasionally faces and forms are seen at night, or a crowd of men throwing stones at the window. . . .
>
> The *emotional attitude* soon changes and becomes more and more exalted. At the same time the delusions become less repressive and more expansive and fantastic. The patient, in spite of persecution, is happy and contented, extravagant and talkative, and boasts that he has been

creases in motor activity. Many catatonics alternate between periods of immobility and periods of frenzied motor activity, which may include violent behavior. (This, too, is illustrated in the case above.) In either form, catatonic schizophrenia often involves medical emergencies. When excited, patients may injure themselves or others; when stuporous, they must be prevented from starving.

Though catatonic immobility suggests passivity, it may in fact be quite "active" and willful. While some patients take on waxy flexibility, others become quite rigid and strenuously resist any effort on the part of others to move their limbs—a feature known as **catatonic rigidity.** McNeil suggests that this ironclad immobility is a response to some subjectively perceived threat, "as if the catatonic fears making a voluntary or willful mistake that would further jeopardize

transformed into the Christ; others will ascend to heaven, have lived many lives, and traversed the universe. They have the talent of poets, have been nominated for President, and have represented the government at foreign courts. The delusions may become most florid, foolish, and ridiculous. A patient may say that he is a star, that all light and darkness emanate from him; that he is the greatest inventor ever born, can create mountains, is endowed with all the attributes of God, can prophesy for coming ages, can talk to the people in Mars; indeed, is unlike anything that has ever existed (1902, pp. 257–258).

The defining characteristics of paranoid schizophrenia are delusions and/or hallucinations of a relatively consistent nature, often related to the themes of persecution and grandeur. The delusions can range from a jumble of vague suspicions to an exquisitely worked-out system of imagined conspiracies. In either case, they are often accompanied by hallucinations—especially auditory hallucinations—supporting the delusional belief. When, in the classic case, the theme is persecution, it is often combined with the theme of grandeur. Thus, as Kraepelin notes, patients may claim immense power, wisdom, and genius. Or, in extreme cases, they may adopt a permanent delusional identity with some famous figure, such as Napoleon or, as we have seen, Christ.*

Paranoid schizophrenia is far more common than either the disorganized or catatonic types. A 1974 survey of more than 8,000 hospitalized schizophrenics found that close to half were diagnosed as paranoid (Guggenheim and Babigian, 1974). Though the active

FIGURE 14.4
This drawing was done by a man diagnosed as suffering from paranoid schizophrenia. Eyes are prominent in the picture, as is a figure watching over the shoulder. The torso of the central figure is surrounded by hands, and the figure in the background is reaching out. Religiosity as well as delusions of persecution and grandeur may be seen in the Christlike figure bestowing a wreath.

---

* Stable delusional identities are apparently rare, however, and contrary to the popular stereotype, they are not necessarily of the magnitude of Christ or Napoleon. When Rokeach was planning the experiment described earlier in this chapter, he did a survey of all the state hospitals in Michigan in an effort to find two or more patients with the same delusional identity. It turned out that he had little to choose from:

The replies revealed that of the 25,000 or so mental patients in the state hospitals of Michigan there were only a handful with delusional identities. There were no Napoleons or Caesars, no Khrushchevs or Eisenhowers. Two people claimed to be members of the Ford family, but not the same person. We located one Tom Mix, one Cinderella, a member of the Morgan family, a Mrs. God, and an assortment of lesser known personages (Rokeach, 1964, p. 36).

In addition, he located six Christs. Of these, however, only three were free of organic brain damage and consistently claimed that they were Christ. These three became the subjects of the study.

phase usually does not appear until after age twenty-five, it is preceded in most cases by years of fear and suspicion, leading to tense and fragile interpersonal relationships. The onset and development of a paranoid schizophrenic episode are illustrated in the following case:

Laura was a 40-year-old married woman. A few weeks prior to her first examination, her husband had noted restlessness and agitation, which he interpreted as being due to some physical disorder. A physician who was consulted prescribed a tonic. Later Laura started to complain about the neighbors. A woman who lived on the floor beneath them was knocking on the wall to irritate her. According to the husband, this woman had really knocked on the wall a few times; he had heard the noises. However, Laura became more and more concerned about it. She would wake up in the middle of the night under the impression that she was hearing noises from the apartment downstairs. . . . Later she became more disturbed. She started to feel that the neighbors were now recording everything she said; maybe they had hidden wires in the apartment. She started to feel "funny" sensations. There were many strange things happening, which she did not know how to explain; people were looking at her in a funny way in the street; in the butcher shop, the butcher had purposely served her last, although she was in the middle of the line. During the next few days she felt that people were planning to harm either her or her husband. In the neighborhood she saw a German woman whom she had not seen for several years. Now the woman had suddenly reappeared, probably to testify that the patient and her husband were involved in some sort of crime.

Laura was distressed and agitated. She felt unjustly accused, because she had committed no crime. Maybe these people were really not after her, but after her husband. In the evening when she looked at television, it became obvious to her that the programs referred to her life. Often the people on the programs were just repeating what she had thought. They were stealing her ideas. She wanted to go to the police and report them. At this point the husband felt the patient could not be left alone, and after a brief telephone conversation with the family doctor, a consultation with [a psychiatrist] was arranged (Arieti, 1974a, pp. 165–166).

Two Related Categories: Brief Reactive Psychosis and Schizophreniform Disorder

A high school graduate with two years of college, Jane held a responsible job in a small business. She had been married for five years. All her friends considered her well adjusted—so well adjusted that one of her friends felt that Jane could take the news that her husband was having an affair with another woman. After hearing the friend's story, Jane wept uncontrollably for several hours. Then she went to her bedroom and climbed into bed. Attempts to talk to her or to get any response from her were ignored. She simply remained curled up under the covers, either weeping or mumbling incoherently. Her husband and the friend who had told her the

news pleaded with her to respond. Occasionally, they would leave her alone for a few hours, hoping she would begin behaving normally again. Finally, after she had been in bed for twenty-four hours and shown no signs of recovery, her husband got in touch with a psychiatrist, who hospitalized her. Within several days, Jane began responding to the approaches of the ward personnel and friends, and after four days, she was back home. A week later, she returned to work with no apparent residual signs of psychosis.

What was the diagnosis that this patient received upon admission to the hospital? Since she was apparently out of touch with reality and unable to function, she might be called schizophrenic. However, in view of the shock she had received, her response might also seem normal—or at least different from the disorder that we call schizophrenia. Until recently, such cases—with rapid onset, short duration, and a clear precipitating event—were classified as "acute schizophrenic episode," a subtype of schizophrenia. Today they are specifically distinguished from the schizophrenic disorders. If the episode lasts for less than a month and follows a recognizable stressor—something that would disturb almost anyone, such as the news that one's spouse has been unfaithful—it is called **brief reactive psychosis.** If it lasts for more than a month but less then six months, with or without a precipitating trauma, it is called **schizophreniform disorder.** If it lasts for more than six months, it is relabeled as schizophrenia. Jane's diagnosis, then, would be brief reactive psychosis.

Why these careful distinctions? Recall our discussion, earlier in the chapter, of the dimensions of schizophrenia. As we saw, Kraepelin and Bleuler believed that process cases were primarily biogenic and reactive cases primarily psychogenic, and many researchers today suspect that they were right. Hence there is now a trend toward separating process and reactive cases diagnostically, reserving the term "schizophrenia" for process cases and finding some other way to classify reactive cases. It is this trend that is responsible for the new nonschizophrenic categories "brief reactive psychosis" and "schizophreniform disorder."

It is important to note that during the active phase, neither brief reactive psychosis nor schizophreniform disorder need differ from schizophrenia in symptomatology. The primary criterion for differential diagnosis is the length of the episode. There are also certain other ways in which these three disorders differ from one another. As we saw, brief reactive psychosis, by definition, follows a severe psychological trauma; both onset and recovery are extremely rapid, and recovery is virtually complete. There is usually more emotional turmoil associated with brief reactive psychosis than with schizophreniform disorder or schizophrenia. Schizophreniform disorder, which in duration lies between brief reactive psychosis and schizophrenia, is intermediate in other respects as well. It may or may not be preceded by an identifiable trauma; it often involves a prodromal phase rather than a sudden plunge from normal functioning into active-phase psychosis; finally, recovery is slower and not necessarily complete. After a brief reactive psychosis, the person is generally his or her "old self" again; after an episode of schizophreniform disorder, the person will have more difficulty adjusting—but still not as much difficulty as a person recovering from a schizophrenic episode. The distinction between brief reactive psychosis and schizophreniform disorder is, then, primarily quantitative. The same is true of the distinction between these two disorders on the one hand and schizophrenia on the other hand. Nevertheless, the contrast may reflect an important difference in etiology and prognosis.

DELUSIONAL DISORDERS

Of the three major categories of functional psychosis, the delusional disorders, sometimes called paranoia, are the most frequently portrayed in novels, movies, and television dramas. This type of psychosis is also the one most likely to involve violence to others. The reasons are made clear in the following case:

> Frank W., a thirty-two-year-old electrician, came to the clinic complaining of difficulties in his social life. Frank did his job competently. He seldom missed work and was never late. His co-workers found him somewhat quiet at times, but they noted nothing unusual about his behavior. The problem that brought him to the clinic was the threatened breakup of his current romance. Since his divorce five years earlier, Frank had dated five successive women. On each occasion, he had been more interested in the relationship than the woman had been, and each of the previous four relationships had ended in a serious heartbreak for him. When the most recent woman in his life began suggesting that they both date other people, Frank sought professional counseling.
>
> At first the therapist noted little out of the ordinary. Soon, however, it became apparent that Frank had a much more serious problem than his shaky romance. The therapist's suspicions were first aroused when he offered Frank a cup of coffee from the clinic "coffee station." Frank used a number of delaying tactics to avoid drinking his coffee until he had seen another person pour a cup of coffee from the same pot and take a drink of it. He was also wary of the one-way mirror in the counseling room, and he absolutely refused to allow the therapist to tape-record their sessions. Finally, after several sessions, Frank told the therapist about the people who regularly followed him to the clinic. Ultimately it came out that Frank was convinced that he was being pursued by a group of people bent on killing him. Through an elaborate system of safeguards, he had been able to thwart them so far, but much of his private life was devoted to these efforts at self-protection. Recently, he had begun planning strategies of reprisal.

This patient's major symptom, a system of delusions, is something that we have already discussed under the heading of paranoid schizophrenia. In paranoid schizophrenia, however, the delusional system is simply one item in a cluster of abnormalities, all of which may function independently of one another. In the **delusional disorders,** on the other hand, the delu-

The person with a delusional disorder creates a delusional system whose content may take any of a number of forms. For instance, a persecutory delusional system involves the person's belief that other people are threatening him or her. (Charles Gatewood/The Image Works)

sional system is the fundamental abnormality. Indeed, in some cases, the delusional system is the *only* abnormality; in all other respects the person appears quite normal. Other patients may show some disturbances of mood, but only as a *consequence* of the delusional system. (For example, they may explode in anger at complete strangers, but only because they suspect those strangers of spying on them, flirting with their spouses, or whatever.) It is assumed, in other words, that if there were no delusions, there would be no abnormality. Furthermore, whatever other symptoms the person shows, they do not include the characteristic symptoms of schizophrenia, such as hallucinations, loosening of associations, incoherence, or thought broadcasting. Finally, unlike the delusions of the paranoid schizophrenic, the delusions seen in this disorder are not truly bizarre; they involve things that *could* happen. For example, the person may claim to be pursued by enemies, but not by enemies from outer space.

Frank's case illustrates the restricted nature of the abnormality in this syndrome. The patient's work record and intellectual functioning were good. He spoke coherently and seemed to reason logically enough. Even those who worked with him daily had apparently failed to notice any outward signs of psychosis. Aside from his delusions, his only apparent problem was in his social relationships, especially with women, and this was presumably a function of the distrustfulness generated by his delusions.

As for the content of the delusions, *DSM-III-R* lists five specific categories. The classic type, just seen in the case of Frank, is the *persecutory type,* involving the belief that one is being threatened or maltreated by others. In the *grandiose type,* as the name indicates, the person believes that he or she is endowed with some extraordinary power or knowledge. In the *jealous type,* the delusion is that one's sexual partner is being unfaithful. In the *erotomanic type,* the victim believes that some person of high status—the president of the company or of the United States—is in love with him or her. Finally, the *somatic type* involves the false conviction that one is suffering from some physical abnormality or disorder.

With the delusional disorders, differential diagnosis can be a problem. On one side they border on paranoid schizophrenia. Indeed, some investigators (e.g., Buss, 1966) have claimed that they are simply variants of schizophrenia, though genetic evidence indicates that there is a difference between the two patterns. (For example, the relatives of victims of delusional

disorder are *not* at greater risk for schizophrenia than the general population [Kendler and Davis, 1981].) On the other side, the delusional disorders border on paranoid personality disorder (Chapter 11). According to *DSM-III-R,* the difference here is that people with paranoid personality disorder are simply abnormally suspicious; they do not embrace actual delusions, beliefs that are patently false and indefensible. Furthermore, the suspicions of the paranoid personality are more realistic than psychotic delusions. For example, the belief that the coffee in a mental health clinic has been poisoned in anticipation of one's arrival is beyond the scope of the paranoid personality. Again, however, these are distinctions that are easier to make in a diagnostic manual than in an actual patient.

As defined by the narrow criteria outlined above— a delusional system unaccompanied by any further independent signs of schizophrenia—paranoid disorders are extremely rare. Estimates of prevalence vary from 1 percent of the mental hospital population (McNeil, 1970) to only one case in several thousand patients (Sullivan, 1956), depending on the purity of symptomatology demanded by the diagnostician. It is possible, of course, that many more exist. In the course of our daily lives we have all probably encountered a few candidates for this diagnostic label: jealous husbands, ignored geniuses, self-styled prophets, people who telephone radio talk shows to describe in detail some scheme for solving the world's problems—a scheme that the world has so far stubbornly refused to adopt. Because such people tend, apart from their isolated delusional systems, to have relatively good contact with reality, many of them remain within the community and never see a therapist. Those who present themselves for treatment often do so not of their own volition but at the insistence of others, such as beleaguered spouses.

SUMMARY

Two groups of functional psychoses, the schizophrenic disorders and the delusional disorders, have been the subject of this chapter. Schizophrenia is the label given to a group of psychoses characterized by bizarre behavior, social withdrawal, and severely distorted thought, perception, and mood. It is a relatively common disorder that was first identified as a diagnostic category by Kraepelin, but it was given its present name, meaning "split mind," by Eugen Bleuler.

Among the symptoms of schizophrenia, the disorganization of thought processes has traditionally been considered primary. Thought disorders are frequently marked by various kinds of delusions, or patently false beliefs. Disorders of language are also extremely common among schizophrenics. They typically experience a loosening of associations, so that their speech tends to slip from one topic to another and as a result is marked by poverty of content. Words may be made up (neologisms) or combined on the basis of sound (clanging) or simply thrown together in an incoherent jumble (word salad). In addition, schizophrenics seem to have difficulty handling abstract concepts.

The disorganization of thought and language, however, is only one facet of schizophrenia, and a number of experts now regard the breakdown of selective attention as the basic pathology instead. That is, schizophrenics seem unable to decide what they want to focus on or to concentrate on it without interference from irrelevant stimuli in the environment. This perceptual disorder, which makes a jumble of all incoming sensory information, may give rise to the other schizophrenic symptoms. Perceptual distortions may also take the form of hallucinations (usually auditory). Disorders of mood often occur, with affect becoming blunted or flat (depending on how apathetic the person is) or inappropriate. Motor behavior may be excessive and violent, deficient (as in catatonic immobility), or simply bizarre. Finally, most schizophrenics show extreme social withdrawal, accompanied by disturbance in the sense of self and by lack of volition.

Schizophrenia follows a fairly regular course, involving three stages: (1) the prodromal phase, marked by a gradual social withdrawal and deterioration of functioning; (2) the active phase, marked by overt signs of psychosis; and (3) the residual phase, in which gross psychotic symptoms recede but functioning remains impaired. In some cases, however, onset and recovery are extremely rapid, so that the prodromal and residual stages are abbreviated or simply skipped. Complete recovery is, unfortunately, rare.

Schizophrenics are classified into subgroups according to various dimensions, all of which parallel one another to some extent: the process-reactive dimension (the onset of process schizophrenia is gradual, whereas reactive schizophrenia is precipitated by some traumatic event); the good-poor premorbid adjustment dimension (in which schizophrenics are classified on the basis of their social adjustment before

the active phase of their disorder); the chronic-acute dimension (the acute schizophrenic is in the active phase of his or her first schizophrenic episode); the positive-negative symptoms dimension (in which either positive symptoms, such as the presence of hallucinations, or negative symptoms, such as absence of affect, predominate); and the paranoid-nonparanoid dimension (reflecting the presence or absence of delusions of persecution and/or grandeur). In addition to correlating with one another to some degree, all these dimensions are related to prognosis for recovery. Characterization of a disorder as reactive, good-premorbid, acute, positive-symptom, or paranoid, for example, suggests greater likelihood of recovery than assignment to the opposite ends of these continua.

Schizophrenics may also be classified into subtypes according to symptomatology. The five subtypes are (1) the residual subtype, whose members have passed beyond the active phase of their disorder; (2) the disorganized subtype, characterized by incoherent language, disturbed affect, and withdrawal from reality; (3) the catatonic subtype, characterized by extremes of motor behavior (i.e., immobility or hyperactivity); (4) the paranoid subtype, characterized by delusions and/or hallucinations of persecution and grandeur; and (5) the undifferentiated subtype, a category reserved for patients who fit into none or more than one of the other subtypes.

When symptoms of schizophrenia are short-lived, and especially when their onset is precipitated by some psychological trauma, they are classified not as schizophrenia but as brief reactive psychosis (duration of less than a month) or schizophreniform disorder (duration of one to six months). Many investigators suspect that biological factors play a lesser role in these brief, reactive psychoses than in the longer-lasting, process schizophrenias.

The delusional disorders, another category of psychosis, resemble paranoid schizophrenia in that their most prominent symptom is a system of delusions. In the delusional disorders, however, the delusions are the fundamental abnormality, from which any other abnormalities emanate, and in many cases they are the patient's only symptom. Furthermore, if the patient does have other symptoms, they do not include the characteristic symptoms of schizophrenia (e.g., hallucinations, loosening of associations, and incoherence). Finally, the delusions are more plausible and less bizarre than those found in paranoid schizophrenia. Their content may be of the persecutory, grandiose, jealous, erotomanic, or somatic type.

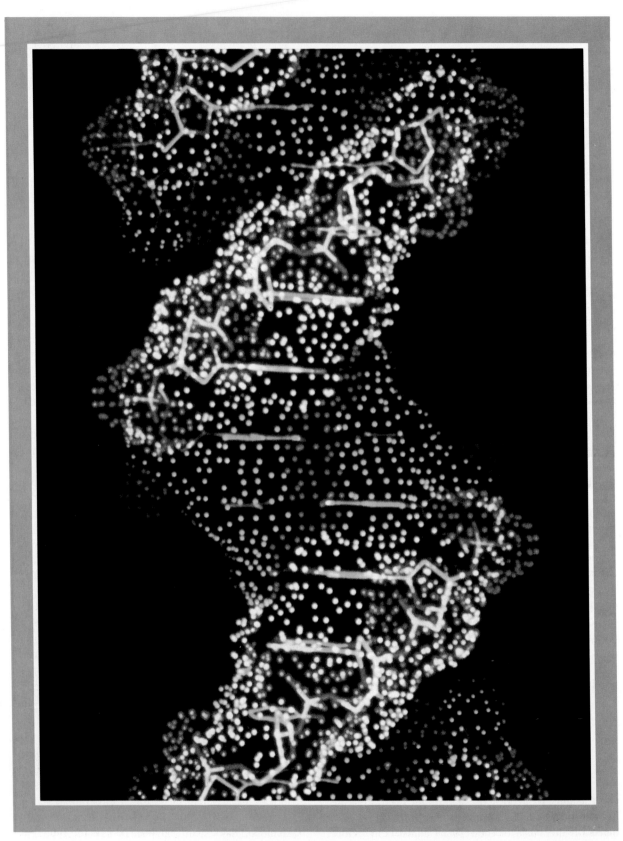

Perspectives on Schizophrenia

We have described the symptoms of schizophrenia and paranoia, but we have not yet raised the question of why. What causes people to act in such bizarre and self-defeating ways? It is with this question—the question of etiology—that the bulk of scientific writing on the functional psychoses is concerned. And it is this question that is the subject of our present chapter. Since the schizophrenic disorders have been much more thoroughly researched than the paranoid disorders, our discussion will confine itself to theories of schizophrenia.

PROBLEMS IN THE STUDY OF SCHIZOPHRENIA

If schizophrenia is as widespread and debilitating as the last chapter asserted, why don't we appropriate the necessary funds, hire a team of researchers, and

simply go to work until we have found both cause and cure? Unfortunately, it is not so easy. Schizophrenia is a slippery research problem. We do not know whether it is a single disorder or a group of disorders. Furthermore, it has many and varied symptoms, not all of which turn up in any single patient. Researchers have attacked the problem from a multitude of directions, but only in recent years have they been able to arrive at any firm conclusions—and so far, only a few. A brief examination of the questions surrounding research in this area will show why.

What Is to Be Studied?

Historically, a nagging problem in schizophrenia research has been diagnostic disagreement. Researchers must learn from one another, each launching his or her work from findings produced by others. But this presupposes that everyone is talking about the same thing, and with schizophrenia, this has not always been the case.

In a number of studies conducted in the sixties (e.g., Beck et al., 1962; Sandifer et al., 1964), the percentage of agreement among professionals on a general diagnosis of schizophrenia ranged from only 53 percent to 74 percent. Worse yet, when attempts were made to specify the subcategory of schizophrenia, the rate of agreement generally dropped to between 35 and 50 percent. In other words, if Dr. Green in one hospital and Dr. Brown in another hospital were both publishing papers on paranoid schizophrenia, only 35 to 50 percent of the patients in each hospital would be comparable to those studied in the other hospital. On a cross-national basis, interjudge reliability has been even poorer. In one experiment (Cooper et al., 1972), groups of psychiatrists in New York and in London were shown identical videotapes of doctor-patient interviews and were asked to diagnose the patients on the basis of those tapes. In London the diagnoses of schizophrenia and of mood disorder were given with approximately equal frequency. In New York the diagnosis of schizophrenia was given *nine times* more frequently than that of mood disorder.

According to the investigators, these results were due to cross-national differences in the relative emphasis given to disturbances of thought and mood. In cases involving both kinds of disturbance, the American psychiatrists saw the thought disturbance as the primary symptom, whereas the English psychiatrists gave more weight to the mood disturbance. Stephens (1978) offers a less subtle explanation; in the United States, he claims, there is a tendency to diagnose almost all nonorganic psychoses as schizophrenia. Whatever the reason, there has obviously been a profound cross-national disagreement over this category.

It must be kept in mind that as long as there is no laboratory test for schizophrenia, diagnostic agreement will never be perfect. Indeed, as one study has shown, diagnostic agreement is higher on schizophrenia than on several well-established physical conditions, such as angina and emphysema, when those conditions must be diagnosed without benefit of laboratory tests (Falek and Moser, 1975). Furthermore, interjudge reliability on schizophrenia has improved in recent years. Diagnostic criteria still differ from country to country; but in the United States, at least, with the acceptance of *DSM-III*'s more specific and stringent criteria, reliability has increased and is expected to increase further through use of *DSM-III-R*.

A more serious problem today is disagreement over the primary pathology in schizophrenia—a controversy already touched upon in Chapter 14. Consider the analogy of a leg fracture. The fracture will produce pain, a bent leg, and also a limp. But of these three symptoms, only the first two are primary—direct results of the broken bone. The limp is a secondary symptom, a strategy adopted to cope with the primary symptom of pain. Likewise in schizophrenia there is little doubt that of the recognized symptoms of the disorder, some are primary and others merely reactions to the primary symptoms. But which is which? Is social withdrawal the primary pathology, as some theorists believe, or do schizophrenics withdraw simply because their thought disorders make it difficult for them to communicate with others? Are delusions a primary symptom, or are they, as suggested earlier, merely the schizophrenic's way of explaining the chaos of his or her thoughts? Answering these questions is crucial to research on schizophrenia. Until we know what the basic disorder is, we stand little chance of discovering its cause. But as yet, the riddle remains unsolved.

Problems in Experimentation

The study of schizophrenia is impeded not just by unanswered questions about the nature of the disorder but also by standard research problems. These problems have already been described in general in Chapter 6, but since they are a particular hindrance in the area of schizophrenia, they merit a brief review.

As we saw, the most common scientific procedure for determining the effect of a given set of conditions is the **randomized groups design,** with subjects randomly assigned either to the **experimental group,** which is then exposed to whatever conditions are being studied, or to the **control group,** which is not exposed to the conditions. The two groups are then compared to determine the effects, if any, of the conditions.

For obvious reasons, this method cannot be used for etiological research in schizophrenia. The alternative, then, is to gather evidence ex post facto—that is, to compare groups of people who are already schizophrenic with groups of normal people on whatever variable we are interested in: socioeconomic background, size of brain ventricles, or whatever. But with this method, it is difficult to identify cause-and-effect relationships. Researchers may find clear correlations—it is well established, for example, that schizophrenia correlates with low socioeconomic status—but how do they determine the *direction* of the causal relationship? On the one hand, it seems likely that the hardships of life in the lower socioeconomic strata might contribute to the development of schizophrenia. On the other hand, it may be that because schizophrenics adapt poorly to life, they tend to gravitate to the lower socioeconomic strata.

This chicken-and-egg problem is actually secondary. Before that is the question of whether there is in fact a causal relationship between these two variables, or whether both are the result of an unidentified *third variable*. In research on schizophrenia there are two third variables that are notoriously difficult to control. Most of the schizophrenics available for research purposes are (1) hospitalized and (2) taking antipsychotic drugs. Consequently, any interesting differences that turn up between these subjects and non-hospitalized, nonmedicated controls may well be a function *not* of schizophrenia but of the medication or of the overcrowding, poor diet, difficult sleeping conditions, lack of exercise, and lack of privacy that are routine conditions of hospitalization.

Researchers today are keenly sensitive to such problems, but that does not mean they can get around them. It is one thing to know that the best subjects for one's glucose metabolism experiment would be schizophrenics with no history of hospitalization or of antipsychotic medication; it is another thing to find such subjects. In some cases, one can control for third variables via the research design. Certain investigators, for example, have compared hospitalized schizophrenics with hospitalized nonschizophrenics as well as with normal controls. But many researchers must settle for taking these third variables into account in drawing their conclusions—which of course renders their conclusions less firm.

PERSPECTIVES ON SCHIZOPHRENIA

There are three basic schools of thought as to the etiology of schizophrenia: first, that it is caused by environmental stress; second, that it is caused by genetically transmitted abnormalities; third, that it is caused by an interaction between these two forces. We shall consider these positions in order, the environmental theories first.

One difficulty in studying schizophrenia is that most schizophrenics studied have been medicated and hospitalized patients. Long-term medication and confinement may produce pathology that is mistaken for the disorder itself. (Roy Zalisky/Black Star)

The Psychodynamic Perspective

Schizophrenia as Regression   While Freud devoted his attention primarily to the anxiety, somatoform, and dissociative disorders, he also wrote about the psychoses at various points in his career. His most influential idea regarding schizophrenia was that this disorder was a form of regression. According to Freud, schizophrenics are people whose egos are not strong enough to cope effectively with unacceptable id impulses. Overwhelmed by anxiety, they simply give up the fight and regress to the early oral stage, a period in which there is as yet no separation between ego and id and therefore no struggle between the two. This regression to an egoless phase accounts for the schizophrenic's break with reality, since it is the ego that mediates between the self and reality.

To this day, anxiety-motivated regression is still the major theme of psychodynamic writing on schizophrenia. However, later psychodynamic theorists have departed from Freud's position in two respects. First, like almost all writers on the subject, they believe that there are several kinds of schizophrenia, some more biologically based than others. Second, as to a psychological base, they tend to stress the role of interpersonal factors much more than Freud did. A good example of the latter trend is Harry Stack Sullivan (1962), who devoted much of his theoretical writing to schizophrenia. According to Sullivan, the cause of the schizophrenic's anxiety is not id impulses but a damaging mother–child relationship. To Sullivan and many other post-Freudians, schizophrenia represents a gradual withdrawal from other people. This process begins in early childhood, with anxious and hostile interactions between parent and child. Scared off from intimacy with others, the child takes refuge in a private world of fantasy. This initiates a vicious cycle, for the more the child withdraws, the less opportunity he or she has to develop the trust, confidence, and skills necessary for establishing close bonds with others, and the fewer the bonds, the greater the anxiety. The spiral continues until, in early adulthood, the person is faced with a new and more taxing set of social demands—work, marriage, and so forth. In the face of these challenges, the person becomes so swamped with anxiety that he or she withdraws completely, closing down those mental faculties (e.g., communication, perception, reasoning) that are the bridge to the world of other people. It is this final withdrawal that we call the schizophrenic "break," though according to psychodynamic writers it is only the culmination of a gradual disengagement from human relationships.

Psychoanalysis for Schizophrenics   Psychoanalysis—or, for that matter, any conventional psychodynamic "talk" therapy—requires a psychological coherence and emotional strength that is beyond the grasp of most schizophrenics. Freud himself believed that psychoanalysis was of little use for schizophrenic patients. It was Sullivan who pioneered psychodynamic treatment for schizophrenia and established its outlines. They differ from those of conventional psychoanalysis in that, in order to overcome the patient's detachment, the patient–therapist relationship is warmer and more nurturant, as in humanistic-existential therapies. For those schizophrenics who receive psychodynamic treatment—and they are a very small minority—this basic pattern still holds today (Arieti, 1974b). As with nonpsychotic patients, the psychoanalyst interprets the unconscious meaning of the patient's words and actions, but in an especially gradual, gentle, and supportive manner. At the same time, the therapist is likely to take a more "activist" approach with schizophrenic patients, helping them to solve practical problems. Thus the therapist acts simultaneously as an analyst, probing the patient's unconscious, and as a sort of second parent, offering the esteem and affection that schizophrenic patients presumably need in order to emerge from their frightened withdrawal and reenter the real world.

Family Theories

It is generally agreed that the family has a greater impact on a person's psychosocial development than does any other element of society. Hence it would seem logical that if schizophrenia is caused by psychosocial factors, the family would be a foremost cause. As we have just seen, Sullivan placed the major burden of causation on the family. So do many other theorists, psychodynamic and otherwise. In some cases, such as the following, this conclusion is almost irresistible:

> Will J., a nineteen-year-old youth, fluctuated between states of catatonic stupor and wild excitements that, in those preshock and pretranquilizer days, were difficult to manage. With the help of a special nurse, Will began to improve,

but clearly became worse after each of his mother's semiweekly visits. Despite Will's desperate condition, his mother would spend her time with him seeking to have him pray with her and in admonishing him to remember to move his bowels regularly, to take his vitamins, to do deep breathing exercises, and so forth. When Mr. J., a dignified industrialist, was asked to persuade his wife to return to their home in another state and leave their son's care to the hospital staff, he said that it would not be possible; he had given up trying to get his wife to permit Will to have some independence and grow up, and now that Will was so desperately ill, she would never leave him. When the hospital decided to ban her visits temporarily, she sent imploring notes to her son daily, and when these were returned to her, she sent him a box of chocolates. The brand had been selected carefully, for instead of the customary brown paper "trays," these contained white ones, on each of which Mrs. J. had carefully printed a message such as "eat your prunes at breakfast," "breathe deeply five times each hour," "say your prayers morning and night" (Lidz, 1973, p. 8).

In a case like Will's, many psychologists would suspect that the family had played some role in the develop-

ment of the disorder. Such a view is encouraged by the fact that the members of a schizophrenic's immediate family are very likely to manifest some form of psychopathology. But is there an actual family *type* that tends to produce schizophrenia? Some theorists believe there is.

Family Type   Arieti (1974a) sees the schizophrenic's family milieu as one in which the child is deprived of all security and is submerged in an atmosphere of anxiety and hostility. In the creation of such an atmosphere, the relationship between the parents is of course particularly decisive. Lidz (1973) claims that a great number of schizophrenic children come from families that fall into one of two categories: the **schismatic family,** in which parental discord has divided the family into opposing factions; and the **skewed family,** which remains reasonably calm but only because one spouse is totally dominated by the other. In both situations the child is denied the emotional support necessary for a sense of security and self-worth. Furthermore, role modeling may become extremely problematic, particularly in the schismatic family, where identification with one parent might an-

Some theorists believe that certain kinds of disordered family relationships are at the root of schizophrenia. (James H. Karales/Peter Arnold)

Helping Schizophrenics by Family Management

Schizophrenic episodes are considered to be partly—though not totally—triggered by environmental stresses, and stresses from within the family figure high on the list of suspects (Leff, 1976). The scenario often goes like this: patients are diagnosed, treated, and released (generally on drug therapy) to the family—where ordinary frictions such as arguments often cause their symptoms to recur. Home life is simply too stressful for most schizophrenics, according to Dr. Ian Falloon, who directed a study of the effects of family life on schizophrenics. Conditions in most families tend to make schizophrenics "overexcited and overstimulated," he says.

Recently a study by Falloon and his colleagues (1982) showed that if families are taught to talk out and attempt to solve their problems, the recovery rate of family members suffering from mental illness improves dramatically. The study compared two groups, each of eighteen schizophrenics living with their families. The patients in both groups received the standard drug treatment for schizophrenia. In the experimental group, the researchers counseled the families as well, spending several weeks in the patients' homes studying the family's problems. The families were taught a step-by-step method to work out problems and cope with crises—from planning a dinner menu to dealing with the loss of a job to confronting death. The researchers also briefed the families on schizophrenia. "Family members then understand why the patient acts strangely and can see ways to support him," Falloon observes. In the two groups studied, after nine months only one member of the experimental group suffered a relapse, compared with eight of the controls. These results were sustained through two years of follow-up (Falloon et al., 1985).

In another study of family management training (Hogarty et al., 1986), 103 patients living with relatives found to be high in "expressed emotion" (critical, very emotionally involved with the patient) were randomly assigned to one of four aftercare treatment programs: (1) family treatment and medication; (2) behavioral social-skills training for the patient and medication; (3) a combination of these treatments; and (4) medication only. Of the medication-only patients, 41 percent relapsed within one year, compared with 20 percent of the family-treatment patients, 19 percent of those who had received social-skills training, and none of those who had received the combined treatment. Relapse was most delayed in patients whose families learned to become less critical and less emotionally involved with them. Thus it would seem that when families learn to interact more calmly with a schizophrenic member, he or she is much less likely to experience relapse.

tagonize the other and thus cause even greater hostility.

In 1948, Frieda Fromm-Reichmann coined the term **schizophrenogenic mother** to describe the type of mother who was capable of inducing schizophrenia in her children. In Fromm-Reichmann's view, such mothers were typically cold, domineering, rejecting, and yet overprotective. The father, meanwhile, was faulted mainly for his passivity in not interfering in the pernicious mother–child relationship. Subsequent investigations (e.g., Caputo, 1968), however, have suggested that the fathers are as responsible as the mothers for the hostile, aggressive atmosphere that seems to permeate homes of many schizophrenic children.

To sort the parents of schizophrenics into such "types" involves considerable interpretation. Something that can be measured more objectively is what the family members of a schizophrenic actually *say* about the patient. In a number of studies (Brown et al., 1972; Vaughan and Leff, 1976; Vaughan et al., 1984) families of hospitalized schizophrenics were rated on "expressed emotion," or EE, toward the patient. The rating was based on two factors—the level of criticism and the level of emotional overinvolvement—in the remarks made by a key relative (e.g., the father, the mother, the spouse) in an interview regarding the patient shortly after his or her admission. Nine months after these patients were discharged, they were followed up to see who had relapsed. Interestingly, of all the factors on which the patients varied, the family EE was the best single predictor of relapse: patients who lived with high-EE relatives were three to four times more likely to have been rehospitalized within nine months than patients who lived with low-EE relatives. Of course, this finding says nothing about the original cause of the schizophrenia. Yet if a negative and emotionally charged family atmosphere is related to later breakdowns, it may also have had some relation to the original one.

Parent–Child Communications   Many family theorists feel that the heart of the interpersonal disturbance lies in the matter of communications between parent and child. Consider, for example, the messages passed from mother to son in the following account:

> A young man who had fairly well recovered from an acute schizophrenic episode was visited in the hospital by his mother. He was glad to see her and impulsively put his arm around her shoulders, whereupon she stiffened. He withdrew his arm and she asked, "Don't you love me any more?" He then blushed, and she said, "Dear, you must not be so easily embarrassed and afraid of your feelings." The patient was able to stay with her only a few minutes more and following her departure he assaulted an aide (Bateson et al., 1956, p. 251).

Bateson and his co-workers offer this case as an example of what they call **double-bind communication,** which they feel may be a strong causative agent in schizophrenia. In the double-bind situation the mother gives the child mutually contradictory messages (for example, both rejection and affection in the case just cited), meanwhile implicitly forbidding the child to point out the contradiction. Thus whichever message the child acts upon, he or she is the loser. Bateson and his colleagues propose that the type of mother most likely to engage in double-bind communication is one who finds closeness with her child intolerable but who also finds it intolerable to admit this to herself. Thus she pushes the child away, but when the child withdraws, she accuses the child of not loving her.

The most current research in this area has focused on a broader range of communications, and communications among the entire family rather than just between mother and child. It is now well established that families of schizophrenics tend to have unusual communication patterns (Wynne et al., 1975). Their verbal exchanges are variously described as blurred, muddled, vague, fragmented, or incomplete (Friedman and Friedman, 1970; Hassan, 1974; Lewis et al., 1981). In one study (Doane et al., 1981) it was found that "communication deviance" (CD) in parents, measured according to the number of deviant or idiosyncratic responses on a test such as the TAT or Rorschach, was a good predictor of whether their adolescent children would be diagnosed as schizophrenic five years later. The recent finding (Miklowitz et al., 1986) that "communication deviance" seems to correlate with "expressed emotion"—relatives that are high-EE are also high-CD—has given added impetus to this line of research.

Yet, however well supported, these findings are still subject to the interpretation problems outlined at the beginning of our chapter. Given that schizophrenia in the child correlates with deviant communications in the family, there may still be no causal relationship between the two factors, for both may be the result of a third variable, such as a shared genetic defect (Reiss, 1974). Furthermore, even if there is a causal relationship between the two, we are faced with the chicken-and-egg problem: while the disturbed family communications may have fostered the child's disorder, it is equally possible that the child's disorder has fostered the troubled communications (Mishler and Waxler, 1968). Indeed, evidence suggests that what psychological researchers regard as vague and fragmentary parental communications are actually techniques that these parents have evolved, over years of experience, to make themselves understood by a severely disturbed child (Liem, 1974).

There is one further problem: If the total family setting is of major importance in the etiology of schizophrenia, why does one child in the family grow up schizophrenic while another develops normally? Bowen (1960) hypothesizes that one child may be selected as the focal point toward which both parents direct their emotional immaturity, thus achieving an uneasy stabilization of their own relationship. It has also been suggested that this "focal child" may be selected from among the others because he or she is weaker or less intelligent or otherwise vulnerable (Mosher et al., 1971). But we do not know for certain

The mutually contradictory messages involved in double-bind communications have been thought to be implicated in schizophrenia, but researchers often disagree on which messages qualify as double-binds. (Sylvia Johnson/Woodfin Camp & Associates)

whether this is the case. Studies of the families of schizophrenics are extremely difficult to conduct and to interpret, both because of the multitude of uncontrollable variables and because of ethical problems: the invasion of the family's privacy and the implication that the parents are to blame.

The difficulty in doing research with families of schizophrenics has not advanced the cause of family theories. In the late 1950s and early 1960s family theories were the "rage" in schizophrenia research. Ambitious, plausible, and bolstered by vivid case material (see above), formulations such as Bateson's "double-bind" won many followers. Today, for lack of evidence, they have far fewer defenders, and family research tends to confine itself to more verifiable factors such as "expressed emotion" and "communica-

tion deviance." Yet most experts have not discarded the idea that the family may figure in the etiology of schizophrenia—only the claim that the family *alone* can engender the disorder. The majority would agree that if a child is predisposed to schizophrenia by some other factor, such as a genetic abnormality, then the emotional climate of the family can influence whether that predisposition is actually translated into schizophrenia.

The Behavioral Perspective

Two principles are central to the behavioral perspective on schizophrehia (Liberman, 1982a). The first is that schizophrenic symptomatology is not actually discontinuous with normal experience. All people have to deal, at various times, with physiological overarousal, information overload, and disordered thoughts. Schizophrenics simply experience these problems more acutely and more frequently, and consequently have reduced coping skills. From this continuity hypothesis follows the second principle: that what schizophrenics need is not a "cure" for a "disorder" but rather a way of bolstering their competence, their ability to deal with life. Such retraining has been the primary concern of behaviorists in regard to schizophrenia.

Learned Inattention   The most comprehensive interpretation of schizophrenia within the behavioral tradition is that of Ullmann and Krasner (1975). According to these investigators, schizophrenia is a learned behavior and consists primarily of attention problems. Schizophrenics are people who, because of a disturbed family life or other environmental misfortunes, have not learned to respond, through reinforcement, to the social stimuli to which most of us respond. Hence they cease to attend to these stimuli and begin taking their behavioral cues from other, idiosyncratically chosen stimuli. (They may also have been exposed to models for such responses.) In consequence, they tend to become objects of disciplinary action and social rejection, leading to additional feelings of alienation and to the belief that others are out to "get" them. Hence their behavior becomes even more bizarre. And if, as may well happen, they are rewarded for bizarre responses—through attention, sympathy, and release from responsibilities—then such responses are likely to become habitual.

There is some support for this hypothesis. It has been shown, for example, that like the learned behaviors of normal people, the "crazy" behaviors of schizophrenics are often produced in situations where they will lead to rewards. (Recall, in Chapter 14, the disorganized schizophrenic who would produce his word salad and clang associations only if a staff member was within earshot.) Schizophrenics have also been found to be capable of engaging in impression management—that is, many can "look good" or "look bad" depending on the requirements of the situation (Braginsky et al., 1969). Yet the fact that schizophrenics can turn on and off bizarre behavior according to the availability of reinforcement does not prove that these oddities were originally produced through reinforcement. Indeed, this is very slight evidence for a comprehensive theory, and even among behaviorists there is little support for the idea that schizophrenia is caused by differential reinforcement. Rather, most behaviorists invoke learning theory not in the etiology but in the treatment of schizophrenia.

Relearning Normal Behavior   Whatever the root cause of schizophrenic behavior, it may be that mental health settings inadvertently encourage such behavior by reinforcing "craziness" and not reinforcing adaptive responses. If this is the case, then reversing that reinforcement pattern should lead to improvement. Such is the goal of the behavioral treatment strategies that have been developed in the past twenty-five years.

DIRECT REINFORCEMENT   Many behavioral treatments are straightforward applications of the principles of operant conditioning. That is, they attempt to change behavior by changing the consequences of behavior. Let us look at a specific case.

> Mr. C.'s most obnoxious behaviors were: urinating and defecating on the floor, shouting, swearing, name-calling, begging cigarettes, demanding other things, striking at other patients. It . . . seemed evident that Mr. C.'s inappropriate conduct usually was followed by some kind of staff attention. Two procedures for eliminating Mr. C.'s disruptive behavior were [implemented]. 1. Social attention should no longer be given following inappropriate behavior. 2. Social attention and cigarettes . . . would be the consequence of socially acceptable behavior (Sushinsky, 1970, p. 24).

Modest though it was, this treatment program proved effective. In two weeks, Mr. C.'s "obnoxious" behaviors disappeared. Furthermore, he was now striking up conversations, participating in rehabilitation therapy, and even insisting on buying his own cigarettes.

Procedures that involve the giving or withholding of tangible reinforcers, such as the cigarettes in the case of Mr. C., are surrounded by a number of ethical and legal questions that are as yet unresolved. (These issues will be discussed in Chapter 22.) There is no question, however, that such procedures can change behavior. In one of the earliest operant-conditioning studies, Ayllon and Haughton (1962) reported increases in attending meals on time and in the performance of both simple and complex tasks when food was contingently given or withheld. Other researchers have succeeded in instituting or increasing speech in mute and near-mute patients through the use of such simple reinforcers as fruit, chocolate, milk, cigarettes, and magazines (Baker, 1970, 1971; Thomson et al., 1974).

THE TOKEN ECONOMY   Some hospitals have extended operant-conditioning procedures to entire wards, using a system called the token economy. In a **token economy** patients are given tokens or points or some other kind of generalized conditioned reinforcer in exchange for performing certain target behaviors, such as personal grooming, cleaning their rooms, or doing academic or vocational-training tasks. The patients can then exchange the tokens for any number of backup reinforcers, such as cigarettes, snacks, coffee, new clothes, or special privileges. The procedure is very much like that which operates outside the hospital: we earn money by performing certain tasks and then exchange this money for the privileges and goods that we want. (Token economies are described in more detail in Chapter 21.)

SOCIAL-SKILLS TRAINING   As we have seen, most schizophrenics are socially inept: they avoid eye contact, speak little to others, show emotions unconnected with the situation, and so forth. Needless to say, such social handicaps impede the schizophrenic's post-hospitalization readjustment—his or her ability to make friends, to hold down a job, and in general to obtain those things that most of us associate with happiness. To alleviate this problem, behavioral programs often include **social-skills training,** in which patients are taught conversation skills, eye contact, appropriate physical gestures, smiling, and improved

In a token economy, appropriate behaviors are rewarded with tokens that can then be "spent" for various needs, privileges, and rewards. A private room in this state hospital in California can be "rented" for five tokens. The aim of such a system is to produce the kinds of behaviors (such as proper grooming and social cooperation) needed in the outside world by reinforcing them as the outside world does. (John Oldenkamp/I.B.O.L.)

intonation—generally those characteristics that make one attractive to others (Bellack et al., 1976).

At the other end of the spectrum are people who are indeed communicative but in the wrong way. These people may also need social-skills training. Wallace and his colleagues (1973), for example, tell of Joe C., a twenty-two-year-old hospitalized patient whose history included firing a gun at his sister, smashing innumerable household items, punching holes in walls, and severely assaulting other patients. Through role playing, Joe was taught to respond to potentially frustrating situations by using appropriate verbal responses rather than physical aggression. This emphasis on problem solving has been widely adopted in social-skills training. One social-skills program that was developed in California, for example, involves the role playing of two hundred interpersonal scenes. These are designed to help patients interact more effectively with their families, with friends, within the hospital, and within the larger community (Wallace et al., 1980; Liberman, 1982b). Cognitive, problem-solving, and social skills are fostered through modeling, coaching, and positive feedback.

How effective are these behavioral treatments? Without doubt, the best-designed and most elaborate test of the usefulness of behavioral therapy for schizophrenics is that conducted by Gordon Paul and his staff (Paul and Lentz, 1977). During a five-year period, the progress of long-term chronic schizophrenics was measured under three different treatment conditions: (1) a behavioral program consisting of an overall token economy coupled with individualized behavioral treatments; (2) a milieu treatment program based on humanistic principles (a method that will be described shortly); and (3) a traditional "custodial care" hospital program. The behavioral program proved most effective in decreasing bizarre, violent, and assaultive behavior and increasing adaptive behavior. In addition, the behavioral program led to a greater release rate. Once returned to the community, however, all patients fared equally well. (See Chapter 21 for a more complete discussion of this study.)

As this study suggests, most of the schizophrenics helped by behavioral therapy are simply helped, not cured. This is in keeping with the goal of most behavioral programs: enhanced functioning. Some behavioral programs have very modest objectives—for example, to help schizophrenic patients live happier and more useful lives within a hospital or some other protective setting. It is in the attainment of specific goals such as these that behaviorists may ultimately make their greatest contribution to the treatment of schizophrenia.

The Humanistic-Existential Perspective

Schizophrenia and Alienation   Humanistic and existential writers have directed their attention primarily to the "neurotic" disorders. Nevertheless, a few attempts have been made to apply the humanistic-existential model to the problem of schizophrenia. The writer who has contributed the most in the area is R. D. Laing, whose theories we have already touched on in Chapter 4.

Laing's most original contribution was to challenge the standards by which people were labeled schizophrenic:

> The concept of schizophrenia as a form of madness implies a concept of sanity as the norm against which madness is judged. . . . The psychiatrist seems to us in varying degrees sane, and the patients in varying degrees mad. This is because the psychiatrist's behavior is assumed axiomatically to be the yardstick against which the abnormality of the patient is scaled (1964, pp. 185 and 189).

Yet according to Laing, the schizophrenic may be more sane than the psychiatrist. Laing shares the radical existential view that in industrial societies the "normal" state of mind is that of alienation, in which individuals suppress their true feelings and adopt a false self, a robotlike identity programmed to pursue trivial goals and conform to distorted values. Schizophrenics are people who, because of severe psychological stress, find themselves unable to continue this masquerade. Their false, socially acceptable self crumbles, forcing them to retreat into their own minds in the effort to relocate the true self. Schizophrenia, then, is not insanity but rather "hypersanity," a voyage from our own mad reality into another reality in the existential search for an authentic identity.

THE ANTIPSYCHIATRIC MOVEMENT   In defending the schizophrenic experience against the presumptions of conventional psychiatry, Laing is supported by the so-called **antipsychiatric movement,** a group of theorists, including Thomas Szasz, who contend that the state called "insanity" is simply a label fabricated by society to justify the exploitation of persons so labeled. According to this group, psychiatrists are little more than society's police officers, enforcing compliance with social norms and locking up in mental hospitals people who fail to comply. Psychiatry's preoccupation with finding out what sort of "disease" such people have is, in their view, entirely unjustified, if not a fraud. At the same time, it is extremely destructive, for it allows psychiatrists to exert control over people and also results in the labeling of those people as mentally ill—a label that may destroy their chances of ever leading a normal life (Scheff, 1975).

R. D. Laing, the British existential psychiatrist, has argued that schizophrenia is not "madness," but a strategy for living in an intolerably stressful situation.

The antipsychiatry group are thus primarily polemicists. What they have offered is less a theory of schizophrenia than a critique of society's handling of the "schizophrenic"—and of all the so-called mentally ill. However, this critique is in many respects consistent with humanistic-existential interpretations and treatment.

Milieu Therapy and Other Therapeutic Communities   From a radical viewpoint such as Laing's, the ultimate treatment for all mental disorders would be a drastic restructuring of society so that distorted values and dehumanizing conditions would be eliminated. But since this ideal is unlikely to be attained, humanistic-existential therapists have concentrated on designing small communities aimed at fostering the personal growth of immediate members. Depending on the degree to which their designers view schizophrenia as an actual "disturbance" requiring "cure," these communities range from mild to radical departures from the traditional mental hospital.

Predating the more radical residential communities are various forms of **milieu therapy,** some of which have produced promising results (Artiss, 1962; Cumming and Cumming, 1962). Like treatment in a traditional mental hospital, milieu therapy takes place in a residential community and is conducted by mental health professionals with fairly conventional notions of what constitutes normal and abnormal behavior. Unlike most mental hospital therapies, however, milieu therapy programs place as few restraints as possible on the patients and actively encourage them to take part in a wide variety of activities. Patients are expected to take responsibility for their own behavior, to participate in their own rehabilitation and that of others, and to help in the making of decisions that affect the entire community.

Therapeutic communities have their own special problems, particularly when the diffusion of power is carried too far. Clearly defined leadership and clearly defined roles may have certain disadvantages, but their absence has other disadvantages. In the words of one therapeutic community director, such programs are vulnerable to "cliques, withdrawal, and disillusionment" (Wilmer, 1976, p. 338). Even with these drawbacks, however, milieu therapy, as one type of therapeutic community, has been shown to be more effective than traditional custodial care in hospitals (Cumming and Cumming, 1962; Paul and Lentz, 1977).

Considerably more radical is the type of residential community first founded by Laing in London in 1965, under the name of Kingsley Hall, and since imitated by another community, Soteria House in San Jose, California. These communities differ from milieu therapy and from all other types of mental health facilities in two basic respects. First, there is little role differentiation between patients and staff. Soteria House, for example, selects its staff not on the basis of their knowledge or experience in working with schizophrenics but rather on the basis of their ability to "tune into the patients' altered state of consciousness" (Mosher, 1972, p. 233). Residents are regarded not as patients and staff but simply as people, those who are "up" helping those who are "down." The second major difference is in the attitude toward psychotic behavior. In keeping with Laing's theories (1967), a schizophrenic reaction is viewed not as a breakdown but as a potential "breakthrough"—an experience which the individual has a valid reason for going through and which has meaning for the individual. The role of the staff in relation to the schizophrenic residents is "similar to that of the LSD-trip guide" (Mosher, 1972, p. 233), supporting them and working *with* them as they go through their process of growth. Although occasional positive reports have been published (Mosher and Menn, 1978), there has been little systematic evaluation of the more radical therapeutic communities.

The humanistic-existential perspective has performed a service to mental health by insisting on the validity of the individual's experience, schizophrenic or otherwise, and by questioning such matters as the ethics of labeling and commitment, the effectiveness of traditional treatments, and the overall social significance of the disease model of mental illness. However, the radical existential view of schizophrenia as a "hypersanity" with which psychiatry has no right to meddle is emphatically rejected by adherents of most other perspectives. Indeed, Laing himself has modified his views, claiming that he never completely opposed psychiatry (Laing, 1979) and conceding that schizophrenia may be due in part to biochemical disturbances (Sedgwick, 1982). Not just Laing's formulation but all exclusively psychosocial theories have become increasingly difficult to defend as evidence accumulates that biological abnormalities are in fact involved in schizophrenia. To this biological evidence we now turn.

The Neuroscience Perspective

Undoubtedly one of the most exciting areas of abnormal psychology today is neuroscience research in schizophrenia. A vast amount remains to be done, but from the evidence already accumulated, it is clear that schizophrenia is, at least in part, genetically inherited. It is also known that many cases are related to irregularities of brain structure and biochemical activity. These findings, which have revolutionized schizophrenia research in the last two decades, derive from many different kinds of studies. We shall examine the most important.

Genetic Studies   The idea that schizophrenia might be passed from parent to child goes back at least as far as the eighteenth century. By the late nineteenth century, when biogenic theories were popular, the genetic hypothesis was endorsed by Kraepelin, Bleuler, and many other experts on schizophrenia. But it was not until about twenty-five years ago that researchers were able to design studies sophisticated enough actually to test the hypothesis scientifically. The evidence produced by these studies, as noted above, is extremely persuasive. In the words of David Rosenthal, one of the world's foremost authorities on the genetics of abnormal behavior, "the issue must now be considered closed. Genetic factors do contribute appreciably and beyond any reasonable doubt to the development of schizophrenic illness" (1970, pp. 131–132).

The studies leading up to this conclusion are—in order of chronology and sophistication—family, twin, and adoptive studies.

FAMILY STUDIES   Family studies of the genetics of schizophrenia clearly indicate that the more closely one is related to a schizophrenic, the more likely one is to develop schizophrenia. Figure 15.1 shows the data published by Gottesman in 1978. As may be seen from this graph, the child of one schizophrenic parent has a 13.8 percent chance, and the child of two schizophrenic parents a 36.6 percent chance, of becoming schizophrenic, as compared with a prevalence of 1 to 2 percent in the general population—a striking differential.

Yet family studies, no matter how striking or unanimous their findings, cannot be considered good tests of a genetic hypothesis, for the reason that we have discussed in earlier chapters—that is, that any psychological similarity between parent and child or sibling and sibling could be the product of a shared environment rather than of shared genes. If the child of a schizophrenic parent is about fourteen times more likely to become schizophrenic than the child of a normal parent, this could be due to the fact that the child was raised by a schizophrenic—or that he or she was exposed to the same environmental conditions that produced schizophrenia in the parent. In any case, it does not prove that the differential is a function of genetic inheritance.

The family studies, then, were only the beginning. Their major value was to spur other researchers to design better studies—studies in which genetic and environmental variables could be separated.

TWIN STUDIES   A great deal more precision on the question of genetics versus environment can be achieved in twin studies. As was pointed out in Chapter 5, these studies are based on the difference between monozygotic (MZ) and dizygotic (DZ) twins in the degree of genetic similarity. Any pair of twins tend to share a highly similar environment. However, MZ twins, having developed from the same sperm and the same ovum, have 100 percent of their genes in common. DZ twins, like any pair of siblings, have

FIGURE 15.1
Relatives of schizophrenics are at greater risk of developing the disorder themselves. (Adapted from Gottesman, 1978.)

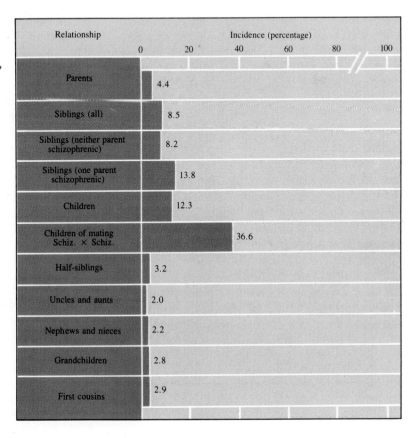

only approximately 50 percent of their genes in common. Hence a wide disparity in concordance rates between MZ and DZ twins would seem to be a function of genetic factors alone.

In the case of schizophrenia, such a disparity in concordance rates does indeed exist. In twin studies conducted over the past twenty years, the mean concordance rate for schizophrenia in MZ twins is approximately 47 percent, three times greater than the 15 percent mean concordance rate for DZ twins (Gottesman, 1978; Kessler, 1980). As more recent studies have improved in research methodology, the concordance rates for both MZ and DZ twins have dropped. Nevertheless, the MZ–DZ concordance ratios found in these studies generally lie between 3:1 and 5:1.

Such data must be considered strong evidence for the genetic hypothesis. However, as we saw in Chapter 5, twin studies too are subject to objections. To begin with, the researcher is dealing with a small sample. (There simply are not that many MZ schizophrenic twins in the world.) Second, as we saw, some researchers (e.g., Lidz, 1976) feel that MZ twins share not only a more similar genotype but also a more similar environment than DZ twins, in that the MZ twins are always the same sex, tend to be dressed alike, are often confused with each other, and so forth. Hence it is possible that here too the differential may be due to environment rather than (or as well as) genes. Even the twin studies, then, cannot be considered altogether conclusive.

ADOPTIVE STUDIES   It is only within the past two decades that researchers have developed studies in which environmental influences can be distinguished from genetic influences with truly scientific precision. These are the adoptive studies: studies of children who were adopted away from their biological families in infancy and who thus have the genetic endowment of one family and the environmental history of another. If such a study could show that children who were born to schizophrenic mothers[*] but were adopted in infancy by psychologically normal families still developed schizophrenia at the same rate as those children who were born of one schizophrenic parent and were

not adopted away, then this would indeed by very strong evidence for the genetic hypothesis.

Such studies have been done, and such were the findings. In a pioneering study, Heston (1966) located forty-seven adoptees who had been born to hospitalized schizophrenic mothers. He also selected a control group of fifty individuals adopted through the same foundling homes and matched for age, sex, type of placement, and length of time in child-care institutions. From a large variety of sources, mostly first-hand interviews, information was gathered on all these subjects. A dossier was then compiled on each subject, all identifying information was removed, and diagnoses were made by several independent psychiatrists. The results were that schizophrenia was found only in the children of schizophrenic mothers. The age-corrected[†] rate for schizophrenia among this group was 16.6 percent, about the same rate as for children who are born of a schizophrenic parent and not adopted away (see Figure 15.1). Heston also found that about half the children born of schizophrenic mothers exhibited signs of major psychosocial disability, such as mental deficiency, antisocial personality, or "neurotic" disorders.

Another study that has produced immensely influential findings was begun in Denmark by Rosenthal and his colleagues in 1963 (Rosenthal et al., 1968). The scope of this project is truly astounding. Through various central registries that have been maintained by the Danish government for some fifty years, the investigators identified 5,500 adoptees and 10,000 of their 11,000 biological parents. Then they identified all of those biological parents, called the *index parents,* who had at some time been admitted to a psychiatric hospital with a diagnosis of either schizophrenia or affective psychosis.[‡] The 76 adopted-away children of these parents (*index children*) were then matched with a control group of adopted children whose biological parents had no history of psychiatric hospitaliza-

---

[*] Studies of children of schizophrenic parents often limit their subjects to children of schizophrenic mothers, since paternity can never be established with absolute certainty.

[†] An *age-corrected* figure is a figure adjusted to take into account the age of the subjects being studied. For example, a subject who is only eighteen years old at the time when the study is done may develop schizophrenia at a later time. The figures are adjusted slightly to allow for this possibility.
[‡] The most important difference between the design of this study and that of Heston's study is that the majority of the Danish index parents were not hospitalized until some time after the birth of their children, thus eliminating the possibility that a mother's abnormal condition might have affected her child's gestation or birth.

tion. So far, three of the index children have been diagnosed as having chronic or process schizophrenia. No such diagnoses have been made among the controls. Perhaps of greater interest is the finding, derived from extensive interviews and psychological testing, that 21.9 percent of the index children, compared with 6.3 percent of the control children, were diagnosed as having schizophrenic characteristics (Haier et al., 1978).

Using the same Danish records, the same investigators (Kety et al., 1968, 1975, 1978) did another study from a slightly different perspective. In the same group of 5,500 adoptees from Copenhagen, 33 were identified as having psychiatric histories that warranted a diagnosis of schizophrenia. A matched control group of nonschizophrenic adoptees was selected from the same records. Then 463 biological and adoptive parents, siblings, and half-siblings were identified for both the index and control groups. A search through a variety of state and agency records revealed that 21 of these biological and adoptive relatives could be labeled schizophrenic. The incidence of schizophrenia among the adoptive relatives, those who shared only a common environment with the adoptees, was low and about the same for both the index and control groups. On the other hand, the incidence among the biological relatives, those who shared only a common genetic endowment with the adoptees, was significantly higher for the index group (8.7 percent) than for the control group (1.9 percent).

Note that the diagnoses of biological and adoptive relatives were based on information in official records, not on diagnostic interviews. To evaluate whether the same pattern would be found when relatives were interviewed, more than 90 percent of the living relatives who resided in Denmark, Norway, or Sweden were interviewed. The pattern of results was the same, although, overall, a higher percentage of relatives of all types showed schizophrenic symptoms. But most important, there was still very little difference between the frequency of schizophrenia in adoptive relatives of index cases (5.4 percent) compared with control cases (7.7 percent), whereas there was a highly significant difference between the frequency of schizophrenia in biological relatives of index cases (21.4 percent) compared with control cases (10.9 percent) (Kety et al., 1975). Thus adopted children who later become schizophrenic are much more likely to have biological, rather than adoptive, relatives with schizophrenia. This is persuasive evidence that there is a biological component to schizophrenia.

RESEARCH EXTENSIONS FROM GENETIC FINDINGS: HIGH RISK STUDIES   A vast number of studies have been conducted with children who have been born to schizophrenic parents and who have shown at least some symptoms of schizophrenia. These studies have revealed a wealth of information, but they are almost always contaminated by serious methodological problems. If, for example, you wanted to identify significant events in the background of a child who is now showing schizophrenic symptomatology, your theoretical notions might well bias your attention toward certain details of the child's history. Furthermore, if you interview people who have known the child—parents, grandparents, and so forth—their recollection will usually be influenced by what they know of the child's present condition. In short, retrospective information is often highly questionable. In addition, some of your subjects would probably already have experienced hospitalization and drug therapy, factors that would affect their responses to present testing.

The solution would be to conduct a longitudinal study, testing and interviewing a large random sample of children at regular intervals over a period of time. Then when certain of these children became schizophrenic, you would already have on file a reliable record of their physiological, psychological, and social histories and could begin searching for correlations. There is one problem with such a project, however. As we have seen, something over 1 percent of the general population becomes schizophrenic. Hence in order to end up with a reliable sample of schizophrenics, you would have to do longitudinal studies of thousands of children—a prohibitively expensive and time-consuming project.

In the early 1960s, Mednick and Schulsinger made a clear breakthrough in schizophrenia research by devising a longitudinal project that would largely resolve all of the problems outlined above (Mednick, 1970). Recognizing the impossibility of studying a random sample of normal children, the investigators selected instead a group of children who were at risk for schizophrenia—that is, children born of schizophrenic mothers. A number of previous studies had demonstrated that about 50 percent of the children of schizophrenic mothers could be expected eventually to show deviant behavior and that about 15 percent would become schizophrenic. Thus by choosing 200 normally functioning young children of schizophrenic mothers, the investigators were able to predict that the number who would become schizophrenic would be large enough to permit meaningful comparisons with low-risk control children—that is, children of nonschizophrenic mothers (Figure 15.2).

Mednick lists the following advantages of this research design over that of previous studies:

1. The children have not yet experienced the confounding effects of the schizophrenic life, such as hospitalization and drugs.
2. No one—teacher, relative, child or researcher—knows who will become schizophrenic, which eliminates much bias from testing and diagnosis.
3. Our information is current; we do not have to depend on anyone's recollection.
4. We have two built-in groups of controls for the children who become ill: the high-risk subjects who stay well and the low-risk subjects (1971, p. 80).

Considering its longitudinal nature, the Mednick project is still in its infancy; nevertheless, some fascinating preliminary data have already been published. As of 1971, 27 of the 200 high-risk children had been identified as mentally ill. Five critical differences appeared

to separate these children from those high-risk children who were still normal and from the control subjects:

1. The mothers of the deviant children were more severely schizophrenic, and they were hospitalized while their children were at a younger age.
2. School reports showed that the deviant children were more domineering, aggressive, and unmanageable in class.
3. On a word-association test, the deviant children quickly drifted away from the stimulus. The word "table," for example, might elicit a sequence of associations such as "chair, top, leg, girl, pretty, sky."
4. Galvanic skin responses (GSRs) of the deviant group were quite different from those of the other two groups.
5. Complications during pregnancy or birth had occurred for 70 percent of the deviant children

FIGURE 15.2

In this research design for the study of "high-risk" and "low-risk" children, Mednick (1970) gathered comparative data at three levels. At the first level, the distinguishing characteristics of children with and without schizophrenic mothers were studied. At the second level, the high-risk children who became deviant were compared with those who did not. At the third level, the characteristics of high-risk children who became schizophrenic were compared with those who were deviant but not schizophrenic, with those who did not become deviant, and with "low-risk" control children. (Adapted from S. Mednick, "Breakdown in Individuals at High Risk for Schizophrenia: Possible Predispositional Perinatal Factors." *Mental Hygiene,* 1970, 54, 50–63.)

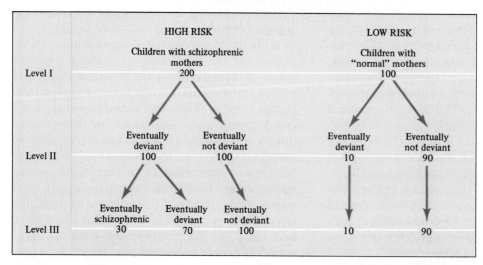

as compared with 15 percent of the nondeviant high-risk group and 33 percent of the controls.

Between 1972 and 1974, all children in the study went through an intensive diagnostic assessment. Among the high-risk group, seventeen were diagnosed as schizophrenic, but only one low-risk child was so diagnosed. However, one difference that had earlier distinguished deviant children in the high-risk group had disappeared. Those in the high-risk group who were diagnosed as schizophrenic did not show more drift on the word-association task than did those who did not become schizophrenic (Griffith et al., 1980).

This project has inspired many other similar projects, and there is now intense activity in high-risk research. Recent results from the Mednick and other projects have revealed that in comparison with low-risk children, high-risk children commit more criminal offenses (Kirkegaard-Sørensen and Mednick, 1975) and are more likely to show adjustment problems (Hanson et al., 1976) and poor attention (Asarnow et al., 1977). In addition, the EEG patterns of high-risk children tend to differ from those of low-risk children (Itil, 1977). As for children who later developed schizophrenia, their mothers were more likely to have become schizophrenic at an early age, to have been institutionalized for much of the child's first five years of life (Parnas et al., 1985), to have experienced childbirth-precipitated psychosis, and to have had unstable relationships with men (Talovic et al., 1980). Also, of the group who later became schizophrenic, the boys were described by their schoolteachers as behaving inappropriately and being disciplinary problems, the girls as apathetic, withdrawn, and isolated (John et al., 1982).

These are only preliminary findings. The full results of today's high-risk studies will not be in for at least another ten years. It is hoped, however, that those results will ultimately help us to identify the earliest signs of schizophrenia and to devise preventive treatments for children showing those signs, so as to stem the development of the disorder.

Brain Structure Studies   As we mentioned in Chapter 5, the development of computer-assisted tomography (the CT scan) has enabled researchers to take sophisticated X-rays of the brain and thus to identify structural abnormalities. A number of studies using the CT scan have found that in chronic schizophrenics the brain ventricles—that is, the cavities containing the cerebrospinal fluid—tend to be enlarged (Revely, 1985; Seidman, 1983) and that this ventricular enlargement is related to cognitive impairment (Golden et al., 1980; Johnstone et al., 1976), poor response to drug treatment (Weinberger, Bigelow, et al., 1980), poor premorbid adjustment (Weinberger, Cannon-Spoor, et al., 1980), and more negative than positive symptoms (Andreasen et al., 1982). Such a pattern of results strengthens the theory, described in the previous chapter, that there are two different schizophrenic disorders, one of which—the so-called Type II (Crow et al., 1982)—is associated with diffuse brain damage and is closer to Kraepelin's idea of dementia praecox.

These CT scan findings have been supported by postmortem analyses of schizophrenic brains (Brown et al., 1986) and by MRI, or magnetic resonance imaging, another technique described in Chapter 5. Using MRI, one group of researchers found that schizophrenics had atypically small frontal lobes, as well as small cerebrums and skulls (Andreasen et al., 1986). What this suggests is that some type of early developmental abnormality—again, probably only in Type II patients—has retarded the growth of both the brain and the skull.

Biochemical Research: The Dopamine Hypothesis   Some biochemical abnormality has long been suspected of causing schizophrenia. For reasons mentioned earlier in this chapter—particularly interference by third variables such as hospitalization and drugs—the progress in biochemical research has been slow and difficult. However, it has produced some plausible hypotheses.

The biochemical theory that has attracted the most attention in the past decade is the **dopamine hypothesis,** which posits that schizophrenia is associated with excess activity of those parts of the brain that use dopamine as a neurotransmitter. The major line of evidence for the dopamine hypothesis comes from research on the antipsychotic drugs (the phenothiazines and butyrophenones). These drugs have been dramatically effective in controlling schizophrenic symptoms. An interesting finding is that the antipsychotic drugs are most effective on Bleuler's primary symptoms such as thought disorder and withdrawal (two of the "four A's"—association and autism—mentioned in Chapter 14), are moderately effective on Bleuler's secondary symptoms such as hallucinations, and are ineffective on neurotic symptoms such as anxi-

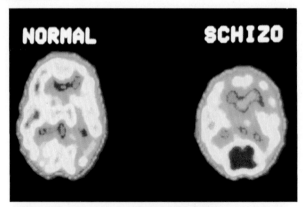

These CT scans of a normal brain (left) and a schizo-phrenic's brain (right) reveal the diffuse brain damage associated with chronic "Type II" schizophrenia. (N.I.H./Science Source/Photo Researchers)

ety (Paul, 1977). These drugs, in other words, seem to act on fundamental schizophrenic symptoms, and therefore many researchers feel that their chemical activity should provide a clue to the chemical activities underlying schizophrenia. The drugs work by blocking the brain's receptor sites for dopamine. That is, they reduce the activity of those parts of the brain that use dopamine to transmit neural impulses (Snyder, 1976). Hence the dopamine hypothesis: that schizo-phrenia is connected to excess dopamine activity.

Another piece of evidence involves the stimulants amphetamine and methylphenidate, both of which are known to increase dopamine activity in the brain. As we saw in Chapter 12, amphetamines can produce psychotic states similar to schizophrenia, and so can methylphenidate (Snyder, 1972, 1976). Furthermore, when these drugs are given to schizophrenic patients, the patients' symptomatology becomes more dramatic (Van Kammen, 1977). Here, then, we see another connection between schizophrenia and increased lev-els of dopamine activity. A final link has been provided by postmortems. Mackay and his colleagues (1982) found increased brain dopamine and an increased num-ber of dopamine receptors in the postmortems of forty-eight schizophrenic patients. Many of these pa-tients, however, had been taking antipsychotic drugs, which may have produced these results.

This focus on dopamine has suggested a conceptual link between schizophrenia and Parkinson's disease (Chapter 16), an organic brain disorder that produces uncontrollable bodily tremors. Parkinson's disease is known to be caused, in part, by a deficiency of dopa-mine in certain parts of the brain, and the drug L-dopa, which increases dopamine levels, is quite ef-fective in reducing tremors in Parkinson's patients. However, L-dopa can also produce schizophrenia-like symptoms (Celesia and Barr, 1970). Conversely, antipsychotic drugs often produce a Parkinson's-like movement disorder as a side effect.

Thus many lines of evidence converge to support the dopamine hypothesis. It is mostly indirect evi-dence, however. Other than the postmortem data, which are open to alternative interpretations, we have no direct evidence that schizophrenics do in fact expe-rience increased dopamine activity. Furthermore, as we noted in Chapter 14, the dopamine hypothesis applies only to Type I schizophrenics, those with posi-tive symptoms (Haracz, 1982). At the same time, there is some evidence *against* the dopamine hypothe-sis (Alpert, 1975; Biederman et al., 1977; Crow et al., 1976). There is also the confusing fact that the antipsychotic drugs, with their dopamine-blocking ef-fect, relieve the symptoms not just of schizophrenia but of all the major psychoses: mania, depression, drug-induced psychoses, schizophreniform disorder, and so on (Meltzer, 1979). In addition, schizophrenics who do respond to these drugs improve gradually over a period of about six weeks. Yet it takes only a few hours for the drugs to block dopamine receptors in the brain. If schizophrenia were merely the result of activity in these neural tracts, it should improve dramatically within a few hours (Davis, 1978). This suggests that excess dopamine activity, if in fact it underlies schizophrenia, is probably not its ultimate cause. What is further suggested by these findings is that the biological explanation of schizophrenia, if it is ever arrived at, will be a highly complex one, probably involving a *combination* of biochemical im-balances—and different combinations both for differ-ent types of schizophrenia and for different phases of any single case of schizophrenia (e.g., Davis, 1975).

Chemotherapy   We have spent a good deal of space in this chapter discussing the various forms of psychotherapy used with schizophrenics. The most common treatment for schizophrenia, however, is not psychotherapy but chemotherapy—treatment via drugs. The vast majority of schizophrenic patients are on a daily regimen of one of the phenothiazines, the antipsychotic drugs mentioned in the last section. And this is the only therapy that many patients re-ceive.

Since their introduction in 1952, the antipsychotic

drugs have virtually revolutionized the study and treatment of schizophrenia. We have already discussed the drugs' impact on biochemical research. When the drugs were introduced, researchers had little idea of how they worked. But the fact that they did work, and so well, prompted investigations of their biochemical effects—a line of research that has led so far to the dopamine hypothesis and may ultimately yield a comprehensive biochemical explanation of schizophrenia.

The impact of the antipsychotic drugs on the treatment of schizophrenics has been even greater. These drugs, as noted above, are very effective. They reduce agitation, hallucinations, delusions, and indeed all the primary and secondary symptoms of schizophrenia (Lipton and Burnett, 1980). As a result, they have permitted us to "open up" our mental hospitals to some degree, releasing patients who would otherwise have spent long periods, if not their entire lives, in the hospital. In the twenty years after the introduction of antipsychotic drugs, the population of the state mental hospitals was cut to less than half (Lipton and Burnett, 1980) and the length of hospitalization for a psychotic episode was reduced by about two-thirds. The drugs also help to prevent relapses. Patients who continue medication after release from the hospital have about a 32 percent chance of suffering a relapse within the year, compared with a 70 percent chance for patients who discontinue medication (Hogarty, 1977).

At the same time, there are good arguments against the antipsychotic drugs. To begin with, they can have debilitating side effects, the most serious being **tardive dyskinesia,** a muscle disorder that causes patients to grimace and smack their lips uncontrollably. Tardive dyskinesia usually appears in patients who have had more than six months of continuous treatment with antipsychotic drugs. The condition is very resistant to treatment, even after the drug is discontinued.

There is also evidence that many patients would not need antipsychotic drugs if they were in better treatment programs. Patients at Soteria House, described above, receive no drugs, and they apparently do as well as patients who are hospitalized and medicated (Mosher and Menn, 1978). Likewise, when a group of young schizophrenics with good prognoses were given an excellent milieu therapy and no drugs for at least a month in a study conducted by the National Institute of Mental Health, about 30 percent improved sufficiently to be released (Gunderson, 1977).

However, the major criticism of the antipsychotic drugs is that they do not cure schizophrenia. Even with the medication, as we saw, a third of released patients relapse within the year. And even those who do not relapse to the point of rehospitalization often continue to require special care. In truth, the chances of a person's attaining full and permanent recovery after a schizophrenic episode have not been significantly increased by the advent of antipsychotic drugs (Lehmann, 1975). This does not mean, however, that the drugs have no value. At the moment, we have no cure for schizophrenia, and no preventive measures. All we have are drugs that alleviate the symptoms. Therefore, just as with illnesses such as hypertension and diabetes, when cause and cure are unknown, we go on using symptom-relieving drugs while in the meantime researchers continue to seek cause and cure.

The Diathesis-Stress Model

For a time, the breakthroughs in genetic research tended to discredit the environmental theories. In the words of two researchers, the burden of proof was shifted "from showing that genes are important to showing that environment is important" (Gottesman and Shields, 1976, p. 367). But while the genetic findings are virtually incontrovertible, they are obviously not the whole story. As Seymour Kety (1970), one of the foremost genetic researchers, has pointed out, schizophrenia cannot be entirely controlled by genes, for if it were, the concordance rate for MZ twins would be 100 percent. Not only is it not 100 percent; as we saw, it is only about 40 to 50 percent. This leaves ample maneuvering space for what can only be environmental influence.

These facts have led most schizophrenia researchers to adopt what is called the **diathesis-stress theory,** which states that what is genetically inherited is a diathesis, or predisposition, to schizophrenia, but that this predisposition must be combined with environmental stress for the disorder actually to develop. Given a biological predisposition, a painful parent–child relationship might precipitate schizophrenia, but so might birth injury, puberty, a serious physical illness, repeated rejection, prolonged poverty, or any other form of stress. In an influential paper, Zubin and Spring (1977) proposed that a predisposition to schizophrenia can be produced in a variety of ways—through inheritance, physical disease, or maturational processes. Whether a person actually has a schizophrenic episode depends on the stresses encountered and on the person's coping skills.

These explanations appeal to common sense and help to reconcile a great many different research findings, such as the role of birth injury and parental absence found in the high-risk studies. At the same time, the diathesis-stress model is simply a model, not an answer, and it leaves many riddles unsolved. If a predisposition to schizophrenia is inherited, what is the nature of the genetic defect? And what stresses are most likely to convert it into schizophrenia? In an extensive review of the research, Mirsky and Duncan (1986) listed the stresses that are now hypothesized to be associated with the development of schizophrenia. They include (1) feelings of clumsiness and being "different" as a result of attentional deficits, (2) increased dependence on parents as a result of being impaired, (3) poor academic performance and poor coping skills, again as a result of the basic organic impairment, (4) stressful family interactions, including high "expressed emotion," (5) "communication deviance" in the family, leading to difficulty in communicating with people outside the family and hence to increased isolation, and (6) frequent hospitalization of a parent or other family members. Emphasis on stressful family interactions receives support from the research findings discussed in the box on page 380.

Some investigators (e.g., Rabkin, 1980) question whether schizophrenics do in fact have histories of greater stress than other people. Certain studies (e.g., Brown and Birley, 1968) show that in the three months preceding hospitalization, schizophrenics have experienced more crises, great and small, than normal people within a comparable period. But as the investigators themselves concede, these crises look more like triggering events than like actual causal factors (Brown et al., 1973). It is also possible that the difference lies less in raw numbers of stressful events than in the attitude toward such events. On the evidence of one study (Serban, 1975), it appears that problems that most of us would greet with mild worry or annoyance arouse much more anxiety in schizophrenics. Especially for chronic schizophrenics, the investigator notes, "the surrounding world is a source of turmoil. . . . Everything appears to represent either an insurmountable demand which society places on them, or worry induced by frustrated expectations" (Serban, 1975, p. 405). But to what extent is this overreaction a result rather than a cause of schizophrenia? As usual, we do not know.

This last finding raises once again the problem of primary versus secondary symptoms. Of all the questions facing schizophrenia researchers, this is the most pressing, for only by locating the primary symptoms will researchers know what they should be studying. As we saw in Chapter 14, many experts feel that the root problem in schizophrenia is a breakdown of selective attention. Others believe that the basic pathology lies in the way schizophrenics process *all* incoming information, attentional deficits being only one facet of the problem. A third theory is that the critical factor is the level of arousal of the autonomic nervous system and that it is this that causes the attention problem (Venables, 1964). A fourth position, connected to the family theories, is that the basic flaw is faulty communication patterns, leading to poor correspondence between language and reality, which in turn leads to poor reality contact. Finally, as mentioned earlier, there are those who believe that social withdrawal, again stemming from family interactions, is the fundamental pathology. Until researchers can determine which of these problems is in fact primary, their efforts will be dispersed in many different directions.

SUMMARY

Research into the causes of schizophrenia has been hampered by a number of problems. There is no consensus on what the basic disorder is or on whether schizophrenia is a disease or merely a label that is attached to people who act in certain ways. Even when researchers agree on a conceptual level, they often disagree as to who fits the category. *DSM-III-R* has eliminated some of these diagnostic differences by establishing more specific and widely accepted criteria for what constitutes schizophrenia. Yet serious difficulties remain, especially that of discriminating between primary symptoms and mere reactions to primary symptoms.

Two major problems hamper investigations into the origins of schizophrenia. First, after a correlation is established between two variables, there is no clue as to the direction of a causal relationship between the two—if indeed there is one. Second, it is possible that both factors are the result of an unidentified cause, a third variable—such as hospitalization or drugs. Also, the expectations of researchers can influence their assessment of the effectiveness of different treatments.

A number of perspectives have been offered on

the etiology of schizophrenia, some stressing the environmental origins of the disorder, some the hereditary influences, and others the interaction between environmental stress and genetic abnormalities.

Initially, the psychodynamic perspective emphasized the environmental causes of schizophrenia. According to Freud, schizophrenia is a form of regression; schizophrenics are people who are overwhelmed by anxiety because their egos are not strong enough to cope with unacceptable id impulses. Later psychodynamic theorists came to believe that there are several kinds of schizophrenia—some primarily biological in origin—and to stress the role of interpersonal factors more strongly than Freud did. In treating schizophrenics, psychodynamic therapists act both as analysts, probing the patient's unconscious, and as "second parents," offering support and esteem.

Family theorists believe that a specific type of family tends to produce schizophrenics. Those who believe that the parental relationship is the crucial factor point to two types of families, the schismatic family and the skewed family. One study found a relationship between the "expressed emotion" (EE—high levels of criticism and emotional overinvolvement) within the family and rehospitalization of the schizophrenic member. Theorists who focus on parent–child communication believe that double-bind communication—mutually contradictory messages from the mother—may be a causative agent in schizophrenia. "Communication deviance" (CD) in the parents has been found to be a good predictor of schizophrenia in adolescent children—and to correlate with high EE. Because of interpretation problems, recent studies have tended to focus attention on the communication patterns among all members of the family and to see the emotional climate of the family as causative only if the child is otherwise predisposed to schizophrenia.

The behavioral perspective views schizophrenics as people with inadequate coping skills who need retraining. Ullmann and Krasner provide the most comprehensive behavioral interpretation of schizophrenia, terming it a learned behavior consisting primarily of attention problems. Schizophrenics are seen as people who have received little or no reinforcement for socially acceptable responses and who may be receiving powerful rewards for bizarre responses. Behavioral treatments aim at reversing this pattern. Treatments include direct reinforcement, token economies, and social-skills training.

Of the few humanistic and existentialist writers who have directed their attention to schizophrenia, R. D. Laing is the most outspoken. Laing challenges the labeling process, claiming that our society is a poor standard of sanity. Laing is supported by the antipsychiatric movement, a group of critics who believe that "insanity" is simply a label used by society to exploit and suppress people so labeled, and that psychosis should be treated as a disruption of social or interpersonal relations. The humanistic-existential and antipsychiatric schools propose treatment strategies based on the establishment of a nurturant environment to promote healing and growth. These strategies range from milieu therapy, which encourages patients to take responsibility for their own behavior, to Laing's radical Kingsley Hall community, which does not distinguish between the roles of patients and staff. In recent years, however, Laing has modified his views, acknowledging that schizophrenia may have a biochemical basis.

The neuroscience perspective has convincingly indicated that genetic factors contribute to the development of schizophrenia. While this theory is not new, it was not until family, twin, and adoptive studies were conducted that biological and environmental variables could be separated. Preliminary results of a longitudinal study of high-risk children (those born to schizophrenic parents) offer additional indications of the importance of genetic factors in schizophrenia. The CT scan and MRI technique are making it possible to study abnormalities in the brain structure of chronic schizophrenics.

Biochemical research focuses on the biological abnormality that is genetically transmitted and produces schizophrenic behavior. Progress in this area has been slow, but it has produced some plausible hypotheses based on the role of neurotransmitters. One promising but problematic theory ascribes schizophrenia to excess dopamine activity within the brain. It seems likely that any biological explanation of schizophrenia will involve a combination of biochemical imbalances.

The most common treatment for schizophrenia is not psychotherapy but chemotherapy—treatment with drugs. While drugs, particularly the various phenothiazines, are effective in relieving schizophrenic symptoms, they do not cure the disorder, and side effects have made their use controversial.

Most researchers now recognize that environmental and genetic factors interact in the etiology of schizophrenia. Hence many adopt the diathesis-stress model, which states that a predisposition to schizophrenia is inherited but that the disorder must be triggered by environmental stresses, such as poor coping skills and high "expressed emotion" and "communication deviance" within the family.

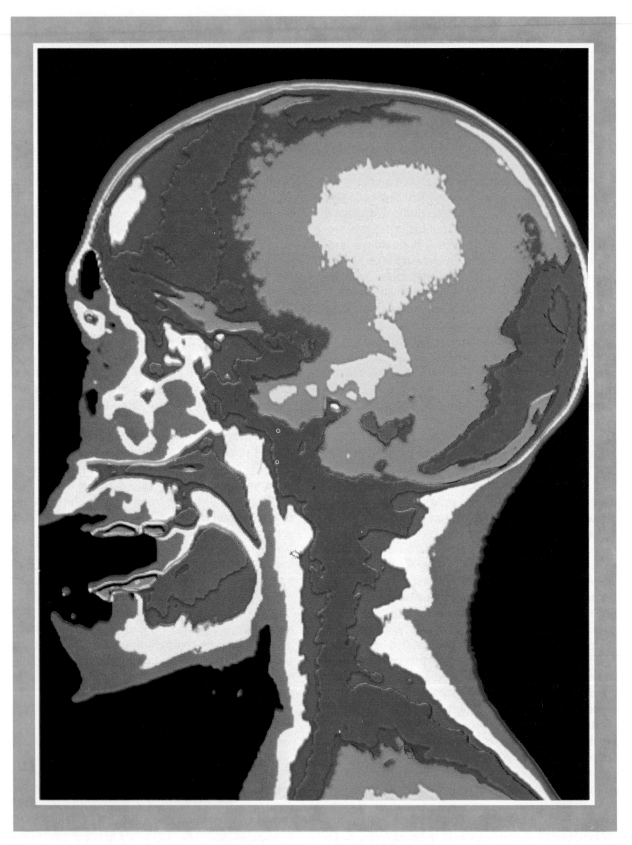

CHAPTER 16

Organic Brain Disorders

PROBLEMS IN DIAGNOSIS

Biogenic versus Psychogenic Disorders
Specifying the Organic Impairment
Specifying the Site of the Damage

**ORGANIC BRAIN DISORDERS
CLASSIFIED BY ETIOLOGY**

Cerebral Infection
Brain Trauma
Vascular Accidents
Brain Tumors

Degenerative Disorders
Nutritional Deficiency
Endocrine Disorders
Toxic Disorders

THE EPILEPSIES

Etiology
Personality and Intellectual Characteristics
Precipitation of Seizures
Types of Epilepsy

The last eight chapters have been devoted to disorders that have long been considered psychogenic: schizophrenia, anxiety, depression, and other disorders. Historically, psychologists have traced these conditions to the individual's relations to his or her experience and environment. Current theories have now begun to recognize the role of biological factors in some of these disorders: certain people may be genetically vulnerable to schizophrenia, for example. But scientists have not established direct connections between the biological factors in most of these conditions and their psychological effects. The **organic brain disorders,** in contrast, are by definition biogenic. They are clusters of behavioral problems that are directly traceable to the destruction of brain tissue or to biochemical imbalances in the brain. This is not to say, however, that these disorders are "purely" biological. The form an organic syndrome takes depends in part on psychosocial factors. Two people suffering from the same organic syndrome may exhibit different symptoms because of their experiences and/or environmental circumstances. Just as psychogenic disorders can sometimes be treated with

organic therapies, such as drugs, so organic disorders can sometimes be treated with psychological therapies. Nevertheless, the distinction between psychogenic and organic disorders is an important one.

Although we pay more attention to functional disorders in this book, the organic brain syndromes constitute a major health problem. At present they account for one-fourth of all first admissions to mental hospitals in the United States. In this chapter we will first examine the difficulties of diagnosing organic brain disorder. Then we will discuss the symptoms and the causes (those that are known) of the major organic brain disorders.

PROBLEMS IN DIAGNOSIS

There are four major problems in the diagnosis of organic brain disorder: (1) deciding whether the disorder is in fact organic; (2) if it is, determining the cause of the brain pathology; (3) if the brain damage is localized (i.e., restricted to a specific area of the brain), determining the location; and (4) deciding how psychosocial factors influence the manifestation of symptoms and whether psychological therapy can modify the impact of the organic pathology. As we shall see, none of these decisions is a simple matter.

Biogenic versus Psychogenic Disorders

The major symptoms of brain disorder are listed below. Not all symptoms occur in all disorders; there is considerable variety in symptom pattern.

1. *Impairment of orientation.* The person may be unaware of his or her own body and surroundings, unable to tell who he or she is, what the date is, and so forth.

2. *Impairment of memory.* The person may forget events of the distant past or, more typically, of the very recent past and may invent stories to fill in these memory gaps. The ability to learn and retain new information may also be disrupted. (Memory impairment may be the most common symptom of brain disorder.)

3. *Impairment of other intellectual functions, such as comprehension and production of speech, calculation, and general knowledge.* The person may be unable to define simple words, do ordinary calculations, name the president of the United States, and the like.

4. *Impairment of judgment.* The person ceases to be able to make appropriate decisions—cannot decide what to have for lunch, when to keep clothes on and when to take them off, and so forth.

5. *Lability or shallowness of affect.* The person passes quickly and inappropriately from apathy to hostility or from laughing to weeping.

6. *Loss of mental and emotional resilience.* The person may function well under ordinary circumstances but when emotionally stressed, mentally taxed, or physically fatigued may experience a significant decline in the ability to solve problems, make decisions, learn and remember new material, and control emotions.

The interesting thing about this list is how closely the symptoms of organic brain disorder resemble those of psychogenic disorders. Disorientation, impaired intellectual functioning, and inappropriate affect are well-recognized symptoms of schizophrenia, for example. Diagnosis in such cases may not be easy, at least initially. Differences in the natural history, course, and presenting signs and symptoms of a disorder help clinicians identify it as an organic condition.

Consider, for example, the following case:

> This girl, who had had seizures since infancy, at the age of 17 went into a psychotic state which developed rapidly in the course of a few days. There were first a tendency to make odd and inappropriate remarks, and bizarre behavior such as sitting the whole of a morning with a newspaper, apparently reading it but in answer to questions being unable to say even what was in the headlines. She then kept her eyes closed, her mouth in a fixed smile; in the night she was found kneeling naked in a position of prayer, apparently having been there for some time, as she was very cold. Admitted to the hospital, she remained negativistic and catatonic. At times she would eat if a piece of bread was put into her hand; at other times the food had to be put into her mouth. She had to be taken to the toilet, but would walk with assistance; if pushed too hard she would become aggressive (Slater and Beard, 1971, pp. 140–141).

A patient with such symptoms might well be diagnosed initially as a catatonic schizophrenic. In fact, investigation showed that there was damage within the right temporal lobe of her brain, which had been the cause of her seizures as well as her catatonic-like behavior.

Thus there may be overlap between the symptoms of organic and functional disorders. Furthermore, the symptoms of an organic disorder may be complicated by emotional disturbances developing *in response to* the organic impairment. For example, if a man who is unknowingly suffering from an organic brain disorder suddenly finds that his cognitive skills are deteriorating—that he is continually making mistakes on the job or repeatedly taking the wrong bus to get home—he is likely to become anxious, depressed, or defensive. Thus by the time he is seen by a diagnostician, his primary symptoms—the symptoms of the organic impairment—may well be obscured by an overlay of secondary functional disturbances.

Before the development of modern diagnostic tests (such as the CT scan), it was exceedingly difficult to differentiate between organic and psychogenic disorders. It was not unknown for an autopsy to reveal that a patient whose symptoms had been curiously resistant to several years of psychotherapy had actually been suffering from a brain tumor (Waggoner and Bagchi, 1954; Patton and Sheppard, 1956). Such an unfortunate case was that of the composer George Gershwin. Young and seemingly healthy, Gershwin one day lost consciousness momentarily while conducting a concert of his works. In the months that followed, he began to act peculiarly; he was irritable, restless, and suffered from painful headaches. At the urging of his family he entered a hospital for a complete physical examination; he was released, the physicians insisting that he was "a perfect specimen of health" (Ewen, 1956, p. 298). He then began daily treatment with a psychotherapist, who decided that what Gershwin needed was rest and seclusion. The rest seemed to help, for about a month. Then Gershwin collapsed and went into a coma. He was rushed to a hospital, where exploratory surgery located an inoperable brain tumor. Gershwin died that same day, at the age of thirty-eight.

The reverse mistake—diagnosing a psychological problem as an organic disorder—also occurs, especially with elderly patients. Psychiatrists may presume that an elderly patient is growing senile and diagnose dementia (an organic disorder) when in fact the person is suffering from depression brought on by the loss of a spouse, health problems, difficulties with the tasks of everyday living, and so on (Gurland et al., 1980).

The differential diagnosis of functional and psychological disturbances is crucial. Many organic disorders can be treated, but only if they are recognized for what they are. Misdiagnosis can be fatal. Sound practice calls for a diagnostician to rule out organic factors before concluding that a disorder is psychological in origin. Diagnosticians can draw on a number of resources: direct observation of the patient, a detailed history of the onset and progress of the symptoms, interviews with the patient's family and physician. In addition, diagnosticians usually put the patient through a series of tests: neurological tests to assess reflexes, which may be faulty if there is damage to the nervous system; EEGs, brain CT scans (Chapter 7), and chemical analyses of cerebrospinal fluids; and finally, neuropsychological tests, such as the Halstead-Reitan Battery (Chapter 7) and others that are specifically designed to detect organic impairment. Newer technologies, such as PET (positron emission tomography) and NMR (nuclear magnetic resonance) scans promise even better detection of brain pathology (Chapter 7).

Modern medical technology, such as the electroencephalograph, has made it easier to differentiate between functional and organic brain disorders. (David York/Medichrome/The Stock Shop)

Specifying the Organic Impairment

If a man appears in an emergency room with a revolver in his hand and bullet holes on either side of his head, the physician on duty will have little difficulty determining the source, to say nothing of the existence, of organic brain damage. In most cases, however, it is even more difficult to specify the source of the organic impairment—tumor, poisoning, infection, "stroke," whatever—than to distinguish between psychogenic and biogenic pathology. And like the psychogenic–biogenic distinction, the accurate identification of a biogenic disorder is essential, as it is on this decision that treatment is based. A physician, of course, does not wish to treat for a brain tumor only to discover that the patient is suffering from lead poisoning.

Several possible sources of confusion can make diagnosis difficult. In the first place, the symptoms of the various organic brain disorders overlap considerably. If it is determined that a patient's amnesia is biogenic, this condition could still be due to a number of possible brain pathologies, each requiring different treatment. Second, just as different organic brain disorders may result in the same symptoms, so the same etiology may produce widely different symptomatologies, depending on *location* in the brain. A brain tumor may cause a speech disorder in one patient, double vision in another, and emotional lability in a third. Indeed, the source of the brain pathology is only one of the many factors determining the patient's behavioral responses to the disease. The patient's age, general physical condition, prior intellectual achievements, premorbid personality, emotional stability, and social situation—as well as the location and extent of the brain damage—will affect the symptoms. A patient who feels alone in the world or who is basically rigid and pessimistic or to whom a serious medical problem may spell financial ruin may respond to unwelcome symptoms with panic or total dejection. On the other hand, a patient who is happily married, well insured, and blessed with a resilient disposition may show a surprisingly moderate response to what is actually a severe impairment. From this bewildering array of variables the diagnostician must ferret out the single primary variable: the source of the brain pathology.

There is one final problem in determining the source of organic brain syndromes. As with so many of the functional disorders, there are many organic brain disorders about which we simply know very little. Unfortunately, it often happens that the better-understood syndromes—those whose causes, symptoms, course, and prognosis we can chart with substantial accuracy—are those that occur least frequently, while many of the most common organic disorders remain somewhat baffling. For example, brain poisoning due to the ingestion of toxic mushrooms is both very well understood and very rare, while the senile degenerative disorders, which affect about half of all older persons confined to nursing homes, remain something of a mystery.

Specifying the Site of the Damage

We mentioned earlier the matter of determining the location of the brain damage. This is the third important problem in diagnosis. In the case of some disorders (e.g., cerebral syphilis and the senile degenerative disorders), the problem may not apply, for the damage is often relatively diffused throughout the brain. But with many other disorders, such as "strokes" and brain tumors, and damage may be restricted to one specific area, leaving the rest of the brain relatively unaffected. When this is the case, it is essential to determine what the specific area is, for this information may have important implications for treatment. Obviously, surgeons are in a better position to operate on a brain tumor when they know where the tumor is located.

Physiological measures such as the EEG can sometimes give vague hints as to the location of the brain pathology. Another hint is often found in the patient's behavioral symptoms. In many cases, CT and PET scans (Chapter 7) can be used to locate the brain damage if the damaged area is large enough. (These techniques offer little help in the identification of diffuse disorders, however.) As we saw in Chapter 5, certain areas of the brain are known to control certain behaviors. This knowledge may enable diagnosticians to generate hypotheses about the location of lesions on the basis of test scores and/or behavior patterns. The physician who can discover exactly where the brain is damaged can direct rehabilitation more effectively, either by retraining the patient to use the impaired functions or by teaching the patient to use intact abilities to compensate for the loss of impaired ones.

Patterns of Disability: Aphasia, Apraxia, and Agnosia   In some cases of organic brain disorder, the symptoms are restricted to a specific aspect of behavior. (These are sometimes called "focal symptoms.") One such condition is **aphasia,** or language impairment. The diagnosis of aphasia depends on fluency of speech, comprehension, and the ability to repeat phrases and sentences (Cummings, 1985). Patients with **fluent aphasia** produce streams of incoherent speech (syllables are reversed, word order is jumbled, and so on). Patients with **nonfluent aphasia** have difficulty initiating speech and respond to questions with one-word answers, short phrases, and long pauses. Such patients are further differentiated by their ability to comprehend speech (ranging from good to poor) and their ability to repeat speech correctly (also ranging from good to poor).

The location of brain damage that produces the aphasias is known. In most individuals (99 percent of right-handers and about 60 percent of left-handers), language is controlled largely by the left hemisphere. Aphasia is caused by damage to this hemisphere. Fluent aphasia is produced by damage closer to the rear of this hemisphere, nonfluent aphasia by damage closer to the front of the hemisphere. When damage is limited to the left frontal lobe, comprehension is usually preserved; when damage extends to the posterial lobe, comprehension is impaired.

Another major class of disability is **apraxia,** impairment of the ability to perform voluntary movements in a person who has normal primary motor skills (strength, coordination, etc.) and who understands the nature of the movement to be performed. For example, a patient may try to write with a pair of scissors or to light a match by striking the wrong end (Hécaen and Albert, 1978).

A third class of disability is **agnosia,** disturbed sensory perception. When Dr. P., a distinguished professor of music, developed visual agnosia, he developed a number of "eccentricities" (Sacks, 1985). He often failed to recognize his students' faces, yet when they spoke, he knew immediately who they were. At the same time, he saw faces that didn't exist: he would pat fire hydrants and parking meters as if they were the heads of children and begin animated conversations with pieces of furniture. An opthalmologist examined Dr. P. and, finding nothing wrong with his eyes, recommended he see a neurologist. The neurologist found him "a man of great cultivation and charm, who talked well and fluently, with imagination and humor" (p. 8). At first he couldn't imagine why Dr. P. had been referred to the clinic. Gradually, however, the patient's "eccentricities" began to assume a pattern. He was able to see, but not to make sense of his perceptions. "Visually, he was lost in a world of lifeless abstractions" (p. 13). Able to identify a cube, a dodecahedron, and other complex geometric forms, he was baffled by a rose.

> "About 6 inches in length," he commented. "A convoluted red form with a linear green attachment."
> "Yes," I [the neurologist] said encouragingly, "but what do you think it *is*, Dr. P.?"
> "Not easy to say." He seemed perplexed. . . .
> "Smell it," I suggested, and he again looked somewhat puzzled, as if I'd asked him to smell a higher symmetry (p. 12).

An ordinary glove produced a similar response.

> "A continuous surface," he announced at last, "infolded on itself. It appears to have"—he

hesitated—"five outpouchings, if that is the word" (p. 13).

On one occasion, as he was preparing to leave the neurologist's office, Dr. P. reached for his wife's head and tried to lift her, mistaking his wife for a hat. Interestingly, although Dr. P.'s visual sense was totally impaired, his musical sense remained intact. He was able to function in everyday life by composing eating songs, dressing songs, and bathing songs, which guided his actions. Dr. P. was found to have a massive tumor in the visual-processing region of his brain.

Dr. P.'s case was unusual. Such impairments rarely appear in isolation. Most patients show a combination of disabilities (along with a confusing overlay of secondary psychological symptoms, such as anxiety and depression, developed in response to the new disabilities). Thus it is the rare case in which the diagnostician can accurately specify one spot, and one spot alone, in which the damage has occurred. Nevertheless, an educated guess must be made as to the site or sites of the pathology.

In diagnosing an organic brain syndrome, the clinician classifies the syndrome according to its etiology—trauma, infection, poisoning, or whatever. And accordingly it is by etiology that these brain syndromes will be discussed in the remainder of our chapter. (The one exception to this classification system is epilepsy, which, because its etiology is in some cases unknown, is classified by its symptomatology.)

ORGANIC BRAIN DISORDERS CLASSIFIED BY ETIOLOGY

Cerebral Infection

Behavior disorders may result from infections that damage and destroy the neural tissue of the brain. There are four major categories of brain infection: cerebral abscess, encephalitis, meningitis, and neurosyphilis.

Cerebral Abscess   A **cerebral abscess,** like an abscess in any other part of the body, is an infection that becomes encapsulated by connective tissue. It cannot drain and heal like an infection on the outside of the body, but simply continues to grow inside the body. Brain abscesses can result when an infection in some other part of the body travels to the brain or when some foreign object (e.g., a bullet, a piece of shrapnel) enters the brain, introducing germs.

Symptoms of cerebral abscess vary widely. In the early stages of the infection, the patient may experience chills, fever, stiffness of the neck, loss of appetite, and sometimes convulsions. Once the infection becomes closed off by the connective tissue, however, the symptom picture changes. As the abscess grows within the tissue, it presses against neighboring brain structures and interferes with their functioning, in much the same way as a brain tumor. Hence the later symptoms of brain abscess are similar to those of brain tumor or any other cause of increased intracranial pressure: headache, nausea, vomiting, problems with vision, and in some cases marked personality changes. As the pressure in the brain continues to build, it may produce extreme lethargy and eventually stupor; the patient becomes mute and motionless.

The usual treatment for cerebral abscess consists of surgical drainage or removal of the abscess and administration of antibiotic drugs. Even after this treatment, however, the patient may continue to have behavioral problems. The nature and severity of the problems will depend on the size and location of the abscess and on the age of the patient at the time of the infection.

Encephalitis   In the United States, **encephalitis,** a generic term meaning any inflammation of the brain, was a more serious problem earlier in this century than it is today. One form, **epidemic encephalitis** (also called *von Economo's disease,* after the Viennese physician who first identified it), was particularly widespread following World War I. Its most striking symptoms were profound lethargy and prolonged periods of sleep, often for days or even weeks at a time. For this reason, the disease was often called "sleeping sickness." In their periods of wakefulness, however, patients might become extremely hyperactive, irritable, and then breathless and unable to sleep. Other symptoms included convulsive seizures and delirium—a state of excitement and disorientation marked by incoherent speech, restless activity, and often hallucinations. Furthermore, striking psychological aftereffects could be observed in victims who survived the disease, especially in children, who are more susceptible to it than are adults. After an episode of epidemic encephalitis, a child who had been cheerful

and affable before the episode might demonstrate a marked moral deterioration, including such offensive behaviors as lying, cheating, cruelty, and sexual aggression. In short, such children came to resemble young sociopaths—a condition that often persisted into adulthood.

The virus responsible for epidemic encephalitis, while still active in certain areas of Asia and Africa, is now virtually unknown in Europe and America. However, there remain scores of other viruses that can cause various types of encephalitis, most of which are grouped under the general heading of **unspecified encephalitis.** Typically transmitted by such animals as mosquitoes, ticks, and horses, these viruses induce many of the same symptoms that we have described as typical of epidemic encephalitis: lethargy, irritability, convulsions, and the like.

Meningitis   Another type of infection is **meningitis,** an acute inflammation of the **meninges,** the membranous covering of the brain and spinal cord. Meningitis may be caused by bacteria, viruses, protozoa, or fungi. As in cerebral abscess, these foreign bodies may be introduced into the brain either through an infection elsewhere in the body or by an exogenous agent such as a bullet. Among the psychological symptoms usually observed in the various forms of meningitis are drowsiness, confusion, irritability, inability to concentrate, memory defects, and sensory impairments. In milder cases the primary infection may be effectively eradicated, but residual effects such as motor and sensory impairments and, in infants, mental retardation are not uncommon. In more severe cases, meningitis progresses rapidly from drowsiness to coma to death. Autopsies is such cases generally reveal that the brain is swollen and covered with pus and that the pressure from the swelling has caused the gyri (the convolutions in the surface of the brain) to flatten against the inside of the skull.

Neurosyphilis   **Neurosyphilis,** the deterioration of brain tissue as a result of syphilis, was once more common than any of the forms of encephalitis. As we have seen in Chapter 1, it was not until the late nineteenth century that the degenerative disorder called **general paresis** was finally linked with syphilis. Throughout the previous centuries syphilis had raged unchecked through Europe, taking a fantastic toll in infant mortality, blindness, madness, and death.

Among its more famous victims were Henry VIII, along with most of his many wives, and probably Columbus. Indeed, it is thought that the disease was introduced into Europe by Columbus's crew, who were apparently infected by the natives of the West Indies (Kemble, 1936). Nearer our own times, Lord Randolph Churchill, father of Winston Churchill, and Al Capone both suffered gruesome deaths from neurosyphilis.

Syphilis begins when the spirochete known as *Treponema pallidum* invades the victim's body through tiny skin lesions or, more commonly, through the mucous membranes in the mouth or genital areas. The transmission almost invariably occurs during sexual intercourse (genital or anal) or oral–genital contact with a syphilitic sexual partner. Once contracted, the disease runs a well-defined course:

Stage 1: About ten to twenty days after the disease has been contracted, a chancre, or sore, appears at the site of the infection—the genitals, the mouth, or the anus. Unfortunately, the chancre is often painless and disappears without treatment, so that many people either do not recognize this early warning sign or conclude that they have recovered once the chancre disappears.

Stage 2: About three to six weeks after the appearance of the chancre, the victim develops a copper-colored rash that covers the body and may be accompanied by fever, headaches, and other indispositions. This symptom also passes quickly. Thereafter the spirochetes may eventually be eliminated from the body or, in less fortunate individuals, they simply multiply, carrying the individual into the decisive third and fourth stages of the disease.

Stage 3: In the third stage, called the latent stage, which may last anywhere from ten to thirty years, the spirochetes slowly and insidiously invade the vital organs of the body.

Stage 4: Whatever damage has been done during the latent period now becomes apparent in any of a wide variety of organ failures, including heart attack, blindness, or—if the spirochetes have infiltrated the brain—general paresis.

General paresis develops in approximately 3 percent of untreated syphilitics. Its onset is usually marked by a vague but pervasive slovenliness of behavior. The person begins to show up late for work, ignores the feelings of others, dispenses casual insults, loses interest in his or her appearance, evades responsibilities, and so forth. As the disease becomes more advanced, a number of better-defined symptoms

make their appearance, including tremors, slurring of speech, deterioration of handwriting, a shuffling gait, and, almost invariably, disturbances of vision. One very common indication is the so-called Argyll Robertson sign: the pupil of the eye makes an accommodation to distance but not to light.

This physical deterioration is accompanied by an equally grave deterioration of the personality as the individual becomes increasingly sloppy, indifferent, and callous. Memory losses begin to appear. At the same time the individual may become severely depressed or, on the other hand, expansive, delusional, and euphoric. When the disease has progressed to this stage, the only possible treatment is custodial. In the final stage preceding death, both body and mind are virtually nonfunctional. The individual is paralyzed, inarticulate, cut off from reality, and subject to frequent convulsive seizures.

While syphilis is normally contracted through sexual acts, it may also be transmitted by a syphilitic mother to her unborn child as blood—in this case containing the syphilitic spirochetes—passes from one to the other across the placenta. If the child lives (many syphilitic fetuses are stillborn), he or she stands a good chance of developing **juvenile paresis,** the childhood form of general paresis. While the juvenile paretic may seem normal at birth, the same symptoms of intellectual and physical deterioration seen in general paresis generally appear sometime between the ages of five and twenty. Like general paresis, juvenile paresis is irreversible, usually resulting in death approximately five years after the onset of symptoms.

With the development of such early detection procedures as the Wassermann test and with the advent of penicillin, the incidence of syphilis decreased dramatically in the late 1940s and the 1950s. The reward for this conquest is that at present general paresis accounts for less than 1 percent of all first admissions to mental hospitals in the United States.

Brain Trauma

Behavior disorders ranging from mild to totally disabling can result from **trauma,** or severe injury to brain tissue produced by jarring, bruising, or cutting. Although automobile and motorcycle accidents are the most frequent causes of brain trauma, alcoholics and epileptics are subject to it too, as they are particularly prone to head injuries due to falls. Any extreme physical force suddenly applied to the head, whether from an automobile windshield or an ill-aimed baseball bat, may result in brain damage. There are approximately 200 traumatic head injuries a year per 100,000 population (Kalsheek, 1980). A high percentage of these injuries occur in young men. Brain trauma is subdivided into three categories: concussions, contusions, and lacerations.

Concussions   In the case of a **concussion,** the blow to the head simply jars the brain, momentarily disrupting its functioning. The result is a temporary loss of consciousness, often lasting for only a few seconds or minutes, after which the individual is typically unable to remember the events immediately preceding the injury. A familiar instance of concussion is a knockout in a boxing match. The fighter loses consciousness, falls to the floor of the ring (probably hitting his head a second time), and may then show some reflexive twitching of the arms or legs.

Concussions may involve posttraumatic symptoms lasting for as long as several weeks. (In general, the longer the person remains unconscious after the blow, the more severe the posttraumatic symptoms and the longer they will last.) In addition to headaches and dizziness, the person may display apathy, depression, general memory difficulties, inability to concentrate, insomnia, irritability, fatigue, and a decreased tolerance for noise, light, heat, alcohol, and exertion.

In most cases of minor concussion, observable or even subjectively noticeable mental deficits disappear within the span of a few days to a few months. Nevertheless, the neurological consequences of even mild injuries include permanent brain changes. These changes are often not clinically significant. Head injury, however, is cumulative. Even after what may appear to be complete recovery, one's threshold for the severity of subsequent head injury necessary to produce lasting damage is lowered (Symmonds, 1962). In other words, a series of fairly minor blows to the head can produce damage much like that of a major injury.

Contusions   In a **contusion** the trauma is severe enough so that the brain is not simply jarred; it is actually shifted out of its normal position and pressed against the skull, so that the sensitive neural tissue is bruised. The results of a contusion are more severe than those of a concussion. Individuals who experience contusions typically lapse into a coma lasting for several hours or even days, and afterward may

suffer convulsions and/or a temporary speech loss. Furthermore, on awakening from the coma, they may fall into a state of disorientation called **traumatic delirium,** in which they may imagine, for example, that the hospital staff are enemies or kidnappers. Other patients may simply wander away if they are not carefully watched. These symptoms generally disappear within a week or so, but a very severe contusion or repeated contusions (such as boxers often suffer) can result in permanent emotional instability and intellectual impairment. Again, the length of the period of unconsciousness is a good predictor of the severity and duration of the posttraumatic symptoms.

The number of injuries a person suffers is also a factor in the severity of symptoms. Repeated concussions and contusions, such as those incurred by boxers, can result in cumulative damage. The effects can be manifested years later, in dementia pugilistica (better known as the punch-drunk syndrome), which involves memory lapses, loss of coordination, dizziness, tremors, and other physical and psychological impairments. One recent study of a small sample of former prizefighters found that 87 percent exhibited abnormalities on at least two of four measures (Casson et al., 1984). Structural changes in the brains of former boxers have also been identified, including neuronal degeneration and the formation of neurofibrillary tangles not unlike those found in Alzheimer's disease (Lampert and Hardman, 1984). Indeed, some people speculate that head injury may play a role in the later development of Alzheimer's disease (Mortimer et al., 1985).

Lacerations   **Lacerations,** produced when a foreign object, such as a bullet or a piece of metal, enters the skull and directly ruptures and destroys brain tissue, constitute the most serious form of brain trauma. The effects of a brain laceration depend greatly on the exact site of the damage. Lacerations in certain areas of the brain result in death or in extremely debilitating impairments of intellectual, sensory, or motor functioning; damage to other sites may lead to only relatively minor consequences. Periodically the newspapers report a case in which a person who has been shot in the head simply resumes normal functioning after the external wounds have healed and goes about daily business with a bullet or two lodged in the brain. Such cases, however, are exceedingly rare. Normally, a cerebral laceration results in some form of physical impairment or personality change, whether major or minor.

The following classic case, reported in 1868, illustrates the subtle, variable, and unpredictable nature of the effects of cerebral laceration:

> Phineas P. Gage, age 25 and strong and healthy, was the popular foreman of a railroad excavation crew. While he was working at a site, a premature explosion drove a tamping iron into the left side of his face and up through his skull. Gage, thrown onto his back by the force of the blast and by the entry of the rod, convulsed. However, he quickly regained speech and was placed in a cart, in which he rode in a sitting position for three-quarters of a mile to his hotel. He got out of the cart by himself and was able to walk up a long flight of stairs to his room. Although bleeding profusely, he remained fully conscious during the doctor's ministrations. And soon afterward he appeared completely recovered physically. However, his personality had undergone a radical change. The equilibrium between his intellectual faculties and his instincts seemed to have been destroyed. He was now inconsiderate, impatient, and obstinate, and yet at the same time capricious and vacillating in decision-making. He also began indulging in the grossest profanity. The change in temperament was so extreme that his employers had to replace him as foreman. To his friends he was simply "no longer Gage" (adapted from Harlow, 1868, pp. 330–332, 339–340).

Vascular Accidents

A third category of organic brain disorders includes those due to endogenous **vascular accidents,** in which blockage or breaking of cranial blood vessels results in injury to the brain tissue. Vascular accidents

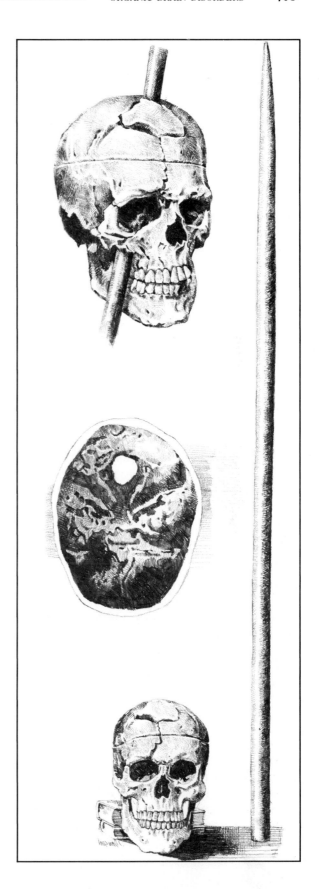

FIGURE 16.1

The cerebral laceration suffered by Phineas Gage is illustrated in these drawings, which are adapted from original sketches done by Dr. Harlow, the physician who attended Gage. The drawings at the bottom and right show the relative sizes of the skull and the tamping iron that passed through it. The top drawing shows the position in which the iron lodged and the large section of the skull that was torn away and later replaced. The middle sketch, an upward view of the inside of the skull, shows the hole made by the iron, partially filled in by new bone deposit. Gage's survival of the accident is considered remarkable; however, as noted in the text, he underwent profound personality changes.

fall into two categories: cerebral occlusion and cerebral hemorrhage.

Cerebral Occlusion   A major cause of psychological symptoms, including aphasia, apraxia, and agnosia, is occlusion of cerebral vessels. When a clot develops in one of the blood vessels feeding the brain, circulation in that vessel is cut off. The result is that the portion of the brain served by that blood vessel can no longer take in nourishment or dispose of chemical wastes and consequently cannot function properly. An occurrence of cerebral occlusion is technically labeled a **cerebrovascular accident (CVA),** which is known in everyday language as a "stroke."

The two most common causes of CVA are embolus and thrombus. An **embolus** is a ball of substance such as fat, air, or clotted blood, which breaks loose from the side of a blood vessel or in some other way enters a blood vessel and floats upward in the bloodstream until its size no longer permits it to pass. At that point it clogs the vessel, producing an occlusion. A **thrombus** is a buildup of fatty material coating the inside of the vessel at the site of the eventual occlusion. As the thrombus becomes larger, the blood flow is gradually reduced until it is completely stopped. When a CVA results from an embolus, the disorder has a sudden onset and typically results in dramatic symptoms: the patient may collapse or suddenly become paralyzed or unable to talk. A CVA produced by a slowly developing thrombus, on the other hand, may take months or even years to produce noticeable impairment.

The most common form of organic brain disorder, CVAs are found in 25 percent of routine autopsies. This does not mean that the CVA was necessarily the cause of death. Many people apparently have what are called "silent strokes"—small CVAs that occur in less critical regions of the brain and thus have less noticeable effect on behavior. In other cases, CVAs are immediately fatal. And in still other cases, the patient lives, but with a variety of aftereffects, the most common being aphasia, agnosia, apraxia, and paralysis, usually of one limb or of one half of the body.

These disabilities (whether they result from CVAs or from any other organic brain disorder) are almost invariably accompanied by some degree of disturbance, partly organic and partly a functional response to the new impairment. One possible reaction is emotional lability: the patient may pass from laughing to

weeping in an instant. Another response that is sometimes seen is a **catastrophic reaction** (Goldstein, 1948): patients, utterly bewildered by their inability to perform elementary tasks long since taken for granted—walking across a room, forming a sentence, reading a magazine—react, understandably, with disorganization and sometimes violent fury. Later, as a means of coping with the impairment, patients may develop seemingly odd habits. To compensate for memory losses, for example, some people may make elaborate inventories of their belongings and may react with anger if something is moved from its proper place. A catastrophic reaction is more frequently seen in patients who have brain damage to the left rather than the right cerebral hemisphere. Those with right-hemisphere lesions tend to show the opposite reaction: they minimize the problem, appear indifferent to it, and joke about it (Gainotti, 1972: Sackeim et al., 1982). Again, the response depends greatly on the premorbid personality. People with compulsive tendencies are generally intolerant of any reduction in their mental acuity and may become depressed in response. Likewise, people with suspicious natures, exacerbated by their sudden helplessness, may develop paranoid symptoms, accusing others of making fun of them, of stealing their belongings, and so forth. The symptomatology, then, is the result not just of a specific disorder in a specific part of the brain but of this disorder *working on* a specific personality.

Some of the behavioral impairments resulting from CVAs may disappear spontaneously, while some others can be remedied through rehabilitation therapy. And as the disability is remedied, so in most cases is the attendant emotional disturbance. Some CVA patients recover completely, but most continue to labor under some form of impairment for the rest of their lives. In general, the younger the patient and the smaller the area of brain damage, the better the chance of recovery.

Cerebral Hemorrhage   A **cerebral hemorrhage** occurs when a blood vessel ruptures, causing blood to spill out of the vessel onto brain tissue, damaging or destroying it. The most frequent cause of a hemorrhage is an intracranial aneurysm. **Aneurysms** are enlargements or bulges in the blood vessel wall, often at points where the vessels branch off. Aneurysms are thought to be caused by congenital weakness of the vessel. These bulges may vary in size from that of a pea to that of a plum. Aneurysms may be asymptomatic throughout life and are found in 2 percent of autopsied adults (Merritt, 1967). The aneurysm causes damage to the brain when its swelling causes it to rupture.

As with other causes of damage to the brain, the specific effects of a cerebral hemorrhage depend on the location and extent of damage. Usually the patient lapses into a coma, which is sometimes accompanied by convulsions. Victims of extensive hemorrhaging usually die within two to fourteen days. Those who survive the hemorrhage may suffer paralysis, speech difficulties, and/or severe psychological impairment, such as loss of memory or impaired judgment.

The experience of a brain hemorrhage, with subsequent speech and memory disturbances, is described in the following personal account. Undoubtedly the account itself suffers from distortions and memory gaps of which the patient, a neuroanatomist, was probably not aware:

> I found that I was extremely tired. I did not feel quite well, and I was conscious of a tingling and numbness in my right arm. . . . I found the lucid formulation of my train of reasoning impossible. I felt almost desperate: I searched for the dictionary for expressions which at other times were familiar and while so doing I forgot what I wanted to say. . . . My condition now seemed to me critical. . . . It was obvious to those about me that I had difficulty in finding certain words. . . . I became suspicious, and I began to think I had had a slight stroke. . . .
>
> My impediment of speech recurred, and was more apparent. I fumbled for phrases, my speech became uncertain and indistinct. . . . I was very tired and even rather dizzy.
>
> Next morning, after a good sleep, I got up and went, half-dressed, to the toilet. . . . I turned giddy, and fell down. I did not lose consciousness, but I felt very vague. . . . Supporting myself and swaying on my feet, I crept away. . . . However, I could still walk, dress myself, and even take my breakfast. My secretary told me later that I had looked very absent-minded, and had spread the butter on my sugar instead of my bread (Forel, 1937, pp. 288–290).

Brain Tumors

Brain tumors may be categorized in two ways. *Primary* tumors are those that originate in the brain itself; *secondary* tumors are those that originate in

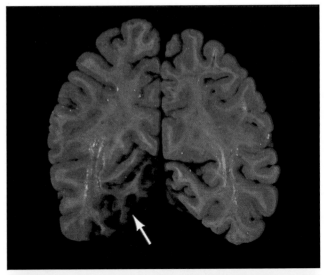

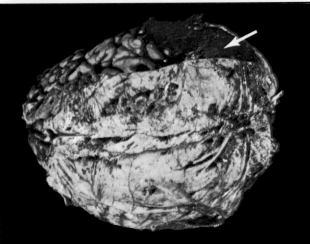

(Top) A brain section showing the atrophy of tissue (arrow) resulting from a cerebral hemorrhage. (Bottom) In this photograph of a hemorrhaged brain, part of the dura (the membrane covering the brain) has been cut away to show the position of the blood clot (arrow) between the dura and the cortex. (California Medical Publications, all rights reserved)

portions of the body outside the brain and then travel to the brain, usually through the vascular system. Brain tumors are also commonly classified into three types: intracerebral, extracerebral, and metastatic. **Intracerebral tumors** grow within the brain, destroy normal brain tissue, and replace that tissue with abnormal tumor cells. In addition, they tend to grow larger than the tissue replaced, thus producing signs of increased intracranial pressure due to the added mass. **Extracerebral tumors** grow outside the brain but inside the skull, typically on such support tissues as the meninges. Intracerebral tumors are more common in adults; extracerebral tumors, in children. **Metastatic brain tumors** (those that have spread by body fluids from an original source) are secondary tumors that develop most commonly from cancer of the lung, breast, stomach, or kidney; they make up only 5 percent of all brain tumors.

Although the actual cause of tumors has not yet been determined, their clinical course is clear. For some reason, a few cells begin to grow at an abnormally rapid rate, destroying the surrounding healthy brain tissue and resulting in a wide variety of psychological symptoms. Because of the inexplicable cellular growth, brain tumors are referred to technically as **intracranial neoplasms**—that is, new growths within the brain.

In most cases, the first signs of brain tumor are subtle and insidious—headaches, visual problems, neglect of personal hygiene, indifference to previously valued activities, and failures of judgment and foresight. With the progressive destruction of brain tissue, the patient eventually develops at least one of the more obvious symptoms: abnormal reflexes; blunting of affect; disorientation in regard to time, place, and/or person; poor memory and concentration; double vision; and jerky motor coordination. The kind and severity of symptoms are directly related to the location of the tumor in the brain: the functions controlled by that section will probably be impaired earlier and more severely than other functions. However, as the tumor grows, pressing against other sections, their functioning too will be affected.

Any tumor that continues to grow undetected and untreated in the brain will eventually cause extreme physical distress (splitting headaches, vomiting, seizures), along with personality changes that may reach psychotic proportions. Just before death, the patient may become overtly psychotic and finally lapse into a coma.

Tumors can be removed surgically, and in many cases they are. However, since the surgery itself can cause additional permanent brain damage, the physician may choose to avoid it. Surgeons are especially reluctant to operate on the language areas and on the major motor areas. In such cases, radiation treatment is used, though this too may destroy brain tissue. In other cases, surgery and radiation are used in combination, both to remove the growth and to prevent future growths.

Degenerative Disorders

Degenerative disorders are those organic brain syndromes characterized by a general deterioration of intellectual, emotional, and motor functioning as a result of progressive pathological change in the brain. Degenerative disease can be classified according to the region of the brain that is damaged (Cummings and Benson, 1983). Disorders caused by deterioration of the cerebral cortex (the higher regions of the brain; see Figure 16.2) are characterized by memory disturbances, impaired comprehension, naming difficulties, and environmental disorientation. Until the late stages of the disease, gait, posture, muscle tone, and reflexes are usually unimpaired. Alzheimer's disease is such a disorder. Disorders caused by deterioration of the subcortical or lower regions of the brain (outside the cerebral cortex) are characterized by difficulty in solving problems, forgetfulness, alterations in affect or mood, and motor disturbances. Huntington's chorea and Parkinson's disease are disorders of this type. Still other disorders are caused by vascular disease that affects both the cortical and subcortical regions of the brain. These disorders are characterized by abrupt onset, stepwise deterioration, and focal symptoms (such as aphasia), as in multi-infarct dementia.

Aging and Dementia   Psychologists used to think that senility was a final stage of aging that would occur in everyone who lived long enough. Today we know that senile dementia is the result of a degenerative brain disorder that affects only a small minority of the aged. Approximately 4 percent of people over sixty-five have definite signs of dementia (Mortimer et al., 1981). Prevalence rises with age, however: of people over eighty, about 20 percent have dementia (Gurland et al., 1980). Why this should be so is not known. Most older people (80 percent or more) have little or no evidence of these diseases—no pronounced loss of memory or impaired judgment and reasoning. Nevertheless, when degenerative disorders strike, their victims are most often middle-aged or elderly.

Almost all old people experience some psychological changes simply as a function of aging. Although the precise biological processes are still not clear, it seems that all behavior mediated by the central nervous system slows down as the body ages (Birren, 1974; Salthouse, 1985). Old people in general experience a slowing of motor reactions, a lessened capacity to process complex information, and decreased efficiency in memory and in the learning of new material. These changes are part of the *normal* process of aging; they are no more pathological than wrinkles or gray hair. By contrast, the degenerative diseases of late life, known collectively as **senile dementias,** are pathological; they are the direct result of a severe organic deterioration of the brain. Dementias account for more hospital admissions and for more in-patient hospital days than any other psychiatric disorder among elderly people (Cummings and Benson, 1983). The two most common senile dementias are Alzheimer's disease and multi-infarct dementia.

The diagnosis of these two senile dementia syndromes is complicated. A host of treatable problems, including other illnesses, reactions to medications, and depression, can mimic the symptoms of dementia. Furthermore, Alzheimer's disease is difficult to distinguish from multi-infarct dementia, since they have many of the same clinical signs. No sure medical test is yet available to confirm the presence of either disease; diagnosis can be confirmed only through post-mortem examination. To make matters even more confusing, it is not uncommon for both types of degeneration to appear together in the same patient. A final source of diagnostic confusion is one we mentioned earlier: the symptoms in any individual case of organic brain disorder have everything to do with the patient's premorbid personality and psychosocial history, the availability of outside supports, and any number of other intangible factors. This is particularly true of the senile dementias.

Alzheimer's Disease   The most common form of dementia, and one of the most tragic, is **Alzheimer's disease.** Autopsies of patients with this disorder reveal both **neurofibrillary tangles** (twisted and distorted nerve fibers) and **senile plaques** (microscopic lesions in the neurons). Alzheimer's can occur as early as age forty, but its prevalence increases with age. Estimates suggest that about 1.5 million Americans over age sixty-five are victims of this degenerative disorder.

The primary symptoms of Alzheimer's disease are cognitive deficits—particularly loss of memory for recent events. A patient, for example, may be able to give you the lineup of his favorite baseball team sixty years ago, complete with batting averages and runs batted in, but does not remember what he ate for lunch. As the disease worsens, there is loss of memories of distant events as well. The characteristic early signs of the disease are irritability and failure of concentration and memory, with mild difficulty in recalling names and words. Patients may also experience difficulties in spatial orientation and perceptual problems.

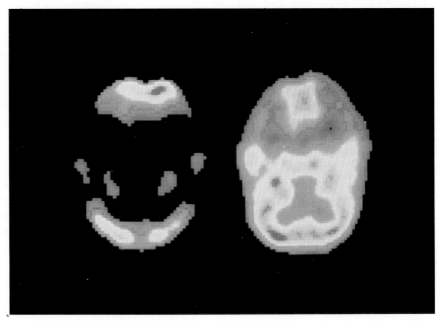

A PET scan showing a normal brain (right) and the brain of a victim of Alzheimer's disease (left). The degeneration of brain tissue is readily apparent. (NIH/Science Source/Photo Researchers)

One aspect of the tragedy of Alzheimer's disease is the strain it puts on relatives and other caregivers, who must meet the helpless patient's every need and cope with the deterioration in his or her behavior. (Ron Cooper/EKM-Nepenthe)

The cognitive deficits of Alzheimer's disease result in increasing problems in adaptation for patients and for their families (Zarit et al., 1985; see the box on p. 414). While patients' symptoms vary considerably, the general pattern is for complex behavior, such as managing personal finances or playing bridge, to be affected first, and more basic activities of daily living, such as dressing and bathing, to be disrupted later. Patients often engage in behavior that is disturbing and stressful for family members or other caregivers. Agitated and restless, they may ask the same question over and over again. Some reverse night and day; some forget that they have turned on the water in the tub or lit the stove; some wander off and get lost. A rare patient may become violent. Eventually patients reach a point where they are physically weakened. They may be bedridden and have little awareness of their surroundings. The rate of progression of the disease is highly variable. In some persons, severe impairment and death occur between three and five years of onset, while other patients decline more slowly, and live fifteen years or more after the onset of the disease.

The cause of the widespread deterioration of brain tissue characteristic of Alzheimer's disease is not known, but several theories have been advanced. Some researchers believe that early-onset Alzheimer's (cases occurring between age 40 and 60), in par-

ticular, may have a genetic component (Mortimer et al., 1981). Recent biochemical theories note that many Alzheimer's patients have deficits in the neurotransmitter acetylcholine and have suggested that this substance may be important to cognitive functioning (Roth, 1980). Other researchers have focused on the possible role of slow-acting viruses, such toxic substances as aluminum, and a breakdown in the immune system. As we noted earlier, head trauma may also play a role in the disease. Research along these lines may someday enable physicians to prevent or slow the progress of Alzheimer's disease.

At present, however, there is no cure for Alzheimer's. In some cases, changes in the patient's environment or behavioral therapy procedures may help to control some of its symptoms. Tranquilizing medications may be useful as well, although they are not consistently effective and may have the paradoxical effect of making symptoms worse. The most common treatment is custodial care, often in a nursing home. However, patients may be cared for in the home during most of the course of the disorder if resources are available to the family. Such help might include giving family members information about the disease, providing concrete suggestions for solving problems the patient is causing the family, counseling family members individually, organizing family support groups, and so on. Such help often enables family

Genetic Defects and Alzheimer's Disease

Researchers were not startled when a 56-year-old man and his 52- and 54-year old sisters all complained of failing memories and were diagnosed as having Alzheimer's disease (Kolata, 1986b). The literature was already filled with histories of cases in which Alzheimer's—especially early onset Alzheimer's—seemed to be a family problem. Estimates of the number of cases of Alzheimer's tied to hereditary factors range from a low of 10 to a high of 70 percent. But while some cases of Alzheimer's are clearly the result of inheritance, in many cases there is no family history of the disease. Then, in 1987, scientists in several nations approaching the problem of Alzheimer's from different perspectives came to the mutual conclusion that genetic defects are a factor in at least some forms of Alzheimer's disease.

The first announcement of a genetic link came from Dr. Peter St George-Hyslop of Massachusetts General Hospital in Boston. He and an international group of colleagues had used molecular biological techniques on blood samples of four families who had experienced a total of 145 cases of Alzheimer's over eight generations (St George-Hyslop et al., 1987). After cutting up the deoxyribonucleic acid (DNA)—the genetic coding substance that makes up the 23 human chromosomes—in the samples with restriction enzymes, biologists used molecular probes to identify gene segments (markers) on the chromosome so closely related to Alzheimer's that the disease and the gene segments were inherited together.

Researchers began their studies with chromosome 21 because of that chromosome's role in Down's syndrome (see Chapter 19). The brains of Down's syndrome victims show the same build-up of plaques as those of Alzheimer's sufferers, and almost all those born with Down's syndrome develop the symptoms of Alzheimer's in later life. After three years of tests, a pattern had clearly emerged: Genetic markers for Alzheimer's were found on two locations on chromosome 21, and the genes involved appear to be autosomal dominant. That is, sooner or later, anyone with the gene develops the disease. Moreover, the probes seemed to focus on the genetic materials corresponding to the senile plaques found in the brains of Alzheimer's patients (Wietgrese et al., 1985).

In what Dr. Robert G. Rohwer of the University of North Carolina has called "a beautiful convergence of two different approaches to the same problem,"

other researchers in both the United States and Great Britain were uncovering a link between chromosome 21 and specialized proteins found in the brains of Alzheimer's patients. In 1986, Peter Davies and Benjamin Wolozin of Albert Einstein College of Medicine in New York announced that they had found a protein called A68 in the spinal fluid of 8 out of 9 patients diagnosed as having the "classic" symptoms of Alzheimer's, but not in any patients without those symptoms. These results offer the promise of faster, more accurate diagnoses of Alzheimer's, but questions remain as to whether A68 is a cause or a symptom (*Science,* 1986).

Several months later scientists at the National Institute of Health in Maryland reported locating a genetic marker for the production of amyloid proteins on chromosome 21 near the markers for Alzheimer's. These proteins form the senile plaques in Alzheimer's patients and are also found in the brains of many aged mammals. Unlike the subjects in the study by St George-Hyslop et al., the NIH study dealt with three patients who had no family history of Alzheimer's disease. The NIH study also found the same abnormal duplication of amyloids in two Down's syndrome patients, reinforcing speculation that the two disorders are related and have a common genetic basis (Goldgaber, 1987).

Despite these breakthroughs, many questions remain. What specific genes are responsible for the amyloid proteins and Alzheimer's in general? (Each segment under consideration is large enough to hold up to 500 genes.) Does the close proximity of the markers for amyloids and Alzheimer's mean that this region of chromosome 21 is particularly unstable? Or is the relationship merely coincidental? Will new genetic tests for Alzheimer's show that previous estimates of the percentage of Alzheimer's attributable to inheritance were low only because many of those genetically destined for Alzheimer's don't live long enough to show symptoms? Is Alzheimer's the result of a dominant gene—one that causes all those with the gene to contract the disease—as the St George-Hyslop et al. study suggests? Or are such genes responsible for only early-onset Alzheimer's, with other forms at least partly dependent on what the NIH report called "faulty regulatory mechanisms and environmental stress"?

members to care for the patient at home much longer than they otherwise could, without sacrificing their own health or well-being.

Multi-Infarct Dementia   When an area of the brain ceases to function because a blood clot has cut off its blood supply—in other words, because the person has suffered a CVA—that area is called an *infarct*. And as the name indicates, **multi-infarct dementia** is the cumulative effect of multiple small strokes, which eventually close down many of the brain's faculties. Multi-infarct dementia used to be called cerebral arteriosclerosis. This, however, was a misnomer. **Cerebral arteriosclerosis** is a hardening of the walls in the blood vessels of the brain—a condition that simply slows blood flow throughout the brain. By contrast, the disorder we are considering is usually due to discrete blood clots (i.e., CVAs) that cut off circulation of blood altogether to discrete parts of the brain.

Certain physiological signs—blackouts, heart problems, symptoms of kidney failure, hypertension, and retinal sclerosis (a scarring of the retina of the eye)—suggest to the physician that multi-infarct dementia is the proper diagnosis. The prominent psychological symptoms are similar to those of Alzheimer's disease: language and memory defects, emotional lability, declining interest in personal hygiene. The clinical course of multi-infarct dementia is a stepwise deterioration, with evidence of vascular disease (*DSM-III-R*). In Alzheimer's, by contrast, deterioration tends to be smooth and gradual. Multi-infarct dementia poses similar problems of care for families.

Alzheimer's disease and multi-infarct dementia are cortical and mixed cortical-subcortical disorders, respectively; nearly all of their victims are elderly. The degenerative disorders to which we now turn—Huntington's chorea and Parkinson's disease—fall into the subcortical category; their victims may be middle-aged or, in the case of Huntington's, young adults.

Huntington's Chorea   **Huntington's chorea** is one of the very few neurological disorders definitely known to be transmitted genetically. Passed on by a dominant gene from either parent to both male and female children, Huntington's cannot be detected at birth. Indeed, whether a person has been unlucky enough to inherit Huntington's cannot currently be determined until after the age of thirty, when the symptoms typically appear. Forty to seventy cases of Huntington's chorea have been estimated to occur in every 1 million population (Cummings and Benson, 1983).

The primary site of the damage that causes Huntington's chorea is the basal ganglia, clusters of nerve-cell bodies located deep within the cerebral hemispheres and responsible primarily for posture, muscle tonus, and motor coordination. However, the first signs of the disease are not so much motor impairments as vague behavioral and emotional changes. The patient may become slovenly and indifferent to everyday social amenities. Furthermore, his or her moods may become unpredictable and inconsistent, running the gamut from obstinacy, passivity, and depression to inexplicable euphoria. Intellectual functions, particularly memory and judgment, are also disrupted. As the disease progresses, delusions, hallucinations, and suicidal tendencies commonly appear (Boll et al., 1974).

In addition to these psychological problems, the patient will eventually begin to show the characteristic motor symptoms—that is, the involuntary spasmodic jerking of the limbs to which the term *chorea* (from the Greek *choreia*, meaning "dance") refers. This sign appears to indicate irreversible brain damage (James et al., 1969). The victim's behavior becomes increasingly bizarre: the person may smack tongue and lips involuntarily, spit, bark out words (often obscenities) explosively, and walk with a jerky or shuffling gait. Eventually the victim of Huntington's loses complete control of bodily functions. Death is the inevitable result, occurring an average of fourteen years after the onset of symptoms. Recent advances in biogenetic research have led to the identification of the gene that causes Huntington's disease, and development of a practical test to identify carriers. Genetic engineering offers hope for the eventual treatment for afflicted persons.

Parkinson's Disease   First described in 1871 by James Parkinson (who himself suffered from it), **Parkinson's disease,** also involves damage to the basal ganglia, particularly the region known as the substantia nigra. The cause of this condition is unknown, although it has been attributed to a variety of factors, including encephalitis, heredity, viruses, toxins, deficient brain metabolism, and head trauma. The illness occurs most frequently in persons between the ages of fifty and seventy.

The primary symptom of Parkinson's is tremor, occurring at a rate of about four to eight movements per second. The tremors are usually present during rest periods, but tend to diminish or cease when the patient is sleeping. Interestingly, patients can often abruptly stop the tremors, at least temporarily, if someone orders them to do so, and for a short time they may even be able to perform motor activities requiring very fine muscular coordination. Such remissions are always temporary, however, and the patient once again lapses into the typical rhythmic jerking of arms, hands, jaws, and/or head.

Another highly characteristic sign of Parkinson's is an expressionless, masklike countenance, probably due to increased muscle tonus resulting from damage to the basal ganglia. Parkinson's patients also tend to walk, when they *can* walk, with a distinctive slow, stiff gait, usually accompanied by a slight crouch.

Approximately 40 to 60 percent of Parkinson's disease patients also experience psychological disturbances. These include a general mental deficit involving memory, learning, judgment, and concentration, as well as apathy and social withdrawal. (Such disturbances are not always easily distinguishable from those experienced by many old people who have no such pathological condition; see the box on p. 414). In more severe cases there may be highly systematized delusions and severe depression, including suicidal tendencies. However, it is difficult to determine whether these symptoms are due directly to the brain pathology or simply to patients' distress over their physical helplessness.

Parkinson's is unusual among degenerative disorders in that it can be treated with some success. Cells in the substantia nigra are involved in the synthesis of the neurotransmitter dopamine. Because these cells are lost in Parkinson's, a deficit of dopamine results. L-dopa, a drug that increases the amount of dopamine, can in most cases control the tremor and other motor symptoms for several years, though it cannot cure the disease. Unfortunately, the beneficial effects of this medication decline with long-term use.

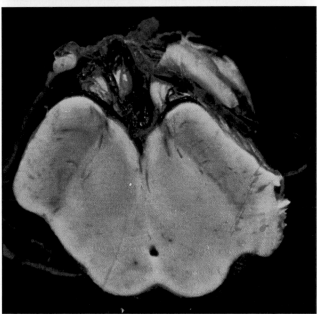

(Top) A section of the midbrain from a normal brain. (Bottom) A midbrain section from a Parkinsonian brain, showing the tissue degeneration caused by the disorder. This degeneration occurs on both macroscopic and microscopic levels, and the etiology is unknown. (Top, California Medical Publications, all rights reserved; bottom, courtesy, R. Rowan, M.D.)

Nutritional Deficiency

Malnutrition—or, specifically, insufficient intake of one or more essential vitamins—can result in neurological damage and consequently in psychological disturbances. The most common conditions of this kind are Korsakoff's psychosis, pellagra, and beriberi.

Korsakoff's Psychosis   Victims of **Korsakoff's psychosis,** which is considered irreversible, invariably have a history of alcoholism. Alcoholics have notoriously bad diets, and it is generally agreed that the primary pathology in this disorder is due to a

The Problems of Aging

When society idealizes "growing old gracefully," it asks a great deal of the aging person, for the over-sixty-five years often bring the most stressful changes of a person's life. Consider the following life changes, at least several of which confront every old man and woman:

Retirement

Many people look forward to the period of their lives when they will be free from the demands of the clock and the commuter train. And some do find their retirement years to be "golden"—particularly those who are healthy, happily married, financially comfortable, and well equipped with interests that they are eager to pursue. However, many others, cut off from the activity that has lent them an identity for a lifetime, feel bereft. Many miss their friends from the job and the camaraderie of the workplace.

Poverty

People who have no money worries in their old age are a minority. While most older people are better off today than their counterparts of the past, many still find that their pensions, social security checks, and savings do not allow them the comforts or even the necessities that they once took for granted. The deprivations may be subtle, such as not being able to buy one's grandchild a special graduation present, or they may be starkly obvious, such as cold and hunger. In either case, the experience of having less money than one is accustomed to is stressful. Old women are more likely to be living in poverty than old men. Typically they have not worked as steadily as their husbands, have not earned as high salaries, and have accumulated fewer retirement benefits, but live longer.

Loneliness

Many people in the over-sixty-five years must survive the death of a spouse, one of the most traumatic changes that can occur in the life of a human being. The surviving partner may be ill equipped to live alone, and other choices—such as living with one's children—may be unattractive or unavailable. To compound the problem, the longer people live, the more likely they are to see their friends die one by one, leaving them more isolated every year.

Physical Changes

Older people must accept the unpleasant fact that in a society that overvalues the looks and concerns of youth, they no longer look young. Both men and women may be chagrined at their deepening wrinkles and sagging bodies. In addition, old people may begin to notice that their bodies just don't seem to work as well as they used to: eyes and ears are not as keen as they were. Worse still, more than 80 percent of those over sixty-five suffer from some form of chronic illness: heart disease, arthritis, problems with digestion and sleep, and so on.

An old man or woman may feel stress from every one of these sources. Add to these circumstances the generally negative attitude of the larger society toward the aged—where even the fact of aging must be hidden under a euphemism ("senior citizens")—and it is hardly surprising that depression and anxiety are common among old people.

And what becomes of old people who respond to such stresses with anxiety or depression? The most pernicious result is that they may be labeled "senile" without showing real signs of organic brain pathology. It is easy for family members, nursing home personnel, and even doctors and nurses who deal with the aging to make this mistake. Consider the woman of eighty who seems sad and withdrawn, who complains about her health and reminisces about her past, who talks to herself because she has no other audience, who begins to neglect her appearance and hygiene because she has nowhere to go and no one to see, and whose memory doesn't seem what it used to be. Our reaction is too often to conclude that "Aunt Jane's mind is wandering" rather than "Aunt Jane is depressed." This error has sinister ramifications. For while depression is something that we have ways of treating, senility is not. The senile are generally put away in nursing homes or in the back wards of general hospitals, where they are likely to deteriorate further.

Given the stresses associated with aging, it is not surprising that some older people experience depression, anxiety, and other psychological problems. Sometimes, of course, psychotherapy may be helpful. But greater support from society as a whole—and the recognition that even normal aging can be stressful in our day and age—would seem to be in order.

deficiency of vitamin B$_1$, or thiamine (Redlich and Freedman, 1966; Brion, 1969).

There are two classic behavioral signs of Korsakoff's psychosis, anterograde amnesia and confabulation. **Anterograde amnesia** is the inability to incorporate new memories, and **confabulation** is the tendency to fill in memory gaps with invented stories. In response to questioning, for example, patients may placidly offer a nonsensical account of why they are in the hospital, if indeed they even admit that the place is a hospital. Such patients usually seem calm and affable, while at the same time their total unawareness of the fantastic quality of their stories reveals a psychotic impairment of judgment. This impairment gradually spreads to other aspects of psychological functioning. In addition to these memory deficits, many alcoholics experience a more generalized intellectual decline. Like the degenerative diseases discussed above, chronic alcoholism can lead to deficits in most cognitive abilities (Cummings and Benson, 1983).

Pellagra   **Pellagra,** caused by a severe deficiency of the B vitamin niacin, is most common in geographical areas where the population subsists primarily on corn meal. In the early 1900s, pellagra accounted for about 10 percent of all admissions to state mental hospitals in some areas of the United States, particularly the South (Millon, 1969), but since that time improvements in the average American's diet have virtually eliminated this syndrome in our society. The early physical symptoms of pellagra are skin rash and diarrhea. These symptoms are generally accompanied by depression, anxiety, and eventually delirium and hallucinations leading to death. Massive vitamin therapy, if instituted in time, can halt the progress of the disease.

Beriberi   Like Korsakoff's psychosis, **beriberi** is due to thiamine deficiency. It often appears in association with other disorders, such as chronic alcoholism, pellagra, pernicious anemia, and diabetes. The most prominent clinical signs of beriberi include lack of appetite, insomnia, disturbances in memory and concentration, irritability, and above all, extreme lassitude. (The name of the disease comes from the Singhalese word *beri,* meaning "weakness.") This disorder has been a particular problem in such areas as the Far East, where polished rice constitutes a major portion of the diet.

Endocrine Disorders

The **endocrine glands** are responsible for the production of hormones. When released into the bloodstream, the hormones affect various bodily mechanisms, such as sexual functions, physical growth and development, and the availability of energy. Disturbances in the endocrine system, and particularly in the thyroid and adrenal glands, can give rise to a variety of psychological disorders.

Thyroid Syndromes   Overactivity of the thyroid gland—a condition called **hyperthyroidism,** or **Graves' disease**—involves an excessive secretion of the hormone thyroxin, which gives rise to a variety of physical and psychological difficulties. Psychological symptoms accompanying the disorder may include severe apprehension and agitation, hallucinations, excessive motor activity, sweating, and other symptoms suggestive of anxiety.

Opposite in both cause and effect is **hypothyroidism,** sometimes referred to as **myxedema,** in which underactivity of the thyroid gland results in deficient production of thyroxin. Hypothyroidism may be due to iodine deficiency, a problem that has become much less common in the United States since the advent of iodized table salt. Individuals suffering from hypothyroidism are frequently sluggish, have difficulties with memory and concentration, and appear to be lethargic and depressed. Again, however, symptomatology depends greatly on premorbid personality. (The same is true of hyperthyroidism.)

Another condition resulting from thyroid deficiency is **cretinism,** caused by a thyroid that has not developed, has been injured, or has undergone degeneration. When the deficiency occurs during the prenatal or perinatal period, the unwelcome result is mental retardation (Chapter 19). Cretinism has become relatively rare as a result of public health measures designed to prevent, detect, and treat it. With early treatment, normal intellectual and personality functioning can usually be restored.

Adrenal Syndromes   The **adrenal glands** are a pair of ductless glands located above the kidneys and consisting of an outer layer called the **cortex** and an internal portion called the **medulla.** Chronic underactivity of the adrenal cortex gives rise to **Addison's disease,** which involves both physical and psychological changes. Again, the psychological symptoms vary considerably according to the individual's premorbid adjustment. Some patients simply appear moderately depressed and withdrawn; others experience debilitating extremes of depression, anxiety, irritability, and invalidism. Appropriate medical therapy can alleviate the symptoms of even a severe case of Addison's disease, restoring the individual to normal functioning. Such was the case with President John F. Kennedy, who suffered from Addison's.

When the adrenal cortex is excessively active, several disorders may arise, one of which is **Cushing's syndrome.** This relatively rare disorder usually affects young women. Like the other endocrine disorders, Cushing's syndrome involves both physical symptoms—in this case, obesity and muscle weakness—and psychological difficulties, especially extreme emotional lability, with fluctuations in mood ranging from total indifference to violent hostility.

Toxic Disorders

Various plants, gases, drugs, and metals, when ingested or absorbed through the skin, can have a toxic or poisonous effect on the brain. Depending on the individual, the toxic substance, and the amount ingested, the results of such brain poisoning range from temporary physical and emotional distress to psychosis and death. However, one sign that is almost always present in the toxic disorders is delirium.

Mushroom Toxins   The ingestion of certain species of mushrooms can cause extreme physical illness as well as a number of psychological symptoms. For example, most mushrooms of the genus *Amanita* cause hallucinations, delirium, and periods of extreme excitement alternating with periods of sleep. Such symptoms are typically transitory. However, certain members of this genus, along with the genus *Galerina,* can be fatal.

Lead   Much more common than mushroom poisoning is lead poisoning. The excessive ingestion of lead causes a condition called **lead encephalopathy,** in which fluid accumulates in the brain, causing extreme pressure. Early symptoms include abdominal pains, constipation, facial pallor, and sometimes convulsions and bizarre behaviors such as hair pulling.

In severe cases, the symptoms may be similar to those of psychosis, including delirium and hallucinations. The most common victims of lead poisoning are children, who may become mentally retarded as a result.

In recent years, consumer advocacy groups have identified a number of sources of lead contamination, including old lead-lined water pipes, lead-based paint on children's toys and furniture, old plaster walls, candles with lead-core wicks, certain electric tea kettles that release lead from soft solder joints when heated, pottery glazes from which acetic foods (e.g., grape juice) can leach lead, exhaust from automobiles that burn leaded gasoline, and industrial pollution. As may be seen from this list, the issue of metal poisoning often involves a conflict between the needs of industry and the needs of the individual.

Other Heavy-Metal Toxins   The "industry vs. the individual" conflict also crops up in two of the more common varieties of heavy-metal poisoning, mercury and manganese poisoning. Victims of these toxic disorders are usually those whose jobs bring them into close daily contact with mercury and manganese. However, other victims are simply unwitting citizens whose food or air has been contaminated by industrial wastes containing metallic toxins. One notorious source of such poisoning is fish taken from waters polluted by mercury wastes from nearby factories. In Japan, for example, thousands of people have been permanently paralyzed and brain-damaged as a result of eating mercury-contaminated fish (Kurland et al., 1960).

Early signs of brain damage due to mercury poisoning are memory loss, irritability, and difficulty in concentration. As the disease progresses, the individual typically develops tunnel vision (that is, loss of peripheral vision), faulty motor coordination, and difficulty in speaking and hearing. In extreme cases, these symptoms lead to paralysis, coma, and death. Manganese poisoning is manifested in motor and speech impairments, restlessness, and emotional instability. Some clinicians believe that the personality changes that accompany both types of poisoning are often simply pathological exaggerations of the individual's premorbid personality traits.

Psychoactive Drugs   As we have seen in Chapter 12, abuse of psychoactive drugs such as alcohol, narcotics, and amphetamines can cause severe psychological disturbances. Other drugs have also been implicated in organic brain damage. In recent years, for example, the inhalation of aerosol gases and fumes of certain glues has become a popular means of getting "high" among adolescents. Unfortunately, the toxins in these gases and fumes tend to accumulate in the vital organs and may cause permanent damage not only to the liver and kidney but also to the brain, which in turn may result in severe physiological deterioration and, in extreme cases, death.

Carbon Monoxide   Carbon monoxide, an odorless, tasteless, and invisible gas usually inhaled with automobile exhaust fumes, combines with the hemoglobin in the blood in such a way as to prevent the blood from absorbing oxygen. The usual result of this process is a swift and rather painless death, which makes carbon monoxide inhalation a favored means of suicide. Patients who survive, however, suffer a number of psychological consequences, typically including apathy, confusion, and memory defects. While these symptoms may clear up within two years, some patients suffer permanent mental impairment (Kolb, 1973).

THE EPILEPSIES

It is estimated that about 0.5 percent of the American population suffers from the disease called epilepsy. **Epilepsy** is actually a generic term covering a variety of organic disorders characterized by irregularly occurring disturbances in consciousness, in the form of seizures or convulsions. These seizures appear to be due to a disruption in the electrical and physiological activity of the discharging cells of the brain. About 85 percent of epileptics manifest brain-wave abnormalities in EEG recordings. However, the remaining 15 percent of epileptics have normal EEGs— a fact that suggests that the abnormal discharges may occur too infrequently for detection by this instrument or that the disturbance takes place so deep within the brain that it is not detectable by surface electrodes.

In most cases, epilepsy, regardless of its type, can be controlled with medication. In some very severe cases, however, surgery may be considered in order to remove the portion of the brain responsible for

Tighter federal regulations now minimize the risk of lead poisoning, but many older buildings still contain layers of lead-based paint. Small children, who tend to put everything in their mouths, may suffer lead poisoning from eating just a few chips of paint containing lead. (Jeff Albertson/Stock, Boston)

the seizures. In such cases, the affected area can often be localized by EEG studies (Rasmussen and Branch, 1962).

Etiology

As we have seen, convulsions occur in a number of brain syndromes—neurosyphilis, acute alcohol or other drug intoxication, tumors, encephalitis, trauma, and multi-infarct dementia. Though such seizures are labeled **symptomatic** or **acquired epilepsy,** indicating that they are symptoms of the brain damage caused by these other pathologies, the appropriate diagnosis is not epilepsy but rather the primary organic condition. About 77 percent of all cases of epilepsy, however, have no known cause (Kolb, 1973);

such cases are called **idiopathic epilepsy,** and it is this type of epilepsy that we will discuss in the following section. Idiopathic epilepsy usually has its onset between the ages of ten and twenty, though it may also appear in early childhood. Though in some rare cases it "runs in families," the genetic factor is considered relatively unimportant.

Personality and Intellectual Characteristics

For many years the clinical lore attributed a certain type of personality to all epileptics. It is now generally accepted that there is no single, stereotypic epileptic personality (Tizard, 1962). Some forms of epilepsy may be connected to certain personality traits. For example, there is a growing belief that epilepsy originating in the temporal lobe (partial seizure with complex symptomatology, also called partial complex, or psychomotor, epilepsy) is associated with such personality disturbances as emotionalism, compulsiveness, and a concern with issues of conscience, and it is possible that these traits are somehow biologically connected to the organic condition underlying the epilepsy. On the other hand, many epileptics show no psychological abnormalities whatsoever. And in those who do, such abnormalities are likely to be, at least in part, a response to the social stigma attached to epilepsy and to the embarrassment and inconvenience of the seizures.

As for the intellectual characteristics of epileptics, as a group their functioning is in the low-normal range, though many have IQ scores that are well above average (Kolb, 1973). There have been many famous epileptics—including, for example, Julius Caesar, Feodor Dostoevsky, and Vincent van Gogh.

Precipitation of Seizures

Factors that may precipitate an epileptic attack include blows to the head, high fevers, rapid breathing **(hyperventilation),** low blood sugar level **(hypoglycemia),** alcohol, fatigue, highly charged emotional situations, and sleep deprivation. In some cases, what seems to be a very mild or innocuous stimulus can provoke an epileptic seizure; for example, certain musical notes or lights flickering at certain frequencies have been known to set off seizures in susceptible individuals. Other known precipitative factors are pro-longed reading and, in women, hormonal changes during the menstrual period.

Once the attack has been precipitated, many epileptics experience a warning sign known as the **aura.** The aura may take many different forms. Some patients always note a strong aroma or small involuntary movements before the onset of convulsions; others simply become aware of a diffuse fear or "funny feeling," a sensation of dizziness, or sudden cramps. Despite its frightening aspects, the aura does permit epileptics to prepare for the attack and thereby reduce the chances of their being injured.

Types of Epilepsy

Epilepsy is classified into several different types. The best known are petit mal (absence) and grand mal (tonic-clonic), which are generalized seizures; partial seizures with motor symptoms (Jacksonian); and partial complex seizures with motor, mental, and sensory symptoms (psychomotor).

Petit Mal (Absence)   The seizure of **petit mal** (literally, "small illness"), or absence, generally lasts for only a few seconds and involves only a brief, and not necessarily total, loss of consciousness. During the attack sufferers remain immobile, become completely unaware of their surroundings, and simply stare straight ahead. A loss of muscle tone may or may not accompany the seizure. After the attack, unaware that anything has happened, they simply resume whatever they were doing before the seizure. Such attacks can occur as often as a hundred times a day, but usually their occurrence is much less frequent, in which case the individual may not even require treatment.

Grand Mal (Tonic-Clonic)   What most people think of when they think of epilepsy is **grand mal** (literally, "great illness"), or tonic-clonic, epilepsy. This, the most common and the most dramatic of the epilepsies, involves a generalized seizure throughout the brain. There are thought to be four stages of grand mal, the first of which is the aura phase, which may or may not occur. The second stage is the **tonic phase,** in which the person's body becomes very rigid—with arms flexed, legs outstretched, and fists clenched—and undergoes strong muscular contractions. During this phase, which may last for as long as a minute, breathing ceases. In the third stage, or **clonic phase,** breathing resumes and the muscles begin to contract and relax in a rhythmic way, causing the body to jerk in violent and rapid generalized spasms. In this stage there is some danger that the patient may be injured because of the violent jerking movements. The clonic phase also lasts about a minute, after which the convulsions dissipate. In the last stage, the **coma,** the muscles slowly relax while the patient remains unconscious. When patients regain consciousness, they are typically somewhat confused, have headaches, and feel quite exhausted and sleepy. In severe cases, such attacks may occur as often as several times a day.

Dostoevsky, a grand mal epileptic, eventually came to believe that his condition was a sort of divine gift, for in the aura stage he felt that he received a transcendent vision of life's ultimate meaning. However, most epileptics experience the disease not as a gift but as a handicap. What a grand mal attack can be like for the ordinary person is well portrayed in the following account by Margiad Evans, a writer who suffers from this form of epilepsy:

> The food was on the table, the oil-stove lit. I picked up the coffee percolator to fill it. Just as I reached the sink and was standing in the doorway, I found I could not move, could not remember what I wanted to do. It seemed a long time that I stood there (actually perhaps a few seconds) saying to myself, "This is nothing. It will be all right in a moment and I shall remember *all the rest.*" Then I felt my head beginning to jerk backwards and my face to grimace. Then the percolator fell from my hand into the sink. But still some dogged part of me kept saying, "All this is really controllable." I was still conscious and felt violent gestures and spasms were shooting all over me, even till I felt my knees give and I fell down on the concrete floor. As I went, it shot through me, the astonishment: "As bad as this then?"
>
> The next thing I remember was the B_____s' kitchen and Betty B_____ . . . giving me tea and talking to me in the tone mothers use to little children coming out of nightmares (quoted in Kaplan, 1964, pp. 346–347).

The sense of helplessness engendered by such a seizure—the experience of having one's body go completely out of control and of awakening with no knowledge of what has passed—can, over time, become psychologically crippling, especially if it is combined with constant expressions of sympathy by others, encouraging the epileptic to settle back into an invalid role. Furthermore, society for some reason attaches a special stigma to epilepsy, with the result that epileptics often suffer not only from a conviction of helplessness but also from shame and embarrassment, the feeling of being somehow "marked." It is no surprise, then, that this disorder is sometimes accompanied by secondary psychological disturbance. However, now that there are drugs that can control seizures in most cases, such disturbances tend to be less severe, though epileptics still have the problem of dealing with the social stigma.

Jacksonian Epilepsy (Partial Seizure with Motor Symptoms)   First described by the neurologist Hughlings Jackson, **Jacksonian epilepsy** begins with a muscular twitching or a tingling in the hands and feet, which may then spread to other parts of the body. The part of the brain where the seizure originates is thought to be quite localized, and treatment sometimes involves removal of that portion of the brain. The Jacksonian seizure is often a prelude to a full-scale tonic-clonic seizure.

Psychomotor Epilepsy (Partial Seizure with Complex Symptomatology)   An attack of **psychomotor epilepsy,** preceded by an aura, usually involves nothing more dramatic than a loss of contact with reality lasting anywhere from a few seconds to several minutes. During this time the person may appear quite normal and may engage in some rather mechanical activity. After the attack has passed, the person will resume his or her former business and will be amnesic for the episode.

During these attacks, some psychomotor epileptics may engage in bizarre, schizophrenic-like behavior, such as public disrobing and urination, ambiguous responses to hallucinations and paranoid delusions, and possibly violent aggression as well (Standage, 1973). Some of these symptoms, such as delusions, are occasionally seen between seizures as well (Bear and Fedio, 1977; Gloor et al., 1982). Violent behavior is extremely rare, however, and is almost always precipitated by an attempt to restrain the victim. For example, a well-intentioned but naive attendant may wish to halt certain harmless but inappropriate acts that a person performs during a seizure. In response, the epileptic may strike out. Even this kind of aggression occurs infrequently, however.

SUMMARY

The organic brain disorders differ from most of the other syndromes discussed in this book in that they are definitely biogenic. There are five major symptoms of organic brain disorder: impairment of orientation, of memory, of general intellectual functioning, of judgment, and of control over affect or mood. Since these symptoms overlap with those of functional disorders, differential diagnosis is often extremely complicated. And since many organic syndromes have similar symptom pictures, specifying the precise pathology involved is doubly difficult. Finally, when disorders are localized, the diagnostician must try to determine what specific area of the brain has been affected, and though the patient's behavioral deficits provide good clues, this too is a tricky decision.

Most organic brain syndromes are classified by etiology. These classifications include cerebral infection, in the form of abscess, encephalitis, meningitis, or neurosyphilis; brain trauma, including, in order of increasing severity, concussions, contusions, and lacerations; vascular accidents, including cerebral occlusion ("strokes") and cerebral hemorrhage, both of which commonly result in multiple disabilities; brain tumors; degenerative disorders, including Alzheimer's disease, multi-infarct dementia, Huntington's chorea, and Parkinson's disease; nutritional deficiencies (especially of B-complex vitamins), including Korsakoff's psychosis, pellagra, and beriberi; endocrine disorders, including disturbances in thyroid and adrenal functioning; and toxic disorders, in which the brain is essentially poisoned, whether by mushrooms, heavy metals (e.g., lead, mercury, and manganese), psychoactive drugs, or carbon monoxide.

A final category of organic brain disorder, epilepsy, is classified by symptomatology rather than etiology, as the etiology of this disorder, when it occurs in the absence of other brain disorders, is unknown. The four types of epilepsy, all of which are usually treatable, are petit mal (absence), grand mal (tonic-clonic), Jacksonian (partial), and psychomotor (partial complex).

PART 6

Developmental Disorders

The Disorders of Childhood and Adolescence

The developmental disorders of children and adolescents include problems of eating—overeating and self-starvation—and of eliminating, sleeping, speaking, paying attention and learning, as well as disorders characterized by feelings of anxiety and depression and those characterized by antisocial conduct. These disorders are called "developmental" because they involve serious divergences from the usual path of childhood or adolescent development. Some children fail to develop age-appropriate behavior—four-year-olds who do not speak, eight-year-olds who are terrified of going to school on their own—or they persist in a behavior more appropriate to a younger child—eight-year-olds who wet their beds, fifteen-year-olds who are afraid of ghosts and cannot sleep without a light on. Other children develop an expected form of behavior on time but problematically—the three-year-old who speaks, but with a stutter; the six-year-old who reads, but who sometimes perceives letters or entire words as reversed.

Some of the developmental disorders of children and adolescents resemble adult anxiety and personality disorders. Despite this similarity, the disorders of children and adolescents are worth studying separately. Most differ from adult disorders in important ways and in fact have no counterpart in adult psychopathology. Learning disabilities, hyperactivity, and elimination disorders, for example, are problems of childhood. Sometimes even disorders that have the same name—"depression," for example—manifest themselves differently in children and adults.

A second important reason for studying developmental disorders apart from adult disorders is that the age of the individual, a relatively unimportant matter in the assessment of most adult disorders, is of critical importance in the assessment of developmental disorders. If one did not know which forms of behavior normally occur at the various points in development from infancy through adolescence, no one could say whether the boy who attacks his baby brother with uncontrolled rage is normal or not. Tantrums mean one thing in a three-year-old and quite another in a thirteen-year-old.

Third, the period from infancy through adolescence is filled with so many rapid changes that the most normal of children may develop temporary psychological problems. Because children are vulnerable to these "normal" problems, it can be difficult for parents to decide when the problems are no longer normal and require treatment. The lines between normal and abnormal are blurred even further by the perceptions of parents, teachers, and doctors; prevailing cultural norms strongly influence the acceptability of a child's

behavior. Many parents and doctors today are fairly relaxed about masturbation, for example, but a few generations ago a child who masturbated was considered to be well on the way to moral degeneracy.

Fourth, the courses and outcomes of children's and adolescents' disorders differ from those of adults. The less severe disorders of childhood are often quite transitory. Children are more likely to recover from phobias, for example, in part because children develop so rapidly and in part because they depend on and respond so readily to their social environment.

Finally, unlike troubled adults, most children do not think of themselves as having psychological problems. They ordinarily do not seek therapy on their own, and require the intervention of their parents or other adults if they do get it. Children depend on adults to recognize their problems and to see that they get help.

We begin with general issues in childhood psychopathology—the prevalence of childhood disorders, their classification and diagnosis, and their long-term consequences. Then we turn to the individual patterns observed in disorders of eating, elimination, sleep, speech, attention, anxiety, depression, and conduct. Finally, we examine several perspectives on these disorders, including the psychodynamic, behavioral, humanistic-existential, family theory, and neuroscience perspectives.

The diagnosis of a childhood disorder depends not only on the behavior involved but on the age of the child. An occasional tantrum is normal in a toddler, but might well be a sign of disorder in an older child or adolescent. (Judith D. Sedwick/The Picture Cube)

GENERAL ISSUES IN CHILDHOOD PSYCHOPATHOLOGY

Prevalence

We do not know exactly how many children and adolescents in the United States have developmental disorders, but statistics suggest that 7 to 15 percent of children have some form of disorder (Knopf, 1984). Surveys in the United States and Great Britain have shown that 7 percent of children have moderate to severe disorders and 15 percent, mild disorders.

When do the troubles begin? Are some ages more likely than others to be difficult? A summary of information on children who had treatment at mental health clinics provides some answers to these questions. Admission rates begin to increase gradually at about age six or seven—a phenomenon that is probably related to a child's beginning school. Problems that can be ignored or endured at home may not be tolerated in the classroom, and a child may be referred for treatment by a teacher. It also seems that the stress of starting school itself may create or exacerbate psychological problems. After age seven, clinic admissions peak at nine to ten years of age and again, even more strongly, at fourteen to fifteen years of age (Rosen et al., 1964). The reasons for the peak at nine to ten years of age are not clear. Some theorists suggest that developmental stresses and environmental demands, particularly those associated with school, are especially difficult at this point in development. The even higher peak at ages fourteen to fifteen probably reflects the inherent difficulties of adolescence. Nearly 20 percent of adolescents in Western and developing countries have emotional disorders. In every age group, clinic admission rates are higher for boys than for girls, sometimes two or three times higher (Eme, 1979). Disorders themselves are also more prevalent among boys, sometimes five times higher, a difference that is not yet clearly understood (Knopf, 1984). In short, the prevalence of disorders increases with age and is greater among boys than among girls.

Classification and Diagnosis

The system most widely used to classify childhoood and adolescent disorders—as well as those of adults— is *DSM-III-R*. Its approach is to identify syndromes and then to name the most characteristic feature of each syndrome. For example, a child who has no real friends, who lies, cheats, steals, and bullies, and who shows no remorse over these actions is diagnosed as having a "conduct disorder, undersocialized, aggressive."

As we said in Chapter 7, *DSM-III-R* sets forth highly specific diagnostic categories, especially for childhood disorders. These diagnostic categories are designed to be used on more than one axis (see Chapter 7). For example, a child might be diagnosed as "Axis I: separation anxiety disorder" or "Axis II: developmental language disorder." The advantage of multiple axes is that they give researchers and therapists more information.

But any diagnostic label must be used cautiously with children, for several reasons. First, as we have said, children change rapidly. Second, because they do change so rapidly, children's behavior may not fit neatly into any one category or may fit more than

one. A victim of child abuse, for example, may show the symptoms of several disorders, and an adolescent may be both withdrawn *and* violently aggressive (Rutter and Shaffer, 1980).

The Long-Term Consequences of Childhood Disorders

Is it true that the better we understand childhood disorders, the better chance we have of preventing people from developing disorders in adulthood? To answer this question, we have to raise two others:

1. Do childhood disorders actually predict adult disorders?

2. If so, can childhood disorders be nipped in the bud through early treatment, so that they will *not* develop into adult disorders?

The answer to the first question is a qualified no. Seriously antisocial behavior in childhood predicts adult disorders in about half of the cases, although psychologists still cannot identify the children who are likely to improve (Robins, 1979). Thus antisocial behavior in childhood is often—though by no means always—followed by a lifetime of personal distress, problems with the law, and problems in holding a job and in maintaining relationships with others. On the other hand, children who are severely withdrawn and anxious are likely to improve within a year or two and often become quite normal adults. This pattern is typical of most of the milder kinds of childhood disorders.

Some researchers have found connections between childhood and later disorders. In one study, researchers assessed the psychological adjustment of forty-two adults who had been treated in childhood for psychological problems. Over 75 percent were judged at least mildly disturbed, and 40 percent were diagnosed as having psychiatric problems. Of a control group of people who had gone to the same school but had not been treated for psychological problems in childhood, only 15 percent were judged mildly disturbed, and none was considered to have a psychiatric problem (Waldron, 1976). The difference between the two groups is striking, and similar differences have been found by other researchers (O'Neal and Robbins, 1958; Weiss et al., 1978; Janes and Hesselbrock, 1978).

But these studies themselves raise questions. The subjects were clinic patients and may not have represented the progress of other children with psychological disorders. They also were treated for their disorders, and the process of labeling and diagnosis may have made them more vulnerable to adult disorders. Of course, the treatment may also have made them *less* vulnerable to adult disorders.

This gray area leads us to our second question: Can treatment of childhood and adolescent disorders prevent the development of adult disorders? A review of research on the short-term improvement of children treated or not treated for conduct disorders, "neurotic disorders," and psychotic disorders found that treatment made no significant difference (Levitt, 1971). A more recent review found psychotherapy to be about as successful with children as with adults

(Casey and Berman, 1985). Children who received psychotherapy did better than children who received none, and all types of therapy—play and nonplay, individual and group, children only and children plus parents—seemed equally effective. Psychotherapy was a less effective treatment for problems in social adjustment than for problems of other kinds, and it was less effective for boys than for girls.

In short, we have to qualify our answers to both our questions. *Some* childhood disorders (usually the severe and antisocial ones) predict adult disorders some of the time, and some (usually the milder disorders) do not. *Some* childhood disorders respond well to treatment, and some do not. But the fact that at least some do respond well suggests that children and adolescents with disorders stand a better chance of becoming well-functioning adults if they receive treatment.

Children sometimes overeat and become obese because it is the "normal" behavior in their family. (Rick Smolan)

DISORDERS OF CHILDHOOD AND ADOLESCENCE: INDIVIDUAL PATTERNS

Eating Disorders

Since Freud's time, psychologists have interpreted eating as a crucial part of development, because children's feelings about eating are bound up with their feelings about those who feed and sustain them—their parents and others. Eating may symbolize being loved and cared for, or—if there is anxiety connected with mealtime—it may be a focus of conflicting feelings. Because eating is so closely bound to a person's emotional life, psychologists assume that eating disorders mirror emotional problems. We shall discuss two eating disorders in this section—obesity and anorexia nervosa.

Obesity   In children as in adults, **obesity** may be defined as an excessive amount of fat on the body. Though different people have different notions as to what is excessive, most investigators consider a child obese if his or her weight is 40 percent higher than the median weight for children of the same height. By this definition, somewhere between 2 and 15 percent of children in the United States are obese (Rodin, 1977).

We have already discussed obesity in Chapter 9, and what we said there probably applies as well to children as to adults. Like some obese adults, children may be overresponsive to environmental cues for eating and underresponsive to negative feedback from their stomachs. Likewise, Hilde Bruch's classification of obesity into three categories—normal, developmental, and reactive—has been applied to children as well as to adults (Bruch, 1957). A child may become obese not because of any emotional problem but because overeating is the "normal" thing to do in his or her family and ethnic group; this is "normal" obesity. In the second, "developmental" pattern, obesity may occur as a function of family problems, especially of problems between the parents. When parents are in conflict with each other, they often attempt to satisfy their own needs through their children. The response of the mother, in particular, may be to overprotect and overfeed the child. As a result, the child becomes obese and remains so by overeating whenever he or she is subject to stress and frustration. In the third, or "reactive," pattern, obesity may develop in response to some acute emotional stress (e.g., the death of a parent or the birth of a sibling), and in this case overeating may function as a form of consolation and reassurance.

Regardless of its causes, obesity, like so many of the other disorders that we will discuss in this chapter, has a snowball effect. Children who are obese (or who wet their pants in school or who stutter) are children who are made fun of. Guilt, rejection, self-contempt, and exclusion from peer-group activities then become sources of further stress, causing such children to overeat (or wet their pants or stutter) even more than before.

Anorexia Nervosa   Although obesity may have ill effects on physical as well as psychological health, far more dangerous is its opposite, **anorexia nervosa,** defined as a severe restriction of food intake caused by a fear of gaining weight. Anorexia is overwhelmingly a disease of adolescent girls and young women. From 85 to 95 percent of anorexics are female, and in most cases the onset is between ages twelve and eighteen, though it may also occur in prepuberty or as late as age thirty. Anorexia is a relatively rare disorder, with annual incidence probably less than 1 in 100,000 population, but it is apparently becoming more common (Bemis, 1978).

Predictably, the most dramatic physical sign of an-

Most people go on occasional "eating binges," stuffing themselves with a favorite food; but bulimia—a pattern of binge eating followed by self-induced vomiting—is a serious eating disorder. (Susan Rosenberg/Photo Researchers)

orexia is weight loss. Bliss and Branch (1960) cite the case of a woman whose weight dropped from 180 to 60 pounds. However, most clinicians consider a loss of 25 percent of body weight sufficient, along with other signs, for a diagnosis of anorexia (Feighner et al., 1972). The weight loss is normally accompanied by **amenorrhea,** suspension of menstrual periods, and by other physical signs as well.

In behavioral terms, the anorexic usually follows one of two patterns: either she simply refuses to eat, or she eats (sometimes voraciously) and then either vomits spontaneously or induces vomiting. Some patients report that they are so repelled by food that they never experience normal sensations of hunger, but they are the exceptions. Most anorexics clearly have normal appetites, at least in the early stages of the disorder (Bruch, 1973). Indeed, they may become quite preoccupied with food, collecting cookbooks, preparing elaborate meals for others, and going through sporadic episodes of **bulimia,** or uncontrolled binge eating, followed by self-induced vomiting. (The binge-and-purge cycle of bulimia is also found among people of normal weight, and *DSM-III-R* recognizes it as a distinct disorder.)

In combination with extreme weight loss, fear of obesity is perhaps the most typical feature of anorexia. One investigator has said that anorexia might more appropriately be called "weight phobia" (Crisp, 1967). Despite overwhelming evidence from the mirror to the contrary—protruding ribs and pelvis, skeletal faces, claw-like hands—anorexics insist that they are too fat and need to lose weight. This distorted image of the body, this image of oneself as fat in the face of grossly contradictory evidence, and the anorexic's iron determination to correct her body by self-denial are important in the development of the disorder. Some anorexic women have been obese in the past (Crisp, 1970), and anorexia often follows a period of dieting common among teenage girls. But this more reasonable calorie counting eventually hardens into a program of determined starvation, as in the following case:

> At fifteen Alma had been healthy and well-developed, had menstruated at age twelve, was five feet six inches tall, and weighed one hundred twenty pounds. At that time her mother urged her to change to a school with higher academic standing, a change she resisted; her father suggested that she should watch her weight, an idea that she took up with great eagerness, and she began a rigid diet. She lost rapidly and her menses ceased. That she could be thin gave her a sense of pride, power, and accomplishment. She also began a frantic exercise program, would swim by the mile, play tennis for hours, or do calisthenics to the point of exhaustion. Whatever low point her weight reached, Alma feared that she might become "too fat" if she regained as little as an ounce. . . .
>
> When she came for consultation [at age twenty] she looked like a walking skeleton, scantily dressed in shorts and a halter, with her legs sticking out like broomsticks, every rib showing, and her shoulder blades standing up like little wings. . . . Alma insisted that she looked fine and that there was nothing wrong with being so skinny (Bruch, 1978, pp. 1–2).

Because it so often occurs in adolescence, the point in development when secondary sexual characteristics emerge and when many people embark on sexual relationships, some clinicians interpret anorexia as a way of avoiding an adult sexual role and especially the possibility of pregnancy. The fact that amenorrhea sometimes *precedes* the weight loss (Halmi, 1974) and therefore may be psychogenic rather than the result of malnutrition supports this hypothesis. But even if anorexia does not aim to suppress sexuality, that undoubtedly is its effect. Menstruation stops, the sex drive disappears, and breasts and hips shrink. Many anorexic women barely look female, much less sexually attractive.

Another suspected cause of anorexia is family warfare, with self-starvation serving as a daughter's weapon against her parents. Few actions can bring parents to surrender as quickly as their child's refusal to eat. Disturbed relationships between parents and anorexic children are often seen, a connection that supports the family hypothesis. But the disturbed relationships may be the effect rather than the cause of the anorexia (Bemis, 1978). Families are not usually harmonious when one member is starving herself to death. Whatever the cause of anorexia, family therapy, as we shall see later in the chapter, is one of the most promising forms of treatment.

Elimination Disorders

Like eating, toilet training may be an arena of intense conflict for a child. Toilet training is one of the first points in development at which children have to comply with demands that run counter to their natural impulses. Sometimes these demands are extreme, for our society insists that children achieve control over elimination at an early age. When children fail to pass this developmental milestone, they are diagnosed as having either enuresis (lack of bladder control) or encopresis (lack of bowel control).

Enuresis   **Enuresis** usually is defined as a lack of bladder control past the age when such control is usual. In this country, most children achieve daytime control between the ages of two and three and nighttime control a year later. Individual children do vary greatly, however, in the ages at which they achieve control. Most children who fall behind in bladder control have trouble with nighttime control—bedwetting. Daytime wetting is much less common and may be the sign of a more serious psychological problem. Whatever the pattern, enuresis is more common in boys than in girls.

Although various clinicians diagnose enuresis at different ages, *DSM-III-R* proposes that the dividing line between late but normal bladder control and enuresis is age five. Similarly, although various clinicians diagnose enuresis by different frequencies, *DSM-III-R* proposes that children between five and six years old who wet their beds twice a month and older children who wet their beds once a month be diagnosed as enuretic.

Enuresis may be primary or secondary. Children with *primary enuresis* have never achieved bladder control; whenever they have to urinate, day or night, they wet themselves. Primary enuresis may last until middle childhood, and occasionally it lasts into adolescence or beyond. Some authorities (e.g., Bakwin and Bakwin, 1972) have suggested that the condition may stem from organic, possibly genetic, abnormalities.

Children with *secondary enuresis* have lost the bladder control they once had, almost always as a result of stress. The birth of a baby brother or sister, with the jealousy and insecurity it often provokes, is probably the most common cause. Whether treated or not, secondary enuresis is usually temporary.

Enuresis may or may not be a serious problem. Most enuretic children are not emotionally disturbed (Werry, 1979b). But one longitudinal study found certain personality correlates with enuresis. Among the 153 children studied at an Israeli kibbutz, two high-risk personality patterns emerged (Kaffman and Elizur, 1977). About 30 percent of the enuretic children were aggressive, easily frustrated, responded negatively to discipline, and resisted adjusting to new situations. A smaller number were dependent, unassertive, and had little motivation toward mastery. Delayed toilet training seemed to increase the risk of enuresis in high-risk but not low-risk children. Even if the enuresis itself is not a serious problem, this disorder, like obesity, can *cause* serious problems. Children who wet their pants at school are likely to be ridiculed by their schoolmates, to the detriment of their self-esteem and social adjustment. Their parents, weary of changing wet sheets and clothes, may react with anger and rejection, adding to the children's problems.

Encopresis   A pattern of toilet-training failure that involves a lack of bowel control rather than of bladder control is called **encopresis.*** In some ways encopresis resembles enuresis. It too is classified as either primary (control is never achieved) or secondary (control is mastered and then lost). In the primary form, it too may have an organic basis. It too is more common in boys than in girls. Finally, even more than enuresis, encopresis can earn a child mockery from peers and wrath from parents, compounding whatever problems he or she has.

Encopresis, which occurs in approximately 1 percent of the general population (*DSM-III-R*), is much less common than enuresis. When it is involuntary rather than deliberate, encopresis is often the result of constipation or impaction of the feces with subsequent overflow.

In the following case, secondary encopresis occurred with enuresis:

> Carl, third of five children, was seven years old and in the second grade when he was seen by a counselor. His parents reported that he wet his pants every day and each night and that he soiled himself three to four times a week. The investigator found that Carl had been successfully toilet-trained by the age of three. He had had a few daytime "accidents" at the time of the birth of a younger sister when he was three, but thereafter his toilet habits remained good. About six months before Carl's visit to the clinic, his mother began to toilet-train the youngest daughter in the family. Quite suddenly, Carl began wetting his pants every day and night and having bowel movements in his pants about three times a week.
>
> On investigation, Carl's mother was found to have singled him out as a "problem" child ever since her difficult and painful pregnancy. Early in childhood, he had been involved in aggressiveness against his two older brothers, but since the birth of his two younger sisters, he had generally sought them out as companions and playmates in preference to his brothers. In consequence, he was ridiculed as a sissy by his brothers and his parents. When his mother began to toilet-train his youngest sister by reading to her for long periods as she sat on the potty and showing her similar attentions, Carl began to have problems with elimination.
>
> Both Carl and his parents were seen in weekly therapy sessions for more than a year. A long-standing pattern of considering Carl a "problem" child and thus the scapegoat for problems in the parents' marriage (which were considerable) proved difficult to alter. Finally, consistent use of praise and other positive reinforcement resulted in Carl's resuming proper toilet habits (adapted from Leon, 1977, pp. 27–42).

---

* Sometimes it involves both; about one-fourth of encopretic children are also enuretic (*DSM-III-R*).

Sleep Disorders

Children's sleep disorders include sleepwalking, insomnia, night terrors, anxiety dreams, and other problems. In this section, we focus on sleepwalking, night terrors, and anxiety dreams.

Sleepwalking, also called **somnambulism,** occurs in 1 to 6 percent of the general population (*DSM-III-R*), but it is far more common in children than in adults. Sleepwalking does not seem to indicate a serious psychological problem in children (Kales et al., 1966). Children who sleepwalk typically fall asleep, then get out of bed an hour or two later without actually waking up and perform some complex action such as making a sandwich, rearranging the furniture, or getting dressed and leaving the house. (Few go far, however.) The episode lasts from a few minutes to half an hour, and the child then returns to bed. In the morning, the child has no memory of the episode.

Night terrors, also called *pavor nocturnus,* are a harrowing kind of bad dream found almost exclusively among children. Children in the throes of night terrors show extreme autonomic arousal (rapid breathing and

Sleep disturbances in children are usually temporary responses to stress, seldom persisting beyond the age of about six. (Erika Stone/Peter Arnold)

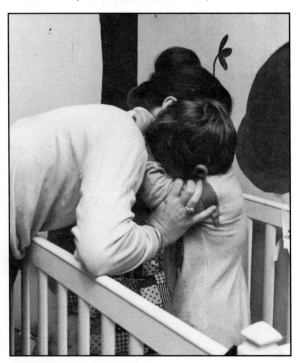

heartbeat, etc.) and violent movements. When awakened, they are confused, disoriented, and difficult to calm. They cannot seem to pull themselves out of their dream. Eventually they do go back to sleep, and in the morning they usually do not remember the episode.

Far less dramatic is the **anxiety dream,** or garden-variety nightmare, which is common in adults as well as children. Physiological responses are milder and verbalizing more subdued in anxiety dreams than in night terrors (Keith, 1975). When awakened, children calm quickly and usually can relate their dreams in detail—describe the monster, for example, and the size of its fangs, the look of its den, and so forth.

Most children go through periods of sleep disturbances, especially between the ages of four and six, when they are adjusting to school. As with elimination problems, it often is hard for clinicians to draw the line between normal and abnormal sleep disturbances. In most children, sleep disturbances are normal, temporary responses to stress.

Speech Disorders

Childhood speech disorders may take many forms. Psychological problems appear to be implicated in only two of them, delayed speech and stuttering.

Delayed Speech   Most children say their first words within a few months after their first birthday. By eighteen to twenty-four months, they put together two- and three-word sentences. Individual children vary widely in the age at which they speak, and a few months' delay rarely signals a developmental disorder. Some normal children begin to speak quite late. Albert Einstein, for example, did not speak until he was three years old. But a prolonged delay may signal an organic or functional disorder. In some cases, failure to speak is an early sign of autism (Chapter 18), deafness, mental retardation, or another specific form of brain damage.

Stuttering   **Stuttering** is the interruption of fluent speech through blocked, prolonged, or repeated words, syllables, or sounds. Many people stutter sometimes, and hesitant speech is common in young children. Therefore, as with so many other childhood disorders, it often is difficult to decide when stuttering is a serious problem. Persistent stuttering occurs in about 1 percent of the population and in about four times as many boys as girls. It is most likely to appear between the ages of two and seven (with peak onset at around age five) and seldom appears after age eleven (*DSM-III-R*).

Many children outgrow stuttering as their motor skills and confidence increase. Even those who do not outgrow it completely eventually tend to stutter less or only in stressful situations. About 40 percent of children are estimated to overcome stuttering before they start school, and 80 percent overcome it by late adolescence (Sheehan and Martyn, 1970).

Organic theories of stuttering are popular in some quarters. One organic theory, for example, holds that stuttering stems from a problem with the physical articulation of sounds in the mouth and larynx (Agnello, 1975; Kerr and Cooper, 1976). But many psychologists today think that stuttering is psychogenic. Stuttering may be created unwittingly by parents who become so alarmed at their children's mild speech hesitations that they make the children anxious about speaking (Johnson, 1955). The children's anxiety further disturbs their speech, which in turn makes them more anxious, and so on, until a chronic problem has been created. Other theorists emphasize factors other than parents' overconcern, but almost all agree that anxiety is important in creating, maintaining, and aggravating stuttering.

Attention Deficit Disorders

In almost every elementary school, there are a few children who cannot sit still, cannot finish any task they begin, cannot focus their attention for longer than a minute or two—who fidget, interrupt, butt into other children's games, explode in frustration if made to wait their turn, and generally drive teachers to despair. A few decades ago researchers began to suspect that such children's behavior pattern, characterized primarily by excess motor activity and short attention span, might be due to brain damage. It was known, for example, that certain kinds of brain infection produced restless motor activity. Furthermore, many of the children who manifested this pattern also showed "soft," or ambiguous, neurological signs that could suggest brain damage, and a small percentage of them showed definite signs of neurological impairment. On this evidence, the disorder was labeled *minimal brain dysfunction* (MBD). Still, no one could say

what exactly the dysfunction was. At the same time, there was (and still is) a strong trend away from labeling disorders according to etiology when that etiology was not definitely established. Hence the syndrome was eventually given a new name, descriptive rather than etiological—*hyperactivity*. Although this term is still in common use, in *DSM-III-R* it has been replaced. It has been noted that many children show all the symptoms described above *except* for the excessive motor activity, the very symptom for which the disorder was originally named (Sandberg et al., 1978). Furthermore, an analysis of the performance of hyperactive children on a variety of tasks indicated that the basic problem was a failure of *sustained* attention (Douglas and Peters, 1979). Thus, it seemed, the factor that united all these children was not the motor problem but the *attention* problem. Accordingly, *DSM-III-R* includes all forms of this disorder under a broad category titled "attention deficit disorder," with two subcategories—one for those who show both hyperactivity and attention problems and the other for those who show only the attention problems. We shall concentrate on the first category, since it is the more common.

Attention deficit disorder with hyperactivity is a commonly diagnosed disorder. It is the most common behavior disorder seen by child psychiatrists (Ross, 1981) and the most common cause of childhood referral to mental health clinics (Wender, 1971). It affects between 2 and 5 percent of the elementary school population (Lambert et al., 1978), with boys greatly outnumbering girls. It is a controversial diagnosis; some experts believe that it is too readily applied to children whom parents and teachers find difficult to control.

We have already described the typical behavior of the hyperactive child.* Its most salient features are incessant restlessness and an extremely poor attention span, leading in turn to impulsive and disorganized behavior. These handicaps affect almost every area of the child's functioning. Even the most trivial human accomplishments—setting a table, playing a card game—depend on the ability to set goals, plan ahead, organize one's behavior, and postpone gratification. It is this ability that is most strikingly absent in the hyperactive child. Thus the characteristic motor be-

---

* For the sake of convenience, we will use the term "hyperactive" to describe children showing what *DSM-III-R* now calls "attention-deficit hyperactivity disorder."

havior of these children is often distinguished less by its excessiveness as by its haphazard quality. Normal children are exceedingly active, but their getting up and down and running back and forth is usually directed toward some goal. By contrast, the incessant activity of hyperactive children seems purposeless and disorganized. Furthermore, a normal child can, if motivated, sit still and concentrate; a hyperactive child has difficulty doing so.

This inability to focus and sustain attention has a ruinous effect on academic progress. Hyperactive children have great difficulty following instructions and finishing tasks; frequently they cannot even remember what they set out to do. Consequently, while often intelligent, they have severe learning problems. They are also extremely disruptive in the classroom, making incessant demands for attention. (Often it is not until such children enter school that their problem is recognized. What parents can put up with, a teacher with twenty-five pupils and a set of lessons to complete usually cannot.) Hyperactive children also show poor social adjustment. They disrupt games, get into fights, refuse to play fair, and throw temper tantrums. Such behavior does not make them popular.

Attention deficits with hyperactivity are usually variable. The child may seem greatly improved one week and then much worse the next week. The disorder also varies situationally. In many cases, hyperactive children function adequately on a one-to-one basis but fall apart in group situations; hence they may do well at home but not at school—another reason why the disorder often goes undiagnosed until school age.

What happens to hyperactive children as they grow up? The prognosis for the disorder is not clear, since there have not yet been enough long-term follow-up studies. What research we have indicates that the motor restlessness tends to decline in adolescence, while the attention problem usually persists, often into adulthood. To the extent that aggressiveness accompanies hyperactivity in childhood, an individual may have social behavior problems in adolescence (Loney et al., 1979). Even if symptoms disappear completely, the problems *created* by the childhood disorder—academic underachievement, negative self-image, parent–child conflicts, lack of friends—reduce the individual's chances for social and occupational success as an adult. However, improved treatments (to be discussed later in this chapter) may lead to improved prognosis.

Children diagnosed as having **attention deficit disorder without hyperactivity** show the same behaviors described above, minus the motor restlessness. (Indeed, they may be noticeably underactive.) Since this disorder has only recently been isolated as a separate category, we know less about it than about attention deficit with hyperactivity. It too seems to be common, and more common in boys than in girls. (In fact, the high prevalence of 2 to 5 percent reported for attention deficit with hyperactivity may be due in part to the past practice of lumping together the hyperactive and nonhyperactive forms.)

Learning Disabilities

Some children who have normal or even superior intelligence and adequate schooling nevertheless are diagnosed as "learning disabled" because they have great trouble acquiring a certain skill and lag significantly behind other children their age in some area of intellectual development. These children have specific developmental disorders in reading, writing, spelling, speaking, calculating, or other skills needed to do well in school. No one knows precisely how many children are learning disabled. Estimates are that up to 10 percent of the general population of the United States may have reading problems (Meir, 1971). Boys generally outnumber girls, sometimes by a factor of 2 to 3, among children with learning disabilities.

Learning disabilities is an umbrella term, coined in the 1960s (Kirk, 1963), to cover the many children who were failing school subjects but who did not fit neatly into any existing category of handicap (Gelfand et al., 1982). Even today, clinicians do not agree on the definition of learning disabilities, and they continue to struggle to define the term. One of the difficulties they face is the fact that nearly half of all learning disabled children also can be labeled brain dysfunctional or hyperactive (Benton and Pearl, 1978).

The most recent legal definition of learning disability is presented in the Education for All Handicapped Children Act:

> Specific learning disability means a disorder in one or more of the basic psychological processes involved in understanding or in using language, spoken or written, which may manifest itself in an imperfect ability to listen, think, speak, read, write, spell, or to do mathematical calculations. The term includes such conditions as perceptual handicaps, brain injury, minimal brain dysfunction, dyslexia, and developmental aphasia. The term does not include children who have learning problems which

are primarily the result of visual, hearing, or motor handicaps, of mental retardation, or of environmental, cultural, or economic disadvantage (Sections 5[b] [4] of Public Law 94–142).

In part to help researchers investigate learning disabilities, *DSM-III-R* has established diagnostic categories for such academic skills disorders as reading disorder, arithmetic disorder, and expressive writing disorder. In the case of reading disorder, also called **dyslexia,** children cannot identify letters or words, or their reading is distorted. Children with arithmetic disorder, sometimes called *dyscalcula,* cannot do the arithmetic that is expected at their age. Children with writing disorder are far below their peers in their writing ability and specifically in their spelling, grammar, and organization of thoughts into sentences and paragraphs. Finally, children with articulation disorder consistently fail to use the sound of *r, sh, th, f, z, l,* or *ch* when they speak, and so their speech is babyish and imperfect.

Diagnostic categories aside, children with learning disabilities may show signs of underlying problems of several kinds. Some have problems in visual and auditory perception. In fact, more learning disabled children have problems with visual perception than any other kind of problem. They may be unable to copy words from the blackboard or to recognize the distinctions between circles and triangles. For example, a learning disabled child may see the capital letter *A* as three unrelated lines (Lerner, 1976). Some children with problems of visual perception have trouble focusing on lines of type or words on a page, or they may not be able to tell *M* from *N* or *dig* from *dog*.

Children with problems of auditory perception may have trouble distinguishing the sounds of words or syllables, or they may have trouble identifying the sound of, say, a doorbell and distinguishing it from other sounds, or they may not be able to make simple associations between the words they hear (Gelfand et al., 1982). Children with perceptual problems usually have problems in more than one system—visual, auditory, and haptic (touch and movement). Because many learning disabled children have perceptual problems, some theorists have suggested that their underlying problem is neurological.

Some learning disabled children have memory and other cognitive problems, too. They cannot remember from one moment to the next or from one day to the next what they have struggled so hard to learn in school. Although this kind of forgetting happens to virtually everyone at some time or other, it is especially common among certain learning disabled children and a source of continual frustration to them and to their teachers. Learning disabled children may also show cognitive deficits such as difficulty with sequential thinking and inability to use organization strategies. Research on the memory and cognitive aspects of learning disabilities has been of recent interest.

Some children with learning disabilities have trouble focusing their attention and seem hyperactive. They may have short attention spans and find it difficult to focus on important stimuli to the exclusion of irrelevant stimuli. Research suggests that learning disabled children usually can recall less central information than nonhandicapped children do but *more* irrelevant information (Pelham and Ross, 1977; Tarver et al., 1976). Both learning disabled and nonhandicapped children tend to get better at focusing their attention with age, although learning disabled children may lag two to four years behind. This finding supports the hypothesis that learning disabled children have developmental delays.

Because learning disabled children do poorly in school, they are often seen as failures by their teachers, peers, and family members. As a result, learning disabled children usually have formed negative self-images by age nine, and such images tend to worsen with time (Wenar, 1983). Learning disabled children, especially girls, tend to be less popular with other children than nonhandicapped children, and their teachers may have less positive attitudes toward them. Social problems may develop as frustration and anxiety lead the children to act in ways that alienate others. Such problems may also result from the fact that the same cognitive problems that prevent these children from learning academic skills may prevent them from accurately perceiving and dealing with social situations.

The definitions, causes, and symptoms of learning disabilities often merge confusingly. Children with the same symptoms may have different underlying disorders, and the same disorder may produce different symptoms in different children. People have attributed learning disabilities to birth injuries, genetic defects, dietary deficiencies, environmental problems, and poor teaching (Gelfand et al., 1982). Others have suggested that learning disabilities are only an extreme variation of normal development. But the precise causes of learning disabilities remain unknown. What is more, it is unlikely that any single factor will be found to explain all forms of learning disabilities. Ap-

Separation anxiety disorder, in which the child dreads being parted from the parents, occurs in most babies in our culture at around the age of one year, and often recurs in older children as a result of some kind of stress. (Olive R. Pierce/Stock, Boston)

proaches to treatment are extremely varied. Some learning disabled children who are also hyperactive are treated with drugs or special diets. A variety of instructional techniques have been devised for classroom use. The outlook for children affected by learning disabilities is as variable as the conditions that gather under the umbrella term. It is hoped that future research will shed more light on this perplexing group of disorders.

Anxiety Disorders

Most of the disorders discussed elsewhere in this book are not confined to adults. Conversion disorders, organic brain disorders, stress-related physical disorders (e.g., asthma), and, increasingly, drug addiction can appear in children and adolescents as well as in adults. And when they do, the child is given the same diagnosis as the adult, for *DSM-III-R* in general does not differentiate between childhood and adult versions of a single disorder. There are a few exceptions to this rule, however, and anxiety disorders constitute one of them. Because the object and expression of childhood anxiety may differ markedly from those of

adult anxiety, *DSM-III-R* includes a separate list of "anxiety disorders of childhood or adolescence."* As we shall see, these disorders, like the anxiety disorders discussed in Chapter 8, are differentiated from one another primarily according to the object of the anxiety.†

Separation Anxiety Disorder   Separation anxiety—intense fear and distress upon being separated from parents (or other caretakers)—is seen in almost all children toward the end of the first year of life. It peaks at about twelve months and then gradually disappears. In some children, however, it does not disappear but persists well into the school years. Or, in the more typical pattern, it disappears on schedule and then reappears, at full intensity, some time later in childhood, usually after the child has undergone

---

* This list does not include all the anxiety disorders appearing in childhood, but rather those that occur *only* in childhood. Phobia, for example, is not included in this list. A dog-phobic child is given the same diagnosis as a dog-phobic adult.
† The following descriptions of childhood anxiety disorders are based on *DSM-III-R*.

some kind of stress, such as the death of a pet or a move to a new school or new neighborhood. This condition, essentially a phobia of being parted from parents, is known as **separation anxiety disorder.**

In extreme cases, children with this disorder cannot be separated from their parents by so much as a wall and will shadow them from room to room. In most cases, however, all that the child asks is to be allowed to stay at home, with the parent in the house. But even with their parents present, children with this disorder may be haunted by fears of horrible things—kidnapping, automobile accidents, attacks by monsters—that may befall them or their parents if they are separated. They generally have sleeping problems as well, since sleep means separation, and consequently they may reappear night after night to crawl in bed with the parents. (If banished from the parents' bedroom, they are likely to camp outside the door.)

Children with this disorder are typically clinging and demanding, putting considerable strain on their parents. Parent–child conflicts, then, are common with separation anxiety disorder and of course exacerbate it, since the parents' annoyance makes the child all the more fearful of abandonment.

In addition to family conflicts, these children also suffer in other areas. They may refuse to attend school,* and consequently their academic progress comes to a halt. Furthermore, since they cannot go to school or camp or other children's houses, they make no friends or lose the friends they had.

It is not yet known how common this disorder is, but it seems to occur in both sexes with equal frequency. It may appear at any time during childhood—usually, as we noted earlier, after some traumatic incident—and tends to persist for several years, with fluctuating intensity.

Avoidant Disorder   As the term suggests, **avoidant disorder,** parallel to avoidant personality

---

* According to *DSM-III-R,* the "school refusal" of the child with separation anxiety disorder is not the same thing as *school phobia,* another childhood anxiety disorder. The object of school-phobic children's fear is specifically school and school alone, and the child would continue to be afraid even if accompanied by a parent. The child with separation anxiety disorder fears separation, and school is feared only because it means separation. However, this distinction is difficult to make, and many school-phobia cases also involve separation anxiety.

disorder (Chapter 11) in adults, is an extreme fear and avoidance of strangers. Like separation anxiety, fear of strangers is normal in very young children, beginning around eight months. But most children grow out of it by age two and a half. They may still be standoffish with people they don't know—averting their gaze, pretending not to hear questions, and so forth—but eventually they warm up to the new person and resume their normal behavior. Children with avoidant disorder, on the other hand, do not "warm up" even after prolonged contact with a new person. When addressed by a stranger, they may be struck mute. When a new person enters the room, they may take refuge behind a piece of furniture. When pushed into a situation with many new people, they will simply withdraw into a corner, blushing and embarrassed, until rescued.

Such children, unlike those with separation anxiety disorder, are often well adjusted at home and have good relationships with their parents. But at school they are painfully withdrawn. This behavior may interfere with their academic progress, and of course it interferes with their social adjustment. They make few if any friends, and their resulting loneliness may give rise to depression and low self-esteem.

Overanxious Disorder   Like the fears of adults suffering from generalized anxiety disorder (Chapter 8), those of children ensnared in **overanxious disorder** are not focused on any specific object, but are generalized and diffuse, so that almost any situation may engender worry and anxiety. In particular, such children are plagued by anticipatory anxiety, fears of what *might* go wrong. Will they be picked for the baseball team? If so, will they get hurt playing ball? Will they be invited to so-and-so's birthday party? If so, will the birthday child like the gift they bring?

As these worries suggest, such children tend to have severe doubts about their own capabilities and likeableness—doubts that lead them to constant approval-seeking. This complex of worry and self-doubt may be the result of family dynamics. There is some evidence that overanxious disorder is more common in families where parental love is made conditional on consistently "good" behavior.

Whatever its cause, the pervasive anxiety of these children tends to breed failure. Anticipatory anxiety, because it robs behavior of its spontaneity, often creates the very problems that were anticipated. Terrified lest they fail the test or be excluded from the neighborhood skating party, overanxious children run a higher risk of failing and being excluded. Such failures tend to lead to further anxiety and further failure—the familiar vicious cycle.

Childhood Depression

Depression in children and adolescents shares essential features with depression in adults. As we discussed in Chapter 10, depression is characterized by a sad or hopeless mood, loss of interest in usual activities, fatigue, insomnia, poor appetite, and so on. But children express their depression differently from adults—by clinging to their parents, refusing to go to school, or expressing exaggerated fears (of their parents' death, for example). Older children may sulk, withdraw from family activities, and retreat to their rooms. They may have trouble in school, become slovenly, or engage in delinquent acts. Surveys suggest, however, that the clear-cut kinds of depression seen in adults are unusual among children (Rutter and Garmezy, 1983). Depression is often part of other emotional or conduct disorders, but is not necessarily the predominant symptom.

Survey evidence indicates that unhappiness and misery are not uncommon among children. Ten to 12 percent of ten-year-olds investigated in one survey were often "miserable, unhappy, tearful, or distressed" (Rutter et al., 1981). Depression increases sharply in adolescence. When the ten-year-olds were surveyed again at age fourteen or fifteen, the incidence of depression among them now corresponded to a rate of 40 percent of the general population (Rutter, 1979). Whereas childhood depressive disorders (as opposed to other disorders in which depressive feelings are present) are somewhat more common among boys, in adolescence such disorders are much more common among girls. Grief reactions and unusually elevated moods (hypomania) are also more prominent in adolescents than in children (Rutter and Garmezy, 1983).

Adolescents feel suicidal and attempt or commit suicide far more often than children do. Statistics from the United States and Britain show that suicide is rare in children under twelve. The suicide rate rises sharply during adolescence and continues to rise throughout the life span, peaking in old age (Rutter and Garmezy, 1983). Because follow-up studies of children who were diagnosed as depressed indicate that they tend to have episodes of mood disorder as adults (Cantwell, 1982), early detection and treatment may be important preventive measures.

Conduct Disorders

As with anxiety, *DSM-III-R* distinguishes between adult and childhood manifestations of antisocial behavior. As we saw in Chapter 11, antisocial personality disorder in adults is characterized by a lack of moral scruples and a failure to sustain close relationships with others; it is highly resistant to treatment and tends to persist over the years. Some teenagers fit the description of antisocial personality in every respect except age. In other cases, antisocial behavior in the young takes somewhat different forms. Accordingly, *DSM-III-R* lists three categories of **conduct disorders,** childhood disorders involving antisocial behavior.

DSM-III-R lists thirteen criteria for conduct disorders. Three of them must be present in a disturbance of conduct for at least six months. The criteria include the following: stealing, running away from home, telling lies, or being truant from school. More aggressive acts include setting fires, breaking into homes or cars, or destroying property. Some actions involve physical confrontation, such as being physically cruel to people or animals, forcing someone into sexual activity, initiating fights, using a weapon in a fight, or mugging.

The first category is **conduct disorder, solitary aggressive type.** Characterized by a lack of emotional attachments and by aggressive antisocial behavior, children in this category are the closest parallel to adult antisocial personalities. They may lie, steal, set fires, break into houses, and constantly get into fights with other children. What is most striking about them, however, is not just their aggressive behavior but their callousness. We normally think of children and young teenagers as emotionally vulnerable creatures. Adults may be hardened against others; children, no. Nevertheless, children who fit this category are precociously devoid of feelings. They often have no real friends, and the associates they do have they will betray in a moment if it is to their advantage to do so. Likewise, they typically show little attachment to their families, and the feeling is often mutual. The parents of such children are often neglectful and inconsistent in discipline, and may themselves be antisocial personalities. Many children in this category are institutionalized as juvenile delinquents and convicted and imprisoned for criminal activity as adults (Henn et al., 1980).

A second category, **conduct disorder, group type,** differs markedly from the other two in that it includes normal emotional attachments. Children in this category have friends; indeed, they typically belong to a gang and are decent and loyal to other members. Furthermore, they often have normal emotional ties to their families. Toward the rest of the world, however, their behavior is as antisocial as that of "undersocialized" children. Aggressive behavior may or may not be part of the pattern. The distinction between this pattern and that of the solitary conduct disorders is similar to the distinction we drew in Chapter 11 between the "normal" criminal and the antisocial personality. And as with the normal criminal, it is arguable that the child (or, usually, teenager) who falls into this pattern has no psychological abnormality, but is simply socialized into a deviant value system.

The third category, **conduct disorder, undifferentiated type,** includes children or adolescents with a combination of features so that they cannot be classified solely as one of the other two types.

Regardless of specific diagnosis, children with conduct disorders are cause for grave social concern. Whether in gangs or on their own, these children commit many crimes—a large percentage of them serious. Police records show that in 1986 in New York City alone, there were 7,340 felony arrests (including murder, rape, and robbery) in the under-sixteen age group (New York Police Department, Public Affairs Division, 1987).

PERSPECTIVES ON THE DISORDERS OF CHILDHOOD AND ADOLESCENCE

The Psychodynamic Perspective

Because of its emphasis on the childhood determinants of adult behavior, the psychodynamic perspective probably interests itself more than any other perspective in the behavior disorders of childhood.

The symptoms of the solitary aggressive type of conduct disorder resemble those of the adult antisocial personality—random acts of aggression and violence and lack of emotional attachments. (Harvey Wang)

Conflict and Regression   It may be said as a general rule that psychodynamic theorists interpret childhood developmental disorders as stemming from a conflict between, on the one hand, the child's sexual and aggressive impulses and, on the other hand, the prohibitions imposed by the parents and by the developing superego. For example, nightmares and night terrors may result when forbidden wishes, repressed during the waking hours, surface in the child's dreams. This process can then give rise to insomnia, as the child refuses to go to sleep for fear that the unacceptable desire will once again be reenacted in dreams.

In much the same way, encopresis can be interpreted as a disguised expression of hostility. If the child and the parents are engaged in a power struggle over toilet training or anything else, the child needs some release for aggressive feelings. To express them directly would arouse too much anxiety, so instead, he or she inflicts on the parents the annoyance and mess of cleaning up dirty pants.

Enuresis, on the other hand, is usually interpreted as a sign of regression. As we saw earlier, secondary enuresis is often precipitated by the birth of a sibling. In such cases, according to psychodynamic theory, the wetting constitutes an envy-motivated regression to the new baby's level—a way of letting parents know that older children need as much attention as new babies. Even if the stressor is something altogether different, such as the death of a grandparent or the beginning of school, it is still interpretable as regression: a retreat to an earlier and less threatening period of development.

Anorexia, too, is often associated with regression by psychodynamic writers. As we saw earlier, anorexia has been interpreted as a strategy for avoiding adult sexuality. According to psychodynamic theorists, the young woman, unable to meet the demands of the mature genital stage, regresses to a more primitive stage of development. Here, however, she is caught in a dilemma, for among very young children, according to Freudian theory, eating is associated with sexual pleasure; indeed, it may also be associated with pregnancy. (For lack of better information, many small children do believe that women become pregnant via the mouth.) Hence the young woman, to avoid the disturbing sexual thoughts associated with food, refuses to eat (A. Freud, 1958; Szyrynski, 1973).

This classic psychodynamic interpretation has been challenged by ego psychologists who feel that anorexia has less to do with repressed instincts than with the adolescent's drive for autonomy. Bruch, for example, see anorexia as a "desperate struggle for a self-respecting identity" (1978, p. 1) on the part of a girl whose wishes have for years been brushed aside by her mother. What the daughter wants is not important; mother "knows better." At first the girl submits to this psychological bullying, becoming the perfect, well-behaved daughter. Eventually, however, she strikes back by refusing to eat. This refusal constitutes both a rejection of the mother and a last-ditch attempt at self-determination. In effect, the girl is saying, "I will control my own life, even if it means starving to death." In support of this view, anorexic girls have repeatedly been described as shy, conscientious, and obedient prior to the onset of the disorder (Bruch, 1973; Char and McDermott, 1970; Story, 1976).

Treatment   For children as for adults, psychodynamic theorists feel that the best treatment is one that allows patients to bring to the surface and "work through" their unconscious conflicts. However, the specific procedures for achieving this result are tailored to fit the child's emotional and intellectual level and therefore differ somewhat from adult psychotherapy.

The technique of Anna Freud (1965), who was the best-known exponent of child psychoanalysis, is probably closest to traditional adult psychoanalysis. Like adults, children are seen four or five times a week, but instead of lying on a couch, they usually play in the presence of the therapist. And as with adults, the therapist provides interpretations. For example, if a child commented, "You must see a lot of kids in this office," the therapist might respond, "Would you like to have me all to yourself?" However, interpretations are geared to the child's level and are aimed at clarifying feelings as well as promoting insight. Furthermore, the child is given more affection, support, and encouragement than an adult would receive.

In treating children, psychodynamic therapies go far afield from traditional psychoanalysis. In informal sessions, often once or twice a week, the child is encouraged to vent emotional problems through symbolic fantasy. A very popular technique for this purpose is **play therapy.** Here, instead of asking young patients what the problem is, the therapist provides them with drawing materials and toys, on the assumption that whatever is troubling them will be expressed in their drawings and games. Typically the therapist's office looks something like a small-scale nursery schoolroom, with blocks, paints, and clay. Other essentials are toys for expressing aggression and dolls and puppets for play-acting family conflicts.

Whatever their methods, therapists treating children usually have a good deal of contact with parents. In some cases, the parents may be drawn in as "co-therapists," adopting at home techniques taught to them by the therapist. In other cases, all members of the family may be involved in therapy. Whatever the techniques used, the therapist's conversations with parents may help to resolve family conflicts that have been maintaining the child's problem.

While such methods are characteristic in general of psychodynamic treatment of children, the specific approach varies with the tastes of the therapist, the age of the child, and the nature of the problem. With an anorexic whose life is in danger, a highly directive approach may be used; with an enuretic child, a looser, less directive approach. In treating a preschooler, the therapist may have regular contact with the parents; in treating an adolescent at war with her parents, the therapist may severely limit conversations with the parents, so as not to forfeit the child's trust. In all cases, the technique will depend on the child's needs.

The Behavioral Perspective

In treating children, as in treating adults, behaviorists focus directly on the problem behavior. What situations elicit this behavior? What consequences maintain this behavior? And how can the child's environment be changed so that the behavior will change accordingly?

Inappropriate Learning   Behaviorists state that behavior disorders in children usually stem from either inadequate learning or inappropriate learning, concepts that have already been discussed in Chapter 3.

For example, inadequate learning—that is, a failure to learn relevant cues for performing desired behaviors—may play a role in primary enuresis. In other words, the child may never have learned to identify the physiological cues associated with a full bladder. Ross (1981) suggests that inadequate learning may also figure in regressive enuresis if the toileting was newly learned and had not yet been completely mastered. Since praise from parents may have helped the child to master the response, premature removal of this positive reinforcement could lead swiftly to the extinction of the behavior. To counteract this process, social reinforcement (i.e., praise) should be resumed until internal reinforcers—pride in accomplishment, for example—are strong enough to maintain the newly developed response.

As for the development of problems through inappropriate learning—that is, the reinforcement of undesirable behavior—the behaviorist's prime example would be the conduct disorders. Children with conduct disorders often come from poor and violence-ridden city neighborhoods, where being "tough" with others may be the quickest route to social prestige, especially within a gang. In addition, there is little doubt that modeling plays some role in the conduct disorders. Aside from the influence of gangs, parents may themselves be models of antisocial behavior, especially through indifferent and abusive treatment of the child. Movies and television may provide further models for aggression.

In Chapters 3 and 8 we have already discussed the importance of avoidance learning—the reinforcement of avoidance behavior by the cessation or avoidance of an aversive stimulus such as anxiety—in the development of phobias. According to behavioral theory, this sequence would be as applicable to the defensive behavior accompanying separation anxiety and shyness as to any other phobia. Furthermore, in the case of these two disorders, the extra parental attention and special privileges associated with staying home may directly reinforce the maladaptive behaviors.

Treatment   In attempting to replace the child's maladaptive responses with adaptive behaviors, behavior therapists use the entire behavioral repertoire: reinforcement, extinction, punishment (usually in the form of the withdrawal of rewards), modeling, respondent conditioning, and so on. To begin with the simplest technique, respondent conditioning, a classic example is the treatment of nocturnal enuresis by means of the so-called Mowrer pad. This device, invented by the psychologist O. H. Mowrer, is a liquid-sensitive pad connected by a battery to an alarm. Any moisture on the pad sounds the alarm, awakening the child (Mowrer and Mowrer, 1938). Although theoretically the child should learn to awaken in anticipation of the alarm, many children learn instead to sleep throughout the night, neither awakening nor wetting. Behavioral techniques can also be applied to teach toilet habits in more sophisticated ways. Richard Foxx and Nathan Azrin (1973) reported toilet training children successfully after only one day of intensive instruction and practice. In their procedure, thirty-four children ranging in age from twenty to thirty-six months were reinforced with praise, hugs, and special treats for successfully mastering each step in using the toilet: approaching the potty chair, lowering the pants, sitting down, etc. At a four-month follow-up, the children averaged about one accident a week, compared with six accidents a day before training.

In treating childhood anxiety disorders, behaviorists have used systematic desensitization (Wolpe, 1958). In this process, just as with adults, the child is taught to engage in relaxation or another response incompatible with anxiety while he or she is being gradually exposed to the feared stimuli, usually by imagining them at the therapist's request. A predecessor of this technique was Mary Cover Jones's famous desensitization of the boy Peter to his fear of furry animals by bringing a rabbit successively closer and closer to him while he was eating candy (Chapter 3).

Modeling has also proved very valuable in the treatment of phobias. The child is given the opportunity

The Problem of Child Abuse

Child abuse in the United States today is only partly explained by the social and psychological ills of the modern world and its breakdown of values. Children suffered under the old values, too, and have been victimized in every era and in most of the world's cultures. Although child abuse is not a psychological disorder, it puts the child at risk for a number of disorders.

Although laws were passed to protect children from abusive parents as early as 1735 in Massachusetts and the Society for the Prevention of Cruelty to Children was established in 1874 in the United States, public concern over child abuse has waxed and waned over the last century. Only recently, over the past two decades, has child abuse been identified as a serious social problem requiring tough legislation, treatment, and preventive measures. Thousands of children die or suffer irreversible damage every year despite media coverage and public outrage over the problem.

Incidence Today

More than 200,000 cases of child abuse are reported in the United States each year. Although estimates of actual incidence vary, most experts agree that cases are greatly underreported (President's Commission on Mental Health, 1978). Abuse may include emotional neglect and failure to meet a child's basic physical needs as well as sexual abuse and physical violence. Underreporting of child abuse has several causes, including the abusers' shame, the inability of small children to seek help outside the family, the reluctance of some medical practitioners to turn their clients over to the law, and the ongoing American tradition of accepting family violence. One survey indicates that up to 4 million American children have been kicked or punched at least once in their lives, up to 2.3 million have been beaten senseless, and up to 1.8 million have been attacked with a gun or knife (Gelles, 1979; Wickes-Nelson and Israel, 1984).

The Cause of Child Abuse

Although some researchers emphasize the psychological and some the social causes of child abuse, most agree that the problem has multiple, interacting causes. Factors that may predispose a person to child abuse include the experience of childhood abuse and the parent's immaturity, dependency, rigidity, sense of powerlessness, and lack of self-confidence. Two types of mothers emerge: those who keep babies they do not want and those who get pregnant in order to establish identities separate from their own neglectful or abusing parents. A child who fails to meet the unrealistic expectations of a mother desperate to be loved may become the target of abuse (Walsh, 1977). Although psychosis is seldom found in either abusing parent, drug or alcohol dependence and personality disorders are frequently seen. **Folie à deux** is the term Williams (1983) uses for a pathological pattern in which the two parents collude, presenting to the world the picture of an ideal family while repeatedly abusing a child.

The social-pathology view of child abuse points to unemployment and poverty as the major contributing factors. Critics argue that abuse is better reported among the poor because the poor are more visible to the social agencies they depend on. Although greater visibility may account for part of the high incidence of child abuse in impoverished families, it cannot account for all of it: child abuse remains a problem that is disproportionately represented in poor families. The chronic stress of poverty, in fact, is one of the factors that most strongly affect the interaction between parents and children (Gil, 1970). Animal mothers under stress have been observed to attack their own offspring as well as predators, and human mothers, too, may misdirect their aggression (Williams, 1976). The effect of chronic stress on the family surely decreases both parents' ability to cope with or adapt to unpredictable events and may account for the pattern of repeated abuse in families. The relationship between stress and child abuse, however, is not a simple one of cause and effect. One or more of the following factors is usually present when a stressful parent becomes a child abuser (Straus, 1980): marital discord; family history of violence; dominance of the husband or male caretaker; low income, education, and occupation; approval of physical punishment; and social isolation.

In sum, although abusers may suffer from specific psychological problems, ranging from alcoholism to personality disorder, and although they may share certain predisposing social characteristics, none of these factors, singly or in combination, has proved to be a necessary or sufficient cause of child abuse (Williams, 1983). That is, although risk factors can be identified, these do not predict that a caretaker or parent will become an abuser.

The Victims

Abuse can occur at any age and is seldom a one-time experience for the victim—and the more often a child is beaten, the less likely are the effects to be reversible. Repeated abuse often causes permanent gastrointestinal, neurological, sensory, orthopedic, and other damage. It leads to growth retardation and a host of emotional problems. The reported annual deaths from abuse are 6,000 but the actual number may be as high as 50,000 (Center for the Improvement of Child Caring, 1977; Roberts, 1974). Up to 30 percent of surviving abused children have brain damage and are candidates for further cruel treatment because they are even less likely than abused children who remain cognitively unimpaired to meet the irrational demands of their caretakers. Repeated head injuries cause mental handicaps, cerebral palsy, and other chronic disorders (Williams, 1983). A ten-year longitudinal study showed that abused children have a 6 to 10 percent chance of death and a 90 percent chance of developmental retardation (Elmer and Gregg, 1967). Neglect, too, has serious long-term consequences, and undernourished children fare even worse than well-nourished physically abused children (Martin, 1976).

The victims of abuse also show multiple social and emotional problems, ranging from hyperactivity and aggression (25 percent) to extreme passivity (75 percent) (Gray and Kempe, 1976). If abused children survive cigarette burns, poisoning, extremes of temperature, laceration, and punching or kicking, they tend to approach the world with a joyless vigilance, low self-esteem, and a readiness to change their behavior rapidly to adapt to their environment.

Sexually abused children also show emotional disturbance. Many victims of incest and other forms of sexual abuse have initial symptoms of anxiety and depression and feelings of fear, anger, hostility, guilt, and shame. The long-term effects on adult women may include a negative self-concept, self-destructive behavior (including substance abuse), sexual maladjustment, and depression. Although studies so far are not conclusive, it appears that abuse by fathers or stepfathers has an even more negative effect than abuse by other perpetrators (Browne and Finkelhor, 1986).

Finally, according to Charles Wenar (1983), children themselves play a role in abuse, insofar as they are difficult to care for before abuse occurs or have other characteristics that make them likely to become the targets of abuse, including prematurity, mental retardation, physical handicaps, and congenital malformations. All these factors can cause a parent to view the child as "different." Perhaps prolonged separation of mothers and neonates hospitalized for low birth weight or other congenital problems weakens the bond between mother and infant or makes the mother especially anxious. Even if this is so, many parents of "difficult" children or of neonates from whom they are separated because of the baby's placement in a special-care facility do not become abusers.

Prevention and Treatment

The treatment and prevention of child abuse are complicated issues requiring an understanding of its multiple causes. All fifty states now have legislation to prosecute offenders, but neither legal nor preventative measures and programs has curbed the problem. Studies by the National Center on Child Abuse and Neglect have contributed to the development of educational programs, greater vigilance of teachers and other professionals, and parents' support groups, including the Voluntary Intervention and Treatment Program (VITP), which is funded by the Center, and Parents Anonymous, a self-help group. The courts have shown greater willingness to remove children from homes where their repeated abuse is likely. In some cases, removal is the only treatment to safeguard the children from further violence. Ironically, abused children have fewer treatment opportunities than child abusers, who are likely to have damaged their charges repeatedly before they are stopped by legal controls or are able to change their behavior through programs designed to teach them parenting skills.

to watch the therapist or another person play with a dog, handle a snake, or deal in a carefree manner with whatever it is that the child fears so intensely (Rosenthal and Bandura, 1978).

A training program that incorporates modeling, rehearsal, prompts, and social reinforcement has been designed to teach hyperactive children to think before they act (Meichenbaum and Goodman, 1971). In this "think aloud" program, a child watches and listens to an adult both perform a task and talk specifically about what he is doing. Then the child does the same thing under the adult's specific guidance. In the following phases, the child performs the task as he first talks aloud to himself, then whispers to himself, and finally talks silently to himself. After progressing from simple sensorimotor tasks through the solving of complex problems, the hyperactive child can better control his behavior by talking to himself. This approach has been successful with children who have been aggressive or disruptive or who have cheated in school.

Operant-conditioning programs have been successful in the treatment of attention deficit disorders. Patterson (1965) has reported success with a classroom program combining extinction of problem behaviors, such as the distracting of one's schoolmates, with reinforcement of more positive behaviors, such as remaining seated at one's desk long enough to finish a task. In altering the disruptive social behavior of the hyperactive child, such operant techniques have proved as effective as drugs (O'Leary and Pelham, 1978). Operant techniques have also been used in the treatment of anorexia nervosa: when anorexic patients are hospitalized and their privileges are made contingent upon eating, they almost invariably gain weight. But once they are released from hospital treatment programs, they tend to relapse unless programs involving the family are also developed (Van Buskirk, 1977). Parents, teachers, and other adults are a critical part of most behavioral programs.

One application of operant conditioning that has proved useful for certain behavior disorders is the token economy, a technique that we have already mentioned in earlier chapters. With children it is used just as with adults. Desirable behavior is rewarded with stars or points or some token that the child can save and later exchange for candy, a turn with a special toy, or some other coveted reward. Tokens seem particularly suitable in working with children, since they provide a tangible signal for reinforcement. Token systems have proved successful in institutions for delinquent children (Braukmann and Fixsen,

1975). Furthermore, O'Leary (1978) reports that token systems can also work well in schoolroom settings.

The Humanistic-Existential Perspective

Although humanistic and existential clinicians have written relatively little on the specific psychological problems of the child, most of them, like the psychodynamic theorists, believe that the genesis of psychopathology lies in the experiences of childhood.

Denial of Self   In explaining the evolution of psychological disorders, humanists and existentialists typically emphasize the loss of self-integrity in childhood. As we saw in Chapter 4, Rogers (1951) claimed that to win social approval, children often deny aspects of their experience that are inconsistent with the values of their parents and other people whose approval they seek. Similarly, Moustakas (1959) argues that a child's psychological difficulties are caused by the denial of his or her unique self. Rogers and Moustakas seem to agree that although the child's problems begin with the judgments of others, the child comes to internalize these judgments and gradually restricts his or her own self-image in order to conform to them.

Another concept that seems to have some bearing on this process is Laing's notion of mystification (1965). By **mystification,** Laing means a habitual mode of interaction between parent and child that causes the child to doubt the adequacy or legitimacy of his or her own thoughts, feelings, and perceptions. As described by Laing, these doubts appear much more profound and radical than those discussed by Rogers and Moustakas. This difference is probably due to the fact that Laing's primary concern is with the development of schizophrenia, whereas Rogers and Moustakas concentrate on less severe disorders. Nevertheless, the humanistic-existential consensus is that psychological disorder takes root when the child, responding to the disapproval of others, begins to reject important parts of the self.

Treatment   According to the humanistic-existential perspective, a useful mode of treatment for troubled children is play therapy. At first glance, humanistically oriented play therapy resembles other forms of play therapy, but there are important differences.

Unlike psychodynamic therapists, who often regard play as the symbolic expression of unconscious conflicts which must then be worked through, humanistic therapists see the play itself as the therapy. If it helps young clients to express their feelings and to deal with their problems, then it has done its job. Accordingly, humanistic therapists, unlike many psychodynamic therapists, generally do not offer interpretations. Axline (1969), following the guidelines of Rogers' client-centered therapy, argues that the therapist's role is simply to help children rediscover what they really feel and to provide a positive relationship within which they can pursue their innate drive for self-actualization. Actually, many psychodynamic clinicians use play therapy in much the same way; in the treatment of children, there is considerable overlap between the two schools.

Family Theory

In the view of Haley (1963), Satir (1967), and several other theorists, the family is a miniature social system in which each member plays a major role. Childhood developmental disorders, when seen within this frame of reference, take on a somewhat different meaning. When a child develops a problem, the problem is interpreted as symptomatic of difficulties within the family as a unit. The child may have the symptoms, but it is the family that has the problem.

Consider the case of one highly intelligent boy of fourteen who was referred for treatment because he was doing very poorly in school. When the family was seen together, problems between the boy's mother and father soon became apparent. The mother repeatedly undercut the father, making invidious comparisons between him and his son. For his part, the father was quite gruff with his wife. And despite his apparent concern about his son's academic difficulties, he also made it clear, through indirect remarks, that he doubted the virility of any boy who spent too much time with his schoolbooks. The boy, then, was caught in a struggle between his parents. He wanted to do well in order to please his mother. Yet by succeeding academically, he would become a sissy in his father's eyes. Worse yet, he would give his mother one more reason to prefer the boy to his father, thus further endangering the father–son relationship. Hence the boy's academic problems.

According to family therapists, such family psychopathology underlies many childhood disorders and must be dealt with if the child's problems are to be relieved. This is not to suggest that psychodynamic and behavioral therapists ignore family dynamics. On the contrary. However, rather than concentrating on the present family interaction, a psychodynamic therapist handling the above case might search for deeper conflicts, possibly connected to oedipal desires, while the behavioral therapist might emphasize the reinforcement patterns of the one-to-one relationship between father and child and between mother and child rather than exploring the complex triangular interaction among the three family members.

An adolescent disorder that has been treated with some success through family therapy is anorexia nervosa. Minuchin and his co-workers (1978), who have been working with anorexics for several years, claim that the families from which these girls come tend to share the same characteristics: overprotectiveness, rigidity, and a superficial "closeness" covering a good deal of unexpressed anger and resentment. According to these investigators, the girl's anorexia serves an important function for the family. It gives them a "safe" target for the expression of frustration and thus makes it possible for them to avoid open conflict over their true grievances. Since it performs this essential service, the anorexia is subtly and unwittingly encouraged by the family.

Thus in order to relieve the anorexia, the family problems must first be relieved. To this end, the investigators propose "family therapy lunch sessions." Minuchin (1974) describes one such session with a hospitalized anorexic teenager and her parents. First the therapist allows both parents to try to get their daughter to eat. Inevitably they fail, and the therapist points out to them why, in terms of intrafamily struggles, the child is responding in this way. Then the therapist, who interprets the girl's refusal to eat as a fight for independence within the family, tells the patient she has triumphed over the parents and can savor that triumph, but that to stay alive she must eat. After a time this strategy begins to work; the patient begins eating surreptitiously. Once the patient is released from the hospital, the parents are instructed to use behavior modification techniques at home. The girl must eat enough to gain a certain amount of weight each week. If she falls short of the goal, she must remain in bed.

Minuchin reports that approximately 85 percent of those on whom this family therapy has been tried show a lasting recovery (Minuchin et al., 1978)—a far better success rate than other therapies have

Preventing Childhood Disorders

The rights of children became an issue of intense professional and public concern in the seventies, a concern echoed worldwide when the United Nations declared 1979 the International Year of the Child. A decade earlier the public health model had been established as a full-scale plan to reduce mental illness in the United States in a three-stage program of prevention: prevention of new cases of disorder, shortening the duration of existing cases, and rehabilitation. Although programs of prevention, hand in hand with the global emphasis on child welfare, have met with positive public attitudes and set nationwide goals, children in the United States still lack adequate health care and suffer a range of emotional disorders. The following issues, defined by the Children's Defense Fund, challenge the child advocacy movement and frustrate the efforts of mental health professionals to reduce the prevalence of childhood disorders:

1. Over 17 percent of American children—10 million—are poor. Poverty is thus more widespread among children than among any other group in America, including the elderly. In 1979 one in every six preschoolers lived in a family at or below the poverty line.

2. An estimated 570,000 children are born annually to teenagers. Seven of ten mothers under fifteen years of age receive no prenatal care in the first three months of pregnancy; over one-fifth receive no such care at all or receive it very late.

3. Ten million children, or one in six, get virtually no health care.

4. Only about one-sixth of our poorest children receive the periodic screening to which they are entitled, and when they are screened, about 40 percent of the detected problems go untreated.

5. The national commitment to preschool intervention remains precarious. Head Start and other programs must continuously struggle for funding.

6. American policy still does not reflect the fact that only one in seventeen families is the stereotypic traditional family. Most mothers work outside the home. Still, licensed day care can take care of only 10 percent of the needs. The debate over standards for day care drags on. By 1990 at least 1 million more day care placements and 1.6 million child-care workers will be needed.

7. At least half a million children live in out-of-home placement, and many will grow up there. Tens of thousands are placed inappropriately and then forgotten.

8. Mental health care for children is shockingly inadequate. Few resources and staff are available for children. Those in foster care and

---

achieved. Whether other childhood disorders would also yield more easily to family therapy remains to be investigated.

The Neuroscience Perspective

There have been a number of heated disputes between biogenic and psychogenic theory in the area of childhood disorders. Biological causes have been proposed for enuresis and encopresis. Likewise, some researchers (e.g., Travaglini et al., 1976) be-

lieve that anorexia may be due to disturbances in the hypothalamus. However, of all the disorders that we have discussed in this chapter, the ones that seem most likely to have a biological basis are the attention deficit disorders.

As we saw earlier, the term *minimal brain dysfunction* is no longer widely used to describe the attention deficit disorders, for lack of "hard" neurological evidence. And some researchers feel that these disorders are psychogenic. However, the neuroscience perspective has contributed a controversial drug treatment for the disorder. Most children with atten-

correctional facilities receive little of the care they require. Funding patterns work against treatment of children in the least restrictive setting. Children are inappropriately hospitalized for lack of alternatives, and institutions are not of adequate quality (adapted from Edelman, 1981).

Added to these social problems are widespread child abuse and an infant mortality rate that exceeds those of thirteen other nations and is twice as high for nonwhites as for whites in this country (Knopf, 1984). Ten percent of American schoolchildren are affected by some form of psychological disorder (Bower, 1969). The variables related to psychopathology in children show the interaction of heredity and environment, including the nationwide environmental challenges identified by the Children's Defense Fund. Poverty, for example, is related to delinquency, learning disabilities, child abuse, and disruptive behavior. Parental influence, a stronger variable in childhood emotional disorders, cuts across social classes and reflects genetic as well as environmental factors: the children of disturbed parents are more likely to suffer some form of disorder (Knopf, 1984).

Can our society prevent childhood disorders? Prevention requires that funds be channeled from treatment programs—whose resources are inadequate to meet the needs of children who are already enmeshed in disorder—into genetic counseling, prenatal care, and control of environmental toxins or into programs to prevent diagnosable mental disorders. Prevention represents an enormous financial commitment, and even its proponents disagree about the goals to be set. Those who believe that social conditions are powerful causal factors support prevention programs that deal with competence, quality of life, and problems in living (Cowen, 1980; Albee, 1982). Other professionals argue that programs should not spend funds to improve social conditions because we have no hard evidence that social factors cause mental illness (Lamb and Susman, 1981). In addition to this theoretical debate and the question of cost are such ethical issues as sterilization, family planning, and evaluation of parents (Wicks-Nelson and Israel, 1984). Does early intervention mean that impoverished nonwhite families will be judged by middle-class white values? Even if screening techniques became less expensive and value-free, most school systems are not equipped to deal with severe learning disabilities or emotional disorder.

Existing child-care programs try to provide proper nutrition as well as to build cognitive and social skills. Many more such services will be needed as the number of working mothers continues to climb. Such pilot programs as PACE (Parent and Child Education), which teaches emotionally disturbed mothers better coping and parenting skills and enrolls their preschoolers in nursery day care, and the Vermont Child Development Project, a day care program for children at risk for childhood disorders, recognize that mental health care must address the needs of the family as a whole. Such projects have shown that developmental gains can be made but have been unable to prove that early identification of disorders leads to improved adjustment later on (Knopf, 1984). If the life chances, psychological adjustment, and emotional development of children are to be improved, far more resources than are now available must be devoted to helping families whose children are at risk.

---

tion deficit disorders have a seemingly "paradoxical response" to stimulant drugs—above all, to amphetamines. Whereas amphetamines can be expected to "speed up" normal people, so that they behave something like hyperactive children, the same drugs slow down hyperactive children, so that they behave more like normal people. Not only does the drug reduce excess motor activity; it also increases children's ability to pay attention and concentrate, so that they may be able to function in a normal classroom for the first time. Approximately 35 percent of children with attention deficit disorders show a dramatic improvement with amphetamines, while another 35 percent show moderate improvement (Safer and Allen, 1976). Recent studies suggest that the effect may not be so paradoxical after all. Many normal children show improved attention after taking amphetamines (Kolata, 1978).

A large percentage of children diagnosed as having attention deficit disorders are now on daily doses of amphetamines, usually either Dexedrine or Ritalin. Some investigators have voiced strong objections to this widespread use of chemotherapy. For one thing, the drugs may have adverse side effects, including weight loss, insomnia, and high blood pressure. Second, they do not actually cure the disorder. General behavior may improve, but academic performance usually does not (Safer and Allen, 1976), and the prognosis for the child remains the same. No drug can compensate for the accumulated deficits in problem-solving skills in the child. Such skills must be taught after attention has been improved by medication, thus requiring a combination of approaches (Pelham et al., 1980). Third, if parents, schools, and physicians become accustomed to using drugs for "problem children," the possibilities for abuse are frightening. It is all too easy to imagine medication being administered to *all* problem children, including those whose disruptive behavior is a response to family conflicts or simply to a boring school program. Finally, even for those children who do have attention deficit disorders and who are clearly helped by amphetamines, the drugs may become a social handicap. Drugs mean illness; children who must take pills every day are likely to be branded as "sick" or "freaky" by others and eventually by themselves, so that their self-esteem suffers. This problem is reflected in the following statement by an eight-year-old boy:

> Last year my teacher was always saying, "Did you take your pill, David?" and pretty soon the other kids started saying it and then that dumb Susan Nielson wrote her poem on me and this is the poem. I heard it a million times already:
>
> > *David Hill*
> > *Did you take the pill*
> > *That makes you work*
> > *And keeps you still?*
> > *Take your pill, Hill.*
>
> And in baseball when I swing out, and I almost always do, the kids all yelled it. Sometimes I wish I could go to another school and start over (Ross and Ross, 1976).

These objections are important, and it is generally agreed that drugs must be prescribed with great caution. And, as mentioned earlier, some behavioral programs have been as effective as drug therapy (O'Leary and Pelham, 1978). Nevertheless, since amphetamines do, in general, have beneficial effects on the adjustment of children with attention deficit disorders, they are still widely used, often in conjunction with behavior therapy programs.

SUMMARY

The developmental disorders of childhood and adolescence are characterized by problems in achieving or failure to achieve age-appropriate behavior at various stages of development. Developmental disorders deserve study in their own right because most have no counterparts in adult psychopathology or differ significantly in course and outcome, because the age of a child often is of critical importance for diagnosis, and because children depend on adults for treatment.

Childhood disorders can be grouped into eight basic patterns: eating disorders, elimination disorders, sleep disturbances, speech disturbances, attention deficit disorders, anxiety disorders, depression, and conduct disorders.

Emotional difficulties among children in this country tend to peak during three stressful stages—ages six and seven, nine and ten, and fourteen and fifteen. But sometimes the distinctions between normal and abnormal behavior in children are blurred. Whether a certain form of behavior is considered normal or abnormal depends on the attitudes of authority figures, changing cultural norms, and the child's age.

The most widely used classification system of developmental disorders is *DSM-III-R,* which sets forth diagnostic categories designed to be used on multiple axes. No diagnosis of developmental disorders is foolproof, despite the increasing sophistication of diagnostic methods.

Eating disorders are assumed to mirror emotional problems, because children depend on others for food. Two eating disorders are obesity and anorexia nervosa.

The elimination disorders—enuresis and encopresis—apparently develop out of children's conflicts between their natural impulses and the demands of toilet training, or they may have an organic basis.

Sleep disturbances are considered abnormal only when they are not transient responses to stress. Childhood sleep disorders include sleepwalking, insomnia, night terrors, and anxiety dreams.

Delayed speech and stuttering are the only speech disorders considered to be manifestations of psychological disturbances, though a prolonged delay in speaking is regarded as a possible indication of an organic or functional disorder. Stuttering is believed to be the result of anxiety or articulation problems.

Attention deficit disorders include hyperactivity and

attention problems (the most common cause of referrals to mental health clinics). They also include learning disabilities, a catchall term to describe the problems of children with normal intelligence who do poorly in reading, spelling, calculating, and other academic skills.

Childhood anxiety disorders are differentiated by the object of the anxiety. They include separation anxiety disorder, avoidant disorder, and overanxious disorder.

Childhood depression shares some features with adult depression, although it manifests itself in different ways, as in clinging, irrational fears, and delinquency. The prevalence of depression rises during adolescence. During adolescence, too, the prevalence of suicide rises sharply.

Included in childhood conduct disorders are four categories of antisocial behavior: conduct disorder, undersocialized, aggressive; conduct disorder, undersocialized, nonaggressive; conduct disorder, socialized, aggressive; and conduct disorder, socialized, nonaggressive.

The five major perspectives on developmental disorders offer different interpretations and treatments. According to the psychodynamic perspective, developmental disorders originate in a conflict between a child's impulses on the one hand and parents' prohibitions and the developing superego on the other hand. Treatment aims at allowing the child to bring unconscious conflicts to the surface and to deal with them. Treatment procedures depend on a child's emotional and intellectual level, the nature of the problem, and the therapist's perspective.

Behaviorists focus on actual problem behaviors and the environmental variables that have conditioned them. They believe that children's behavioral problems usually stem from either inadequate or inappropriate learning. For example, in inadequate learning in toilet training, the child may never have learned to identify the physiological cues associated with a full bladder; moreover, if parents discontinue praise

for bladder and bowel control too early, before the child develops such internal reinforcers as pride, the behavior that was praised may be extinguished. In inappropriate learning, undesirable behaviors become reinforced. For example, children may model their behavior after violent figures on television, antisocial parents, or neighborhood toughs. Parents can also reinforce such problems as separation anxiety by providing special attention or favors to the child too shy or frightened to go to school. The behavioral treatment for both conduct and anxiety disorders makes use of the entire behavioral repertoire: reinforcement, extinction, withdrawal of rewards, modeling, and respondent conditioning. For example, the Mowrer pad for treating enuresis is a respondent-conditioning technique. Systematic desensitization is effective in teaching relaxation to children with anxiety disorders; modeling, in treating phobias. The "think aloud" program incorporates modeling, rehearsal, prompts, and social reinforcement to help hyperactive children to think before they act.

Humanistic-existential clinicians, like psychodynamic theorists, generally emphasize the childhood origins of adult behavior. They consider the loss of feelings of integrity crucial in the evolution of psychological disorders. Many use play therapy, which allows children to express their feelings and to deal with their problems.

Family theorists see developmental disorders as symptoms of difficulties within the child's family. Their treatment involves an exploration of the interaction among all family members.

The neuroscience perspective ascribes some developmental disorders to biological factors. Because many attention deficit disorders have responded to medical treatment, they are assumed to be the developmental disorders most likely to have biological causes. Even so, there are strong arguments against using drugs to treat children's psychological disturbances.

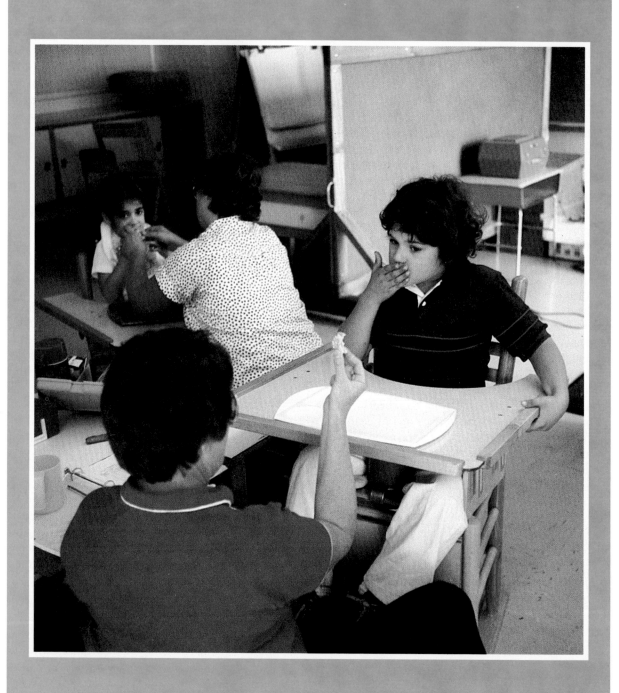

Childhood Autism

The developmental disorders discussed in Chapter 17—disorders of eating and elimination, sleeping and speaking, attention and anxiety, depression and antisocial behavior—are called *specific* because the children who have them are not disabled by them. Children may stutter or wet their beds or refuse to eat, but they continue to function relatively well in other areas of their lives. But the problems of an autistic child are *pervasive*—they encompass all aspects of the child's functioning. Autism affects intelligence, speech, movement, social relationships—everything. In this chapter we first describe the development and symptoms of this serious disorder and then present current thinking on its cause and treatment.

PERVASIVE DEVELOPMENTAL DISABILITY

People have long recognized that some children behave in markedly unusual ways, some of them from early infancy. For many years such children were labeled "psychotic" or "schizophrenic," because their symptoms were severe and in some ways resembled those of adult schizophrenics. In 1943 Leo Kanner described a new kind of "psychotic" disorder among children, recognizable from infancy. Because its main symptom seemed to be the inability to relate to anyone outside of oneself, Kanner called the syndrome **early infantile autism,** from the Greek *autos,* "self." Kanner proposed that autism, which became apparent by the time a child was two and one-half years old, was inborn and distinct from other psychotic disturbances of childhood.

About 20 in every 10,000 children today are diagnosed as autistic, and 5 are disabled enough to meet Kanner's original criteria (Wing, 1981). Clinicians have observed that autism does not always show itself by age two and one-half and that it is a more varied disorder than Kanner recognized. The term *autism* today describes a range of pervasive developmental disabilities in social relationships, speech, movement, and intellect. Some autistic children are clearly abnormal from birth, others not until they are several years old. Some autistic children are more severely affected than others.

Every psychotic child, like every normal child, is

unique. Four symptoms, however, are almost invariably present in any child diagnosed as autistic: disturbed social relationships, cognitive deficits, language deficits, and disturbed motor behavior.

Disturbance in social relationships, sometimes identified as the cardinal trait of autism, may take the form of total withdrawal. Or, at the other extreme, the child may form an obsessive attachment to an inanimate object. However the child behaves, his or her pattern of relating to family members is decidedly abnormal.

Cognitive deficits are typical of autism; most autistic children are mentally retarded. This condition, like "simple" mental retardation, tends to be stable over time.

Autistic children also show distinct abnormalities in speech. They may be totally mute, or their speech may be bizarre. Often it seems simply incoherent or nonsensical.

The most striking oddity of autistic children, however, is their abnormal motor behavior. These behaviors can vary considerably, ranging from a total lack of movement (catatonia) to tics, tremors, and posturing. Most typical, however, is a limited repertoire of movements that the child repeats endlessly, with no observable goal.

Taken together, these symptoms add up to a pattern of severe disability. Unfortunately for these children and their families, autism even in its milder forms is a very serious disorder. Unfortunately also, our knowledge of its causes is still limited.

Classification: Autism and Childhood Schizophrenia

As we have said, clinicians once thought that autism in children was the same disorder as schizophrenia in adults. If it were not the same, the thinking went, it was at least very similar. But today most specialists in children's psychoses distinguish between autism and childhood schizophrenia (although some of them use different names for the two syndromes). Schizophrenia in children is now thought to be rare, and most psychotic disorders in children are considered instances of autism. Moreover, follow-up studies of autistic children have shown that as adults they bear little resemblance to adult schizophrenics (DeMeyer et al., 1981). Most clinicians consider that the two disorders differ in the following ways (DeMeyer et

al., 1981; Rimland, 1964; Rutter, 1968, 1972; Kolvin et al., 1971; Kernberg, 1979; Wing, 1972):

1. *Age at onset:* The symptoms of autism usually appear earlier than those of schizophrenia, which usually appear at age six or later.

2. *Premorbid adjustment:* The autistic child may appear disturbed from birth, whereas the schizophrenic child usually experiences a period of normal or near-normal development and then regresses.

3. *Autistic aloneness:* Whereas autistic children are severely withdrawn, most schizophrenic children do respond, however inappropriately, to their social environment and to physical contact.

4. *Preservation of sameness:* Most autistic children strongly resist any change in their physical surroundings or their daily routines. Fewer schizophrenic children have such an urge.

5. *Perception of environment:* Schizophrenic children have distorted perceptions of their environment, but autistic children seem "overselective" in their perceptions, as if they have a kind of tunnel vision that permits them to attend only to small parts of their environment.

6. *Hallucinations and delusions:* Hallucinations and delusions, along with other features of schizophrenic thinking (Chapter 14), are common in schizophrenic children but not in autistic ones.

7. *Language:* Autistic children who can speak use their speech uncommunicatively, whereas schizophrenic children use their speech to communicate bizarre thoughts.

8. *Intellectual abilities:* Autistic children are far more likely than schizophrenic children to be severely mentally retarded.

9. *Family history of schizophrenia:* Schizophrenia is rare in parents and siblings of autistic children but is present in about 10 percent of the parents of schizophrenic children.

10. *Sex ratio:* Three to four times as many boys as girls are autistic, but equal numbers of boys and girls are schizophrenic.

Diagnostic Criteria for Childhood Autism and Childhood Schizophrenia

According to *DSM-III-R*, autism is a "pervasive developmental disorder" that is characterized by distortions in most of the basic psychological functions that begin during childhood. A child's development is not merely delayed in some way, as it would be if the child were just slow to walk or talk. The child's development is distorted or clearly abnormal: the child walks, but only on tiptoe, or talks, but only in echoes of what others say. Here, briefly, are the diagnostic criteria for childhood autism:

1. Impaired reciprocal social interactions, marked by at least two of the following: lack of awareness of others' existence, failure to seek comfort from others at times of distress, failure to imitate others, abnormal or no social play, and impaired ability to form friendships.

2. Impaired communication, marked by at least one of the following: no developmentally appropriate form of communication, abnormal or no nonverbal communication, absence of imaginative activity, abnormally formed speech (repetitive, stereotyped, etc.), impaired ability to converse with others, abnormally produced speech (monotone, high pitch, etc.).

3. Restricted activities and interests, marked by at least one of the following: stereotyped body movements, preoccupation with parts of objects, distress over changes in trivial aspects of environment, unreasonable insistence on sameness of routines, no developmentally appropriate imaginative play, restricted patterns of interest.

4. Onset during infancy or childhood.

In contrast, *DSM-III-R* has no specific category for childhood schizophrenia. To be diagnosed as schizophrenic, children must meet the same general criteria as adults:

1. Bizarre delusions or hallucinations or extreme incoherence of speech or thought.

2. Deterioration from an earlier level of functioning.

3. Continuous signs of disorder for at least six months.

All of these differences between autism and schizophrenia have led clinicians to distinguish between the two disorders. Clinicians also increasingly accept the argument (Kernberg, 1979) that adult schizophrenia is continuous with childhood schizophrenia, especially in view of the findings on hallucinations and delusions and on the family history of schizophrenia. *DSM-III-R*, in fact, has no separate category for childhood schizophrenia—as is the case with many other disorders that affect adults and children alike. It describes one schizophrenic syndrome and says that it may appear in both adults and children. The accompanying box describes *DSM-III-R*'s characterization of autism.

THE SYMPTOMS OF CHILDHOOD AUTISM

Although the prevalence of autism is a relatively low 20 per 10,000 children, as we have said, the number of children *diagnosed* as autistic has grown enormously since Kanner first described the syndrome in 1943. No one really knows whether this increase in diagnosed cases is a result or a cause of growing interest in autism, but there is no question that interest in it has grown, perhaps because its symptoms form such a distinctively disturbing pattern.

Autistic children shrink from any kind of contact with other people, living almost entirely in an isolated world of their own. (F. Hers/Viva/Woodfin Camp & Associates)

Social Isolation

As we've noted, the very term *autism* suggests an inability to transcend the self. Some autistic children essentially withdraw from all social contact, into a state of what has been called "extreme autistic aloneness." Some autistic infants fuss and cry constantly, despite all attempts to soothe them. Many others do not demand attention from others—an unusual trait for an infant—and are difficult to hold and cuddle because they stiffen or go limp when they are picked up. The recoil from personal contact is even sharper in older children. They avoid looking anyone in the eye and may even act as if other people did not exist. If they form any attachments at all, they may be obsessive attachments to inanimate objects—a garden hose, a vacuum cleaner, or something equally improbable. Autistic children may exhibit rage, panic, inconsolable crying, and other apparently inexplicable responses to nothing that an observer can identify. Tantrums are common. Autistic children either do not respond to their social surroundings at all or they respond inappropriately.

Cognitive Deficits

Most autistic children are mentally retarded. About 70 percent have an IQ of less than 70. The most severely retarded are likely to have the most seriously impaired social relationships and speech as well (Wing, 1981). Autistic children differ significantly from nonautistic mentally retarded children in cognition. Autistic children do quite a bit better, for example, on tests of sensorimotor ability, such as finding hidden figures, than on tests of social understanding and language; retarded children tend to perform more evenly on all such tests (Shah and Frith, 1983). When autistic children receive therapy to improve their social relationships, their mental retardation does *not* improve as well (Rutter, 1983). Therefore, autistic children's mental retardation is a primary cognitive problem, not merely a result of their social withdrawal.

Autistic children cannot see the world from another's point of view, and in this way they differ from both normal and retarded children. In one study, for example, autistic, normal, and retarded children between the ages of six and sixteen were given the following task concerning two dolls, Sally and Ann (Baron-Cohen et al., 1985). Sally, they were shown, put her marble in her basket and left. While Sally was gone, Ann took the marble out of the basket and hid it in her box. When Sally returned, the children were asked where Sally would look for the marble. Over 80 percent of both the normal and retarded children answered, "In the basket," but only 20 percent of the autistic children gave the obviously correct answer. It was not that they could not remember, but that they could not put themselves in one doll's place and figure out what she would have seen. This inability to take another's point of view, a cognitive ability that normally increases with age, probably contributes to the autistic child's social isolation.

Language Deficits

Not only are the cognitive and social abilities of autistic children disturbed, but their speech is disturbed as well. More than half do not speak at all. Others babble, whine, scream, or simply echo what other people say (**echolalia**). Some autistic children aimlessly repeat snatches of songs, television commercials, or other bits of overheard language. Those who do speak can communicate only a limited number of ideas (Wetherby, 1986; Wing, 1981): such children may speak, but they say little that can be understood. Others who speak use pronouns strangely. A boy may refer to himself as "you," "he," or "Michael." Still others speak repetitively or extremely literally.

In essence, autistic children cannot communicate *reciprocally,* cannot engage in the usual give and take of conversation.

The severity of an autistic child's language problems is an excellent indicator of the child's prognosis. Children most likely to benefit from treatment have developed some meaningful speech by the age of five (Rutter and Lockyer, 1967; Havelkova, 1968; Fish et al., 1968; Goldfarb, 1963). A child's intellectual development is another excellent indicator of his or her prognosis. Many of the autistic children who are not mentally retarded (about one-fourth of autistic children) also are those who have begun to speak meaningfully by age five and adjust better as adults than others.

Ritualistic Motor Activity

Unusual motor behavior is a characteristic feature of autism. Although physical movements may be more or less disturbed, most autistic children tend to repeat a limited number of movements endlessly, ritualistically, and without any clear goal. These self-stimulating movements—twirling, tiptoeing, hand flapping, rocking, tensing parts of the body—may involve the fine or gross muscles of the hands, face, trunk, arms, and legs. Left to themselves, unstimulated by others, most autistic children—especially those who are institutionalized—spend as much as 90 percent of their time in these bizarre forms of self-stimulation (Lovaas et al., 1971).

Some of these repetitive movements cause autistic children physical harm. Head banging, face slapping, and hand biting are not uncommon. Autistic children have even been known to pull out their hair, bite off the ends of their fingers, and chew their shoulders down to the bone. Not only is such mutilation horrifying to others, but the children themselves sometimes cry out from the pain their behavior causes.

The urge to perform these strange motor behaviors is apparently very strong. In one study, for example, autistic children who had not eaten in twenty-four hours and who were moving ritualistically either would not respond or delayed in responding to a sound that signaled that food was available (Lovaas et al., 1979; Lovaas et al., 1971). When they were not repeating their stereotyped movements, however, the same children responded immediately to the same signal.

Preservation of Sameness

Autistic children are usually anxious and obsessive about keeping their surroundings utterly unvarying. Toys must always be put in the same place on the same shelves. Breakfast must be an unvarying ritual

Like this boy, most autistic children engage in bizarre, self-stimulating, ritualistic motor activities such as constant arm waving. (David M. Grossman)

The Separate Universe of the Autistic Child

Autism literally means "self-ism." A prime distinguishing feature of autism is extended periods of self-absorption. Whereas schizophrenic children are unable to respond appropriately to reality, autistic children seem to inhabit a totally different world, a world closed to everyone but themselves. And across the frontiers dividing that world from ours, little communication is possible. This striking feature of autism—along with autistic children's typically good motor coordination and love of manipulating objects—is well illustrated in the following quotation, a father's description of his autistic child's play:

> His little hands hold the plate delicately, his eyes surveying Its smooth perimeter, and his mouth curls in delight. He is setting his stage. This is the beginning of his entry into the solitude that has become his world. Slowly, with a masterful hand, he places the edge of the plate on the floor, sets his body in a comfortable and balanced position, and snaps his wrist. The plate spins with dazzling perfection. It revolves on itself as if set in motion by some exacting machine . . . as indeed it was.
>
> This is not as isolated act, a mere aspect of some childhood fantasy . . . it is a great and skilled activity performed by a very little boy for a very great and expectant audience . . . himself.
>
> As the plate moves swiftly and spins hypnotically on its edge, he bends over it and stares squarely into its motion.
>
> For a moment, his body betrays a just-perceptible motion similar to the plate's. His eyes sparkle. He swoons in the playland that is himself.
>
> . . . Seldom does he cry or utter tones of discomfort. His contentment and solitude seem to suggest a profound and inner peace. He is seventeen months old and seems to be contemplating another dimension (Kaufman, 1975, p. 43).

of egg first, vitamin pill second, and then toast. In the bath, the face always must be washed first, then the arms, and so on. If the child senses that any step in the intricate ritual has been skipped, he or she may respond with a tantrum. Clinicians have noted that many normal children, when they are about two and one-half years old, insist on unvarying sameness in routines. They have suggested, therefore, that the development of autistic children may have stalled at this point.

All of these problems—the ritual behaviors, the self-absorption and bizarreness, the intellectual and social deficits—appear in the following case, reported by the child's mother:

> Peter nursed eagerly, sat and walked at the expected ages. Yet some of his behavior made us vaguely uneasy. He never put anything in his mouth. Not his fingers nor his toys—nothing. . . .
>
> More troubling was the fact that Peter didn't look at us, or smile, and wouldn't play the games that seemed as much a part of babyhood as diapers. While he didn't cry, he rarely laughed, and when he did, it was at things that didn't seem funny to us. He didn't cuddle, but sat upright in my lap, even when I rocked him. But children differ and we were content to let Peter be himself. We thought it hilarious when my brother, visiting us when Peter was 8 months old, observed that "that kid has no social instincts, whatsoever." Although Peter was a first child, he was not isolated. I frequently put him in his playpen in front of the house, where the school children stopped to play with him as they passed. He ignored them too. . . .
>
> Peter's babbling had not turned into speech by the time he was three. His play was solitary and repetitious. He tore paper into long thin strips, bushel baskets of it every day. He spun the lids from my canning jars and became upset if we tried to divert him. Only rarely could I catch his eye, and then saw his focus change from me to the reflection in my glasses. It was like trying to pick up mercury with chopsticks.
>
> His adventures into our suburban neighborhood had been unhappy. He had disregarded the universal rule that sand is to be kept in sand-boxes, and the children themselves had punished him. He walked around a sad and solitary figure, always

carrying a toy aeroplane, a toy he never played with. At that time, I had not heard the word that was to dominate our lives, to hover over every conversation, to sit through every meal beside us. That word was autism.

Peter's mother took him to various doctors and therapists and finally he was sent to a special school, where he spent nine years.

> I'm not qualified to discuss the programme at the [school]. It apparently gave Peter the help he needed. . . . Peter has made a marginal adjustment, but a "near-miracle" nevertheless, according to his psychiatrist.
>   Peter chose his own vocation. He tunes pianos, giving them the same devotion that many teenage boys give to their cars. At present he needs help with transportation and arrangements. He does his own bookkeeping. He is happy in his work and happy to be home again. We have found a programme for him, where young adults with a history of emotional difficulties meet for recreation and group therapy. I'm sure this is a factor in his continuing improvement (Eberhardy, 1967).

The only unrepresentative feature of this case is Peter's adult adjustment, which, as his psychiatrist indicated, was atypically good. Some few autistic children, perhaps as many as 5 percent (Kernberg, 1979), improve enough by the time they are grown to hold down jobs and even live alone, though they are still aloof and still have poor social judgment and language difficulties. As for the remainder—that is, nearly all autistic children—most do improve with treatment, acquiring some language, self-help, and social skills, but such skills are rarely enough to allow them to live outside a special residence when they reach adulthood, let alone on their own (DeMyer et al., 1981). The accompanying box provides a glimpse into the private world of an autistic child.

PERSPECTIVES ON CHILDHOOD AUTISM

Before we examine various ideas about the causes and treatments of autism, we should say that no single cause has been acknowledged and no single known treatment completely *cures* autism. Although a variety of treatments can help many autistic children to escape the diagnosis of autism, they still have problems (Or-

nitz, 1973; Margolies, 1977). The authors of a review (Ornitz and Ritvo, 1976) of studies on treatments for autism suggested that autistic children benefit most from behavior therapy and special education aimed at developing language and other skills (Schopler and Reichler, 1971).

The Neuroscience Perspective

Evidence that organic factors are at least partly responsible for childhood autism has been accumulating rapidly. Much recent research supports the theory that the autistic child does not perceive the world in the same way that the normal child does. (We consider these cognitive theories in the following section.) But whereas cognitive theorists concentrate on determining how the autistic child's perception is impaired, biological theorists try to determine whether that perceptual impairment is organic and, if so, what specific organic defect is responsible.

Genetic Research   As we noted in Chapter 15, a great deal of sophisticated and productive research has been carried out on the genetics of schizophrenia. But so far there have been fewer genetic or twin studies of autism, in the latter case because it has been difficult to find large enough samples of twins. Researchers who scoured Great Britain, for example, found eleven pairs of monozygotic (MZ) twins and ten pairs of dizygotic (DZ) twins in which at least one twin was autistic (Folstein and Rutter, 1977). Of the MZ group, four of eleven were concordant. Of the DZ group, none were concordant. Even when a twin with an autistic MZ twin was *not* diagnosed as autistic, he or she was likely to be markedly impaired in language or cognition. (MZ and DZ twins are discussed in Chapter 6.) But the sample was not large enough to form the basis of firm scientific evidence. The fact that several of the autistic children seemed to have suffered brain damage at birth made it difficult for the researchers to say to what extent their impairment was inherited. Despite these drawbacks, the study suggests that autism has some genetic component.

In sum, there is some evidence, not yet conclusive, that genetic factors figure in the development of autism. But the picture remains obscure, and given the difficulties of locating sets of twins, it is unlikely to be clarified soon.

Biochemical Studies Researchers today are investigating the role of neurotransmitters in autism, as they have been doing with schizophrenia. It is now well established that many autistic children have abnormally high levels of serotonin and dopamine (Goldstein et al., 1976; Hanley et al., 1977; Takahashi et al., 1976). Whatever their role in the development of autism, these two neurotransmitters may play a role in its treatment. When autistic children receive stimulants such as the amphetamines, which increase dopamine, their symptoms of hyperactivity, ritualistic behavior, and self-stimulation get worse (Young et al., 1982). Dopamine-inhibiting drugs such as the phenothiazines mitigate many of the symptoms of autism, including self-mutilation and repetitive motions, although they are less effective with autism than with schizophrenia (Campbell et al., 1982; Kernberg, 1979). Drugs that reduce serotonin also hold promise. In one study (Geller et al., 1982), for example, fenfluramine (which reduces serotonin) was given to two autistic boys, a three-year-old and a five-year old, for three months. Both improved noticeably in their speech, social behavior, and IQ scores (the three-year-old's IQ nearly doubled). When the drug treatment was stopped, these gains held for at least six weeks, but after three months they were diminishing. Although this approach is new and untested, it holds out hope that some autistic children someday may benefit from drug therapy.

Certain allergies also produce symptoms similar to those of autism, such as screaming, head banging, and mutism (Rimland and Meyer, 1967). Consequently, some clinicians have tried to treat autism as they treat these allergies. They have tried orthomolecular therapy, which includes special diets (especially low-carbohydrate diets), and megavitamin therapy. A few have reported that some autistic children improve when they take large daily doses of vitamin B_6 (Rimland, 1973, 1974). To try to test this relationship, a group of researchers found sixteen "autistic-type" children who seemed to respond to B_6 and had their behavior carefully observed when the children were taking vitamins and when they were taking a placebo (Rimland et al., 1978). The naive observers noted a deterioration in the behavior of eleven of the children when they were taking, it was later revealed, a placebo. But sixteen is still a small sample, and most of the children were only loosely characterized as autistic. More research will be needed before the orthomolecular approach can be established as more than an interesting possibility.

Congenital Disorders and Birth Complications Some cases of autism seem to involve congenital disorders—that is, disorders acquired during prenatal development but not transmitted genetically. The prevalence of autism is disproportionately high in children who had congenital rubella (German measles). An astonishingly large number—8 to 10 percent—of such children are autistic (Chess et al., 1971).

Other cases of autism (and also of childhood schizophrenia) may be connected to complications of pregnancy and birth, for the prevalence of such complications is higher in schizophrenic and autistic children than in the general population (Kolvin et al., 1971; Lotter, 1966; Taft and Goldfarb, 1964). But such complications are not necessarily independent of genetic factors. In a longitudinal study of children with schizophrenic parents, the researcher found that the pregnancies had involved more difficulties than normal and that the babies had had lower birth weights and more abnormalities than babies in a control group (Mednick, 1971).

In a recent study of identical seventeen-year-old triplet boys who had a mild form of autism, researchers found that although the boys were generally quite similar, the severity of their problems differed (Burgoine and Wing, 1983). At birth the triplet with the most severe problems had weighed the least, had been slightly blue and needed oxygen, and had stayed longest (four and one-half weeks) in an incubator. At the age of one year he had had pneumonia and again was in the hospital, this time for nearly a month. The triplet with the least severe problems had weighed the most at birth and had had the fewest problems after he was born. This study adds support for the idea that birth complications and problems in infancy are implicated at least in the severity of autism.

Finally, a family study of autism found that the siblings of the most severely retarded autistic children were most likely to be autistic or mentally retarded themselves. This finding suggests that only the autism associated with severe mental retardation may be genetic (Baird and August, 1985).

Neurological Studies If, as the studies on biochemical and congenital factors suggest, autism involves organic defects, then the defects probably lie in the central nervous system. In the case of autism, at least, a good deal of circumstantial evidence supports this supposition. In the first place, most of the characteristic signs of autism—impaired language de-

Idiot Savants

An **idiot savant** (French for "wise idiot") is a person who despite generally diminished mental skills shows astonishing proficiency in one isolated skill. This extremely rare condition was until recently thought to be associated with retardation, but it is likely that idiots savants are actually autistic, not retarded. The abilities of idiots savants are often so wildly exaggerated by the press that the phenomenon is often regarded with some skepticism. Scientists too, however, have observed and described idiots savants (e.g., Scheerer et al., 1945; Viscott, 1970).

How do these remarkable skills develop? Perhaps by way of compensation. Just as the blind may develop particularly keen hearing, so a child who is retarded in most skills may compensate by becoming "overproficient" in one salvaged skill. Alternatively, the source of idiots savants' abilities may be purely biological. That is, one area of the brain may be rendered abnormally efficient by the same structural change that rendered the rest of the brain abnormally inefficient. Another possibility is that when such abilities appear in association with autism, they are produced by the intense concentration typical of autistic children. These children can focus their attention on a single object for hours and days on end. Perhaps, in rare cases, this superhuman concentration produces special abilities. Whatever its source, the idiot savant phenomenon makes an enigmatic disorder seem even more enigmatic.

In almost all reported cases, the skill in question is based on memory or calculation. There have been several reports of children who, if given a date, could say immediately what day of the week it fell on. Others can recite columns of numbers from the telephone book after one reading. Recently, however, an English psychiatrist, Lorna Selfe (1978), reported the case of an idiot savant with a truly creative ability—drawing.

Nadia, the second of three children born to a Ukrainian couple living in England, was clearly abnormal from an early age. She did not speak. Indeed, she did not seem even to notice other people, with the exception of her mother and a few others. Occasionally she would burst into violent tantrums, screaming for two or three hours at a stretch, but most of her days were spent tearing paper into thin strips or performing some other ritualistic activity. The diagnosis was autism.

When Nadia was three years old, her mother had to be hospitalized for several months. When the mother returned, the child was overjoyed. Inexplicably, she began to draw. What she drew was equally inexplicable—figures of astonishing beauty and sophistication. For the next three years Nadia produced drawing after drawing. She refused to use color; only a ball-point pen would do. She would draw on any kind of paper she could find, including boxes. Most of her subjects were taken from picture books, horses and roosters being particular favorites. She would sketch with the utmost concentration, then sit back, survey the result, and wiggle her hands and knees with pleasure.

At the same time Nadia was being taken the round of clinics and special schools for treatment of her linguistic and social handicaps. She was enrolled in several special programs but made no progress. Then, around age six and a half, she began speaking—and stopped drawing. At the time when this case was written up, Nadia was ten years old. She had acquired a small vocabulary, was responsive to a limited circle of people, and could even handle simple mathematics. When asked to draw a picture, she could produce one, but it had none of the genius of her earlier work. As mysteriously as it had appeared, her remarkable artistic talent had vanished.

A rooster drawn by Nadia when she was about three and a half.

velopment, mental retardation, bizarre motor behavior, under- and overreactivity to sensory input, responsiveness to touch and movement as opposed to auditory and visual stimuli—are related to the functioning of the central nervous system. Second, seizure disorders, known to originate in the central nervous system, are often seen in autistic children, especially as they grow older. In one study, for example, 25 percent of a relatively large sample of autistic children developed seizures during adolescence, often after having tested normal on neurological examinations during childhood (Rutter and Lockyer, 1967; Rutter, 1971). Third, neurological examinations of autistic children sometimes reveal abnormalities such as poor muscle tone, poor coordination, drooling, and hyperactivity. DeMyer and her colleagues (1973) claim that three-fourths of the autistic children they have observed showed such neurological signs.

Finally, there are many reports that autistic children have abnormal EEGs. EEGs of psychotic children are difficult to obtain, for the test requires a degree of cooperation on the part of the subject—cooperation that is not always forthcoming in the severely disturbed child. Nevertheless, two studies have reported EEGs of unusually low amplitude in autistic children—a finding that suggests abnormally high arousal (Kolvin et al., 1971; Hutt et al., 1965). Other researchers have found other abnormalities in 50 to 80 percent of autistic children (Creak and Pampiglione, 1969). These studies have been contradicted by various other studies, which have found different degrees and different kinds of EEG abnormality. Nevertheless, though variable and circumstantial, the accumulated evidence strongly suggests a neurological impairment in autistic children.

The search for the specific defect that causes the autistic child's neurological abnormalities has prompted a number of hypotheses. Rimland (1964) has proposed that the reticular formation in the brainstem of the autistic child may be failing to provide the proper degree of arousal. DeMyer and her co-workers (1973) have suggested that localized damage within the cerebral cortex, the outermost layer of the brain, may be responsible for both the verbal and perceptual dysfunctions. A more recent hypothesis, based on the pattern of cognitive and linguistic defects characteristic of autism, is that the dysfunction lies in the left hemisphere of the brain (Prior, 1979; Blackstock, 1978). Cognitive functions that seem to be mediated by the left hemisphere (language, sequential processing, analytic skills) are almost always

either weak or missing in autistic children, whereas functions thought to be controlled by the right hemisphere (visual-spatial skills, recognition without analysis) are much closer to normal. The peculiarities of autistic language—its concreteness, its repetitiveness, its mechanical, automatic quality—also support the left-hemisphere hypothesis, for these traits are associated with the operations of the right hemisphere. In other words, the language we find in autistic children may result from the right hemisphere's efforts to do what it can without support from the left.

In sum, as research continues, the biological hypothesis is becoming increasingly convincing. At this moment it does seem probable that many autistic children are the victims of some organic defect that causes them to fail socially and intellectually. But we are still far from identifying the exact nature of that organic defect.

The Cognitive Perspective

No one denies that autistic children suffer profound cognitive problems that affect their capacity to imitate and comprehend, to be flexible and inventive, to form and apply rules, and to use information (Werry, 1979a)—problems that render these children almost incapable, in other words, of coping with the world. Cognitive theories hold that the cognitive problems of autistic children are primary and cause their social problems (Rutter, 1983). Family theories (considered below), in contrast, hold that the social problems are primary and cause the cognitive problems.

Cognitive theorists have tried to pinpoint the basic cognitive defect in autism. Some hold that the basic problem lies in modulating and integrating input from different senses (Ornitz, 1974; Ornitz and Ritvo, 1968; Ritvo, 1976). Some experimental evidence supports this position. It is known, for example, that autistic children may be either oversensitive or undersensitive to sounds. Sometimes they act as if they were deaf, but at other times they startle at relatively ordinary sounds (Hintgen and Coulter, 1967; Prior and Gajzago, 1974; Prior et al., 1976). The same holds true for their visual perception. There is some evidence that these perceptual abnormalities underlie autistic children's social insensitivity (Hermelin and O'Connor, 1970).

A second argument to focus on sensory perception suggests that the autistic child's basic defect is in understanding sounds (Rutter, 1968, 1971). In this view, autism is comparable to other language disorders, such as **aphasia,** the loss or impairment of speech as a result of brain damage, and differs from them only in that the autistic child's defective understanding of sounds is accompanied by other perceptual problems. The experimental evidence cited in the previous paragraph supports this view as well. Furthermore, autistic children's speech is retarded early in the progress of the disorder and is one of its defining symptoms. In further support of the idea that autism involves a primary language impairment is the pattern of cognitive abilities autistic children typically show. As we have said, they usually do far better on sensorimotor tasks such as finding hidden figures, on visual motor tasks, and on rote memory than on verbal and conceptual tasks. Finally, one of the strongest arguments in favor of this hypothesis is that an autistic child's language ability is one of the best predictors of the child's chances of benefiting from treatment. A strange case in which improvement in language ability was accompanied by loss of another ability is described in the box on idiots savants.

Another cognitive hypothesis is that autistic children are overselective in their attention (Lovaas et al., 1979). Because of a perceptual defect, they can process and respond to only one stimulus at a time, be it visual, tactile, or whatever. Experimental evidence to support this interpretation has come from tests of autistic children in finding hidden figures (Shah and Frith, 1983). They do well on such tests because they focus directly on each part and are not easily distracted by the overall picture. But they do not do well at deriving meaning from stimuli with several parts. This kind of impairment may well account for the social and intellectual retardation of the autistic child. According to Lovaas, much of a child's intellectual and emotional development is based on the association of paired stimuli, through the process of respondent conditioning. Thus as children mentally pair their mother with food and cuddling, they come to love her. But if children process only the stimulus of the food or the cuddling and do not pair it with their mother's presence, they do not positively associate it with her.

Other cognitive theorists argue that autism is the product not of a single, basic perceptual defect but of a cluster of perceptual defects (Wing, 1969, 1972). This line of investigation has led to some interesting kinds of treatment that circumvent the child's presumed cognitive defects. Some behavior therapists,

One cognitive view of autism maintains that a perceptual defect permits autistic children to attend to only one stimulus at a time. As a result, they cannot make associations between one stimulus and another, which might explain their social and intellectual impairment. (Constantino Manos/Magnum)

for example, have taught autistic children sign language, which takes advantage of their sensitivity to touch and movement and circumvents their insensitivity to spoken language (Webster et al., 1973). Other researchers have tried to develop reinforcers more effective than auditory rewards, such as the therapist's saying "Good!" Newsom and his colleagues (1974) found that lights flashing on and off after a correct response were more effective reinforcers than spoken praise or even food. The treatments emerging from this line of investigation—treatments based on a combination of cognitive and behavioral theory—appear promising.

The Behavioral Perspective

Although most behaviorists do not believe that autism is *caused* by faulty learning, they do believe that learning can be a valuable tool in its treatment. Therefore they have focused their efforts primarily on therapy rather than on theory.

Reconditioning Adaptive Responses   The major techniques of behavioral therapy for psychotic children are direct reinforcement (e.g., giving a cookie to the child who refrains from engaging in the undesirable behavior or engages in a desirable behavior), extinction (e.g., withdrawing attention in response to undesirable behavior), and punishment (e.g., administering a spanking in response to unacceptable behavior). By means of these techniques, adaptive behaviors are reinforced while maladaptive behaviors are either punished or simply allowed to extinguish.

Reports indicate that all three techniques are effective, but that their effectiveness depends greatly on what behavior is being eliminated. For example, self-mutilating responses such as head banging will eventually extinguish if social attention is withdrawn when the head banging occurs. In one case, however, it took nearly eight days and 1,800 head bangs before the response dropped out (Simmons and Lovaas, 1969). Another problem with extinction procedures is that some behaviors seem to be maintained by internal rather than external rewards, in which case withdrawing social attention or food will have little if any effect. For example, psychotic children's ritualistic motor behaviors—which, as we have seen, they will prefer over food even when they are hungry—are highly resistant to extinction through the withdrawal of food or attention (Reuter et al., 1974), apparently because they satisfy an internal need for stimulation (Litrownik, 1969).

Of course, if extinction doesn't work, the therapist can resort to punishment, usually in the form of spankings or, in cases of extreme self-destructive behavior, electric shock. O. I. Lovaas has conducted research on the use of electric shock in treating autistic children, and as he points out, it is extremely effective in eliminating self-mutilating behavior: "Seemingly independently of how badly the child is mutilating himself or how long he has been doing so, we can essentially remove the self-destructive behavior within the first minute" (1970, p. 38). But even though this immediate effect may be desired in some cases—the case of self-mutilation, for example—moral, ethical, and legal concerns frequently limit the use of aversive procedures. Applying punishment to disturbed children in any context is understandably controversial. Many people believe that punishing a psychotic child for undesirable behaviors only compounds the problem (Bettelheim, 1967). In response, Lovaas argues that psychotic children are more likely to respond to therapy when they are treated like people—that is, rewarded, punished, and generaly held responsible for their behavior—rather than like patients. Lovaas has also pointed out that if self-destructive behavior is *not* eliminated by some kind of treatment, the child

may spend long periods of time tied down in restraints, unable to take part in any other kind of therapy.

Another potential problem in eliminating inappropriate behaviors is **symptom substitution,** the replacement of a suppressed maladaptive behavior by a new maladaptive behavior. Once a child's rocking behavior is eliminated, for example, he or she may suddenly begin hyperventilating (Reuter et al., 1974). What this seems to mean is that once we have eliminated a behavior in which a child has been engaging frequently and at long stretches, we can't expect the child simply to sit quietly and wait for someone to teach a new, appropriate behavior with which to fill the vacuum. Hence, with childhood psychosis as with drug addiction and sexual deviation, most behavioral treatment programs aim simultaneously at eliminating old, inappropriate behaviors and at fostering new, appropriate behaviors to take their place (e.g., Simmons and Lovaas, 1969; Wolf et al., 1964).

Procedures for developing appropriate responses in psychotic children have first and foremost focused on establishing people as secondary reinforcers—that is, the child must first see people as being important and valuable. The therapist can often bring the child to understand the significance of other people through respondent conditioning, by pairing praise (social reinforcement) with primary positive reinforcers such as food or with primary negative reinforcers such as pain relief (Lovaas et al., 1965). Next, through shaping and modeling—with the use of social reinforcement as well as direct reinforcers such as food—the child is taught new responses such as toileting, speaking, and playing with other children (Lovaas et al., 1966; Wolf et al., 1964). Once having learned these basic skills, the child can be placed in a group learning situation (Koegel and Rincover, 1974) and thus will be able to learn by observing others.

As in eliminating inappropriate behaviors, so in developing appropriate behaviors there are problems in maintaining the change. Follow-up reports indicate that responses learned in the treatment laboratory often do not generalize to the school or the home (Nordquist and Wahler, 1973; Koegel and Rincover, 1977). And some children, especially those who are returned to institutions after their treatment, relapse completely. There is no question that institutions foster such relapses, since in many institutional settings patients are expected to act in an inappropriate fashion and no rewards are given for acting otherwise. For example, one therapist who was visiting an institution decided to look up a child with whom he had worked

Sometimes food is an effective direct reinforcement in behavioral therapy programs designed to elicit adaptive responses from autistic children. (Alan Carey/The Image Works)

with considerable success. He found her crouched in a corner, flapping her hand and making bizarre sounds. As soon as she saw the therapist, she got up, walked over, and said, "Hi, how are you?" She continued to talk and act appropriately while the therapist was there. After he left, she presumably returned to her corner.

Recent efforts to get around this problem have involved keeping the child at home and directing treatment efforts at the parents as well as at the child. The parents are actually trained to act as behavioral therapists. Such home therapy can apparently be very successful (Lovaas et al., 1973). Once the parents see the child improving as a result of their efforts, they are likely to try even harder, with the result that the child will make further gains.

Most behavior therapists have no illusion that they are transforming psychotic children into normal children (Margolies, 1977). Rather, their aim is to provide these children with enough adaptive responses so that they can graduate from custodial care to a more useful and fulfilling existence, albeit in a "special" class. Critics of behavioral therapy for psychotic children have claimed that its products are no better than performing robots (Bettelheim, 1967), and in some instances this seems to be the case. For example, one psychotic child, when asked, "What did you have for breakfast?" would tell you that she had had "eggs, toast, jelly, juice, and milk" even on days when she had had no breakfast at all. In short, she had no understanding of the concept; she was simply responding with a programmed answer to a specific question. In many other instances, however, behavioral treatment has resulted in the development of responses that are spontaneous as well as appropriate. Substantial gains have been made in eliminating self-mutilating and bizarre motor behavior and developing language, self-help, and social skills (Lovaas et al., 1973). Perhaps the most effective way to help autistic children is to give them structured, organized education for at least as long as normal children are educated, by teachers skilled in teaching children with such pervasive handicaps (Wing, 1981).

The Psychodynamic Perspective

For years the accepted wisdom was that children became autistic because they had been raised by cold, detached, overintellectual parents—"emotional refrigerators," in the words of Kanner and Eisenberg (1955). The idea that pathological family relationships cause childhood autism has been explored by many researchers (Bateson et al., 1956; Kanner and Eisenberg, 1955; Eisenberg and Kanner, 1956; Singer and Wynne, 1963), including some who have no allegiance to psychodynamic theory (Ferster, 1961). In general, this theory has been eclipsed by the findings of more recent research.

The foremost publicist of family theory has been Bruno Bettelheim, whose theory of autism is detailed in his book *The Empty Fortress* (1967). Autism, Bettelheim argues, is a child's response to an extreme situation in which parents reject the child and fail to respond to the child's slightest attempts to influence the environment. The parents fail to provide stimulation during the first six months of life, when social relationships begin to form, and during the next three months, when language and locomotion begin. Because of this lack of stimulation, the child has no basis on which to form emotional attachments or to develop proper language and motor skills. Most important, because the parents are unresponsive, the child feels unable to control the external world. The child therefore withdraws into fantasy and tries to impose some order and constancy on the world by insisting on sameness.

Bettelheim's argument has been challenged by many other investigators, especially because the brothers and sisters of autistic children are usually normal. More recent research has not supported the idea that parents of autistic children are cold and aloof (Cox et al., 1975; Kolvin et al., 1971; Rutter, 1971). What is more, those studies that have shown that parents handle their autistic children differently from their normal children do not answer the question of cause and effect. Although it is possible that unresponsive parents produce autistic children, it is equally possible that autistic children produce unresponsive parents. Remember, for example, the studies of disturbed communication (Wynne et al., 1975) in the families of schizophrenic children (Chapter 15). Although some clinicians interpret these studies to support the hypothesis that disturbed family relationships produce schizophrenia, others say that a child's schizophrenia *causes* the disturbances in family relationships (Liem, 1974).

The mother of Peter, the autistic boy described earlier, reflects on a social worker's accusation of coldness:

> How could I be anything but cold after years of trying to warm up this icy child of mine? Even with your own son, friendship is a two-way street. We hadn't rejected Peter; he had rejected us. Even rejection was too strong a word. Peter accepted us as he did the furniture, as tools to get what he wanted. He simply didn't recognize us as people (Eberhardy, 1967, p. 260).

As we pointed out in Chapter 15, family theories of schizophrenia have lost considerable ground in recent years—and so have family theories of autism. As the evidence for biological causes mounts, many investigators feel that the family theory should be abandoned, for to cling to it without scientific support is to impose a needless burden of guilt on parents who already have burdens enough.

Rebuilding the Ego   Psychodynamic treatment generally requires that the child be removed from the home and placed in a residential treatment facility, a famous example being the Sonia Shankman Orthogenic School in Chicago, founded by Bettelheim. In such a residence the child is provided with a counselor who is constantly available and sympathetic—a steady, reliable image that the child can internalize. The basis of this treatment is constant responsiveness to the child's needs on the part of the counselor and the staff. Thus, in an example cited by Sanders (1974), when a new child was being shown around the school and said "mashed potatoes" during a visit to the kitchen, the kitchen staff responded by giving him a special serving of mashed potatoes at every meal.

In this way the child learns what, according to psychodynamic theory, he or she could not learn at home: that by communicating through speech and movement, he or she can influence the environment. Once this foundation is laid, the child can begin to develop emotional attachments and to build a stable personality.

A major problem in evaluating psychodynamic treatments is the general lack of concrete suggestions for actual therapy (Wieland, 1971). Another problem is that such evaluations as do exist generally lack any methodological strictness. For example, Bettelheim (1967), in evaluating the progress of some forty children treated at his school, claimed that 42 percent had made a "good" adjustment—a figure that compares very favorably with the usual follow-up reports of good adjustment for only 5 to 15 percent of autistic children (DeMeyer et al., 1973). The children on whom Bettelheim reported, however, were evaluated by Bettelheim himself. Thus the possibility arises that his expectations and hopes may have colored his judgments. And Bettelheim's subjective criteria for what constituted "improvement" have made it difficult for other researchers to evaluate his treatment. Furthermore, over 65 percent of Bettelheim's forty patients had evidenced functional speech by the age of five—a factor which, as we have noted, indicates a good prognosis. Hence these children were much more likely to benefit from treatment than the average autistic child. A survey of parents of autistic children on the effectiveness of different treatments indicates that psychotherapy and residential treatment are not as effective as operant conditioning (Rimland, 1977). A possible explanation of the varying treatment results from study to study is a difference in diagnostic populations. Only recently has there been a widely accepted set of diagnostic criteria for autism, and therefore the autistic children on whom Bettelheim was reporting may have had a somewhat different symptomatology from that of the children in the studies discussed by DeMyer and her colleagues.

SUMMARY

Autism is a pervasive developmental disorder that affects virtually all aspects of a child's functioning.

Autism, named in the 1940s, today is considered to appear in infancy or childhood and to affect individual children with symptoms that vary in severity. Despite these variations, nearly all autistic children are mentally retarded, speak abnormally or not at all, move bizarrely, and do not form close relationships with their parents or anyone else.

Autism was once thought to be the same as schizophrenia in adults. But today it is thought to be quite different from schizophrenia. Autism is the main pervasive disorder of childhood, whereas childhood schizophrenia is rare. The two conditions differ in age of onset, premorbid adjustment, autistic aloneness, preservation of sameness, perception of the environment, hallucinations and delusions, language, intellectual abilities, family history, and sex ratio.

The symptoms of autism include extreme social isolation, characterized by withdrawal, an inability to form attachments to others, and bursts of inexplicable emotion.

Autistic children are mentally retarded, and the most severely mentally retarded have the most impaired social relationships. Autistic children cannot see the world from another person's point of view and do better on tests of rote memory and sensorimotor skills than on those involving verbal or social comprehension.

Autistic children either do not speak at all or speak abnormally—in howls or babbles or in echolalia. They cannot communicate reciprocally. The severity of an autistic child's language problems is a good indicator of his or her prognosis.

Many autistic children perform repeated ritualistic movements, such as twirling, flapping their hands, or banging their heads. Some stay totally still; others have tremors. The ritualistic movements may be self-mutilating, but they are so compelling that many children engage in them rather than eating or doing other things.

Autistic children also are anxiously obsessive about keeping their surroundings and their routines utterly unvarying. When they perceive even a trivial change, they often become upset.

The neuroscience perspective suggests that organic factors are partly responsible for childhood autism. Autism may have a genetic component. It clearly has a biochemical component, as levels of serotonin and dopamine are elevated, and some children have benefited from drug therapy. Some children develop autism during prenatal life; many children who were exposed to rubella as fetuses become autistic, for example. Autism is also associated with high levels of complications in pregnancy and birth. Neurological studies suggest that the defect responsible for autism lies in the central nervous system, perhaps in the left hemisphere of the brain.

According to the cognitive perspective, autistic children's profound problems, which prevent them from imitating others, comprehending, forming and applying rules, using information, or thinking flexibly and inventively, are primary and cause their social problems. Some cognitive theorists suggest that autistic children cannot modulate or integrate sensory input, such as sights and sounds. Autistic children are overselective in their attention and do not do well at deriving meaning from stimuli with several components.

According to the behavioral perspective, inappropriate learning is not the cause of autism, but learning can be a valuable tool in its treatment. Behavior therapists use such techniques as direct reinforcement, extinction, and punishment. Although punishment is controversial, it can be effective in preventing children from mutilating themselves. Shaping and modeling are used to eliminate inappropriate behavior, to develop appropriate behavior, and to help autistic children maintain their gains.

The psychodynamic perspective has lost popularity in recent years and has not been widely supported by scientific evidence. It holds that children become autistic because their parents are cold and detached "emotional refrigerators." The cause of autism is laid to faulty family relationships and a failure to provide necessary stimulation to the child during infancy. Therapy usually entails removing the child from the family and aims at rebuilding his or her ego, that is, laying a new foundation of personality on which development can proceed more normally.

Mental Retardation

M ental retardation, the name we give to a condition of impaired intelligence and adaptive functioning, is not a single disorder with a single cause. It may be due to genetic abnormalities, to damage to the brain at birth, or—some experts believe—to deprivation in childhood. Its manifestations are as varied as its causes. The mentally retarded in this country range from people who grow up, marry, and live on their own, going to work during the week and to the movies on Saturday night much like anyone else, to people who cannot learn, speak, or care for themselves in any way.

Although there are no absolute statistics on the prevalence of mental retardation, *DSM-III-R* estimates that mental retardation affects approximately 1 percent of the U.S. population. However imprecise this estimate, it signifies an enormous problem for society.

DEFINING MENTAL RETARDATION

The most widely accepted current definition of **mental retardation** is that offered by the *Manual on Terminology and Classification in Mental Retardation*, published by the American Association on Mental Deficiency (AAMD):[*]

---

[*] The *DSM-III-R* definition of retardation was written in accordance with the AAMD definition. *DSM-III-R* states: "The essential features [of mental retardation] are: (1) significantly subaverage general intellectual functioning, accompanied by (2) significant deficits or impairments in adaptive functioning, with (3) onset before the age of 18. The diagnosis is made regardless of whether or not there is a coexisting mental or physical disorder."

Mental retardation refers to significantly subaverage general intellectual functioning existing concurrently with deficits in adaptive behavior, and manifested during the developmental period (1977, p. 11).

Several things should be noted about this definition. First, the diagnosis is based on current functioning. Many earlier definitions of mental retardation stressed the person's intellectual potential—what he or she *could* achieve—a prediction often based on unproved assumptions. Today diagnosticians confine their judgments to the person's present behavior.

Second, and very important, the definition requires that the person diagnosed as mentally retarded show serious deficits in *both* intellectual and adaptive functioning. That is, a child whose measured intelligence is below average but who still successfully engages in adaptive behavior—dressing herself, making friends, and so forth—would not necessarily be judged retarded.

Third, the definition emphasizes the developmental period. A child's progress is judged to be normal or delayed in comparison with norms for his or her specific age group.

Finally, the AAMD definition says nothing about cause. Earlier diagnostic criteria often stated that mental retardation was organically based and incurable. But in most cases the cause of retardation is unclear. Today, therefore, diagnosis does not depend on cause. Thus a child who does poorly in school, who scores very low on intelligence tests, and who has difficulty adjusting to the school environment may be considered retarded even though there is no evidence of organic impairment.

Levels of Retardation

All human beings, no matter how bright or accomplished, are limited in some way; all human beings also have potentials whose limits we do not yet know. The AAMD definition of retardation recognizes that some people's intellectual functioning is clearly limited in comparison with that of most other people. The degree of that limitation and what it may mean for an individual's potential to live in society are described in terms of four levels of retardation—mild, moderate, severe, and profound—based on scores achieved on standard intelligence tests and on estimates of adaptive behavior. Intelligence test scores have an approximately normal distribution, with a mean of 100 and

a standard deviation of about 16 points (see Figure 1.1 on p. 3). The four levels of retardation all fall in the area of the distribution that is more than two standard deviations below the mean. Each level represents one standard deviation on the normal curve of the distribution of intelligence test scores.

The following descriptions of the characteristics of and potential for each of the four levels are based on Robinson and Robinson (1976), Baroff (1974), and MacMillan (1982). These writers emphasize some important trends in recent thinking about retardation. One is that chronological age must be taken into account along with IQ in order to obtain an accurate estimate of any individual's potential for functioning. A mildly retarded six-year-old and a mildly retarded twenty-year-old may have the same IQ, but in view of their ages, we will evaluate their skills differently. Another recent trend puts emphasis on what retarded people *can* do as opposed to what they cannot—an orientation fostered by recent laws that have greatly expanded public education programs for retarded people. Now that there are more services aimed at developing the retarded person's potential, clinicians have begun to think more seriously, and more optimistically, about what that potential may be.

Mild Retardation (Binet IQ 52 to 67)   Of approximately 6.5 million people who are labeled retarded, 6 million, or more than 90 percent, fall into the category of mild retardation. The mildly retarded are people who, as adults, can often lead productive lives with relatively little help. Most can hold a job and have friends; some can also marry and raise children. Mildly retarded people generally need someone who can occasionally act as an advisor, particularly in regard to budgeting and money management. As very young children, they develop more slowly and need help longer with self-care tasks such as eating, dressing, and toilet training. Language, fine-motor skills, and social skills also develop more slowly, though they do develop. By adolescence, a mildly retarded person can function independently in most areas of life. He or she can speak fluently, and with proper education can usually read easy material and do simple arithmetic.

Moderate Retardation (Binet IQ 36 to 51) Moderately retarded people are those who can learn to care for themselves but are not fully independent.

They can work in sheltered workshops and have friends, though they rarely marry or become parents. Moderately retarded children of five to seven can do simple tasks, such as opening boxes and stringing beads; can feed themselves with cup and spoon, cooperate with dressing, and begin toilet training; and can use some words and recognize shapes. By adolescence, they have good self-care skills and can carry on simple conversations, read a few words, and do simple errands and household tasks. In the past, moderately retarded persons were often institutionalized, but today many live in the community, in special residences or with their families.

Severe Retardation (Binet IQ 20 to 35)   Severely retarded people can learn some self-care skills and with proper training can learn to perform tasks in a sheltered workshop or a daytime activity center. Training is especially valuable at the severely retarded level, since it can make the difference between institutionalization and a more productive and happy life in a family or residence group. Severely retarded people do, however, require considerable supervision. They can understand, but have considerable difficulty expressing themselves in language, and their reading and number skills are not sufficient for normal daily living. In adolescence, such people may have a mental age of five to six years (see Figure 19.1) and can usually perform most self-care tasks, with help in certain areas, such as bathing.

Profound Retardation (Binet IQ below 20)   Profoundly retarded people can carry out some day-to-day self-care activities and can sometimes perform tasks in a daytime activity center, but they will always require extensive supervision and help. Language is a severe problem; they may understand a simple communication but have little or no ability to speak. Many profoundly retarded people remain institutionalized, usually because of severe behavior problems or multiple physical handicaps. Because of increased susceptibility to disease, people in this category often die in childhood or adolescence.

Systems of Classification

Over the years, people concerned with the study and treatment of mental retardation have proposed

Learning to get along with others is an important part of the education of every child, whether retarded or normal. (Bruce Roberts/Rapho/Photo Researchers)

various systems of classification. From the outset, attempts at classification led to confusion and controversy, largely because causation and levels of function were lumped together. Today the trend is to deal with these issues as separate but interrelated factors.

Such is the policy of the AAMD manual, which today is the most widely used guideline for the diagnosis of retardation. The manual has two systems of

FIGURE 19.1
A drawing of a man on a horse done by a twelve-year-old retarded boy with an IQ of 33. It indicates a developmental level comparable to that of a normal child of four to six years. The retarded child goes through the same developmental stages as a normal child, but goes more slowly, and ultimately does not reach as high a level.

classification, the biomedical system, which groups cases by causation, and the functional system, which groups cases according to behavior.

The Biomedical System The biomedical system, which treats mental retardation as a secondary effect of a physical condition, is designed to distinguish groups according to demonstrated or presumed etiology. Because this classification is based entirely on organic factors, however, not all persons in a particular group will be functioning at the same level. (Nor will all necessarily be retarded.) The biomedical classification system is divided into ten major groupings: (1) infections and intoxications, (2) trauma and physical agents, (3) metabolism and nutrition, (4) gross brain disease (postnatal), (5) unknown prenatal influence, (6) chromosomal abnormalities, (7) gestational disorders, (8) psychiatric disorders, (9) environmental influences, and (10) other conditions (AAMD, 1977). Each group is further divided into a number of subgroups and specific syndromes. For example, phenylketonuria, a disease we will discuss shortly, is a specific syndrome that falls within the amino acid disorders, which in turn constitute a subgroup of the disorders of metabolism and nutrition.

The Functional System The functional system distinguishes among the four levels of functioning described earlier—mild, moderate, severe, and profound retardation. It is based on two criteria for determining retardation: "subaverage general intellectual functioning" and "deficits in adaptive behavior."

Intellectual functioning is evaluated on the basis of standard IQ tests, such as the Stanford-Binet and the Wechsler scales (see Chapter 7). The assessment of adaptive behavior covers a number of areas—intellectual, emotional, motivational, social, and motor behavior—with the emphasis depending on the person's age. During infancy and early childhood, sensorimotor, language, self-help, and social skills are considered particularly significant—walking, talking, feeding oneself, dressing, using the toilet, playing with others. During the school years, skills essential to academic functioning and social interaction are emphasized— reading and arithmetic, use of language, ability to play games and make friends. During adulthood, the focus is on overall social adjustment—ability to be self-supporting and to conform to the standards of the community. Thus the focus of testing varies with developmental level.

The functional system has been criticized on a number of counts. Particularly open to attack are the tests of adaptive functioning. A number of rating scales have been developed for this purpose—the Vineland Social Maturity Scale and the AAMD Adaptive Behavior Scale are two examples—but because adaptive behavior is a rather hazy concept, such tests tend to produce fairly crude measures. For want of better instruments, diagnosticians often rely heavily on the intelligence tests. This practice has lent weight to complaints about the "tyranny of the IQ." The IQ tests have been harshly criticized as tools for the assessment of retardation. Errors in testing can produce IQ differences of up to 10 points, which, by shifting the child from one "level" to another (for example, from mild to moderate retardation), can make a substantial difference in the treatment he or she receives. Furthermore, many people believe the most commonly used IQ tests to be biased in favor of white middle-class children, a point we discussed in Chapter 7. (See the box on p. 469.)

How the Systems Are Related Though the biomedical and functional systems are independent, there are certain well-established links between causality and level of functioning. Most mildly retarded individuals show no evidence of brain injury or other organic anomalies. A child functioning at this level, for example, might be culturally disadvantaged and educationally retarded. At the other extreme, severely retarded persons more frequently have genetic disorders or neurological damage. Among the profoundly retarded, neurological damage and physical impairments (e.g., blindness, deafness, paralysis) are often so severe that the person has to be confined to bed or to a wheelchair. In sum, the lower the level of functioning, the higher the probability of organic impairment.

ORGANIC FACTORS

In some cases, a specific biological factor can be identified as contributing to mental retardation. But the mechanism by which that factor produces retardation is seldom understood. We know, for example, that most people with Down's syndrome have an extra

IQ Tests, the Mentally Retarded, Minorities, and the Law

The use of IQ tests in the educational placement of mildly retarded children (who are sometimes called the "educable" mentally retarded, or EMR) has been the subject of considerable controversy in recent years. The controversy is not merely abstract or theoretical: it has been the focus of two lawsuits in federal courts. Plaintiffs have charged that IQ tests are biased against minority children, that they systematically underestimate their abilities, and that this bias leads to a disproportionately large representation of minority students in EMR classes.

The battle has been fought in federal courts in California and Illinois. Though the issues were virtually identical in the two cases, the outcomes were not. In 1979, the California public schools were enjoined from using standardized IQ tests in the placement of minority schoolchildren in EMR classes (*Larry P.* v. *Riles,* 1979). The court became convinced, after hearing extensive expert testimony from both sides, that the rights of minority children under the Constitution and various federal antidiscrimination statutes were violated by the use of the tests. A federal judge in Illinois, on the other hand, after hearing very similar testimony and considering the same legal theories, permitted the Chicago public schools to use the tests condemned by the California judge (*PASE* v. *Hannon,*

1980). The Illinois judge based his decision that the tests were not biased primarily on his personal examination of the test items, rather than on the expert testimony that was presented. In both the California and Illinois cases, the losing sides appealed. The ultimate legal outcome is uncertain, and the matter may well reach the U.S. Supreme Court.

Both the scientific and legal issues involved in these cases are extremely complex. The concept of "test bias" itself can be defined in a variety of ways (Anastasi, 1982), and, in principle at least, a test can be biased under some definitions and yet be unbiased under others. Another important question, of course, is whether placement in an EMR class benefits children so placed, or whether, as the plaintiffs in these lawsuits charged, such placement "stigmatizes" the children and impedes their educational progress. The data on this question are not unequivocal (Lambert, 1981).

Even if the tests can be shown to have a discriminatory impact, it is not yet clear whether, on that account alone, their use would be unlawful. It may be necessary to show an "intent" to discriminate to prove a violation of the rights of minority children. The law in this area is not yet settled (Bersoff, 1981).

chromosome, but we do not know how that chromosome actually damages the nervous system. Furthermore, individuals may have the same medical diagnosis yet be at very different levels of retardation. Finally, there is the problem of differential diagnosis. It is not always clear whether a diagnosis of retardation, autism, emotional disturbance, or learning disability is appropriate in any given case. All four conditions may result in generally impaired or deficient behavior and development, and the conditions are not mutually exclusive. Mental retardation and emotional disturbance, for example, may be present in the same person.

The AAMD manual lists more than a hundred organic or genetic anomalies associated with retarda-

tion. Obviously, it is beyond the scope of this chapter to describe in detail all or even most of these conditions. We will discuss only some of the more common and better-known syndromes.

Chromosomal Anomalies

The best-known and the most common condition in the category of chromosomal anomalies is **Down's syndrome,** which occurs in approximately 1 of every 900 births (MacMillan, 1982). The syndrome is named after Langdon Down, the British physician who first described it. For many years, however, it was known as "mongolism," the term coined by Down in reference to the slanting eyes and flat nose that characterize most people with this condition, making them look faintly like the peoples of northeastern Asia, who were once called Mongoloids. Other typical traits are a small, round head; an extra fold of skin on the upper eyelids; a small mouth with drooping corners; a thickened, protruding tongue; short, stubby fingers; poor muscle tone; and, in almost all cases, mental retardation. (Most people with Down's syndrome have IQs of 50 or less.) However, not all victims have all these characteristics. Nor does there appear to be any direct relationship between the number of physical characteristics and the level of retardation.

It was not until 1959 that the genetic basis of Down's syndrome was identified. The normal human cell has twenty-three pairs of chromosomes. But the French geneticist Jerome Lejeune and his colleagues found that individuals with Down's syndrome almost always have an extra chromosome in pair 21, or **trisomy 21** (see Figure 19.2). This extra chromosome is thought to be caused by an error in cell division in the mother's ovum. The likelihood of this occurrence seems to be directly related to the mother's age: the older a woman is, the greater the chances that she will conceive a Down's syndrome child. For women aged twenty-nine or under, the chances are

about 1 in every 1,500 births, but for women over the age of forty-five, the chances are about 1 in 30 (MacMillan, 1982). The clinical procedure called **amniocentesis** can identify chromosomal abnormalities in the developing fetus. A pregnant woman, given such diagnostic information, may choose to undergo an abortion. Thus the birth of Down's syndrome babies is now preventable.

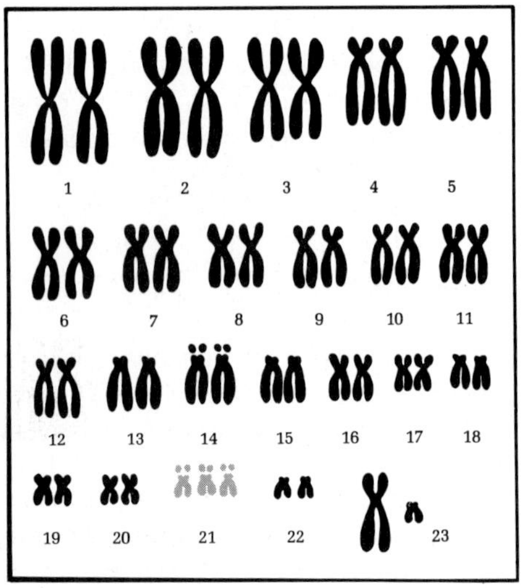

Because such children are susceptible to serious cardiac and respiratory diseases, their life expectancy is shorter than average. Modern medicine has increased their survival rate considerably, however. Today a Down's syndrome child who survives the first few months has a good chance of living into adulthood.

Less common than Down's syndrome, and found only in males, is another chromosomal abnormality known as **Klinefelter's syndrome.** In this case, there is an extra X chromosome in pair 23. Individuals with Klinefelter's syndrome have underdeveloped testes and are sterile. About 25 percent of them also show mental retardation, usually of the mild category.

Metabolic Disturbances

Another form of genetic defect results in metabolic disturbances. One of the best known is **phenylketonuria (PKU),** which occurs in about 1 in every 13,000 to 20,000 live births (MacMillan, 1982). The cause of PKU appears to be a defective recessive gene, which leaves the child deficient in phenylalanine 4-hydroxylase, a liver enzyme that is needed to metabolize the amino acid phenylalanine. In consequence, phenylalanine and its derivatives accumulate in the body and eventually cause serious damage to the developing central nervous system. The result is usually severe retardation, hyperactivity, and erratic and unpredictable behavior. Seizures and severe eczema are also common. Fortunately this disorder can be detected soon after birth. Most states now require the testing of newborn infants for PKU. A special low-phenylalanine diet from infancy to at least age six can often prevent or at least minimize neurological damage in children found to have the disorder (MacMillan, 1982).

Another metabolic disorder is **Tay-Sachs disease.** This disorder, transmitted by a recessive gene, is a defect of lipid metabolism, due to the absence of the enzyme hexosominidase A in the cerebral tissues. It is usually detected between four and eight

FIGURE 19.2
The chromosomes of a male child with Down's syndrome. In most cases (as in this one), the presence of an extra chromosome in the twenty-first pair causes the abnormality. More rarely, the trisomy occurs in the twenty-second pair.

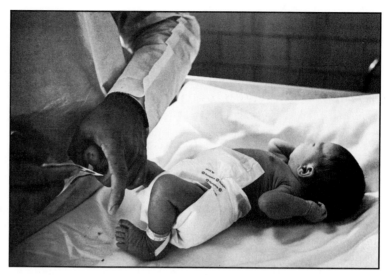

Testing for phenylketonuria, a physician samples blood from the heel of a newborn. Most states now require such a test. If the genetic defect is detected, a special diet can minimize its effects, which include severe retardation. (Lawrence Frank)

months and is confined largely to children of Eastern European Jewish ancestry. It is characterized by progressive deterioration to the point of complete immobility, but with isolated episodes of convulsions. There is no treatment for Tay-Sachs disease. Even under intensive hospital care, only 17 percent of afflicted infants survive beyond four years, and death is virtually certain before the age of six (Aronson and Wolk, 1965).

Other Organic Factors

Other organic factors associated with mental retardation include congenital anomalies, such as infections and hormonal imbalances, neurological damage from drugs and other toxins, and physical trauma from childbirth injuries or child abuse.

Congenital Factors   Some cases of mental retardation occur when a fetus contracts a disease such as rubella (German measles) or syphilis from its mother. Children affected by congenital rubella may be born with several impairments, including brain lesions, which usually result in mental retardation. The earlier in her term the mother contracts the disease, the greater the risk to the fetus. Congenital syphilis, under certain circumstances, causes hydrocephalus, excessive cerebrospinal fluid, which results in retardation. Thanks to widespread immunization for rubella

and premarital and prenatal blood tests for syphilis (which responds to penicillin), both of these congenital diseases are now rare.

Thyroxine deficiency, a congenital hormonal imbalance, causes cretinism, a condition marked by serious mental retardation and physical disabilities. If a pregnant woman's diet lacks iodine—now widely available in iodized salt—or if the thyroid of the fetus is damaged during birth, thyroxine deficiency will result. Mental retardation can be prevented only if the deficiency is detected and treated with thyroid extract during the first year of the infant's life.

Drugs and Other Toxins   Toxic substances taken by the mother and communicated to the fetus during pregnancy or ingested by the child during infancy or childhood can cause neurological damage and consequent retardation. One of the most common forms of poisoning associated with retardation is lead poisoning. Lead-based paint, though its use is now prohibited, is still to be found on the walls of some lower-income housing. If that paint is flaking and if the flakes, which have a sweet taste, are eaten by a child on a regular basis, lead deposits will accumulate in various tissues and interfere with brain-cell metabolism, resulting in permanent damage. Retardation is usually severe (Koch, 1971).

Drugs taken by the mother during pregnancy may also result in malformation of the fetus. The drug thalidomide, for example, produced retardation and severe limb malformation in children whose mothers took this prescription drug. Recent research (Kaminski et al., 1978) indicates that children of women who regularly drink large quantities of alcoholic beverages during pregnancy have a high incidence of retardation and of physical abnormalities.

Physical Trauma   Physical trauma may occur during childbirth or as a result of accident or child abuse. Two sources of brain damage during delivery are head injuries and hypoxia. If labor is rapid and the baby's head compresses and reexpands so quickly that it hemorrhages, or if labor is slow and high- or mid-forceps delivery injures the brain, retardation can occur. Hypoxia, or insufficient oxygenation of the baby's blood, can result if anesthesia is improperly administered, the mother is hypertensive, labor is prolonged, or the umbilical cord ruptures. Oxygen deficiency, for even short periods, can result in mental retardation. Unfortunately, physical trauma from accident or child abuse can occur at any time during infancy and childhood. Head injuries from repeated beatings, for example, can result in irreversible brain damage and retardation in a child with no congenital or birth defects.

ENVIRONMENTAL FACTORS

Among the mildly retarded—who, as we have seen, constitute the vast majority of the retarded population—the contribution of organic factors is least clear, and it is here that environmental factors are believed to have their greatest impact.

The crucial question is that of cause and effect. No one doubts that a poor environment can prevent the full development of intellectual abilities already limited by organic factors. What we do not know is whether a poor environment can be *alone or primarily* the cause of retardation. Research on human beings has definitely shown a relationship between environmental deprivation and retardation, but whether that relationship is one of cause and effect remains unclear.

Cultural-Familial Retardation

Retardation for which no organic cause can be found is widely thought to have been caused, or at least

fostered, by the home environment. This condition, called **cultural-familial retardation,** is closely related to poverty and its effects:

> The majority of the mentally retarded are the children of the more disadvantaged classes of our society. This extraordinarily heavy prevalence in certain deprived population groups suggests *a major causative role, in some way not yet fully delineated,* for adverse social, economic, and cultural factors. These conditions may not only mean absence of the physical necessities of life, but the lack of opportunity and motivation . . . (President's Panel on Mental Retardation, 1962; italics added).

According to this view, children who lack a stable home, proper parental attention and care, intellectual stimulation, and adequate language models and who are exposed to low expectations for life advancement and feelings of hopelessness and despair suffer a kind of mental impoverishment that is not organic but that is measurable with intelligence tests (Garber and McInerney, 1982). Inadequate food and lack of medical care can also, in this view, affect intellectual and adaptive functioning. For example, a child whose hearing problem goes undetected or untreated will probably learn far more slowly than his or her classmates and thus is more likely to end up among the retarded population.

The cultural-familial perspective also links severe deficits in cognitive development to an impoverished environment. Such deficits are sometimes called pseudoretardation, on the assumption that poverty-related emotional disturbances in children can cause impaired intellectual functioning (Reiss et al., 1982a). Although every aspect of poverty, including substandard housing, inferior education, and discrimination, can contribute to emotional disturbance and thus to impaired learning and the motivation to learn, it is the absence of rich verbal communication, stimulation, and variety in the households of the very poor that are thought to be most closely associated with poor intellectual development.

Verbal ability, an important component of measurable intelligence, is seldom encouraged—and may even be suppressed—in impoverished homes. Poor parents tend to talk less often to their infants than middle-class parents do to theirs (Tulkin and Kagan, 1972), a fact that almost certainly influences the child's cognitive development. The parents themselves—or the single parent—are often deficient in language and

The lack of stimulation in an impoverished home environment can inhibit verbal and cognitive development in children. As a result of such deprivation, children may be inappropriately labeled mentally retarded. (Charles Gatewood/The Image Works)

therefore unable to teach the kind of communication skills that are basic to success in the classroom. Impoverished parents tend to speak in shorter sentences, for example, and to use simpler syntax and vocabulary than their middle-class counterparts. The impoverished child not only lacks role models for appropriate verbal communication but, once in school, frequently is inattentive, so that cognitive development and learning are further deterred. Inattention may result from the child's earlier responses to the unbearable noise level in an overcrowded home: the child simply tunes out family arguments and blaring radios and TV sets. Unfortunately, the child who learns to deaden attention simply in order to survive the overload of noise at home is also learning inattention, which is extremely maladaptive in the classroom from kindergarten on. The middle-class child, by comparison, not only is more ready for the demands of school but also can selectively attend to the right verbal cues. When traffic noises contend with the teacher's instructions, for example, the verbally prepared child can screen out the honking horns, whereas the inattentive child may hear only jumbled noise.

Language development, which is basic to cognitive development and general intellectual functioning, can also be impaired by a physical environment that is barren of interesting, varied objects. After all, a vocabulary of names and relational terms requires a collection of complex objects to name and manipulate. Moreover, the disadvantaged environment may restrict a child's developing memory function by restricting stimulation. The consequences are an inability to understand time sequences and an inappropriate orientation to the present. Pseudoretarded children who enter school with these verbal and cognitive deficiencies are frequently unable to understand or speak formal English and therefore may soon be labeled mentally retarded by the school system.

The more traditional view is that living in such conditions does in fact bring about a genuine condition of retardation, not simply pseudoretardation. "Poverty, malnutrition, and mental retardation form an especially unholy trinity, with an ever-tightening chain of evidence connecting the first with the second and both with the third" (Kramer, 1976, p. 33). A diet poor in protein and vitamins has also been linked to lowered intellectual functioning (Eichenwald and Fry, 1969). Poor nutrition can produce retardation through either the mother's diet (prenatally) or the infant's diet (postnatally). Inadequate medical care is associated with an increased incidence of prematurity, illness, and other problems related to retardation.

Attitudes among the poor may also play a role here. Children of poor families tend to have lower self-esteem and more difficulty in accepting personal responsibility than do middle-class children (Ausubel and Ausubel, 1963; Battle and Rotter, 1963). These attitudinal differences are also found among adults and are reflected in child-rearing practices. Poor parents have lower expectations of success than middle-class parents and are less likely to feel that children's progress is affected by parents' efforts (Garber and McInerney, 1982). And the parents' skepticism is apparently seconded by the schools. Teachers have been shown to expect less of poor children; consequently, neither child nor teacher is motivated to try, and low achievement may become a self-fulfilling prophecy (Rosenthal and Jacobson, 1966). Thus the deprivation that begins at home usually continues at school and is compounded by the fact that the poorest school facilities of all serve the poorest neighborhoods and rural districts.

Environmental Deprivation

Institutionalization and its effects have been studied as a type of stimulation deprivation, particularly in relation to parental care. The pioneering work in this area was done by René Spitz (1945). Spitz found that children cared for in an institutional setting by professional nurses showed an average loss in developmental quotient from 124 to 72 within a year. In research done even earlier, Skeels and Dye (1938–39) found that the IQs of thirteen mentally retarded children increased an average of 27.5 points over two years after they were moved from an overcrowded orphanage to living conditions in which they became the center of attention. They also found that twelve average to dull-normal children who remained at the orphanage decreased in IQ by an average of 26.2 points during the same two years. There has been considerable debate over the meaning and methodology of both these studies. Nevertheless, more recent research has confirmed the negative impact of institutions that provide severely impoverished environments. In comparisons of children reared at home and in institutions, those who lived at home, whether retarded or not, seemed to show improved mental development, especially in language, which seems to be a prime casualty of institutionalization (Dennis, 1973). On the other hand, much seems to depend on the kind and quality of institutional care. Kibbutz children in Israel and children in well-staffed, high-quality residences seem to suffer little or no deprivation (Kohen-Raz, 1968; Moyles and Wolins, 1971).

Much research has been done with animals to determine what the effects of various types of deprivation might be. Studies have shown that rats raised with little or no stimulation show adverse effects, ranging from decreased problem-solving ability to fear of exploration to reduction in the size of the brain (DeNelsky and Dennenberg, 1967; Hebb, 1947; Rosenzweig, 1966). In one study, both brain-injured and normal rats were raised in an environment rich in stimulation; others were raised in an environment lacking stimulation. As might be expected, the normal rats did better than the brain-injured animals within each environment. A more striking finding was that the brain-injured rats raised in the "rich" environment did better than the normal animals raised in the "poor" environment (Schwartz, 1964).

Other researchers have investigated more specific types of deprivation. Using monkeys as subjects, Harlow (1964) and his co-workers studied social deprivation. They found that the most extreme form of social isolation (no contact whatever) led to severe disruption in social behavior. If the isolation was maintained through the first twelve months of life, the deficits could not be completely remedied by later experience. The longer the animals experienced social isolation, the greater the incidence of stereotyped, bizarre, and self-destructive behavior. In general, then, it seems that adequate stimulation in many areas is necessary for normal development. But just what constitutes "adequate" stimulation is far from clear.

ISSUES FOR THE FAMILY

It is now a publicly proclaimed ideal that retarded children should not be shut away as lost causes but rather kept at home, if possible, and given the opportunity to develop their potential. However, the task of raising a retarded child poses a serious challenge for the family.

Parental Reactions

Parents' reactions to the news that their child is mentally retarded vary widely, depending on such factors as individual personality, the stability of the marriage, and socioeconomic status. Some reactions, however, are extremely prevalent—namely, denial, anger, guilt, and intense disappointment. This is not the looked-forward-to child, the heir, the embodiment of hopes and dreams for the future. In consequence, parents may feel extreme ambivalence toward the child, veering between their normal impulse to love and their understandable reaction of anger and shame (Schild, 1971). Some parents view the birth of a retarded child as a punishment for "sins" on their part (Kramm, 1963). Solnet and Stark (1961) have likened the reaction to the grief felt at the death of a child. Olshansky (1962) sees the parents of a retarded child as suffering from chronic sorrow. Not all parents respond this way; much depends on their personalities and attitudes and on the quality of the professional help and advice they receive.

Some parents go from doctor to doctor, seeking additional opinions. Many professionals consider this so-called shopping behavior wasteful and destructive, since it consumes the parents' time, energy, and money—precious resources that they should be devoting to learning how to raise this special child (Anderson, 1971). Often, however, the professionals themselves contribute to "shopping" behavior. When parents have been given conflicting diagnoses, they will continue to seek a definitive opinion. Some diagnosticians may even withhold the truth intentionally, in the mistaken belief that they are sparing the parents grief or simply because they cannot bear to tell them. Kanner describes one such case:

> I once had a long-distance telephone call from a physician in a small town, who asked me to see a six-year-old boy who was markedly retarded. For several years, he had "played along" with Billy's parents, who were his personal friends. He minimized, if not ridiculed, their apprehensions. When Billy did not begin to talk long past the expected time, he reminded the parents of a cousin of his who had not talked until the age of four years but then made up for lost time and eventually graduated from high school and college. He advised: "If Billy won't talk, just don't give him the things he wants unless he asks for them verbally." When this method did not work and the parents wondered whether they should have Billy tested, he said some unkind words about "all that psychology stuff." But when Billy was to be enrolled in the first grade, the school authorities refused to accept him. The heartbroken parents were enraged at the physician who, they felt, had either been inexcusably ignorant or had knowingly betrayed their trust in him. When I saw them, they asked again and again: "Why didn't he tell us?" (1969).

In the not so distant past, physicians often advised parents to remove the retarded child to an institution *at birth*. The mother would be prevented from seeing the child, and the father, other family members, and even the family clergyman would be enlisted to persuade her that this was best for the child (Aldrich, 1947). Given the continuing prevalence of negative and stigmatic attitudes about mental retardation, many parents are probably still advised to consider residential placement as a primary alternative by professionals who emphasize the "hopelessness" of the child's condition and the "burden" his or her care will mean for the family. Such advice, especially when presented to parents who have not yet accepted or adjusted to the situation, can have devastating effects on all concerned: "Considerable pain and lasting damage can be inflicted by insensitive counselors who abruptly announce a diagnosis or give professional advice characterized by a lack of respect for the parents and for the child" (Robinson and Robinson, 1976, p. 415).

Parents who are given reliable, honest information about the child's condition and who have the support of committed professionals will have a far easier time adjusting to their problems and dealing with them. Family disruption will be minimized, and resources can be concentrated on doing the best that can be done for the child and for the family as a unit.

Child-Rearing Problems

Current approaches favor an effort to care for the retarded child (even the profoundly retarded child) within the community. The family is encouraged to manage and rear the child at home. Parents who assume the responsibility for the day-to-day care of a retarded child inevitably have many questions about child-rearing techniques. Furthermore, the presence of a retarded child in the home puts strains on the family. If parents are to raise a retarded child at home, they need supportive training and counseling.

The retarded child, of course, has many of the same needs as a normal child: to be fed and kept warm, clean, and dry; to be loved and cuddled and played with; to be given structure, discipline, and training in keeping with his or her abilities. Like normal children, retarded youngsters must have social interaction with other children and with adults in order to develop interpersonal skills. Again like normal children, they need to be encouraged to be as independent as possible. But the retarded child does have special needs and problems. The child may suffer from physical handicaps. Learning will be slower and achievement more limited. The child may experience social rejection and be subjected to ridicule. Some recent efforts to teach parents simple behavioral techniques that can be used at home in the early years (Baroff, 1974) have benefited both child and parents. Reinforcing attempts at speech and rewarding the attainment of new steps in complex behaviors such as

Retarded children have many of the same needs as normal children. They need to be given opportunities to learn, for example, and to be encouraged to be as independent as possible. (Leonard Speier)

eating or using the toilet can make parents feel they are doing something concrete to help their child.

The retarded adolescent presents additional concerns to family and community. Parents must deal with sensitive issues and must walk a narrow line between the child's need for independence and his or her lack of maturity. They must help the child to deal with physical changes, with sexual feelings, with threats to self-esteem (an especially difficult task if the child is aware of being "different"), and with interaction with members of the opposite sex and a peer group that is outgrowing him or her. The extent to which these problems become an issue depends, of course, on the level of retardation. They are of greatest concern for parents of mildly and moderately retarded individuals.

Problems for the Retarded Adult

As the adolescent nears adulthood, family and community must consider carefully the extent to which he or she will be able to live independently. Although parents may be confident of their ability to provide for a young retarded child, they become uneasy when they think about the stresses and demands placed on the retarded adult. One of the most complex issues is that of sex and marriage.

Historically, attitudes toward the mentally retarded person's sexual development have favored complete desexualization, physically, intellectually, and emotionally (Perske, 1973). It was incorrectly believed that the mentally retarded had abnormal sex drives—that they were likely to be child molesters, for example. Any relationships between retarded men and women were discouraged, and involuntary sterilization was common. Today a more humane approach is taken. The trend is toward the belief that each retarded individual has the right to sexual development and that he or she can be taught sexual behavior appropriate to his or her level of functioning. In keeping with this trend, state laws prohibiting marriage for the retarded and permitting sterilization without consent are being challenged (Krischef, 1972).

Severely retarded adults are often incapable of a long-term relationship with a person of the opposite sex. But with proper guidance and supervision, mildly or moderately retarded adults can have emotional and/or sexual relationships without destructive consequences (Perske, 1973). Some programs exist to teach retarded young adults "dating skills": how to ask for and accept a date, how to behave appropriately in a social situation, and so on. Those who are able to maintain a social relationship should demonstrate a certain amount of self-sufficiency before contemplating marriage. Studies show that with some support and assistance from families or social agencies, many mildly retarded people are able to marry and maintain themselves as functioning units in society (Andron and Strum, 1973).

Emotional Disturbance

Most parents undertaking the job of raising a retarded child are better prepared to deal with the child's intellectual and adaptive deficits than with the emotional difficulties that often accompany them. Retarded people suffer the full range of emotional disturbances found in nonretarded people (Szymanski and Tanguay, 1980), but with higher frequency (Phillips and Williams, 1975). Mild disturbances, such as nonassertiveness, inadequate self-confidence, and low-level depression, are especially common. Serious disorders, such as schizophrenia, alcoholism, and severe behavioral problems, are rarer but still occur in as many as 10 to 20 percent of the retarded population.

Why are retarded people more subject to emotional disturbance than the nonretarded? A likely reason is simply their social position: the fact that many people prefer to avoid them, that even those who care for them often treat them like children long after they have reached adulthood, that they must watch others succeed where they themselves fail, that they cannot have the same privileges as others. The day when a retarded teenager sees his younger brother come home with a driver's license—something that he himself can never have—can be a bitter one, and the cumulative impact of these small, day-to-day sorrows can have grave emotional consequences.

The reaction may take many forms. Some retarded people become depressed, while others strike back angrily. Still others escape into a fantasy world, becoming sufficiently withdrawn to be labeled schizophrenic. Such problems may be closely linked to the person's intellectual deficits, but in many cases it is clear that the emotional problem is the result of an intellectual *strength*—that is, the person's painfully accurate perception of his or her social handicaps—rather than of intellectual weakness.

The mental health needs of retarded people are often overlooked, partly as a result of what is called "diagnostic overshadowing" (Reiss et al., 1982b). Just as a 6-inch line, when set alongside a 12-inch line, can look smaller than it actually is, so the emotional difficulties of retarded people can easily be overshadowed by their more obvious intellectual and adaptive problems, with the result that the emotional component is never dealt with. In recognition of this

Working around the house. A certain amount of self-sufficiency is important before marriage is contemplated, but studies show that with assistance, retarded people are able to marry and maintain themselves in society. (Leonard Speier)

shortcoming, researchers are now giving closer attention to the emotional and social behavior of retarded people, and recent years have seen the establishment of several model mental health programs for retarded children and adults (Reiss et al., 1982b). (See the accompanying box, which discusses the dual diagnosis of mental retardation and emotional disorder.)

SOCIETY AND MENTAL RETARDATION

In the past twenty-five years there have been tremendous changes in the field of mental retardation. To begin with, parent groups—above all the National Association for Retarded Citizens (NARC), founded in 1950—have vigorously lobbied federal and state gov-

Dual Diagnosis

Many mentally retarded people have the added burden of mild to severe emotional disorders. Although some counseling programs have been successful in helping retarded children and adults to cope with stress, depressive symptoms, and low self-esteem, many other dually diagnosed individuals remain institutionalized without proper treatment, and deinstitutionalized retarded adults who require mental health care may not get it. Too many community mental health centers are either uninterested or too poorly staffed to address their needs.

Disorders that are often seen in mentally retarded persons include depression, schizophrenia, antisocial behavior, and such personality problems as the mismanagement of anger, social discomfort, and lack of self-confidence. Steven Reiss (1985) estimates that 15 to 20 percent of mentally retarded people suffer from emotional disturbances. They not only are disproportionately affected by psychological disorders but have more difficulty than nonretarded people in adjusting to everyday stress. However, mentally retarded people with IQs over 50 show symptoms of disorder that are similar to symptoms of people with normal intelligence. Depressed mentally retarded patients, for example, report the same clinically expected symptoms: on the emotional level, they feel sad and lonely; on the cognitive level, they blame themselves and have difficulty making decisions; on the physical level, they suffer from sleep disturbances and loss of appetite. Mentally retarded people are very much at risk for the mood disorders (Sovner and Hurley, 1983; Reid, 1972a, 1972b). Fortunately, new measures for diagnosing depression in mentally retarded adults have been developed (Kadzin et al., 1983), and a recent study has found that their depression is strongly associated with the lack of social support they experience and their poor social skills (Reiss and Benson, 1985).

Although it is generally agreed that psychoanalysis is not effective in treating dually diagnosed people, other therapies work very well. For example, Prouty (1976) and his colleagues have developed a method called pretherapy, which is based on Carl Rogers' client-centered therapy. Matson has shown that training dually diagnosed retarded people to improve their social skills helps relieve symptoms of depression and a wide range of other problems. Benson has applied cognitive therapy in teaching anger-management techniques to mentally retarded adults.

Despite the availability of effective therapies, dually diagnosed people still have difficulty finding the services they need, whether in state institutions, where there are still too few special residential units, or in outpatient programs, where not enough support is given through community-based mental health facilities. A major problem is that the dually diagnosed fall through a crack in the service-delivery system—between the agencies that serve mentally retarded people and those that serve the mentally ill. Efforts of concerned mental health professionals today are therefore aimed at educating their colleagues about the need to provide services for the "whole person" (Reiss et al., 1982a) and encouraging the public at large to respond with increased sensitivity to the special problems of dually diagnosed children and adults.

---

ernments and have obtained, in consequence, not only large increases in funding but also legislation guaranteeing the right of retarded people to a free education geared to their abilities. Second, these same parent organizations, along with other advocacy groups, have increasingly taken their grievances to the federal and state courts, whose decisions have substantially altered the treatment of retarded people in this country. Finally, the number of professionals in the field of mental retardation has expanded greatly, a reflection of the discovery that retarded people respond well to behavior therapy. This finding generated a new mood of hope, attracting to the field a large number of young clinical psychologists. At the same time, several university-affiliated centers for training and research have been established to train these professionals and teach them to work in interdisciplinary teams.

Public Policy

This new activism has brought about sweeping changes in public policy toward mentally retarded people. Whereas retarded people once were truly third-class citizens, today certain principles have been established which, though by no means fully put into practice, are nevertheless guiding public institutions toward granting full citizens' rights to the retarded population. There are five basic principles. First, the principle of *independent living* holds that services for retarded people must be designed to enable them to live with the maximum independence possible as productive members of the society. Second, the principle of *individual programming* requires that services for retarded people be tailored to the individual—what he or she needs and can do—rather than based on textbook descriptions of the capabilities of retarded people. Third is the principle of *timely progress reviews*—a mentally retarded person, once routed into a given program, should not be left there indefinitely but should have his or her progress evaluated regularly, with at least one comprehensive medical, psychological, and educational review per year. Fourth, the principle of *normalization* asserts that life circumstances for the retarded person should be as nearly like those of nonretarded people as possible. Insofar as possible, services should be provided by the person's own community. For example, the education of mentally retarded children should be handled by the local school district, not the state institution. Finally, the principle of *human rights,* already implied in the other four, affirms that as human beings, retarded people have the right to be protected against abuse, whether physical or verbal, to receive a free and appropriate education, to be given treatment if they are institutionalized, and to live in the least restrictive environment consistent with their handicaps.

Institutionalization

The movement for institutional care of the mentally retarded began in a spirit of great hope and optimism. Edouard Seguin (1866), the driving force behind the establishment of state and private training schools, saw these facilities as links in the chain of common schools. His idea was that retarded people could be sent, temporarily, to institutions to be trained, and then returned to their homes and communities as more successful, contributing citizens. Optimism dwindled somewhat when it became apparent that not all students could return to the community. Indeed, comparatively few ever left the training schools. By 1890, long-term custodial care of the retarded had become the major function of the state institutions

(Fernald, 1893). Still, the emphasis was on training, on developing new ways of preparing retarded persons for a more self-sufficient life, and on establishing new programs that enabled retarded persons to board out and work in special industries. Such programs, it was hoped, would lead to the return of greater numbers of the mentally handicapped to the community.

By the second decade of the twentieth century, the increased financial burden of a greatly enlarged institutional population, along with an extremely naive notion of genetics, brought this hopeful era to a sad end. Soon after the turn of the century, various authorities, including the British Royal Commission, had been suggesting that mental retardation might be transmitted genetically. But it was not until 1912, with the publication of Henry H. Goddard's famous study *The Kallikak Family,* that this idea began to achieve wide acceptance. In his treatise, Goddard, the director of a school for the "feeble-minded," traced the family tree of a young girl in his school—a history that in his view constituted conclusive evidence of the genetic basis of retardation:

> How do we account for this kind of individual? The answer is in a word "Heredity,"—bad stock. We must recognize that the human family shows varying stocks or strains that are as marked and that breed as true as anything in plant or animal life (p. 12).

The solution, obviously, was selective breeding: mentally retarded people should be segregated from the society and sterilized, so as not to pollute healthy stock. Of course, we know today that the "feeble-mindedness" that Goddard saw in the Kallikak family could well have had nothing whatever to do with heredity.

With the spread of the "bad stock" idea, interest in the education of retarded people, and consequently the funding for such education, rapidly diminished, for why spend money training these people if they are not going to return to the community? There followed a long period of dismal custodial care, with thousands of retarded people living lives that were at best idle and forgotten and at worst utterly deplorable.

In many parts of the country this period is only now coming to an end. The change is due in part to the publication in the 1960s of a number of exposés with shocking pictures and accounts of life in the institutions. More lasting have been the effects of two other developments of the same period. First was the adoption of the concept of normalization: the idea that the life circumstances (treatment, housing, etc.) of the retarded should be as nearly like those of nonretarded people as possible. This concept, introduced in the late sixties, not only has forced an improvement in the handling of retarded people but also reflects and encourages a new attitude, expressed by Chambers:

> Mentally retarded people are people. When strong reasons exist to treat them differently from other people, they should be provided the necessary services, restraint, or protection through means that intrude as little as possible on their freedom to live the life that others are permitted to live (1976, p. 486).

The second important development has been a series of court decisions with regard to the mentally disabled, particularly *Wyatt* v. *Stickney* in 1972. *Wyatt* v. *Stickney* (to be discussed further in Chapter 22) was a class-action suit filed on behalf of a retarded boy, Ricky Wyatt, who was living at the Partlow State School in Alabama. However, its real purpose was to challenge the state's right to house mentally retarded people (and mentally disturbed people in general) against their will in horrible circumstances, and then to offer them no treatment for the condition that presumably necessitated their institutionalization. The court ruled that when a person is involuntarily institutionalized, he or she has a constitutional right to treatment. This decision has not utterly revolutionized the treatment of the mentally retarded, as many had hoped. Indeed, it has been challenged by later rulings. Still, it set a crucial precedent, forcing states to reevaluate their institutions for the retarded, to release some patients, and to create humane treatment programs for those who could not be released.

Residential Alternatives

The release of patients from state institutions has been made possible by one of the most important developments in public policy in regard to mentally retarded people: the expansion of residential alternatives to institutionalization. Until recently, families had to choose between two extremes: the retarded family member either stayed at home or was sent away to a large institution. In the sixties, however, communities began to recognize the need for intermediate residential arrangements. The guiding principle of this development is to place the retarded person in the least restrictive environment consistent with his or her handicaps. In other words, the person should be subject to no restraints or supervisory attentions that are not truly necessary.

Today there are several different kinds of residential arrangements for retarded people, at carefully spaced levels of restrictiveness. Many mildly retarded adults with independent-living skills and jobs live in their own apartments, with no restraints at all. Other mildly retarded people live in small group homes called **supported living arrangements (SLAs),** where supervision is generally provided only in the evening. Many moderately retarded people, along with mildly retarded people who have behavioral or emotional problems, live in **community living facilities (CLFs),** small to medium-size residential centers with round-the-clock supervision. For many severely retarded people, the appropriate choice may be the **intermediate care facility (ICF),** a nursing home located in a community setting and ideally providing close supervision. (Unfortunately, many ICFs have proved to offer less than ideal care in practice. Often they are little more than institutions located within the community.) Finally, the state institution, the most restrictive placement, is still the usual choice for profoundly retarded people.

As increasing numbers of SLAs, CLFs, and ICFs are being established, more and more mildly and moderately retarded people are being moved out of the state institutions and into these facilities. This is an extremely heartening development. Large institutions, as we have seen in previous chapters, can have damaging effects on the people they are supposed to care for, not only because so many of them offer dreary and even cruel living conditions but, in a subtler sense, because they do not allow patients to use the skills they have. Those skills, consequently, tend to disappear. The great virtue of the residential alternatives for retarded people is that they challenge and encourage residents actually to use and develop their coping abilities.

Employment

New federal and state laws provide that retarded people must have opportunities for useful employment, whether or not in the types of jobs nonretarded

Exclusionary Zoning and the Mentally Disabled

In July, 1980, a building in Cleburne, Texas was purchased for development as a group home for thirteen mentally retarded men and women. The city then told the developer that under local zoning laws, a group home for the retarded could not be operated at that site without a special use permit. The developer applied for such a permit, but the city council denied it. The developer then sued the city in federal court, claiming that exclusion of the mentally retarded was a violation of the constitutional guarantee of equal protection of the law.

Ultimately, the case reached the U.S. Supreme Court, which in 1985 decided that the zoning ordinance was unconstitutional as applied to the particular facility in question (*City of Cleburne* v. *Cleburne Living Center,* 105 S.Ct. 3249). The Court determined that the exclusion of the proposed group home was not based on any legitimate governmental interest. Instead, the Court found that the exclusion was simply a manifestation of "irrational prejudice" against the mentally retarded. The Court came to this conclu-sion because the zoning law that excluded the proposed group home *permitted* apartment houses, fraternity and sorority houses, dormitories, hospitals, and nursing homes. The city could not explain why a group home for the retarded would cause any more noise, traffic, or other disturbance than the fraternity houses, apartment houses, hospitals, etc., that were permitted in that district. By eliminating any rational basis for the exclusion, the Court deduced that irrational prejudice must be the motivation for the exclusion. The U.S. Constitution's equal protection clause does not permit laws which are nothing but manifestations of such prejudice.

The *Cleburne* case does not invalidate all zoning ordinances excluding homes for the mentally disabled, however. It was a narrow decision based on the specific facts of that case. Nevertheless, zoning obstacles to the development of group homes will surely be easier to overcome as a result of the *Cleburne* decision.

---

people hold. In practice, this means that whatever their residential placement, retarded people must be offered planned daytime programs. In the case of severely and profoundly retarded people, such daytime activities may be very simple, but many mildly retarded people and some moderately retarded people do hold paying jobs, some in ordinary work environments, others in special work centers, called **sheltered workshops,** tailored to their needs.

It has long been assumed that retarded people belong to America's socioeconomic surplus population—that most of them either can't or don't want to work or, if they do work, that they are the first to lose their jobs when the payroll is being cut. Recent information suggests that this is no longer the case. Studies show that many, if not most, retarded people do want to work (Friedman, 1976). Furthermore, when properly placed, they make good employees and consequently are not necessarily the first to be fired when jobs become scarce (Halpern, 1973). Interestingly, research also indicates that when they are fired, it is often not because of a failure to do the job, but because of a lack of social skills—talking too much or too little, for example, or saying the wrong things in the wrong situations. Greenspan and Shoultz, in their study of this problem, cite the following example:

> This incident involved a mildly mentally retarded woman who worked as a chambermaid in a large hotel. She was under considerable pressure to clean a certain number of rooms per day and was frustrated, therefore, when guests would sleep late. Her way of coping with this dilemma was to bang on a guest's door and say, "All right, get your fucking ass out of bed." Not surprisingly, this behavior was reported and the client was fired (1981, pp. 32–33).

The problem, in other words, was not a lack of attention to the job she was assigned to do, but a failure to appreciate the subtle social rules surrounding that job. The obvious conclusion is that vocational training for retarded people must cover social skills as well as vocational skills—and training programs now tend to include them.

These formerly institutionalized retarded people now work at Riverside Industries. Retarded people make good employees, but their job training must teach social skills as well as vocational skills. (Lionel J.M. Delevigne/Stock, Boston)

PREVENTION AND TREATMENT

One of the most significant developments in the field of mental retardation is the idea that treatment can make a decisive difference in the lives of mentally retarded persons. Whereas early detection of chromosomal and congenital abnormalities is available to help couples at risk and expectant parents, who may then seek counseling about the pregnancy, the new hope in the therapeutic community is to improve the quality of life of mentally retarded and pseudoretarded children and adults. The most promising results have been found in the areas of early intervention, education, behavior therapy, and counseling.

Prevention

Genetic analysis and counseling constitute a major breakthrough in the prevention of mental retardation. Couples at risk for abnormal births can be identified, informed of the risk, and advised how to proceed. The gene for Tay-Sachs disease, for example, occurs in about one of every thirty people of Eastern European Jewish descent. If one carrier marries another, their chances of having a child with the disease are one in four. A simple blood test can identify carriers, who can then get advice from a genetic counselor.

Genetic analysis can also identify abnormalities in the developing fetus. If Down's syndrome or another abnormality is detected by amniocentesis, the parents may choose to terminate the pregnancy. Amniocentesis is now routinely recommended for mothers over the age of thirty-five.

Early Intervention

When a child already has a condition that could lead to retardation, early intervention can do much to minimize its effects. We have already described several medical procedures that fall under this heading, including low-phenylalanine diets for PKU children and thyroid treatments for infants with missing or damaged thyroid glands. Remedial efforts also include psychological therapies. In infant stimulation therapy, for example, babies who are mentally handicapped (e.g., Down's syndrome children) or who seem at high risk for retardation (e.g., children of poor, low-IQ mothers) are played with intensively several hours a day to stimulate their language acquisition, problem-solving skills, and achievement motivation. Most infant stimulation programs also train the mother in techniques for fostering the child's development (Pines, 1982a).

Infant stimulation programs capitalize on the extraordinary flexibility of the very young brain. Parents do most of the teaching, aided and guided by a special-education teacher, a physical therapist, a speech/

language therapist, a social worker, an occupational therapist, and other child-development specialists who observe the child periodically at home or in a school setting, and who suggest and demonstrate activities to be added to the child's regimen (Brody, 1982a).

The key to the children's development is the amount of stimulation, exercise, and encouragement they receive as they strive to master the mental, physical, emotional, and social skills that come more easily to nonretarded youngsters. In its earliest stages, infant stimulation sharpens the child's senses by exposing him or her to different sounds, sights, colors, textures, and tastes. Special attention paid to the development of motor skills enables the youngster to achieve some physical independence.

Infant stimulation activities may be as simple as mothers talking to and making eye contact with their babies. Mothers may aid the babies' fine-motor coordination by providing pegs, puzzles, and other objects to pick up and manipulate. They may encourage use of the long muscles (Down's syndrome children are often strikingly "loose jointed" and have poor muscle tone), helping the babies sit up and lift their heads. Activities and equipment become more sophisticated as the child progresses. Many "graduates" of early intervention programs are able to feed and dress themselves, talk fluently, and participate in most children's activities. Some have learned to read and have acquired other academic skills (Pines, 1982a).

Unfortunately, only a small fraction of the children who need help have access to early intervention. Funds for such programs are scarce, and not all parents have the time, stamina, and patience needed for such an intensive commitment. A typical early intervention program requires that someone work with the child four or five mornings a week, year round, for two and a half years, at which time the child should be ready for a preschool program.

Education

For many years mentally retarded children were essentially excluded from the public school system. Then, in the early seventies, decisions in a number of class-action suits required that local school systems provide special education for retarded children. Finally, in 1975, this requirement became effective nationwide when Congress passed Public Law 94–142, guaranteeing to every citizen under the age of twenty-

one a free public education appropriate to his or her needs.

P.L. 94–142 has been responsible for a great increase in special-education programs since the late seventies. These programs are carefully tailored to the individual, in keeping with the requirement that public education be "appropriate" to each child's needs. Typically, the school system will have what is called an individualized education program (IEP). The school holds a multidisciplinary conference to identify the handicaps of children requesting special education and to review the progress of those already receiving such services. The committee then formulates, in writing, an IEP for each child, and the appropriate services are provided.

The new law has stimulated some highly innovative thinking. One concept, for example, is the "cascade system." Nine educational programs, beginning with a regular classroom in a regular school and ending with a hospital setting, are designed to accommodate individual needs and to provide for progression from one level to another. Upward mobility is the goal, and it is to be achieved by constant periodic evaluation, so that assignment to a particular cascade level does not become a life sentence. Many retarded children, given modified tasks, can stay in the regular classroom and thus remain with their peers. Other children may spend part of the school day in the regular class and part in a special class. Children who need more help and guidance may attend a special day school or live in a residential school. At all levels, the emphasis is on individual programs tailored to each child's needs and modified continuously as the child develops.

Such programs, however, are by no means the norm. Though P.L. 94–142 mandates special education for all handicapped children, Congress has not provided full funding for the implementation of the new law, and many communities have been unable or unwilling to find the necessary funds. Some school districts have raised local taxes to pay for special education, but others are still taking their time about putting the law into practice. Furthermore, recent court decisions have raised some questions regarding the extent of the services that school systems must provide. A case in point is *Board of Education of the Hendrick Hudson School District* v. *Rowley,* involving a deaf girl whose request for a sign-language interpreter as part of her IEP was rejected by the school district. Deciding in favor of the school district, the U.S. Supreme Court ruled that while P.L. 94–142 requires that handicapped children be given a "basic floor of opportunity" in the education system, it does not specify the *level* of education to be provided. In other words, beyond a certain point it is up to the school district to determine how special the special-education program will be. The *Rowley* decision, combined with current economic pressures, suggests that full implementation of P.L. 94–142 will be a long and gradual process, with a number of lawsuits along the way.

Behavior Therapy

Of all the new programs and services for the retarded, almost none has generated more enthusiasm than the application of learning principles to training and behavior management. Behavioral techniques are being used extensively and with good success in the home, in schools and workshops, in institutional settings, and with both children and adults. They can be taught to parents, teachers, therapists, and hospital staffs, and they can be used for a variety of purposes.

The three basic techniques of behavior therapy are shaping (reinforcing successive approximations of desirable behavior), chaining (teaching the person to finish the task and then gradually expanding the number of steps required to finish), and stimulus control (teaching that a behavior should occur in some situations but not in others). These methods have proved extremely successful in the training of retarded people in many areas, including verbal behaviors, academic learning, classroom social behaviors (e.g., sitting and talking only at the appropriate time), self-care behaviors, social skills, and work habits such as promptness and task completion. In early childhood, one of the most important applications has been language acquisition (Grabowski and Thompson, 1977). Research into patterns of language acquisition by both normal and retarded children has yielded information that has allowed for the construction of step-by-step behavioral sequences to teach both speech and comprehension among the mentally retarded. Another area in which behavior therapy has been very useful is the counseling of parents of young retarded children. With relatively brief training, parents can learn how to teach their children academic subjects at home, how to shape the children's behavior, and how to structure the family living situation in the best way possible for the child. In middle childhood years and in adoles-

cence, behavioral techniques are useful in teaching children to read, to use the toilet, to behave appropriately in play and peer-interaction situations, and to learn appropriate sexual behaviors.

In daytime adult programs, behavior therapy has been quite successful in teaching retarded people the vocational and social skills necessary for holding a job. Often tasks or settings that seem too complicated for a retarded person can in fact be mastered given appropriate teaching techniques. Token economies have been especially successful in vocational training programs, improving job performance rates (Rusch and Mithaug, 1980) and on-the-job social behavior (Eilbracht and Thompson, 1977), and inculcating work habits such as arriving on time, punching in and out, and taking breaks and lunch periods at the right times.

For more severely retarded individuals, especially those confined to institutions, behavior therapy is considered one of the most appropriate and effective techniques (Grabowski and Thompson, 1977; Matson and Andrasik, 1982). It has been used in teaching self-help skills (Watson and Uzzell, 1981) and in decreasing hyperactivity (Alabiso, 1975) and self-destructive behavior (Favell, 1982). The results, for both patients and staff, can be startling. Incontinence, for example, is a persistent problem in institutions for the severely retarded. Cleaning up not only consumes most of the staff's time but makes assignment to these wards undesirable, so that patients receive little friendly attention from the staff. Furthermore, patients who are incontinent generally cannot leave the ward. Toilet training not only improves the patients' hygiene and comfort and promotes positive interactions with the staff but opens new worlds; toilet-trained people can go out of the ward to other parts of the building or onto the grounds for outdoor recreation (McCartney and Holden, 1981).

The behavioral perspective's recent emphasis on cognitive behavior therapy is also reflected in treatment for the retarded. Thus even moderately retarded children have been successfully taught to delay rewards (Franzini et al., 1980) and to monitor their own behavior in order to achieve self-control (Litrownik et al., 1978).

Counseling

As we saw earlier, mentally retarded people not only suffer the same kinds of emotional disorders that affect nonretarded people but are more likely to experience emotional disorders and are less able to cope with stress. For these reasons, many mentally retarded children and adults can benefit from counseling.

Counselors who treat mentally retarded clients recognize that their patients are often painfully aware of their own limitations and may try to hide them from the therapist. Some of the negative social conditions that contribute to a mentally retarded person's depressive symptoms and low self-esteem are rejection and ridicule, segregation from peers of normal intelligence, restricted opportunities, and infantilization (Reiss, 1985). The therapist or counselor also recognizes that the mentally retarded patient is usually unskilled in verbal communication and may lapse into silence for fear of being rejected. The patient, however, may interpret the therapist's silence as disapproving or critical of the patient's thoughts and feelings. Because mentally retarded patients who need help in coping with stress or require treatment for emotional disorders also have shorter attention spans than nonretarded patients, they may benefit from visits that are briefer and more frequent than the traditional hour-long sessions. Thus flexibility both in the therapeutic approach and in the treatment schedule is the first requirement for success.

Recent directives for counseling mentally retarded clients focus on the tasks of the initial interview, in which the patient's needs are assessed and appropriate therapy is chosen (Hurley and Hurley, 1986). These tasks include identifying the client's problem, assessing his or her level of cognitive functioning, and explaining what the client can expect during therapy. During the interview the clinician reassures the patient by clearly explaining the purpose of the meeting. Because many mentally retarded patients have been shuttled between service agencies in the past, they may be reluctant to express their emotional difficulties for fear that they are being sent to the new therapist for punishment. The counselor therefore tries to create a positive attitude and win the client's trust. In assessing cognitive ability, the therapist avoids threatening questions, such as "Did you understand what I just said?" and instead encourages the client to give his or her version of an idea or remark. Responsive listening is especially helpful to mentally retarded patients preparing for therapy. Rather than merely listening in silence, the therapist acknowledges the client's feelings, saying, for example, "You felt very bad when you lost the bus ticket" or "You wanted your sister to praise you." These methods, as well as gestures such as offering toys or refresh-

ments, can help counselors communicate with their retarded clients.

SUMMARY

The judgment of mental retardation depends on the standards of a given society; therefore, we have no universally accepted definition of mental retardation and no absolute statistics on its prevalence.

According to the most accepted definition, that of the American Association on Mental Deficiency, *mental retardation* refers to subaverage intellectual functioning coupled with deficits in adaptive behavior for a person's age or developmental level. The AAMD delineates four levels of retardation describing the degree of limitation and what it means for an individual's potential in society. These four levels—mild, moderate, severe, and profound—are based on standard intelligence test scores and estimates of adaptive behavior.

The category of mild retardation encompasses nearly 90 percent of all those labeled retarded. As adults the mildly retarded can often lead productive lives, provided they have some help. Moderately retarded people are those who can learn to care for themselves but are not fully independent. Severely retarded people require considerable supervision; they lack basic language and number skills, but can learn some self-care skills and can perform some tasks in a sheltered environment. Profoundly retarded people can sometimes learn to carry out some self-care activities and perform some tasks, but will always require supervision, in part because they experience great difficulty in speaking.

The major system of classifying mental retardation is provided by the AAMD manual, which covers both causation and function. The biomedical system of classification focuses on organic causes of retardation, as indicated by medical findings and medical history. It recognizes ten major categories of physical disorders. The functional system focuses on behavior, comparing an individual's intellectual and adaptive functions with age-appropriate norms for the general population. The functional system is essentially descriptive and is used to develop remedial programs; it is limited in that it says little about causation, and the measuring tools necessary for its use are far from exact. A correlation of the biomedical system and the functional system indicates that the lower the level of functioning, the higher the probability of organic impairment.

Many organic or genetic anomalies are associated with retardation, though the actual process by which they cause retardation is seldom understood. Five major syndromes consist of chromosomal anomalies, metabolic disturbances, congenital infections, reactions to toxins, and the results of physical trauma.

Environmental factors are believed to have the greatest causative role in mild retardation, but the effects of environmental factors are not entirely clear. Cultural-familial retardation is believed to be fostered by poverty and its effects—parental neglect or instability, absence or suppression of verbal communication, lack of stimulation, and physical conditions, such as inadequate housing, nutrition, or medical care. Institutionalization has also been studied as a type of stimulation deprivation contributing to retardation.

In recent years, changing attitudes, new legislation, and the development of new facilities and programs have greatly extended opportunities to mentally retarded people. It is now believed that retarded children should be helped to grow up at home whenever possible. Raising a retarded child poses a significant challenge to the family. Parental reactions to the diagnosis that a child is retarded are highly individual, but they usually include denial, anger, guilt, and intense disappointment. Such emotions, coexisting with feelings of love, typically result in extreme ambivalence toward the child. Uncertainties in the diagnosis often add to the parents' problems. It appears that families adjust best if they are given reliable, honest information and the help of committed professionals. In the child's early years, parents can use simple behavioral techniques to teach eating and self-care behaviors. Parents must help the mildly or moderately retarded adolescent to cope with physical changes, sexual feelings, and peer relationships. In adulthood, the concern of the community and family determines the extent to which the retarded person can function independently. It is now believed that many mildly retarded people can marry and maintain themselves, with some support and assistance.

Recent legislation at the federal and state levels recognizes that the retarded person has needs and rights similar to those of other members of society. Five basic principles now serve as guides for public institutions and agencies providing services: (1) retarded people should be helped to achieve independent living; (2) they should receive individual programming, with (3) timely progress reviews. (4) The principle of normalization asserts that the retarded should be treated as normally as possible and that services should be provided by the person's own community; finally, (5) the principle of human rights affirms that retarded people have rights, such as the right to a free and appropriate education, and the right to live in the least restrictive environment appropriate to their capabilities.

The principle of normalization, especially, has led to release of many retarded people from institutions, and to the development of various kinds of residential arrangements for retarded people, among them supported living arrangements, community living facilities, and intermediate care facilities. Legislation has had a similarly beneficial effect on the education of mentally retarded children; many retarded children are now served by special-education programs within local public school systems. Behavioral techniques are being used successfully with both children and adults in a wide variety of settings. Based on the conditioning principles of reinforcement and extinction, behavioral techniques are considered among the most effective ways of treating severely retarded people. Since recent legislation requires that retarded persons have opportunities for useful employment, many retarded adults hold jobs, either in ordinary work environments or in sheltered workshops. Recent findings show that retarded people want to work and that when properly placed they make good employees.

Efforts are being made to prevent mental retardation (for example, through genetic counseling and improved prenatal care) and to minimize the effect of retardation when it occurs (for example, through infant stimulation programs).

Dually diagnosed people have special needs for mental health care. Current studies suggest that such nonpsychoanalytic therapies as pretherapy and client-centered therapy significantly improve the life chances of mentally retarded children and adults who have psychological disorders.

PART 7

Dealing with Disorder

CHAPTER 20

Approaches to Treatment: Individual Psychotherapy

Centuries ago, when people had spells of depression or problems within their families, they might go to a relative or perhaps a priest and receive some sympathy and a dose of conventional wisdom. Today, while many people still take their problems to friends, relatives, members of the clergy, or even bartenders (see the box on page 491), many others turn to professional counselors. For in the last half-century the therapeutic function of church and family has been turned over, in large measure, to the institution of psychotherapy.

A succinct but comprehensive definition of **psychotherapy** has been offered by Lewis Wolberg:

Psychotherapy is the treatment, by psychological means, of problems of an emotional nature in which a trained person deliberately establishes a professional relationship with the patient with the object of (1) removing, modifying, or retarding existing symptoms, (2) mediating disturbed patterns of behavior, and (3) promoting positive personality growth and development (1977, p. 3).

Psychotherapy often includes the same kind of comfort and advice that we get from our friends, but it differs in that it involves a formal relationship and, furthermore, a business relationship. In addition, many forms of psychotherapy aspire to the level of science. That is, they claim to be based upon, and aim to contribute to, the accumulation of empirically verifiable laws of behavior—a goal undreamed of by our friends and relatives.

In this chapter and the next, we shall describe the major current approaches to the treatment of abnormal behavior. Chapter 21 will cover group and community therapies, along with biological treatment; the present chapter will cover individual psychotherapy, in its psychodynamic, humanistic-existential, and behavioral forms. First, however, we shall briefly consider the institution of psychotherapy as a whole.

THE DIVERSITY OF PSYCHOTHERAPIES

Though it is possible to frame a one-sentence definition of psychotherapy, this term actually encompasses an immense variety of techniques, ranging from dream analysis to reading assignments to instructions for talking back to rude waiters. Therapists differ in their professional training, in their conception of the therapist's role, and in their personal "styles." The result is a vast assortment of therapeutic approaches.

Two differences deserve special attention. The first has to do with the basic approach to bringing about change in the client's behavior. London (1964) divides psychotherapy into two categories: insight therapy and action therapy. **Insight therapy** is based on the theory that behavior problems arise when people fail to understand the motives underlying their actions, and especially when they refuse to confront conflicts between different motives. Accordingly, the goal of insight therapy, as the name indicates, is to increase patients' awareness of why they do what they do, the assumption being that once they understand their behavior, they will be able to control it better. In **action therapy,** on the other hand, there is little or no discussion of motives. The therapist focuses directly on the patient's problem behavior and attempts to correct it by teaching the patient new skills. We have already seen numerous examples of both of these kinds of therapy. Psychodynamic therapy and humanistic-existential therapy, in their classic forms, are insight therapies, differing only in the kinds of insights at which they aim. Behavioral therapy, on the other hand, is generally action therapy. As we shall see later in this chapter, there is a growing

trend toward integration of these two approaches, with each school now willing to learn from the successes of the other. Nevertheless, as a matter of emphasis, the difference between insight and action therapies is still quite valid.

Another important distinction has to do with the scientific status of psychotherapy. Some therapists regard psychotherapy as an applied science, in which one can achieve a predicted result by controlling a certain number of variables. In the words of Gordon Paul, such therapists ask themselves, "What treatment, by whom, is most effective for this individual, with that specific problem, under which set of circumstances?" (1969a, p. 62). This question is answered according to scientific evidence accumulated from past treatments, and the results of the present treatment, once it is completed, are added to that body of evidence, in the effort to refine our scientific understanding of human behavior. At the same time, other therapists feel that to conduct treatment in this way is to mistake human beings for experimental animals. According to this latter group, psychological treatment is not only a science but also an "art"—something that depends more on empathy and intuition than on empirical analysis. Behaviorists generally regard therapy as an applied science, while psychodynamic and humanistic-existential therapists are more likely to see it as in some measure an "art." There are numerous exceptions to this rule, and most therapists would probably take an intermediate position. Again, however, this is a valid dimension of difference among therapeutic approaches.

In addition to these two important distinctions—action versus insight, science versus art—there are many other areas of disagreement within contemporary psychotherapy. Since World War II the field has expanded at an astounding rate. One indication of this growth is the increase in the number of clinical psychology programs accredited by the American Psychological Association. In 1947, there were 29 such programs; in 1962, 60; in 1986, 143 (Sears, 1947; Ross, 1962; American Psychological Association, 1986). In other words, the number of accredited programs quintupled in thirty-nine years. With this growth has come the kind of diversification we have mentioned. Freudian psychoanalysis and its derivatives, which once held unquestioned dominance over the field, now compete with behavioral therapy. Both schools, in turn, have been challenged by the humanistic-existential therapies. And from each of these major

Nonprofessional Helpers: The Therapist Behind the Bar

Only a small fraction of people who need mental health consultation actually take their problems to professional practitioners. A survey conducted in 1960 (Gurin et al., 1960) revealed that less than a fifth of those who saw themselves as having psychological problems went to mental health professionals; clergy and physicians handled the problems of two-thirds of these people. It seems possible that the proportion of informal help today is far greater. There is increasing recognition that neighbors, hairdressers, work supervisors, bartenders, cab drivers—and even seatmates on buses and planes—sometimes engage in a helping relationship with an individual or individuals who are troubled.

People seek out nonprofessional help for a number of reasons. Professional help is often costly; such services may be inaccessible or may not suit a particular person's ideology; therapy may carry some sort of stigma in the community; or the individual may simply not want to admit that the problem requires professional attention. In any case, most people find it more comfortable to seek solace and advice from a trusted person in a natural setting.

As might be expected, the kinds of problems people discuss and the kinds of help they receive vary with the context. One study (Cowen, 1982) focused on four groups engaged in giving informal interpersonal help: hairdressers, divorce lawyers, industrial supervisors, and bartenders. The investigators found that the major problems discussed with hairdressers involved children, health, and marriage; bartenders most often heard about marital, job, and money problems. Divorce lawyers tended to deal with anger at the spouse, depression, and problems with spouse contacts, while supervisors dealt mainly with problems with fellow workers, advancement opportunities, and job restlessness. Such problems are, in fact, similar to those handled by mental health professionals.

The "strategies" that the nonprofessionals used to help their troubled clients and customers ranged from acceptable to naive, by professional mental health standards. Listening and offering support and sympathy were major responses on the part of all the groups; the lawyers tended, in addition, to ask questions, give advice, point out consequences of bad ideas, and propose alternatives. The hairdressers, more than the other groups, also made use of the less acceptable strategy of changing the topic or telling people to count their blessings. Both hairdressers and bartenders also accented a lighthearted approach, which may or may not be appropriate strategy, depending on the severity of a person's unhappy mental state.

All four categories of helpers felt comfortable with their role. For the most part they were happy to listen to people's problems and accepted the fact that the "therapy" they perform is part of the job—and sometimes the most important aspect of it. One hairdresser put it this way: "To be perfectly truthful, I regard myself a B− hairdresser. But my business is booming. Mostly that's because I listen to people, care about their personal concerns, and try to be helpful. The guy down the street is really an A+ hairdresser—one of the best in town. But he's going to go out of business because he can't stand people and is incapable of listening sympathetically to *anyone's* problems" (Cowen, 1981, p. 390).

All four groups view their efforts as moderately effective. They make no claims to being experts. Unquestionably, they provide a useful service simply by listening to people's problems. We have all realized how therapeutic it is at times simply to "talk out" our problems. Beyond that, some risk is attached to attempts to give advice or to make light of potentially serious problems. Consider how a suicidal person might feel if his or her despair were laughed at or discounted. Also, some troubled people may be misled into thinking that informal help is adequate, and therefore fail to seek the professional guidance they may in fact need. It is important, then, that people from all walks of life be informed about what symptoms are serious and when professional help is truly called for.

therapeutic schools, several specialized treatment approaches have evolved: rational-emotive therapy, Gestalt therapy, cognitive restructuring, and so on. Today there are well over 200 schools of psychotherapy, each with its own program for solving human problems.

As psychotherapy has diversified, it has changed in other ways as well. For one thing, it has become vastly more popular. Approximately 5 percent of the population makes at least one voluntary mental health visit in a given year (Horgan, 1985). That is one of every twenty people; obviously, psychotherapy is no longer the private preserve of the "crazy." Consequently, the stigma attached to psychological treatment has greatly diminished. Though we still do not find political candidates discussing their therapy, ordinary citizens are increasingly willing to consult a therapist, and to tell their friends that they do.

As the stigma of psychological treatment has diminished, so has its mystique. With each new therapeutic school challenging the others, the actual methods employed by different schools have been placed more and more squarely before the public. And this exposure has resulted in a good deal of critical questioning. Today the assessment of therapy—does it work? if so, how? is it cost-effective?—is receiving unprecedented emphasis. Many of these challenges come not just from the public but also from the third-party payers who pick up a good part of this country's psychological treatment bill: insurance companies, industrial health plans, and the government. Whoever the challenger, therapists must now justify their techniques.

This is a welcome development, for it forces professionals to demonstrate that their techniques actually work, and work better than alternative techniques. Later in this chapter we will describe a number of studies measuring the relative effectiveness of alternative therapies for specific problems. Such studies—and there will be more of them—are the outcome of the current demand for accountability, an outcome from which future patients can only benefit.

In earlier chapters, we have discussed a number of specific treatments. In the remainder of this chapter, we shall try to pull together these threads and present a unified summary of each of the current approaches to treatment. It is possible to categorize them in this way, despite their great diversity. Though individual styles may differ, therapists, because of their training, approach therapy with assumptions that correspond at least roughly to one or another of the theoretical perspectives outlined in preceding chapters. Other therapists regard themselves as "eclectic" practitioners who integrate across approaches. To be eclectic, however, therapists must be familiar with the different perspectives. Each broad perspective has some internal unity. In addition to its repertory of techniques, it has its own notion of what the focus of treatment should be (e.g., the client's past, the client's present subjective world, the client's environmental reinforcements), what the client's role should be (e.g., sitting back and taking a pill or actively making new "life choices"), and finally, what the therapist's role should be (e.g., expressing unconditional acceptance or climbing out onto fire escapes with clients in order to help them overcome fear of heights). It is these broad treatment approaches that we will now outline.

THE PSYCHODYNAMIC APPROACH TO TREATMENT

Psychoanalysis, as developed and practiced by Freud, is not widely used today. It is, however, the grandfather of all current psychodynamic approaches. Hence we shall give this technique first consideration and then discuss some of its modern variants.

Freudian Psychoanalysis

As we saw in Chapter 2, Freud's experience with his patients led him to conclude that the source of "neurosis" was anxiety experienced by the ego when unacceptable unconscious drives threatened to break through into the conscious mind. In order to deal with this threat, the ego had recourse to a number of defense mechanisms, the most important of which was repression—the pushing back of the impulse into the unconscious. But while the impulse could be buried, the effort involved weakened the ego considerably. Furthermore, some anxiety remained, forcing its victims into various self-defeating postures and generally making them miserable. Thus, according to Freud, the proper treatment for neurosis was to coax the unconscious impulse out into consciousness so that the patient could at last confront it. Once confronted and "worked through," this material—be it castration anxiety, hatred of one's mother, or what-

This is Freud's office in Vienna, with the famous couch on which his patients reclined while he analyzed them. Freud sat at the head of the couch, out of the patient's view, and urged the patient to talk freely about the past. The couch technique was designed to make the patient comfortable (note the pillows and coverlets) and free of the inhibition that might have accompanied confronting the analyst face to face. (Edmund Engleman)

ever—would lose its power to terrorize the ego. Self-defeating defenses could accordingly be abandoned, and the ego would then be free to devote itself to more constructive pursuits. As Freud succinctly put it, "where id was, there shall ego be."

It is on this theory that the techniques of psychoanalysis are founded. In the first place, because the trouble is thought to be within the client's psyche, which the analyst is helping the client to explore, psychoanalysis is strictly a one-to-one client–analyst relationship. The client often lies on a couch, the better to relax, and thus to loosen the restraints on the unconscious. And the analyst typically sits outside the client's field of vision. What the client then does is talk—usually for fifty minutes a day, three to four days a week, over a period of several years. The client may talk about his or her childhood, since it is there that the roots of the problem presumably lie, but present difficulties are also discussed. The analyst remains silent much of the time, in order to facilitate the client's exploration. When the analyst does speak, it is generally to *interpret* the client's remarks—that is, to point out their possible connection with unconscious material. This dialogue between client and therapist turns on four basic techniques: free association, dream interpretation, analysis of resistance, and analysis of transference.

Free Association   As we pointed out in Chapter 1, Freud early in his career became dissatisfied with hypnosis. He decided that the purpose of dislodging repressed material from the unconscious could be better achieved by **free association,** whereby the patient, while lying on the couch, is asked to verbalize whatever thoughts come to mind, in whatever order they come. The primary directive to clients is that they must in no way structure or censor their remarks in order to make them appear logical, coherent, mature, morally sound, or otherwise admirable. The rationale behind this technique is that the unconscious has its own logic and that if clients report their thoughts exactly as they occur, the connective threads between verbalizations and unconscious impulses will be revealed. When such connections do become clear, the analyst points them out to the client, thus cutting through defenses and furthering the client's access to unconscious motivations.

Dream Interpretation   A second important tunnel to the unconscious is dreams. Freud believed that in sleep, the ego's defenses were lowered, allowing unconscious material to make its way into dreams. But defenses are never completely abandoned, even in sleep, and therefore the repressed impulses reveal themselves in dreams only in symbolic fashion. For example, a threatening figure such as a TV gangster might represent the client's father as perceived through the eyes of childhood. Thus a dream has two levels of content: (1) **manifest content,** the material of the dream as seen and reported by the individual, and (2) **latent content,** the unconscious material that is being expressed in disguised fashion through the symbols contained in the dream. For example, one patient, a new mother who (like most new mothers) was up at all hours of the night tending to her baby, reported to her analyst a dream in which she gave birth to identical twin boys, one of whom then died. According to the analyst, the latent content of this dream was that the woman, while she loved her newborn son, also wished him dead for destroying her peace of mind. However, the ego's defenses

against this aggressive id impulse were still in partial operation during the dream. So the ego and the id "compromised" on the manifest content, multiplying the baby into two identical babies and killing off only one (Ildiko Mohacsy, personal communication, 1975).

This is a simplified example, for dream interpretation normally involves free association. After the dream is reported, the analyst asks the patient to free-associate to its contents, and the resulting associations—memories, emotions, signs of mounting defenses—are taken as clues to the unconscious meaning of the dream.

Analysis of Resistance   As clients are guided toward the unwelcome knowledge of their unconscious motivations, they may begin to show **resistance,** using various defenses to avoid confronting painful memories or unsavory impulses. Resistance can be manifested in a number of ways. Clients may break up a fruitful train of thought by changing the subject; they may suddenly fail to remember the upshot of an episode from childhood; they may disrupt the ses-

Psychoanalytic methods encourage the patient to report his or her dreams and then to free associate to the dream material. In light of the patient's associations, the analyst interprets the dream, revealing its latent content, which will presumably center on unconscious conflicts. (*The Dream,* Henri Rousseau; Collection, Museum of Modern Art, New York; Gift of Nelson A. Rockefeller.)

sion by making jokes or by trying to pick a quarrel with the analyst; they may even begin missing appointments. It is then the analyst's job to point out that the patient is showing resistance and possibly also to interpret the resistance by suggesting what it is that the patient is trying not to discover.

Analysis of Transference   As the psychoanalysis progresses, with the client revealing to the analyst truths that he or she may never have revealed to anyone else, the relationship between the two partners becomes understandably complex. In his own practice, Freud noted that while he was noncommittal and neutral, many of his patients began responding to him with very strong and often very mixed feelings—sometimes with a childlike love and dependency, at other times with bitter hostility and rebellion. Freud interpreted this phenomenon as a **transference** onto him of his clients' childhood feelings toward important people in their lives—above all, their feelings toward their parents.*

Transference is an essential component of the therapeutic process. In fact, traditional psychoanalysts maintain that in order for the therapeutic process to be successful, clients must go through a stage, called *transference neurosis,* of reenacting with the analyst their childhood conflicts with their parents. Such conflicts typically include unsatisfied dependency needs along with feelings of anger and hatred—emotions that the clients have repressed and that may currently be subverting their adult relationships. The belief is that once these central emotions are brought out, clients have reached the core of the neurosis. With the analyst's help, clients at last face up to the emotional conflicts left over from childhood and can evaluate them realistically, thus depriving them of their power, as shadowy and fearful presences, to manipulate the clients' behavior into self-defeating patterns. This is a prime example of what analysts mean by the term "working through"—that is, identifying the

___

* Transference occurs in everyone. Analysts, though they make every effort to remain objective, are nevertheless subject to **countertransference,** whereby they project onto the client emotions originating in their own personal histories. One of the reasons psychoanalysts are required to undergo analysis themselves before attempting to practice it is so that they can identify their areas of emotional vulnerability and thus better control for countertransference.

many manifestations of a basic conflict and then dealing with each of them in the light of one's new understanding of their origin and meaning.

Post-Freudian Variations in Psychodynamic Therapy

At present Freud's techniques are rigorously followed by only a small percentage of psychodynamic therapists. The others, although they may retain the Freudian vocabulary, practice a considerably modified form of psychoanalysis, often based not simply on Freud's theory but also on the theories of his followers. As we saw in Chapter 2, many post-Freudian thinkers rejected Freud's contention that the id was the primary motivating force in human development. Instead of the id, Adler stressed the drive for superiority and the influence of social relationships; Jung, the richness and creative potential of the unconscious; Horney, the sociocultural environment; Erikson, the power of the ego and the formation of the ego identity; Sullivan, like Adler, development through interpersonal relations. All these concerns, along with those of other post-Freudians, have contributed to making psychodynamic therapy what it is today.

What is psychodynamic therapy today? This can be stated only in broad generalizations, as techniques vary from therapist to therapist. Like psychoanalysis, its primary concern is with unconscious motivations and their effects on the person's adaptation, and its goal is insight into these motivations. However, it differs from traditional psychoanalysis in several important respects. First, today's psychodynamic therapist generally takes a more active part than the psychoanalyst, dealing with the client face to face (the couch is seldom used) and speaking, interpreting, directing, and advising much more extensively than Freud would have considered appropriate. Second, while the client's past history is certainly not ignored, psychotherapy generally pays more attention to the client's present life, especially his or her personal relationships. Finally, psychodynamic therapy is briefer and less intensive than orthodox psychoanalysis. Therapist and client typically meet once or twice a week for anywhere from a few months to a few years. This broad category of therapy is probably the most common form of psychological treatment in the United States (Parloff, 1976).

We shall examine very briefly two specific forms

of this post-Freudian psychotherapy: ego psychology and Sullivanian therapy.

Ego Psychology   We pointed out in Chapter 2 that a major revision of Freudian theory was that of the ego psychologists, a loosely formed group including, among others, Heinz Hartmann and Erik Erikson. The basic contention of ego psychology is that ego is at least as important as id in controlling human behavior. As we have seen, Freud's conceptualization of the psyche was one in which the ego, borrowing its energy from the id, merely served as a sort of reality-oriented mediator of the id's sexual and aggressive strivings. In contrast, the ego psychologists argue that the ego has substantial energy of its own and that its functions—memory, judgment, perception, problem solving, planning—serve constructive purposes independent of id strivings. A second fundamental premise of ego psychology is the critical importance of interpersonal relationships, and especially the mother–child relationship. As we saw, Erikson advanced his theory of psychosocial development—development through interaction with others—as a revision of Freud's theory of psychosexual development.

The contributions of the ego psychologists have been more theoretical than practical; in therapy, they tend to adapt Freudian methods to their own individual techniques. In general, like orthodox Freudians, they rely on free association, interpretation of dreams, analysis of resistance, and analysis of transference. Unlike orthodox Freudians, however, they tend to be more active, trying to help individuals cope with their present social world, rather than concentrating exclusively on the inner workings of their psyches. Ego psychologists stress the present as opposed to the past, the development of identity as opposed to the replay of childhood experience. They regard the therapy situation as the home base from which the client may venture out to engage in new experiments in living—and not just as a setting for reexperiencing the formative events of childhood.

Sullivanian Therapy   Harry Stack Sullivan's contributions to psychotherapy deserve special mention, for Sullivan went even further than the ego psychologists in emphasizing the interpersonal. As we saw in Chapter 2, Sullivan proposed that psychological disturbance was essentially interpersonal disturbance, a disruption in the individual's way of relating to others.

Sullivan thought such disruptions were usually due to self-protective styles of relating to others—characteristics developed in childhood and carried over into adult life, much to the detriment of the individual's interpersonal relations. Accordingly, Sullivanian therapists emphasize the client's relations with family members (past and present), with other significant figures, and with the therapist.

Aside from this interpersonal emphasis, the Sullivanians also differ from the Freudians in taking a more active role in therapy. They not only respond to but initiate topics of discussion. In particular, Sullivanian therapists adapt their demeanor to the client's personality and to his or her needs at the moment. Thus a Sullivanian therapist may appear detached, empathetic, concerned, demanding, or even verbally aggressive (up to a point), depending on his or her understanding of what the client needs.

Psychodynamic Therapy: Pros and Cons

In the entire field of psychology there is perhaps no issue more controversial than the value of psychodynamic treatment. The psychiatric literature contains many testimonials to the insights and personality changes achieved through psychoanalysis. From other quarters, however, psychodynamic therapy has been criticized.

A common objection, as we pointed out in Chapter 2, is that psychodynamic therapy is based on a theory that is difficult to validate scientifically. In recent years there has been considerable interest among researchers in testing the theory, and many of Freud's insights *have* been empirically supported (Fisher and Greenberg, 1977). Furthermore, psychodynamic clinicians have historically been careful observers of their patients, and have passed on many valuable clinical observations to other investigators. Yet it remains true that most psychodynamic and especially psychoanalytic writing, including reports on treatment, rests more on intuition and personal judgment than on scientific measures.

A second criticism has to do with the multiplicity of psychodynamic theories. Almost all psychodynamic theorists would agree that a successful therapy depends on the attainment of insight. But insight into what? In fact, patients develop insights according to the theory that their therapist espouses. And this makes the central mechanism of psychodynamic therapy look less like insight—a confrontation with something that is truly there—than a form of persuasion, in which the patient is won over to the therapist's belief system (Bandura, 1969; London, 1964).

This charge is basically unanswerable. (And it applies to all therapies, though it is a special problem with the insight therapies.) At the same time, recent research has shown that psychodynamic methods do in fact lead patients to discover important things about themselves; that central interpersonal conflicts can be reliably identified in psychodynamic therapy (Luborsky et al., 1986); that when they are, patients become more involved in the therapy session and more expressive (Silberschatz et al., 1986); and that the more positive the patients' immediate response at such moments, the more likely he or she is to improve (Luborsky et al., 1986). Conceivably, the specific insights may depend on the therapist's training, but something like insight does seem to occur, and to have therapeutic effects.

A third criticism of psychodynamic therapy is that it is "elitist," since, by its very nature, it seems to exclude a large number of patients. Some are barred purely on financial grounds. Though more and more health plans are now including some coverage for psychotherapy, psychodynamic treatment, because it tends to take longer than other therapies, is rarely paid for in full, or even in large part, by health plans. Second, psychodynamic therapy is generally limited to people with "neurotic" disorders, thus leaving out vast numbers of psychotics. Finally, because psychodynamic therapy is such a highly verbal enterprise, it tends to work best for those who are articulate and well-educated (Luborsky and Spence, 1978). Indeed, the patients most likely to benefit from this kind of therapy—as from any verbal therapy—are the so-called YAVIS patients: young, attractive, verbal, intelligent, and successful (Schofield, 1964). In other words, those who tend to succeed at psychodynamic therapy are those who tend to succeed at most things in life.

The fact that most psychodynamic therapy today is briefer than traditional psychoanalysis is in part a response to the financial objection. But the "elitist" charge is arguably irrelevant. Central air conditioning benefits only people who can afford it and who live in hot climates, but no one claims that it doesn't cool houses. Likewise, even if psychodynamic therapy benefits only verbal middle-class neurotics, it *does* benefit them.

THE HUMANISTIC-EXISTENTIAL APPROACH TO TREATMENT

While humanistic and existential therapists tend to be highly individualistic in their techniques, they share the common objective of helping patients to become more truly "themselves"—to seek meaning from life and then to make deliberate choices in order to live more meaningfully. In keeping with this therapeutic goal, the humanistic-existential approach to treatment differs from both the psychodynamic and behavioral approaches in that it maximizes clients' sense of freedom, discourages them from engaging in deterministic thinking (e.g., "passing the buck" to a stern father, a cruel wife, a dreary job), turns them face-front toward the future, and asks them to "become"—to choose their own destiny. This approach further differs from the two other treatment philosophies in that it places greater emphasis on intimacy in the client–therapist relationship, with the therapist attempting to enter the client's phenomenological world and the client drawing strength from the warmth and honesty of the therapeutic relationship.

Client-Centered Therapy

The best-known and most popular humanistic therapy is Carl Rogers' (1951) **client-centered therapy.** The fundamental principle of this treatment approach, which we have already outlined in Chapter 4, is that human beings are innately good and innately motivated to actualize their potential. Self-actualization, however, depends on the social environment. People often absorb from their families and peers unrealistic "conditions of worth"—requirements that they be something other than what they are in order to be loved. This forces them to screen out large portions of their experience, those portions that violate the conditions of worth. Though they may want to show anger or affection, to try out for the baseball team or stay home and write poetry, they do not do so because the conditions of worth forbid it. Thus the unfolding of the self is impeded, and the individual becomes poorly adjusted and generally unhappy.

According to Rogers, the only way to solve this problem is to eliminate unrealistic conditions of worth. The means to this end is client-centered therapy. As the name indicates, this treatment is focused di-

In client-centered therapy—and, indeed, in any form of psycho-therapy—empathy between thera-pist and client is crucial. (Michael Weisbrot & Family/Stock, Boston)

rectly on the client's individual personality, not on any system of theories or laws regarding human behavior in general. In the effort to reconcile clients to their true selves, the therapist attempts to see the world through their eyes so that they will come to regard their own experience of the world as a thing of value. The therapist's ability to do this depends on three basic factors. The first is unconditional positive regard. In contrast to the partial and conditional acceptance that children typically receive from their parents, the therapist offers total acceptance, hoping by this means to induce clients to accept the totality of their experience.

Second, and perhaps most important, the therapist must offer empathic understanding. Rogers (1980) often described this process as "hearing" the clients— that is, resonating on all possible levels to what they are communicating. Most clients, in Rogers' opinion, have scant experience of being "heard":

> I have had the fantasy of a prisoner in a dungeon, tapping out day after day a Morse code message, "Does anybody hear me? Is anybody there?" And finally one day he hears some faint tappings which spell out "Yes." By that one simple response he is released from his loneliness; he has become a human being again. There are many, many people living in private dungeons today, people who give

no evidence of it whatsoever on the outside, where you have to listen very sharply to hear the faint messages from the dungeon (1980, p. 10).

Therapists, once they "hear" the client, "mirror" back the message—that is, they state the feelings that they are picking up. This process allows clients to clarify their feelings and, since the feelings are mirrored back to them without any disapproval, to accept their feelings.

The third requirement of client-centered therapists is what Rogers (1980) called "congruence," or "real-ness"—that is, the ability to realize and to verbalize what they are experiencing at a given moment:

> Sometimes [in therapy] a feeling "rises up in me" which seems to have no particular relationship to what is going on. Yet I have learned to accept and trust this feeling in my awareness and to try to communicate it to my client. For example, a client is talking to me and I suddenly feel an image of him as a pleading little boy, folding his hands in supplication, saying, "Please let me have this, please let me have this." I have learned that if I can be real in the relationship with him and express this feeling that has occurred in me, it is very likely to strike some deep note in him and to advance our relationship (1980, p. 15).

As these remarks indicate, the touchstones of Rogerian therapy are empathy and intuition. While the psychodynamic therapist will, to some extent, remain outside the client's experience, so as to be able to interpret it, the Rogerian therapist tries to close the gap between therapist and client and "be with" the client as completely as possible.

Existential Therapy

We have pointed out in Chapter 4 that existential psychology differs somewhat from humanistic psychology in the approach to the question of freedom. While the humanists assume that an integrated personality will automatically use its freedom by bringing into full flower all its potentialities, the existentialists less optimistically stress the difficulty of accepting and exercising freedom. Where the humanists speak of self-actualization, the existentialists speak of anguish and self-confrontation. In short, the existentialists tend to regard freedom less as a gift than as a moral challenge.

As popularized by such figures as Frankl, van den Berg, and Rollo May (Chapter 4), existential therapy encourages patients to take responsibility for their symptoms as something that they themselves have chosen and to show them that they are free—indeed, almost obligated—to choose better ways of coping, ways that will give meaning to their lives. Whatever the presenting complaint, the existential therapist will consistently turn his or her patients' attention to the here and now, emphasize the active rather than the passive aspects of their mode of "becoming," and urge them to formulate for themselves a system of values that will give their lives an ultimate meaning. For the existentialists, this meaningfulness is tightly bound to interpersonal relationships, which, if they are honest and open, can infuse life with the sense of worth and direction that the existentialists seek.

Existential therapy is based on the phenomenological approach—an emphasis that has become even more pronounced as a result of van den Berg's writings (Chapter 4). In keeping with van den Berg's approach, existential therapists will try to elicit, as clearly and specifically as possible, a picture of the patient's "lived world." To increase their access to that realm, therapists may "bracket" their theoretical assumptions at the outset of therapy—that is, state their assumptions and then lay them aside as completely as they can. Having cleared away these impediments, the therapist can then presumably enter into the patient's phenomenological universe, seeing the world as the patient sees it. This process is related to the "empathic understanding" of the Rogerian therapist, but there is a marked difference in tone. The existentialists are less distinctively warm than the Rogerians. Rather, they see themselves as practitioners of a new, "human" science and regard the therapeutic process as a sort of heroic partnership, therapist and client together facing the facts of life in a world where human values, because of social constraints, are hard to locate and harder still to pursue.

Gestalt Therapy

The founder of **Gestalt therapy,** Frederick (Fritz) Perls (1951, 1970), was trained in Europe as a Freudian psychoanalyst. As his career progressed, he repudiated large portions of Freudian theory. Thus Gestalt therapy is both an outgrowth of and a departure from psychoanalysis. On the Freudian side, Perls adhered to the theory that psychological disturbance is the result of unresolved conflicts left over from the past—conflicts that must be located and worked through. Furthermore, Perls, like Freud, believed in the symbolic content of dreams and made extensive use of dream interpretation. On the other hand, Perls' handling of childhood conflicts, repressed impulses, dreams, and all the other Freudian materials is decidedly un-Freudian in that all these matters are brought to bear solely on the present, the *now,* in which clients choose what they will become and whether or not

Fritz Perls, the founder of Gestalt therapy. Perls believed that when clients act out their conflicts and confront their feelings, they learn to control them rather than be controlled by them. (Deke Simon)

they will allow their past to control their future. In short, Perls detached a number of Freudian concepts from Freud's deterministic view of human behavior and redirected these concepts toward humanistic-existential ends: freedom, responsibility, openness, the active control of one's "becoming."

In Gestalt therapy, clients are asked to unearth their past conflicts and reenact them in the consulting room. If, for example, the client is still disturbed, at the age of forty, over the way his father treated him when he was ten, then the therapist assumes the role of the father and has the client act out the conflict—reopen the quarrel and perhaps this time close it as well. Clients are encouraged to "act out" as violently and as vividly as they need to—to swear, kick the chair, yell, weep, and so on. In this way, Perls argued, clients confront their feelings, take responsibility for them, and learn to control them rather than being controlled by them. And by doing so, clients unify their feelings and their behavior into a new whole and begin living a more spontaneous, open, and honest life—a life of decisive feeling and decisive action.

Gestalt therapy has been influential, particularly in the group therapy movement, where it has helped people to understand and accept their own feelings and to be able to deal with others more openly. (Group therapy will be discussed in Chapter 21.)

Humanistic-Existential Therapy: Pros and Cons

The humanistic-existential therapies enjoyed great popularity during the 1960s, when their philosophy converged with the political sentiments of the time. Today they still have a faithful, if smaller, following. Client-centered therapy remains popular, in part because of its simplicity. Client-centered therapists do not have to interpret obscure symbols, as in psychodynamic therapy, or implement highly precise treatment techniques, as in behavior therapy. What they must do is be empathic and warm—surely an appealing style of therapy to most people.

As an insight therapy, humanistic-existential treatment is credited with many of the same virtues as psychodynamic treatment—that it deals with the person as a whole rather than with fragments of behavior, that it goes to the root of the patient's problem, and that it leads to genuine self-knowledge. Furthermore, humanistic-existential therapists claim that they offer their patients a sense of hope that no deterministic

psychology, whether behavioral or psychodynamic, can offer. In addition, both client-centered and existential therapy deserve credit for according the maximum possible respect to the patient's own point of view.

Humanistic-existential treatment is also subject to the same criticisms as psychodynamic treatment, the criticisms of insight therapy as a whole: that the treatment is long and costly, that it is appropriate only for "neurotic" disorders, and that it benefits only a certain sector of the population—the YAVIS patients described above. Finally, like psychodynamic therapy, humanistic-existential therapy has feen faulted for being unscientific and therefore hard to evaluate empirically.

To this final criticism the existentialists reply that the scientific standards being invoked are those of natural science, which they regard as inadequate for the study and treatment of human beings. In their view, they are pursuing a new science, which takes into account those facts of human life that differentiate it from plant and animal life. As for the humanists, Rogers and his followers have actually made strenuous efforts to subject their theory and therapy to scientific testing. Their major research tool has been the Q-sort, which, as we saw in Chapter 7, measures the subject's self-image and "ideal self."

Research with the Q-sort (Rogers, 1959; Rogers and Dymond, 1954) has supported Rogers' argument that patients seeking therapy tend to have both an extremely negative self-image and unrealistically high ideals for themselves. It has also shown that client-centered therapy helps to close this gap, improving the self-image and cutting the ideal self down to realistic proportions. Client-centered therapists have also attempted to identify the qualities that make a therapist more effective. Rogers, for example, was among the first to tape-record his therapy sessions in an attempt to encourage analysis of the therapeutic process. This practice led to a great surge in research on the therapy process, embracing therapies of all perspectives, and many of the results have supported Rogers' claims. In particular, the therapist's warmth, empathy, and "congruence," especially when evaluated by the patients, have all been frequently associated with successful therapeutic outcomes (Beutler et al., 1986; Orlinsky and Howard, 1986).

Despite the efforts of people such as Rogers, humanistic-existential therapy is likely to remain a less than perfectly mapped territory. Humanistic-existential therapists, in general, concern themselves with helping clients, not with generating data. As for the existentialists, they are at least as committed to philosophy and morality as to what most psychologists understand by the term "science."

THE BEHAVIORAL APPROACH TO TREATMENT

Like the techniques of psychodynamic therapy, the techniques of behavior therapy have already been examined to some degree in earlier chapters. And in Chapter 3 we discussed in detail the principles on which behavior therapy is based. The most fundamental of these principles is that all behavior, whether psychotic, "neurotic," or normal, is governed by the same laws. Consequently the goal of therapy is to use those laws—learning and other experimentally derived principles—to teach people with behavioral problems the skills they need in order to enhance their functioning (Bootzin, 1975). Behavior, then, is not regarded by the behaviorists as a symptom or a signpost pointing to the true target, an underlying conflict. On the contrary, the behavior itself is the target, and the therapist aims at it directly.

What this means is that behaviorists place considerably less emphasis on a person's past than do psychodynamic therapists. This is not to say that they ignore the client's history altogether. They recognize that past learning has important implications for current functioning. However, they point out that a maladaptive behavior is maintained not by past conditions but by current conditions, which may be very different from the circumstances that originally produced the behavior. (This is one reason for behaviorists' skepticism regarding the curative power of insight into the past.) Consequently, treatment emphasizes the conditions that elicit and reinforce the problem behavior in the present.

Another consequence of the direct approach of behavior therapy is that it focuses less on the inner life than do other forms of therapy. Again, it should not be assumed that behaviorists ignore this aspect of experience. However strict the empiricism of the early behaviorists, modern behaviorism has been so influenced by its cognitive school that there is now almost no behavioral therapist who does not take self-defeating expectations and attitudes into account in treatment. Nevertheless, the behaviorists' approach to the client's thoughts differs substantially from that of psychodynamic and humanistic-existential therapists. While the insight therapists tend to regard thoughts as elusive clues to deep-seated conflicts, the behaviorists consider these internal events relatively accessible and tend to take them at face value. To them, cognitions are simply covert responses, subject to the same laws of learning as overt responses and therefore equally open to change (e.g., Wolpe, 1978). Thus while the behaviorists definitely take the inner life into account, it is handled in the same direct manner as the outer life.

As the behaviorists' goal is pragmatic—the building of skills—so is their therapeutic manner. While insight therapists aim at creating a special emotional climate in which patients can discover their own truths, the behaviorists devote the therapeutic hour to giving instructions, analyzing goals, implementing strategies, modeling appropriate behaviors, and providing reinforcement for goal attainment. Most behavior therapists will also be supportive, but they tend to regard the establishment of a sympathetic client–therapist relationship as a first step to the remaining, essential steps of behavioral or cognitive retraining. The relationship, in other words, is not central to behavior therapy in the same way that it is to the insight therapies.

Behavioral treatments tend to be multicomponent "packages." As we saw in Chapter 10, for example, behavioral therapy for depression may include training in relaxation, time management, parenting, coping skills, and social skills, along with cognitive restructuring. However, these complex treatment programs are based on relatively few and simple principles. When the primary goal is a change in overt behavior, treatment usually takes the form of operant conditioning. When the primary goal is a change in emotion (i.e., in the patient's attraction or aversion to given stimuli), treatment generally centers on respondent conditioning. When the primary goal is a change in cognition, the therapist will tend to use the recently developed techniques of cognitive restructuring. Any given treatment plan may well embrace all these goals. Hence the multicomponent approach. But for the sake of clarity, we will consider each principle separately.

Operant Conditioning

Operant conditioning, as we have seen, is learning via consequences. Under certain stimulus conditions, we produce a certain response, and the fact that this response is followed by positive or negative consequences provides an incentive for us to repeat or avoid that same response when next we are faced with those same stimulus conditions. Operant behavior, then, involves three components: (1) the stimulus or cue for a certain response, (2) the response, and (3) the consequences. Behavior therapists have found that by altering any of these components, they can change maladaptive patterns of behavior.

Contingency Management   The manipulation of the consequences of a response in order to change the frequency of that response is called **contingency management.** Throughout earlier chapters, we have seen applications of this technique. As we have noted, retarded children can be taught to tie their shoes, feed themselves, speak, and master many other skills through the administration of rewards (Thompson and Grabowski, 1977). Autistic children can be induced to stop banging their heads if head banging is followed by electric shock (Bucher and Lovaas, 1968). Likewise, reinforcement for achieving academic goals has produced large gains in classroom programs (Kelley and Stokes, 1982). All these are examples of contingency management. Other examples abound in everyday life. Children are persuaded to clean up their rooms, employees to arrive at work on time, and spouses to take out the garbage through this time-honored method of influencing other people's behavior.

Contingency management, then, is a familiar technique requiring no further explanation here. We shall, however, examine two special applications of the technique: contingency contracting and time-out from positive reinforcement.

CONTINGENCY CONTRACTING   **Contingency contracting** is a highly specific contingency management system in which a contract is drawn up indicating that for desirable behavior X, the subject will be given reward X; for desirable behavior Y, reward Y; and so on. Along with other behavior modification techniques, this procedure has the great advantage of being usable outside the consulting room—in the classroom, the home, and so forth. Some therapists have used contracts to help clients lose weight and maintain their weight loss, with rewards for those who stuck to their diet contracts for a specified number of days per week (Craighead et al., 1981). Contingency contracting has also been used to establish truces between delinquent teenagers and their parents. For instance, the contract might state that in return for

doing certain specific household chores, the teenager will receive a weekly allowance of $10; in return for maintaining a certain academic average, the young person is permitted to go out one night per weekend; in return for being home from school by 4:30, he or she is allowed to go to and from school on the bus, rather than being driven by the parents, and so forth. Penalties for deviation from the rules will also be specified. The usefulness of the contract is enhanced by having the child participate in specifying the contingencies, the rewards, and the penalties. Such contracts have had some success with conduct disorders (Stuart, 1971; Patterson, 1974). This is a hopeful sign, for as we pointed out in Chapter 17, conduct disorders have proved highly resistant to other kinds of treatment.

TIME-OUT FROM POSITIVE REINFORCEMENT   Though punishment by means of the direct application of aversive stimuli is not widely used in behavior therapy, the withdrawal of rewards is used. One common technique, especially in the treatment of children, is **time-out from positive reinforcement.** Children who engage in an undesirable behavior are temporarily removed to a neutral environment, such as an empty room, where they can receive no reinforcement.

This technique is cousin to the time-honored practice of sending naughty children to their rooms. There are important differences, however. First, the time-out room contains no reinforcers—indeed, that is the whole point of it—whereas most children can find in their rooms a wealth of reinforcers (e.g., toys, books, records) to comfort them in their exile. Second, families seldom have clear rules for when children are sent to their rooms or when they are released; children are simply sent off when they have gone "too far" and are released when they are thought to have had "enough." By contrast, time-out is instituted in response to a clearly defined behavior (e.g., temper tantrums) and is terminated when the child terminates the behavior (e.g., as soon as the child has calmed down); hence there is no ambiguity as to how further removals to the time-out room can be avoided. Finally, when children are sent to their rooms, this punishment is usually imposed in anger, and for some children, parental anger seems to be reinforcing. (It is, after all, a form of attention.) Time-out is imposed dispassionately; the only "punishment" is the unavailability of reinforcers. Hence the child does not have the pleasure of irritating authority figures.

Time-out, like contingency contracting, can be used at home (Patterson and Gullion, 1968) and has proved quite effective in eliminating tantrums and head banging in psychotic children (Wolf et al., 1964). It is also useful in inducing children to sit still and pay attention during various kinds of treatment, such as speech therapy (Risley and Wolf, 1967). Yet despite its success, time-out is coming under increasing government regulation, largely because of its similarities to frequently abused practices such as seclusion. This problem will be discussed in Chapter 22, along with other legal issues that affect behavior therapy.

Stimulus Control   Behaviorists have found that operant behavior is controlled not only by the rewards or punishments that follow it but also by the stimuli that precede it. Our environment is filled with "cues for reinforcement," which, without thinking about it, we are constantly obeying. For many people, finishing a meal is a cue for smoking. For others, sitting down in front of the television is a cue for snacking. And just as behavior can be changed by controlling its consequences, it can also be changed by controlling its cues—a procedure known as stimulus control.

In **stimulus control** one establishes a highly predictable relationship between a given stimulus and a given response by eliminating all other stimuli associated with that response and all other responses associated with that stimulus. The object is to create a situation in which that stimulus, and no other, will automatically elicit that response, and no other. If this object is attained, then the frequency of the response can be controlled by controlling the frequency of exposure to the stimulus.

What does this mean in concrete terms? Imagine a woman who is overweight and wants to decrease the frequency of her eating behavior. She would be told to confine all eating behavior to one location and not to combine it with any other activities, such as television watching, reading, or socializing (Ferster et al., 1962). This program, if carefully followed, would eventually eliminate all other cues for eating and thereby eliminate impulsive and random eating behavior.

To decrease a behavior, as we just saw, patients are instructed to confine the behavior to one cue. To increase a behavior, on the other hand, patients are instructed to confine the cue to one behavior— in other words, to banish all other activities from the stimulus condition in which the target behavior is sup-

In the behavioral approach to psychotherapy a "time-out room" is often used, especially with children. The room contains no reinforcers. (Elizabeth Crews)

posed to take place. Insomniacs, for example, often use their beds at night for a number of activities besides sleeping—reading, television watching, telephone conversations, and so forth. To reestablish the bed as a cue for sleeping, insomniacs in one program were given the following instructions:

1. Lie down intending to go to sleep *only* when you are sleepy.
2. Do not use your bed for anything except sleep; that is, do not read, watch television, eat, or worry in bed. Sexual activity is the only exception to this rule. . . .
3. If you find yourself unable to fall asleep, get up and go into another room. Stay up as long as you wish and then return to the bedroom to sleep. Although we do not want you to watch the clock, we want you to get out of bed if you do not fall asleep immediately. Remember the goal is to associate your bed with falling asleep *quickly!* If you are in bed more than about 10

Most people needn't resist enjoying an ice cream cone. But, a patient with an eating disorder may employ the concept of stimulus control to ignore all but one of the environmental cues that encourage him or her to eat. This behavioral approach to psychotherapy encourages the establishment of a predictable relationship between a specific stimulus and a specific response. For example, if the patient learns to eat only when seated at a table, the urge to eat impulsively and randomly can be decreased. (Alan Carey/The Image Works)

minutes without falling asleep and have not gotten up, you are not following this instruction.
4. If you still cannot fall alseep, repeat Step 3. Do this as often as is necessary throughout the night.
5. Set your alarm and get up at the same time every morning irrespective of how much sleep you got during the night. This will help your body acquire a consistent sleep rhythm.
6. Do not nap during the day (Bootzin and Nicassio, 1978).

Following this program, an experimental group of thirty-one subjects were able to reduce the time it took them to fall asleep from an average of eighty-five minutes to an average of thirty-six minutes.

Incompatible Behavior   Another technique that has proved helpful in decreasing problem behaviors is to engage instead in an **incompatible behavior**— that is, a behavior that makes the problem behavior difficult or impossible to perform. The classic example is gum chewing for people trying to stop smoking. Another useful application of this principle is the substitution of muscle relaxation for muscle tension in anxiety-producing situations.

There are several procedures for inducing deep muscle relaxation, but perhaps the most commonly used is Jacobson's (1938) "progressive relaxation." In this technique, the client, going from muscle group to muscle group within the body, is instructed to contract the muscles as tightly as possible, to hold them that way for about ten seconds, and then to release them, thus achieving a state of relaxation. The object is to teach the person, first, how to distinguish between tension and relaxation, and second, how to achieve the latter. With practice in this technique, many people, as soon as they feel themselves going tense, can relax their bodies—a great aid in combating anxiety. Progressive relaxation has proved useful in controlling reactions to stress in depressives (Lewinsohn et al., 1980b) and in alleviating insomnia (Borkovec, 1982). In most cases, however, relaxation is used as one component of a more comprehensive treatment, the best example being systematic desensitization, which we will describe shortly.

Modeling   Modeling, whereby a person learns a new behavior by imitating another person performing that behavior, clearly involves more than stimulus, response, and consequences. As we saw in Chapter 3, modeling depends on symbolic processes—above all, it seems, on the desire of the imitator to be like the model and win his or her approval. Thus children learn to brush their teeth by watching their parents and older siblings brush their teeth, students learn to speak French by listening to their teachers speak French, and so on.

The same principles can be put to good use for the relief of problem behaviors. If therapists can capture their patients' attention and regard, they can begin teaching new adaptive behaviors simply by demonstrating these behaviors themselves. Rosenthal and Bandura (1978) reported a very high success rate for the treatment of phobias through modeling. For example, Bandura and his co-workers (1967) were able to eliminate dog phobias in children by allowing them, in a number of successive sessions, to watch another child (dubbed "Fearless Peer") approach a dog, touch it, pet it, and eventually engage in active play with it.

Other programs have combined modeling with practice sessions, in which the patient is guided gradually toward the successful completion of the target behavior, with much reinforcement along the way. This, actually, is how we learn most of our skills in real life—not just by modeling but by *practicing* our imitation of the model and by being rewarded for it. Such guided participation has proved effective in eliminating snake phobia (Bandura et al., 1974), in relieving compulsions (Rachman and Hodgson, 1980), and in teaching social skills (Bellack et al., 1983).

It should be added that all psychological therapies—behavioral, psychodynamic, humanistic-existential, whatever—involve some degree of modeling. Whatever else therapists offer their clients, they also provide an example, and the fact that they are not alcoholic or chronically depressed or afraid of snakes is an important factor in helping their clients overcome these problems.

Respondent Conditioning and Extinction

The operant conditioning techniques discussed in the preceding section are aimed primarily at inducing overt behavior changes. The respondent conditioning techniques that we will discuss in the present section are aimed at changing emotion—the degree to which we like, dislike, or fear certain stimuli—and thereby at changing behavior. As we saw in Chapter 3, respondent conditioning is a type of learning in which a previously neutral stimulus comes to elicit a response similar to that elicited by another stimulus with which it has been paired. All human beings, every day of their lives, are subject to respondent conditioning, sometimes with unfortunate results, so that they develop fears and desires that interfere with their functioning. When this happens, the individual can therapeutically *unlearn* the maladaptive response. This can be done either by removing the stimuli that reinforce the response (extinction) or by pairing the response with incompatible positive or negative stimuli. Among the many techniques that employ these principles, we shall discuss four: systematic desensitization, flooding, aversion therapy, and covert sensitization.

Systematic Desensitization   Perhaps the earliest example of the therapeutic use of respondent conditioning was the famous experiment in which Mary Cover Jones cured the furry-animal phobia of a little boy named Peter by giving him candy and then bringing a rabbit closer and closer to him (Chapter 3). **Systematic desensitization** is a similar technique, in which patients are exposed to an anxiety-producing stimulus while in a relaxed state. This gives the patient the chance to confront the stimulus without feeling anxiety. As a result, the anxiety is allowed to extinguish.

First named and developed as a formal treatment procedure by Joseph Wolpe (1958), systematic desensitization is based on the premise that if a response antagonistic to anxiety (such as relaxation) can be made to occur in the presence of anxiety-provoking stimuli, the bond between these stimuli and anxiety will be weakened. Systematic desensitization involves three steps. In the first step, the therapist trains the client in muscle relaxation, usually Jacobson's progressive relaxation, described above. In the second step, therapist and client construct a **hierarchy of fears**—that is, a list of anxiety-producing situations in the order of their increasing horror to the client. The following, for example, is the hierarchy of fears established for someone who was plagued by fears of dying (listed from most to least frightening):

1. Seeing a dead man in a coffin.
2. Being at a burial.
3. Seeing a burial assemblage from a distance.
4. Reading the obituary notice of a young person who died of a heart attack.
5. Driving past a cemetery (the nearer, the worse).
6. Seeing a funeral (the nearer, the worse).
7. Passing a funeral home (the nearer, the worse).
8. Reading the obituary notice of an old person.
9. Being inside a hospital.
10. Seeing a hospital.
11. Seeing an ambulance
    (Wolpe and Wolpe, 1981, p. 54).

Once the relaxation response and the hierarchy of fears have both been established, then the two can be combined in the third step, the actual desensitization. In some cases, the desensitization is conducted **in vivo**—that is, the client practices relaxing while confronting the feared stimuli in the actual situation, as in the Mary Cover Jones experiment. Most desensitization, however, takes place in the consulting office and relies on imagery. Clients are asked to relax and then to imagine themselves experiencing, one by one, the anxiety-producing stimuli listed in their hierarchies, starting with the lowest hierarchy item and moving upward. The process continues until the client signals that his or her relaxation has given way to anxiety. When this happens, the client is instructed to stop imagining whatever scene it was that produced the anxiety, to rest, to reestablish the state of relaxation, and to reimagine the scene that produced the anxiety. (If the client still cannot imagine this scene without experiencing anxiety, a few intermediate scenes may be reinserted before the scene so as to make the progression more gradual.) This process continues until the client can vividly imagine the scene at the top of the hierarchy and still remain relaxed. The entire treatment takes anywhere from 2 to 200 sessions, the median being 11.5 to 29, depending on the complexity of the problem (Wolpe, 1976).

The success of this technique depends, of course, on the carrying over of the relaxed response from the imagined situation to the actual situation. In most cases it appears that this transfer does in fact take place. Wolpe (1958, 1973, 1976) has described the successful use of systematic desensitization in the treatment of a wide variety of problems. It has been effective with phobias, recurrent nightmares, and complex interpersonal problems involving various fears—of social and sexual intimacy, aggressive behavior, social disapproval, rejection, and authority figures (e.g., Kazdin and Wilson, 1978). In a review of seventy-five articles describing the systematic desensitization of approximately a thousand individuals, Gordon Paul concluded, "For the first time in the history of psychological treatments, a specific therapeutic package reliably produced measurable benefits for clients across a broad range of problems in which anxiety was of fundamental importance" (1969b, p. 159). In all, this has proved a remarkably versatile and successful treatment.

Flooding   **Flooding** might be described as a cold-turkey extinction therapy. Unlike the gradual exposure paired with relaxation that constitutes systematic desensitization, flooding involves prolonged exposure to the feared stimulus—or, if that is not possible, then to vivid representations of the stimulus—in a situation that does not permit avoidance (Aronson, 1979). Like systematic desensitization, the technique

Through systematic desensitization, these people are learning not to fear dogs. The patients first are helped to relax; then they are presented with a series of progressively more frightening pictures of dogs. If the patients are able to remain relaxed while viewing the pictures, they should be able to generalize this response to the real world and soon be able to observe and touch real dogs without fear. (*The New York Times*)

depends on the therapist's first finding out exactly what it is that the client most fears.

Flooding has proved to be particularly useful in the elimination of obsessive-compulsive rituals (Rachman and Hodgson, 1980). As we saw in Chapter 8, obsessive-compulsive rituals usually have to do with one of two themes: contamination and checking. When the fear is contamination, flooding involves having clients actually "contaminate" themselves by touching and handling dirt or whatever substance they are trying to avoid, all the while preventing them from carrying out their anxiety-alleviating rituals (in this case, usually hand washing). The hoped-for result is that they will realize that the thing they fear actually poses no real threat.

A variant of flooding is **implosive therapy** (also called *imaginal flooding*), in which the feared stimuli, instead of being confronted, are merely imagined (Levis, 1985; Stampfl, 1961). First, as usual, the therapist obtains from the client a careful description of the fears in question. Then the client is asked to sit back and imagine highly vivid anxiety-provoking scenes based on that description. The scenes are usually embellished, in addition, with painful details taken from the client's past history, with stimulus cues based on psychodynamic theory, and with whatever gruesome additions the therapist's imagination can provide. Hogan (1968) has provided the following example of a scene used in implosive-therapy research with snake phobics:

> [Imagine that the snakes are] touching you, biting you, try to get that helpless feeling like you can't win, and just give up and let them crawl all over you. Don't even fight them anymore. . . . And now there is a big giant snake, it is as big as a man and it is staring at you and it is looking at you; it's ugly and it's black and it has got horrible eyes and long fangs, and it is coming towards you. . . . Horrible, evil, ugly, slimy, and it's looking down on you, ready to strike at you (p. 429).

Repugnant as this sounds, it is often effective. Implosive therapy has not been evaluated as thoroughly as systematic desensitization, but in a few comparative studies it proved approximately as successful as systematic desensitization in relieving snake phobias (Levis and Hare, 1977).

Aversion Therapy   As we have seen in earlier chapters, **aversion therapy,** whereby a maladaptive response is paired with an aversive stimulus such as electric shock or a nausea-producing drug, has been used extensively in the treatment of sexual deviations, homosexuality, and alcoholism. Such therapy, particularly when it involves electric shock, seems extremely harsh to many people, including many clinicians. Nevertheless, a number of clients consider it far preferable to the behavior they are trying to eradicate. Furthermore, the mere fact that it seems to work in cases where other therapies do not is a strong argument for its use. As we saw in Chapter 18, electric shock has succeeded, where all other techniques have failed, in eliminating self-mutilation in autistic children—something that is a prerequisite for any genuine treatment of such children (Bucher and Lovaas, 1968).

Covert Sensitization   A possible alternative to aversion therapy is covert sensitization. **Covert sensitization** is to aversion therapy as implosive therapy is to flooding. That is, rather than actually encounter-

ing the aversive stimulus, the person simply imagines it. In covert sensitization, clients are asked to conjure up in their minds the image of an extremely painful or revolting stimulus, along with a visualization of the behavior that they are trying to eliminate (Cautela, 1966, 1967). For example, a therapist treating a problem drinker might ask the client to imagine having a pleasurable first and second drink at a party, then becoming progressively more drunk, then becoming violently ill, then vomiting on his clothing and his hostess's Oriental rug, and so forth.

Such therapy, like other forms of aversion therapy and like the extinction therapies, is most successful when it is part of a "package" in which, at the same time that maladaptive behaviors are being eliminated, adaptive behaviors are being built up to replace them. For example, alcoholics undergoing behavior therapy will typically receive treatment not only to eliminate the alcohol dependence but also to build up skills such as stress management and assertiveness, on the assumption that mastery of these skills will allow the clients to solve constructively the problems that they were previously drowning in drink.

Cognitive Restructuring

Several of the techniques we have just described depend on cognitive processes. Systematic desensitization and covert sensitization both use mental imagery; modeling procedures, as we noted, depend on mental variables—memory, admiration of the model, and so forth. Thus, while not the main focus, cognitive processes do play a part in traditional behavior therapy.

In one school of behavior therapy, however, cognitive processes *are* the main focus. That school is cognitive behaviorism. As we saw in Chapter 3, the central tenet of cognitive behaviorism is that cognitions, or thoughts, are the most important causes of behavior; it is our thoughts, more than any external stimuli, that elicit, reward, and punish our actions and thereby control them. Hence if we wish to change a pattern of behavior, we must change the pattern of thoughts underlying it. To this end, the cognitive behaviorists have developed a variety of techniques to increase coping skills, to develop problem solving, and to change the way clients perceive and interpret their worlds (e.g., Kendall and Hollon, 1979). One important set of techniques, called **cognitive restructuring,** has developed from procedures first suggested by cognitive therapists such as Albert Ellis and Aaron T. Beck.

Several individual treatments fall under the heading of cognitive restructuring. Perhaps the oldest is **rational-emotive therapy,** developed by Albert Ellis (1962). Ellis' basic contention is that emotional disturbances are the result not of objective events in people's lives but of the irrational beliefs that guide their interpretations of those events. For example, it is not failure that causes depression but rather failure filtered through the belief that one should be thoroughly competent, adequate, intelligent, and achieving in all possible respects. Likewise, it is not threatening situations that generate anxiety but rather threatening situations interpreted according to the irrational belief that if something is or may be dangerous or frightening, one should be very upset about it. To combat such beliefs, Ellis and his followers point out in blunt terms the irrationality of the client's thinking, model more realistic evaluations of the client's situation (e.g., "So what if your mother didn't love you. That's *her* problem!"), instruct the client to monitor and correct his or her thoughts, rehearse the client in appraising situations realistically, and give homework assignments so that new ways of interpreting experience can be strengthened.

Similar in theory if not in tone is Aaron Beck's (1976) **cognitive therapy.** Like Ellis, Beck holds that emotional disorders are caused primarily by irrational thoughts. We have already described Beck's interpretation and treatment of depression in Chapter 10. In his view, this disturbance is the result of a "cognitive triad" of (1) self-devaluation, (2) a negative view of life experiences, and (3) a pessimistic view of the future. To change such cognitions, Beck adopts a less didactic and more Socratic approach than Ellis, questioning patients in such a way that they themselves gradually discover the inappropriateness of their thoughts.

A more recent variant of cognitive restructuring is **self-instructional training,** developed by Donald Meichenbaum and his colleagues (Meichenbaum, 1975, 1977; Meichenbaum and Cameron, 1973; Meichenbaum and Goodman, 1971). Instead of focusing on general beliefs or attitudes, like Beck and Ellis, these investigators concentrate on "self-talk," the things that people say to themselves before, during, and after their actions. And instead of assessing this self-talk in terms of its rationality or irrationality, they simply try to change it in such a way that instead of defeating the person, it helps him or her to *cope* with

threatening situations. In self-instructional training, therapists will typically model "cognitive coping exercises." First, they will voice defeating self-sentences, so as to alert clients to the kinds of thoughts that trigger and reinforce maladaptive behavior. Then they will "answer back" with more constructive self-talk, thus showing patients how they can combat defeating thoughts. For example, a model in nail-biting treatment might say, "There I go again. Just this one nail, then I'll stop. . . . I knew the treatment wouldn't help me. I just can't control myself. Cut it out. You always make excuses for yourself. Take a slow, deep breath. Relax. Just think of myself sucking my finger in front of everyone. What a picture! . . ." (Meichenbaum, 1975). Finally, clients are asked to practice pairing the behavior with self-talk and reinforcement through graduated performance assignments.

Though differing in tone and emphasis, these three therapies share the same basic goal: to change behavior by changing the thoughts that produce the behavior. But if the cognitive therapists attempt to dig *beneath* behavior to mental processes, what differentiates them from the insight therapists? The essential difference is that they do not seek the deep-seated causes of the patient's cognitions. Their goal is simply to identify those cognitions and then to change them, using well-tried behavioral techniques such as modeling, behavioral rehearsal, and reinforcement. Thus while they focus on mental processes, they still rely on behavioral procedures for altering these processes (Bandura, 1977; Mahoney and Arnkoff, 1978).

Behavior Therapy: Pros and Cons

A commonly voiced criticism of behavior therapy is that it is superficial. Because it does not dwell on the patient's past, does not have insight as a primary goal, and does not concern itself with philosophical issues, it seems shallow to those who feel that therapy should lead to greater self-acceptance and self-understanding. This is a criticism that cannot really be answered. Though many behavior therapists believe in the value of self-understanding, they also feel that it is too vague and grandiose an ideal to serve as a treatment goal. The goal of behavior therapy is simply to provide people with the skills they need in order to deal more effectively with life. If this leads to self-understanding, so much the better. But patients look-

Symptom Substitution

If a problem behavior is merely the "symptom" of an underlying disorder, as the psychodynamic perspective and medical model suggest, then would it not make sense that as soon as one symptom is treated and removed, the underlying disorder, remaining untreated, would simply manifest itself in a new symptom? This notion of "symptom substitution" has for many years been a focus of controversy between the behavioral and psychodynamic perspectives. Psychodynamic theorists, as we have seen, hold strongly to the view that to treat a problem like bedwetting without dealing with the psychic conflicts that presumably underlie this behavior is like treating a fever without treating the infection that is causing it. In contrast, behaviorists hold that a person's problem is whatever problem behaviors he or she has and that searching for a "deeper" problem is unwarranted.

It is probable that in some cases—despite the therapist's efforts to teach the client new, adaptive behaviors to replace the old, maladaptive behavior—symptom substitution does take place. The problem, however, is that we can never know whether a symptom that appears after the termination of treatment is actually a replacement or "stand-in" for the symptom at which the treatment was aimed. The new symptom might easily be a response to new environmental pressures; alternatively, this "new" symptom could actually have been there all the while, along with the treated behavior, but might have simply been ignored because it was not as dramatic or as troublesome as the treated behavior (Bandura, 1969). In short, the question of whether symptom substitution takes place can never be definitively answered, because we have no precise way of determining whether a new symptom, if it does appear, is in fact a substitution.

Nevertheless, it is possible to evaluate whether the client's general functioning improves or gets worse after direct treatment of a problem. Research on this question supports the behaviorists. Most studies report substantial improvement in other areas of functioning (e.g., Bandura et al., 1969; Sloane et al., 1975). Far from producing new maladaptive behaviors, behavioral treatment for the "symptoms" generally results not only in relief from the "symptom" but in extra behavioral benefits (e.g., renewed self-confidence, improved marital relations, increased ability to deal effectively with stress) as well.

ing for treatment that is specifically aimed at self-understanding must look elsewhere.

A more serious version of the "superficiality" charge suggests that behavior therapy can do patients harm by treating their symptoms in a simplistic way and ignoring related or "deeper" problems. In such a case, a patient might undergo "successful" treatment for a problem, only to have another psychological problem appear later because of a neglected underlying condition. This phenomenon, called "symptom substitution" by the critics of behavior therapy, has generally been disconfirmed. (See box above.)

Other critics of behavior therapy argue that it denies individual freedom—that behavior therapists move in and take control of the patient's behavior, manipulating it according to their own values. Actu-ally, all psychotherapies involve some control on the part of the therapist, whether that control is directed toward insight or self-actualization or reconditioning. Likewise, in all therapies the therapist's values play an important part. Indeed, in this respect the only important difference between behavior therapy and the insight therapies is that in the latter the therapist's values are often implicit, whereas the clear spelling out of treatment goals in behavior therapy tends to make the therapist's values clearer to the patient from the start.

How well does behavior therapy do in achieving its goal of behavior change? According to the evidence, quite well. We have already discussed the effectiveness of individual treatment methods. In general, behavior therapy has a good record in treating anxiety and phobias (Emmelkamp, 1986), sexual dysfunction (LoPiccolo and LoPiccolo, 1978), insomnia (Bootzin and Nicassio, 1978), obesity (Brownell, 1982), alcoholism (Nathan et al., 1978), and other problems (Kazdin and Wilson, 1978). For depression, both cognitive and traditional behavioral therapy have been shown to be effective, in about equal measure (Berman et al., 1985; Miller and Berman, 1983).

Aside from the fact that it often works, behavior therapy has other advantages as well. It tends to be faster and less expensive than other therapies. Its techniques can be taught to paraprofessionals and nonprofessionals, so that therapy can be extended beyond the consulting room to hospital wards, classrooms, and homes. Finally, because behavior therapy is precise in its goals and techniques, it can be reported, discussed, and evaluated with precision.

EFFECTIVENESS: WHAT WORKS BEST?

In recent years many comprehensive reviews of psychotherapy outcome studies have appeared, and the results indicate that, on the average, people who receive psychotherapy do better than about 80 percent of those who receive no treatment (Lambert et al., 1986). Furthermore, the effects of psychotherapy have been shown to be as powerful as, or more powerful than, drug treatment. In other words, psychotherapy, in general, works. But do some psychotherapies work better than others?

This is an issue that has been hotly debated for more than three decades. The controversy began in 1952, when the behaviorist Hans Eysenck published a review of psychotherapy outcome studies in which he concluded that the improvement rate for patients who underwent psychodynamic therapy was approximately the same as for people who received no formal treatment at all but simply "waited out" the problem. According to Eysenck, about two-thirds of "neurotics" got better within two years whether they were treated or not. In other words, the patients who underwent psychodynamic therapy could have stayed home and saved their money. In Eysenck's view, the only kind of treatment that worked was behavioral therapy.

Eysenck's article stimulated a good deal of bitter discussion, along with much research aimed at checking his conclusions. The findings, for the most part, have not supported his claims. For one thing, spontaneous remission (i.e., recovery without treatment) is apparently not as common as he judged it to be. In a review of seventeen studies of untreated "neurotics," Bergin and Lambert (1978) found that the median rate of spontaneous remission was 43 percent, considerably lower than Eysenck's figure of 66 percent. Second and more important is the finding, reported by two comprehensive reviews of psychotherapy outcome studies (Luborsky et al., 1975; Smith et al., 1980), that psychodynamic therapy *does* result in greater improvement than no treatment and that in fact psychodynamic, behavioral, and humanistic-existential therapies are approximately equal in effectiveness, with a slight edge to the behavioral. (See Figure 20.1.) The case is by no means closed, however, for many people question the methodological adequacy of the psychodynamic outcomes studies included in the two reviews just cited. In most of these studies the patient's improvement was measured not by any objective yardstick, such as testing or behavioral observation, but by the therapist's overall impression, which in turn was based in part on the patient's self-report—both extremely indirect and bias-prone measures. Yet the same finding of equivalent effectiveness, at least for psychodynamic and behavioral therapies, emerged from a methodologically excellent study undertaken at the Temple University Outpatient Clinic (Sloane et al., 1975). In this study "neurotic" patients seeking treatment at the clinic were matched for age, sex, and severity of problem. They were then randomly assigned to three different conditions: (1) behavior therapy (mostly systematic desensitization), (2) short-term psychodynamic therapy, and (3) a waiting list for treatment. After four months the subjects' improvement was measured via psychological tests, reports from the patients' close associates, and interviews of the patients by blind independent raters—raters who were not involved in treating the subjects and did not know which experimental condition they had been assigned to. The results showed that of those on the waiting list, 48 percent had improved; of those in *either* the psychodynamic or behavioral treatment group, 80 percent had improved. Again a tie.

Other comparative evaluations (e.g., Kazdin and Wilson, 1978) have found behavioral therapy somewhat more successful, but these too are open to question. For example, a review of 143 outcome studies (Shapiro and Shapiro, 1982) found both cognitive and behavioral treatments more than twice as effective

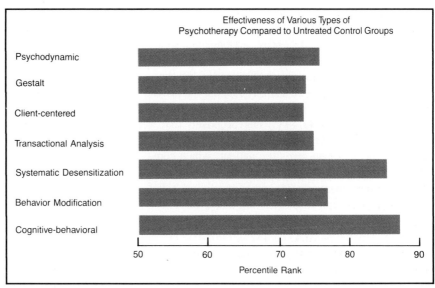

FIGURE 20.1
Is psychotherapy effective? Researchers who reviewed 475 studies think the answer is yes. Clients receiving each of the types of psychotherapy shown in this graph were compared with untreated control groups. The bars indicate the percentile rank that the average treated client attained on outcome measures when compared with control subjects for each type of therapy. Thus the average client receiving psychodynamic therapy scored more favorably on outcome measures than 75 percent of the untreated controls. (Adapted from Smith et al., 1980.)

as either psychodynamic or humanistic therapy, but many of the behavioral and cognitive "treatments" documented in these studies involved college-student volunteers with problems much less severe than those that would turn up in a therapist's office.

In sum, because of the hazards of making comparisons between studies with different methodologies, the results are not really in as regards relative effectiveness. The different therapies need to be much more thoroughly evaluated—a process that is well under way in the behavioral and cognitive camps but is only beginning in the psychodynamic and humanistic therapies.

One trend that has facilitated comparative effectiveness studies is the creation of manuals for specific therapies. For example, Beck and his colleagues (1979) have developed a detailed manual for the administration of cognitive therapy with depressives. This manual has made it possible to train many therapists in this technique and thus to conduct large-scale outcome studies—studies that, incidentally, have

shown cognitive therapy to be at least as effective as drugs in treating acute depression and more effective than drugs in reducing the likelihood of further depressive episodes (Hollon and Beck, 1986). Such studies have in turn prompted others to create manuals so that their methods can be legitimately tested.

INTEGRATION AND ECLECTICISM

In the history of all disciplines, periods of differentiation and competition between theoretical schools are followed by periods of integration, in which different theories mingle, make truces, and learn from one another. Psychology is now in a period of integration (Beutler, 1983; Garfield, 1980; Goldfried, 1980; Orlinsky and Howard, in press).

This development is due in part to the research just discussed. With the provisional finding that all the psychotherapies work, and may work equally well, defensiveness among adherents of different approaches has diminished. Today, writings on treatment tend to emphasize not the differences among the psychotherapies but their similarities and the therapeutic importance of these shared qualities: the provision of support, the giving of information, the raising of hopes. Frank (1961, 1983) has proposed that a central ingredient of all psychotherapies is merely the hope that the therapist gives the patient, which combats demoralization. In support of this suggestion is the finding that many patients experience some relief from their problems after just an initial interview (Howard et al., 1986).

With the recognition of common ground has come a tendency to enlarge that common ground by trading ideas across perspectives. Already some years ago it was found that most therapists regarded themselves not as adherents of a specific perspective but as "eclectic" practitioners (Garfield and Kurtz, 1976), choosing the techniques that served them best from whatever source. Today there is even a *Journal of Integrative and Eclectic Therapy.*

In 1984 a behaviorist, H. Arkowitz, and a psychoanalyst, S. B. Messer, published a book titled *Psychoanalytic Therapy and Behavior Therapy: Is Integration Possible?* Possible or not, it is being tried.

As was noted earlier, behaviorism has been profoundly affected by cognitive theory, and in the process has become increasingly interested in "mental events." Mahoney (1980), a prominent cognitive behaviorist, has even proposed that behavior therapists should start to pay attention to cognitive variables lying outside awareness, and look for ways to bring them into awareness—a concern that would sound familiar to Freud. Conversely, psychodynamic therapists have become more interested in promoting direct behavior change. As with the behaviorists, this shift came originally from within the school—from ego psychology, with its emphasis on the active, adaptive functions of the ego. But today there is a conscious willingness in many quarters to incorporate into psychodynamic therapy the strengths of behaviorism. Wachtel (1977), for example, has suggested that the ideal therapy might involve, first, a psychodynamic "working through" of the patient's problem, with the goal of insight, and then a behavioral treatment aimed at changing the maladaptive behaviors involved in that problem. As we have seen, this is the basic design of many current therapies for sexual dysfunction (Chapter 13).

The integrative trend is seen not just in therapy but in the highest reaches of theory. For example, Kohut's **self psychology** (Chapter 2), one of the most influential recent advances in psychodynamic thought, is not distant from humanistic psychology. In his idea that the crux of personality development is empathy between parent and child and in his consequent belief that empathy in treatment is more effective than interpretation in strengthening the patient's self, Kohut was undoubtedly influenced by Rogers (Kahn, 1985).

This does not mean that the different perspectives have lost their distinctiveness. For one thing, many practitioners want no part of integration. And as for those to whom it appeals, behaviorists may become more introspective and psychodynamic therapists more practical-minded without forsaking the methods in which they were trained. But the differences are blurring somewhat. Action and insight, art and science, are crossing over—a process that makes textbook definitions harder to frame, but that probably is helping patients.

SUMMARY

In psychotherapy—the psychological treatment of emotional problems—the therapist's aim is to establish a relationship with the patient to (1) remove or modify symptoms, (2) mediate disturbed patterns of behavior, and (3) promote positive personality growth. Insight therapy tries to help clients understand their behavior so that they can change or control it; action therapy focuses not on motives but on the problem behavior itself, in an attempt to correct it. Some therapists see psychotherapy as an applied science, whereas others regard it as both a science and an art that depends largely on empathy and intuition.

All psychodynamic therapy is based to some extent on Freudian psychoanalytic theory. In psychoanalysis, the client or patient talks, and the analyst interprets possible connections with unconscious material. The process relies on free association, dream interpretation, analysis of resistance, and analysis of transference. Most psychodynamic therapists today practice a modified form of psychoanalysis that includes neo-Freudian approaches. Two examples are ego psychology, which stresses the importance of interpersonal relationships and of the ego as a source of energy, and Sullivanian therapy. Critics of psychodynamic therapies say that it cannot be validated scientifically, works better for neurotics than for psychotics, is more effective with the articulate, well-educated client, and is prohibitively expensive. Other critics have countered that psychodynamic methods do lead to insight and self-discovery and do identify interpersonal conflicts. Briefer treatment schedules are provided today in response to the financial objection.

Humanistic and existential therapies share the goal of helping clients to become more truly "themselves." Rogers' client-centered therapy aims to remove unrealistic conditions of worth—clients' view that they must be something other than themselves in order to be loved. The therapist relies on warmth, unconditional positive regard, and empathy to promote self-actualization. Existential therapy stresses the acceptance and exercise of freedom through the phenomenological approach. Gestalt therapy helps patients to act out unresolved conflicts, confront their feelings, and become more honest, open, spontaneous, and decisive in dealing with others. Humanistic-existential therapies, like psychodynamic therapies, are criticized as being difficult to validate by scientific measures.

Behavior therapy uses the principles of learning to help patients to change maladaptive behavior. Although earlier behaviorists took a strictly empirical approach to treatment, most behavioral therapists now take account of self-defeating attitudes or expectations, viewing such cognitions as covert responses that, like overt behavior, are subject to the laws of learning. Operant-conditioning techniques are used when the goal is to change overt behavior; respondent-conditioning and extinction techniques are used when the aim is to change emotional responses, such as fear or aversion, that lead to maladaptive behavior.

Operant techniques include contingency management (for example, contingency contracting and time-out from positive reinforcement), stimulus control, engaging in an incompatible behavior, and modeling. Respondent techniques include systematic desensitization, flooding, aversion therapy, and covert sensitization. Cognitive therapists use cognitive restructuring, including rational-emotive therapy, cognitive therapy, and self-instructional training, to change the thought patterns that underlie behavior. Behavior therapy is effective in teaching people better skills to deal with life and is often less expensive and faster than insight therapies. It is criticized for denying the client's freedom and uniqueness and for being superficial.

Since Eysenck's review of therapy effectiveness in 1952, the value of different therapies and of psychotherapy itself has been debated, and assessment measures have been criticized for their reliance on self-reports. Recent studies show, however, that people who receive psychotherapy do better than 80 percent of those who receive no treatment. In comparing therapies, Eynsenck concluded that only behavioral techniques brought clear results, but other studies have suggested that psychodynamic, behavioral, and humanistic-existential therapies are roughly equally effective. Very recent studies indicate that cognitive therapy is as effective as or more effective than drug therapy for acute episodes of depression. Psychotherapies are now in a period of integration: as ideas are traded across perspectives, therapists are becoming more eclectic. Psychodynamic therapists may emphasize behavior change along with the goal of insight, and behaviorists may attend not only to cognitive events representing covert responses but to cognitive variables lying outside awareness.

Approaches to Treatment: Biological Therapy, Group Therapy, and Community-Based Services

In Chapter 20 we discussed individual psychotherapy, in which therapist and client meet alone to discuss the client's problem. This is the traditional way of handling nonpsychotic patients. At the same time, other kinds of treatment are often used in addition to, or in place of, individual therapy. One is biological treatment, especially drug therapy. Another is

group and family treatment, less expensive and, according to some writers, more realistic than individual psychotherapy, since it retains the interpersonal context that is the setting (and, in some cases, at least the partial cause) of psychological disturbance. Finally, some patients must be institutionalized, and accordingly, special treatments must be designed for the institutional setting. In this chapter we will discuss these three categories of treatment—biological, group, and institutional—along with the broader subject of community-based mental health services, which attempt to organize and administer the various forms of treatment for a given population.

BIOLOGICAL THERAPIES

As we saw in our chapters on depression and schizophrenia, the last decade has seen a rapid accumulation of evidence that both of these disorders are related to biochemical abnormalities, particularly in the action of neurotransmitters. These advances have influenced the study of "neurotic" disorders as well. Biogenic theories—and consequently biological therapies—have risen dramatically in prestige, and neuroscience research is now one of the best-funded, most active, and most exciting areas of abnormal psychology. We shall examine three major biological treatments: drugs, electroconvulsive therapy, and psychosurgery.

Drugs

Most of the advances in neuroscience are taking place in **psychopharmacology,** the study of the drug treatment of psychological disorders. With each new advance in our understanding of brain chemistry, new drugs are developed. In turn, the action of those drugs tells us more about the biochemistry of psychological disturbance.

Three major categories of drugs are used in treating abnormal behavior (see Table 21.1). We shall discuss four types: antianxiety, antipsychotic, antidepressant, and antimanic drugs.

Antianxiety Drugs   At least once a year, one of every ten adults in the United States uses one of the **antianxiety drugs** (Uhlenhuth et al., 1983), also called **minor tranquilizers,** the most common being Tranxene (chlorazepate), Librium (chlordiazepoxide hydrochloride), and Valium (diazepam). In most cases, these drugs are prescribed by family doctors for people who are not in psychological treatment but are simply going through a hard time in their lives. Indeed, half the users of such drugs are people who are medically ill; the drug is prescribed to control the patient's emotional reactions to the illness (Uhlenhuth et al., 1983). However, antianxiety drugs are also often used in conjunction with psychological treatment, particularly for anxiety disorders, stress-related physical disorders, and withdrawal from alcohol and other drugs. Recently a newer antianxiety drug, Xanax, has proved very helpful in the treatment of panic disorders (Klerman, 1986), as have antidepressants.

Antianxiety drugs are not without problems. For one thing, they have side effects, the most common being fatigue, drowsiness, and impaired motor coordination—reason enough for users to avoid driving. Another unwelcome effect of these drugs, especially when taken in large doses, is that once the drug treatment is terminated, the symptom that they were prescribed to eliminate may return with redoubled strength. Thus the person is likely to resume taking the drug—in larger and larger doses, because of tolerance—in order to suppress the now-magnified symptom. This is particularly true in the case of insomnia and nightmares, for which antianxiety drugs are often prescribed. Finally, antianxiety drugs can be very dangerous or even fatal when taken in combination with other central nervous system depressants, especially alcohol.

However, the most common criticism of the antianxiety drugs is that they invite people to avoid solving their problems. As Freud pointed out, anxiety is a *signal.* Or, to use Schwartz's disregulation model (Chapter 9), anxiety is part of a negative feedback loop—an alarm bell telling us that something needs adjusting, either in the environment or in our response to it. By taking antianxiety drugs, we suppress the signal, but we do not solve the problem. Indeed, the problem may become more serious as a result of our ignoring it. Taking antianxiety drugs, then, is something like turning off a fire alarm because we can't stand the noise.

Even when drugs are used in conjunction with psychotherapy, there is some question as to their usefulness. Learning, as psychologists have discovered, is state-dependent (Ho et al., 1978; Overton, 1966). What we learn in a given biological or psychological state does not fully generalize to other states. Thus if, while taking antianxiety medication, we learn new skills for dealing with stress, this does not mean that these skills will necessarily survive the withdrawal of the medication.

In sum, antianxiety drugs, while they may be useful on a short-term basis in certain situations, can also be counterproductive. To an extent, we *need* to expe-

TABLE 21.1 MAJOR PSYCHOTHERAPEUTIC DRUGS

Category	Chemical Structure or Psychopharmacologic Action	Generic Name	Trade Name
Antipsychotics (also called "major tranquilizers" or "neuroleptics")	Phenothiazines	Chlorpromazine	Thorazine
	Aliphatic	Thioridazine	Mellaril
	Piperidine	Trifluoperazine	Stelazine
	Piperazine		
	Thioxanthenes		
	Aliphatic	Chlorprothixene	Taractan
	Piperazine	Thioxthixene	Navane
	Butyrophenones	Haloperidol	Haldol
	Dibenzoxazepines	Loxapine	Loxitane
	Dihydroindolines	Molindone	Moban
	Rauwolfia alkaloids	Reserpine	Sandril
	Benzoquinolines	Tetrabenazine	
Antidepressants	Tricyclic antidepressants (TCAs)		
	Tertiary amines	Amitriptyline	Elavil
		Imipramine	Tofranil
		Doxepin	Sinequan
	Secondary amines	Desipramine	Norpramin
		Nortriptyline	Pamelor
		Protriptyline	Vivactil
	Monoamine oxidase inhibitors (MAOIs)	Phenelzine	Nardil
		Tranylcypromine	Parnate
		Pargyline	Eutonyl
		Isocarboxazid	Marplan
Antimanic drugs		Lithium	Eskalith
		Carbamazapine	Tegretol
Antianxiety drugs (also called "anxiolytics" or "minor tranquilizers")	Benzodiazepines	Chlordiazepoxide	Librium
		Diazepam	Valium
		Chlorazepate	Tranxene
		Oxazepam	Serax
		Lorazepam	Activan
	Triazolobenzodiazepine	Alprazolam	Xanax
	Triazolam	Halcion	
	Propanediol carbamates	Meprobamate	Miltown
	Barbiturates	Phenobarbital	Luminal

rience our anxiety in order to alert us to problems, to motivate us to solve them, and to test the effectiveness of our solutions.

Antipsychotic Drugs   As their name indicates, the **antipsychotic drugs** (also called **major tranquilizers** or **neuroleptics**) are used to relieve symptoms of psychosis—confusion, withdrawal, hallucinations, delusions, and so forth. The most common

antipsychotic drugs are the phenothiazines, which we have already discussed briefly in Chapter 15. As with so many other drugs, the therapeutic use of the phenothiazines was discovered by accident. Phenothiazine, the nucleus of this group of compounds, was first synthesized in 1883 by a German research chemist and was used to treat infections of the digestive system in animals. That the drug also had psychoactive properties was not understood until sixty years later, when the antihistamines, which also have a phenothiazine base, were discovered. Antihistamines, it was found, not only helped to relieve colds and allergies (their major use today) but also had tranquilizing effects. This discovery prompted chemists to look again at the other phenothiazines. In 1950 a French drug company produced a new phenothiazine derivative called chlorpromazine, advertised as a potent tranquilizer. Four years later chlorpromazine was marketed in the United States under the trade name Thorazine. It was an overnight success. Within eight months of its appearance, it had been used by approximately 2 million patients (*Hospital and Community Psychiatry,* 1976). Today the vast majority of psychotic patients in the United States take either Thorazine or one of the other phenothiazines, such as Stelazine (trifluoperazine), Prolixin (fluphenazine), or Mellaril (thioridazine), on a daily basis.

No one disputes that phenothiazines actually work—that they reduce schizophrenic symptoms (Andrews et al., in press). They have also had a great impact on schizophrenia research. It was the effort to find out how the phenothiazines worked that led biochemical researchers to the dopamine hypothesis, which at this point seems the most promising of the etiological theories. At the same time, by reducing disruptive behavior in schizophrenic patients, phenothiazines have radically altered the conditions under which these patients live. Patients who would have been in straitjackets thirty years ago are now free to roam hospital grounds. And many patients are sufficiently calm and functional to be released altogether, though they must go on taking the drug.

This is not to say that the phenothiazines are without drawbacks. In producing calm, they often produce fatigue and apathy as well, reducing the patient to a "zombielike" state. Capitalizing on this effect, some hospitals have been known to use high doses of Thorazine for "patient management"—that is, to control patients who are making trouble. (Such high doses usually tranquilize patients to the point where they can barely move for several days.) Phenothiazines also tend to produce constipation, blurred vision, dry mouth, and muscle rigidity and tremors. In some cases, these side effects can be relieved by other drugs. However, there is an additional side effect that has so far proved resistant to treatment. That is **tardive dyskinesia,** a muscle disorder in which patients grimace and smack their lips uncontrollably. Tardive dyskinesia usually appears in patients over forty after at least six months of continuous treatment with antipsychotic drugs. Unlike other side effects, it does

not disappear when the drug is discontinued. On the contrary, it usually surfaces when the drug dosage is reduced or when the drug is withdrawn altogether. Estimates of the incidence of tardive dyskinesia in chronically hospitalized schizophrenics are as low as 0.5 percent and as high as 40 percent (Crane, 1973)—a range that suggests faulty reporting.

Finally, it should be stressed that phenothiazines alone cannot solve the problem of schizophrenia. Patients who are released from the hospital under the calming influence of phenothiazines usually make only a marginal adjustment to life on the outside. And sometimes, once outside, they stop taking the drugs. In many cases they have to be readmitted, only to be released and readmitted again. Thus although phenothiazines have definitely reduced the number of chronically hospitalized schizophrenics, it has been argued that they have merely replaced long-term institutionalization with "revolving door" admission. This outcome, however, is due less to an unkept promise—no one ever claimed that the phenothiazines cured schizophrenia—than to a lack of services for released patients, a problem that we will address later in this chapter.

Antidepressant and Antimanic Drugs   Antidepressant drugs, as the name indicates, are used to elevate mood in depressed patients. The first important class of antidepressants to gain a wide following were the **MAO inhibitors,** including phenelzine (Nardil) and tranylcypromine (Parnate). The name of this class of drugs is derived from the fact that they interfere with the action of the enzyme monoamine oxidase (MAO). MAO serves to degrade certain neurotransmitters, including norepinephrine and serotonin, in the nervous system. As we saw in Chapter 10, deficiencies of both norepinephrine and serotonin have been implicated in depression. By blocking the action of MAO, the MAO inhibitors presumably correct this deficiency. However, it has never been satisfactorily established that the MAO inhibitors are actually more effective than placebos in relieving depression (Davis et al., 1967). Furthermore, these drugs can have adverse effects on the brain, the liver, and the cardiovascular system, and when combined with certain other drugs or foods—especially foods prepared by fermentation (e.g., beer, some varieties of cheese, and wine)—can result in severe illness and even death.

Because of all these problems, the MAO inhibitors have been largely replaced in recent years by another class of antidepressants, the **tricyclics,** so named for their three-ringed molecular structure. Commonly used tricyclics are imipramine (Tofranil) and doxepin (Sinequan). The tricyclics seem to produce, by a different route, the same effect that the MAO inhibitors are thought to produce: an increase in the level of certain neurotransmitters, including norepinephrine and serotonin. Unlike the MAO inhibitors, however, the tricyclics have substantial evidence to support their effectiveness, particularly with endogenous depressions (Akiskal and McKinney, 1975; Andrews et al., 1983). They, too, have some unpleasant side effects, similar to those of the phenothiazines: drowsiness, blurred vision, constipation, dry mouth. But presumably because tricyclics are taken in smaller doses than phenothiazines, these side effects are milder, and they do not include tardive dyskinesia. Another disadvantage is that the tricyclics do not begin to take effect for about two to four weeks—which, to a severely depressed person, is a long time to wait for relief. Still, these drugs have proved remarkably successful with many patients, and they are now a widely used treatment for depression. New, quicker-acting antidepressants have recently been introduced, but it is not yet known whether they will be as effective as the tricyclics.

Another mood-altering drug that has caused some excitement in recent years is the antimanic medication, **lithium.** Lithium is administered as lithium carbonate, a natural mineral salt that has no known physiological function (Berger, 1978). Yet for some reason this simple salt is capable of ending swiftly and effectively about 70 percent of all manic episodes. In some cases, it also terminates depressive episodes, particularly in bipolar patients (Bassuk and Schoonover, 1977; Berger, 1978; Segal et al., 1976). At the moment, its great virtue is preventive: when taken regularly, in maintenance doses, it is generally effective in eliminating or at least diminishing mood swings in bipolar disorder. Prescribing maintenance doses, however, is somewhat tricky, since for most patients the effective dosage is close to the toxic dosage, and a toxic dose can cause convulsions, delirium, and, in rare cases, death (Lydiard and Gelenberg, 1982). An overdose is generally preceded by clear warning signs, such as nausea, alerting the patient to discontinue the drug. Still, because of its potential dangers, patients who take lithium must have regular blood tests to monitor the level of the drug in their systems.

Electroconvulsive Therapy

For reasons that are not completely understood, electric shock seems to help in relieving depression. This type of treatment, known as **electroconvulsive therapy (ECT),** involves administering to the patient a shock of approximately 70 to 130 volts, thus inducing a convulsion similar to a tonic-clonic (grand mal) epileptic seizure. Typically, therapy involves about nine or ten such treatments, spaced over a period of several weeks, though the total may be much lower or higher.

This technique was first discovered in the thirties (Bini, 1938). Since that time it has become clear that, like antidepressants, the shock affects the levels of norepinephrine and serotonin in the brain, but theories as to its exact mode of operation are as various and incomplete as those regarding the antidepressants. At present all we know is that electric shock apparently *does* work, and quite well, for many depressed patients, especially endogenous cases (Greenblatt, 1977; NIMH, 1985; Scovern and Kilmann, 1980). In 1980 approximately 33,000 patients—that is, about 2.4 percent of all psychiatric admissions—received ECT (NIMH, 1985).

Like other biological treatments, ECT has its complications. The most common side effect is memory dysfunction, both anterograde (the capacity to learn new material) and retrograde (the capacity to recall material learned before the treatment). Research indicates that in the great majority of cases, anterograde memory gradually improves after treatment (Squire and Slater, 1978). As for retrograde memory, there is generally a marked loss one week after treatment, with nearly complete recovery within seven months after treatment. In many cases, however, some subtle memory losses, particularly for events occurring within the year preceding hospitalization, will persist beyond seven months (Squire et al., 1981). And in very rare cases (e.g., Roueché, 1974), such persisting losses are not subtle, but comprehensive and debilitating. The probability of memory dysfunction is less if ECT is confined to only one hemisphere of the brain (Squire and Slater, 1978), the one having less to do with language functions—as we saw in Chapter 5, this is usually the right hemisphere—and this approach has proved as effective as bilateral shock (Horne et al., 1985).

Another problem with ECT is that although the treatment is painless (the patient is anesthetized before the shock is administered), many patients are mortally afraid of it. And in some cases, ward personnel have made use of this fear, again for "patient management," telling patients that if they don't cooperate, they will have to be recommended for an ECT series.

These problems have made ECT an extremely controversial issue in recent years. Defenders of ECT point out that many studies have found it highly effective—more effective, in fact, than antidepressants (NIMH, 1985; Birmingham University Clinical Psychiatry Committee, 1965; Greenblatt et al., 1966). Furthermore, unlike antidepressants, it works relatively quickly—an important advantage with suicidally depressed patients. On the other hand, ECT has vociferous critics, who consider it yet another form of psychiatric assault on mental patients. These writers (e.g., Costello, 1976) point out that most of the studies of ECT's effectiveness have used poor methodology—for example, raters who knew what treatments the subjects had received—and therefore prove nothing. In support of this view, the voters of Berkeley, California, in 1982 passed a referendum making the administration of ECT a misdemeanor punishable by a fine of up to $500 and six months in jail. While the ban was later reversed by the courts, the fact that the voters passed it indicates the strength of opposition to this treatment.

Though the controversy over ECT is not settled, it has already had its impact on practice. State legislatures have established legal safeguards against the abuse of ECT, and in general the technique is being used less frequently than it was a decade ago. At the same time, a 1985 National Institute of Mental Health Consensus Conference concluded that ECT *was* an effective treatment for endogenous and delusional depressions and should be used, particularly in cases where other treatments, such as antidepressants, have failed.

Psychosurgery

Psychosurgery is surgery aimed at reducing abnormal behavior. In 1935, two Portuguese physicians, Egas Moniz and Almeida Lima, developed what is called the **prefrontal lobotomy.** In this surgical procedure an instrument is inserted into the frontal lobe and rotated, thus destroying a substantial portion of brain tissue. The theory behind this technique was that in extremely disturbed patients, activity in the frontal lobe was intensifying emotional impulses originating in lower parts of the brain, especially the thalamus and hypothalamus. Presumably, if some of the connections between the frontal lobe and these lower regions could be severed, behavior would improve. This was the goal of the operation.

In the 1940s and early 1950s thousands of lobotomies were performed, and some patients undoubtedly benefited from them. Others, however, emerged from surgery in a vegetative state, in which they remained permanently; others were hostile, childlike, lethargic, or generally devoid of affect; some suffered recurring convulsions; some died (Redlich and Freedman, 1966). It was therefore with considerable relief that mental health professionals welcomed the phenothiazines in the 1950s as a safer method of calming the severely disturbed. Lobotomy is now resorted to only very rarely.

In recent years, however, researchers have developed more refined psychosurgical techniques—techniques that destroy less brain tissue and therefore produce fewer and milder side effects. In one procedure, called **stereotactic subcaudate tractotomy,** a small localized area of the brain is destroyed by radioactive particles inserted through small ceramic rods. The site varies with the nature of the disturbance. For depressed patients, it is the frontal lobe; for aggressive patients, it is the amygdala, a structure in the lower part of the brain.

These techniques are used only for severely disturbed patients who have not responded to other treatments. Psychosurgery has been found to be effective with severe depression, anxiety, and obsessions (Bridges and Bartlett, 1977). Nevertheless, it is still extremely controversial. Its defenders claim that the benefits are substantial and the side effects relatively mild. Other observers doubt both claims and feel that the public should be very wary of such radical and irreversible treatments. In particular, many writers, including many psychosurgeons, feel that surgical procedures for controlling aggression should be regarded with the gravest suspicion, as procedures that could easily be abused (Valenstein, 1973).

Evaluation

The major objection to drugs, other than their side effects, is that they do not cure disorders but only suppress symptoms. Ideally, anxiety, depression, and schizophrenia should be attacked at their roots, and in some cases, such as anxiety, drugs are a poor substitute for psychotherapy. But in other cases, we do not know what the roots of the problem are, or how to attack them, and in the meantime the patient requires some relief. Antidepressants are surely preferable to suicide or, for that matter, to unrelieved misery. Likewise, the antipsychotic drugs are preferable to straitjackets, and they have unquestionably introduced a calmer atmosphere in modern mental hospitals.

This latter improvement should not be regarded lightly, for it has made other, nondrug therapies possible. And as a number of researchers have found, drug therapy combined with psychotherapy can be more effective than either of these treatments alone. The reason, according to Klerman (1986), is that each therapy may bolster the other, the drugs making the patient willing and able to engage in psychotherapy, and the psychotherapy increasing the patient's motivation to take the drugs and building on their positive effects.

Unfortunately, however, many patients, particularly those in institutions, receive *only* drugs. Drugs are far easier and less expensive to administer than psychotherapy. Consequently, when budgets are cut back, it is the psychotherapy that is eliminated, not the drugs. And it is arguable that by calming the patients, drugs have encouraged such cutbacks, as well as making the need for better treatments seem less urgent.

As for ECT, its risks, in the form of memory loss, have already been discussed. Nevertheless, it is apparently an effective treatment for severe endogenous depression that has not responded to other forms of treatment.

The risks of psychosurgery are far graver, but they must still be weighed against the patient's problem. If, for example, a man is subject to uncontrollable fits of violence, so that he must be kept locked in solitary confinement, is he better or worse off if surgery eliminates his rage attacks but leaves him sexually impotent? On the one hand, it can be said that the surgery has enabled him to function in *some* capacity; on the other hand, it can be argued that his physicians should have gone on looking for some other, less risky treatment. Psychosurgery is a treatment of last resort, but even as a last resort, it will undoubtedly remain controversial.

GROUP AND FAMILY THERAPY

Unquestionably one of the most significant changes in psychological treatment in recent years has been the group therapy movement. Treatment in groups has the obvious advantage of saving time and money. Instead of seeing only one client per hour, the therapist can handle perhaps eight or ten. This means that each client pays less for the therapist's time. It also

In recent years, group therapy has shown a marked increase. In addition to its financial advantages for the client, this approach offers several psychological benefits—among them, the security of belonging to a close-knit group, the chance to practice new interpersonal skills, and the comforting knowledge that one's problems are not unique. (Baron Wolman/Woodfin Camp & Associates)

means that more people, in absolute terms, can receive help—an important advantage in a society where mental health professionals are in short supply.

However, cost efficiency alone does not account for the spectacular rise of group therapy. Rather, the popularity of this type of treatment is due primarily to the current belief that many psychological difficulties are basically interpersonal difficulties—problems in dealing with other people—and that consequently these difficulties must be worked out in an interpersonal context—that is, with other people. These other people may be one's "significant others"; thus a couple or an entire family may be treated together. Or the members of a group may have nothing more in common than the fact that they are all human beings with problems.

The number of different kinds of group therapy is staggering. There are behavioral groups, psychodynamic groups, and many, many varieties of humanistic groups. What specifically does group treatment have to offer? Irwin Yalom (1975) has listed ten factors that help to promote therapeutic change in this type of treatment. They are:

1. *Information.* From the group leader the clients can acquire information about psychological disturbance, psychodynamics, reinforcement contingencies, and so on. Clients may also receive advice and direct guidance as to their specific problems from both the group leader and the other members of the group.

2. *Hope.* Like most other kinds of therapy, group therapy instills in clients the hope that they can change, and this hope has great therapeutic value.

3. *Universality.* Clients often enter therapy believing that they are "unique in their wretchedness" (Yalom, 1975, p. 10)—that no one else could possibly have thoughts or feelings as frightening and unacceptable as theirs. In the group they make the comforting discovery that such problems are relatively common.

4. *Altruism.* Group members help one another with advice, encouragement, and sympathy. In the process, the givers learn that they have something to offer their fellow human beings, while the receivers learn that they are not alone. This exchange of social support is perhaps the chief virtue of group therapy.

5. *Corrective recapitulation of the family group.* The group is like a family, with leaders representing parents and other members representing siblings. Thus the group, as a sort of new family, may help to heal wounds and ease inhibitions produced by the client's original family.

6. *Development of social skills.* Corrective feedback from other group members may help to correct flaws in the client's interpersonal behavior (e.g., a sarcastic tone of voice, a condescending manner).

7. *Imitative behavior.* The group leader and other members of the group may serve as useful models for new kinds of behavior.

8. *Interpersonal learning.* By interacting with the group, clients may gain insight into themselves and revise their ideas of the kinds of relationships they want to have. Furthermore, the group may serve as a social laboratory in which to try out new "selves" and new kinds of relationships.

9. *Group cohesiveness.* The sense of belongingness and intimacy that develops within the group as a whole may give clients both comfort and courage.

10. *Catharsis.* Within the protective atmosphere of the group, members may feel free to express emotions that they have been bottling up, to the detriment of their behavior, for years.

Not all these factors are unique to group therapy; information is conveyed, hope instilled, behavior modeled, and catharsis achieved in individual therapy as well. Furthermore, not all these factors will be equally important in every form of group therapy. Nevertheless, this list helps to show the mechanisms by which group therapy in general operates. And in the following section, it will help us differentiate among modes of group treatment.

Psychodynamic Approaches to Group Treatment

In psychodynamic theory, as we have seen, childhood conflicts are seen as the key to psychological disturbance, and insight into these conflicts is considered the key to therapeutic change. Hence, not surprisingly, psychodynamic group therapy stresses items 5 and 8 of Yalom's list—corrective recapitulation of the family group and interpersonal learning. There are many variations on the psychodynamic group. For example, there are psychoanalytically inspired groups that focus on interpretation, working through of transference, and dealing with resistance, much as would be done in psychoanalysis with individuals (e.g., Slavson, 1964). The following case study illustrates how transference might be interpreted within group therapy. The patient always had had problems explaining his actions to his alcoholic father.

> Half an hour after he entered a therapy group, this mild, soft-spoken man had three men, who had long been in the group, sitting silently and respectfully listening to his detailed disclosure of what had brought him to the group. This behavior was unnatural for the group members, who usually interacted more freely. The therapist saw that the patient had at once begun to act out a piece of transference and was enjoying being the father or master artist to these men, who listened intently. He was bringing a piece of his past into the group, like a calling card. Instead of commenting on the general mood of the group, which would have been appropriate enough, the therapist pointed out, in terms of transference, that the patient had introduced this air of the powerful father controlling the men and that the three men were encouraging him to do so. The mood changed at once and the members resumed interacting more freely (Day and Semrad, 1971, p. 572).

Some psychodynamic therapists recommend the use of group and individual therapy in combination so that the issues raised in each can be dealt with in the other (Caligor et al., 1984).

Psychodrama   A specialized form of psychoanalytically oriented group therapy is psychodrama, developed in the 1920s by J. L. Moreno, a Viennese psychiatrist. Participants in **psychodrama** act out their emotional conflicts in company with other group members, often on an actual stage. If a male member of the group is terrified of women, for example, he may be put on the stage with a female member of the group, playing his mother, and will be asked to act out a childhood scene with her. If necessary, other members may enter the play as his father, his brothers, or his sisters. Presumably the sources of the client's fear of women will emerge in the family drama.

This basic pattern may then be varied in a number of ways (Starr, 1977; Yablonsky, 1976). Three common techniques are **role reversal,** in which actors switch parts; the **double technique,** in which the therapist gets up on the stage and acts out a client's part at the same time that the client does; and **mirroring,** in which group members portray one another on the stage. In each case, the goal is to show clients how they actually behave and why they behave in that way. The usefulness of this technique has not been lost on therapists of other persuasions. As we shall see, several kinds of therapy involve role playing (Kipper, 1981).

According to Moreno (1946), psychodrama has several advantages over conventional therapy. First, many feelings can be acted out but not adequately described or explained. Second, the therapeutic acting out helps to prevent irrational and destructive acting out in everyday life. Third, role taking, especially in a family drama, encourages clients to reveal the deepest roots of their problems, which can then be discussed within the group. Finally, like almost all forms of group therapy, psychodrama enables clients to learn from one another.

Behavioral Approaches to Group Treatment

Most behavioral group therapy is directed toward a very specific goal. In consequence, behavioral groups are less likely than other kinds of groups to depend heavily on the vague and uncontrollable variable called "group process," the sum of the interactions within the group, as the major mechanism of change. This does not mean that the group format serves no significant purpose in behavioral group therapy—only that its importance varies. At one end of the continuum, groups of clients may be brought together to undergo relaxation training or systematic desensitization in the same place at the same time; here the group format is simply a convenience, aimed at saving the therapist's time and the client's money. Further along the continuum, there are many kinds of special-purpose groups—for example, groups to stop smoking or to lose weight—in which the group plays a more important role. While instructions and exercises provided by the group leader constitute the major therapeutic tools, social support from group members serves as a valuable source of reinforcement. At the far end of the continuum is social-skills training, where the group format is of great importance, since the clients use one another to rehearse the new interpersonal skills that they are learning. Thus the degree of dependence on group interaction ranges from small to great. It should be added, however, that the kinds of therapy that behaviorists do in groups could be (and are) done, without much change of technique, in individual counseling as well. This could not be said of most psychodynamic and humanistic groups.

In general, behavioral groups concentrate on items 1, 6, and 7 of Yalom's list: information, corrective feedback on social behavior, and opportunities for modeling. We shall describe social-skills training, which combines these three elements and which, as we saw above, makes greater use of group interaction than do other varieties of behavioral groups.

Social-Skills Training and Assertiveness Training
Social-skills training, mentioned in earlier chapters, is based on the premise that many behavior problems are due not (or not only) to deep-rooted emotional conflicts but to a lack of expertise in dealing with certain interpersonal situations—giving and receiving criticism, accepting and offering compliments, approaching members of the opposite sex, and so forth. In social-skills training, useful responses to such situations are taught through what is called **behavioral rehearsal,** in which the therapist tells clients how to perform the target behavior, models the behavior for them, and then has them practice the behavior repeatedly in little skits that simulate the situations they find troubling.

Social-skills training may be conducted on either an individual or a group basis. When it is conducted in groups, the participants are people with similar interpersonal problems, and the training focuses on those particular problems. With a group of juvenile delinquents, for example, the therapist would concentrate on how to respond to authority figures, how to react to aggression, how to act in a job interview, and so forth (Sarason, 1976). With clients whose major complaint is shyness, sessions would be devoted to practice in starting a conversation, asking for a date, responding to a request for one's phone number, and other shyness-provoking situations (Zimbardo, 1977). Additional social-skills programs have been designed for, among others, depressives (Sanchez and Lewinsohn, 1980) and chronic psychotic patients (Hersen et al., 1975; Hogarty et al., 1986).

One form of social-skills training that has become quite popular in recent years is **assertiveness training.** Assertiveness is often defined as the ability to stand up for one's rights without violating other people's rights. It is actually somewhat broader than that, however. It can perhaps best be characterized as a style of behavior based on the assumption that one's own feelings and opinions *count.* Andrew Salter (1949), one of the earliest therapists to discuss assertiveness, drew up for his clients a list of rules that nicely summarize an assertive approach to life. They are: (1) Verbally express your feelings; that is, let people know when you are happy, sad, determined, angry, and so forth. (2) Show your emotions nonverbally. If you are happy, smile and look happy; if angry, scowl. (3) When you disagree with someone, contradict that person. Do not sit quietly. (4) Use the pronoun "I" as much as possible. (5) Express agreement when praised. (6) Improvise; live for the moment.

Such an agenda, if followed relentlessly and without regard to circumstances, might produce overbearing behavior. However, as an antidote to a state of anxious passivity, it is quite useful. As assertiveness training has developed in the hands of later therapists, it has incorporated several of Salter's rules.

In group assertiveness training, clients discuss their particular problems with assertiveness and then, under the therapist's guidance, role-play more assertive responses in those situations. In the following dialogue, for example, "Sally" is rehearsing a more forthright way of dealing with her boss. "Louis," a group member who has problems being a boss, has volunteered to play the boss:

> *Louis:* What were you hired for? (speaks in a good firm voice)
> *Sally:* Typist. Now I'm doing record keeping, have no lunch hour. I'm answering phones all day (complaining tone of voice).
> *Louis:* What do you want?
> *Sally:* I really can't handle all this work you pile on me (voice is cracking and she is close to tears).
> [*Therapist*]: What did you want? What are your goals?
> *Sally:* I want him to know there's too much work for one person. We need an extra person.
> [*Therapist*]: Did you tell him that? (Fodor, 1980, p. 530)

In many cases, the therapist will first model the assertive response. In all cases, the client's role playing is followed by feedback from the therapist and the other group members. Then it is practiced again and again until the client feels comfortable with it. In addition to these group exercises, clients are usually given "homework" assignments. (For example, someone who is overly aggressive may be "assigned" to practice making a complaint at a restaurant in a more effective manner.) Problems encountered while carrying out these tasks will be brought back to the group session, and especially troubling situations will be re-rehearsed.

The major therapeutic tools in this kind of treatment are modeling, rehearsal, and reinforcement. However, assertiveness training is also an extinction therapy, in that the clients learn that no catastrophe will ensue if they express their true feelings and prevent people from taking advantage of them. In addition, most assertiveness training involves some cognitive therapy. Clients are asked to discuss and reexamine their fear of rejection, their sense that it is "wrong" to complain, their tendency to define themselves in terms of others' approval, and other assertiveness-squelching attitudes and emotions.

Humanistic Approaches to Group Treatment

Of all the theoretical schools, it is the humanistic perspective that has interested itself most intensely in the unique possibilities of group therapy, as opposed to individual therapy. And it is this perspective that has contributed most to the group therapy movement. (Conversely, the rise of group therapy in the last two decades has contributed greatly to the influence of humanistic psychology.) In humanistic groups, more than in any other kind, it is the *group* experience that is foremost. To return to Yalom's list, the emphasis is on items 4 and 8, altruism (or social support) and interpersonal learning. The major therapeutic gains are expected to come from (1) developing intimacy and cooperation by virtue of being part of a mutually supportive group and (2) finding out about oneself by interacting candidly with others. In addition, many humanistic groups also stress Yalom's item 10, emotional catharsis, on the assumption that this is both therapeutic for the client and conducive to intimacy within the group as a whole.

Encounter Groups, T-Groups, and Gestalt Groups   The earliest forms of humanistic group therapy were the **encounter group,** originating in

such human-potential centers as California's Esalen Institute, and the **sensitivity-training group,** or **T-group,** first introduced in the late forties to help group leaders improve the functioning of groups by the use of democratic methods and then later to help business executives improve their relations with their co-workers. Originally the encounter group was the more radical of the two, encouraging touching exercises, yelling, weeping, and other unrestrained shows of emotion. In contrast, the T-group limited itself to somewhat more subdued verbal interchanges. However, as the group therapy movement has grown, the distinctions between the two types have blurred considerably.

A third tributary of humanistic group treatment was Gestalt therapy. As we saw in Chapter 20, Gestalt therapy offers clients the opportunity to finish their "unfinished business"—to dredge up unresolved emotional conflicts, act them out, and take responsibility for the feelings involved. Such therapy has been conducted not only in individual counseling but also in groups, where participants help one another work through their emotional crises. Gestalt groups, in their pure form, differ from T-groups in that they encourage unrestrained emotional outpourings. (In this respect the Gestalt group is closer to the encounter group.) And Gestalt groups differ from both encounter groups and T-groups in that they concern themselves with their participants' past histories, whereas the other two kinds of groups generally confine discussion to the "here and now"—that is, the emotions and perceptions occurring within the group at that particular moment. Here again, however, there has been much cross-fertilization, and the distinctions among the different kinds of groups are no longer clear-cut.

The central goals of humanistically oriented group therapy are, predictably, personal growth—that is, understanding of and experimentation with one's own behavior—and increased openness and honesty in personal relations. Note that the emphasis is positive rather than negative, as is typical of humanistic psychology. The members are there not to become less sick but to become more well. Indeed, hundreds of people join groups not because they feel they are psychologically disturbed but simply because they find their lives somewhat lacking in intensity or intimacy.

During a typical session, group members may talk about the problems they encounter in their outside lives, but the emphasis usually shifts to the members' reactions to one another, which they are encouraged to express with complete candor. Love, anger, warmth, suspicion—whatever a member feels toward another member he or she is free to voice. And the other member is free to respond in kind, so that both can gain practice in expressing their emotions honestly, achieve some insight into how they affect other people, and eventually learn how to work out interpersonal conflicts with patience, tolerance, and sympathy.

During such interchanges, the group leader (sometimes called the "facilitator") straddles a fence between directing and participating. On the one hand, the leader is fair game for the other participants; he or she is not to be the "expert," as in other therapies. On the other hand, the leader must also make sure that each person is allowed a fair say and that no member is made a scapegoat by the group (Aronson, 1972).

Such are the basic themes of the humanistic group, but they are subject to hundreds of variations. Some groups are conducted as marathons, lasting as long as an entire weekend, with only short breaks, if any, for sleep. This has been called the "pressure cooker" approach to therapeutic change. Presumably, by exposing clients to one another for hours on end, without distractions or interruptions, the marathon creates a continual buildup of emotional intensity and thus hastens the process of self-revelation. There are numerous other techniques as well. Some groups are conducted in the nude, others in swimming pools. Some use "warming up" exercises, such as **eyeball-to-eyeball,** in which participants pair off and stare into each other's eyes for a minute or more, or **blind mill,** in which participants close their eyes and wander around the room, communicating only by touch. Such maneuvers are designed to jolt participants out of the polite conventions of normal social intercourse and force them to interact more honestly and spontaneously.

An interesting recent variant is the **large community group,** which, in contrast to the usual 10-person gathering, includes anywhere from 50 to 2,000 people, under several leaders. Community groups will typically convene for one long session, perhaps a weekend, perhaps one or two weeks, breaking up regularly into smaller groups during the course of the session. Client-centered therapists have been in the forefront of the community group movement (e.g., Bozarth, 1981), but the format has been tried by group leaders of many persuasions. One popular example is Marriage Encounter, an organization that convenes large groups of married couples for a single weekend devoted to improving communication and increasing intimacy within the marriage. Marriage Encounter has now reached approximately 1.5 million couples worldwide.

Family Therapy and Marital Therapy

Family therapy is group therapy with a naturally rather than an artificially constituted group. Family therapy originated in the 1950s, around the same time as humanistic group therapy, and it often follows many of the same principles. Above all, family therapy, like the humanistic group, emphasizes group process rather than individual pathology. The assumption is that while one member of the family may have symptoms, the disturbance lies not in the symptomatic individual but in the family unit as a whole.

There are a variety of approaches to family therapy. One is the **communications approach** (Satir, 1967; Watzlawick et al., 1967), or **strategic approach** (Watzlawick et al., 1974), which developed as an extension of the double-bind theory of schizophrenia. As we saw in Chapter 15, the double-bind theory holds that an important cause of schizophrenia is childhood exposure to mutually contradictory messages from parents. According to communications theorists, such messages contribute not just to schizophrenia but to most forms of family disturbance. In family therapy, communications-minded therapists try to pinpoint contradictory messages, show the message givers what they are communicating, and indicate how this message undercuts the one they claim to mean. In general, the therapist's effort is to prod family members into telling one another what they actually feel and what kind of relationship they really want.

Often, in order to shake up a faulty communication system, the therapist will use a technique known as **paradoxical intention.** That is, the therapist will instruct the family members to engage in whatever maladaptive pattern of behavior they are already engaging in. For example, if a father is constantly interrupting his daughter, the therapist will tell the father that in the next session he is to interrupt the daughter every time she begins to speak. This stratagem has a way of upsetting the maladaptive pattern and thus forces patients to find other, and perhaps more useful, ways of dealing with their problems.

A second approach to family therapy is the **systems approach,** represented by the more psychody-

The assumption behind family therapy is that disturbance in one family member indicates a problem within the family as a whole. The two basic treatments in family therapy are the communications approach, which seeks to clarify contradictory messages among family members, and the systems approach, which focuses on the interlocking roles that family members perform. (Michael Weisbrot & Family)

namic and group process traditions. We have already discussed the application of systems theory to sexual counseling (Chapter 13). In family therapy, systems-minded therapists analyze the family unit as a set of interlocking roles (Ackerman, 1958; Minuchin and Fishman, 1981). Like any group, family members create roles for one another: the disciplinarian, the scapegoat, the one who needs looking after, the one who is expected to take care of everyone else, and so on. These roles satisfy certain needs; furthermore, individual members must go on fulfilling their roles in order for the others to continue in their roles. Consequently, any effort on the part of an individual member to abandon his or her role will meet with formidable resistance from the rest of the family. According to adherents of systems theory, such roles are the key to family disturbance. Indeed, some therapists contend that the reason one family member becomes "sick" is that the family role system requires a sick member (Minuchin, 1974). Systems-oriented family therapy thus concentrates on analyzing roles, along with the psychological purposes that they serve, and encouraging members to fashion more comfortable and flexible roles for themselves.

A more pragmatic psychoeducational-behavior approach has been used recently to help prevent relapses in schizophrenics. As we saw in Chapter 15, a good predictor of whether or not a schizophrenic

patient, once discharged from the hospital, will have to be rehospitalized is the family "EE," or expressed emotion, measured according to the level of criticism and the degree of emotional overinvolvement indicated by remarks made by key family members when they are interviewed about the patient. In an interesting experiment, a group of researchers (Falloon et al., 1982, 1985) conducted therapy with the families of eighteen newly discharged schizophrenic patients, the aim being to reduce EE. The families were taught new ways of expressing positive and negative emotions and of solving problems and handling crises. The importance of the patients' continuing to take their medication was also stressed. At the end of nine months, only one patient in this group had had a major relapse, compared with eight of eighteen patients in a control group receiving individual therapy, without family counseling. The experimental group also showed fewer schizophrenic symptoms and required less medication than the control group, and these differences still obtained at a two-year follow-up. Other, similar experiments have produced similar results (Gurman et al., 1986), suggesting that schizophrenics can be greatly helped merely by a calmer atmosphere at home.

Marital therapy, in which the group consists simply of a married couple, follows essentially the same lines as family therapy. Troubled marriages almost invariably involve unclear communications; indeed, in some cases, communication has broken down altogether. Thus the establishment of an honest dialogue between the two partners is of top priority in almost all marital therapy. However, roles too are of great concern to marital therapists. Many marriages have a designated "strong" partner and a designated "weak" partner. Others will have a dogged, responsible partner and a naughty, "spoiled" partner. As in family therapy, such roles and the needs they fulfill will be analyzed, and the partners will be urged to try out more honest and satisfying ways of relating to each other.

A relatively recent entry into the field of family and marital counseling is behavior therapy. One behavioral view of family and marital distress is that it is the result of "coercion" (Patterson and Hops, 1972)—that is, the reciprocal use of aversive stimuli—to influence the other person's behavior. The opposite of coercion is "reciprocity," the mutual use of positive reinforcement to influence the other person's behavior. In coercive marriages, for example, spouses get each other to do things by means of complaints, accusations, and the like. In reciprocal marriages, on the other hand, spouses get what they want out of each other by selectively reinforcing desirable behavior with compliments, thanks, and more tangible rewards. Through the use of contingency contracting, behavioral rehearsal, and other techniques, behavior therapists (e.g., Weiss et al., 1973; Jacobson and Margolin, 1979) try to teach families and married couples how to convert from coercion to reciprocity and also how to improve their skills for solving problems and settling conflicts.

Just as group therapy is seen as having certain advantages over individual therapy, so some have suggested that multiple-family and multiple-couple groups may achieve more than therapy with a single family or a single married couple. Marriage Encounter, as we have seen, has a multiple-couple format. Multiple-family therapy, though less common, has also been tried. One of the first experiments with this technique was a remarkable project conducted by Murray Bowen (1976) in the late 1950s. Bowen had the families of a number of schizophrenics move into the hospital with their schizophrenic members. During their stay the families all participated in joint therapy sessions, in which each family had its turn being the focus of therapy while the others observed. Bowen claims that the experiment was extremely valuable not only in teaching the families that their miseries

were not unique (Yalom's item 3, universality) but also in giving them the opportunity to try out one another's solutions to interpersonal problems. Others have since used this type of therapy with many kinds of dysfunctional families and have reported positive results, though the technique has not yet been systematically evaluated (Strelnick, 1977).

Peer Self-Help Groups

An interesting phenomenon of the past few decades is the increase in **peer self-help groups**—that is, groups of people who share a special problem and meet to discuss that problem without the help of mental health professionals. We have already examined one such group, the one from which most of the others are descended—Alcoholics Anonymous (Chapter 12). When AA was founded in the 1930s, the idea that people with similar problems could obtain from one another as much help as they could obtain from experts was a novel one. Today it is much more widely accepted, and self-help groups have been organized to deal with hundreds of problems—groups for dieters, stutterers, drug addicts, former mental patients, dialysis patients, cancer patients, families of cancer patients, spouses of alcoholics, children of alcoholics, parents of hyperactive children, single parents, widows, widowers, and so forth. More than anything else, these are social support groups (Yalom's item 4). Some groups (e.g., AA, Weight Watchers) use social support, along with other techniques, to help members to overcome a specific behavioral problem. In others, social support is itself the primary goal, along with the important secondary goal of giving members an opportunity to air their problems. A group of mastectomy patients, for example, may discuss everything from problems with buying clothes to postoperative sexual inhibitions to fear of death. The group may not actually *solve* these problems for any individual member, but it can offer her encouragement, a sympathetic ear, and the knowledge that she is not alone. For almost anyone with a serious problem, such support may be very helpful, but for people without other sources of social support (e.g., the single, the widowed, the elderly) it can be absolutely crucial. In both kinds of groups, the goal-directed type and the pure emotional-support type, the assumption is that no one can help you or understand you better than someone who has been through what you have been through.

Members of peer self-help groups, such as this union sponsored "stress workshop," offer one another support in dealing with problems they have in common. (Jane Scherr/Jeroboam)

This assumption may be correct to some degree, for in many instances self-help groups have apparently brought about therapeutic gains as great as those of professional mental health services. As Stuart (1977) has pointed out, this fact is all the more remarkable when we consider that such groups have developed at a time when professional mental health services have become considerably more varied, sophisticated, and available. It is hard to tell, however, whether the success rates claimed by self-help groups are accurate, for most of the evaluation studies of these groups have been methodologically flawed (e.g., lacking in controls for placebo effect or evaluator bias) (Lieberman and Bond, 1978). Nevertheless, self-help groups are undoubtedly the best bargain in the therapy market, and they probably reach many people who would not seek professional help.

Evaluation

What group and family therapy *may* offer clients has already been detailed in Yalom's list. Does it in fact offer these things? And if so, do they actually produce beneficial changes in behavior? Two large and systematic reviews of group therapy outcome literature (Bednar and Kaul, 1978; Kaul and Bednar, 1986) conclude that group therapy in general results in more improvement than either no treatment or placebo treatment (i.e., treatment in which the client's problem merely receives attention) and that some of the improvements do persist over time. Several qualifications must be added, however. First, the improvements in question were usually positive changes in attitude and self-concept, but not necessarily in actual behavior. Second, the methodology of many of the studies reviewed was poor. In most cases the rating was done by the therapist and client, not by a blind, independent rater, and it was done primarily on the basis of the client's self-report, not on the basis of observed behavior. Third, group therapy is far too vast and heterogeneous a field to be summed up in a single evaluation. Any general verdict that embraces everything from assertiveness training to Gestalt marathons cannot be very meaningful.

Outcome studies of specific forms of group and family therapy present a mixed picture. The results from social-skills training and assertiveness training are very good (Curran and Gilbert, 1975; Goldsmith and McFall, 1975; Upper and Ross, 1977). Likewise, marital and family therapy appear to be generally successful—more so, in some cases, than individual therapy. In a thorough review of the research in this area, Gurman and Kniskern (1978) found that out of thirty studies comparing marital/family therapy to individual or group treatment of the "identified patient" (i.e., the symptomatic member of the family), twenty-two—or 73 percent—found marital or family therapy to be superior. Behavior therapy with married couples and families has produced similarly good results (Gurman et al., 1986; Jacobson, 1979). This finding strongly suggests that when a person comes to a therapist complaining of marital or family problems, it is the marriage or the family that should be treated, rather than the individual alone.

Outcome studies of humanistic groups are less heartening. Some follow-up studies have reported heartfelt endorsement (e.g., Bozarth, 1981). At the same time, many people have raised questions about the usefulness of such groups. Do the skills learned in the group actually generalize to the client's outside life? If so, are they really adaptive to life outside the group? (The extreme bluntness encouraged in encounter groups, for example, might be a handicap rather than a benefit in normal social intercourse.) Finally, what are the chances that intense encountering will be actually harmful to more vulnerable group members, increasing rather than decreasing their psychological distress?

A partial answer to these questions has been provided by a comprehensive study of the long-term effects of seventeen encounter groups (Lieberman et al., 1973). The group participants were college students, 206 of them in all. Fifteen of the groups were conducted by experienced group leaders; two had no leader, but simply followed tape-recorded instructions. Each of the groups lasted a total of thirty hours, though the time was distributed differently from group to group. (Some groups spent their thirty hours on a few marathons; others met weekly for two-hour sessions, and so forth.) The orientation of the groups varied with the preferences of the leaders. Some used a psychoanalytic approach; some used Gestalt or other techniques. Before entering the group, immediately after leaving the group, and then several months later, the participants were asked to fill out extensive self-report questionnaires. On the basis of their answers, they were classified as having undergone positive change, no change, or negative change as a result of their group experience. The percentages were as follows:

Positive change:	33 percent
No change:	38 percent
Negative change:	16 percent
Dropouts:	13 percent

In other words, only one-third of the participants found that their lives actually improved as a result of having taken part in the group. It should be added

that almost half of the positive-change subjects (14 percent of the total) reported *great* benefits from the group experience. It should also be added, however, that half of the negative-change subjects (8 percent of the total) had to be rated as "casualties"—people who as a direct result of the group experience became more psychologically distressed than before and remained so eight months after the termination of the group. Thus for every two people who benefited from the group, one was harmed by it; for every two people who greatly benefited from the group, one was greatly harmed by it; and the most commonly reported result was no change. This is not a good showing, particularly in comparison with other kinds of therapy.

Later research on encounter groups has produced mixed results. On the positive side, Kaplan (1982) found that only 2.3 percent of encounter group participants could be called casualties. On the negative side, a follow-up study of people who had been through Marriage Encounter found that while 80 percent of the sample reported that the experience had improved their marriages, 9.3 percent showed evidence of "potentially serious negative effects" (Lester and Doherty, 1983).

The results of these studies also suggest how encounter groups might be improved. It seems that leaders who devote more time to explaining and interpreting what is happening in the group, and who stress "caring" over confrontation, produce better results (Lieberman et al., 1973). It is also clear that encounter groups should be avoided by anyone who is experiencing serious psychological distress, that people who experience negative effects should be referred for follow-up therapy, and that group leaders should be better trained to identify participants who need referral.

THERAPEUTIC ENVIRONMENTS WITHIN INSTITUTIONS

It has been argued that because group therapy, like ordinary life, places the individual within a social context, the skills learned in group therapy should be easily transferable to ordinary life. But is this in fact the case? The group is separate from and different from the average client's everyday social environment. Hence generalization may not be so easy after all. Furthermore, the client's everyday social environment may actually undermine whatever he or she is learning in the group.

One partial solution to this problem, at least for institutionalized patients, is to make the *entire* environment therapeutic. In most institutions, therapy, if it is provided, is fitted into one time slot during the day; for the rest of the day, the client is mostly left alone. In a **therapeutic environment,** on the other hand, the institutional environment is arranged in such a way that all the patient's interactions with that environment, day and night, will serve some therapeutic purpose.

Psychodynamic Therapeutic Environments

One of the earliest therapeutic communities was a residence for juvenile delinquents established by Aichhorn (1935) in Vienna at the end of World War I. In several respects this residence was markedly different from other juvenile facilities of that and the present day. First, the purpose of the program was treatment rather than simply custody. Second, the institutional environment was manipulated for therapeutic purposes. (For example, boys were assigned to living cottages according to the type and severity of their psychological problems.) Third, the staff made every attempt to create a warm, accepting environment for the residents. Fourth, aggressive behavior was permitted, even encouraged, unless there was a possibility of serious harm to one of the residents. The idea was to create an environment that would repair early damage to the psyche and strengthen the ego and superego. Aichhorn's school has long since closed its doors, but it engendered a number of like-minded institutions both in Europe and in the United States. One of the best-known was Fritz Redl's Pioneer School for delinquent boys, which opened in Detroit in 1946. Another famous psychodynamic residence, already discussed in Chapter 18, was the Sonia Shankman Orthogenic School in Chicago, founded by Bruno Bettelheim for the treatment of autistic children.

The assumption behind most of these psychodynamic facilities was that since their patients (usually either delinquent or psychotic children) did not benefit greatly from intensive individual therapy, the best treatment would be reeducation through identification with an adult. Obviously, this approach requires an extremely high ratio of staff to patients; the Orthogenic School, for example, had almost one-to-one cov-

erage. Such an arrangement is extremely expensive and cannot accommodate many patients. (Pioneer School, for example, never housed more than five boys.) For this reason and others, strictly psychodynamic facilities are now rare, though many therapeutic residences still use psychodynamic techniques in individual counseling.

Behavioral Therapeutic Environments

Many times in this book we have presented evidence for the power of systematic reinforcement to change specific behaviors. Such evidence has encouraged psychologists to expand their reinforcement programs. If rewards can change a patient's manner of eating or speaking, why not structure that patient's environment so that in *all* areas of his or her life appropriate behavior is reinforced and inappropriate behavior extinguished? The result has been the token economy.

As we have seen in earlier chapters, **token economies** are institutional programs in which a wide range of behaviors are rewarded with tangible conditioned reinforcers, or tokens, that patients can then use to "buy" backup reinforcers. In the typical token-economy ward, there is a board listing various desirable behaviors and their token rewards. There is also a canteen where patients can exchange their tokens for backup reinforcers. Some institutions even have department store catalogs from which patients can order their rewards. In many cases, however, tokens are spent not on tangible rewards but on privileges—television time, access to the telephone, overnight passes, and so forth.

The advantages of the token system are many:

1. Tokens can be dispensed for small gradations of improvement and for each step in the process of shaping complex behaviors, as backup reinforcers often cannot. You cannot give a patient a weekend pass for each successful rehearsal of improved interpersonal behavior. However, you can give one token for each successful rehearsal and a weekend pass for twenty tokens.

2. Tokens constitute visible proof of improvement. As such, they help the staff to identify patients who are not responding, so that they can be helped. Tokens also allow staff to spot those

patients who *are* responding and to praise them accordingly.

3. Tokens allow staff to control the timing of reinforcement. In general, reinforcement is most powerful when it immediately follows the target behavior. There are certain times, however—such as the middle of a meal—when it may not be convenient to give the patient a trip to town in reward, say, for good table manners or active socializing. Tokens, on the other hand, can be dispensed at any time.

4. Tokens, since they are exchangeable for a wide variety of backup reinforcers, are resistant to satiation. Patients who are tired of candy bars or cigarettes can simply switch to some other reward.

5. Tokens get around the problem of differences in individual tastes. A program that offered only snacks and television time would have problems not only with satiation but also with the fact that some people don't care about snacks or television. Tokens, however, can appeal to almost any patient, since patients can spend them on whatever they like.

A final advantage, at least according to the advocates of token economies, is that such a program simulates life in the community, as other kinds of therapeutic environments generally do not. The behaviors that token economies attempt to increase are those that people most need (and that chronic patients most lack) in order to make their way in normal society—work skills, social interaction, and hygiene and grooming. Like the real world, the token economy offers reinforcement when such behaviors are present and does not offer reinforcement when such behaviors are missing. This means that the token economy runs a somewhat "tighter ship" than other therapeutic environments, but in this sense too it resembles life on the outside.

It should be noted that most directors of token economies do not just wait around for patients to develop the behaviors that are slated for token rewards. Most token economies are part of multifaceted programs, involving social-skills training and other kinds of behavioral interventions as well as token reinforcement. (See the box on pages 534–535.)

Humanistic-Existential Therapeutic Environments

The humanistic-existential perspective's contribution to the idea of the therapeutic environment is milieu therapy (also called the therapeutic community). Milieu therapy arose in the 1940s and 1950s (e.g., Maxwell Jones, 1953) as a reaction to the type of custodial care typically offered to chronic patients: care that tended to reinforce withdrawal (and hence chronic hospitalization), since withdrawn behaviors posed fewer problems for the staff. In a sense, the emergence of milieu therapy was a case of history repeating itself. Just as moral therapy (Chapter 1) developed in the nineteenth century as an antidote to custodial neglect, so milieu therapy, based on many of the same principles as moral therapy, developed in the twentieth century as a solution to the same problem.

As we saw in Chapter 15, **milieu therapy** is essentially an institutional environment designed to maximize the independence, self-respect, and activity level of severely disturbed patients. One of the most distinctive qualities of milieu therapy is its democratic nature. Everyone in the community is valued as a therapeutic agent: the patients for one another, the staff for the patients, and the patients for the staff. The atmosphere is warm, open, and, above all, busy, involving the patients in occupational therapy, recreational activities, self-governmental meetings, and other projects.

The major use of milieu therapy has been with schizophrenics, in residences such as Soteria House and Kingsley Hall (Chapter 15). However, other kinds of programs have also been affected by the principles underlying milieu therapy. Particularly influential has been the idea that disturbed people, if given the opportunity, can run their own lives and that the experience of doing so may have a powerful healing effect. The patient-administered wards that now exist in some mental hospitals and the self-governing halfway houses that have been established for former mental patients in numerous communities are both products of this idea.

Evaluation

Do therapeutic environments achieve their goal of enabling patients to transfer new skills to life outside the institution? With regard to psychodynamic programs this is hard to say, for the number of patients is small and the outcome data consist mainly of case histories (e.g., Bettelheim, 1967). Milieu programs too are small and generally are not subjected to systematic evaluation. Yet there has been at least one careful outcome study of milieu therapy. As we saw in Chapter 15, Paul and Lentz (1977) conducted a long-term comparative study of the effectiveness of three programs for chronic mental patients: custodial care, milieu therapy, and a multifaceted behavioral program involving a token economy. The experimenters found that milieu therapy was superior to custodial care both in changing in-hospital behavior and in getting patients discharged.

As for the token economy, Paul and Lentz found that just as the milieu program produced greater behavioral change and higher discharge rates than custodial care, so the token economy surpassed the milieu program on both scores. This is by no means the only evidence for the effectiveness of the token economy. There is a vast literature on this treatment strategy, including several comprehensive reviews (e.g., Kazdin, 1977, 1982). In general, these studies support the conclusions of Paul and Lentz: token economies—and above all, token economies in conjunction with other forms of behavior therapy—are capable of producing extensive changes in behavior. This is true for hospitalized mental patients (e.g., Ayllon and Azrin, 1968; Atthowe and Krasner, 1968) as well as for retarded people (e.g., Welch and Gist, 1974), juvenile delinquents (e.g., Kirigin et al., 1982), and even ordinary children in their classrooms (e.g., O'Leary, 1978).

But what happens once the patients leave the token economy? Most outcome studies have not done extensive follow-up. Those that have are not heartening. In general, it appears that generalization does *not* occur automatically to any significant extent. When the tokens disappear, so do the improvements in behavior (Kazdin and Bootzin, 1972).

Though discouraging, this fact is perhaps not surprising. While the token economy may be more like ordinary life than other therapeutic environments, the differences between the two settings are still vast, especially as regards the manner of reinforcement. In the token economy, reinforcement is immediate and predictable; furthermore, patients can choose what reinforcers they want. In ordinary life, on the other hand, reinforcement is often slow in coming and unpredictable in form and timing. Patients who are used to collecting a candy bar as a reward for having a civil conversation may be quite bewildered to find that on the outside all they get is a smile or handshake, if that. And as a result, the conversations may come to an end.

Such considerations have persuaded many therapists that instead of merely hoping for generalization, they must program it into the treatment (Stokes and Baer, 1977). There have been numerous efforts to do so. In some programs, patients, before being discharged, are gradually weaned from tokens to extra privileges and social approval—in other words, reinforcers closer to what they will encounter on the outside (Schaefer and Martin, 1969). In other programs, patients have been taught to reinforce themselves for appropriate behavior once they are released (Kanfer and Phillips, 1970). Another solution has been to place greater emphasis on work skills, since a person who can work is one who is going to receive predictable and regular reinforcement in the form of a paycheck. (Furthermore, paychecks, like tokens, can be spent on reinforcers of one's choice.) In the best-run programs, such as the Paul and Lentz program, this generalization training is part of a comprehensive aftercare program. Even so, it must be noted that many patients will remain in the aftercare program, as was the case with the Paul and Lentz patients.

COMMUNITY-BASED SERVICES

The State Institution

As we saw in Chapter 1, one of the fruits of the Enlightenment was the widespread development of large hospitals for the mentally disturbed. Most of these hospitals, both in the United States and elsewhere, were built in relatively isolated rural or suburban areas. There were a number of reasons for this decision. First, it was thought that patients would recover sooner if they were removed from the stresses of community life and allowed to repose in the fresh country air. A second reason was economy; land was far less expensive in the countryside. Furthermore, until fairly recently, most of these state mental hospitals had large farms attached to them, where the patients, as part of their "therapy," worked to produce their own food. A third and equally important reason for transferring these patients to remote locations was that no one wanted to see them. Mental

Solving the "Chronic Problem": The Paul and Lentz Study

Of all the psychologically disturbed, those who receive perhaps the least attention are chronic psychotic patients. These are essentially forgotten people; no one knows how to solve their problems, and many have ceased to care. For this reason, among others, Paul and Lentz's (1977) comparative study of treatments for chronic patients, already briefly described in this chapter, is of great importance. Gordon Paul first became interested in the "chronic problem" in the mid-1960s, while working as a consultant to the state mental hospitals of Illinois. These hospitals, like state institutions throughout the country, had back wards filled with chronic schizophrenics—people who had stagnated there for years and would presumably continue to do so until they died. Could such patients, given appropriate treatment, return to some kind of independent life in the community? If so, what *was* the appropriate treatment? These were the questions that Paul set out to answer.

With the help of his colleagues at the University of Illinois, Paul selected three groups of twenty-eight patients each, matched for age, sex, and other variables. One group, the control group, remained in custodial care at the state hospital. The remaining two groups were transferred to adjacent units of a new mental health center, where one embarked on a program of milieu therapy and the other a token-economy-based program of behavior therapy—the two treatment strategies that research suggested might hold some promise for chronic patients. Each program was to run for three years, with the goal of releasing its patients to relatively independent living (e.g., at home or with a foster family). The object of the study was to see which of the treatment conditions did best at achieving this goal.

The original plan was to use typical chronic patients. However, by the time the study got under way, the deinstitutionalization movement was also under way, with the result that there were no "typical" chronics left in the state hospitals. All patients who could meet certain very minimal standards had been transferred to community shelter-care programs. Hence the pool from which Paul drew his subjects consisted of only the most dysfunctional patients. Just how dysfunctional they were became clear in the first week of the program. At any given moment, fully 90 percent of the patients were behaving bizarrely. Some were mute; others screamed for hours on end. Many were incontinent. Worse yet, some smeared their feces on the walls or threw them at the staff. At meals it was the rare patient who used silverware, and some habitually buried their faces in their food. Physical assaults were not uncommon. At the first meeting of the behavioral group, a staff member narrowly escaped being stabbed by a naked patient armed with a knife that she had stolen from the kitchen. The experimenters clearly had their work cut out for them.

How were the programs designed? To begin with, the hospital program consisted of typical custodial care: patients were treated like sick people, given high doses of antipsychotic medication, and essentially left to their own devices. (Though formal therapy was offered, it occupied less than 5 percent of the patients' waking hours.) Nothing much was either given to them or expected of them.

This was precisely the environment that the experimental programs aimed to avoid. In both the milieu and behavioral units, subjects were treated as "residents," not patients. Appropriate behavior was expected of them, and they spent 85 percent of their waking hours learning, in formal treatment situations, how to produce it. In return, they received prompt, courteous, and friendly attention from the staff.

Similar in these respects, the two experimental programs differed sharply in other respects. The milieu program was organized around the principles outlined in Chapter 15. The major emphasis was on the residents' assuming responsibility, at both an individual and a group level. The unit was organized as a community, with an executive council elected from among the residents. The community in turn was divided into three living groups. Both the living groups and the executive council had wide decision-making powers. (It was the residents, for example, who decided how to punish assaultive behavior.) And though some of their rulings were unwise, the staff honored them all the same, on the theory that residents would learn from their mistakes.

Another matter emphasized in the milieu program was clear, plentiful, and positive communication. This was the staff's major tool for influencing the residents' behavior. To elicit appropriate behavior, staff members communicated positive expectations (e.g., "I know you'll remember to comb your hair tomorrow,

Charlie"), and to maintain appropriate behavior, they responded to it with praise. As for inappropriate behavior, it was never ignored. On the contrary, staff members were instructed to remain with the offending resident, providing negative feedback for the behavior in question and voicing expectations of more appropriate behavior.

While the milieu program relied on trust and encouragement as the two major rehabilitative forces, the behavioral program relied on operant conditioning. Appropriate behavior was elicited through prompting, verbal instruction, modeling, and shaping; when it appeared, it was systematically reinforced with praise and tokens. Inappropriate behavior, on the other hand, was generally ignored. (In addition, of course, it resulted in failure to earn tokens.) This operant-conditioning program embraced every conceivable aspect of the residents' lives. Before breakfast, for example, the residents underwent an "appearance check." If they met the eleven criteria for good appearance—proper use of make-up; clean fingernails; hair combed; teeth brushed; all appropriate clothing on; clothing buttoned, zipped, tucked; clothing clean and neat; body clean; no odor; shaven; hair cut appropriately—they were given a token and praised. If not, they were given no token and were told what to do in order to earn the token next time. Likewise, there were specific criteria for appropriate bedmaking, bathing, mealtime behavior, classroom participation, and social behavior during free periods, and tokens were accordingly disbursed or withheld. (If the behavior was still being shaped, the resident did not have to meet all the criteria—only those that he or she had already met plus one.)

The earning of these tokens was serious business, for they were used to purchase not only luxuries such as cigarettes but also necessities such as meals. Breakfast cost three tokens, lunch six tokens, dinner five, and those who did not have the price of admission were turned away. If residents missed enough consecutive meals to pose a health problem, they were eventually given a free meal—the so-called "medical meal." This consisted of all the elements of the regular meal puréed together in a blender and dyed purple-gray—a nutritious but unappetizing mush. As this example illustrates, life in the behavioral unit was not soft.

How the subjects progressed in the three programs is documented by voluminous observational notes. (In the experimental programs, each resident's behavior was observed and recorded at least once every hour of every day!) The notes tell an interesting story. At the end of the first seven months, the behavioral subjects and, to a somewhat lesser extent, the milieu subjects had made substantial improvements,

enough to qualify most of them for release to shelter-care facilities. However, the goal of the program was not shelter care, but independent living. So the treatment continued—and began to encounter difficulties. The major problem was that the frequency of assaults, both on staff and on other patients, steadily increased, especially in the milieu unit. (At one point, the milieu unit was averaging *320 assaults per week.*) This, of course, interfered with treatment. Though the program was extended to four and a half years, at the end of that time the average improvement in the behavioral unit was roughly the same as at the end of the first seven months, while in the milieu unit it was somewhat inferior to what it had been at the end of the first seven months.

This does not mean that the treatments failed. On the contrary, the improvements were still substantial enough so that the behavioral unit was able to release 98 percent of its residents and the milieu program 71 percent of its residents, compared with 45 percent for the hospital program. (Of these, only five residents—three behavioral and two milieu—were able to take up independent living; the rest went to shelter-care facilities.) And after eighteen months of follow-up and aftercare, only two of the seventy-four released patients, both behavioral, had had to be rehospitalized. This study, then, definitely benefited its subjects. Furthermore, it is of great value as a piece of careful research, establishing two important principles. First, even the most dysfunctional chronic patients, with the longest histories of hospitalization (Paul's subjects averaged seventeen years apiece), can, with appropriate treatment, improve sufficiently to be released from the hospital. Second, the most useful treatment for this purpose is apparently a behavioral program based on the token economy.

It would be encouraging to report that public hospitals have taken the Paul and Lentz study to heart and developed effective token economies for their seriously disturbed patients. Unfortunately, this is not the case. A 1986 survey of 152 Veterans Administration medical centers found that only ten had programs similar to the one developed by Paul and Lentz; these programs served only 1.01 percent of all psychiatric patients treated in the VA system (Boudewyns et al., 1986). Among the reasons suggested for the scarcity of these programs are (1) pressures to reduce the amount of time each patient stays in the hospital, and consequently the amount of inpatient services; and (2) the reliance of the token economy on the services of nurses' aides, who are among the most poorly paid employees and thus often resist the imposition of additional duties. As long as these conditions prevail, the lessons learned by the Paul and Lentz study are likely to remain theoretical.

patients were considered unsightly and dangerous—an attitude that is still widely held today.

Whatever the reasons, the isolation of the large state mental hospitals did not contribute to their effectiveness. Very few competent professionals were willing to take poorly paid jobs in remote areas, and as a result, staffing became a serious problem. (It was not uncommon to find hospitals with over a thousand patients and only one or two psychologists or psychiatrists on the staff.) The consequence, of course, was that care was custodial rather than remedial. Furthermore, the very fact that patients were removed from their communities proved counterproductive. Families, friends, and jobs give people a sense of identity, provide an incentive to be "normal," and can often be mobilized to aid in psychological treatment. Isolation from their communities cuts patients off from these informal therapeutic benefits. Finally, the remoteness of the mental hospitals made it impossible for patients to engage in any kind of *partial* treatment, such as outpatient counseling or work-release programs. It was all or nothing—hospitalization or no treatment. Consequently, thousands of patients who might have benefited from less drastic intervention were hospitalized, with all the damaging effects that psychiatric hospitalization involves—the loss of one's moorings in reality, the temptation to fall into the "sick" role, the tremendous social stigma, the crushing loss of self-esteem.

The Exodus to the Community

The disadvantages of the state mental hospitals were known to many people, but the alternatives were few, and the system continued more or less unchanged until the mid-1950s. Then the phenothiazines were introduced into American mental hospitals. Under the influence of these drugs, many patients became considerably calmer—calm enough, it seemed, to reenter the society. Around the same time, evidence of the damaging effects of hospitalization—the effects listed above—began to accumulate (e.g., Goffman, 1961; Scheff, 1966). It soon became conventional wisdom that hospitalization was bad; patients should be treated within their communities. And with phenothiazines, releasing patients into the community now seemed possible. Finally, many state officials thought that it would be less expensive to treat patients in the community than to maintain them in mental hospitals.

Thus the exodus from the hospitals began. Starting in the late 1950s, mental institutions discharged more and more patients every year. Not only acute patients but also chronic patients—people who had spent the better part of their lives in mental hospitals—were given supplies of pills and either sent home or placed in community facilities (Pollack and Taube, 1975). Throughout the country, the resident population of the mental hospitals dwindled. In Illinois, for example,

A typical state hospital—a large, barracks-like building in a suburban location. Today, the trend is away from housing large numbers of patients in such institutions, and the number of hospitalized patients has shrunk considerably. (Paul Fusco/Magnum)

the inpatient population dropped from 47,000 to 13,000 in the twenty years from 1955 to 1975 (Cohen and Appleby, 1976). Since then, the trend has continued. From 1973 to 1983 the inpatient population of state and county mental hospitals dropped by 53 percent (Greene et al., 1986). With fewer patients to serve, many of the hospitals were either closed or converted into other kinds of mental health facilities (Rieder, 1974).

Of course, most of the newly released patients still required some kind of treatment. Furthermore, if other people were to be saved from hospitalization, alternative services had to be created. Thus while the mental hospitals were gradually emptying, mental health professionals devoted their energies to developing psychological services within the communities. Perhaps the most important of these is a totally new kind of service known as the **community mental health center.**

The Community Mental Health Center

In 1963, as part of President Kennedy's drive for a "bold new approach" to mental illness, Congress passed the Community Mental Health Centers Act. The law provided for the establishment of one mental health center for every 50,000 people. In these centers, anyone, rich or poor, from the center's **catchment area** (i.e., its area of geographical coverage) would receive the psychological services he or she required without having to leave the community. Furthermore, the centers were to implement programs for the prevention of mental disturbance; to educate other community workers, such as teachers, clergy, and police, in the principles of preventive mental health; to train professionals and nonprofessionals to work in the centers; and finally, to carry out research. In this section we will describe how some of these services are provided. It should be kept in mind that our examples are drawn primarily from the best, most innovative programs. The more usual programs will be described in the evaluation section.

Outpatient Services   The outpatient service, the first place to which the disturbed person turns for help, is the most heavily used service of the community mental health center. Partly because the community mental health centers have offered such services and partly because of the mounting popularity of psy-

Community mental health centers, such as this one in Brooklyn, New York, were set up by Congress in 1963 to serve catchment areas of 50,000 people each. Their outpatient services are the most heavily used, but they also offer inpatient services, emergency services, and consultation. (Hazel Hankin)

chotherapy, the use of outpatient counseling has risen dramatically in the last few decades. In the twenty years from 1955 to 1975, for example, outpatient care increased *twelvefold,* from 379,000 to 4.6 million clinical episodes (Kiesler, 1982a).

The goal of outpatient care is to provide help without disrupting the patient's normal routine. Here people can receive psychotherapy once or twice a week without leaving their families (indeed, their families can be brought into the therapy) and without abandoning their schooling, their work, their friends, their turf—all the things that give them a sense of identity. Furthermore, the services are convenient and available, only a short trip away. And many community mental health centers have additional satellite operations—storefront offices and traveling teams—that attempt to bring help even closer to all the members of the community. Thus people with problems can receive therapy quickly and conveniently and still be home in time for dinner—a fact that encourages them to see their problems as natural and solvable rather than hideous and extreme.

Another goal of the community mental health center's outpatient services was the provision of aftercare (for example, weekly therapy or perhaps just monthly checkups) for people who have been discharged from the hospital—a crucial matter that we have already touched upon. In the community center, it was thought, patients could be treated by the same people who had treated them in the hospital—people who remembered their names and their problems. In some community mental health centers, that is in fact what happens. In most others, however, such ideal aftercare never went beyond the stage of hopeful planning.

Because of tightened public budgets, the number of centers set up fell short of the need, and those that were provided had to curtail their services; aftercare was a common casualty of such cutbacks. Consequently, despite the success of the community mental health centers in other respects, the provision of truly adequate aftercare services is an endeavor that in most communities remains to be undertaken.

Inpatient Services   While effective outpatient services can reduce the need for hospitalization, some patients still have to be hospitalized, either because they pose a threat to themselves and others or because they lack family or other resources to support them in their difficulties. In such cases, the community mental health center provides hospitalization, usually in a general hospital in the community. Because these

FIGURE 21.1

The percentage of cases treated by inpatient and outpatient facilities in 1955 and 1983. The two circles illustrate the dramatic increase in outpatient treatment in the twenty-eight-year period.

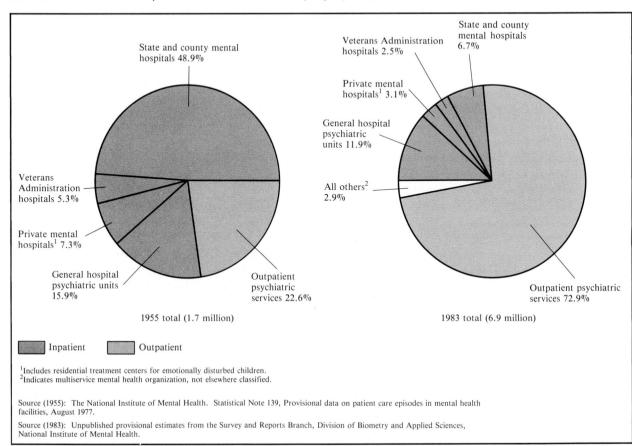

1955 total (1.7 million)

1983 total (6.9 million)

Inpatient   Outpatient

[1]Includes residential treatment centers for emotionally disturbed children.
[2]Indicates multiservice mental health organization, not elsewhere classified.

Source (1955): The National Institute of Mental Health. Statistical Note 139, Provisional data on patient care episodes in mental health facilities, August 1977.

Source (1983): Unpublished provisional estimates from the Survey and Reports Branch, Division of Biometry and Applied Sciences, National Institute of Mental Health.

facilities are readily and quickly available, because family and friends can easily visit, and because (in some cases) coordinated aftercare can be provided, it is hoped that this system of hospitalization can speed up the patient's release. Furthermore, in many centers patients can receive partial hospitalization through the innovative systems of the day hospital and the night hospital. In the **day hospital,** patients are hospitalized only on a nine-to-five basis. During the day they take part in the hospital's therapeutic activities; then at night they return home to their families, their friends, their poker games, and so on. In the **night hospital,** the system is the opposite. From nine to five, patients go to work or to school; then in the evening they return to the hospital. In both cases, the emphasis is once again on preserving the patient's normal lives, so that they will not fall into the role of the chronic patient.

Day hospitals, first introduced at the Meninger Clinic in 1949 and now numbering over a thousand nationwide, seem to be particularly successful (Greene, 1981; Straw, 1982). They are, obviously, more cost-effective than full-time hospitalization. Furthermore, because they ease the burden on the family, they can be the crucial deciding factor between the family's retaining the patient at home and throwing up their hands and turning the patient over to an institution. Finally, day hospitals seem to be helpful in preventing full-time rehospitalization. In one study, a group of chronic schizophrenics, upon release from full-time hospitalization, were randomly assigned either to drug treatment alone or to drug treatment combined with day hospitalization as aftercare. Of the ten day hospitals involved, six were more effective than drug treatment alone in preventing rehospitalization. Interestingly, those six were low-cost centers that focused primarily on offering a "sustained non-threatening environment" and favored occupational therapy over psychotherapy (Lin et al., 1979).

Emergency Services   Before the advent of the community mental health center, emergency psychological services were virtually nonexistent. The public mental hospitals, as we have seen, were usually miles away from major population centers, and even communities that were rich in mental health services generally provided such services only during ordinary work hours, and almost never on weekends or holidays. People who did not time their psychological emergencies to fit this schedule usually either spent the night in jail, sat for hours in the local hospital emergency room, or simply weathered the crisis alone.

To solve this problem, many community mental health centers have established various kinds of emergency services. In some cases a satellite storefront clinic will remain open at night for emergencies. Here the troubled person can come for an informal talk (and possibly a tranquilizer) and make an appointment to go to the regular outpatient clinic in the morning. Other community centers provide teams of mental health workers to serve in the emergency rooms of the community's general hospitals so that acute psychological problems can be given the same swift attention as acute physical problems. In addition to filling the obvious need for emergency psychological services, the presence of these mental health professionals in hospital emergency rooms has had the beneficial side effect of sensitizing the rest of the emergency room staff to the psychological responses of people involved in automobile accidents, rape, fires, and other life-threatening situations. In this way the psychological trauma can be dealt with at the same time as the physical trauma, thus obviating or at least minimizing posttraumatic stress disorders.

In other communities, the community mental health center runs a twenty-four-hour service for police referrals. Until recently, for example, the Chicago police, in handling people who obviously needed psychological supervision—usually they were seriously disturbed people, with psychotic symptoms, who lived alone and had no social supports—referred them to the state hospital. Then, with the establishment of an emergency service at the community mental health center, they were taken to the community center. In a two-year follow-up comparing the patients referred to the state hospital in the three months before the establishment of the emergency service to the patients referred to the community mental health center in the three months after the establishment of the emergency service, researchers found that the latter group had fewer subsequent hospital admissions and spent fewer total days in the hospital (Sheridan and Teplin, 1981).

Consultation   A chronic problem in the delivery of psychological services is that there are simply not enough mental health workers to go around. One solution to this problem is consultation, whereby mental health professionals, instead of working with specific cases themselves, advise other types of profession-als—physicians, teachers, police, clergy, and the like—on how to deal with the psychologically troubled people they encounter in the course of their work. For example, if a teacher is having great difficulty with a particular child, the school could ask a psychologist from the community mental health center to observe the child in question during a class hour and then to advise the teacher, and perhaps other teachers at the same time, on how to deal with the behavior problem. This type of consulting service is being given increasing attention by community mental health centers, not only because it saves professional time but also because it allows behavior problems to be handled at the moment and in the context in which they occur.

A good example of the usefulness of the consultation approach was a program in which a group of New York City police officers were trained by mental health professionals in how to intervene in family quarrels (Bard, 1970). It is a little-known fact that family quarrels are a major source of assaults and homicides—crimes that the public tends to assume occur in the streets. Domestic quarrels are dangerous not only for the family members involved but also for the police officers who are called in to handle them. Hence New York City's innovative consultation program. In one precinct, eighteen police officers received 160 hours of training—including lectures, demonstrations, and behavioral rehearsal—in how to intervene effectively in family quarrels. These trained officers then worked as family-crisis intervention teams in that precinct. In contrast to police officers in a neighboring district, who witnessed and suffered the same amount of violence normally involved in such calls, the trained team members were able to decrease the number of assaults on family members, did not themselves suffer a single assault, and did not witness a single family homicide in 1,388 family-crisis calls. The spectacular success of this program has led to the adoption of similar programs by police departments all over the United States and provides strong support for the effectiveness of providing consultation services to other human service agencies.

Halfway Houses

Another type of community service that has proliferated in recent years is the halfway house, a service closely related to the partial hospitalization programs offered by many community mental health centers. A **halfway house** is a residence for people (e.g., ex-drug addicts or newly released mental patients) who no longer require institutionalization but still need some support in the trying process of readjusting to community life. In the halfway house these people live together, talk out their difficulties with one another, and relearn appropriate social skills.

The best halfway houses are small residences, with perhaps fifteen to twenty acute patients (Cannon, 1975). There may be a psychologist or psychiatrist who visits regularly, but the live-in staff usually consists of a paraprofessional, such as a graduate student in psychology, who advises the residents on practical problems (e.g., how to plan the week's menu, how to enforce rules) and acts as an informal counselor. Many halfway houses set up stores, janitorial services, and other moneymaking enterprises that support the members and at the same time train them to support themselves on their own once they leave the house. For many people, these residences appear far preferable to a cold-turkey return to the community. Early reports indicate that small halfway houses do a good job of reducing the chances of rehospitalization. For chronic patients who have lived in smaller halfway houses, the recidivism rate after one year of independent living (i.e., one year after leaving the halfway house) is estimated at 20 percent (Cannon, 1975), whereas the recidivism rate for chronic patients in general after one year on their own is about 40 to 50 percent (Rog and Raush, 1975).

Long-Term-Care Facilities

Closer to hospitalization are **long-term-care facilities,** which, while they resemble halfway houses in being smaller than hospitals and located in the community, differ in that they are not a bridge between the institution and independent living. Their purpose, as their name indicates, is long-term care, for patients who presumably will never, or not soon, achieve independent living.

There are several kinds of long-term care facilities, but by far the most common is the nursing home (Shadish and Bootzin, 1981). A high percentage of the residents of this country's intermediate-care nursing homes (i.e., nursing homes without intensive medical supervision) are not old people but former mental patients. Indeed, in 1977, over $2 billion was paid out to nursing homes for the care of mental patients (Kiesler, 1982a). Thus, despite a national emphasis on deinstitutionalization, a large proportion of funds for mental health continues to be spent on custodial care, although in settings located more centrally in the community.

Alternatives to Hospitalization

Day hospitals, night hospitals, and halfway houses are all attempts to cut down on the amount of time that the patient spends in the hospital. But the fact is that most acute patients do not need hospitalization at all. As we saw earlier, the experience of psychiatric hospitalization can actually harm them, whereas all it usually offers by way of help is medication, the opportunity to consult a mental health professional, and a chance to rest for a few weeks, after which they are typically discharged. Couldn't we offer patients these things without hospitalizing them? Recently a number of innovative programs have attempted to do just that.

In one program, operating out of southwest Denver, patients seeking hospitalization are sent instead to one of six participating families in the community, who house the patients as their guests for a small fee. If the families encounter problems, psychiatric nurses are available to them on a twenty-four-hour basis. Patients requiring a day or two of close supervision are sent to an "intensive observation" apartment, staffed by a psychology student and his or her spouse. Here the patient can receive rapid tranquilization, if it is necessary, and is looked after around the clock. As a last resort, hospital beds are available, but they are rarely used. Within a few weeks most patients are back home, with no record of psychiatric hospitalization (Polak, 1978).

A second, more experimental program was part of a study that took place in Madison, Wisconsin (Test and Stein, 1978). Patients seeking psychiatric hospitalization were randomly assigned to either (1) brief hospitalization (the median stay was seventeen days), with typical aftercare, or (2) a community treatment program not involving hospitalization. In the latter program the staff helped the patients find an acceptable community residence if staying at home was not feasible, and they gave them assistance in finding jobs or places in sheltered workshops if they were unemployed. They also created an individually tailored

Halfway houses for former drug addicts, such as Daytop Village in New York City, exist to ease the process of readjusting to community life without drugs. (Jason Lauré/Woodfin Camp & Associates)

treatment program for each patient, based on an assessment of what coping skills that particular patient was lacking. Treatment took place *in vivo*—that is, in the patients' homes, places of work, and neighborhood haunts. For fourteen months the staff maintained daily contact with the patients, calling them, dropping by, offering suggestions, and in general actively helping them make their way in the community. At the end of the fourteen-month experimental period and again upon follow-up one and a half years later, the community treatment patients showed better adjustment (e.g., fewer days unemployed) than the hospitalized patients. Upon two-year follow-up, however, the advantage of the community treatment program began to narrow. This finding suggests that community treatment, if it is to be successful, must maintain active involvement with patients long after their crises have passed.

Such an effort has been made in a third experimental program, Tucson's Treatment Network Team, organized to serve chronic mental patients who live in the community. Such patients are often extremely unwilling to go to the hospital—indeed, to any traditional kind of mental health facility—for help, and many of them are also uninterested in traditional kinds of help. Yet they still need some assistance. Hence the Treatment Network Team, which assigns its members to individual patients and trains them to place the patients in settings consistent with their needs. Through this representative, who stays in close touch with them, the patients can then receive whatever services they need—medication, crisis intervention, family counseling, informal advice—when and where they need them. A study of the program found that this flexible service-delivery approach did increase patient participation, and that the patients who participated improved substantially more than those who received typical hospital and outpatient care (Santiago et al., 1985).

Hot Lines

As we saw earlier, some community mental health centers have devoted considerable energy to providing emergency psychological services. But face-to-face emergency counseling is simply one part of a whole new trend toward crisis intervention, the handling of severe emotional stress on the spot. Another important innovation in this area is the development of telephone **hot lines**—that is, round-the-clock telephone services where people who are in trouble can call and receive immediate comfort and advice, usually from trained but nonprofessional volunteers. The prototype is the suicide-prevention hot line, the most famous of which is the Los Angeles Suicide Prevention Center, established by Shneidman and Farberow in 1958. That service has since spawned many other varieties of hot lines—numbers for people with drinking, gambling, or drug problems, for rape victims, for child-abusing parents, for troubled teenagers. There are even so-called Dial-a-Shoulder numbers, where volunteers take calls from people who simply

need a kindly ear to listen to their troubles. But the most influential services have been those for drug problems, teenage problems, and suicide prevention. Since 1960, more than 180 suicide-prevention and 600 youth and/or drug hot lines have been established in the United States (Trowell, 1979).

Aside from providing a kindly ear, a major function of hot-line volunteers is to give callers information on community services where they can obtain help and to try to induce them to use these services. In some cases, the volunteer can make an appointment for the caller then and there. Not all hot-line conversations are unqualified successes, however. Indeed, volunteers on suicide hot lines often have no idea, once they have hung up the phone, whether the caller will keep the clinic appointment he or she has just made or jump out the nearest window. Thus working on a hot line is sometimes frustrating and depressing. At the same time, these services can be of help to people who need immediate assistance and have no one else to turn to.

Prevention

In psychology there are three levels of prevention: **primary prevention,** the goal of which is to prevent disorders from developing; **secondary prevention,** which aims at early detection and early treatment, so that minor disorders do not become major ones; and **tertiary prevention,** which attempts to minimize the damage, to both the victim and the society, of a major disorder.

Among the services dispensed by community mental health centers we have already seen many instances of preventive effort. Halfway houses, day hospitals, night hospitals, and experimental noninstitutional treatments are all instances of tertiary prevention, just as hot lines and outpatient services are categorized as secondary prevention. But a frequent criticism of community mental health centers is that they have not exerted themselves to engage in primary prevention—that is, to attack community problems that breed psychological disturbance, such as racism, poverty, and drug use (Holden, 1972). This is a huge order. However, the National Mental Health Association (Long, 1986) has recently outlined four specific areas as having immediate potential for preventing psychological disorders. First is the provision of family planning and prenatal care services, along with information on health and parenting, to ensure that babies are healthy and wanted. Second is the prevention of teenage pregnancies, through sex education, contraception and health services, and counseling on responsible decision making. Third is the promotion of academic mastery and psychosocial skills in the early grades by bringing mental health strategies into the schools. A final need is the extension of support, information, and training to people in stressful situations, such as families with an alcoholic or schizophrenic member. The idea is to create a healthier society, one with fewer built-in stresses—or stresses that seem unmanageable—for we know that whatever the biological correlates of psychological disorder, stress still makes a great difference.

Evaluation

Since they are relatively new, it is difficult to evaluate the community services described in this section. Those services that exist have unquestionably made psychological help more widely and quickly available to the population at large, and this is their great advantage over mental hospitals. The hospitals see people only after they have reached the breaking point; community centers can reach out to people long before they reach that point. Furthermore, for those who do have to be hospitalized, community-based services such as day hospitals, night hospitals, and halfway houses demonstrably help to prevent recurrence, as we have seen.

The major criticism of community services is not that what they are doing is wrong but that they are not doing enough. As we just saw, they have barely begun the job of primary prevention, and even in secondary and tertiary prevention a huge amount remains to be done. As we pointed out, our examples were drawn from the better-funded, better-staffed, and more carefully thought-out programs. But such programs are still comparatively rare. Many community mental health centers offer only the standard services, such as psychotherapy and short-term hospitalization; the promising newer services—consultation, day hospitals, night hospitals—are far less available. The same is true of innovative emergency care. A large percentage of psychiatric emergencies still end up in general hospitals without specialized psychiatric staff or separate psychiatric inpatient facilities, for no such services are available (Hendryx and Bootzin, 1986).

Similarly, the halfway houses that we have described are the smaller, better-run ones, whereas many of what are called halfway houses are actually large "shelter-care" facilities where patients may get nothing more than the same sort of custodial treatment that they received in the hospital. Indeed, some of the so-called halfway houses are merely seedy hotels where patients see a social worker for perhaps a few minutes a week and spend the rest of their time in front of a television set. Likewise, many of the nursing homes that house mental patients are uncannily like state mental hospitals (Bootzin and Shadish, 1983). In the extreme case, some patients released to "community care" simply roam the streets and sleep on doorsteps. The community, in other words, can be as neglectful as the mental hospital. (See the box on p. 544.)

In recent years thousands of mentally ill people have been released from institutions without adequate provision for follow-up care and have ended up living in the streets. (David Grossman)

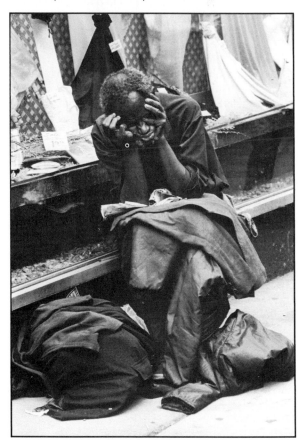

The Homeless and Mentally Ill

Shifting the care of chronic mental patients from state hospitals to the community is called "deinstitutionalization," but many city dwellers call it "dumping." In cities across the country, hundreds of thousands of patients thought capable of functioning on medication outside the institution have been released. Of the estimated 45,000 homeless in New York City today, at least a third are thought to be suffering from mental disorders, most of them from schizophrenia (Goleman, 1986a, 1986b). And in a southwestern city, a study of homeless men recruited from the lines of a soup kitchen and tested on the MMPI found that half showed evidence of either severe alcoholism or severe psychopathology (Kahn et al., 1987). Community services in every urban dumping ground are insufficiently staffed and funded to see that the homeless and mentally ill are properly housed, put to work, or looked after.

Where do they live? Some are placed in cheap single-room-occupancy (SRO) "hotels"—miserable warrens of tiny, filthy, dilapidated rooms. Community services to the chronic mentally ill may consist of a welfare check and occasional visits by a social worker to dispense major tranquilizers and other medications. Otherwise, they are typically on their own. By day, they drift through the streets or hang around the lobby of the SRO; by night, they sleep in roach-infested rooms. They are rarely missed when they die.

Still worse, many former mental patients can find no housing at all, especially in cities where urban renovation has claimed SROs for development and emptied the buildings.

Many of the homeless—the street people, vagrants, or bag people—are not mentally ill but are instead the victims of economic conditions, such as unemployment, cuts in government programs and services, and the rising costs of city housing; as the economic picture worsens, those who were only marginally getting by become homeless. Yet thousands of psychologically disordered people also have nowhere to live. Some spend their days wandering from neighborhood to neighborhood; others travel around one or a few blocks; all sleep where they can—in doorways, in parks, in subways and train stations, in refrigerator cartons, if they can find one, for the little shelter they offer against the rain and winter weather. They carry their belongings in shopping bags or roll grocery carts along the sidewalks.

In New York City the problem has grown to staggering proportions over the past decade. Mental health care professionals there have recognized the need for outreach programs flexible enough to support the diverse needs of that city's homeless and mentally ill population. The broad spectrum concept in current parlance is "supportive housing" and is similar to milieu therapy. Mental health care workers have the task of seeing that the homeless eat, get and take medication, keep appointments, are trained in social skills, and where possible find jobs. Success depends on compassionate nonprofessional workers, or guardians, who do most of the work but are tied, with as little red tape as possible, to psychiatric services. Because most of the mentally ill on the streets suffer from schizophrenia, they cannot seek community services on their own. The guardians, however, can help them apply for the assistance they are entitled to but are unable to request without help in communicating with agency interviewers, filling out forms, and offering proof of identity.

Supportive housing has had good success so far in New York and may provide a model for other urban centers overwhelmed by the bureaucratic and financial problems involved in processing a large, heterogeneous population of the homeless and mentally ill. Since deinstitutionalization following the Community Mental Health Care Act of 1963, the fundamental problem has been that no one has really wanted the responsibility for chronic mental patients. Yet simple humanity requires that something be done to lessen the obvious plight of these people, whose families are seldom willing to take them in and whose middle-class neighbors see them as a nuisance.

Because of the continuing inadequacy of community services, the move toward deinstitutionalization has been slowed. There is now considerable evidence that hospitalization, when necessary, should be brief (Braun et al., 1981; Caton, 1982; Straw, 1982)—perhaps two to three weeks—and that experimental alternatives such as day hospitals and halfway houses are preferable. But these facts have only partially been acted upon. It is true, as stated earlier, that the population of the state mental hospitals has been greatly reduced. So has the average length of hospitalization. Even in settings where, traditionally, most patients were lifetime residents (e.g., state and county mental hospitals, VA psychiatric hospitals), the average length of stay is now less than three months. And in general hospitals, which account for most psychiatric admissions, the average length of stay is less than twelve days (Kiesler, 1982b). At the same time, however, the number of mental hospital admissions has not only not decreased but has actually *increased* since the advent of deinstitutionalization (Kiesler, 1982b). And the hospitals are still devouring most of the public funds for mental health. In 1977, the amount paid under Medicaid to state, county, and private mental institutions was $558 million—more than the total federal cost of all the country's 600 community mental health centers.

The solutions to these problems can come only with time and—more important—with money. The shift in emphasis from mental hospitals to community services has proved a great boon to state budgets. For example, in 1973 it cost the state of Illinois less than $3,500 to house a patient for one year in a representative shelter-care home; by contrast, the annual cost of keeping a patient at any of the three state mental hospitals serving the same area ranged from $8,200 to $21,000 (Kohen and Paul, 1976). Logically, the money saved by keeping patients out of mental hospitals should have been reinvested in community services, but in many cases this has not been done. Though people are still being discharged from mental hospitals as quickly as possible, the community services that were supposed to take responsibility for these people after discharge often do not exist. Or if they exist, they may be inferior to hospital care. Hence the "revolving door" syndrome, mentioned earlier: whatever gains the person has made in the hospital are lost in the community, and the person is readmitted. In sum, while there is little doubt that comprehensive community-based care is an excellent idea, it is still far from a reality.

SUMMARY

In addition to the psychotherapies discussed in Chapter 20, other treatments available to people with psychological disorders include biological therapy, group therapy, and community-based services. The biological approach has received increased professional approval and support in the last decade, following evidence of the biochemical bases of such major disorders as schizophrenia and depression. Most advances have been in psychopharmacological, or drug, treatment. Other major treatments are electroconvulsive therapy (ECT) and psychosurgery. The three main categories of drugs are antianxiety drugs (minor tranquilizers), antipsychotic drugs (major tranquilizers), and antidepressant drugs. Antianxiety drugs, including Librium, Tranxene, Valium, and Xanax, provide effective temporary relief from panic attacks or anxiety, but they can be harmful if they are taken regularly or to avoid problem solving. Antipsychotic drugs, including the phenothiazines, help to reduce symptoms of schizophrenia but may produce side effects of apathy, fatigue, and motor disturbances. Antidepressant drugs include MAO inhibitors and tricyclics; lithium carbonate works effectively to relieve symptoms of mania, particularly in patients with bipolar disorder. ECT, like antidepressant drugs, affects levels of norepinephrine in the brain: the risk of memory dysfunction is lower if only one hemisphere is treated. ECT remains controversial despite its effectiveness in many cases of severe endogenous depression. Psychosurgery is used only as the last resort for severely disturbed or violent patients.

The popularity of group and family therapy is due largely to the belief that many psychological difficulties are basically interpersonal and must be worked out in an interpersonal context. Ten factors have been identified that help to promote therapeutic change in this type of treatment: information, hope, universality, altruism, corrective recapitulation of the family group, development of social skills, imitative behavior, interpersonal learning, group cohesiveness, and catharsis. Different kinds of groups stress different factors as the key to change.

Psychodrama is a psychodynamic approach to group treatment in which participants act out their emotional conflicts using such techniques as role reversal, the double technique, and mirroring. Most behavioral group therapy is directed toward a goal. Social-skills training and assertiveness training are forms of behavioral therapy that are most compatible with the group interaction process. Assertiveness training uses the therapeutic tools of modeling, rehearsal, and reinforcement; it is an extinction therapy, and to some extent a cognitive therapy, insofar as clients lose their fear of expressing feelings and examine their attitudes through interaction with the group.

The humanistic perspective has contributed most to the group therapy movement. The two original humanistic groups were the encounter group and the sensitivity-training or T-group. A third form is Gestalt therapy, in which the participant acts out unresolved emotional conflicts, taking responsibility for the feelings involved. The central goals of humanistically oriented group therapy are personal growth and increased honesty and openness in personal relations, accomplished through free interchange among group members. Of the ten factors that promote change, humanistic approaches emphasize altruism (social support), interpersonal learning, and catharsis.

Family therapy follows many humanistic principles and stresses the group process rather than the pathology of any individual member. The communications (strategic) approach developed out of the double-bind theory of schizophrenia and strives to treat family disturbances arising from the contradictory messages that parents may be giving their children. Paradoxical intention is a technique used to change maladaptive patterns, forcing the family members to find more appropriate ways of communicating and solving problems. The systems approach sees family disturbances as arising from a set of interlocking family roles and encourages family members to adopt more flexible roles. In an effective new psychoeducational-behavioral approach to preventing relapses of schizophrenia, family members are taught new ways of expressing positive and negative emotions and solving family problems. Marital therapy, in which the group consists of a married couple, follows essentially the same lines as family therapy, attempting to establish an honest dialogue between the two partners. Behavior therapy, a more recent entry into the field of family and marital counseling, is aimed at teaching families and couples how to solve problems and settle conflicts through reciprocity rather than coercion.

In peer self-help groups, people who share a given problem meet to discuss it without the guidance of a mental health professional. The groups provide social support (e.g., AA, Weight Watchers).

Evaluations of the effectiveness of specific forms of group therapy have yielded mixed results; social-skills training, assertiveness training, marital and family therapy, and behavior therapy all appear to be generally successful. Outcome studies of humanistic-existential groups indicate that their effectiveness is more modest than that of other kinds of therapy. People who are in serious psychological distress should avoid encounter groups, and those who experience negative effects should be referred for follow-up therapy by group leaders who have been trained to identify participants who need referral.

The major goal of therapeutic environments within institutions is to increase the likelihood that therapeutic gains will generalize from the therapeutic setting to life on the outside so that the patient can reenter society. Psychodynamic therapeutic environments assume that the best treatment for the patient is reeducation through identification with an adult. Behavioral therapeutic environments seek to reinforce appropriate behavior and extinguish inappropriate behavior through the use of token economies in conjunction with other interventions, such as social-skills training. The humanistic-existential version of the therapeutic environment is milieu therapy, which provides an institutional environment designed to maximize the independence, self-respect, and activity level of severely disturbed patients.

Evaluations of therapeutic environments indicate that token economies, especially when used in conjunction with other forms of behavioral therapy, are most effective both in changing in-hospital behavior and in getting patients discharged. Milieu therapy is less effective but is superior to custodial care. However, follow-up studies of token economies indicate that the behavior elicited in the hospital is not generalized to ordinary life to any great extent. This finding has prompted efforts to program such generalization into the token economy by teaching patients to reinforce themselves for appropriate behavior, teaching work skills, and providing aftercare programs.

Hospitalization of the mentally disturbed was much more widespread before the late 1950s than it has been since. The introduction of drugs that render mental patients relatively calm, combined with growing awareness of the adverse effects of the isolation and primarily custodial care typical of state institutions, has led to the release of vast numbers of patients to their homes or to community facilities.

Community mental health centers developed in the mid-1960s after Congress passed the Community

Mental Health Centers Act. These centers provide treatment for large numbers of outpatients and seek to save others from hospitalization. Services consist of outpatient services (including aftercare), inpatient services (including day hospitals and night hospitals), emergency services (including police referrals), consultation, halfway houses, long-term-care facilities, various alternatives to hospitalization (including the experimental Tucson Treatment Network Team), and hot lines. Day hospitals have had notable success, whereas aftercare services have been generally disappointing.

The prevention of psychological disorders requires intervention efforts on three levels: (1) primary (pre-venting disorders from developing in the first place), (2) secondary (early detection and treatment), and (3) tertiary (minimizing the effects or shortening the duration of existing major disorders). Community services are difficult to evaluate because many are so new. They have been criticized for falling short of prevention goals, especially primary prevention. Although these services have made help at the community level more widely available, community mental health centers do not always meet the needs of the specific communities they serve. Community mental health care is an excellent idea, but it is far from being a reality.

CHAPTER 22

Legal Issues in Abnormal Psychology

PSYCHOLOGICAL DISTURBANCE AND CRIMINAL LAW

The Insanity Defense
Competency to Stand Trial

CIVIL COMMITMENT

Procedures for Commitment
Standards for Commitment

PATIENTS' RIGHTS

The Right to Treatment
Other Rights of Mental Patients

POWER AND THE MENTAL HEALTH PROFESSION

I n recent years the overlap between the concerns of mental health and those of law has been increasingly brought to public attention. When we read newspaper accounts of bizarre crimes—such as attempts to assassinate the pope and President Reagan—we take it for granted that a psychiatrist or psychologist will be called on to make judgments about the defendant's sanity and possibly to give "expert testimony" at the trial. In other widely publicized court cases—such as that of Kenneth Donaldson, who sued officials of the state of Florida for wrongfully keeping him in a mental institution for fourteen years—the mental health system itself has been on trial.

These court cases are only the most obvious illustrations of the fact that the diagnosis and treatment of disturbed people have important legal implications. For one thing, people who are judged to be out of contact with reality may be relieved of legal responsibility for crimes that they commit. For another thing, such people, if they are institutionalized for their own or for society's protection, may also be relieved of many of their constitutional rights.

Mental health law, the branch of law that deals

with such matters, has been changing at a rapid pace. In recent years nearly all states have substantially revised their laws regarding the commitment and treatment of the psychologically disturbed (Monahan and Loftus, 1982), and more changes can be expected. The issues that these new laws are attempting to settle are essentially three:

1. *Psychological disturbance and criminal law.* Can psychologically disturbed persons be held guilty of breaking the law? Can such people be given a fair trial? If they are not tried or are acquitted by reason of insanity, what then should the state do with them?

2. *Civil commitment.* Under what circumstances can persons who have committed no crime but appear to be severely disturbed be involuntarily institutionalized by the state?

3. *Patients' rights.* Once a person is institutionalized, what are his or her rights concerning living conditions, psychological treatment, and so forth?

Most of this chapter will be devoted to an examination of these three legal issues. Then, in a final section, we will address ourselves to the larger issue of the power of the mental health profession—how that power is used and how, in recent years, it has been challenged.

PSYCHOLOGICAL DISTURBANCE AND CRIMINAL LAW

Abnormal behavior, as we saw in Chapter 1, can be defined as a violation of the society's norms. Many social norms, however, are not just standards of behavior but legal requirements. Hence abnormal behavior may also be illegal behavior, ranging from drug abuse to theft to murder. Most people agree that when deeply disturbed people commit such crimes, they should not be treated in the same way as ordinary lawbreakers. But how they should be treated is another question altogether—one that is surrounded by controversy.

The Insanity Defense

Though psychologists may question the concept of free will, criminal law does not. The business of criminal law is to fix blame for and to penalize socially intolerable conduct. For the law to carry out these functions, it must assume that human beings freely choose their actions. (If they didn't, how could we justifiably blame or punish them?) Thus when a court pronounces someone guilty, it is making both a judgment of fact *and* a moral judgment: the defendant not only committed the crime but is also morally responsible for it and can therefore be punished for it.

Nevertheless, the law does acknowledge that certain people may commit crimes not out of free choice but because mental disturbance has somehow deprived them of free choice. For such people, there is a loophole known as the **insanity defense,** whereby the defendant admits to having committed the crime but nevertheless pleads not guilty, stating that because of insanity he or she was not morally responsible at the time of the crime. Though guilty in fact, the defendant claims to be innocent in moral terms, and therefore exempt from punishment.

The insanity defense, then, is intended to protect the mentally disturbed from the penalties that we impose on the mentally sound. At the same time, as Alan Stone (1975) has pointed out, it serves to protect the moral prestige of the law. By making exceptions of people who cannot be held responsible for their actions, the insanity defense implies that every other defendant does have the capacity to choose "between good and evil."

Legal Tests of Insanity   If the defendant pleads insanity, how is the jury to decide whether that plea is justifiable? What, in other words, is the legal test of insanity? This question has haunted the courts for many years and has been answered in a variety of ways.

For the purpose of modern law, the first important ruling on this matter was the so-called irresistible impulse decision, handed down by an Ohio court in 1834. According to this test, defendants are acquitted if, as a result of mental illness, they could not *resist* the impulse to do wrong. The main problem with this test is obvious: How is the jury to distinguish between resistible and irresistible impulses? (From the point of view of psychoanalytic or behavioral theory, *is* there any difference?) But as we shall see, this distinction is no more difficult to draw than the distinctions required by other tests of insanity (La-Fave and Scott, 1972).

Historically, the second important test is the so-called M'Naghten rule, handed down by an English court in 1843. The defendant in this case, Daniel M'Naghten, claimed that he had been commanded by the voice of God to kill the English prime minister, Sir Robert Peel; he then killed Peel's secretary by mistake. In acquitting M'Naghten, the court ruled that defendants are legally insane and therefore not criminally responsible if, as a result of a "disease of the mind" and consequent impairment of reason, they either (1) did not know what they were doing or (2) did not know that what they were doing was wrong. (Hence the commonly heard question "Did the defendant know right from wrong?") Thus while the irresistible impulse test stresses the matter of self-control, the M'Naghten test singles out one aspect of self-control, cognition, and makes the test of insanity rest on that. For this it has been criticized.

According to some authorities (e.g., Bromberg, 1965; Weihofen, 1957) cognitive activity cannot be separated from emotion or from any other mental activity; the mind is an integrated whole, not a collection of separate compartments. To this argument legal scholars have responded that while the mind may be integrated, it is not an undifferentiated blob; almost all psychological theories recognize the existence of distinguishable mental processes. Furthermore, the M'Naghten rule has the virtue of limiting the insanity defense to those people who are perceived by the public as truly "insane." All of us have difficulty, in varying degrees, with resisting impulses, but very few of us commit misdeeds because we do not know what we are doing or because we do not know that they are misdeeds. By reserving the insanity defense for people who *are* in this extreme situation and who therefore cannot reasonably be expected to comply with the law, the M'Naghten test, in the eyes of some legal scholars (e.g., Livermore and Meehl, 1967), serves the purpose of excusing the truly excusable and preserving the moral authority of the law.

The most recent formulation of the insanity defense is that adopted by the American Law Institute (ALI) in its Model Penal Code of 1962:

1. A person is not responsible for criminal conduct if at the time of such conduct as a result of mental disease or defect he lacks substantial capacity either to appreciate the criminality of his conduct or to conform his conduct to the requirements of law.
2. As used in the Article [of the code], the terms "mental disease or defect" do not include an abnormality manifested only by repeated criminal or otherwise antisocial conduct (sec. 4.01).

Many legal scholars feel that the ALI test is the best that can be hoped for. What makes it so attractive, in their opinion, is that it places the burden of assigning moral responsibility squarely on the shoulders of the jury. Aside from the difficulties already mentioned, a major problem with both the irresistible impulse and M'Naghten tests is that they are worded in such a way that they almost require mental health professionals, rather than the jury, to decide the case. How is a jury of ordinary citizens to determine whether a defendant was under the influence of an irresistible impulse, or knew what he or she was doing, or knew that it was wrong? These questions, it would seem, can be answered only by experts. As for the ALI rule, to a degree it incorporates both the irresistible impulse criterion ("conform his conduct to the requirements of law") and the M'Naghten criterion ("appreciate the criminality of his conduct"). At the same time,

however, it states these criteria in broader terms and adds the phrase "substantial capacity." The result is a test that *can* be applied without expert knowledge. In effect, the ALI rule asks the jury, "Can the defendant be justly blamed for his or her misbehavior?" In the opinion of many legal scholars, this is the question that should be asked—and of the jury, not the mental health profession.

The ALI test has been adopted by all federal circuit courts of appeal and by about half of the states. Other states are still using the M'Naghten test, with or without a supplemental irresistible impulse test (Weiner, 1985).[*]

A New Verdict—Guilty but Mentally Ill   Several scholars have expressed concern that as the concept of mental illness has been expanded beyond its original limits, encompassing only the grossly psychotic, to its present scope, embracing potentially a very substantial fraction of the population, so many defendants may escape responsibility for their crimes that the deterrent effect of the criminal law may be weakened (Gaylin, 1982; Nesson, 1982). The deterrent effect is not compromised when an obviously psychotic person is found not guilty by reason of insanity; but when someone who appears to be "sane" is found to lack criminal responsibility, the authority of criminal law may seem to be diminished. The Hinckley verdict has been cited as an example of just such a case. (See the box on p. 552.) As the law professor Charles Nesson wrote, "For anyone who experiences life as a struggle to act responsibly in the face of various temptations to let go, the Hinckley verdict is demoralizing, an example of someone who let himself go and who has been exonerated because of it" (Nesson, 1982, p. A19).

This concern has led to consideration of a new verdict of "guilty but mentally ill," not to replace the traditional insanity verdict but to provide an intermediate verdict between "guilty" and "not guilty by reason of insanity." It would be appropriate in cases in which the defendant knew what he or she was doing and

---

[*] A fourth test, known as the Durham test, states that the defendant is not criminally responsible "if his unlawful act was the product of mental disease or mental defect." As is obvious from the wording, this test, more than any of the others, forces the jury to rely on expert testimony. For this reason, the Durham test has been replaced in most of those jurisdictions that had adopted it.

The Hinckley Case

Ye people of England exult and be glad
For ye're now at the mercy of the merciless mad
This bit of doggerel, which appeared in the *Times* of London in 1843, expressed the public outrage when Daniel M'Naghten was acquitted by reason of insanity after he had tried to kill the prime minister of England (Monahan, 1981). Evidence was introduced at the trial in an attempt to show that M'Naghten suffered delusions of persecution.

Many Americans felt similar outrage in 1982, when John W. Hinckley, Jr., was found not guilty by reason of insanity following his attempt to assassinate President Ronald Reagan in 1981. An ABC opinion poll indicated that 76 percent of the public felt that the verdict was unjust. An Indianapolis paper ran a headline declaring "Hinckley Insane, Public Mad" ("Insane on All Counts," 1982). Many people thought the assassination attempt was too deliberate and cold-blooded to be attributed to insanity.

On March 30, 1981, Hinckley had loaded his gun with "Devastator" bullets—the kind that explode on impact—and set off to stalk the president. According to a letter found later in Hinckley's Washington hotel room, his avowed motive was to commit a historical deed that would "gain [the] love and respect" of Jodie Foster, a teenage actress whom Hinckley had written to but never met.

Hinckley's trial focused on his sanity at the time of the act. Clearly, he had pulled the trigger; he had been caught with the gun in his hand. The prosecution did not need to prove that he had committed the shooting, but the legal burden *was* on the prosecution to prove "beyond a reasonable doubt" that the defendant had the mental capacity to know that the criminal act was wrong and to control his actions at the time.

The jury was presented with mountains of conflicting evidence from expert witnesses called by both sides. The defense witnesses portrayed Hinckley as driven by a delusion of achieving a "magical union" with Jodie Foster and suffering from a severe form of schizophrenia, as well as numerous other mental problems. The psychiatrists called by the prosecution testified that Hinckley made a conscious choice to shoot Reagan and had no "compelling drive" to do so. They depicted Hinckley as selfish and manipulative and suffering from only some minor personality disorders.

The jury's verdict of not guilty by reason of insanity stunned the courtroom, including the judge and Hinckley himself, who had fully expected conviction. Many jurors who were questioned afterward about how they had reached their verdict stated simply that the prosecution had not proved beyond a reasonable doubt that Hinckley had the mental capacity to be responsible for his crime.

The nation's outrage at the verdict in the Hinckley case has taken some concrete forms. Several states have passed or are pressing to pass laws establishing a new verdict, "guilty but mentally ill," which will allow treatment for the criminally insane but confine them within the penal system. Some states now call for the defense to prove that the defendant is insane rather than requiring the prosecutor to prove sanity. Three states (Idaho, Montana, and Utah) have even abolished the insanity defense.

Abolition of the plea is a radical and perhaps unwise step. As one of the psychiatrists who testified in the Hinckley case said, "the insanity plea is necessary to maintain our view of a moral justice. . . . In a sense, it is the mark that separates us from the wild beasts" (quoted in *The New York Times*, July 1, 1982, p. A15). The publicity surrounding the Hinckley case should not be allowed to obscure the fact that the insanity defense is in fact rarely invoked and rarely successful when used. Research in several states indicates that it is successful in less than 1 percent of felony cases (Weiner, 1985). It is safe to assume that the great majority of defendants who use the plea successfully are truly deserving of its protection.

that it was wrong, but who nonetheless had some form of mental illness. The defendant convicted by this verdict would serve time and receive treatment within the penal system. Michigan was the first state to adopt the "guilty but mentally ill" verdict (in 1975); about ten states have followed suit (Weiner, 1985).

John W. Hinckley, Jr.'s, successful use of the insanity defense following his attempt to assassinate President Ronald Reagan set off a storm of controversy. The uproar obscured the fact that an extremely small number of defendants are found not guilty by reason of insanity. (AP/Wide World Photos)

Procedural Aspects of the Insanity Defense

The Hinckley case stirred interest in two procedural aspects of the insanity defense: the burden of proof of insanity (or sanity), and procedures used to determine whether a defendant who was acquitted should be committed to a mental hospital or released back into the community.

As a general rule, the prosecution must prove beyond a reasonable doubt all elements of a criminal offense—including both the physical act and the requisite mental state, which in a murder case is the intent to kill (LaFave and Scott, 1972). When defendants raise the insanity defense, must they prove that they were insane at the time of the crime, or must the prosecution instead prove that they were sane?

Roughly half the states place the burden on the prosecution to prove sanity, and prove it beyond a reasonable doubt, once the defense has presented some evidence, such as psychiatric testimony, suggesting insanity (Weiner, 1985). The federal rules of criminal procedure under which Hinckley was tried also required the prosecution to prove sanity beyond a reasonable doubt. Partly because of the Hinckley verdict, the federal rules were changed in 1984 to place the burden of proving insanity on the defendant (Weiner, 1985).

What is to be done with defendants who are acquitted by reason of insanity? In the past, defendants acquitted of serious charges by reason of insanity were usually subjected to long-term confinement in a mental hospital, often a high-security hospital with the physical appearance of a prison. As a result of mental health law reform in the last fifteen years, however, commitment following acquittal on the grounds of insanity is no longer automatic in many states. While a defendant may be committed briefly for evaluation, prolonged hospitalization is now often permitted only under standards of ordinary civil commitment ("Commitment Following an Insanity Acquittal," 1981). As we will see later, these standards typically require a finding that the person is *now* mentally ill and dangerous. Since a great deal of time may have elapsed between the commission of the offense and the acquittal, the defendant may have experienced a change in mental condition. Thus it is entirely possible that a particular defendant's condition may not meet commitment criteria at the postacquittal commitment hearing.

Precisely this possibility alarmed many people, including a majority of U.S. Supreme Court justices, and in 1983 the Court ruled that it *is* permissible to automatically commit insanity acquittees, who could then be hospitalized until they proved themselves no longer dangerous. Further, the Court ruled that they could be hospitalized for longer than they could have been imprisoned had they been convicted (*Jones* v.

United States, 103 S.Ct. 3043). This more cautious approach to the release of insanity acquittees was probably the result, in part at least, of the Hinckley verdict and its aftermath.

The Argument against the Insanity Defense
In the abstract, it seems only fair to provide an escape hatch such as the insanity defense for people who violate the law as a result of psychological disturbance. In reality, however, the insanity defense poses very thorny problems, both practical and moral.

For one thing, how can a jury accurately determine whether the case conforms to the court's definition of insanity? To rule on a person's sanity is to arrive at a subjective judgment that is extremely difficult to make. Furthermore, it is important to note that the jury is required to make a *retrospective* judgment. The question is not the defendant's current mental state, which the jury might at least guess at by observing his or her courtroom behavior, but the defendant's mental state at the time of the crime.

In most cases, the jury must rely on testimony of psychological professionals, but this, in fact, is no solution. In the first place, psychiatrists and psychologists have as much difficulty with retrospective diagnoses as other people. Second, they often produce diametrically opposed diagnoses of the same defendant—an absurdity of which the trial of John Hinckley was only the most recent example. Of the forty-one witnesses called at that trial, seven were psychiatrists and eleven others also were physicians. Often even the testimony of the experts called by one side was contradictory. Third, even if the "expert" witnesses could agree, their opinion, as we saw above, is only partially relevant. The court is there not to make a scientific judgment but to make a legal judgment— whether the defendant should be held legally responsible for the crime. This is a judgment that only the jury, not the mental health profession, is empowered to make. But because the jury has so little concrete information to go on, that judgment may be erroneous.

A second criticism of the insanity defense, based on a totally different point of view, is that of Thomas Szasz (1963). According to Szasz, the problem with the insanity defense is not that it is difficult for the jury to evaluate but that the special circumstance that it attempts to deal with—insanity—does not exist. As we saw in Chapter 1, Szasz claims that mental illness is a myth perpetuated by an arrogant profession. In his opinion, all behavior is of a purposeful and therefore responsible nature. If people act in socially offensive or hostile ways, they do so because they *mean* to act in socially offensive or hostile ways. To label them insane is to deny their behavior any meaning or value and thus, by extension, to deny that there is any conflict between the individual and society. Szasz proposes that the courts get out of the business of judging people on their intentions and judge them instead on their behavior. If a person has committed hostile and dangerous acts, "he should be punished, not treated—in jail, not in a hospital" (1977, p. 135).

Szasz's stance brings us to the third major criticism of the insanity defense: that those who successfully plead it sometimes end up in a worse situation than if they had been convicted of their crimes. As we pointed out earlier, people who are pronounced not guilty by reason of insanity are usually not set free like others who are acquitted of crimes. Rather, they are often committed to mental hospitals and are kept there until such time as experts testify that they are no longer dangerous. Such testimony is usually very long in coming; indeed, it may never come. Thus while people convicted of crimes are deprived of their liberty for a specific period of time—after which, by law, they are free—people acquitted by reason of insanity often are given **indeterminate sentences**—sentences with no limit—and may languish for the rest of their lives in a mental hospital before a staff member decides that they are no longer dangerous.[*]

These considerations, among others, have led to widespread criticism of the insanity defense, and not just by extremists such as Szasz. As the box on page 552 indicates, three states—Idaho, Montana, and Utah—actually abolished the insanity defense in the early 1980s. It remains to be seen if the courts will decide that such a defense is in fact constitutionally required.

---

[*] While lifetime hospitalization may have been the fate of insanity acquittees in the past, it is rarely so now. Research indicates that those acquitted on the insanity plea in New York State, for example, spend less time in institutions, on the average, than persons convicted on similar charges spend in prison (Pasework et al., 1982).

Competency to Stand Trial

The number of people confined in mental hospitals as a result of successful insanity pleas is small in comparison with the number who are there because they are judged mentally unfit even to be tried. In most states, defendants, in order to stand trial, must understand the nature of the proceedings against them and must be able to assist counsel in their own defense. When defendants do not meet these requirements, the trial is delayed, and the defendants are sent to a mental health facility in hope of restoring their competency. As with the insanity defense, the purpose is to protect the defendant and at the same time to preserve the court's reputation for justice. The courts would not inspire public trust if they tried people who were obviously out of touch with reality.

Incompetency to stand trial must not be confused with legal insanity. The insanity defense has to do with the defendant's mental state at the time of the crime; competency to stand trial has to do with the defendant's mental state at the time of the trial. Furthermore, while the insanity defense concerns moral responsibility for crime, competency to stand trial is merely a question of ability to understand the charges and to confer fairly reasonably with one's attorney. Thus a person who is judged competent to stand trial can still successfully assert an insanity defense. Even people diagnosed as psychotic may be competent to stand trial; many are lucid enough to meet the competency requirements (Roesch and Golding, 1980).

Incompetency, then, is a very limited concept. However, the rule is often applied in a very loose fashion. Both prosecutors and defense attorneys have been accused of abusing the competency issue (Rappeport, 1978; Stone, 1975). Prosecutors who fear that their cases are too weak can use it to keep the defendant incarcerated, thus accomplishing the same purpose that would be gained by a conviction. On the other hand, defense attorneys may use the competency proceedings in order to delay the trial, in the hope that some of the prosecutor's witnesses may become unavailable to testify or simply in order to convince the defendant that they are doing all they can (Rappeport, 1978).

For the defendants, the consequences may be grave. Once ruled incompetent, they are often denied bail, cut off from their jobs, friends, family, and other social supports, and confined in a hospital for the criminally insane, when in fact they may never have committed the crimes they are charged with. And until recently they often remained in the hospital for years, since there was often no means of restoring their competency. In 1972, however, this particular abuse was ruled unconstitutional by the U.S. Supreme Court in the case of *Jackson* v. *Indiana* (92 S.Ct. 1845). The defendant in this case was a mentally retarded deaf-mute who had been charged with robbery. Judged incompetent to stand trial, he was being held in a state hospital indefinitely, since there was no way to render him competent to stand trial. The Court ruled that when a person is detained solely on the grounds of incompetency to stand trial, the detention can last only as long as it takes to determine whether the defendant is likely to become competent to stand trial in the foreseeable future. If the likelihood is poor or nil, the defendant must be either committed to an institution according to the state's ordinary civil commitment procedures or released. (See "Civil Commitment," below).

Competency and Antipsychotic Medication

One controversy surrounding the competency issue has to do with antipsychotic drugs (Graber and Marsh, 1979; Stone, 1975). If defendants fulfill the competency requirements only when under the influence of antipsychotic drugs, are they in fact competent to stand trial? On the one hand, it seems almost unfair not to try such patients if in fact the drugs render them lucid enough to be tried. On the other hand, these drugs, as we have seen, often render people somewhat groggy and passive—surely an inappropriate state to be in at one's own trial. Furthermore, antipsychotic medication might well affect the defendant's chances of successfully pleading the insanity defense. The "crazier" the defendant seems during the course of the trial, the more likely it is that the jury will accept the insanity plea. But whatever crazy behavior the defendant normally exhibits may well be reduced by the medication. Should we then allow defendants to undergo trial without medication, so that the jury can see them in their "true" state? But even if this were the most direct route to justice (which is questionable), many defendants could not be tried because they would not be competent to stand trial without the medication. This catch-22 is only one of the many problems in mental health law that courts and state legislatures have had to resolve. In recent years nearly all states have adopted the view that competency achieved by medication is acceptable (Weiner, 1985).

CIVIL COMMITMENT

Criminal commitment accounts for only a small percentage of those committed to our mental hospitals. The remainder are there as a result of **civil commitment**—that is, not because they were charged with a crime but because the state decided that they were disturbed enough to require hospitalization. About 55 percent of admissions to public mental hospitals are involuntary; at psychiatric units of general hospitals, only 15 percent of admissions are involuntary (Brakel, 1985). It is in regard to involuntary commitment that the legal questions are most numerous and serious.

Procedures for Commitment

The U.S. Constitution provides that the government may not deprive a person of life, liberty, or property without "due process of law." Involuntary commitment to a mental hospital is clearly a deprivation of liberty. What in the way of "due process," or legal procedures, is required before a person may be subjected to involuntary commitment? This is a question that the U.S. Supreme Court has not fully considered. Many lower courts have addressed it, but the answers they have given vary from jurisdiction to jurisdiction.

A useful way to approach the problem is to consider the rights that a defendant has in a criminal trial and then to ask whether a person faced with the possiblity of involuntary civil commitment should have the same rights. Among other things, the following are guaranteed to persons accused of serious crimes: (1) a jury trial, (2) the assistance of counsel, (3) a right not to be compelled to incriminate themselves, and (4) the requirement that guilt be proved "beyond a reasonable doubt." Should these rights also apply to involuntary civil commitment?

The Right to a Jury Trial   Let us take first the right to a jury trial. Today states typically require a formal judicial hearing before commitment (though the

hearing may follow a brief period of emergency commitment). In fifteen states the defendant has a right to have a jury at such a hearing. Other states make no provision for a jury; the decision is rendered by the judge or perhaps a lower judicial officer.

The argument against a jury trial is that juries are expensive and time-consuming, and furthermore, that it is not in the best interests of mentally distressed people to have their psychological condition formally debated before a jury. The argument for a jury trial is that distressed or otherwise, these people stand to lose their liberty, and that in a matter so serious, the judgment must come from the citizenry, just as in a criminal trial, for this is the best protection against oppression. (Keep in mind that many civil libertarians do feel that involuntary patients in mental institutions are akin to prisoners.) However, since the U.S. Supreme Court has ruled that jury trials are not required in juvenile cases, it is unlikely that the Court will require them in commitment cases (Brakel, 1985).

The Right to the Assistance of Counsel   In most states a person who is threatened with involuntary commitment does have the right to be represented by counsel at the commitment hearing. However, there is much disagreement about what lawyers are supposed to do for their clients at such hearings. In criminal trials, defense attorneys have a clear role: they are the adversaries of the prosecutor, and they are supposed to do everything they legally can to get their clients acquitted. It is not their job to worry about the legal question of the defendant's guilt or innocence. Should lawyers at commitment hearings behave in the same way—that is, as advocates for their clients' wishes? Or should they act instead as "guardians," pursuing their clients' best interests as they, the lawyers, see them? If we assume that some people are too disturbed to know what their best interests are, then lawyers who take the advocate role run the risk of acting against their clients' best interests. If, on the other hand, they take the guardian role, they may well act in direct opposition to the clients' wishes, deferring instead to the judgment of expert witnesses who claim hospitalization is necessary. Apparently most lawyers at commitment hearings do precisely that—a practice that is bitterly criticized by those who feel that clients should be allowed to decide what their best interests are (Reisner, 1985).

The Right against Self-Incrimination   Defendants at criminal trials have the right to remain silent, and their silence may not be used against them. The prosecutor is not even permitted to comment on their silence to the jury (Israel and LaFave, 1975). Should the same rule apply at a commitment hearing? Some people would say yes, that people threatened with commitment should have the same protections as those threatened with imprisonment, for they have as much, if not more, to lose. Others would say that since silence may be a symptom of serious mental disturbance, it is completely inappropriate to exclude it from the evidence. Should psychiatrists, for example, be barred from testifying that their diagnosis of psychotic depression is based in part on the patient's muteness (Brooks, 1974)? Like the matter of a jury, protection against self-incrimination has been variously interpreted by the states.

The Standard of Proof   Finally, a jury can convict a defendant only if the prosecution has proved guilt "beyond a reasonable doubt." The degree of certainty is called the **standard of proof.** The "beyond a reasonable doubt" standard is a very high one—perhaps a 90 to 95 percent certainty. Should this requirement also apply to commitment hearings? There are other possibilities. In most civil proceedings (e.g., lawsuits), the standard of proof is the "preponderance of evidence"—in other words, "more likely than not," or at least 51 percent certainty (Stone, 1975). A third possibility is the far lower standard of proof used in medical diagnosis, where any evidence whatsoever—theoretically even a 5 to 10 percent certainty—may lead to diagnosis of illness. Which of these standards should apply in the case of involuntary commitment?

To consider this question, we must consider the seriousness of two possible errors: (1) a **false positive,** or unjustified commitment, and (2) a **false negative,** a failure to commit when commitment is in fact justified and necessary.[*] In a criminal trial, a false positive—that is, the conviction of an innocent person—is considered a far more serious error than a

---

[*] These terms are taken from the medical diagnostic vocabulary. A *false positive* is an incorrect diagnosis of illness; a *true positive,* a correct diagnosis of illness; a *false negative,* an incorrect diagnosis of no illness; a *true negative,* a correct diagnosis of no illness.

false negative—that is, the acquittal of a guilty person. Hence the extremely high standard of proof in criminal trials: "When in doubt, acquit."

In a civil proceeding, a false positive (the complainant's unjustifiably winning the lawsuit) is considered approximately as serious as a false negative (the complainant's unjustifiably losing the lawsuit). Therefore the standard of proof falls in the middle: 51 percent certainty. In medical diagnosis, on the other hand, a false positive (a false diagnosis of illness) is considered a negligible error compared with the extremely serious mistake of a false negative (a false diagnosis of no illness). Imagine, for example, that a person is being tested for cancer and the physician finds only a few slightly suspicious cell changes. If the diagnosis is a false positive, this fact will emerge in the course of further testing, and the diagnosis will be changed, with no harm done. But a false negative diagnosis may well eliminate the chance of the cancer's being treated at an early and perhaps curable stage; in other words, a great deal of harm will have been done. Thus the extremely low standard of proof in medicine—"When in doubt, diagnose illness"—seems quite logical.

Which standard should apply at a commitment hearing? The answer depends on what we see as the purpose of commitment. Generally the law recognizes two justifications for involuntary commitment: the good of the patient and the good of society. At first glance, it would seem that when commitment is undertaken for the good of society (i.e., to protect people from harm by the patient), the criminal standard of proof should be used, since the issue in both cases is the same: public safety versus individual liberty. By the same token, it would seem that when commitment is sought for the good of the patient (e.g., so that he or she can be treated), the medical standard of proof should be applied. However, critics of civil commitment (e.g., Ennis and Emery, 1978) argue that the medical standard should never be used, since commitment cases, no matter what their stated purpose, are never analogous to medical diagnosis. According to these writers, so-called good-of-the-patient commitments are often undertaken more for the sake of others (e.g., the patient's family) than for the sake of the patient. Moreover, unlike medical diagnosis, a diagnosis to commit cannot be disproved, deprives the patient of liberty, stigmatizes the patient, and does not necessarily lead to treatment. For these reasons, among others, critics of commitment insist

The Limits of Confidentiality

On October 27, 1969, a man named Prosenjit Poddar killed a young woman named Tatiana Tarasoff. Two months earlier, Poddar had told his therapist that he intended to commit the crime. Although the therapist then notified the police—who detained Poddar briefly but released him upon finding him "rational"—neither Tatiana Tarasoff nor her family was informed of Poddar's threat. After the crime, the young woman's parents brought suit against the therapist and the hospital that employed him, charging that they should have been warned about the man's intentions. The California Supreme Court agreed, holding that "when a therapist determines . . . that a patient presents a serious danger of violence to another, he incurs an obligation to use reasonable care to protect the intended victim against such danger."

In effect, this ruling meant that psychotherapists have obligations to the society at large that override their obligations to their own patients. Traditionally, the relationship between therapist and patient has been considered privileged: information supplied by the patient is held in strict confidence by the therapist. According to this ruling, however, the therapist must divulge such information if the patient is "dangerous"; the police and the family of the threatened victim must be warned. As the court stated in its opinion, "the protective privilege ends where the public peril begins."

But where does the public peril begin? The prediction of "dangerousness" is an uncertain (if not impossible) task. As a dissenting opinion in this case pointed out, psychotherapists find it difficult enough to diagnose mental illness itself without also having to predict whether a patient will or will not be dangerous at some time in the future.

The *Tarasoff* decision was widely denounced by mental health professionals. The psychiatrist Alan Stone, for example, wrote that "the imposition of a duty to protect, which may take the form of a duty to warn threatened third parties, will imperil the therapeutic alliance and destroy the patient's expectation of confidentiality, thereby thwarting effective treatment and ultimately reducing the public safety" (Stone, 1976, p. 368). Under circumstances of reduced confidentiality, a patient who felt a compulsion to do violence might well be reluctant to confide it to a therapist. Potentially dangerous patients might be unwilling to seek therapy at all, for fear that they would ultimately be dealt with by the police. On the other side, therapists, to avoid lawsuits, would be encouraged to report all threats of violence to potential victims and to the police—or even to seek the commitment of "dangerous" patients to avoid possible harm to others and to themselves. Since the vast majority of patients who express violent intentions do not act on them, the "innocent victims," ironically, may be patients—not those whom they threaten.

There may be a brighter side to *Tarasoff,* however. David Wexler, professor of law at the University of Arizona, has argued that the decision could have a positive impact on treatment (1981). Since 80 to 90 percent of persons threatened by patients in therapy are family members or lovers (MacDonald, 1967), the prospective victim might be encouraged to participate in "conjoint," or family, therapy with the patient. By directly discussing the patient's anger and the potential victim's role in precipitating violence, therapy may thereby reduce the likelihood of such violence.

Source: *Tarasoff* v. *Regents of California,* 17 Cal. 3d 425, 131 Cal. Rptr. 14 (1976).

that no matter what the reason for commitment, the "beyond a reasonable doubt" standard should be used. It should be added that in general, civil libertarians are extremely skeptical of procedures that are purportedly "for the good of the patient." Their skepticism extends beyond the lowered standard of proof to the nonjury hearing, the "guardian" lawyer, and the lack of protection against self-incrimination. In their opinion, an expressed attitude of concern for patients assumes that they are "guilty" and leads directly to a violation of their civil rights. If these people are threatened with loss of liberty as a result of socially offensive behavior, then they are in the same position as alleged criminals and should be accorded the same rights.

Unlike the other three procedural questions we

have discussed, the standard of proof at commitment hearings *has* been dealt with by the U.S. Supreme Court. In the 1979 case of *Addington* v. *Texas* (99 S.Ct. 1804) the defendant was a man whose mother had filed a petition to have him committed. The commitment was approved by a Texas court according to the "preponderance of evidence" standard. The defendant then appealed the decision, arguing that the need for hospitalization should be proved "beyond a reasonable doubt." The Supreme Court quickly rejected the "preponderance of evidence" standard (and by implication any less stringent standard) because of the liberty interest at stake. The Court also rejected the criminal "beyond a reasonable doubt" standard, however, for several reasons. The Court observed that unlike the wrongfully convicted criminal defendant, who would languish in prison until his sentence had been served, the wrongfully civilly committed person would probably be discharged, as doctors would recognize that hospitalization was unwarranted. Thus the false positive error is less serious in the civil context than in the criminal context because of the greater opportunity to correct the error. The consequences of a false negative error were also seen as different in the two contexts. A truly guilty criminal defendant benefits from a wrongful acquittal, whereas a truly mentally ill person who is not ordered to get treatment suffers from the absence of the needed treatment. The Court thus used some of the notions underlying the medical decision rule as grounds for rejecting the "beyond a reasonable doubt" standard. The Court adopted an intermediate standard of proof, called "clear and convincing evidence," as the proper standard for commitment hearings. It corresponds to approximately "75 percent sure," higher than the ordinary civil standard but lower than the criminal one. This decision is to some extent a victory for the proponents of the criminal standard, in that it at least rules out the civil and medical standards and moves the required degree of certainty that much closer to the criminal standard. At the same time, it remains to be seen how jurors and judicial officers will interpret this standard of proof.

Standards for Commitment

So far we have dealt only with the procedures for commitment; we must now consider the *standards* for commitment. What must be proved in order to justify involuntary commitment?

Until recently, mental illness alone, or mental illness and "need for treatment," were sufficient grounds for involuntary commitment in many states. However, judges and legislators have read the literature critical of the concept of mental illness, and over the years there has been a trend toward requiring that the procommitment forces show something in addition to mental illness—usually dangerousness to self or others (Monahan and Loftus, 1982).

The Definition of Dangerousness   Is dangerousness confined to the threat of physical harm to oneself or others? What about emotional harm, such as schizophrenic parents may inflict on their children? What about economic harm, such as people in a manic episode may bring down upon their families by spending their life savings on foolish business ventures? What about harm to property? Various courts and legislatures have taken different positions on this matter. Some states, for example, do consider a threat of harm to property sufficient (Brakel, 1985).

The Determination of Dangerousness   Whatever the definition of dangerousness, determining it is an extremely difficult matter. To say that someone is dangerous is to predict future behavior. The rarer an event, the harder it is to predict accurately. Hence if dangerousness is defined as homicide or suicide, both of which are rare events, the prediction of dangerousness will inevitably involve many unjustified commitments as well as justified ones. Consider, for example, the following hypothetical case:

> A man with classic paranoia exhibits in a clinical interview a fixed belief that his wife is attempting to poison him. He calmly states that on release he will be forced to kill her in self-defense. The experts agree that his condition is untreatable. Assume that statistical data indicate an eighty percent probability that homicide will occur (Livermore et al., 1968).

What should the court do? Instinctively, it would seem correct to "play it safe" and commit the patient. (See the box on p. 558.) However, as the authors of this case point out, even accepting an 80 percent probability of homicide as sufficient to commit means committing twenty nonhomicidal people for every eighty homicidal ones. Perhaps society could accept such a ratio. But the fact is that an 80 percent probability is unrealistically high. Murder is very rare: in any year, only one person in 8,000 commits murder (Beck, 1985), and mental patients without arrest records are no more likely than the general public to commit murder (Monahan, 1981). Further, very few patients threatened with commitment will calmly state in a clinical interview that they intend to commit murder once they are released. In many cases, for example, the evidence for possible future homicide is a report from a family member that in the past the patient has threatened homicide, perhaps in a moment of extreme anger. In such a case, the probability of homicide would be very low—probably less than 1 percent. Is this a ratio that society can accept? If in criminal law it is better that ten guilty people go free than that one innocent person suffer (Blackstone, 1769), how can we say that in cases of civil commitment it is better for ninety-nine harmless people to be locked up than for one dangerous person to go free?

In addition to the rarity of dangerous behavior, several other factors tend to swell the number of false positives in predictions of dangerousness (Monahan, 1976). These factors include:

1. *Lack of corrective feedback.* Since patients who are judged to be dangerous are institutionalized, there is no opportunity to find out whether they would in fact have been dangerous if released.

2. *Differential consequences to the predictor.* False negatives (people who are released and turn out to be dangerous) create very bad publicity; false positives (people who are committed when in fact they are harmless) do not.

3. *Unreliability of the criterion.* The only hard evidence for a prediction of dangerousness is the patient's past record of *detected* violence, which may be very unrepresentative. Knowing this, clinicians may tend to "play it safe."

4. *Powerlessness of the subject.* Until recently, people erroneously committed on the grounds of dangerousness had little power to oppose this decision.

All of these factors encourage mental health professionals to err in the direction of overpredicting danger-ousness. Do they in fact do so? Every study of predictions of dangerousness has yielded far more false positives than false negatives (e.g., Kozol et al., 1972). But as Monahan (1978) has pointed out, such studies themselves may not be highly valid, for they are based on predictions from an institutional context applied to a real-world context. In most of these studies, mental health professionals were asked to predict the likelihood of dangerous behavior in patients about to be released from institutions. Since there is considerable evidence that human behavior is situation-specific, changing as we move from classroom to work to home, it is no surprise that predictions of real-world behavior based on institutional behavior have turned out to have poor validity.

Furthermore, this is not actually the kind of prediction that is made at commitment hearings. At such hearings, mental health professionals are called upon to predict real-world behavior on the basis of reports of the patient's prior real-world behavior and of interviews with the patient. In other words, at least part of their information comes from the same context as the one for which they are predicting. Such predictions should have higher validity than cross-context predictions. Do they? No study has addressed this question, and it is hard to imagine how any study *could* address it. Theoretically, one could have mental health professionals evaluate the dangerousness of a large number of people threatened with commitment, then release all those people and keep track of them to find out whether they bore out the predictions made for them. But the knowledge to be gained from such an experiment would not justify the hazard to society. Thus we have little means of determining the validity of the predictions of dangerousness made by mental health professionals at commitment hearings.

Some prominent psychiatrists (e.g., Sadoff, 1978; Stone, 1975) have suggested that dangerousness, in the sense of propensity to physical violence, is actually an inappropriate criterion for commitment. Several arguments have been advanced to support this view. First, mental patients as a class are not particularly dangerous; they seem no more likely, or perhaps only slightly more likely, than the general population to engage in criminal activity, violent or nonviolent (Monahan, 1981). Second, we cannot use the justification of treatment, since there is no effective treatment for dangerousness. Third, as we have seen, there is little evidence that mental health professionals can accurately predict dangerousness.

The "Thank You" Proposition   What, then, *should* the courts use as a basis for commitment decisions? In place of dangerousness, Stone (1975) has offered the "thank you" proposition. It runs as follows. If a person is suffering from mental illness, if a treatment is available to relieve that illness, and if the patient refuses treatment on grossly irrational grounds (e.g., "Don't come near me—I'm radioactive"), then the involuntary commitment for the sake of providing that treatment is justified. After the treatment is provided, the patient will be grateful that his or her wishes were disregarded, just as children who are forced to go to school are grateful, as adults, that education was forced on them. Stone's proposition has been criticized on the grounds that most involuntarily treated patients do *not* in fact become grateful for their treatment (Ennis and Emery, 1978). Research on this issue has yielded mixed results (Roth, 1979). Nevertheless, the proposition does at least have the virtue of stressing the patient's welfare—a matter that is not prominently featured in the dangerousness rule. Critics of involuntary commitment would respond that many wrongs have been inflicted on patients because of someone's judgment of what is in the patient's best interest. A version of Stone's proposition was adopted by the American Psychiatric Association in its model commitment law in 1983 (Stromberg and Stone, 1983).

Expert Testimony in Civil Commitment   Whatever the standard for involuntary commitment, whether dangerousness or the expectation of gratitude, expert testimony will continue to be called for. As we saw earlier, many legal scholars feel that criminal courts rely too much on the opinions of mental health professionals. The same problem exists at commitment hearings. To say what mental health professionals should and should not rule upon in commitment cases requires certain fine distinctions, but they are distinctions that must be made. At commitment hearings psychologists and psychiatrists may be asked, "How dangerous is this patient?" Though they may have only limited ability to respond to this question, it is still not an improper question to put to them. However, expert witnesses are frequently asked not only how dangerous patients are but whether they are *too dangerous to be released;* this is not a proper question for the expert witness to answer. How dan-

gerous a person must be in order to be deprived of his or her freedom is not a mental health question but a legal and moral question. It involves weighing the individual's interest in liberty against the society's interest in public safety, and the weighing of these competing interests is the business not of the mental health profession but of the court (Morse, 1978). Similarly, if involuntary commitment is sought on the basis of the "thank you" proposition, the proper question for the expert witness would seem to be "What is the probability that the patient will later be grateful for having been treated involuntarily?" or at a minimum, "How effective is the treatment likely to be?" How high that probability must be in order to justify involuntary treatment is again a legal and moral issue that only the courts or the legislatures can decide.

The Case against Involuntary Commitment   Just as some people have argued against the insanity plea, some argue that civil commitment itself should be abolished (Szasz, 1963; Morse, 1982b). They maintain that individuals who engage in criminal activity should be dealt with by the criminal justice system; those who do not should simply be left alone. "Disturbed" persons who truly were dangerous would ultimately find themselves subject to the criminal justice system. This, the proponents argue, would be a benefit—both because of the greater procedural safeguards of the criminal process (trial by jury, etc.) and because of the fixed sentences of the criminal system (in contrast to the indeterminate "sentences" of the mental health system).

Those who argue that there should be *no* involuntary commitment are in the minority, however, and proponents of commitment find flaws in the argument for abolition, at least insofar as it relies on a comparison between commitment and imprisonment. Although the criminal justice system would seem to offer more protection to individual rights, the widespread practice of plea bargaining often acts to negate these legal safeguards (Brooks, 1974). Any procedural protections a defendant has may mean little in a system in which over 90 percent of all defendants plead guilty (Alschuler, 1979) because of the risk of a stiffer sentence if they assert their right to a trial. The "fixed sentences versus indeterminate sentences" distinction is also not completely compelling, as modern commitment statutes often put limits on involuntary commitment, though these limits are usually subject to extension through further judicial review (Brakel, 1985).

Nevertheless, the argument against involuntary commitment has gained a certain measure of support, particularly among civil libertarians. From this point of view, no innocent persons should be confined in institutions against their will, no matter how "crazy" their behavior in some eyes or how convincingly it can be argued that they need therapy.

PATIENTS' RIGHTS

Until recently, people who were deprived of their liberty on the grounds that they were mentally ill and dangerous were usually deprived of most of their other civil rights as well. Once institutionalized, they were largely at the mercy of the institution, which decided for them what privileges and duties they should have and what treatments, if any, they should undergo. (The abuses that could result from this system were suggested by a popular movie, *One Flew Over the Cuckoo's Nest.*) Today there is a strong trend toward guaranteeing patients certain basic rights, especially the right to treatment, the right to refuse certain types of treatment, and the right to decent living conditions.

The Right to Treatment

For decades the need for treatment has served as a justification, explicit or implicit, for involuntary commitment. However, it was not until the 1960s that the courts suggested that involuntary mental patients had a constitutional right to treatment. And it was not until 1972 that this right was spelled out, by an Alabama federal court in the case of *Wyatt* v. *Stickney,* which has already been discussed briefly in Chapter 19. In this case, the state of Alabama was accused of failure to provide adequate treatment for those confined in its hospitals for the mentally disabled and retarded. As it turned out, treatment was not all that these hospitals failed to provide. In the two institutions where the case originated, conditions were shocking. The wards were filthy, dark, and chaotic. The food was barely edible. (The state at that time spent less than fifty cents a day on food for each patient.) As for treatment, both of the institutions had well over a thousand patients for every psychologist. Needless to say, no treatment was being given under these conditions. As one expert witness put it, these were neither treatment facilities nor even facilities for "care" or "custody," since these words imply safekeeping. Rather, they were storage facilities.

In deciding the case against the state, the court ruled that it was a violation of due process to deny

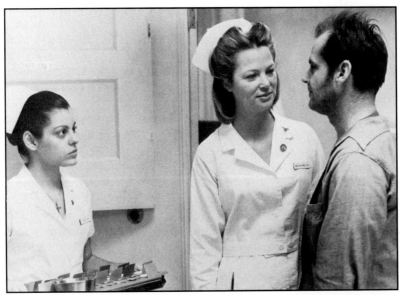

A scene from the movie *One Flew Over the Cuckoo's Nest,* in which the two characters MacMurphy, a pseudo-patient in a mental institution, and Nurse Ratched, a powerful figure in the institution, were in frequent conflict over the patients' rights. (Museum of Modern Art Film Still Archive)

people their liberty on the grounds that they needed treatment and then to provide no treatment. The court went on to state that all Alabama mental institutions must provide (1) an individualized treatment program for each patient, (2) skilled staff in sufficient numbers to administer such treatment, and (3) a humane psychological and physical environment. This decision, then, established the right to treatment, at least in Alabama. Although binding only in Alabama, the *Wyatt* decision has influenced mental health procedures across the country. Several states have passed revised mental health codes that incorporate most aspects of the *Wyatt* decision.

The next major case to touch upon the right-to-treatment issue was the highly publicized 1975 case of *O'Connor* v. *Donaldson.* Kenneth Donaldson had been institutionalized involuntarily in 1957 on the petition of his father. His father claimed that Donaldson had delusions that people were poisoning his food. This testimony, along with the fact that Donaldson had been institutionalized for three months thirteen years earlier, led the judge to conclude that Donaldson should be committed. He was sent to a Florida state mental hospital, and there he remained for fourteen years. During this time he was given no treatment that could realistically be expected to cure or improve his "condition." He petitioned repeatedly for his release. Finally, under threat of a lawsuit, the hospital authorities discharged him. He then sued them for damages and ultimately settled for $20,000. The U.S. Supreme Court ruled that "a finding of mental illness alone cannot justify a State's locking a person up against his will and keeping him indefinitely in simple custodial confinement" (*O'Connor* v. *Donaldson,* 95 S.Ct. 2486, 1975).

Though it has been hailed as a victory for right-to-treatment advocates, the *Donaldson* ruling, strictly speaking, has to do with the right to liberty rather than the right to treatment. (And even on the right to liberty it is somewhat vague. For example, if a person is found to be dangerous as well as mentally ill, can he or she then be subjected to simple custodial confinement?) However, it does at least lend indirect support to the view that involuntary patients have a constitutional right to treatment (Ennis and Emery, 1978).

The U.S. Supreme Court did not directly address the right-to-treatment issue until 1982, in the case of *Youngberg* v. *Romeo.* The lawsuit had been initiated on behalf of Nicholas Romeo, a resident of a state institution for the retarded in Pennsylvania. Romeo had been injured on numerous occasions, both by his own violence and by other residents. On several occasions he was placed in physical restraints to prevent harm to himself and others. The Supreme Court held that involuntarily committed mentally retarded persons—and presumably mentally ill persons as well—have a constitutional right to "conditions of reasonable care and safety, reasonably non-restrictive confinement conditions, and such training as may be required by these interests" (*Youngberg* v. *Romeo,* 102 S.Ct. 2452, 2463 [1982]). The Court emphasized, however, that treatment decisions made by professionals are "presumptively valid" and that courts should not second-guess the judgment of professionals responsible for the care of patients (102 S.Ct. 2462). Thus this decision provides a subtle shift in emphasis from absolute patient rights to support for decisions made by mental health professionals.

The Court did not decide whether there is a constitutional right to treatment per se, apart from any impact such treatment may have on safety and freedom from restraints. This is a question that remains to be addressed in a future Supreme Court decision.

Other Rights of Mental Patients

The Right to Refuse Treatment   If people in mental institutions have a right to treatment, do they also have a right to refuse treatment? We have already discussed one answer to this question: Stone's "thank you" proposition, which states that if treatment is refused on irrational grounds, it should be administered involuntarily, for the patient's own good. However, Stone's proposition seems to assume that treatment will be effective and that it will not have harmful side effects—a very unsafe assumption. As we have seen in earlier chapters, the history of psychological treatment is replete with unpleasant surprises. When iproniazid was introduced as a treatment for depression, no one knew that it caused liver damage. When chlorpromazine was put on the market, no one knew that it could cause tardive dyskinesia. Thus there is no reason to assume that when patients refuse treatment, they are refusing something that will truly work for their good. Furthermore, as civil rights advocates have pointed out, to deprive mental patients of any control over treatment is to make them vulnerable to any number of abuses.

But what if a patient's refusal does in fact seem grossly irrational? Or what if it is not grossly irrational but nevertheless infringes on the rights of others? Assume that a depressed suicidal patient refuses electroconvulsive therapy (ECT), insisting instead on antidepressant drugs, which may not be as effective. Should the hospital assign one of its staff members to watch over the patient day and night to make sure she doesn't commit suicide? If so, what about the rights of the other patients, who are then deprived of that staff member's services? One might answer at this point that since the woman made the choice, she should not be given special treatment; if she commits suicide, that is her decision. But surely the hospital has the duty to prevent suicides on its premises, particularly since it cannot be therapeutic for other patients to watch people kill themselves (Stone, 1975). Should the patient be coerced into receiving a particular treatment because less elaborate security measures would then be required? As this example indicates, the right to refuse treatment is an extremely difficult question.

State statutes and regulations vary considerably (Reisner, 1985), but the general rule is that involuntary patients may be required to undergo "routine" treatment, which may include psychotropic medication. More controversial forms of treatment, such as ECT, are usually regulated more closely, and consent from the patient or next of kin or, in some states, a court order may be required.

The U.S. Supreme Court had the opportunity in 1982 to decide whether involuntary mental patients have a constitutional right to refuse antipsychotic medication, but it chose not to take that opportunity. This remains a controversial and still unsettled issue.

The Right to a Humane Environment   As we saw above, the decision in the case of *Wyatt* v. *Stickney* affirmed not only the right to treatment but also the right to a humane environment. What the court meant by a humane environment is spelled out in the decision. The following is only a partial list of the minimum requirements:

1. Patients have a right to privacy and dignity.

2. An opportunity must exist for voluntary religious worship on a nondiscriminatory basis.

3. Dietary menus must be satisfying and nutritionally adequate to provide the recommended daily dietary allowances.

Nutritionally adequate meals must not be withheld as punishment.

4. Within multipatient sleeping rooms, screens or curtains must be provided to ensure privacy. Each patient must be furnished with a comfortable bed, a closet or locker for personal belongings, a chair, and a bedside table.

5. Toilets must be installed in separate stalls to ensure privacy. If a central bathing area is provided, showers must be separated by curtains to ensure privacy.

6. Patients have a right to wear their own clothes and to keep and use their own personal possessions.*

7. Patients have the same rights to visitation and telephone communications as patients at other public hospitals.*

8. Patients have an unrestricted right to send and receive mail.*

9. Patients have a right to regular physical exercise several times a week as well as a right to be out of doors at regular and frequent intervals.

10. An opportunity must exist for interaction with members of the opposite sex (*Wyatt* v. *Stickney,* 1972, pp. 379–383).

In addition, the *Wyatt* decision addressed the matter of work requirements imposed on institutionalized patients. For years mental institutions have used patients as a supplementary work force. Throughout the country mental patients clear tables, wash dishes, scrub floors, feed other patients, and otherwise help to maintain the institution in which they live. For their work they often receive some reward—perhaps a small allowance or special privileges—but this reward in no way approximates the compensation that would be expected for such work in the outside world. The *Wyatt* ruling declared this practice unconstitutional. The court ruled that patients may not be required to do any work aimed at maintaining the institution in which they live. If, however, they *volunteer* for

---

* The asterisks indicate rights that may be abridged if, in the judgment of a mental health professional, their exercise is detrimental to the patient's safety or welfare.

A modern mental hospital. In recent years the courts have established that patients have a legal right to a humane physical and psychological environment. (Jim Pozarik/Liaison)

such work, they must be given at least minimum-wage compensation for it. The point is that involuntary patients, by definition, do not ask to be committed to an institution. If the society chooses to commit them and then compels them to work without pay, then their position is essentially that of slaves. (Indeed, this practice has been referred to as "institutional peonage.") Subsequent rulings by other courts have reaffirmed the *Wyatt* position on this matter. And though in many states mental patients are still assigned unpaid jobs in the hospital kitchen or laundry, the practice may well be on its way out.

Behavior Therapy and Patients' Rights   Almost every issue raised in this chapter is the subject of intense debate between those concerned primarily

with the constitutional rights of mental patients and those concerned primarily with what they consider the "best interests" of such patients. The issue of a humane environment is no exception. On the one hand, it seems indisputable that if a society confines people to mental hospitals against their will, either to protect itself or to help them, then the people in question should be free from forced labor and should be provided with simple amenities that the rest of us take for granted—a comfortable bed, privacy in the bathroom, nourishing meals, and so forth. To treat them otherwise would appear to be quite improper. On the other hand, the guarantee of these rights may directly conflict with a mode of therapy that has proved most effective with long-term institutionalized patients: behavior therapy.

As we saw in earlier chapters, behavioral tech-

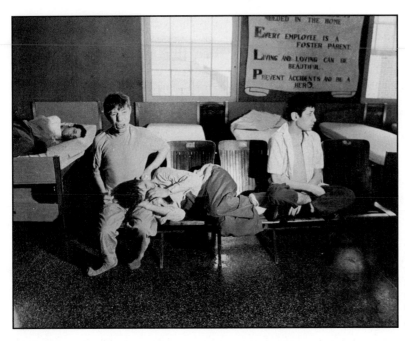

Despite recent attempts to honor the right of patients to a humane and stimulating environment, many institutions remain as barren as this ward for severely retarded children. (Leonard Speier)

niques for chronic patients tend to be contingency management techniques, the most widespread and useful being the token economy. The principle on which these techniques work is that patients are given certain reinforcers as rewards for socially desirable behaviors. However, in many cases these reinforcers are the very same items and activities that such decisions as *Wyatt* have affirmed are absolute rights. If patients have an absolute right to stall showers or to curtains around their beds, you cannot offer them these things in return for shaving or making their beds or completing a reading program. They are entitled to them no matter what they do. A related problem arises with the ban on compulsory labor. Many token economies have used institution-maintaining work as a target response that earns reinforcers. However, if such work must be compensated by the minimum wage, then institutions may prefer to hire nonpatient labor rather than encourage patients to acquire work skills. In sum, "patients' rights" may make contingency management within institutions more difficult (Wexler, 1981).

Another aspect of behavior therapy that is now being carefully restricted is the use of aversive techniques. As we saw in Chapter 20, aversive techniques are not widely used either inside or outside institutions, but in extreme cases psychologists have used hand slapping and even electric shock to suppress severely self-injurious behavior. Such practices are coming under increasing legal regulation. In the *Wyatt* decision, for example, the court ruled that electric shock could be used only "in extraordinary circumstances to prevent self-mutilation leading to repeated and possibly permanent physical damage to the resident and only after alternative techniques have failed" (*Wyatt* v. *Stickney,* 1972, pp. 400–401).

To the dismay of many behavior therapists, the courts have tended to regard time-out as a punishment procedure requiring extensive regulation. As we saw in Chapter 20, time-out is technically not a punishment technique but an extinction technique. It does not involve the application of aversive stimuli; it removes the patient from the presence of reinforcing stimuli. But perhaps out of fear that patients will simply be locked up in time-out rooms indefinitely, like prisoners in solitary confinement, the courts have severely limited the use of time-out, and some have prohibited it altogether. Behavior therapists point out that time-out procedures are often the most effective and least intrusive procedures available to deal with violent behavior. If time-out is prohibited, the alternatives are often physical restraints or large doses of sedatives. The *Romeo* case, described earlier, however, suggests that therapists will be given considerable latitude in using emergency management procedures. It has been suggested (Wexler, 1982) that if time-out procedures are used only to prevent or interrupt seriously dangerous or destructive behaviors, they will continue to be allowed. The use of time-out in nonemergency situations is still being debated.

Many behavior therapists feel that their techniques have been unfairly singled out by the courts. To some extent this may be true. In the last decade there have been a couple of notorious cases in which mental patients have been cruelly abused in programs masquerading as behavioral aversion therapy. In one case, mentally ill prisoners at the Iowa Security Medical Facility were punished for minor rule violations by injections of apomorphine, a drug that induces continuous vomiting for about fifteen minutes (*Knecht* v. *Gillman,* 1973). The supposed justification for this program was that an aversion to antisocial behavior was being conditioned. However, the rule infractions that resulted in this treatment—failure to get out of bed, giving cigarettes against orders, talking, swearing, lying—are not serious antisocial actions that threaten society. What the hospital administrators were in fact doing was using an extremely cruel punishment to terrify mental patients into cooperating with rules. Such procedures do not constitute behavior therapy; behaviorists find them as appalling as anyone else would. Nevertheless, because this and other abusive programs have been "justified" by their administrators as applications of behavioral psychology, the courts have cast an extremely suspicious eye on behavioral techniques in general.

There are other reasons for the emphasis on behavior therapy in the recent patients' rights decisions. For one thing, because many behavioral techniques are still relatively new, they have come under close scrutiny (Paul and Lentz, 1977). Another likely reason for the attention that the courts have given to behavior therapy is its highly specific and concrete nature. It is far easier to weigh the dangers of a procedure in which identifiable actions are performed and concrete things are given or withheld than it is to evaluate a vague process such as insight therapy. Finally, while much less intrusive than medication, electronconvulsive therapy, or psychosurgery, behavior therapy may cause patients some distress. They may have to do things that are difficult for them, or they may be deprived of something that they want, or in rare cases they may actually experience physical pain. This makes behavior therapy easier to criticize, no matter how positive its results. By contrast, psychodynamic

therapy may be of no help to chronic patients, but it is hard to say how such therapy could cause them pain either.

If in fact the courts severely limit behavior therapy for institutionalized patients, they may be working against these patients' best interests. As we saw in Chapter 15, there is good evidence that at least with chronic schizophrenics, a token economy in combination with individualized behavioral programs results in a greater increase in adaptive behavior, a greater decrease in bizarre and violent behavior, and a higher rate of release than either of the other two treatments available to such patients, milieu therapy and traditional custodial care (Paul and Lentz, 1977).

Could contingency management procedures be modified in such a way as to conform to decisions such as *Wyatt?* For example, instead of making breakfast contingent upon bedmaking, you might provide a very plain breakfast noncontingently and then offer a fancy breakfast as a reward for bedmaking (Wexler, 1981). It remains to be seen, however, whether chronic patients would appreciate such gradations of desirability in reinforcers. Often it is primary reinforcers that are most effective with chronic mental patients.

Another possibility is that the superior effectiveness of behavior therapy, at least with chronic patients, will eventually encourage the courts to ease some restrictions. So far the courts have been concerned primarily with the adequacy of treatment. When they start to focus on the *results* of treatment—establishing the right to effective treatment—the courts may find that the effective treatments have been severely restricted by previous patients' rights decisions. Should this happen, some of those restrictions may have to be eased.

POWER AND THE MENTAL HEALTH PROFESSION

The thrust of most of the recent court decisions discussed in this chapter is the same: to limit the power of the mental health profession. Yet despite these restrictions, the power of psychological professionals is still immense. To begin with, it is the psychiatric profession that declares, in the form of the *DSM,* which among the countless variations of human behavior are abnormal. This is a momentous decision—and one that psychiatrists have a questionable right to make. Many homosexuals, for example, find it bitter to recall that in 1973 the American Psychiatric Association *voted* on the normality of their sexual preference. Presumably, if a condition were severe enough to be labeled abnormal, it should not require a vote.

Whether or not psychiatrists are qualified to make such decisions, they do in fact make them, and the decisions carry tremendous weight. The very word *abnormal,* as used in psychology, implies a need for change. Thus included in the power to decide what behavior is abnormal is the power to decide who and what needs changing in our society. Again, do mental health professionals have the right to make this decision? Many people feel that the major cause of psychological disturbance in our society is not individual genes or parent–child relationships but poverty. What is the probability that mental health professionals—who are largely middle-class people of middle to high income—will be especially sensitive to this problem?

Finally, as we have seen, psychological professionals are often the ones who determine whether people identified as mentally disturbed should be institutionalized and whether those who are currently institutionalized should be released. It is hard to imagine a one-to-one relationship in our society that involves greater power than this, for what situation in our society involves a greater loss of power than involuntary commitment?

These powers held by the mental health profession are now being disputed. Numerous groups—women, ethnic minorities, the poor—have asked why a professional class made up largely of affluent white males should be given such broad authority. It has been argued that the mental health profession suffers from a tradition of paternalism that permits a handful of "experts" to determine the fate of a large part of the rest of the population. Just as the consumer movement has demanded of the automobile industry that cars be equipped with safety devices and of food manufacturers that harmful chemicals be removed from packaged foods, so a "consumer" movement has made demands on the mental health profession. In this case, the demands have been for a sharing of information between professionals and lay people, so that those who need therapy can give it their *informed consent.* This implies, of course, the right to say no and the right to question the therapist. Patients for whom ECT is recommended should be told that their memory may be impaired by the procedure; those for whom drugs are prescribed should be told about side effects. Alternative treatments—and alternatives to treatment—should be discussed. When information is shared in this way, power is diffused and abuses are less likely.

SUMMARY

Mental health law is the branch of law that deals with both the legal responsibility and the constitutional rights of those people judged to be disturbed. These rapidly changing laws deal with three major issues: psychological disturbance and criminal responsibility, civil commitment, and patients' rights.

Since abnormal behavior may also be illegal behavior, the criminal responsibility of psychologically disturbed persons must be determined. The insanity defense is designed to protect those who commit crimes because of mental disturbance—and to enable the court to regard all other defendants as responsible for their actions. The important legal precedents on which the test of insanity is based are the "irresistible impulse" decision of 1834 and the M'Naghten rule, handed down by a British court in 1843. The American Law Institute's formulation of the insanity defense (1962) specifies that the defendant must "conform his conduct to the requirements of law" and "appreciate the criminality of his conduct." This formulation places the burden of assigning moral responsibility on the jury rather than on mental health professionals. Recently, especially in the wake of the Hinckley case, changes in the insanity defense have been advocated, such as a new verdict of "guilty but mentally ill." Moreover, the Hinckley case was largely responsible for the shift in the burden of proof in insanity cases from the prosecution to the defense.

There are three major arguments against the insanity defense. First, the jury is asked to make a judgment that is both subjective and retrospective and that conforms to a court's definition of insanity. A second criticism, based on the views of Thomas Szasz, contends that what a jury is asked to judge—insanity—does not exist, and that courts should judge people on their behavior rather than on their intentions. The third criticism is that those who successfully plead insanity may end up in a worse situation than if they had been convicted of their crimes, because commitment to a mental hospital is in essence an indeterminate sentence.

Another means of protecting the defendant and preserving the courts' reputation for justice is the judgment of competency—defendants must understand the nature of the proceedings against them and be able to assist counsel in their own defense. Though a limited concept, incompetency is often abused by prosecutors to keep defendants incarcerated and by defense attorneys to delay a trial. One controversy surrounding the competency challenge is whether defendants are competent to stand trial if they fulfill the competency requirement only when under the influence of antipsychotic drugs.

Involuntary commitment to a mental hospital raises serious legal questions. The Supreme Court has failed to establish specific legal procedures necessary before a person may be involuntarily committed, and lower courts have differed on the issue. A person faced with involuntary civil commitment does not have the same legal rights that a defendant has in a criminal trial. According to current laws, jury trials are not required in commitment cases; in most states a person threatened with commitment has the right to be represented by counsel at the commitment hearing, although the role of the attorney is by no means clearly defined; the right to avoid self-incrimination has been variously interpreted by the states. Unlike these three procedural questions, the standard of proof required for civil commitment has been spelled out by the Supreme Court: a person cannot be involuntarily committed to a mental institution without "clear and convincing" evidence that he or she is committable. Typically, statutes require that to be committable, a person must be found mentally ill and dangerous. "Dangerous," however, is rarely defined with specificity, and predictions of such behavior are open to error. It has been argued that dangerousness is an inappropriate criterion for commitment because mental patients as a class are not particularly dangerous, there is no effective treatment for "dangerousness," and there is no evidence that mental health professionals can accurately predict "dangerousness."

Whatever the standard for involuntary commitment—the "thank you" proposition has been offered, suggesting that patients will be grateful later for treatment they refuse today—the role of mental health professionals at commitment hearings will continue. Distinctions must be made between mental health questions, which psychologists and psychiatrists are qualified to answer, and legal and moral questions, which should be determined by the courts.

The third major issue in mental health law is patients' rights. There is a strong trend toward guaranteeing certain basic rights to all patients, including the right to treatment, the right to refuse treatment, and the right to decent living conditions. The right to treatment is being increasingly asserted, although judicial decisions are by no means clear. The amount of control a patient has over treatment depends to some degree on whether that patient is committed voluntarily or involuntarily. According to the *Wyatt v. Stickney* decision in 1972, patients are ensured of the right to a humane environment and to compensation for work performed in the institution. These rights may conflict with some techniques used in behavior therapy; rights and amenities that are legally guaranteed can no longer be offered or withheld to reinforce desired behavior. Also, it is now questionable whether certain behavioral techniques are legal.

The mental health profession has the power to determine what is "abnormal" and whether people judged to be abnormal should be institutionalized. Most court decisions discussed in this chapter have tended to limit this power; these legal decisions and challenges from numerous advocate groups indicate that the relationship between the mental health profession and society is in transition.

REFERENCES

Abel, G., J. Rouleau, and **J. Cunningham-Rathner.** Sexually aggressive behavior. In W. Curran, A. L. McGarry, and S. A. Shah, eds., *Modern legal psychiatry and psychology.* Philadelphia: Davis, 1984.

Abraham, K. Notes on psychoanalytic investigation and treatment of manic-depressive insanity and applied conditions (1911). In *Selected papers of Karl Abraham, M.D.* D. Bryan and A. Strachey. trs. London: The Hogarth Press, 1948.

Abraham, K. The first pregenital stage of the libido (1916). In *Selected papers of Karl Abraham, M.D.* D. Bryan and A. Strachey. trs. London: The Hogarth Press, 1948.

Abramowitz, S. I. Psychosocial outcomes of sex reassignment surgery. *Journal of Consulting and Clinical Psychology,* 1986, *54,* 183–189.

Abramson, L. Y., G. I. Metalsky, and **L. B. Alloy.** The hopelessness theory of depression: A metatheoretical analysis with implications for psychopathology research. *Psychological Review.* In press.

Abramson, L. Y., and **M. E. P. Seligman.** Modeling psychopathology in the laboratory: History and rationale. In J. D. Maser and M. E. P. Seligman, eds., *Psychopathology: Experimental models.* San Francisco: W. H. Freeman, 1977.

Abramson, L. Y., M. E. P. Seligman, and **J. D. Teasdale.** Learned helplessness in humans: Critique and reformulation. *Journal of Abnormal Psychology,* 1978, *87,* 49–74.

Ackerman, N. *The psychodynamics of family life.* New York: Basic Books, 1958.

Adams, H. E., M. Feuerstein, and **J. L. Fowler.** The migraine headache: A review of parameters, theories, and interventions. *Psychological Bulletin,* 1980, *87,* 217–237.

Agnello, J. G. Voice onset and voice termination features of stutters. In L. M. Webster and L. C. Furst, eds., *Vocal tract dynamics and dysfluency.* New York: Speech and Hearing Institute, 1975.

Agras, S., D. Sylvester, and **D. Oliveau.** The epidemiology of common fears and phobias. Unpublished manuscript, 1969.

Aichhorn, A. *Wayward youth.* London: Putnam, 1935.

Akiskal, H. S. Sub-affective disorders: Dysthymic, cyclothymic and bipolar II disorders in the borderline realm. *Psychi-atric Clinics of North America,* 1981, *4,* 25–46.

Akiskal, H. S. Dysthymic disorder: Psychopathology of proposed chronic depressive subtypes. *American Journal of Psychiatry,* 1983, *140,* 11–20.

Akiskal, H. S., R. M. A. Hirschfeld, and **B. I. Yerevanian.** The relationship of personality to affective disorders. *Archives of General Psychiatry,* 1983, *40,* 801–810.

Akiskal, H. S. and **W. T. McKinney.** Overview of recent research in depression. *Archives of General Psychiatry,* 1975, *32,* 285–305.

Alabiso, F. Operant control of attention behavior: A treatment for hyperactivity. *Behavior Therapy,* 1975, *6,* 39–42.

Albee, G. W. IQ tests on trial. *The New York Times,* February 12, 1978, E13.

Albee, G. W. Preventing psychopathology and promoting human potential. *American Psychologist,* 1982, *37*(9), 1043–1050.

Alcoholism Council of Greater New York. Some facts of alcoholism in industry, 1987.

Aldrich, C. Preventive medicine and mongolism. *American Journal of Mental Deficiency,* 1947.

Aldrich, C. K. The clouded crystal ball: A 35-year follow-up of psychiatrists' predictions. *American Journal of Psychiatry,* 1986, *143,* 45–49.

Alexander, A. B. Asthma. In S. N. Haynes and L. Gannon, eds., *Psychosomatic disorders: A psychophysiological approach to etiology and treatment.* New York: Praeger, 1981.

Alexander, B. K., and **P. F. Hadaway.** Opiate addiction: The case for an adaptive orientation. *Psychological Bulletin,* 1982, *92,* 367–381.

Alexander, F., Emotional factors in essential hypertension. *Psychosomatic Medicine,* 1939, *1,* 153–216.

Alexander, J. F. and **B. V. Parsons.** Short term behavioral intervention with delinquent families: Impact on family process and recidivism. *Journal of Abnormal Psychology,* 1973, *81,* 219–225.

Allderidge, P. Hospitals, madhouses and asylums: Cycles in the care of the insane. *British Journal of Psychiatry,* 1979, *134,* 321–334.

Allen, M. G. Twin studies of affective illness. *Archives of General Psychiatry,* 1976, *33,* 1476–1478.

Alloy, L. B., and **L. Y. Abramson.** The judgment of contingency in depressed and nondepressed students: Sadder but wiser? *Journal of Experimental Psychology: General,* 1979, *108,* 441–485.

Alloy, L. B., L. Y. Abramson, and **D. Viscusi.** Induced mood and the illusion of control. *Journal of Personality and Social Psychology,* 1981, *41,* 1129–1140.

Allport, G. W. *Pattern and growth in personality.* New York: Holt, Rinehart and Winston, 1961.

Alpert, M. Tremography as a measure of extrapyramidal function in study of the dopamine hypothesis. In Friedhoff, A., ed., *Catecholamines and behavior,* Vol. 1. New York: Plenum Press, 1975, 167–185.

Alschuler, R. Plea bargaining and its history. *Law and Society Review,* 1979, *13,* 211–245.

American Association on Mental Deficiency. *Manual on terminology and classification in mental retardation,* 1977 revision. Washington, D.C.: American Association on Mental Deficiency, 1977.

American Psychiatric Association. *Diagnostic and statistical manual of mental disorders (DSM-II),* 2nd ed. Washington, D.C.: American Psychiatric Association, 1968.

American Psychiatric Association. *Diagnostic and statistical manual of mental disorders (DSM-III),* 3rd ed., Washington, D.C.: American Psychiatric Association, 1980.

American Psychiatric Association. *Diagnostic and statistical manual of mental disorders (DSM-III-R),* 3rd ed. rev. Washington, D.C.. American Psychiatric Association, 1987.

American Psychiatric Association membership upholds decision of trustees bid to drop homosexuality from list of mental disorders. *The New York Times,* April 9, 1974, p. 12.

American Psychological Association. APA-approved doctoral programs in clinical, counseling, and school psychology: 1982. *American Psychologist,* 1982, *37,* 1374–1376.

American Psychological Association. APA-accredited doctoral programs in professional psychology: 1986. *American Psychologist,* 1986, *41,* 1357–1363.

American Psychological Association. *Guidelines for computer-based tests and interpretations.* Washington, D.C.: American Psychological Association, 1986.

Anastasi, A. *Psychological testing*, 5th ed. New York: Macmillan, 1982.

Anderson, K. A. The "shopping" behavior of parents of mentally retarded children: The professional person's role. *Mental Retardation*, 1971, *9*, 3–5.

Andreasen, N. C., and **W. M. Grove.** Thought, language and communication in schizophrenia: Diagnosis and prognosis. *Schizophrenia Bulletin*, 1986, *12*, 348.

Andreasen, N. C., P. McDonald-Scott, W. M. Grove, M. B. Keller, R. W. Shapiro, and **R. Hirschfeld.** Assessment of reliability in multicenter collaborative research with a videotape approach. *American Journal of Psychiatry*, 1982, *139*, 876–882.

Andreasen, N., H. A. Nasrallah, V. Dunn, S. C. Olson, W. M. Grove, J. C. Ehrhardt, J. A. Coffman, and **J. H. W. Crossett.** Structural abnormalities in the frontal system in schizophrenia: A magnetic resonance imaging study. *Archives of General Psychiatry*, 1986, *43*, 136–144.

Andreasen, N. C., and **S. Olsen.** Negative v. positive schizophrenia: Definition and validation. *Archives of General Psychiatry*, 1982, *39*, 789–794.

Andreasen, N.C., W. Schefner, T. Reich, R. M. A. Hirschfeld, J. Endicott, and **M. B. Keller.** The validation of the concept of endogenous depression. *Archives of General Psychiatry*, 1986, *43*, 246–251.

Andreasen, N. C., M. R. Smith, C. G. Jacoby, J. W. Dennert, and **S. A. Olsen.** Ventricular enlargement in schizophrenia: Definition and prevalence. *American Journal of Psychiatry*, 1982, *139*(3), 292–302.

Andrews, G., M. S. Armstrong, H. Brodaty, D. Hadzi-Pavlovic, P. R. Harvey, P. Holt, C. Tennant, and **K. Vaughn.** Treatment outlines for the management of schizophrenia: The Quality Assurance Project. *Australian and New Zealand Journal of Psychiatry*. In press.

Andrews, G., M. S. Armstrong, H. Brodaty, D. Hadzi-Pavlovic, W. Hall, P. R. Harvey, D. J. Sansom, C. C. Tennant, P. Weeks, J. Grigor, B. J. Hughson, G. Johnson, and **L. G. Kiloh.** A treatment outline for depressive disorder: The Quality Assurance Project. *Australian and New Zealand Journal of Psychiatry*, 1983, *17*, 129–146.

Andron, L., and **M. Strum.** Is "I do" in the repertoire of the retarded? *Mental Retardation*, 1973, *11*, 31–34.

Anesheusel, C. S., and **J. D. Stone.** Stress and depression: A test of the buffering model of social support. *Archives of General Psychiatry*, 1982, *39*, 1392–1396.

Arana, G. W., R. J. Baldessarini, and **M. Ornstein.** The dexamethasone suppression test for diagnosis and prognosis in psychiatry. *Archives of General Psychiatry*, 1985, *42*, 1193–1204.

Arentewicz, G., and **G. Schmidt.** *The treatment of sexual disorder.* New York: Basic Books, 1983.

Arieti, S. *Interpretation of schizophrenia.* New York, Basic Books, 1974a.

Arieti, S. An overview of schizophrenia from a predominantly psychological approach. *American Journal of Psychiatry*, 1974b, *131*(3), 241–249.

Aring, C. D. The Gheel experience: Eternal spirit of the chainless mind! *Journal of the American Medical Association*, 1974, *203*, 998–1001.

Arkowitz, H., and **S. B. Messer,** eds. *Psychoanalytic therapy and behavior therapy: Is integration possible?* New York: Plenum Press, 1984.

Aronson, E. *The social animal.* San Francisco: W. H. Freeman, 1972.

Aronson, S. M., and **B. W. Volk.** The nervous system sphingolipidoses. In C. H. Carter, ed., *Medical aspects of mental retardation.* Springfield, Ill.: Charles C Thomas, 1965.

Artiss, K. L. *Milieu therapy in schizophrenia.* New York: Grune & Stratton, 1962.

Asarnow, R. F., R. A. Steffy, D. J. MacCrimmon, and **J. M. Cleghorn.** An attentional assessment of foster children at risk for schizophrenia. *Journal of Abnormal Psychology*, 1977, *86*, 267–275.

Atthowe, J. M., Jr., and **L. A. Krasner.** Preliminary report on the application of contingent reinforcement procedures (token economy) on a "chronic" psychiatric ward. *Journal of Abnormal Psychology*, 1968, *73*, 37–43.

Ausubel, D. P., and **P. Ausubel.** Ego development among segregated Negro children. In A. H. Passow, ed., *Education in depressed areas.* New York: Bureau of Publications, Teachers College, Columbia University, 1963.

Ax, A. F. The physiological differentiation between fear and anger in humans. *Psychosomatic Medicine*, 1953, *15*, 433–442.

Axline, V. M. *Play therapy,* rev. ed. New York: Ballantine, 1969.

Ayllon, T., and **N. H. Azrin.** *The token economy: A motivational system for therapy and rehabilitation.* New York: Appleton-Century-Crofts, 1968.

Ayllon, T., and **E. Haughton.** Control of the behavior of schizophrenic patients by food. *Journal of the Experimental Analysis of Behavior*, 1962, *5*, 343–352.

Baekeland, F., L. Lundwall, B. Kissin, and **T. Shanahan.** Correlates of outcome in disulfiram treatment of alcoholism. *The Journal of Nervous and Mental Disease*, 1971, *153*(1), 1–9.

Baird, T. D., and **G. J. August.** Familial heterogeneity in infantile autism. *Journal of Autism and Developmental Disorders*, 1985, *15*, 315–321.

Baker, R. The use of operant conditioning to reinstate the speech of mute schizophrenics: A progress report. In L. Burns and J. L. Worsley, eds., *Behavior therapy in the 1970's.* Bristol, Eng.: John Wright, 1970.

Baker, R. The use of operant conditioning to reinstate speech in mute schizophrenics. *Behavior Research and Therapy*, 1971, *9*, 329–336.

Bakwin, H., and **R. M. Bakwin.** *Behavior disorders in children.* Philadelphia: W. B. Saunders, 1972.

Ball, J. C., J. W. Shaffer, and **D. N. Nurco.** Day to day criminality of heroin addicts in Baltimore: A study in the continuity of offense rates. *Drug and Alcohol Dependence*, 1983, *12*, 119–142.

Bandura, A. *Principles of behavior modification.* New York: Holt, Rinehart and Winston, 1969.

Bandura, A. Social learning analysis of aggression. In E. Ribes-Inesta and A. Bandura, eds., *Analysis of delinquency and aggression.* Hillsdale, N.J.: Erlbaum, 1976.

Bandura, A. Self-efficacy: Toward a unifying theory of behavioral change. *Psychological Review*, 1977, *84*, 191–215.

Bandura, A. The self system in reciprocal determinism. *American Psychologist*, 1978, *33*, 344–358.

Bandura, A. Self-efficacy mechanism in human agency. *American Psychologist*, 1982, *37*, 122–147.

Bandura, A. Representing personal determinants in causal structures. *Psychological Review*, 1984, *91*, 508–511.

Bandura, A., E. B. Blanchard, and **B. Ritter.** Relative efficacy of desensitization and modeling approaches for inducing behavioral, affective, and attitudinal changes. *Journal of Personality and Social Psychology*, 1969, *13*, 173–199.

Bandura, A., J. E. Grusec, and **F. L. Menlove.** Vicarious extinction of avoidance behavior. *Journal of Personality and Social Psychology*, 1967, *5*, 16–23.

Bandura, A., R. W. Jeffery, and **C. L. Wright.** Efficacy of participant modeling as a function of response induction aids. *Journal of Abnormal Psychology*, 1974, *83*, 56–64.

Bandura, A., and **R. Walters.** *Social learning and personality development.* New York: Holt, Rinehart and Winston, 1963.

Bard, M. *Training police as specialists in family crisis intervention.* Washington, D.C.: U.S. Government Printing Office, 1970.

Barker, R. G., and **H. F. Wright.** *Midwest and Its Children.* Evanston, Ill.: Row, Peterson, 1955.

Barlow, D. H. Behavioral conception and

treatment of panic. *Psychopharmacology Bulletin.* In press.

Barlow, D. H., and G. G. Abel. Sexual deviation. In W. Craighead, A. Kazdin, and M. Mahoney, eds., *Behavior modification: Principles, issues, and applications.* Boston: Houghton Mifflin, 1976.

Barlow, D. H., G. Abel, E. Blanchard, and M. Mavissakalian. Plasma testosterone levels in male homosexuals: A failure to replicate. *Archives of Sexual Behavior,* 1974, *3,* 73–76.

Barlow, D. H., J. Vermilyea, E. B. Blanchard, B. B. Vermilyea, P. A. DiNardo, and J. A. Cerny. The phenomenon of panic. *Journal of Abnormal Psychology,* 1985, *94,* 320–328.

Barnes, G. E., and H. Prosen. Parental death and depression. *Journal of Abnormal Psychology,* 1985, *94,* 64–69.

Baroff, G. S. *Mental retardation: Nature, cause, and management.* Washington, D.C.: Hemisphere, 1974.

Baron-Cohen, S., A. M. Leslie, and U. Frith. Does the autistic child have a "theory of mind"? *Cognition,* 1985, *21,* 37–46.

Barraclough, B. M., B. Nelson, J. Bunch, and P. Sainsbury. The diagnostic classification and psychiatric treatment of 100 suicides. Proceedings of the Fifth International Conference for Suicide Prevention, London, 1969.

Bassuk, E. L., and S. C. Schoonover. *The practitioner's guide to psychoactive drugs.* New York: Plenum, 1977.

Bateson, G., D. Jackson, J. Haley, and J. Weakland. Toward a theory of schizophrenia. *Behavioral Science,* 1956, *1,* 251–264.

Battle, E. S., and J. B. Rotter. Children's feelings of personal control as related to social class and ethnic group. *Journal of Personality,* 1963, *31,* 482–490.

Baucom, D. H., and P. A. Aiken. Effect of depressed mood on eating among obese and nonobese dieting and nondieting persons. *Journal of Personality and Social Psychology,* 1981, *41,* 577–585.

Bear, D. M., and P. Feido. Quantitative analysis of interietal behavior in temporal lobe epilepsy. *Archives of Neurology,* 1977, *34,* 454–467.

Beck, A. T. *Depression: Clinical, experimental, and theoretical aspects.* New York: Harper & Row, 1967.

Beck, A. T. *Cognitive therapy and the emotional disorders.* New York: International Universities Press, 1976.

Beck, A. T., and M. S. Hurvich. Psychological correlates of depression: I. Frequency of "masochistic" dream content in a private practice sample. *Psychosomatic Medicine,* 1959, *21,* 50–55.

Beck, A. T., A. J. Rush, B. F. Shaw, and G. Emery. *Cognitive theory of depression.* New York: Guilford Press, 1979.

Beck, A. T., and S. Valin. Psychotic depressive reaction in soldiers who accidentally killed their buddies. *American Journal of Pychiatry,* 1953, *110,* 347–353.

Beck, A. T., C. H. Ward, M. Mendelson, J. Mock, and J. Erbaugh. Reliability of psychiatric diagnoses 2: A study of consistency of clinical judgments and ratings. *American Journal of Psychiatry,* 1962, *119,* 351–357.

Beck, J. C. Psychiatric assessment of potential violence. In J. C. Beck, ed., *The potentially violent patient and the* Tarasoff *decision in psychiatric practice.* Washington, D.C.: American Psychiatric Press, 1985.

Beck, S. J. *Rorschach's test. I: Basic processes,* 3rd ed. New York: Grune & Stratton, 1961.

Becker, J. V., L. J. Skinner, and G. G. Abel. Sequelae of sexual assault: The survivor's perspective. In J. G. Green and I. R. Stuart, eds., *The sexual aggressor.* New York: Van Nostrand, 1983.

Becker, J. V., L. J. Skinner, G. G. Abel, and J. Cichon. Level of postassault sexual functioning in rape and incest victims. *Archives of Sexual Behavior,* 1986, *15,* 37–49.

Bednar, R. L., and T. J. Kaul. Experimental group research: Current perspectives. In S. L. Garfield and A. E. Bergin, eds., *Handbook of psychotherapy and behavior change: An empirical analysis,* 2nd ed. New York: Wiley, 1978.

Bedrosian, R. C., and A. T. Beck. Principles of cognitive therapy. In M. J. Mahoney, ed., *Psychotherapy process: Current issues and future directions.* New York: Plenum, 1980.

Begelman, D. A. Ethical and legal issues of behavior modification. In M. Hersen, R. Eisler, and P. Miller, eds., *Progress in behavior modification.* Vol. I. New York: Academic Press, 1975.

Bell, A. P., and M. S. Weinberg. *Homosexualities: A study of diversity among men and women,* New York: Simon and Schuster, 1978.

Bell, A., M. S. Weinberg, and S. K. Hammersmith. *Sexual preference.* Bloomington, Ind.: Indiana University Press, 1981.

Bell, D. S. The experimental reproduction of amphetamine psychosis. *Archives of General Psychiatry,* 1973, *39*(1), 35–40.

Bellack, A. S., M. Hersen, and J. M. Himmelhoch. A comparison of social skills training, pharmacotherapy and psychotherapy for depression. *Behavior Research and Therapy,* 1983, *21,* 101–108.

Bellack, A. S., M. Hersen, and S. M. Turner. Generalization effects of social skills training in chronic schizophrenia: An experimental analysis. *Behaviour Research & Therapy,* 1976, *14,* 391–398.

Bellak, I. *The Thematic Apperception Test*

and the Children's Thematic Apperception Test in clinical use. New York: Grune & Stratton, 1954.

Bem, D. J., and D. C. Funder. Predicting more of the people more of the time: Assessing the personality of situations. *Psychological Review,* 1978, *85,* 485–501.

Bemis, K. Current approaches to the etiology and treatment of anorexia nervosa. American Psychological Association, *Psychological Bulletin,* 1978, *85,* 593–617.

Bender, L. A visual motor gestalt test and its clinical use. *Research monograph of the American Orthopsychiatric Association,* 1938, *3,* xi and 176.

Benjamin, H. *The transsexual phenomenon.* New York: Julian Press, 1966.

Bentler, P. M., and C. Prince. Psychiatric symptomology in transvestites. *Journal of Clinical Psychology,* 1970, *26*(4), 434–455.

Bentler, P. M., R. W. Shearman, and C. Prince. Personality characteristics of male transvestites. *Journal of Clinical Psychology,* 1970, *26,* 287–291.

Benton, A. L., and D. Pearl, eds. *Dyslexia: An appraisal of current knowledge.* New York: Oxford University Press, 1978.

Berg, M. Influence of age and ABO blood groups in the precipitation of bleeding peptic ulcer. *GUT,* 1969, *10,* 1029–1030.

Berger, P. A. Medical treatment of mental illness. *Science,* 1978, *200,* 974–981.

Bergin, A. E., and M. J. Lambert. The evaluation of therapeutic outcomes. In S. L. Garfield and A. E. Bergin, eds., *Handbook of psychotherapy and behavior change: An empirical analysis,* 2nd ed. New York: Wiley, 1978.

Bergler, E. Analysis of an unusual case of fetishism. *Bulletin of the Menninger Clinic,* 1947, *2,* 67–75.

Berlin, F. S. Sex offenders: A biomedical perspective and a status report on biomedical treatment. In J. G. Green and I. R. Stuart, eds., *The sexual aggressor.* New York: Van Nostrand, 1983.

Berman, J. S., C. Miller, and P. J. Massman. Cognitive therapy versus systematic desensitization: Is one treatment superior? *Psychological Bulletin,* 1985, *97,* 451–461.

Bernstein, I. Learned taste aversion in children receiving chemotherapy. *Science,* 1978, *200,* 1302–1303.

Bersoff, D. Testing and the law. *American Psychologist,* 1981, *36,* 1047–1056.

Bettelheim, B. *The empty fortress.* New York: Free Press, 1967.

Beutler, L. *Eclectic psychotherapy: A systematic approach.* New York: Pergamon Press, 1983.

Beutler, L. E., M. Crago, and T. G. Arizmendi. Research on therapist variables in psychotherapy. In S. L. Garfield and A. E. Bergin, eds., *Handbook of psychotherapy and behavior change: An eval-*

uative analysis, 3rd ed. New York: Wiley, 1986.

Bieber, I. A discussion of "homosexuality": The ethical challenge. *Journal of Consulting and Clinical Psychology,* 1976, *44,* 163–166.

Bieber, I., H. J. Dain, P. R. Dince, M. G. Drellich, H. C. Grand, R. H. Gundlach, M. W. Kremer, A. H. Rifkin, C. B. Wilbur, and T. B. Bieber. *Homosexuality: A psychoanalytical study.* New York: Random House, 1962.

Biederman, J., R. Rimon, R. Ebstein, R. H. Belmaker, and J. T. Davidson. Cyclic AMP in the CSF of patients with schizophrenia. *British Journal of Psychiatry,* 1977, *130,* 64–67.

Bini, L. Experimental researches on epileptic attacks induced by the electric current. *American Journal of Psychiatry,* 1938. Supplement 94, 172–183.

Birmingham University Clinical Psychiatry Committee. Clinical trial of the treatment of depressive illness: Report to the Medical Research Council. *British Medical Journal,* 1965, *5439,* 881–886.

Birnbaum, K. *Die psychopathischen verbrecker,* 2nd ed. Leipzig: Thieme, 1914.

Birren, J. E. Translations in gerontology—From lab to life: Psychophysiology and speed of response. *American Psychologist,* 1974, *29,* 808–815.

Blackstock, E. G. Cerebral asymmetry and the development of early infantile autism. *Journal of Autism and Childhood Schizophrenia,* 1978, *8,* 339–353.

Blackstone, W. *Commentaries on the laws of England* (1769).

Blair, C. D., and R. I. Lanyon. Exhibitionism: Etiology and treatment. *Psychological Bulletin,* 1981, *89*(3), 439–463.

Blane, L., and R. H. Roth. Voyeurism and exhibitionism. *Perceptual and Motor Skills,* 1967, *24,* 391–400.

Blashfield, R. An evaluation of the *DSM-II* classification of schizophrenia as a nomenclature. *Journal of Abnormal Psychology,* 1973, *82,* 382–389.

Blashfield, R. K., and J. G. Draguns. Evaluative criteria for psychiatric classification. *Journal of Abnormal Psychology,* 1976, *85,* 140–150.

Bleuler, E. *Dementia praecox or the group of schizophrenias* (1911). J. Zinkin, tr. New York: International Universities Press, 1950.

Bleuler, M. E. The long term course of schizophrenic psychoses. In L. C. Wynne, R. L. Cromwell, and S. Matthyse: *The nature of schizophrenia: New approaches to research and treatment.* New York: Wiley, 1978.

Bliss, E. W., and C. H. Branch. *Anorexia nervosa: Its history, psychology, and biology.* New York: Hoeber Medical Book, 1960.

Block, J. *The Q-sort method in personality assessment and psychiatric research.* Springfield, Ill.: Charles C Thomas, 1961.

Bloom, B. L., S. J. Asher, and S. W. White. Marital disruption as a stressor: A review and analysis. *Psychological Bulletin,* 1978, *7,* 488–498.

Blumer, D., and A. E. Walker. The neural basis of sexual behavior. In D. F. Benson and D. Blumer, eds., *Psychiatric aspects of neurological disease.* New York: Grune & Stratton, 1975.

Boals, G. F., D. R. Peterson, L. Farmer, D. F. Mann, and D. L. Robinson. The reliability, validity and utility of three data models in assessing marital relationships. *Journal of Personality Assessment,* 1982, *46,* 85–95.

Bockoven, J. S. *Moral treatment in American psychiatry.* New York: Springer, 1963.

Bogen, J. E., E. D. Fisher, and P. J. Vogel. Cerebral commissarotomy: A second case report. *Journal of the American Medical Association,* 1965, *194,* 1328–1329.

Boll, T. J., R. Heaton, and R. M. Reitan. Neuropsychological and emotional correlates of Huntington's chorea. *Journal of Nervous and Mental Disease,* 1974, *158,* 61–69.

Bootzin, R. R. *Behavior modification and therapy: An introduction.* Cambridge, Mass.: Winthrop Press, 1975.

Bootzin, R. R. The role of expectancy in behavior change. In L. White, B. Tursky, and G. Schwartz, eds., *Placebo: Clinical phenomena and new insights.* New York: Gilford Press, 1985.

Bootzin, R. R., and M. Engle-Friedman. Sleep disturbances. In B. Edelstein and L. Carstensen, eds., *Handbook of clinical gerontology.* New York: Pergamon Press, 1987.

Bootzin, R. R., M. Engle-Friedman, and L. Hazlewood. Sleep disorders and the elderly. In P. Lewinsohn and L. Teri, eds., *Coping and adaptation in the elderly.* New York: Pergamon Press, 1983.

Bootzin, R. R., and D. Max. Learning and behavioral theories. In I. L. Kutash and L. B. Schlesinger, eds., *Handbook on stress and anxiety.* San Francisco: Jossey-Bass, 1980.

Bootzin, R. R., and P. M. Nicassio. Behavioral treatments for insomnia. In M. Hersen, R. M. Eisler, and P. M. Miller, eds., *Progress in Behavior Modification,* Vol. 6, New York: Academic Press, 1978.

Bootzin, R. R., and W. R. Shadish. *Evaluation of mental health long term care facilities.* Final report to the Illinois Department of Mental Health and Developmental Disabilities. Northwestern University, 1983.

Borkovec, T. D. Insomnia. *Journal of Consulting and Clinical Psychology,* 1982, *50,* 880–895.

Borkovec, T. D., T. W. Lane, and P. H. VanOot. Phenomenology of sleep among insomniacs and good sleepers: Wakefulness experience when cortically asleep. *Journal of Abnormal Psychology,* 1981, *90,* 607–609.

Boss, M. Flight from death—mere survival: And flight into death-suicide. In B. B. Wolman and H. H. Krauss, eds., *Between survival and suicide.* New York: Gardner Press, 1976.

Boudewyns, P. A., T. J. Fry, and E. J. Nightingale. Token economy programs in VA medical centers: Where are they today? *Behavior Therapist,* 1986, *6,* 126–127.

Bourne, P. G. *Addiction.* New York: Academic Press, 1974.

Bowen, M. Principles and techniques of multiple family therapy. In P. J. Guerin, ed., *Family therapy: Theory and practice.* New York: Gardner Press, 1976.

Bowen, M. A. A family concept of schizophrenia. In D. D. Jackson, ed., *The etiology of schizophrenia.* New York: Basic Books, 1960.

Bower, E. M. *The early identification of emotionally handicapped children in school.* Springfield, Ill.: Thomas, 1969.

Bower, E. M. Mental health. In R. Ebel, ed., *Encyclopedia of educational research,* 4th ed. New York: Macmillan, 1969.

Bowlby, J. *Separation: Anxiety and anger.* New York: Basic Books, 1973.

Boyd, J. H., and M. M. Weissman. Epidemiology of affective disorders: A reexamination and future directions. *Archives of General Psychiatry,* 1981, *38,* 1039–1045.

Bozarth, J. D. The person-centered approach in the large community group. In G. M. Gazda, ed., *Innovations to group psychotherapy,* 2nd ed. Springfield, Ill.: Charles C. Thomas, 1981.

Brady, J. P., and D. L. Lind. Experimental analysis of hysterical blindness. In L. P. Ullmann and L. Krasner, eds., *Case studies in behavior modification.* New York: Holt, Rinehart and Winston, 1968.

Brady, J. V. Ulcers in "executive" monkeys. *Scientific American,* 1958, *199,* 95–100.

Brady, J. V., R. W. Porter, D. G. Conrad, and J. W. Mason. Avoidance behavior and the development of gastroduodenal ulcers. *Journal of Experimental Analysis of Behavior,* 1958, *1,* 69–73.

Braginsky, B. M., D. D. Braginsky, and K. Ring. *Methods of madness: The mental hospital as a last resort.* New York: Holt, Rinehart and Winston, 1969.

Brakel, S. J. Involuntary institutionalization. In S. J. Brakel, J. Parry, and B. A. Weiner, eds., *The mentally disabled and the law,* 3rd ed. Chicago: American Bar Foundation, 1985.

Brandsma, J. M., M. C. Maultsby, and R. J. Welsh. *Outpatient treatment of al-*

coholism: A review and comparative study. Baltimore: University Park Press, 1980.

Braukmann, C. J. and **D. L. Fixsen.** Behavior modification with delinquents. In M. Hersen, R. M. Eisler, and P. M. Miller, eds., *Progress in behavior modification,* Vol. 1. New York: Academic Press, 1975.

Braun, P., G. Kochansky, R. Shapiro, S. Greenberg, J. E. Gudeman, S. Johnson, and **M. R. Shore.** Overview: Deinstitutionalization of psychiatric patients, a critical review of outcome studies. *American Journal of Psychiatry,* 1981, *138,* 736–749.

Brewin, C. R. Depression and causal attributions: What is their relation? *Psychological Bulletin,* 1985, 98, 297–309.

Bridges, P. K., and **J. R. Bartlett.** Psychosurgery: Yesterday and today. *British Journal of Psychiatry,* 1977, *131,* 249–260.

Brion, S. Korsakoff's syndrome: Clinicoanatomical and physiopathological considerations. In G. A. Talland and N. C. Waugh, eds., *The pathology of memory.* New York: Academic Press, 1969.

Brodie, H. K. H., N. Gartrell, G. Doering, and **T. Rhue.** Plasma testosterone levels in heterosexual and homosexual men. *American Journal of Psychiatry,* 1974, *131*(1), 82–83.

Brody, J. E. Personal health. *The New York Times,* December 22, 1982a, C6.

Brody, J. E. Remembering the Hyatt disaster: Emotional scars persist a year later. *The New York Times,* July 6, 1982b, C1, C4.

Bromberg, W. *Crime and the mind.* New York: Macmillan, 1965.

Brooks. A. *Law psychiatry and the mental health system.* Boston: Little, Brown, 1974.

Brown, G. W. The social etiology of depression—London studies. In R. A. Depue, ed., *The psychobiology of the depressive disorders.* New York: Academic Press, 1979.

Brown, G., and **J. L. Birley.** Crises and life changes and the onset of schizophrenia. *Journal of Health and Social Behavior,* 1968, *9,* 203–214.

Brown, G. W., J. L. T. Birley, and **J. K. Wing.** Influence of family life on the course of schizophrenic disorders: A replication. *British Journal of Psychiatry,* 1972, *121,* 241–258.

Brown, R., N. Colter, J. A. N. Corsellis, T. J. Crow, C. D. Frith, R. Jagoe, E. C. Johnstone, and **L. Marsh.** Postmortem evidence of structural brain changes in schizophrenia. *Archives of General Psychiatry,* 1986, *43,* 36–42.

Brown, G., T. Harris, and **J. Peto.** Life events and psychiatric disorders: Part II. Nature of causal link. *Psychological Medicine,* 1973, *3,* 159–176.

Browne, A., and **D. Finkelhor.** Impact of child sexual abuse: A review of the research. *Psychological Bulletin,* 1986, *99,* 66–77.

Brownell, K. D. Obesity: Understanding and treating a serious, prevalent, and refractory disorder. *Journal of Consulting and Clinical Psychology,* 1982, *50,* 820–840.

Brownell, K. D. Public health approaches to obesity and its management. *Annual Review of Public Health,* 1986, *7,* 521–533.

Brownell, K., G. A. Marlatt, E. Lichtenstein, and **G. T. Wilson.** Understanding and preventing relapse. *American Psychologist,* 1986, *41,* 765–782.

Brozan, N. Coping with travail of Alzheimer's disease. *The New York Times,* November 29, 1982, B12.

Bruch, H. *The importance of overweight.* New York: Norton, 1957.

Bruch, H. *Eating disorders: Obesity, anorexia nervosa and the person within.* New York: Basic Books, 1973.

Bruch, H. *The golden cage: The enigma of anorexia nervosa.* Cambridge, Mass.: Harvard University Press, 1978.

Bruner, J. S. *Beyond the information given.* New York: Norton, 1973.

Bucher, B., and **O. I. Lovaas.** Use of aversive stimulation in behavior modification. In M. R. Jones, ed., *Miami symposium on the prediction of behavior, 1967: Aversive stimulation.* Coral Gables, Fla.: University of Miami Press, 1968.

Buchsbaum, M. S., J. Cappelletti, R. Ball et al. Positron emission tomographic image measurement in schizophrenia and affective disorders. *Annals of Neurology,* 1984, *15,* 5157–5165.

Buchsbaum, M. S., D. H. Ingvar, R. Kessler, R. N. Waters, J. Cappelletti, D. P. van Kammen, A. C. King, J. L. Johnson, R. G. Manning, R. W. Flynn, L. S. Mann, W. E. Bunney, L. Sokoloff. Cerebral glucography with positron tomography: Use in normal subjects and in patients with schizophrenia. *Archives of General Psychiatry,* 1982, *39,* 251–259.

Buckner, H. T. The transvestic career path. *Psychiatry,* 1970, *33*(3), 381–389.

Burgess, A. W., A N. Groth, and **M. P. McCausland.** Child sex initiation rings. *American Journal of Orthopsychiatry,* 1981, *51,* 110–119.

Burgoine, E., and **L. Wing.** Identical triplets with Asperger's syndrome. *British Journal of Psychiatry,* 1983, *143,* 261–265.

Burish, T. G., W. H. Redd, and **M. P. Carey.** Conditioned nausea and vomiting in cancer chemotherapy: Treatment approaches. In T. G. Burish, S. M. Levy, and B. E. Meyerowitz, eds., *Cancer, nutrition, and eating behavior: A biobehavioral perspective.* Hillsdale, N.J.: Erlbaum, 1985.

Buss, A. H. *Psychopathology.* New York: Wiley, 1966.

Butcher, J. N. Present status of computerized MMPI reporting devices. In O. Buros, ed., *Eighth mental measurements yearbook.* Highland Park, N.J.: Gryphon Press, 1978.

Butler, J. M. and **G. V. Haigh.** Changes in the relation between self-concepts and ideal concepts consequent upon client-centered counseling. In C. R. Rogers and R. F. Dymond, eds., *Psychotherapy and personality change.* Chicago: University of Chicago Press, 1954.

Caligor, J., N. D. Fieldsteel, and **A. J. Brok.** *Individual and group therapy: Combining psychoanalytic treatments.* New York: Basic Books, 1984.

Campbell, M., L. T. Anderson, A. M. Small, R. Perry, W. H. Green, and **R. Caplan.** The effects of haloperidol on learning and behavior in autistic children. *Journal of Autism and Developmental Disorders,* 1982, *12,* 167–175.

Cannon, M. S. The halfway house as an alternative to hospitalization. In Zusman and E. Bertsch, eds., *The future role of the state hospital.* Lexington, Mass.: Lexington Books, 1975.

Cannon, W. B. *Bodily changes in pain, hunger, fear and rage.* New York: Appleton, Century, 1936.

Cantwell, D. P. Childhood depression: A review of current research. In B. B. Lahey and A. E. Kazdin, eds., *Advances in clinical child psychology.* New York: Plenum Press, 1982.

Caputo, D. V. The parents of the schizophrenic. In E. G. Mishler and N. E. Waxler, eds., *Family processes and schizophrenia.* New York: Science House, 1968.

Carroll, B. J., et al. A specific laboratory test for the diagnosis of melancholia. *Archives of General Psychiatry,* 1981, *38,* 15–22.

Carroll, E. M., D. B. Rueger, D. W. Foy, and **C. P. Donahoe, Jr.** Vietnam combat veterans with posttraumatic stress disorder: Analysis of marital and cohabitating adjustment. *Journal of Abnormal Psychology,* 1985, *94,* 329–337.

Casey, R. J., and **J. S. Berman.** The outcome of psychotherapy with children. *Psychological Bulletin,* 1985, *98,* 388–400.

Casson, I. R., O. Seigel, R. Sham, E. A. Campbell, M. Tarlau, and **A. DiDomenico.** Brain damage in modern boxers. *Journal of the American Medical Association,* 1984, *251,* 2663–2667.

Caton, C. L. M. Effect of length of inpatient treatment for chronic schizophrenia. *American Journal of Psychiatry,* 1982, *139,* 856–861.

Cautela, J. R. Treatment of compulsive

behavior by covert sensitization. *Psychological Record,* 1966, *16,* 33–41.

Cautela, J. R. Covert sensitization. *Psychological Reports,* 1967, *20,* 459–468.

Cavallin, H. Incestuous fathers: A clinical report. *American Journal of Psychiatry,* 1966, *122*(10), 1132–1138.

Celesia, G. G., and A. N. Barr. Psychosis and other psychiatric manifestations of levodopa therapy. *Archives of Neurology,* 1970, *23,* 193–200.

Chambers, D. The principle of the least restrictive alternative: The constitutional issues. In M. Kindred, J. Cohen, D. Penrod, and T. Shaffer, eds., *The mentally retarded citizen and the law: President's Committee on Mental Retardation.* New York: Free Press, 1976.

Chapman, L. J., and J. P. Chapman. Illusory correlation as an obstacle to the use of valid psychodiagnostic signs. *Journal of Abnormal Psychology,* 1969, *74,* 271–287.

Char, W. F., and J. F. McDermott. Treating anorexia nervosa. *Medical Insight,* 1970, *2,* 41–49.

Chess, S., S. J. Korn, and P. B. Fernandez. Psychiatric disorders of children with congenital rubella. New York: Brunner/Mazel, 1971.

Chodorow, N. *The reproduction of mothering: Psychoanalysis and the sociology of gender.* Berkeley: University of California Press, 1978.

Christiansen, K. O. Threshold of tolerance in various population groups illustrated by results from the Danish criminologic twin study. In A. V. S. de Reuck and R. Porter, eds., *The mentally abnormal offender.* Boston: Little, Brown, 1968.

Christoffel, H. Male genital exhibitionism. In S. Lorand and M. Bolint, eds., *Perversions: Psychodynamics and therapy.* New York: Random House, 1956.

Ciompi, L. Catamnestic long-term study on the course of life and aging of schizophrenics. *Schizophrenia Bulletin,* 1980, *6,* 606–617.

Cisin, I., and D. Calahan. The big drinkers, *Newsweek,* July 6, 1970, p. 57.

Clark, D. M., and J. D. Teasdale. Diurnal variation in clinical depression and accessibility of memories of positive and negative experiences. *Journal of Abnormal Psychology,* 1982, *9,* 87–95.

Cleckley, H. M. *The mask of sanity.* St. Louis: Mosby, 1976.

Clinthorne, J. K., I. H. Cisin, M. B. Balter, G. D. Mellinger, and E. H. Uhlenhuth. Changes in popular attitudes and beliefs about tranquilizers: 1970–1979. *Archives of General Psychiatry,* 1986, *43,* 527–532.

Cohen, B. D., G. Nachmani, and S. Rosenberg. Referent communication disturbances in acute schizophrenia. *Journal*

of Abnormal Psychology, 1974, *83*(1), 1–13.

Cohen, E., J. A. Motto, and R. H. Seiden. An instrument for evaluating suicide potential: A preliminary study. *American Journal of Psychiatry,* 1966, *122,* 886–891.

Cohen, L., and L. Appleby. Preliminary evaluation of Chicago's Subregion 5 long-term care facilities. Paper presented at the International Association of Psychosocial Rehabilitation Services. Oct. 1976, Chicago.

Cohen, M., and T. Seghorn. Sociometric study of the sex offender. *Journal of Abnormal Psychology,* 1969, *74,* 249–255.

Cohen, S., and K. S. Ditman. Prolonged adverse reactions to lysergic acid diethylamide. *Archives of General Psychiatry,* 1963, *8,* 479.

Cohen, S., and T. A. Wills. Stress, social support, and the buffering hypothesis. *Psychological Bulletin,* 1985, *98,* 310–357.

Combs, B. J., D. R. Hales, and B. K. Williams. *An invitation to health: Your personal responsibility.* Menlo Park, Calif.: Benjamin/Cummings, 1980.

Commitment following an insanity acquittal. *Harvard Law Review,* 1981, *94,* 604–625.

Conger, J. J. The effects of alcohol on conflict behavior in the albino rat. *Quarterly Journal of Studies on Alcohol,* 1951, *12,* 1–29.

Conte, J. R., and L. Berliner. Sexual abuse of children: Implications for practice. *Social Casework,* 1981, *62,* 601–606.

Cook, M., S. Mineka, B. Wolkenstein, and K. Laitsch. Observational conditioning of snake fear in unrelated rhesus monkeys. *Journal of Abnormal Psychology,* 1985, *94,* 591–610.

Cooper, J. E., R. E. Kendell, B. J. Gurland, L. Sharp. J. R. M. Copeland, and R. Simon. *Psychiatric diagnosis in New York and London: A comparative study of mental hospital admissions.* New York: Oxford University Press, 1972.

Cooper, J. R., F. E. Bloom, and R. H. Roth. *The biochemical basis of neuropharmacology,* 5th ed. New York: Oxford University Press, 1986.

Costa, E., and A. Guidotti. Endogenous ligands for benzodiazepine recognition sites. *Biochemical Pharmacology,* 1985, *34,* 3399–3403.

Costello, C. G. Electroconvulsive therapy: Is further investigation necessary? *Canadian Psychiatric Association Journal,* 1976, *21,* 61–67.

Costello, C. G. Fears and phobias in women: A community study. *Journal of Abnormal Psychology,* 1982, *91,* 280–286.

Coursey, R. D., M. Buchsbaum, and B. L. Frankel. Personality measures

and evoked responses in chronic insomniacs. *Journal of Abnormal Psychology,* 1975, *84,* 239–250.

Cowen, E. L. The wooing of primary prevention. *American Journal of Community Psychology,* 1980, *8,* 258–284.

Cowen, E. L. Help is where you find it: Four informal helping groups. *American Psychologist,* 1982, *37*(4), 385–395.

Cox, A., M. Rutter, S. Newman, and L. Bartak. A comparative study of infantile autism and specific developmental language disorders: II. Parental characteristics. *British Journal of Psychiatry,* 1975, *126,* 146–159.

Coyne, J. C. Toward an interactional description of depression. *Psychiatry,* 1976a, *39,* 14–27.

Coyne, J. C. Depression and the response of others. *Journal of Abnormal Psychology,* 1976b, *85,* 186–193.

Craighead, L. W., A. J. Stunkard, and R. M. O'Brien. Behavior therapy and pharmacotherapy for obesity. *Archives of General Psychiatry,* 1981, *38,* 763–768.

Crane, G. E. Persistent dyskinesia. *British Journal of Psychiatry,* 1973, *122,* 395–405.

Creak, E. M., and G. Pampiglione. Clinical and EEG studies on a group of 35 psychotic children. *Developmental Medicine and Child Neurology,* 1969, *11,* 218–227.

Crisp, A. H. The possible significance of some behavioral correlates of weight and carbohydrate intake. *Journal of Psychosomatic Research,* 1967, *2,* 117–131.

Crisp, A. H. Premorbid factors in adult disorders of weight, with particular reference to primary anorexia nervosa (weight phobia). *Journal of Psychosomatic Medicine,* 1970, *14*(1), 1–22.

Critchlow, B. The powers of John Barleycorn: Beliefs about the effects of alcohol on social behavior. *American Psychologist,* 1986, *41,* 751–764.

Cromwell, R. L., and P. R. Dokecki. Schizophrenic language: A disattention interpretation. In S. Rosenberg and J. H. Koplin, eds., *Developments in applied psycholinguistics research.* New York: Macmillan, 1968.

Crook, T., and J. Eliot. Parental death during childhood and adult depression: A critical review of the literature. *Psychological Bulletin,* 1980, *87,* 252–259.

Crooks, R., and P. Baur. *Our sexuality,* 3d ed. San Francisco: Benjamin/Cummings, 1987.

Crow, T. J., A. J. Cross, E. C. Johnstone, and F. Owen. Two syndromes in schizophrenia and their pathogenesis. In F. A. Henn and H. A. Nasrallah, eds., *Schizophrenia as a brain disease.* New York: Oxford University Press, 1982.

Crow, T. J., E. C. Johnstone, and H. A. McClelland. The coincidence of schizophrenia and Parkinsonism: Some neurochemical implications. *Psychological Medicine*, 1976, *6*, 227–233.

Crowe, R. An adoptive study of psychopathy: Preliminary results from arrest records and psychiatric hospital records. In R. Fieve, D. Rosenthal, and H. Brill, eds., *Genetic research in psychiatry*. Baltimore: Johns Hopkins University Press, 1975.

Crumbaugh, J. D., and L. T. Maholick. An experimental study in existentialism: The psychometric approach to Frankl's concept of noogenic neurosis. *Journal of Clinical Psychology*, 1964, *20*, 200–207.

Cummings, C., J. R. Gordon, and G. A. Marlatt. Relapse: Prevention and prediction. In W. R. Miller, ed., *The addictive disorders: Treatment of alcoholism, drug abuse, smoking, and obesity*. New York: Pergamon Press, 1980.

Cummings, J. L. *Clinical neuropsychiatry*. Orlando, Fla.: Grune & Stratton, 1985.

Cummings, J. L., and D. F. Benson. *Dementia: A clinical approach*. Boston: Butterworths, 1983.

Curran, J. P., and F. S. Gilbert. A test of the relative effectiveness of a systematic desensitization and an interpersonal skills training program with date anxious subjects. *Behavior Therapy*, 1975, *6*, 510–521.

Curtiss, S. R. *Genie: A psycholinguistic study of a modern-day "wild child."* New York: Academic Press, 1977.

Custer, R. L., and R. F. Custer. *Characteristics of the recovering compulsive gambler: A survey of 150 members of Gamblers Anonymous*. Paper presented at the fourth annual Conference on Gambling, Reno.

Custer, R. L., and H. Milt. *When luck runs out*. New York: Facts on File, 1985.

Cutter, H. S. G., R. E. Boyatzis, and D. D. Clancy. Effectiveness of power motivation training in rehabilitating alcoholics. *Journal of Studies on Alcohol*, 1977, *38*, 131–141.

Dain, N. *Concepts of sanity in the United States, 1789–1895*. New Brunswick, N.J.: Rutgers University Press, 1964.

Dana, R. H. *A human science model for personality assessment with projective techniques*. Thomas, 1982.

Datel, W. E., and J. A. Gengerelli. Reliability of Rorschach interpretations. *Journal of Projective Techniques*, 1955, *19*, 372–381.

Davis, H. The self-schema and subjective organization of personal information in depression. *Cognitive Therapy and Research*, 1979, *3*, 415–425.

Davis, J. M. Critique of single amine theories: Evidence of a cholinergic influence in the major mental illnesses. In D. X. Freedman, ed., *Biology of the major psychoses*. New York: Raven Press, 1975.

Davis, J. M. Dopamine theory of schizophrenia: A two-factor theory. In L. C. Wynne, R. L. Cromwell, and S. Matthysse, eds., *The nature of schizophrenia*. New York: Wiley, 1978.

Davis, J. M., G. Klerman, and J. Schildkraut. Drugs used in the treatment of depression. In L. Efron, J. O. Cole, D. Levine, and J. R. Wittenborn, eds., *Psychopharmacology, A review of progress*. Washington, D.C.: U.S. Clearinghouse of Mental Health Information, 1967.

Davison, G. C. Homosexuality: The ethical challenge. Presidential Address, Annual Convention of the Association for the Advancement of Behavior Therapy, Chicago, 1974.

Day, M., and E. Semrad. Group therapy with neurotics and psychotics. In H. Kaplan and B. Sadock, eds., *Comprehensive group psychotherapy*. Baltimore: Williams & Williams, 1971.

Dean, C. W., and E. de Bruyn-Kops. *The crime and consequences of rape*. Springfield, Ill.: Charles C Thomas, 1982.

de Catanzaro, D. *Suicide and self-damaging behavior: A sociobiological perspective*. New York: Academic Press, 1981.

DeMyer, M. K., S. Barton, W. E. DeMyer, J. A. Norton, J. Allen, and R. Steele. Prognosis in autism: A follow-up study. *Journal of Autism and Childhood Schizophrenia*, 1973, *3*, 199–246.

DeMyer, M. K., J. N. Hingtgen, and R. K. Jackson. Infantile autism reviewed: A decade of research. *Schizophrenia Bulletin*, 1981, *7*, 388–451.

DeNelsky, G. Y., and V. H. Dennenberg. Infantile stimulation and adult exploratory behavior: Effects of handling upon tactual variation seeking. *Journal of Comparative and Physiological Psychology*, 1967, *63*, 309–312.

Dennis, W. *Children of the Créche*. New York: Appleton-Century-Crofts, 1973.

Depue, R. A., and R. M. Kleiman. Free cortisol as a peripheral index of central vulnerability to major forms of polar depressive disorders: Examining stress-biology interactions in subsyndromal highrisk persons. In R. A. Depue, ed., *The psychobiology of the depressive disorders*. New York: Academic Press, 1979.

Depue, R. A., and S. M. Monroe. The unipolar-bipolar distinction in the depressive disorders. *Psychological Bulletin*, 1978, *85*, 1001–1029.

Depue, R. A., J. F. Slater, H. Wolfstetter-Kausch, D. Klein, E. Goplerud, and D. Farr. A behavioral paradigm for identifying persons at risk for bipolar depressive disorder: A conceptual framework and five validation studies. *Journal of Abnormal Psychology*, 1981, *90*, 381–438.

Derry, P. A., and N. A. Kuiper. Sche-

matic processing and self-reference in clinical depression. *Journal of Abnormal Psychology*, 1981, 286–297.

Derry, P. A., and N. A. Kuiper. Schematic processing and self-reference in clinical depression. *Journal of Abnormal Psychology*, 1981, *90*, 286–297.

DeSilva, P., S. Rachman, and M. E. P. Seligman. Prepared phobias and obsessions: Therapeutic outcome. *Behaviour Research and Therapy*, 1977, *15*, 65–77.

Deutsch, A. *The mentally ill in America*. 2nd ed. New York and London: Columbia University Press, 1949.

Developments in the law—civil commitment of the mentally ill. *Harvard Law Review*, 1974, *87*, 1190–1406.

Devins, G. M., Y. M. Binik, D. J. Hollomby, P. E. Barre, and R. D. Guttmann, Helplessness and depression in end-stage renal disease. *Journal of Abnormal Psychology*, 1981, *90*, 531–545.

de Young, M. *Sexual victimization of children*. Jefferson, N.C.: MacFarland, 1982.

Diamond, E. L. The role of anger and hostility in essential hypertension and coronary heart disease. *Psychological Bulletin*, 1982, *92*, 410–433.

Di Cara, L., and N. Miller. Instrumental learning of vasomotor responses by rats: Learning to respond differentially in the two ears. *Science*, 1968, *159*, 1485–1486.

Didion, J. In bed. In *The white album*. New York: Simon and Schuster, 1979.

Doane, J., K. West, M. J. Goldstein, E. Rodnick, and J. Jones. Parental communication deviance and affective style as predictors of subsequent schizophrenia spectrum disorders in vulnerable adolescents. *Archives of General Psychiatry*, 1981, *38*, 679–685.

Dohrenwend, B. S., and B. P. Dohrenwend. Hypotheses about stress processes linking social class to various types of psychopathology. *American Journal of Community Psychology*, 1981, *9*, 146–159.

Dole, V., and M. Nyswander. Methadone maintenance treatment: A ten-year perspective. *JAMA*, 1976, *235*, 2117–2119.

Douglas, V. I., and K. G. Peters. Toward a clearer definition of the attentional deficits of hyperactive children. In G. A. Hale and M. Lewis, eds., *Attention and cognitive development*. New York: Plenum, 1979.

Dragstedt, L. R. Gastric secretion and duodenal ulcer. In T. K. Shnitka, J. Gilbert, and R. C. Harrison, eds., *Gastric secretion: Mechanisms and control*. New York: Pergamon, 1967.

DSM-III casebook: A learning companion to the diagnostic and statistical manual of mental disorders (3rd ed.). Robert L. Spitzer et al. (eds.). Washington, D.C.: American Psychiatric Press, 1981.

Drake, R. E., and G. E. Vaillant. A validity study of axis II of DSM III. *American Journal of Psychiatry*, 1985, *142*, 553–558.

Duke, M. P., and **M. C. Mullins.** Preferred interpersonal distance as a function of locus of control orientation in chronic schizophrenics, non-schizophrenic patients, and normals. *Journal of Consulting and Clinical Psychology*, 1973, *41*(2), 230–234.

Dunbar, H. F. *Emotions and bodily changes.* New York: Columbia University Press, 1935.

Dunham, H. W. *Community and schizophrenia: An epidemiological analysis.* Detroit: Wayne State University Press, 1965.

Durkheim, E. *Le suicide.* Paris: Librarie Felix Alcan (1897). J. A. Spaulding and G. Simpson, trs. Glencoe, Ill.: Free Press, 1951.

Dyer, K., W. P. Christian, and **S. C. Luce.** The role of response delay in improving the discrimination performance of autistic children. *Journal of Applied Behavior Analysis*, 1982, *15*, 231–240.

Eberhard, G. Peptic ulcer in twins: A study in personality, heredity, and environment. *Acta Psychiatrica Scandinavica*, 1968, Suppl. 205.

Eberhardy, F. The view from "the couch." *Journal of Child Psychology and Psychiatry*, 1967, *8*, 257–263.

Edelman, M. W. Who is for children? *American Psychologist*, 1981, *36*(2), 109–116.

Edman, G., M. Asberg, S. Levander, and **D. Schalling.** Skin conductance habituation and cerebrospinal fluid 5-hydroxyindoleacetic acid in suicidal patients. *Archives of General Psychiatry*, 1986, *43*, 586–592.

Edwards, A. L. The relationship between the judged desirability of a trait and the probability that the trait will be endorsed. *Journal of Applied Psychology*, 1953, *37*, 90–93.

Edwards, G., C. Hensman, A. Hawker, and **V. Williamson.** Alcoholics Anonymous: The anatomy of a self-help group. *Social Psychiatry*, 1967, *1*, 195–204.

Egeland, J. A., and **A. M. Hostetter.** Amish study, I: Affective disorders among the Amish. *American Journal of Psychiatry*, 1983, *140*, 56–61.

Egeland, J. A., et al. Bipolar affective disorders linked to DNA markers on chromosome 11. *Nature*, 1987, *325*, 783–787.

Eich, E. Paper presented at the convention of the American Psychological Association. Washington, D.C., 1986.

Eichenwald, H. F., and **P. C. Fry.** Nutrition and learning. *Science*, 1969, *163*, 644–648.

Eilbracht, A., and **T. Thompson.** Behavioral intervention in a sheltered work activity setting for retarded adults. In T. Thompson and J. Grabowski, eds., *Behavior modification of the mentally retarded.* 2nd ed. New York: Oxford University Press, 1977.

Eisenberg, L., and **L. Kanner.** Early infantile autism. *American Journal of Orthopsychiatry*, 1956, *26*, 556–566.

Eisenberg, M. M. *Ulcers.* New York: Random House, 1978.

Ellington, R. J. Incidence of EEG abnormality among patients with mental disorders of apparently nonorganic origin: A criminal review. *American Journal of Psychiatry*, 1954, *3*, 263–275.

Ellis, A. Rational psychotherapy. *Journal of General Psychology*, 1958, *59*, 35–49.

Ellis, A. *Reason and emotion in psychotherapy.* New York: Lyle Stuart, 1962.

Ellis, A. The treatment of a psychopath with rational therapy. In S. J. Morse and R. I. Watson, eds., *Psychotherapies: A comparative casebook.* New York: Holt, Rinehart & Winston, 1977.

Ellis, H. *Studies in the psychology of sex.* 7 vols. Philadelphia: Davis, 1899–1928.

Elmer, E., and **G. S. Gregg.** Developmental characteristics of abused children. *Pediatrics*, 1967, *40*, 595–602.

Eme, R. F. Sex differences in childhood psychopathology: A review. *Psychological Bulletin*, 1979, *86*, 574–595.

Emmelkamp, P. M. G. Behavior therapy with adults. In S. L. Garfield and A. E. Bergin, eds., *Handbook of psychotherapy and behavior change: An evaluative analysis,* 3rd ed. New York: Wiley, 1986.

Endicott, J., and **R. L. Spitzer.** A diagnostic interview: The schedule for affective disorders and schizophrenia. *Archives of General Psychiatry*, 1978, *35*, 837–844.

Engel, B. T. Stimulus-response and individual-response specificity. *Archives of General Psychiatry*, 1960, *2*, 305–313.

Engel, B. T., and **A. F. Bickford.** Response specificity: Stimulus response and individual response specificity in essential hypertension. *Archives of General Psychiatry*, 1961, *5*, 478–489.

Engel, G. L. Conversion symptoms. In C. M. MacBryde and R. S. Blacklow, eds., *Signs and symptoms: Applied pathologic physiology and clinical interpretation,* 5th ed. Philadelphia: Lippincott, 1970.

Engle-Friedman, M., E. A. Baker, and **R. R. Bootzin.** Reports of wakefulness during EEG identified states of sleep. *Sleep Research*, 1985, *14*, 121.

Ennis, B. J., and **R. D. Emery.** *The rights of mental patients.* New York: Avon Books, 1978.

Epstein, H. A sin or a right? *The New York Times Magazine*, September 8, 1974, pp. 91–94.

Erdelyi, M. H. *Psychoanalysis: Freud's cognitive view.* New York: W. H. Freeman, 1985.

Erdelyi, M. H., and **B. Goldberg.** Let's not sweep repression under the rug: Toward a cognitive psychology of repression. In J. F. Kihlstrom and F. J. Evans, eds., *Functional disorders of memory.* Hillsdale, N.J.: Erlbaum, 1979.

Erikson, E. *Childhood and society.* New York: Norton, 1950.

Erikson, Kai T. *Everything in its path: Destruction of community in the Buffalo Creek flood.* New York: Simon and Schuster, 1976.

Evans, D. A. P., L. Horwich, R. B. McConnel, and **M. R. Bullen.** Influence of the ABO blood groups and secretor status on bleeding and on perforation of duodenal ulcer. *GUT*, 1968, *9*, 319–322.

Evans, R. B. Childhood parental relationships of homosexual man. *Journal of Consulting and Clinical Psychology*, 1969, *33*, 129–135.

Ewen, D. *Journey to greatness: The life and music of George Gershwin.* New York: Holt, Rinehart and Winston, 1956.

Exner, J. E. *The Rorschach: A comprehensive system.* Vol. 1. New York: Wiley, 1978.

Exner, J. E. *The Rorschach: A comprehensive system.* Vol. 2. New York: Wiley, 1982.

Exner, J. E. *The Rorschach: A comprehensive system.* Vol. 3. New York: Wiley, 1986.

Eysenck, H. J. The effects of psychotherapy: An evaluation. *Journal of Consulting Psychology*, 1952, *16*, 319–324.

Fabian, W. D., Jr., and **S. M. Fishkin.** A replicated study of self-reported changes in psychological absorption with marijuana intoxication. *Journal of Abnormal Psychology*, 1981, *90*, 546–553.

Fadiman, J. The transpersonal stance. In M. J. Mahoney, ed., *Psychotherapy process: Current issues and future directions.* New York: Plenum, 1980.

Falek, A., and **H. M. Moser.** Classification in schizophrenia. *Archives of General Psychiatry*, 1975, *32*, 59–67.

Falloon, I. R. H., J. L. Boyd, C. W. McGill, M. Williamson, J. Razani, H. B. Moss, A. M. Gilderman, and **G. M. Simpson.** Family management in the prevention of morbidity of schizophrenia. *Archives of General Psychiatry*, 1985, *42*, 887–896.

Falloon, Ian R., J. L. Boyd, C. W. McGill, et al. Family management in prevention of exacerbation of schizophrenia: A controlled study. *New England Journal of Medicine*, 1982, *306*(24), 1437–1440.

Farberow, N. L., and **R. E. Litman.** A comprehensive suicide prevention program. Suicide Prevention Center of Los Angeles, 1958–1969. Unpublished final report DHEW NIMH Grants No. MH 14946 and MH 00128. Los Angeles, 1970.

Falkner, B., H. Kushner, G. Onesti, and **E. T. Angelakos.** Cardiovascular characteristics in adolescents who develop essential hypertension. *Hypertension*, 1981, *3*, 521–527.

Favell, J. E. The treatment of self-injurious behavior. *Behavior Therapy*, 1982, *13*, 529–554.

Feighner J. P., E. Robins, S. B. Guze, et al. Diagnostic criteria for use in psychiatric research. *Archives of General Psychiatry*, 1972, 57–63.

Feinberg, M., J. C. Gillin, B. J. Carroll, and **J. F. Greden.** EEG studies of sleep in the diagnosis of depression. *Biological Psychiatry*, 1982, *17*, 305–316.

Fenichel, O. *The psychoanalytic theory of neurosis.* New York: Norton, 1945.

Fernald, W. E. The history of the treatment of the feeble-minded. *Proceedings of the National Conference on Charities and Correction*, 1893, *20*, 203–221.

Ferster, C. B. Positive reinforcement and behavioral deficits of autistic children. *Child Development*, 1961, *32*, 437–456.

Ferster, C. B. Classification of behavioral pathology. In L. Krasner and L. P. Ullmann, eds., *Research in behavioral modification.* New York: Holt, Rinehart and Winston, 1965.

Ferster, C. B. A functional analysis of depression. *American Psychologist*, 1973, *28*, 857–870.

Ferster, C. B., J. I. Nurnberger, and **E. B. Levitt.** The control of eating. *Journal of Mathematics*, 1962, *1*, 87–109.

Figley, C. R. Combat as disaster: Treating combat veterans as survivors. Presented at the Annual Meeting of the American Psychiatric Association, Chicago, 1979.

Finch, J. R., J. P. Smith, and **A. D. Pokorny.** Vehicular studies. Paper presented at meetings of the American Psychiatric Association, May 1970.

Finkelhor, D. *Sexually victimized children.* New York: Free Press, 1979.

Finkelhor, D., and **S. Araji.** Explanations of pedophilia: A four factor model. *The Journal of Sex Research*, 1986, *22*, 145–161.

Fish, B., T. Shapiro, and **M. Campbell,** et al. A classification of schizophrenic children under five years. *American Journal of Psychiatry*, 1968, *124*, 109–117.

Fish, J. F. The classification of schizophrenia. *Journal of Mental Science*, 1957, *103*, 443–465.

Fisher, S., and **R. P. Greenberg.** *The scientific credibility of Freud's theories and therapy.* New York: Basic Books, 1977.

Flender, H., ed. *We were hooked.* New York: Random House, 1972.

Flor-Henry, P. Lateralized temporal-lim-

bic dysfunction and psychopathology. *Annals of the New York Academy of Sciences*, 1976, *280*, 777–797.

Flor-Henry, P., D. Fromm-Auch, and **D. Schopflocher.** Neuropsychological dimensions in psychopathology. In P. Flor-Henry and J. Grozelier, eds., *Laterality and psychopathology.* Amsterdam: Elsevier, 1983.

Fodor, I. G. The treatment of communication problems with assertiveness training. In A. Goldstein and E. B. Foa, eds., *Handbook of behavioral interventions.* New York: 1980.

Folstein, S., and **M. Rutter.** Genetic influences and infantile autism. *Nature*, 1977, *265*, 726–728.

Foltz, E. L., and **F. E. Millet.** Experimental psychosomatic disease states in monkeys: I. Peptic "ulcer-executive" monkeys. *Journal of Surgical Research*, 1964, *4*, 445–453.

Ford, C. S., and **F. A. Beach.** *Patterns of sexual behavior.* New York: Ace Books, 1951.

Forel, A. *Out of my life and work.* B. Miall, tr. London: Allen and Unwin, 1937.

Forsyth, R. P. Mechanisms of the cardiovascular responses to environmental stressors. In P. A. Obrist, A. H. Black, J. Brener, and L. U. Di Cara, eds., *Cardiovascular psychophysiology: Current issues in response mechanisms, biofeedback and methodology.* Hawthorne, N.Y.: Aldine, 1974.

Foucault, M. *Madness and civilization.* Richard Howard, tr. New York: Random House, 1965.

Foxx, R. M., and **N. H. Azrin.** *Toilet training the retarded: A rapid program for day and night time independent toileting.* Champaign, Ill.: Research Press, 1973.

Frank, G. *The Boston strangler.* New York: New American Library, 1966.

Frank, J. D. *Persuasion and healing: A comparative study of psychotherapy.* Baltimore: Johns Hopkins University Press, 1961.

Frank, J. D. The placebo in psychotherapy. *Behavioral and Brain Sciences*, 1983, *6*, 291–292.

Frankl, V. E. *The doctor and the soul.* New York: Knopf, 1955.

Frankl, V. E. *Man's search for meaning.* Boston: Beacon Press, 1962.

Frankl, V. E. Paradoxical intention and dereflection. *Psychotherapy: Theory, Research, and Practice*, 1975a, *12*, 226–237.

Frankl, V. E. *The unconscious god: Psychotherapy and theology.* New York: Simon & Schuster, 1975b.

Franzini, L. R., A. J. Litrownik, and **M. A. Magy.** Training trainable mentally retarded adolescents in delay behavior. *Mental Retardation*, 1980, *18*, 45–47.

Frazier, T. W. Avoidance conditioning of

heart rate in humans. *Psychophysiology*, 1966, *3*, 188–202.

Freedman, B., and **L. J. Chapman.** Early subjective experience in schizophrenic episodes. *Journal of Abnormal Psychology*, 1973, *82*(1), 46–59.

Freud, A. *The ego and mechanisms of defense.* New York: International Universities Press, 1946.

Freud, A. Adolescence, *Psychoanalytic Study of the Child*, 1958, *13*, 255–278.

Freud, A. *Normality and pathology: Assessment of development.* New York: International Universities Press, 1965.

Freud, S. The defense neuropsychoses (1894). In J. Strachey, ed., *The standard edition of the complete psychological works of Sigmund Freud*, Vol. I. London: The Hogarth Press, 1953.

Freud, S. The questioning of lay analysis (1926). In J. Strachey, ed., *The standard edition of the complete psychological works of Sigmund Freud*, Vol. XX. London: The Hogarth Press, 1953.

Freud, S. Three essays on sexuality (1905). In J. Strachey, ed., *The standard edition of the complete psychological works of Sigmund Freud.* Vol. III. London: The Hogarth Press, 1953.

Freud, S. Notes upon a case of obsessional neurosis (1909). In J. Strachey, ed., *The standard edition of the complete psychological works of Sigmund Freud.* Vol. X. London: The Hogarth Press, 1955.

Freud, S. Mourning and melancholia (1917). In J. Rickman, ed., *A general selection from the works of Sigmund Freud.* Garden City, N.Y.: Doubleday, 1957

Freud, S. *The interpretation of dreams* (1900). J. Strachey, ed. and tr. New York: Wiley, 1961.

Freud, S. Analysis of a phobia in a five-year-old boy (1909). In J. Strachey, ed., *The standard edition of the complete psychological works of Sigmund Freud.* Vol. X. London: The Hogarth Press, 1962.

Freud, S. Studies on hysteria (1895). In J. Strachey, ed., *The standard edition of the complete psychological works of Sigmund Freud.* Vol. II. London: The Hogarth Press, 1962.

Freud, S. *An autobiographical study.* J. Strachey, ed. and tr. New York: Norton, 1963.

Friedman, C., and **A. Friedman.** Characteristics of schizogenic families during a joint family story-telling task. *Family Process*, 1970, *9*, 333–354.

Friedman, M., and **R. H. Rosenman.** *Type A behavior and your heart.* New York: Knopf, 1974.

Friedman, M., C. E. Thoresen, J. J. Gill, D. Ulmer, L. Thompson, L. Powell, V. Price, S. R. Elek, D. D. Rabin, W. S. Breall, G. Piaget, T. Dixon, E. Bourg, R. A. Levy, and **D. L. Tasto.** Feasibility of altering Type A behavior pattern after myocardial infarction. Recurrent coronary prevention project study: Methods, baseline results and preliminary findings. *Circulation*, 1982, *66*, 83–92.

Friedman, P. Overview of the institutional labor problem: The nature and extent of institutional labor in the United States. In M. Kindred, J. Cohen, D. Penrod, and T. Shaffer, eds., *The mentally retarded citizen and the law: President's Committee on Mental Retardation*. New York: Free Press, 1976.

Friedrich, L. K., and **A. H. Stein.** Aggressive and prosocial television programs and the natural behavior of preschool children. *Monographs of the Society for Research in Child Development*, 1973, *38* (Serial No. 151).

Fromm, Erich. *Greatness and limitations of Freud's thought*. New York: Harper & Row, 1980.

Frosch, W. A., E. S. Robbins, and **M. Stern.** Untoward reactions to lysergic acid diethylamide (LSD) resulting in hospitalization. *The New England Journal of Medicine*, 1965, *273*(23), 1236.

Frye, J. S. and **R. A. Stockton.** Discriminant analysis of posttraumatic stress disorder among a group of Viet Nam veterans. *American Journal of Psychiatry*, 1982, *139*, 52–56.

Gagnon, J. H. *Human sexualities*. Chicago: Scott, Foresman, 1977.

Gainotti, G. Emotional behavior and hemispheric side of the lesion. *Cortex*, 1972, *8*, 41–55.

Gallemore, J., and **W. Wilson.** Adolescent maladjustment or affective disorder? *American Journal of Psychiatry*, 1972, *129*, 608–619.

Garber, H. L., and **M. McInerney.** Sociobehavioral factors in mental retardation. In P. T. Legelka and H. G. Prehm, eds., *Mental retardation: From categories to people*. Columbus, Ohio: Charles E. Merrill, 1982.

Garcia, J., B. K. McGowan, F. R. Ervin, and **R. A. Koelling.** Cues: Their relative effectiveness as a function of the reinforcer. *Science*, 1968, *160*, 794–795.

Garcia, J., K. W. Rusiniak, and **L. P. Brett.** Conditioning food-illness aversions in wild animals: *Caveant canonici*. In H. Davis and H. M. B. Hurwitz, eds., *Operant–Pavlovian interactions*. Hillsdale, N.J.: Erlbaum, 1977.

Gardner, H. *Frames of mind: The theory of multiple intelligences*. New York: Basic Books, 1984.

Garfield, S. L. *Psychotherapy: An elective approach*. New York: Wiley, 1980.

Garfinkel, B. D., A. Froese, and **J. Hood.** Suicide attempts in children and adolescents. *American Journal of Psychiatry*, 1982, *139*, 1257–1261.

Garfinkel, L. Changes in the cigarette consumption of smokers in relation to changes in tar/nicotine content of cigarettes smoked. *American Journal of Public Health*, 1979, *69*, 1274–1276.

Garmezy, N. Process and reactive schizophrenia: Some conceptions and issues. *Schizophrenia Bulletin*, 1970, *2*, 30–67.

Gartrell, N. K. Hormones and homosexuality. In W. Paul, J. D. Weinrich, J. C. Gonsiorel, and M. E. Hotveot, eds., *Homosexuality*. Beverly Hills, Calif.: Sage, 1982.

Gawin, F. H., and **H. D. Kleber,** Abstinence symptomatology and psychiatric diagnosis in cocaine abusers. *Archives of General Psychiatry*, 1986, *43*, 107–113.

Gaylin, W. *The killing of Bonnie Garland*. New York: Simon and Schuster, 1982.

Gazzaniga, M. S. One brain—two minds? *American Scientist*, 1972, *60*, 311–317.

Gebhard, P. H. Incidence of overt homosexuality in the United States and Western Europe. In J. M. Livingood, ed., National Institute of Mental Health Task Force on Homosexuality: Final Report and Background Papers. Rockville, Md.: National Institute of Mental Health, 1972.

Gebhard, P. H., J. H. Gagnon, W. B. Pomeroy, and **C. V. Christenson.** *Sex offenders*. New York: Harper & Row, 1965.

Gelfand, D. M., W. R. Jenson, and **C. J. Drew.** *Understanding child behavior disorders*. New York: Holt, Rinehart and Winston, 1982.

Geller, E., E. R. Ritvo, B. J. Freeman, and **A. Yuwiler.** Preliminary observations on the effect of fenfluramine on blood serotonin and symptoms in three autistic boys. *The New England Journal of Medicine*, 1982, *307*(3).

Gelles, R. J. Violence toward children in the United States. *American Journal of Orthopsychiatry*, 1978, *48*(4), 580–592.

Gil, D. *Violence against children: Physical abuse in the United States*. Cambridge: Harvard University Press, 1970.

Gilbert, D. G. Paradoxical tranquilizing and emotion-reducing effects of nicotine. *Psychological Bulletin*, 1979, *36*, 643–661.

Gilligan, C. *In a different voice*. Cambridge, Mass.: Harvard University Press, 1982.

Giorgi, A. *Psychology as a human science: A phenomenologically based approach*. New York: Harper & Row, 1970.

Gist, R. and **S. B. Stolz.** Community response to the Kansas City hotel disaster. *American Psychologist*, 1982, *37*(10), 1136–1139.

Glass, D. C., L. R. Krakoff, R. Contrada, W. F. Hilton, K. Kehoe, E. G. Mannucci, C. Collins, B. Snow, and **E. Elting.** Effect of harrassment and competition upon cardiovascular and plasma catecholamine responses in Type A and Type B individuals. *Psychophysiology*, 1980, *17*, 453–463.

Gleser, G. C., B. L. Green, and **C. Winget.** *Prolonged psychological effects of disaster: A study of Buffalo Creek*. New York: Academic Press, 1981.

Gloor, P., et al. The role of the limbic system in experiential phenomena of temporal-lobe epilepsy. *Annals of Neurology*, 1982, *12*, 129–144.

Goddard, H. H. *The Kallikak family*. New York: Macmillan, 1912.

Goffman, E. *Presentation of self in everyday life*. New York: Doubleday, 1959a.

Goffman, E. The moral career of the mental patient. *Psychiatry: Journal for the Study of Interpersonal Processes*, 1959b, *22*, 123–131.

Goffman, E. *Asylums: Essays on the social situation of mental patients and other inmates*. New York: Doubleday, 1961.

Goldberg, L. R. The effectiveness of clinicians' judgments: The diagnosis of organic brain damage from the Bender-Gestalt Test. *Journal of Consulting Psychology*, 1959, *23*, 25–28.

Goldblatt, M., and **H. Munitz.** Behavioral treatment of hysterical leg paralysis. *Journal of Behavior Therapy and Experimental Psychiatry*, 1976, *7*(3), 259–263.

Golden, C. J., J. A. Moses, J. A. Coffman, W. R. Miller, and **F. D. Strider.** *Clinical neuropsychology: Interface with neurologic and psychiatric disorders*. New York: Grune and Stratton, 1983.

Golden, C. J., J. A. Moses, Jr., R. Zelazowski. Cerebral ventricular size and neuropsychological impairment in young chronic schizophrenics. *Archives of General Psychiatry*, 1980, *37*, 619–626.

Goldfarb, W. Self-awareness in schizophenic children. *Archives of General Psychiatry*, 1963, *8*, 47–60.

Goldfried, M. R. Psychotherapy as coping skills training. In M. J. Mahoney, ed., *Psychotherapy process: Current issues and future directions*. New York: Plenum, 1980.

Goldgaber, D., M. I. Lerman, et al. Characterization and chromosomal localization of a cDNA encoding brain amyloid of Alzheimer's disease. *Science*, 1987, *235*(4), p. 877.

Goldsmith, J. B., and **R. M. McFall.** Development and evaluation of an interpersonal skill-training program for psychiatric patients. *Journal of Abnormal Psychology*. 1975, *83*, 51–58.

Goldstein, A. Opioid peptides (endorphins) in pituitary and brain. *Science*, 1976, *193*, 1081–1086.

Goldstein, K. *Aftereffects of brain injuries in war: Their evaluation and treatment*. New York: Grune & Stratton 1948.

Goldstein, M., D. Mahanand, J. Lee, et al. Dopamine-β-hydroxylase and endogenous total 5-hydroxindole levels in autistic patients and controls. In M. Coleman, ed., *The autistic syndrome.* Amsterdam: North-Holland, 1976, 57–63.

Goleman, D. To expert eyes, city streets are open mental wards. *The New York Times,* November 4, 1986a, c1, c3.

Goleman, D. For mentally ill on the street, a new approach shines. *The New York Times,* November 11, 1986b, c1, c3.

Golin, S., P. D. Sweeny, and **D. E. Shaeffer.** The causality of causal attributions in depression: A cross-lagged panel correlation analysis. *Journal of Abnormal Psychology,* 1981, *90,* 14–22.

Gomberg, E. S. L. Women, sex roles, and alcohol problems. *Professional Psychology,* 1981, *12*(1), 146–155.

Goodwin, D. W., F. Schuisinger, L. Hermansen, S. B. Guze, and **G. Winokur.** Alcohol problems in adoptees raised apart from alcoholic biological parents. *Archives of General Psychiatry,* 1973, *28,* 238–243.

Gorenstein, E. E. Frontal lobe functions in psychopaths. *Journal of Abnormal Psychology,* 1982, *91,* 368–379.

Gorenstein, E. E., and **J. P. Newman.** Disinhibitory psychopathology: A new perspective and a model for research. *Psychological Review,* 1980, *87,* 301–315.

Gotlib, I. H. and **L. A. Robinson.** Responses to depressed individuals: Discrepancies between self-report and observer rated behavior. *Journal of Abnormal Psychology,* 1982, *91,* 231–240.

Gottesman, I. I. Schizophrenia and genetics: Where are we? Are you sure? In L. C. Wynne, R. L. Cromwell, and S. Matthysse, eds., *The nature of schizophrenia: New approaches to research and treatment.* New York: Wiley, 1978.

Gottesman, I., and **J. Shields.** A critical review of recent adoption, twin and family studies of schizophrenia: Behavioral genetics perspectives. *Schizophrenia Bulletin,* 1976, *2*(3), 360–398.

Gough, H. C. A sociological theory of psychopathy. *American Journal of Sociology,* 1948, *53,* 359–366.

Gove, W. R. The current status of the labelling theory of mental illness. In W. R. Gove, ed., *Deviance and mental illness.* Beverly Hills, Calif.: Sage Publications, 1982.

Graber, G. C., and **F. H. Marsh.** Ought a defendant be drugged to stand trial? *The Hastings Center Report,* 1979, *9,* 8–10.

Grabowski, J., M. L. Stitzer, and **J. E. Henningfield.** *Behavioral intervention techniques in drug abuse treatment.* Rockville, Md.: National Institute on Drug Abuse, 1984.

Grabowski, J., and **T. Thompson.** Development and maintenance of a behavior modification program for behaviorally retarded institutionalized men. In T. Thompson and J. Grabowski, eds.,

Behavior modification of the mentally retarded, 2nd ed. New York: Oxford University Press, 1977.

Graham, D. T. Health, disease, and the mind-body problem: Linguistic parallelism. *Psychosomatic Medicine,* 1967, *39,* 52–71.

Gray, J., and **R. S. Kempe.** The abused child at time of injury. In H. P. Martin, ed., *The abused child: A multidisciplinary approach to developmental issues and treatment.* Cambridge, Mass.: Ballinger, 1976, pp. 57–65.

Greaves, G. B. Multiple personality: 165 years after Mary Reynolds. *Journal of Nervous and Mental Disease,* 1980, *168,* 577–596.

Green, R. Guidelines to the management of the transsexual patient. *Roche Reports,* 1971, *11*(8), 3, 6.

Green, R. Sexual identity of 37 children raised by homosexual or transsexual parents. *American Journal of Psychiatry,* 1978, *135*(6), 692–697.

Green, R., J. Barclay Mandel, M. E. Hotvedt, J. Gray, and **L. Smith.** Lesbian mothers and their children: A comparison with solo parent heterosexual mothers and their children. *Archives of Sexual Behavior,* 1986, *15,* 167–184.

Greenblatt, M. Efficacy of ECT in affective and schizophrenic illness. *American Journal of Psychiatry,* 1977, *134,* 1001–1005.

Greenblatt, M., H. Freeman, E. Meshores, et. al. Comparative efficacy of anti-depressant drugs and placebo in relation to electric shock treatment. In M. Rinkel, ed., *Biological Treatment of Mental Illness.* New York: Page and Co., 1966.

Greene, L. R. Psychiatric day treatment as alternative to and transition from full time hospitalization. *Community Mental Health Journal,* 1981, *17,* 191–202.

Greene, S., M. J. Witkin, J. Atay, A. Fell, and **R. W. Manderscheid.** State and county mental hospitals, United States, 1982–83 and 1983–84, with trend analysis from 1973–74 to 1983–84. *Mental health statistical note No. 176.* DHHS Publication No. (ADM) 86–1478, 1986.

Greenspan, S., and **B. Shoultz.** Why mentally retarded adults lose their jobs: Social competence as a factor in work adjustment. *Applied Research in Mental Retardation,* 1981, *2,* 22–38.

Greer, S. Study of parental loss in neurotics and sociopaths. *Archives of General Psychiatry,* 1964, *11,* 177–180.

Gregory, I., and **E. Rosen.** *Abnormal psychology.* Philadelphia: W. B. Saunders, 1965.

Griffith, J. J., S. A. Mednick, F. Schulsinger, and **B. Diderichsen.** Verbal associative disturbances in children at high risk for schizophrenia. *Journal of Abnormal Psychology,* 1980, *89,* 125–131.

Grinspoon, L. *Marihuana reconsidered,* 2nd ed. Cambridge, Mass.: Harvard University Press, 1977.

Guggenheim, F. G., and **H. M. Babigian.** Catatonic schizophrenia—Epidemiology and clinical course—7-year register study of 798 cases. *The Journal of Nervous and Mental Disease,* 1974, *158*(4), 291–305.

Gunderson, J. G. Drugs and psychosocial treatment of schizophrenia revisited. *Journal of Continuing Education in Psychiatry,* 1977, 25–40.

Gunderson, J. G. *Borderline personality disorder.* Washington, D.C.: American Psychiatric Press, 1984.

Gunderson, J. G., J. H. Autry, L. R. Mosher, and **S. Birchsbaum.** Special report: Schizophrenia, 1973. *Schizophrenia Bulletin,* 1974, *2,* 15–54.

Gurin, G., J. Veroff, and **S. Feld.** *Americans view their mental health: A nationwide interview survey.* New York: Basic Books, 1960.

Gurland, B., L. Dean, P. Craw, and **R. Golden.** The epidemiology of depression and delirium in the elderly: The use of multiple indicators of these conditions. In J. O. Cole and J. E. Barrett, eds., *Psychopathology in the aged.* New York: Raven Press, 1980.

Gurman, A. S., and **D. P. Kniskern.** Research on marital and family therapy: Progress, perspective, and prospect. In S. L. Garfield and A. E. Bergin, eds., *Handbook of psychotherapy and behavior change: An empirical analysis,* 2nd ed. New York: Wiley, 1978.

Gurman, A. S., D. P. Kniskern, and **W. M. Pinsof.** Research on the process and outcome of marital and family therapy. In S. L. Garfield and A. E. Bergin, eds., *Handbook of psychotherapy and behavior change: An evaluative analysis,* 3rd ed. New York: Wiley, 1986.

Gustavson, C. R., J. Garcia, W. G. Hankins, and **K. W. Rusiniak.** Coyote predation control by aversion conditioning. *Science,* 1974, *184,* 581–583.

Gutmann, M. C., and **H. Benson.** Interaction of environmental factors and systemic arterial blood pressure: A review. *Medicine,* 1971, *50,* 543–553.

Haier, R., D. Rosenthal, and **P. H. Wender.** MMPI Assessment of psychopathology in the adopted-away offspring of schizophrenics. *Archives of General Psychiatry,* 1978, *35,* 171–175.

Haley, J. *Strategies of psychotherapy.* New York: Grune & Stratton, 1963.

Hall, H. H. Hypnosis and the immune system: A review with implications for cancer and the psychology of healing. *American Journal of Clinical Hypnosis,* 1983, *25,* 92–103.

Halmi, K. A. Anorexia nervosa: Demographic and clinical features in 94 cases. *Journal of Psychosomatic Medicine*, 1974, *36*, 18–25.

Halperin, D. A. Psychodynamic strategies with outpatients. In L. D. Hankoff and B. Einsidler, eds., *Suicide: Theory and clinical aspects*. Littleton, Mass.: PSG Publishing, 1979.

Halpern, A. General unemployment and vocational opportunities for EMR individuals. *American Journal of Mental Deficiency*, 1973, *78*, 123–127.

Hamburger, C. The desire for change of sex. *Acta Endocrinologica*, 1953, *14*, 361–375.

Hammen, C., and R. de Mayo. Cognitive correlates of teacher stress and depressive symptoms: Implications for attributional models of depression. *Journal of Abnormal Psychology*, 1982, *91*, 96–101.

Hammen, C., T. Marks, A. Mayol, and R. de Mayo. Depressive self-schemas, life stress, and vulnerability to depression. *Journal of Abnormal Psychology*, 1985, *94*, 308–319.

Hanley, H. G., S. M. Stahl, and D. X. Freedman. Hyperserotonemia and amine metabolites in autistic and retarded children. *Archives of General Psychiatry*, 1977, *34*, 521–531.

Hanson, D. R., I. I. Gottesman, and L. L. Heston. Some possible childhood indicators of adult schizophrenia inferred from children of schizophrenics. *British Journal of Psychiatry*, 1976, *129*, 142–154.

Haracz, J. L. The dopamine hypothesis: An overview of studies with schizophrenic patients. *Schizophrenia Bulletin*, 1982, *8*, 438–469.

Hare, R. D. *Psychopathy: Theory and research*. New York: Wiley, 1970.

Harlage, S., K. Howard, and E. Ostrov. The mental health professional and the normal adolescent. In D. Offer, E. Ostrov, and K. I. Howard, eds., *Patterns of adolescent self-image*. New York: Jossey-Bass, 1984.

Harlow, H. F. Early social deprivation and later behavior in the monkey. In H. H. Garner and J. E. P. Toman, eds., *Unfinished tasks in the behavioral sciences*. Baltimore, Md.: Williams and Wilkins, 1964.

Harlow, J. Recovery from the passage of an iron bar through the head. *Publication of the Massachusetts Medical Society*, 1868, *2*, 327–340.

Harris, S. E. Schizophrenics' mutual glance patterns. *Dissertation Abstracts*, 1968, *29B*, 2202.

Harrow, M., and L. S. Grossman. Outcome in schizoaffective disorders: A critical review and reevaluation of the literature. *Schizophrenia Bulletin*, 1984, *10*, 87–108.

Harrow, M., L. S. Grossman, M. L. Silverstein, H. Y. Meltzer, and R. L. Kettering. A longitudinal study of

thought disorder in manic patients. *Archives of General Psychiatry*, 1986, *43*, 781–785.

Hartmann, H. *Ego psychology and the problem of adaptation*. New York: International Universities Press, 1939.

Hartogs, R. Discipline in the early life of sex-delinquents and sex-criminals. *New Child*, 1951, *9*, 167–173.

Hassan, S. A. Transactional and contextual invalidation between the parents of disturbed families: A comparative study. *Family Process*, 1974, *13*, 53–76.

Hathaway, S. R., and J. C. McKinley. A multiphasic personality schedule (Minnesota): 1. Construction of the schedule. *Journal of Psychology*, 1940, *10*, 249–254.

Hathaway, S. R., and J. C. McKinley. *Minnesota Multiphasic Personality Inventory: Manual*. New York: The Psychological Corporation, 1943.

Havelkova, M. Follow-up study of 71 children diagnosed as psychotic in pre-school age. *American Journal of Orthopsychiatry*, 1968, *38*, 846–857.

Havighurst, R. J. Suicide and education. In E. S. Shneidman, ed., *On the nature of suicide*. San Francisco: Jossey-Bass, 1969.

Haynes, S. N. Muscle-contraction headache: A psychophysiological perspective of etiology and treatment. In S. N. Haynes and L. Gannon, eds., *Psychosomatic disorders: A psychophysiological approach to etiology and treatment*. New York: Praeger Publishers, 1981.

Hebb, D. O. The effects of early experience on problem solving at maturity. *American Psychologist*, 1947, *2*, 306–307.

Hécaen, H., and M. C. Albert. *Human neuropsychology*. New York: Wiley, 1978.

Hedlund, J. L. MMPI clinical scale correlates. *Journal of Consulting and Clinical Psychology*, 1977, *45*, 739–750.

Heim, N. Sexual behavior of castrated sex offenders. *Archives of Sexual Behavior*, 1981, *10*, 11–19.

Heim, N., and C. J. Hursch. Castration for sex offenders: Treatment or punishment? A review and critique of recent European literature. *Archives of Sexual Behavior*, 1979 8(3), 281–304.

Heiman, J. R., L. LoPiccolo, and J. LoPiccolo. The treatment of sexual dysfunction. In A. Gurma and D. Kniskern, eds., *Handbook of family therapy*. New York: Brunner/Mazel, 1981.

Helzer, J. E., I. F. Brockington, and R. E. Kendell. Predictive validity of DSM III and Feigner definitions of schizophrenia. *Archives of General Psychiatry*, 1981, *38*, 791–797.

Henderson, D., and R. D. Gillespie. *Textbook of psychiatry for students and practitioners*, Ivor R. C. Batchelor, ed. London and New York: Oxford University Press, 1969.

Hendryx, M., and R. R. Bootzin. Psychiatric episodes in general hospitals without psychiatric units. *Hospital and Community Psychiatry*, 1986, *37*, 1025–1029.

Henn, F. A., R. Bardwell, and R. L. Jenkins. Juvenile delinquents revisited: Adult criminal activity. *American Journal of Psychiatry*, 1980, *37*, 1160–1163.

Herd, J. A., R. T. Kelleher, W. H. Morse, and S. A. Grose. Sympathetic and parasympathetic activity during behavioral hypertension in the squirrel monkey. In P. A. Obrist, A. H. Black, J. Brener, and L. V. Di Cara, eds., *Cardiovascular psychophysiology*, Chicago: Aldine, 1974.

Herman, C. P., and D. Mack. Restrained and unrestrained eating. *Journal of Personality*, 1975, *43*, 647–660.

Herman, C. P., and J. Polivy. Anxiety, restraint and eating behavior. *Journal of Abnormal Psychology*, 1975, *84*, 666–672.

Hermelin, B., and N. O'Connor. *Psychological experiments with autistic children*. Oxford: Pergamon Press, 1970.

Hersen, M., and D. H. Barlow. *Single case experimental designs: Strategies for studying behavior change*. New York: Pergamon Press, 1976.

Hersen, M., S. M. Turner, B. A. Edelstein, and S. G. Pinkston. Effects of phenothiazines and social skills training in a withdrawn schizophrenic. *Journal of Clinical Psychology*, 1975, *31*, 588–594.

Heston, L. L. Psychiatric disorders in foster home reared children of schizophrenic mothers. *British Journal of Psychiatry*, 1966, *112*, 819–825.

Hibscher, J. A., and C. P. Herman. Obesity, dieting, and the expression of "obese" characteristics. *Journal of Comparative and Physiological Psychology*, 1977, *91*, 374–380.

Hill, R. B., and F. Kern. *The gastrointestinal tract*. Baltimore: Williams and Wilkins Co., 1977.

Hintgen, J. N., and S. K. Coulter. Auditory control of operant behaviour in mute autistic children. *Perceptual and Motor Skills*, 1967, *25*, 561–565.

Hiroto, D. J. and M. E. P. Seligman. Generality of learned helplessness in man. *Journal of Personality and Social Psychology*, 1975, *31*, 311–327.

Hirsch, S. R., C. Walsh, and R. Draper. Parasuicide: A review of treatment intervention. *Journal of Affective Disorders*, 1982, *4*, 299–311.

Hirschfeld, R. M. A., and C. K. Cross. Epidemiology of affective disorders: Psychosocial risk factors. *Archives of General Psychiatry*, 1982, *39*, 35–46.

Ho, B. T., D. W. Richard, and D. L. Chute, eds., *Drug Discrimination and State Dependent Learning*. New York: Academic Press, 1978.

Hodgson, R. J. The alcohol dependence

syndrome: A step in the wrong direction? *British Journal of Addiction*, 1980, *75*, 255–263.

Hoehn-Saric, R. Neurotransmitters in anxiety. *Archives of General Psychiatry*, 1982, *39*, 735–742.

Hoffer, A., and H. Osmond. The relationship between mood and time perception. *Psychiatric Quarterly Supplement*, 1962, *36*, 87–92.

Hoffman, A. LSD discoverer disputes "chance" factor in finding. *Psychiatric News*, 1971, *6*(8), 23–26.

Hogan, D. R. The effectiveness of sex therapy: A review of the literature. In J. LoPiccolo and L. LoPiccolo, eds., *Handbook of sex therapy*. New York: Plenum, 1978.

Hogan, R. A. The implosive technique. *Behavior Research and Therapy*, 1968, *6*, 423–431.

Hogarty, G. E. Treatment and the course of schizophrenia. *Schizophrenia Bulletin*, 1977, *3*, 587–599.

Hogarty, G. E., C. M. Anderson, D. J. Reiss, S. J. Kornblith, D. P. Greenwald, C. D. Javna, and M. J. Madonia. Family psychoeducation, social skills training, and maintenance chemotherapy in the aftercare treatment of schizophrenia: I. One-year effects of a controlled study on relapse and expressed emotion. *Archives of General Psychiatry*, 1986, *43*, 633–642.

Holden, C. Nader on mental health centers: A movement that got bogged down. *Science*, 1972, *177*, 413–415.

Holland, J. G. Behaviorism: Part of the problem or part of the solution? *Journal of Applied Behavior Analysis*, 1978, *11*, 163–174.

Hollingshead, A. B., and F. C. Redlich. *Social class and mental illness*. New York: Wiley, 1958.

Hollon, S. D., and A. T. Beck. Cognitive and cognitive behavioral therapies. In S. L. Garfield and A. E. Bergin, eds., *Handbook of psychotherapy and behavior change: An evaluative analysis*, 3rd ed. New York: Wiley, 1986.

Holmes, T. H., and R. H. Rahe. The social readjustment rating scale. *Journal of Psychosomatic Research*, 1967, *11*, 213–218.

Holmes, T. S., and T. H. Holmes. Short-term intrusions into the life style routine. *Journal of Psychosomatic Research*, 1970, *14*, 121–132.

Holtzman, W. H., and S. B. Sells. Prediction of flying success by clinical analysis of test protocols. *Journal of Abnormal and Social Psychology*, 1954, *49*, 485–490.

Hooker, E. The adjustment of the male overt homosexual. *Journal of Projective Techniques*, 1957, *21*(1), 18–31.

Horgan, C. M. Specialty and general ambulatory mental health services. *Archives*

of *General Psychiatry*, 1985, *42*, 565–572.

Horne, R. L., M. M. Pettinati, A. Sugerman, and E. Varga. Comparing bilateral to unilateral electroconvulsive therapy in a randomized study of EEG monitoring. *Archives of General Psychiatry*, 1985, *42*, 1087–1092.

Horney, K. *The neurotic personality of our time*. New York: Norton, 1937.

Horney, K. *Our inner conflicts*. New York: Norton, 1945.

Horney, K. *Feminine psychology*. Harold Kelman, ed. New York: Norton, 1967.

Hospital and Community Psychiatry, 1976, *27*(7), 505.

Howard, K. I. The convergent and discriminant validation of ipsative ratings from three projective instruments. *Journal of Clinical Psychology*, 1962, *18*, 183–188.

Howard, K. I., S. M. Kopta, M. S. Krause, and D. E. Orlinsky. The dose–effect relationship in psychotherapy. *American Psychologist*, 1986, *41*, 159–164.

Hughes, J. R., and D. Hatsukami. Signs and symptoms of tobacco withdrawal. *Archives of General Psychiatry*, 1986, *43*, 289–294.

Hull, J. G., and C. F. Bond, Jr. Social and behavioral consequences of alcohol consumption and expectancy: A meta-analysis. *Psychological Bulletin*, 1986, *99*, 347–360.

Hunt, M. *Sexual behavior in the 1970's*. New York: Dell, 1974.

Hurley, A. D., and Hurley, F. J. Counseling and psychotherapy with mentally retarded clients I. The initial interview. *Psychiatric Aspects of Mental Retardation Reviews*, 1986, *5*, 22–26.

Hutchings, B., and S. A. Mednick. Registered criminality in the adoptive and biological parents of registered male criminal adoptees. In R. R. Fieve, D. Rosenthal, and H. Brill, eds., *Genetic research in psychiatry*. Baltimore: Johns Hopkins University Press, 1975.

Hutt, C., S. J. Hutt, D. Lee, and C. Ounsted. A behavioral and electroencephalographic study of autistic children. *Journal of Psychiatric Research*, 1965, *3*, 181–197.

Hypertension Detection and Follow-Up Program Cooperative Group. Five year findings of the Hypertension Detection and Follow-Up Program. I. Reduction in mortality of persons with high blood pressure, including mild hypertension. *Journal of the American Medical Association*, 1979, *242*, 2562–2571.

Insane on all counts. *Time*, July 5, 1982, 22.

Insel, T. R., T. Zahn, and D. L. Murphy. Obsessive-compulsive disorder: An anxiety disorder? In A. H. Tuma and

J. D. Maser, eds., *Anxiety and the anxiety disorders*. Hillsdale, N.J.: Erlbaum, 1985.

Institute of Medicine. *Sleeping pills, insomnia, and medical practice*. Washington, D.C.: National Academy of Sciences, 1979.

Institute of Medicine. *Marijuana and health*. Washington, D.C.: National Academy Press, 1982.

Isaacs, W., J. Thomas, and I. Goldiamond. Application of operant conditioning to reinstate verbal behavior in psychotics. *Journal of Speech and Hearing Disorders*, 1960, *25*, 8–12.

Israel, J. H., and W. F. LaFave, *Criminal procedure*, 2nd ed. St. Paul, Minn.: West, 1975.

Itil, T. M., Qualitative and quantitative EEG findings in schizophrenia. *Schizophrenia Bulletin*, 1977, *3*(1). 61–79.

Jackson, D. N., and S. Messick. Acquiescence and desirability as response determinants on the MMPI. *Education and Psychological Measurement*, 1961, *21*, 771–790.

Jacobs, P. A., M. Brunton, and M. M. Melville. Aggressive behavior, mental subnormality, and the XYY male. *Nature*, 1965, *208*, 1351–1352.

Jacobs, T. J., and E. Charles. Life events and the occurence of cancer in children. *Psychosomatic Medicine*, 1980, *42*, 11–24.

Jacobson E. *Progressive relaxation*. Chicago: University of Chicago Press, 1938.

Jacobson, N. S. Behavioral treatments for marital discord: A critical appraisal. In M. Hersen, R. R. Eisler, and P. M. Miller, eds., *Progress in behavior modification*, Vol. 8. New York: Academic Press, 1979.

Jacobson, N. S., and G. Margolin. *Marital therapy: Strategies based on social learning and behavior exchange principles*. New York: Brunner/Mazel, 1979.

James, W. E., R. B. Mefford, and I. Kimbell. Early signs of Huntington's chorea. *Diseases of the Nervous System*, 1969, *30*, 556–559.

Jampala, V. C., F. S. Sierles, and M. A. Taylor. Consumers' views of DSM III: Attitudes and practices of U.S. psychiatrists and 1984 graduating psychiatric residents. *American Journal of Psychiatry*, 1986, *143*, 148–153.

Janes, C. L., and R. M. Hesselbrock. Problem children's adult adjustment predicted from teachers' ratings. *American Journal of Orthopsychiatry*, 1978, *48*, 300–309.

Jarvik, L. F., V. Klodin, and S. S. Matsuyama. Human aggression and the extra Y chromosome: Fact or fantasy? *American Psychologist*, 1973, *28*(8), 674–682.

Jellinek, E. M. *Phases in the drinking his-*

tory of alcoholics. New Haven, Conn.: Hillhouse Press, 1946.

Jemmott, J. B., III, and **S. E. Locke.** Psychosocial factors, immunologic mediation, and human susceptibility to infectious disease: How much do we know? *Psychological Bulletin,* 1984, *95,* 78–108.

Johannsen, W. J., S. H. Friedman, T. H. Leitschuk, and **H. Ammons.** A study of certain schizophrenic dimensions and their relationship to double alternation learning. *Journal of Consulting Psychology,* 1963, *27,* 375–382.

John, R. S., S. A. Mednick, and **F. Schulsinger.** Teacher reports as a predictor of schizophrenia and borderline schizophrenia: A Bayesian decision analysis. *Journal of Abnormal Psychology,* 1982, *91,* 399–413.

Johnson, J. E., and **T. P. Petzel.** Temporal orientation and time estimation in chronic schizophrenics. *Journal of Clinical Psychology,* 1971, *27*(2), 194–196.

Johnson, S. M., G. Wahl, S. Martin, and **S. Johansson.** How deviant is the normal child? A behavioral analysis of the preschool child and his family. In R. D. Rubin, J. P. Brady and J. D. Henderson, eds., *Advances in Behavior Therapy,* Vol. 4. New York: Academic Press, 1973.

Johnson, W. *Stuttering in children and adults.* Minneapolis: University of Minnesota Press, 1955.

Johnston, L. D., P. M. O'Malley, and **J. G. Bachman.** *Drugs and American high school students, 1975–1983.* Rockville, Md.: National Institute on Drug Abuse, 1984.

Johnstone, E. C., T. J. Crow, C. D. Frith, et al. Cerebral ventricular size and cognitive impairment in chronic schizophrenia. *Lancet,* 1976, *2,* 924–926.

Jones, D. R., and **D. A. Dowd.** Development of elevated blood pressure in young genetically hypertensive rats. *Life Sciences,* 1970, *9,* 247–250.

Jones, E. Rationalization in Everyday Life. In *Papers on Psychoanalysis.* New York: Wood and Co., 1963.

Jones, E. E., and **S. Berglas.** Control of attributions about the self through self-handicapping strategies: The appeal of alcohol and the role of unachievement. *Personality and Social Psychology Bulletin,* 1978, *4,* 200–206.

Jones, M. *The therapeutic community: A new treatment method in psychiatry.* New York: Basic Books, 1953.

Jones, M. *Maturation of the therapeutic community.* New York: Human Sciences Press, 1978.

Jones, M. C. A laboratory study of fear: The case of Peter. *Pedagogical Seminary,* 1924, *31,* 308–315.

Jones, M. M. Conversion reaction: Anachronism or evolutionary form? A review of the neurologic, behavioral, and psychoanalytic literature. *Psychological Bulletin,* 1980, *87,* 427–441.

Jung, C. G. Fundamental psychological conceptions. In Mary Barker and Margaret Game, eds., *A Report of Five Lectures.* London: Institute of Medical Psychology, 1935.

Kaffman, M., and **E. Elizur.** *Infants who become enuretics: A longitudinal study of 161 kibbutz children.* Monographs of the Society for Research in Child Development, 1977, *42*(2).

Kahn, E. Heinz Kohut and Carl Rogers: A timely comparison. *American Psychologist,* 1985, *40,* 893–904.

Kahn, M. W., M. Hannah, C. Hinkin, C. Montgomery, and **D. Pitz.** Psychopathology on the streets: Psychological assessment of the homeless. *Professional Psychology* (in press).

Kahn, R. L. Stress: From 9 to 5. *Psychology Today,* 1969, *3*(4), 34–38.

Kales, A., M. J. Paulson, A. Jacobson, and **J. Kales.** Somnambulism: Psychophysiological correlates. *Archives of General Psychiatry,* 1966, *14,* 450–457.

Kallmann, F. J. Twin and sibship study of overt male homosexuality. *American Journal of Human Genetics,* 1952, *4,* 136–146.

Kalsheek, W. D. The national head and spinal cord injury survey: Major findings. *Journal of Neurosurgery* (suppl.), 1980, *53,* 19–31.

Kaminski, M., C. Rumbau, and **D. Schwartz.** Alcohol consumption in pregnant women and the outcome of pregnancy. *Alcoholism: Clinical and Experimental Research,* 1978, *2*(2), 155.

Kandel, D. Adolescent marihuana use: Role of parents and peers. *Science,* 1973, *181,* 1067–1069.

Kandel, D. B., M. Davies, D. Karus, and **K. Yamaguchi.** The consequences in young adulthood of adolescent drug involvement. *Archives of General Psychiatry,* 1986, *43,* 746–754.

Kandel, E. R. From metapsychology to molecular biology: Explorations into the nature of anxiety. *American Journal of Psychiatry,* 1983, *140,* 1277–1293.

Kanfer, F. H., and **S. M. Hagerman.** Behavior therapy and the information-processing paradigm. In S. Reiss and R. R. Bootzin, eds., *Theoretical Issues in Behavior Therapy.* New York: Academic Press, 1985.

Kanfer, F. H., and **J. S. Phillips.** *Learning foundations of behavior therapy.* New York: Wiley, 1970.

Kanin, E. J. Date rapists: Differential sexual socialization and relative deprivation. *Archives of Sexual Behavior,* 1985, *14,* 219–231.

Kannel, W. B., M. J. Schwartz, and **P. M. McNamara.** Blood pressure risk of coronary heart disease: The Framingham study. *Diseases of the Chest,* 1968, *56,* 43.

Kanner, L. Autistic disturbances of effective content. *Nervous Child,* 1943, *2,* 217–240.

Kanner, L. The children haven't read those books: Reflections on differential diagnosis. *Acta Paedopsychiatrica,* 1969, *36*(1), 2–11.

Kanner, L., and **L. Eisenberg.** Notes on the follow-up studies of autistic children. In P. Hoch and J. Zubin, eds., *Psychopathology of childhood.* New York: Grune & Stratton, 1955.

Kantor, R. E., J. M. Wallner, and **C. L. Winder.** Process and reactive schizophrenia. *Journal of Consulting Psychology,* 1953, *17,* 157–162.

Kaplan, B., ed. *The inner world of mental illness.* New York: Harper & Row, 1964.

Kaplan, H. S. *The new sex therapy: Active treatment of sexual dysfunctions.* New York. A Brunner/Mazel Publication published in cooperation with Quadrangle/ The New York Times Book Co., 1974.

Kaplan, H. S. Hypoactive sexual desire. *Journal of Sex and Marital Therapy,* 1977, *3,* 3–9.

Kaplan, R. E. The dynamics of injury in encounter groups: Power, splitting, and the mismanagement of resistance. *International Journal of Group Psychotherapy,* 1982, *32,* 163–187.

Kaufman, B. Reaching the "unreachable" child. *New York,* Feb. 3, 1975, pp. 43–49.

Kaul, T. J., and **R. L. Bednar.** Experiential group research: Results, questions, and suggestions. In S. L. Garfield and A. E. Bergin, eds., *Handbook of psychotherapy and behavior change: An evaluative analysis,* 3rd ed. New York: Wiley, 1986.

Kayne, N. T., L. B. Alloy, D. Romer, and **J. Crocker.** Predicting depression and elation reactions in the classroom: A test of an attributional diathesis-stress theory of depression. *Journal of Abnormal Psychology.* In press.

Kazdin, A. E. *The token economy: A review and evaluation.* New York: Plenum Press, 1977.

Kazdin, A. E. *History of behavior modification: Experimental foundations of contemporary research.* Baltimore: University Park Press, 1978a.

Kazdin, A. E. Methodological and interpretive problems of single-case experimental designs. *Journal of Consulting and Clinical Psychology,* 1978b, *46,* 629–642.

Kazdin, A. E. *Research design in clinical psychology.* New York: Harper & Row, 1980.

Kazdin, A. E. The token economy: A decade later. *Journal of Applied Behavior Analysis,* 1982, *15,* 431–446.

Kazdin, A. E., ed. Special issue: Psychotherapy research. *Journal of Consulting and Clinical Psychology,* 1986, *54,* 1–118.

Kazdin, A. E., and **R. R. Bootzin.** The token economy: An evaluative review. *Journal of Applied Behavior Analysis,* 1972, *5,* 343–372.

Kazdin, A. E., J. L. Matson, and **M. S. W. Senatore.** Assessment of depression in mentally retarded adults. *American Journal of Psychiatry,* 1983, *140,* 1040–1043.

Kazdin, A. E., and **T. Rogers.** On paradigms and recycled ideologies: Analogue research revisited. *Cognitive Therapy and Research,* 1978, *2,* 105–117.

Kazdin, A. E., and **G. T. Wilson.** *Evaluation of behavior therapy: Issues, evidence and research strategies.* Cambridge, Mass.: Ballinger, 1978.

Keith, P. R. Night terrors: A review of the psychology, neurology and therapy. *Journal of the American Academy of Child Psychiatry,* 1975, *14*(3), 477–489.

Keith-Spiegel, P., and **D. Spiegel.** Affective states of patients immediately preceding suicide. *Journal of Psychiatric Research,* 1967, *5,* 89–93.

Kelley, M. L., and **T. F. Stokes.** Contingency contracting with disadvantaged youths: Improving classroom performance. *Journal of Applied Behavior Analysis,* 1982, *15,* 447–454.

Kelly, J. A., and **R. S. Drabman.** The modification of socially detrimental behavior. *Journal of Behavior Therapy and Experimental Psychiatry,* 1977, *8,* 101–104.

Kemble, J. *Idols and invalids.* New York: Doubleday, 1936.

Kendall, P. C., and **S. D. Hollon, eds.** *Cognitive-behavioral interventions: Theory, research, and procedures.* New York: Academic Press, 1979.

Kendall, P. C., and **S. D. Hollon, eds.** *Assessment strategies for cognitive-behavioral interventions.* New York: Academic Press, 1981.

Kendell, R. E. *The classification of depressive illnesses.* New York: Oxford University Press, 1968.

Kendler, K. S., and **K. L. Davis.** The genetics and biochemistry of paranoid schizophrenia and other paranoid psychoses. *Schizophrenia Bulletin,* 1981, *7,* 689–709.

Kernberg, O. F. *Borderline conditions and pathological narcissism.* New York: Jason Aronson, 1975.

Kernberg, P. F. Childhood schizophrenia and autism: A selective review. In Leopold Bellak, ed., *Disorders of the schizophrenic syndrome.* New York: Basic Books, 1979.

Kerr, S. H., and **E. B. Cooper.** Phonatory adjustment times in stutterers and non-stutterers. Unpublished manuscript, 1976.

Kessler, S. The genetics of schizophrenia: A review. In *Special report:* Schizophrenia 1980, *Schizophrenia Bulletin,* 1980, 14–26.

Kety, S. S., D. Rosenthal, P. H. Wender, and **F. Schulsinger.** The types and prevalence of mental illness in the biological and adoptive families of adopted schizophrenics. In D. Rosenthal and S. S. Kety, eds., *The transmission of schizophrenia.* Oxford: Pergamon Press, 1968.

Kety, S. S., D. Rosenthal, P. H. Wender, and **F. Schulsinger.** Mental illness in the biological and adoptive families of adopted schizophrenics. *American Journal of Psychiatry,* 1971, *128,* 302–306.

Kety, S. S., D. Rosenthal, P. H. Wender, F. Schulsinger, and **B. Jacobsen.** Mental illness in the biological and adoptive families of adopted individuals who have become schizophrenic: A preliminary report based upon psychiatric interviews. In R. Fieve, D. Rosenthal, and H. Brill, eds., *Genetic research in psychiatry.* Baltimore: Johns Hopkins University Press, 1975.

Kety, S. S., D. Rosenthal, P. H. Wender, F. Schulsinger, and **B. Jacobsen.** The biologic and adoptive families of adopted individuals who became schizophrenic: Prevalence of mental illness and other characteristics. In L. C. Wynne, R. L. Cromwell, and S. Matthysse, eds., *The nature of schizophrenia.* New York: Wiley, 1978.

Keyes D. *The minds of Billy Milligan.* New York: Random House, 1981.

Kiesler, C. A. Mental hospitals and alternative care. *American Psychologist,* 1982a, *37,* 349–360.

Kiesler, C. A. Public and professional myths about mental hospitalization. *American Psychologist,* 1982b, *37,* 1323–1339.

Kihlstrom, J. F., and **W. Nasby.** Cognitive tasks in clinical assessment: An exercise in applied psychology. In P. C. Kendall and S. D. Hollon, eds., *Assessment strategies for cognitive-behavioral interventions.* New York: Academic Press, 1981.

Kinsey, A. C., W. B. Pomeroy, and **C. E. Martin.** *Sexual behavior in the human male.* Philadelphia: Saunders, 1948.

Kinsey, A. C., W. B. Pomeroy, C. E. Martin, and **P. H. Gebhard.** *Sexual behavior in the human female.* Philadelphia: W. B. Saunders, 1953.

Kipper, D. A. Behavior simulation interventions in group psychotherapy. In G. M. Gazda, ed., *Innovations to group psychotherapy,* 2nd. ed. Springfield, Ill.: Charles C. Thomas, 1981.

Kirigin, K., C. J. Braukmann, J. D. Atwater, and **M. M. Wolf.** An evaluation of teaching-family (Achievement Place) group homes for juvenile offenders. *Journal of Applied Behavior Analysis,* 1982, *15,* 1–16.

Kirk, S. A. Behavioral prognosis and remediation of learning disabilities. *Proceedings, Conference on Exploration into the Problems of the Perceptually Handicapped Child, First Annual Meeting.* Vol. 1. Chicago, April 6, 1963.

Kirkegaard-Sörensen, L., and **S. A. Mednick.** Registered criminality in families with children at high risk for schizophrenia. *Journal of Abnormal Psychology,* 1975, *84,* 197–204.

Klajner, R., C. P. Herman, J. Polivy, and **R. Chhabra.** Human obesity, dieting, and anticipatory salivation. *Physiology and Behavior,* 1981, *27,* 195–198.

Klein, D. F. Psychopharmacology and the borderline patient. In J. Mack, ed., *Borderline states in psychiatry.* New York: Grune & Stratton, 1975.

Kleist, K. Schizophrenic symptoms and cerebral pathology. *Journal of Mental Science,* 1960, *106,* 246–253.

Klerman, G. I. Drugs and psychotherapy. In S. L. Garfield and A. E. Bergin, eds., *Handbook of psychotherapy and behavior change: An evaluative analysis,* 3rd ed. New York: Wiley, 1986.

Klerman, G. L., B. Rounsaville, E. Chevron, G. Neu, and **W. M. Weissman.** *Manual for short-term interpersonal psychotherapy (IPT) of depression.* Unpublished manuscript. New Haven, CT: Yale University, 1979.

Klonoff, H. Marijuana and driving in real-life situations. *Science,* 1974, *186,* 317–323.

Knopf, I. J. *Childhood psychopathology: A developmental approach.* Englewood Cliffs, N.J.: Prentice-Hall, 1984.

Koch, R. Prenatal factors in causation (general). In R. Koch and J. C. Dobson, eds., *The mentally retarded child and his family.* New York: Brunner/Mazel, 1971.

Koegel, R. L., and **A. Rincover.** Treatment of psychotic children in a classroom environment: I. Learning in a large group. *Journal of Applied Behavior Analysis,* 1974, *7,* 45–59.

Koegel, R. L., and **A. Rincover.** Research on the difference between generalization and maintenance in extra-therapy responding. *Journal of Applied Behavior Analysis,* 1977, *10,* 1–12.

Koestler, A. *The ghost in the machine.* New York: Macmillan, 1968.

Kohen, W., and **G. L. Paul.** Current trends and recommended changes in extended-care placement of mental patients: The Illinois system as a case in point. *Schizophrenia Bulletin,* 1976, *2,* 575–594.

Kohen-Raz, R. Mental and motor development of kibbutz, institutionalized, and home-reared infants in Israel. *Child Development,* 1968, *39,* 489–504.

Kohut, H. Forms and transformations of narcissism. *Journal of the American Psychoanalytic Association,* 1966, *14,* 243–272.

Kohut, H. *The analysis of the self.* New York: International Universities Press, 1971.

Kohut, H. Thoughts on narcissism and narcissistic rage. *Psychoanalytic Study of the Child,* 1972, *27,* 360–400.

Kohut, H. *The restoration of the self.* New York: International Universities Press, 1977.

Kohut, H., and **E. S. Wolf.** The disorders of the self and their treatment: An outline. *International Journal of Psychoanalysis,* 1978, 59, 413–425.

Kolata, G. B. Childhood hyperactivity: A new look at treatments and causes. *Science,* 1978, *199,* 515–517.

Kolata, G. Manic depression: Is it inherited? *Science,* 1986a, *232,* 575–576.

Kolata, G. Researchers hunt for Alzheimer's disease gene. *Science,* 1986b, *232,* 448–450.

Kolb, L. C. *Modern clinical psychiatry,* 10th ed. Philadelphia: W. B. Saunders, 1982.

Kolodny, R. C., W. H. Masters, J. Hendryx, and **G. Toro.** Plasma testosterone and the semen analysis in male homosexuals. *New England Journal of Medicine,* 1971, *285,* 1170–1174.

Kolodny, R. C., W. H. Masters, R. M. Kolodner, and **T. Gelson.** Depression of plasma testosterone levels after chronic intensive marihuana use. *The New England Journal of Medicine,* 1974, *290*(16), 872–874.

Kolvin, I., C. Ounsted, M. Humphrey, and **A. McMay.** The phenomenology of childhood psychoses. *British Journal of Psychiatry,* 1971, *118,* 385–395.

Korsten, M. A., and **C. S. Lieber.** Medical complications of alcoholism. In J. H. Mendelson and N. K. Mello, eds., *The diagnosis and treatment of alcoholism.* New York: McGraw-Hill, 1985.

Kovacs, M., A. J. Rush, A. T. Beck, and **S. D. Hollon.** Depressed outpatients treated with cognitive therapy or pharmacotherapy. *Archives of General Psychiatry,* 1981, *38,* 33–39.

Kozal, N. J., R. A. Crider, M. D. Brodsky, and **E. H. Adams.** *Epidemiology of heroin: 1964–1984.* Rockville, Md.: National Institute on Drug Abuse, 1985.

Kozol, H., R. Boucher, and **R. Garofolo.** Diagnosis and treatment of dangerousness. *Crime and Delinquency,* 1972, *18,* 371–392.

Kraepelin, E. *Clinical psychiatry: A textbook for physicians.* A. Diffendorf, tr. New York: Macmillan, 1902.

Kraepelin, E. *Textbook of psychiatry* (1883). New York: Macmillan, 1923.

Krafft-Ebing, R. von *Psychopathia sexualis* (1886), F. S. Klaf, tr. New York: Bell, 1965.

Kraft, D. P., and **H. Babigian.** Somatic delusion or self-mutilation in a schizophrenic woman: A psychiatric emergency room case report. *American Journal of Psychiatry,* 1972, *128*(7), 127–129.

Kraines, S. H. Manic-depressive syndrome: A physiologic disease. *Diseases of the Nervous System,* 1966, *27,* 573–582.

Kramer, J. R. The right not to be mentally retarded. In M. Kindred, J. Cohen, D. Penrod, and T. Shaffer, eds., *The mentally retarded citizen and the law: President's Committee on Mental Retardation.* New York: Free Press, 1976.

Kramm, E. R. *Families of mongoloid children.* Washington, D.C.: U.S. Government Printing Office, 1963.

Krischef, C. H. State laws on marriage and sterilization. *Mental Retardation,* 1972, *10,* 29–38.

Kuiper, N. A., L. J. Olinger, and **M. R. MacDonald.** Depressive schemata and the processing of personal and social information. In L. B. Alloy, ed., *Cognitive processes in depression.* New York: Guilford Press, 1987.

Kupferman, I. Localization of higher functions. In E. R. Kandel and J. H. Schwartz, eds., *Principles of neuroscience.* New York: Elsevier/North Holland, 1981.

Kurland, L. T., S. N. Faro, and **H. Siedler.** Minamata disease. The outbreak of neurologic disorder in Minamata, Japan, and its relationship to the ingestion of seafood contaminated by mercuric compounds. *World Neurology,* 1960, *1,* 370–395.

Lacey, J. I. Psychophysiological approaches to the evaluation of psychotherapeutic process and outcome. In E. A. Rubinstein and M. B. Parloff, eds., *Research in psychotherapy.* Washington, D.C.: American Psychological Association, 1959.

Lacey, J. I., J. Kagan, B. C. Lacey, and **H. A. Moss.** The visceral level: Situational determinants and behavioral correlates of autonomic response patterns. In P. H. Knapp, ed., *Expression of the emotions in man.* New York: International Universities Press, 1963.

LaFave, W. F., and **A. Scott.** *Criminal law.* St. Paul, Minn.: West, 1972.

Laing, R. D. Is schizophrenia a disease? *International Journal of Social Psychiatry,* 1964, *10,* 184–193.

Laing, R. D. Mystification, confusion and conflict. In I. Boszormenyi-Nagy and J. L. Framo, eds., *Intensive family therapy.* New York: Hoeber Medical Division, Harper & Row, 1965.

Laing, R. D. *The politics of experience.* New York: Pantheon, 1967.

Laing, R. D. Round the bend. *New Statesman,* July 20, 1979.

Lamb, H. R., A. P. Sorkin, and **J. Zusman.** Legislating social control of the mentally ill in California. *American Journal of Psychiatry,* 1981, *138*(3), 334–339.

Lambert, M. J., D. A. Shapiro, and **A. E. Bergin.** The effectiveness of psychotherapy. In S. L. Garfield and A. E. Bergin, eds., *Handbook of psychotherapy and behavior change: An evaluative analysis,* 3rd ed. New York: Wiley, 1986.

Lambert, M., S. de Julio, and **D. Stein.** Therapists interpersonal skills. *Psychological Bulletin,* 1978, *83,* 467–489.

Lambert, N. Psychological evidence in *Larry P. v. Wilson Riles:* An evaluation by a witness for the defense. *American Psychologist,* 1981, *36,* 937–952.

Lampert, P. W., and **J. M. Hardman.** Morphological changes in brains of boxers. *Journal of the American Medical Association,* 1984, *251,* 2676–2679.

Lang, A. R. Addictive personality: A viable construct? In P. K. Levison, D. R. Gerstein, and D. R. Maloff, eds., *Commonalities in substance abuse and habitual behavior.* Lexington, Mass.: Lexington Books, 1983, 157–235.

Lang, P. J. Stimulus control, response control, and desensitization of fear. In D. Levis, ed., *Learning approaches to therapeutic behavior change.* Chicago: Aldine, 1970.

Lanyon, R. I. Theory and treatment in child molestation. *Journal of Counseling and Clinical Psychology,* 1986, *54,* 176–182.

Laudenslager, M. L., S. M. Ryan, R. C. Drugan, R. L. Hyson, and **S. F. Maier.** Coping and immunosuppression: Inescapable but not escapable shock suppresses lymphocyte proliferation. *Science,* 1983, *221,* 568–570.

Lazarus, A. A. Learning theory and the treatment of depression. *Behavior Research and Therapy,* 1968, *6,* 83–89.

Ledwidge, B. Cognitive behavior modification: A step in the wrong direction? *Psychological Bulletin,* 1978, *85,* 353–376.

Leff, J. P. Schizophrenia and sensitivity to the family environment. *Schizophrenia Bulletin,* 1976, *2*(4).

Lehmann, H. E. Psychopharmacological treatment of schizophrenia. *Schizophrenia Bulletin,* 1975, *13,* 27–45.

Lemere, F., and **W. Voegtlin.** An evaluation of the aversion treatment of alcoholism. *Quarterly Journal of Studies on Alcohol,* 1950, *11,* 199–204.

Lenneberg, E. H. *Biological foundations of language.* New York: Wiley, 1967.

Leon, G. R. Anxiety neurosis: The case of Richard Benson. *Case histories in deviant behavior,* 2nd ed. Boston: Holbrook Press, 1977.

Leonard, C. V. Depression and suicidality.

Journal of Consulting and Clinical Psychology, 1974, *42*, 98–104.

Le Shan, L. An emotional life-history pattern associated with neoplastic disease. *Annals of New York Academy of Sciences*, 1966, *125*, 780–793.

Le Shan, L. In E. M. Weyer, and H. Hutchins, eds., *Psychophysiological aspects of cancer*. New York: New York Academy of Sciences, 1966, pp. 780–793.

Lester, M. E., and W. J. Doherty. Couples' long-term evaluations of their marriage encounter experience. *Journal of Marital and Family Therapy*, 1983, *9*, 183–188.

Levis, D. J. Implosive theory: A comprehensive extension of conditioning theory of fear/anxiety to psychology. In S. Reiss and R. R. Bootzin, eds., *Theoretical issues in behavior therapy*. New York: Academic Press, 1985.

Levis, D. J., and N. Hare. A review of the theoretical rationale and empirical support for the extinction approach of implosive (flooding) therapy. In M. Hersen, R. M. Eisler and P. M. Miller, eds., *Progress in behavior modification*, Vol. 4. New York: Academic Press, 1977.

Levitt, E. E. Research on psychotherapy with children. In A. E. Bergin and S. L. Garfield, eds., *Handbook of psychotherapy and behavior change*. New York: Wiley, 1971.

Lewine, R. R. J. Sex differences in schizophrenia: Timing or subtypes? *Psychological Bulletin*, 1981, *90*, 432–444.

Lewinsohn, P. M. Clinical and theoretical aspects of depression. In K. S. Calhoun, H. E. Adams, and K. M. Mitchell, eds., *Innovative treatment methods of psychopathology*. New York: Wiley, 1974.

Lewinsohn, P. M., and M. Graf. Pleasant activities and depression. *Journal of Consulting and Clinical Psychology*, 1973, *41*, 261–268.

Lewinsohn, P. M., H. Hoberman, L. Teri, and M. Hautzinger. An integrative theory of depression. In S. Reiss and R. Bootzin, eds., *Theoretical issues in behavior therapy*. New York: Academic Press, 1985, pp. 331–359.

Lewinsohn, P. M., and J. Libet. Pleasant events, activity schedules, and depression. *Journal of Abnormal Psychology*, 1972, *79*, 291–295.

Lewinsohn, P. M., W. Mischel, W. Chaplin, and R. Barton. Social competence and depression: The role of illusory self-perceptions. *Journal of Abnormal Psychology*, 1980a, *89*, 203–212.

Lewinsohn, P. M., J. L. Steinmetz, D. W. Larson, and J. Franklin. Depression-related cognitions: Antecedent or consequence. *Journal of Abnormal Psychology*, 1981, *90*, 213–219.

Lewinsohn, P. M., J. M. Sullivan, and S. J. Grosscup. Changing reinforcing events: An approach to the treatment of depression. *Psychotherapy: Theory, Research, and Practice*, 1980b, *17*, 322–334.

Lewinsohn, P. M., M. A. Youngren, and S. J. Grosscup. Reinforcement and depression. In R. A. Depue, ed., *The psychobiology of the depressive disorders*. New York: Academic Press, 1979.

Lewis, J. M., E. H. Rodnick, and M. J. Goldstein. Intrafamilial interactive behavior, parental communication deviance, and risk for schizophrenia. *Journal of Abnormal Psychology*, 1981, *90*, 448–457.

Liberman, R. P. What is schizophrenia. *Schizophrenia Bulletin*, 1982a, *8*, 435–437.

Liberman, R. P. Assessment of social skills. *Schizophrenia Bulletin*, 1982b, *8*, 62–81.

Liberman, R. P., and T. Eckman. Behavior therapy vs. insight-oriented therapy for repeated suicide attemptors. *Archives of General Psychiatry*, 1981, *38*, 1126–1130.

Lidz, T. *The origin and treatment of schizophrenic disorders*. New York: Basic Books, 1973.

Lidz, T. Commentary on "A Critical review of recent adoption, twin, and family studies of schizophrenia: Behavioral genetics perspectives." *Schizophrenia Bulletin*, 1976, *2*(3), 402–412.

Lieberman, M. A., and G. R. Bond. Self-help groups: Problems of measuring outcome. *Small Group Behavior*, 1978, *9*, 222–241.

Lieberman, M. A., I. D. Yalom, and M. B. Miks. *Encounter groups: First facts*. New York: Basic Books, 1973.

Liebowitz, M. R., J. M. Gorman, A. J. Fyer, M. Levitt, D. Dillon, G. Levy, I. L. Appleby, S. Anderson, M. Palij, S. O. Davies, and D. F. Klein. Lactate provocation of panic attacks: II. Biochemical and physiological findings. *Archives of General Psychiatry*, 1985, *42*, 709–719.

Liem, J. H. Effects of verbal communications of parents and children: A comparison of normal and schizophrenic families. *Journal of Consulting and Clinical Psychology*, 1974, *42*(3), 438–450.

Lifton, R. J. On death and dying: The Hiroshima disaster. *Psychiatry*, 1967, *27*, 191–210.

Lin, M. W., E. M. Caffey, C. J. Klett, G. E. Hogarty, and H. R. Lamb. Day treatment and psychotropic drugs in the aftercare of schizophrenic patients. *Archives of General Psychiatry*, 1979, *36*, 1055–1066.

Lindemalm, G., D. Körlin, and N. Uddenberg. Long-term follow-up of "sex change" in 13 male-to-female transsexuals. *Archives of Sexual Behavior*, 1986, *15*, 182–210.

Lindzey, G., C. S. Hall, and M. Manosevitz. *Theories of personality: Primary sources and research*, 2nd ed. New York: Wiley, 1973.

Linehan, M. M., J. L. Goodstein, S. L. Neilson, and J. A. Chiles. Reasons for staying alive when you are thinking of killing yourself: The Reasons for Living Inventory. *Journal of Consulting and Clinical Psychology*, 1983, *51*, 276–286.

Lion, J. R. A comparison between DSM III and DSM II personality disorders. In J. R. Lion, ed., *Personality disorders: Diagnosis and management*, 2nd ed. Baltimore: Williams and Wilkins, 1981.

Lipton, M. A., and G. B. Burnett. Pharmacological treatment of schizophrenia. In L. Bellak, ed., *Disorders of the schizophrenic syndrome*. New York: Basic Books, 1980.

Litrownik, A. J. The relationship of self-stimulatory behavior in autistic children to the intensity and complexity of environmental stimulation. Unpublished master's thesis, University of Illinois, Champaign-Urbana, Ill., 1969.

Litrownik, A. J., J. L. Freitas, and L. R. Franzini. Self-regulation in mentally retarded children: Assessment and training of self-monitoring skills. *American Journal of Mental Deficiency*, 1978, *82*, 499–506.

Little, K. B., and E. S. Shneidman. The validity of MMPI interpretations. *Journal of Consulting Psychology*, 1954, *18*, 425–428.

Little, K. B., and E. S. Shneidman. Congruencies among interpretations of psychological test and anamnestic data. *Psychological Monographs*, 1959, *73*, No. 6 (Whole No. 476).

Livermore, J. M., C. P. Malmquist, and P. E. Meehl. On the justifications for civil commitment. *University of Pennsylvania Law Review*, 1968, *117*, 75–96.

Livermore, J. M., and P. E. Meehl. The virtues of M'Naghten. *Minnesota Law Review*, 1967, *51*, 789–856.

London, P. *The modes and morals of psychotherapy*. New York: Holt, Rinehart and Winston, 1964.

London, P. *Behavior control*. New York: Harper & Row, 1969.

Loney, J., J. Kramer, and R. Milich. The hyperkinetic child grows up: Predictors of symptoms, delinquency, and achievement at follow-up. Presented as part of symposium, K. D. Gadow, Chair., *Psychosocial Aspects of Drug Treatment for Hyperactivity*. Annual Meeting of the American Association for the Advancement of Science, Houston, Texas, January 7, 1979.

Long, B. B. The prevention of mental-emotional disabilities: A report from a National Health Association Commission.

American Psychologist, 1986, *41,* 825–829.

LoPiccolo, J. Direct treatment of sexual dysfunction in the couple. In J. Money and H. Musaph, eds., *Handbook of sexology.* Amsterdam: Excerpta Medica, 1977.

LoPiccolo, J. Diagnosis and treatment of male sexual dysfunction. *Journal of Sex and Marital Therapy,* 1985a, *4,* 215–232.

LoPiccolo, J. Guidelines for treatment of sex offenders. Unpublished paper. 1985b.

LoPiccolo, J. Personal communication, 1986.

LoPiccolo, J., and J. Heiman. The role of cultural values in the prevention and treatment of sexual problems. In C. B. Qualls, J. P. Wincze, and D. H. Barlow, eds., *The Prevention of sexual disorders.* New York: Plenum, 1978.

LoPiccolo, J., and P. Hogan. Multidimensional behavioral treatment of sexual dysfunction. In O. Pomerleau and J. P. Brady, eds., *Behavioral medicine: Theory and practice.* Baltimore: Williams and Wilkins, 1979.

LoPiccolo, J., and W. C. Lobitz. Behavior therapy of sexual dysfunction. In L. A. Hammerlynck. L. C. Handy, and E. J. Mash, eds., *Behavior change: Methodology, concepts and practice.* Champaign, Ill.: Research Press, 1973.

LoPiccolo, J., and L. LoPiccolo, eds. *Handbook of sex therapy.* New York: Plenum, 1978.

LoPiccolo, J., and W. E. Stock. Treatment of sexual dysfunction. *Journal of Counseling and Clinical Psychology,* 1986, *54,* 158–167.

Loraine, J. A., D. A. Adamopoulos, E. E. Kirkham, A. A. Ismail, and G. A. Dove. Patterns of hormone excretion in male and female homosexuals. *Nature,* 1971, *234,* 552–555.

Lotter, V. Epidemiology of autistic conditions in young children: I. Prevalence. *Social Psychiatry,* 1966, *1*(3), 124–137.

Lovaas, O. I., J. P. Berberich, B. F. Perloff, and B. Schaeffer. Acquisition of imitative speech in schizophrenic children. *Science,* 1966, *151,* 705–707.

Lovaas, O. I., R. L. Koegel, and L. Schreibman. Stimulus overselectivity in autism: A review of research. *Psychological Bulletin,* 1979, *86,* 1236–1254.

Lovaas, O. I., R. Koegel, J. Simmons, and J. Long. Some generalization and follow up measures on autistic children in behavior therapy. *Journal of Applied Behavior Analysis,* 1973, *6,* 131–166.

Lovaas, O. I., A. Litrownik, and R. Mann. Response latencies to auditory stimuli in autistic children engaged in self-stimulatory behavior. *Behavior Research and Therapy,* 1971, *2,* 39–49.

Lovaas, O. I., B. Schaeffer, and J. Q. Simmons. Building social behavior in autistic children by use of electric shock. *Journal of Experimental Research in Personality,* 1965, *1,* 99–109.

Lubin, B., R. M. Larsen, and J. D. Matarazzo. Patterns of psychological test usage in the United States: 1935–1982. *American Psychologist,* 1984, *39,* 451–454.

Luborsky, L., P. Crits-Christoph, and J. Mellon. Advent of objective measures of the transference concept. *Journal of Consulting and Clinical Psychology,* 1986, *54,* 39–47.

Luborsky, L., B. Singer, and L. Luborsky. Comparative studies of psychotherapies: Is it true that everyone has won and all must have prizes? *Archives of General Psychiatry,* 1975, *32,* 995–1008.

Luborsky, L. and D. P. Spence. Quantitative research on psychoanalytic therapy. In S. L. Garfield and A. E. Bergin, eds., *Handbook of psychotherapy and behavior change: An empirical analysis,* 2nd ed. New York: Wiley, 1978.

Lucas, C., P. Sansbury, and J. G. Collins. A social and clinical study of delusions in schizophrenia. *Journal of Mental Health,* 1962, *108,* 747–758.

Luisada, P. V. *The PCP psychosis: A hidden epidemic.* Presented at the VI World Congress of Psychiatry, Honolulu, Hawaii, August 1977.

Luparello, T. J., E. R. McFadden, H. A. Lyons, and E. R. Bleecker. Psychologic factors and bronchial asthma. *New York State Journal of Medicine,* 1971, *71,* 2161–2165.

Lydiard, R. B., and A. J. Gelenberg. Hazards and adverse effects of lithium. *Annual Review of Medicine,* 1982, *33,* 327–344.

Lyght, C. E., ed. *The Merck manual of diagnosis and therapy,* 11th ed. Rahway, N.J.: Merck Sharpe and Dohme Research Laboratories, 1966.

Lykken, D. I. A study of anxiety in the sociopathic personality. *Journal of Abnormal and Social Psychology,* 1957, *55*(1), 6–10.

Lynch, J. J. *The broken heart: The medical consequences of loneliness.* New York: Basic Books, 1977.

Lynch, J. J., S. A. Thomas, D. A. Paskewitz, K. L. Melinow, and J. M. Long. Interpersonal aspects of blood pressure control. *Journal of Nervous and Mental Disease,* 1982, *170,* 143–153.

MacDonald, A. Bisexuality: Some comments on research and theory. *Journal of Homosexuality,* 1981, *6,* 21–35.

MacDonald, J. Homicidal threats. *American Journal of Psychiatry,* 1967, *124,* 475.

Mackay, A. V. P., L. L. Iversen, M. Rossor, E. Spokes, E. Bird, A. Arregui, I. Creese, and S. Snyder. Increased brain dopamine and dopamine receptors in schizophrenia. *Archives of General Psychiatry,* 1982, *39,* 991–997.

MacMillan, D. L. *Mental retardation in school and society.* 2nd ed. Boston: Little, Brown, 1982.

McBroom, P. *Behavioral genetics.* National Institute of Mental Health Science Monographs. Washington, D.C.: DHEW Publication (ADM)80–876, 1980.

McCartney, J. R., and J. C. Holden. Toilet training for the mentally retarded. In J. L. Matson and J. R. McCartney, eds., *Handbook of behavior modification with the mentally retarded.* New York: Plenum, 1981.

McClelland, D. C. The impact of power motivation training on alcoholics. *Journal of Studies on Alcohol,* 1977, *38,* 142–144.

McClelland, D. C., W. N. Davis, R. Kalin, and E. Wanner. *The drinking man.* New York: Free Press, 1972.

McCord, W., and J. McCord. *The psychopath: An essay on the criminal mind.* New York: Van Nostrand, 1964.

McCord, W., J. McCord, and J. Gudeman. *Origins of alcoholism.* Stanford, Calif.: Stanford University Press, 1960.

McGarvey, B., W. F. Gabrielli, P. M. Beutler, and S. Mednick. Rearing social class, education, and criminality: A multiple indicator model. *Journal of Abnormal Psychology,* 1981, *90,* 354–364.

McGhie, A., and J. Chapman. Disorders of attention and perception in early schizophrenia. *British Journal of Medical Psychology,* 1961, *34,* 103–116.

McLean, P. D., and A. R. Hakstian. Clinical depression: Comparative efficacy of outpatient treatments. *Journal of Consulting and Clinical Psychology,* 1979, *47,* 818–836.

McNally, R. J., and S. Reiss. The preparedness theory of phobias and human safety-signal conditioning. *Behaviour Research and Therapy,* 1982, *20,* 153–159.

McNeal, E. T., and P. Cimbolic. Antidepressants and biochemical theories of depression. *Psychological Bulletin,* 1986, *99,* 361–374.

McNeil, E. B. *The psychoses.* Englewood Cliffs, N.J.: Prentice-Hall, 1970.

McReynolds, P. Historical antecedents of personality assessment. In P. McReynolds, ed., *Advances in psychological assessment,* Vol. 3. San Francisco: Jossey-Bass, 1975.

McWhirter, D. and A. W. Mattisom. *The male couple.* Englewood Cliffs, N.J.: Prentice-Hall, 1984.

Maher, B. A., ed. *Contributions to the psychopathology of schizophrenia.* New York: Academic Press, 1977.

Maher, B. A., and W. B. Maher. Psychopathology. In E. Hearst, ed., *The first century of experimental psychology.* Hillsdale, N.J.: Lawrence Erlbaum, 1979.

Maher, B. A., and W. B. Maher. Psychopathology: II. From the eighteenth century to modern times. In G. A. Kimble and K. Schlesinger, eds., *Topics in the history of psychology,* Vol. 2. Hillsdale, N.J.: Erlbaum, 1985b.

Maher, W. B., and **B. A. Maher.** Psychopathology: I. From ancient times to the eighteenth century. In G. A. Kimble and K. Schlesinger, eds., *Topics in the history of psychology,* Vol. 2. Hillsdale, N.J.: Erlbaum, 1985a.

Mahler, M. S. *The selected papers of Margaret S. Mahler.* Vol. 2. New York: Aronson, 1979.

Mahler, M. S., F. Pine, and **A. Bergman.** *The psychological birth of the human infant.* New York: Basic Books, 1975.

Mahoney, M. J. *Cognition and behavior modification.* Cambridge, Mass.: Ballinger, 1974.

Mahoney, M. J. Psychotherapy and the structure of personal revolutions. In M. J. Mahoney, ed., *Psychotherapy process: Current issues and future directions.* New York: Plenum, 1980.

Mahoney, M. J., and **D. Arnkoff.** Cognitive and self-control therapies. In S. L. Garfield and A. E. Bergin, eds., *Handbook of psychotherapy and behavior change: An empirical analysis,* 2nd ed. New York: Wiley, 1978.

Maier, S. F., M. E. P. Seligman and **R. L. Solomon.** Pavlovian fear conditioning and learned helplessness. In B. A. Campbell and R. M. Church, eds., *Punishment.* New York: Appleton-Century-Crofts, 1969.

Maletzky, B. M., and **J. Klotter.** Smoking and alcoholism. *American Journal of Psychiatry,* 1974, *131*(4), 445–447.

Malitz, S., B. Wilkens, and **H. Esecover.** A comparison of drug-induced hallucinations with those seen in spontaneously occurring psychoses. In L. J. West, ed., *Hallucinations.* New York: Grune & Stratton, 1962.

Malmo, R. B., and **C. Shagass.** Physiologic study of symptom mechanisms in psychiatric patients under stress. *Psychosomatic Medicine,* 1949, *11,* 25–29.

Mann, J. J., M. Stanley, P. A. McBride, and **B. S. McEwen.** Increased serotonin Z and β-adrenergic receptor binding in the frontal cortices of suicide victims. *Archives of General Psychiatry,* 1986, *43,* 954–959.

Margolies, A. Behavioral approaches to the treatment of early infantile autism: A review. *Psychological Bulletin,* 1977, *84,* 249–264.

Marks, I. Clinical phenomena in search of laboratory models. In J. D. Maser and M. E. P. Seligman, eds., *Psychopathology: Experimental models.* San Francisco: W. H. Freeman and Company, 1977.

Marlatt, G. A., and **J. R. Gordon.** *Relapse prevention: Maintenance strategies in addictive behavior change.* New York: Guilford Press, 1985.

Marshall, D. S. Sexual behavior on Mangaia. In D. S. Marshall and R. C. Suggs, eds., *Human sexual behavior.* New York: Basic Books, 1971.

Martin, H. P. *The abused child: A multidisciplinary approach to developmental issues and treatment.* Cambridge, Mass.: Ballinger, 1976.

Maser, J. D., and **M. E. P. Seligman, eds.** *Psychopathology: Experimental models.* San Francisco: W. H. Freeman and Company, 1977.

Masling, J. M. The influence of situational and interpersonal variables in projective testing. *Psychological Bulletin,* 1960, *57,* 65–85.

Masserman, J. H. *Principles of dynamic psychiatry,* 2nd ed. Philadelphia: W. B. Saunders Company, 1961.

Masters, W. H., and **V. E. Johnson.** *Human sexual response.* Boston: Little, Brown, 1966.

Masters, W. H., and **V. E. Johnson.** *Human sexual inadequacy.* Boston: Little, Brown, 1970.

Masters, W. H., and **V. E. Johnson.** *Homosexuality in perspective.* Boston: Little, Brown, 1979.

Masterson, J. *Psychotherapy of the borderline adult.* New York: Brunner/Mazel, 1976.

Matarazzo, J. D. Computerized clinical psychological test interpretations. *American Psychologist,* 1986, *41,* 14–24.

Matson, J. L., and **F. Andrasik.** *Treatment issues and innovations in mental retardation.* New York: Plenum, 1982.

Matthews, K. A., D. C. Glass, R. H. Rosenman, and **R. W. Bortner.** Competitive drive, pattern A, and coronary heart disease: A further analysis of some data from the Western Collaborative Group Study. *Journal of Chronic Diseases,* 1977, *30,* 489–498.

Maugh, T. H. Marijuana "justifies serious concern." *Science,* 1982, *215,* 1488–1489.

May, R. Contributions of existential psychotherapy. In R. May, E. Angel, and H. F. Ellenberger, eds., *Existence: A new dimension in psychiatry and psychology.* New York: Basic Books, 1958.

May, R. *The discovery of being: Writings in existential psychology.* New York: W. W. Norton, 1959, p. 37.

May, R. Existential bases of psychotherapy. In R. May, ed., *Existential psychology.* New York: Random House, 1961.

Mednick, S. A. Breakdown in individuals at high risk for schizophrenia: Possible predispositional perinatal factors. *Mental Hygiene,* 1970, *54,* 50–63.

Mednick, S. A. Birth defects and schizophrenia. *Psychology Today,* 1971, *4,* 48–50.

Meehl, P. E. *Clinical versus statistical prediction.* Minneapolis: University of Minnesota Press, 1954.

Meichenbaum, D. H. Self-instructional methods. In F. H. Kanfer and A. P. Goldstein, eds., *Helping people change: A textbook of methods.* New York: Pergamon Press, 1975.

Meichenbaum, D. H., ed. *Cognitive behavior modification: An integrative approach.* New York: Plenum Press, 1977.

Meichenbaum, D. H., and **R. Cameron.** Training schizophrenics to talk to themselves: A means of developing attentional controls. *Behavior Therapy,* 1973, *4,* 515–534.

Meichenbaum, D. H., and **J. Goodman.** Training impulsive children to talk to themselves: A means of developing self control. *Journal of Abnormal Psychology,* 1971, *77,* 115–126.

Meichenbaum, D. H., and **M. E. Jaremko, eds.** *Stress reduction and prevention.* New York: Plenum Press, 1983.

Meier, J. H. Prevalence and characteristics of learning disabilities in second grade children. *Journal of Learning Disabilities,* 1961, *4,* 1–16.

Meissner, W. *The borderline spectrum.* New York: Aronson, 1984.

Meissner, W. W., J. E. Mack, and **E. V. Semrad.** Classical psychoanalysis. In A. M. Freedman, H. I. Kaplan, and B. J. Sadock, eds., *Comprehensive textbook of psychiatry II.* Baltimore: Williams and Wilkins, 1975.

Mellsop, G., F. Varghere, S. Joshua et al. The reliability of axis II of DSM III. *American Journal of Psychiatry,* 1982, *139,* 1360–1361.

Meltzer, H. Y. Biochemical studies in schizophrenia. In L. Bellak, ed., *Disorders of the schizophrenic syndrome.* New York: Basic Books, 1979.

Mendel, W. M. *Schizophrenia: The experience and its treatment.* San Francisco: Jossey-Bass, 1976.

Mendlewicz, J., and **J. D. Rainer.** Adoption study supporting genetic transmission in manic-depressive illness. *Nature,* 1977, *168,* 327–329.

Menninger, K. *Man against himself.* New York: Harcourt, 1938.

Merritt, H. H. *A textbook of neurology,* 4th ed. Philadelphia: Lea and Febiger, 1967.

Merton, R. K. *Social theory and social structure,* 2nd ed. Glencoe, Ill.: Free Press, 1957.

Messenger, J. C. Sex and repression in an Irish folk community. In D. S. Marshall and R. C. Suggs, eds., *Human sexual behavior.* New York: Basic Books, 1971.

Messer, S. B. Behavioral and psychoanalytic perspectives at therapeutic choice points. *American Psychologist,* 1986, *41,* 1261–1272.

Metalsky, G. I., L. Y. Abramson, M. E. P. Seligman, A. Semmel, and **C. Peterson.** Attributional styles and life events in the classroom: Vulnerability and invulnerability to depressive mood reactions. *Journal of Personality and Social Psychology,* 1982, *43,* 612–617.

Meyer, J. K., and D. J. Peter. Sex reassignment: Follow-up. *Archives of General Psychiatry,* 1979, *36,* 1010–1015.

Meyer, R. J., and R. J. Haggerty. Streptococcal infections in families: Factors altering individual susceptibility. *Pediatrics,* 1962, *29,* 539–549.

Meyerowitz, B. E. Psychosocial correlates of breast cancer and its treatments. *Psychological Bulletin,* 1980, *87,* 108–131.

Miklowitz, D. J., A. M. Strachan, M. J. Goldstein, J. A. Doane, K. S. Snyder, G. E. Hogarty, and I. R. H. Falloon. Expressed emotion and communication deviance in the families of schizophrenics. *Journal of Abnormal Psychology,* 1986, *95,* 60–66.

Miller, G. The magical number seven, plus or minus two: Some limits of our capacity for processing information. *Psychological Review,* 1956, *63,* 81–97.

Miller, L. L., ed. *Marihuana: Current research.* New York: Academic Press, 1975.

Miller, N. E. Learning of visceral and glandular responses. *Science,* 1969, *163,* 434–445.

Miller, N. E. Comments on strategy and tactics of research. In A. E. Bergin and H. H. Strupp, eds., *Changing frontiers in the science of psychotherapy.* New York: Aldine-Atherton, 1972.

Miller, R. C., and J. S. Berman. The efficacy of cognitive behavior therapies: A quantitative review of the research evidence. *Psychological Bulletin,* 1983, *94,* 39–53.

Miller, W. R., and R. K. Hester. Inpatient alcoholism treatment: Who benefits? *American Psychologist,* 1986, *41,* 794–805.

Millon, T. *Modern psychopathology.* Philadelphia: W. B. Saunders, 1969.

Millon, T. *Disorders of personality.* New York: Wiley, 1981.

Millon, T. *Millon Clinical Multiaxial Inventory manual,* 3rd ed. Minneapolis: National Computer Systems, 1982.

Millon, T. *Millon Clinical Multiaxial Inventory: Second edition* (MCMI-II). Minneapolis: National Computer Systems, 1985a.

Millon, T. The MCMI provides a good assessment of DSM-III disorders: The MCMI-II will prove even better. *Journal of Personality Assessment,* 1985b, *49,* 379–391.

Mineka, S., M. Davidson, M. Cook, and R. Keir. Observational conditioning of snake fear in rhesus monkeys. *Journal of Abnormal Psychology,* 1984, *93,* 355–374.

Mintz, S., and M. Alpert. Imagery vividness, reality testing and schizophrenic hallucinations. *Journal of Abnormal Psychology,* 1972, *79*(3), 310–316.

Minuchin, S. *Families and family therapy.* Cambridge, Mass.: Harvard University Press, 1974.

Minuchin, S., and H. C. Fishman. *Family therapy techniques.* Cambridge, Mass.: Harvard University Press, 1981.

Minuchin, S., B. L. Rosman, and L. Baker. Psychosomatic families: Anorexia nervosa in context. Cambridge, Mass.: Harvard University Press, 1978.

Mirsky, A. F., and C. C. Duncan. Etiology and expression of schizophrenia: Neurobiological and psychosocial factors. *Annual Review of Psychology,* 1986, *37,* 291–319.

Mischel, W. *Personality and assessment.* New York: Wiley, 1968.

Mischel, W. Toward a cognitive social learning reconceptualization of personality. *Psychological Review,* 1973, *80,* 252–283.

Mischel, W. On the interface of cognition and personality: Beyond the person-situation debate. *American Psychologist,* 1979, *34,* 740–754.

Mischel, W., and P. K. Peake. Beyond deja vu in the search for cross-situational consistency. *Psychological Review,* 1982, *89,* 730–755.

Mishler, E. G., and N. E. Waxler. Family interaction processes and schizophrenia: A review of current theories. In E. G. Mishler and N. E. Waxler, eds., *Family processes and schizophrenia.* New York: Science House, 1968.

Mohr, J. W., R. E. Turner, and M. B. Jerry. *Pedophilia and exhibitionism.* Toronto: University of Toronto Press, 1964.

Monahan, J. The prevention of violence. In J. Monahan, ed., *Community mental health and the criminal justice system.* New York: Pergamon Press, 1976.

Monahan, J. Prediction research and the emergency commitment of dangerous mentally ill persons: A reconsideration. *American Journal of Psychiatry,* 1978, *2,* 547–548.

Monahan, J. *The clinical prediction of violent behavior.* Rockville, Md.: NIMH, 1981.

Monahan, J. and E. Loftus. The psychology of law. In M. Rosenzweig and L. Porter, ed., *Annual review of psychology,* Vol. 33. Palo Alto: Annual Reviews, 1982.

Money, J., N. A. Borrow, and F. C. Clarke. Autism and auto-immune disease—a family study. *Journal of Autism and Childhood Schizophrenia,* 1971, *1,* 146–160.

Money, J., and C. Primrose. Sexual dimorphism and dissociation in the psychology of male transsexuals. *Journal of Nervous and Mental Disease,* 1968, *147,* 472–486.

Monroe, L. J. Psychological and physiological differences between good and poor sleepers. *Journal of Abnormal Psychology,* 1967, *72,* 255.

Montague, A. Chromosomes and crime. *Psychology Today,* 1968, *2*(5), 43–49.

Moore, J. *Roads to recovery.* New York: Guilford Press, 1985.

Mora, G. Mind-body concepts in the middle ages: Part II. The Moslem influence, the great theological systems and cultural attitudes toward the mentally ill in the late middle ages. *Journal of the History of the Behavioral Sciences,* 1980, *16,* 58–72.

Moran, E. Varieties of pathological gambling. *British Journal of Psychiatry,* 1970, *116,* 593–597.

Moreno, J. L. *Psychodrama.* New York: Beacon, 1946.

Morgan, C. D., and H. A. Murray. A method for investigating fantasies: The Thematic Apperception Test. *Archives of Neurology and Psychiatry,* 1935, *34,* 289–306.

Morrison, J. R. Changes in subtype diagnosis of schizophrenia: 1920–1966. *American Journal of Psychiatry,* 1974, *131,* 674–677.

Morse, S. J. Law and mental health professionals: The limits of expertise. *Professional Psychology,* 1978, *9,* 389–399.

Morse, S. J. A preference for liberty: The case against the involuntary commitment of the mentally disordered. *California Law Review,* 1982, *70,* 55–106.

Mortimer, J. A., L. R. French, J. T. Hutton, and L. M. Schuman. Head injury as a risk factor for Alzheimer's disease. *Neurology,* 1985, *35* 264–267.

Mortimer, J. A., L. M. Schuman, and L. R. French. Epidemiology of dementing illness. In J. A. Mortimer and L. M. Schuman, eds., *The epidemiology of dementia.* New York: Oxford University Press, 1981.

Mosher, L. R. A research design for evaluating a psychosocial treatment of schizophrenia. *Hospital and Community Psychiatry,* 1972, *23,* 229–234.

Mosher, L. R., and Menn, A. Z. Community residential treatment for schizophrenia: Two-year follow-up. *Hospital and Community Psychiatry,* 1978, *29,* 715–723.

Mosher, L. R., W. Pollin, and J. R. Stabenau. Identical twins, discordant for schizophrenia: Neurologic findings. *Archives of General Psychiatry,* 1971, *24,* 422–430.

Moustakas, C. E. *Psychotherapy with children.* New York: Harper & Row, 1959.

Moustakas, C. E. *Loneliness.* New York: Prentice-Hall, 1961.

Moustakas, C. E. *Loneliness and love.* Englewood Cliffs, N.J.: Prentice-Hall, 1972.

Moustakas, C. E. *The touch of loneliness.*

Englewood Cliffs, N.J.: Prentice-Hall, 1975.

Mowrer, O. H. Learning theory and the neurotic paradox. *American Journal of Orthopsychiatry*, 1948, *18*, 571–610.

Mowrer, O. H. and **W. M. Mowrer.** Enuresis: A method for its study and treatment. *American Journal of Orthopsychiatry*, 1938, *8*, 436–459.

Moyles, E. W., and **M. Wolins.** Group care and intellectual development. *Developmental Psychology*, 1971, *4*, 370–380.

Mucha, T. F., and **R. F. Reinhardt.** Conversion reactions in student aviators. *American Journal of Psychiatry*, 1970, *127*, 493–497.

Murphy, E., J. Lindesay, and **E. Grundy.** 60 years of suicide in England and Wales: A cohort study. *Archives of General Psychiatry*, 1986, *43*, 969–976.

Murphy, G. E., and **R. D. Wetzel.** Suicide risk by birth cohort in the United States, 1949 to 1974. *Archives of General Psychiatry*, 1980, *37*, 519–523.

Murstein, B. I. Assumptions, adaptation level and projective techniques. *Perceptual and Motor Skills*, 1961, *12*, 107–125.

Myers, J. K., and **L. L. Bean.** *A decade later: A follow-up of social class and mental illness.* New York: Wiley, 1968.

Myers, J. K., M. M. Weissman, G. L. Tischler, C. E. Hozer III, P. J. Leaf, H. Orvaschel, J. C. Anthony, J. H. Boyd, J. D. Burke, M. Kramer, and **R. Stoltzman.** Six-month prevalence of psychiatric disorders in three communities. *Archives of General Psychiatry*, 1984, *41*, 959–967.

Nathan, P. E. Alcoholism. In H. Leitenberg, ed., *Handbook of behavior modification and behavior therapy.* Englewood Cliffs, N.J.: Prentice-Hall, 1976.

Nathan, P. E., G. A. Marlatt, and **T. Loberg, eds.** *Alcoholism: New directions in behavioral research and treatment.* New York: Plenum, 1978.

Nathan, P. E., P. Robertson, and **M. M. Andberg.** A systems analytic model of diagnosis. IV: The diagnostic validity of abnormal affective behavior. *Journal of Clinical Psychology*, 1969, *25*, 235–242.

National Academy of Sciences, 1983. *See* Lang, A. R., 1983.

National Council on Alcoholism. *Facts on alcoholism.* New York, 1986.

National Institute of Mental Health. *Electroconvulsive therapy: Consensus development conference statement.* Bethesda, Md.: Office of Medical Applications of Research, 1985.

National Institute on Drug Abuse. *National household survey on drug abuse.* Rockville, Md., 1983.

Neisser, V. *Cognitive psychology.* Englewood Cliffs, N.J.: Prentice-Hall, 1967.

Nesson, C. A needed verdict: Guilty but insane. *The New York Times*, July 1, 1982, A19.

Neugebauer, R. Treatment of the mentally ill in medieval and early modern England: A reappraisal. *Journal of the History of the Behavioral Sciences*, 1978, *14*, 158–169.

Newsome, C. D., E. A. Carr, and **A. Rincover.** *Identifying and using sensory reinforcers.* Paper presented at Western Psychological Association, San Francisco, April 1974.

Nielson, P. E. A study in transsexualism. *Psychiatric Quarterly*, 1960, *34*, 203–235.

Nisbett, R. E. Taste, deprivation, and weight determinants of eating behavior. *Journal of Personality and Social Psychology*, 1968, *10*, 107–116.

Nisbett, R. and **L. Ross.** *Human inference: Strategies and shortcomings of social judgment.* Englewood Cliffs, N.J.: Prentice-Hall, 1980.

Nisbett, R. E., and **T. D. Wilson.** Telling more than we can know: Verbal reports on mental processes. *Psychological Review*, 1977, *84*, 231–259.

Nordquist, V. M., and **R. G. Wahler.** Naturalistic treatment of an autistic child. *Journal of Applied Behavior Analysis*, 1973, *6*, 79–87.

Norman, D. A. *Memory and attention.* New York: Wiley, 1976.

Norton, G. R., B. Harrison, J. Hauch, and **L. Rhodes.** Characteristics of people with infrequent panic attacks. *Journal of Abnormal Psychology*, 1985, *94*, 216–221.

Noyes, R., Jr., J. Clancy, R. Crowe, P. R. Hoenk, and **D. J. Slymen.** The familial prevalence of anxiety neurosis. *Archives of General Psychiatry*, 1978, *35*, 1057–1059.

Noyes, R., R. R. Crowe, E. L. Harris, B. J. Hamra, C. M. McChesney, and **B. R. Chaudhrey.** Relationship between panic disorder and agoraphobia. *Archives of General Psychiatry*, 1986, *43*, 227–232.

Nunnally, J. *Psychometric theory*, 2nd ed. New York: McGraw-Hill, 1978.

Nunes, D. The anguish behind the three faces of Eve. *N.Y. Post*, September 15, 1975, *4*, 26.

O'Connor, J. F. and **L. O. Stern.** Results of treatment in functional sexual disorders. *New York State Journal of Medicine*, August 1972, *72*,(15), 1927–1934.

O'Hara, M. W., L. P. Rehm, and **S. B. Campbell.** Predicting depressive symptomatology: Cognitive-behavioral models and post partum depression. *Journal of Abnormal Psychology*, 1982, *91*, 457–461.

Öhman, A., U. Dimberg, and **L. G. Öst.** Animal and social phobias: Biological constraints on learned fear responses. In S. Reiss and R. R. Bootzin, eds., *Theoretical issues in behavior therapy.* New York: Academic Press, 1985.

O'Leary, K. D. The operant and social psychology of token systems. In A. C. Catania and T. A. Brigham, eds., *Handbook of applied behavior analysis: Social and instructional processes.* New York: Irvington, 1978.

O'Leary, K. D., and **T. D. Borkovec.** Conceptual, methodological, and ethical problems of placebo groups in psychotherapy research. *American Psychologist*, 1978, *33*, 821–830.

O'Leary, K. D., and **G. T. Wilson.** *Behavior therapy—application and outcome.* Englewood Cliffs, N.J.: Prentice-Hall, 1975.

O'Leary, S. G., and, W. E. Pelham. Behavior therapy and withdrawal of stimulant medication in hyperactive children. *Pediatrics*, 1978, *61*, 211–217.

O'Neal, P., and **L. N. Robbins.** The relation of childhood behavior problems to adult psychiatric status: A thirty-year follow-up study of 150 subjects. *American Journal of Psychiatry*, 1958, *114*, 961–969.

Olshansky, S. Chronic sorrow: A response to having a mentally defective child. *Social Casework*, 1962, *43*, 191–194.

Oltman, J., and **S. Friedman.** Parental deprivation in psychiatric conditions. *Disturbances of the Nervous System*, 1967, *28*, 298–303.

Olton, D. S., and **A. R. Noonberg.** *Biofeedback: Clinical applications in behavioral medicine.* Englewood Cliffs, N.J.: Prentice-Hall, 1980.

Orlinsky, D. E., and **K. I. Howard.** Processes and outcome in psychotherapy. In S. L. Garfield and A. E. Bergin, eds., *Handbook of psychotherapy and behavior change: An evaluative analysis*, 3rd ed. New York: Wiley, 1986.

Orlinsky, D. E., and **K. I. Howard.** A generic model of psychotherapy. *Journal of Integrative and Eclectic Psychotherapy.* In press.

Ornitz, E. M. Childhood autism: A review of the clinical and experimental literature. *California Medicine*, 1973, *118*, 21–47.

Ornitz, E. M. The modulation of sensory input and motor output in autistic children. *Journal of Autism and Childhood Schizophrenia*, 1974, *4*, 197–215.

Ornitz, E. M., and **E. R. Ritvo.** Perceptual inconstancy in early infantile autism. *Archives of General Psychiatry*, 1968, *18*, 76–98.

Ornitz, E. M., and **E. R. Ritvo.** The syndrome of autism: A critical review. *The American Journal of Psychology*, 1976, *133*, 27–65.

Overton, D. A. State-dependent learning produced by depressant and atropine-like drugs. *Psychopharmacologia*, 1966, *10*, 6–31.

Parke, R. D., L. Berkowitz, J. Leyens, S. West, and **R. Sebastian.** The effects of repeated exposure to movie violence on aggressive behavior in juvenile delinquent boys: A field experimental approach. In L. Berkowitz, ed., *Advances in experimental social psychology*, Vol. 8. New York: Academic Press, 1975.

Parker, N. Twins: A psychiatric study of a neurotic group. *Medical Journal of Australia*, 1964, *2*, 735–741.

Parloff, M. B. Shopping for the right therapy. *Saturday Review*, February 21, 1976, pp. 14–20.

Parnas, J., T. W. Teasdale, and **H. Schulsinger.** Institutional rearing and diagnostic outcome in children of schizophrenic mothers: A prospective high-risk study. *Archives of General Psychiatry*, 1985, *42*, 762–769.

Pasewark, R. A., M. L. Pantle, and **H. J. Steadman.** Detention and rearrest rates of persons found not guilty by reason of insanity and convicted felons. *American Journal of Psychiatry*, 1982, *139*, 892–897.

Patterson, G. R. Interventions for boys with conduct problems: Multiple settings, treatments, and criteria. *Journal of Consulting and Clinical Psychology*, 1974, *42*, 471–481.

Patterson, G. R., and **M. E. Gullion.** *Living with children.* Champaign, Ill.: Research Press, 1968.

Patterson, G. R., and **H. Hops.** Coercion: A game for two: Intervention techniques for marital conflict. In R. Ulrich and P. Mountjoy, eds., *The experimental analysis of social behavior.* New York: Appleton-Century-Crofts, 1972.

Patton, R. B., and **J. A. Sheppard.** Intercranial tumors found at autopsy in mental patients. *American Journal of Psychiatry*, 1956, *113*, 319–324.

Paul, G. L. Outcome of systematic desensitization I: Background procedures and uncontrolled reports of individual treatment. In C. M. Franks, ed., *Behavior therapy: Appraisal and status.* New York: McGraw-Hill, 1969a.

Paul, G. L. Outcome of systematic desensitization II: Controlled investigation of individual treatment technique variations and current status. In C. M. Franks, ed., *Behavior therapy: Appraisal and status.* New York: McGraw-Hill, 1969b.

Paul, G. L., and **R. J. Lentz.** *Psychosocial treatment of chronic mental patients: Milieu versus social-learning programs.* Cambridge, Mass.: Harvard University Press, 1977.

Paul, W. M., J. C. Gonsiorek, and **M. E. Hotvedt, eds.** *Homosexuality.* Beverly Hills, Calif.: Sage, 1982.

Pauly, I. B. The current status of the change of sex operation. *Journal of Nervous and Mental Disease*, 1968, *147*, 460–471.

Paykel, E. S. Life stress. In L. D. Hankoff and B. Einsidler, eds., *Suicide: Theory and clinical aspects.* Littleton, Mass.: PSG Publishing, 1979b.

Paykel, E. S. Recent life events in the development of the depressive disorders. In R. A. Depue, ed., *The psychobiology of the depressive disorders.* New York: Academic Press, 1979a.

Paykel, E. S., and **J. Tanner.** Life events, depressive relapse, and maintenance treatment. *Psychological Medicine*, 1976, *6*, 481–485.

Peck, C. P. A public mental health issue: Risk-taking behavior and compulsive gambling. *American Psychologist*, 1986, *41*, 461–465.

Pelham, W. E., and **A. O. Ross.** Selective attention in children with reading problems: A developmental study of incidental learning. *Journal of Abnormal Child Psychology*, 1977, *5*, 1–8.

Pelham, W. E., R. W. Schnedler, N. C. Bologna, and **J. A. Contreras.** Behavioral and stimulant treatment of hyperactive children: A therapy study with methylphenidate probes in a within-subject design. *Journal of Applied Behavior Analysis*, 1980, *13*, 221–236.

Peplau, L. What homosexuals want in relationships. *Psychology Today*, March 1981, 28–38.

Perls, F. S. Four lectures. In J. Fagan and I. L. Shepherd, eds., *Gestalt therapy now: Therapy, techniques, applications.* Palo Alto, Calif.: Science and Behavior Books, 1970.

Perls, F. S., R. F. Hefferline, and **P. Goodman.** *Gestalt therapy: Excitement and growth in the human personality.* New York: Julian Press, 1951.

Perry, J. C., and **G. L. Klerman.** Clinical features of the borderline personality disorder. *American Journal of Psychiatry*, 1980, *137*, 165–173.

Perske, R. About sexual development. *Mental Retardation*, 1973, *11*, 6–8.

Persons, J. B., and **P. A. Rao.** Longitudinal study of cognitions, life events, and depression in psychiatric in-patients. *Journal of Abnormal Psychology*, 1985, *94*, 51–63.

Petzel, T. P., and **J. E. Johnson.** Time estimation by process and reactive schizophrenics under crowded and uncrowded conditions. *Journal of Clinical Psychology*, 1972, *28*(3), 345–347.

Phillips, E. L., M. M. Wolf, D. L. Fixsen, and **J. S. Bailey.** The achievement place model: A community-based, family-style, behavior modification program for predelinquents. In E. Ribes-Inesta and A. Bandura, eds., *Analysis of delinquency and aggression.* Hillsdale, N.J.: Erlbaum, 1976.

Phillips, L., and **N. Williams.** Psychopathology and mental retardation. *American Journal of Psychiatry*, 1975, *132*, 1265–1271.

Pinel, P. *A treatise on insanity* (1801). D. D. Davis, tr. New York: Hafner, 1967.

Pines, M. Infant-stim. It's changing the lives of handicapped kids. *Psychology Today*, June 1982a, 48–52.

Pines, M. Recession is linked to far-reaching psychological harm. *The New York Times*, April 6, 1982b, C1.

Pitman, R. K., and **P. S. Moffett.** Somatization disorder (Briquet's syndrome) in a male veteran. *Journal of Nervous and Mental Disease*, 1981, *169*(2).

Polak, P. R. A comprehensive system of alternatives to psychiatric hospitalization. In L. I. Stein and M. A. Test, eds., *Alternatives to mental hospital treatment.* New York: Plenum, 1978.

Polivy, J., and **C. P. Herman.** Clinical depression and weight change: A complex relation. *Journal of Abnormal Psychology*, 1976, *85*, 338–340.

Polivy, J., and **C. P. Herman.** Dieting and binging: A causal analysis. *American Psychologist*, 1985, *40*, 193–201.

Pollack, E. S., and **C. A. Taube.** Trends and projections in state hospital use. In J. Zusman and E. Bertsch, eds., *The future role of the state hospital.* Lexington, Mass.: Lexington Books, 1975.

Prange, A. J., Jr., M. A. Lipton, C. B. Nemeroff, and **I. C. Wilson.** Minireview—The role of hormones in depression. *Life Sciences*, 1977, *20*, 1305–1318.

Prange, A. J., Jr., I. C. Wilson, C. W. Lynn, B. A. Lacoe, and **R. A. Stikeleather.** L-Tryptophan in mania—contribution to a permissive hypothesis of affective disorders. *Archives of General Psychiatry*, 1974, *30*, 56–62.

Premack, D. Reinforcement therapy. In D. Levine, ed., *Nebraska Symposium on Motivation.* Lincoln: University of Nebraska Press, 1965.

President's Commission on Mental Health. *Report to the president.* Washington, D.C.: U.S. Government Printing Office, 1978.

President's Panel on Mental Retardation. *A proposed program for national action to combat mental retardation.* Washington, D.C.: U.S. Government Printing Office, 1962.

Preu, P. W. The concept of the psychopathic personality. In J. McV. Hunt, ed., *Personality and the behavior disorders*, Vol. 2. New York: The Ronald Press, 1944.

Price, R. H. *Abnormal behavior: Perspectives in conflict*, 2nd ed. New York: Holt, Rinehart and Winston, 1978.

Prince, M. *The dissociation of personal-*

ity. New York: Longmans, Green, 1905.

Prince, V. Transsexuals and pseudotranssexuals. *Archives of Sexual Behavior,* 1978, *7*(4), 263–272.

Prior, M. R. Cognitive abilities and disabilities in infantile autism: A review. *Journal of Abnormal Child Psychology,* 1979, *7,* 357–380.

Prior, M., and **C. Gajzago.** Early signs of autism. *Medical Journal of Australia,* August 1, 1974.

Prior, M., C. Gajzago, and **D. Knox.** An epidemiological study of autistic and psychotic children in the four eastern states of Australia. *Australian and New Zealand Journal of Psychiatry,* 1976, *10*(2), 173–184.

Pritchard, M. Homosexuality and genetic sex. *Journal of Mental Sciences,* 1962, *108,* 616–623.

Prochaska, J. O., and **C. C. DiClemente.** Stages and processes of self-change of smoking: Toward an integrative model of change. *Journal of Consulting and Clinical Psychology,* 1983, *51,* 390–395.

Prochaska, J. O., and **C. C. DiClemente.** *The transtheoretical approach: Crossing traditional boundaries of therapy.* Homewood, Ill.: Dow Jones/Irwin, 1984.

Prouty, G. Pre-therapy—A method of treating preexpressive psychotic and retarded patients. *Psychotherapy: Theory Research, and Practice,* 1976, *13,* 290–294.

PsychoSources: *A psychology resource catalog.* New York: Bantam, 1973.

Quay, H. C. Psychopathic personality as pathological stimulus seeking. *American Journal of Psychiatry,* 1965, *122,* 180–183.

Rabkin, J. G. Stressful life events and schizophrenia: A review of the research literature. *Psychological Bulletin,* 1980, *87*(2), 408–425.

Rachman, S. Sexual fetishism: An experimental analogue. *Psychological Record,* 1966, *16,* 293–296.

Rachman, S. *Fear and courage.* San Francisco: Freeman, 1978.

Rachman, S. J., and **R. J. Hodgson.** *Obsessions and compulsions.* Englewood Cliffs, N.J.: Prentice-Hall, 1980.

Rada, R. T. Psychological factors in rapist behavior. In R. T. Rada, ed., *Clinical aspects of the rapist.* N.Y.: Grune and Stratton, 1978.

Rahe, R. H., and **R. J. Arthur.** Life change and illness studies. *Journal of Human Stress,* 1978, *4,* 3–15.

Raker, J. W., A. F. Wallace, and **J. F. Raymer.** *Emergency medical care in disasters.* Disaster Study No. 6, National Academy of Sciences, Washington, D.C.: National Resources Council Publication No. 457, 1956.

Rapaport, D., M. Gill, and **R. Schaefer.** *Diagnostic psychological testing.* New York: International Universities Press, 1968.

Rapee, R. Differential response to hyperventilation in panic disorder and generalized anxiety disorder. *Journal of Abnormal Psychology,* 1986, *95,* 24–28.

Rappeport, J. R. The psychiatrist and criminal justice. In J. P. Brady and H. K. H. Brodie, eds., *Controversy in psychiatry.* Philadelphia: W. B. Saunders, 1978.

Raps, C. S., C. Peterson, K. E. Reinhard, L. Y. Abramson, and **M. E. P. Seligman.** Attributional style among depressed patients. *Journal of Abnormal Psychology,* 1982, *91,* 102–108.

Rasmussen, T., and **C. H. H. Branch.** Temporal lobe epilepsy: Indications for and results of surgical therapy. *Postgraduate Medicine,* 1962, *31,* 9–14.

Ray, O. S. *Drugs, society, and human behavior.* St. Louis, Mo.: Mosby Company, 1983.

Redd, W. H., T. G. Burish, and **M. A. Andrykowski.** Aversive conditioning and cancer chemotherapy. In T. G. Burish, S. M. Levy, and B. E. Meyerowitz, eds., *Cancer, nutrition, and eating behavior: A biobehavioral perspective.* Hillsdale, N.J.: Erlbaum, 1985.

Redlich, F. C., and **D. X. Freedman.** *The theory and practice of psychiatry.* New York: Basic Books, 1966.

Rees, L. The importance of psychological, allergic, and infective factors in childhood asthma. *Journal of Psychosomatic Research,* 1964, *7,* 253–262.

Reid, A. H. Psychoses in adult mental defectives. I. Manic depressive psychoses. *British Journal of Psychiatry,* 1972a, *120,* 205–212.

Reid, A. H. Psychoses in adult mental defectives. II. Schizophrenic and paranoid psychoses. *British Journal of Psychiatry,* 1972b, *120,* 213–218.

Reid, J. B., ed. *A social learning approach to family intervention. Volume II: Observation in home settings.* Eugene, Oreg.: Castalia Publishing, 1978.

Reid, J. B., and **G. R. Patterson.** The modification of aggression and stealing behavior of boys in the home setting. In E. Ribes-Inesta and A. Bandura, eds., *Analysis of delinquency and aggression.* Hillsdale, N.J.: Erlbaum, 1976.

Reid, W. H. The antisocial personality and related symptoms. In J. R. Lion, ed., *Personality disorders: Diagnosis and management,* 2nd ed. Baltimore: Williams and Wilkins, 1981.

Reisner, R. *Law and the mental health system.* St. Paul: West, 1985.

Reiss, D. Competing hypotheses and warring factions: Applying knowledge of schizophrenia. *Schizophrenia Bulletin,* 1974, No. *8,* 7–11.

Reiss, S. The mentally retarded, emotionally disturbed adult. In M. Sigman, ed., *Children with emotional disorders and developmental disabilities.* New York: Grune & Stratton, 1985.

Reiss, S., and **B. A. Benson.** Psychosocial correlates of depression in mentally retarded adults: I. Minimal social support and stigmatization. *American Journal of Medical Deficiency,* 1985, *89,* 331–337.

Reiss, S., G. W. Levitan, and **R. J. McNally.** Emotionally disturbed mentally retarded people: An underserved population. *American Psychologist,* April 1982a, *37*(4).

Reiss, S., G. W. Levitan, and **J. Szysko.** Emotional disturbance and mental retardation: Diagnostic overshadowing. *American Journal of Mental Deficiency,* 1982b, *86*(6), 567–574.

Reiss, S., R. A. Peterson, D. M. Gursky, and **R. J. McNally.** Anxiety sensitivity, anxiety frequency, and the prediction of fearfulness. *Behavior Research and Therapy,* 1986, *24,* 1–8.

Rekers, G. A., and **O. I. Lovaas.** Behavioral treatment of deviant sex-role behaviors in a male child. *Journal of Applied Behavior Analysis,* 1974, *7,* 173–190.

Reuter, K. E., A. D. Walsh, J. A. Buck, and **A. J. Litrownik.** Comparison of instructions, timeout, and punishment for controlling self-stimulatory behavior in autistic-like preschoolers. Papers presented at Western Psychological Association meeting, San Francisco, April 1974.

Reveley, M. A. CT scans in schizophrenia. *British Journal of Psychiatry,* 1985, *146,* 367–371.

Rieber, Q., and **V. Sigusch.** Psychosurgery on sex offenders and sexual "deviants" in West Germany. *Archives of Sexual Behavior,* 1979, *8*(6), 523–527.

Rieder, R. A. Hospitals, patients, and politics. *Schizophrenia Bulletin,* 1974, *11,* 9–15.

Rimland, B. *Infantile autism.* New York: Appleton-Century-Crofts, 1964.

Rimland, B. High-dosage levels of certain vitamins in the treatment of children with severe mental disorders. In D. Hawkins and L. Pauling, eds. *Orthomolecular Psychiatry.* San Francisco, Calif.: W. H. Freeman, 1973.

Rimland, B. An orthomolecular study of psychotic children. *Orthomolecular Psychiatry,* 1974, *3,* 371–377.

Rimland, B. Comparative effects of treatment on child's behavior (drugs, therapies, schooling, and several non-treatment events). *Institute for Child Behavior Research,* Publication 34, 1977.

Rimland, B., et al. Vitamin B$_6$ on autistic children: A double blind cross-over study. *American Journal of Psychiatry,* 1978, *35,* 472–475.

Rimland, B., and D. I. Meyer. Malabsorption and the celiac syndrome as possible causes of childhood psychosis: A brief discussion of evidence and need for research. Unpublished manuscript, Institute for Child Behavior Research, San Diego, 1967.

Rimm, D. C. and J. C. Masters. *Behavior therapy: Techniques and empirical findings.* New York: Academic Press, 1979.

Risley, T., and M. M. Wolf. Establishing functional speech in echolalic children. *Behavior Research and Therapy,* 1967, *5,* 73–88.

Ritvo, E. R., ed. *Autism: Diagnosis, current research, and management.* New York: Spectrum, 1976.

Ritzler, B., and G. Rosenbaum. Proprioception in schizophrenics and normals: Effects of stimulus intensity and interstimulus interval. *Journal of Abnormal Psychology,* 1974, *83*(2), 106–111.

Roach, M. Another name for madness. *The New York Times Magazine,* January 16, 1983, 22–31.

Roazen, Paul. *Freud and his followers.* New York: Knopf, 1974.

Robins, L. N. Follow-up studies. In H. C. Quay and J. S. Werry, eds., *Psychopathological disorders of childhood,* 2nd ed. New York: Wiley, 1979.

Robins, L. N., J. E. Helzer, J. Croughan, and K. S. Ratcliff. National Institute of Mental Health diagnostic interview schedule. *Archives of General Psychiatry,* 1981, *38,* 381–389.

Robins, L. N., J. E. Helzer, M. M. Weissman, H. Orvaschel, E. Gruenberg, J. D. Burke, and D. A. Regier. Lifetime prevalence of specific psychiatric disorders in three sites. *Archives of General Psychiatry,* 1984, *41,* 949–958.

Robins, N. L. *Deviant children grow up.* Baltimore, Md.: Williams and Wilkins, 1966.

Robinson, N. M., and H. B. Robinson. *The mentally retarded child, a psychological approach,* 2nd ed. New York: McGraw-Hill, 1976.

Rodin, J. Bidirectional influences of emotionality, stimulus responsivity and metabolic events in obesity, In J. D. Maser and M. E. P. Seligman, eds., *Psychopathology: Experimental models.* San Francisco: W. H. Freeman, 1977.

Rodin, J. Research on eating behavior and obesity: Where does it fit in personality and social psychology? *Personality and Social Psychology Bulletin,* 1977, *3,* 335–355.

Rodin, J. Current status of the internal-external hypothesis for obesity: What went wrong? *American Psychologist,* 1981, *36,* 361–372.

Rodin, G., and K. Voshort. Depression in the medically ill: An overview. *American Journal of Psychiatry,* 1986, *143,* 696–705.

Roesch, R., and S. L. Golding. *Competency to stand trial.* Urbana: University of Illinois Press, 1980.

Rog, D. J., and H. L. Rausch. The psychiatric halfway house: How is it measuring up? *Community Mental Health Journal,* 1975, *11,* 155–162.

Rogentine, G. N., Jr., B. H. Fox, D. P. Van Krammen, J. Rosenblatt, S. Boyd, and W. E. Bunney, Jr. *Psychological and biological factors in short term prognosis of malignant melanoma: A validation study.* Paper given at the 35th Annual Meeting of the American Psychosomatic Society, Washington, D.C.: March, 1978.

Rogers, C. R. *Client-centered therapy: Its current practice, implications and theory.* Boston: Houghton Mifflin, 1951.

Rogers, C. R. Persons or science? A philosophical question. *American Psychologist,* 1955, *10,* 267–278.

Rogers, C. R. A theory of therapy, personality, and interpersonal relationships, as developed in the client-centered framework. In S. Koch, ed., *Psychology: A study of a science,* Vol. 3. New York: Basic Books, 1959.

Rogers, C. R. *On becoming a person.* Boston: Houghton Mifflin, 1961.

Rogers, C. R. *A way of being.* Boston: Houghton Mifflin, 1980.

Rogers, C. R., and R. F. Dymond, eds. *Psychotherapy and personality change: Coordinated studies in the client-centered approach.* Chicago: University of Chicago Press, 1954.

Rohr, C. C., and J. Densen-Gerber. Adolescent drug abuse: An evaluation of 800 inpatients in the Odyssey House program. Paper presented at American Psychiatric Association annual meeting, Washington, D.C., May 3–7, 1971.

Rokeach, M. *The three Christs of Ypsilanti.* New York: Random House, 1964.

Rorschach, H. *Psychodiagnostics: A diagnostic test based on perception.* New York: Grune & Stratton, 1942.

Rose, R. J., and M. A. Chesney. Cardiovascular stress reactivity: A behavioral-genetic perspective. *Behavior Therapy,* 1986, *17,* 314–323.

Rosen, B. M., S. K. Bahn, and M. Kramer. Demographic and diagnostic characteristics of psychiatric outpatients in the U.S.A., 1961. *American Journal of Orthopsychiatry,* 1964, *24,* 455–467.

Rosenhan, D. L. The contextual nature of psychiatric diagnosis. *Journal of Abnormal Psychology,* 1975, *84,* 442–452.

Rosenman, R. H., R. J. Brand, C. D. Jenkins, M. Friedman, R. Straus, and M. Wurm. Coronary heart disease in the Western Collaborative Group study: Final follow-up experience of 8½ years. *Journal of the American Medical Association,* 1975, *8,* 872–877.

Rosenthal, D. *Genetic theory and abnormal behavior.* New York: McGraw-Hill, 1970.

Rosenthal, D. *Genetics of psychopathology.* New York: McGraw-Hill, 1971.

Rosenthal, D., P. H. Wender, S. S. Kety, F. Schulsinger, J. Welner, and L. Ostergaard. Schizophrenics' offspring reared in adoptive homes. In D. Rosenthal and S. S. Kety, eds., *The transmission of schizophrenia.* Oxford: Pergamon Press, 1968.

Rosenthal, R., and L. Jacobson. Teachers' expectancies: Determinants of pupils' I.Q. gains. *Psychological Reports,* 1966, *19,* 115–118.

Rosenthal, T., and A. Bandura. Psychological modeling: Theory and practice. In S. L. Garfield and A. E. Bergin, eds., *Handbook of psychotherapy and behavior change: An empirical analysis,* 2nd ed. New York: John Wiley, 1978.

Rosenzweig, M. R. Environmental complexity, cerebral change and behavior. *American Psychologist,* 1966, *21,* 321–332.

Ross, A. O. *Child behavior therapy: Principles, procedures and empirical basis.* New York: Wiley, 1981.

Ross, D. M., and S. A. Ross. *Hyperactivity: Research, theory, and action.* New York: Wiley, 1976.

Ross, S. APA approved doctoral programs in clinical and in counseling psychology, 1962. *American Psychologist,* 1962, *17,* 501–502.

Roth, L. A commitment law for patients, doctors, and lawyers. *American Journal of Psychiatry,* 1979, *136,* 1121–1127.

Roth, M. The phobic anxiety-depersonalization syndrome. *Proceedings of the Royal Society of Medicine,* 1959, *52,* 587–595.

Roth, M. Senile dementia and its borderlands. In J. O. Cole and J. E. Barrett, eds., *Psychopathology in the aged.* New York: Raven Press, 1980.

Roueché, B. Annals of medicine: As empty as Eve. *The New Yorker,* September 9, 1974, pp. 84–100.

Ruderman, A. J. Dysphoric mood and overeating: A test of restraint theory's disinhibition hypothesis. *Journal of Abnormal Psychology,* 1985, *94,* 78–85.

Ruderman, A. J., and G. T. Wilson. Weight, restraint, cognitions, and counterregulation. *Behaviour Research and Therapy,* 1979, *17,* 581–590.

Rusch, F. R., and D. E. Mithaug. *Vocational training for mentally retarded adults: A behavior analytic approach.* Champaign, Ill.: Research Press, 1980.

Rush, A. J., A. T. Beck, M. Kovac, and S. Hollon. Comparative efficacy of cognitive therapy and imipramine in the treatment of depressed outpatients. *Cog-*

nitive Therapy and Research, 1977, *1,* 17–37.

Russell, D. E. H. *The secret trauma: Incest in the lives of girls and women.* New York: Basic Books, 1986.

Rutter, D. R. Visual interaction in psychiatric patients. *British Journal of Psychiatry,* 1973, *153*(57), 193–202.

Rutter, D. R., and **G. M. Stephenson.** Visual interaction in a group of schizophrenic and depressive patients. *British Journal of Social and Clinical Psychology,* 1972, *11*(1), 57–65.

Rutter, M. Concepts of autism: A review of research. *Journal of Child Psychology and Psychiatry,* 1968, *9,* 1–25.

Rutter, M. The description and classification of infantile autism. In D. W. Churchill, G. D. Alpern, and M. K. DeMyer, eds., *Infantile autism.* Springfield, Ill.: Charles C. Thomas, 1971.

Rutter, M. Childhood schizophrenia reconsidered. *Journal of Autism and Childhood Schizophrenia,* 1972, *2*(44), 315–337.

Rutter, M. *Changing youth in a changing society: Patterns of adolescent development and disorder.* London: Nuffield Provincial Hospitals Trust, 1979.

Rutter, M. Cognitive deficits in the pathogenesis of autism. *Journal of Child Psychology and Psychiatry,* 1983, *24,* 513–531.

Rutter, M., and **N. Garmezy.** Developmental psychopathology. In E. M. Hetherington, ed., *Handbook of child psychology.* Vol. 4: *Socialization, personality, and social development.* New York: Wiley, 1983.

Rutter, M., and **L. Lockyer.** A five to fifteen year follow-up of infantile psychosis: I. Description of sample. *British Journal of Psychiatry,* 1967, *113,* 1169–1182.

Rutter, M., and **D. Shaffer.** DSM-III: A step forward or back in terms of the classification of child psychiatric disorders? *Journal of the American Academy of Child Psychiatry,* 1980, *19,* 371–394.

Rutter, M., J. Tizard, and **K. Whitmore, eds.** *Education, health, and behavior.* Huntington, N.Y.: Krieger, 1981.

Rycroft, C. Introduction to M. Prince, *Dissociation of Personality.* New York: Oxford University Press, 1978.

Sachar, E. J. Neuroendocrine dysfunction in depressive illness. *Annual Review of Medicine,* 1976, *27,* 389–396.

Sackeim, H. A., J. W. Nordlie, and **R. C. Gur.** A model of hysterical and hypnotic blindness: Cognition, motivation, and awareness. *Journal of Abnormal Psychology,* 1979, *88,* 474–489.

Sackeim, H. A., et al. Hemispheric asymmetry in the expression of positive and negative emotions: Neurologic evidence. *Archives of Neurology,* 1982, *39,* 210–218.

Sacks, O. *The man who mistook his wife for a hat and other clinical tales.* New York: Summit Books, 1985.

Sadoff, R. L. Indications for involuntary hospitalization: Dangerousness or mental illness? In W. E. Barton and C. J. Sanborn, eds., *Law and the mental health professions.* New York: International Universities Press, 1978.

Safer, D. J., and **R. P. Allen.** *Hyperactive children: Diagnosis and management.* Baltimore: University Park Press, 1976.

Saghir, M. T., and **E. Robins.** Homosexuality: I. Sexual behavior of the female homosexual. *Archives of General Psychiatry,* 1969, *20,* 192–201.

Saghir, M. T., E. Robins, and **B. Walbran.** Homosexuality: II. Sexual behavior of the male homosexual. *Archives of General Psychiatry,* 1969, *21,* 219–229.

St. George-Hyslop, P., et al. The genetic defect causing familial Alzheimer's disease maps on chromosome 21. *Science,* 1987, *235,* 885–889.

Salter, A. *Conditioned reflex therapy.* New York: Farrar, Strauss, 1949.

Salthouse, T. A. Speed of behavior and its implications for cognition. In J. E. Birren and K. W. Scale, eds., *Handbook for the psychology of aging.* Englewood Cliffs, N.J.: Prentice-Hall, 1985.

Salzman, C., and **J. Lieff.** Interviews with hallucinogenic drug discontinuers. *Journal of Psychedelic Drugs,* 1974, *6*(3), 329–332.

Sanchez, V., and **P. M. Lewinsohn.** Assertive behavior and depression. *Journal of Consulting and Clinical Psychology,* 1980, *48,* 119–120.

Sandberg, S. T., M. Rutter and **E. Taylor.** Hyperkinetic disorder in psychiatric clinic attenders. *Developmental Medicine and Child Neurology,* 1978, *20,* 279–299.

Sanders, J. An autistic child in residential treatment. Paper presented at American Psychological Association meeting, New Orleans, September 1974.

Sandifer, M. G., Jr., C. Pettus, and **D. Quade.** A study of psychiatric diagnosis. *Journal of Nervous and Mental Disease,* 1964, *139,* 350–356.

Santiago, J. M., F. McCall-Perez, and **L. J. Bachrach.** Integrated services for chronic mental patients: Theoretical perspective and experimental results. *General Hospital Psychiatry,* 1985, *7,* 309–315.

Sarason, I. G. A modeling and informational approach to delinquency. In E. Ribes-Inesta and A. Bandura, eds., *Analysis of delinquency and aggression.* Hillsdale, N.J.: Erlbaum, 1976.

Sarrel, P. Biological aspects of sexual functioning. In R. Gemene and C. C. Wheeler, eds., *Progress in sexology.* New York: Plenum, 1977, 227–244.

Sartorius, N., A. Jablensky, and **R. Shapiro.** Cross-cultural differences in the short-term prognosis of schizophrenic psychoses. *Schizophrenia Bulletin,* 1978, *4,* 102–112.

Satir, V. *Conjoint family therapy,* rev. ed. Palo Alto, Calif.: Science and Behavior Books, 1967.

Schachter, S. Eat, eat. *Psychology Today,* 1971, *4*(11), 44–47; 78–79.

Schachter, S. Pharmacological and psychological determinants of smoking. *Annals of Internal Medicine,* 1978, *88,* 104–114.

Schachter, S. Recidivism and self-cure of smoking and obesity. *American Psychologist,* 1982, *37,* 436–444.

Schachter, S., and **L. Gross.** Manipulated time and eating behavior. *Journal of Personality and Social Psychology,* 1968, *10,* 98–106.

Schachter, S., and **B. Latané.** Crime, cognition, and the autonomic nervous system. In D. Levine, ed., *Nebraska Symposium on Motivation,* Vol. 12. Lincoln: University of Nebraska Press, 1964.

Schaefer, H. H., and **P. L. Martin.** *Behavioral therapy.* New York: McGraw-Hill, 1969.

Schaeffer, J., T. Andrysiak, and **J. T. Ungerleider.** Cognition and long-term use of ganja (cannabis). *Science,* 1981, *213,* 465–466.

Schecter, M., E. Jeffries, P. Constance, B. Douglas, M. Maynard, R. Nitz, B. Willoughby, W. Boyko, and **A. McLeod.** Changes in sexual behavior and fear of AIDS. *The Lancet,* June 9, 1984, 1293.

Scheff, T. J. *Being mentally ill: A sociological theory.* Chicago: Aldine, 1966.

Scheff, T. J. *Labeling madness.* Englewood Cliffs, N.J.: Prentice-Hall, 1975.

Schild, S. The family of the retarded child. In R. Koch and J. C. Dobson, eds., *The mentally retarded child and his family.* New York: Brunner/Mazel, 1971.

Schildkraut, J. The catecholamine hypothesis of affective disorders: A review of supporting evidence. *American Journal of Psychiatry,* 1965, *122,* 509–522.

Schildkraut, J. J. Neuropharmacological studies of mood disorders. In J. Zubin and F. A. Freyhan, eds., *Disorders of mood.* Baltimore: Johns Hopkins Press, 1972.

Schmauk, F. J. Punishment, arousal, and avoidance learning in sociopaths. *Journal of Abnormal Psychology,* 1970, *76,* 443–453.

Schmeck, H. M., Jr. The biology of fear and anxiety: Evidence points to chemical triggers. *The New York Times,* September 7, 1982, C7.

Schmidt, G., and **E. Schorsch.** Psychosurgery of sexually deviant patients: Review and analysis of new empirical findings. *Archives of Sexual Behavior*, 1981, *10*(3), 301–323.

Schmidt, H. O., and C. P. Fonda. The reliability of psychiatric diagnosis: A new look. *Journal of Abnormal and Social Psychology*, 1956, *52*, 262–267.

Schmidt, W. Cirrhosis and alcohol consumption: An epidemiological perspective. In G. Edwards and M. Grant, eds., *Alcoholism: New knowledge and new responses*. London: Croom Hall, 1977.

Schneider, K. *Clinical psychopathology*. New York: Grune and Stratton, 1959.

Schofield, W. *Psychotherapy, the Purchase of Friendship*. Englewood Cliffs, N.J.: Prentice-Hall, 1964.

Schopler, F., and R. J. Reichler. Psychobiological referents for the treatment of autism. In D. W. Churchill, G. D. Alpern, and M. K. DeMyer, eds., *Infantile autism*. Springfield, Ill.: Charles C. Thomas, 1971.

Schover, L. R., and J. LoPiccolo. Treatment effectiveness for dysfunctions of sexual desire. *Journal of Sex and Marital Therapy*, 1982, *8*(3), 179–197.

Schreiber, F. *Sybil*. New York: Warner, 1974.

Schuckit, M. A., and V. Rayses. Ethanol ingestion: Differences in blood acetaldehyde concentrations in relatives of alcoholics and controls. *Science*, 1979, *203*, 54–55.

Schulsinger, F. Psychopathy: Heredity and environment. *International Journal of Mental Health*, 1972, *1*, 190–206.

Schulsinger, R., J. Knop, D. W. Goodwin, T. W. Teasdale, and U. Mikkelson. A prospective study of young men at high risk for alcoholism: Social and psychological characteristics. *Archives of General Psychiatry*, 1986, *43*, 755–760.

Schuster, R. Trust: Its implication in the etiology and treatment of psychopathic youths. *International Journal of Offender Therapy and Comparative Criminology*, 1976, *20*, 128–133.

Schwartz, B. A., G. Guilbaud, and H. Fischgold. Études électroencéphalographiques. Le sommeil de nuit: I, L'"insomnie" chronique. *Presse Med*, 1963, *71*, 1474.

Schwartz, G. E. Psychosomatic disorders and biofeedback: A psychobiological model of disregulation. In J. D. Maser and M. E. P. Seligman, eds., *Psychopathology: Experimental models*. San Francisco: Freeman, 1977.

Schwartz, G. E. Psychobiological foundations of psychotherapy and behavior change. In S. L. Garfield and A. E. Bergin, eds., *Handbook of psychotherapy and behavior change*. New York: Wiley, 1978.

Schwartz, G. E., D. A. Weinberger, and J. A. Singer. Cardiovascular differentiation of happiness, sadness, anger, and fear following imagery and exercise. *Psychosomatic Medicine*, 1981, *43*, 343–364.

Schwartz, M. F., and W. H. Masters. The Masters and Johnson program for dissatisfied homosexual men. *American Journal of Psychiatry*, 1984, *141*, 173–181.

Schwartz, S. Effect of neonatal cortical lesions and early environmental factors on adult rat behavior. *Journal of Comparative and Physiological Psychology*, 1964, *57*, 72–77.

Scovern, A. W., and P. R. Kilmann. Status of electroconvulsive therapy: Review of the outcome literature. *Psychological Bulletin*, 1980, *87*, 260–303.

Sears, R. R. Clinical training facilities: 1947. *American Psychologist*, 1947, *2*, 199–205.

Sedgwick, P. Antipsychiatry from the sixties to the eighties. In W. R. Gove, ed., *Deviance and mental illness*. Beverly Hills, Calif.: Sage Publications, 1982.

Segal, D. S., J. Yager, and J. L. Sullivan. *Foundations of biochemical psychiatry*. Boston: Butterworths, 1976.

Seguin, E. *Idiocy: And its treatment by the physiological method*. New York: Wood, 1866.

Seidman, L. J. Schizophrenia and brain dysfunction: An integration of recent neurodiagnostic findings. *Psychological Bulletin*, 1983, *94*, 195–238.

Sekuler, R., and R. D. MacArthur. Alcohol retards visual recovery from glare by hampering target acquisition. *Nature*, 1977, *270*, 428–429.

Selfe, L. *Nadia: A case of extraordinary drawing ability in an autistic child*. New York: Academic Press, 1978.

Seligman, M. E. P. Phobias and preparedness. *Behavior Therapy*, 1971, *2*, 307–320.

Seligman, M. E. P. *Helplessness: On depression, development, and death*. San Francisco: Freeman, 1975.

Seligman, M. E. P. A learned helplessness point of view. In L. P. Rehm, ed., *Behavior therapy for depression: Present status and future directions*. New York: Academic Press, 1981.

Selling, L. S. *Men against madness*. New York: Greenberg, 1940.

Sells, S. B., D. D. Simpson, L. F. Savage, and M. R. Lloyd. Evaluation of drug abuse treatments based on the first year after DARP (IBR Report No. 77–14). Institute of Behavioral Research. Texas Christian University, Fort Worth, Texas, Sept. 1977.

Selye, H. *The stress of life*. New York: McGraw-Hill, 1956.

Selye, H. *Stress without distress*. Philadelphia: Lippincott, 1974.

Semans, J. H. Premature ejaculation: a new approach. *Southern Medical Journal*, 1956, *49*, 353–357.

Serban, G. Stress in normals and schizophrenics. *British Journal of Psychiatry*, 1975, *126*, 397–407.

Shadish, W. R., and R. R. Bootzin. Nursing homes and chronic mental patients. *Schizophrenia Bulletin*, 1981, *7*, 488–498.

Shah, A., and U. Frith. An islet of ability in autistic children: A research note. *Journal of Child Psychology and Psychiatry*, 1983, 24, 613–20.

Shapiro, D., and I. B. Goldstein. Biobehavioral perspectives on hypertension. *Journal of Consulting and Clinical Psychology*, 1982, 841–858.

Shapiro, D. A., and D. Shapiro. Meta-analysis of comparative therapy outcome studies: A replication and refinement. *Psychological Bulletin*, 1982, *92*, 581–604.

Shapiro, S. A. *Contemporary theories of schizophrenia*. New York: McGraw-Hill, 1981.

Shearn, D. Operant conditioning of heart rate. *Science*, 1962, *137*, 530–531.

Sheehan, J. G., and M. Martyn. Stuttering and its disappearance. *Journal of Speech and Hearing Research*, 1970, *13*, 279–289.

Sheehan, S. *Is there no place on earth for me?* Boston: Houghton Mifflin, 1982.

Sher, K. J., and R. W. Levinson. Risk for alcoholism and individual differences in the stress-response-dampening effect of alcohol. *Journal of Abnormal Psychology*, 1982, *91*, 350–367.

Sher, K. J., and K. S. Walitzer. Individual differences in the stress-response-dampening effect of alcohol: A dose-response study. *Journal of Abnormal Psychology*, 1986, 95, 159–167.

Sheridan, E. P., and L. A. Teplin. Police-referred psychiatric emergencies: Advantages of community treatment. *Journal of Community Psychology*, 1981, *9*, 140–147.

Shiffman, S. Relapse following smoking cessation: A situational analysis. *Journal of Consulting and Clinical Psychology*, 1982, *50*, 71–86.

Shneidman, E. S., and N. L. Farberow. Attempted and completed suicide. In E. S. Shneidman, N. L. Farberow, and R. E. Litman, eds., *The psychology of suicide*. New York: Science House, 1970a.

Silberschatz, G., P. B. Fretter, and J. T. Curtis. How do interpretations influence the process of psychotherapy? *Journal of Consulting and Clinical Psychology*, 1986, *54*, 646–652.

Silver, R. L., and C. B. Wortman. Coping with undesirable life events. In J. Garber and M. E. P. Seligman, eds., *Human helplessness: Theory and applications*. New York: Academic Press, 1980.

Simeons, A. T. W. *Man's presumptuous brain: An evolutionary interpretation of psychosomatic disease.* New York: Dutton, 1961.

Simmons, J. Q., and **O. I. Lovaas.** Use of pain and punishment as treatment techniques with childhood schizophrenics. *American Journal of Psychotherapy,* 1969, *23,* 23–36.

Simons, A. D., G. E. Murphy, J. L. Levine, and **R. D. Wetzel.** Cognitive therapy and pharmacotherapy for depression: Sustained improvement over one year. *Archives of General Psychiatry,* 1986, *43,* 43–48.

Sims, E., E. Danforth, E. Horton, G. Bray, J. Glennon, and **L. Salans.** Endocrine and metabolic effects of experimental obesity in man. *Recent Progress in Hormonal Research,* 1973, *29,* 457–496.

Sines, J. O. Selective breeding for development of stomach lesions following stress in the rat. *Journal of Comparative and Physiological Psychology,* 1959, *52,* 615–617.

Sines, J. O. Physiological and behavioral characteristics of rats selectively bred for susceptibility to stomach lesion development. *Journal of Neuropsychiatry,* 1963, *4,* 396–398.

Singer, M., and **L. C. Wynne.** Differentiating characteristics of the parents of childhood schizophrenics, childhood neurotics, and young adult schizophrenics. *American Journal of Psychiatry,* 1963, *120,* 234–243.

Sizemore, C. C., and **E. S. Pittillo.** *I'm Eve.* Garden City, N.Y.: Doubleday, 1977.

Skeels, H. M., and **H. B. Dye.** A study of the effects of differential stimulation on mentally retarded children. *AAMD Proceedings,* 1938–39, *44,* 114–136.

Skinner, B. F. *Science and human behavior.* New York: Free Press, 1965.

Sklar, L. S., and **H. Anisman.** Stress and cancer. *Psychological Bulletin,* 1981, *89,* 369–406.

Sklar, L. S., and **H. Anisman.** Stress and coping factors influence tumor growth. *Science,* 1979, *205,* 513–515.

Slater, E., and **P. W. Beard.** The Schizophrenia-like psychoses of epilepsy. In J. Shields and I. J. Gottesman, eds., *Man, mind and heredity: Selected papers of Eliot Slater on psychiatry and genetics.* Baltimore: Johns Hopkins Press, 1971.

Slavson, S. R. *A textbook in analytic group psychotherapy.* New York: International Universities Press, 1964.

Sloane, R. B., F. R. Staples, A. H. Cristol, N. J. Yorkston, and **K. Whipple.** *Psychoanalysis versus behavior therapy.* Cambridge: Harvard University Press, 1975.

Smith, M. L., G. V. Glass, and **T. J. Miller.** *The benefits of psychotherapy.* Baltimore: Johns Hopkins, 1980.

Snyder, C. R. *Alcohol and the Jews.* New York: Free Press, 1958.

Snyder, J. J. Reinforcement and analysis of interaction in problem and nonproblem families. *Journal of Abnormal Psychology,* 1977, *86,* 528–535.

Snyder, S. H. Catecholamines in the brain as mediators of amphetamine psychosis. *Archives of General Psychiatry,* 1972, *27,* 169–179.

Snyder, S. H. The dopamine hypothesis of schizophrenia: Focus on the dopamine receptor. *American Journal of Psychiatry,* 1976, *133*(2), 197–202.

Snyder, S. H. The true speed trip: Schizophrenia. In D. Goleman and R. J. Davidson, eds., *Consciousness: Brain, states of awareness, and mysticism.* New York: Harper & Row, 1979.

Snyder, S. H. *Biological aspects of mental disorder.* New York: Oxford University Press, 1980.

Solnet, A. J., and **M. H. Stark.** *Mourning and the birth of a defective child.* New Haven, Conn.: Yale University School of Medicine, Department of Pediatrics and Child Study Center, 1961.

Solomon, R. L. The opponent-process theory of acquired motivation: The costs of pleasure and the benefits of pain. *American Psychologist,* 1980, *35,* 691–712.

Solomon, R. L., and **J. D. Corbit.** An opponent-process theory of motivation: I. Temporal dynamics of affect. *Psychological Review,* 1974, *81,* 119–145.

Sorosky, A. D., E. M. Orintz, N. B. Brown, and **E. R. Ritvo.** Systematic observations of autistic behavior. *Archives of General Psychiatry,* 1968, *18,* 439–449.

Soskin, W. F. Influence of four types of data on diagnostic conceptualization in psychological testing. *Journal of Abnormal and Social Psychology,* 1959, 58, 69–78.

Southwick, L., C. Steele, A. Marlatt, and **M. Lindell.** Alcohol-related expectancies: Defined by phase of intoxication and drinking experience. *Journal of Consulting and Clinical Psychology,* 1981, *49,* 713–721.

Sovner, R., and **A. D. Hurley.** Do the mentally retarded suffer from affective illness? *Archives of General Psychiatry,* 1983, *40,* 61–67.

Spitz, R. A. Hospitalism: An inquiry into the genesis of psychiatric conditions in early childhood. *Psychoanalytic Study of the Child,* 1945, *1,* 53–74.

Spitzer, R. L. More on pseudoscience in science and the case for psychiatric diagnosis: A critique of D. L. Rosenhan's "On Being Sane in Insane Places" and "The Contextual Nature of Psychiatric Diagnosis." *Archives of General Psychiatry,* 1976, *33,* 459–470.

Spitzer, R. L., J. Endicott, and **M. Gib-**

bon. Crossing the border into borderline personality and borderline schizophrenia. *Archives of General Psychiatry,* 1979, *36,* 17–24.

Spitzer, R. L., and **J. L. Fleiss.** A reanalysis of the reliability of psychiatric diagnosis. *British Journal of Psychiatry,* 1974, *125,* 341–347.

Spitzer, R. L., A. E. Skodol, M. Gibbon, and **J. B. W. Williams.** *Psychopathology: A case book.* New York: McGraw-Hill, 1983.

Squire, L. R., and **P. C. Slater.** Bilateral and unilateral ECT: Effects on verbal and nonverbal memory. *American Journal of Psychiatry,* 1978, *135,* 1316–1320.

Squire, L. R., P. C. Slater, and **P. L. Miller.** Retrograde amnesia and bilateral electroconvulsive therapy. *Archives of General Psychiatry,* 1981, *38,* 89–95.

Stampfl, T. G. Implosive therapy: A learning-theory derived psychodynamic therapeutic technique. Paper presented at a colloquium of the University of Illinois, 1961.

Standage, K. F. Schizophreniform psychosis among epileptics in a mental hospital. *British Journal of Psychiatry,* 1973, *123,* 231–232.

Starr, A. *Psychodrama: Rehearsal for living.* Chicago: Nelson-Hall, 1977.

Steel, C. M., L. Southwick, and **R. Pagano.** Drinking your troubles away: The role of activity in mediating alcohol's reduction of psychological stress. *Journal of Abnormal Psychology,* 1986, *95,* 173–180.

Stengel, E. *Suicide and attempted suicide.* Baltimore, Md.: Penguin, 1964.

Stenstedt, A. A study of manic-depressive psychosis: Clinical, social, and genetic investigations. *Acta Scandinavica Supplementum,* 1952, *79.*

Stephens, J. H. Long term prognosis and followup in schizophrenia. *Schizophrenia Bulletin,* 1978, *4*(1), 25.

Steptoe, A. Psychophysiological processes in disease. In A. Steptoe and A. Mathews, eds., *Health care and human behavior.* New York: Academic Press, 1984.

Steptoe, A., D. Melville, and **A. Ross.** Behavioural response demands, cardiovascular reactivity and essential hypertension. *Psychosomatic Medicine,* 1984, *46,* 33–48.

Stilling (1846). Cited in H. Barden, *Neuromelanin.* In Benjamin B. Wolman, ed., *International encyclopedia of psychiatry, psychology, psychoanalysis, and neurology,* Vol. 8. New York: Van Nostrand Reinhold/Aesculapius, 1977.

Stokes, T. F., and **D. M. Baer.** An implicit technology of generalization. *Journal of Applied Behavior Analysis,* 1977, *10,* 349–368.

Stone, A. A. *Mental health and law: A system in transition.* Rockville, Md.: National Institute of Mental Health, 1975.

Stone, A. The Tarasoff decision: Suing psychotherapists to safeguard society. *Harvard Law Review*, 1976, *90*, 358.

Stone, M. *The borderline syndromes.* New York: McGraw-Hill, 1980.

Story, I. Caricature and impersonating the other: Observations from the psychotherapy of anorexia nervosa. *Psychiatry*, 1976, *39*, 176–188.

Straus, M. A. Stress and child abuse. In C. Henry Kempe and R. E. Helfer, eds., *The battered child*, 3rd ed. Chicago: University of Chicago Press, 1980, pp. 86–103.

Strauss, J. S., W. T. Carpenter, and **J. J. Bartko.** The diagnosis and understanding of schizophrenia: II. Speculations on the processes that underlie schizophrenic symptoms and signs. *Schizophrenia Bulletin*, 1974, *11*, 61–76.

Strauss, M. E. Behavioral differences between acute and chronic schizophrenics: Course of psychosis, effects of institutionalization, or sampling biases? *Psychological Bulletin*, 1973, *79*, 271–279.

Strauss, M. E., W. C. Foureman, and **S. D. Parwatikar.** Schizophrenics' size estimations of thematic stimuli. *Journal of Abnormal Psychology*, 1974, *83*(2), 117–123.

Straw, R. B. *Meta-analysis of deinstitutionalization in mental health.* Unpublished doctoral dissertation, Northwestern University, 1982.

Strelnick A. H. Multiple family therapy: A review of the literature. *Family Process*, 1977, *16*, 307–325.

Stricker, G. Some issues in psychodynamic treatment of the depressed patient. *Professional Psychology: Research and Practice*, 1983, *14*, 209–217.

Stromberg, C. D., and **A. A. Stone.** A model state law on civil commitment of the mentally ill. *Harvard Journal on Legislation*, 1983, *20*, 275–396.

Stuart, R. B. Behavioral contracting within the families of delinquents. *Journal of Behavior Therapy and Experimental Psychiatry*, 1971, *2*, 1–11.

Stuart, R. B. Self-help group approach to self-management. In R. B. Stuart, ed., *Behavioral self-management: Strategies, techniques and outcome.* New York: Brunner/Mazel, 1977.

Stunkard, A. J., and **C. Koch.** The interpretation of gastric motility: I. Apparent bias in the reports of hunger by obese persons. *Archives of General Psychiatry*, 1964, *11*, 74–82.

Sullivan, H. S. *Clinical studies in psychiatry.* New York: Norton, 1956.

Sullivan, H. S. *Schizophrenia as a human process.* New York: Norton, 1962.

Suomi, S. J. Relevance of animal models for clinical psychology. In P. C. Kendall and J. N. Butcher, eds., *Handbook of research methods in clinical psychology.* New York: Wiley, 1982.

Sushinsky, L. An illustration of a behavioral therapy intervention with nursing staff in a therapeutic role. *Journal of Psychiatric Nursing and Mental Health Services*, 1970, *8*(5), 24–26.

Symmonds, C. P. Concussion and its sequelae. *Lancet*, 1962, *1*, 1–5.

Szasz, T. S. *The myth of mental illness.* New York: Harper & Row, 1961.

Szasz, T. S. *Law, liberty, and psychiatry.* New York: Macmillan, 1963.

Szasz, T. *Psychiatric slavery.* New York: Free Press, 1977.

Szymanski, L. S., and **P. E. Tanguay,** eds., *Emotional disorders of mentally retarded persons.* Baltimore: University Park Press, 1980.

Szyrynski, V. Anorexia nervosa and psychotherapy. *American Journal of Psychotherapy*, 1973, *27*, 492–505.

Taft, L., and **W. Goldfarb.** Prenatal and perinatal factors in childhood schizophrenia. *Developmental Medicine and Child Neurology*, 1964, *6*(1), 32–43.

Taft, R. The ability to judge people. *Psychological Bulletin*, 1955, *52*, 1–28.

Takahashi, S., H. Kanai, and **Y. Miyamoto.** Reassessment of elevated serotonin levels in blood platelets in early infantile autism. *Journal of Autism and Childhood Schizophrenia*, 1976, *6*(31), 7–26.

Talovic, S. A., S. A. Mednick, F. Schulsinger, and **I. R. H. Falloon.** Schizophrenia in high-risk subjects: Prognostic maternal characteristics. *Journal of Abnormal Psychology*, 1980, *89*, 501–504.

Tart, C. T. *States of Consciousness.* New York: Dutton, 1975.

Tarver, S. G., D. P. Hallahan, J. M. Kauffman, and **D. W. Ball.** Verbal rehearsal and selective attention in children with learning disabilities: A developmental lag. *Journal of Experimental Child Psychology*, 1976, *22*, 375–385.

Test, M. A., and **L. I. Stein.** Training in community living: Research design and results. In L. I. Stein and M. A. Test, eds., *Alternatives to mental hospital treatment.* New York: Plenum, 1978.

Thigpen, C. H., and **H. Cleckley.** *The three faces of Eve.* New York: McGraw-Hill, 1957.

Thompson, J. K., G. J. Jarvie, B. B. Lahey, and **K. J. Cureton.** Exercise and obesity: Etiology, physiology, and intervention. *Psychological Bulletin*, 1982, *91*, 55–79.

Thompson, S. C. Will it hurt less if I control it? A complex answer to a simple question. *Psychological Bulletin*, 1981, *90*, 89–101.

Thompson, T., and **J. Grabowski.** *Behavior modification of the mentally retarded*, 2nd ed. New York: Oxford University Press, 1977.

Thomson, N., D. Fraser, and **A. McDougall.** The reinstatement of speech in near-mute chronic schizophrenics by instructions, imitative prompts and reinforcement. *Journal of Behavior Therapy and Experimental Psychiatry*, 1974, *5*, 83–89.

Thoresen, C. E., M. Friedman, J. K. Gill, and **D. K. Ulmer.** The recurrent coronary prevention project. Some preliminary findings. *Acta Medica Scandinavia*, 1982, *660* (suppl.), 172–192.

Thoresen, J. Lesbians and gay men: Complements and contrasts. Paper presented at the Society for the Scientific Study of Sex. Philadelphia, April 7, 1984.

Thorne, F. C. The etiology of sociopathic reactions. *American Journal of Psychotherapy*, 1959, *13*, 319–330.

Tinklenberg, J. R. A clinical view of the amphetamines. *American Family Physician*, 1971a, *4*(5), 82–86.

Tinklenberg, J. R. Marihuana and crime (a consultant's report prepared for the National Commission on Marihuana and Drug Abuse), October 1971b.

Tinklenberg, J. R. What a physician should know about marihuana. *Rational Drug Therapy* (American Pharmacology and Experimental Therapeutics), 1975.

Tinklenberg, J. R., and **K. M. Woodrow.** Drug use among youthful assaultive and sexual offenders. *The Association for Research in Nervous and Mental Disease: Aggression*, 1974, *52*, 209–224.

Tizard, B. The personality of epileptics: A discussion of the evidence. *Psychological Bulletin*, 1962, *59*, 196–210.

Tollefson, D. J. The relationship between the occurrence of fractures and life crisis events. *Master of Nursing Thesis*, 1972, University of Washington, Seattle.

Tolman, E. C. Cognitive maps in rats and men. *Psychological Review*, 1948, *55*, 189–208.

Tolman, E. C., and **C. H. Honzig.** "Insight" in rats. *University of California Publications in Psychology*, 1930, *4*, 215–232.

Torgersen, S. Genetic factors in anxiety disorders. *Archives of General Psychiatry*, 1983, *40*, 1085–1089.

Torgersen, S. Genetic factors in moderately severe and mild affective disorders. *Archives of General Psychiatry*, 1986, *43*, 222–226.

Travaglini, P., et al. Some aspects of hypothalamic-pituitary function in patients with anorexia nervosa. *Acta Endocrinologica*, 1976, *81*, 252–262.

Trowell, I. Telephone services. In L. D. Hankoff and B. Einsidler, eds., *Suicide: Theory and clinical aspects.* Littleton, Mass.: PSG Publishing, 1979.

Tucker, J. A., R. E. Vuchinich, and **M. B. Sobell.** Alcohol consumption as a self-handicapping strategy. *Journal of Abnormal Psychology*, 1981, *90*, 220–230.

Tulkin, S. R., and J. Kagan. Mother-child interaction in the first year of life. *Child Development*, 1972, *43*, 31–41.

Tulving, E. and Z. Pearlstone. Availability versus accessibility of information in memory for words. *Journal of Verbal Learning and Verbal Behavior*, 1966, *5*, 381–391.

Uhde, T. W., P. P. Roy-Byrne, B. J. Vittone, J. P. Boulenger, and A. M. Post. Phenomenology and neurobiology of panic disorder. In A. H. Tuma and J. D. Maser, eds., *Anxiety and the anxiety disorders*. Hillsdale, N.J.: Erlbaum, 1985.

Uhlenhuth, E. H., M. B. Balter, G. D. Mellinger, I. H. Cisin, and J. Clinthorne. Symptom checklist syndromes in the general population. *Archives of General Psychiatry*, 1983, *40*, 1167–1173.

Ullmann, L. P., and L. Krasner, eds., *Case studies in behavior modification*. New York: Holt, Rinehart and Winston, 1965.

Ullmann, L. P., and L. Krasner. *A psychological approach to abnormal behavior*, 2nd ed. Englewood Cliffs, N.J.: Prentice-Hall, 1975.

U.S. Bureau of the Census. *Statistical abstract of the United States*. Washington, D. C.: Government Printing Office, 1986.

U.S. Department of Health and Human Services. *The fourth special report to the United States Congress on alcohol and health*. Washington, D.C.: Alcohol, Drug Abuse, and Mental Health Administration, January, 1981.

U.S. Department of Health, Education, and Welfare. *Prevalence of selected chronic respiratory conditions*. Vital and Health Statistics, Series 10, No. 84, 1970.

U.S. Public Health Service. *Smoking and health*, Report of the Advisory Committee to the Surgeon General of the Public Health Service. Washington, D.C.: Department of Health, Education, and Welfare, 1964.

Upper, D., and S. M. Ross. Behavioral group therapy: I. Emotional, avoidance, and social skills problems of adults. In M. Hersen, R. M. Eisler, and P. M. Miller, eds., *Progress in behavior modification*, Vol. 5. New York: Academic Press, 1977.

Vaillant, G. E. A 10-year follow-up of remitting schizophrenics. *Schizophrenia Bulletin*, 1978, *4*, 78–85.

Vaillant, G. E., and E. S. Milofsky. The etiology of alcoholism: A prospective view point. *American Psychologist*, 1982, *37*, 494–503.

Valenstein, E. S. *Brain control*. New York: Wiley, 1973.

Van Buskirk, S. S. A two-phase perspective on the treatment of anorexia nervosa. *Psychological Bulletin*, 1977, *84*, 529–538.

van den Berg, J. H. What is psychotherapy? *Humanitas 1971*, win, *7*(3), 321–370.

Vanden-Bos, G. R., ed., Special issue: Psychotherapy research. *American Psychologist*, 1986, *41*, 111–215.

Van Kammen, D. P. Y-Aminobutyric acid (Gaba) and the Dopamine hypothesis of schizophrenia. *American Journal of Psychiatry*, 1977, *134*, 138–143.

Van Wyk, P. Psychosocial development of heterosexual, bisexual, and homosexual behavior. *Archives of Sexual Behavior*, 1984, *13*, 506–544.

Vaughn, C. E., and J. P. Leff. The measurement of expressed emotion in the families of psychiatric patients. *British Journal of Social and Clinical Psychology*, 1976, *15*, 157–165.

Vaughn, C. E., K. Snyder, S. Jones, W. B. Freeman, and I. R. H. Falloon. Family factors in schizophrenic relapse: A replication in California of British research on expressed emotion. *Archives of General Psychiatry*, 1984, *41*, 1169–1177.

Velten, E. A laboratory task for the induction of mood states. *Behavior Research and Therapy*, 1968, *6*, 473–482.

Venables, P. H. Input dysfunction in schizophrenia. In B. A. Maher, ed., *Progress in experimental personality research*. New York: Academic Press, 1964.

Vernon, P. Psychological effects of air raids. *Journal of Abnormal and Social Psychology*, 1941, *36*, 457–476.

Visintainer, M. A., J. R. Volpicelli, and M. E. P. Seligman. Tumor rejection in rats after inescapable or escapable shock. *Science*, April 1982, *216*(23), 437–439.

Wachtel, P. *Psychoanalysis and behavior therapy: Toward an integration*. New York: Basic Books, 1977.

Waggoner, R. W., and B. K. Bagchi. Initial masking of organic brain changes by psychic symptoms. *American Journal of Psychiatry*, 1954, *110*, 904–910.

Waldron, S. The significance of childhood neurosis for adult mental health: A follow-up. *American Journal of Psychiatry*, 1976, *133*, 532–538.

Walker, B. B. Treating stomach disorders: Can we reinstate regulatory processes? In W. Whitehead and R. Holzl, eds., *Psychophysiology of the gastrointestinal tract*. New York: Plenum, 1983.

Walker, J. I. and J. O. Cavenar. Vietnam veterans: Their problems continue. *Journal of Nervous and Mental Disease*, 1982, *170*, 174–180.

Wallace, C. J., C. J. Nelson, R. P. Liberman, R. A. Aitchison, D. Lukoff, J. P. Elder, and C. Ferris. A review and critique of social skills training with schizophrenic patients. *Schizophrenia Bulletin*, 1980, *6*, 42–63.

Wallace, C. J., J. R. Teigen, R. P. Liberman, and V. Baker. Destructive behavior created by contingency contracts and assertive training: A case study. *Journal of Behavior Therapy and Experimental Psychiatry*, 1973, *4*, 273–274.

Walsh, T. Premature parenting and child abuse. Paper presented at the Workshop on Teen Parenthood, March 8, 1977. Onondaga Community College, New York.

Wardle, J. Dietary restraint and binge eating. *Behavioural Analysis and Modification*, 1980, *4*, 201–209.

Wasserman, M. D., C. P. Pollak, A. J. Spielman, and E. D. Weitzman. Theoretical and technical problems in the measurement of nocturnal penile tumescence for the differential diagnosis of impotence. *Psychosomatic Medicine*, 1980, *41*, 575–585.

Watson, C. G. and C. Buranen. The frequency and identification of false positive conversion reactions. *Journal of Nervous and Mental Disease*, 1979, *167*, 243–247.

Watson, J. B. Psychology as the behaviorist views it. *Psychological Review*, 1913, *20*, 158–177.

Watson, J. B., and R. Rayner. Conditioning emotional responses. *Journal of Experimental Psychology*, 1920, *3*, 1–14.

Watson, L. S., and R. Uzzell. Teaching self-help skills to the mentally retarded. In J. L. Matson and J. R. McCartney, eds., *Handbook of behavior modification with the mentally retarded*. New York: Plenum, 1981.

Watzlawick, P., J. Beavin, and D. Jackson. *Pragmatics of human communication: A study of interaction patterns, pathologies, and paradoxes*. New York: Norton, 1967.

Watzlawick, P., J. Weakland, and R. Fisch. *Change: Principles of problem formation and problem resolution*. New York: W. W. Norton, 1974.

Webb, L. J., R. S. Gold, E. E. Johnstone, and C. C. DiClemente. Accuracy of *DSM III* diagnoses following a training program. *American Journal of Psychiatry*, 1981, *138*, 376–378.

Webster, C. D., H. McPherson, L. Sloman, M. A. Evans, and E. Kuchar. Communicating with an autistic boy by gestures. *Journal of Autism and Childhood Schizophrenia*, 1973, *3*, 337–346.

Wechsler, D. *The measurement and appraisal of adult intelligence*, 4th ed. Baltimore, Md.: Williams and Wilkins, 1958.

Weihofen, H. *The urge to punish.* London. V. Gollancz, 1957.

Weinberger, D. R., L. B. Bigelow, and **J. E. Kleinman.** Cerebral ventricular enlargement in chronic schizophrenia: Its association with poor response in treatment. *Archives of General Psychiatry,* 1980, *37.*

Weinberger, D. R., L. E. DeLisi, G. P. Perman, S. Targum, and **R. J. Wyatt.** Computed tomography in schizophreniform disorder and other acute psychiatric disorders. *Archives of General Psychiatry,* 1982, *39,* 778–783.

Weinberger, D. R., et al. Poor premorbid adjustment and CT scan abnormalities in chronic schizophrenia. *American Journal of Psychiatry,* 1980, *137,* 1410–1413.

Weiner, B. A. Mental disability and the criminal law. In S. J. Brakel, J. Parry, and B. A. Weiner, eds., *The mentally disabled and the law,* 3rd ed. Chicago: American Bar Foundation, 1985.

Weiner, D. B. The apprenticeship of Philippe Pinel: A new document, "Observations of Citizen Pussin on the Insane." *American Journal of Psychiatry,* 1979, *136,* 1128–1134.

Weiss, E., and **O. English.** *Psychosomatic Medicine.* Philadelphia: W. B. Saunders, 1943.

Weiss, G., L. Hechtman, and **T. Perlman.** Hyperactive as young adults: School, employer and self-rating scales, obtained during a ten-year follow-up evaluation. *American Journal of Orthopsychiatry,* 1978, *48*(3), 430–445.

Weiss, J. M. Effects of coping behavior in different warning-signal conditions on stress pathology in rats. *Journal of Comparative and Physiological Psychology,* 1971, *77,* 1–13.

Weiss, J. M. Psychosomatic disorders. In J. D. Maser and M. Seligman, eds., *Psychopathology: Experimental models.* San Francisco: W. H. Freeman, 1977.

Weiss, J. M. A model for neurochemical study of depression. Paper presented at the annual meeting of the American Psychological Association, Washington, D.C., August, 1982.

Weiss, J. M., H. I. Glazer, and **L. A. Pohorecky.** Coping behavior and neurochemical changes: an alternative explanation for the original "learned helplessness" experiments. In G. Serban and A. Kling, eds., *Animal models of human psychobiology.* New York: Plenum Press, 1976.

Weiss, R. L., H. Hops, and **G. R. Patterson.** A framework for conceptualizing marital conflict: A technology for altering it, some data for evaluating it. In L. A. Hamerlynck, L. G. Handy, and E. J. Mash, eds., *Behavior change: The Fourth Banff Conference on Behavior Modification.* Champaign, Ill.: Research Press, 1973.

Weissman, M. M. Epidemiology of suicide attempts, 1960 to 1971. *Archives of General Psychiatry,* 1974, *30,* 737–746.

Welch, M. W., and **J. W. Gist.** *The open token economy system: A handbook for a behavioral approach to rehabilitation.* Springfield, Ill.: Charles C. Thomas, 1974.

Wenar, C. *Psychopathology from infancy through adolescence: A developmental approach.* New York: Random House, 1983.

Wender, P. *Minimal brain dysfunction in children.* New York: Wiley-Interscience, 1971.

Wender, P. H., S. S. Kety, D. Rosenthal, F. Schulsinger, J. Ortmann, and **I. Lunde.** Psychiatric disorders in the biological and adaptive families of adopted individuals with affective disorders. *Archives of General Psychiatry,* 1986, *43,* 923–929.

Werry, J. S. The childhood psychoses. In H. C. Quay and J. S. Werry, eds., *Psychopathological disorders of childhood,* 2nd ed. New York: Wiley, 1979a.

Werry, J. S. Psychosomatic disorders, psychogenic symptoms, and hospitalization. In H. C. Quay and J. S. Werry, eds., *Psychopathological disorders of childhood,* 2nd ed. New York: Wiley, 1979b.

Wesson, D. R., and **D. E. Smith.** Barbiturate use as an intoxicant: A San Francisco perspective. Testimony to be presented to the subcommittee to investigate juvenile delinquency. December 15, 1971.

Wetherby, A. M. Ontongeny of communicative functions in autism. *Journal of Autism and Developmental Disorders,* 1986, *16,* 295–316.

Wexler, D. B. *Mental health law: Major issues.* New York: Plenum, 1981.

Wexler, D. B. Seclusion and restraint: Lessons from law, psychiatry, and psychology. *International Journal of Law and Psychiatry,* 1982, *5,* 285–294.

White, R. W., and **N. F. Watt.** *The abnormal personality.* New York: The Ronald Press, 1973.

Whitehead, W. E., and **L. S. Bosmajian,** Behavioral medicine approaches to gastrointestinal disorders. *Journal of Consulting and Clinical Psychology,* 1982, *50,* 972–983.

Whitlock, F. A. The aetiology of hysteria. *Acta Psychiatrica Scandinavica,* 1967, *43,* 144–162.

Whittaker, J. O. Alcohol and the Standing Rock Sioux tribe: A twenty-year follow-up study. *Journal of Studies on Alcohol,* 1982, *43,* 191–199.

Whybrow, P. C., H. S. Akiskal, and **W. T. McKinney, Jr.** *Mood disorders: Toward a new psychobiology.* New York: Plenum Press, 1984.

Whybrow, P. C., and **A. J. Prange.** A hypothesis of thyroid-catecholamine-receptor interaction. *Archives of General Psychiatry,* 1981, *38,* 106–113.

Wickes-Nelson, R., and **Israel, A. C.** *Behavior disorders of childhood.* Englewood Cliffs, N.J.: Prentice-Hall, 1984.

Widiger, T. A., J. B. W. Williams, R. L. Spitzer, and **A. Frances.** The MCMI as a measure of *DSM-III. Journal of Personality Assessment,* 1985, *49,* 366–378.

Wieland, I. H. Discussion of treatment approaches. In D. W. Churchill, G. D. Alpern, and M. K. DeMyer, eds, *Infantile autism.* Springfield, Ill.: Charles C. Thomas, 1971.

Wietgresse, S., et al. Cloning of a gene whose expression is increased in scrapie and in senile plaques in human brain, *Science,* 1985, *230,* 1177–1179.

Williams, A. F., M. A. Peat, D. J. Cronch, J. K. Wells, and **B. S. Finkle.** Drugs in fatally injured young male drivers. *Public Health Reports,* 1985, *100,* 19–25.

Williams, E. An analysis of gaze in schizophrenics. *British Journal of Social and Clinical Psychology,* 1974, *13,* 1–8.

Williams, G. J. R. Child abuse. Edited by C. E. Walker and M. C. Roberts. *Handbook of clinical child psychology.* New York: Wiley, 1983, pp. 1219–1248.

Williams, R. B., Jr., J. D. Lane, C. M. Kuhn, W. Melosh, A. D. White, and **S. M. Schanberg.** Type A behavior and elevated physiological and neuroendocrine responses to cognitive tasks. *Science,* 1982, *218,* 483–485.

Williams, R. L. Danger: Testing and dehumanizing black children. *Clinical Child Psychology Newsletter,* Spring 1970.

Wilmer, H. A. Origins of a Jungian-oriented therapeutic community for schizophrenic patients. *Hospital and Community Psychiatry,* 1976, *27,* 338–372.

Wilson, G. T., and **K. D. O'Leary.** *Principles of behavior therapy.* Englewood Cliffs, N.J.: Prentice-Hall, 1980.

Wilson, J. P. *Identity, ideology and crisis: The Vietnam veteran in transition. Part I.* Unpublished monograph. Cleveland State University, 1977.

Wilson, M. Female homosexuals' need for dominance and endurance. *Psychological Reports,* 1984, *55,* 79–82.

Wing, L. The handicaps of autistic children: A comparative study. *Journal of Child Psychology and Psychiatry,* 1969, *10,* 1–40.

Wing, L. *Autistic children: A guide for parents and professionals.* New York: Brunner/Mazel, 1972.

Wing, L. Language, social, and cognitive impairments in autism and severe mental retardation. *Journal of Autism and Developmental Disorders,* 1981, *11,* 31–44.

Winnicott, D. W. *Through paediatrics to psycho-analysis: The collected papers of*

D. W. Winnicott. London: Tavistock, 1958.

Winokur, G. The validity of neurotic-reactive depression: New data and reappraisal. *Archives of General Psychiatry*, 1985, *42*, 1116–1122.

Witkin, H. A., S. A. Mednick, F. Schulsinger, E. Bakkestom, K. O. Christiansen, D. R. Goodenough, K. Hirchhorn, C. Lunsteen, D. R. Owen, J. Philip, D. B. Ruben, and M. Stocking. Criminality in XYY and XXY men. *Science*, 1976, *193*, 547–555.

Witzig, J. S. The group treatment of male exhibitionists. *American Journal of Psychiatry*, 1968, *25*, 75–81.

Wolberg, L. R. *The technique of psychotherapy*. New York: Grune & Stratton.

Wolf, M. M., T. Risley, and M. L. Mees. Application of operant conditioning procedures to the behavior problems of an autistic child. *Behavior Research and Therapy*, 1964, *1*, 305–313.

Wolf, S. Cardiovascular disease. In E. D. Wittkower and H. Warnes, eds., *Psychosomatic medicine: Its clinical applications*. New York: Harper and Row, 1977.

Wolf, S., and H. G. Wolff. *Human gastric functions*. New York: Oxford University Press, 1947.

Wolff, P. H. Ethnic differences in alcohol sensitivity. *Science*, 1972, *175*, 449–450.

Wolpe, J. *Psychotherapy by reciprocal inhibition*. Stanford, Calif.: Stanford University Press, 1958.

Wolpe, J. *The practice of behavior therapy*. New York: Pergamon Press, 1969.

Wolpe, J. *The practice of behavior therapy*, 2nd ed. New York: Pergamon Press, 1973.

Wolpe, J. *Theme and variations: A behavior therapy casebook*. Elmsford, N.Y.: Pergamon Press, 1976.

Wolpe, J. Cognition and causation in human behavior and its therapy. *American Psychologist*, 1978, *33*, 437–446.

Wolpe, J., and D. Wolpe. *Our useless years*. Boston: Houghton-Mifflin, 1981.

Woodruff, R. A., P. J. Clayton, and S. B. Guze. Is Everyone Depressed? *American Journal of Psychiatry*, 1975, *132*, 627–628.

Wynne, L. C., M. T. Singer, J. J. Bartko, and M. L. Toohey. Schizophrenics and their families: Recent research on parental communication. In J. M. Tanner, ed., *Psychiatric research: The widening perspective*. New York: International Universities Press, 1975.

Yablonsky, L. *Psychodrama: Resolving emotional problems through role-playing*. New York: Basic Books, 1976.

Yalom, I. D. *The theory and practice of group psychotherapy* (2d ed.). New York: Basic Books, 1975.

Yeaton, W. H. and L. Sechrest. Critical dimensions in the choice and maintenance of successful treatments: Strength, integrity, and effectiveness. *Journal of Consulting and Clinical Psychology*, 1981, *49*, 156–167.

Young, J. G., M. E. Kavanagh, G. M. Anderson, B. A. Shaywitz, and D. J. Cohen. Clinical neurochemistry of autism and associated disorders. *Journal of Autism and Developmental Disorders*, 1982, *12*, 147–165.

Youngren, M. A., and P. M. Lewinsohn. The functional relation between depression and problematic interpersonal behavior. *Journal of Abnormal Psychology*, 1980, *89*, 333–341.

Zafiropoulou, M., and F. M. McPherson. "Preparedness" and the severity and outcome of clinical phobias. *Behavior Research and Therapy*, 1986, *24*, 222–222.

Zarit, S. H., N. K. Orr, and J. M. Zarit. *The hidden victims of Alzheimer's disease: Families under stress*. New York: New York University Press, 1985.

Zax, M., and G. Stricker. *Patterns of psychopathology: Case studies in behavioral dysfunction*. New York and London: Macmillan, 1963.

Zigler, E., and J. Levine. Premorbid adjustment and paranoid-nonparanoid status in schizophrenia: A further investigation. *Journal of Abnormal Psychology*, 1973, *82*(2), 189–199.

Zigler, E., and J. Levine. Age on first hospitalization of schizophrenics: A developmental approach. *Journal of Abnormal Psychology*, 1981, *90*, 458–467.

Zigler, E., and L. Phillips. Psychiatric diagnosis and symptomatology. *Journal of Abnormal and Social Psychology*, 1961, *63*, 69–75.

Zilbergeld, B., and C. R. Ellison. Desire discrepancies and arousal problems in sex therapy. In S. L. Leiblum and L. A. Pervin, eds., *Principles and practice of sex therapy*. New York: Guilford, 1980.

Zilboorg, G., and G. W. Henry. *A history of medical psychology*. New York: Norton, 1941.

Zimbardo, P. *Shyness*. Reading, Mass.: Addison-Wesley, 1977.

Zimmerman, M., W. Coryell, and B. Pfohl. The validity of the dexamethason suppression test as a marker for endogenous depression. *Archives of General Psychiatry*, 1986, *43*, 347–355.

Zimmerman, M., W. Coryell, B. Pfohl, and D. Stangl. The validity of four definitions of endogenous depression. II. Clinical demographic familial, and psychosocial correlates. *Archives of General Psychiatry*, 1986, *43*, 234–244.

Zinner, S. H., P. S. Levy and E. H. Kass. Familial aggregation of blood pressure in childhood. *New England Journal of Medicine*, 1971, *284*, 401–404.

Zubin, J., and B. Spring. Vulnerability—New view of schizophrenia. *Journal of Abnormal Psychology*, 1977, *86*, 103–126.

CREDITS AND ACKNOWLEDGMENTS

CHAPTER 2
Page 31 Erdelyi, M. H. and B. Goldberg, "Let's Not Sweep Repression Under the Rug: Toward a Cognitive Psychology of Repression." In J. F. Kihlstrom and F. J. Evans (eds.) *Functional Disorders of Memory.* Hillsdale, N.J.: Erlbaum, 1979. Reprinted with permission.

CHAPTER 4
Page 83 Rogers, Carl, from *A Way of Being.* Copyright © 1980, Houghton Mifflin Company, used by permission.
Page 90 Figure 4.2, Drawing by Weber; © 1982 The New Yorker Magazine.

CHAPTER 5
Page 102 Figure 5.1, *Psychology Today: An Introduction,* Sixth Edition by Richard Bootzin, Gordon Bower, Robert Zajonc, and Elizabeth Hall. New York: Random House, 1986, page 55.

CHAPTER 6
Page 126 Curtiss, S. R., from *Genie: A Psycholinguistic Study of a Modern-Day "Wild Child."* New York: Academic Press, 1977. Reprinted by permission.
Page 130 Figure 6.1, Reprinted with permission from *Journal of Behavior Therapy and Experimental Psychiatry,* 8, Kelly, J. A. and R. S. Drabman, "The Modification of Socially Detrimental Behavior, Copyright © 1977 by Pergamon Journals, Ltd.

CHAPTER 7
Page 138 Reprinted with permission from the *Diagnostic and Statistical Manual of Mental Disorders,* Third Edition, Revised. Copyright 1987 American Psychiatric Association.
Page 149 Figure 7.1, © 1957 United Feature Syndicate, Inc.
Page 153 Figure 7.2, Wechsler Adult Intelligence Scale Copyright © 1955 by the Psychological Corporation. All rights reserved.
Page 159 From the "Bender® Visual Motor Gestalt Test" published by the American Orthopsychiatric Association, 1938©.

CHAPTER 8
Page 169 Leon, Gloria Rakita, from *Case Histories of Deviant Behavior: An Interactional Perspective.* Second Edition. Copyright © 1977 by Allyn and Bacon, Inc., Boston. Reprinted by permission.

Page 182 Goldblatt, M., and H. Munitz, "Behavioral Treatment of Hysterical Leg Paralysis," *Journal of Behavior Therapy and Experimental Psychology,* 1976, 7 (3), 259–263. Reprinted by permission.
Page 185 Masserman, J. H., from *Principles of Dynamic Psychiatry,* Second Edition. W. B. Saunders Company, Philadelphia, 1961. Reprinted by permission.
Page 186 Nunes, Donnell, from "The Anguish Behind the Three Faces of Eve," *New York Post,* September 15, 1975. Reprinted by permission.
Page 187 Keyes, Daniel, from *The Minds of Billy Milligan.* New York: Random House, 1981. Used with permission.

CHAPTER 9
Page 212 From "In Bed," *The White Album,* by Joan Didion. New York: Simon & Schuster, 1979. Copyright 1979 by Joan Didion.

CHAPTER 10
Pages 229, 231, 232 Spitzer, R. L. et al., from *Psychopathology: A Case Book.* New York: McGraw-Hill, 1983. Reprinted by permission.
Page 229 "Depression: The Shadowed Valley," from the series *The Thin Edge.* Copyright © 1975 by the Educational Broadcasting Corporation. Reprinted by permission.
Pages 233, 235 Kolb, L. C. from *Modern Clinical Psychiatry,* Tenth Edition. Philadelphia: W. B. Saunders Company, 1982. Reprinted by permission of Dr. Lawrence C. Kolb.
Page 242 Seligman, M. E. P., table from *Helplessness.* W. H. Freeman & Company, 1975. Reprinted by permission.

CHAPTER 11
Page 267 Figure 11.1, Courtesy of C. Scott Moss.
Page 269 Cleckley, Hervey, from *The Mask of Sanity,* Fifth Edition. The C. V. Mosby Company, St. Louis, 1976. Reprinted by permission.

CHAPTER 12
Page 284 Table 12.1, Ray, Oakley, from *Drugs, Society, and Human Behavior,* Second Edition. The C. V. Mosby Company, St. Louis, 1976. Reprinted by permission.
Page 285 Table 12.2, Ray, Oakley, slightly modified from *Drugs, Society, and Human Behavior.* Second Edition. The C. V. Mosby Company, 1983. Reprinted by permission.

Page 303 Figure 12.1, Gawin, F. H., and H. D. Kleber, Abstinence symptomotology and psychiatric diagnosis in cocaine abusers. *Archives of General Psychiatry,* 1986, 43, 107–113.
Page 308 Figure 12.2, Courtesy, Schering Corporation
Page 309 Flender, H., from *We Were Hooked.* Random House, 1972. Reprinted by permission.

CHAPTER 13
Page 340 Jones, E., in L. Trilling and S. Marcus (eds.), *The Life and Work of Sigmund Freud.* Doubleday Anchor, 1963. Reprinted by permission of Sigmund Freud Copyrights Ltd. and the Hogarth Press.

CHAPTER 14
Page 354 Figure 14.1, Courtesy Al Vercoutere, Camarillo State Hospital.
Page 364 Copyright © 1986 by the New York Times Company. Reprinted by permission.
Page 369 Figure 14.4, Courtesy Al Vercoutere, Camarillo State Hospital.

CHAPTER 17
Page 429 Leon, Gloria Rakita, from *Case Histories of Deviant Behavior: An Interactional Perspective,* Second Edition. Copyright © 1977 by Allyn and Bacon, Inc., Boston. Reprinted by permission.
Pages 444–445 Adapted from M. W. Edelman, Who is for Children?, *American Psychologist,* 1981, 36(2), 109–116.

CHAPTER 18
Page 454 Eberhardy, Frances, from "The View from the Couch," *The Journal of Child Psychology and Psychiatry, 8.* Copyright © 1967 by Pergamon Press, Ltd. Reprinted by permission.
Page 457 Selfe, Lorna, from Nadia: Case of Extraordinary Drawing Ability in an Autistic Child. Copyright © 1978 by Academic Press Inc. (London) Ltd. Reprinted by permission.

CHAPTER 21
Page 517 Table 21.1, Klerman, G. E. 1986. Drugs and Psychotherapy. In S. L. Garfield and A. E. Bergin (eds.), *Handbook of Psychotherapy and Behavior Change.* New York: Wiley. Reprinted by permission of John Wiley & Sons, Inc.

Chapter Opening Photo Credits

Chapter 1 Geoff Gove; **Chapter 2** Nancy Brown/The Image Bank; **Chapter 3** Elyse Lewin/The Image Bank; **Chapter 4** Eric A. Roth/Picture Cube; **Chapter 5** Alexander Tsiaras/Science Source/Photo Researchers; **Chapter 6** Dan McCoy/Rainbow; **Chapter 7** Nicholas Foster/The Image Bank; **Chapter 8** Werner H. Müller/Peter Arnold; **Chapter 9** David Glaubinger/Jeroboam; **Chapter 10** Phil Schofield; **Chapter 11** Jim Smith; **Chapter 12** Mike Stuckey/Comstock; **Chapter 13** Barbara Alper; **Chapter 14** Eric Simmons/Stock, Boston; **Chapter 15** NIH/Science Source/Photo Researchers; **Chapter 16** Howard Sochurek/Woodfin Camp & Associates; **Chapter 17** Phillip Wallick/Jeroboam; **Chapter 18** Alan Carey/The Image Works; **Chapter 19** Owen Franken/Stock, Boston; **Chapter 20** Russ Kinne/Comstock; **Chapter 21** Stacy Pick/Stock, Boston; **Chapter 22** Comstock.

ABAB design. An experimental research design that seeks to confirm a treatment effect by showing that behavior changes systematically with alternate conditions of no treatment (A) and treatment (B).

acquiescence set. A test-taking attitude in which subjects tend to agree with a statement regardless of its applicability to them.

acquired dysfunction. A sexual dysfunction that is present at the time of diagnosis but has not persisted since an individual's earliest sexual experiences.

acrophobia. The fear of high places.

action therapy. The approach to psychotherapy that focuses on correcting problem behaviors by teaching the patient new skills.

active phase. The second stage of schizophrenia, during which the patient begins showing prominent psychotic symptoms.

addiction. A physiological dependence on a drug developed through continual use in increasing dosage.

Addison's disease. A disease caused by chronic underactivity of the adrenal cortex, which results in both physical and psychological changes.

adrenal cortex. The outer layer of the adrenal glands.

adrenal glands. A pair of ductless endocrine glands located above the kidneys.

adrenal medulla. The inner part of the adrenal glands.

affective disorders. See *mood disorders*.

agitated depression. A form of depression characterized by incessant activity and restlessness.

agnosia. Disturbed sensory perception.

agoraphobia. The fear of open places.

alternating personality. A form of multiple personality in which two identities alternate with each other, each having amnesia for the thoughts and actions of the other.

altruistic suicide. Durkheim's classification of a suicide that occurs because individuals are totally immersed in their culture's value system—a value system that tells them that under certain circumstances it is either necessary or at least honorable to commit suicide.

Alzheimer's disease. A severe organic brain disorder that results from atrophy of the cerebral cortex and the basal ganglia. Symptoms include impairment of memory and concentration, facial paralysis, involuntary movements and convulsions, physical aggression, hallucinations, and rapid intellectual decline.

amenorrhea. The suspension of menstrual periods. This condition often accompanies anorexia nervosa.

amnesia. The partial or total forgetting of past experiences, which can be associated with organic brain syndromes or hysteria.

amniocentesis. A clinical procedure that can identify abnormal chromosomes in the developing fetus.

amphetamines. A group of synthetic stimulants, the most common of which are Benzedrine, Dexedrine, and Methedrine.

analogue experiment. A research method that reproduces, under controlled conditions, the essential features of naturally occurring psychopathology or its treatment.

anal stage. In psychodynamic theory, the second stage of psychosocial development in which the focus of the child is on the pleasurable feelings of retaining and expelling the feces; occurs in the second year of life.

aneurysm. A blood vessel breakage in which a weak part of the vessel wall balloons out and ruptures.

anniversary suicide. The ending of one's life on a date that has some special, personal meaning, such as a birthday, a wedding anniversary, or Christmas.

anomic suicide. Durkheim's classification of a suicide that takes place when the equilibrium of a society is severely disturbed, as, for example, in war or economic collapse.

anomie. Robert Merton's term for a feeling of normlessness that exists in disadvantaged groups. Such a feeling may contribute to the development of antisocial personalities in members of such groups.

anorexia nervosa. Chronic failure to eat for fear of gaining weight; characterized by an extreme loss of appetite that results in severe malnutrition, semistarvation, and sometimes death.

anterograde amnesia. The loss of memory for events following a trauma.

antianxiety drugs (minor tranquilizers or neuroleptics). Drugs used to reduce tension and anxiety. They are used by normal people during times of stress, by neurotics, by people with stress-related physical disorders, and by people withdrawing from alcohol and other drugs.

antidepressant drugs. Drugs used to elevate mood in depressed patients.

antipsychiatric movement. A group of theorists who contend that "insanity" is simply a label fabricated by society in order to justify the exploitation of persons so labeled.

antipsychotic drugs (major tranquilizers or neuroleptics). Drugs used to relieve symptoms such as extreme agitation, hyperactivity, and hallucinations and delusions in psychotic patients.

antisocial behavior. Behavior that violates the rights of others, usually associated with an antisocial personality.

antisocial personality disorder. A chronic indifference to and violation of the rights of others.

anxiety. A state of increased physiological arousal and generalized feelings of fear and apprehension.

anxiety dream. A nightmare, common in adults and children. Children who experience such dreams frequently may be harboring fears that can be relieved through therapy.

aphasia. A language impairment generally attributable to damage in the dominant hemisphere of the brain.

apraxia. Impairment of the ability to perform voluntary movements in a person who has normal primary motor skills and who understands the nature of the movement to be performed.

assertiveness training. A behavior modification technique whereby clients are taught how to assert themselves properly with other people and thus avoid being either passive or overaggressive.

asthma. A respiratory disorder in which the body's air passageways narrow, causing coughing, wheezing, and shortness of breath. The condition is usually associated with allergies or with an organic problem, but some cases may be related to stress.

attention deficit disorder with hyperactivity. A childhood disorder characterized by an inability to focus attention and restlessness.

attention deficit disorder without hyperactivity. A childhood disorder characterized by an inability to focus attention, but without the restlessness.

aura. A warning sign experienced before the onset of a migraine or an epileptic attack.

aura phase. The first stage of a grand mal seizure, in which the victim experiences a warning sign of the onset, such as an aroma, involuntary

movements, or diffuse fear. This stage does not always occur.

authenticity. The striving to live according to one's own vision of the truth; one of the three central themes of existential psychology.

autism. A childhood disorder involving severe social and language impairment, motor disturbance, and retardation.

autonomic nervous system (ANS). That part of the nervous system which governs the smooth muscles, the heart muscle, the glands, and the viscera, and controls their functions, including physiological responses to emotion.

aversion therapy. A behavior modification technique in which the patient's maladaptive response is paired with an aversive stimulus such as an electric shock or a nausea-producing drug; often used in the behavioral treatment of homosexuality, sexual deviations, and alcoholism.

avoidance learning. A variant of escape behavior whereby an organism, having encountered an aversive stimulus, will arrange its responses in the future so as to prevent any further encounter with the stimulus.

avoidant disorder. A childhood disorder that parallels *avoidant personality disorder* in adults and is characterized by an extreme fear and avoidance of strangers.

avoidant personality disorder. A disorder in which the individual withdraws from social contact out of fear of rejection.

barbiturates. A group of powerful sedative drugs whose major effects are to alleviate tension and bring about relaxation and sleep.

becoming. The dynamic process of self-creation; one of three central themes of existential psychology.

behavior deficit. A condition that results when a certain behavior occurs at a lower frequency than is appropriate to the situation, with resulting impairment of an individu-

al's social, intellectual, or practical skills.

behavior excess. A condition that results when certain behavior occurs at a higher frequency than is adaptive, according to what is appropriate to the situation.

behavior genetics. The genetic study of psychological disorders.

behavior therapy. A treatment for specific problems that uses the principles of learning theory.

behavioral medicine. Research and applications that focus on the relationship between mental and physical health.

behavioral rehearsal. A method of social skills training in which the therapist tells clients how to perform the target behavior, models the behavior for them, then has them practice the behavior in skits that simulate the situations they find troubling.

being-in-the-world. The relationship between the individual and the world; one of the three central themes of existential psychology.

beriberi. A disease caused by a thiamine deficiency. Clinical signs include poor appetite, insomnia, memory disturbances, and extreme lassitude.

biofeedback training. A technique by which subjects, with the help of various machines, can monitor and control their own biological processes such as pulse, blood pressure, and brain waves.

biogenic psychosis. A severe mental disorder that can be attributed to a physical cause.

biogenic theory. The view that mental disturbance is due to organic disorders.

bipolar disorder. A mood disorder involving both manic and depressive episodes.

blind mill. A "warming-up" exercise in some humanistic group therapies in which participants close their eyes and wander around the room communicating only by touch.

blocking. A condition sometimes experienced by schizophrenics. In the midst of talking, they fall silent, with no recollection of what they were talking about.

blood alcohol level. The amount of alcohol in the bloodstream, expressed in terms of the number of milligrams of alcohol per 100 milliliters of blood.

blunted affect. An affective abnormality among schizophrenics in which the individual shows little emotion.

borderline personality disorder. A disorder marked by instability and abrupt shifts in emotion and behavior.

brain tumor. A new growth within the brain. *Primary* tumors originate in the brain; *secondary* tumors originate outside the brain and travel to it through the vascular system.

brief reactive psychosis. A schizophrenic episode with rapid onset, a duration of less than two weeks, and a clear precipitating event.

bulimia. Excessive overeating or uncontrolled binge eating followed by self-induced vomiting.

case study. A research design that focuses on a single individual for description and analysis.

castration anxiety. In psychodynamic theory, the male child's fear that his penis will be cut off as punishment for his sexual desire of his mother.

catastrophic reaction. A condition in which the victim of aphasia, bewildered by his or her inability to perform elementary tasks, responds with disorganization and sometimes violent fury.

catatonic negativism. The tendency of some catatonic schizophrenics to consistently do the opposite of what is requested of them.

catatonic posturing. The bizarre postures sometimes assumed by catatonics during a stupor (see *catatonic stupor*).

catatonic rigidity. An "active" form of catatonic stupor in which the individual resists any attempts by others to move his or her limbs.

catatonic schizophrenia. A form of schizophrenia characterized by a marked disturbance in motor behavior—the slowing down of motion and eventual cessation of all adaptive behavior, or alternating periods of immobility and extreme agitation.

catatonic stupor. An extreme form of withdrawal in which the individual retreats into a completely immobile state, showing a total lack of responsiveness to stimulation.

catchment area. The area of geographical coverage of a community mental health center.

catecholamine hypothesis. The biochemical theory that increased levels of the neurotransmitter norepinephrine produce mania, while decreased levels produce depression.

central nervous system (CNS). That part of the nervous system made up of the brain and spinal cord.

cerebral abscess. A brain infection that becomes encapsulated by connective tissue; one of the four major categories of brain infection.

cerebral arteriosclerosis. A hardening of the walls of the blood vessels in the brain.

cerebral hemorrhage. A rupture of a vessel wall in the brain; blood then spills directly onto brain tissue, damaging or destroying it.

cerebrovascular accident (CVA, "stroke"). The formation of a blood clot in one of the blood vessels feeding the brain which cuts off circulation in the vessel.

chromosome. Threadlike structure in all the cells of the body that carries genes in a linear order.

civil commitment. The commitment of an individual to a mental institution because the state has decided that he or she is disturbed enough to require hospitalization.

clanging. A characteristic speech pattern of schizophrenics in which a series of words are used together because they rhyme or sound similar, without regard to logic.

claustrophobia. The fear of closed places.

client-centered therapy. A therapeutic procedure developed by Rogers in which the therapist provides a safe environment for the patient by mirroring the patient's own perceptions and offering unconditional positive regard, thus releasing the patient from the necessity of defending his or her unrealistic self-image.

clinical evidence. Observations of patients in therapy.

clonic phase. The third stage of grand mal seizure in which muscles contract and relax rhythmically while the body jerks in violent spasms.

cocaine. A natural stimulant made from the coca plant which produces feelings of euphoria and omnipotence.

coconscious. A type of multiple personality disorder in which the subordinate personality is fully aware of the dominant personality's thoughts and actions.

cognition. Mental processes such as emotion, thought, expectation, and interpretation.

cognitive appraisal (interpretation of the stimulus). According to cognitive behaviorists, the process by which a person evaluates a stimulus in accordance with his or her memories, beliefs, and expectations before responding. It accounts for the wide variation in responses to the same stimulus.

cognitive behaviorism. The school of behaviorism that proposes that the study of cognitive events should be incorporated into behavioral research.

cognitive restructuring. A behavioral therapy procedure that attempts to alter clients' ways of perceiving their lives in order to change their behavior.

cognitive therapy. A cognitive restructuring technique which holds that emotional disorders are caused primarily by irrational thoughts; patients are encouraged to discover the inappropriateness of their thoughts.

collective unconscious. According to Jung, the unconscious life of all human beings, which is composed of many common elements and not just sexual strivings as Freud contended.

coma. In a grand mal seizure, the final stage in which the muscles slowly relax while the patient remains unconscious.

communications approach (strategic approach). One of two basic approaches to family therapy; family members are encouraged to tell one another what they actually feel and what kind of relationship they really want.

community living facility (CLF). A small to medium-size residential center in which moderately retarded people and mildly retarded people with behavioral or emotional problems live and supervision is provided around the clock.

community mental health center. A facility designed to provide a variety of psychological services for everyone within a specified area.

compulsion. An action which an individual may consider irrational but feels compelled to do.

computerized axial tomography (CT). A series of x-rays of the brain, used in testing for organic impairment.

concordant. A genetic term that means sharing the same disorder.

concussion. A head injury caused by a blow to the head that jars the brain and momentarily disrupts functioning.

conditioned reflex. A basic mechanism of learning whereby if a neutral stimulus is paired with a nonneutral stimulus, the organism will eventually respond to the neutral stimulus as it does to the nonneutral stimulus.

conditioned reinforcer (secondary reinforcer). A stimulus or need that one learns to respond to by associating it with a primary reinforcer.

conditioned response. A simple response to a neutral stimulus that is the result of repeatedly pairing the neutral stimulus with another nonneutral stimulus that would have naturally elicited the response.

conditioned stimulus. The neutral stimulus that elicits a particular response as a result of repeated pairings with a nonneutral or unconditioned stimulus that naturally elicits that response.

conditions of worth. According to Rogers, the values incorporated by the child that dictate which of his or her self-experiences are "good" and which are "bad."

conduct disorder, group type. A childhood disorder characterized by the predominance of conduct problems occurring mainly as a group activity with peers. Aggressive physical behavior may or may not be present.

conduct disorder, solitary aggressive type. A childhood conduct disorder characterized by a lack of emotional attachments and by aggressive antisocial behavior.

conduct disorder, undifferentiated type. This subtype of childhood disorder with a mixture of features that cannot be classified as either solitary aggressive type or group type.

conduct disorders. Childhood disorders involving antisocial behavior.

confabulation. A tendency to fill in memory gaps with invented stories.

confounding. In a research study, a phenomenon that occurs when two or more causal factors are operating on the same thing simultaneously, interfering with accurate measurement of the causal role of either one.

contingency contracting. A technique of behavioral therapy in which a contract is drawn up indicating that for desirable behavior X, the subject will receive reward X, and so on.

contingency management. A technique of behavior therapy that manipulates the consequences of a response in order to change the frequency of that response.

continuity hypothesis. A theory which sees pathological depression and normal sadness as two points on a continuum of mood reactions.

continuous amnesia. The forgetting of all events after a specific period and up to the present, including events that occur after the onset of amnesia.

control group. Those subjects in an experiment who are not exposed to whatever conditions are being studied. See *randomized groups design.*

control techniques. The three methods by which the independent variables in an experiment can be controlled: manipulating, holding conditions constant, and balancing.

contusion. A head injury in which the brain is shifted out of its normal position and pressed against one side of the skull, thus bruising the neural tissue.

conversion disorder. The loss or impairment of some motor or sensory function for which there is no organic cause. Formerly known as *hysteria* or *hysterical neurosis.*

correlational research designs. Research studies that seek to find the relationships between subjects' characteristics and their performance. Such studies effectively meet two of the objectives of the scientific method—description and prediction, but the results of correlational studies should not be used to make causal inferences.

cortex. An outer layer of an organ.

co-twin. A term used by genetic researchers to refer to the twin of the index case.

countertransference. In a psychoanalytic relationship, the analyst's projection onto the client of emotions which originated in his or her own personal history. (Cf. *transference.*)

covariation of events. The first condition to be met before causality can be demonstrated. Two events must vary together; when one changes, the other must also change.

covert sensitization. A behavioral technique to change the affect of a stimulus by pairing an imagined stimulus with imagined dire consequences.

cretinism. A congenital hormonal imbalance caused by a thyroxine deficiency and marked by mental retardation and physical disabilities.

cultural-familial retardation. Retardation resulting from, or at least fostered by, the individual's home environment. It is believed to be related to the effects of poverty.

Cushing's syndrome. A disease caused by an excessively active adrenal cortex; it usually affects young women and involves both physical and psychological difficulties.

cyclothymia. Mild, persistent bipolar disorder, involving recurring cycles of mania and depression.

day hospital. A partial hospitalization service in which the patient is treated on a nine-to-five basis and then returns home for the night.

defense mechanisms. Psychic stratagems that reduce anxiety by concealing the source of anxiety from the self and the world.

degenerative disorder. An organic brain syndrome in which intellectual, emotional, and motor functioning appear to deteriorate as a function of advancing age.

delirium tremens. A severe withdrawal symptom experienced by alcoholics when their blood alcohol level drops suddenly. Known as the DTs, the condition consists of severe trembling, heavy perspiring, feeling disoriented, and experiencing delusions.

delusion. An irrational belief that a person will defend with great vigor despite overwhelming evidence that the belief has no basis in reality. Delusions are among the most common schizophrenic thought disorders.

delusional disorders. A form of schizophrenia in which the delusional system is the basic or even the only abnormality.

demand characteristics. A methodological problem in which a subject's response is strongly determined by the research setting.

denial. The refusal to acknowledge the source of distress.

dependent personality disorder. A disorder marked by low self-esteem and extreme dependence on others.

dependent variables. In a research study, the factors used to measure the effect (if any) of the independent variables.

depressant. A drug that acts on the central nervous system to reduce pain, tension, and anxiety, to relax and disinhibit, and to slow down intellectual and motor reactivity.

depression. An emotional state characterized by intense and unrealistic sadness.

depth interview. A psychodynamic assessment method in which subjects are encouraged to talk about their past, particularly about sexual and aggressive impulses during childhood.

depth psychology hypothesis. Freud's view that almost all mental activity happens unconsciously.

description. The first objective of the scientific method. The procedures by which events and their relationships are defined, classified, catalogued, or categorized.

descriptive validity. The degree to which an assessment device provides significant information about the current behavior of the people being assessed.

detoxification. A medical treatment for alcoholism consisting of getting the alcohol out of the alcoholic's system and supervising his or her withdrawal symptoms.

dexamethasone suppression test (DST). A laboratory test used to identify people suffering from endogenous depression. In depressed individuals, dexamethasone suppresses cortisol secretion for at least twenty-four hours. Cortisol secretion of individuals with endogenous depression returns to high levels within twenty-four hours despite administration of dexamethasone.

diagnosis. The classification and labeling of a patient's problem within one of a set of recognized categories of abnormal behavior.

diathesis. A constitutional predisposition toward a disorder.

diathesis-stress theory. The belief that certain genes or gene combinations may lead to a diathesis or predisposition toward a disorder and that if this is combined with certain kinds of environmental stress, abnormal behavior will result.

disaster syndrome. A pattern of response to severe physical trauma involving three stages—shock, suggestibility, and recovery.

discrimination. The process of learning to distinguish among similar stimuli and to respond only to the appropriate one.

disorganized (hebephrenic) schizophrenia. A form of schizophrenia characterized by childlike behavior, such as giggling wildly, making faces, and assuming absurd postures.

displacement. A defense mechanism that involves the transfer of emotion from an unacceptable object to a safer one.

disregulation model. A model proposed for understanding stress-related physical disorders. When the body's regulatory systems fail to operate properly at any of four stages in the model, disease develops.

dissociative disorders. Disorders resulting from the splitting off of some psychological function from the rest of the conscious mind.

dizygotic twins (DZ twins, fraternal twins). Twins who develop from two eggs fertilized by two different sperm and who have only approximately 50 percent of their genes in common.

dopamine hypothesis. The hypothesis that schizophrenia is associated with excess activity of those parts of the brain that use dopamine as a neurotransmitter.

double-bind communication. Mutually contradictory messages from mother to child; believed by some to be a causative agent in schizophrenia.

double-blind. A procedure in scientific research that seeks to minimize the influence of subjects' and experimenters' expectations. Both the subject and the experimenter are unaware of what treatment is being administered, that is, whether they are in the experimental group or the control group.

double technique. A technique used in psychodrama in which the therapist acts out a client's part at the same time that the client does.

Down's syndrome. A form of mental retardation caused by an extra chromosome. Individuals with this condition usually have IQs of 50 or less and distinctive physical characteristics, such as an extra fold of skin on the upper eyelid, a flat nose, and poor muscle tone.

dream interpretation. A psychoanalytic technique in which patients report their dreams as accurately as possible and the therapist interprets the elements of the dreams as symbols of unconscious wishes and conflicts.

drug-induced insomnia. A pattern of disrupted slumber without any deep sleep, created by prolonged barbiturate use.

dyslexia. Partial impairment of reading ability.

dyspareunia. A kind of sexual dysfunction characterized by pain during intercourse. Men may suffer from this disorder but it is more typically a female problem.

dysthymia. A mood disorder involving mild, persistent depression over an extended period of time.

early infantile autism. A disorder in children in which the primary symptom, apparent from infancy, seems to be the inability to relate to anything beyond the self.

echolalia. A speech deficit characteristic of autistic children, in which the child aimlessly repeats words or phrases without regard to their meaning.

ego. In Freudian theory, the psychic component of the mind which mediates between the id, reality, and the superego.

ego ideal. In Freudian theory, the composite picture of values and moral ideals held by the superego.

ego identity. Erikson's belief that the ego does more than just assimilate values of a parent, that it goes on to form an integrated, unique, and autonomous "self."

ego psychologists. The second generation of Freudian theorists who believe in less deterministic and less biologically oriented psychology and who argue that the ego has its own energy and autonomous functions apart from the id.

egoistic suicide. Durkheim's classification of a suicide that results from the individual's lack of a supportive social network (community or family).

electroconvulsive therapy (ECT). The administering of an electric shock to the patient, which induces a convulsion; used in the treatment of depression.

electroencephalogram (EEG). A record of brain wave activity obtained by connecting sensitive electrodes to the skull which pick up and record the minute electrical impulses generated by the brain.

electromyograph (EMG). The changes in the electrical activity of muscles, recorded by a polygraph.

elimination of plausible alternative causes. The third condition to be met before causality can be demonstrated. The proposed causal relationship can be accepted only after other likely causes have been ruled out.

embolus. A ball of fat, air, or clotted blood which breaks loose from the side of a blood vessel or in some other way enters a blood vessel and floats upward in the bloodstream until its size restricts its movement. When it clogs the vessel, a cerebral vascular accident (CVA), or stroke, occurs.

encephalitis. Inflammation of the brain; one of the four major categories of brain infection.

encopresis. A childhood developmental disorder in which episodes of defecating alternate with longer periods of fecal retention.

encounter group. A humanistic form of group therapy that emphasizes personal growth and increased openness and honesty in personal relations by means of free and candid expression within the group.

endocrine glands. Glands responsible for the production of hormones that, when released into the bloodstream, affect various bodily mechanisms such as physical growth and development.

endocrine system. The system of endocrine, or ductless, glands—such as the hypothalamus and the pituitary—that is closely integrated with the central nervous system and is responsible for the production of hormones.

endogenous depression. A depression that seems to have no connection with an external precipitating event.

enuresis. A lack of bladder control past the age when such control is normally achieved. Children with *primary enuresis* have never achieved bladder control. Those with *secondary enuresis* experience a loss of control that had been achieved.

epidemic encephalitis. A brain infection characterized by profound lethargy and prolonged periods of sleep; often called "sleeping sickness."

epilepsy. A generic term for a variety of organic disorders characterized by irregularly occurring disturbances in consciousness in the form of seizures or convulsions. The seizures are due to a disruption in the electrical and physiochemical activity of the discharging cells of the brain.

erectile disorder. The absence or weakness of the physiological changes that produce an erection.

error variation. In scientific research, the differences that remain among subjects despite balancing through random assignment. Because of these differences, subjects' responses may differ regardless of the effects of the independent variable.

essential hypertension. Chronically

high blood pressure for which no organic cause can be found.

exhibitionism. Sexual gratification through displaying one's genitals to an involuntary observer.

existential frustration. In Frankl's view, when people cannot find meaning in their lives they suffer from existential frustration, a major source of abnormal behavior.

exorcism. The practice of expelling evil spirits from a person believed to be possessed by such demons. It was thought that this would cure a person of aberrant behavior.

experimental group. Those subjects in an experiment who are exposed to whatever conditions are being studied. See *randomized groups design.*

experimenter effects. A methodological problem in which researchers inadvertently influence the subjects' responses or perceive the subjects' behavior in terms of their own biases.

external validity. The degree to which research results can be generalized, or applied, to different populations, settings, and conditions.

extinction. A process in which a conditioned response is reduced to its preconditioned level. Previously reinforced responses are no longer reinforced.

extracerebral tumor. A tumor that grows outside the brain but inside the skull.

eyeball-to-eyeball. A "warming-up" exercise for some humanistic group therapies in which participants pair off and stare into one another's eyes for a minute or more.

false negative. An incorrect diagnosis of no illness; in commitment hearings, a failure to commit when commitment is justified and necessary.

false positive. An incorrect diagnosis of illness; in commitment hearings, an unjustified commitment.

family therapy. The therapeutic technique in which an entire family is seen together so that destructive roles and attitudes can be exposed and treated.

feedback. A process in which information is returned to a system in order to regulate that system.

female sexual arousal disorder. The absence or weakness of the physiological changes in women that normally accompany the excitement phase of sexual arousal.

fetishism. Sexual gratification via inanimate objects or via some part of the body to the exclusion of the person as a whole.

fixation. A psychic mechanism in which an individual experiences anxiety at a certain stage of development and fails to progress beyond that stage.

flat affect. A subjective feeling or tone in which there is no emotional response to one's surroundings or to other people.

flooding. A respondent conditioning technique in which extinction is achieved by confronting the anxiety-producing stimulus.

fluent aphasia. A speech disability in which patients produce streams of incoherent speech, including reversed syllables and jumbled word order.

folie à deux. A term used to describe a pathological pattern in which both parents collude, presenting to the world the picture of an ideal family while repeatedly abusing a child.

free association. A psychoanalytic technique whereby the patients verbalize whatever thoughts come to mind, without structuring or censoring their remarks.

functional analysis. Thorough analysis of the frequency of particular behaviors, the situations in which they occur, and their consequences.

functional psychosis. A severe mental disorder that cannot be attributed to known physical causes.

galvanic skin response (GSR). The changes in the electrical resistance of the skin, recorded by a polygraph.

gender identity. The individual's sense of being a man or a woman.

gene. The unit of heredity carried on the chromosome that carries the instructions, inherited from the parents at conception, about the proteins that the body should produce. The proteins, in turn, determine the hereditary characteristics of the person—height, hair and eye color, and so on.

general paresis. A final stage of syphilis, involving the gradual and irreversible breakdown of physical and mental functioning.

generalizability. The ability of research results to be applied to different populations, settings, and conditions.

generalization. The process by which an organism, conditioned to respond in a certain way to a particular stimulus, will also respond to similar stimuli in the same way.

generalized amnesia. The forgetting of all past experiences.

generalized anxiety disorder. A chronic state of diffuse, unfocused anxiety.

generalized dysfunction. A sexual dysfunction that occurs in all sexual situations.

genital stage. According to Freud, the final phase of mature sexuality, by which he meant heterosexual genital mating.

genotype. That unique combination of genes which represents one's biological inheritance from one's parents.

Gestalt therapy. An existential-humanistic form of therapy in which the patients act out past conflicts with the therapist in order to confront their feelings and learn to take responsibility for them.

glove anesthesia. A form of hysterical neurosis in which the individual reports a numbness in his or her hand from the tips of the fingers to a clear cut-off point at the wrist.

grand mal. The most common and most dramatic of the epilepsies, involving a generalized seizure throughout the brain, with violent convulsions and loss of consciousness.

Graves' disease. See *hyperthyroidism.*

halfway house. A residence for people who no longer require institutionalization but who still need some support system in readjusting to community life.

hallucination. A sensory perception that occurs in the absence of any appropriate external stimulus.

hallucinogens. A class of drugs that act on the central nervous system to cause distortions in sensory perception.

hebephrenic schizophrenia. See *disorganized schizophrenia.*

helplessness-hopelessness syndrome. The depressed persons' conviction that they are both unable to help themselves and unlikely to be helped by external forces.

heroin. An addictive narcotic drug derived from morphine.

hierarchy of fears. In systematic desensitization, a list of anxiety-producing situations in order of their increasing horror to patients.

hierarchy of needs. Maslow's concept of a series of needs that must be satisfied one by one in the process of development before the adult can begin pursuing self-actualization.

histrionic personality disorder. A personality disorder involving the exaggerated display of emotion.

homosexuality. Sexual activity directed toward one's own sex.

hormones. Chemical messengers that are released directly into the bloodstream by the endocrine glands and that affect sexual functioning, physical growth and development, and emotional responses.

hot line. Round-the-clock telephone service where people in trouble can call and receive immediate comfort and advice from trained volunteers.

humanistic-existential perspective. A diverse approach to abnormal psychology whose proponents generally agree that behavior is both willed and purposive and that human beings choose their lives and therefore are responsible for their lives.

humors. In Hippocrates' view, humans possessed four vital fluids, or humors: phlegm, blood, black bile, and yellow bile. The balance of these humors in each individual influenced personality.

Huntington's chorea. A fatal presenile disorder which is transmitted genetically. The symptoms include spasmodic jerking of the limbs, bizarre behavior, and mental deterioration.

hypertension (high blood pressure). Chronic elevation of the blood pressure due to constriction of the arteries; a stress-related physical disorder.

hyperthyroidism (Graves' disease). Overactivity of the thyroid gland which causes excessive secretion of the hormone thyroxin. The disorder is accompanied by anxietylike symptoms.

hyperventilation. Rapid breathing.

hypnosis. An artificially induced sleeplike state in which the subject is highly susceptible to suggestion.

hypochondriasis. A disorder in which a person converts anxiety into a chronic preoccupation with his or her bodily functioning.

hypoglycemia. A low blood-sugar level.

hypothesis. A tentative explanation for behavior; it attempts to answer the questions "how?" and "why?". Scientific research often begins with a hypothesis.

hypothyroidism (myxedema). Underactivity of the thyroid gland which results in deficient production of thyroxin, due possibly to inadequate iodine consumption. Symptoms include lethargy and depression.

hysteria. A physical disability for which no organic cause can be found.

hysterical neurosis. See *conversion disorder.*

id. According to Freud, the sum of biological drives with which a person is born.

identification. In psychodynamic theory, the incorporation of the same-sexed parent's values, standards, sexual orientation, and mannerisms, as part of the development of the superego.

idiographic research. Research built on the individual, such as the *case study.*

idiopathic epilepsy. A convulsive disorder for which there is no known cause; the disorder usually has its onset between the ages of ten and twenty.

idiot savant ("wise idiot"). A child who, despite generally diminished skills, shows astonishing proficiency in one isolated skill.

implosive therapy. A behavior modification technique to extinguish anxiety by maximizing the client's anxiety through imagined fear-producing situations and holding the anxiety at this pitch until the anxiety extinguishes.

inappropriate affect. A subjective feeling or tone in which emotional responses are totally unsuited to the immediate context.

inappropriate stimulus control. Disruption in the relationship between stimulus and response, either a response occurring in the absence of an appropriate stimulus or a stimulus failing to elicit an appropriate response.

incest. Sexual relations between members of the immediate family.

incidence. The number of new cases of a disorder reported during a specific time period.

incompatible behavior. An operant conditioning technique that aims to make a problem behavior difficult to perform. People may learn to use relaxation as a means of controlling stress.

independent variables. The factors in a research study that are manipulated by the experimenter.

indeterminate sentence. A period of incarceration with no limit, often given to those defendants acquitted by reason of insanity.

index case (proband case). In genetic family studies, the individual in the family who has the diagnosed case of the disorder being studied.

individual response specificity. The principle that people seem to have characteristic patterns of autonomic nervous system response, which carry over from one kind of stress to another.

inhibited female orgasm. A sexual disorder in which orgasm is either greatly delayed or does not occur at all.

inhibited male orgasm. A sexual disorder in which ejaculation is either greatly delayed or does not occur at all.

insanity defense. A defendant's plea that he or she is not guilty of a crime because of insanity.

insight therapy. The approach to psychotherapy that attempts to increase patients' awareness of their behavior so that they can better control it.

insomnia. The chronic inability to sleep.

intellectualization. The avoidance of unacceptable feelings by repressing these feelings and replacing them with an abstract intellectual analysis of the problem.

intelligence quotient (IQ). A score on an intelligence test that is computed by dividing the subject's mental age by his or her chronological age and then multiplying by 100.

intelligence test. A psychological assessment technique effective in predicting success in school.

interjudge reliability. A criterion for judging the reliability of psychological tests. The test should yield the same results when scored or interpreted by different judges.

intermediate care facility (ICF). A nursing home in a community setting in which severely retarded people live and supervision is close.

internal consistency. A criterion for judging the reliability of psychological tests. Different parts of a test should yield the same result.

internal validity. The extent that the results of an experiment can be confidently attributed to the effects of the independent variable.

interview. An assessment method consisting of a face-to-face conversation between subject and examiner.

intracerebral tumor. A tumor that grows within the brain, destroying normal brain tissue and replacing it with abnormal tumor cells.

intracranial neoplasm. A new growth within the brain; the technical term for brain tumor.

introspection. A method of psychological study in which trained observers report their own mental activities under controlled conditions.

isolation. In Freudian theory, a defense mechanism that separates feelings from the events to which they are attached. The feelings are repressed, and the events are viewed without emotion.

in vivo desensitization. A procedure in which phobic patients are led through the actual situations that arouse their anxieties, usually accompanied by a therapist. The goal is for patients to learn to relax in the presence of anxiety-causing stimuli.

Jacksonian epilepsy. A form of epilepsy in which the origin of the seizure is localized in one part of the brain.

juvenile paresis. Irreversible syphilis that the child contracts in the womb from a syphilitic mother.

Kleinfelter's syndrome. A condition that affects only men in which the nondisjunction of the sex chromosomes results in an extra X chromosome in pair 23, causing underdeveloped testes, sterility, and sometimes mild mental retardation.

Korsakoff's psychosis. An irreversible nutritional deficiency due either to alcohol poisoning or to vitamin B deficiency associated with alcoholism; characterized by anterograde amnesia and confabulation.

la belle indifférence. A characteristic of conversion disorder in which the person does not seem at all disturbed by his or her disability.

laceration. A serious kind of brain damage, in which a bullet or piece of metal enters the skull and directly ruptures and destroys brain tissue.

large community group. A variant of humanistically oriented group therapy. Anywhere from 50 to 2,000 people convene with several leaders for sessions lasting from one weekend to two weeks.

latency. The dormancy of a particular behavior or response.

latent content. In psychoanalytic theory, the unconscious material of a dream that is being expressed in disguised fashion through the symbols contained in the dream.

lateralization. The localization of functions in either the left or the right hemisphere of the brain.

law of effect. Thorndike's formulation of the importance of reward in the learning process which states that responses that lead to satisfying consequences are strengthened and therefore are likely to be repeated, while responses with unsatisfying consequences are weakened and therefore unlikely to be repeated.

lead encephalopathy. A toxic disorder due to excessive ingestion of lead, which causes fluid to accumulate in the brain and results in extraordinary intracranial pressure.

learned helplessness. In behavioral theory, the depressive's inability to initiate adaptive responses, possibly due to a helplessness conditioned by earlier, inescapable trauma.

learning. A relatively enduring change in behavior caused by experience or practice.

lesbianism. Female homosexuality.

libido. In psychoanalytic theory, the energy of the life instinct, which Freud saw as the driving force of personality.

lithium. A mood-altering drug used to control manic episodes.

localized amnesia. The blocking out of all events occurring during a circumscribed period of time; the most common pattern of psychogenic amnesia.

logotherapy. Frankl's technique for dealing with the spiritual aspect of psychopathology, in which the therapist confronts patients with their responsibility for their existence and their obligation to pursue the values inherent in life.

longitudinal or developmental studies. A scientific research design in which a group of subjects is studied several different times over an extended period of time.

long-term-care facilities. Facilities within a community that are designed to meet the needs of patients who will not live independently. These facilities are smaller than hospitals.

major depression. A type of major mood disorder characterized by major depressive episodes occurring without intervening manic episodes.

major depressive episode. An extended period of intense depression that usually begins and ends gradually and causes a radical change in all aspects of the individual's functioning.

mania. An emotional state characterized by intense and unrealistic feelings of elation.

manic episode. An extended period of intense mania that usually begins and ends suddenly and causes a radical change in an individual's social functioning.

manifest content. In psychoanalytic theory, the content of a dream as seen and reported by the individual. (Cf. latent content.)

MAO inhibitors. The first important class of antidepressants; their effectiveness has never been established.

marital therapy. A therapeutic procedure that aims at pinpointing the role expectations and patterns of communication between the cou-

ple, encouraging each member to examine his or her role and the role he or she imposes on the other.

masochism. Sexual gratification through pain inflicted on oneself.

medical model. The conceptualization of psychological abnormality as a group of diseases analogous to physical diseases.

medulla. The internal portion of the adrenal glands.

meninges. The membranous covering of the brain or spinal cord.

meningitis. A brain infection involving an acute inflammation of the meninges, characterized by drowsiness, confusion, irritability, and sensory impairments; one of the four major categories of brain infection.

mental retardation. A condition that is manifested during the period and is characterized by intellectual ability that is significantly below average and by a serious deficiency in adaptive behavior.

metastatic brain tumor. A secondary tumor, usually developing from cancer of the lungs, breast, stomach, or kidney, that is spread to the brain by body fluids.

methadone. A synthetic narcotic that satisfies the craving for narcotics but does not produce narcotic euphoria.

migraine. A stress-related disorder characterized by episodes of severe headache, usually localized in one side of the head.

milieu therapy. An institutional group therapy in which severely disturbed patients live together in an atmosphere designed to maximize their independence, their activity level, and their sense of dignity.

mind-body problem. The issue of the relationship between the psychic and somatic aspects of human functioning.

mirroring. A technique used in psychodrama in which group members portray one another.

modeling. In behavioral theory, the learning of a new behavior by imitating another person performing that behavior.

monozygotic twins (MZ twins, identical twins). Twins who develop from a single fertilized egg and have exactly the same genotype; they are always of the same sex, have the same eye color and blood type, and so on.

mood disorders. Disturbances of mood in which feelings of sadness or elation become intense and unrealistic.

moral therapy. A treatment procedure developed in the early nineteenth century based on providing a pleasant and relaxed atmosphere for the mentally ill.

morphine. An addictive narcotic derived from opium.

multi-infarct dementia. The cumulative effect of multiple small strokes, eventually closing down many of the brain's faculties.

multiple-baseline design. An experimental research design in which treatment is introduced at different intervals across subjects, behaviors, or situations.

multiple personality. An extreme form of dissociative reaction in which two or more complete behavior organizations, each well-developed and highly distinct, are found in one individual.

muscle-contraction headaches (tension headaches). Stress-related headaches that range from mild to severe and generally affect both sides of the head.

mutism. The cessation of speech; often a characteristic of catatonic schizophrenia.

mystification. As used by R. D. Laing, a habitual mode of interaction between parent and child that causes the child to doubt the adequacy or legitimacy of his or her own thoughts, feelings, and perceptions.

narcissism. The erotic preoccupation with one's own body.

narcissistic personality disorder. A disorder characterized by a grandiose sense of self-importance, often combined with periodic feelings of inferiority.

narcotics. A class of drugs that induces relaxation and reverie and provides relief from anxiety and physical pain.

natural group designs. Research studies designed to see whether systematic differences exist between groups of people who have been treated "naturally."

negative feedback. Feedback in which the turning on of one component of a system leads to the turning off of another component, in order to regulate the system.

negative reinforcement. A conditioning procedure in which a response is followed by the removal of an aversive event or stimulus, which has the effect of promoting the response.

negative symptoms. In schizophrenia, the absence of something, including poverty of speech, flat affect, withdrawal, and inattention.

neologisms. A schizophrenic speech pattern in which new words are formed by combining parts of two or more regular words or in which common words are used in a unique fashion.

nervous system. The vast electrochemical conducting network that extends from the brain through the rest of the body and carries information, in the form of electrical impulses, from the brain to the rest of the body and back to the brain.

neurofibrillary tangles. Twisted and distorted nerve fibers, present in victims of Alzheimer's disease.

neurons. The cells of the nervous system. They connect motor and receptor cells and transmit information throughout the body.

neuroscience perspective. A perspective that focuses on the biological aspects of abnormal behavior.

neuroses. Conditions in which maladaptive behaviors serve as a protection against a source of unconscious anxiety.

neurosyphilis. Deterioration of brain tissues as a result of infection by the spirochete *Treponema palli-*

dum, one of the four major categories of brain infection.

neurotransmitters. A group of chemicals that facilitate the transmission of electrical impulses between nerve endings in the brain.

night hospital. A partial hospitalization service in which the patients go to their jobs from nine to five and then return to the hospital for the night.

night terror. A particularly harrowing variety of bad dream experienced by a child, which occurs in the deepest stage of sleep, stage 4.

noncontingent reinforcement. Arbitrary reinforcement unrelated to behavior.

nonfluent aphasia. A speech disability in which patients have difficulty initiating speech and respond to questions with one-word answers, short phrases, and long pauses.

norms. The rules in any society that define "right" and "wrong." Norms guide most of our actions, and are an important standard for defining abnormality.

nuclear magnetic resonance (NMR). A diagnostic technique in which the body is surrounded by a magnetic field and radio waves are employed to produce an image.

null hypothesis. The assumption that the independent variable had no effect on the differences between experimental groups.

obesity. An excessive amount of fat on the body. Each culture sets its own standard for ideal body weight, so what is considered obese in one culture may be desirable in another.

object relations theorists. Recent psychodynamic theorists who believe that the most powerful determinant of psychological development is the child's relationship with the mother. See *separation-individuation.*

obsession. A thought or image that an individual may consider irrational but which recurs repeatedly, compelling the person to dwell on it.

obsessive-compulsive disorder. Invo-

luntary dwelling on an unwelcome thought (*obsession*) and/or involuntary repetition of an unnecessary action (*compulsion*).

obsessive-compulsive personality disorder. Excessive preoccupation with trivial details, to the detriment of both spontaneity and effectiveness.

Oedipus complex. According to Freud, the desire that all male children have during the phallic stage to do away with the parent of the same sex in order to take sexual possession of the parent of the opposite sex, a crucial stage of development which determines the child's future sexual adjustment.

operant behavior. In behavioral theory, a class of complex behavior in which an organism acts upon the environment in order to achieve a desired result; all operant behavior is the result of conditioning. (Cf. *respondent behavior.*)

operant conditioning (instrumental conditioning). The process by which an organism learns to associate certain results with certain actions it has taken.

operational definition. In science, a set of specific criteria that identifies a concept.

opium. A chemically active substance derived from the opium poppy; one of the narcotics.

oral stage. In psychoanalytic theory, the first stage of psychosocial development in which the mouth is the primary focus of libidinal impulses and pleasure; occurs in the first year of life.

organic brain disorders. Behavioral problems that are directly traceable to the destruction of brain tissue or to biochemical imbalance in the brain.

overanxious disorder. A condition in which the child's fears are generalized and diffuse, so that almost any situation may engender worry and anxiety.

panic attack. An attack of almost unbearable anxiety, usually lasting several minutes though possibly continuing for hours.

panic disorder. A disorder characterized by recurrent panic attacks.

paradoxical intention. A technique of existential therapy in which patients are asked to indulge or exaggerate their symptoms in order to prove to patients that they control their symptoms rather than having their symptoms control them.

paranoid-nonparanoid dimension. The classification of schizophrenics according to the presence (paranoid) or absence (nonparanoid) of delusions of persecution and/or grandeur.

paranoid personality disorder. A personality disorder defined by suspiciousness in almost all situations and with almost all people.

paranoid schizophrenia. A form of schizophrenia characterized by consistent delusions and/or hallucinations, often related to themes of persecution and grandeur.

parasympathetic division. That division of the autonomic nervous system which decreases physical arousal and is usually dominant under less emotional conditions. It regulates breathing, heart rate, blood pressure, stomach and intestinal activity, and elimination. (Cf. *sympathetic division.*)

paresis. (See **general paresis.**)

Parkinson's disease. A presenile psychosis involving degenerative lesions of midbrain nerve tracts responsible for relaying motor impulses. Symptoms include tremors, a masklike countenance, stiff gait, and withdrawal.

passive-aggressive personality disorder. Indirectly expressed resistance to demands made by others.

pedophilia. Child molesting—that is, gratification, on the part of the adult, through sexual contacts with children.

peer self-help groups. Groups of people who share a special problem and meet to discuss that problem without the help or guidance of a mental health professional.

pellagra. A disease caused by severe deficiency of the B vitamin niacin. It occurs most often in areas where corn is a major part of the diet of the population. Symptoms include depression, anxiety, delirium, and hallucinations.

penis envy. In psychoanalytic theory, the female child's feeling that she has been born unequipped with a penis because of her sexual desire toward her father; female counterpart of castration anxiety.

perceptual conscious. In Freudian theory, the first level of the mind's consciousness which contains whatever requires no act of recall.

peripheral nervous system. The network of nerve fibers that leads from the central nervous system to all parts of the body and carries out the commands of the CNS. It has two branches: the somatic nervous system and the autonomic nervous system.

person variables. Each person's stable traits. Adherents of the psychometric approach hold that personality issues mainly from person variables.

personality disorder. An inflexible and maladaptive pattern of behavior that causes significant impairment in social or occupational functioning, presumably adopted at an early age.

petit mal. An epileptic seizure lasting only a few seconds and involving a brief loss of consciousness.

phallic stage. In psychoanalytic theory, the third stage of psychosocial development in which pleasure is derived from masturbation, the stroking and handling of the genitals; occurs from the third to the fifth or sixth year of life.

phenomenological approach. A therapeutic procedure in which the therapist attempts to see the patient's world from the vantage point of the patient's own internal frame of reference.

phenotype. The unique combination of observable characteristics that results from the combination of a person's genotype with the environment.

phenylketonuria (PKU). A genetic defect caused by a deficiency in a liver enzyme, phenylalanine 4-hydroxylase, which results in severe retardation, hyperactivity, and erratic behavior.

phobia. An intense and debilitating fear of some object or situation that actually presents no real threat.

phobic disorder. A psychological disorder characterized by both a phobia and by avoidance of the phobic stimulus.

placebo control groups. In a research study, a group of subjects given a treatment designed to affect only their expectations of change. A way of minimizing the effects of expectations of subjects and experimenters.

play therapy. A psychodynamic technique which encourages children to vent their conflicts through symbolic play rather than verbal expression.

pleasure principle. In Freudian theory, the tendency of the id to devote itself exclusively to the immediate reduction of tension.

polygenetic trait. A complex characteristic that is the product of the interaction of many genes.

polygraph. A physiological recording device equipped with sensors which, when attached to the body, can pick up subtle physiological changes in the form of electrical impulses. The changes are recorded on a moving roll of paper.

positive regard. As defined by Rogers, people's need for affection and approval from those most important to them, particularly parents.

positive reinforcement. A situation in which a response is followed by a positive event or stimulus which increases the probability that the response will be repeated.

positive symptoms. In schizophrenia, the presence of something, including hallucinations, delusions, bizarre behavior, and incoherent thought patterns.

positron-emission tomography (PET). A means of examining the brain. The patient is injected with a radioactively labeled sugar solution, and the path of the radioactive particles through the brain is traced.

posttraumatic stress disorders. A form of anxiety disorder that results from exposure to intensely traumatic events, including assault, rape, natural disasters, and wartime combat. Victims may reexperience the traumatic event in recollections or in nightmares, may show diminished responsiveness to their present surroundings, and may suffer physical symptoms and intense irritability. Generally appearing shortly after the trauma, the symptoms usually disappear within six months, but some may last for years.

posttraumatic stress syndrome. A disorder characterized by the development of anxiety, depression, disturbing recollections and dreams, emotional numbing, or other problems following a psychologically traumatic event.

poverty of content. A characteristic of schizophrenic speech in which words are used correctly but communication is poor.

preconscious. In Freudian theory the second level of the mind's consciousness which consists of whatever the person can remember without great difficulty.

prediction. One of the objectives of the scientific method: the ability to predict the relationship between events.

predictive validity. The degree to which a test's findings are consistent with the subject's future performance.

prefrontal lobotomy. A surgical procedure in which a cut is made between the frontal lobes (the thought center) and the thalamus (the emotional center) of the brain.

premature ejaculation. Ejaculation that occurs before a couple would prefer it to.

premorbid adjustment. The level of social and sexual adjustment before the onset of a disorder.

prevalence. The frequency of a disorder in a particular population.

primary gain. In neurosis, the relief

from anxiety through the use of a defense mechanism.

primary prevention. The first level of prevention of psychological disorder, the goal of which is to prevent disorders from developing.

primary process thinking. In Freudian theory, one of the id's methods of self-gratification which involves conjuring up a mental image of the source of satisfaction.

primary reinforcer. A stimulus or need that one responds to instinctively, without learning.

principle of reinforcement. Skinner's term for Thorndike's law (see *Law of Effect*), which he considered the basic mechanism for predicting and controlling human behavior.

process-reactive dimension. The classification of schizophrenics according to whether the onset of symptoms is gradual (process) or abrupt and precipitated by some traumatic event (reactive).

process schizophrenia. Those cases of schizophrenia in which onset is gradual.

prodromal phase. The initial stage of schizophrenia, during which the individual generally becomes withdrawn and socially isolated.

prognosis. The prediction of the course of a patient's illness.

projection. A defense mechanism whereby unacceptable impulses are first repressed, then attributed to others.

projective personality test. An assessment technique used to draw out, indirectly, individuals' true conflicts and motives by presenting them with ambiguous stimuli and allowing them to project their private selves into their responses.

proprioceptive discrimination. The ability to discriminate the orientation of one's body in space. Schizophrenics do poorly on this kind of task.

psychiatric diagnosis. The classification of a patient's problem within the taxonomy of psychological disturbances developed by the psychiatric profession.

psychoactive drug. A drug that alters one's psychological state.

psychoactive substance dependence. A diagnostic category of *DSM-III-R* that covers all physiological and psychological manifestations of drug use.

psychoanalysis. The psychodynamic therapy method that relies heavily on the techniques of free association, dream interpretation, and analysis of resistance and transference: the aim is to give patients insight into their unconscious conflicts, impulses, and motives.

psychodrama. A psychoanalytically oriented form of group therapy in which members get on a stage and together act out their emotional conflicts. The purpose is for the clients to confront their feelings and also to get at the unconscious roots of these feelings, which are then examined according to Freudian theory.

psychodynamic perspective. A school of thought based on the assumption that human behavior is a function of events occurring within the mind and is explainable only in terms of those mental events.

psychogenic fugue. A dissociative episode in which a person flees his or her anxiety-ridden identity and environment, not returning for days, weeks, or even years. Upon "waking up," the person remembers nothing about the particular fugue period.

psychogenic theory. The view that mental disturbance is due primarily to emotional stress.

psychological assessment. The systematic analysis of a person and his or her life situation.

psychological dependence. The psychological need for a drug that is not physiologically addictive.

psychological test. An assessment technique in which the subject is presented with a series of stimuli to which he or she is asked to respond.

psychometric approach. A method of psychological testing that aims at locating and measuring stable underlying traits.

psychomotor epilepsy. A form of epilepsy in which the individual loses contact with reality but appears normal and performs some mechanical activity. After the attack has passed, the person will be amnesic for the episode.

psychoneuroimmunology. The specialized discipline that studies the interaction between psychological factors and the immune system, mediated by the central nervous system.

psychopathology. Abnormal psychology.

psychopharmacology. The study of the drug treatment of psychological disorders.

psychophysiological disorders. Physical disorders that are thought to be due to emotional factors and that are also scientifically traceable to a clear organic cause.

psychoses. A class of severe psychological disorders in which a person's perception of reality is drastically distorted.

psychosexual development. Freud's theory that personality development takes place in a series of stages, in each of which the child's central motivation is to gratify the drive for pleasure in a different bodily zone.

psychosocial development. Erikson's theory of personality development, consisting of a series of chronological stages extending from birth to death.

psychosurgery. Surgery aimed at reducing abnormal behavior.

psychotherapy. A systematic and structured series of interactions between a therapist and a client. The goal is to produce in the client emotional, cognitive, or behavioral changes.

punishment. In behavioral theory, the process for suppressing behavior whereby a response is followed by an aversive stimulus.

random assignment. A balancing control technique that involves assigning subjects randomly to the different groups in the experiment.

randomized groups design. A scientific procedure for finding out the effect of a given set of conditions. The method involves assigning subjects at random to two groups: one group is exposed to the conditions being studied (*experimental group*), the other not (*control group*), and the two groups are then compared to determine the effects, if any, of the conditions.

random sample. A way of selecting subjects for research studies so that a representative sample is achieved. In a random sample, every element of a population has an equal chance of being included in the sample.

rape. Forced sexual intercourse with a nonconsenting partner.

rational-emotive therapy. The "talking cure" method of Albert Ellis in which the patient is helped to establish more pragmatic goals for the unrealistic ones he or she has set.

rationalization. A defense mechanism in which socially acceptable reasons are offered for something that is done for unconscious and unacceptable reasons.

reaction formation. A state in which a person represses feelings that are arousing anxiety and then vehemently professes the exact opposite of these feelings.

reactive depression. The type of depression that is clearly linked to a precipitating event in the person's environment.

reactive schizophrenia. Those cases of schizophrenia in which onset is sudden and apparently precipitated by some traumatic event.

reality principle. In Freudian theory, the way in which the ego seeks to gratify the desires of the id, with safety as its main concern.

regression. A defense mechanism that involves the return to an earlier, less threatening developmental stage that one has already passed through.

reliability. The degree to which a measurement device yields consistent results under varying conditions.

representativeness. The degree to which a research sample's characteristics match those of the population under study.

repression. A defense mechanism in which unacceptable id impulses are pushed down into the unconscious and thereby forgotten.

residual phase. The third phase of schizophrenia, during which behavior is similar to that seen during the prodromal phase.

resistance. In psychoanalytic theory, a defense mechanism on the part of the patient to avoid confronting certain memories and impulses.

respondent behavior. In behavioral theory, that behavior which is elicited by specific stimuli, both unlearned and conditioned. (Cf. *operant behavior.*)

respondent conditioning (classical conditioning). The process of learning a conditioned response.

response set. A test-taking attitude that leads subjects to distort their responses, often unconsciously.

retarded depression. A type of depression in which there is little spontaneous motor activity; movement is slow and deliberate, with a minimum number of gestures and little verbalization.

role reversal. A technique used in psychodrama in which actors switch parts.

sadism. Sexual gratification through infliction of pain on others.

sadomasochism. The pairing up of a sadist and a masochist to satisfy their mutually complementary sexual tastes.

schema. A structured body of information that is stored in the mind and helps a person to organize and process newly learned information.

schismatic family. A family type in which parental discord has divided the family into opposing factions; believed by some to tend to produce schizophrenia.

schizoaffective disorder. A syndrome

intermediate between schizophrenia and the mood disorders in which individuals suffer a manic or a depressive episode while showing the symptoms of schizophrenia.

schizoid personality disorder. A personality disorder marked by social withdrawal and isolation.

schizophrenia. A group of psychoses marked by severe distortion and disorganization of thought, perception, and affect, by bizarre behavior, and by social withdrawal. Also called schizophrenic disorders.

schizophreniform disorder. A schizophrenic episode that lasts for more than two weeks but less than six months, with or without a precipitating event.

schizophrenogenic mother. The type of mother believed by some to be capable of inducing schizophrenia in her children.

schizotypal personality disorder. A disorder marked by odd speech, behavior, thinking and/or perceptions.

seasonal affective disorder (SAD). A mood disorder characterized by depression during the winter.

secondary gains. In neurosis, the extra attention and "babying" that an adult receives when responding inappropriately to anxiety.

secondary prevention. The second level of prevention of psychological disorder, the goal of which is to detect and treat disorders at an early stage, so that minor disorders do not develop into major ones.

secondary process thinking. In Freudian theory, the remembering, reasoning, and evaluating done by the ego in mediating between the id and reality.

selective amnesia. The forgetting of certain events that occurred during a circumscribed period of time.

self. The individual's image of himself or herself.

self-actualization. According to Rogers, the fulfillment of all an individual's capabilities.

self-instructional training. A cognitive restructuring technique that seeks to change people's behavior by changing what they say to them-

selves before, during, and after their actions.

self psychology. The view proposed by Kohut, as a result of his work with patients suffering from narcissistic personality disorder, that the development of the self depends on the child's receiving two psychological supports from the parents: confirmation of the child's sense of "greatness" and confirmation of the child's sense of calmness and infallibility.

self-report personality inventory. An assessment technique in which subjects are asked direct questions about their personality and feelings; that is, subjects assess themselves.

senile dementia. A pathological degenerative disorder resulting from severe organic deterioration of the brain.

senile plaque. A microscopic lesion in the neurons of the brain, present in victims of Alzheimer's disease.

sensitivity-training group (T-group). A humanistic form of group therapy that emphasizes personal growth and self-understanding, and improving relations with others.

separation anxiety disorder. Intense fear and distress upon being separated from parents or other caretakers.

separation–individuation. The four-stage process, outlined by Mahler, by which the infant separates psychologically from the mother. Beginning at five months of age, the infant undergoes "differentiation" (distinguishing between his or her own and the mothers' bodies), "practicing" (physically escaping from the mother), "rapprochement" (alternatively pushing away and clinging to the mother), and "object constancy" (internalizing the image of the mother and consolidating his or her own personality).

sexual dysfunction. A class of disorders that prevent the individual from having or enjoying coitus.

shame aversion therapy. A behavioral technique to eliminate deviant sexual arousal that involves the patient's performing a deviant act in

the therapist's office while the therapist observes and comments.

shaping. A type of operant conditioning used often with children, whereby the subject is reinforced for successive approximations of target behavior.

sheltered workshop. A special work center, designed to meet the needs of the retarded people who are employed there.

single-case experiment. Research that focuses on behavior change in one person, but, unlike the *case study,* methodically varies the conditions surrounding the person's behavior and monitors the behavior under the changing conditions.

situational dysfunction. A sexual dysfunction that only occurs in certain situations.

situational variables. The environmental stimuli that precede and follow any given action by a person.

skewed family. A family type in which one spouse is totally dominated by the other; believed by some to tend to produce schizophrenia.

sleepwalking (somnambulism). A dissociative disorder in which the person walks while asleep. It is much more common in children than in adults.

social desirability set. A test-taking attitude in which subjects distort their responses in order to ascribe to themselves qualities that will make them look good.

social phobias. The fear of performing certain actions when exposed to the scrutiny of others.

social role. The result of the labeling process in which an individual is accorded a role within the society and rewarded for behavior consistent with that role, whatever it may be.

social-skills training. A behavioral therapy that teaches people basic techniques for engaging in satisfying interactions with others.

somatic nervous system. That part of the peripheral nervous system that senses and acts on the external world, relaying to the brain information picked up by the sense organs and transmitting the brain's messages to the skeletal muscles, which move the body.

somatic weakness. A theory suggesting that a psychophysiological complaint is most likely to develop in a person's weakest or most vulnerable organ system.

somatization disorders. Complaints or symptoms of physical disorder for which there is no demonstrable organic cause.

somatoform disorders. Conditions in which psychological conflicts take on a somatic or physical form. These disorders include hypochondriasis, somatization disorder, and conversion disorder.

standard of proof. The Supreme Court has declared that a person cannot be involuntarily committed to a mental institution without "clear and convincing" evidence that he or she is committable. To be committable, a person must be found mentally ill and dangerous.

statistical inference. A technique used by researchers to try to determine whether differences between experimental groups are due to the independent variable. It begins by assuming the *null hypothesis* and then using probability theory to determine the likelihood of having obtained the experimental results if the independent variable had had no effect. If the likelihood is small, the result is judged to be statistically significant and the independent variable is assumed to have had an effect.

statutory rape. Sexual intercourse with a minor, which usually occurs in the absence of force.

stereotactic subcaudate tractotomy. A psychosurgical technique in which a small localized area of the brain is destroyed by radioactive particles inserted through small ceramic rods.

stereotypy. The act of engaging in purposeless actions repetitively for hours; a behavior sometimes shown by schizophrenics.

stimulants. A class of drugs whose major effect is to provide energy, alertness, and feelings of confidence.

stimulus control. An operant conditioning technique in which a predictable relationship is established between a given stimulus and a given response by eliminating all other stimuli associated with that response and all other responses associated with that stimulus.

stimulus satiation. A behavioral technique to reduce the attractiveness of a stimulus by providng an overabundance of it.

stimulus specificity. The principle that different kinds of stress produce different patterns of physiological response.

structural hypothesis. Freud's belief that the mind can be divided into three basic forces: the id, the ego, and the superego.

stuttering. The interruption of speech fluency through blocked, prolonged, or repeated words, syllables, or sounds.

sublimation. A defense mechanism by which impulses are channeled away from forbidden outlets and toward socially acceptable ones.

superego. In Freudian theory, that part of the mind in which the person has incorporated the moral standards of the society.

supported living arrangement (SLA). A small group home in which mildly retarded persons live and supervision is provided in the evening.

sympathetic division. That division of the autonomic nervous system which becomes dominant in times of stress and which heightens the body's arousal, causing blood pressure, heart rate, perspiration, and adrenalin to increase, pupils to dilate, and salivation and digestive functions to diminish. (Cf. parasympathetic division.)

symptomatic epilepsy (acquired epilepsy). Convulsions that are a function of brain damage caused by other pathologies, such as neurosyphilis, alcohol or drug intoxication, tumors, encephalitis, or trauma.

symptom substitution. The replacement of a suppressed maladaptive behavior by a new maladaptive behavior.

synapse. The gap between two neurons across which nerve impulses pass.

syndrome. The distinct cluster of symptoms that tends to occur in a particular disease.

synergistic effect. The combined effect of two drugs is greater than the effect of either drug when taken alone.

systematic desensitization (reciprocal inhibition). A behavioral therapy in which the patient, in a relaxed state, is presented with the anxiety-arousing stimulus while the therapist prevents the anxiety response and the negatively reinforcing behavior from taking place.

systems approach. One of two basic approaches to family therapy; the family unit is analyzed as a set of interlocking roles.

systems theory. An approach to understanding sexual dysfunction based on the view of relationships as a system of interlocking needs. Sexual dysfunction, although distressing to a couple, has a function in their overall relationship.

tardive dyskinesia. A muscle disorder caused by the antipsychotic drugs, the phenothiazines.

Tay-Sachs disease. A genetic disorder of lipid metabolism marked by the absence of the enzyme hexosominia A in cerebral tissues; causes mental retardation, muscular deterioration, convulsions, and death before the age of six.

tertiary prevention. The third level of prevention of psychological disorder, the goal of which is to minimize the damage, to both the victim and society, of a major disorder.

test-retest reliability. A criterion for reliability in psychological testing: the test should yield the same results when administered to the same person at different times.

therapeutic environment. The arrangement of an institutional environment in such a way that all the patient's interactions with that environment will serve some therapeutic purpose.

third-variable problem. In scientific research, an alternative factor, not considered by the researchers, that may be causing the covariation of the two factors being investigated.

thrombus. A buildup of fatty material coating the inside of a blood vessel. If a thrombus becomes too large, it blocks the flow of blood through the vessel. A thrombus in the brain can cause impairment.

time–order relationship. The second condition to be met before causality can be demonstrated. The presumed cause must occur before the presumed effect.

time-out from positive reinforcement. An operant conditioning technique whereby the subject is "punished" for undesirable behavior by being temporarily removed from the situation and placed in a neutral environment where he or she can receive no reinforcement.

token economy. A behavior modification procedure, based on operant conditioning principles, in which patients are given artificial rewards for socially desirable behavior; the rewards or tokens can then be exchanged for a range of rewards which the patients choose.

tolerance. The physiological condition in which the usual dosage of a drug no longer provides the desired "high."

tonic phase. The second stage of a grand mal seizure in which the person's body becomes very rigid and undergoes strong muscular contractions, and breathing is suspended.

traits. Enduring patterns of relating to, perceiving, and thinking about the environment and oneself.

tranquilizers. A group of drugs that produce mild calm and relaxation. They can be addictive and have side effects. Among the most popular tranquilizers are Tranxene, Librium, and Valium.

transference. In psychoanalytic theory, the process by which patients identify the therapist with important people in their lives, usually with their parents, and project on to the therapist their relationship with those people.

transsexualism. Gender identification with the opposite sex.

transvestism. Sexual gratification through dressing in the clothes of the opposite sex.

trauma. A severe physical injury to the body from an external source; or a severe psychological shock.

traumatic delirium. The state of disorientation that a patient suffering from contusion may experience upon awakening from the coma.

trephining. An ancient and crude surgical technique that involved cutting a hole in the skull of a person.

tricyclics. A class of antidepressants that seem to increase the level of certain neurotransmitters, including norepinephrine and serotonin.

trisomy 21. A condition in which there are three rather than the pair of chromosomes in pair 21 in the human cell.

ulcer. An open sore in the wall of the stomach or in a portion of the small intestine produced by abnormally high levels of gastric activity; a stress-related physical disorder.

unconditioned response. A natural, unlearned response to a stimulus.

unconditioned stimulus. A stimulus which elicits a natural or unconditioned response.

unconscious. In Freudian theory, the largest level of the mind's consciousness which contains all memories not readily available to the perceptual conscious, either because they have been forgotten or repressed.

understanding. The third objective of the scientific method. The identification of the cause or causes of a phenomenon.

unspecified encephalitis. A brain infection typically transmitted by mosquitoes, ticks, and horses. The disorder is characterized by lethargy, irritability, convulsions, and the like.

vaginismus. The spasmodic contractions of the outer third of the vagina, which render intercourse either impossible or very painful.

validity. The measure of how consistent a test is with other sources of information about the same subject.

valuing process. In Carl Rogers' theory, people judge experiences as self-enhancing or not enhancing. Self-enhancing experiences are sought after, and negative experiences are avoided.

vascular accident. An organic brain disorder in which blockage or breaking of cranial blood vessels results in injury to the brain tissue.

voyeurism. Sexual gratification through clandestine observation of other people's sexual activities or sexual anatomy.

waxy flexibility. A condition that catatonic schizophrenics occasionally exhibit in which their limbs can be moved around and "arranged" by another person and will remain in whatever position is imposed.

will-to-meaning. In existential philosophy, the struggle of human beings to find some reason for their troubled, complicated, and finite existence.

withdrawal symptoms. Temporary psychological and physiological disturbances resulting from the body's attempt to readjust to the absence of a drug.

word salad. A schizophrenic speech pattern in which words and phrases are combined in a disorganized fashion, seemingly devoid of logic and meaning and even associational links.

NAME INDEX